THE ANCIENT GREEKS

'*The Ancient Greeks* is a valuable new textbook . . . Written in a lucid and approachable style, the book is extensively illustrated with figures and maps. *The Ancient Greeks* along with its companion the *Ancient Greece* sourcebook will make an excellent resource for students registered in ancient Greek history courses as well as the wider public interested in this fascinating period of Greek history.'

Zinon Papakonstantinou, *University of Illinois at Chicago, USA.*

'This volume admirably fulfils its professed aims in providing both the student reader and other interested parties with a comprehensive introduction to the history and culture of the Greek world c. 800–323 BC. . . . The focus is not merely on historical sources but also a wide array of archaeological materials - many of which appear as illustrations - together with numerous tables, maps and plans. There is, in short, everything one could wish for (and more!) when teaching a course in Greek history.'

Joseph Skinner, *University of Liverpool, UK.*

This work offers students a comprehensive introduction to the history and culture of the ancient Greek world for the period c. 800–323 BC. It provides critical background to the key historical developments of the time: the Persian Wars, the rise of Athens and its empire in the fifth century and the subsequent Peloponnesian War, and the emergence of Macedon as a world power under Philip and Alexander. A chapter dedicated to Sparta provides students with crucial understanding of this important but enigmatic kingdom. However, *The Ancient Greeks* moves beyond political history to include social sections on women, religion, the city-state, and slaves, offering extensive coverage of the social and religious environment.

The book is lavishly illustrated, with over 180 illustrations, maps and photographs, and it includes a chronological table and a glossary of key terms. With close referencing to *Ancient Greece: Social and Historical Documents from Archaic Times to the Death of Alexander* (third edition) and accompanied by a companion website, this volume provides invaluable support for students of ancient Greek history and civilization, and offers a comprehensive introduction for the interested reader.

Matthew Dillon is Associate Professor of Classics and Ancient History, School of Humanities, at the University of New England, Australia. His main research interests are ancient Greek history and religion.

Lynda Garland is a professor and Head of the School of Humanities at the University of New England, Australia. Her main research interests are in the areas of ancient history and Byzantine Studies.

THE ANCIENT GREEKS

History and culture from archaic times to
the death of Alexander

Matthew Dillon and Lynda Garland

Routledge
Taylor & Francis Group

LONDON AND NEW YORK

First published 2013
by Routledge
2 Park Square, Milton Park, Abingdon, Oxon OX14 4RN

Simultaneously published in the USA and Canada
by Routledge
711 Third Avenue, New York, NY 10017

Routledge is an imprint of the Taylor & Francis Group, an informa business

British Library Cataloguing in Publication Data
A catalogue record for this book is available from the British Library

Library of Congress Cataloging in Publication Data
The ancient Greeks : history and culture from archaic times to the death of Alexander/
Matthew Dillon, Lynda Garland.
p. cm.
Includes bibliographical references and index.
1. Greece—History—To 146 B.C. 2. Greece—Civilization—To 146 B.C.
I. Garland, Lynda, 1955– II. Title.
DF214.D55 2012
938—dc23
2011051367

ISBN: 978–0–415–47144–2 (hbk)
ISBN: 978–0–415–47143–5 (pbk)

Typeset in Baskerville MT
by Swales & Willis Ltd, Exeter, Devon

Printed and bound in Great Britain by
CPI Group (UK) Ltd, Croydon, CR0 4YY

FOR ALL OUR STUDENTS,
PAST, PRESENT AND FUTURE

CONTENTS

CONTENTS

3   Religion in the Greek world

4   Women, sexuality, and the family

5   Labour: slaves, serfs and citizens

CONTENTS

CONTENTS

FIGURES

FIGURES

MAPS

TABLES

PREFACE

Fifteen years after the first publication of the sourcebook *Ancient Greece: Social and Historical Documents from Archaic Times to the Death of Socrates*, when we were finalising the third edition of that work, now expanded in its historical range down to the death of Alexander III 'the Great' of Macedon, we decided that it was finally time to provide the sourcebook with a related textbook so that students could use the two in tandem. This new definitive historical study of the period c. 800–323 BC gives students the full background to the texts translated in *Ancient Greece*, thus providing a comprehensive suite of materials for the study of Greek political history and society. This seemed to us particularly important because the sourcebook, like its companion sourcebook, *Ancient Rome: From the Early Republic to the Assassination of Julius Caesar* which appeared late in 2005, has been so widely used at Australian and overseas institutions; it has been prescribed for units and courses at institutions as diverse as University College London, the University of Leeds, the University of Wales (Lampeter), the University of Florida, the University of Pennsylvania, the University of Kansas, the University of Oregon, the University of Queensland, Universität Regensburg, Cornell University, Loyola University, Université de Louvain, as well as being a recommended text at Trinity College Dublin, the University of Victoria in Canada, the University of Auckland, the University of Edinburgh, Universität Heidelberg, the University of Manchester, Birkbeck College in London, the University of Sasktachewan and the University of Cambridge, particularly since the second edition in 2000. Seeing that the sourcebook has had such a wide circulation it seemed a good idea to present this same audience with the background history of Greek politics and society which we teach our own students in Australia at the University of New England, specifically drawing on the texts featured in the sourcebook, in part because we had not to date found a work which completely satisfied all the needs of students in our different Ancient History courses and units relating to archaic and classical Greek history and which clearly commented on the information presented by the ancient sources themselves.

This textbook has the same chapter titles and subheadings as *Ancient Greece*, and provides students with the necessary background knowledge and details for an understanding of each historical period and social phenomenon of the archaic and classical Greek world. Accordingly, many of the extensive comments accompanying individual documents have been reduced in scope and size in *Ancient Greece* itself and the background and contextual information is now given in this textbook. The aim has been not only to give a wide range of material from ancient sources, but to accompany this with a detailed historical overview; as with the sourcebook we have tried to give a view of the Greek world as a whole, not focusing merely on Athens and Sparta but on the lesser-known centres of Greek civilisation and culture as well, with the aim of keeping the reader continually in mind of the geographical and chronological scope of Greek history and civilisation. To this end we have provided numerous maps, charts and illustrations: history is not merely a study of literary sources, and in this book we have tried to supplement the historical and literary sources with depictions of the most important and relevant pieces of art and architecture to help students conceptualise the visual and special background to the most important social and political events, as well as personalities and ideologies, in the Greek world.

We give a special thanks to all our students over the last fifteen years, not just at the University of New England, but those who have used the sourcebook, *Ancient Greece* and its companion *Ancient Rome*, in Australia, New Zealand, Britain, Ireland, Germany, the United States and elsewhere. Finally, we would like to thank all those who have made comments and suggestions to help us improve these and hope that this textbook will prove to be equally as useful as the sourcebook to students of Ancient History.

Armidale, Australia
December 2011

GLOSSARY

acropolis	citadel, the highest part of a city (plural: acropoleis)
agema	the Macedonian guard
agoge	the Spartan system of education
agora	the market square, civic centre of a city-state
agoranomoi	market magistrates at Athens
aisymnetes	an elected tyrant
Amphiktyonic Council	representatives of the twelve states responsible for the upkeep and welfare of the sanctuary and games at Delphi
Amphiktyonic League or amphiktyony	an association of cities responsible for administering a sanctuary
amphora	a large vase, usually of pottery, used for storing and transporting liquids (plural: amphorai)
apoikia	a colony or settlement (plural: apoikiai)
architheoros	the leader of a sacred embassy
archon	a magistrate; the most important archonship in Athens was the eponymous archonship (the holder gave his name to the year)
Areiopagos	a hill west of the acropolis; the council of the Areiopagos which was composed of ex-archons met here
asylia	immunity, protection against reprisals
atimia	loss of citizen rights (adjective: atimos, plural: atimoi)
axon	wooden tablets recording the laws of Drakon and Solon (plural: axones)
boeotarch	a chief magistrate of the Boeotian League
boule	the council of a city
bouleuterion	meeting place of a boule, council chamber
chiliarch	a Macedonian commander (of 1000 men)
choregos	a wealthy citizen who financed a dramatic chorus for a festival
Companions	nobles serving in the cavalry in the Macedonian army
dekarchy	a government of ten men
demagogue	a popular leader or speaker (a fourth-century term)
deme	a village; Kleisthenes divided Attica into 140 units called demes
demos	the people of a city, the citizens; sometimes the assembly (Spartan: damos)
dikasterion	a jury-court (plural: dikasteria)
dokimasia	the scrutiny of a candidate's qualifications for office or citizenship

ekklesia	the assembly of adult male citizens
Eleven, the	the police-commissioners at Athens
emporion	a trading station (plural: emporia)
ephebe	a young man between 18 and 20 years prior to becoming a full citizen (plural: epheboi)
ephebeia	the military training system for ephebes
ephor	a Spartan magistrate; five were elected annually
Epigonoi	the successors of Alexander the Great
epimetelai	supervisors
epoptes	the highest grade of initiate at Eleusis (plural: epoptai)
erastes	lover (male)
eromenos	beloved (male)
eunomia	good order
eupatridai	nobles, aristocrats
euthyna	the examination of an official's conduct or accounts at the end of his term (plural: euthynai)
genos	a clan, group of families (plural: gene)
gerousia	a council of twenty-eight elders (gerontes) in Sparta plus the two kings
gnorimoi	the notables, wealthy
graphe paranomon	a charge brought against the proposer of a supposedly illegal decree
gymnasiarch	a supervisor responsible for running a gymnasium
harmost	a governor imposed by Sparta
hegemon	a leader or commander (as of the League of Corinth)
hektemoroi	'sixth-parters', poor Athenian farmers who paid one-sixth of their produce to a wealthy landowner prior to Solon
heliaia	a court (generally of appeal) at Athens
hellenotamiai	financial officials of the Delian League
helot	a Spartan serf
herm	stone surmounted by the head of Hermes with an ithyphallos (plural: hermai)
hetaira	a courtesan, higher-class prostitute (plural: hetairai)
hetaireia	a club, association of citizens (plural: hetaireiai)
hieromnemones	representatives on the Delphic Amphiktyonic Council
hieron	a sanctuary, temple
hieropoioi	sacred officials, temple overseers
hippeis	cavalry; the second of Solon's four property-classes in Athens; in Sparta a bodyguard of 300 protecting the king in battle
homoioi	'peers': a term used in Sparta for full citizens, the Spartiates
hoplite	a heavy-armed infantryman
horos	a boundary-stone (plural: horoi)
hydria	a large pottery vessel for holding water (plural: hydriai)
hypaspistai	Macedonian shield-bearers; a brigade of guards
isonomia	equality of political rights
kanephoros	a young unmarried woman who carried a ceremonial basket in religious processions (plural: kanephoroi)

kleros	an allotment of land (plural kleroi; Spartan: klaros)
kolakretai	Athenian financial officials
komos	a band of revellers; a celebratory procession
krater	a large vase for mixing wine and water
krypteia	a force of young Spartans which waged war on the helots
kylix	a drinking-cup, often used at symposia (plural: kylikes)
Lakedaimon	Sparta; the Spartans were known as Lakedaimonians
Lakonia	Sparta's immediate countryside; 'Lakonian' often means Spartan
liturgy	a public duty imposed on wealthy citizens in Athens, such as financing a dramatic chorus or paying for the maintenance of a trireme for a year (the trierarchia)
medise	to support or collaborate with the Persians
metic	an immigrant, foreign resident
metoikion	the tax on metics
metropolis	a mother-city (of a colony)
mystagogos	someone who introduced others to the Eleusinian Mysteries
mystes	an initiate, especially at the Eleusinian Mysteries (plural: mystai)
nauarchos	an admiral
neodameis	new citizens (in Sparta); enfranchised helots
nomos	a law
nomothetes	a legislator
nothoi	illegitimate children
oikistes	the founder of a colony (plural: oikistai)
oikos	a household, consisting of family, slaves and property (plural: oikoi)
oligarchy	the rule of a few ('oligoi') men within a polis
Olympiad	the four-year period between one Olympic Games and the next
ostracism	a procedure in the assembly that exiled a selected Athenian for ten years
paidagogos	a slave responsible for escorting a boy to his school
paideia	education
palaistra	a wrestling-court
parthenos	a young, unmarried girl
Parthenos	epithet of the virgin goddess Athena
peltast	a lightly armed soldier (pelte: a shield)
penestai	Thessalian serfs
pentakosiomedimnoi	the 500 bushel-class, the first of Solon's four property-classes in Athens
perioikoi	neighbours; peoples subject to Sparta in the Peloponnese
pezetairoi	foot-guards in the Macedonian army
phalanx	a military formation of rows of hoplites
phoros	tribute contribution (eg, to Athens from members of the Delian League), literally 'burden'
phratry	a brotherhood with social and religious associations which recognised a common ancestor
phroura	garrison

phrourarch	commander of a garrison
phyle	a tribe; Kleisthenes organised the Athenians into ten tribes (plural: phylai)
polemarch	a war leader, senior military officer; one of the archons in Athens
poletai	Athenian financial officials
polis	a city-state (plural: poleis)
politeia	constitution; (by extension) citizenship, political rights (plural: politeiai; 'patrios politeia': ancestral constitution)
polites	citizen (plural: politai)
probouleusis	recommendations made to the assembly by the Council after preliminary discussion
proedros	president (e.g., of a council)
proskynesis	prostration, obeisance, performed by the Persians towards their king but reserved by the Greeks as a mark of respect to the gods
prostates	champion, leader of a political party; patron of metics
proxenos	a citizen responsible for promoting and protecting the interests of ambassadors and visitors from another city in his state
prytaneion	town-hall, where the prytaneis dined during their term of office
prytany	one-tenth of the Athenian administrative year, during which the representatives of one of the ten tribes (the fifty prytaneis) presided in the boule and assembly
Pythia	the priestess at Delphi
Relatives	an elite corps of Persians
rhapsode	a bard, minstrel
rhetra	a constitutional law
sarcophagus	a stone receptacle for a corpse: the terms means 'flesh-eating' (plural: sarcophagi)
sarissa	the basic Macedonian weapon, a six-metre pike
satrap	a Persian governor
seisachtheia	the 'shaking-off of burdens', by which Solon resolved the agrarian crisis in Athens
skolion	a drinking song (plural: skolia)
skytale	a stick used by Spartans for recording messages while on campaign
sophist	an intellectual who taught young men how to employ rhetoric
Spartiate	a full Spartan citizen
stamnos	a type of pottery used to store liquids (plural: stamnoi)
stasis	civil dissension, factional disturbance; a party or faction
stele	a slab; an inscription, such as a gravestone or decree (plural: stelai)
strategia	the command or office of a general
strategos	a general (plural: strategoi); straegos autokrator: supreme commander
symposium	a drinking-party (plural: symposia)
synoikismos	the union of several towns to form a single state (synoecism)
syssitia	public messes at Sparta (also pheiditia)

tagos	the chief magistrate of Thessaly
theoria	a sacred embassy (singular: theoros)
theoroi	sacred envoys
thetes	the lowest of Solon's four property-classes (singular: thes)
Thirty, the	the oligarchs who ruled Athens 404/3
tholos	the round house; the headquarters of the prytaneis
tresantes	literally 'tremblers', Spartans accused of cowardice in battle
trierarch	the commander of a trireme
trireme	a warship with 170 rowers
trittys	a regional division of Attica (plural: trittyes)
tyrant	a ruler with no hereditary right to rule
tyrannos	a tyrant (plural: tyrannoi)
zeugitai	the third of Solon's four property-classes

CHRONOLOGICAL TABLE

c. 1250	The 'Trojan War'
c. 1200–1125	Destruction of Mycenean centres in Greece
c. 1200–1000	Greek colonisation of the Asia Minor coast
c. 825	Establishment of an emporion at Al Mina
776	Traditional date for the first Olympic Games
c. 750–725	Foundation of Pithekoussai
c. 740–c. 720	Spartan conquest of Messenia: 'First Messenian War'
734	Foundation of Sicilian Naxos
669/8	Argive defeat of the Spartans at Hysiai
c. 680–640	Reign of Gyges of Lydia
c. 650	Second Messenian War
664–610	Reign of Psammetichos I; establishment of Naukratis
c. 658–c. 585	Kypselid tyranny at Corinth
656/5?–556/5?	Orthagorid tyranny at Sikyon
c. 640	Theagenes becomes tyrant of Megara
632?	Attempted tyranny of Kylon at Athens
631	Foundation of Cyrene
621/0	Drakon law-giver at Athens
607/6	Athenian and Mytilenaean dispute over Sigeion
594/3	Solon's archonship and nomothesia (law-giving)
590–580	Pittakos made aisymnetes (elected tyrant) of Mytilene
c. 575	Marriage of Kleisthenes' daughter to Megakles of Athens
570–526	Amasis king of Egypt
561/0–556/5	Peisistratos' first tyranny at Athens and expulsion
560–546	Croesus king of Lydia
559–556	Miltiades the elder, tyrant of the Chersonese
556/5	Peisistratos' second tyranny at Athens and expulsion
546/5	Peisistratos' third tyranny at Athens; Cyrus defeats Croesus
c. 537	Battle of Alalia
532–522	Polykrates sole tyrant of Samos
530	Accession of Cambyses to the Persian throne
527	Death of Peisistratos; rule of the Peisistratidai at Athens
525/4	Kleisthenes' archonship at Athens
522	Darius seizes power in Persia
521 or 520	Kleomenes becomes king of Sparta

514/13	Harmodios and Aristogeiton assassinate Hipparchos at Athens
c. 513	Darius' Scythian expedition
511/0	Expulsion of the Peisistratidai from Athens
508/7	Isagoras' archonship at Athens; reforms of Kleisthenes
505	Beginning of tyranny at Gela
499	Ionian revolt
494	Battle of Lade and sack of Miletos
493/2	Themistokles' archonship at Athens
c. 491	Gelon becomes tyrant of Gela
491 or 490	Death of Kleomenes of Sparta
490	First Persian expedition against Greece; battle of Marathon
488/7	First ostracism at Athens (Hipparchos, ?grandson of Hippias)
486	Death of Darius; accession of Xerxes as king of Persia
485	Gelon becomes tyrant of Syracuse
483	Discovery of new vein of silver at Laureion, Attica
480	Second Persian invasion; the Carthaginians invade Sicily
	Battles of Thermopylai, Artemision, Salamis and Himera
479	Battles of Plataea and Mykale
478/7	Delian League founded under Athens' leadership
	Hieron becomes tyrant of Syracuse
c. 469–466	Persians defeated at the Eurymedon River
466	End of the Deinomenid tyranny at Syracuse
?465/4	Revolt of Thasos; helot revolt in Messenia
462/1	Reforms of Ephialtes at Athens
c. 460	Start of First Peloponnesian War
c. 460	Athenian expedition to Egypt
458/7	Battles of Tanagra and Oionophyta
454/3	First tribute-quota lists; League treasury moved to Athens
451	Five Years' Peace
447	Building of the Parthenon begun in Athens
446	Revolts of Euboea and Megara; Thirty Years' Peace
440–439	Revolt of Samos
437/6	Foundation of Amphipolis with Hagnon as oikistes
435–433	War between Corinth and Corcyra
431	Second Peloponnesian War begins with the 'Archidamian War'
429	The plague; death of Perikles
428–427	Revolt of Lesbos; the 'Mytilene debate'
426	Spartan foundation of Herakleia in Trachis
425	Athenian success at Pylos
422	Death of Kleon and Brasidas at Amphipolis
421	Peace of Nikias between Athens and Sparta and their allies
415–413	Sicilian Expedition
413	Spartan fortification of Dekeleia in Attica
411	The Four Hundred take power at Athens
406	Athenian naval victory at Arginousai
405	Athenian fleet defeated at Aigospotamoi; Athens besieged
	Dionysios I becomes tyrant of Syracuse

404	Capitulation of Athens; Rule of Thirty instigated at Athens
	Artaxerxes II becomes king of Persia
403	Thrasyboulos and the democrats take the Piraeus
	King Pausanias effects reconciliation at Athens; end of the Thirty
401	Failed rebellion of Cyrus against Artaxerxes II
	Sparta attacks Persian possessions in Asia Minor
399	Sparta defeats Elis and regains access to Olympic festival
	Execution of Socrates
397	Conspiracy of Kinadon revealed and crushed at Sparta
	Konon works with Pharnabazos against the Spartans in Asia Minor
395	Athens commences rebuilding the Long Walls and Piraeus walls
	Tithraustes bribes the Greeks to oppose Sparta (or soon after)
	Athens' alliance with Boeotia
	Persia, Athens, Thebes and Corinth oppose Sparta in the Corinthian War
394	Persian fleet and Konon defeat the Spartans at Knidos in Asia Minor
	Sparta abandons the war against Persia in Asia Minor; Agesilaos II returns to Greece
	Agesilaos defeats Thebans and allies at Koroneia in Boeotia
386	The King's Peace ends the Corinthian War to Sparta's advantage
381	Sparta seizes the Kadmeia and occupies Thebes
379	Pelopidas frees Thebes and institutes a democracy
377	Athens forms the Second Athenian Confederacy
375	Thebans under Pelopidas defeat Spartan force at Tegyra
371	Spartan peace conference
	Sparta invades Boeotia and is defeated by the Thebans under Pelopidas at Leuktra
370	Messenian helots freed; Messenian exiles return
	Iason of Pherai assassinated
370–367	Megalopolis founded as capital of Arkadia
369	Messene founded as capital of Messenia
368	Alliance between Dionysios I and Athens
367	Dionysios II becomes tyrant of Syracuse
362	Battle of Mantineia; Epaminondas killed; Theban hegemony ends
359	Philip becomes king of Macedon
358	Philip defeats Illyrians and begins transformation of Macedon
357	'Social War' commences
	Philip marries Olympias of Epirus; seizes Amphipolis, Pydna and Potideia
	Third Sacred War commences
357–356	Olynthos allies with Philip
356	Alexander future king of Macedon born to Olympias and Philip
355	End of Social War
354	Philip captures Methone and loses right eye
353	Philip's alliance with Boeotian League
352	Philip elected archon of Thessaly for life
351	Philip intervenes in Euboea
	Demosthenes delivers his *First Philippic* speech

350	Philip threatens Olynthos
349	Olynthos appeals to Athens; Demosthenes delivers *First, Second* and *Third Olynthiacs*
348	Olynthos destroyed by Philip
346	Two Athenian embassies to Philip; Peace of Philokrates
	Third Sacred War ends with destruction of Phokis by Philip
344	Demosthenes delivers his *Second Philippic* speech
343	Trial of Aeschines (*On the Embassy*); acquitted
	Persians reconquer Egypt and rule it harshly
343–342	Philip intervenes in Euboea
341	Demosthenes delivers his *Third Philippic*
340	Philip unsuccessfully attacks Perinthos and Byzantium; captures Athenian grain fleet
339	Philip in Phokis for the Fourth Sacred War
338	Thebans persuaded by Demosthenes to join Athens
	Philip defeats the Athenians and Boeotians at Chaironeia in Boeotia
	Demosthenes delivers funeral oration for the Athenian dead
338–337	Philip marries Kleopatra Eurydike, ward of Attalos; Olympias retires to Epirus
337	Formation of the League of Corinth with Philip as hegemon
336	Parmenion invades Asia Minor as a prelude to Philip's planned campaign
	Assassination of Philip II of Macedon; Alexander III 'The Great' elected king
	Aeschines indicts Ktesiphon for proposal to award Demosthenes a crown
	Kleopatra Eurydike, wife of Philip, murdered
	Darius III becomes king of Persia
335	Alexander campaigns in the north
	Destruction of Thebes by Alexander
334	Alexander crosses the Hellespont into Asia Minor
	Alexander defeats Darius at Granikos
	Capture of Sardis
333	Alexander defeats Darius at Issos
332	Darius' first offer of peace
	Siege of Tyre
331	Alexander frees Egypt from Persian control; founds Alexandria
	Alexander visits Siwah and apparently hailed as Zeus-Ammon's son
	Darius' second offer of peace
	Alexander defeats Darius at Gaugamela
330	Persepolis burnt
	Darius assassinated; Bessos becomes Persian king as Artaxerxes V
	Sparta defeated by Antipater
	Philotas executed; Parmenion assassinated
	Trial of Ktesiphon (Demosthenes *On the Crown*); Aeschines goes into exile
329	Bactrian revolt (ends in 327)
	Bessos captured and handed over to Darius' relatives
328	Alexander murders Kleitos the Black
327	Rock of Sogdiana captured

SOME USEFUL DEFINITIONS

Athenian months

Hekatombaion (June/July)
Metageitnion (July/August)
Boedromion (August/Sept.)
Pyanopsion (Sept./Oct.)
Maimakterion (Oct./Nov.)
Posideion (Nov./Dec.)

Gamelion (Dec./Jan.)
Anthesterion (Jan./Feb.)
Elaphebolion (Feb./March)
Mounichion (March/April)
Thargelion (April/May)
Skirophorion (May/June)

The ten Athenian tribes in their official order

Erechtheis (I)
Aigeis (II)
Pandionis (III)
Leontis (IV)
Akamantis (V)

Oineis (VI)
Kekropis (VII)
Hippothontis (VIII)
Aiantis (IX)
Antiochis (X)

Attic coinage

6 obols (ob.) = 1 drachma (dr.)
100 dr. = 1 mina
2 minas = 1 stater
60 minas = 1 talent (T.)

Measurements of capacity

1 kotyle (jug) = 285cc
12 kotylai = 1 chous (3.4 litres)
12 choes = 1 metretes (41 litres)
192 kotylai = 1 medimnos (55 dry litres)

Measurements of distance

1 daktylos (finger) = approx. $7/10$ in; 1.9 cm.
24 daktyloi = 1 cubit (approx. 1 ft 5 in; 45 cm.)
1 orguia = 1 fathom (approx. 6 ft; 1.80 metres)
100 orguiai = 1 stade (approx. 606 ft; 180 metres)

ABBREVIATIONS

Ael.	Aelian
Aesch.	Aeschylus
Aeschin.	Aeschines
Alc.	Alcaeus
Alcm.	Alcman
Anac.	Anacreon
Anax.	Anaximenes
Anaxag.	Anaxagoras
Andoc.	Andocides
Androt.	Androtion
Antiph.	Antiphon
Ar.	Aristophanes
Archil.	Archilochos
Arist.	Aristotle
Arr.	Arrian
Ath.	Athenaeus
Ath. Pol.	*Athenaion Politeia*
Bacchyl.	Bacchylides
Const. Spart.	*Constitution of the Spartans*
Curt.	Curtius Rufus
Dein.	Deinarchos
Dem.	Demosthenes
Diod. Sic.	Diodorus Siculus
Diog. Laert.	Diogenes Laertius
Etym. Magn.	*Etymologicum Magnum*
Eur.	Euripides
Hdt.	Herodotos
Herakl.	Herakleitos
Hes.	Hesiod
Hom.	Homer
Hyper.	Hypereides
Isoc.	Isocrates
Just.	Justin
Lys.	Lysias
Men.	Menander

Nic. Dam.	Nicholas of Damascus
Paus.	Pausanias
Philem.	Philemon
Philoch.	Philochoros
Pind.	Pindar
Pl.	Plato
Plut.	Plutarch
Polyb.	Polybios
Schol. Ar.	Scholiast to Aristophanes
Simon.	Simonides
Soph.	Sophocles
Steph. Byz.	Stephen of Byzantium
Theophr.	Theophrastos
Theopomp.	Theopompos
Thgn.	Theognis
Thuc.	Thucydides
Tyrt.	Tyrtaeus
Xen.	Xenophon
Xen. Kol.	Xenophanes of Kolophon

1

THE POLIS

The Greek city-state

Introduction

The polis, or 'city-state' (plural: poleis), was the basis of Greek civilisation and society in the archaic and classical periods. The polis was a city, but it was also a state in its own right, hence polis is often translated as city-state. This term includes whatever territory the polis controlled outside of its city walls, as the polis consisted of both the city itself and the countryside surrounding it, which could make the city self-sufficient in terms of agricultural produce. Each Greek polis was ideally a self-governing settlement, a community of citizens, which prized its independence and resented and opposed attempts by other cities to impose their will on it. As a result poleis were often at war with each other, and there could be intense and long-lasting hostility between neighbouring cities. While Greek writers can describe barbarian settlements as 'poleis', in Aristotle's view the polis was the factor differentiating Greeks from barbarians. Civilised people lived in a polis, and civilisation in his view revolved around those adult Greek males who were citizens of a polis: while women, children, metics (foreigners) and slaves lived within a polis, they were not citizens (Arist. *Politics* 1252b28–1253a, 1279a22–b10: doc. 1.1). The institutions of a polis were extremely sophisticated and it would normally possess its own army, laws, coinage, political system, patron deities and festivals, taxation and commercial system and possibly its own calendar, weights and measures, and alphabet. Despite this a polis, according to Aristotle, should not become too big, as all citizens should be able to know one another and have a role in politics. The size of the citizen body should therefore be large enough to function as a political entity, but be limited to approximately 10,000 citizens (this does not of course include women, slaves and others) so that they can be acquainted with each other and make decisions on this basis (Arist. *Politics* 1326a40–b24: doc. 1.3). Polis life presupposed a high level of urbanisation and a 'face-to-face' society where the individual citizen actively participated in the life of the city.

Of all the Greek city-states, most is known of the city of Athens, but Athens was only one of some 1500 poleis that existed in the Greek world between c. 750 and 200 BC. Some 600 of these were situated in mainland Greece, with another 400 as colonies or hellenised communities around the shores of the Mediterranean coastline or the Black Sea. In the hellenistic period, following Alexander the Great's conquests, there would also be 300 or so hellenistic poleis founded in the Near East and as far east as India. Even after the Roman conquest of the Mediterranean, some city-states still existed in the sixth century AD and Greek city-state culture lasted over 1200 years. Poleis were not therefore confined to the Greek mainland, and by the early sixth century BC could be found from southern Spain

Figure 1.1 Each polis (city) had its own laws, army, calendar – and often coinage. Aegina's coinage was the preferred currency for transactions between Greek city-states of the mainland and islands until Athenian coinage took over this role in the fifth century BC. This silver coin from Aegina weighs 12.21 g, has a diameter of 17mm and dates to 600–550 BC. It is decorated with the turtle, Aegina's symbol, and an incuse ('stamped into') square. Photo © Yale University Art Gallery, 2001.87.6879.

and France to Phasis and Tanais at the eastern end of the Black Sea and Cyrene on the north coast of Africa.

Poleis were continually being founded, or destroyed by enemy activity, and possibly no more than 850–1000 cities were ever in existence at any one time. There must also have been many cities whose names are not found in the sources and which are now lost to the historical record. In the classical period (479–323) the total population of these cities may have amounted to 7.5 million people.

Because Athens produced great writers, playwrights and historians, many of whose works are still extant, more is known about Athens than about any other Greek city: historians like Herodotos, Thucydides and Xenophon; dramatists like Aeschylus, Sophocles, Euripides and Aristophanes; philosophers like Plato and Aristotle, as well as the sculptors Phidias and Praxiteles flourished in Athens in the classical period, even though not all of these were Athenian. As a result sources from Athens outweigh all the written evidence for the other Greek cities together. This, however, does not mean that Athens was the most important city; at the very least it shared this distinction with Sparta, and to every citizen his own city was the centre of his world. While Athens is the capital of Greece today, it was in no sense the political capital of the ancient Greek world. For a brief period in the second half of the fifth century it dominated the Aegean and can be said to have had an empire (the so-called 'Athenian Empire'), following the establishment of which Sparta, Athens' friend and ally in the Persian Wars, gradually became Athens' enemy. The two cities fought a bitter contest, the Peloponnesian War, from 431 to 404 BC. When Athens lost the war, Sparta claimed the Athenians' empire, but the resulting Spartan hegemony over much of Greece did not last and Sparta's former allies, Thebes and Corinth, were soon at loggerheads with it. Hence modern perceptions of the classical Greek world dualise the two great but contrasting cities, Athens and Sparta, but this is but a partial view of what was a Mediterranean-wide phenomenon (the polis), a civilisation in which each polis possessed its own individual identity and self-government.

Sources

Nearly every piece of writing from the ancient Greek world is related in some way to the polis and the role that it played in the life and perception of its citizens. Philosophers, historians, orators, geographers and comic poets provide invaluable information about the workings of Greek poleis and their political and social systems. The framework for the social and political history of the city-states is given by contemporary historians, who were primarily concerned with charting the details and outcomes of conflicts between the different poleis. The earlier of the two main fifth-century historians, Herodotos, who was writing his *Histories* in the 430s and 420s, is the most important source for the history of archaic Greece from the mid-sixth century down to 479. His primary theme was the conflict between the Greeks and Persians in 490 and 480–479 and the ways in which the earlier histories of these two states had ended in war. While he discusses political reforms and reformers in the context of his wider narrative his interest is more in persons and events than in narrating constitutional developments, though he does discuss topics such as the tyranny in Corinth, the liberation of Athens from the tyranny of the Peisistratidai and Kleisthenes' reforms in Book 5, and Spartan kingship in Book 6, and he relies primarily on oral traditions for his sources. His travels included Egypt, the Black Sea, Cyrene and the Greek cities of southern Italy as well as poleis throughout the Greek mainland.

His younger contemporary, Thucydides, in his *History of the Peloponnesian War* between Sparta and Athens and their allies, much of which he spent in exile from Athens after he failed to save Amphipolis from the Spartan general Brasidas in 422, gives a detailed account of events between 432 and 411, with Book 1 serving as an introduction to the conflict. The section known to modern scholars as the 'Archaeology' (Thuc. 1.1–9) provides information on the early history of Greek poleis, in particular Athens and Sparta, and he gives important details of the colonisation of Sicily in Book 6 as a prelude to Athens' attempt to conquer Sicily in 416–415. Thucydides' narrative, which is incomplete, was continued by Xenophon in his *Hellenika*, a history of Greece from 411 to 362 BC, which deals in detail with the various struggles between the Greek city-states, particularly Sparta, Athens and Thebes and their allies. Xenophon, like Thucydides, spent some time in exile from Athens, and displays distinct oligarchic (anti-democratic) and pro-Spartan tendencies in his narrative.

Aristotle shows a considerable interest in discussing the constitutions of Greek poleis, and was said to have written 158 such constitutions, including one on Athens. The *Athenaion Politeia* (*Constitution of the Athenians*) has been attributed to him on these grounds, but is more probably the work of one of his pupils. The treatise, probably composed c. 320, deals with the changes to Athens' constitutions down to 403 BC and the workings of Athenian democracy at the time of writing. The author was a moderate supporter of oligarchy and his work is invaluable for constitutional developments in Athens. Unfortunately Aristotle's constitutions are lost but he does provide valuable information on systems of government within Greek poleis and useful details about the constitutional government of specific cities in his *Politics*. Aristotle's successor at the Academy, Theophrastos, theorises in his *Laws for Eresos*, his home

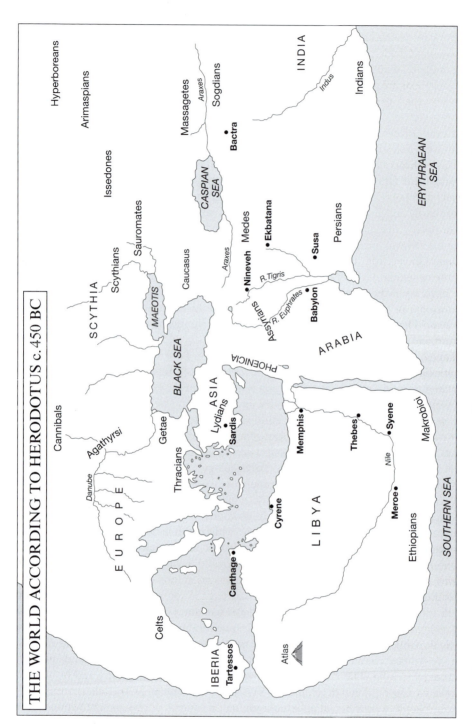

THE WORLD ACCORDING TO HERODOTUS c. 450 BC

Hyperboreans

Arimaspians

INDIA

Massagetes

Araxes

Issedones

Sogdians

• **Bactra**

Indus

Indians

CASPIAN SEA

Sauromates

SCYTHIA

Scythians

Medes

• **Ekbatana**

ERYTHRAEAN SEA

• **Nineveh**

Araxes

• **Susa**

Persians

Caucasus

MAEOTIS

R. Tigris

Assyrians

R. Euphrates

• **Babylon**

Cannibals

Agathyrsi

Getae

BLACK SEA

PHOENICIA

ARABIA

Thracians

Danube

Lydians •

ASIA

• **Sardis**

EUROPE

Celts

• **Cyrene**

• **Memphis**

• **Thebes**

• **Syene**

Makrobioi

LIBYA

Nile

Carthage •

• **Meroe**

Ethiopians

IBERIA

Tartessos

Atlas

SOUTHERN SEA

Map 1.1 The world according to Herodotos. Based on M. Grant, *The Routledge Atlas of Classical History*, fifth edition, Routledge, 1994, p. 24.

town, about the best ways in which officials can be appointed and incidentally gives examples of the practices of a number of Greek cities in selecting their magistrates.

Literary compositions describing the foundation and the workings of cities other than Athens have almost entirely been lost. However, archaeologists have discovered a number of epigraphic texts, such as state decrees or laws inscribed on stone, not only from Athens (where such texts are an invaluable source for Athenian political history) but from a variety of poleis across the Greek world, where many of these inscriptions provide the only information available about a particular city and its government. Issues addressed in such decrees include regulations concerning a city's officials, constitution or relationships with other poleis, provisions for indirect taxation and customs duties, the settlement of new territory, criminal and sacred law, alliances and treaties, commendations and honours for outstanding citizens and foreigners, trade and commerce (particularly the import of grain), piracy and the duties of financial officials.

The Greek identity

The Greeks themselves, according to Herodotos (1.56.2–3), thought that they were a single people, descended from Deukalion's son Hellen after the 'flood'. They had in common their origin, language, culture, and religious beliefs (Hdt. 8.144: doc. 3.91). While there were many Greek dialects, such as Doric (Sparta, Crete), Ionic (Athens and much of Asia Minor), Aeolion (Boeotia and Thessaly) and Arkadian (central Peloponnese), the Greeks shared a common language and no Greeks seem to have had great trouble understanding any other, however much Athenian comic poets might make fun of others' accents on stage. They accepted that, while different cities had their own patron deities and festivals, they shared the same main religious sites, such as the oracles at Delphi, Oropos and Didyma and the same panhellenic festivals as at Olympia, and that their religion (gods, temples, sacrifices, oracles and festivals) bound them together. And the same 'culture' underpinned them all – from the Homeric poems to chariot-racing. They also had a clearly defined idea of who was 'Greek', as opposed to barbarian (or more correctly non-Greek speaking: the Persians, even though they possessed a highly sophisticated culture, were still 'barbarians' to the Greeks). Only Greeks could participate at panhellenic festivals, where victors were proclaimed by their name and polis – an essential qualification for being 'Greek' was to live in a polis. The location was unimportant: of the known victors at Olympia, 177 out of 736 came from outside mainland Greece. As the poet Poseidippos is recorded as saying (*F* 30): 'there is only one Hellas but there are many poleis.'

Aristotle considers that one of the factors that divided the Greeks from the rest of the world was their geographical location and climate, and both their climate and environment were superior to all others. In his view Europeans were spirited but lacked intelligence; Asiatics were intelligent but lacked spirit. 'The Greek race, however, lying between these regions, shares the characteristics of both. It is spirited and intelligent, and for this reason remains at liberty and attains the highest political development, while it is able to rule everyone else, if it can achieve political unity.' Greeks in other words combine both intelligence and spirit. As a result they can attain the highest degree of political development and are implicitly justified in enslaving and ruling others (Arist. *Politics* 1327b23–33: doc. 1.2). In fact, except in times of great crisis, Greek unity was difficult to achieve: while the Greeks saw themselves as part of a single 'people' and could unite when faced with an outside enemy, as when between the Persian Wars the Hellenic League was formed in 481 to combat Xerxes (Hdt. 7.145.1–2: doc. 11.24), most Greeks identified themselves as a member of their city-state rather than

5

Figure 1.2 The Parthenon on the Athenian acropolis. Photo © Nigel Fletcher-Jones, 2011. http://nigel-fletcherjones.artistwebsites.com.

as 'Greek' and had no compunction about going to war with and even exterminating other Greek cities or selling their inhabitants into slavery. In 510 Sybaris in southern Italy was destroyed by its neighbour Croton and never reinhabited; the Spartans razed Plataea in 427; in 416/15 Athens blockaded the island of Melos, killed all the adult males and sold the women and children into slavery (Thuc. 5.116.2–4: doc. 5.4); and Alexander the Great in 335 sacked Thebes, killing over 6000 Thebans and selling 30,000 as slaves (Plut. *Life of Alexander* 11.9–12.6: doc. 15.4).

What was a polis?

While the Mycenaean world had to some degree been a city-state culture, following the destruction of Mycenaean civilisation there was a gap of some three centuries before the emergence of the polis in the late Geometric period, c. 750. Inspired by a growth in both population and prosperity, during the Dark Age in Greece and in the archaic period which followed, small communities came together to create larger urban groups, each consisting of an area of agricultural land, centred around a single city which controlled the government of the territory. This process of the amalgamation of villages into a single city-state was known as synoikismos (synoecism), which means 'coming to live together' and was a process which created more complex and developed political and social structures to cope with the challenges which arise from large numbers of people living together. Athens' 'mythical' synoikismos under Theseus (which probably took place c. 700) is described by Thucydides (Thuc. 2.15.1–2: doc. 1.56), and the process was still taking place in parts of Greece in 471–470 when Elis synoecised into a single polis (Diod. Sic. *Library of History* 11.54.1: doc. 1.55). Most

6

Greek cities had a foundation myth: the Thebans traced their foundation back to Kadmos, and Athens to Erechtheus, in the same way as colonies traced their foundation back to an oikistes (founder), who was celebrated as a hero.

Audiences of the Homeric poems, arguably in their final form c. 700–650, would have recognised contemporary poleis in Odysseus' visit to Scheria on Phaeacia, the idealised kingdom of Alkinoos (Hom. *Odyssey* 6.1–12: doc. 2.5), and in the cities described on Achilles' shield (*Iliad* 18.490–540). Certainly the late eighth-century colonies founded in Sicily, such as Syracuse in 734 and Megara Hyblaia in 728 (the earliest definite examples), were poleis from the time of their foundation. Important elements in determining the site of a polis were the water-supply and defensive possibilities, such as a citadel or other high ground. The term polis originally seems to have meant a fortified settlement, and in the classical period the term is sometimes used instead of acropolis, or 'high city', the citadel which was probably the earliest inhabited part of a polis, as at Athens and Thebes. Most Greek cities have such an area of high ground within them, which sheltered the inhabitants in times of attack and was the site of important temples, like the Parthenon and temple of Athena Nike at Athens (Figs 1.2, 1.3). It was also where the state treasures were stored and most public inscriptions set up. The first usages of the term 'polis' occur c. 650, and 'polis' is used by Archilochos, referring to Paros' proposed settlement on Thasos (Steph. Byz. , Lexikon *s.v.* Thasos: doc. 2.25), by Tyrtaeus about Sparta (Tyrt. 4, 10: docs 6.6, 6.9), and in a law from Dreros on Crete concerning the tenure of the 'kosmos', a magistrate, which appears to be the earliest Greek law which has survived intact (Meiggs and Lewis 2: doc. 1.45).

Size and territory

The geo-political reality of the Greek world was favourable to the growth of poleis, with different regions clearly divided from each other by mountain ranges or by the sea. The size of a polis was often determined by its physical environment: that is, a community would often come to dominate the surrounding area as marked out by geographical features such as mountains, rivers, or the ocean, while the amount of territory which a polis possessed naturally determined the size to which the polis could expand. This was clearly the case when colonies were established: when settlers founded a colony on new territory, they were generally isolated within a native population and on limited territory, perhaps based within a fortified town. If they wished their settlement to expand they would need to deal in some way with the earlier inhabitants, either by conquest or negotiation. Similarly Greek poleis often went to war with their neighbours to gain territory for expansion and increased agricultural land, as Sparta did in Messenia.

Population and territory could vary quite widely between different poleis: the smallest may have had as few as 1000 or less inhabitants and a territory of anything from 10 to 25 km^2. A prosperous polis did not need to have a large amount of surrounding countryside: the island of Aegina, south of Athens, had only 85 km^2 but in the archaic period was extremely prosperous and a main trading centre for the Aegean as well as the first polis to coin metal currency (Aeginetan coinage was to be the standard currency in the sixth century; Fig. 1.1): it was also a long-standing enemy of Athens (doc. 11.23 [Arist.] *Ath. Pol.* 22.7). In contrast, one of the larger poleis, such as Athens, could have had a population of approximately 200,000 or more inhabitants and a territory of 2500 km^2. Any estimation of Athens' population is problematic, but it seems reasonable to suppose that in the fifth century Athens had some 30,000 citizens, about one-third of whom, with their families, would have lived in Athens itself, with the rest based in the Attic countryside. In addition as a large trading centre Athens attracted large numbers of foreigners wishing to exploit the trading and mercantile activities which Athens provided. These foreigners were known as metics, and there were about 10,000 of them in Athens in late fifth and early fourth-century Athens. In addition, the citizens and the foreigners would have owned slaves, and thus the population of Athens was many times greater than the number of citizens.

With small to medium-sized poleis the border of their territory would have been no more than a day's walk away from the city (a radius of no more than 30 km from the polis), and it would have been normal for citizens to live in the city and visit their farms on a regular basis, or live on the farm and visit the city regularly for markets and civic duties, such as taking part in the assembly. Even in Athens it was not unusual for landowners to live in Athens and visit their estates at intervals, while in the fourth century the farmers who lived in Attica would walk into Athens four times a month to vote and exercise their political rights: Attica was unusual in this respect in that, according to Thucydides (2.16.1), in 431 more than half the Athenians lived outside of the city. Athens was an unusually large polis and, as well as the city, consisted of several important urban areas, such as Eleusis, and various villages (demes) scattered throughout the territory of Attica like Acharnai, which may itself have had a population of nearly 10,000 (much larger than many other cities in Greece). Athens itself consisted of two parts. There was the city itself, clustered around the acropolis, and the Piraeus, the harbour of Athens, where many of the foreigners lived. City-states could also have a number of demes, or villages, throughout their territory as centres of population, though Athens was unusual in having as

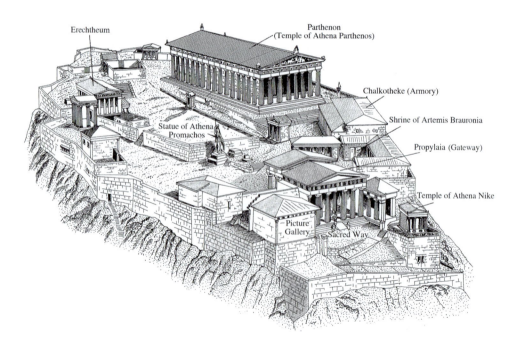

Figure 1.3 A reconstruction drawing of the Athenian acropolis. Many of the temples were constructed during the period when Perikles was very influential in the Athenian ekklesia. Drawing by Neslihan Yılmaz. Charles Gates, *Ancient Cities*, second edition (Routledge 2011), p. 255. Used with permission.

many as 140. The largest poleis in terms of territory, such as Sparta, which possessed more than 8000 km² after its capture of Messenia, or Syracuse in the time of Dionysios I with more than 10,000 km², would have had a number of dependent poleis in their territory: these would have been self-governing, but deferring to the dominant city in military and foreign policy matters. So a polis did not necessarily possess political independence (autonomia): the cities of the perioikoi in the Peloponnese were politically dependent upon Sparta, and the members of the Delian League were dominated by Athens as the Peloponnesian League was by Sparta. Poleis could even be dominated by foreign powers: the King's Peace of 386 made all Greeks accept Persian sovereignty of all Greek poleis in Asia Minor, though these cities still possessed their own internal government.

The army in city-states was made up of the citizens themselves and there was a very strong relationship between those who defended the polis and those who had political power. In Athens, both the citizens and the metics, the foreigners living in Athens, could be called upon to serve in a military capacity. The hoplites and the cavalry had to provide their own equipment, but would receive a small daily allowance while on service, as did their slaves. But in Athens the navy was the most important. The rowers of the navy were drawn from the least wealthy group in society, the thetes, and because the Athenian empire of the fifth century depended greatly upon the navy, the thetes became very politically prominent in the democracy of the fifth century.

Without existing records, one of the least problematic ways of calculating populations at any point in a city's history is from the number of troops that it was able to put into the field in a hoplite setting. A hoplite (heavy-armed infantryman; Fig. 1.4) had to be able to afford to provide his own armour (as opposed to a cavalryman who provided his own horse, and the lower property classes of the city who at Athens rowed in the fleet), and hoplites are generally estimated at 10 per cent of the population including women and children. Hence, from the fact that, in the crisis of the Second Persian War when every available man would have been under arms, Corinth fielded 5000 hoplites, it can be deduced that the city's total population was approximately 50,000. Similarly Megara's 3000 hoplites at the battle of Plataea

Figure 1.4 The 'Macmillan aryballos', named after its donor to the British Museum, is a Corinthian perfume bottle with the lid in the shape of a lion's head, found in Corinth, Greece. It is only 6.88 cm high, and the frieze of hoplites is a bare 2 cm high, but it depicts seventeen hoplites, each with armour, shield, spear and crested helmet. All of the shields are decorated with the favourite symbol of the hoplite, in some cases with birds of good omen. In the lower register are scenes of a hunt for hares and racing horses. This vase is also the work of the Chigi Painter, dating to about 640 BC, and belongs to the Protocorinthian phase of Corinthian pottery. British Museum GR 1889.4–18.1, London. Drawing by J. Etherington.

suggests a total population of 30,000. Plataea in contrast was a much smaller city with some 1000 inhabitants judging from the number of hoplites, and the smallest cities may have had as few as 300 adult male citizens. Athens' forces at the beginning of the Peloponnesian War included 300 triremes (warships), 1200 cavalry, and 13,000 hoplites and 16,000 others on garrison duty, though these included metics (Thuc. 2.13.3–5: doc. 1.10). Aristotle thought that the maximum size for a city was for it to have 10,000 citizens, so it could be self-sufficient, but the citizens would be able to know each other (Arist. *Politics* 1326a40–b24: doc. 1.3).

The government of the city-state

Aristotle's statement that 'man is a political animal' in fact should be translated as 'man is a polis animal' or 'man is a creature who lives in a polis' (Arist. *Politics* 1253a 2–3: doc. 1.1). In Aristotle's view, without the polis there could be no civilisation, and the essential factor was that every citizen (polites) played a role in the workings and government of his polis through exercising his political rights; a man without a city was as hopeless as an 'isolated piece in a board-game like draughts'. This immediately leads Aristotle into a discussion of what types of government can exist within a polis, and the city's system of government is the defining factor by which he distinguishes one polis from another. He considers that the options for government, the supreme authority in the polis, consist of either the rule of the one, the few, or the many. These alternatives mean that a city is governed by one man, and so is either a monarchy (an inherited kingship) or a tyranny (non-inherited one-man rule); by the few, and so government by an aristocracy (the rule of the best, or the nobles); or an oligarchy (the rule of the few or an elite); or by the many, or the people as a whole, which is constitutional government or 'politeia' (the ideal) or a democracy.

In any of these types of government, the demos, the people in assembly, was seen as having the right to speak and vote, and one of the reasons for the need for the city to be of a certain size was so that citizens could know each other and make sound decisions both in the appointment of magistrates and other political offices, and in lawsuits in the courts. The polis had to be large enough to be self-sufficient, but should not grow any larger than would allow citizens to form a 'face-to-face' society: 'a polis is of best size when it has a population large enough for a self-sufficient lifestyle but one that can be seen at a glance' (Arist. *Politics* 1326a40–b24: doc. 1.3). Thucydides, even in 411 after drastic losses (8.66.3), emphasised the large number of Athens' inhabitants and the fact that not all the citizens were known to each other. In Sicily, the tyrant Hieron's foundation of Aetna planned for 10,000 citizens (Diod. Sic. 11.49.1–2; Pind. *Pythian* 1: doc. 7.58).

Whatever the type of government, nearly every polis would have possessed an assembly, even those ruled by an oligarchy or tyranny. It would also have been normal for a polis to have had a council (boule), while there would also have been magistrates elected by the people or chosen by lot, and lawcourts (dikasteria). The constitutions of poleis could change over time, and often did, with warring factions (staseis) within a city fighting for political control. Most cities would have possessed opposing groups of citizens with different ideas about government, such as democrats against oligarchs, or two sets of oligarchs, and a large number of cities at some point in their history experienced civil war; Syracuse between 670 and 279 BC suffered no less than twenty-seven periods of civil unrest.

In the 320s Athens was seen as being under its eleventh constitution ([Arist.] *Ath. Pol.* 41.2: doc. 1.4), a democratic one at that point in time. However, in the past it had seen a monarchy, periods of tyranny between 561/0 and 510, and oligarchic rule in 411 and

404. The author of the *Athenaion Politeia* sees the Athenian constitution as having, with occasional exceptions, become increasingly democratic over time from the earliest period down to 322/1, with democracy defined as the people's ability to vote for decrees in the assembly and control the lawcourts. At Athens, which was ruled by a form of 'direct' democracy, every citizen was expected to participate by voting and speaking in the assembly, and by standing for office or for membership of the council, the boule, with political offices being rotated through the whole citizen body. Offices therefore were not dependent on property qualifications, and should not, except for the generalship (strategia), be held more than once by the same person. Furthermore, where possible office-holders should be paid to allow even the poorest citizen to play a political role. This is seen at Athens as 'liberty', along with liberty in practice, by which every citizen may live as he chooses: anything else would be slavery (Arist. *Politics* 1317a40–b4: doc. 1.5). Theophrastos, Aristotle's pupil and successor in the Academy, the school of philosophy founded by Plato, continues with a dissertation on the best ways in which to elect magistrates, and his work provides evidence for magistracies and election practices in states other than Athens, and the detail and sophistication of such systems even in the smallest poleis such as Karystos and Kythnos (Theophr. *Laws for Eresos*: doc. 1.6), and shows how some cities more than others valued experience and skill in those they elected to office.

Athens: 'the violet-crowned city'

The features and amenities of Greek poleis

In the case of most poleis, with the notable exception of Sparta, fortifications were one of the most important amenities. Even if many of the citizens lived outside the walls, as did a large number of the Athenians, they could retreat behind these walls when their city was under attack: Attica, though a single city, was unusual in having as many as 140 demes, or villages, with more than half of the citizens living outside the walls. Even so, in the Peloponnesian War, many of these countrymen poured into the city, the consequent over-crowding being one of the causes of the devastating plague of 429 (Thuc. 2.14.1–2: doc. 13.5). A water-supply was also essential, and well-houses or fountain-houses formed a particular type of monumental architecture in cities such as Athens, Corinth and Megara (Paus. *Description of Greece* 1.40.1: doc. 7.20; Figs 7.2, 9.4). If the city had an acropolis, or citadel, this might be fortified separately and contain the most important temples and treasury, as at Athens and Corinth.

A polis contained the city's political institutions and administration, cult areas, defence, education and entertainment, as well as facilities such as a harbour and a market-place (agora), the hub of the city where citizens would meet to chat and shop, and where they gossiped and exchanged news and views before attending meetings of the political assembly. Consequently, a polis included not only a place for the assembly to meet, which might be the agora or theatre (in Athens this was the role of the Pnyx, a small hill close to the acropolis where the assembly met), but a chamber where the council could meet (the bouleuterion). There was also need for offices for magistrates and spaces to be used for court proceedings. Another essential feature was the prytaneion, where the prytaneis, or officials responsible for executive duties at any particular time, could meet and dine, and where ambassadors to the city could be entertained. It was here that the eternal flame burned on an altar to Hestia, goddess of the hearth, from which founders of colonies took fire to light in the prytaneion of the colony they were establishing (*Etymologicum Magnum* 694.28–31: doc. 2.4). Public heroes and victors at the panhellenic games also dined here at no expense (Xen. Kol. *F* 2: doc. 1.78).

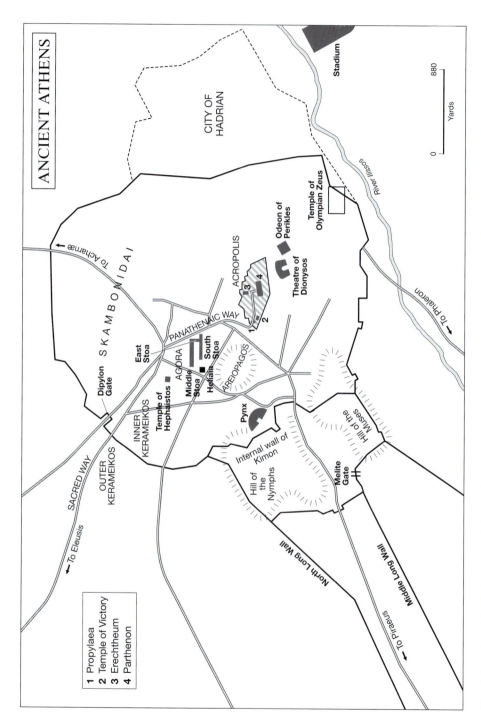

ANCIENT ATHENS

1 Propylaea
2 Temple of Victory
3 Erechtheum
4 Parthenon

To Acharnae

SKAMBONIDAI

Dipylon
Gate

SACRED WAY

To Eleusis

OUTER
KERAMEIKOS

INNER
KERAMEIKOS

Temple of
Hephaistos

East
Stoa

AGORA

Middle
Stoa

South
Stoa

Heliaia

PANATHENAIC WAY

AREIOPAGOS

Pynx

Internal wall of
Kimon

Hill of
the
Nymphs

Hill of the
Muses

Melite
Gate

North Long Wall

Middle Long Wall

To Piraeus

ACROPOLIS

3

4

2

1

Odeon of
Perikles

Theatre of
Dionysos

Temple of
Olympian Zeus

CITY OF
HADRIAN

Stadium

River Ilissos

To Phaleron

0   880

Yards

Map 1.2 Ancient Athens. Based on M. Grant, *The Routledge Atlas of Classical History*, fifth edition, Routledge, 1994, p. 26.

Cities such as Athens contained costly buildings and temples which deliberately advertised Athens' place at the head of the Delian League. At the same time governments, especially in Athens, provided facilities for the use of all citizens, so that even the poorest could enjoy not just the use of temples and shrines, but religious participation in sacrifices and festivals, where the cost was born by the city, and amenities such as gymnasia, wrestling-schools (palaistrai) and public baths ([Xen.] *Constitution of the Athenians* 2.9–10: doc. 1.8). Athens, from c. 500 BC, also contained a theatre sacred to Dionysos on the south slope of the acropolis where dramatic contests in honour of the god were performed twice a year at the expense of the richer citizens: the five-day City Dionysia in March and the shorter Lenaia in January.

The Athenians were exceptionally proud of their city and the comic poet Aristophanes laughs at them for their willingness to be flattered by envoys quoting Pindar's famous description of Athens as 'violet-crowned and famed in song' (Pind. *F* 64), and Thucydides admits that, compared to Sparta, Athens in the future would appear from its visible remains to be twice as powerful as it was in reality (Thuc. 1.10.2: doc. 1.7). In the second half of the fifth century Athens, rich and imperialistic, was certainly the most splendid of all Greek cities, even

Figure 1.5 Pheidias' cult statue of Athena (Doc. 1.12) no longer survives, but is described in the ancient sources and was reproduced in several smaller copies. This Roman reproduction in Pentelic marble is 105 cm high: Pheidias' original, of gold and ivory (chryselephantine), stood 12 m high. National Archaeological Museum, Athens, inv. No. 129. Photo © Hellenic Ministry of Culture and Tourism / Archaeological Receipts Fund.

if rivalled by some of the Greek colonies in Sicily and southern Italy, such as Syracuse and Akragas. Under Perikles a building programme of some size was put into place, to express Athens' success and imperial status, and in 431 prior to the Peloponnesian War Thucydides records Perikles informing the Athenians of their available resources: 600 hundred talents a year as tribute from their allies, a reserve of 6000 talents on the acropolis, and countless precious dedications in their temples, worth some 500 talents (Thuc. 2.13.3–5: doc. 1.10). The gold on the statue of Athena in the Parthenon alone weighed 40 talents and the purchase of materials such as gold and ivory for the cult statue, which may have cost between 700 and 1000 talents, was regularly itemised (*IG* I^3 458a: doc. 1.12; Fig. 1.5). Inventories of the Parthenon's treasures were made every four years by the treasurers involved to guard against embezzlement, with every item clearly identified and where possible weighed: these show the nature of dedications, including beds, bread-baskets, foot-stools and musical instruments, which were thought appropriate offerings to the goddess Athena and were an important part of the city's resources (*IG* I^3 351: doc. 1.11). Payments for improving Athens' water supply were a concern of the assembly (*IG* I^3 49: doc. 1.14) and even olive trees, sacred to Athena with olive oil one of Athens' more important exports, were protected by law: no more than two olive trees could be dug up per year, except for specific religious usages, or the malefactor would be fined 200 drachmas per tree (Dem. 43 *Against Makartatos* 71: doc. 1.15; Fig. 1.10).

The workings of Athenian democracy

Athens was unusual even among Greek democracies in that the assembly and the lawcourts were seen as the two most important institutions in Athens' democratic constitution. All political decisions were made and decrees passed in the assembly after the agenda had first been considered in the council, and all citizens over 18 years of age were voting members of the assembly in the fifth century (the age limit was raised to 20 years in the fourth). Even political institutions such as the assembly reflected the religious beliefs which underpinned all aspects of the polis, and assembly meetings began with a prayer, curse and sacrifice demonstrating the degree to which religion was a concern to the whole community. Popular participation was the keynote of Athenian democracy and every citizen was expected to play a part in regularly attending the assembly, speaking when appropriate, and voting. As a result arrangements had to be in place so that even the poorest citizens had the time to exercise their political rights. Citizens were also expected to take a turn in holding political office, as in becoming a member of the council. A majority of Athenian citizens did serve on the council at least once in their lives, so it was a representative body; members could only serve twice and had to be at least thirty years of age. Anyone who wished would have been able to gain a position, even the a-political Socrates who was a member of the boule in 406, being the only prytanis (executive member of the boule) who voted against the unconstitutional proposal to acquit or condemn all six generals from the battle of Arginousai by a single vote (Xen. *Hellenika* 1.7.9–15: doc. 1.20).

Citizen participation

Perikles, in his Funeral Oration for the first Athenian casualties of the Peloponnesian War in 431, specifically addresses Athens' democratic ideals, which ensured that nearly every citizen took a part in running the state. All citizens were in a state of total equality, whatever their personal circumstances: in fact he expected everyone to participate in politics, articulating clearly that poverty in itself was nothing to be ashamed of and no deterrent for office. Athens was free and independent through the efforts of successive generations of citizens and now self-sufficient, he tells his audience, both in war and in peace. It was Athens' political institutions and way of life that made it so great and, despite Sparta's military ethos, the dead whom he is praising showed no less courage than did the Spartans in laying down their lives for their country. Perikles praises Athens, in implicit contrast to Sparta, for its past military achievements, and for the uniqueness of its constitution, in as much as it is run by the majority of its citizens, with positions decided on merit and with no-one being prevented by poverty or obscurity from taking part in public life:

> [E]ven those primarily concerned with their own business are not deficient in their knowledge of the city's affairs; indeed, we are unique in considering the man who takes no part in the affairs of the city not as one who minds his own business, but as one who is totally useless . . .
>
> (Thuc. 2.37.1–43.2: doc. 1.17)

Significantly the term for a man who took no part in the affairs of the city, or a 'private person' was 'idiotes', a 'private' citizen, from which modern European languages derive the word 'idiot'.

The assembly and council

The assembly (ekklesia) met regularly, once a month in the fifth century and four times a month in the fourth century (*Ath. Pol.* 43.3), and approximately 6000 citizens, the quorum needed for an ostracism (docs 10.11–12), appear to have regularly attended. The Pnyx, just outside the city where assemblies took place, would have been able to hold 6000 seated people (they sat on the ground or on cushions), and there were wooden seats for the 500 councillors. Less than 5000 citizens were accustomed to attend during the Peloponnesian War (Thuc. 8.72.1), but considering the number of citizens on military service or rowing in the navy, this still seems a remarkable rate of attendance. Many of these citizens would have needed compensation for losing a day's income from their business or trade while at the meeting of the assembly, and there was apparently even in the first phase of the Peloponnesian War (431–421) some difficulty in getting citizens into the assembly area on time because they were too busy gossiping: a vermilion-painted rope was used by the public slaves (the Scythian archers, Fig. 1.6) to pull in late-comers, the mark on their clothes serving as a comment on their tardiness (Ar. *Acharnians* 17–39: doc. 1.18). To encourage attendance and ensure that a quorum was reached for each meeting, pay for attending meetings was introduced in 403: only the first 6000 to arrive were paid. Initially this was one obol a day, or a sixth of a standard day's wage, but this clearly was not enough as it soon had to be raised to two obols and then three, at a cost of some 3000 drachmas, or half a talent, per assembly meeting. In the later fourth century this pay had risen to a drachma for an ordinary meeting and nine obols for a kyria (sovereign) assembly ([Arist.] *Ath. Pol.* 41.2–3: doc. 1.24).

From 508 BC the council (boule) had 500 members, fifty from each of the ten tribes, with each tribe presiding for one-tenth of the year: the members of a tribe in their time of executive government were known as prytaneis, and each tenth of the year a 'prytany', and the meeting place of these executive officers was the prytaneion, or town hall. For each day one of the prytaneis, known as the epistates, was chosen by lot to preside over that day's business

Figure 1.6 A Scythian archer used at Athens for policing duties, mainly in the ekklesia (docs 1.11, 1.18). Note the tight-fitting long sleeved shirt and trousers, as well as the distinctive hat; his left hand rests on his quiver. A red-figure amphora of about 510–500 BC, with a height of 24.4 cms and a diameter of 28.3 cms, by the Euphronios Painter. Louvre, Paris, G106. Drawing by J. Etherington.

and over the assembly if it was meeting on that day. The prytaneis had to give written notice of the agenda for each meeting of the council and written notice of assembly meetings. During each prytany in the fourth century there were four assembly meetings (and so forty in total for a year), one of which was kyria (sovereign), or the most important of the four. At this there were standard items brought forward: a vote as to whether the magistrates appeared to be performing their duties in an appropriate manner, and discussion on the food supply and defence of the city. At this meeting it was also customary to bring impeachments and ensure that the inventories of confiscated properties and claims to estates and heiresses be read out for interested parties to take note of. At the second assembly meeting of the month anyone who wished could address the assembly, while the other two meetings dealt with any remaining business, including compulsory discussions of sacred matters such as embassies ([Arist.] *Ath. Pol.* 43.1–6: doc. 1.16). Meetings began early in the morning with religious preliminaries such as a prayer and sacrifice, and were generally over by midday: in cases of disturbance the archers, public slaves, were there to keep order. Voting was generally by show of hands, and speakers wore a wreath, as did the councillors as a badge of office, demonstrating the religious significance of their role in participating in the business of the city.

The standard procedure at assembly meetings was that speakers would be called for by a herald who issued a general invitation, 'Who would like to speak?' (Aeschin. 1 *Against Timarchos* 26–32: doc. 1.42), with older citizens being given the chance to speak first. Speeches would be made for or against a particular motion, which would then be voted upon by a show of hands; where a particular number of votes was required black and white pebbles would be tossed into urns. The assembly could be critical and boo or jeer at a speaker for his inexperience, as they did with Demosthenes' initial attempts at oratory, or because they disagreed with his views (Plut. *Life of Demosthenes* 6.1–5: doc. 14.43). Despite clear rules of process assembly procedures could be derailed. Following heavy casualties after the naval victory at Arginousai in 406, when the generals were unable to rescue sailors who had been shipwrecked, the council had agreed that an unconstitutional motion be put to the assembly that all six generals who had returned to Athens should be acquitted or condemned en bloc, and the decision should be reached not by a show of hands but by the use of voting urns: the majority in the assembly, swayed by mass anger, insisted that this motion be approved, and all six generals were condemned to death: the only dissenter out of the fifty prytaneis, who refused to put the motion to the vote, was Socrates, at this time a member of the council. The condemned included Perikles' son by Aspasia, and the citizens later regretted their actions, but it was too late. The proposers of this illegal motion were then condemned in their own turn when the assembly reflected on its action (Xen. *Hellenika* 1.7.9–15: doc. 1.20).

Officials in Athens

In Athens, as a direct (not a representative) democracy, it was considered that any citizen was capable of holding office, with the exception of generals, financial officials and supervisors of the water supply, as these were considered to need experience or a skill-base. As a result these were elected by a show of hands in the assembly. Many officials, too, were supported by public slaves who were skilled in specific duties, such as the drafters of inscriptions. But the rest of each year's officials, however, were chosen by lot, in the same way as the five hundred councillors for each year, with fifty councillors selected in this way from each tribe from those who were nominated. As Aristotle states: one principle of liberty is that everyone is governed and governs in turn (Arist. *Politics* 1317a40–b4: doc. 1.5).

One of the consequences of having citizens undertaking full-time civic duties was of course the need for them to be paid for their time. Pay for members of the council, the bouleutai, was introduced possibly in the 450s and was certainly in place by 412/11; in the fourth century the payment was 5 obols a day, with an extra obol for the food for the prytaneis who dined in the prytaneion. The nine archons each received four obols a day for food and had to keep a herald and flautist ([Arist.] *Ath. Pol.* 41.2–3, 62.2: doc. 1.24). The *Athenaion Politeia* also estimates that no less than 20,000 people were maintained every year when Athens was at the head of the Delian League in the fifth century. This is of course an exaggeration because it includes the 6000 jurors who only served intermittently and were not paid a full wage even when they did serve on a jury, and those on military service, but it does itemise the 500 councillors, guards of the acropolis and dockyards, jailers and 1400 officials at home and abroad, which may be a fairly realistic estimate ([Arist.] *Ath. Pol.* 24.3: doc. 1.23). Certainly, immediately prior to the revolution of 411 participation in public affairs was supposedly restricted to not more than 5000 citizens (Thuc. 8.65.3). However, the passage does outline the essential quality of the Athenian system, payment to citizens for performing their citizen duties, and there were numerous officials in the fourth century appointed to oversee the details of the smooth running of the city: these included ten repairers of shrines, ten city-controllers to supervise the hiring out of flute-girls and the cleanliness of the city (including the removal of dead bodies, dumping of excrement, and overflowing pipes), ten market-controllers, ten measure-controllers, 35 grain-guardians and ten harbour-inspectors, all of whom oversaw merchandise, weights and measures, prices and trading in the market generally ([Arist.] *Ath. Pol.* 50.1–51.4: doc. 1.25).

The dikasteria (lawcourts)

One of the reasons for the importance of the lawcourts in a democracy was because the qualifications of officials could be challenged before they entered office, through the dokimasia (examination), while all officials had also to submit to examination (euthyna) at the end of their term. As a result the courts had jurisdiction over both incoming and outgoing magistrates, in this way monitoring any possible misconduct, and after c. 415 those who had proposed legislation in the assembly which was considered unconstitutional or contrary to existing legislation could be prosecuted in the courts through a graphe paranomon (a legal action against the proposer of a decree which was contrary to existing legislation): the penalty was a fine which could be trivial, or so great as to lead to loss of citizenship. To the orator Isocrates, the euthyna, or auditing of officials' accounts in the lawcourts, when the people could review the actions of magistrates during their year of office and take action against those that had performed badly, was the essence of democracy: 'how could anyone discover a democracy with more stability or more justice than this one – which put the most competent men in charge of its government, but gave the people absolute power over them?' (Isoc. 7 *Areiopagitikos* 26–7: doc. 1.19). Such audits were often the chance for political rivals to take revenge on each other, but one case in which a miscarriage of justice did take place occurred when the hellenotamiai, who administered the funds of the Delian League, were accused of embezzlement: all were executed but one, who was reprieved when it was discovered what had actually happened to the funds: all the others had already been executed, though innocent (Antiph. 5 *On the Murder of Herodes* 69–71: doc. 1.21). Aeschines in 330 makes clear that every official had to undergo this audit, whether political, military or religious – even the priests and priestesses in charge of the Eleusinian Mysteries. Even trierarchs, wealthy Athenians who had undertaken to cover the expenses of a trireme for a year, had to undergo the euthyna, though the funds they were handling were their own. Members of the council and of the Areiopagos, the council of ex-archons, had to submit to audit, and various restrictions were in place to make sure that this happened. No one was allowed to leave the country, or make a dedication or a will, before the audit took place, just in case they might be found to be a defaulter (Aeschin. 3 *Against Ktesiphon* 17–21: doc. 1.22).

Six thousand Athenian citizens, 600 from each of the ten tribes, served as jurors in classical Athens. Each of the jurors was assigned by lot to one of the ten courts and juries were chosen by lot from those that turned up on the day: anyone over the age of 30 could serve, though it appears that many jurors were older citizens who engaged in jury-service for additional

Figure 1.7 An Athenian bronze pinakion: a juror's identification ticket, with the name of a juror, Demophanes, son of Phili . . . (the rest of the name is lost), of the deme Kephisia. It is from the fourth century BC and has a length of 10 cm. Agora Museum B822, Athens. Drawing by J. Etherington.

support; each received an identification ticket (Fig. 1.7). Public cases needed a minimum of 501 jurors, private suits a minimum of 201, though it was not uncommon for 401 to be called if a large amount of property was in dispute, while in cases of a graphe paranomon or critical cases like the mutilation of the hermai all 6000 jurors might be summoned for the one case. Jurors would not have received a living wage, not least because the courts did not sit every day and selection on a particular day was a matter of chance; in addition jury pay, instituted by Perikles, was initially two obols a day, raised to three (half a day's pay for a craftsman) in 425 or 424. This, however, would have been a useful addition to a family's income, and must have been a considerable burden on the state. Aristophanes' estimate of 150 talents a year is excessive, as it imagines every juror sitting for 300 days a year, though juries did not meet on assembly or festival days (Ar. *Wasps* 655–64: doc. 1.28). However, the courts were a great expense to the city and at least at one point in the fourth century had to be suspended for financial reasons. Jurors and their attitudes are frequently satirised by Aristophanes: Philokleon ('Kleon-lover'), an old man obsessed with the part he plays on a jury, is passionately addicted to condemning everyone and has to have a 'court' set up at home to keep him away from the dikasteria. One of the family dogs is accusing of stealing a cheese: the proposed penalty if the case is proved is a figwood dog collar (Ar. *Wasps* 836–62, 894–7: doc. 1.26).

The litigants themselves presented their cases to the court, and the jurors could only vote yes or no after hearing the speeches for both sides. If found guilty, both prosecutor and defendant would then suggest a penalty and the jurors would vote between those. A famous example is the trial of Socrates for introducing new divinities and refusing to believe in the gods of the city; the prosecution asked for the death penalty, while Socrates proposed that he be given public maintenance by the state, which so annoyed the jurors that even though his friends persuaded him to change this to a fine, he was condemned to execution (Pl. *Apology* 36b–e: doc. 3.86). For private suits only the victim or members of his family could bring a case: for public suits any citizen was entitled to initiate a prosecution. While it was possible to employ a speechwriter, the litigants had to appear and present their case in person and none of the participants had any legal training. The emphasis once again was that any citizen had the right both to propose a law and to bring a suit against anyone who appeared to be acting against the interests of the Athenian people. As the people formed the assembly and staffed the courts there was no higher power or court of appeal.

While the dramatisations of Aristophanes may seem to trivialise court proceedings, the courts, and the people as an integral part of the system, had a tremendous amount of power and nearly all prominent Athenians faced trial in the courts and some were condemned over mishandling of their offices: Miltiades was fined fifty talents and died in prison of gangrene, Aristeides, Themistokles and Kimon were ostracised, and Ephialtes was assassinated. Perikles was to die of the plague in 429, but he and his associates had also faced prosecution and fines, and on one occasion, in 430, Perikles was deposed from the strategia and fined, though later reelected: political life in Athens was not a sinecure.

In 416/15, when the graphe paranomon (indictment against measures contrary to law) was introduced as a result of the mutilation of the hermai, anything proposed to or passed by the assembly could be formally reviewed in a court of law. From 355 all such questions were decided in the lawcourts. If an insufficient number of votes was received by one party the penalty could be atimia: loss of citizen rights. This was the verdict in the legal battle between Demosthenes and Aeschines 'On the Crown' / 'Against Ktesiphon' in 333 (Dem. 18 *On the Crown* 60–9: doc. 14.46), the only case for which we have the speeches of both sides recorded. As a result of this trial Aeschines was forced to go into exile at Rhodes.

Rich and poor in Athens

One of the principles of Athenian democracy was that the wealthy should finance some of the city's expenses, especially those for civic activities such as theatrical performances and festivals. It is this that the 'Old Oligarch' is complaining of when he states that the rich have to pay for the pleasures of the poor ([Xen.] *Constitution of the Athenians* 2.9–10: doc. 1.8; Fig. 1.8). Obviously some citizens, like Nikias who rented out 1000 slaves to work in the silver mines, were extremely wealthy, but on the whole even the richest of the property classes defined by Solon, the pentakosiomedimnoi or 500-bushel-men, needed only 75–145 acres of grain-growing land to qualify. One of the most ostentatious of the Athenians, Alkibiades, apparently paid 70 minas for a beautiful dog and cut off its tail to give the Athenians something to talk about, while he also entered seven chariots for the same race at the Olympic festival in 416, winning three places (Plut. *Life of Alkibiades* 11.1–12.1: doc. 3.27). After the mutilation of the hermai, in which he was suspected of involvement, his property was sold, including bedroom furniture which contained 12 Milesian-made couches (*IG* I³ 421h: doc. 1.32). Demosthenes criticises the politicians of the later fourth century for their ostentation and extravagance in private, contrasting these with the great public figures of the fifth, like Themistokles and Miltiades, whose houses were the same size as everyone else's, and Athens' revenues were directed into its splendid buildings and the treasury so that Athens could afford to make war: in his own time, he implies, politicians are so corrupt that 'some of them have constructed houses that are more splendid than many public buildings, and some have acquired more land than all of you in this court possess between you' (Dem. 23 *Against Aristokrates* 206–9: doc. 1.35). This need not be taken literally but clearly the litigant believes that his statements will find favour with a jury, and Athens in the fourth century did have problems in financing military campaigns and the Athenians were not erecting buildings of such magnitude and importance as the great temples of Perikles' time.

The majority of Athenians were clearly not wealthy, and some of them were so poor that they could not afford a slave and found it hard to make a living. Disabled persons were given a small pension of an obol a day by the council if they could show that they were unable to earn a living: late in the fourth century eligibility for public support was restricted to those with property less than 300 drachmas (3 minas). One such tradesman asserts in court that he is so poor that he is unable even to have a slave to help him, that he maintained his mother

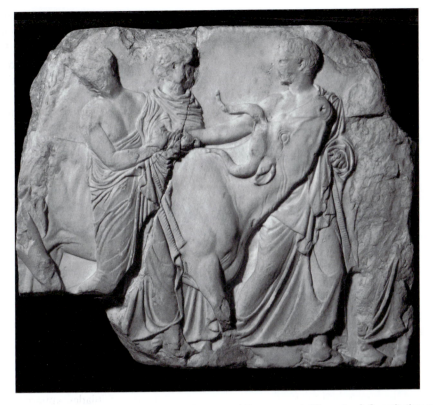

Figure 1.8 'The city sacrifices numerous victims at public expense': [Xenophon] *Constitution of the Athenians* 2.10 (doc. 1.8). This marble relief from the Parthenon Frieze shows one of the many sacrificial victims at the annual festival of the Panathenaia: the meat would be distributed amongst all the citizens, making a welcome addition to their diets. Parthenon Frieze, slab XLIV (129–31) from the south frieze, 100 cm high. British Museum 1816,0610.86 (Parthenon Frieze slab XLIV), London. Image © The Trustees of the British Museum.

until two years earlier and as yet has no children, and requests that his pension be continued (Lys. 24 *On the Refusal of a Grant to an Invalid* 6: doc. 1.33). Another citizen is characterised as a 'penny-pincher' in Theophrastos' *Characters*. He owns a slave, but if this unfortunate breaks a pot or a plate the cost is taken out of his rations, and he forbids his wife to lend even such small items as salt, a lamp-wick, herbs or cakes for sacrifice (Theophr. *Characters* 10: doc. 1.34). While this character is obviously the stereotype of a confirmed miser, it does suggest that many citizens lived frugally and on the margins of a subsistence income.

Liturgies

One way in which redistribution of wealth took place was through the process of liturgies, by which richer individuals financed certain state activities, often in this way buying gratitude from the people and thus political influence. The threshold for liturgy service was three talents, and in the fourth century there were more than 97 annual liturgical appointments, and over 118 in a Great Panathenaic year, and this did not include some 300 trierarchs. The defendant in Lysias 21 (*On a Charge of Taking Bribes* 1–5: doc. 1.30), who appears to have been charged with corruption, lists a number of liturgies that he performed over the last ten years, which he claims had cost him ten talents, four times as much as he needed to have paid. These included paying for successful dramatic choruses, Pyrrhic dances (dances in armour) and choruses at the Great and Lesser Panathenaia, games, sacred embassies and processions of maidens such as the arrhephoria (cf. Paus. *Description of Greece* 1.27.3: doc. 3.62). In addition he had contributed to special taxes, such as the eisphora, a levy imposed on the wealthy from time to time to meet special military costs, and on trierarchies. A trierarch was expected to outfit and maintain a trireme for a year, including the pay of the 170 rowers, and had to command the ship himself. The cost, approximating to a talent (6000 drachmas), was considerable, and in the fourth century was often shared between two people, as in the list of fourth-century records of the shipyard superintendents at the Piraeus (*IG* II² 1609 lines 83–111: doc. 1.31), where each item of equipment, such as timbers for making oars that came with the ship was recorded. While some trierarchs reused existing equipment many of them would equip their ship from scratch, and there was intense competition to be the captain of the first or best equipped trireme of the year.

Citizenship

Citizenship was the basis of the membership of every Greek polis. Whether the government was a tyranny, oligarchy or democracy, the main duty of a citizen was to play a part in the politics and government of his polis, as in attending the assembly and voting on issues brought forward there and being elected to office, and the obligation to defend his polis against outside attack. This could be dependent upon the citizen's property qualification, and in Athens the hoplite had to afford his own armour and the hippeus (cavalryman) provided his own horse, while the poorer citizens, the thetes, rowed in the navy. While only adult males were citizens per se with political rights, females and underage children had legal rights such as inheritance, and these were guarded for them by their male relatives. Citizens were the land-holders (non-citizens were not permitted to own land), and the city (polis) was made up of hundreds or thousands of landowners, each of whom was a citizen (polites), with politeia meaning both citizenship and constitution: the two were synonymous. Whatever the type of government in place, all citizens had a share in the polis and its governance, the size of the polis allowing for such individual participation, which, in its most extreme forms, was either a radical democracy or a tyranny.

Male citizens would generally have been in the minority in any Greek polis, compared to women, metics and slaves, but it was this minority that mattered. In all poleis, including of course Athens and Sparta, citizenship was a matter of descent, whether from one or both parents, and this was rigidly monitored so that non-citizens should not share in the rights and duties which belonged only to citizens. Citizenship within a polis granted the right to take part in political affairs and the obligation to bear arms on the city's behalf and there were a range of political, judicial and social rights which were seen as the special prerogative of the original inhabitants of the polis. Athenian citizens, for example, described themselves as autochthonous: they had sprung from the very soil itself and had always lived in Attica. It was their state and they did not want to share decision making with outsiders. This became especially important with the coming of Athenian democracy, when citizens were entitled to various financial payments, such as jury pay and pay for serving on the boule, while officials received state pay. There was even some rudimentary social welfare, with disabled citizens receiving a small allowance. As a result of these privileges, and the desire to restrict the citizen body to pure Athenians, ability to prove citizenship was vital (cf. Dem. 57 *Against Euboulides* 30–1, 33–5, 40–2: doc. 5.63).

Phylai and gene

In every polis, there were smaller groups to which citizens would belong, which could be territorial, as in deme membership, or could be based on kinship groups, and citizenship could depend not only on the possession of citizen parents, but on membership of tribes and phratries, which were based on kinship relationships. Most cities were composed of several tribes (phylai), which were in turn composed of phratries, brotherhoods based on ancestry and social and religious ties, and finally gene (singular: genos), or extended families. These gene are mainly seen as politically active in the case of noble families, such as the Philaidai, the family of Miltiades the Elder, and the Alkmeonidai, the family of Kleisthenes (Tables 9.2, 10.1). Various groups of Greeks had different tribes to which their members belonged and membership of a tribe was essential in claiming citizenship. The traditional Ionian tribes were the Geleontes, the Argadeis, the Hopletes and the Agikoreis as in pre-Kleisthenic Attica; the Dorian tribes were the Hylleis, the Pamphyloi and the Dymanes, as attested at Sparta and Sikyon and on Crete (Hdt. 5.68.1: docs 7.5, 10.1). After Kleisthenes reformed the four Attic tribes into ten, these became the units for army enrolment, election for magistracies or the council, jury service and festival competitions. There were also strong religious obligations and each tribe had its own officials and shrines, while some religious duties even in the late fifth century remained linked to the old Ionian tribes: these included sacrifices of two unblemished oxen to Zeus Phratrios and Athena Phratria by the Geleontes, obviously in connection with phratry membership within the tribe (Sokolowski 10: doc. 3.12).

Phratry membership

Before Kleisthenes' reforms every citizen belonged to a phratry, which was the criterion for citizenship. Following his reforms in 508/7 citizenship depended on membership of a deme, but nevertheless, in the fifth century it is still reasonable to assume that all or most citizens belonged to a phratry as well as a deme, as grants of citizenship could include the right to choose one's own phratry, while in cases where citizenship was in dispute defendants regularly demonstrate their membership of a phratry as well as a deme (cf. [Arist.] *Ath. Pol.* 21.1–6: doc. 10.7; cf. 10.16). Although each citizen had to be able to demonstrate descent from citizen parents, there were mechanisms by which outsiders could be naturalised, that is granted citizenship, in very specific cases. After Plataea was destroyed by Sparta in 427, the Athenian assembly passed a decree conferring citizenship on the Plataeans, with reservations: the Plataeans were not to be eligible for the archonships or family-based priesthoods, but would be distributed among the Athenian demes and tribes ([Dem.] 59 *Against Neaira* 104: doc. 1.37). The right of citizenship could also be granted to individual non-citizens: when Perikles' legitimate sons died, his son by the metic Aspasia (who came from the city of Miletos) was granted citizenship as a special exemption from his own law. For individuals who had done great service to the Athenian people, enrolment in a phratry accompanied the grant of citizenship: when Thrasyboulos of Kalydon was honoured in 409 for his part in Phrynichos' assassination, the assembly voted that he should be granted citizenship and enrolled in the tribe and phratry of his choice (*IG* I³ 102: doc. 13.30). Similarly the metics who supported him in 403 were granted citizenship by a decree of the assembly and assigned to the ten tribes (*IG* II^2 10: doc. 5.43).

Inscriptional evidence on the phratries primarily concerns eligibility for membership, and young boys were presented annually for enrolment in their phratry at the Apatouria. The three days of ceremonies consisted of communal feasting, sacrifices to Zeus and Athena of the phratry (Zeus Phratrios and Athena Phratria), and the admission of the youths to the phratry accompanied by ritual sacrifices, including the dedication of a lock of hair, symbolising the passage from childhood to adulthood. As with membership of a deme, the phratry members, under the supervision of the president, or phratriarch, and a priest, voted on the eligibility of the boys for membership. If someone had been fraudently brought forward as a candidate for admission, the person who attempted to have him enrolled was fined 100 drachmas. In one such phratry, that of the Dekeleians, in order to ensure that only those eligible were admitted, each child's name, together with his father's name and deme, and his mother's father's name and deme, were to be recorded and publicly displayed (*IG* II^2 1237: doc. 1.40). In Drakon's law on involuntary homicide, in the absence of closer family members it is at the discretion of the phratry members of the victim that the offender is to be admitted back into the country (*IG* I^3 104: doc. 8.3). There is also evidence for phratries in Dorian states such as Cyrene, in Naples in Italy, founded by the Chalkidians, Pithekoussaians and Athenians, and at Elis, where membership of a phratry appears to have been an important factor in the possession of citizen rights (Buck no. 61: doc. 1.50). Aristotle considers an increase in the number of phratries, as at Cyrene, as a feature of extreme democracy, as more people can be involved and old associations broken down (Arist. *Politics* 1319b19–27: doc. 10.16).

Hetaireiai

Many aristocratic Athenians would also have belonged to clubs, hetaireiai, some of which were political, some purely social; these are also found elsewhere in Greece, as on Mytilene and at Cyrene (Meiggs and Lewis 5: doc. 2.28). The hetaireiai could be an important asset in acquiring power: Kylon, when attempting to become tyrant of Athens, gathered together a hetaireia of his own age to support him (Hdt. 5.71.1–2: doc. 7.21), while on Lesbos Alcaeus called on his hetaireia, relatives and friends, to celebrate on Pittakos' death (Alc. 332: doc. 7.27). Membership of a hetaireia appears to imply both common dining and united military action, and when Kleisthenes in Athens was losing out in struggle against Isagoras to attract the hetaireiai in his bid for political power, he turned to the people instead and brought them into his own hetaireia (Hdt. 5.65.5–67.1: doc. 10.1). The support of a hetaireia was still important when Perikles was in competition with Thucydides, son of Milesias, as to which of the two should be ostracised and Perikles was the victor because he was able to defeat the hetaireia formed against him (Plut. *Perikles* 14.1–3: doc. 12.27), and the *Athenaion Politeia* implies that membership of a hetaireia was generally confined to aristocrats, who were in favour of oligarchy after Athens' defeat by Sparta in 404, while non-members wanted democracy ([Arist.] *Ath. Pol.* 34.2–35.4: doc. 13.40).

Deme membership

In the fifth century boys were registered as deme members after their eighteenth birthday, and in the fourth century this took place at 20 years, after two years of military service. At this point an Athenian citizen could attend the assembly, and stand for election as a magistrate and serve as a juror when over 30. Prior to 451/0 it was only necessary to prove that one's father was an Athenian citizen ([Arist.] *Ath. Pol.* 26.4: doc. 1.36): following Perikles' citizenship law a potential citizen had to be able to prove that both his parents were of citizen birth. This may have been because Athenians, especially the poorer ones, were finding it difficult to find husbands for their daughters, with Athenians marrying metics or other foreigners, but also because it was perceived that citizenship was a privilege as well as a right, with many advantages both financial and social, which should not be diluted by non-Athenians. Henceforth penalties were severe for those who attempted to foist a non-citizen onto the citizen body. A foreigner convicted of living with an Athenian woman as her husband was sold into slavery and his property confiscated, while an Athenian living with a foreign woman was fined 1000 drachmas. Similarly, anyone marrying off a non-Athenian woman to a citizen lost his citizen rights and had his property confiscated ([Dem.] 59 (*Against Neaira*) 16, 52: doc. 4.56).

Enrolment on their deme's register of citizens (the pinax ekklesiastikos) was an essential procedure for Athenian youths in their transition to citizenhood. The process was that a meeting of all deme members was called and these then voted on whether the boys were the correct age and eligible for membership. If a youth was considered to have fraudulently claimed deme membership, he had the right of appeal and would be prosecuted in court by five demesmen. If the case was upheld he was sold into slavery ([Arist.] *Ath. Pol.* 42.1–2: doc. 1.38). The onus was also on the deme to ensure that the youths were the correct age: if the council, on examining the new members, considered any to be too young, the demesmen were fined.

Demes held their own religious festivals and collected and spent revenue. Some demes like Acharnai and Eleusis could be relatively large and have their own shrines, theatre, cults and festivals, as well as separate magistrates and courts. The demarch (deme-leader, or 'mayor') supervised the deme's affairs along with various other civil, religious and military functionaries, and the institution continued in Greek colonies: the magistrates at Naples in Italy were known as demarchs (Strabo *Geography* 5.4.7: doc. 2.35). One of the duties of the demarchs was to collect the tithes for Eleusis and hand these over to the priests at Eleusis (*IG* I^3 78: doc. 3.38). An inscription of the tiny deme Plotheia of the tribe Aigeis (*IG* I^3 258: doc. 10.19), which had a demarch and two treasurers, lists the interest on the deme's financial capital and the deme assembly's decision on what this interest is to be used for, the financing of five festivals and an immunity fund, as well as sacrifices by the deme as part of the Athenian people as a whole. The officials to handle the money are to be elected by lot and one of their duties is to lend out the sums at the best possible interest. Another inscription of the deme Skambonidai, of the tribe Leontis, provides for participation in the Synoikia festival and the distribution of meat from the sacrifices to deme members (the demarch's perquisite is the skin). From this inscription it is clear that deme officials, like those in Athens, also underwent an audit (euthyna) at the end of their period of office (*IG* I^3 244: doc. 10.20).

The less than ideal citizen

If citizenship was a right and a privilege, it could be revoked for inappropriate conduct, or, in some states, for falling below a property qualification. Both are true of Sparta, where citizens could be deprived of citizen rights for demonstrating cowardice, or for being unable, for reasons of financial hardship, to pay their mess contribution. At Athens too there were citizens who did not live up to the ideal, as expounded by Perikles in his Funeral Oration, and Theophrastos gives a lively portrait of a typical coward on military service, who pretends that he has forgotten his sword and hides it, and spends his time tending a wounded friend rather than engaging with the enemy (Theophr. *Characters* 25: doc. 1.41). One of the obligations of a Greek citizen was to bear arms, and if necessary die on behalf of his country, and cowardice negated this duty. Aeschines lists the reasons for which citizens were debarred from address-ing the assembly. These include those who have treated their mother or father with violence ('people whom he ought to respect like the gods themselves'); those who have not done mili-tary service, or thrown away their shield in order to run away faster; those who have acted as a pathic, or male 'prostitute'; and those who have squandered their possessions or inherit-ance. In Aeschines' view, Solon considered that however awkward the speech delivered by an upright citizen to the assembly, his advice would be of use to the city, while someone who had squandered his inheritance or prostituted himself could have nothing to say which could benefit his fellow citizens. As a result Solon had forbidden such persons from mounting the platform and addressing the people (Aeschin. 1 *Against Timarchos* 26–32: doc. 1.42).

There were also strict regulations against committing 'hubris', that is when the stronger acted violently towards the weaker, regulations intended to protect men, women, children and even slaves against inappropriate and aggressive or demeaning treatment. As this was regarded as a public rather than private crime, any Athenian, not merely the victim or a member of his or her family, could bring the charge, with the court deciding on the penalty. If the penalty happened to be a fine, and the victim a free man, the offender was imprisoned until the fine was paid (Dem. 21 *Against Meidias* 47: doc. 1.43). The same attitude was dis-played towards those who had been accused of maltreating their parents or evading military service: they could be prosecuted by any citizen, and if the penalty was financial (it could also be corporal) they were to be kept in prison until the fine was discharged (Dem. 24 *Against Timokrates* 105: doc. 1.44).

City-states and their laws

Unless dependent on a larger polis, as for example the members of the Delian League under Athenian control, a polis, whatever its constitution, would normally pass legislation, prac-tise a system of justice, mint coinage, and collect taxes and revenues. The polis would also through its citizen body decide on matters of war and peace; make alliances and treaties; found colonies; and organise festivals and sacrifices to its deities. As part of Athens' empire-building league members were prohibited from continuing to mint their own coinage and use their own weights and measures, and were obliged to go to war at Athens' bidding (*IG* I^3 1453: doc. 13.13). The same was true of the perioikoi in the Peloponnese who had to go to war at Sparta's command.

In order for government to function there needed to be laws in place regulating the work-ings of the political system: how citizenship was to be defined and awarded; when and how often the assembly and council should meet; how magistrates and councillors should be elected; about the processes of legislation and judicial procedures; and how the constitution should be safeguarded. There would need to be criminal and inheritance law; regulations for trade, markets and other economic activities; and provisions for the sale of priesthoods, financing of sacrifices, conduct of festivals and upkeep of amenities in the city. There might also be restrictions on displays of mourning, sumptuary laws, regulations on divorce, mar-riage, adoption, provisions for orphans and heiresses, intermarriage with foreigners, and sexual crimes such as rape, adultery and male prostitution.

For most states other than Athens, inscriptions are generally the only existing form of information about their constitutions and laws, except where authors such as Aristotle, in his

Politics, have commented on different forms of constitutional government, or historians such as Herodotos found it appropriate to include anecdotal information about other poleis in their works. Perhaps the earliest surviving Greek law inscribed on stone dates to c. 650 BC and is also one of the earliest texts in which the term 'polis' is found. It comes from the temple of Apollo Delphinios at Dreros, a small Dorian town on the north coast of Crete, and is one of a number of texts from across the Greek world banning the re-election of magistrates, which implies that there may have been a popular assembly which in some way participated in this procedure. In this instance, the kosmos, who is presumably the chief magistrate of the city (similar to the eponymous archon at Athens), may not hold office again for the next ten years: if he does all his decisions will be rescinded and he will be fined and lose his right to hold office. A similar ban is found at Gortyn, also in Crete, and was in place at Athens where most magistracies, though not the strategia (the position of strategos, general), could only be held once in the classical period. The emphasis on the rotation of offices was also typical of oligarchies, which feared that one of their number might become tyrant, as of democracies, and the Cretan cities were typically ruled by oligarchies. At Dreros the main kosmos, along with a board of other officials (also called kosmoi), were elected annually from one particular clan (Meiggs and Lewis 2: doc. 1.45), with the council, perhaps representing the people as a whole, ratifying the election.

The two boulai of Chios

The island of Chios, off the Asia Minor coastline, promulgated a set of laws in the second quarter of the sixth century which give some clues as to its constitution and political development at that time (Meiggs and Lewis 8C: doc. 1.46). Chios was known for being the earliest Greek state to acquire barbarians as chattel-slaves, rather than serfs (Theopomp. *F* 122: doc. 5.51, cf. doc. 5.2), and for the production of fine wines. This inscription deals with a right of appeal from a verdict of the magistrates to a 'council of the people', perhaps representing the body of the assembly as a whole, which presumably supplemented an aristocratic council. This council can be compared to the Solonian one of 400, established in Athens in 594/3, to decide on and organise the agenda for the assembly ([Arist.] *Ath. Pol.* 8.4: doc. 8.19). This 'public council' at Chios met monthly, was elective (with fifty members chosen from each tribe) and heard appeals.

Indirect taxation at Cyzicus

Cyzicus, though a small community on the sea of Marmara, was wealthy as a result of its location near the island of Prokonnesos, which was rich in marble. Its gold coinage, staters worth 28 Athenian drachmas, formed one of the main currencies of the Greek world until the time of Philip of Macedon. One of the most informative documents on indirect taxation in the ancient world was inscribed at Cyzicus in the sixth century, and demonstrates the sophistication of taxation systems in even relatively small Greek poleis. The sons and descendents of two public benefactors, Medikes and Aisepos, are granted by the assembly public maintenance in the prytaneion (i.e., the right to dine daily free of charge) and immunity from all indirect taxation in the city. The only indirect taxes that they will still have to comply with include the tax for the use of the public scales, the tax on the sale of horses, the tax on the sale of slaves, the tax of 25 per cent, and the nautos, which may be a tax on the movement of goods by boat. Clearly there was a complex system in place implying a very sophisticated system of administration (*SIG* [3] 4, lines 5–12: doc. 1.47).

Settlement of new territory

Some of the most important laws, including those for the establishment of colonies, concern the regulations for the settlement of new territory. A late sixth-century law from western Lokris, probably referring to Naupaktos, deals with inheritance rights in a newly settled area. Lots of apportioned land can only be sold in cases of real necessity, exchange has to take place in the presence of magistrates, and there are clearly defined inheritance laws. Crops are immune from seizure. A selected body of 101 men are allowed to decide that, under pressure of war, 200 additional settlers may be invited: otherwise there are strict prohibitions about any further proposed division of land, and anyone who does so will be accursed, with his family, his house destroyed and his property confiscated. The original settlement is clearly well established, and there are magistrates, a council of elders, and a 'select council', together with an assembly (Meiggs and Lewis 13 A & C: doc. 1.48).

Bilateral agreements

An example of an agreement of bilateral judicial rights (isopoliteia) is recorded on a mid-fifth-century tablet from western Lokris, in which the two small cities of Oiantheia and Chaleion guarantee that the citizens of each will have reciprocal rights when on the other state's territory. If a citizen of one resides in the other state for more than a month he will be subject to the state's legal procedures. In particular, no person or property is to be seized to enforce claims, and if anyone attempts this he shall in turn be seized. The property of foreigners, i.e., the residents of the other city, can be seized at sea, but not from the other state's harbour, and the penalty for any unlawful seizure is to be four drachmas, or, if kept for more than ten days, one and a half times the value of the property taken. The inscription also defines the legal rights of foreigners in law suits; if cases concerning them are in dispute the 'foreigner' may choose a jury from the best citizens (not including his proxenos or host), fifteen men in cases involving a mina or more, or if less, nine men. Where citizens bring a case against each other the magistrates shall choose the jurors, after swearing the 'five-fold oath' (Buck no. 58: doc. 1.49).

Oligarchy at Elis

Elis, which hosted the Olympic festival, traditionally had a very oligarchic government: Aristotle (*Politics* 1306a) in fact states of it that its gerousia was an oligarchy within an oligarchy. The body of the citizens was small in numbers and very few ever became councillors, because there were only ninety councillors, and they had life-membership and the election was 'dynasteutic' – confined to certain families. However, a sixth-century Eleian law permits the assembly to override the judgement of a magistrate, and the people's decision ('rhetra') is to be final. Any constitutional changes may be made with the approval of the whole council of 500 and a full assembly of the people (Buck no. 64: doc. 1.51). In addition, there appear c. 500 BC to have been magistrates (basileis) whose duty it was to ensure that the phratry, family and property of an accused man were immune from seizure or prosecution. If they did not do so, there were themselves liable to a fine, which was to be enforced by the hellenodikas (judge), while the demiourgoi (officials) were to exact the fines which had not been paid. No one was permitted to intentionally mistreat a man accused of a charge involving a fine, under penalty of a 10 mina fine himself (Buck no. 61: doc. 1.50).

Alliances

Many of the agreements between cities were alliances, like that of Sparta and Aetolia (Meiggs and Lewis 67 (bis): doc. 6.61). The Eleians and Heraians c. 500 bound themselves to a hundred-year alliance. They agreed to join in war to assist the other, and if this did not happen the defaulter was to dedicate a talent of silver to Olympian Zeus, while anyone who went against this covenant would be liable to the same fine (Meiggs and Lewis 17: doc. 1.52). Similarly the two Cretan towns of Knossos and Tylissos forged an agreement, fragments of which have been found both in a shrine of Artemis at Tylissos and at Argos. Argos was involved because the city was believed to have founded a number of colonies in Crete, including probably these two cities, and in this inscription Tylissos, the smaller of the two cities, is being protected against its neighbour. In this section of the inscription regulations for the division of plunder and export of goods are laid down for the two states (Meiggs and Lewis 42B: doc. 1.53).

Proxenoi

A proxenos (plural: proxenoi) was a citizen who hosted visitors from a particular city at his own expense and saw to the interests of the citizens of that state in his own city: the position could be hereditary, and numerous decrees express the appreciation of citizens of one state towards their proxenos in another city. One such example is a commendation in 408/7 of a proxenos for Athenians on the island of Skiathos in the north-western Aegean. Oiniades is proclaimed a proxenos and benefactor of the Athenians, together with his descendents; the authorities (council, generals and magistrate) of Skiathos are to ensure his safety, and he is invited for dinner on the following day in the Athenian prytaneion (*IG* I³ 110: doc. 1.54). Similarly Hegelochos of Taras is named proxenos and benefactor in 411 by the Eretrians when Eretria revolted from Athens, and he and his son were granted public maintenance and front seats at the games (Meiggs and Lewis 82: doc. 13.29)

Leagues, unions and federations

Each polis was an independent entity, but sometimes poleis could be part of a larger organisation such as a league or federation, which might be dominated by a more powerful city, such as Athens or Sparta. One example was the Hellenic League, when Greek cities united against the Second Persian invasion, thirty-one of which are mentioned on the Serpent Column dedicated after their victory at Delphi (Hdt. 7.145.1–2: doc. 11.24; Meiggs and Lewis 27: doc. 11.49). Following the Greeks' successful defeat of the Persians, the Delian League was founded in 478 BC, with the aim of continuing the war and freeing Ionian Greek cities still under Persian domination. Members could choose to pay taxes to the league treasury or contribute armed forces and they swore to have the same friends and enemies as the Athenians. Athens soon began to assume the leadership of the allies and utilise the league's navy for its own purposes, essentially creating an empire in which the various city-states were self-governing as long as they remained loyal to Athens. The Second Athenian Confederacy, a maritime self-defence league, was founded in 377 BC and was led by Athens; but Athens would never recover the full extent of the power it had wielded in the fifth century (Tod 2.123: doc. 14.15).

The Peloponnesian League, dominated by Sparta, did not exact tribute payments from the allies (except in times of war), and foreign policy was discussed in league meetings rather than imposed, though states had to send troops to participate in wars when required. The league protected member states, while Sparta itself was protected from attack by this ring of oligarchic allies. Like the Delian League, it turned into an empire after Athens' defeat in 404 (Diod. Sic. *Library of History* 14.10.1–2: doc. 13.37).

Synoecism

On a much smaller scale, cities could decide to synoecise into a larger community, like Elis in 471/0 (Diod. Sic. *Library of History* 11.54.1: doc. 1.55). This could involve emigration from neighbouring settlements to a new polis (or an existing one), as in Megalopolis in Arkadia in 368, where a number of cities in southern Arkadia synoecised into a new city founded by the Theban Epameinondas (Paus. *Description of Greece* 8.27.1–2: doc. 14.21). In many cases this had happened in the city's distant past, in the same way as Athens was described to have synoecised in the time of Theseus, when Athens became the single political centre of Attica, with all the council chambers (bouleuteria), and governments from population centres throughout Attica becoming centralised into the one city, an event celebrated by the Synoikia festival, still held in Thucydides' own time (Thuc. 2.15.1–2: doc. 1.56).

The Boeotian federation

There were also federations uniting poleis with common interests in a particular region, such as the Boeotian confederacy dominated by Thebes. The poleis had a common council, magistrates and army commanded by boeotarchs ('commanders of Boeotia'); the cities were divided into eleven electoral districts, of which each supplied to the federal army approximately 1000 hoplites and 100 cavalry, and one boeotarch and 60 councillors to the federal government which met at Thebes. While the individual cities were self-governing, their constitutions, which were moderately oligarchic, were modelled on the same pattern and governed by a council divided into four sections, like that of the federation itself (Thuc. 5.38.1–3: doc 1.57; *Hellenica Oxyrhynchia* 16.1–4: doc. 1.58). Similar regional leagues existed in Phokis, Lokris, Thessaly, Arkadia and Achaia in the fourth century.

Religious leagues

Other leagues were founded for religious purposes, when cities of similar ethic background would meet to celebrate common festivals. One such was the Panionian ('all-Ionian') league (koinon) in which twelve Ionian cities from the islands and Asia Minor met at a common temple, the Panionian on Cape Mykale, to celebrate the Panionia, in honour of Poseidon Helikonios (Hdt. 1.142.1–4, 1.148.1: doc. 1.59). Similarly the six (later five) Dorian cities of south-west Asia Minor and Rhodes shared a temple and festival in honour of Triopian Apollo: Halikarnassos was originally a member but was thrown out when an athlete from Halikarnassos refused to dedicate his bronze tripod, the prize for victory, in the temple, and instead took it home (Hdt. 1.144.1–3: doc. 1.60).

Amphiktyonies

There were also amphiktyonies, which were set up to support a specific sacred site, as for the Olympian and Pythian festivals. The Amphiktyonic League was originally founded for the administration of Demeter's temple at Anthele and then Apollo's temple at Delphi. The amphiktyony was responsible for the conduct of the Pythian Games and care of the finances of the sanctuary and the upkeep of the temple. There were twelve member states and the amphiktyony was able to impose sanctions and fines on those who attacked the sanctuary and were involved in the 'sacred wars', such as the Third Sacred War as a result of which the Phokaians sacked Delphi in 356 (Diod. Sic. *Library of History* 16.23.1–5: doc. 14.32).

Trade and commerce

The Greeks did not have a concept of economic theory or practice in the modern sense: subsistence – breaking even at the end of the year, or making a profit – was the concern of the individual economic unit such as the family or the small business, such as the family farm. Agriculture was the basis for the economy of all city-states, even Athens, although it became increasingly dependent on grain imports during the fifth century, and the majority of city-states would have been based on a subsistence economy. When faced with starvation, the

Figure 1.9 Corinth was Greece's largest exporter of pottery until Athens overtook it in the fifth century BC. This vase is the famous 'Hunt Krater', which is 27 cm high and dates to around 575–550 BC. Corinth remained wealthy throughout the classical period because of its advantageous trading position on the Isthmus. British Museum GR 1772.3–20.6 (Vase B37), London. Drawing by J. Etherington.

31

main option open to city-states was that of migration. Poverty and the inability to function economically was one of the most important motives behind the colonisation movement in which Greeks from the mainland and Asia Minor sent out colonies from the extreme eastern end of the Black Sea to the coastline of France and Spain – and to Italy, Sicily, Egypt, the Propontis, Thrace, Africa – in fact to any region where there might be space and fertile land to support a significant part of their population which could not survive at home (Map 2.1). The foundation of colonies throughout the Mediterranean and Black Sea gave rise to inter-city trade and the development of cities such as Corinth which became centres of trade and commerce.

While Athens at the end of the fifth century was the great maritime power, importing goods from all over the known world, Corinth, which previously had been the wealthiest city in Greece, would have closely rivalled Athens in terms of wealth. This wealth was based on its control of the two harbours, serving the western and eastern Mediterranean respectively and on the traffic across the Isthmus on the 'diolkos', the stone road especially constructed to transport ships or their cargoes the six kilometres from one side of the Isthmus to the other (Strabo *Geography* 8.2.1: doc. 7.61). Because of its unique position Corinth had from an early period controlled important trade routes, including the land route to and from the Peloponnese: the Bakchiads of Corinth, the oligarchic family whom the Kypselids overthrew c. 658, were already extremely wealthy from Corinthian trade (Strabo *Geography* 8.6.20: doc. 1.62), and Thucydides confirms that the Corinthian economy had continued to boom throughout its history (Thuc. 1.13.2, 1.13.5: doc. 1.61). Until the mid-sixth century Corinth was a major exporter of black-figure pottery (Fig. 1.9) and had settled many colonies and emporia, trading posts, under the tyrants Kypselos and Periander, founding Epidamnos, Syracuse, Ambracia, Corcyra, Anaktorion, Apollonia in Illyria, and Potidaea.

Market regulations

Trade and commerce were so integral to the economy of many states that their financial and market regulations were officially recorded on stone. These include commercial treaties, laws for the prevention of piracy, and regulations for banking, deposits and credit, customs duties and harbour taxes, the insurance of cargoes, exchange rates and the validation of foreign currency, as well as laws specifying conditions for retail trade, for example in wine and oil. While the evidence for trade and for taxation in this period has to be drawn from the available documents, which are primarily epigraphic or from speeches delivered in courts of law, it is possible to obtain a clear impression of some of the economic priorities of Greek cities. Most important was the protection of the grain supply, not only for Athens, but also for other Greek cities which were unable to be self-sufficient either in general or in a particular year. The primary concern of any city was that there would always be enough grain (the staple diet) to feed the city's inhabitants. The city of Teos in about 470 recorded curses to be pronounced publicly three times every year by their magistrates against those who endangered the community. These envisaged threats included the manufacture of poisonous drugs, the prevention of the import of grain, and treason, robbery and piracy (Meiggs and Lewis 30: doc. 1.65). Piracy was always a concern of trading states and, according to Thucydides, in some areas such as Aetolia and Acarnania it was still a very profitable lifestyle, and not considered in disrepute (Thuc. 1.5.1–6.2). Life could also be difficult for the individual trader: the Berezan 'lead letter' was written c. 500 by a trader in the Black Sea, Achillodoros, whose cargo had been confiscated by Matasys, and whom Matasys was attempting to seize as a slave. Matasys seems to have had what he considered to be an outstanding claim on

Anaxagoras whom he states to have been Achillodoros' owner. So, as Anaxagoras owed him money, he considered he was justified in seizing his slave Achillodoros as compensation. Achillodoros' letter to his son advises him of this attempted injustice and tells him to inform Anaxagoras and the rest of the family and appeal to their city's magistrates to sort out the issue immediately (Chadwick 35–6: doc. 1.64).

Public benefits

As the polis was made up of citizen members, it was not unusual for any unexpected profits to be divided between citizens rather than banked centrally by the polis itself as a future resource. When a rich vein of silver was discovered at Laureion in Attica in 483/2 some speakers in the assembly suggested that the windfall, which amounted to a hundred talents, should be divided amongst the people, and it was only on Themistokles' advice that the money was used to construct a fleet which was then prepared to face the Persians in 480/79 ([Arist.] *Ath. Pol.* 22.7: doc. 11.23). The island of Siphnos was rich in gold and silver mines and every year the islanders would share out the profits among themselves. Herodotos comments that they were so wealthy that with one-tenth of the yield they were able to afford to build one of the richest treasuries at Delphi (Hdt. 3.57.1–2: doc. 1.63). Thasos also possessed gold mines both on the island and on the Thracian coast, producing an annual revenue of up to two or three hundred talents in total, but unlike Siphnos it had used its wealth to construct a fleet and strong fortifications (Hdt. 6.46.2).

Legislation on trade

There was legislation to stop corruption and consumer exploitation, as with the wine trade at Thasos, which not only regulated when wine could be sold, but specifically prevented adulteration and retail dealing (the selling of wine 'by the jug'), in terms which imply that these were a common occurrence. The jars, pithoi, had to be stamped with a seal for the sale to be valid and all pithoi had to be of a regulation size. The inscription is also concerned with foreign competition and the import of foreign wines into the Thasian-controlled area of the Thracian mainland is forbidden, with the owner and helsman of the vessel importing the prohibited cargo both being liable to the same penalties as for adulterating the wine with water (Pleket *Epigraphica* I, no. 2: doc. 1.66). Herodotos ponders the question of what happened to all the earthenware jars of wine exported from throughout Greece and Phoenicia to Egypt, and records the 'solution': all mayors (demarchs) had to collect the empties and send them to Memphis so they could be used for conveying water to the desert areas of Syria (Hdt. 3.6.1–2: doc. 1.67).

Athenian trade

The most specific evidence for the economy of a city-state of course derives from Athens. During the period of the Athenian empire in the second half of the fifth century Athens controlled eastern Mediterranean trade, importing all its needs, such as timber (for ship-building), copper, flax and iron, and using its control of the sea to restrict exports to its enemies ([Xen.] *Constitution of the Athenians* 2.11–12: doc. 1.69). Perikles had earlier stated in his Funeral Oration: 'because of the city's size, all kinds of things are imported from all over the earth, so that it seems just as natural to us to enjoy the goods of other men as those of our own

Figure 1.10 Harvesting olives (doc. 1.15). One man is in the tree shaking the ripe olives off; two beat the tree with sticks to loosen the fruit (a method still used in Greece), another gathers the olives. The two naked figures are probably slaves. A black-figure neck amphora dating to 530–510 BC, it is attributed to the Antimenes Painter and stands 40 cm high. British Museum 1837,0609.42 (Vase B226), London. Drawing by J. Etherington.

production' and Athens clearly had access to not only necessities but the luxury goods available throughout the Greek world (Thuc. 2.38.2: doc. 1.17). The orator Andocides provides information on customs duties at Athens, which were levied at 2 per cent on all traffic through the Piraeus. Just like most other taxes these were not collected centrally by government officials, but were farmed out to the highest bidder. In 399 BC the orator states that previously a plot had been hatched to keep the price artificially low at 30 talents, when possible rivals for the contract got together and shared in the proceeds. The fair price now in place was 36 talents, at which the tax-collectors were still able to make a reasonable profit, while still saving the Athenian people six talents. On this estimate the volume of traffic through the Piraeus was approximately 1800 talents (nearly 11 million drachmas, or the equivalent annual wage for 30,000 citizens). This was even after the loss of Athens' empire to Sparta, and the trade would presumably have been considerably greater prior to 405/4 BC (Andoc. 1 *On the*

Mysteries 133–4: doc. 1.68). Aristophanes' *Wasps*, produced in 422, estimates Athens' income as 2000 talents from the tribute, taxes, one-per-cents, court deposits, mines, market-taxes, harbour dues, rents for public land and confiscations, and the sum of 2000 talents appears a reasonable estimate for the Peloponnesian War period (Ar. *Wasps* 655–64: doc. 1.28). In 425/4 the tribute had theoretically amounted to some 1460 talents (*IG* I³ 71).

During the Peloponnesian War, probably c. 425, Athens had decreed that all its allies had to use Athenian coinage, weights and measures throughout the empire and all other currencies previously minted and used by the allies were now prohibited (*IG* I³ 1453: doc. 13.13). The standardisation of currency and prevention of adulteration was vital for the protection of trade and in the fourth century there were ten measure-controllers, five for the city and five for the Piraeus whose responsibility it was to ensure that all weights and measures conformed to the accepted standard ([Arist.] *Ath. Pol.* 50.1–51.4: doc. 1.25). In 375/4 Athens possessed a 'tester' of silver coinage, a public slave whose duty it was to sit in the market among the bankers' tables and test all foreign currency for false weight or counterfeit. A similar slave was also to be established in the Piraeus 'for the shipowners and merchants' (Bogaert *Epigraphica* 21: doc. 1.70). The seriousness of the role is shown by the fact that if the tester did not follow his instructions, or was absent from his post, he was given fifty blows of the whip.

The grain trade

Grain (wheat and barley, especially barley which comprised the basic diet, as barley bread or barley porridge) was the most important foodstuff in ancient Greece, and any problems involving the food supply of the polis related to the provision of grain. Since the growing of grain was the responsibility of families and households on their own farms, there was no central governmental production or provision for any failure in supply and so states such as Athens encouraged imports of grain, normally wheat, by various decrees and regulations which offered incentives to merchants and traders to carry grain to Athens rather than other goods. In addition states which supplied Athens with grain were treated with great diplomacy, as in the case of Spartocids who ruled in the eastern Crimea and who had control of large supplies of grain. In the fifth and fourth centuries grain was imported into Greece from the Black Sea, Egypt, Libya and Sicily, and this trade took place in the sailing season which generally lasted from March to October. According to Demosthenes (20 *Against Leptines* 31–2: doc. 1.74) Athens imported 400,000 medimnoi a year (22 million litres) from the Black Sea region alone, with Sicily and Egypt also major suppliers. Severe food shortages, such as the one which occurred about 330–326, were however unusual, and generally famine could be relieved by supplies from within the area or were the result of siege as at Athens in 405–404 BC.

Athens' dependence on grain imports

Herodotos makes the first explicit reference to the grain trade when he describes the Persian monarch Xerxes at Abydos in 480 BC noticing the grain ships sailing from the Black Sea through the Hellespont to mainland Greece, taking cargoes to Aegina and the Peloponnese. On being told that these ships were taking grain to his enemies, he told his men to leave them unmolested – they were transporting supplies for the Persians themselves when they arrived in Greece (Hdt. 7.147.2–3: doc. 1.71). Sicily, colonised by Greek cities from the late eighth century, was another important source: Herodotos also records that Gelon, tyrant of Syracuse, had planned to come to the aid of the Greeks and feed the entire Greek army with

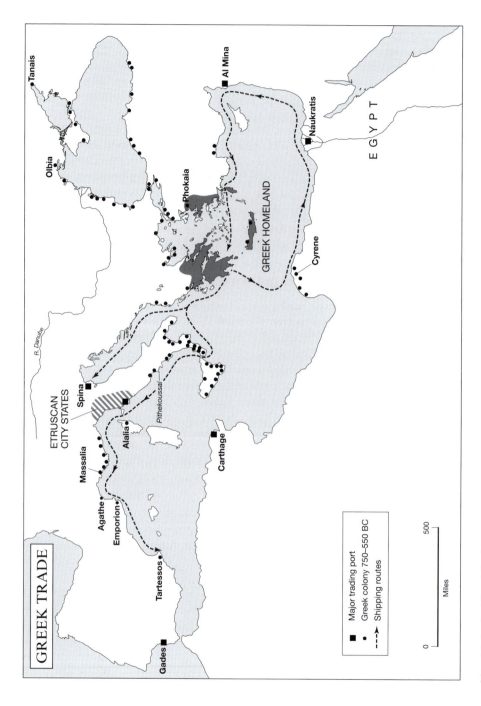

Map 1.3 Ancient Greek trade.

grain from Sicily if he were made commander (7.158.4–5; cf. 7.165–6: doc. 7.44). The main factor in Athens' surrender at the end of the Peloponnesian War was that after his victory at the battle of Aigospotamoi in 405 the Spartan admiral Lysander had been able to prevent the grain ships from sailing down the Hellespont to Athens and as a result large numbers of Athenians were dying of starvation by the time peace was finally made in 404 BC (Xen. *Hellenika* 2.2.10–11, 2.16–23: doc. 13.35).

The grain market

According to the *Athenaion Politeia*, in fourth-century Athens there were ten agoranomoi (market-controllers), five for Athens and five for the Piraeus, whose duty it was to see that all merchandise was unadulterated and that goods were in an acceptable condition. There were also ten 'measure-controllers' responsible for weights and measures and grain-guardians whose original numbers had increased from ten to thirty-five (twenty for Athens and fifteen for the Piraeus) such was the importance of grain to Athens' citizens. Their task was to check that the grain sold in the market was available at a reasonable price and that bakers' loaves were of the regulation weight and not sold at a price too high above that of grain. Ten harbour-inspectors, elected by lot, also supervised the Piraeus markets and ensured that two-thirds of the grain brought by sea arrived at the grain market ([Arist.] *Ath. Pol.* 50.1–51.4: doc. 1.25). So important was the question of the grain supply that it was a fixed item on the agenda of the main (kyria) assembly meeting every month which dealt, among other things, with the grain supply, defence and whether the officials were governing appropriately ([Arist.] *Ath. Pol.* 43.4: doc. 1.16).

Laws on the import of grain and maritime loans

The Athenians did everything they could to assist the transport of crucial commodities such as grain into the Piraeus. In the fourth century it was illegal to lend money on a ship if it was not going to be bringing grain back to Athens on its return trip, or to lend money for transporting grain if the destination was not to be Athens. A merchant was not permitted to bring a case to recover any money so lent, nor was an offical allowed to bring this sort of case to trial (Dem. 35 *Against Lakritos* 51: doc. 1.72). Many merchants took out loans to finance all or part of their trading expeditions. The money would be given on short-term loan, such as a few weeks or however long the trip would take, at a high rate of interest. Contracts were put in writing and the lender of the finance carried all the risk of the venture. Bottomry loans (loans on the 'bottom' or keel of a ship) were a popular way of financing a venture; if the ship failed to complete the voyage, the borrower owed nothing (so the loss of the ship cancelled the loan), and if successful he repaid the loan at high interest, which could be as much as 30 per cent or more, from the sale of the cargo.

In his speech for the prosecution in this lawsuit, Demosthenes describes a situation in which two merchants have borrowed money for a voyage to Mende or Skione on the Chalkidike peninsula. There they planned to outlay the funds to purchase 3000 jars of wine, which they would then transport for sale to the Bosphoros or Black Sea. At the Black Sea they would ship a return cargo of grain for sale back in Athens. Within twenty days of their return to Athens they would repay the loan on the cargo (Dem. 35 *Against Lakritos* 10–13: doc. 1.73). In a further speech which concerned the grain supply in 355 BC, Demosthenes emphasises the importance of imported grain from the Black Sea which, he states, is equal in amount to that from all other sources. Leukon, the ruler of the Cimmerian Bosphoros, or Crimea, had

Figure 1.11 The boxers Xenophanes does not praise (doc. 1.78). Two boxers fight, while on the right a judge holds ready a twitch to punish either of them for breaking the rules. This scene is on an Athenian red-figure kylix (cup) painted by the Triptolemos Painter and dating to about 490 BC. The height of the cup is 13.5 cm, and the diameter of the cup itself 32.3 cm. The Toledo Museum of Art 1961.26, Toledo. Drawing by J. Etherington.

given the Athenians priority in loading and exempted from taxes any merchants taking grain to Athens. For this reason the Athenians had granted him a golden crown and citizenship and given him and his sons immunity from liturgies and war-taxes (the eisphora) (Dem. 20 *Against Leptines* 31–2: doc. 1.74).

The main famine in the Greek world during the classical period took place c. 330–326, and was relieved by the colony of Cyrene in North Africa, founded by the island of Thera in 631 (Meiggs and Lewis 5: doc. 2.28). The colony sent fifty-one shipments of grain to forty-one Greek states, as well as to Olympias and Kleopatra, mother and sister of Alexander the Great. Most shipments are of 5000 to 10,000 medimnoi (275,000 to 550,000 dry litres), though Athens received 100,000 and Olympias 72,600. Recipients included Corinth, Rhodes, Megara, Delphi and Aegina as well as smaller cities and islands (Tod 2.196: doc. 1.75).

The super-stars of the city-state

Poleis typically showed their appreciation of benefactors by awarding them dining rights in perpetuity in the prytaneion (town-hall), where the prytaneis in office dined every evening. Athens granted this to the descendants of the tyrannicides Harmodios and Aristogeiton, and to Kleon after his victory over the Spartans at Pylos (*IG* I³ 131: doc. 9.41; Ar. *Knights* 162–67: doc. 1.29). Similar privileges were granted to the descendants of benefactors at Cyzicus (*SIG*³ 4: doc. 1.47). Victors at the four panhellenic festivals, at Olympia, Delphi, the Isthmus and Nemea, were awarded wreaths: olive at Olympia, bay at Delphi, pine at the Isthmus and celery at Nemea. However there were more material rewards on their return home, and they also received perpetual dining rights as the 'super-stars' of their polis, and could on occasions also be granted a state pension or monetary reward. Their victory was seen to bestow glory on their polis as well. According to Plutarch, Solon laid down that a victor at the Isthmian festival was awarded 100 drachmas and a victor at Olympia 500 (Plut. *Solon* 23.3). The Sicilians were known for their luxurious lifestyle and when Exainetos of Akragas won the stadion at the Olympic Games in 412 he was conducted into his city by a procession of 300 chariots each of which was drawn by two white horses, all the chariots belonging to citizens of Akragas (Diod. Sic. *Library of History* 13.82.5–8: doc. 1.76). Athletes and their achievements could be larger than life; Milon, who could lift and carry a four-year old steer around the stadium at Olympia and then eat it single-handed, was presumably the exception rather than the rule, though other athletes engaged in similar feats (Ath. *Deipnosophistae* 10.412d–413a: doc. 1.77).

Philosophers could carp at this implication that athletes were the greatest benefactors of their cities. Xenophanes of Kolophon criticises cities for awarding wrestlers, boxers, runners and pankrationists seats of honour at festivals, public maintenance, and costly gifts in their admiration for strength rather than wisdom (Xen. Kol. *F* 2: doc. 1.78; Fig. 1.11). Socrates at his trial in 399 BC suggested that the best reward for a man of his talents would be maintenance in the prytaneion:

> Well, what suits a poor man who has benefited the city and who needs leisure for giving you exhortation? There is nothing more appropriate for such a person, gentlemen, than maintenance in the prytaneion, which is far more appropriate in fact for me than for any of you who has won at the Olympics with a horse or pair or team; such a person makes you seem to be successful, but I really do, and he does not need the maintenance, whereas I do.
>
> (Pl. *Apology* 36b–e: doc. 3.86)

The polis was fundamental to Greek civilisation, with the body of citizens seeing themselves as equivalent to their polis: where modern scholars speak of the polis of Athens, the Greeks spoke of 'the Athenians' and it was both a social and religious association rather than a geographical entity. Thucydides has Perikles in the Funeral Oration (doc. 1.17) speak of the Athenians having to view their city as if they were its 'lover': 'you must actively keep before you the power of this city day by day, and become her lovers'.

The Greeks themselves were unable to conceive of civilisation without the polis and the disagreements between the various poleis provide the material for most of Greek history. It was also within the polis that Greek culture and civilisation flourished and it was the framework within which the Greeks lived and through whose institutions they expressed their identity. The Greek without a polis was indeed, as Aristotle suggested, 'tribeless, lawless, hearthless'.

2

COLONISATION

Table 2.1 Important Greek colonies

Colony	Mother-city	Foundation date
Abdera (Thrace)	1. Klazomenai	654
	2. Teos	c. 545
Abydos	Miletos	675
Akrai	Syracuse	663
Akragas (Sicily)	Gela	580
Alalia (Corsica)	Phokaia	c. 565
Al Mina	Euboea and others	c. 825
Alexandria (Eschate)	Macedonia	329
Alexandria (Egypt)	Macedonia	332–331
Alexandria (Oxiana)	Macedonia	c. 328
Ambracia (Epirus)	Corinth	c. 625
Amphipolis	Athens	437
Anaktorion	Corinth and Corcyra	c. 620
Apollonia in Illyria	Corinth	588
Apollonia in Libya	Thera	c. 600
Barka (Africa)	Cyrene	c. 560–550
Berezan (Black Sea)	Miletos	647
Boukephala	Macedonia	326
Byzantium (Bosphoros)	Megara	659 or 668
Camarina (Sicily)	Syracuse	598
Catana (Sicily)	Chalkis	729
Chalcedon (Bosphoros)	Megara	676 or 685
Chersonese (Thrace)	Athens	559–556
Corcyra	1. Eretria	8th century
	2. Corinth	734
Croton (Italy)	Achaea	c. 710
Cumae (Italy)	Chalkis and Eretria	c. 725
Cyrene (Africa)	Thera	631
Cyzicus (Black Sea)	1. Corinth (?)	756
	2. Miletos	675
Elea	Phokaia	535
Emporion (Spain)	Massalia	early 6th century
Epidamnos (Epirus)	Corcyra and Corinth	627
Gela (Sicily)	Rhodes and Crete	688
Herakleia Pontica (Black Sea)	Megara	c. 560
Herakleia Trachinia	Sparta	426
Himera (Sicily)	Zankle	c. 648
Kasmenai (Sicily)	Syracuse	643

Lampsakos	Phokaia	654
Lemnos (N. Aegean)	Athens	c. 500
Leontinoi (Sicily)	Chalkis and Naxos	729
Leukas	Corinth	c. 625
Lipara (N. of Sicily)	Knidos	c. 580
Lokri Epizephyrioi	Opountian Lokris	7th century
Massalia (France)	Phokaia	c. 600
Megara Hyblaia (Sicily)	Megara	728
Methone	Eretria	730
Naukratis	Miletos and others	c. 610
Naxos (Sicily)	Chalkis	734
Neapolis (Italy)	Cumae	c. 600
Neapolis (Thrace)	Thasos	before 600
Odessos (Thrace)	Miletos	560
Olbia (Black Sea)	Miletos	647
Olynthos	Chalcidice	479
Phaselis (A. Minor)	Rhodes	688
Phasis	Miletos	c. 550
Pithekoussai (Italy)	Chalkis and Eretria	750–725
Poseidonia (Italy)	Sybaris	625–600
Potidaea (Chalkidike)	Corinth	c. 600
Rhegium (Italy)	Chalkis	730–720
Samothrace (N. Aegean)	Samos	c. 700
Selinous (Sicily)	Megara Hyblaea	628
Selymbria (Black Sea)	Megara	before 688
Sigeion (Hellespont)	Athens	c. 600
Sinope (Black Sea)	Miletos	(1) before 756; (2) 631
Siris (Italy)	Kolophon	670
Sybaris (Italy)	Achaea	c. 720
Syracuse (Sicily)	Corinth	733
Taras (Italy)	Sparta	706
Thasos (N. Aegean)	Paros	c. 680
Thourioi (Italy)	Athens and others	444/3
Torone (Chalcidice)	Chalkis	710
Trapezous (Black Sea)	Sinope	756
Zankle (Sicily)	Cumae and Euboea	c. 730–720

Source: Adapted and expanded from the list of A.J. Graham, 'The Colonial Expansion of Greece', in the *Cambridge Ancient History*, III (3), 1982, pp. 160–2, who also gives the date of the earliest archaeological material found at each site.

Introduction

The Greek city-states were energetic and prolific colonisers (see Table 2.1). Whether for reasons of over-population, crop failure or drought, political pressures or trade, Greek cities in the archaic and classical periods sent out colonies around the whole coastline of the Mediterranean and Black Sea. The Greek world at this period was not simply confined to mainland Greece: it comprised an intricate web of colonies and trading stations around the edges of their known world, from the far east of the Black Sea to the south of Spain. In the words of Plato's Socrates, the Greeks lived around the shores of the Mediterranean and Black Sea like 'ants or frogs around a pond' (Pl. *Phaedo* 109a–b: doc. 2.37).

Even in Mycenaean times, when the rulers of the Mycenaean cities took over the commercial thalassocracy which had been established by Minoan Crete, the Mycenaean Greeks ruled an empire from the palace at Knossos in Crete. They were settled on many of the Aegean islands and along the coastline of Asia Minor from as early as the fifteenth century BC, trading goods with Egyptians, Phoenicians and the palace centres of their own homeland. One of the main areas of Mycenaean settlement in Asia Minor was around Miletos, from where the Greeks had dealings with the Hittite kingdom based at Hattusas, as well as on the larger islands of Rhodes and Cyprus. The Hittite ruler corresponded with a Great King of Ahhiyawa (or 'Achaea': Homer frequently calls the Greeks 'Achaeans'), who was presumably the ruler of Mycenae, and wrote to him as an equal about problems caused in Asian Minor by renegade Mycenaeans with designs on Hittite territory.

After the fall of the Mycenaean kingdoms and Troy, c. 1200, during what is sometimes called the 'Dark Ages', Greeks continued to prosper in their settlements in Asia. Trading contacts were to some extent maintained during this period and the next main wave of colonisation began c. 800 BC. The term Hellene (or 'Greek') is never used by Homer and throughout the history of archaic and classical Greece individual cities were responsible for their own programmes of trade and colonisation: they were more likely to be at loggerheads over the settlement of fertile regions than working in unity (Thuc. 1.3.1–3: doc. 2.1). But despite the network of trading routes across the Mediterranean between colonies and their mother-cities, Solon, in the sixth century, still considered sea journeys to be dangerous and the life of a seafarer an unsafe one: he describes a merchant as wandering 'the fishy sea desiring in his ships to bring home gain, tossed by dreadful winds, quite unsparing of his life' (Solon *Poem* 13: doc. 5.56; Fig. 2.1).

Sources

While the archaeological record is of course important, there are many literary accounts of the foundation of specific colonies, to which historians such as Herodotos and

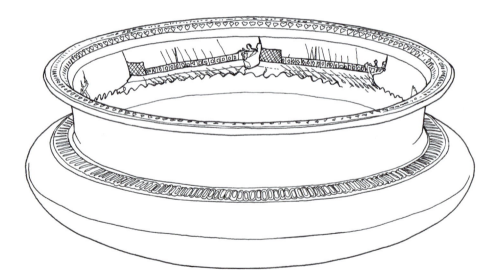

Figure 2.1 On the inside of this vessel several ships are depicted. These are probably meant to represent pentekonters, ships with fifty rowers, such as those used in the colonisation of Cyrene (doc. 2.29). This is a particularly fine Athenian black-figure dinos, with a height of 17.3 cm and a diameter of 36 cm, dating to about 500 BC. Hermitage Museum, St Petersburg, Russia. Drawing by J. Etherington.

Thucydides had access in writing their accounts. Herodotos provides valuable information regarding colonies of relevance to his narrative, as when the Phokaians and Teians fled from Persian domination for political motives, and the Therans colonised Cyrene; these are often part of his entertaining digressions. He himself travelled widely to the Black Sea, Egypt, Phoenicia, Palestine, Cyrene and southern Italy, where, at Thourioi, Perikles' resettlement of Sybaris, he died. Thucydides is the main source for the foundation of colonies in Sicily, giving a detailed account of settlements in Sicily, and their dispossession by later arrivals, as an introduction to his account of the Sicilian Expedition in 415/14 BC (6.3.1–5.3: doc. 2.12). The details of the rivalry between Corinth, her colony Corcyra, and Corcyra's colony Epidamnos form part of his discussion of the causes of the Peloponnesian War (1.24.1–26.2: doc. 2.8).

Historians like Thucydides had access to the works of earlier authors, including logographers such as Hekataios of Miletos (*F* 1: doc. 16.1), of whom they made use in compiling their accounts. Thucydides may well have taken much of his material on the settlement of Sicily from Antiochos of Syracuse, who wrote a history of Sicily in nine books, as well as, it appears, an account of the foundation of Greek colonies in southern Italy (*F* 2: doc. 16.2), a subject which was also addressed by Timaios of Sicily. Authors such as Antiochos and Timaios are now only preserved in fragments, references in the works of later historians, who made use of the earlier works and quoted from or paraphrased them. Tales, in prose or verse, of the foundations of colonies were a popular literary genre, and Polybios in his *Histories* (9.1.4) states that his work on the rise of Rome would not appeal to those interested in accounts of colonies or the foundations of cities, such as were written by Ephoros, who composed a history of Kyme, his home-city on the northern coast of Asia Minor. Xenophanes of Kolophon in the mid-sixth century BC composed an account in verse on the foundation of his city Kolophon in Asia Minor, which was established c. 1200–1000 (*Poem* A1: doc. 2.2), as well as one on the settlement of Elea in Italy, a Phokaian colony founded c. 540. These works reminded the colonists of their mother-city (their metropolis) and place of origin, and reinforced their perception that they were as much a part of the Greek world as the Greek mainland. Indeed, these works were possibly read or recited annually at festivals commemorating the city's foundation. Not all, of course, can be accepted as factual, and many are closer to legend than historical narrative, while foundation stories by different authors do not always agree in all their details. Antiochos states that he is recording the most trustworthy tales concerning Greek cities in Italy (implying that there were others current), and Strabo relates differing versions of the way in which the partheniai from Sparta came to settle Taras in 706 BC, as recorded by Antiochos and Ephoros (*Geography* 6.3.2–3: doc. 2.23). Similarly Herodotos relates two accounts of the events preceding the successful settlement of Cyrene by the Therans, the official version of the Cyrenaeans and Therans and one of his own (Hdt. 4.150.2–159.4: doc. 2.29).

The 'age of colonisation'

In the period between 800 and 600 BC numerous colonies were sent out by Greek city-states in mainland Greece and Asia Minor and hence this period is sometimes known as 'the age of colonisation', as this was when the majority of colonies were established. This, however, was not the only time during which the cities of mainland Greece and Asia Minor sent out colonial settlements, and several major foundations were made in the fifth century and later, while colonisation was still taking place as late as 200 BC. These colonies were established throughout the Mediterranean, to both the east and west of Greece, as well as around the coastline of the Black Sea, with Greek colonies settled as far east as modern Marseilles (Massilia) in southern France and Emporion in Spain, and as far west as Phasis (at the eastern end of the Black Sea). There were also important settlements in North Africa at Cyrene and in Egypt, where the profitable trading centre at Naukratis was shared by Greeks from a number of cities and islands, many of whom settled there. By the sixth century important colonies flourished in Sicily and southern Italy, Egypt and North Africa, the Black Sea, France and Spain, while there was a long history of settlement by Greeks in western Asia Minor (Anatolia). All of these were an integral part of the Greek world and Greek culture, and recognised as such, with the colonists sharing in the religious ceremonies of their mother-city and competing on equal terms and with equal success at the panhellenic festivals.

It was not necessarily the largest and most important cities in the Greek world that decided to send out colonies – often it was the smaller and less prosperous islands and cities, hit by a crisis in food-production or drought which they could only survive by ridding themselves of surplus population – that established some of the most successful colonies. For example, the small drought-ridden island of Thera was responsible for settling Cyrene in Africa (Meiggs and Lewis 5: doc. 2.28; cf. docs 2.29–30; Fig. 2.2) and the Aegean island of Paros for the colonisation of Thasos, for its rich gold mines, and the Thracian mainland opposite (Archil. *FF* 20–21, 102: doc. 2.27), while the relatively small city of Chalkis on the island of Euboea, along with the neighbouring city of Eretria, became one of the most prolific of colonisers, even rivalling the great trading centres of Corinth and Miletos (docs 2.11–12).

Figure 2.2 The temple complex of Apollo and surrounding area at Cyrene. The sacred pool can be seen clearly, fed by a natural spring; the complex is a UNESCO World Heritage Site. Photo © Sebastià Giralt.

The great colonisers

Whatever the reason for the initial venture into colonisation, the mother-cities that sent out colonies tended to display a preference for settlements in particular areas, depending to some degree upon their economic needs. Miletos and Megara, for example, established most of the colonies around the Black Sea for trading purposes, Miletos founding some 90 settlements in the region (Anaximenes of Lampsakos *F* 26: doc. 2.16), with Megara settling both Chalkedon and Byzantium, which between them controlled trade from the Black Sea through the Bosporos (Hdt. 4.144.1–2: doc. 2.15). Colonisation of the Black Sea and Propontis region began in the eighth century, but increased exponentially in the seventh, with the area exporting grain to mainland Greece from the end of the sixth century. Corinth, whose wealth was founded on trade, possessed a network of commercial colonies around the Corinthian gulf founded between 733 and c. 585. The most important were Syracuse, Ambracia, Corcyra, Anaktorion and Apollonia in Illyria (with Corcyra), Leukas, and Potidaea. They also sent additional settlers to Epidamnos (Thuc. 1.24.1–26.2: doc. 2.8). Along with its colonies, Corinth founded the majority of the Sicilian and Italian colonies in 'Magna Graecia' (Greater Greece), as the area was known (docs 2.10–12). Chalkidike, the three-pronged peninsula where there were numerous colonies, mostly sent out by Chalkis, was so named because of its mother-city. In the west Chalkis also founded Pithekoussai and Cumae (with Eretria), Sicilian Naxos, Catana, Leontinoi, Zankle and Rhegium. Pithekoussai, where there was iron, was the earliest Greek colony in the west, founded probably c. 750–725, on the island of Ischia off the west coast of Italy. The famous 'Nestor's cup' was found there, which has one of the oldest examples of writing in Greek and demonstrates that the inhabitants had a knowledge of Nestor as the elderly counsellor of the Greeks in the *Iliad* (11.632–7): 'Nestor's cup was good to drink from, but whoever drinks from this cup will immediately be seized with desire for beautifully-crowned Aphrodite' (Meiggs and Lewis 1: doc. 2.10).

Sicily was settled soon after Pithekoussai, and Greeks competed with the indigenous Sikels, Carthaginians and each other for prime land on this fertile and prosperous island: traditional foundation dates for some of its cities are: Naxos 734; Syracuse 733; Zankle c. 730–720; Rhegium c. 730–720; Leontinoi 729; Catana 729; Gela 688; Akrai 663; Himera c. 648; Kasmenai 643; Selinous 628; and Camarina 598. The city of Naples or Neapolis (which is the Greek for 'New City'), on the west coast of Italy, which was founded in about 660, long retained its Greek character (Strabo *Geography* 5.4.7: doc. 2.35). The emperor Augustus himself attended the contests, while the emperor Nero performed here in musical events and addressed the crowd in Greek. Some parts of southern Italy and Sicily were still Greek-speaking in the eleventh and twelfth centuries AD.

The Delphic oracle

One of the most important duties for the founder of a colony, the oikistes (plural: oikistai), was of course that of consulting Delphi to enquire whether the foundation would be successful. In fact the Sicilian Greeks when departing to take part in panhellenic festivals sacrificed at the altar of Apollo Archagetes or Archegetes (the Founder) at Sicilian Naxos, the first Greek settlement in Sicily (Thuc. 6.3.1: doc. 2.12), and many colonies claimed that Apollo was himself their oikistes. While the resettlement of Sybaris in southern Italy as the new city of Thourioi was primarily an Athenian foundation, with an Athenian oikistes, Lampon, the colony was soon in discord in 434/3 as to which was their mother-city and who their oikistes:

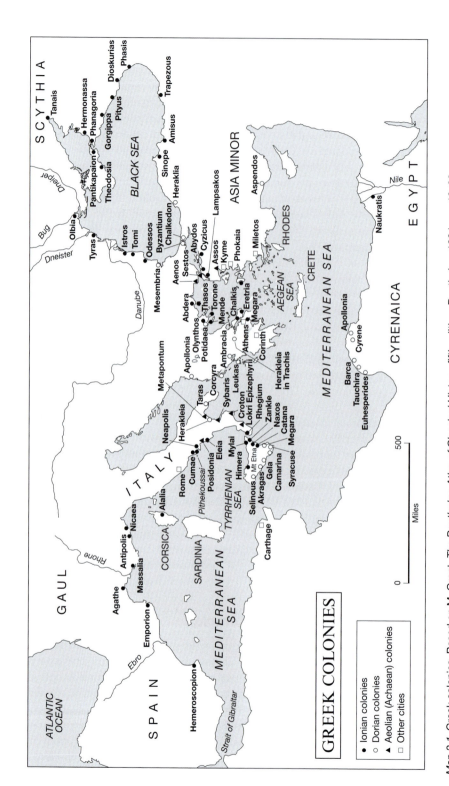

Map 2.1 Greek colonies. Based on M. Grant, *The Routledge Atlas of Classical History*, fifth edition, Routledge, 1994, pp. 19–20.

Delphi was consulted on this issue and the god himself declared that he was the founder, thus resolving the conflict. In later times consultation of the god at Delphi was thought to be an essential part of the colonisation process (Lucian *Astrology* 23: doc. 2.3), although many of the earlier oracles appear to be apocryphal and were 'forged' retrospectively to legitimise the settlement.

Early foundation oracles

While it is possible that founders of these colonies in the archaic period consulted Delphi, in reality the oracle did not take on panhellenic status until much later and there are no foundation oracles recorded in the eighth- and seventh-century sources. Furthermore, despite the details contained in many of these oracles as recorded, it is not likely that the priests at Delphi actually suggested possible destinations: the role of the oracle was simply to ratify that the settlement had the god's approval. When, however, it became customary to consult Delphi, colonies already founded felt the need to ensure that their credentials were equally as impeccable as those of later settlements. In Herodotos' account the consultation of Delphi is presented as being so important that any failure to do so automatically resulted in the colony's failure. The Spartan Dorieus on his first attempt to establish a colony was at fault for not consulting Delphi, and thus failed in his attempted African settlement. On his second attempt, while he did consult Delphi about the possibility of establishing a colony at Eryx in western Sicily and the oracle gave its approval, he landed in southern Italy before reaching Sicily, his actual destination. In Italy he became involved in the war between Sybaris and Croton and was killed in the fighting. He failed because he had not followed Delphi's instructions absolutely and did not go straight to Sicily (Hdt. 5.42.2–45.1: doc. 2.22).

Similarly, the colonisation of Cyrene was recorded as not running smoothly until Delphi's instructions were followed precisely; a spontaneous declaration by the Pythia was ignored at first (whether by Grinnos or Battos – Herodotos gives two different versions of the initial consultation), and when the colony finally departed it settled on the island of Platea off the Libyan coast, not in Libya itself. When after two years without success the colonists returned to Delphi, the priestess responded curtly: 'If you know Libya, feeder of sheep, better than I, I who have been there, though you have not, I much admire your wisdom' (Hdt. 4.150.2–159.4: doc. 2.20). Realising that the oracle was going to insist that its directions were fulfilled to the letter, the colonists returned to Libya, and on this occasion were successful. That this response of the oracle was spontaneous is improbable and it can be argued that all the oracles associated with Cyrene were probably invented in the sixth century. Later generations, of course, believed in these foundation oracles completely, and the fourth-century inscription dealing with a new group of colonists from Thera at that period speaks of the original founders taking out the colony 'in accordance with the injunction of Apollo the Founder (Archagetas)' (Meiggs and Lewis 5: doc. 2.28); Pindar too speaks of Apollo's 'oracles for Cyrene's lord' (Pind. *Pythian Ode* 5: doc. 2.30).

Delphi and the oikistes

Founders were seen as having a special relationship with the god Apollo through their consultation of the oracle at Delphi (Fig. 2.3). The fourth-century inscription preserves the detail that Apollo spontaneously told Battos to settle Cyrene and Pindar's ode focuses on this as of major importance: 'From him even loud-roaring lions fled in fear, when he let loose on them his speech from overseas; and Apollo Archagetas gave the wild beasts to dread fear, so his oracles for Cyrene's lord should not be unfulfilled' (Pind. *Pythian Ode* 5: doc. 2.30).

A further prophecy from Delphi in the reign of Battos' grandson, Battos the Fortunate, when the Cyrenaeans were allocating more land to new settlers, advised all Greeks to settle there with them, because, 'Whoever comes to lovely Libya after the land has been apportioned, I say will later regret it' (Hdt. 4.159.3: doc. 2.29). The settlement continued to be successful and kings descended from Battos, the Battiad dynasty, ruled Cyrene until a democracy took over c. 440. Similarly the Parians preserved the tradition that Archilochos' father in the early seventh century had consulted Delphi prior to Paros' settlement on Thasos, receiving the foundation oracle, 'Report to the Parians, Telesikles, that I bid you found a far-seen city on a lofty island' (Step. Byz. *Lexikon*: doc. 2.25). Before the partheniai set off to Taras in southern Italy, traditionally founded in 706, the Spartans themselves were said to have consulted Delphi about the colony, and the Pythia responded with advice on the specific site to be settled: 'I have given you Satyrion, and the rich land of Taras to dwell in and become a bane to the Iapygians' (Strabo *Geography* 6.3.2–3: doc. 2.23).

Historical foundation oracles

Fifth-century consultations, in contrast, are historical: the Spartans consulted Delphi in their foundation of Herakleia, with the god, it is recorded, specifying who should be allowed to

Figure 2.3 The temple of Apollo at Delphi in which the Pythian priestesses delivered oracles to enquirers. Many cities sent embassies here to seek approval for their colonisation ventures. In the early age of colonisation, however, cities did not do this, but later invented accounts that they had done so. Photo © Sarah C. Murray.

take part ('any of the other Greeks who wished to join them, except the Ionians and Achaeans and some other races'; Thuc. 3.92.1–93.2: doc. 2.24). Similarly Epidamnos consulted Delphi when it received no help from its mother-city Corcyra (Thuc. 1.24.1–26.2: doc. 2.8) and it was on Apollo's advice that prior to the Peloponnesian war the Epidamnians took the Corinthians, who had founded Corcyra in the late eighth century, rather than the Corcyraeans, as their 'oikistai'. Delphi's role in such consultations was mainly confirmatory. Founders were already clear in their own minds as to their plans and the oracle would either agree to the suggestion or not, rather than suggest possible destinations. But, as one of the primary responsibilities of the oikistes, the consultation of Delphi was considered an essential factor in the success of the new settlement and colonies preserved their foundation oracles with pride.

The oikistes

One of the first essentials for any potential colony was that it should have a founder (oikistes) or founders (oikistai) if more than one group was involved in the settlement. The founder was often chosen because of his line of descent: when Knidos founded Lipara in 580 BC, the founder, Pentathlos, was chosen because he traced his descent back to Hippotes, a descendant of Herakles (Diod. Sic. *Library of History* 5.9.1–5: doc. 2.14). The name Miltiades, too, may have suggested in fourth-century Athens that its possessor was an auspicious choice to settle a colony in the Adriatic (*IG* II² 1629: doc. 2.21), in memory of the Miltiades who earlier founded the Athenian colony in the Chersonese (Hdt. 6.103.1: doc. 9.27). If a colony was a joint initiative of two different states it was customary for a founder to represent each group, as in Sicily where Antiphemos (Antiphamos in the Doric dialect) from Rhodes and Entimos from Crete founded Gela; when Gela later founded Akragas, Aristonous and Pystilos were the joint oikistai, with each representing one of the original groups. Zankle (modern Messina) was settled by Perieres of Cumae and Krataimenes of Chalkis. Interestingly the site had already been settled by pirates from Cumae, and although the colony was a Euboean initiative, sent from Chalkis and the rest of Euboea, one of the founders chosen was from the original 'mother-city' of Cumae. Zankle chose three founders, Euklides, Simos and Sakon, when it sent out its own colony to Himera, perhaps because the settlers were from different regions, Chalkidians and the Myletidai, a group of exiles from Syracuse, as well as Cumae (Thuc. 6.3.1–5.3: doc. 2.12). If a colony needed a further wave of settlement, it automatically asked its city of origin for an oikistes to oversee the process.

Sacred fire from the prytaneion

While this is nowhere specifically mentioned as one of the duties of the oikistes, Greek colonists apparently took with them fire from their mother-city, in order that the first fire lit in the new city was kindled from the one burning in the prytaneion (town-hall) in their old home (*Etym. Magn.* 694.28–31: doc. 2.4). In this way the new colony and its oikistes ensured that they maintained the cultural identity and social and religious links of the new foundation with its mother-city.

The selection of the oikistes

Founders were often chosen because they had links, such as family ties, with a particular site. It was also possible for founders to be elected from the citizen body, and when the tyrant Dionysios II regained power at Syracuse in 346 BC, at a time when Carthage was also preparing for an attack on Sicily, the Sicilian Greeks appealed to Corinth, which had founded Syracuse, for assistance. Plutarch notes that the Corinthians 'always took care of the cities they had founded as colonies and Syracuse in particular' (Plut. *Life of Timoleon* 1.1–2.2, 3.1–2: doc. 7.53). In this case they searched for a suitable commander, and possible candidates were recorded by the magistrates prior to holding an election. A number of volunteers put themselves forward for the honour and the choice of Timoleon to lead the resettlement was clearly a public decision, based on his integrity and the success of his past career. His first duty was to rid Sicily of Dionysios II and other tyrants. When Dionysios surrendered to Timoleon, he was dispatched in relative poverty (one ship and a small amount of treasure) to Corinth. The same treatment was meted out to Leptines of Apollonia, who was sent to Corinth on the grounds that it was 'a good thing to have the tyrants of Sicily in the mother-city where they could be seen by the Greeks living the lowly life of exiles' (Plut. *Life of Timoleon* 22.7–24.2: doc. 7.55). Timoleon then, in his resettlement of the depopulated city of Syracuse, not only divided up the land and sold the existing houses for

Figure 2.4 In Sicily, the Greeks erected and decorated magnificent temples to the gods. On this metope from Temple E at Selinous, Zeus and Hera are shown together: he is lifting up her veil as part of their wedding ceremony. The carving dates to about 450 BC. Museo Archeologico, Palermo, Sicily. Photo © Giovanni Dall'Orto/Wikimedia Commons.

1000 talents, and the statues of the tyrants as well (excepting only that of Hieron who was seen as a 'beneficent' ruler), but also repopulated a large proportion of Greek Sicily such as Akragas and Gela under new oikistai, protected it from the Carthaginians and established new laws and a constitution: 'to these settlers,' Plutarch writes, 'Timoleon not only provided security and calm after so long a period of warfare, but also was so committed to supplying them with everything else they needed that he was revered as founder' (Plut. *Life of Timoleon* 35.1–3, 39.3–7: doc. 7.56).

Epameinondas, as founder of two new cities in the Peloponnese, appears to have been chosen by popular acclaim. After the Thebans' victory over the Spartans at Leuktra in 371 BC in which he played the leading part, two new foundations, both primarily his responsibility, took place in the Peloponnese. These were Megalopolis in Arkadia, and Messene at the base of Mount Ithome to be the home of the Messenian helots, both those who had recently been freed from Spartan domination and those who had long been living in exile. The Arkadians synoecised at Epameinondas' instigation in order to create a city which they could defend against the Spartans, and Pausanias relates that Epameinondas 'could fairly be called their oikistes; for it was he who encouraged the Arkadians to undertake synoicism and sent 1000 picked Thebans and Pammenes to defend them' (Paus. *Description of Greece* 8.27.1–2: doc. 14.21).

The duties of the oikistes

Homer's *Odyssey* describes the main duties of an early oikistes: he was expected to define the city's limits, and to wall the site if necessary, divide up the agricultural land equitably between the settlers, build houses and erect temples to the gods on their own land (*Odyssey* 6.1–12: doc. 2.5; Figs 2.4, 2.6). Setting aside land for the gods and building their shrines and temples was one of the oikistes' most important duties, and Pindar describes how Battos at Cyrene 'built greater groves for the gods, [and] made a straight-cut level path for Apollo's processions, which shield men from ill...' (*Pythian Ode* 5: doc. 2.30). When discussing the foundation of Naukratis in Egypt, Herodotos primarily concentrates on the religious precinct, the Hellenion, which was jointly dedicated by all the Greek settlers, and on the other religious foundations established by specific Greek cities: the Aeginetans set up a precinct for Zeus, the Samians one to Hera, and the Milesians one to Apollo. Each group in this way continued the worship of their city's deity in their new settlement (Hdt. 2.178.1–181.2: doc. 2.31). Religious links went right back to the original founders of the mother-city: as late as the fifth century, Cyrene, as a colony of Thera, celebrated the Karneia because in ancient times the Spartans had supposedly founded Thera: the festival, like the cult of Apollo Karneios, was inherited from Sparta by Thera and from Thera by Cyrene.

The founder was clearly meant to ensure that the colony was defensible. At Messene, Epameinondas in 369 BC consulted diviners before deciding on a site for the new helot capital. After the omens proved propitious he turned to the actual construction, had stone brought, and sent for workmen experienced at laying out streets and constructing houses, temples and walls. After a whole day of sacrifices, with each group (Argives, Thebans and Messenians) making offerings to their primary deity and heroes, the men started work on the walls, temples and houses, to the accompaniment of music (Paus. *Description of Greece* 4.26.5–27.11: doc. 14.22). Diodorus adds the usual details that Epameinondas divided up the land equally and granted citizenship to all those who wished it (Diod. Sic. *Library of History* 15.66.1: doc. 14.23).

The settlement at Brea

When the Athenians colonised the site of Brea between 445 and the late 430s (*IG* I³ 46: doc. 12.31) – the actual site is unknown but it is thought to have been near Amphipolis in Thrace – the first responsibility laid upon the oikistai was to ensure that the colonists were organised to embark in timely fashion, and in this case the settlers were to be at Brea within thirty days of arriving at Athens. The founders' next task at the site itself was to sacrifice and obtain good omens on behalf of the colony. Once this divine approval was obtained for the actual site they then oversaw the election of ten men (geonomoi), one from each tribe, to distribute the land. Demokleides, who appears to have been the primary oikistes, had full powers to establish the colony 'as seems best to him', while Aeschines, who was presumably the treasurer of the expedition, provided for any expenses. Precincts already set apart for the gods were left as they were, and others were not consecrated, so the site appears to have been previously settled and the original shrines were preserved. Founders, whether of a new colony or a resettlement, had tremendous responsibilities: they were to make sure that the colonists arrived safely, decide on the details of the actual site and obtain the gods' blessing for the foundation, set up the new city, ensure that land was divided up equitably and the holdings agriculturally viable, and that houses were built, the citizens were self-sufficient, and the whole settlement protected from attack by local populations.

The cult of oikistai

The role of founder was so important that founders had the status of heroes and were revered in their settlements with annual festivals and foundation ceremonies: from Gela, settled in 688 BC, there is a cup dedicated in the fifth century to the Rhodian founder Antiphamos (or Antiphemos), showing that his cult was in existence some 200 years after the colony was founded (Graham 1983, 21–2n.7: doc. 2.6). Cyrene, founded in 631 by settlers from Thera still, Pindar in the mid-fifth century relates, honoured the original king, Battos as a hero, who was 'blessed amongst men while he lived, and afterwards a hero worshipped by the people' (Pind. *Pythian* O*de* 5: doc. 2.30), and Miltiades the Elder was honoured with an annual festival after his death by the Greeks of the Chersonese (Hdt. 6.38.1). The funeral of Timoleon who expelled the tyrants and recolonised Syracuse cost 200 minas at public expense and was attended by thousands of Sicilians: he was buried in the agora and his tomb surrounded with porticoes and made into a gymnasium, named the Timoleonteion in his honour (Plut. *Life of Timoleon* 39.3–7: doc. 7.55).

The founder was seen as the protector of his foundation, even after death, hence his cult. But if the founder was considered not to be performing this role, he could be replaced. When the Spartan Brasidas gained control of the Athenian colony at Amphipolis, where he was killed in battle, the inhabitants decided to forget the previous Athenian founder, Hagnon, and pay honours to Brasidas instead: they enclosed his tomb (presumably in a public place like the agora), sacrificed to him as a hero, and established annual games and sacrifices in his honour (Thuc. 5.11.1: doc. 2.7). Hagnon 'could no longer,' they thought, 'be honoured with similar benefit or contentment' because he had failed in his role as their defender and they clearly considered, following Brasidas' victory and no doubt with the encouragement of a pro-Spartan faction in the city, that a Spartan oikistes would be far more successful in protecting the colony. So colonies could change their founder if they thought this expedient for political or military reasons, and although Sicilian Naxos in conjunction with the Chalkidians (their own mother-city) decided to found Leontinoi and Catana, Catana later chose another founder for itself, Euarchos (Thuc. 6.3.3: doc. 2.12). Colonies could also revere the founder of an earlier epoch in their city's history, as well as their own founder, and when the Teians founded Abdera, after abandoning their homeland to escape Persian rule, they honoured as a hero Timesios of Klazomenai who had been driven out by the Thracians in an earlier attempt at establishing a colony there (Hdt. 1.168.1–169.1: doc. 2.13): apart from the case of Hagnon who did not protect his foundation, everyone who attempted to settle the site should be remembered.

The colonists' oath

An oath of loyalty to the settlement was expected in many cases, and it was the responsibility of the oikistes to ensure that all colonists were committed to the new settlement: when the fourth-century Therans arrived at Cyrene, they swore the same oath as the original settlers in 631 BC, and were assigned to a tribe, phratry and nine hetaireiai (brotherhoods), thus giving them identified affiliations in their new home. The sworn agreement was inscribed on a stele and placed in the temple of Apollo (Meiggs and Lewis 5: doc. 2.28). These later arrivals then possessed citizenship and were allocated land. According to Herodotos, there were still distinct groups among the settlers five generations after the initial settlement, and Demonax of Mantineia was called in to settle the groups' differences: to achieve this he divided them into three tribes consisting of the Theraeans and perioikoi, the Peloponnesians and Cretans, and the islanders (Hdt. 4.161). An oath was also taken by the settlers who colonised Notion, Kolophon's port, under Athenian protection (*IG* I^3 37: doc. 13.8). The Kolophonians who assembled to establish the colony swore: 'I shall act and speak and advise as fittingly and best I can concerning the people of the Athenians and concerning the colony'; they also swore that they would support democratic rule. When a community in Lokris settled additional territory c. 525–500 (Meiggs and Lewis 13 A & C: doc.1.48), rules were again laid down to protect the new and the established settlers. The settlement already possessed a temple, assembly and elders, and land was now allocated to the new colonists. This land was to be sold only if absolutely necessary, while strict regulations for inheritance were laid down, with crops being immune from seizure.

As part of their commitment to their colony, founders were generally expected to remain in the colony they established, at least in the eighth to sixth centuries. However, in the fifth century, when the Spartans established Herakleia in Trachis, the three okistai, Leon, Alkidas and Damagon, perhaps representing three different Peloponnesian groups, do not seem to have remained long in the colony and Spartan magistrates were installed in their place (Thuc. 3.92.1–93.2: doc. 2.24); similarly Hagnon did not remain in Amphipolis, and returned to Athens by 430/29 to take another role as strategos, but was honoured until the Spartan victory outside the city when he was discarded as the founder (Thuc. 5.11.1: doc. 2.7).

Mother-cities and their colonies

In Aristophanes' *Lysistrata*, a comedy in which the women of Greece go on a sex-strike to force their husbands to put an end to the Peloponnesian War, the heroine Lysistrata advises the Athenians to make the best use of their colonies for the good of their mother-city, or metropolis (Ar. *Lysistrata* 582–6: doc. 4.66):

All the cities that are colonies of this country
You must certainly see that these are lying like flocks of wool
All separate; you should take the wool from all of these
Bring it here and gather it into one, and then make
A huge ball, and then out of it weave a cloak for the people.

Certainly those mother-cities which engaged heavily in colonial ventures, like Corinth and Miletos, did so to gain economic and trading advantages for themselves, often specialising in the intensive colonisation of a particular area. In order for this to prove to be to the mother-city's advantage it was important that colonies felt bound to their mother-city and maintained cultural and religious links with it. This was nearly always the case (Corcyra was an exception; Thuc. 1.24.1–26.2: doc. 2.8), although colonists did not retain citizen-rights in their mother-city. Only in Athenian cleruchies, where colonists from Athens were sent out by Perikles and others to act almost as a substitute garrison, was citizenship retained. The mother-city was also expected to retain a strong feeling of responsibility for its colonies, however long ago their date of foundation. This feeling was, generally, reciprocated and is one reason why Greek colonists took with them fire from the prytaneion in their mother-city, to light the first fire in their new settlement thereby reinforcing their religious and cultural links with their homeland (*Etym. Magn.* 694.28–31: doc. 2.4).

The Phokaians provide an extreme example of the ties that settlers could feel for their homeland – to such an extent indeed in this case that half the colonists decided to return home. When abandoning their city, they took all of their movable possessions with them, including of course their temple statues and dedications, 'except what was of bronze, or stone, or paintings', and threw a lump of iron into the sea, swearing an oath that they would never return until this floated (Hdt. 1.164: doc. 2.13). But a large contingent regretted abandoning their city and their customs, and returned despite having to live under Persian rule and break their oath. Considering that the Phokaians had already colonised Corsica, Massilia in France and Emporion in Spain, this bout of homesickness shows that even cities with a history of colonisation could have misgivings about what awaited them and regrets for what they left behind.

The oikistes and the mother-city

The oikistes was of course supplied by the mother-city, and when a colony sent out a colony of its own, the oikistes still came from the original mother-city: when Corcyra, a colony of Corinth, colonised Epidamnos, the oikistes Phalios came from Corinth (Thuc. 1.24.1–26.2: doc. 2.8), and when the inhabitants of Hyblaian Megara in Sicily were forced to relocate by Gelon of Syracuse, Pamillos the oikistes came from Megara, the city which had founded Trotilos, Thapsos and Megara Hyblaia (Thuc. 6.3.1–5.3: doc. 2.12). Similarly, when a city was under threat, for example when Syracuse was under tyrannical rule and facing Carthaginian aggression, the colony appealed to its mother-city, in this case Corinth, for a new 'oikistes', Timoleon. Of all the mainland Greek cities, the great trading centre Corinth, like Miletos, was one of the most dynamic in terms of the establishment of colonies and Plutarch comments on the Corinthians' care for their colonies (Plut. *Life of Timoleon* 1.1–2.2, 3.1–2: doc. 7.53). The Corinthians in the fourth century, acting for the second time as Syracuse's 'oikistai', organised the recolonisation of Sicily to revive agriculture and protect Syracuse and the rest of Greek Sicily in the face of Carthaginian expansion. They proclaimed at the panhellenic games that they were inviting all Syracusans and other Sicilian Greeks in exile to return and resettle Syracuse,

Figure 2.5 The theatre at the Greek city of Taormina (Tauromenion) in Sicily; it has a magnificent setting and view with Mount Etna in the background. Photo © Peter Marik.

and that land would be allocated equitably. Envoys were also sent to Asia Minor and the islands, and Sicilians in exile were invited to come to Corinth where they would be provided with safe passage, a general and ships, all at Corinth's expense. As the numbers were insufficient, the call was extended both to Corinthians and the rest of the Greeks and some 10,000 colonists set sail from Corinth. Under Timoleon's leadership Sicily was resettled with the total number of colonists from Corinth and elsewhere in Greece totalling some 60,000 (Plut. *Life of Timoleon* 22.7–24.2: doc. 7.55). Doubtless the prosperity which returned to Sicily as a result of its repopulation meant that Corinth was well repaid for its apparently altruistic gesture.

Colonies and their relationship to their mother-city

When a colony was suffering factional strife with an exiled group attacking the city, the mother-city could be asked to intervene and find a resolution, and they were in general expected to do so, although in the case of Epidamnos, Corcyra refused to become involved in any process of arbitration (Thuc. 1.24.1–26.2: doc. 2.8). Similarly it appears that Argos was responsible for colonising at least part of Crete, which was the reason why it was involved in a treaty defining the relationship between the two Cretan cities of Knossos and Tylissos (Meiggs and Lewis 42B: doc. 1.53). It was of course possible, as in the case of Corinth and Corcyra, that relations could become dysfunctional, and colonies even revolted from their mother-city, as Camarina did from Syracuse (Thuc. 6.5.3: doc. 2.12). There was a similar relationship in the case of Neapolis which rebelled from its mother-city Thasos, in order to remain allied with Athens when Thasos revolted after the Sicilian Expedition. An Athenian decree commends the Neapolitans, 'because they are colonists of the Thasians and though besieged by them and the Peloponnesians they did not choose to revolt from the Athenians' (*IG* I³ 101: doc. 13.31). Normally, however, the mother-city and its allies were expected to come to the aid of a colony which was under attack, as in the provisions for Athens' fifth-century colony at Brea: 'if anyone wages war against the colonists' territory, the [allied] cities shall come to their aid as quickly as possible in accordance with the agreements' (*IG* I³ 46: doc. 12.31). In warfare and political alliances colonies were expected to take their lead from their mother-city; in the Peloponnesian War the Athenians were afraid that their tributary ally Potidaea, a colony of Corinth, would be persuaded by Corinth to revolt against them, and hence instructed the inhabitants to demolish part of their wall and give hostages (Thuc. 1.56.1–57.1: doc. 2.9).

Mother-cities also expected that their colonies would not only maintain links with them, but view them with a certain respect. Colonies were supposed to grant their mother-cities specific honours, and one of the reasons why the Corinthians decided to help Epidamnos, the colony of Corinth's colony Corcyra, was because they had been angered by Corcyra's refusal to give 'the Corinthians the customary honours in their common festivals, nor served Corinthians with the first portion of the sacrifices, as the other colonies did' (Thuc. 1.25.4: doc. 2.8). This failure or refusal to pay it the due observances in their festivals and sacrifices angered Corinth in its role as mother-city. Other cities expected participation by their colonies in their festivals as well: the decree regarding the settlement of Brea specifies that the colonists were to participate in the festival of the Great Dionysia at Athens and bring a cow, panoply and model phallus for the phallophoria (*IG* I³ 46: doc. 12.31; cf. *IG* I³ 34: doc. 13.17).

Usages inherited from the mother-city

This close relationship between mother-city and colony was reinforced by the existence of stories narrating the colony's settlement and the foundation oracles attributed to Delphi. In ordinary administrative matters, too, colonists retained the accustomed practices of their original city. Dorian colonies kept Doric legal usages as well as the Doric dialect, as in the case when Antiphemos of Rhodes and Entimos of Crete (both Dorian areas) founded Gela. Similarly, when Gela's colony Akragas sent out a colony of its own, it established this settlement in accordance with its own constitution: 'in about 108 years after their own foundation the people of Gela founded Akragas, naming the city after the Akragas river, and making Aristonous and Pystilos the founders, giving it the same usages as those of Gela', and when exiles from Syracuse joined the Chalkidians in the foundation of Himera, they 'mainly' kept to Chalkidian usages, although the dialect was a mixture of Chalkidian and Doric, suggesting that there was some intermingling of Chalkidian and Doric practices to satisfy both groups (Thuc. 6.3.1–5.3: doc. 2.12). It appears that Dorian foundations retained their customs of dining in common messes and having communal property shared between all members of the community, as on the island of Lipara, where holdings were reallocated by lot every twenty years (Diod. Sic. *Library of History* 5.9.1–5: doc. 2.14). Furthermore, in Dorian settlements at least, it may have been customary for the mother-city to supply the colony's magistrates: Potidaea, founded somewhere between 625–585, was still receiving annual magistrates from its mother-city, Corinth, in the 430s, over one and a half centuries since its foundation (Thuc. 1.56.1–57.1: doc. 2.9). In the same way, another Dorian foundation, Herakleia Trachinia, received its magistrates from its mother-city Sparta (Thuc. 3.92.1–93.2: doc. 2.24). In this case, however, the magistrates were not popular, and it was their harsh and often unjust government that caused the decline of the settlement in the face of the Thessalians' aggression.

The colonisation of the west: Italy and Sicily

There were, of course, a number of factors behind the foundation of colonies, both private and public. The economy of the Greek city-state was such that, apart from Athens which in the fifth and fourth centuries depended on importing grain from the Black Sea to feed its large population, it expected to be self-sufficient in terms of production. A typical city was seen as composed of a collection of individual households (oikoi) (Arist. *Politics* 1253b–1254a24: doc. 5.1). The agricultural norm was a subsistence economy in which each family grew enough for its needs until the next harvest, with barter being used for items which could not or had not been produced during that season. Even in Athens, two-thirds of the citizens lived in the countryside of Attica, coming into Athens regularly to perform their civic duties such as attending the assembly, but working the land as small-scale famers. The economy of a city-state was primarily rural and the household unit dependent on small-scale, low-status cultivation and on family labour. In a period when the stock-piling of essential supplies by a central authority was un-thought of, a drought, unseasonable weather or crop failure could 'bankrupt' a city in a single season and its agricultural resources were insufficient to maintain all of the inhabitants until the next harvest.

'Land-hunger' as a motive for colonisation

While many settlements were the result of careful and strategic planning based on the mother-city's needs and goals for future expansion, it was often the case that the dispatch of a colony

Figure 2.6 The Temple of Concord at Agrigento (Akragas), constructed in the fifth century BC. There are several temples at this site attesting to the power and wealth of the Greek cities in Sicily. The whole complex of temples is a UNESCO World Heritage Site. Photo © James Helland.

was an *ad hoc* response to an unexpected crisis with regard to the annual harvest. 'Land-hunger' is frequently cited as one of the decisive factors in colonisation and cities with growing populations found the acquisition of additional agricultural land to support their population a major incentive, even without a crisis at hand. This was clearly, according to Ephoros, one of the reasons for the settlement of the fertile island of Sicily (Ephoros *F* 137: doc. 2.11). Certainly, most colonies, whatever the reason for their foundation, still needed agricultural resources at their new site in order to be self-sufficient without the aid of their mother-city, as well as a viable harbour, access to water and a defensible site in case of aggressive local inhabitants or acquisitive neighbours. Mineral resources and raw materials for manufacture in some cases may well have been another prime motive for settlement, as well as the ability to access or control trade routes and maintain communication with the mother-city.

Even relatively small cities like Chalkis in Euboea undertook a wide-spread colonisation programme and Chalkis was responsible for the colonising not only of Chalkidike in the north of Greece, but of Pithekoussai and Cumae (with Eretria), the earliest Greek colonies in the west, probably founded c. 750–725, although they were the colonies in Italy furthest from Greece. The discovery that iron was smelted at Pithekoussai has been taken to mean that it was this metal which brought the colonists here. This need not have been a primary motive for their settlement, but, along with sufficient, fertile agricultural land the presence of iron for their own use may well have been an additional incentive for the colony, just as the island's position off the west coast of Italy may have been attractive for reasons not just of trade but of defensibility against Etruscans and other enemies (Meiggs and Lewis 1: doc. 2.10).

The colonisation of Sicily

Compared to mainland Greece, Sicily had immense agricultural potential and was extremely prosperous when not under threat from the Carthaginians: one of its traditional epithets was 'spacious' (*IG* I³ 1178: doc. 12.33), and it was attractive because of its fertile land. But, while Ephoros considers that 'land-hunger' was one of the motivating forces behind the colonisation of Sicily, his account shows that the original founder Theokles (Thoukles in the Dorian dialect), an Athenian who saw its potential, was unable to persuade his fellow-citizens to take advantage of this excellent land, and so took with him a range of colonists from other cities – Chalkidians, Ionians and Dorians, with most of the Dorians being Megarians. The Chalkidians founded Naxos (in 734 BC) and the Megarians Megara Hyblaia, named after their own home town, thus beginning the successful process of the colonisation of Sicily (Ephoros *F* 137: doc. 2.11). In other words, while Athens was not tempted to acquire extra agricultural land at this point, the chance of such an acquisition was, for most cities with a large population, too attractive to pass up.

Thucydides' account of the dramatic development of colonisation within Sicily up to his own time (Thuc. 6.3.1–5.3: doc. 2.12), which possibly derives from the narrative of Antiochos of Syracuse, details a number of motives behind the establishment of colonies in Sicily in the period 734–598 BC. The most important of these was clearly the wish to acquire additional agricultural land. In fact, not only did these colonies once founded send out colonies of their own to other parts of Sicily, but many of the original settlers were displaced by later arrivals from Greece or southern Italy attracted by the island's prosperity. It was not unusual for colonies, once established, to send out further colonies, which suggests that there was something of a race to seize spots for valuable land, or trading posts, before potential rivals arrived. This was particularly the case in Sicily and shows the prosperous nature of the island and the dynamic growth of Greek settlement there. Syracuse, founded by Corinth in 733, itself founded Akrai, Camarina and Casmenae; Gela, established by founders from Rhodes and Crete in 688, founded Akragas (Agrigentum) in 580; Megara Hyblaia, founded by Megara in 728, settled Selinous in 628; and Selinous went on in the sixth century to found Herakleia Minoa. Cultivation of land was also important at Lipara, an island to the north of Sicily, where half the colonists farmed and the other half provided defence from pirates (Diod. Sic. *Library of History* 5.9.1–5: doc. 2.14). In this case the colonists on the island came from Knidos on Rhodes, and joined 500 settlers left from an earlier colony. These farmed the land in common, following the communal lifestyle common to Dorian societies such as Sparta and Crete.

Political motives: Phokaia and Teos

There were often political reasons behind the foundation of a colony, and on many occasions this occurred because the mother-city was threatened by Persian domination or the aggression of local inhabitants or other Greeks. Both Phokaia and Teos dispatched colonies to avoid Persian domination (they were 'unable to endure slavery'), and in these cases the entire population of the home city departed rather than just a settled number of colonists (Hdt. 1.163.1–169.1: doc. 2.13). It was the Phokaians, according to Herodotos, who were the first to undertake long voyages and discover the Adriatic, Etruria and Spain, and so their departure for the west was to an area with which they were long familiar: Massalia, on the southern coast of France, was also a Phokaian colony, founded c. 600 BC. However, in the event of their mass exodus c. 565 BC, while half of the Phokaians settled at their existing colony on Corsica, at Alalia, the other half of the Phokaians soon returned home out of homesickness. Those who did not return home asked the Chians to sell them the Oinousai islands: the Chians obviously feared them as trade rivals (or possibly, in view of their later career) as pirates, and refused, and so they continued on to Corsica. After founding a settlement there they relocated following a naval battle against a combined force of Carthaginians and Etruscans c. 537 BC to the safer haven of Rhegium, from where they later founded Elea (Hdt. 1.163.1–169.1: doc. 2.13). Another case in point is Teos, which like Phokaia had been threatened by the Persian general Harpagos. As a result the entire population left c. 545 BC for Thrace, where they founded the city of Abdera, a site earlier unsuccessfully colonised by Timesios of Klazomenai. Other peoples of Asia Minor left to found colonies elsewhere to avoid Persian rule, and not long after the Teians' settlement, Aristagoras of Miletos, in attempting to escape Darius following the failure of the Ionian Revolt in 494, tried to settle the site of Amphipolis but was driven out by the Edonians (Thuc. 4.102.2). The Samians and other Ionians who left their homes because of the Persians were more successful in 486 BC, taking over Zankle in Sicily after driving out the original setters (Thuc. 6.4.5–6: doc. 2.12).

The Black Sea and Propontis

Mixed motives for colonisation

Most cities sending out colonies did so from a variety of motives: while some may have found that their population had outgrown the available agricultural land, or were impelled by drought or bad harvests in a particular year to take emergency measures to remove some of their surplus population, trading considerations in general played a very important role in the colonisation movement. Of course the availability of agricultural land at a particular site was essential for all colonies, even centres founded especially for trade (emporia), because all settlements had to be agriculturally self-sufficient and capable of producing enough food for their inhabitants. But not all colonies were founded because the mother-city was incapable of sustaining its current population. From the fact that Miletos on the coast of Asia Minor sent out dozens of colonies along the coast of the Black Sea (Anaximenes of Lampsakos *F* 26: doc. 2.16), it is clear that most of these were established as trading stations, which promoted Miletos' development into a great mercantile centre. None of these colonies around the Black Sea, except perhaps the early settlement of Sinope on the south shore, was founded to relieve Miletos of surplus population, and by the beginning of the fifth century these settlements had become very important centres of trade, especially with regard to the export of grain and slaves. Sinope had been founded in the mid-eighth century by Miletos probably for agricultural purposes, while other inducements included its strategic commercial position. Minerals and fish were perhaps a further incentive (Pseudo-Skymnos *Geographical Description* 986–97: doc. 2.17). The area was of great importance to Miletos: when the colony at Sinope founded initially by Habrondas in the mid-eighth century was taken over by the Cimmerians, the Milesians later re-established it in 631 BC (Pseudo-Skymnos *Geographical Description* 986–97: doc. 2.17). Sinope then established other colonies in the area, Kerasous, Kotyora and Trapezous, taking land from barbarians for this purpose, and the colonies paid Sinope tribute in return.

Even neighbouring foundations by the same city could have entirely different motives for their settlement: Megara was responsible for the foundation of Chalcedon (on the Asian side of the Bosphoros) in 685 or 676 and Byzantium (on the European side) some seventeen years later. The Persian Megabazos thought those at Chalcedon quite strange and 'blind' indeed to have passed up the opportunities for controlling trade in and out of the Black Sea inherent in the later site. The earlier settlers at Chalcedon, however, appear to have been looking for agricultural land (Hdt. 4.144.1–2: doc. 2.15).

Colonies and trading networks

One of the main advantages for mother-cities was the trading networks that their colonies could create to their mutual advantage. The great colonising cities, like Corinth and Miletos, were clearly taking every chance to establish a network of colonies and trading stations to underwrite their wealth and prosperity, and were not concerned to rid themselves of surplus population. Corinth was proverbially 'wealthy' (Thuc. 1.13.2, 1.13.5: doc. 1.61), and Miletos' interest in the Black Sea, an area vital for the grain supply, was obviously commercial, although metals as well as grain may have been an initial incentive. By the end of the sixth century grain was certainly being purchased by colonists from the native inhabitants to send to the older cities of the mainland and the Asia Minor coast (Hdt. 7.147.2–3: doc. 1.71). Miletos had an important impact on this area with numerous colonies and emporia (trading centres) around the coastline of the Black Sea including Sinope, Amisos (with Phokaia), Apollonia Pontika, Berezan, Kepoi, Istros, Odessos, Olbia, Phasis, Theodosia, Tieion, Tomis, Tyros and possibly Myrmekion, Hermonassa and Nymphaion. From Berezan comes the well-known 'lead letter' which tells how one business rival seized the cargo and employee of another on the grounds of an outstanding claim (Chadwick 35–6: doc. 1.64).

Xenophon and the 'Ten Thousand'

One example of an attempt to found a colony as a private venture without reference to a particular mother-city occurred c. 400 BC, when Xenophon and his 'Ten Thousand'

Figure 2.7 Dolphin-shaped bronze coins from Olbia, fifth–fourth century BC. The coins are 25mm long and 13mm high from fin-top to bottom. Dolphins are very common in the Black Sea. Yale University Art Gallery, 2001.87.9802 and 2007.182.93.

Greeks reached the Black Sea coastline after fighting their way across Asia Minor, following the death of Cyrus whom Xenophon and the Greek mercenaries were supporting in his coup against his brother, Artaxerxes II, king of Persia (404–358 BC). On their arrival at the Black Sea, Xenophon contemplated the army's establishing a colony there, with their current numbers reinforced by other Greek inhabitants from the Black Sea area. The idea was scuttled by the intrigues of Cyrus' seer Silanos, who passed round to the troops the report that 'Xenophon wanted the army to settle there and found a city to achieve fame and power for himself'. Xenophon, as the organiser of the settlement, would have had the honour of being the oikistes. While most of the army in any case wanted to return home, Xenophon relates that some of them were attracted to this proposition and it appears that this group of soldiers could easily have established a viable settlement and without any opposition. Xenophon's idea while thwarted was definitely a practical proposition, and it is interesting that it was merchants from Greek colonies in the locality, seeing these potential settlers as rivals in trade, that paid for provisions to allow the mercenaries to sail home (Xen. *Anabasis* 5.6.15–19: doc. 2.20). As a body of 10,000 adult males, they would have founded a city of exactly the size that Aristotle thought most appropriate (Arist. *Politics* 1326a40–b24: doc. 1.3).

Political and strategic reasons for colonisation: Sparta and Athens

'Ad hoc' colonisation

The very real possibility of relocating an entire population for political reasons is graphically shown in Themistokles' threat to his Peloponnesian allies in the second Persian War (480 BC) that all the inhabitants of Athens would sail off to settle in Italy if the Peloponnesians withdrew to the Isthmus and did not stay to face the Persian fleet at Salamis. In Herodotos' version Themistokles was taunted as being a man 'without a city' by the Corinthian commander Adeimantos because the Athenians had abandoned Athens to the Persians. He leveraged the situation by remarking that, although the Athenians had evacuated their city for the common good, if the Peloponnesians withdrew behind the Isthmus and abandoned the rest of Greece, the Athenians would take their 200 triremes and sail safely out of the Persian sphere to Siris in Italy, where they would found a new Athens. Plutarch has an alternative account where it is the Spartan commander Eurybiades who provokes Themistokles, who then retorts:

> We have the greatest city in Greece, our two hundred triremes, which are now ready to help you, if you want to be saved by them, but if you go away and betray

us again, the Greeks will soon hear that the Athenians have acquired a city as free
and land no worse than that we cast off.

(Plut. *Life of Themistokles* 11.5: doc. 11.37)

As a result of this threat, which was clearly a very real one, the Peloponnesians stayed to fight
at Salamis, and the Persian fleet was defeated. Colonies could be founded by anyone with
enough ships and manpower to win and hold the land they desired: in the ill-fated Sicilian
Expedition Nikias raised the spirits of the Athenians prior to their retreat from Syracuse
with the suggestion that if they wished they could settle down there and found their own city
(Thuc. 7.77.4).

Spartan colonisation

Mother-cities naturally settled colonies for political and strategic reasons, and there are examples from both Athens and Sparta, although neither was given to extensive colonisation in the
normal way. Athens' main colonies were at Sigeion, founded in the late seventh century, on the
Asian shore of the Hellespont (Hdt. 5.94.1–95.2: doc. 2.18), and the Chersonese, which was
settled by Miltiades in the time of Peisistratos c. 559–556, but more for personal reasons than
for reasons of state (Herodotos 6.10 3.1–4: doc. 9.27). Athens had less need for colonies than
most by the fifth century, as the city had the Attic countryside as well as tribute from its allies
and a constant grain supply from the Black Sea. Similarly Sparta, in the archaic period, solved
any 'land-hunger' problems by annexing the territory of its neighbours the Messenians in the
First and Second Messenian Wars, thus acquiring a vast tract of agricultural land and a subject
population to farm it (Strabo *Geography* 8.4.10: doc. 6.52). While there was a tradition that the
Spartans were the original founders of Thera, for which reason Cyrene maintained Spartan
usages and festivals (Pind. *Pythian* Ode 5: doc. 2.30), there is no evidence from the historical
period about the foundation.

Sparta's eighth-century foundation of Taras in south-eastern Italy was not to acquire extra
land but was intended to be a solution to a political problem at home. It aimed to rid the city
of a group of 'partheniai', who for some reason no longer possessed citizen rights: sources
suggest that these may have been Spartans who did not take part in the First Messenian War
or who were of mixed birth and unhappy with their lack of citizen privileges (Strabo *Geography* 6.3.2–3: doc. 2.23). The partheniai successfully settled Taras in c. 706 BC and the colony
was clearly one of willing volunteers, who continued to maintain their links with Sparta and
retained their Dorian traditions. The Spartan king Archidamos III (360–338) was killed fighting there in Italy, after Taras requested help against the Lucanians in 343 BC. He arrived
there with a fleet and army in 342, and was still battling on the colony's behalf when he was
defeated at Manduria in Apulia in 338 BC.

Dorieus and Spartan colonisation

Colonies could also be sent out for personal motives by one or more disgruntled individuals, with or without approval by their state. A colonising venture was organised by Dorieus,
son of the Spartan king Anaxandridas, who attempted to establish a colony in the western
Mediterranean, when his half-brother Kleomenes was made king of Sparta c. 521/0 BC.
Although Kleomenes was the elder of the two brothers, Dorieus was the son of Anaxandridas' first wife, and felt he had the better claim. While his reasons for departure were private
ones, his venture was officially sanctioned at Sparta, and he had others with him who wished

to leave Sparta and try their luck elsewhere. He was granted these companions from among the Spartan citizens and attempted, unsuccessfully, to establish a settlement in Libya. He returned to the Peloponnese, and before making his next attempt consulted Delphi about the possibility of successfully establishing a colony at Eryx in western Sicily. He then sailed west and en route helped Croton in its war against Sybaris, but was killed in battle (Hdt. 5.42.2–45.1: doc. 2.22). However, one of Dorieus' companions, Euryleon, did succeed in setting up a brief tyranny at Selinous in 507/6 (Hdt. 5.46). In somewhat similar circumstances, Miltiades the Elder appears to have founded his colony in the Chersonese because of his unwillingness to remain in Athens under the rule of Peisistratos, although presumably he had the tyrant's approval for his undertaking as other Athenians went with him as colonists. He was succeeded as tyrant by his nephews Stesagoras and Miltiades the Younger, who was sent out officially as tyrant after being archon in 524/3 BC, to ensure Athenian control of traffic through the Hellespont. In this case it appears that a settlement for 'private' reasons later became a foundation officially controlled from Athens (Hdt. 6.103.1–4: doc. 9.27).

Herakleia in Trachis

The later Spartan colony, the fifth-century foundation of Herakleia in Trachis, had a strategic motive behind it, and it was settled by Sparta in 426 during the Peloponnesian War because it was ideally suited as a strategic base to station a fleet which was then well situated to attack Euboea, as well as handy for access to Thrace (Thuc. 3.92.1–93.2: doc. 2.24). It was also hoped that the settlement would stop some of the locals who were in conflict with each other allying themselves with the Athenians. However, hostility from the Thessalians and the inequitable government of the Spartan magistrates soon saw most of the colonists returning home.

Athenian colonies and cleruchies

During the Peloponnesian War the Athenians also established colonies and cleruchies, colonies at sites such as Thourioi in southern Italy and Brea, as well as cleruchies on the territory of rebellious allies, with the Athenian settlers (unlike normal colonists) retaining their Athenian citizenship and acting as a garrison for Athens. Plutarch (*Life of Perikles* 11.4–6: doc. 12.25) records that Perikles established cleruchies in the Chersonese, on Andros and Naxos, and in Thrace, amounting between them to 2750 settlers. Other colonists were sent to the new settlement of Sybaris (renamed Thourioi) in Italy (where Herodotos was to die). Thourioi was not an entirely Athenian refoundation, but the oikistes, Lampon, was from Athens and its constitution was democratic, with ten tribes, as at Athens. Perikles' rationale according to Plutarch was to remove the unemployed from the city, relieve poverty, and prevent rebellion from conquered territories:

> In this way he lightened the city of an idle mob, who were trouble-makers because they had leisure, and relieved the poverty of the people, and by sending out settlers to live alongside the allies installed both fear and a garrison to prevent their rebellion.

However Plutarch's notion of an 'idle mob' of Athenian citizens is anachronistic and need not be taken seriously (see p. 436). In 437/6 BC Hagnon led the Athenian colony to Amphipolis in Thrace, a valuable site for Athens as it provided timber (needed for the fleet) and controlled silver mines in the region, as well as commanding important trade routes and the crossing of the Strymon river. This was just the latest in a series of attempts to settle the site: there were several earlier attempts, the first of these by Aristagoras of Miletos, and thirty-two years later the Athenians sent out 10,000 colonists to 'Nine Ways' (Ennea Hodoi), as Amphipolis was then known, who drove out the Edonians, but who were destroyed by the Thracians at Drabeskos. Finally, twenty-nine years later, under Hagnon, the Athenians finally succeeded. Brea, which may have been sited near Amphipolis, was settled between 445 and 430 by colonists from Athens taken from the two lowest property classes, the zeugitai and the thetes. This was clearly a measure by the Athenians to settle urban poor on properties outside of Athens, who if they were prosperous could then join the hoplite class (*IG* I³ 46: doc. 12.31), thus not only providing for citizen colonists but making sure that the most needy were targeted. The decree provided for their defence and they had to maintain their religious and cultural links with Athens by participating in the festival of the Great Dionysia at Athens.

In 427 BC during the Peloponnesian War the Athenians also founded a colony at Notion, Kolophon's port (*IG* I³ 37: doc. 13.8), after a pro-Athenian group at Notion fled the city following a take-over by the pro-Persian party. The Athenian general Paches placed Notion in the power of those who remained loyal to Athens, and a number of settlers from Athens, under the command of oikistai, together with all the exiled Kolophonians they could find who had settled themselves elsewhere, were established at Notion as an Athenian colony. These Kolophonians swore loyalty to Athens and to a democratic constitution, and one of the oikistai's first duties was to set up the decree and oath taken at Athens on a stele in the new colony. Other colonies of Athens were established on the territory of defeated opponents: when Melos sided with Sparta in 416/15 BC the Athenians took the island, and enslaved the women and children after killing all the adult males. Five hundred colonists were later sent out from Athens to settle the island (Thuc. 6.62.3–4: doc. 5.4). This practice continued in the fourth century and *IG* II² 1609 (doc. 1.31) describes a list of trierarchies in 371/0 or 366/5 in which a number of the ships carried cleruchs under the leadership of their founders Euktemon and Euthios: the destination is not known.

Thasos

Paros in about 680 BC colonised Thasos in the northern Aegean for its gold, but it was also a viable settlement agriculturally (Archil. *F* 21: doc. 2.27). Earlier colonised by the Phoenicians, the island of Thasos was 'rich in gold' (obviously the primary motive for the colony), but also possessed fertile land and vineyards, and a regulation regarding the wine trade, obviously of great importance to Thasos, controlled the retail sale of wine (Pleket *Epigraphica* I, no. 2: doc. 1.66). There were extremely rich sources of gold on the Greek mainland north of the island, where the colonists took control. That the gold was an incentive for the settlement is seen by the fact that when Thasos unsuccessfully rebelled against Athenian control, probably in 465, it lost control of the mainland and mines (Thuc. 1.100.2–101.3: doc. 12.9), and one of Archilochos' complaints about the island concerned the troubles brought about by the quest for gold: his father, Telesikles, had led the colony from Paros (Archil. *FF* 20: doc. 2.27). Herodotos estimates that the revenue from these mines brought great wealth and that Thasos had an annual revenue of 200 or 300 talents (Hdt. 6.46.2).

The Thasians had trouble with natives on the mainland and it was in a battle against one tribe, the Saians, that the lyric poet Archilochos threw away his shield, an unheroic feat which he later celebrated in his poetry (Archil. *F* 5: doc. 2.26). Tradition recorded that when he visited Sparta, the Spartans were so shocked by this boasting of his cowardice that they expelled him from the city. He also, according to later sources, visited Italy, which he compares favourably to the rugged and mountainous island of Thasos that he describes as 'an ass's backbone, covered with forest', and complains that the quest for gold had brought miseries on the Parian colonists (Archil. *FF* 20, 21: doc. 2.27). Obviously he did not settle on Thasos and appears to have served as a mercenary soldier. He was said to have been killed in a battle against the Naxians. His satirical poetry was considered the equal of Homer's, and after his death he was worshipped as a hero on the island of Paros.

The Greeks at Cyrene

Drought at Thera

When the inhabitants of the small island of Thera suffered a seven-year drought in which all but one of the trees on the island died (probably a detail invented for dramatic effect), they sent off colonists to Cyrene in order to reduce the surplus population. According to the fourth-century inscription concerning a further wave of settlers, which quotes the original decree, the colonists were only taken from families where there was more than one son, so there was no mass conscription of settlers. On the other hand, refusal to go, or the concealment of someone who refused to go (even if a family member), incurred the death penalty and confiscation of property. Wax images were burnt and oaths sworn by everyone on the island, including women and children, whether staying or going, that they would all abide by their oath to send out this settlement: those that kept the oath would have good fortune both for themselves and their descendants (Meiggs and Lewis 5: doc. 2.28). The seriousness of the oaths taken is reflected in the burning of wax-images as a form of sympathetic magic, and clearly the colonists were not volunteers; similar curses were laid on any of the Phokaians who changed their mind and returned to Phokaia under Persian rule (Hdt. 1.165.1–3: doc. 2.13).

The extent of the problem caused by the drought and crop failure is seen by the number

Figure 2.8 A silver didrachma from Cyrene showing the silphium plant on its reverse; this was one of the main export products of the city. On the obverse of the coin there is a head of Zeus Ammon; the shrine of the Egyptian god Ammon, whom the Greeks identified with Zeus, was in the Egyptian desert to the east of Cyrene. This didrachma has a diameter of 21mm. Yale University Art Gallery, 2007.182.146.

of settlers involved: Herodotos speaks of two pentekonters of colonists, or some 100 settlers, who were to remain away for a minimum of five years: after that they were allowed to return (Hdt. 4.150.2–159.4: doc 2.29). This extraneous population was clearly carefully considered as sufficient to redress the balance of the seven-year drought, and the expectation was that over a five-year period the agricultural economy of the island of Thera would have improved enough to allow these settlers to return home. Should, however, they prosper in Africa, relatives could join them there, be granted some of the unallocated land and share in civic rights and stand for office. The settlement of course eventually prospered, and the colonists, once they were established, married local women from Libya; other settlers joined them two generations later and there was a further wave of colonists from Thera in the fourth century. Similarly, according to Strabo (6.257), Rhegium in Sicily was founded on advice from Delphi after Chalkis suffered a bad harvest and 'dedicated' a tenth of its inhabitants as colonists to the god Apollo: clearly again the departure of one-tenth of the citizens relieved the city of just enough population to allow it to survive the crisis.

Just as trading centres needed where possible to be able to support their inhabitants agriculturally, those settlements founded to solve problems of overcrowding in their mother-city were obviously not averse to engaging in trade whenever possible, and maintained close trading links with their mother-city. Cyrene in Libya, for example, although founded after the island of Thera suffered a severe drought, was noted for the production of the medicinal plant silphium

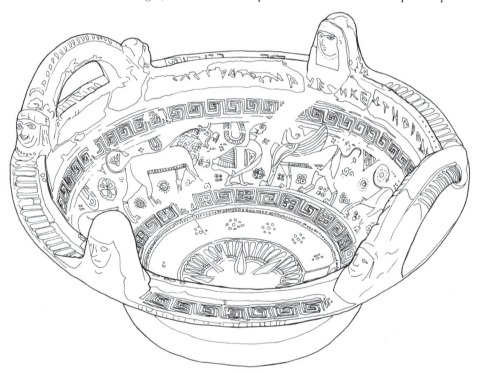

Figure 2.9 This bowl by the Naukratis Painter was discovered in the Greek sanctuary of the goddess Aphrodite at Naukratis, in Egypt. Along the rim has been scratched an inscription that indicates that Sostratos dedicated it to Aphrodite. The Greek traders at Naukratis continued to worship their own gods and to build temples to them (doc. 2.31). British Museum Gr 1888.6–1.456, London. Drawing by J. Etherington.

which was prized widely throughout Greece. Silphium became the main export of the colony, and it even appeared on Cyrene's coinage (Fig. 2.8): a Spartan cup depicts King Arkesilas II of Cyrene, of the mid-sixth century, supervising its weighing, although the commodity is often thought to be wool (Fig. 6.2). Clearly there was also an element of luck involved here in finding the best site. The Therans were guided by natives to Irasa, a region in Libya which possessed a spring sacred to Apollo and 'where (the natives told the colonists) the sky has holes in it', and this annual rainfall was obviously an advantage in cultivation, whether of silphium or subsistence crops.

The Greeks in Egypt: traders and mercenaries

Al Mina and Tell Sukas

Al Mina, the most important emporion, trading depot, in the eastern Mediterranean, was located in northern Syria, at the outlet of the Orontes river. The site was settled by the Greeks about 825, or perhaps even earlier, and it is thought to have been an emporion, rather than a settlement of Greeks living among the local people, as in a colony proper. The remains of numerous warehouses have been uncovered there, mostly dating to after c. 700, and the site was exclusively commercial. The Euboean element is dominant in the archaeological finds until c. 700, possibly corresponding to the destruction of the site at that date; after this date Corinthian ware takes over, suggesting a change in the composition of the community. This emporion would have resumed the trade which the Mycenaeans had conducted with the Levant until the eleventh century BC, and the site prospered until the establishment of Seleukia, Antioch's port, which replaced it in 301 BC. Another Greek emporion seems to have been established 70 kilometres to the south, at Tell Sukas, but this had a shorter history, c. 850–500. Greek traders at these sites were seeking copper, as well as manufactured goods such as dyed Phoenician cloth, worked gold and silver, ivories and bronzes.

Naukratis

Another important emporion in the eastern Mediterranean was Naukratis in the Delta region of the Nile. The primary reason for settlement in Egypt was again trade, with grain from Egypt exchanged for Greek wines, although Herodotos has an unusual angle on the story on how the wine-jars were disposed of, recording that the Egyptians used them to store water in desert regions (Hdt. 3.6.1–2: doc. 1.67). Bacchylides speaks of 'wheat-bearing ships across the gleaming sea bringing immense wealth from Egypt' (*F* 20b). Naukratis was established during the reign of Psammetichos I (664–610), who used Greek mercenaries (initially raiders or pirates) to establish himself in power in Egypt. Psammetichos then settled these Carian and Ionian mercenaries in settlements called the 'Camps' on opposite sides of the Nile at the Pelousian mouth, near Boubastis, and trained Egyptian boys in Greek, who later became interpreters. Herodotos tells us that he saw the ruins of their houses and hauling-engines for the ships.

King Amasis (570–526) later moved the settlement to Memphis and granted the Greek traders the city of Naukratis, where both those who settled there and other Greek merchants were allowed to worship at the religious shrines (Fig. 2.9). The Aeginetans, Samians and Milesians set up precincts to their own particular deities, while the Hellenion, the most important of these shrines, was jointly dedicated by Chios, Teos, Phokaia and Klazomenai (the Ionians),

Rhodes, Knidos, Halikarnassos and Phaselis (the Dorians), and Mytilene (the Aeolians): these cities provided for the operation of Naukratis as a trading centre and a wide variety of Greek states were involved in this commercial enterprise. Naukratis, Herodotos relates, was powerful because it was the only trading station in Egypt, to which all merchant ships were diverted. The wealth of Egypt was underrepresented in the donations from Naukratis towards the 300 talents needed to rebuild the temple at Delphi after it burned down: Amasis donated 1000 talents of alum and the Greeks of Egypt 20 minas (Hdt. 2.152.3–154.5, 178.1–181.2: doc. 2.31).

Greeks descended from these earlier settlers served on the expedition of Psammetichos II to Ethiopia in 591 BC, en route carving graffiti on the colossal statues of Ramesses II at Abu Simbel (Fig. 2.10). Those mercenaries who record their names without ethnics (places of origin) were born in Egypt, while the others, like Helesibios the Teian, may have been born in Egypt as well, but were simply more conservative in continuing to use their fathers' ethnics, reflecting their family's place of origin (Meiggs and Lewis 7: doc. 2.32).

Access to sufficient supplies of grain was one of the most important motivations for setting up emporia, and Athens in particular was in the fifth century dependent on grain from the Black Sea (as well as from Sicily and Egypt). In the fourth century, having lost their empire, the Athenians attempted to establish a colony to serve as a trading station in the area of the Adriatic, specifically to secure a grain supply (*IG* II² 1629: doc. 2.21): the actual site has not been identified. Led by a Miltiades, the colonists were transported in nine ships, plus some additional quadriremes. The potential for trade was also a consideration, but the main object

Figure 2.10 Greek mercenaries in the employ of King Psammetichos II of Egypt served with the Egyptian forces in Nubia in 591 BC, and some of them carved their names on the legs of the 20m high statues of Ramesses II at his mortuary complex at Abu Simbel (doc. 2.32). Photo © Diana I. Chen.

was to set up a trading station to supply grain, and provisions were made to provide safe anchorage for any ships sailing along that coastline and defences against Etruscan fleets in the area.

Greeks and indigenous populations

Naturally the network of Greek colonies across the Mediterranean and Black Sea was not without its effects on existing local populations, and the settlers, who often displaced native groups, brought Greek culture with them. A colony often faced problems before it was successfully established and when colonies were founded the Greeks often had to fight the native inhabitants for the land they wanted. In some cases they had to make several attempts before they could find a place to settle. In other cases Greek settlers competed against each other for sites, as the Athenians and Mytilenaians did at Sigeion, where in 607/6 the Athenian general Phrynon was killed in single combat with Pittakos, later tyrant of Mytilene, in a dispute over possession of the site: the dispute was referred to the arbitration of Periander, tyrant of Corinth, who awarded Sigeion to Athens (Hdt. 5.94.1–95.2: doc. 2.18). The fertility of Sicily was such that a number of colonies which were displaced by subsequent waves of settlers, relocated elsewhere on the island, and there was often no feeling of mutual solidarity between Greek colonies even in areas where the locals were hostile: in Sicily, where there were both the local tribes, the Sikels and Sikani, and the Carthaginians to deal with, the Greeks fought not only against these two groups, but also against each other. Some even sided with the Carthaginians in order to gain territory from rival Greek cities, as Egesta did, co-operating with Carthage in the horrendous sack of Selinous in 409 (Diod. Sic. *Library of History* 13.57.1–58.2: doc. 13.32).

The 'hellenisation' of the Mediterranean coastline

The Greeks brought with them not only their language, literacy, art and architecture, but all that made a city Greek, and they were to have a particular impact on the West. The Euboean colonists from Chalkis and Eretria, for example, who founded Pithekous-

Figure 2.11 Both sides of a silver tetradrachma (four drachma) coin, of about 409–406 BC from Akragas (modern Agrigento), Sicily. The obverse (front) shows a chariot being driven by winged Nike, a goad in her right hand; the reverse shows two eagles devouring a pregnant hare: the omen which is described in Aeschylus' *Agamemnon*. Photo © CNG Coins.

sai and Cumae in western Italy took the 'Chalkidic' alphabet, their form of the Greek alphabet, with them and this influenced the alphabet used by the Etruscans and later by the Romans which has lasted in Europe to the present day. Southern Italy and Sicily were beautified with Greek temples and theatres, which still stand and where the plays of the greatest dramatists of the time were presented. The temples of Juno and Concordia at Akragas (Fig. 2.6), and those of Hera, built c. 550 and c. 450 at Paestum in Italy, rival any constructed on the Greek mainland, with the possible exception of the Parthenon, and the theatres at Taormina, Egesta, Syracuse, Catania, Morgantina and Tindari in Sicily are evidence of the extent to which settlers in 'Magna Graeca' (Greater Greece) demonstrated a love of dramatic entertainment, developed but not exclusively performed in Athens.

Athletics were an important part of the culture that the colonists took with them. As proof of this, the Greeks from the colonies had great successes in the Olympic and other panhellenic games, and their rulers employed the most eminent poets to eulogise their successes. Pindar, for example, wrote two odes celebrating the victory of Arkesilas IV of Cyrene in the four-horse chariot race at Delphi in 462 BC, and another for Telesikrates, victor in the foot-race in full armour in 474 (Pind. *Pythian Ode* 5: doc. 2.30). Hieron, tyrant of Syracuse, was victorious in the four-horse chariot race at Delphi in 482, 478 and 470, and in the same event at Olympia in 468, and his successes were celebrated by both Pindar and Bacchylides (docs 7.57–9; Fig. 7.3).

Colonies, in Sicily in particular, were visited by the most eminent of Greek scholars – Plato, for example, spent much time in Sicily hoping to create the 'perfect' philosopher-king out of Dionysios II of Syracuse, and his view of the luxurious lifestyle of Sicily is given in his *Seventh Letter* (doc. 7.52). Significantly Aeschylus and Herodotos both died in colonies in the Greek west: little else could demonstrate the extent to which this area was as integral a part of the Greek world as Athens or Sparta, and Aeschylus' epitaph, in 456/5, notes that he was buried at Gela (*F* 2: doc. 11.11). He had visited Sicily at least once before and composed his play (now lost), *The Women of Aetna*, to celebrate Hieron's foundation of the new city of Aetna. He may also have written *Prometheus Bound* while in Sicily and produced his *Persians* there at Syracuse. There was also a later tradition in which Euripides was recorded as having taken part in a diplomatic mission to Syracuse. Naples, on the west coast of Italy, which was founded prior to 650 BC, had a mixed Greek and Italian population, and employed both Greek and Italian names for their magistrates, but preserved Greek culture in their use of gymnasia, wrestling-courts (ephebeia), phratries and Greek names. They also, in Strabo's time, celebrated a musical and athletic competition every four years, which Strabo considered the equal of those in Greece itself (*Geography* 5.4.7: doc. 2.35). Similarly, the city of Emporion on the east coast of Spain, a trading centre founded between 600 and 575 BC, had a constitution which combined both Greek and local usages, which, Strabo comments, was the case in many other colonies (*Geography* 3.4.8: doc. 2.36).

The Greek impact on indigenous populations

Greek culture also had an impact on local populations in other ways. Greek colonies, as a result of their commercial interchanges and other contacts with local populations, might 'go native' to some degree, and this resulted in colonies not always retaining a purely Greek character. Herodotos speaks of 'Scythian Greeks', perhaps the result of Greek-native inter-marriages and acculturisation, and the Gelonoi, and possibly the Kallipidai, on the Black

Sea coast were examples of Greeks dispossessed by later Greek settlers, who joined Scythian tribes, forming a Hellenic-Scythian culture (Hdt. 4.16–17, 108–9: docs 2.33–4). In many cases intermarriage with local populations assisted the smooth foundation of the colony: Euxenos, the oikistes of the Phokaian colony at Massalia (modern Marseilles in southern France), married a Celtic princess (Arist. *F* 549), and the daughter of one of the kings of Cyrene was said to have married the Egyptian king Amasis, although in another version the bride was the daughter of a wealthy citizen (Hdt. 2.181.1: doc. 2.31). Miltiades the Younger clearly acculturated: he married a daughter of the Thracian king Oloros, and only fled the Chersonese in advance of Darius' attack (Hdt. 6.34.1–41.4), while the Therans who settled in Libya were an all-male contingent and must have planned to marry local women, as they did after founding Cyrene. In many cases it is apparent that the natives became at least partially hellenised by their contacts with the Greeks: Skyles, the Scythian king, with a Greek mother, was said to have lost his throne because of his addiction to Greek culture (Hdt. 4.78.3–80.5). In several colonies it is clear that there was interaction between Greeks and the indigenous people. The colonists and their mother-cities could of course make use of their locale to gain valuable amenities, not just minerals and other resources but also manpower and expertise which was of use in military engagements: in the fifth and fourth centuries Abdera (founded by Teos c. 545), like other Greek cities in the vicinity, seems to have hired Thracian peltasts for its armies, in the same way as Philip of Macedon and his son Alexander used Thessalian cavalry to the best advantage in all their most important engagements.

While, according to Socrates, the Greeks lived around the coastline of the Mediterranean and Black Sea like 'ants or frogs around a pond' (Pl. *Phaedo* 109a–b: doc. 2.37), by the end of the fourth century the focus had changed for good. Alexander's conquests across Asia and his foundations of new 'Greek' cities shifted the centre of the known world eastwards away from the Aegean, and soon not Athens or Sparta but Alexandria in Egypt became the cultural hub of the Greek world. Following the opening up of the Near East by Alexander's conquests the east attracted thousands of settlers from Greece as administrators, merchants or mercenaries in the new empires carved out of the old Persian Empire. Greeks in the 'old world', the mainland and Magna Graecia, were now frogs croaking around a backwater. Even so some of the western colonies in southern Italy remained Greek-speaking until at least the twelfth century AD. In the east, one of Alexander's foundations, Alexandria on the river Oxos (modern Khanoum in Afghanistan), which lay thousands of kilometres from Greece, possessed all the necessities of Greek civilisation, including a gymnasium and theatre, while Boukephala, the city named for his favourite horse, Boukephalos, established at the furthest reach of Alexander's conquests still exists today on the river Jhelum in Pakistan.

3

RELIGION IN THE GREEK WORLD

Introduction

When the Athenians replied to the Spartan ambassadors in 479 BC, Herodotos has them state that there are two characteristics that give the Greeks their particularly unique identity: the fact that they have 'the same blood and the same language', a common ethnicity and linguistic system. The Athenians underlined the fact that the Greeks as a people have the same religion, with the same sacrificial system, as well as temples (such as that of Zeus at Olympia), shared by all the Greeks in common. Other aspects of their culture were also distinctly Greek: for example, their common polis system and its political institutions, their artistic and material culture, clothing and sports. But Herodotos thought that religion and language were the common bonds between the Greeks as a people, and religion made up such a large part of

Figure 3.1 The 'Gigantomachy': the Olympian gods fight against the Giants. In the centre the twins Apollo and Artemis attack a Giant who flees toward his comrades on the right. On the left, a lion, partisan of the gods, attacks a Giant. This scene is from the north frieze of the Treasury of the Siphnians at Delphi, dating to around 525 BC; height: 64 cm. Several states, including Athens, had treasuries at Delphi in which they housed their dedications to the god Apollo. These treasures were plundered by the Phokaians in the fourth century BC. Archaeological Museum, Delphi. Courtesy of Delphi Archaeological Museum. Photo © Adrian Lazar Adler.

their daily lives, influenced their attitudes and even political decisions to such a degree, and was so intrinsic a theme of their material arts that his assessment is surely correct: religion defined 'Greekness' and the Greek identity (Hdt. 8.144.2: doc. 3.91).

Sources

Herodotos notes that Homer and Hesiod were responsible for recording the stories of the gods (Hdt. 2.53). These could have been in oral circulation for many centuries, and perhaps even went back to the Mycenaean period. Homer's *Iliad* and *Odyssey* provide an opportunity to see the gods both at play and at war, and the picture presented of the squabbling Olympians is not always a flattering one, as Xenophanes of Kolophon complained (Xen. Kol. *F* 11: doc. 3.4). Hesiod's seventh-century work, *Theogony* (*Genealogy of the Gods*) is the principal source for myths about the gods written in this period (Hes. *Theogony*: doc. 3.1). There was no single body of sacred texts for the ancient Greeks. In the fourth century Apollodoros wrote a work *On the Gods*, of which fragments survive. But for the historian of the archaic and classical periods, the nature of the evidence is scattered. Because, however, religion was crucial to the politics and society of the time, there are numerous references to the gods, attitudes towards them, and religious practices in works of history, drama and litigation. In addition, individual cult centres had specific rules, which might be inscribed on stone, and these yield valuable information about the nature of the cult. Extremely important epigraphic evidence are the records of the cures which were said to have taken place in the cult of Asklepios at Epidauros, and which the priests there had inscribed on stone in the fourth century BC (*IG* IV² 1, no. 121–2: doc. 3.43). Iconography should not be overlooked, and there is a wealth of architecture and its decoration, painted vases, religious stelai and reliefs all providing an insight into what the ancient Greeks believed. Caution needs to be exercised with some of this iconography as it presents a 'snapshot' only of an aspect of a religious rite, with no accompanying text, and interpretation can be difficult.

The Olympian religion and its critics

Greek religion was polytheistic; this is a Greek term, with 'poly' meaning many, and 'theistic' coming from the Greek word theos (plural: theoi) for god. The Greek gods were believed to be anthropomorphic, having human form and characteristics (Fig. 3.1), and as such were corporeal: that is, they were beings of 'flesh and blood', though in fact it was ichor which flowed in their veins, the divine equivalent of human blood. They could be injured, as when Diomedes spears Aphrodite on the battle ground of Troy. Xenophanes and some of the other sixth-century philosophers, particularly those from Ionia, either criticised existing assumptions about the gods or came up with new ideas about them. For Xenophanes it was ridiculous that the gods could behave as badly as humans, and more importantly it was clear that mortals had created the gods 'in their own image': if oxen and horses and lion had the ability to fasten gods, they too would make gods in their own form (Xen. Kol. *F* 11: 3.4, *FF* 15–16: doc. 3.5). Herakleitos scoffs at those who pray to statues, which in his view had as much efficacy as 'gossiping to houses' (Herakl. *F* 5: doc. 3.6). At the very heart of Greek religion was the act of animal sacrifice, accompanied by prayer and often taking place at a religious festival. The Pythagoreans rejected the eating of animals because of their belief in metempsychosis (namely, that one can be reborn as another living thing), a belief which was rejected by most Greeks without question but which Empedokles expounds (*F* 117: doc. 3.73). But there were other grounds for objecting to animal sacrifice: it was often used as a purificatory ritual, to atone for sin and crime, and Herakleitos thought this ridiculous: how could the crime of murder, involving bloodshed, be washed away with further blood (Herakl. *F* 5: doc. 3.6)?

These gods can be broadly defined as 'Olympian' and 'chthonic'. Twelve major gods lived on Mount Olympos, but also came down to visit the Greeks, being thought of as present at sacrifices, and appearing occasionally to individuals (such occasions were known as epiphanies). The Athenians showed twelve Olympians on the east frieze of the Parthenon, watching the preparations for the Panathenaic festival (Table 3.1).

Then there were the chthonic deities, beings of the underworld, of whom the most important was Hades, god of the dead. Mythical heroes of the past, such as Amphiaraos and Trophonios, were considered to have power after their death and were thought of as dwelling and presiding under the ground, and so were also chthonic in nature (Paus. *Description of Greece* 9.39.5–14: doc. 3.48).

Gaia ('Earth') was the original Greek deity in the remote past but her cult was much overshadowed in the archaic and classical period. She created Uranos (Ouranos, 'Sky') who became her consort and was castrated by his son Kronos, who cast his testicles into the sea, with Aphrodite emerging from the resulting foam. Kronos married his sister Rheia, but frightened by a prophecy that he would be overthrown by his children, he swallowed them all whole. But his sister-wife Rheia saved the last and greatest, Zeus, by giving Kronos a rock wrapped in swaddling clothes instead of Zeus (Hes. *Theogony* 466–91: doc. 3.2). Zeus rescued his brothers (Hades, Poseidon) and sisters (Demeter, Hera, Hestia), and overcame his father, who was imprisoned in Tartaros in Hades. The term Titans was employed for those gods who ruled prior to Zeus and the other Olympians. There was also the race of Giants, descended from Gaia and Kronos; the Olympians had to fight them in order to cement their own authority. This myth is known as the Gigantomachy, 'Battle with the Giants,' and is shown on the sixth-century treasury of the Siphnians at Delphi (Fig. 3.1). The Erinyes, chthonic deities, were primarily responsible for punishing family crime: they famously pursue Orestes after he kills his mother (they are also known as the Eumenides). The Greek pantheon was therefore made up of Olympian gods, Titans, Giants, the Erinyes, nymphs and various heroes; living men could not aspire to divinity,

Table 3.1 The twelve major Olympian gods

Aphrodite	Goddess of love and marriage (Fig. 3.15)
Apollo	God of prophecy, oracles and healing (son of Zeus and Leto) (Fig. 3.1)
Ares	God of carnage, and indiscriminate slaughter in war, despised by all the other gods
Artemis	Goddess of nature and of hunting (daughter Zeus and Leto) (Figs 3.1, 4.5)
Athena	Virgin goddess of wisdom and knowledge, and a warrior goddess; she sprang fully armed and adult from the head of Zeus after he had intercourse with the goddess Metis (wisdom) whom he then swallowed; Hephaistos split his head open with an axe to allow for the 'birth' (Figs 1.5, 6.5, 8.1, 12.4, 13.3, 13.4)
Demeter	Goddess of agriculture, and of a blessed afterlife (Fig. 3.7)
Dionysos	God of wine, ecstasy and possession, especially worshipped by women known as maenads
Hephaistos	God of blacksmithing and metallurgy (son of Zeus and Hera) (Fig. 8.1)
Hera	Goddess of marriage and motherhood (Fig. 2.4)
Hermes	Messenger god, patron of thieves
Poseidon	God of sea and earthquakes
Zeus	The youngest of the siblings, who, as the one who had overthrown his father, came to be the ruler. He was the most powerful of the gods, and ruled over his brothers and sisters and their offspring. Originally a weather god, his main weapon was the lightning bolt (Figs 2.4, 3.16, 4.12)

Figure 3.2 A female griffin breast-feeding its baby; this is a bronze sheet of Corinthian workmanship dating to 640–630 BC and discovered at Olympia. Olympia Museum B104, Olympia. Photo © Olympia Archaeological Museum, Hellenic Ministry of Culture and Tourism, 7th Ephorate of Prehistoric and Classical Antiquities and Archaeological Receipts Fund.

but Lysander the Spartan admiral was accorded extraordinary divine honours as a living hero by the city of Samos (Plut. *Life of Lysander* 18.1–10: doc. 13.38), and Alexander, who proclaimed himself the son of Zeus Ammon, became a god while alive (Arr. *Expedition of Alexander* 7.29.3–4, 30.2–3: doc. 15.45). There were various deities worshipped only in certain places, generally local heroes whose cults centred on the place where their bones were buried, such as Oedipous and Orestes (Soph. *Oedipus at Colonus* 1518–34: doc. 3.45; Hdt. 1.67.2–68.6: doc. 3.46). New gods could be introduced to the pantheon, but sometimes met with opposition: one of the charges brought against Socrates was that he had introduced 'new gods'.

The nature of humanity

Myths about the behaviour of half-humans such as the centaurs (creatures mainly equine but with human heads), and the cruel and lawless deeds of the one-eyed Cyclopes and other creatures, underlined for the Greeks what made a human being wholly human and the Greeks were conscious of the special gifts of humanity. Sophocles could write, 'much exists that is wonderful, but there is nothing as wonderful as man!' Man ploughs and controls the very earth; he is intelligent and dominates the beasts; his inventiveness has led him to escape the elements and cure illnesses: it is only against death that he is helpless. But Sophocles observed that mortals were prone to both evil and good, and that as the gods have sworn to uphold justice the evil man will be an outcast from his city (Soph. *Antigone* 332–3: doc. 3.7).

The nature of the gods

Zeus, head of the Olympians, was the major Greek god. His huge statue, made by the Athenian sculptor Pheidias, sat enthroned in his temple at Olympia, and the ancient Greek joke was that if he stood up he would take the roof off the temple. Pausanias describes the statue and also mentions two other important cult statues: those of Athena in the Parthenon and

Table 3.2 Mythical creatures

Centaurs	Half-horse and half-man; they were invited to Peirithous' wedding, became drunk and attempted to rape the bride and other women guests; this was a famous myth (Centauromachy) shown on the Parthenon metopes. The contrast between them and mortals highlighted what constituted the values of civilisation
Griffins	Beasts with the body of a lion, head of an eagle; they guarded gold in the mysterious regions to the north; they appear frequently in Greek art (Fig. 3.27)
Sphinx	The sphinx had the head of a woman, a lioness's body and eagle's wings, and sometimes appeared on top of Athenian grave stelai. Used by the gods to punish mortals in myth, she was associated especially with the city of Thebes, where she committed suicide or was killed by Oedipus when he guessed her riddle

the healing deity Asklepios at Epidauros (Paus. *Description of Greece* 5.11.1, 5.11.8–11: doc. 3.3). Cult statues were housed in temples, usually in the central section (the 'cella' or 'naos'). Worshippers would approach the statues with their prayers, and even touch them in supplication while they prayed. If they were life-size statues of goddesses, they would receive a new garment every year, woven and presented by women of the city. Such statues are the ultimate expression of the anthropomorphic nature of the gods; the statues were man-made, but a few, such as the ancient wooden statue of Athena in the Erechtheum on the Athenian acropolis, were thought to have been made by the gods and to have fallen from heaven, and as such were considered to be particularly sacred. Not only did the Greeks believe that their gods looked like humans, they considered that they were capable of behaviour, at least in myth, which was very much like that of humans. Many stories are recorded in the Homeric poems, the *Iliad* and the *Odyssey*, in which the gods are devoted to their own interests and willing to use mortals for their own ends, and even willing to persecute them: Poseidon, for instance, makes Odysseus' life a misery and delays his return home to Ithaka after the hero has killed Poseidon's son Polyphemos, one of the Cyclopes. Yet Pindar has a more positive attitude than Xenophanes on the similarities between mortals and gods: the gods and mortals come from the same mother (Earth), and there are positive similarities: mortals resemble the gods in 'greatness of mind or outward form', and so he praises the spark of divinity in mortals, even though they are separated from the gods (Pind. *Nemean* 6.1–7: doc. 3.8).

Sacrifice and public worship

The many deities of ancient Greece were worshipped in two main ways, through prayer and, more importantly, animal (but not human) sacrifice. Numerous Athenian vases, as well as others from elsewhere in Greece, show animal sacrifices at some stage in the proceedings, but only one, the famous Viterbo vase, depicts the actual killing of the animal at a sacrifice. The Greeks shied away from depicting the moment of death of the sacrificial victim, although they did describe it in literature. This reluctance to record the animal's death pictorially may have been a result of some feeling of guilt over the destruction of the beast.

Of the literary sources, the best and most detailed account of animal sacrifice is that found in Homer's *Odyssey*, describing a sacrifice made by Nestor, king of Pylos – the elderly hero who figures prominently in the *Iliad* – to Athena (Hom. *Odyssey* 3.430–63, 470–3: doc. 3.9). Several key elements in the ritual of every sacrifice are made clear in this description. It was a domestic cow that was to be sacrificed: usually sacrifices were of domestic animals, but Xenophon in establishing his temple for Artemis at Skillous in Sparta laid down that the goddess at her festival receive both victims from the sacred herd and animals killed in the hunt (Xen. *Anabasis* 5.3.9: doc. 3.52), but as Artemis was a hunting deity this is understandable. At a sacrifice an animal was killed and parts burnt for the gods, and the rest consumed by the participants: a sacrifice was essentially a meal shared between worshippers and a god or gods. In fact, every time a domestic animal was slaughtered it was in a sacrificial context, with the gods sharing in the meat so obtained. In this way the gods were thanked for the bounty of the herd and to show them honour.

Athena was to be the beneficiary of the sacrifice Homer describes and he has her coming to attend the sacrifice herself. First the cow was decorated, in order to make its appearance more pleasing to the goddess, so that she 'would rejoice when she saw the offering' (Hom. *Odyssey* 3.438: doc. 3.9): the blacksmith hammered gold over the beast's horns. In a similar vein, young Athenian women are shown on Athenian vases decorating sacrificial victims with ribbons or tasselled cords, to make them more beautiful to the deity (Fig. 3.3).

The sacrificial victims

Victims also had to be free of blemish or disease as the gods were felt to deserve only the very best offerings. 'Unblemished' or 'of high quality' are the terms specifically used in the Athenian calendar of state sacrifices (*LSCG Suppl.* 10, lines 50, 70: doc. 3.12). Similarly, on the first and seventh days of every month, each of the two Spartan kings received 'a perfect victim' to sacrifice to Apollo (Hdt. 6.57.2: doc. 6.26). Olympian gods generally received victims of any colour, but chthonic (underworld) deities preferred black-skinned beasts, symbolising the darkness of their domains. Animals sacrificed to the Olympian gods had their throats cut upwards, but those for chthonic deities were killed with their throats held downwards. Many chthonic deities (such as heroes and the dead), however, received 'bloodless' offerings of milk, olive oil and honey.

Purity was an important aspect of sacrifice: those officiating at a sacrifice had to have clean hands, and so 'water for the hands in a basin adorned with flowers' is brought to the sacrifice (Hom. *Odyssey* 3. 440: doc. 3.9). 'Moral' purity was also important and at Athens adulterous women could not attend state sacrifices ([Dem.] 59 (*Against Neaira*) 87: doc. 4.57). At the sacrifice described by Homer, one of the participants brings barley grains in a basket, which were to be strewn over the victim's head, possibly to make it assent to its sacrifice to the goddess. When women held or carried on their heads baskets during a sacrificial ceremony, this is one item the basket would have contained (Fig. 3.14).

However, the modern notion that the Greeks wanted the victim to go willingly to its slaughter is overstated and it was not always the case that the victim went peacefully to its death. Of course it was easier for the whole procedure if the animals were quiet, but on the Parthenon frieze several of the beasts in the procession are portrayed as quite lively. This could be quite deliberate, to indicate the healthiness of the beasts: certainly their size is emphasised. At Delphi, however, the goat sacrificed before an oracular enquiry had to assent to its destruction by nodding its head (after it was sprinkled with water) as a sign that the Pythia was able to prophecy (Plut. *Moralia* 51.438a–c: doc. 3.22).

Sacrificial prayers

Prayers accompanied the sacrifice to Athena in the *Odyssey*, as its purpose was to gain a favour from the goddess: if the sacrifice was pleasing and accepted the prayer would

Figure 3.3 Two young women decorate cows for sacrifice with knotted cords to make them more pleasing to the god to whom they are to be sacrificed. An Athenian red-figure skyphos, fifth century BC. British Museum E284, London. Drawing by J. Etherington.

hopefully be fulfilled. Or there might not be a particular request associated with a sacrifice, but worshippers at a later time of need or crisis could remind the god of the sacrifices which had been made to it. The washing of hands and tossing of grain was followed by the slaughter of the beast. Presiding over the sacrifice in the *Odyssey* was the aged Nestor; he did not perform the act of killing the beast, which was carried out by his sons, Thrasymedes who stuns the cow, and Peisistratos who cuts its throat. At most sacrifices, even when a priest was present, there would have been a professional butcher – a mageiros – to kill and then dismember the beast. In Menander's *Dyskolos* the mageiros taking the sacrificial sheep from Athens to Pan's rural shrine has to, literally, drag it every inch of the way from the city (Men. *Dyskolos* 393–406: doc. 3.10). When Thrasymedes has felled the cow, its head is raised and Perseus holds a bowl under its neck to catch the blood as Peisistratos cuts the throat. The blood would later be poured onto the altar; images of altars on Athenian vases are frequently bloodstained and this was obviously considered a mark of piety as it bore witness to the number of sacrifices that had been made there or to the fact that a sacrifice had recently taken place. An Athenian vase shows the goddess Athena standing behind her altar as a sacrifice is made to her: this should not be imagined as the cult statue of the goddess (which would be inside her temple) but is as in Nestor's sacrifice: it is an epiphany of the goddess who has come down from Mount Olympos to receive her sacrifice. The viewers do not seem to be

78

aware of her presence. Sacrifice did not take place inside the temple, but outside, due to the nature of sacrifice: it was bloody and messy, and temples were not designed for sacrifice to take place inside.

The procedure

Prior to the actual killing, Nestor cut some hair from the head of the cow and cast it into the fire: this is like a first-fruits offering and marks the commencement of the ritual of slaughter. As the axe descends, the women cry out, making an ululation, either to drown out the victim's screams or to call the god's attention to the sacrifice: perhaps both. It is a special duty performed by the women, and Nestor's wife is foremost amongst the screamers.

Athena as the presiding deity is attended to first in the butchering and apportioning of shares. The thigh-bones are cut out, covered in fat, and raw pieces of meat put upon them; these are then burnt and Nestor pours a libation of 'sparkling wine' over them. This is Athena's share. There was a myth that gods and mortals had met to agree what share of the sacrifice the gods should receive and that they had been deceived by an offering of bones overlaid with fat, although in many sacrifices, including that here, the gods received more. Another description of a sacrifice, in a comedy, has the gods receiving the blood, gall-bladder, bones and spleen, from a victim which apparently was all skin and bones (Men. *Samia* 399–404: doc. 3.11).

Next the entrails were placed on skewers and roasted in the fire and eaten. The rest of the meat was then roasted, though it was also possible to boil it in a cauldron; the participants then sat down to dine on meat and wine. Sacrifice was at the heart of Greek religion and was so important that cities passed decrees about when sacrifices would occur and to which deities, inscribing on stone when sacrifices were to occur, to which god or goddess, and the nature of the victim (as in *LSCG Suppl.* 10: doc. 3.12). It was important to record these details so that the community would not overlook a particular sacrifice, for if this happened it was believed that the gods concerned would be angered and as a result withhold their favour.

Sacrifices were often made on behalf of the state but could also be offered by an individual family (Men. *Dyskolos* 393–406: doc. 3.10), or by a group of friends (Antiph. 1 *Prosecution of the Stepmother* 16: doc. 4.52). A priest or priestess did not need to preside over a sacrifice or be present at it unless the cult law of a sanctuary expressly made this condition. Individuals sacrificed to gods for a range of personal reasons, and one of the most common was when individual hoplites sacrificed and examined the beast's entrails prior to setting out for war, when the entrails of the sacrificed beast would be used to look for good omen (Fig. 3.5). The Spartans always sacrificed before a campaign, and sacrificed a she-goat just before they went into battle (Xen. *Constitution of the Spartans* 13.8: doc. 6.17). Personal sacrifices also occurred for marriage, childbirth, sickness and whenever the need arose. When gods were called upon to witness oaths, this would have been accompanied by sacrifices to those gods (Tod 20: doc. 3.13).

Many types of animals could be sacrificed depending on the deity to whom the sacrifice was being made, and on the family budget. Athena received a cow at Nestor's sacrifice, the cult of the war-god Enyalios on Rhodes required that a boar, dog and goat be offered to the god (*LSCG Suppl.* 85: doc. 3.51), while the Athenian sacrificial calendar mentions sheep, rams, oxen and pigs (*LSCG Suppl.* 10: doc. 3.12). This inscription also lists the prices to be paid for the victims, not in order to attempt to budget for the cost of the sacrifices but to ensure that beasts of sufficient quality were purchased. Sacrificial victims did not have to be large animals, and Asklepios was happy even with roosters (Pl. *Phaedo* 118: doc. 3.88). Festivals with sacrifices were important for dietary reasons, as at public sacrifices held by cities the ordinary people shared in the meat. At Athens, 'the city sacrifices numerous victims at public expense, but it is the people who banquet and who are allocated the victims' ([Xen.] *Constitution of the Athenians* 2.9: doc. 1.8). Perikles in praising the Athenian way of life in 431 BC pointed to the sacrifices and festivals held throughout the year as a major form of relaxation and recreation (Thuc. 2.38.1: doc. 1.17), and such sacrifices took place at the local (deme) level as well as at city festivals (*IG* I³ 258, 244: docs 10.19–20). The author of the *Oeconomicus* attributed to Aristotle recommended that slaves be allowed to share in sacrifices ([Arist.] *Oeconomicus* 1344b15), and the naked men in sacrificial scenes on Athenian vases are almost certainly slaves there to help with the sacrificial tasks. Sacrifices forged an essential bond with the gods for both individuals, families and communities, who by participating in this ritual were able to communicate to the gods their thanks for past favours and requests for benefits in the future.

Divination: omens and oracles

Athena was believed to be present on the sandy beach of Pylos when Nestor made his sacrifice to her. In Greek thought, the gods were always potentially present, and the Greeks believed that their deities took a keen interest in the lives and affairs of mortals. Like many ancient – and modern – peoples the Greeks looked to their gods for advice, both in momentous affairs of state and in their private, individual concerns. They did this through the art of manteia, divination. Lacking any sacred texts for Olympian religion, there was little written advice on how to ascertain the will of the gods. The Greeks knew that there was divine law and justice, and their own human laws gave them a framework of reference for the definition of good and evil behaviour (Soph. *Antigone* 441–70: doc. 4.69), but the Greeks firmly believed that the gods were interested in what they as mortals were doing or planning to do and so, before undertaking major projects, they sought to ascertain the gods' opinion about and approval for their proposed course of action. Hesiod counsels that bird omens are to be taken seriously in order to avoid any transgressions against the gods (Hes. *Works and Days* 826–8: doc. 3.14).

Lucian could note in the second century AD that the earlier Greeks: 'would not found cities, or surround themselves with walls, or kill anyone, or get married, before they had learnt all the details from the diviners' (Lucian *Astrology* 23: doc. 2.3). It was considered vital to consult the god Apollo at Delphi through his priestess medium, the Pythia, before sending out a colony. Herodotos blamed the failure of Dorieus' colonisation ventures on his failure to consult Delphi before his first attempt, and then for not explicitly following the oracle's instructions after he had subsequently consulted it about his second planned settlement (Hdt. 5.42.2, 5.43.1, 5.45.1: doc. 2.22). Similarly the Delphic oracle features prominently in Herodotos' detailed account of the foundation of Cyrene (Hdt. 4.150.2–159.4: doc. 2.29). In the fifth century, the Spartans consulted Delphi and obtained the god's approval before establishing a colony of strategic importance at Herakleia (Thuc. 3.92.5: doc. 2.24).

Means of divination

There were several types of divination; it was a techne (skill), practised primarily by professionals, supposedly taught to mortals by Prometheus. His 'lessons' included how to interpret dreams, doubtful utterances, and 'signs by the way'. Divination by the flight of birds (oionomanteia), and the inspection of the entrails after sacrifice (hieroskopia) were also said to

Figure 3.4 According to myth, Herakles had contested control of the Delphic oracle by attempting to seize the tripod the Pythia sat upon. Here Apollo and Herakles fight for possession of the tripod. Herakles was unsuccessful, but the story was a popular artistic motif. It is shown here on a bronze plaque that decorated a tripod leg dedicated at Olympia, and dates to the sixth century BC. Olympia Museum B1730, Olympia. Drawing by J. Etherington.

have been taught by him (Aesch. *Prometheus Bound* 484–95: doc. 3.16). Dreams were thought to be messages from the gods which should be acted upon, while from the fifth century on there were dream manuals containing descriptions of dreams which could be consulted for a possible interpretation. When Theophrastos' 'Superstitious Man' has a dream he goes off to 'the dream interpreters, the prophets and the omen-diviners to ask which god or goddess he should pray to' (Theophr. *Characters* 16.11: doc. 3.72).

Forms of divination involving 'doubtful utterances' refer to the fact that things which one heard were believed to be potentially significant and ominous, while in 'signs by the way' what one encountered when going along could be a sign of what was to happen in the future. Sneezing was considered a sign of good luck (Hom. *Odyssey* 17.541; Xen. *Anabasis* 3.2.9), while having a weasel cross one's path was extremely unfortunate. The 'Superstitious Man' takes action when he sees a snake or a weasel, or hears an owl hoot, considering these to be omens, and goes to the diviners if a mouse eats a hole in a sack of barley (Theophr. *Characters* 16.3–7: doc. 3.72).

Birds were very important in divination, being seen as messengers of the gods, and the future could be predicted according to their movement, flight and behaviour. This seems to have been the oldest type of divination known to the ancient Greeks, and the word for bird, oionos, came to mean 'omen'. A sixth-century inscription from Ephesos shows how complex the art of divination could be and is clearly part of a sophisticated system of bird divination which has only partly survived (*LSAM* 30: doc. 3.15); for example, Poseidippos in the third century BC wrote several poems on interpreting bird omens. At Ephesos, the direction in which the bird was flying and the way it raised its wing were used to determine whether the omen was favourable or unfavourable. The inscription is fragmentary and there were probably many more interpretations of different bird movements set out than those that now survive; the type of bird itself might have been specified. Teiresias, the famous mythical diviner of Thebes, learnt of the wrath of the gods against his city from his 'ancient seat of divination' where he could hear the sounds of the birds and their fighting which held prophetic meaning for him (Soph. *Antigone* 998–1011: doc. 3.18). The Ephesos inscription also strongly suggests that there was an official place from which bird movements were observed and it is possible that the practitioners of the skill went there with a specific question in mind for the gods, which would be answered, they thought, by a bird being sent by the gods to fly in a specific way or direction. Birds gave good omens at Alexander the Great's foundation of Alexandria in Egypt (Plut. *Life of Alexander* 26.1–10: doc. 15.16).

The heroes of Homer's *Iliad* and *Odyssey* did not practise entrail examination (hieroskopia), but simply roasted and ate them together with the rest of the meat; however, the evidence of

Figure 3.5 A hieroskopia scene in which an Athenian hoplite departing for war examines the entrails of a sacrificed beast. The Scythian on the left and the woman (the hoplite's wife) raise their hands at the entrails: it is clearly a good omen, which they accept (docs 3.16–17). The youth holding the entrails is deliberately depicted small to indicate that he is a slave. This scene is a common one on vases, in this case an Athenian red-figure amphora, by the Kleophrades Painter, dating to around 500–475 BC. The height of the vase is 63.3 cm, and the height of the register with the scene is 25 cm; Martin von Wagner Museum der Universität Würzburg L507. Drawing by J. Etherington.

Athenian vase paintings shows that by the sixth century BC entrails were consulted at sacrifices (Fig. 3.5). Prometheus states that it is the smoothness of the entrails (the heart, kidneys, lungs, spleen, gall bladder and the liver, with its constituent parts), the colour of the gall bladder, and the 'speckled symmetry of the liver's lobe' that are all good omens (Aesch. *Prometheus Bound* 493–5: 3.16). In contrast the absence of the lobe of the liver was one of the most common ill-omens associated with the examination of entrails; Aegisthus notes the lobe's absence in the sacrificial entrails he is examining, and can tell from the appearance of the liver's portal veins and the gall bladder that misfortune is at hand (Eur. *Electra* 826–9: doc. 3.17) – and in fact Orestes, who is present at the sacrifice, is about to kill him with a blow from the sacrificial axe. Spartans routinely and regularly consulted sacrificial entrails while on military campaign, and an absence of the liver's lobe was always taken as a bad sign, and could even lead to the abandonment of a military campaign. Even worse, when Teiresias attempts to consult the will of the gods by examining the entrails of a sacrificial animal, the gall bladder 'melted into air' and the fat dripped off the thighs, a portent of the gods' anger at Kreon's decision to have Antigone entombed in a cave, which is going to lead to the suicide of his own son and wife (Soph. *Antigone* 1009–10: doc. 3.18).

The Delphic oracle

A popular form of divination, and certainly the most portentous, was to consult the gods directly, to hear their will in 'their own words'. The most famous oracular sanctuary in ancient Greece was at Delphi, where the god of prophecy, Apollo, made known the will of Zeus through the medium of a woman, a priestess known as the Pythia. Apollo also had an oracular centre at Didyma in Asia Minor, as had Zeus at Dodona, while as Zeus Ammon he also had an oracle at the Siwah oasis in western Egypt, known and consulted by the Athenians by the last two decades of the fifth century, and famously by Alexander the Great to confirm his divine birth (Arr. *Expedition of Alexander* 3.3.1–4.5: doc. 15.17). Enquirers were able to put their questions directly to the priestess or priest of these oracular shrines and receive a direct oral reply back, in intelligible prose or poetry, which gave them advice for or against a particular course of action.

In classical times, there were three priestesses at any one time at Delphi, who took it in turns to serve on the one day of the month when the oracular centre was open for consultations: official embassies and private enquirers needed to plan their trip ahead. The Pythian priestesses were chosen through divine inspiration by the priests at Delphi, irrespective of their social and economic class. Although she did not take drugs, chew laurel leaves or hallucinate, the Pythia did have to prepare herself. On the day of the month on which she was to prophesy, she first bathed in the Kastalian spring, and drank from it. Reports of a chasm at Delphi from which emanated gases which inspired the priestess can be safely discounted. The enquirers had to make their questions known to the priests in advance, so that the Pythia had advance warning of what was to be asked of her and the extent to which she was guided in her replies by the priests is matter for conjecture only. Certainly, in her own mind, her replies may well have been dictated by the god. The priestess delivered her oracular responses either in plain prose or in the Homeric poetic lines known as hexameters. She gave her responses clearly and in an articulate manner, and enquirers often wrote the responses down. The two oracles given by the Pythia to the Athenians prior to the Persian War were both in hexameters (Hdt. 7.140.1–311.22, 7.141.1–143.2: docs 11.21–2).

At Delphi, the procedure began with a payment for consultation, and the sacrifice of a cake, the pelanos, and of a goat. The price of the pelanos could vary from state to state and it

Figure 3.6 Aigeus, father of Theseus, consulting the Delphic priestess Themis, seated on her lidded tripod; she is sedate and calm. The central column indicates that she is in the temple; she holds a bowl which might represent the water she has drawn from the Kastalian spring where she bathed to purify herself before delivering Apollo's oracles. She also holds a laurel sprig, Apollo's symbol. This is a well-known scene on an Athenian red-figure kylix (cup), attributed to the Kodros Painter, and dating to about 440 BC, with a diameter of 32 cm. Antikensammlung Staatliche Museen Berlin F 2538, Berlin. Drawing by J. Etherington.

seems the Delphians honoured the people of the city of Phaselis by setting down a discounted price of the pelanos in Delphic coinage; there were money-changers available to change different currencies (*LSCG Suppl.* 39: doc. 3.23). A goat was then to be sacrificed, and its head was doused with water to encourage it to nod and assent. On one occasion described by Plutarch, which occurred in his own lifetime, the goat was unwilling and the priests 'nearly half-drowned' it before it nodded its head. But the Pythia was unwilling to descend, that is to go into the temple, down its interior steps to a sunken chamber known as the abaton, 'secret place', where she sat on her tripod. She ranted and raved incomprehensibly until she rushed out, threw herself down and died a few days later. What Plutarch makes clear is that this was an unusual situation and that the priests should not have gone ahead once the goat had shown its unwillingness. Normally, the Pythia would have sat on her tripod and given an intelligible reply to her enquirers (Plut. *Moralia* 51.438a–c: doc. 3.22; Figs 3.4, 3.6).

Various celestial phenomena were believed to have a divinatory significance. When some type of sign, perhaps a comet or solar flare, had appeared above Athens, it was a disturbing enough celestial event for the Athenians to seek the advice of the Delphic oracle. Their enquiry is recorded in a speech of Demosthenes, as is the reply given by the Pythia. Athens wished to know to which god they 'should sacrifice or pray' so that 'the sign' would be advantageous to them, that is, well omened. Many of the enquiries to Delphi and other oracles were along these lines: some disturbing event had occurred and the city, or individual, wanted to know what gods they needed to placate. Many of the Pythia's replies were therefore of a 'prescriptive' nature, providing a ritual prescription to deal with the matter under enquiry. In this case the Athenians were instructed to perform various good-omened sacrifices (that is, if the entrails were unpropitious in the sacrificial beast, they had to then use another victim). So many sacrifices were to be made that the streets should be full of the smell of the cooking sacrifices, everyone was to wear wreaths and raise their hands in adoration, relatives were to make offerings to their dead and the city was to sacrifice and make offerings to the 'hero-founder', Erechtheus, the ancient king of Athens, who traditionally received rams and bulls (Dem. 43 *Against Makartatos* 66: doc. 3.19). The Athenians were said to be named after him in that he was born out of the earth and all the Athenians descended from him; they were autochthonous, 'sprung from the very soil' of Attica, not immigrants, and as such they were often termed the Erechtheidai ('offspring of Erechtheus').

The Pythia, however, might give a riddling response, as on the occasion when Croesus sent ambassadors to enquire as to whether he should make war against the Persians, whereupon the response was that if he did so, 'he would destroy a great empire' (Hdt. 1.53.1–54.2: doc. 3.20; see also Hdt. 1.90–1; Amphiaraos, Herodotos notes, gave the same response). Croesus attacked and the Persians defeated him; sending again to Delphi he reprimanded the oracle, but received the reply that it had been up to him to send a second embassy to ask exactly what the response had meant. Not only states but individuals as well could consult the Delphic oracle, and the childless couple Xouthos and his wife Kreousa consulted first Trophonios' oracle at Lebadeia, and then Delphi (for the procedure at Lebadeia: Paus. *Description of Greece* 9.39.5–14: doc. 3.48). On seeing her there on her own Ion, one of the Delphic priests, asked Kreousa whether she had come to enquire of the oracle concerning 'crops for the land or children?' Women, therefore, could consult the oracle in their own right (Eur. *Ion* 299–306: doc. 3.21). Naturally, omens might occur when it was simply impossible to consult Delphi: so when an eclipse of the full moon occurred at Syracuse when the Athenians had decided to withdraw, Nikias followed his own inclination and the interpretation of the professional seers (manteis) with him, and decided not to move, with disastrous results (Thuc. 7.50.3–4: doc. 3.24).

Festivals

Festivals were an intrinsic aspect of Greek religion, and public sacrifices generally occurred at these. They were held by various organisations, by the religious fraternities known as phratries, demes in Attica, cities, panhellenic sanctuaries and specific ethnic groups, such as those of Dorians or Ionians (Hdt. 1.142.1–4, 1.144.1–3, 1.148.1: docs 1.59–60). There were four panhellenic festivals attended by individuals from throughout the Greek world: at Olympia, Corinth (the Isthmia), Nemea and Delphi (the Pythia), all of which held both musical and athletic contests, except for the Olympian festival, which focused on athletics. These four festivals formed a periodos, a circuit. The prizes at these games were simply wreaths or sprigs of vegetation, but athletes were competing for the honour of victory, though it was also the case that the cities of victorious chariot drivers and athletes granted them honours, awarding them dining rights in the town hall, as well as other privileges. Socrates, condemned to death for impiety, suggested that as his punishment he should have daily maintenance in the prytaneion ('town hall'), like victors at the Olympic festival (Pl. *Apology* 36b–e: doc. 3.86; cf. 1.76)

Any Greeks could attend and participate in the panhellenic festivals, and states sent official embassies to make sacrifices to the gods at these, to prove the piety of their cities and to honour the gods. Sacrifices whether by the state or a local unit of government, or by leagues, or the Greeks as a whole, took place at festivals. Cities sent sacred delegations, for example, to Delphi and attendance at these festivals was taken seriously. When the island of

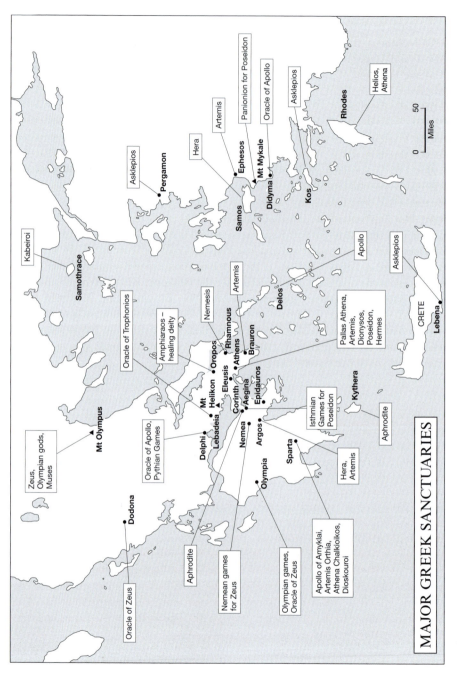

MAJOR GREEK SANCTUARIES

Zeus, Olympian gods, Muses

Mt Olympus

Dodona

Oracle of Zeus

Kabeiroi

Samothrace

Asklepios

Pergamon

Hera

Samos

Artemis

Ephesos

Panionion for Poseidon

Oracle of Apollo

Mt Mykale

Didyma

Asklepios

Kos

Rhodes

Helios, Athena

Oracle of Trophonios

Amphiaraos – healing deity

Nemesis

Rhamnous

Oropos

Athens

Artemis

Brauron

Pallas Athena, Artemis, Dionysos, Poseidon, Hermes

Delos

Apollo

Asklepios

CRETE

Lebena

Mt Helikon

Eleusis

Delphi

Lebadeia

Oracle of Apollo, Pythian Games

Aphrodite

Corinth

Aegina

Nemea

Epidauros

Isthmian Games for Poseidon

Kythera

Aphrodite

Nemean games for Zeus

Argos

Sparta

Hera, Artemis

Olympia

Olympian games, Oracle of Zeus

Apollo of Amyklai, Artemis Orthia, Athena Chalkioikos, Dioskouroi

0   50
Miles

Map 3.1 Major Greek sanctuaries. Based on M. Grant, *The Routledge Atlas of Classical History*, fifth edition, Routledge, 1994, p. 18.

Andros sent a choir to compete at the Pythian festival at Delphi an inscription makes detailed provisions for all the participants during the visit. The personnel are listed and given food and monetary allowances, the costs of the pelanos and sacrifices for consulting the Delphic oracle are specified, and a team of five men are appointed to supervise the others and to fine them if they misbehave (*LSCG Suppl.* 38: doc. 3.25). All the details of the visit have been worked out and the inscription is promulgated as a state decree, indicating the official interest in ensuring that the visit was a success.

Involvement in the competition at these panhellenic festivals was a matter of civic pride, but individual competitors often had to pay their own expenses. Alkibiades from his own personal resources in 416 BC entered more individual chariot teams (seven all told) than anyone ever before, but he was so admired by Athens' allies that various states defrayed the cost of his tents, sacrificial animals, wine and food (Plut. *Life of Alkibiades* 11.1–12.1: doc. 3.27; Thuc. 6.15.3: doc. 13.23). His victories considerably enhanced his political reputation at Athens. Victorious athletes would be greeted rapturously on their return to their home cities, and part of a city wall might even be demolished to allow a huge procession to make its way into the city in their honour (see p. 39).

Ethnic festivals

Festivals could also be celebrated at an ethnic level. The Ionians, for example, held a festival on Delos in honour of Apollo that only Ionians could attend, with boxing, dancing and singing (Thuc. 3.104.1–4: doc. 3.28). Each city had its own festivals, and of these the Panathenaia (the 'all-Athenian') at Athens is the best-known example in honour of Athena as guardian of the city of Athens. In the fifth century, the Athenians required their allies to attend the festivals of the Panathenaia and Dionysia (*IG* I³ 46: doc. 12.31). Aristophanes' *Frogs* has the god Dionysos making fun of one of the less successful, fat and flabby, runners in the torch race, which was a feature of the first day of the Great Panathenaia (Ar. *Frogs* 1089–98: doc. 3.29). Every fourth year in the Great Panathenaia the festival included games, as well as competitions in music and poetry (such as recitations of the Homeric poems), with some of the events, such as the torch race, only open to Athenians. The most significant feature of the festival was the procession carrying a new robe, the peplos, decorated with scenes of the battle between the gods and the giants, for the statue of Athena, which began at the Dipylon gate and made its way through the agora to the acropolis and which is depicted on the Parthenon frieze. Prizes at the festival consisted of amphorai of olive oil, Athena's own gift to Athens (Fig. 13.3), and the festival concluded with a hecatomb, the sacrifice of a hundred oxen, and a feast for all citizens on the last night. At Troizen a festival for Poseidon was celebrated by the cities Hermione, Epidauros, Aegina, Athens, Prasieis, Nauplion and Orchomenos Minyeios, while all the Italian Greeks attended the festival of Hera at Lakinion and the Boeotians celebrated a festival of their own called the Daidala at Plataea. The purpose of these 'ethnic' festivals was to underline the shared identity of the ethnic groups and to draw neighbouring cities into religious celebrations, which fostered good relations with each other.

Sparta celebrated several festivals, including the Karneia for Apollo (*IG* V 1.222: doc. 3.30), and the Gymnopaidiai: it was just when the men's choruses were performing at this festival that news came of the Spartan defeat by the Thebans at Leuktra in 371 BC, but the ephors decided that, to use the modern expression, the 'show must go on' (Xen. *Hellenika* 6.4.16: doc. 14.18). Their celebration of festivals with dances and singing to entertain the gods proves that Sparta was not a cultural desert.

Sacred truces

Greeks considered their right to go to panhellenic sanctuaries and worship there as an important part of their Greek identity. Truces allowed pilgrims to travel in safety to festivals throughout the Greek world and under the terms of the 'Peace of Nikias' in 421 BC, the right of all Greeks to travel to panhellenic sanctuaries and attend festivals was guaranteed (Thuc. 5.18.1–3: doc. 3.26). Major sites, such as Olympia and Eleusis, proclaimed sacred truces for the pious pilgrims who wished to participate at their festivals and these truces came into effect for the period immediately before, during and after the major celebration at these sites. Prior to the celebration of the Eleusinian Mysteries, an annual event, messengers would be sent out throughout the Greek world to announce a sacred truce under the terms of which all who wished were to be allowed to travel to and return from Eleusis in safety (see *IG* I³ 6B: doc. 3.36). Festivals allowed communities to come together to offer up communal worship of the gods in return for the gods' continued support of the community. At Athens and other cities, these festivals were considered so important that the state made the various arrangements for the event, to ensure that it was conducted properly. The gods were believed to watch the festivities, and they are shown on the east frieze of the Parthenon casually waiting in expectation of the beginning of Athena's festival. A procession is being organised, in which animals are being brought up for sacrifice, and young women are receiving or have received the items they will carry in the procession. When it arrived on the acropolis, having made its way through Athens witnessed by crowds of thousands, the sacrifices would commence. Athens as a community would honour its main deity, Athena, and pray that she would continue to safeguard their city.

The Eleusinian Mysteries

The Eleusinian Mysteries had two celebrations, the Lesser and the Greater, held annually at different times of the year, the Lesser at Agrai and the Greater at Eleusis in the territory of Attica. These were secret celebrations, and those who took part were bound to silence: there was a 'golden key' which locked their tongues and 'great reverence for the gods' kept silent those who participated (*Homeric Hymn to Demeter* line 479; Soph. *Oedipus at Colonus* 1051–2: doc. 3.31). This secrecy means that many aspects of the cult are not understood. Yet historians agree on one point: that the *Homeric Hymn to Demeter*, written in the seventh century, which recounts the abduction of Demeter's daughter Persephone by her uncle Hades into the underworld, where she became his consort, and her mother's wanderings in searching for her which led her to Eleusis contains themes which were reflected in significant ways in the ritual of the Greater Mysteries.

   Those who were initiated into the Mysteries were known as mystai (singular: mystes), and groups of mystai were initiated by an initiated cult person known as the mystagogos, 'leader of the mystai', responsible for overseeing their initiation. Some scholars have suggested that each individual initiate had their own mystagogos but this is based only on an unnecessary restoration in a single inscription. Children, however, were excluded from the Eleusinian Mysteries and all the mystai were adults except for the one 'child of the hearth', whose role was to propitiate the goddess on behalf of all the initiates (*IG* I³ 6C, line 25: doc. 3.37). He was probably taking the place of Demophon in the myth, to whom Demeter was granting immortality by laying him in the fire each night until his mother discovered this and intervened. Perhaps children were excluded because the mysteries involved a comprehension of the rites, and an understanding of the revelation, which was at the core of the ceremony.

Figure 3.7 Demeter on the right instructing the youth Triptolemos in the art of agriculture, which he taught to the rest of humanity (doc. 3.31). Persephone with a lighted torch looks on from the left. This relief is carved on a large stone from Eleusis, and dates to around 440–430 BC. National Archaeological Museum, Athens, inv. no. 126. © Hellenic Ministry of Culture and Tourism/Archaeological Receipts Fund.

The Eleusinian myth

According to the *Homeric Hymn to Demeter*, Demeter roamed the world with Hekate looking for her daughter until, totally exhausted, she came to Eleusis, and was cared for by the local residents. There she fasted and drank only the kykeon. While modern authors have attempted to reconstruct this as a hallucinogen to help explain the mystic experience of the initiates, it was clearly simply a refreshing concoction of water, ground grain and the pennyroyal herb (kykeon: *Homeric Hymn to Demeter* 208–9: doc. 3.31). After an initially pleasant stay, spoilt by Metaneira's interference in Demeter's nocturnal process to make her son Demophon immortal, Demeter withdrew within herself, withheld her gift of fertility from the soil, and humanity began to starve. As a result the gods became worried too, for without worshippers they would have no sacrifices or offerings. Eventually an agreement was worked out whereby Persephone would spend spring and summer in the upper world, returning to Hades and the underworld for winter, for which her absence was believed to be responsible. Demeter in gratitude for the Eleusinians' help gave to them ceremonies ensuring a happy afterlife for the participants and better hopes for the current life. The Mysteries could be as old as the Mycenaean Age, but certainly existed by the time the hymn was composed. When Athens took over Eleusis, probably in the seventh or sixth century, the cult was adapted to tie it closely into Athenian religious life.

What occurred at the Lesser Mysteries is unknown, and it is not certain if they were essential preparation for the Greater Mysteries and perhaps involved rites of purification to

Table 3.3 The Boedromion calendar

Boedromion 14	The sacred chests (kistai) containing cultic items were transported from Eleusis to Athens
Boedromion 15	The archon basileus summoned the initiates to the Painted Stoa in Athens; a sacred herald invited everyone to be initiated, except non-Greek speakers and murderers
Boedromion 16	The mystai journeyed to the sea and washed a piglet they brought with them, which was probably sacrificed later that day
Boedromion 17 Boedromion 18 }	Days of rest and fasting
Boedromion 19	The pilgrimage from Athens to Eleusis; the priestesses carried the kistai in ritual procession back to Eleusis (*IG* I³ 79: doc. 3.39); there was ritual abuse of mystai as they crossed streams, in order to make pilgrims laugh and undergo catharsis, washing away their worries
Boedromion 20	The night of the re-enacted search for Persephone, when the initiation in the telesterion ('initiation hall') and drinking of the kykeon took place, and the hierophant emerged from an inner sanctum (the anaktoron) to reveal the sacred items
Boedromion 21	A day of rest
Boedromion 22	The mystai made libations to the dead
Boedromion 23	The initiates returned to Athens

prepare mystai for the Great Mysteries. They were compulsory according to an ancient scholiast, and the fact that if there were large numbers of participants the Lesser Mysteries would be held twice would strengthen the argument that the Lesser Mysteries were a compulsory preliminary for initiation into the Great. The Boedromion calendar was a very specific calendar of events for the Great Mysteries, and several days were set aside for ritual preparation for initiation, days which would have heightened the sense of expectation amongst those about to be initiated, and prepared them to receive the promise of a better afterlife.

The celebration of the Mysteries

On the day after the initiates had walked from Athens to Eleusis there was a night-time celebration including the actual initiation. There may well have been a nocturnal search with torches for Persephone, imitating Demeter's search for her daughter in the hymn. In the darkened hall called the telesterion the secret of a blessed afterlife was then revealed to the initiates. The mystai may have drunk the kykeon during the rites, just as Demeter herself did at Eleusis. The contents of the kistai, the hiera ('sacred objects'), may well have been revealed to the initiates: and since Demeter was connected with agriculture, there may well also have been an agricultural symbolism in the objects revealed to the initiates. Perhaps they were shown something as simple as an ear of wheat: an ordinary enough item, but redolent with ideas of the seed, the ground and the emergence of a new plant. Initiates did not need to have any theological understanding, and the rites were apparently explained in simple terms: an initiate had to be able to understand Greek, however, so there must have been at least some simple explanation, or perhaps the rule was simply to keep the rites for Greeks and not the 'barbaroi' (barbarians, 'non-Greeks'). Christian writers such as Clement and Tertullian were critical of these 'pagan' rites and attributed sexual overtones to them, but such criticism has no evidence to support it.

Those who were being initiated had eschatological hopes, a word derived from 'eschatos', 'final', meaning that they had hopes concerning an afterlife, the 'finality' of human existence. So in Aristophanes' play *Frogs* Dionysos and his slave Xanthias (both presumably initiates) visit the Eleusinian 'section' of Hades and there they see the 'pious mystai' chanting, dancing and tossing their garlanded heads and certainly having a better time than Achilles was having in the underworld judging by his complaints to Odysseus (Ar. *Frogs* 312–36: doc. 3.32; Achilles: Hom. *Odyssey* 11.489–91: doc. 3.53). As Sophocles writes, those who have been initiated are 'thrice blessed', while for those who have not been all that Hades holds is 'wretchedness' (Soph. *F* 837: doc. 3.33). Even Diagoras is there in the *Frogs*, chanting away; this is meant to be ironic and comic, for he was an atheist who in the fifth century trivialised the Mysteries by telling people about them, attempting to dissuade people from being initiated. He was therefore sentenced to death and there was a reward of one talent for the person who killed Diagoras and, the scholiasts add, two talents if he was brought in alive.

The secrecy concerning events in the telesterion was therefore taken very seriously. In 415 BC, two significant events occurred at Athens just prior to the sailing of the Athenian expedition to Sicily (Thuc. 6.27.1–28.2: doc. 13.24). Throughout the city the stone block hermai, which stood at the entrance to public buildings and houses, were mutilated (their erect phalluses, seen as symbols of good luck, were smashed off). This gave rise to the report, in connection with similar incidents that had occurred earlier, that young men had parodied the Eleusinian Mysteries in private celebrations in their houses by holding their own version of their rites, and amongst those accused was Alkibiades. His enemies linked the mutilation of the hermai with this mocking of the Mysteries and argued that it was part of a plot to overthrow the democracy and establish him as tyrant. Alkibiades denied the charges, but a formal prosecution was brought against him. He successfully defended himself and the expedition sailed, but once he was away along with most of his supporters, he was tried in his absence and found guilty, the punishment being death. He therefore fled from Sicily and took refuge at Sparta (where he was said to have fathered Leotychidas, son of King Agis, doc. 4.24). Alkibiades' removal as one of the three commanders had a very negative affect on Athenian chances in Sicily and must have been a major contributor to their eventual defeat there, as indeed was Nikias' over-inclination to listen to the seers on the expedition when he catastrophically delayed the retreat of the expedition because of an eclipse of the full moon (Andoc. 1 *On the Mysteries* 11–12: doc. 3.34; Thucydides 6.1.1, 15.2–4: doc. 13.23; Thucydides 6.27.1–28.2: doc. 13.24; Thucydides 7.50.3–4: doc. 3.24). That religious matters could bring down a powerful and popular politician shows precisely how seriously the Athenians took their beliefs.

The Great Mysteries were certainly popular and the remains of the initiation hall, the telesterion, today show that it could seat 3000 individuals. Given that there were at least 30,000 Athenian male citizens, it is probable that most Athenians were initiates, especially bearing in mind that women and adult slaves of both genders, as well as non-Athenians, could participate. Clearly this was the largest cult group experience of the ancient Greek world, and the procession from Athens to Eleusis must have been a staggering one, with thousands of people spread out over the 21-kilometre walk from Athens to Eleusis. During the Peloponnesian War after the Spartan fortification at Dekeleia (doc. 9.23) the initiates had to go by sea instead, but in 407 BC, Alkibiades, now returned to Athens, led out the army by land to protect the mystai during their procession to Eleusis (Xen. *Hellenika* 1.4.20–1: doc. 3.35). The initiates made their way by foot and in carts and wagons, except in the fourth century when the Athenian orator and statesmen Lykourgos specifically enacted that all the mystai had to walk from Athens to Eleusis, regardless of their wealth. One of the supernatural visions during the Persian invasions was the sound of mystic cries and the sight of a cloud of dust at Eleusis arising as if from the marching of 30,000 men (the citizen body comprised approximately 30,000), indicating that the majority of Athenians may well have been initiates (Hdt. 8.65, cf. 5.97.2; Plut. *Themistokles* 15.1, *Phokion* 28.1–2); cf. Poseidonios *FGH* 87 *F*36.51; Paus. 1.36.3). As with other panhellenic festivals, such as the Olympian, Pythian, Nemean and Isthmian, the Mysteries encouraged participation from non-Athenians by declaring a 'sacred truce' for both the Lesser and Greater Mysteries (*IG* I^3 6B: doc. 3.36). The length of the truce for the Mysteries was fifty-five days, covering the period before, during and after the celebration itself, and cities which did not observe the truce were not allowed access to the Mysteries.

In order to be initiated, the initiates had to pay various fees to cult personnel and in addition there were sums of money to be paid to the goddesses. The amounts were carefully specified in an Athenian decree so that there would be no over-charging by cult personnel, while initiates could plan ahead with a clear understanding of the expenses of initiation (*IG* I^3 6C: doc. 3.37). The Eumolpidai and the Kerykes were the Eleusinian priestly families in charge of the Mysteries, receiving five obols as a fee from each initiate. Initiation was not expensive and this, and the better hopes for the afterlife which the cult promised, largely explain the cult's popularity. Non-Greeks, as long as they could understand Greek, women and slaves could all participate, and slaves may have had their fees paid for by their masters, or been able to save up the sum involved. It is possible to imagine that men who initiated their wives and slaves wanted them all to be together in the blessed afterlife in Hades promised for those who took part in the Mysteries.

The first-fruits

The Athenians provided 'first-fruit' offerings to the goddesses Demeter and Persephone and decreed that their allies do so as well. Accordingly, a tithe (dekate) or 10 per cent of the first of the harvest was to be dedicated to the goddesses and brought to Eleusis. The Athenians offered these first-fruits by 'ancestral custom', and had also received an oracle from Delphi instructing them to do so: perhaps they had consulted it on this matter. A fifth-century Athenian decree sets out the details: 1/600th of every measure of barley and 1/1200th of every measure of wheat was to be collected and storage pits for this grain were to be constructed at Eleusis. A draft decree concerning similar provisions for olive oil was also to be drawn up and presented at a later stage to the assembly. The Athenians also decreed that all Greek cities were to be encouraged to make offerings to the goddesses in this way. The fact that fines of 1000 drachmas a day were to be charged against the hieropoioi (sacred officials) for failing to receive the grain brought to Athens for the goddesses shows how seriously the matter was taken (*IG* I^3 78: doc. 3.38). Presumably this grain was sold and the proceeds helped to underwrite the costs of the cult and its practices. Demeter was the goddess of agriculture, who had given this gift to humanity, and the Athenians, following the general principle of thanksgiving in Greek religion, showed their appreciation to the goddess by making the donation of first-fruits compulsory for all their allies. Specifically, she had entrusted the task of spreading the knowledge of agriculture to one of the royal family at Eleusis, Triptolemos, who set out on this task (Fig. 3.7).

The pilgrimage from Athens to Eleusis was made mostly by foot; when the bridge over the Rhetos stream was constructed in 422 BC it was specifically so that the priestesses could cross

Figure 3.8 A maenad holding the thyrsos in one hand, and a panther in another; she wears a pan-ther skin shawl, a snake as a headband, and goes barefoot (doc. 3.41). She is painted on an Athenian white-ground cup, 14 cm in diameter, by the Brygos Painter, dating to about 480–470 BC. Staatliche Antikensammlungen und Glyptothek 2645, Munich. Drawing by J. Etherington.

it in safety without endangering the kistai they were carrying on their heads (*IG* I³ 79: doc. 3.39). Wagons were not to be driven across the bridge: it was specifically narrow in order to prevent this: it was a walking bridge. Eschatologically, the mysteries enabled the mystai to escape from the dreary underworld of Homeric Hades to one of happiness and joy. They learnt the origins of agriculture, came away with a better attitude to this life, and could look forward to a blessed afterlife. It is no wonder that the Eleusinian Mysteries remained popular throughout the Hellenistic and Roman periods until the rites were finally abolished in the fourth century AD.

Maenads and Dionysos

Women were involved in many fertility festivals which excluded men, such as the Thes-mophoria and the Haloa, in which they entreated Demeter's help for human fecundity and agricultural prosperity. Women were also particularly devoted to Dionysos, the god of wine and ecstasy. Herakleitos, critical of blood sacrifice (*F* 5: doc. 3.6) was scathing as well towards 'night-wanderers' (perhaps nocturnal devotees of certain cults), magicians, Bacchan-ts, maenads and mystai (*F* 14: doc. 3.40). In many parts of Greece (but not Athens) women celebrated a festival for the god every two years in which they took to the hills, abandoning their domestic chores, to drink and dance, and enter into a state of mania, 'possession' or 'madness' by the god. They were thought of being one with the god, in a state of enthousi-asmos (literally 'in the god'). Euripides in his play the *Bacchae* ('women Bacchants') depicted them in the hills near Thebes, and recounted the punishment which was meted out to

93

Pentheus, king of Thebes, by his mother and aunts, when he attempted to prevent the women from worshipping Dionysos. The message of the play was that the women *had* to honour the god or he would be displeased. While in the play the women are depicted as being able to tear wild animals apart, maenads of the archaic and classical periods restricted themselves to drinking wine and wearing fawn skins, handling tame snakes and tossing their heads back, with their hair 'let down to their shoulders' in enthusiastic dances, while holding a staff known as the thrysos (a staff made of fennel, Eur. *Bacchae* 704–6: doc. 3.41; Fig. 3.8).

Asklepios the Healer

Apollo was the god of disease and sicknesses, and was believed to send plagues as a punishment on both individual mortals and entire communities. In such cases it was normal to consult Delphi, and the Pythia would prescribe a ritual that would avert the wrath of the god and so end the plague. At the very beginning of the *Iliad*, Apollo sends a plague against the Greeks at Troy when they dishonoured his priest, with the opening lines of the epic concerning the way in which Apollo attacks the Greeks (and their dogs) with arrows symbolising the plague. In classical Greece it was his son Asklepios who was seen as the primary god of healing, and Asklepios had major sanctuaries (Asklepieia: singular, Asklepieion) at Epidauros in southern Greece, Kos in the Aegean and Pergamon in Asia Minor; there was also an Asklepieion at Lebena on Crete. The other main healing deity was Amphiaraos whose shrine the Amphiaraion was at Oropos, roughly half-way between Athens and Thebes. His cult was introduced into Athens at the Piraeus in the late 420s, and from there into the city itself, where he had a sanctuary at the foot of the acropolis and its substantial remains can still be seen there today (*IG* II² 4960a: doc. 3.42).

The abaton and ritual practices

Asklepios' cult was one of faith-healing. Individuals slept overnight in his sanctuary, in a special building known as an abaton. They hoped (following preliminary prayer and sacrifice)

Table 3.4 Important non-Olympian gods

Amphiaraos	Healing hero with shrine at Oropos
Asklepios	Healing god (Fig. 3.9)
Hades	God of the underworld (and so a 'chthonic' deity), brother of Zeus and Poseidon
Hekate	Goddess of magic and sorcery; dogs were her special agents
Kabeiroi	Mystery gods worshipped on the Aegean island Samothrace; especially thanked by sailors saved in shipwreck
Nemesis	Goddess of punishment
Nymphs	Female deities of trees, springs and caves
Pan	Anthropomorphic god, but with goats' legs and horns; he appeared to Philippides on his run to Sparta in 490 BC (Fig. 5.4)
Persephone	Daughter of Demeter and closely associated with her Eleusinian cult (Fig. 3.7)
Sabazios	Eastern god imported and adapted in the fourth century
Trophonios	Chthonic oracular hero at Lebedeia

that the god would appear to them in a dream and lay his healing hands on them, or give them verbal instructions on how they were to be cured. This process of sleeping in the shrine is known by modern scholars as incubation (Fig. 3.9). Cures which took place under such circumstances were recorded at some of Asklepios' cult centres, especially at Epidauros in the Peloponnese. While some of the accounts of cures are exaggerated and have been 'improved' in the telling, the fact remains that the sick people who went to these shrines did so because they believed that Asklepios would take a personal interest in their sickness and cure them. Not everyone was cured, as even the Greeks recognised, but enough recovered from their illnesses (for whatever reason) for the cult to remain popular for hundreds of years (*IG* IV^2 1, no. 121–2: doc. 3.43).

In Aristophanes' comedy, *Wealth*, the god Asklepios cures Wealth (Ploutos) so that Wealth will in future, now that he is able to see, distribute riches fairly rather than indiscriminately, as at present when the undeserving often become rich. In this play the procedure for being cured is given in detail, though rituals would have varied at different healing shrines. After cakes and offerings were set out for the god, the sick would then lie down for the night in the abaton, having prayed that the god would appear to them in a dream and perform a cure. At the shrine of Amphiaraos at Oropos, men and women slept on different sides of the shrine and this was presumably normal practice. Snakes were associated with Asklepios and in the *Wealth* they make their appearance alongside the god; Karion in the *Wealth* exclaims at how enormous they were. Snakes also played an active role in the accounts of their cures dedicated by grateful patients at Epidauros:

> Nikasiboula of Messene slept (in the abaton) for the sake of offspring and saw a dream; it seemed to her that the god approached her with a snake creeping behind him, and that she had intercourse with it; and afterwards two sons were born to her within a year.
>
> (doc. 3.43, no. 42)

Dogs also played a part in cures, and one had healed a blind boy, Lyson of Hermione, presumably by licking his eyes while he was 'wide-awake' (doc. 3.43, no. 20). The snake was so much a part of the cult that when Athens decided to introduce the worship of Asklepios to the Piraeus in 420 BC so that Athenians suffering from various ailments would have the opportunity to be cured by him in their own city instead of travelling to Epidauros, one of the sacred snakes was especially imported, brought by an Athenian named Telemachos in his chariot. This Asklepieion in Athens itself provides the setting for Aristophanes' *Wealth*.

The iamata

The thanks-offerings, which individuals dedicated to Asklepios at Epidauros in return for curing them, give specific details of sick individuals' symptoms and cures. Kleo, for example, who had suffered from a lengthy and difficult pregnancy (purportedly five years), dedicated a small stone tablet (iama; plural, iamata) in Asklepios' shrine at Epidauros (doc. 3.43, no. 1). Her dedication explains that she was self-conscious because her offering was a small one, but worshippers believed that it was the principle of giving in thanks for a cure that was important, and so on the tablet she inscribed her thanks to the god, who was 'wonderful', even if the size of her tablet was not. Individual thanksgiving inscriptions such as these became the basis of the long lists of cures which the priests at Epidauros recorded at Asklepios' shrine there in the fourth century BC. It

Figure 3.9 A marble relief from the fourth century dedicated to Asklepios by a grateful woman or her family, from the god's sanctuary in the Piraeus, Athens. Hygieiea stands behind her father as he heals the woman by placing his hands on her shoulders, presumably the location of her ailment; three individuals, on the left, probably the woman's relatives, raise their hands in adoration. Piraeus National Museum 405, Piraeus, Athens. Drawing by Tessa Rickards.

was believed that if the god was not thanked he would be angry at those who had been healed by his intervention and their illness would return to punish their ingratitude.

When Ambrosia of Athens, who was blind in one eye, went round the sanctuary making fun of the iamata, which recorded cures that she considered to be impossible, Asklepios appeared to her in a dream and said he would cure her but that she would have to dedicate a silver piglet in the temple in thanks for the cure and as 'a memorial of her ignorance' (doc. 3.43, no. 4). The god did not require costly offerings, and Socrates, as he lay dying at his execution in 399 BC, asked his friends to remember that he owed a rooster to Asklepios, presumably in gratitude for a quick and painless death (Pl. *Phaedo* 117a–118: doc. 3.87). Cures could be recorded in a number of ways, and at the Asklepieion at Corinth sufferers whose ailments had been relieved thanked the god by dedicating terracotta models of the part of the body that had been healed. At the Corinth museum, the visitor can still see clay models of eyes, breasts and legs offered to Asklepios in thanks for the fact that these had been cured. A woman who was healed at the Asklepieion at Piraeus dedicated a stone tablet there, which depicts the way in which the healing process took place. She is shown lying asleep on a fleece placed on a couch, with Asklepios laying his hands on her. Behind him stands his daughter, Hygieia (literally, Hygiene, i.e. Health). On the left-hand side the woman's family is depicted, including a child, who are worshipping the god by raising their right hand (Fig. 3.9). The dedication of this relief symbolised the family's gratitude towards the god, and this example would have encouraged others who used the shrine to hope for a cure. This principle of thanking a god for a service which that god performed for the worshipper was fundamental to ancient Greek religion, though the usual form which it took were sacrifices in honour of and dedications to the god concerned.

Heroes

Both Asklepios and Amphiaraos were originally 'heroes', rather than gods. In the Homeric poems Asklepios was a human physician who attended to Greeks who were wounded on the battle-field at Troy, while Amphiaraos was a great warrior and part of the Theban myth cycle. Heroes were therefore mortals, who were usually directly descended from the gods, or in some cases possessed a more distant relationship with them. They attained a semi-divine status, and were 'mid-way' in status between gods and mortals, receiving divine honours after death. Heroes such as Herakles and Asklepios became so important in the popular view that they transcended their original status as heroes and became gods, though they were the exception. Heroes generally had a small shrine, known as a heroon, and were chthonic deities, that is, 'of the earth', because they were mortals who had died and been buried. Libations of blood were therefore poured into the ground for them, but they also received 'bloodless offerings' such as wine and milk.

Chthonic cults

Heroes' powers centred around their bones and the location where they had been buried, which accordingly became their shrine; many of these heroic cults were inspired by the discovery of Mycenaean tombs. For the Spartans, Orestes, the son of Agamemnon (leader of the Greek expedition against Troy), was an important hero. There is a detailed account in Herodotos about how in the sixth century the Spartans, as a result of experiencing military defeat, received an oracle from Delphi to bring home the bones of Orestes. After an unsuccessful search, they then made a further enquiry as to where his bones could be found. These were actually in Tegea, and the Pythia delivered an oracle to this effect, which was in the form of a 'riddle' that needed to be interpreted. In fact, they were discovered in the yard of a blacksmith, who was amazed at the size of the coffin and the height of the corpse when he accidentally dug it up, and this confirmed Orestes' super-human status. The bones were taken to Sparta and from then on Sparta defeated Tegea in any military engagements (Hdt. 1.67.2–68.6: doc. 3.46). Possession of the bones meant that the power of the hero now resided in Sparta and could come to its aid.

Another chthonic cult is evidenced by a stone relief from Sparta (fig. 6.7), with an enthroned couple: a large and conspicuous snake behind the throne with its tail curving underneath it indicates that the pair are chthonic deities. Two diminutive worshippers, showing their status in relationship to the enthroned pair, bring offerings: the man has a rooster and a round object, perhaps a pomegranate (symbolic of the underworld), and the woman a flower, and something in her other hand (another pomegranate?). The enthroned woman who looks at the viewer holds out a two-handled cup to receive a libation while both deities raise a hand in recognition of the offerings being made. The human worshippers may be making funerary offerings to a deceased couple, and this relief would then be a grave marker, or the enthroned couple could be an unidentified heroic couple, such as Menelaos and Helen, with the worshippers focused on Helen as a marriage and fertility deity: roosters were offered for fertility purposes in other cults, such as that of chthonic Persephone in Lokris, Italy.

The role of heroes

The main roles of such heroes, if they had been mighty warriors of the past, was to assist in a military capacity the city where they were buried, and Orestes is seen as leading the Spartans to victory over Tegea, which had earlier defeated them in 560. Similarly, Kimon in the fifth century set out on an expedition to find the bones of Theseus and, aided like the Spartans by divination, found them on the island of Skyros and brought them back to Athens so that this ancestral Athenian king could assist his city (Plut. *Kimon* 8.5–7). Sophocles depicts Oedipus in Athens' remote past as indicating to Theseus the spot where he should be buried, promising that his bones will be 'better than many shields and the imported spear of neighbours'. As ex-king of Thebes Oedipus will prove to be a major weapon against one of Athens' chief enemies of the time: Thebes (Soph. *Oedipus at Colonus* 1518–34: doc. 3.45).

Heroes were especially seen as the protectors of cities, and when the Messenian helots were liberated by the Thebans in the fourth century they founded a new capital city, and summoned back their heroes, who were thought of as having been in exile while the Spartans ruled the country, especially Messene herself and Aristomenes, a quasi-legendary figure who had opposed the Spartans in the Second Messenian War (Paus. *Description of Greece* 4.27.6: doc. 14.22). Trophonios, a son of Apollo and a builder, was another hero, but an oracular one, who had been swallowed by the ground after cutting off the head of his brother Agamedes. Consultants had to invoke Agamedes and descend, in special clothing, into an underground cave, which Pausanias describes as a terrifying ordeal. As with Asklepios their experiences had to be inscribed on a tablet which was then dedicated at the shrine (Paus. *Description of Greece* 9.39.5–14: doc. 3.48)

Mortals who had done great deeds during their lifetime could be heroised, that is, be given the status of heroes and venerated after their death, in much the same way as the founders of colonies – oikistai – received sacrifices and honours after death, while athletic festivals could be held in their memory (Thuc. 5.11.1: doc. 2.7) and dedications made to them (Graham 1983, 21–2n.7: doc. 2.6). Kleomedes the boxer was a very different type of hero. He had been disqualified for killing his opponent at the Olympic festival of 492 BC, and, turning 'mad with grief', murdered sixty school children on his return to his home town of Astypalaia. He took refuge in a chest in the sanctuary of Athena but when it was broken open he had disappeared. Whatever the truth behind the story of the missing body, clearly the local people felt that his spirit needed placating (Paus. *Description of Greece* 6.9.6–8: doc. 3.47). When they made enquiry at Delphi the Pythia declared him the 'last of the heroes': perhaps it was felt that the list of mortals being honoured after their death was growing too long. In a similar way, various poltergeists were treated as heroes and venerated after death to keep their anger at bay. One of the companions of Odysseus, Polites (*Odyssey* 10.224), was a poltergeist whose spirit attacked local inhabitants until appeased, according to tradition, by the annual sacrifice of a virgin, which in historical times had been commuted into a non-human sacrifice.

The Greeks in classical times believed that the gods and mortals had much in common, both in intellect and 'outward' form, though unlike gods humans had no knowledge of their destiny (Pind. *Nemean* 6.1–7: doc. 3.8). Man could not of course aspire to be a god, although the Spartan Lysander was accorded many honours which were close to those that might be granted to a hero, a mythical or historical man who after death was paid semi-divine honours. A festival in his honour and a statue of himself dedicated while he was still alive marked Lysander out from his contemporaries (Plut. *Life of Lysander* 18.1–10: doc. 13.38), but it was only with Alexander, son of Zeus Ammon, that a man might declare himself divine (Arr. *Expedition of Alexander* 3.3.1–4.5: doc. 15.17). Herakles seems to have started out as a mortal hero, with various tales attaching to his name over time, including the famous 'Twelve Labours', and despite being hated by Hera he became a god, and according to myth was welcomed into Mount Olympos through the agency of Athena. Spartan and Macedonian kings claimed him as an ancestor.

Sanctuaries and cult regulations

While the Olympian gods were believed to dwell on Mount Olympos which at near 3000 metres lies between Macedonia and Thessaly, the Greeks built for the Olympians and other deities sacred buildings, which could range from relatively small shrines to elaborate and expensive buildings such as Athena's temple, the Parthenon, on the Athenian acropolis (Fig. 1.2). The sanctuary area was called a temenos, a Greek term meaning 'cut off', as it was a piece of land separated from the ordinary (profane) world around it, while the word for temple was hieron, literally 'sacred place'. Temples became the hallmark of Greek civilisation and Herodotos records the Athenians as saying in 479 BC that they would never defect to the Persians, for they had burnt and demolished the Athenians' statues and temples, referring to the destruction of the various sacred buildings on the acropolis which the Athenians for many years left unrepaired as a visible reminder of the Persian sack of their city. Moreover, Herodotos has the Athenians define Greekness in terms of ethnicity and language and the panhellenic sanctuaries, such as Delphi and Olympia, shared by all Greeks (Hdt. 8.144.2: doc. 3.90).

Temples and sanctuaries

Greek temples have become 'emblematic' of Greek civilisation, immediately recognisable and an integral part of the polis. Wherever the Greeks colonised, they built temples. In fact the temples which have been best preserved are those in southern Italy and Sicily, especially at Paestum near Naples, and at Selinounte in Sicily: in these places the wealth of the cities allowed for several large temples to be constructed in one location. Accounts of the foundation of cities routinely mention that one of the first tasks of the founder was to build temples for the gods (Hom. *Odyssey* 6.10: doc. 2.5; Paus. *Description of Greece* 4.27.7: doc. 14.22). Temple and sanctuary were technically the property of the god but managed by human agents, either

Table 3.5 Gods and their major cult centres

Amphiaraos	Oropos (on the border of Attica and Boeotia)
Aphrodite	Corinthian acropolis (Aphrodite was the main deity of Corinth)
Apollo	Delphi (oracular centre; athletic and musical festival); Delos (athletic and musical festival); Sparta (Karneia); Didyma (oracular centre)
Artemis	Aegina (major temple); Argos (major temple); Brauron (Attica: initiation of girls into womanhood); Ephesos (main deity of city); Sparta (Artemis Orthia)
Asklepios	Major healing shrines at Epidauros (Peloponnese), Lebena (Crete), Kos (Aegean island), and Pergamon
Athena	Athenian acropolis, Rhodes (major temple and dream centre), Sparta (Athena Chalkioikos, 'of the Brazen House')
Demeter (and Persephone)	Eleusis (mystery religion); Lokris in Italy (Demeter was the goddess of childbirth)
Hera	Argos and Samos (Hera was the major deity of these cities; major sanctuary)
Kabeiroi	Samothrace
Nemesis	Rhamnous in Attica (major sanctuary)
Poseidon	Isthmia (athletic festival)
Trophonios	Lebedeia (oracular centre)
Zeus	Nemea (athletic festival), Olympia (athletic festival; oracle), Dodona (oracular centre), Siwah (Zeus Ammon)

state officials or more usually priests and priestesses responsible to the city for the sanctuary's maintenance. They were frequently located in a prominent place, as at Athens and Corinth, where the goddesses Athena and Aphrodite had, respectively, their temples on the acropolis, and the Athenian acropolis became the home of several temples, not just the Parthenon, but also the temple of Athena Nike ('Victory'), and the Erechtheum (Fig. 3.11).

A typical temple was made from marble or limestone, and was rectangular in shape, surrounded by cylindrical columns and roofed with terracotta or marble tiles. Each column was made up of a series of cylindrical stones, referred to as 'drums', stacked one upon the other, and this is best illustrated in the case of temples which have been struck by an earthquake where the drums lie in a tumbled line on the ground. The exterior of the temple, which usually faced east, would be adorned with sculptured scenes drawn from Greek mythology and the triangular front and back of the temple roof, the pediments, filled with large statues of the gods. The east pediment of the temple of Zeus at Olympia depicted the chariot race between Pelops and Oenomaus, whom Pelops had to defeat in order to marry his daughter Hippodameia. Zeus stands in the centre with various heroes and heroines around him, with the two rival chariots and riders on either side, and in the corner at each end, a reclining figure, one a river god, the other a diviner. The west pediment showed the drunken brawl between the Lapiths and the centaurs which took place at the wedding of Peirithoos. This centauromachy (battle with the centaurs) was also a theme of the metopes on the Parthenon, and represented the struggle between civilisation and the forces of chaos and barbarianism, particularly, in the case of the temple of Athena Nike, representing the Greek resistance to the Persians. In the case of the Parthenon, the pediments depicted Athens' birth from the head of Zeus and her contest with Poseidon for Attica as the two most important episodes linking Athena to Athens. There were two main types of column which ran around temples, the Doric and the Ionic. Doric columns were simple and unadorned, while Ionic were surmounted by a scroll-like capital (Fig. 3.10).

Above the columns ran a frieze, with single carvings known as metopes separated by dividers known as triglyphs above Doric columns, while above Ionic columns a continuous frieze of carvings ran around the temple. The Doric column and the Ionic were both fluted, with parallel groves running vertically, and the payments for the fluting of columns on the Erechtheum are listed on an Athenian stele (*IG* I³ 476: doc. 5.42) The Corinthian column was a much later development, and much favoured in classicising western architecture of the eighteenth and nineteenth centuries AD.

The acropolis of Athens and its temples

In the sixth century the Athenians had constructed a temple to Athena on the acropolis which was destroyed in the two Persian sackings of the city (480–479). In 447 BC Athens decided to build the goddess a new temple, the Parthenon, the extensive remains of which survive today on the highest point of the acropolis. Perikles' role in the reconstruction was a conspicuous one, and his associate Pheidias oversaw the exterior sculptural decoration of the Parthenon. The temple was constructed of Pentelic marble, quarried at Mount Pentelikos in Attica, a white stone known particularly for its quality, strength, and slightly translucent character. Doric in style, the Parthenon is approximately 69.5 metres by 30.8 metres, with eight columns along the front and seventeen on the sides. The people of Athens took a very close interest in the temple, and all the details concerning it were discussed and voted on by the ekklesia, as in the building accounts for each year of construction (see *IG* I³ 449: doc. 1.13).

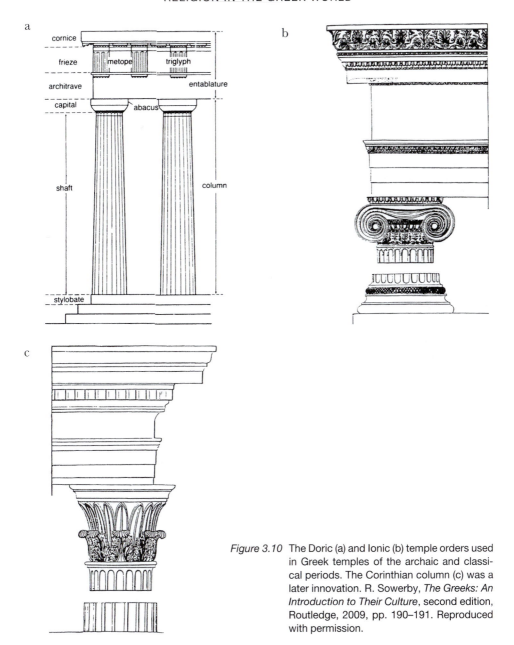

Figure 3.10 The Doric (a) and Ionic (b) temple orders used in Greek temples of the archaic and classical periods. The Corinthian column (c) was a later innovation. R. Sowerby, *The Greeks: An Introduction to Their Culture*, second edition, Routledge, 2009, pp. 190–191. Reproduced with permission.

The temple was converted into a Byzantine church dedicated to the Virgin Mary and then a mosque, and the entire temple would still be intact except for the fact that in AD 1687 the gunpowder magazine which the Turks had stored in the Parthenon was set off by cannonballs fired from the ships of the Venetians who were besieging the city. Thankfully, various European artists had made drawings of the Parthenon frieze, metopes and pediments before the explosion, though there still remains great debate amongst modern art historians regarding the reconstruction of the temple sculptures and their meaning and significance. The temple, dedicated in 438, although construction continued until 431, could be seen for several kilometres around. It housed the chyselephantine (gold and ivory) statue of Athena designed by the Athenian artist Pheidias, who was also responsible for Zeus' statue at his temple at Olympia (Paus. *Description of Greece* 5.11.1, 5.11.8–11: doc. 3.3). Athena's statue was adorned with forty talents of pure gold and Perikles, at the beginning of the Peloponnesian War, advised the Athenians that they could use this in their prosecution of the war (Thuc. 2.13.3–5: doc. 1.10). In addition, the Parthenon served as a treasury (opisthodomos), where the various dedications made to the goddess by private individuals were stored. A board of treasurers who served for four years had to give an exact list of all items stored there at the end of their office (*IG* I³ 351: doc. 1.11). Similarly, in the cult of Enyalios the war-god on Rhodes, a percentage of both the soldiers' pay and the booty they took in war was to be given to the priest of the cult for the temple, and the priest had to report on this to the boule on Rhodes at the end of his term of office and hand the amount over to the incoming priest (*LSCG Suppl.* 85: doc. 3.51).

The Athenian state also housed in the Parthenon the percentage – one-sixtieth – of the tribute (phoros) collected from their allies in the Delian League. The treasury had initially been located on Delos, but appears to have been moved to Athens after the Athenian disaster in Egypt in 454/3 (Thuc. 1.104.1–2, 109.1–110.4: doc. 12.13). The Athenians borrowed these funds during the Peloponnesian War and promised to pay back this money, but were never wealthy enough to do so (*IG* I³ 52: doc. 13.7). Most spectacularly, the Parthenon was unusual, in that around the interior wall ran a frieze, which apparently depicts a procession at the Panathenaic festival in honour of Athena. This showed the gods seated and apparently waiting for the festival to start, with groups of young women holding ritual objects, troops of horsemen and cattle being led for sacrifice.

The acropolis was also the site of the temple of Athena Nike which celebrated the Greek, but especially the Athenian, defeat of the Persians, and the healing sanctuary of Asklepios was at its base. Nestling into its slopes was the theatre of Dionysos, built sometime in the fifth century BC, and in which the great Athenian comedies and tragedies were performed (such as the *Antigone*: doc. 3.7). The most unique of the acropolis structures is the Erechtheum, which was constructed 421–407 BC, the porch of which is strikingly supported by carved statues of six women, caryatids, carrying on their heads what appear to be baskets and who were therefore probably represent basket-bearers in the annual Panathenaic procession (Fig. 3.11). The caryatids were often copied, as for the Forum of Augustus in Rome many centuries later.

The Erechtheum was built in honour of Erechtheus, the early mythical Athenian king; it has four chambers, the purpose of which is unclear, but they held various sacred items, such as the ancient wooden statue of Athena Polias and an altar of Poseidon and Erechtheus, along with the mark of Poseidon's trident. It was here that Poseidon and Athena had their famous contest to decide who would be Athens' deity: Poseidon promised a spring and so struck the rock with his trident, but Athena promised the olive tree: the Athenians chose the latter (the scene was shown on the Parthenon's west pediment). This very same olive tree miraculously regrew after the Persians looted and burnt the acropolis. Poseidon has a magnificent temple at Cape Sounion in Attica.

The role of temples

Greek temples served various purposes. First and foremost, a temple was not a congregational place of worship or the equivalent of a Christian church. People did not gather inside a temple as a group to worship, pray together or sing hymns. Often containing a statue of the deity,

Figure 3.11 The Erechtheum on the Athenian acropolis, with its porch of six young adult women carrying ritual baskets on their heads, as if they are part of a procession; they are caryatids supporting the roof of the Erechtheum porch. One of the six is now in the British Museum and the other five in the Acropolis Museum, Athens. Constructed between 421 BC and 407 BC, it was here that the ancient wooden statue of Athena was kept, and where the mark in the rock which Poseidon blasted with his trident when offering Athens the gift of a fresh water spring could be seen. Athena's rival gift of the olive tree was marked by an actual olive tree, which reshot miraculously after the Persians had looted and burnt the acropolis for a second time in 479 BC. Photo © Azlan Hashim.

a temple was in a sense the house of the god. Zeus' statue at Olympia was one of the seven wonders of the ancient world; Athena's in the Parthenon was equally famous (Paus. *Description of Greece* 5.11.1, 5.11.8–11: doc. 3.3; *IG* I³ 458a: doc. 1.12). Frequently, a temple also contained dedications, items grateful worshippers gave to the gods in return for some favour, such as the silver pig Ambrosia dedicated at Epidauros in thanks for a cure (*IG* IV² 1, no. 121–2: no. 4: doc. 3.43). Many of these could be extremely valuable, and Perikles pointed out to the Athenians that the various dedications made by private individuals and the state housed in the Parthenon were a considerable financial asset which could be used to fight the Spartans (Thuc. 2.13.3–5: doc. 1.10). This points to a crucial factor in Greek religious belief, namely that if the gods helped a worshipper, they expected thanks in return. Similarly, worshippers could build up a 'credit account' with the gods by being pious and making regular sacrifices and then later could remind the gods of these services when they themselves were in need of divine assistance. But the main focus of worship took place outside the temple, at the altar, where beasts were sacrificed to the gods while the worshippers looked on and then feasted in common.

Cult regulations

While there was no overall written code of religious morals, ethics or even myths in ancient Greece, individual cult centres sometimes published cult regulations inscribed on stone outside the sanctuary, warning would-be worshippers of any restrictions on their activities. These regulations governed the behaviour of worshippers at temples and shrines, so that the sanctuaries would not be damaged, items stolen or impious behaviour occur which might offend the gods. Sanctuaries were to be kept clean inside and the outside world kept out: at a sacred spring of the nymphs at Delos a law specifically forbade washing anything in the spring; swimming was prohibited (presumably because of the presence of the nymphs in the water); it was not to be a dumping ground for dung 'or anything else' (*LSCG Suppl.* 50: doc. 3.49). Most importantly temples, as places of sacrifice, needed to be cleaned after this process, and animal by-products such as the mess from entrails or dung had to be kept out or removed after the sacrifice (*IG* I³ 977, 980, 982: doc. 3.50). Xenophon's regulations for his sanctuary of Artemis were inscribed on a stele next to the shrine, and laid down that the possessor had to sacrifice a tithe every year to Artemis and keep the temple in good repair (Xen. *Anabasis* 5.3.13: doc. 3.52).

Many sanctuaries with springs or streams in their grounds or territory had laws imposing fines concerning water use, as water was used to clean and so to purify worshippers. On the Panathenaic frieze, a group of several men is shown carrying large water jugs on their shoulders to be used as part of the sacrificial rituals of the Panathenaic festival. Defecating or urinating in streams, which could themselves be deities, was seen as offensive to the gods. The trees of a sanctuary were also protected from being cut down or lopped by those seeking firewood, and it was a serious crime to cut down olive trees sacred to Athena (Dem. 43 *Against Makartatos* 71: doc. 1.15). Anything which might cause ritual pollution (miasma) at a sanctuary had to be kept away and women who had recently given birth had to wait some days before visiting a temple. Even at the healing sanctuaries of Asklepios, the dying and women in childbirth were removed from the sanctuary grounds. Peisistratos was probably being overscrupulous in removing the graves of the dead from within sight of the temple of Apollo on the sacred island of Delos (Hdt. 1.64.2: doc. 9.17), but when the Athenians purified the island in 426 BC all the graves on the island were removed, and the dying and those about to give birth were henceforth made to leave.

Temple dedications

Temples were generally constructed and paid for by the state, but individuals could also found shrines, often in response to a dream which they had had, or a promise which they had made to the gods if they received divine assistance. Archedamos of Thera showed his personal devotion to the nymphs of the countryside of Vari in Attica by decorating a cave for them, planting them a garden and building them a dancing floor (*IG* I³ 977, 980, 982: doc. 3.50). At Lindos on Rhodes, the cult of the war deity Enyalios was financed by a contribution of one-sixtieth from the pay of all soldiers going on an expedition and, it seems, of any booty gained from these as well, and every year the city's council had to offer up the sacrifice of a boar, dog and goat (*LSCG Suppl.* 85: doc. 3.51). Similarly Xenophon founded a small temple and altar sacred to Artemis, and with 10 per cent of the produce of the land provided food and drink for a festival in honour of the goddess for all men and women in the region, feasting them on barley, bread, wine and dried fruits, as well as a portion of the sacrificial victims from the sacred herd and of the animals killed in the hunt (doc. 3.52).

Cult personnel

Cult personnel, such as priests or priestesses, mainly presided over sacrifices made to the gods at the sanctuary or temple for which they were responsible. The priests of Tylissos and Knossos were specifically instructed by decree to make sacrifices to the gods Poseidon (the priest from Knossos) and Hera (both priests) (Meiggs and Lewis 42B: doc. 1.53). In return for this duty priests would receive specific perquisites: the priest of the Dekeleian phratry (brotherhood) at Athens received from one type of sacrifice a thigh, a side-cut, an ear and three obols of silver, and from another type of sacrifice a thigh, a side-cut, an ear, a cake, a half-kotyle of wine and a drachma of silver (*IG* II² 1237: doc. 1.40). The correct shares of the sacrifice for priests at Athens were specifically laid down in the Athenian sacrificial calendar (*LSCG Suppl.* 10: doc. 3.12), while the democratically elected Myrrhine, priestess of Athena Nike, was to 'receive the legs and hides from public sacrifices' (*IG* I³ 35: doc. 3.65). In the Eleusinian Mysteries, the sacred officials from the clans of the Eumolpidai and the Kerykes received payments from the Eleusinian initiates (*IG* I³ 6C: 3.37; see also doc. 3.25). The Spartan kings, whose role was quasi-religious, received shares of the state sacrifices (Hdt. 6.57.1: doc. 6.26).

Many priesthoods were hereditary in nature, for there was no particular qualification as such for holding a priesthood, and a particular priesthood would be passed down from generation to generation within the same family. The Eumolpidai and the Kerykes clans of Eleusis provide a classic example of such hereditary religious officials (*IG* I³ 6C, lines 20–34: doc. 3.37). When the Plataeans were made Athenian citizens they were not eligible for any of the priesthoods that belonged to a particular Athenian family, but their descendants could be if they married into such priestly families ([Dem.] 59 *Against Neaira* 104: doc. 1.37). In some cults the priesthoods were sold, with the revenue going to the sanctuary or cult. A priest or priestess who bought their priesthood would do so in order to have the sacrificial perquisites, such as the share of the sacrifice that went to the priest or priestess if they were present when a sacrifice was made, and sometimes the sacred law that sold the priesthood stipulated that the priest had to be so present. In addition there was the clear social prestige of being the priest or priestess of a god and so being visible and important on religious occasions: there were no special vestments for cult personnel, but when depicted on vases priests and prestesses always wear elaborate and patterned clothing.

Death and funerary practices

There were two main concepts of the afterlife in ancient Greece: one, the Eleusinian Mysteries, ensured a happy and blessed afterlife for those who were initiated into the cult. The other, traditional, view was one of a gloomy existence in which the psyche, the phantom of the deceased, went to Hades where it joined what Sappho refers to as its 'shadowy corpses' (Sappho 55: doc. 4.3), and it was the desire to escape this that impelled individuals to become initiated into the Eleusinian Mysteries or other mystery cults. If the mysteries had a Mycenaean origin, it is probable that the two versions of the afterlife had always existed side by side. The Homeric afterlife was more suited to the heroic lifestyle of the warrior chieftains of the *Iliad*: as Hades had nothing to offer, it was important to live gloriously and achieve immortality through heroic exploits.

The Homeric afterlife

Homer in Book 11 of the *Odyssey*, a book often termed the Nekyia ('The Consultation of the Dead' or 'Book of the Dead'), describes a ritual for consulting the dead in Hades (Hom. *Odyssey* 11.473–505: doc. 3.53). As a form of divination, this description occurs nowhere else in Greek literature or ritual practice, although the notion that the dead could be consulted about the past, present and future was a common one in historical times. In particular, there was a shrine for consulting the spirits of the dead at Acheron, in the area where Homer has Odysseus consult the dead of Hades: this was a nekuomanteion, an oracle of the dead. Periander as tyrant of Corinth had sent messengers to the oracle at Acheron to ask his wife a question, and her shade appeared and gave them a message, presumably in a dream (cf. doc. 7.14). In the ritual which Homer describes for summoning up the spirits of the dead, Odysseus slaughters two sheep and it is by drinking their blood that the dead can speak to Odysseus and answer his questions.

In order to consult the dead Odysseus engages in a special ritual which does not appear to have classical counterparts but has similarities with chthonic rites, digging a pit, pouring libations of milk and honey, wine, and water, sprinkling barley-meal, and cutting the throats of the victims so their blood flowed into a pit he has dug with his sword. The blood attracts the dead, and on drinking it they remember their past life and can answer Odysseus' enquiries. Odysseus has visited the underworld to consult the blind diviner Teiresias, who was famous in Greek mythology for his prophetic powers, in order to find out how he might return to his home in Ithaka. The scene is shown on a red-figure krater (a vase used for mixing wine and water for symposia) from fourth-century Athens. Odysseus is shown sitting on a pile of rocks, his feet straddling the two sheep he has killed, holding his sword to prevent the dead approaching the blood, while he converses with the head of Teiresias which has appeared from the ground.

It is Achilles' conversation with Odysseus, however, which reveals the reality of the world of the dead. The great hero would rather be a serf (a thes) in the world above, than king over all the dead in the underworld. The dead are simply shadows of their former selves, without their wits and only by drinking the sacrificial blood do they regain any semblance of life or intelligence. Before drinking the blood, Odysseus' own mother cannot recognise her son, and when they have finished speaking, he three times attempted to embrace her but without success: she is simply a shadow without substance. In the underworld Odysseus sees Minos, king of the dead, judging lawsuits among the dead, but Hades was not a place of punishment or reward in popular thought and was simply a destination to which all mortals went after death. Punishments there are only inflicted on those individuals of myth who had offended the gods, such as Tityos who had attempted to rape Leto, mother of Apollo and Artemis (doc. 3.53), Sisyphos, for his deviousness and violation of the sacred laws of hospitality and Tantalos, for killing his own son Pelops and trying to trick the gods into eating his flesh. In addition to Hades, there was also the concept of the aether: of the Athenian dead at Potidaea it is said that the earth has received their bodies and the aether their psychai ('souls'): they have gone to the upper sky. While Achilles languishes in Hades, other Homeric heroes were more fortunate and did not undergo death but were 'translated', taken while still alive, to the mythical utopia of the Elysian fields, perhaps the same as the Islands of the Blest where the weather was always calm and crops and fruit grow abundantly of their own accord (Hom. *Odyssey* 4. 561–9; Pind. *Olympian* 2.68–80: according to whom Achilles resides there).

Funerary rites

Correct performance of burial rites was an important part of the duty owed to family members and to leave bodies unburied was considered a crime against both the gods and mortals as Antigone argues cogently to her uncle Kreon when she is apprehended performing the rites over her brother Polyneikes (Soph. *Antigone*: docs 3.54, 4.69). Cremation was the most popular form of burial at Athens in the last quarter of the fifth century BC, though inhumation (burial) was also practised. The dead were cremated on funeral pyres of wood, and the ash and bones from the pyre collected and placed into an urn, which was then buried. Funerary fashions changed: in archaic Athens larger than life statues of kouroi and kourai, sphinxes, or mounds marked grave sites, but competition for space in the Kerameikos, the cemetery area of Athens, meant that this practice was later abandoned. Classical tombs were often marked by stone reliefs or lekythoi (singular: lekythos, a vessel for holding oil), many of marble rather than of clay like their prototypes. Most common of the lekythoi buried with the dead were the 'white-ground' lekythoi, made of clay and covered with white 'slip' (a fine clay applied while watery), often decorated with scenes which were mythological or funerary in nature, such as scenes of Charon on his boat waiting to transport the dead to Hades.

Other grave goods were buried with the deceased and an obol might be placed in the mouth of the dead, but this practice was by no means universal. Inscribed stelai (singular: stele) marking graves were the norm and there are well over 10,000 epitaphs on stone from classical Athens. These funerary stelai depicted the dead, if male, often in an athletic (Fig. 5.10) or military poses, while women might be shown in their role as priestesses or mothers, or being bade farewell by their husbands and children.

It was a prime duty of the living to care for their ancestral dead and in Athens it was normal for women to make frequent offerings of cakes and libations at family tombs. To these stelai, which were often inscribed with the name of the deceased and some personal detail (*IG* IV 801: doc. 4.36), family and friends would bring offerings of oil in lekythoi which they

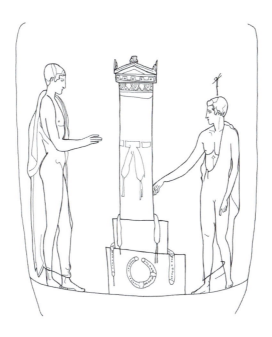

Figure 3.12 A man visits the funerary stele of the deceased, who is shown on the right: a small 'soul' figure hovers above his head to show that he is dead. Note the ribbons tied to the stele, and those on the base, one of which is a filled cylindrical ribbon curved into a circle. This is a particularly magnificent example of a white-ground lekythos (that is, the background colour is white), dating to around 440 BC and attributed to the Achilles Painter; its height is 37.4 cm. The lekythos itself would have been filled with olive oil and left at the stele as part of the ritual of the visit. Stelai were not burial places but commemorated the dead. New York Metropolitan Museum of Art, 1989.281.72. Drawing by J. Etherington.

poured into the ground to the spirit of the deceased. Other libations could be made of milk, honey or wine. A favourite theme on Athenian vases – especially the lekythoi themselves – is of women at home with baskets of coloured ribbons and small lekythoi which they are about to take to the tomb, which the ribbons would then be used to decorate. Another favourite scene shows them at the tomb, with the ribbons and lekythoi in place (cf. Fig. 3.11). When a young girl died unmarried, a marker in the shape of a loutrophoros vase was placed on the tomb to symbolise the unfulfilled hopes of her family. This was a pottery container used for the bridal bath (to bring water from a spring, often a sacred one), and the girl was said to be a bride of Hades, god of the underworld.

Casualties in war

In Greece it was important that the dead were given proper burial, and after a battle a truce would generally be declared so that each side could gather their dead and bury them. Spartan warriors who died in battle were buried on the spot, with the exception of Spartan kings who were taken home to Sparta, and all the Spartans and the helots too were obliged to engage in public mourning on these occasions (Hdt. 6.58.3: doc. 6.26). After battle, the bones of the Athenian dead were gathered up and brought to Athens to be given public burial in the Kerameikos, and it was unusual that the Athenians who died at Marathon were buried on the spot (Thuc. 2.34.1–5: doc. 11.17); their mound can still be seen there today.

It was an inviolable right that the dead be treated with respect. When in the *Iliad* Achilles pierces Hektor's ankles after he has slain him in battle and drags him around the city of Troy, initially refusing him burial, this is a gross act of hubris. Similarly, when Kreon as king of Thebes refuses to allow his nephew Polyneikes to be buried, it sets up a contest between divine law and a man-made law laid down by Kreon to punish traitors to Thebes (Soph. *Antigone* 441–70: doc. 4.69). Antigone refuses to obey Kreon's law, and in the absence of water she pours a libation of dust over his body and laments its naked state (doc. 3.54); Elektra, on a visit to the tomb of her father Agamemnon, prays not for blessings in return for her offerings, but for revenge against his killers, as she pours libations to him at his grave (Aesch. *Libation Bearers* 87–93: doc. 3.55).

The prothesis

As part of the funerary rites the dead would be laid out on a funeral bier from the house, and relatives and friends would gather around the corpse to mourn it prior to its cremation or inhumation: this was known as the prothesis, the laying out of the body (Fig. 3.13). Mourning was gendered and men would raise their hands in grief while women wailed, tore their hair and scratched their faces to draw blood. Practices and behaviour of mourners could be restricted by law, especially in the case of women, whose public grief was sometimes seen as too dramatic or extravagant. At the city of Iulis on the island of Keos (*LSCG* 97A: doc. 3.57), legislation aimed to make funerals less ostentatious, so that wealthy families could not draw attention to themselves for their political or social advantage. But even 300 drachmas, nearly a year's wage at Athens for an ordinary workman, was clearly still a great deal to spend on the clothing and blankets for the deceased, and indicates just how much might have been expended on a funeral in the absence of such a law. The dead man was to be carried to the tomb in silence, this was the ekphora, the carrying out of the body, which was then followed by the interment. The vessels containing the wine and oil to be offered had to be taken back to the house and not left at the tomb, and women had to leave the grave first, clearly so that

Figure 3.13 Geometric terracotta amphora (the 'Dipylon Amphora'), dating to around 750–700 BC, from Attica. This huge amphora, which shows a prothesis (funerary procession) scene, may well have served as a burial monument in the same way as the later stelai did. The figural scene shows, in the abstract form typical of Greek Geometric art, the deceased on a funeral bier. Individuals gather around, their arms and hands held up in gestures of mourning. The deceased appears to be female, as the figure does not have two distinct legs (unlike the deceased depicted on the Dipylon Krater (New York Metropolitan Museum of Art, 14.130.14), who is depicted above martial scenes possibly indicating that he died in battle). National Archaeological Museum, Athens, inv. no. 804. © Hellenic Ministry of Culture and Tourism / Archaeological Receipts Fund.

they would not engage in excessive lamentation. Furthermore, there were strict rules regarding the prevention of pollution, which particularly affected women, and all of those polluted by contact with the dead had to be purified with water.

Beliefs in reincarnation

While cults such as Orphism and the Eleusinian Mysteries had eschatological hopes (hopes of a better afterlife), traditional Greek thought was that the dead were not reborn. An exception to this appears in the beliefs of at least one philosopher, Empedokles, who proclaimed that he had been successively reincarnated as several creatures including a bush, a bird and a fish (*F* 117: doc 3.73). Plato, moreover, expounded a theory of immortality and of the judgement of the deceased, in which souls, after spending a thousand years in the underworld receiving punishments or rewards according to their deserts, chose a new life on earth and were reincarnated. (Pl. *Republic* 614b–615c: doc. 3.58). Herodotos realised that custom played a large role in religious practices, as he notes in his story that the Indians called the Kalliatai who ate their fathers' corpses were horrified at the suggestion that they burn them, while the Greeks who burned their corpses would not eat their fathers' corpses 'for any money' (Hdt. 3.38.1–4: doc. 3.89).

109

Women and their religious role

Women had no political rights and limited judicial ones in the cities of ancient Greece, and nowhere more so than at Athens. However, they did participate in a very full sense in religious cults, celebrations and festivals, and there were several religious activities – such as being maenads in the cult of Dionysos – in which only they were allowed to take part, as well as women-only fertility festivals, such as the Thesmophoria. Furthermore, women served as priestesses to female divinities, the most important of which was Athena Polias ('Guardian of the City') at Athens, who was served by a priestess, and it was to this priestess that worshippers brought their offerings before the altar on the acropolis for sacrifice to the goddess Athena. This priestess of Athena Polias played an important part in Athenian history on at least two occasions, unsuccessfully refusing Kleomenes' admittance to Athena's temple on the acropolis, and supporting the evacuation of Athens in 480 BC prior to the Persian invasion by reporting that the sacred snake there had failed to eat its honey-cake, an omen that signified that Athens should be abandoned (Hdt. 8.41.2–3; cf. doc. 11.36), while the Themistokles decree specifically mentions that 'the priestesses' are to remain on the acropolis when the Athenians abandon their city in 480 (Meiggs and Lewis 23, line 11: doc. 11.35). The Pythia, priestess of Apollo at Delphi, was arguably one of the most important individuals in the whole of Greece, delivering oracles on matters of war, peace, crop failure and phenomena such as earthquakes and lightning-strikes.

Another well-known priestess was that of Hera at Argos. One of these, Chrysis, served the goddess for fifty-six and a half years; Thucydides used her forty-eighth year as priestess in conjunction with the holding of office of the ephor Ainesias at Sparta and the Athenian archon Pythodoros to date the outbreak of the Peloponnesian War (Thuc. 2.2.1; doc. 3.60). One of the duties of priests and priestesses was to look after the temple treasures (as noted above) together with a general custodianship of the temple. When Chrysis left a lighted lamp near some garlands in the temple these unluckily caught alight and the temple burned down, at which she fled (Thuc. 4.133.2; doc. 3.60). At Athens, priestesses were subject to an audit at the end of their term of office, just like public officials, and had to offer prayers to the gods on behalf of the people (Aeschin. 3 *Against Ktesiphon* 17–21: doc. 1.22). Priests and priestesses are often shown on their grave stelai holding a large key, that to the temple of which they were the custodian. Priestesses might also be shown with a cult statue in one hand signifying their care of this and the duties associated with the goddess they served. A priest, in contrast, might also be shown with a sacrificial knife, indicating his role in sacrifices, though often a professional butcher (mageiros) would do the actual killing for him. Priests and priestesses could also act as diviners, examining the entrails of sacrificial animals, though anyone could engage in hieroskopia and a professional did not have to be involved. The overly superstitious man commanded priestesses to perform a purification if he saw 'someone wreathed with garlic at the crossroads' (Theophr. *Characters* 16, no. 12: doc. 3.72).

Girls and cult

The role of young women in cults was important enough for the chorus of women in Aristophanes' play the *Lysistrata* to boast of their religious service as girls in honour of various goddesses (Ar. *Lysistrata* 638–51: doc. 3.61). Serving as arrhephoroi as seven-year-old girls they carried sacred items ('symbols of Athena Polias') on their heads as part of a ritual described by Pausanias and which is partly shown on the east frieze of the Parthenon (Paus. *Description*

Figure 3.14 A kanephoros, a young adult woman carrying a basket containing sacrificial items and paraphernalia. When Harmodios' sister presented herself as a virgin eligible for this duty at the
Athenian Panathenaia, Hipparchos turned her away, as 'she was not fit to take part' (Thuc.
6.56.1: doc. 9.30). These figures are very common – this one is from the late fifth–early
fourth century BC and is 46.7cm high. Yale University Art Gallery, 1998.23.12.

of Greece 1.27.3: doc. 3.62). They ground grain to make sacred cakes to offer as part of a sacrificial ritual to Artemis. Donning a 'saffron coloured robe' they would pretend to be young
bears in the service of the huntress virgin goddess Artemis at the cult site at Brauron in the
Athenian countryside. This rite marked their transition from young bears to young women,
with the next most important stage of their religious life being as basket bearers responsible
for carrying items needed for sacrifices such as the sacrificial knife and grain (Fig. 3.14). On
the Parthenon frieze several young women are shown holding libation vessels and incense
burners.

Women-only festivals

Women in many ways had a full religious life and participated not only in state and family
cults but in their own, and these – in particular the Thesmophoria and Anthesteria – were
state-sponsored and considered of vital importance to the polis as a whole. One particularly personal cult for women was the festival of the Adonia, in which they mourned for the
death of Aphrodite's beloved, the mortal Adonis, who was gored to death by a boar and laid
out in a bed of lettuce by the goddess as he lay dying. The women came together in small
groups, probably of neighbours and friends, and worshipped the goddess of love on their
flat rooftops, where they carried pots of lettuce seeds to symbolise Adonis' death-bed. The
seedlings, quickly withering in their shallow pots, represented his untimely death (Fig. 4.10).
Menander's play *Samia* suggests that a great deal of laughter and enjoyment took place along

111

with an all-night party, and while the festival was only meant for women in this play a young man of the house manages to seduce a young woman who was there celebrating the occasion and Menander gives a colourful depiction of the women's religious activities.

In patriarchal Athens, the women were only allowed to worship Dionysos indoors, whereas in other Greek cities every two years they took to the hills to worship the god. At another festival, the Anthesteria festival, they drew wine in his honour from large vases known as stamnoi, which stood on a table next to a mask of the god attached to a pole. The Thesmophoria was celebrated throughout Greece in autumn by women, in honour of Demeter and Kore (Persephone), and took place in Athens over three days in Pyanopsion (October). Many of the details are debated, but the traditional view of the nature of the festival was that the women left their homes and set up tents in the sacred area on the acropolis. It was a secret all-female citizen celebration for married women, and the rites seem to have been conducted to assist the fertility of the seed for the coming crop. Miltiades' downfall in his attempt to take over the island of Paros seems to have occurred because of his interference with the cult of the Thesmophoria there, and he died in prison of gangrene after being fined fifty talents by the Athenian assembly. Certainly the Parians were concerned enough over the incident to consult Delphi (Hdt. 6.134.1–135.3: doc. 3.59). The sacred animals of Demeter, pigs, were thrown into a pit in the summer, along with serpents and phalloi made of dough. On the first day of the Thesmophoria the women retrieved the remains, and mixed these with grain placed on the altars. On the second day they fasted (they also abstained from sex for three days prior to and for the duration of the festival), and on the third day, the pig remains and seed were symbolically scattered on the fields for fertility. In Aristophanes' play the *Thesmophoriazousai* (*Women at the Thesmophoria*), Euripides calls on Mnesilochos, his elderly relative, to disguise himself in order to defend Euripides, whose 'slander' of women is a stock joke in Aristophanes as is their love of alcohol. Kleisthenes in the play being portrayed as 'effeminate' is permitted to be present, though not a participant in the actual ceremonies, and is shown on the side of the women (doc. 3.64).

Myrrhine, priestess of Athena Nike

Traditional priesthoods of Athens were drawn from aristocratic families, but when the Athenians in about 430 BC established the cult of Athena Nike ('Victory') to honour Athena for her role in defeating the Persians they built her a small temple, with Ionic columns, on the Athenian acropolis. The assembly decided that the priestess for the cult should be chosen democratically from all the Athenian citizen women, 'chosen by lot out of everyone'. Athenian democracy had reached full fruition, now that even a priestess was chosen in democratic style by lot out of the names of those who put themselves forward. The interest which the demos took in religious matters is also made clear in that the decree which made this arrangement also records that it was the decision of the people to build the temple, and names the architect (Kallikrates) as appointed to design it, specifically authorising that the doors were to be the ones he had planned. Also authorised was the construction of a stone altar, on which the sacrifices to the goddess would be made. The priestess was to receive a share in the sacrifices made to the goddess, and a specific annual payment was authorised as well. Myrrhine was the name of the woman chosen, who probably took up office in around 430 BC. Her funerary epitaph boasts that she was the first to serve the goddess Athena Nike and specifically points out that her name, meaning 'myrtle branch', was fortuitous: 'for by divine fortune she was called Myrrhine, 'myrtle wreath' (*IG* I³ 35: doc. 3.65; *IG* I³ 36: doc. 3.66; *SEG* 12.80, line 6: 3.67). Wreaths were worn in religious celebrations, such as by the initiates in the Eleusinian Mysteries (Ar. *Frogs* 330: doc. 3.32). In the *Thesmophoriazousai* the woman myrtle-wreath seller in the Athenian agora complains that she sells only half the myrtle wreaths she used to because of Euripides' tragedies persuading people 'that there aren't any gods' (Ar. *Thesmophoriazousai* 448–51: doc. 4.60). Myrrhine has been tentatively identified with the Myrrhine of the *Lysistrata*, performed at the Lenaia in 411 BC, but this identification is uncertain, and the name is not uncommon (cf. *IG* I³ 1248, found in the Athenian deme Kephale, 'I am the (to)mb of Myrrhine, who died of the plague').

Women at Athens and elsewhere in Greece played an important role in worshipping the gods. As the child-bearing members of the community, their role as conduits of fertility both of themselves, other women and of the very fields of Attica itself found expression in festival and ritual. Their virginity prior to marriage was prized as a special quality for worship in the rites of virgin goddesses such as Athena and Artemis. Participation in cults allowed the women a role other than that of child-bearer and housekeeper. Yet these rites were not simply 'escapist' for them, nor did their husbands permit them to take part so that women had an escape from domesticity and its chores: it was not some type of 'pressure valve' so that women would not go 'crazy' in the house. Rather deities such as Dionysos, Athena and Artemis were believed to require the services of these girls and women.

Personal piety

Each polis had many temples and specific religious observances, in which individuals participated and could play specific roles, whether as priests, priestesses or basket-bearers. Individual Greeks, and family units, also had their own private religious ceremonies and as individuals or private groups could pray, sacrifice and make dedications, all separate from the formal state apparatus of cults and festivals. Xenophanes of Kolophon in Asia Minor in the sixth century BC describes how the gods should be worshipped at a private symposium celebrated at home. Everyone has clean hands and wears a garland; wine is ready and frankincense is burning; the altar is decked with flowers and hymns are sung; and men should now pray to do what is righteous. No mention is made here of an animal sacrifice, and the emphasis is on hymns and worship, moderate drinking, and bearing in mind 'consideration towards the gods' (Xen. Kol. *F* B1, line 22: doc. 3.68).

The family and religious practices

Families celebrated religious events together: Sostratos' mother drags the family though the Athenian countryside to Pan's shrine for a private sacrifice because of an ominous dream she has had. The family is accompanied by the sacrificial butcher, who brings the sheep, and all the cooking and picnic paraphernalia including 'four donkey-loads of stuff' carried by a reluctant slave, along with a flute-girl for entertainment (Men. *Dyskolos* 393–406: doc. 3.10). Many vases depict a hoplite performing a sacrifice before departing for battle, and sacrifices which families had made could be commemorated on stone, and served the same purpose as a dedication, to remind the god of the sacrifice that had been made and to make public the piety of the family.

Individuals and families made their own dedications to the gods to thank them for benefits which they thought the gods had granted them, in the same way as they made dedications to Asklepios in thanks for returning health. Many of the various items dedicated in the temple of Athena on the Athenian acropolis were offered there by private individuals to thank the goddess for answering their prayers, and often an inscription might accompany the dedication (*IG* I³ 351: doc. 1.11). Many such dedications were made in thanks for benefits received or requested, and Akeratos of Thasos in about 500 BC set up a thanks-offering to Herakles, presumably of a statue of the god, in return for his good fortune in having been archon both of Paros and its colony Thasos, and for his participation in many diplomatic missions (Friedländer 143: doc. 3.71).

Dedications

Many of the statues of the gods which survive were the dedications of private individuals in thanks for benefits which they had received. Often the statue, or some other offering, was promised should the prayer made to the deity be answered. The dedications might not necessarily be valuable: women dedicated a dress or other garment to Artemis after they safely gave birth to a child, and inscriptions at this goddess's sanctuary at Brauron in Attica list these, and young married women would also dedicate their bridal veil to Hera (Archil. 326: doc. 4.42). When Amphinomos and his sons from Sybaris in Italy were rescued from shipwreck they dedicated a wooden model of a cow and calf to Athena at Rhodes, presumably where they had been rescued from shipwreck. The model may in fact represent a sacrifice of a cow and a calf which they made in thanks for their safe-keeping (Friedländer 126: doc. 3.69). But family dedications could also serve as a request for assistance in future times: when Kalliteles' descendants made a dedication they specifically asked that the gods give something in return (*IG* I³ 1014: doc. 3.70). Demokydes and Telestodike made a offering 'in common' to Artemis on Paros that 'to their family and livelihood [she] give increase in safety' (Friedländer 144: doc. 4.4; see Fig. 4.6).

While everyone was expected to believe in the gods, individuals, just like cities, could have a favourite or particular god they worshipped. Certain trades, too, had their patron deities;

Figure 3.15 Aphrodite, beautifully dressed and adorned, is seated on a throne, attended by Eros, the winged figure on her left. On her right (not visible here), a woman fills an incense burner. Red-figure lekythos by the Primato Painter, 360–350 BC, found at Paestum (Posidonia), now in the Museo Archeologico Nazionale, Naples, inv. No. 81855. Drawing by J. Etherington.

craftsmen made dedications to Athena and Hephaistos, soldiers to Zeus or Enyalios, mothers to Artemis, and as long as they did not exclude the worship of the other gods these were satisfied. In Euripides' *Hippolytos*, the young hero is punished by Aphrodite because he venerates only Artemis and openly scorns the goddess of love. Furthermore, while individuals could construct altars and shrines to existing gods, the introduction of new gods, such as Asklepios, needed the sanction of the state (*IG* II² 4960a: doc. 3.42), which was concerned to ensure that individuals, by their worship of false gods, or worse no gods at all, did not bring down the wrath of the gods on the state as a whole: hence the importance which was ascribed to trials of philosophers and others who were accused of atheism (see p. 117).

The superstitious citizen

The possible complexities of the private religious life of a fourth-century Athenian is nowhere more apparent than in Theophrastos' comic depiction of the man who is over-given to religion, the 'Superstitious Man', and the passage reads almost like a diary of religious activity. He purifies himself when he sees unlucky omens such as crows or someone wreathed with garlic at the crossroads (the person has been engaged probably in a ritual concerned with Hekate, goddess of magic, with the garlic to ward off evil); when people are purifying themselves in the sea, he is there, and he makes sure he is seen, so that others know he is ritually pure; purification is a particular concern of his. A snake in the house leads him to invoke Sabazios, a deity in whose cult snakes were prominent; this god first appeared in Greece in the fourth century, and incidentally shows perhaps that the man is open to all new religious cults. He founds a hero-shrine in his own house if he sees a sacred snake; clearly many individuals had household shrines, especially women who because of their duties and social conventions could not go out to the temples as often as they liked. Ordinary daily happenings, such as a mouse nibbling a hole in a sack of barley, are construed to be the will of the gods, despite the professional advice of diviners not to take any notice of them; he also consults them if he has a dream. The house must be kept pure in case Hekate has bewitched it, and on the fourth and seventh days it is purified, and the statues of hermaphrodites in the house, which promoted fertility and prosperity, are garlanded. He avoids being contaminated by the pollution of childbirth and death and the sight of a madman or epileptic causes him to spit into his chest to expel any bad 'vibes' that might have affected him. Like many others, he has the family participate in the rituals of Orpheus, in his case every month, probably in the hope of a better afterlife. His might be an extreme case, but attentiveness to the gods and the interpretation of trivial events as reflecting the will of the gods was probably typical of Greeks – though not to this degree (Theophr. *Characters* 16: doc. 3.72).

Socrates and the 'new atheism'

New philosophical thoughts about the gods, the universe and the nature of reality began in the Greek cities of sixth-century Ionia and these ideas often differed from existing traditional beliefs, especially when they concerned the gods. In the sixth century Xenophanes of Kolophon in Asia Minor (570–480 BC) left his native city, probably after its conquest by the Persians, and travelled through the various Greek cities of Sicily for sixty-seven years. He was but one example of the Ionian and, later, other philosophers who made their way through Greece communicating their ideas to those who would listen, in a similar way to the later sophists and Socrates himself, who engaged in dialogues with those eager to learn their ideas. Philosophers also wrote books, and Anaxagoras' work, which dealt with the role of 'Mind' in the creation of the cosmos, was on general sale in Socrates' time for a drachma or less, which made his ideas very accessible to the educated, though he was later prosecuted for impiety and died at Lampsakos (Anaxag. *F* 12: doc. 3.76). Any works which cast a doubt on traditional religious views might be received with hostility. Protagoras of Abdera (490–420 BC), a sophist who taught in Athens and about whom Plato wrote a dialogue (*Protagoras*), claimed that 'man is the measure of all things', and in other words not subject to divine law. Copies of Protagoras' book, which challenged the existence of the gods and commenced with the words, 'Regarding the gods, I have no way of knowing whether they exist or whether they do not. There are many hindrances to knowledge – the obscurity of the topic and the brevity of human life', were collected and burned and he was exiled from Athens (Diog. Laert. *Lives of Eminent Philosophers* 9.51–2: doc. 3.77). While philosophy could be said to have been born in Ionia, Athens became the centre of philosophers and sophists in the fifth century, but their theories did not always meet with a welcome, as indicated by the experiences of Anaxagoras and Protagoras, and Socrates' execution in 399 BC.

Xenophanes

Xenophanes was one of the earliest Ionian philosophers, who theorised about the natural world (the so-called group of natural philosophers) and the nature of divinity. He believed that everything originated from the earth and returned to it, and was also the first to consider the origins of life on earth itself, postulating that all living matter came from earth and water. He believed in only one god and criticised both Hesiod and Homer for presenting stories in which the gods behaved in an immoral and unjust fashion (Xen. Kol. *F* 11: doc. 3.4). In particular he derided belief in the anthropomorphic nature of traditional Greek religious beliefs about their gods: if oxen or horses could sculpt or paint, he argues, they would make gods in their own form as oxen or horses, pointing out that mortals have created gods 'in their own image' (Xen. Kol. *F* 11: doc. 3.5).

Empedokles of Sicily

Other philosophers also developed different conceptions of divinity and for Empedokles of Akragas in Sicily, perhaps influenced by Anaxoragas' presence on the island, 'God' was not physical, but rather 'Mind' which goes 'rushing through the entire cosmos with Its swift thoughts'. For Anaxagoras the divine was too great to be confined within a human-like body and 'Mind' organised and controlled the cosmos, and arranged all that had been, is and will be (Empedokles of Akragas *F* 134: doc. 3.74; Anaxag. *F* 12: doc. 3.76). 'Mind' was not constrained by fate and circumstance, unlike Zeus in traditional Greek thought. His most famous theories were that the sun, moon and stars were red-hot stones and that the sun was a lump of blazing metal larger than the Peloponnese.

Empedokles wrote two books, *Concerning Nature* and *Purifications*, and claimed that thousands sought his assistance with sicknesses. Probably his most important contribution to philosophy was his idea that there were four elements, which were unchangeable and immutable: earth, air, fire and water, which gained wide currency in Greek thought. He was, however, derided for his ideas about reincarnation. Epicharmos was actually a playwright, probably from Syracuse, but he included numerous 'maxims' or pithy sayings of a philosophical nature in his works. His epitaph for himself supposedly read, 'I am a corpse. A corpse is excrement, and excrement is earth. If earth is a god, I am not a corpse but a god' (Epicharmos *F* 64: doc. 3.75).

Diagoras and atheism

But very few Greeks postulated that the gods did not exist, and the vast majority believed in the gods and worshipped them in the traditional ways. Diagoras of Melos, a poet and sophist, was one of the few, and was sentenced to death for trivialising the Mysteries. He apparently joked, when he saw the votive dedications at Samothrace made by those whose lives had been saved at sea, that of course those who had drowned could not make dedications (see p. 114; and doc. 3.69). Attacked by his opponents, he fled Athens and was condemned *in absentia*, by a decree which offered a talent to the person who returned his body to Athens and two talents to anyone who brought him back alive. There was a belief that the community as a whole had to believe in and worship the gods, or the gods would punish the entire community for the disbelief of one or a few people. One of the charges brought against Socrates was that of introducing new gods, and he is parodied in Aristophanes' *Clouds* for worshipping clouds as goddesses and rejecting Zeus (Ar. *Clouds* 365–73: doc. 3.80; *Clouds* 247–8: doc. 3.82); he also had an inner voice he referred to as his daimonion, whose guidance he followed whenever he was in doubt, which may have been seen as a 'new deity' (Pl. *Apology* 31c: doc. 3.85), and like Diagoras he was condemned to death for this and for 'corrupting the youth'.

The sophists

In the fifth century a new intellectual 'movement' developed, that of the sophists, with whom Socrates was unfairly confused. Unlike Socrates, they taught their pupils and listeners for a

Figure 3.16 The 'Artemision Bronze', a slightly over life-sized bronze statue of Zeus recovered from Cape Artemision, off the cost of Euboea, from the fifth century BC. Zeus is shown in the act of hurling a thunderbolt, one of his attributes. There is debate about whether it represents Zeus or Poseidon – some argue that this is Poseidon, and the missing object from his hand is a trident, one of the attributes of the sea god. National Archaeological Museum, Athens, inv. no. X15161. © Hellenic Ministry of Culture and Tourism / Archaeological Receipts Fund.

fee. Protagoras of Abdera had been the first to call himself a sophist and take fees for teaching, which was largely based on the art of persuasive speaking, and he coined the phrase 'to make the weaker argument the stronger'. He was the first to assert that there were two sides to every argument and that each could be made as strong or stronger than the other, regardless of the merits of the case. His views and teachings were hardly such as to endear him with the traditionalists in Athens, who burnt his writings. Like Anaxagoras, he was a friend of Perikles, and formed part of the intellectual milieu of a city at the height of its economic and political power.

Antiphon, a sophist at Athens, was also a speech-writer and prime mover in the oligarchic revolution of 411 BC (although scholars have argued that these might be two different people). He argued that there were natural laws which could not be violated, and while nature had evolved laws that one could not escape, human law was arbitrary and obeyed only by consent. 'Justice' could be defined by the laws in the city of which one happened to be a citizen, so the definition of justice was not a constant but would vary depending on your place of residence. To break the laws of your city was not important provided you were not detected in doing so and avoided disgrace and punishment. Justice was therefore 'relative' (Antiph. *F* 44: doc. 3.78).

The primary concern of the sophists was with the art of rhetoric and persuasion, of seeing both sides to an argument, and of making the weaker argument, even if wrong, prevail in the lawcourts. Hence Socrates, inaccurately portrayed as a sophist in Aristophanes' *Clouds* (first performed in 423 BC), is approached by the debt-ridden farmer Strepsiades who wants Socrates to teach him to construct an argument which will enable him not to have to pay back the debts he has contracted for his extravagant wife and son. In the play, Socrates is also depicted as a natural philosopher, contemplating 'astronomical phenomena' from his position in a basket in the sky, and he tells Strepsiades that 'gods are not current coin with us', and that the 'clouds' are the only real goddesses, with the theories of a number of philosophers such as Anaxagoras being falsely attributed to him (Ar. *Clouds* 218–48: doc. 3.82).

Socrates

Socrates was born in 469 BC, the son of a stone-mason and a midwife. He served on the boule once, during the Arginousai affair of 406 BC, and was the only one to oppose the abrogation of the laws concerning the right of the strategoi at Arginousai to individual trials (Pl. *Apology* 31c–32d: 3.85). In Plato's *Gorgias* (473e) Socrates relates how, when he was chosen by lot as epistates (in charge of presiding for the day over the boule), he caused a laugh by being ignorant of the procedure for putting a motion to the vote; this was the very same day as the Arginousai debate. Similarly he refused to assist the Thirty Tyrants in 403 BC in their execution of innocent citizens. Belonging to the hoplite class, he served in the Athenian army at Potidaea, Amphipolis and Delion in the Peloponnesian War and it was at Potidaea that, in freezing conditions, he wore only his usual short cloak while he stood still for a day contemplating a problem that had occurred to him (Pl. *Symposium* 220b: doc. 3.81); he was a strong believer in 'self-control', as in not succumbing to Alkibiades' advances in 416 (Pl. *Symposium* 219b–d: doc. 4.88). Antiphon questioned Socrates regarding his views, and criticised him for not taking payment for his teaching, but Socrates, who had only this one cloak which he wore day in, day out all year round, responded that true happiness consists in wanting nothing (Xen. *Memorabilia* 1.6.1–3, 6.10: doc. 3.79). He wrote nothing himself, and his views are known from Xenophon and the dialogues of Plato in which Socrates is presented as arguing with his listeners. He was mainly concerned with questions concerning ethics, wisdom and the pursuit of arete (virtue).

Socrates' aim was to elicit definitions from his interlocutors, particularly of terms relating to ethical ideas, such as justice, arete (virtue) and courage, and Socrates states in Plato's *Apology* that one of the reasons for his unpopularity was the fact that a number of upper-class young men attached themselves to him because they enjoyed hearing people cross-questioned, and took him as their model; as a result, people were angry with Socrates for filling young persons' heads with wrong ideas. Xenophon's description of Alkibiades using the 'Socratic method' on Perikles in questioning him on 'what a law is' illustrates how the question and answer technique worked (Xen. *Memorabilia* 1.2.39–46: doc. 3.83).

Socrates was parodied not only in the *Clouds* but by at least four other writers of Old Comedy – Kallias, Ameipsias, Eupolis and Telekleides. The portrayal of Socrates in the *Clouds* is a conflation of the views of various thinkers, including the 'air-theories' of Diogenes of Apollonia, who was said to regard the air as god as well as the rhetorical skills of the sophists. The play is also unfair to the sophists. Clearly they and Socrates and other philosophers were creating quite a 'stir' at Athens, and eventually concerns about their attitudes to the gods played a role in Socrates being brought to trial. But his association with leading pro-Spartan oligarchs such as Kritias must have also played a significant part in his prosecution.

Socrates' trial and execution

Socrates' speech for the defence on the charges of having introduced new gods and corrupted the youth of Athens is recorded in Plato's *Apology*. Here Socrates informed the jurors that the Delphic oracle considered no one to be wiser than himself, even though he considered himself to be wise only in that he knew that he was ignorant. The oracle's meaning was that Socrates' highly limited form of wisdom is the most that human beings can accomplish, and real wisdom is the prerogative of God. Socrates explains his habit of questioning others as his attempt to prove the oracle false. He had, he states, an inner voice, a daimonion, which had spoken to him since childhood, which guided his actions and prevented him from doing wrong. He was too honest, he argued, for politics, and had never been interested in wealth: what he did was to talk to as many people as possible, to persuade them to put their self-interest away and to consider 'how they might become as virtuous and wise as possible'.

Plato has Socrates state that if only thirty (of the 501) jurors had voted the other way he would have been acquitted, and so it seems that 280 voted for conviction and 221 for acquittal. After the prosecution had proposed the death-penalty, it was up to Socrates to propose a counter-penalty that the jury would accept. He at first suggested daily maintenance in the town-hall, the prytaneion, which was far more appropriate for him, he suggested, than for victorious chariot drivers at the Olympics who received this honour (Pl. *Apology*, extracts at docs 3.84–6). His eventual suggestion of a fine of a mina (after an initial suggestion of 100 drachmas), to be guaranteed by his friends, who included Plato and Krito, was reasonable but he had clearly annoyed the jury, as more votes were cast for the death penalty than for his conviction (the vote for death being 360 to 141).

Condemned to death, Socrates refused to allow his friends to arrange for his escape from prison: he had lived in Athens all his life and had obeyed its laws throughout this time and would not countenance the suggestion that he should allow his friends to bribe the jailers to allow him to escape. On the day fixed for the execution, he even asked that the hemlock be brought in, though Krito reminded him that he need not drink it till late at night, and

Socrates dismissed his wife Xanthippe, who was there with their youngest boy, to prevent any final hysterical scenes of lamentation. Socrates cheerfully faced death, praying to the gods that his translation to the other world might be prosperous, and drank the hemlock, scolding his friends for weeping. His last words were to remind Krito to ensure that Asklepios receive a cock: either in gratitude for a quick and painless death, or perhaps because Plato, who was absent on this occasion, was sick that day (Pl. *Phaedo* 117a–118: doc. 3.88). Xenophon, one of Socrates' greatest supporters, was in Asia Minor during this period with Cyrus' army of mercenaries and then leading this 'Ten Thousand' safely out of Asia Minor. In his *Memorabilia* he focuses on Socrates' religiosity, sense of honour, self-discipline and excellence in judging between good and bad – 'exactly what a truly good and happy man should be' (Xen. *Memorabilia* 4.8.11: doc. 3.89). It is perhaps one of history's greatest ironies that it was not a tyranny or an oligarchy but the Athenian democracy that executed Socrates, and this episode perhaps highlights the pressure for conformity that democratic rule had come to exert upon its citizens.

4

WOMEN, SEXUALITY AND THE FAMILY

Introduction

Greek cities like Athens were seen as composed of individual households (oikoi: singular: oikos), made up of citizens and slaves, with males and females within these households having specifically defined and very distinct roles. Probably more implausible and contradictory statements have been made about the position of women in classical Greece than on any other related topic. That being the case, it must be stressed that a detailed and intensive study of the source material is essential to any understanding of the contemporary attitudes involved, especially since any partial use of the evidence can result in a distorted picture of society: each type of ancient evidence – historical sources, tragedy, comedy, lyric poetry, artistic and epigraphic sources – presents a different, and partial, view of the role and position of women. None of these works were specifically intended as a definitive analysis of gender roles in ancient Greece, and almost all of it was, of course, written by men for men. Only an overview of all the important ancient evidence can present a properly faceted picture of the realities of life in the Greek world. Even then there are many areas of family life, social classes and geographical regions which the evidence does not cover. It is important, therefore, to beware of supposing that attitudes towards Athenian women were typical of those towards Greek women as a whole. In fact women in Sparta and in other Doric cities such as Gortyn in Crete appear to have enjoyed considerably more latitude of behaviour and civil rights in some respects than women in Athens seem to have done.

Sources

Due to the fact that the majority of the historical sources were written by Athenians for a primarily Athenian audience, our accounts of historical women are naturally filtered through the perceptions of Athenian males of the classical period. For example, women as a whole play a marginal role in Thucydides' history, as befits gendered life in fifth-century Athens: in fact Thucydides nowhere in his *History* mentions a Greek woman by name. Herodotos, in contrast, is extremely interested in the role played by women in important historical events as well as being concerned with portraying the exotic customs and ways of life of other peoples, along with their perceptions of their own past. He is frequently drawn into descriptions of domestic details of other civilisations, such as dress, food, family life and marriage customs, as well as of sexual practices and gender differences, as in his account of Egyptian life as an inversion of that of other societies (with men, for example, urinating sitting down and women standing up). His portraits of significant Persian women have recently been argued to be generally reliable, and he asks important questions about Greek gender differences as well as those of 'barbarian' cultures: why Ionian women do not eat with or address their husbands; why Spartan men and women take an equal part in mourning; and why Thracian wives want to be buried with their husbands. Greek women are parenthetical to Herodotos' main 'theme' in his *Histories*, and for that reason his account of them is more likely to reflect the values and realities of the time in the various cities with which he deals.

It is not always easy for the reader to ascertain the point-of-attack of any comic composition, especially many centuries after the event. But with some of our texts the real difficulty is that scholars have failed to perceive any humour at all. Just as the epigram of Hipponax of Ephesos on a woman's two best days (Hipponax 68: doc. 4.12) may well not have been intended to be taken literally as misogynistic abuse but rather to be entertainment for a male symposiastic audience, so the work of Semonides of Amorgos (doc. 4.13), who compared women to ten types of animals, should not be taken as a diatribe against women – rather he is poking fun at their behaviour and at the poor men who have to live with them. In the same way Aristophanes is also presenting on stage stereotyped pictures of women often from the perspective of comic inversion. Obviously the Athenians had stock jokes about women and expected references to their drinking, love affairs and what they got up to at the Thesmophoria to be repeated almost ad nauseam in every comedy. These should not be taken literally (after all if they were true, Athenian husbands would hardly have found them funny), and the reader should attempt to work out exactly why the presentations of women and their supposed activities in the *Lysistrata*, *Thesmophoriazousai* (*Women at the Thesmophoria*) and *Ecclesiazousai* (*Women at the Assembly*) appealed to Athenian male audiences.

Classical tragedy is one of the most difficult sources from which to gauge attitudes towards women in fifth-century Athens. It is difficult to tell whether Athenian heroines like Antigone were intended to be, or would indeed have been seen as, representations of contemporary women. The stories as such were already part of the group consciousness, as the plots of tragedy were pre-cast, based on well-known mythological tales. As a result, the poet's point-of-attack has to be deduced from the choice of tale and the way in which the traditional plot has been adapted to reflect contemporary problems. Medea, for example, the witch and barbarian princess who helped Jason to escape from Colchis with the Golden Fleece, is presented by Euripides so as to highlight the problems faced by a wronged wife, who is simultaneously a metic in Athens with no family to defend her rights (Eur. *Medea* 465–95: doc. 4.70). Playwrights could and often did adapt the framework of mythology to suit their plots, and this is an important guide to the 'thesis' or message encapsulated in their play. It seems, for example, that Euripides was the first to present Medea murdering her own children to get revenge on Jason, her children's father, in addition to her escape from Corinth in a chariot sent by the sun god. Similar problems are incurred in the use of speeches in the lawcourts as evidence for the position of women. Such speeches were written to be declaimed before an all-male Athenian jury and deliberately reinforce prevailing ideologies and social conventions. Euphiletos, for example, when using the fact that his wife was allegedly caught in adultery with Eratosthenes as an excuse for his killing, tries to present himself and his family values in such as way as to gain the jury's support (Lys. 1 *On the Murder of Eratosthenes* 6–10: doc. 4.54).

Despite the fact that Plutarch specifically mentions that Sparta's lack of currency deterred the visits of teachers of rhetoric, vagabonds, seers, keepers of hetairai, and workers in gold and silver (*Life of Lykourgos* 9.5: doc. 6.69), there is intriguing evidence that Spartans did not have far to go to associate with ladies of doubtful reputation. When Kinadon and his supporters were arrested for conspiring in 397 against the Spartiates the ephors commanded that the party of guards sent to Aulon also 'bring back the woman who was said to be the most beautiful there, who was thought to be corrupting all the Spartans who visited, whether old or young' (Xen. *Hellenika* 3.3.4–11: doc. 14.5). A traveller, Polemon (*F* 18), in the second century BC, recorded that there was a statue of a hetaira called Kottina, as well as one of a bronze cow, which the lady had dedicated to Athena of the Brazen House; Kottina was so well known that a brothel was named after her (Ath. *Deipnosophistae* 574c–d). The date of the dedication cannot be ascertained, but this does imply despite Plutarch that there were prostitutes in the city of Sparta, and suggests that sources on such topics should be treated with caution.

Sappho of Lesbos

One of the most remarkable facts of Greek civilisation is that one of the earliest and greatest of Greek poets (barring the author(s) of the Homeric poems) was a woman: Sappho of Lesbos. Born c. 620, only incomplete poems and fragments of her work survive and almost nothing is certainly known of her life. Details of her biography have in the past been deduced from her poetry which it has been assumed is autobiographical and speaks for Sappho in the first person, but there are no grounds for most of the assumptions made about her, such as that she was a 'school-mistress' farewelling her pupils who were leaving her to marry. It has generally been assumed that Kleis, 'who resembled golden flowers' and was worth more than all the wealth of Lydia, was Sappho's own daughter, but the character speaking these words need not necessarily be Sappho in her own persona (Sappho *F* 132: doc. 4.4). In this fragment Sappho rejects all the wealth and power of Lydia (home of the wealthy tyrant Gyges: Archil. *F* 19: doc. 7.1), and all masculine values in favour of her lovely daughter, and the emotional bond between women. Similarly in *Fragment* 16 (doc. 4.2) she contrasts male desires (infantry, cavalry, ships) with the more emotional ones of women, as featured by Helen of Troy, 'she that far surpassed mankind in beauty', shown as an autonomous agent in her decision to leave her husband, child and parents for love. Helen reminds Sappho of Anaktoria 'who is no longer near', and this brings the reader back to Sappho's own desires and the ways in which they are the antithesis of masculine aims and ambitions: 'I would rather see her (Anaktoria's) lovely walk and the bright radiance of her face than the Lydians' chariots and fully-armed infantry'.

Sappho was a contemporary of Alcaeus on the island of Lesbos and with him has been regarded both in antiquity and since as one of the greatest lyric poets (Fig. 4.1). She was even known in antiquity as the 'tenth muse'. While the Parian Marble states that she spent some time in exile on Sicily, her poems, unlike those of Alcaeus (who also spent time in exile due to his opposition to the tyrants on Mytilene), show little trace of interest in politics. Her subject is love and passion in an aristocratic and elite setting, for various people and genders, and may have been written for a number of scenarios: the narrators of her poems speak of love for girls and women, which is sometimes returned and sometimes not, and give the feeling of an aristocratic club (the equivalent of the male hetaireia), with shared interests and tastes. She is scathing of an uneducated woman 'who has no share in the roses from Pieria', the Muses' home, of whom there will be no recollection, but like Homer's shades she will go to and fro among the shadowy corpses, forgotten (Sappho *F* 55: doc. 4.3).

Sappho's work is remarkable for the ways in which she is able to express the inner workings of love and desire and the physical effects which these impart: 'for when I look at you

Figure 4.1 The so-called Sappho and Alcaeus vase, an Athenian red-figure vase dating to about 470 BC by the Brygos Painter. The poet Sappho (right) turns and looks at Alcaeus with his harp. Staatliche Antikensammlungen 2416, Munich. Drawing by J. Etherington.

for a moment, then I no longer have the power to speak, but my tongue has broken, at once a subtle fire has stolen under my skin, with my eyes I see nothing, my ears hum, a cold sweat pours over me . . .' (Sappho *F* 31: doc. 4.1). Her epithalamia, or marriage songs, express both the importance of marriage to women and the anxiety and pain caused by leaving home to move to another house and family. Anacreon astutely highlights the intricacies of Sappho's circle and their relationships, when he speaks of a girl in embroidered sandals from Lesbos, with whom he would like to play. Unfortunately, as the punchline emphasises, she is in love – with another girl (Anac. *F* 358: doc. 4.5).

Other female writers in the Greek world

The modern world is fortunate that some of Sappho's corpus of poetry has survived. While there were other women writers in the ancient world, their work has not survived so success-fully. A contemporary of Sappho, Erinna, probably from Rhodes, wrote a poem entitled *Distaff*, and a lament, which exists in fragments, on her friend Baukis, who died shortly before her wedding: Baukis is said to have been a disciple of Sappho. Another female author was Kleobouline of Rhodes, who lived c. 550. She was particularly noted for her riddles and enig-mas in verse, three of which are extant, and was quoted by Aristotle in his *Poetics* (1458a22). Telesilla who flourished c. 510 was from Argos, and was supposed to have foiled Kleomenes in his attack on the city when she led the women, dressed in men's attire, and slaves in a defence of the city (Paus. 2.20.8–10; cf. Hdt. 6.75.3: doc. 6.77). The only two lines of her work which remain ('And Artemis, girls, fleeing from Alphaios. . . .'), were apparently part of a partheneion, a song for a chorus of girls, a genre for which she was famous. A contemporary of Telesilla was Praxilla of Sikyon, who was famous for her skolia (drinking songs) and who also wrote hymns and mythological tales. Only one fragment of her work survives because of the expression to which it gave rise: 'sillier than Praxilla's Adonis'. In her *Hymn to Adonis*, the beloved of Aphrodite who was killed boar-hunting, he is asked in the underworld what he most regrets having left behind. His reply, 'the light of the sun, the next the shining stars and the face of the moon and also ripe cucumbers and apples and pears', was considered somewhat bathetic, in its juxtaposition of the sun, stars, moon and cucumbers (Praxilla *F* 747: doc. 4.6). Another contemporary female poet was Myrtis of Anthedon in Boeotia, none of whose work survives, who was said to have competed with Pindar: Korinna, a later poetess, criticises her on this account (*F* 7), 'I blame clear-voiced Myrtis in that, a woman, she entered into competition with Pindar.' Even Sparta had its female authors: Kleitagora was a Spartan lyric poet mentioned by Aristophanes (twice) in his *Wasps* and his lost play the *Danaids*, while Megalostrata was another Spartan, beloved it is said by the lyric poet Alcman (*F* 59B) who describes her as 'blessed among girls, a golden-haired maiden displaying the gift of the sweet Muses'. Women throughout Greece played an important role in uttering, and presumably adapting, improvising and composing, funerary laments, and so it is not implausible that many developed musical talents and the ability to compose songs, even if few of these have been preserved because of the nature of their authorship.

As well as this small minority of women writers in the archaic and classical Greek world, Athens had educated, non-citizen, women among its residents, often foreign-born hetairai. Certainly the metic Aspasia of Miletos, Perikles' 'partner', is described as edu-cated and articulate, and is mentioned by Aristophanes, Plato and Xenophon, while the philosophers Aeschines and Antisthenes both named a dialogue after her (both are now lost); there was a tradition that she wrote Perikles' speeches for him, including the

Figure 4.2 An Athenian white pyxis (box) showing the details of a marriage procession. The husband takes his wife by the hand, while a flute player goes in front. Dating to about 470–450 BC the pyxis is attributed to the Splanchnopt Painter. A pyxis (plural: pyxides) was a pottery box used by women to hold small personal objects, such as pins, brooches and jewellery. British Museum 1894,0719.1 (Vase D11), London. Drawing by J. Etherington.

important Funeral Oration (doc. 1.17). An important part in the Socratic writings was also played by Diotima of Mantineia, a female diviner featured in Plato's *Symposium*, who explains to Socrates the concept of Platonic love. While she may have been fictional, it is interesting that Plato, who considered that both women and men could act as philosopher-guardians of his ideal city-state (in the *Republic*), felt it appropriate to put this teaching into the mouth of a woman.

Early moralisers and misogynists

Archaic poets frequently focus on women in their domestic role, and it might be argued that this goes back to the Homeric poems, which not only portray the activities of goddesses such as Aphrodite and Athena with full psychological motivation, but treat women characters, especially in the *Odyssey*, with great empathy (so much so that the nineteenth-century author Samuel Butler considered that the composer of the *Odyssey* must have been a woman): some examples of such delicate portraits are seen in Calypso, Penelope, Nausikaa and Helen. Some of the most sensitive depictions of the husband–wife relationship can be seen in these poems, for example, in the bond between Andromache and Hector in the *Iliad*. When Hector farewells his wife, he comments that the fall of Troy and the sufferings of his parents and brothers will not hurt him so much as the thought of Andromache being enslaved and dragged off to Greece (Hom. *Iliad* 6.447–63: doc. 5.67). A similarly close relationship is shown between the couple Penelope and Odysseus at their reunion in the *Odyssey* (23.85–365). When Odysseus in the course of his wanderings is shipwrecked on the island of Phaeacia, the first person he meets is the princess Nausikaa who has gone, at Athena's prompting, to wash the family's clothes (in preparation for her duties in marriage): Nausikaa clearly has reasonable freedom of movement, though accompanied by her slave women on this trip out of town, and the girls remove their veils while playing ball games. Odysseus thanks her for her assistance in directing him to the city and her loan of clothes and wishes her good fortune in the following words, presenting the conjugal relationship in very positive terms (Hom. *Odyssey* 6.182–5: doc. 4.7): 'there is nothing nobler or better than this, when two people, who think alike, keep house as man and wife; causing great pain to their enemies, and joy to their well-wishers; as they themselves know best.'

Hesiod's perceptions of women

This perception is very alien to Hesiod's portrayal of women generally: in contrast to the Homeric poems, Hesiod, writing a work of advice to the typical small farmer in Boeotia c. 700, realises that a woman is essential on a farm and advises the acquisition of a slave woman, but not one nursing a child (because otherwise she will be prevented from following the oxen), before a wife. Both the wife and female slave would have performed the usual female chores of grinding grain and cooking, as well as sharing the farmer's bed. In accounting for all the evils of this world Hesiod depicts the gods' creation of the first woman, Pandora ('the all-endowed'), as a punishment for Prometheus' having stolen fire from Olympos and given it to mortals. Each of the gods gives Pandora a 'gift' so on their behalf she can wreck vengeance on men. Not only was Pandora made innately wily and deceitful, out of curiosity she opened a jar and released all evils, such as toil, sickness and disease, to afflict mankind: only hope remained (Hes. *Works and Days* 57–82: doc. 4.8). This attempt to explain the existence of misfortune and drudgery through the creation of this archetypal woman appears in both his *Theogony* and his *Works and Days*, and Hesiod obviously feels that it says much about womankind. The emphasis is on deceitfulness and deception: Hermes gives Pandora a 'shameless mind and wily nature' and 'lies and crafty words', yet at the same time she is as beautiful as an immortal goddess. She is part goddess, part human and part beast, untrustworthy, yet as necessary to man as fire – needed for the continuation of humankind, but at the same time nothing but trouble, and her arrival signifies the beginnings of all evils on the earth. In his advice to his son and to all farmers, Hesiod makes the point that women are little help, indeed only a trouble in times of poverty, and, while it is possible to avoid marriage altogether to escape this evil, as a result there will be no children to look after you in your old age and inherit the property. So a man should marry, if only to have a son, preferably only one so the land does not have to be divided, who will ensure that the property on which so much work has been expended does not pass into the hands of distant relations.

In Hesiod's view women are seductive and essentially untrustworthy, and he warns against a 'woman who decorates her buttocks' – for she is only after your granary – and suggests that trusting a woman is like trusting thieves. For those who wish to marry, he suggests a girl five years past puberty (the man should be near thirty), after very careful scrutiny of her character and upbringing, and it is best to marry a girl who lives near you so you can ascertain what she is like before you marry her. You should also choose a girl who has not been previously married, so you can teach her 'diligent habits'. He implies that a false step in marriage delights your neighbours, and that while a man acquires nothing better than a good wife, a bad one is 'a parasite, who even if her husband is strong singes him without a torch and brings him to a raw old age' (Hes. *Works and Days* 702–5: doc. 4.9). However, the picture is not without some compensations, and his description of a marriageable young girl (*Works and Days* 519–22), 'a tender maiden who stays indoors with her dear mother, not yet experienced in the works of golden Aphrodite, who washes well her soft body and anoints herself with oil', shows that his view of women's sexuality was not entirely negative and perhaps encapsulates the 'good' wife for whom he exhorts his readers to search (Fig. 4.2).

Theognis and Hipponax

The lesson is repeated in other contemporary poets: Theognis of Megara (traditionally dated to c. 640–600) urges his beloved boy, Kyrnos, with whom he is engaged in a homoerotic relationship, to marry: 'Nothing, Kyrnos, is sweeter than a good wife; I am a witness to the truth of this, and you should become so for me' (in other words, Kyrnos should prove that a wife can be a blessing by marrying). It seems not impossible that the lover here would have some impact on the beloved's choice of wife as well as his decision to marry. At the same time Theognis specifically advises against an elderly husband marrying a young wife: using a boating analogy he describes her as not obeying the rudder, while you should expect her to break her 'mooring cables' and go off at night to find another harbour (Thgn. 457–60, 1225–26; docs 4.10–11). In the Hesiodic tradition, Hipponax, writing c. 540, quips there are only two days when you're happy with a wife: the wedding day and when she's carried out for her funeral – perhaps a joke to be enjoyed at a male symposium (Hipponax 68: doc. 4.12). Whatever might be said about the genres in which these poets are writing (presumably for an all-male audience), there is no doubting the fact that the wife plays an important role in the household, and is the ultimate cause of her husband's happiness or misery. She also by definition has a significant part to play in the economy of the household, and can be the difference between prosperity and ruin. There seems to be no concept of a wife's seclusion in this milieu: or if there is, it is not working properly, and part of life's little enjoyments seems to be taking note of the details of other people's unhappy and ill-matched marriages.

Semonides of Amorgos

Semonides, one of the three great iambic poets of archaic Greece, along with Archilochos and Hipponax, was writing in the mid-seventh century, and appears to have led a colony

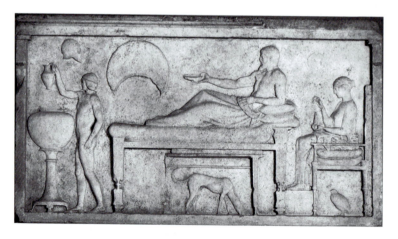

Figure 4.3 A Greek marble funerary stele showing the deceased reclining on a couch, with his dog beneath. His wife sits respectfully behind him and appears to be working: some object was probably painted into her right hand, while a nude slave boy is about to bring the man a pitcher of wine, which he will pour into the shallow drinking vessel the man extends towards him in his right hand. The contrast between the pleasures of a man and the role of his wife (and slave) is made clear. She is certainly the 'bee' wife Semonides wrote about (doc. 4.13). A mirror hangs on a wall behind the woman, while the man's helmet for war is on the left, on his side of the composition. The spatial allocation is made clear in that the woman is relegated to a small section on the far right, while the man occupies most of the scene. This sensitively carved relief with its attention to detail comes from Ionia and dates to about 480–450 BC. © Archaeological Museum, Istanbul.

from Samos to settle on the island of Amorgos. His best known work, *On Women*, portrays ten different types of women, all within the context of married life, created from different animals and elements: the filthy pig, the yapping bitch, the fastidious mare, the wily monkey, the wicked vixen, the stubborn donkey, the disgusting weasel, the hungry earth and the changeable sea. These women in general display a range of characteristics such as extravagance, vanity, laziness, curiosity and greed. The only one of the ten to be praised is the hard-working bee, who gives the household and her husband prosperity and who 'grows old with a husband whom she loves and who loves her'. She typifies the conventional virtues of women: bearing fine children and caring for the household, with her duties focusing on serving her husband (Fig. 4.3). The resolution of the poem is that marriage is a very serious business and not one to be undertaken lightly, for when a man has a wife he can't easily entertain a friend any more, while the woman chosen for her prudence will generally turn out to be a terrible mistake and outrageously extravagant and wasteful. Everyone will then take pleasure in laughing at the deluded husband's mistake and making fun of his married life, as they already do for all their other neighbours. Woman is, indeed, 'the greatest evil that Zeus has made binding us with an unbreakable fetter' – ever since the Greek heroes died for the sake of Helen of Troy. The women whom Semonides describes negatively are blatant in their failure as wives, and one of the problems is not just that the husband has to suffer from having made the wrong choice, but that the faults of each wife are a source of continual amusement to everyone else in the community (Semonides of Amorgos 7: doc. 4.13). Abuse of women particularly stresses the economic burden they are on their husbands, and this appears to have been a common theme of the archaic period. However, while often humorous and generally satirical, the works of Hesiod and others reflect a developing concern over the role and status of women which is reflected in sixth-century legislation, such as that attributed to Solon of Athens (doc. 4.50), in an attempt to restrict women's control of property and general expenditure.

Spartan women and families

Spartan women were unique in Greece: girls were trained in athletics and gymnastics, participated in choruses, sang and danced at religious festivals, and enjoyed far more independence than women elsewhere in Greece, due to the men's full-time participation in the army and life in barracks up until the age of 30. In terms of property and inheritance, heiresses could inherit in their own right and by the fourth century held considerable amounts of property and wealth. Aristotle calculates that in his own time women owned some two-fifths of Spartan land (Arist. *Politics* 1269b39–1270a3: doc. 4.18).

Women and the 'Lykourgan' reforms

Despite the accounts of the austerity and brutality of Spartan life, documents on Spartan women show a very different picture, especially prior to c. 550 when the 'Lykourgan' reforms were probably finally put in place and when Sparta ceased to be known for its fine crafts, such as bronze and ivory work, and musical compositions for choruses and festivals. Most importantly there are the works of Alcman, who was writing c. 630, which were sung by choruses at Sparta. These survive in fragments and he was particularly notable for his songs for girls' choirs (partheneia). In one of these a dawn chorus of eleven girls celebrates the clothing of a cult statue, probably of Artemis Orthia (Alcm. 1: doc. 4.14). Taking part in these choruses was a part of the girls' education system and rites of passage, and played a significant role in their transition to womanhood, while the names of the girls in this particular work suggest that they came from the highest Spartan families: Ainesimbrota ('praise of man'), Timasimbrota ('honour of man'), Astymeloisa ('care for the citadel'). Sparta has not at this point reached its period of austerity: the girls speak of wearing 'excess of purple', golden ornaments and Lydian headbands. The poem is written specifically for this festival occasion, and there is the hint of a contest between the leaders Agido and Hagesichora and their supporters, as well as possible erotic attachments between the girls: Plutarch's *Life of Lykourgos* (17) states that Spartan girls engaged in such relationships. In this chorus there is a clear focus on the girls as articulate, competitive and physically fit: Agido is described as a horse among grazing beasts (such as sheep): a 'strong, thunderous-hoofed prize-winner of winged dreams'. The dancers can be compared to champion racehorses in their strength and beauty, and even if Spartan girls and women did not engage in sexual relationships with each other, there were clearly very strong emotional ties between them.

Xenophon and Plutarch state that the founder of the Spartan regime, 'Lykourgos', wanted Spartan women to be fit and give birth to healthy children. As a result he ensured that they engaged publicly not only in choruses and dancing at festivals, but in gymnastics, athletics and wrestling like the men. In addition, they did not marry until they were between 18 and 20 years of age, considerably later, for example, than girls at Athens. They regularly took a public part in processions, choruses and festivals, with dance and music, and while they may have been instructed in weaving and 'female' tasks, this was primarily the work of slaves. Xenophon provides a useful contrast of the upbringing of Spartan girls with that found in the rest of Greece: girls in Greece generally had a plain diet, with little wine, or only if well diluted, and were expected to sit quietly and work wool, while in Sparta girls, rather than spinning and weaving, took part in physical exercise to toughen them for childbearing (Xen. *Const. Spart.*1.3–8: doc. 4.16). Archaic bronze statuettes show girls, assumed to be Spartan, with long, braided hair, tunics which reach to above the knee and slit at the sides, and often the right shoulder and breast bare (front cover). While other Greeks speak of the Spartan girls exercising naked, their nakedness in Greek terms may have meant the wearing of this short Dorian-style tunic (chitoniskos), split up the sides; Spartan girls were accordingly known as 'thigh-flashers'. To non-Spartans this was exciting and rather risqué: Anacreon exhorts one of his lovers in a clearly erotic context to 'Take off your chiton (tunic) and dress like a Dorian' (Anac. 399: doc. 4.15).

Spartan athleticism

While Aristophanes is clearly making fun of Spartan women and their athleticism in his play *Lysistrata*, in which the women of Greece unite to go on a sex-strike against their husbands until they put an end to the Peloponnesian War, it was true that Spartan women were proud of their fitness. The Spartan Lampito is praised by Myrrhine, one of Lysistrata's Athenian companions: 'What lovely colour you have, what physical vigour! Why you could throttle a bull!' (Ar. *Lysistrata* 77–82: doc. 4.21). Lampito's reply is not as ridiculous as it might sound: 'I think I could, by the two goddesses (a Spartan oath). For I keep in training and practise my buttock-jumps.' Buttock-jumps, 'bibasis', where the participants jumped up touching their buttocks with their feet, were a part of the training for both boys and girls at Sparta; an inscription is recorded for one girl (unnamed) who once did a thousand – the most ever done. This implies a record-keeping system for such feats, and thus a centralised organisation overseeing the girls' athletic training and their individual accomplishments (Pollux *Onomastikon*

4.102: doc. 4.22). The Heraia, an all-woman athletic festival at Olympia in honour of Hera which was already in place in the sixth century, may have been devised specifically for Spartan girls to compete in. The events comprised foot races which took place in the Olympic stadium which was shortened to five-sixths of its length, and there were three age groups for competitors. The festival was organised by sixteen women who also arranged two choruses for the girls who competed: winners received an olive garland and meat from the sacrificial animal and were allowed to erect statues or paintings of themselves.

Such was the concern for eugenics, according to Xenophon, that men too had to marry in their prime, so that they had healthy children, and marriage was expected: it is clear that bachelors suffered penalties (Plut. *Life of Lykourgos* 15.1–3: doc. 6.16), while Aristotle records that men with three sons were exempt from military duties, and those with four from taxation (Arist. *Politics* 1270a29–b6: doc. 6.18). Xenophon also records some unusual family arrangements: if an old man were married to a young wife, he states, he could invite another man in to have children by his wife. This was almost certainly not a normal proceeding, but would perhaps have been an advantage if the elderly husband had no sons to succeed him or to inherit his estate. A Spartan could also, according to Xenophon, ask to share a wife with her husband if he chose not to marry but wanted children, though as humiliating penalties were imposed on those who did not marry the number of these would have been minimal to say the least and Xenophon's account must be treated with caution. The advantage for the wife in this situation would be that she would then have the economic and social status of being in charge of two households, while the husband gained additional brothers for his sons, who, while members of the family and able to extend its influence, would not be able to claim a part of the family estate (Xen. *Const. Spart.*1.3–8: doc. 4.16). Despite its other martial preoccupations, Sparta was as concerned with the preservation of family inheritances and estates as the rest of Greece. Its citizens had to be fit and tough, but in order to be citizens they needed to possess an estate which could cover their mess-dues – hence property had to be a prime consideration in any questions of marriage and inheritance.

The liberty of Spartan women

Nevertheless, Spartan women had considerably more freedom than women elsewhere in Greece, perhaps because the men were so engaged in military activities. They tended to marry later, were frequently in charge of estates and free from male domination, and could engage in activities unheard of elsewhere, not merely athletics and gymnastics, but ones which demanded a control of property and were generally the sphere of men. Kyniska, daughter of Archidamos II, won the chariot race at the Olympic festival in 396 and 392. This was an expensive hobby and clearly, therefore, Spartan women controlled a large proportion of Sparta's wealth as early as 396 (Paus. *Description of Greece* 3.8.1: doc. 4.17). Kyniska was the first woman victor and the occasion was celebrated by the erection of a hero-shrine to her at Sparta and a statue of her by Apelles dedicated at Olympia. Another Spartan woman, Euryleonis, won the same event in 368.

Aristotle, in his *Politics*, identifies three main defects in the Spartan system: the dangers of helot uprisings, the status of women and the disposition of estates. He discusses the lack of control exercised over Spartan women, considering that Spartan men are 'ruled by them', and the problem caused by the number of heiresses and the failure to limit the size of inheritances and dowries, and it appears that through marriage, and the consequent uniting of estates, wealth in Sparta had by his time become concentrated in the hands of a few families, with nearly two-fifths of estates being controlled by women. This had serious consequences in the decline of the number of Spartan citizens, each of whom had to possess an individual estate or lose his citizen rights:

> As things are however it is open to a citizen to bestow an heiress on whatever husband he chooses... the city perished on account of its small population . . . it is better for a city to keep up its male population by seeing that the property is owned on a basis of equality.

Aristotle was something of a chauvinist, and feels aggrieved at women's freedom in Sparta, in contrast to elsewhere. He says that the Spartan women were not trained to a hardihood sufficient to suit their freedom, and therefore they became dissolute and licentious. Interestingly he sees Spartan women and their position as having been one of the problems from the beginning, and one which even forced 'Lykourgos' to give up on them (Arist. *Politics* 1269b39–1270a3: doc. 4.18). Certainly by the third century (Plut. *Life of Agis* 4.1–2: doc. 6.71), most of Spartan wealth was controlled by women, though some noble women were prepared to use this wealth to support the redistribution of land.

Family life in Sparta

Family life was very different in Sparta to elsewhere in Greece, with the possible exception of Crete. Spartan men lived in barracks until they were 30 years of age, and even then dined with their comrades in messes when they were not on campaign. As a result Spartan wives managed the household and property (including helots and the produce from the family's estate) for much of the time, and oversaw the bringing up of their children (boys at least till the age of 7), while their ownership of property in their own right would have given them additional status and authority. Plutarch even records the anecdote that men, who lived in barracks until they were 30, visited their wives by stealth at night, with the result that they might well have had children before they saw their own wives in daylight (Plut. *Life of Lykourgos* 15.5). It might even have been possible for a 7-year old boy to have been sent off to begin his training before his father came to live at home. The emphasis on the training for Spartan girls is directed entirely to their being fit and tough enough to bear strong healthy future Spartan warriors, and childbearing was considered so important that the only women in Sparta whose graves were marked with their names were those who died in childbirth. All new-born babies were taken to the tribesmen, and if the infant seemed weak or deformed it was sent to the 'Place of Exposure', the idea being that any Spartan 'not properly formed with a view to health and strength' should not live. From what is known of Spartan mothers there would have been no demurral (Plut. *Life of Lykourgos* 16.1–2: doc. 4.23). Frequent anecdotes of Spartan wives and mothers stress their strong-mindedness and the concepts of valour and honour that they enforced in their children. They are often depicted as encouraging bravery and discouraging cowardice in their sons, and as rejoicing instead of mourning at a son's glorious death in battle, so committed were they not only to breeding the new generation of soldiers but to ensuring that these did their duty by Sparta. Plutarch even records an anecdote of a mother who killed her son for desertion – on the grounds that he could not have been her son as he was unworthy of Sparta (Plut. *Sayings of Spartan Women (Moralia)* 241a). The mother of Brasidas, who died at Amphipolis in 422 when taking the city from the Athenians, is a case in point: when told that by some Amphipolitans at Sparta that there was no other Spartiate like him, she is supposed to have told them not to say this, for 'Sparta had many better men than he' (Plut. *Life of Lykourgos* 25.8–9: doc. 4.20). Such anecdotes abound: mothers exhort their sons not to throw away their shield (a sign of cowardice), and when told that a son is dead in battle, 'on the spot where he had been positioned', tell their informants to bury him and put his brother in his place (Plut. *Sayings of Spartan Women* 16, 20: doc. 6.18).

Gorgo, daughter of Kleomenes

One of the only Spartan queens of whom sayings are recorded is Gorgo, daughter of Kleomenes I, wife of Leonidas (of Thermopylai fame) and mother of Pleistarchos. As with other Spartan 'quotes' many are no doubt improved by Plutarch to exemplify Spartan austerity and dedication to the state. When some foreign woman came up to her to say, 'You Spartans are the only women who can rule men,' Gorgo replied, 'That is because we are the only ones who give birth to men.' Spartan women were therefore seen as not subservient to male domination, perhaps because they were freed from this by the discipline expected by the state from every Spartan, male and female. At the same time Spartan mothers believed that only Spartan babies grew up to be real men (Plut. *Life of Lykourgos* 14.1–8: doc. 4.19). Gorgo when only 8 or 9 had warned her father against being bribed by Aristagoras of Miletos (Hdt. 5.51.1–3: doc. 6.74), and as Leonidas' wife had advised the Spartans how to uncover a wax tablet from Demaratos secretly warning the Spartans of Xerxes' impending invasion (Hdt. 7.239). In the *Sayings of the Spartans* (Plut. *Moralia* 225a) Gorgo is said to have asked her husband Leonidas when he left for Thermopylai what instructions he had for her: his reply was, 'To marry good men and bear good children.' As far as we know she did not remarry. Gorgo herself would have been a considerable heiress as Kleomenes' only child, and the marriage to her uncle Leonidas, her father's half-brother, would have kept the wealth firmly within the Agiad house, adding to her position and influence within Sparta.

Timaia and Alkibiades

An intriguing vignette of another royal household at Sparta includes the charismatic Alkibiades, who, after escaping from the Athenian fleet en route to Syracuse in 415, was recalled to Athens to answer charges about the mutilation of the hermai. Preferring not to face trial, he fled and finally arrived at Sparta where he allegedly became involved in a romantic intrigue with Queen Timaia while her husband Agis II was on campaign. Timaia's son Leotychidas was thought by some to be the child of Alkibiades and not Agis, and his mother was said to call him Alkibiades in private to her helot women. The Spartans were very attentive to meteorological phenomena, and Agis had apparently left Timaia's bedroom on one occasion after being frightened by an earthquake, and not visited his wife over the next ten months. Leotychidas/Alkibiades was born after the end of this ten month period. If this allegation was true, Alkibiades was in Sparta from 414 to 412, and the earthquake probably that of 413/412, so Leotychidas could only have been between the ages of 12 and 14 at his father's death, and his age, rather than his suspect birth, may have been one of the reasons why Lysander intrigued to have Agis succeeded by his brother Agesilaos rather than Leotychidas, and presumably instigated this story. According to Plutarch in his *Life of Lysander*, Leotychidas' father had always assumed that he was a bastard, though recognising him on his deathbed, but Xenophon's biography of Agesilaos prefers to emphasise that Agesilaos was preferred as king on account of his outstanding qualities, rather than stressing the illegitimacy of Leotychidas, his nephew. Clearly this was a power play stirred up by Lysander, but the fact that the rumour appears to have been known to Plato (*Alkibiades* 1.121b) as well as Xenophon (*Hellenika* 3.3.1–3) implies that it was current in the early fourth century and it was possible that it could have been true: Spartan queens were not so guarded as all that, especially when their husbands were on campaign.

Our accounts of Sparta from Xenophon and Plutarch are arguably biased in favour of Spartan institutions. Nevertheless they do present useful evidence about attitudes towards women in Sparta from the point of view of non-Spartans. Despite the lack of evidence about Spartan women from speeches in court (unlike Athens, where trials often relate to issues such as divorce or sexual misconduct), it is apparent that women at Sparta had a very different way of life from that of their Athenian counterparts, and that this was due to the nature of the two societies. However, as in Athens, property in Sparta had become totally identified as the concern of the oikos, and marriages were arranged along similar lines with property as their guiding motive: one of the kings' prerogatives was deciding on the marriages of heiresses, who had no male relations (Hdt. 6.56–60.1: doc. 6.26). Under these circumstances, it becomes clear that Plutarch's sentimental tales about Spartan weddings and the habits of young married couples are merely romantic fictions if they cut across the important concerns of inheritance and property: in Sparta as elsewhere in Greece, marriage, children and the property were issues that were of paramount importance, and in many ways that may well have been the primary cause of Sparta's decline, as Spartan estates, and thus citizens, became fewer and fewer.

The historical woman

Herodotos and Greek women

One example of Herodotos' interest in non-conventional women is Artemisia, tyrant of Herodotos' own home town, Halikarnassos on the southern coast of Asia Minor, not far from the island of Rhodes. Interestingly, while sometimes considered a 'barbarian', Artemisia was Greek, ruling the polis even though she had a son of age to reign, having taken over after the death of her husband. She commanded five triremes and hers was one of the many Greek contingents that supported Xerxes' campaign against the Greek mainland in 480–479. Herodotos, who must have had detailed knowledge of the circumstances of her participation, makes clear that she joined the expedition not from compulsion, but from 'courage' ('andreia': Hdt. 7.99), and that she took a very active part in events, advising Xerxes not to fight at sea, advice which he appreciated even though he did not follow it. She was also clearly on board and in command of one of her own ships at Salamis, and in order to escape the pursuit of an Athenian ship, once the tide of battle was securely in the Athenians' favour, deliberately rammed one of the ships on her own side, and not even a Persian ship but a Greek ship from the Kalynda on the Asia Minor coast which was fighting for the Persians. The Athenian ship pursuing her lost interest, thinking that she was on the Greeks' side, while Xerxes who was looking on and also considering that she had sunk one of the enemy, commented, 'My men have become women, my women men' (Hdt. 8.87.1–88.3: doc. 4.25). Herodotos criticises neither her involvement in battle, nor her action at Salamis, merely stating that she was lucky that no one from the Kalyndian ship survived to accuse her to set the record straight. He also states more than once that of all Xerxes' advisers Artemisia was the most dependable, and that on his retreat Xerxes entrusted his illegitimate sons to Artemisia to transport them to Ephesos (Hdt. 7.103).

Another Herodotean anecdote concerns the uninhibited behaviour of Athenian widows following their husbands' defeat at the hands of the Aeginetans. In Herodotos' account of the legendary origins of the hostility of these two states, the Aeginetans had stolen from Epidauros two statues of Attic olive wood, representing the deities Damia and Auxesia, which had been set up at Epidauros on the advice of the Delphic oracle to put an end to a crop failure: in return for the wood the Epidaurians promised to pay tribute to Athens. With the Aeginetan seizure of the statues, the tribute ceased and the Epidaurians told the Athenians to demand it of Aegina instead. Accordingly a trireme was sent, but when the Athenians tried to drag away the statues (which fell on their knees to escape capture) the Athenians were struck by a thunderstorm and an earthquake and began madly killing each other; there was only one survivor. When he returned to Athens the wives of the men who had been killed stabbed him to death with their dress pins, and in consequence their style of dress was changed to the unpinned Ionian chiton, while the Argives and Aeginetans, according to Herodotos, began to use even longer pins (Hdt. 5.87.1–88.3: doc. 4.26). Pausanias records that the statues stood there in the kneeling position in his own time. Herodotos is here combining Athenian, Aeginetan and Argive accounts with the purpose of explaining the change in women's dress, projecting back on a mythical episode aetiological traditions explaining changes in customs such as dress codes and the position of the statues. Dress patterns in Aegina do not in fact appear to have changed at this point to include even longer pins, but Herodotos may be extrapolating from pins he had seen dedicated in the sanctuary there. This contrasts with the change in Athens from the Dorian pinned peplos to the Ionian unpinned chiton. The actual change was gradual and took place during the first half of the sixth century, with the chiton appearing in Ionia c. 575.

Each of the accounts is intended to put the narrator's polis in a good light, and Athens comes out of it badly – only one survivor and the women rampaging out of control, with the Athenians changing their women's dress to try to forget a shameful incident, although the defeat had not been at the hands of the Aeginetans but by divine intervention. And there has to be a survivor so that the women can kill him to explain the change in dress. From the Athenian point of view the sacrilegious theft of the statues and refusal to pay cult dues justified the Athenians' long-standing hostility towards Aegina and the compulsory inclusion of Aegina in the Delian League in the 450s. The incident may well be the stuff of legend, but shows that Herodotos considered that at times of crisis women at Athens could take to the streets, and in a more historical setting also records that when a member of the council in 480, Lykidas, suggested that the Athenians, then on the island of Salamis, should consider the proposal of Mardonios that they submit now that their city was occupied by the Persians, the Athenians, including the councillors, stoned him to death, while the women went 'of their own prompting' to Lykidas' house and stoned his wife and children (Hdt. 9.4–5).

That women elsewhere could participate even more actively in warfare is mentioned by Thucydides in the context of the Corcyraean civil war in 427, when women took to the rooftops and threw roof-tiles at the opposition. This seems not to have been an unusual activity in a crisis situation, for women at Plataea went onto their roofs (Greek roofs were flat), and chucked stones and tiles at the invading Thebans in 427 BC (Thucydides 3.74.1: doc. 4.28). Such incidents are seldom recorded in historical sources: after all they do little to enhance the military reputation of the men involved, and are clearly often deliberately left out of the sources. Telesilla's spirited defence of Argos, along with that of the other women dressed in men's attire, is known not from Herodotos, but from Pausanias and Plutarch, presumably from an oral tradition preserved at Argos. Certainly women appear to have worked together in times of uncertainty to protect other women in a religious context: when the Thyiades, maenads, came in their state of possession to Amphissa, during the Third Sacred War, the local women silently protected them as they slept publicly in the market-place, despite the presence of enemy soldiers, and then fed them and escorted them to the borders, with their husbands' permission (Plut. *Fine Deeds of Women* 239e–f: doc. 4.31). In this situation religious obligations to other women engaged in cult practice overcame any normal social taboos about behaviour in public.

Perikles' Funeral Oration

In his Funeral Oration for the Athenians killed in the first year of the Peloponnesian War, Perikles is often considered to be advising seclusion and discretion for the women in his audience – that they should be seen and heard as little as possible, thus reinforcing the conventional ideals of Athenian gender relations:

> I should perhaps say something about the virtue appropriate to women, to those of you who will now be widows, and I shall simply give one brief piece of advice. Your renown will be great if you do not behave in an inferior way to that natural to your sex, and your glory will be to be least mentioned amongst men concerning either your virtue or your faults.

(Thuc. 2.45.2: doc. 4.27)

The conventions of Athenian legal oratory required that women were shown as concerned only with the affairs of their household and essentially restricted to the female sphere within the house, but this is not necessarily a true picture of the lifestyle of Athenian wives, even if it was one with which the jurors in the lawcourts had sympathy. Women, even in Athens, attended festivals, weddings and funerals, visited neighbours, drew water at the fountain-houses, and at the lower end of the social spectrum worked – in the fields or in the markets. On this occasion the female relations of the deceased, both citizens and metics, had followed the funerary procession towards the Kerameikos, accompanying it with their customary laments, to listen to Perikles' praises of their dead and of the glory they had won by their death, prior to the funeral itself. And his words quoted here, towards the end of his speech, are specifically addressed to the newly made widows: he has already spoken to the parents, children and brothers of the deceased.

He advises the widows firstly, that, as women, they will have great renown if they do not behave in a way unnatural to their sex, or inferior to their nature (surely a compliment! – they will have fame if they just behave in the way that comes naturally to them), and that glory on this occasion will belong to those whose behaviour is such that it is least talked of: in other words he is requesting that these young widows not engage in extreme mourning practices and thus make spectacles of themselves. His advice has to be put into historical context. There had been a long tradition of sumptuary laws restricting extravagant mourning practices, from the time of Solon in Athens and elsewhere in the Greek world (*LSCG* 97A: doc. 3.57; Plut. *Life of Solon* 20.2–23.2: doc. 4.50), to try to limit both expenditure and excesses of behaviour at funerals. Many of the widows to whom he is talking would have been relatively young and wealthy, the wives of the cavalrymen killed during the skirmishes of 431 BC, and the custom was for the relatives of the deceased to indulge in lamentations over fate and the injustice of life, even criticising the dead for leaving them, as Andromache does with Hector in another wartime situation (Hom. *Iliad* 24.725–45).

136

The year 431 had not in fact for Athens been a glorious year; little had taken place except for skirmishes, and the Athenians had retreated from the Attic countryside to see it ravaged by the Spartans and their allies, in exchange crowding into the city of Athens and Piraeus to live cooped up in temples and other public spaces. Particularly for those who had abandoned their land, there was little to celebrate and a great deal to lament, and much of this must have fallen on the women who had left their homes for a shanty-town existence in an alien location away from their normal homes and occupations. Even Athenian residents would have seen little that was glorious in the current state of affairs, and under the circumstances it was natural that Perikles would want as little public criticism of the situation as possible: the women of Athens could best help their country's cause by complaining as little as possible and demonstrating the strength of mind, the virtue natural to their sex. None of them, he exhorts them, should behave so as to stand out and be noticeable for their grief and general dissatisfaction with the current situation in Athens.

Aspasia and Perikles

This advice sits somewhat strangely with the prominence given to Perikles' own partner, Aspasia, though it is true that Thucydides does not mention her in his *History*. Perikles had previously been married to a relative, presumably an heiress, whom he later divorced giving her in marriage with her consent to another Athenian. Plutarch implies that this was because he had met Aspasia, but as she was a metic, from Miletos, Perikles was of course unable to marry her anyway: their son, Perikles junior, was only granted citizenship by the assembly after Perikles' legitimate sons had died in the plague. Little is specifically known about Aspasia, even though she is mentioned by Xenophon, Plato and Aristophanes, and much of the anecdote attached to her, such as that she kept a brothel and trained young hetairai, presumably came from the attacks of comic poets on Perikles. Details such as those given by Plutarch, that Perikles kissed her every day when he left and returned home, may well come from such sources (Plut. *Life of Perikles* 24.2–9: doc. 4.29); even his account of her trial for impiety might have stemmed from rumours of her unpopularity, although two friends of Perikles, the sculptor Pheidias and the philosopher Anaxagoras, were also prosecuted on the same charge. The comic dramatists Eupolis and Kratinos attacked her as a 'dog-eyed' concubine and prostitute and Aristophanes in the *Acharnians* even blamed her for the outbreak of the Peloponnesian War claiming that Perikles' Megarian decree, which prevented Megara from trading with Athens or its allies, was retaliation for the Megarian kidnap of some of Aspasia's prostitutes (Ar. *Acharnians* 524–9: doc. 4.95). There may well have been concern over her role both as Perikles' partner and as a metic, a non-citizen foreign woman. She is also portrayed in philosophical works like Plato's *Menexenos* as having taught Perikles and Socrates rhetoric and shown as the centre of an intellectual circle. Antisthenes in his dialogue *Aspasia* uses her to attack Perikles and his family. The most reliable contemporary evidence is that of Xenophon who mentions her twice: in his *Memorabilia* (2.6.36), Socrates quotes Aspasia's good advice on honest match-making, and in the *Oeconomicus* (3.14), Socrates pays compliment to her experience of household management.

Xanthippe and Socrates

If Aspasia had the liberty and education which is ascribed to her, this was the result of her non-citizen status: Athenian women of the time would not have had such freedom to mix with and give advice to men not of their own family. That being said, however, there is also the tradition of Socrates' own wife, Xanthippe, whose name has long been synonymous with that of a nagging wife and a 'shrew' (as in the *Taming of the Shrew*, Act 1, scene 2). As Socrates served as a hoplite, it is likely that Xanthippe was of the same social status, and her name, 'Blond horse', suggests possible aristocratic connections. Socrates and Xanthippe had three sons, Lamprokles, Sophroniskos (after Socrates' father) and Menexenos. The fact that the eldest son Lamprokles is named not for Socrates' father but presumably for Xanthippe's suggests that her family was socially superior. Xanthippe is only mentioned by Plato at the point when she is led away from Socrates' death-bed (Pl. *Phaedo* 59d–60a: doc. 3.87). When Socrates is released from his chains prior to his execution, his friends enter the prison.

> When Xanthippe saw us, she wailed and made the sort of remark you'd expect from a woman: 'Socrates, this is the last time you and your friends will be able to talk together!' Socrates looked at Krito and said, 'Krito, let someone take her home.' And so some of Krito's servants led her away lamenting and beating her breast.

Perhaps Xanthippe had some excuse for her notorious bad temper. Socrates seems to have been considerably older than Xanthippe, as her youngest son was only an infant at the time of Socrates' death when he was approximately 70 years of age. Reports of her bad temper come from Socrates' admirer Xenophon who mentions in his *Memorabilia* (2.2.1–14) that Lamprokles, in a dialogue with his father, complained that no one could put up with his mother's vile temper and that her brutality was worse than a wild beast's. Socrates countered this by listing all the sacrifices made by mothers for their children, with Lamprokles responding that 'she says things that no one in the world could bear to listen to!'

References to her temper also occur in Xenophon's *Symposium*, when Socrates praises the talent of a dancing girl and suggests that her talent is in no way inferior to that of a man, and that therefore any husband should teach his wife what he would like her to know because women should be able to learn anything a man can (perhaps, under the circumstances, not the wisest of advice). At this one of the diners, Antisthenes, retorts:

> So how is it, Socrates, that you think like that and do not train Xanthippe, but live with a wife who is the most difficult to live with of all women in existence, and, I think, of all women past and future as well?
>
> (Xen. *Symposium* 2.8–10: doc. 4.30)

Socrates' response is that just as horse-trainers practised on high-spirited horses, so he chose to marry Xanthippe knowing that, 'if I can stand her, I can easily live with all the rest of mankind.' Later elaborations like that by Plutarch stating that she overturned a dinner-table when Socrates brought home an uninvited guest (Plut. *Moralia* 461d), and by Aelian describing how she trampled on a lovely cake sent to Socrates by Alkibiades, considering it a gift of a beloved to his lover (Ael. *Varia Historia* 11.12), are doubtless just variations on the theme. However, there would have been much to be annoyed by in Socrates, from a wife's point of view: the single ragged cloak, the habit of spending every day in the agora cross-questioning passers-by, his ill-timed irony leading the jurors to condemn him, and his refusal to escape and passive acceptance of death, leaving her with three relatively young sons. What is significant is that Xenophon and Plato, who knew Socrates well, were not afraid to name Xanthippe in their dialogues, despite the convention that citizen women should remain nameless, either because of her relationship to their mentor Socrates, or because she transgressed the boundaries of the behaviour appropriate to citizen women which ensured their anonymity.

Inscriptional evidence

Greek inscriptions are first found in the second half of the eighth century, painted or inscribed on pottery, and funerary texts, or epitaphs, were among the earliest inscriptional material, whether on vessels intended to contain the ashes of the dead or on funerary stelai. The most famous of those from the Greek world are the works of Simonides of Keos on the heroes of

Figure 4.4 The life-size marble statue of the maiden Phrasikleia found at Athens (doc. 4.35). Such statues are known as korai (singular: kore). An inscription on the statue describes Phrasikleia as a maiden who will be called such forever, because she has died and will not be married. The last line records that Aristion of Paros carved the statue; it is of marble from Paros and dates to about 550 BC. National Archaeological Museum Athens 4889, Athens. Photo © Hellenic Ministry of Culture and Tourism / Archaeological Receipts Fund.

139

the Persian Wars; he also wrote epigrams for prominent individuals, including noble women. But the largest group of epitaphs commemorates individuals within the context of the family. Early examples often do little more than record the name of the deceased, while later many of them list virtues specific to the family member. Some of these epitaphs demonstrate that connection and wealth were extremely important to these women and those belonging to them: in the grave stele which speaks to the passer by on her behalf, written by Simonides, Xanthippe boasts not only that she is the 'glorious' wife of Archenautes, but also the great-great-granddaughter of Periander tyrant of Corinth (Simon. 36: doc. 4.32; Hdt. 5.92f.1–92g.1: doc. 7.13). Four generations on, it is this relationship with Periander, 'who once in high-towered Corinth, where he was sovereign, commanded the people' which still defines Xanthippe's perception of why she should not lie in death 'unnamed'. A very similar epitaph, also by Simonides, praises Archedike, wife of the tyrant Aiantides of Lampsakos, and daughter of Hippias, tyrant of Athens (527–510). Hippias had married his daughter to Aiantides shortly before his expulsion from Athens because of Aiantides' connections with Darius, in case Hippias should have to flee to Darius' court at Susa. Significant about the epitaph is its total failure to mention Archedike's husband Aiantides, which would have been unthinkable had he still been in power, and the tyranny must therefore have been overthrown before Archedike's death. So her distinction and rank in this epitaph is based not on the importance of her husband but on her relationship to Hippias 'who was greatest in Greece of those of his time', linked to the fact that she was daughter, wife, sister and mother of tyrants. Nevertheless, written in a city which had removed its tyrants, the epitaph is careful to mention that she was not given to 'unseemly arrogance' (Thuc. 6.59.3: doc. 9.34), implying the status and power with which women like Archedike and Xanthippe were associated and which they saw as their own.

Parents and daughters

Many epitaphs now extant were written for young girls, demonstrating the importance of their role within the family which was prepared to commemorate them with such care (Fig. 4.11): in one perhaps dating to the sixth century, a Thessalian child speaks from her own gravestone relating that she died while an infant and did not reach 'the flower of her youth'. The stone then takes up her story and names her parents, Kleodamos, son of Hyperanor, and Korona who set this up as a monument or memorial to their daughter Thessalia (Friedländer 32: doc. 4.33). Learete of Thasos's epitaph in the early fifth century looks mournfully to the future: 'truly beautiful is the monument which her father erected over dead Learete; for we shall no longer see her alive' (Friedländer 60: doc. 4.34). The beauty of the monument depicting Learete is emphasised – in contrast, the living girl herself will never be seen again. The 'we' speaks both for the father and the passer-by and elicits his sympathy: in the ancient world all reading took place aloud and there was no concept of silent reading, so the passer-by is expected to articulate the words commemorating Learete along with her father. Different again is the memorial of Phrasikleia, a life-size Attic kore, whose statue was found buried next to that of a kouros, Kroisos, dated approximately to 540. The statues are now in the National Archaeological Museum of Athens. It has been suggested that the couple were young members of the Alkmeonid family whose statues were buried when the family went into exile from Attica under the Peisistratid tyranny. The inscription indicates that the statue was made by Aristion of Paros, who is known from other funerary inscriptions. The lotuses with which she is crowned on her elaborately dressed hair and one of which she holds to her breast signify her unmarried state, stressed in the epitaph itself: 'I shall be called maiden for-ever, because I won this name from the gods instead of marriage' (*IG* I³ 1261: doc. 4.35). The reader is perhaps meant to identify Phrasikleia with Persephone as bride of the underworld, but more strongly the tone of a noble house comes through – Phrasikleia will not be able to continue the family succession and has been cut off from life before she can fulfil her honour-able destiny as wife and mother.

Mothers and sons

Three significant epitaphs are written for mothers burying sons. Amphidama, perhaps in the seventh century, set up a pillar at Troizen in memorial of her son Damotimos 'for no children were born in his house', together with the tripod which he won in the footrace at Thebes, signalling his greatest achievement while alive (*IG* IV 801: doc. 4.36). This epitaph is written in the third person, describing Amphidama's actions, from the point of view of an impersonal narrator. Mnesitheos, on a stele from Eretria, however, speaks for himself directly to the passers-by, asking them to come closer to read who is buried at this spot: he is a for-eigner (perhaps a metic) from Aegina, whose mother Timarete has set up the 'imperishable' monument to proclaim eternally his fate to passers-by. While the stele speaks in the persona of Mnesitheos, the words are actually those of Timarete who 'set this up for her dear dead son' (Friedländer 140: doc. 4.37). The implication here may be that as foreigners there are no other family members to do this for him except his mother. On the other hand Echenais erects near Pharsalos in Thessaly a monument for her son Diokles, even though he has a brother who is now 'without laughter' because of the family tragedy. Echenais in her role as woman and mother is 'mourning greatly' both because he was valiant and because of his early death, and instructs all who pass to lament as they continue on their way; the repetition of the epithet valiant (agathos) may imply death in battle, and the stele is intended to provoke eternal remembrance of this heroic son (*IG* IX 2.255: doc. 4.38).

Another case in which a woman took the prominent part in erecting a memorial is that of an unnamed mother, whose sons have erected a monument to their father 'at their moth-er's command' (*IG* I³ 1226: doc. 4.39). This sixth-century stele was found in the wall of Themistokles, erected hastily after the Second Persian War. The epitaph is incomplete, but it appears that the mother's name is not given, as would be normal for an Athenian citizen wife: on the other hand her role in the family is central enough for it to be specifically stated that her sons in remembering their father are acting on her instructions. Another wife who takes responsibility for her husband's memorial is Potalis, wife of Mantitheos from Tanagra in Boeotia. The epitaph praises Mantitheos' expertise in hospitality and horsemanship, two attributes of nobility, and Mantitheos must have been a Boeotian aristocrat, proud of his status and the way he fulfilled his obligations in this regard. If the restoration of Potalis' name beneath this epitaph is correct, she appears later to have been buried with him (Friedländer 74: doc. 4.40). A marble disk from Attica presents an even more unusual phenomenon, a dedication by a sister, who nursed her brother Gnatho in mental illness and who was respon-sible for his burial around 550 – a situation which runs counter to everything that is assumed about the role of women in Athens and the responsibilities which a woman was allowed to assume (*IG* I³ 1210: doc. 4.41). It is not possible to pinpoint the circumstances surrounding this burial (perhaps they were metics rather than citizens), but evidence of this sort suggests that scholars should not make too many assumptions about the state of current knowledge of family life in sixth-century Attica.

Dedications and gifts

Further inscriptional evidence for the priorities and preoccupations of girls and women comes from dedications, and inscriptions on prizes and possessions. It was customary, as part of wedding ritual, for a girl to dedicate her bridal veil to Hera in commemoration of this rite of passage (Fig. 2.4). The veil was the most important part of her costume, symbolising her virginity, and was only removed by the groom after the actual marriage; this 'anakalypteria' or 'uncovering' is depicted on numerous vases and was one of the most formal parts of the ceremony, perhaps not occurring until the bride arrived at the groom's house. An epigram attributed to Archilochos, preserved in the *Greek Anthology*, accompanies the dedication of a wedding veil to Hera, goddess of marriage, in her temple at Paros: 'Alkibia dedicated the sacred veil for her locks to Hera, when she attained lawful wedlock' (Archil. 1210: doc. 4.42). The veil could be magnificently embroidered and its dedication was both a sign of the end of childhood and a thanksgiving for a suitable marriage, as well as evidence of the girl's skill. Garments also made suitable dedications by women, not to garb the cult statue per se, but in thanks for benefits received or requested. In one case the dedication was made by Dyseris, wife of Echekratidas, the ruler of Larissa in Thessaly in the fifth century. Dyseris had designed the garment, with the actual work being done by Praxidike and no doubt it was a splendid creation worthy of both women ([Anac.] *Epigrammata* 7: doc. 4.43). Personal garments were often offered to Artemis, and there are lists of garment dedications from Brauron and Miletos, very suitable gifts in which women could show off their skills in textile manufacture. An offering of clothing was generally made to Artemis by a new mother, while clothes of those who died in childbirth were also dedicated in her temples. Many young mothers would have died in such circumstances as childbirth was dangerous and difficult. Another common type of dedication by women was that of a mirror, seen as typically feminine. Mirrors were frequently dedicated to Artemis Brauronia and to other deities across the Greek world as personal items, as well as ones that could be relatively inexpensive. One example from fifth-century Greek Italy is that of Phillo, daughter of Charmilydas, from Poseidonia, who dedicated a mirror as a tithe to Athena. The mirror stand supported a female bronze statuette on an Ionic capital (Friedländer 166: doc. 4.44).

Very different in scale and intent is the greater than life-size kore dedicated by Nikandra of Naxos in the sanctuary of Artemis on Delos (Fig. 4.5). Perhaps the earliest dedication in the archaic period by a woman, it was carved in Naxos in the mid-seventh century. Nikandra and her family were clearly part of the oligarchic group in power, and Naxos was at this point in virtual control of Delos with many Naxian dedications being erected there, including the famous avenue of lions. The statue represents Artemis rather than Nikandra, and the hole in each hand was probably intended for Artemis' weapons. Nikandra may have been present at Delos on the occasion of the dedication, and the mention of both her father and brother implies that they were well-known Naxians, while Nikandra herself is 'prominent amongst other women'. The occasion for the dedication may have been her marriage, for the inscription specifies that as well as being the daughter of Deinodikes and sister of Deinomenes, she is now the wife of Phraxos, and a dedication to Artemis as goddess of childbirth would have been totally appropriate for a girl making the transition from maidenhood to marriage (Friedländer 46: doc. 4.45). A further dedication to Artemis as goddess of childbirth was made jointly by the married couple Demokydes and Telestodike at Paros, praying that she give increase 'to their family and livelihood . . . in safety' (Friedländer 144: doc. 4.46).

Figure 4.5 The inscription on the statue of Artemis provides details about its purpose: Nikandra the 'most distinguished among women', daughter of Deinodikes of Naxos, the sister of Deinomenes, and wife of Phraxos, dedicated the statue to Artemis (doc. 4.45). It dates to around 650 BC, was dedicated at Delos, and stands at 200 cm high (the statue itself is 175 cm high). National Archaeological Museum 1, Athens. Photo © Sarah C. Murray.

Inscriptions on possessions could also warn against possible theft or misappropriation: Tataia from Cumae in Italy had her ordinary lekythos (generally used for olive oil) marked, 'I am Tataia's flask: whoever steals me will become blind!', while Kephisophon's kylix, or drinking cup, warns the reader, 'if anyone breaks it he shall pay a drachma, because it is a gift from Xenyllos' and so presumably a lover's gift. Even more charming is the kantharos, a deeper and more substantial drinking-cup, given to Eucharis by her husband in fifth-century Thespiai: 'Mogeas gives this cup as a gift to his wife Eucharis daughter of Eutretiphantos, so she may drink her fill.' A final example is that of the Attic black-figure cup won by Melosa, perhaps at Tarentum, in a girl's carding contest: either Melosa herself or the judges of the competition have scratched on its foot: 'I am Melosa's prize; she beat the girls in carding' (Friedländer 177: doc. 4.47).

One further light on Greek funerary practices is that of companion animals: children's tombs in Attica, and particularly in Sicily, often feature the child with a pet bird or Maltese dog (cf. Fig. 4.9). One of Theophrastos' characters (*On petty ambition*) is shown as being vainglorious enough to commemorate his lap-dog, with a monument, pillar and inscription, 'Offshoot of Malta'. This same character has a pet jackdaw that he has trained to hold a little bronze shield as it hops up and down its ladder – perhaps demonstrating the bravery that the character himself has not (Theophr. *Characters* 21: doc. 4.48). Plutarch records, not necessarily authentically, the burial of Xanthippos' dog in a tomb on Salamis (Plut. *Themistokles* 10.8–10: doc. 11.36), but graves of companion animals, and epitaphs recording their virtues, are not unknown in the ancient world.

The legal status of women

Within the oikos women in Athens were always under the protection of a male member of their family, their guardian or 'kyrios': while sons left their father's guardianship when they came of age, girls when they married passed from their father (or brother's) authority into that of their husband. Legally they were always minors and had to be represented by their guardian in any legal situation, while they could not personally enter into contracts of any greater amount than one medimnos of barley (a month's supply) and so could not engage in large business transactions. However, the economic position of Athenian women was clearly protected by law: in the strictest sense of the term they did not themselves own property, though in the event of a family being left without male heirs, the property could not legally be alienated from the orphaned daughters. A woman's property remained always separate from that of her husband, though he had the control of the income from it, with this control passing to her children or their guardians after his death: if the marriage was dissolved without children, he was obliged to repay her dowry and her property was returned to her family. Aristotle makes clear in the *Politics* the Greek view that women never attain the full capacity of reason, which in them never fully matures, and hence they require guardians (*Politics* 1260a12). While apparently evidence of a patronising or paternalistic attitude towards women, nevertheless this is comprehensible in terms of a marriage in which the husband was twice the age of his wife, who at the age of 13 or 14 would suddenly have become the mistress of an household and responsible for all its related activities.

The decision on any marriage was made by the bride's father and the bridegroom or his family: the girl's consent was not necessary. However, marriages between close kin were not uncommon in Greece and in Athens first cousins, uncle and niece, and half-siblings with the same father could marry. In such cases the girl would presumably have been acquainted with her future husband, though a girl marrying her father's brother might have been as much as 30 years his junior. Such marriages were popular because they kept money and land within the kinship group. In his dialogue with Socrates Ischomachos explains how he described to his new bride the rationale behind their marriage:

> Tell me, my wife, have you thought why I took you for my wife and your parents married you to me? You must clearly see that we would have had no problem in finding someone else to sleep with. I on my own behalf and your parents on yours decided who would the best partner of home and children that we could find: and so I chose you and your parents chose me, it seems, as the best to be found.

He is clearly distinguishing the reasons for marriage from those for casual liaisons, and there is no perception that marriage will necessarily put an end to relationships with boys, slaves and prostitutes, or that marriage has been engaged in for sexual pleasure. The main purpose behind the marriage is economic, and both must work to ensure that their property increases. At the same time, if they are lucky enough to have children they will acquire 'the very best of allies and comforters when we are old' (Xen. *Oeconomicus* 7.10–23: doc. 4.63).

Divorce was simple: either side could initiate a divorce and the husband only needed to send his wife away, though the dowry had to be returned with her. Marriages could also be dissolved by the wife's father, particularly if the marriage was childless, and a wife could leave her husband, though in this case she had to register her divorce with the archon. One of the downsides of divorce for wives would have been that the children, and at least the sons, would have remained with their father, though certainly in one case a divorced woman took her daughter with her into her new marriage (Dem. 57 *Against Euboulides* 40–2: doc. 5.63).

The Gortyn law code

While most of the available information about the legal status of women comes from Athens, the Gortyn law code from Crete is evidence for the status of women in a Dorian society and its provisions differ somewhat from Athenian practice. The code dates to c. 450 and seems to be the result of a revision of earlier laws by the legislative body of Gortyn. Women appear to have had more independence, or at least more relaxed inheritance rights than at Athens, and in some cases heiresses could have a say in whom they married. Daughters had a specific portion of the inheritance rather than a dowry decided arbitrarily by their father. A daughter could inherit, even if she had brothers, but only received half a brother's share, and with the exception of any houses and stock animals; she also was able to inherit from both her father and her mother. Thus the girls' portion of the property was calculated in terms of the overall estate, with the amount given not at the discretion of the father, and could be either given at the time of her marriage or at her father's death. This also meant that a girl's 'dowry' was a fixed share of the inheritance.

At Gortyn, an heiress, a girl who had no brothers and was the sole inheritor of her father's estate, was known as a 'patroiokos'. As at Athens she could be married at the age of 12 years, though it appears that women at Gortyn were not so entirely bound up in the survival of the oikos as women in Athens and the girl's inheritance rights were related as much to the tribe as to the individual family. The first candidates for the spouse of the heiress were her father's brothers, then their sons (her paternal cousins), in order of age. If she had no paternal relations, or if none of these wished to marry her – or indeed if she did not want to marry one of them – she could marry 'whomsoever she wishes of those who ask from the tribe'. However in this case she had to hand over half her inheritance (not including the house) to the first rejected applicant. Women at Gortyn could inherit land, and a husband and wife shared the income from any property that they owned jointly, while the woman controlled her own property which could not be sold by her husband or son. A widow with children could take her own property with her on remarriage, while a widow without children kept her property, half what she had woven, and a share of any produce. A divorced wife did slightly less well: she kept her property, half what she had woven, and half the produce from her own property.

Adultery seems to have been punished by a fine, not by death or physical punishment, and the fine depended on the status of the persons concerned. No legal penalties are laid down for the woman involved (though no doubt she suffered some form of public ostracism). The amount of the fine was doubled if the adultery took place in the house of the woman's father, brother or husband, as showing that the woman was a willing partner, and had not been the victim of violence. The fine imposed on the adulterer was 100 staters if the adultery had taken place with a free woman in the house of a relative of hers; 50 if elsewhere; and only 10 if with the wife of an apetairos or 'serf'; if a slave was the offender the penalty was doubled if with a free woman, but only five staters if with another slave. The offender had five days to pay the fine, or the aggrieved party could 'deal with him as they wished'. There were regulations against deliberate entrapment: in the case of a free woman four additional witnesses had to swear that the adulterer had been taken in the act of adultery and not by deceit. The penalty for rape against a free man or woman was 100 staters, and double this if the offender were a slave. Rape by a free man against a serf only accrued a penalty of 5 drachmas (Willetts *The Law Code of Gortyn*: doc. 4.49*).

Dowries, marriage and heiresses in Athens

Plutarch describes legislation attributed to Solon, as archon in 594/3, which dealt with matters of inheritance and issues affecting the status of women. Until this time property could not be alienated from the family, but now Solon allowed men without heirs to make wills and choose their own legatees. He also protected the rights of heiresses, while he may also have had concern for those girls whose family did not wish or were unable to give them a dowry and who might therefore have been tempted to sell them into slavery. Now the only girls who could be so sold as slaves were those that had committed moicheia (fornication). Some of Plutarch's statements in this passage are inaccurate, in that Solon did not abolish dowries, but he perhaps limited the amount of property which a woman could take to her new home (like much of the legislation in Athens which was later attributed to Solon, these laws should probably not be uncritically accepted as belonging to the early sixth century).

This legislation may have been reflecting the concerns of Hesiod and other earlier poets about women's extravagance and unrestrained behaviour in public and, in the measures cited here, is shown as attempting to restrict their expenditure, behaviour in public and the size of their trousseaux, as well as their conduct at funerals. In terms of inheritance, illegitimate sons were no longer obliged to support their fathers. Plutarch himself comments that Solon's laws against adultery were incongruous: an adulterer could be killed if caught in the act, but rapists were only fined 100 drachmas, and 20 drachmas if the victim was an hetaira. The rationale for treating adultery more seriously than rape was supposedly that the woman's affections and loyalty had been seduced away from her household and hence was a far more serious crime (Plut. *Life of Solon* 20.2–23.2: doc. 4.50). This reveals more about Plutarch's inaccuracies as a recorder of Solonian legislation than it does about the legislation itself, if Solon did indeed legislate on social issues. In the classical period Solon was seen as democratising all kinds of Athenian institutions, and one reason put forward for his supposed underwriting the costs of prostitution was that this helped to keep young men away from adulterous affairs with citizen women (Philem. *F* 3: doc. 4.99).

While the giving of a dowry to a daughter, sister or ward so that she could marry was not compulsory in Athens, it was the norm and it appears that fathers found it hard to find their daughters a husband unless a dowry was offered. Several states granted dowries to orphaned daughters of state military heroes and an inscription from Thasos made provision for the children of those who have died in war: boys received a full set of armour worth not less than 3 minas, and the girls a dowry when they turned 14 years of age (Pouilloux (1954) 371, no. 141: doc. 4.58). In Athens the dowry was the girl's share of the family inheritance, and she received this on her marriage, not on her father's death, at which point the land and other remaining property was divided equally between any sons (there was no concept of primogeniture or preferential treatment for the eldest son).

A dowry was not only a way of attracting a suitable husband but provided the new bride with a fund which was secured to her for her protection, and generally consisted of money or valuables, which could include slaves. Wives had no role in handling their own dowry; the money was invested by the husband on her behalf and he was responsible for spending the income. However, it gave the father or girl's male relatives an interest in the marriage, as the dowry had to be returned on divorce and the wife's family could threaten the husband with a potential separation if they were dissatisfied at his behaviour in any way: the dowry also had to be returned to the wife's family if she died childless. Hipparete, Alkibiades' wife, went to live with her brother Kallias, because of her husband's shameful conduct at home with both men and women, but when she attempted to go before the archon to register a divorce, Alkibiades had her carried off, presumably because it would have been extremely inconvenient to repay her 20 talent dowry (120,000 drachmas), 'greater than any other Greek's' ([Andoc.] 4 *Against Alkibiades* 13–15: doc. 4.55). Hence husbands like Alkibiades might think twice before divorcing a wife for a trivial reason, and the threat of a divorce initiated by the father- or brother-in-law might modify a man's behaviour to his wife. As well as using the interest, it was of course also possible for husbands to draw on the capital of the dowry, but the fact that this would have to be repaid should a divorce eventuate must have been a disincentive. If a husband under such circumstances was unable to repay the dowry, he had to pay interest on the sum at the rate of 18 per cent until it was repaid (interest was normally 12 per cent per annum), or be brought to court. Should there be children the husband, at the death of his wife, managed the dowry until his sons were of age to inherit: daughters, however, do not seem to have received a share of their mother's dowry.

Daughters were of course a financial burden to the family, in as much as parents had to go to the expense of providing them with dowries in order to ensure that they could be married. There was, after all, no future for a girl if she remained unmarried (Ar. *Lysistrata* 592–7: doc. 4.66). Through the dowry system girls took money and property out of their families into the family of their husbands and were a drain on their family's estate. It is thus not surprising that girl babies, rather than boys, were at times exposed by their parents. The fact that the birth of a boy was announced by placing an olive crown on the door of the house and a tuft of wool was displayed for a girl (signifying her primary occupation) denotes the difference in the way the two sexes were viewed. The extent to which infanticide was practised in classical Athens is still debated, but there must have been some poorer families who abandoned daughters because of the expense involved in their upbringing. Many of these girls may have been rescued and brought up as slaves or prostitutes, although the legislation attributed to Solon had ensured that unmarried girls could not actually be sold into slavery unless they had committed sexual misconduct. Nevertheless, a study of the inscriptional evidence reveals that daughters could be an integral and much-loved part of a family: epitaphs from all over Greece show that young daughters who had survived the critical first few days of high mortality risk after which they were accepted into the family could be truly mourned by their parents (Fig. 4.11).

The status of women in Athens, as elsewhere in Greece, was to a great degree connected with the preservation of property within the oikos, or household unit, which consisted of family, property and slaves. Complex legislation was involved in ensuring that land and property remained within the family rather than going to outsiders. When citizens died without sons, estates could be left in the possession of epikleroi (singular: epikleros), that is heiresses, daughters who had no brother. The term literally means 'with the estate (kleros)' and the legislation was put in place to ensure that the girl and the estate could not be separated, even though it was not in fact actually under her control. When this situation occurred the nearest male relative had the chance to marry the heiress and claim the estate, to keep it in the family. This practice was not confined to Athens and some of the most detailed regulations in fact are found in the Gortyn law code from Crete. Alternatively the father could betroth his daughter in his will, with the marriage to take place after his death, or adopt a son who then had to be married to the heiress, so that he had in effect to take the girl and the estate together. The heiress's husband was therefore also her adopted brother. Although Solon was credited with having passed legislation allowing Athenians without children to make wills and dispose of their property as they wished instead of it returning to the wider family group, in practice

Figure 4.6 A polychromatic ('many coloured') wooden plaque, 15 cm high and 30 cm in length, discovered along with three others in a cave near the village of Pitsa, Corinth, dating to 540–520 BC. A pregnant woman draped in a blue garment and carrying a sprig of vegetation stands on the very far left. In front of her are other women with ears of grain. Two small boys play musical instruments, while a third brings a sheep to the altar for sacrifice. A woman at the altar carries a basket on her head and pours a libation onto the altar. All their heads are wreathed. A sacrifice is about to take place to the nymphs of the cave for the safe delivery of the pregnant woman's child. National Archaeological Museum inv. No. 16464, Athens. © Hellenic Ministry of Culture and Tourism / Archaeological Receipts Fund.

childless families would generally adopt an heir to ensure the continuation of the family line and property as well as the performance of the customary rites at the family's tombs. This new heir would in such cases renounce any claims to the inheritance of his original family and, if there was a daughter, the newly adopted son married her and their children inherited their grandfather's estate.

If a man without children died intestate (without a will) in Athens, the estate passed first to his brothers and their descendants, then to his sisters and their descendants; next to his paternal uncles and their descendants; and then to his paternal aunts and their descendants. After this inheritance went in the same way on his mother's side of the family. A woman who inherited property in this way could not alienate it and it would have been controlled by her 'kyrios', to be handed down to her children. If an heiress had no other provision for her marriage made for her in her father's will, she too married a relative in the same order as for inheritance where a man died childless, starting with her father's brothers. If the uncle (or other paternal relation) were already married, he could choose to divorce his current spouse, of course returning her dowry with her, to take over the heiress and her estate. If this paternal relation, however, wished to stay married to his current wife, the heiress and estate was then offered to the next nearest paternal relation and, if she were in the class of thetes (the lowest property class in Athens), the next of kin had to give her a dowry in accordance with his class, in addition to her own property: for one of the pentakosiomedimoi, the wealthiest class in Athens, this was 500 drachmas. The archon was specifically responsible for orphans and heiresses and families in danger of dying out, and for the protection of pregnant widows, and was charged to ensure that all these were protected and treated according to law (Dem. 43 *Against Makartatos* 51: doc. 4.51).

The necessity of an heiress marrying her nearest male relative (such as her father's brother) could lead to the dissolution of an existing marriage, since a claimant could choose to divorce his existing wife and marry his wealthy relative. If the heiress was already married and she was without children her marriage could be dissolved and she would have no choice but to marry her nearest relative. It is not quite clear whether this would also apply if she had already borne a son or sons, but it would seem probable that, to prevent this forcible divorce and remarriage, she would need to have two sons, one to inherit his father's estate and the other to inherit the maternal grandfather's, thus ensuring the continuation of both of the individual households. A case in point might be that of Perikles, whose first wife seems to have been an epikleros who already had a son, Kallias the wealthy, by her first husband Hipponikos, but married Perikles nevertheless, perhaps unwillingly. Certainly Perikles' marriage was not a happy one and when he and his wife could no longer live together, Perikles, with her consent, married her to another man and set up house for himself with Aspasia (Plut. *Life of Perikles* 24.2–9: doc. 4.29). Another case in point is described by Demosthenes: Euxitheos' mother had originally been married to Protomachos, by whom she had a daughter. When Protomachos, who was a poor man, inherited an heiress and her estate he wanted to accept this opportunity and therefore felt obliged to marry his wife to someone else. Accordingly he persuaded a friend of his, Thoukritos, to take her. The bride was formally given in marriage by her brother Timokrates of Melite, in the presence of family members and other witnesses. Demosthenes does not explicitly say that the wife's consent was asked for this transfer of her affections, but it does appear as if there was some obligation on the part of the current husband to ensure that she would find an alternative spouse when he married the heiress, and it is perhaps significant that she took her daughter with her into this second marriage (Dem. 57 *Against Euboulides* 40–2: doc. 5.63).

The motive behind the legislation regarding epikleroi was to ensure that the property remained within the family group. The property was not possessed by the new husband, and as with a dowry he administered it until their sons came of age and inherited it. The system was designed so that the children of such a marriage would inherit their grandfather's estate. It could of course make family relationships quite complex: a speech of Lysias concerns an action being brought by a widow against Diogeiton, who was the guardian of her sons' estate as well as being her father and her husband's brother (her uncle). In a group of family and friends she asked Diogeiton how he could have the heart to think it right to treat the children in such a way: 'You are their father's brother, and my father, and their uncle and grandfather . . .' In this particular case the mother accuses her father of embezzlement and produces records to show exactly what her husband had left, suggesting that some women had a strong interest in business matters:

> She convicted him of having recovered seven talents and 4,000 drachmas from bottomry loans and produced the records of these; for in the removal, when he was moving from Kollytos to the house of Phaidros, her sons came upon the register which had been mislaid and brought it to her. And she proved that he had recovered 100 minas which had been lent at interest on a mortgage on land, and another 2,000 drachmas and some very valuable furniture.
>
> (Lys. 32 *Against Diogeiton* 11–15: doc. 4.53)

Another widow is presented by Antiphon, the first orator who composed speeches for other people to deliver in court, as being a murderous wife who persuaded a slave-concubine to poison both the concubine's partner and the wife's husband on the pretext of giving them both a love potion. Antiphon compares this supposed murderess and husband-slayer to Clytemnestra. The motives for the murder are not made clear, but the prosecution is conducted by the son of the deceased (his son by his first wife), while she is defended by her own children from this second marriage implying that there was a conflict within the family. It is perhaps seen to be significant that the wife made a friend of this slave-concubine, who lived in the upper storey of their house, and tricked her into delivering the poison (Antiph. 1 *Prosecution of the Stepmother* 14–20: doc. 4.52).

Adultery

The term moicheia (fornication or adultery) did not only mean having sex with the wife of another citizen. It was also 'moicheia' if you had sex with a man's daughter, unmarried sister or concubine (or indeed his widowed mother). Such seduction of the female members of a family reflected seriously on a man's status and honour. Solon in the early sixth century is credited with introducing legislation permitting an adulterer to be killed if caught in the act; alternatively he could be fined or undergo public humiliation called by Aristophanes the 'radish treatment' or sodomy by radish (this may be an Aristophanic joke about some of the possible forms of public humiliation of an adulterer). The concern was not with the 'sin' of the wife, but that a child which did not belong to the family might usurp rights or property within in. A double sexual standard existed for men and women, for husbands had a number of alternatives to their wives, such as prostitutes, hetairai, slaves or concubines (pallakai), who might even be part of the household. In contrast, sexual misconduct and adultery were inexcusable on the part of a citizen woman, and it was because the chastity of womenfolk was so important an issue that legally an adulterer could be prosecuted, imprisoned or killed.

Figure 4.7 A mother sits on her chair, while her child reaches out its arms to her. It is sitting in the ancient Greek equivalent of a 'highchair', with holes for its legs to dangle through. The scene is shown on an Athenian red-figure stemless kylix cup, attributed to the workshop of the Sotades Painter, and dates to about 460 BC. Musées royaux d'art et d'histoire A 890, Brussels. Drawing by J. Etherington.

The right of a wronged husband to kill an adulterer caught in the act appears to have been the exception to Drakon's law concerning culpable homicide and was reiterated in Solon's legislation; concubines and other women of the family were included in this category as well as wives. But while the wronged husband was allowed to kill the adulterer in the presence of witnesses if he caught him in the act, this could rebound on the husband as the victim's kin might then claim that he had been lured there deliberately in order to be murdered and then prosecute the husband for homicide, as in the case of Eratosthenes, where Euphiletos was charged with the deliberate entrapment and murder of Eratosthenes on the pretext of catching him in adultery with his wife (Lys. 1 *On the Murder of Eratosthenes* 6–10: doc. 4.54, cf. doc. 4.49). Husbands were compelled to divorce adulterous wives, on pain of losing their citizen rights: such wives, having engaged in adultery already, could not be trusted to behave appropriately for the future or to produce citizen children. The wife was only punished by divorce, return in disgrace to her own family, and a form of social ostracism. As someone who had transgressed normative behaviour she was seen as potentially polluting religious rites; if found attending them, she could be made to suffer any penalty whatsoever, 'short of death' by any Athenian citizen ([Dem.] 59 *Against Neaira* 87: doc. 4.57).

Perikles' citizenship law

Perikles' law of 451/0 restricting citizenship to those children born of two Athenian parents meant that mothers as well as fathers transmitted citizenship to their sons and Athenians therefore had to be able to prove their legitimacy in order to have citizen rights: it also made adultery on the part of an Athenian wife the concern of the state, as well as of the family, as if she were to have an affair with a non-citizen the citizen body as a whole would have an 'alien' in its midst. Perikles' concern may have been not so much related to the availability of husbands for citizen girls as an attempt to restrict the citizen body so that benefits such as pay for public duties should only be available to those who were truly citizens ([Arist.] *Athenaion Politeia* 26.4: doc. 1.36). This made adultery a public concern, and, even if an adulterer were not prosecuted by the husband involved, a public action (in the form of a graphe moicheias, an indictment for adultery) could be brought against him by any citizen. From this point, only Athenians were permitted to intermarry, and any foreigner who cohabited with an Athenian woman as her husband was sold into slavery and his property confiscated: anyone could bring the charge and if successful would receive one-third of the property. An Athenian who married a foreign woman was fined 1000 drachmas, and anyone who fraudulently gave a foreign woman in marriage as if she were an Athenian woman lost his citizen rights and his property was confiscated, with the successful prosecutor again receiving a third. This right of intermarriage was closely guarded in Athens and only the Plataeans, after the destruction of their city by Sparta in 427, were admitted to this privilege in recognition of their help against the Persians at Marathon ([Dem.] 59 *Against Neaira* 16, 52, 104: doc. 4.56)

Concubines

Concubines (pallakai) were women who lived with citizens without having gone through a formal marriage process. Many of these would have been slaves or metics, but in cases of poverty, for example when the family might have been unable to provide a dowry for a girl, she might have been handed over as a sort of 'secondary wife'. They were protected by being under their partner's guardianship, with a formal agreement generally being made between the new partner and the woman's family. If a concubine indulged in illicit sexual activity this was classed as adultery (moicheia) just as if she were a wife, sister or daughter of the family. While concubines could become part of the existing household, it was more normal for them to have a separate establishment. Children from such relationships could not inherit their father's estate and did not possess citizen rights, although in the crisis of the Peloponnesian War it appears that the children of citizens by concubines were granted citizenship because of manpower losses. Some concubines were slaves, such as the concubine of Philoneos, who poisoned him in the belief that she was giving him a love-potion, doing so because he was obviously tired of her and intended to put her in a brothel, for the benefit of the wages he would take from her clients. (Antiph. 1 *Prosecution of the Stepmother* 14–20: doc. 4.52). She is obviously a slave, because she was tortured to extract her evidence in court before being executed, but concubines could also be free non-citizen women, such as Aspasia, whose children would be free but not, of course, Athenian citizens.

The working woman at home and abroad

Much has been written about the 'seclusion' of Athenian women. Naturally a citizen woman's duties and responsibilities in the household tended to keep her at home, and it was obviously an 'ideal', particularly one promoted in the lawcourts, that a family be sufficiently economically viable for the wife to be able to stay at home and not work outside the household (Fig. 5.2). Women played an extremely important part in the household economy: they were responsible not only for the care of the children and management of the slaves, but for overseeing all the production of clothes, blankets and materials which contributed very significantly to the household's economy as a whole. In the *Odyssey*, the importance of women's duties in respect to the organisation and storing of supplies is highlighted when Odysseus' son Telemachos intends to travel to Pylos and Sparta in search of news of his father. The treasure chamber in the palace at Ithaka contains not only gold and bronze but chests of clothes too, as well as large jars (pithoi) of wine and olive oil, and the housekeeper Eurikleia, not a slave but a respected woman whose father and grandfather are named, provides him with wine and barley for his journey (Hom. *Odyssey* 2.337–47: doc. 4.59). While very far from the economy of the Mycenaean palace, this would reflect the reality in archaic Greek aristocratic or monarchical households, and supervision of the storeroom and slaves, as part of household duties, would have remained one of the primary responsibilities of wives and housekeepers in the archaic and classical periods.

Figure 4.8 A woman at work: she holds up a distaff in her left hand, and pulls a thread of wool from it, holding it in her right hand between her thumb and finger. Despite working, she is magnificently dressed: she wears a long, decorated chiton, as well as bracelets and earrings. Her hair is bound into a ball and secured with a ribbon. On the right there is an inscription which reads, 'The beautiful girl'. A white-ground oinochoe, with line drawing in red, dating to about 490–470 BC, attributed to the Brygos Painter; it stands at 21.5 cm high. British Museum D13, London. Drawing by J. Etherington.

153

Women's economic role in the home

The care of storerooms was equally important in the classical Greece of Socrates' time. Ischomachos outlines his new wife's duties and expects her to be fully occupied during the daytime in directing the slaves to their inside and outside occupations, storing and distributing items, ensuring that all stores of food are handled properly to remain edible and that there is sufficient clothing for everyone, looking after sick slaves, teaching the slaves how to weave and weaving herself, supervising the slaves in the kitchen, overseeing the housekeeper when she hands out stores, making sure everything is in its right place, and helping to mix and knead in the kitchen and shake and fold clothes and bedding: more than enough to keep her busy (Xen. *Oeconomicus* 7.35–7, 10.10–13: doc. 4.63; Fig. 4.8). Women are often shown on vases supervising slaves in their textile making, including preparing the fleeces, spinning the thread, and weaving cloth on the loom, and so preparing all the woollen goods, including clothes, blankets and hangings, which were made in the household. Ischomachos presents marriage to this unnamed bride as an economic partnership, with the primary duty of both husband and wife within this partnership 'so to act that their possessions are in the best state possible and that as much as possible be added to them by fair and honourable means'. Nothing could better demonstrate the way that the oikos (including of course any estates) was seen as an economic unit.

Naturally, as a woman's major responsibilities lay in the house, conventionally she was expected to stay indoors, but this was not so much for the purposes of 'seclusion' as because the home was the focus of all her duties and responsibilities. Lysias gives the same message in his speech on behalf of Euphiletos, who tells the jurors that his attitude towards his wife changed markedly after they had been married for a while. At first he kept a close, if discreet, eye on her, but once she had a child he trusted her entirely with the running of the household 'and handed over to her all my possessions, believing that this was the greatest sign of marital intimacy' (Lys. 1 *On the Murder of Eratosthenes* 6–10: doc. 4.54). At this point she was the 'best of wives', which the speaker goes on to explain as meaning a clever, economical housewife, precise in her management of everything. A housewife from any era will sympathise with Kalonike who explains to Lysistrata that the reason that the citizen women of Athens are late in attending her summons to discuss their sex-strike is because of their duties at home: 'It's difficult for women to get out of the house. For one will be running around for her husband, another waking up a slave, or with the baby, putting it to bed, or washing it, or feeding it' (Ar. *Lysistrata* 13–19: doc. 4.62; Fig. 4.7).

When Aristarchos lost his property and many of his male relations as a result of the Peloponnesian War he complained to Socrates that he was unable to maintain all the female relatives who had ended up as his responsibility. Socrates enquired whether they were able to cook and make clothing. When Aristarchos assured him that they could, Socrates advised him to put them to work weaving, citing various slave-run businesses of the same type that were making great profits from baking and the manufacture of clothes such as cloaks and tunics. Persuaded by this argument, Aristarchos was then prepared to borrow a little capital to get this scheme underway, as it appeared to have some chance of working, and he used it to buy wool. The success of the scheme was remarkable, with his female relatives happily working through their midday meal, and by their efforts being able to pay for their keep, and his as well. They looked on him as a guardian and all got on well together because they were busily occupied. The only downside, according to Aristarchos, was that they now were critical of him as he was the only one not working for a living (Xen. *Memorabilia* 2.7.6–12: doc.

Figure 4.9 A young boy playing around – balancing on a stool – is about to be joined by a good-sized and enthusiastic dog. As in all societies, pets were an important part of a Greek child's playtime experiences. This playful scene is on a small Athenian red-figure oenochoe (jug) dating to about 425 BC. Louvre, Paris. Drawing by J. Etherington.

4.64). Women's economic contribution to the household in all Greek cities, except Sparta, was clearly centred in the making of all clothes and blankets, supervision of slaves, childcare, cooking, and care of stores and supplies, which was the equivalent of the man's income from outside the household. The role of women in manufacturing textiles was seen as so intrinsic that even goddesses in the Homeric poems are shown weaving, while Penelope, though a queen, spends much of her time in this occupation in the *Odyssey*, and even Helen of Troy back at home in Sparta with Menelaos, after her Trojan adventure, spends her time after dinner in spinning wool (Hom. *Odyssey* 4.120–35).

Women as retail salespersons

Such duties obviously could only be effected by the wife's staying in the home. But as well as these tasks indoors, there are examples of not only metic but citizen women undertaking a regular job in the market. These women would have been from the poorer classes in the community (a very small proportion of Athenians were actually wealthy), when one income was not enough, or where a woman was left widowed, such as the garland seller in Aristophanes'

155

Thesmophoriazousai, first produced in 411 (doc. 4.60): 'My husband died in Cyprus, leaving me with five little children, and it's with difficulty that I've fed them by making garlands in the myrtle-wreath market.' This lady complains that she has managed to date to scrape a living, but now that Euripides has persuaded everyone that the gods do not exist, she is selling only half the wreaths she had previously: wreaths were worn at sacrifices and for libations at symposia. That this complaint need not be taken too seriously is shown by the fact that she has to hurry off to the agora to plait twenty wreaths specially ordered for that day. No stigma is attached to such an occupation, although Euripides is often attacked by Aristophanes because of the 'fact' that his mother used to sell vegetables (this may be an Aristophanic distortion of facts as Euripides' mother was apparently well off, though there is no inherent improbability in the assumption that a citizen woman could sell vegetables). In the *Wasps*, Aristophanes also portrays a citizen bread-seller named Myrtia. When Philokleon knocks over her wares, she calls bystanders to help and summons him before the agoranomoi (market-officials): she's well aware of the value of what she is selling – Philokleon has spoiled 10 obols' worth of loaves and four more loaves (perhaps a day's worth of merchandise) – and proudly proclaims her citizenship: 'I'm Myrtia, daughter of Ankylion and Sostrate!' (*Wasps* 1388–98).

A speech of Demosthenes defends Euxitheos, the son of a seller of ribbons. His deme Halimous has convicted him of being a metic rather than a citizen, partly on the grounds that his mother works in the market, and Euxitheos cites a law stating that anyone who uses against any citizen, male or female, the fact that he or she works in the market can be sued for slander. He admits that his mother sells ribbons (tainiai) in the market and that she is well known for this but states that this has no relevance whatsoever in regard to her status as a citizen or not. In fact, if she were employed in a retail trade as a metic, she would be on the register of those paying the metic tax. Euxitheos also raises the question of another occupation for which women were prominently suited, that of wet-nurse. His mother had been in difficulties with her husband on campaign and two children to raise and so she hired herself out as nurse to Kleinias, son of Kleidikos. From the context it is clear that wet-nurses would normally have been slaves, but Euxitheos states that he could name many other citizen women engaged in the same occupation in times of warfare (Dem. 57 *Against Euboulides* 40–2: doc. 5.63).

When in the *Lysistrata* the acropolis, which the women have seized, is attacked, Lysistrata summons her supporters as, 'You seed-pulse-and-vegetable-market-sellers, you garlic-inn-keeping-bread-sellers! (Ar. *Lysistrata* 456–8: doc. 4.62). These are wives of Athenian citizens, not metics, the only ones with the right to vote in the assembly to stop the war. Lysistrata is seeing these – women working in retail trades in the market – as the backbone of her women citizen troops against male intransigence and war-mongering.

Women's freedom of movement

Some women of course were able to stay at home and did not need to go out to work. However, despite the convention that well-off women did not have to leave their homes, it is quite clear that they did leave the house to visit friends and borrow household items, went regularly to the fountain houses (where Athenian vases often depict them as gossiping and interacting with each other), took part in festivals, and were permitted to attend funerals and weddings. In fact, not only did women attend family funerals, they played a central role in the preparation of the corpse, the washing, anointing and clothing of the deceased, and the mourning and lamentation. It is significant that it was supposedly at Euphiletos' mother's funeral that his wife was seen by Eratosthenes (who allegedly proceeded to seduce her), implying that a funeral was one of the occasions on which a women could be seen by men outside her family. In addition women could of course attend religious festivals, such as the three-day Thesmophoria in October, which was held on the Pnyx and which men were not permitted to attend. Older women also acted as midwives, and elderly relatives and neighbours would be called on to assist younger women in labour. Doubtless there was a great difference of attitude towards a new adolescent bride and an experienced helpmate of long-standing, and greater latitude of behaviour was allowed to older women. On the other hand Euphiletos' wife, who is certainly still young, can go out at night to borrow from a neighbour:

> When I asked why the doors had banged in the night, she told me that the lamp by the baby had gone out, so she had got a light from the neighbours. I made no comment and supposed her story to be true.
>
> (Lys. 1 *On the Murder of Eratosthenes* 14)

Figure 4.10 An Athenian red-figure lekythos (jar for holding oil) dating to about 420–410 BC which shows an imaginery scene from the festival of Adonis (doc. 3.63). Here the goddess Aphrodite herself is handed a 'garden of Adonis' by a winged Eros ('Love'). The goddess is on the lower rungs of a ladder, preparing to take the garden onto a flat houseroof. Here the women will dance and sing in honour of Adonis, killed in the prime of his manhood by a wild boar, and mourned for ever after by the goddess; the women will celebrate the love of men and women. Karlsruhe Badisches Landesmuseum 278, Karlsruhe. Drawing by J. Etherington.

Significantly, the wife had lived in the upper storey of the house prior to the birth of the baby, but at this point the men's and women's quarters were swapped round, 'so that when she had to bath him she did not run the risk of going down the stairs, I used to live upstairs, and the women down below'. In other words, the young mother now had free access to the street (Lys. 1 *On the Murder of Eratosthenes* 9: doc. 4.54). And women in the plays of Aristophanes certainly leave their homes to visit neighbours, even if they were not supposed to. Furthermore, borrowing from the neighbours seems to have been a commonplace: Theophrastos' 'penny-pincher' forbids his wife to lend 'salt, or a lampwick, or cumin, or oregano, or barley, or garlands, or cakes for sacrifice', arguing that these all add up during the course of the year (Theophr. *Characters* 10: doc. 1.34) and even if women were not supposed to leave their homes it is clear from Aristophanes' plays that 'just popping down the street to visit a neighbour' was not meant to count. Achilles' shield in the *Iliad* even depicts women watching a wedding from the doors of their houses, and defending a city from its walls (*Iliad* 18.495–6, 514–15).

There were also priestesses in Athens who held positions of great social and religious importance, involving regular public duties, such as the priestesses of Athena Polias and Athena Nike. Myrrhine, priestess of Athena Nike, was chosen by lot from Athenian citizen women and served for life: inscriptions authorise her annual payment and perquisites (50 drachmas and the legs and hides from public sacrifices: *IG* I³ 35, 36: docs 3.65–6), and she apparently had a prominent seat in the theatre of Dionysos. The priestess of Athena Polias was arguably one of the most important women in the city. The position was always held by a member of the Eteoboutadai clan, thought to be descendants of the original kings of Athens. The position was held for life (one priestess, Lysimache, served for 64 years) and she officiated at the Great Panathenaia, no doubt presenting to the goddess the peplos woven by the girls of Athens and officiating at the sacrifices. She also had charge of the arrhephoroi and the procession for the Skira festival, and was honoured by special seating at the theatre.

Women in drama

Aristophanes in his comedies frequently reverses the gender roles of married couples: the uncouth peasant Strepsiades in the *Clouds* is married to an aristocratic woman who has ruined him and spoiled their son. The audience is meant to be tickled by the contrast between the wife's 'perfume and saffron and sexy kisses, expense and gluttony and Aphrodite Genetyllis' and Strepsiades' odour of 'unfermented wine, dried figs, wool and profit' and he thoroughly regrets the days when he was able to lie around unwashed, at ease among his bees, sheep and pressed olives (Ar. *Clouds* 39–55, 60–74: doc. 4.65). The fact that the wife is described as niece of Megakles, son of Megakles, suggests a relationship to the Alkmeonid clan, and their son Pheidippides has preferred her tastes of chariot racing and high-born family connections to Strepsiades' hopes of his enjoying life with his goats and leather jerkin. While Aristophanes exaggerates the situation beyond rationality, women of high birth with large dowries would have had considerable influence over their sons (who would inherit from them), if not over their husbands, and Strepsiades is unmistakably henpecked and ignored by both wife and son, both of whom are shown as impoverishing him.

Lysistrata, in the play of that name, who unites the women of Greece into forcing their menfolk to make peace by taking over the acropolis and treasury, as well as going on sex-strike until the men agree, describes her husband's reaction when she tries to talk to him about the war and decisions made in the assembly: 'And he'd glare at me and say that, if I didn't weave my web, I'd really have a headache to complain about: "For war should be men's concern!"'

(Ar. *Lysistrata* 507–20, 565–97: doc. 4.66). No doubt this was the conventional response when women attempted to take an interest in politics. Nevertheless, when Lysistrata speaks about the current state of affairs in Athens, she is meant to be taken seriously even though she is a woman, and she clearly articulates that war has an impact on women just as on men. Women contribute to the war effort in sending off their sons as hoplites to die in battle, which even the magistrate who is arguing with her admits is a catastrophe, while young girls are doomed to spinsterhood because of the number of casualties in the war. Her analogy of government to women's work of washing, carding and weaving fleeces is an entertaining fantasy, but the advice on how to deal with pressure-groups aiming for office, maintain the goodwill of metics, and capitalise on the advantages of colonies for the good of the democracy as a whole is sensible and realistic.

There is at present no consensus on whether women attended the theatrical performances at Athens, and it is impossible to be sure whether citizen women were present or how they would have reacted to characters such as Lysistrata on stage. Aristophanes' joke in the *Birds*, that if you had wings you could quickly fly out of the theatre for an assignation with one of the counsellors' wives and then get back again before the end of the performance, suggests that many of citizen women would have stayed at home, but it would be highly unlikely that hetairai and others were prevented from attending and enjoying the entertainment (Ar. *Birds* 785–96: doc. 4.67).

Heroines in Greek tragedy

Many tragedies question traditional gender roles and show women taking part in the masculine arena outside the home. One such is Clytemnestra, long considered one of the most criminal of women, and in the *Odyssey* (24.200) Agamemnon in speaking to Odysseus from the underworld has the chance to express his opinion of his wife: there is 'nothing more deadly or more vile than her,' he states and 'a song of loathing will be hers among men, to make evil the reputation of womankind'. But taking a viewpoint other than that of the murdered Agamemnon, there is something that can be said from Clytemnestra's point of view. In Aeschylus' play *Agamemnon*, part of the *Oresteia* trilogy performed in 458, Clytemnestra, infuriated by the sacrifice of her daughter Iphigeneia to gain favourable winds for the fleet to sail to Troy (Clytemnestra had gone there believing that Iphigeneia had been summoned to Aulis to marry Achilles), had ruled during the ten years of Agamemnon's absence at Troy, and taken his cousin Aegisthos as her lover. Finally she murdered Agamemnon along with his concubine Cassandra on his return. On his arrival, she enticed him to display 'hybris' (inappropriate arrogance) by walking into the house over purple carpets, and while in the bath she threw over him a net-like garment she had specifically woven for the purpose and killed him, according to tradition with an axe, but apparently in the *Agamemnon* with a sword. While in many ways a 'Lady Macbeth' figure, she feels that she has good reason for her actions and her speech to the chorus describes the exultation with which she committed the deed, in language rich in the symbolism of fertility: his murder has given her new life and her third and final stroke is specifically made to Zeus, 'in thanks for prayers accomplished'. As she says, 'this man filled a mixing-bowl of evil curses, which he has returned and drained himself', which he had thoroughly deserved through his killing of her daughter over which she has brooded for ten years. She even speaks of him as a sacrifice to the gods, over which she could pour libation. That her husband and her son Orestes, who is to kill her in a further act of revenge, think differently highlights the gendered viewpoint, which the Athenians may not have agreed with, but which they could not help but respect (Aesch. *Agamemnon* 1377–98: doc. 4.68).

Antigone

Antigone, in Sophocles' play performed perhaps in 442, rebels against the decree of her uncle Kreon, ruler of Thebes, who has proclaimed that her brother Polyneikes, who has attempted to capture Thebes, not be given funerary rites because he has been a traitor. Her father Oedipus had been married to his own mother Iocasta, after having accidently killed his own father without knowing his identity. Iocasta committed suicide on discovering the relationship and Oedipus blinded himself, after which Antigone's two brothers then killed each other fighting over the kingship of Thebes. Even though Polyneikes had technically been the aggressor against the city, Antigone demands the right to perform the female relative's traditional role as mourner on his behalf, thus fulfilling divine laws by giving him proper burial, and in so doing challenges the authority of Kreon as king who has forbidden this. Having performed the correct rites (Soph. *Antigone* 426–31: doc. 3.54), she has been captured and justifies her actions to Kreon in a speech declaring that essentially he is a fool and that there are laws above his: 'I did not consider that your proclamations possessed/such power that you a mortal could override the unwritten and immutable observances of the gods' (Soph. *Antigone* 441–70: doc. 4.69). The family tragedy rolls to a conclusion: Antigone is entombed in a cave. The seer Teiresias sees the wrath of heaven in the omens (Soph. *Antigone* 998–1011: doc. 3.18), but by the time Kreon has her released she has hanged herself; as a consequence of this Kreon's son Haimon, her betrothed, commits suicide as does Kreon's wife Eurydike. Antigone speaks in a way that was presumably unthinkable for a parthenos at Athens, challenging the male hierarchy and the male assumptions regarding power, but in her assertion of divine values she speaks for humankind, and it is not unlikely that an Athenian girl, even if she could not have made this speech, might have taken action to ensure that a brother received proper funerary rites (like Gnatho's sister: doc. 4.41), grieved to think that her 'mother's son should remain a corpse unburied'.

Medea

In the *Medea*, performed in 431, Euripides presents the Greek Jason and the barbarian Medea in conflict over the nature of marriage: having accompanied him from Colchis and ensured him the throne of Iolkos by having his uncle killed, she takes vengeance on Jason for his decision to remarry 'for their sons' advantage' by killing these same sons, as well as Jason's new bride and the bride's father, the king of Corinth. She bewails the sufferings of women in marriage, and their lack of choice and freewill, and lists all the benefits Jason had derived from her and his oaths of fidelity to her, which he has now broken. Medea's main complaint is that even though she has young children she has been cast aside for a new wife, Glauke, princess of Corinth: Medea accepts that had she been childless Jason would have had more reason to renounce her (Eur. *Medea* 465–95: doc. 4.70). Medea clearly (in Athenian terms) has the status of a metic, not a citizen: she has no rights, and no family to defend her. Unlike Clytemnestra, who has a masculine role and status, though she is not without sexuality, Medea insists on her womanhood, and complains about its disadvantages; at one point in the play, where she speaks to the women of Corinth of women's problems, she mentions the lack of choice in marriage, the advantages a man has in an unhappy relationship, and the pain and danger of childbirth: 'I would rather stand three times by my shield than once give birth!' (*Medea* 250–1).

Figure 4.11 The grave stele of a young girl, carrying her favourite pet dove in her left hand, and clasping her chiton in her right. Dating to c. 440 BC, it is carved from Paros marble, and the sculptor evokes brilliantly the youth and innocence of the deceased girl (see docs 4.33–35). From Nea Kallikrateia in the Chalkidike. Archaeological Museum of Thessaloniki Photo © Hellenic Ministry of Culture and Tourism / Archaeological Receipts Fund.

Alcestis

A very different married couple are portrayed in the *Alcestis*, Euripides' earliest surviving work, a play named for its heroine who is notable for her love for her husband, Admetos, king of Pherai in Thessaly, who has been allowed by the Fates to postpone his death provided he can find someone willing to die in his place. No one, not even his elderly parents, is willing to die on his behalf except his wife, who shows the courage he lacks. After lengthy preparations and prayers, described by a maidservant, Alcestis dies after exacting a promise from her husband that he will not marry again. The palace is shortly afterwards disturbed by a visit from a riotous and eventually drunken Herakles, who is highly embarrassed when he realises what has just taken place and offers to confront Hades and reclaim Alcestis, which he succeeds in doing. There are both tragic and comic elements in the play, with the selflessness of Alcestis and her concern for her children (whom she does not want to leave fatherless) contrasted with the vacillation and lack of courage shown by Admetos for whom she dies, and Euripides presents her actions before her death as those of a heroic and noble wife, and a far stronger character than her cowardly husband (Eur. *Alcestis* 150–84, 189–98: doc. 4.71).

In a discussion of Greek tragedy, it is important to take every character and speech in context, and relate them to the overall message of the dramatist: after all not every speech in every play presents the real-life views of the playwright. It is certainly untenable to take speeches from plays and lines as spoken by certain characters and quote them out of context, assuming that they are the opinion of the dramatist, and not primarily that of the character within the dramatic conflict currently being portrayed. An example is the speech of Apollo from Aeschylus' play the *Eumenides* (the *Furies*). Apollo here is defending Orestes, trying to justify his murder of his mother Clytemnestra, by asserting that the mother is only the 'host' of the embryo, not the biological mother: 'The mother is not the true parent of the child/which is called hers. She is a nurse who tends the growth/of young seed planted by its true parent, the male' (*Eumenides* 657–9). But Apollo's argument which entirely fails to convince the jury of Athenian citizens is meant to be weak and untenable: Aeschylus has left it for Athena, not Apollo, to give the casting vote and resolve the conflict by giving the Eumenides a home on her acropolis in Athens. In the same way, when women in tragedy are told, or themselves say, that 'women's place is in the home', the point of the statement very much depends on the character who is making it and why it is made. Nevertheless, plays such as Sophocles' *Antigone* and *Electra*, and Euripides' *Alcestis*, *Electra* and *Medea* are certainly valuable evidence for attitudes towards women in fifth-century Athens, in particular in the context of the kind of conflicts in which dramatists chose to portray them and the ways in which these confrontations are, or are not, resolved.

Homosexuality and pederasty

The sexual relationships of males in the Greek world did not have to be confined to wives, or indeed to women, and no moral or ethical code was transgressed if men kept concubines, visited prostitutes, or engaged in pederastic relationships with boys, or indeed other males as long as the citizen was the active participant in the relationships. If not always the norm, it was not unusual in archaic and classical Greece for an adult male, usually in his twenties, the 'lover' or erastes, to form a relationship with a younger boy, the 'beloved' or eromenos, who would normally be aged between 12 and 18 years; though bearded eromenoi are occasionally shown on Attic vases, conventionally the eromenos should be beardless, with smooth cheeks. The gods themselves are shown as engaging in such relationships with mortals, the most famous example of which was Zeus' abduction of the young Trojan prince Ganymede from Mount Ida to be his cup-bearer (Thgn. 1345–8: doc. 4.74; Fig. 4.12).

Pederastic relationships

While pederastic relationships were part of the rites of passage for wealthy and aristocratic males in many states, these would normally have begun prior to marriage, with the erastes taking a boy as his beloved while in his twenties and then marrying at around the age of 30 years. While Aristotle in the *Politics* (1272a) comments that homosexual activities were introduced in Crete to keep down the birth-rate, and Plato mentions in his *Symposium* (192b) that some male lovers only married under family pressure, this would not have had a serious impact on marriage statistics or the birth-rate. Indeed as men did not marry in Athens until approximately the age of 30, many pederastic relationships may have mutated into friendship by the time the older partner married. In any case Greeks had little concept of homo/hetero-sexuality: the distinction was between being the active as opposed to the passive (woman, male prostitute) partner. In the case of a pederastic relationship the erastes was an older, citizen, male, the eromenos a younger boy, not yet of age to be a citizen. However, the boys grew up to be citizens (and active sexual partners) in their turn: women did not. And the fact that the erastes and beloved are shown standing and facing each other when depicted in sexual activities shows the difference in status between the 'boy', a future citizen, and a woman. Conventionally in Athens the couple engaged in 'intercrural copulation' between the thighs of the eromenos, and the couple are frequently depicted on Attic vases standing facing each other with the lover rubbing his erect penis between the youth's thighs, or touching his genitals and chin (Fig. 4.13).

Pederasty at Sparta

In Sparta pederasty was an important part of the education system, the agoge, and young boys were chosen by older lovers with whom they paired until the lover was married (Xen. *Const. Spart.*2.1–8: doc. 6.49). Institutionalised pederasty was central to the education and military training of Spartan citizens. In other societies it could be an important rite of passage for upper-class adolescent boys, and in Crete in particular (another Dorian society) it appears to have functioned as an initiation ritual into military life, where ritualised rape of an aristocratic eromenos by a worthy erastes was considered an honour. The youth's friends were warned beforehand, and the boy was abducted for a period of no more than two months which were spent hunting and feasting. The beloved was then given the prescribed presents of a suit of armour, an ox (for sacrifice to Zeus) and a drinking-cup as well as other gifts. According to Ephoros, for boys of good ancestry not to be abducted was a disgrace, and these 'parastathentes' were afterwards honoured by being given prestigious places in dances and races and distinctive clothing (Ephoros *F* 149: doc. 4.78). Such homoerotic relationships were fostered by the segregation into messes and barracks typical of Dorian societies such as Crete and Sparta, while the Sacred Band at Thebes, created around 379, was composed of 150 pairs of lovers, who stood by each other in battle, with the band wiped out to a man by Philip of Macedon at Chaironeia in 338, where he saw them after his victory 'all lying in their armour mingled with each other where they had faced and met his sarissas [the long Macedonian spears]', united in death as in life (Plut. *Life of Pelopidas* 18.1–4, 18.7, 19.3–4: doc. 14.17). Plutarch explains that the band until this point had been invincible since 'lovers and beloveds through shame stand firm to protect each other when in danger'.

Of all the sexual relationships in which men could engage that between men was considered the most spiritual, as between equals, and because of the possible educative aspect between the erastes and his younger companion. Plato's *Symposium* and *Phaedrus* deal with this topic, considering this the most superior form of love because of its association with the education of the beloved object. Pederasty was not only viewed without criticism, but Herodotos (1.135) regarded 'copulating with boys' as one of the good things of life that the Greeks had

Figure 4.12 Zeus abducts the young Ganymede, prince of Troy, and takes him to Mount Olympos where he becomes immortal and serves as Zeus' cup-bearer and object of sexual desire. Ganymede holds a rooster, a typical courtship gift of the older bearded male to the younger. Zeus holds a staff in one hand, symbol of his Olympian authority, and the boy in the other. He strides forth purposefully and dramatically prior to the act of rape. Traces of the original colouring remain. This life-size terracotta statue group was the acroterion of a building, as indicated by the triangle base it stands upon, which would have been the apex of a roof gable; it is probably of Corinthian workmanship and dates to about 470 BC. Olympia Museum T2, T2a, Tc 1049, Olympia. © Olympia Archaeological Museum, Hellenic Ministry of Culture and Tourism, 7th Ephorate of Prehistoric and Classical Antiquities & Archaeological Receipts Fund.

taught the Persians. Perhaps the most famous Athenian pederastic relationship was that of Harmodios and Aristogeiton, which resulted in the assassination of the tyrant Hipparchos in 514; the couple and their love-affair were idealised as an aristocratic role model in Athenian drinking-songs (docs 9.43–7). Indeed, Plato in the *Symposium* suggests that tyrants typically attempted to suppress homoeroticism because it gave rise to noble ideals that threatened their rule (Pl. *Symposium* 182c).

It has been noted that no relationship in the Homeric poems matches in depth that between Achilles and Patroklos in the *Iliad*, but there is no sign in the Homeric poem of the couple engaging in a homoerotic relationship, though later Greeks indeed assumed that they were lovers and there was debate about which was the lover and which the beloved. Aeschylus considers Achilles to have been the erastes and Patroklos his beloved, and a fragment of his lost play the *Myrmidons* records Achilles addressing Patroklos, who goes to fight and be killed on Achilles' behalf while he is sulking in his tent: 'And you felt no compunction for my holy reverence of your thighs, ungrateful for our many kisses' (Aesch. *Myrmidons* F135: doc. 4.72). Plato, however, later argues that Achilles and not Patroklos must have been the passive partner in the relationship, the eromenos, because he was the most beautiful of all the heroes of the Trojan War and still beardless, that is, relatively young (Pl. *Symposium* 180a), and this is supported by vase paintings where Patroklos, not Achilles, is shown as bearded.

Homoerotic courtship

The practice of homoeroticism, at least in Athens, appears to have developed during the seventh century, and scenes of homoerotic courtship appear on Attic black-figure vases from the early sixth century, while it was a particularly popular subject for vases in the second half of the sixth century. While it may have been a particular feature of the lifestyle of aristocratic youths, who could afford the necessary presents and had time to attend the gymnasia and palaistrai (wrestling-courts) where athletic nudity may have contributed to the homoerotic ambiance, the subject was still popular in art under the democracy and there was clearly no feeling that the subject was 'class-focused'. In the early sixth century Solon himself, in his poetry, celebrates homoeroticism in the lines: 'When he falls in love with a boy in the lovely flower of youth, desiring his thighs and sweet mouth', and from this period, if not before, homoeroticism was an important part of the social structure of the polis (Solon *Poem* 25: doc. 4.73). In Megara, too, in the sixth century, the poet Theognis addressed much of his poetry to his beloved Kyrnos, both celebrating his youth and beauty and advising him on how to become a good aristocrat. Many of these poems were sung at symposia, drinking parties, and this theme was a popular one, purporting to educate and socialise the young boys present who would have learnt to perform these songs themselves. Boys are compared favourably by Theognis to women: they show gratitude and fidelity, whereas a woman only loves the man who is present. There is no ambiguity about the nature of the relationship, and Theognis specifically contrasts the sort of exercise he will be engaging in with Kyrnos as opposed to the more public exercising which would be taking place at the gymnasium, the scene of many homoerotic encounters: 'Happy the lover who can exercise at home, sleeping all day long beside a beautiful youth!' Theognis can even envisage Kyrnos in his future, when he will no longer have 'smooth cheeks' and be attractive to Theognis, approaching as erastes another young boy to fill the role of eromenos, and hoping that he will find someone as responsive as Theognis has found Kyrnos (Thgn. 1319–68: doc. 4.74).

That such homoerotic expression was not primarily an idealised literary or artistic construct can be seen in epitaphs, inscriptions and graffiti which provide evidence for the reality of the phenomenon. A rough marble slab with crude lettering from Attica, dating to c. 500, is a unique example of an epitaph written by an eromenos for his erastes, who, under love's influence, had sworn a heroic oath to his beloved that he would 'mingle in strife and tearful war' as a result of which he lost his life in proving his courage. The boy then erected this in his memory, and the last line gives the identity of his erastes: 'I am sacred to Gnathios, who lost his life in war' (*IG* I³ 1399: doc. 4.75). The relationship between the older man and younger boy, as at Sparta, may have specifically provided the boy with a role model in bravery and warfare, particularly in hoplite warfare. A fifth-century inscription from the Athenian acropolis states succinctly: 'Lysitheos says he loves Mikion more than anyone in the city since he is brave.' Again in this declaration the beloved is demonstrating that part of the homoerotic ideal is for the young boy to emulate the commitment and experience of his older lover in battle, as demonstrated par excellence in the Sacred Band at Thebes (*IG* I³ 1401: doc. 4.76).

Graffiti from Thera

A very different perception, but one no less sincere in terms of the commitment to homoerotic relationships and sexual conquest, is demonstrated by graffiti dating perhaps to the early to mid seventh century from the island of Thera, at a site some 50 metres distant from the temple of Apollo Karneios. The content is quite clearly sexual, though the sacred setting suggests the possible context of erotic inititation by an older man of a young boy connected with the dances at the Gymnopaidiai, celebrated in the Dorian societies of both Sparta and Thera, where boys danced naked in honour of Apollo. Each of these inscriptions may have been written by the erastes of a young boy who took part in the ceremonial praise of his excellence in the dance, as in: 'Barbax dances well and he gave me pleasure' The relationship between the couples which these inscriptions commemorate may be not so much scurrilous as representative of homoerotic rites of passage, such as those formalised by pederastic abduction on Crete prior to a boy's adoption into manhood (*IG* XII.3 543, 537, 538, 536: doc. 4.77).

Institutionalised homoeroticism

That homoerotic relationships at least in Sparta were institutionalised and involved a sexual component is denied by Xenophon who purports to describe Spartan pederasty as entirely non-sexual. This attempt to show that Lykourgos intended the relationship to be an innocent form of association with a purely educational purpose, rather than a disgraceful 'desire for a boy's body', is not supported by other evidence, and he may well be attempting to play down the relationship between his patron Agesilaos II and Agesilaos' lover Lysander, as a result of whose machinations Agesilaos came to the throne instead of Agis' son Leotychidas (Plut. *Life of Lysander* 24.1–25.3: doc. 13.42). The homosexual practices of Spartans were a constant joke in Attic comedy and according to Aelian (*Varia Historia* 3.10.12) any upstanding Spartan who did not act as an erastes to youths of good character was fined by the ephors, perhaps in the same way as Spartiates who did not marry were penalised, because they were failing in their civic duty (Plut. *Life of Lykourgos* 15.1–3: doc. 6.16). Xenophon contrasts this 'spiritual' association at Sparta with the practices of the Boeotians, who, he says, lived together man and boy as if they were married, and the Eleians, who won youths by means of favours. Unfortunately he gives no details of those Greeks who 'entirely prevent potential erastai from conversing with youths', implying that in some cities such relationships were carefully monitored or restricted, and many fathers would have been concerned to protect their sons from such approaches. But he has said enough to show that homoeroticism was a panhellenic phenomenon and that 'in many cities the laws do not oppose passionate attachments to boys' (Xen. *Const. Spart.*2.12–14: doc. 4.79).

The Eleians were well known for their homoerotic tendencies and the eromenos of the sculptor Pheidias is said to have been an Eleian boy, Pantarkes (Paus. *Description of Greece* 5.11.3), while the young and handsome philosopher, Phaedo of Elis, was enslaved when his city was captured according to Diogenes Laertius and put to work in a male brothel in Athens. He became one of Socrates' associates and gave his name to the *Phaedo*, which relates Socrates' last hours (Pl. *Phaedo* 117a–118: doc. 3.88). Homoeroticism is also linked with courage and shown as motivating brave deeds in a popular song from Chalkis which refers to the heroic deeds of Kleomachos of Pharsalia who died in the Lelantine war against Eretria in the eighth century, and Plutarch adds the detail that Kleomachos' bravery was enhanced by the fact that his eromenos was watching the battle. The song encourages all youths who have grace and noble fathers (the aristocratic dimension of homoeroticism) not to 'grudge brave men converse with your bloom', for courage and 'Eros the limb-relaxer' both flourish in Chalkis (Arist. *F* 98: doc. 4.80).

Skolia

Drinking songs (skolia), like those of Theognis, both promoted homoerotic relationships and associated such relationships with heroic deeds, just as at Athens Harmodios and Aristogeiton were celebrated both as lovers and as tyrannicides (docs 9.43–7). In the sixth century Anacreon wrote many skolia which focused on the pleasures of sex and wine, and youths present at symposia would have learnt and sung these to entertain the company (Anac. *FF* 357, 359, 360, 407: doc. 4.81). From such works it is clear what the Greeks expected of an eromenos: smooth cheeks and slender thighs; the bloom of youth; modesty and a girlish glance; and initial reluctance to accept the proposition followed by fidelity to the lover from thenceforth. It was axiomatic, if unlikely, that the beloved received no sexual pleasure from the erastes and boys are always shown on vases as looking modestly to the ground with no sign of reciprocal passion in response to their lover. The beloved has to be tempted by gifts, normally dogs, hares or roosters, before succumbing to the lover's desires, and only feels gratitude and respect. In his play *Wealth*, however, Aristophanes shows that there could be a fine line between love and prostitution when he describes well-born boys asking their lovers for a good horse or hunting hounds instead of money like prostitutes (Ar. *Wealth* 149–59: doc. 4.104).

The eromenos

In the *Clouds*, Aristophanes presents a contest between 'Right' and 'Wrong', each of which is attempting to show that he can win a lawsuit. In his speech 'Right' praises the good 'old-fashioned' practices, when youths were modest, making sure, when being tutored, that they hid their genitals while seated by putting one thigh forward, brushing the sand when they stood up 'not to leave an impression of youth for their lovers', and ensuring that they did not anoint themselves with oil below their navels, to stop 'down blooming on their genitals as on apples'. Unlike the bold youths of 'today' they did not put on affected voices or flutter their

Figure 4.13 A homoerotic scene with five pairs of male youths, each with a large flower bud between
them, is depicted on a black-figure terracotta sarcophagus produced in the Greek city of
Klazomenai (Asia Minor). The youths are at various stages of courting. It dates to about 510
BC; the sarcophagus itself is 195 cm long and 63–75 cm wide. Antikensammlung Staatliche
Museen 30030, Berlin. Drawing by J. Etherington.

eyelashes at potential lovers (Ar. *Clouds* 973–80: doc. 4.83). In the *Birds*, written during the
Peloponnesian War in 414, Peisthetairos' ideal city is one in which the worst that could happen would be the complaint by the father of a beautiful youth to his neighbour coming home
from the gymnasium after his bath: 'you met my son and you didn't kiss him, or address
him, or embrace him – you didn't even tickle his balls!' (Ar. *Birds* 137–42: doc. 4.84). Eye-
contact was considered the erotic stimulus par excellence, while considerable importance
was attached to the genitals of the youths by their lovers and the depiction of the courtship of
youths in vase-painting frequently involves touching the genitals. The importance of beauty
in youths should not be underestimated: a paiderastes ('lover of boys'), Episthenes, who once
put together an entire army battalion of handsome boys, is recorded by Xenophon (*Anabasis*
7.4.7) as offering on campaign to be executed in place of a beautiful Thracian youth.

Nevertheless, there was a clear distinction between a youth having an accepted erastes
and one who was promiscuously shared by a number of males, and obviously not all fathers
would have approved of approaches to their sons by older men. One of the reasons for young
boys having pedagogues to escort them to and from school was to protect the youths from
unwelcome attentions, and inform the father of the youth of any potential lovers. According
to Aeschines in 346 one of 'Solon's' laws deliberately protected youths from the unwelcome
attention of teachers, specifically laying down the times for school, with no schools or palaistrai to be open before sunrise, ensuring that the boys are superintended at both, and making
sure that any choregos (producer of a dramatic chorus) who might have contact with children

was over 40 years of age (Aeschin. 1 *Against Timarchos* 9–11: doc. 4.85). Similarly legislation was attributed to Solon which forbade slaves to exercise or anoint themselves in the palaistrai (where nudity was de rigueur) or be the lover of a free boy, the penalty for such actions being fifty lashes from the public scourge. The concern was that young Athenian males had sexual relationships only with other free males (Aeschin. 1 *Against Timarchos* 138–9: doc. 5.34).

Male prostitution

While, conventionally at Athens, only intercrural sex should take place between the erastes and eromenos, it is improbable that anal intercourse never took place, and in Dorian societies such as Sparta, Crete and Thera, it was probably the norm. What was disgraceful was to submit to anal intercourse as an adult, and it was axiomatic that an Athenian citizen male was always the active partner in sexual relationships. When Aeschines attacks Timarchos, it is because Timarchos not only engaged in passive anal intercourse as a boy, but continued to do so as a young man, and, worse, received favours for so doing. To engage in male prostitution as a adult, or to force a citizen boy to engage in male prostitution, involved the loss of citizen rights, both for the person who hired the boy out and the person who hired him, while a boy treated in such a way no longer had the obligation to support his father in old age. A male prostitute was unable to become an archon, priest, public advocate, herald, ambassador or public informer, nor was he able to hold any office or speak in the council or assembly (Aeschin. 1 *Against Timarchos* 13–14, 19–20: doc. 4.85). While a citizen could continue as an erastes of boys until any age, as Aeschines admits that he himself has done, terms for passive homosexuals such as katapugon ('male who submits to anal penetration') and euruproktos ('wide-anused') were highly opprobrious, and passive homosexuals, like the much-ridiculed figure Kleisthenes, who is shown by Aristophanes as notoriously effeminate (Ar. *Thesmophoriazousai* 623–33: doc. 3.64) were seen as sexually debauched. Aristophanes finds good material for humour in homosexuality, but his targets are primarily passive homosexuals, male prostitutes and beardless men like Kleisthenes; adult male pathics, who practised passive anal sex, are shown as perverted and shameless. While there were male prostitutes in brothels who paid the prostitute tax, these were presumably slaves or non-Athenians and Herakleia in Pontos apparently had so many male prostitutes that Stratonikos (c. 410–360) called it 'Androcorinth' or 'Male Corinth' (Ath. *Deipnosophistae* 351c–d).

Athenian lovers

Various prominent Athenians are described as being in enthusiastic pursuit of boys. The tragedian Sophocles, in particular, was known as 'boy-loving' and his contemporary Ion of Chios relates how, when Sophocles was a general on Lesbos in 440, he saw him tricking the handsome young wine-pourer at a symposium into kissing him (Ion of Chios *Foundation of Chios* F6: doc. 4.86). Socrates too is portrayed by Plato as passionately attracted to boys, but able to sublimate his passion into a focus on the education of the youths with whom he was in love. His views on 'chaste' love are presented by Xenophon who describes a symposium held by Alkibiades' brother-in-law Kallias in 421, in honour of Kallias' eromenos Autolykos, who had just won a victory at the Olympic Games in the pankration. Autolykos' father, Lykon, was also present, and his invitation was seen as entirely proper. Autolykos is so handsome that his beauty draws the gaze of everyone, but Socrates draws a clear distinction between a relationship with a youth and one with a woman. That with a youth is 'chaste', because 'a youth does not, as a woman does, share with the man in the pleasure of the intercourse, but looks on sober at the other's intoxication by Aphrodite.' From the youth's point of view he will be attracted by and respect an erastes who teaches proper speech and conduct, rather than one who follows him around entreating a kiss or a caress, and Socrates emphasises that the relationship should be spiritual and not physical (Xen. *Symposium* 1.8–9, 8.21–23: doc. 4.87). A rather different view of these celebrated characters is given by the comic poet Eupolis, who the next year in 420 produced his play *Autolykos* on the topic, in which Autolykos was ridiculed as 'Eutresios' ('easily penetrated': *F* 56).

In Plato's *Symposium*, set in 416, Socrates is shown as present at a dinner-party, along with Aristophanes and Alkibiades, to celebrate the victory of the playwright Agathon with his first tragedy: a comic portrait of Agathon is presented by Aristophanes in his *Thesmophoriazousai* (146–67: doc. 16.16). At this party Alkibiades, whose affairs with both sexes were notorious, describes how on several occasions at the gymnasium and in his own home he had tried to seduce Socrates, lying beside and cuddling him the whole night: however, 'when I got up after sleeping with Socrates nothing more had happened than if I had been sleeping with my father or elder brother' (Pl. *Symposium* 219b–d: doc. 4.88). This was seen at the time as evidence of Socrates' considerable strength of character.

As with hetairai and their lovers, young non-citizen boys could receive a considerable income from their relationships with older men. Lysias, in his speech *Against Simon*, describes a case where two Athenians were rivals for the love of a young non-citizen, Theodotos from

Figure 4.14 The interior of an Athenian red-figure kylix (drinking cup) shows a hetaira reaching up to kiss a youth. The outside of the cup is decorated with scenes from a komos (revelry), in which men drink and dance. Dating to about 520 BC, the cup is 10.5 cm high with a diameter of 28.5 cm – a typically large vessel to drink from – and is by the Kiss Painter: 'the kiss' was a favourite theme of his. Antikensammlung Staatliche Museen F2269, Berlin. Drawing by J. Etherington.

Plataea. The defendant admits that his attitude towards the youth might be considered inappropriate for a man of his age by the jury, but shows his opponent as being even more unrestrained in his activities: breaking down the doors of the house, entering the women's quarters, using physical violence and attempting abduction. Simon has apparently stated that he had given Theodotos 300 drachmas as a contract for his sexual services, and that the defendant had seduced the boy away from him, which might well have incited him to serious measures. The 300 drachmas is insignificant compared to the full purchase price of the alleged prostitute Neaira, which was 3000 drachmas ([Dem.] 59 *Against Neaira* 29: doc. 4.98). Theodotos is a slave, as he can be tortured to give evidence in the lawsuit, but the agreed sum does not seem to have been a purchase price; obviously male prostitutes and partners could be as expensive and sought after as much as female ones (Lys. 3 *Against Simon* 4–6: doc. 4.89).

Prostitution

Prostitution was a fact of life in all Greek cities, and so accepted was the practice that at Athens Solon was credited, by comic poets, with having opened brothels staffed by slaves at a price everyone could afford as one of his great democratic achievements (Philem. *F* 3: doc. 4.99). Greek cities had large cohorts of prostitutes (pornai), both female and male, with brothels openly transacting business, street-walkers in the alleyways (sandals have been found with the word akolouthi ('follow') on their soles at Athens), concubines (pallakai) who could be taken into a semi-permanent relationship even by a citizen, and the higher-class hetairai (companions) for hire on demand. In addition, no symposium was complete without entertainment from musicians (flute, lyre or harp players) and dancers, whose skills ranked them above prostitutes, though they were also expected to provide sexual services. The astynomoi (city officials) were supposed to restrict their fees to no more than two drachmas per night and cast lots to decide among rivals who wanted to hire them ([Arist.] *Ath. Pol.* 50.1–51.4: doc. 1.25). Socrates praises the skills of one of these girls who could keep twelve hoops in the air simultaneously (Xen. *Symposium* 2.8–10: doc. 4.30). The street-walkers and brothel-workers were at the bottom of the scale and would primarily have been slaves, though some could have been metic or citizen women who had fallen on hard times. Both male and female prostitutes paid a prostitute tax to the state, and many of these would have been controlled by a pimp, or pornoboskos (Aeschin. *Against Timarchos* 120). The price paid by a client, which could apparently be as low as an obol, meant that everyone could avail themselves of such services. Hetairai (companions) in contrast could be extremely wealthy: they were often educated metics and could choose their clientele, like Theodote (Xen. *Memorabilia* 3.11.4: doc. 4.96), being able to select their own 'friends' and could charge lavishly for their company. These might be the long-term mistresses of one or a select number of citizens and provided intellectual companionship as well as sexual favours. Brothels were considered a standard amenity in Greek cities: when Dionysos plans his trip to Hades in the *Frogs*, he asks Herakles for advice on the best harbours, bread shops, brothels, inns, turnings, springs, roads, cities, rooms, lady innkeepers and where he will find the fewest bed-bugs (Ar. *Frogs* 112–15).

There was no notion of sexual exclusivity: a husband after his marriage could still be the lover of young boys, as well as hiring prostitutes and keeping a concubine. It was not unusual for an erastes or even an eromenos to keep a mistress: Leaina ('lioness'), supposedly tortured to death by Hippias, was said to have been either the mistress of Aristogeiton (Paus. *Description of Greece* 1.23.2) or Harmodios (Ath. *Deipnosophistae* 596f) at the time of the conspiracy

171

against the tyrants, while protagonists in Aristophanes' plays have no trouble in simultaneously pursuing youths and women. In the speech against Neaira the prosecutor clearly states
to an Athenian audience, 'hetairai are kept for pleasure, concubines for the daily care of our
bodies, and wives for legitimate children and the faithful guardianship of our homes' ([Dem.
s] 59 *Against Neaira* 122) and younger men, in particular before they were married at the age
of 30, would have engaged in homoerotic relationships with younger boys and frequented
brothels: the only women off-limits to them were citizen women (cf. [Dem.] 59 *Against Neaira*
16, 52, 104: doc. 4.56).

Pornai

Prostitutes (pornai) are described in a number of opprobrious terms, such as a 'public highway', by seventh- and sixth-century poets, demonstrating both their ubiquitousness and the
unromantic and very pragmatic ways in which they were viewed (Anac. 446; Archil. 209:
doc. 4.90). Prostitutes would primarily have been slaves, and running a brothel was a perfectly acceptable occupation for citizens and metics, and a profitable one: Aspasia, Perikles'
partner, was alleged to conduct such a business and is satirised by comic poets for training
young girls as sex workers and entertainers, and even described as keeping a brothel. The
education and upkeep of young girls for the sex industry was also a perfectly legitimate professions for a citizen or metic, and perhaps babies exposed at birth joined the slaves who were
the trainees in such institutions. The attacks on Aspasia are rather aimed at Perikles, and
she is blamed both for the siege and defeat of Samos as an enemy of her own home Miletos,
and for the outbreak of the Peloponnesian War, because Perikles banned Megarian access
to Athenian harbours when 'the Megarians, garlicked-up like fighting-cocks by this painful
occurrence,/ stole in return two prostitutes of Aspasia's' (Ar. *Acharnians* 524–9: doc. 4.95). The
story became elaborated: according to Plutarch, she was prosecuted c. 438–436 by the comic
poet Hermippos for impiety and for procuring free women for Perikles, but acquitted (Plut.
Life of Perikles 32.1, 5), no doubt Plutarch's misunderstanding of another comic attack on her
in the theatre.

Hetairai in Egypt and Corinth

Hetairai ('companions') were higher-class and managed their affairs independently, in some
cases like Theodote with their mother as their manager. Herodotos recounts the good fortune of Rhodopis, a Greek hetaira in Naukratis in Egypt in the reign of Amasis (c. 570–525)
(Hdt. 2.152.3–154.5, 178.1–181.2: doc. 2.31). He disbelieves the story of Rhodopis earning
enough to be able to build a pyramid worth thousands of talents, but describes the extravagant dedication she made at Delphi, consisting of a tenth of her property, which comprised a
heap of iron-spits each large enough for roasting an ox. Herodotos states that he has himself
seen these, behind the altar dedicated by the Chians, and comments on the renowned fasci-
nations of hetairai at Naukratis and the fact that Rhodopis won a reputation throughout the
Greek world (Hdt. 2.134.1–135.5: doc. 4.91). But the city most renowned for its prostitutes
was Corinth, a great trading state and port. Corinth was known both for its secular and its
sacred prostitutes, hierodouloi, who served the temple of Aphrodite Ourania, and contributed to the city's wealth. There was a proverb that 'not for every man is the voyage to Corinth', as a visit to Corinth could be extremely expensive with captains and sailors in particular
squandering money on the local prostitutes. There were apparently in Roman times more

than 1000 sacred prostitutes, slaves who entertained their clients in the city and gave their earnings to the temple. Strabo records a pun, when a certain hetaira responded to a criticism that she did not engage in women's work such as weaving ('but even so I have already taken down three webs in this short time'). The joke hangs on the word 'histos', which can mean a web set up on a loom, or a ship's mast (and hence a sailor's erection). Prostitutes in Corinth were too busy to spend time weaving (Strabo *Geography* 8.6.20: doc. 4.92). According to the comic playwright Alexis, they also had their own festival in honour of Aphrodite separate to that celebrated by free-born women at Corinth (Alexis *Girl in Love* F255), and they joined in the supplication to the goddess made by Corinthian women at the time of the second Persian invasion; the names of the prostitutes who were involved were recorded on a tablet dedicated to the goddess (Ath. *Deipnosophistae* 573c–d; cf. Simon. 14: doc. 11.43, cf. 15.4).

Sacred prostitutes

One hundred sacred prostitutes were dedicated to Aphrodite by Xenophon of Corinth in thanks for his win in the foot-race and pentathlon at the Olympic festival of 464, a victory recorded by Pindar himself in a skolion sung at the feast at which the victory and dedication was celebrated. The girls are addressed as passive agents: 'To you without the chance of refusal she has granted, O children, that in lovely beds you shall have the fruit of your soft bloom plucked', while he tells Aphrodite that Xenophon has brought her a 'hundred-bodied herd of grazing girls' in fulfilment of his vows (Pind. *F* 122: doc. 4.93). According to Strabo temple prostitutes were also dedicated 'in early times' at the temple of Aphrodite at Eryx in Sicily, as well as at Komana in Pontos, 'a lesser Corinth', in his own day and Athenaeus notes that dedications of sacred prostitutes such as Xenophon's were not uncommon (Ath. *Deipnosophistae* 573e–574a).

Independent sex workers

Alexis of Samos, whose date is unknown, records that the prostitutes who had accompanied Perikles' fleet during its eight-month siege of Samos in 440 did so well out of this excursion that they were able to dedicate a shrine to Aphrodite on the island, known variously as 'in the reeds' or 'in the swamp' (doc. 12.24); these were presumably independent sex workers. There would have been nothing incongruous about sex workers accompanying a fleet or army in Greece, when every hoplite, for example, was attended on campaign by a slave. Like slave dealers they were probably so intrinsic a part of warfare that they are seldom mentioned (Alexis of Samos *Samian Annals* F1: doc. 4.94).

Hetairai in Athens

Well-trained young girls could be assured of a good income. Xenophon describes Socrates' visit to a hetaira called Theodote, who was not unknown to Alkibiades, and who was renowned for her beauty, which was such that she allowed artists to paint her portrait in suggestive but not entirely nude poses. Socrates, famous for his bare feet and single ragged cloak, noted the luxury with which Theodote lived: expensive clothes, her mother also with fine clothes and attendants, good-looking maidservants similarly well-dressed, and a house with lavish furniture. He queries what may have brought her this wealth: a farm; the possession of a rented house; a business with craftsmen? Theodote explains in reply: 'My livelihood

Figure 4.15 Three naked women at their toilette. Their nudity, openly shown on the vase, indicates that they are prostitutes (citizen women would never be depicted naked, but always as modestly dressed). They are at a large basin; the one on the far left is holding her clothes, perhaps to wash them, while in front of her are a pair of slippers, of the 'sensual' kind. The prostitute in the centre is brushing out her thick, shoulder-length hair, holding a brushing device in her left hand and in her right an implement: a short length of wood with what could be a wad of wool on it, perhaps for applying oil to her hair. The third prostitute has her hands in the basin, and might be about to scoop up water to wash her arms and face. This scene is on an Athenian red-figure stamnos which stands at 42 cm high and dates to around 440 BC. Antikensammlung 2411, Munich. Drawing by J. Etherington.

is from any friend I might make who wishes to be generous' (Xen. *Memorabilia* 3.11.4: doc. 4.96). She is clearly a free woman, whose mother oversees her establishment, and she must have been one of many in a society where men were able to associate with anyone they chose and where the role of independent hetaira must have possessed many advantages over that of a wife or concubine.

Towards the end of the fourth century another wealthy hetaira, Phryne from Thespiai, narrowly escaped from being executed for non-traditional religious practices. She was defended by the well-known orator Hypereides, who was also one of her lovers, and in a famous scene, when he felt the sympathies of the jury were not with him or his client, he had her brought into court and ripped open her garments, exposing her breasts to the jurors. They were so stunned by the sight of her beauty and his lamentations at her possible fate, that they viewed her as an attendant, or priestess, of Aphrodite and acquitted her (enraging the prosecutor so greatly that it was said that he never brought another case). The Athenians later felt that they may have been over-enthusiastic on this occasion, and so passed a decree that no defendant should have their body bared during the trial. Athenaeus continues by relating that Phryne was actually 'more beautiful in the parts not usually seen' and so restricted views of herself naked, wearing a tunic when purifying herself in the sea prior to the Eleusinian Mysteries. Apelles painted her as 'Aphrodite rising from the sea' and Praxiteles, another of her lovers, used her as the model for his Aphrodite of Knidos. When he made her the gift of one of his statues, she chose that of Eros and dedicated it in her home town of Thespiai, while her neighbours dedicated a golden statue of her by Praxiteles at Delphi. Her wealth was such that she promised that she would replace the wall around the city of Thebes, razed by Alexander in 335, if the Thebans would inscribe on it: 'though Alexander demolished it, Phryne the hetaira had it rebuilt' (Ath. *Deipnosophistae* 590d–591d: doc. 4.97).

Neaira

Neaira, who was probably born c. 400, was another famous professional. Her alleged career is known from a speech attributed to Demosthenes, but probably written by Apollodoros, which attacks Neaira and her husband Stephanos on the grounds that as a non-Athenian (and an ex-slave and prostitute) Neaira should not have been the wife of an Athenian citizen: furthermore Neaira's daughter had also been married, as if a citizen woman, to two Athenian husbands. The outcome of the case, like most in antiquity, is not known, but if found guilty Neaira would have been sold as a slave and Stephanos fined 1000 drachmas. For giving Neaira's daughter in marriage to a citizen he could also have lost his citizen rights ([Dem.] 59 *Against Neaira* 16, 52: doc. 4.56). According to the prosecution, Neaira and six other young girls were brought up and educated in Corinth by a freedwoman, Nikarete, as her daughters; by pretending they were free-born she could as a result charge high prices for their services. Later, after she had made a considerable profit from their attractions, they were sold, and Neaira was bought for 30 minas (3000 drachmas) by Timanoridas of Corinth and Eukrates from Leukas as their joint slave. Later, when they chose to get married, they offered her her freedom, rebating 5 minas each of the price they had paid for her, as long as she no longer worked in Corinth 'as they did not want to see their own hetaira working in Corinth or in the hands of a brothel-keeper'.

Jumping at this chance to buy her freedom for 20 minas, Neaira contacted her earlier lovers, asking them for money to supplement her savings, and was lucky enough to get an Athenian, Phrynion of Paianeia, to make up the rest of the sum needed. The jurors are reminded that the older ones amongst them will remember his outrageous and extravagant lifestyle. Fourth-century high-class slave prostitutes were not cheap, but if Neaira had belonged to Timanoridas and Eukrates for some five years, perhaps until they chose to marry in their early thirties, she would only have cost them each 100 drachmas a year, probably far less than they would have spent on regular visits to hetairai ([Dem.] 59 *Against Neaira* 18–19, 28–32: doc. 4.98). Some of the tricks engaged in by experienced hetairai to improve the appearance and behaviour of new recruits to their business are ridiculed by the comic poet Alexis, in his *Fair Measure*, which result in their having 'totally different manners and looks from before': cork soles to make them taller, thin slippers and a particular way of holding the head to make them look shorter; bottom-enhancing apparatus to improve the hips; false breasts to give the impression of a small waist; blackened eyebrows; white-lead to whiten the complexion, or rouge to enhance it; the best parts shown naked; and rehearsed laughter to set off lovely teeth (Alexis *Fair Measure* 1: doc. 4.100).

Brothels in Athens

Not only was the institution of public brothels in Athens ascribed to Solon as a great democratic innovation, according to the second-century source Nikander of Kolophon Solon also
instituted the worship of Aphrodite Pandemos (Aphrodite 'of the whole people') at Athens,
financing the cult from the profit of the brothels. The fourth-century comic poet Philemon
praises the fact that even the poorest citizens could afford a prostitute and young men should
therefore not be tempted by 'what did not belong to them', in other words citizen women.
The prostitutes stand there naked, you make your choice and one obol is all it takes, he states
(Philem. *F* 3: doc. 4.99). An 'obol' may be a term for 'dirt cheap', but the profit margin rather
depends on how many clients a prostitute would be expected to entertain during the course
of the day. Six clients would bring in a drachma, the equivalent of a craftsman's wage in the
later fifth century, and Philoneos, who planned c. 420 to put his slave-concubine in a brothel
to get the advantage of her additional income, would surely have considered this a satisfac-
tory supplement (Antiph. 1 *Prosecution of the Stepmother* 14–20: doc. 4.52). The slave Xanthias,
in Aristophanes' *Wasps*, anecdotalises about a prostitute he visited the previous day who
objected to his preferred position, and one obol would certainly have been within the reach
of many slaves (Ar. *Wasps* 500–2: doc. 4.101). Naturally prices would have reflected the skills
and status of the sex worker involved: Corinthian hetairai are described in Aristophanes'
Wealth as ignoring poor men, but turning their anuses immediately to anyone with money:
anal intercourse with prostitutes is frequently depicted on vases, and may have been popular in Corinth. The position was used by sex workers as a means of contraception. Youths,
according to his slave Karion, are only too happy to do the same, not to their lovers, but for
payment. Chremylos corrects him, commenting that that only applies to male prostitutes (Ar.
Wealth 149–59: doc 4.104).

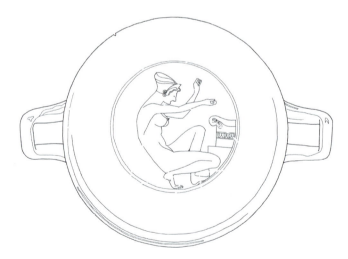

Figure 4.16 A naked woman wearing a cap, almost certainly a prostitute, kneels before an altar. Prostitutes, like citizen women, had religious needs. This scene is on the interior of an Athenian
red-figure kylix by the 'Painter of the Agora Chairias cup', dating to about 510–500 BC. Agora
Museum P23165, Athens. Drawing by J. Etherington.

Prostitutes as such in Athens were almost too easy of access: a fragment of the comic playwright Xenarchos portrays it as disgraceful that despite the availability of a whole range of attractions, prostitutes were being ignored by young men who still had designs on citizen women with all the attendant difficulties of crawling in through holes in the roof or being carried in disguised as a heap of straw. While this harps on the omnipresent comic theme of the licentious and easily seduced nature of Athenian wives, his description of the talent available is graphic: 'very good-looking young girls in the brothels, who can be seen basking in the sun, their breasts uncovered, naked and lined up in rows ready for battle'. Not only can you choose the type you like – thin, fat, round, tall, shrivelled, young, old, middle-aged, fully ripe – you actually have to fight them off as they drag you in with endearments' (Xenarchos *F* 4: doc. 4.103; Fig. 4.15). It is vignettes such as these that add colour to the depiction of women in the Greek world: while many Greek citizen women may seldom have stepped outside the home except to collect water, the sources written by their contemporary menfolk do not entirely deny them a voice or a significant role in the preservation of family property and the economic welfare of the household.

5

LABOUR

Slaves, serfs and citizens

Introduction

The concept of slavery – persons deprived of liberty and in the power of an owner who can buy, sell or mistreat them like a material possession – seems abhorrent in the twenty-first century, but ancient societies considered slavery an economic imperative and ancient Greece was no exception. Although Athens is seen as the cradle of democracy, it was a democracy that specifically excluded women and slaves from political participation and citizen rights and duties. It is arguable that Greek civilisation was based on the labour of slaves and metics (resident foreigners), who undertook both manual and more skilled labour to assist their owners in their trades and professions, on the farm or in the home. It was not the case that slaves undertook menial duties in order to allow citizens to be engaged in higher-order activities such as political duties and responsibilities. Slaves and metics often worked alongside their masters and Athenian citizens engaged in all kinds of trades. Indeed not all of them would have possessed a slave, and if they did the most usual slave would have been a single girl who performed all duties, such as grinding barley and wheat, cleaning, cooking, weaving, and most probably sharing the master's bed.

Sources

Slavery in ancient Greece had a long history. In the Bronze Age, for example, the Linear B tablets record workers of various origins, who presumably were slaves, with many women and children from ethnic communities (for example from Kythera, Chios, Lemnos or Halikarnassos), working in the palace centres like Pylos. These women and children were acquired in war following the death of their menfolk, or perhaps through piracy. Mycenaean society was militaristic and the tale of the Trojan War itself may have been a reflection of raids on Troy and its surrounding region by Mycenaeans for plunder and booty including slaves. The Homeric poems, and in particular the *Iliad*, make clear the fate to which women of a conquered city were destined, and in a prophetic passage that does much to express the miseries of slavery Hector tells his wife Andromache, knowing as he does that Troy is doomed, that he feels for her destiny more than for his parents, his brothers and the rest of the entire city:

> But I do not feel so much grief for the Trojans, nor for Hekabe herself or lord Priam, or my brothers, who many and brave as they are will fall in the dust at the hands of the enemy, as much as for you, when one of the bronze-clad Achaeans leads you off in tears, robbing you of the day of freedom.
>
> (Hom. *Iliad* 6.447–63: doc. 5.67)

Aristotle is the main source for the Greeks' attitude towards the existence of slavery and he rationalises enslavement as necessary for society and the functioning of the city-state (doc. 5.1). Sources which deal with the topic of Greek slavery were of course written by Greek citizens, for Greek citizens, and there is no record from the slave's point of view. However, it is possible to imagine the reaction of slaves under brutal treatment or the endurance of torture in lawsuits in order to force them to give evidence for or against their masters (Xen. *Memorabilia* 2.1.15–17: doc. 5.30; Antiph. 5 *On the Murder of Herodes* 29–32: doc. 5.28). Herodotos in one of his anecdotes presents the viewpoint of a castrated slave, sold as a boy to the Persian court (Hdt. 8.105.1–106.4: doc. 5.2). The fact that slaves ran away and deserted is also clear evidence that many were dissatisfied with their living conditions (Thuc. 7.27.5: doc. 5.25, cf. 5.26), and a number of sources demonstrate the extent to which the helots particularly hated the Spartans (Xen. *Hellenika* 3.3.6: doc. 14.5). However, while accepting slavery as a normal part of life, the Greeks were capable of empathising with the fate of slaves when threatened themselves with the prospect of slavery, as when Xenophon pictured the Athenians' dread of enslavement at the end of the Peloponnesian War (Xen. *Hellenika* 2.2.3–4: doc. 5.7), while Diodorus described the horrendous sufferings of the women and children dragged off from Selinous in Sicily by the Carthaginians (Diod. Sic. *Library of History* 13.57.1–58: doc. 13.32). Doubtless there could be affectionate relationships between elderly slaves and their owners, as frequently portrayed in Athenian tragedy. However, since these are described from the citizen's point of view, often to convince a jury of the speaker's good nature, these should not be accepted uncritically ([Dem.] 47 *Against Evergos and Mnesiboulos* 55–6: doc. 5.14).

More concrete evidence of slave conditions is provided by inscriptions which set out the purchase price of slaves or the wages paid to them for working on state-run projects (*IG* I³ 421, col. I: doc. 5.18), and by works such as Xenophon's *Revenues* which deals in part with the economics of slave-run industries (Xen. *Revenues* 4.14–15: doc. 5.16). There is clearer evidence from historians and orators of the role played by craftsmen and metics in Athens, and the extent to which they were valued by the state. For example, while aristocrats in Greek cities could denigrate craftsmen and professionals, and consider farming to be the only respectable profession (Xen. *Oeconomicus* 4.2–3, 6.8–9: doc. 5.58), obviously most Greeks worked, if not on a farm, then in a variety of trades, with many of them proud of their skills (*IG* I³ 766: doc. 5.64).

Slaves by nature and slaves by circumstance

Interestingly, Greeks saw no philosophical dilemma with regard to the existence and employment of slaves. To Aristotle households (oikoi) were composed by definition of free persons and slaves, with the master–slave relationship being one of the three important relationships which comprised the household, the other two being that between husband and wife and that between father and children. Interestingly the fourth component of the household was the art of money-making which he equated to household management, of which he naturally considered slaves to be an important part. He stated that according to some the rule of the master over the slave, which was the essential component of household management ('oikonomia' or our term 'economy'), was actually a science. Although some considered that the rule of a master was against nature, as it was imposed by force, in his view mankind was divided into slaves by nature and slaves by circumstance. This did not, however, lead to the questioning of slavery: the slave was essentially a possession, belonging totally to his or her master, and 'a human being who by nature belongs not to himself but to another man' and who is 'an instrument of action, distinct from the possessor' (Arist. *Politics* 1253b–1254a24: doc. 5.1).

Despite the fact that a high proportion of slaves were captured in war or through piracy and kidnapping (and hence slaves 'by circumstance'), Aristotle considered that it was both essential and beneficial for society to have rulers and others who were ruled and that at birth people were divided into one of these two categories. The Greeks thought in polarised antitheses – Greeks as opposed to barbarians, men as opposed to women, and freemen as opposed to slaves – and slavery was central to the Greeks' mentality, way of life, and civilisation: much of the economy of the Greek city-state was based on slave labour. Not only was owning slaves in the Greek world free from moral dilemmas, it was quite acceptable to possess Greeks from other city-states as slaves. The Spartan commander Kallikratidas was exceptional in his refusal to enslave the inhabitants of Methymne when he took the city in 406, with the comment that 'while he was leader none of the Greeks should be enslaved if he could help it,' and he only enslaved their Athenian garrison (Xen. *Hellenika* 1.6.13–15: doc. 5.6). In just a few lines Xenophon conveys the scene: all property seized as plunder by the attackers, the inhabitants collected in the agora ready for sale, doubtless with slave-traders waiting their chance for a bargain, the next day the decision to allow citizens to go free, but Athenians and slaves to be sold. The regular consequence of warfare between cities was the acquisition of slaves from the enemy city and this could be extremely lucrative for the victor.

Enslavement and the slave trade

The Homeric poems feature relatively few slaves and nearly all those encountered in the *Iliad* are women captured in warfare, forced to become slaves and concubines to their captors, just as Hector predicts for his wife Andromache the inevitable outcome – a life of bondage including the menial tasks of weaving and fetching water, while tactfully omitting the associated role of concubine. As the hearers know well, Andromache will see her son Astyanax thrown from the walls of Troy, and herself end up as slave and concubine to Neoptolemos, Achilles' son, to whom she will bear several children. In his play the *Andromache*, Euripides shows Andromache as at risk of being assassinated by Neoptolemos' new wife Hermione (Helen of Troy's daughter) through jealousy, because Hermione herself cannot have children. Ten years later he returned to the same topic in his *Trojan Women*, performed in 415 BC, where the Greek herald informs the royal women of Troy to which Greek leaders they have been allocated: Cassandra, prophetess and princess of Troy, to become the slave and concubine of Agamemnon, to be murdered with him by Agamemnon's vengeful wife Clytemnestra; Andromache, wife of 'horse-taming Hector' the defender of Troy, to be the slave of Neoptolemos; the elderly queen Hekabe to be the slave of Odysseus on Ithaka (Eur. *Trojan Women* 235–52, 272–8: doc. 5.68; Fig 5.1).

Despite the fact that dramatists wrote in a way that enabled their Athenian audience to empathise with the enslaved and appreciate the tragedy and pathos inherent in such reversals of fate, slavery was considered an unquestionable part of life in Greece, and Athens itself sold many enemy populations or rebellious allies into slavery. In fact, every Greek must have considered at some point in their lives the possibility of suffering such a fate. This was reflected, for example, in the Athenians' own fears that they would themselves be enslaved when they heard of the Spartan victory at Aigospotamoi when the Athenian fleet was destroyed in 405 BC, putting an end to the Peloponnesian War. At that point they remembered that they had on many occasions during the Peloponnesian War sold the inhabitants of other cities into slavery for questioning their decisions and right to empire. Now, they feared that it was their turn:

Figure 5.1 A scene from the Trojan War myth. During the Greek sack of Troy at the end of the war, the Greek hero Ajax dragged the naked Trojan princess Cassandra, daughter of King Priam of Troy, away from the statue of the goddess Athena to which she had fled for protection; her father stretches out a hand to her hopelessly. She became the sex-slave of Agammenon, and was killed with him by his wife Clytemnestra. The fate of women captured in war was to become slaves (doc. 5.68). A red-figure kalyx krater dating to about 470–460 BC, with a height of 48 cm and a diamter of 49 cm, probably by the Altamura Painter. Museum of Fine Arts 59.178, Boston. Drawing by J. Etherington.

Lamentation passed from the Piraeus along the Long Walls to the city, one man telling the news to another. As a consequence, no one slept during that night, because they were grieving not only for those who were lost, but far more than that for themselves, as they thought that they would now suffer the same as they had done to the Melians [416], who were colonists of the Spartans, after subduing them by siege, and to the Histiaians and Skionaians [421] and Toronaians [422] and Aeginetans [425] and many others of the Greeks.

(Xen. *Hellenika* 2.2.3–4: doc. 5.7; cf. 13.35)

So, while the majority of slaves were from non-Greek civilisations, other Greeks, captured in war or through piracy, did become slaves throughout Greece in the archaic and classical periods. A high proportion of these were women and children, enslaved when their menfolk were killed in battle against other Greek cities or massacred afterwards. There was always the possibility that any Greek might be enslaved, when slavery depended on the outcome of a single battle.

Debt-slavery

It was not the norm to have one's own fellow citizens as chattel-slaves. In some circumstances, however, citizens did become slaves in their own city as a result of debt. This was the case in Athens prior to Solon, who as archon in 594/3 put an end to the practice of debt-slavery in Athens, and henceforth no Athenians could be slaves in their own city. But prior to this ruling, many hektemoroi who had fallen into debt were enslaved and perhaps sold overseas: Solon prided himself on having secured the return of those who had been sold overseas before his archonship, as well as having released those still enslaved in Attica itself (Solon *Poem* 36: doc. 8.12). However, although repudiated in Athens, the practice of debt-slavery continued elsewhere in the Greek world, as at Gortyn in Crete, where it was still in place in the mid-fifth century (Willetts *The Law Code of Gortyn*: doc. 5.27).

The slave trade

Enslavement was a normal consequence of both warfare and piracy, and the slave trade was a profitable profession in the Greek world. Many colonies, especially those around the Black Sea, were an important source of slaves for their mother-cities and the slave markets, particularly those at Byzantium and Ephesos, as well as at Tanais on the river Don. According to Herodotos, some of the Thracians were even accustomed to selling their own children (Hdt. 5.6.1: doc. 5.3), and slaves were one of the main items traded between colonies and native populations. Seuthes, prince of the Odrysian Thracians paid for the service of Xenophon's men in 400 BC by selling his captives in the slave markets of the Greek cities of the coast (Xen. *Anabasis* 7.3.48, 7.4.2). A specialised form of slave trading was that of providing eunuchs for the Persian court, and handsome young boys who were kidnapped or enslaved could expect this fate, or possibly that of ending up in a male brothel. To the Greeks eunuchs were a despicable class, of use only in eastern courts, yet this did not prevent Greek traders castrating young boys for the Persian market, where they were well regarded and often given high positions at court because they were considered to be especially trustworthy. The island of Chios was known from early times to have been engaged in the slave market, purchasing barbarian slaves rather than enslaving other Greeks. Theopompos believed the Chians to have been the first Greeks to institute chattel-slavery (Theopomp. *F* 122: doc. 5.51), while according to Thucydides (8.40.2) there were more slaves on Chios than in any other city except Sparta.

Panionios of Chios

Herodotos recounts an episode from the life of Panionios, a Chian slave-trader, who purchased good-looking boys in the slave markets and castrated them, after which they were sold for large amounts at Sardis or Ephesos, for the Persian market. One of these unfortunates, Hermotimos, reached a high position at Xerxes' court and was able to take his revenge. While on business in Asia Minor he sought out Panionios and invited him to settle at Sardis, professing himself grateful that through his castration he had achieved such a successful career. However, when Panionios and his family had relocated, Hermotimos compelled him to castrate his four sons, who then had to castrate their father (perhaps implying that Panionios had been training up his sons to follow him in his profession), thus getting his revenge for having been made 'a nothing instead of a man': the viewpoint is of course that of the Greek who has been forcibly made a eunuch, tempered with Herodotos' own perceptions (Hdt. 8.105.1–106.4: doc. 5.2). Herodotos also records the story of Periander's actions against Corcyra, where he captured 300 boys and sent them to Sardis to have them castrated in revenge for the Corcyraeans' murder of his younger son, although in the event they ended up on Samos (Hdt. 3.48.2–53.7: doc. 7.14); presumably he would have made a handsome profit through the sale of these children. The practice of castrating Greeks as slaves was viewed with horror, but the profession of slave-trader was seen without prejudice as useful and even valuable, with no negative connotations, just as running a brothel, or training girls to entertain and perform sexual services was accepted without question as a form of employment suitable for Greek citizens.

Slaves captured in war

Greek cities viewed warfare as potentially profitable, not only because agricultural land might be annexed in victory, but because it provided an opportunity to take slaves either for personal use or for sale in the slave markets. In addition, there was the practice of demanding a ransom from the captured soldier's family. The standard ransom for a hoplite enemy captured in war was two minas (or the equivalent of 200 days work for a skilled workman in the fifth century). This was an incentive which appealed to all cities in their consideration of foreign policy towards their neighbours – certainly Greek city-states, with their citizen armies, never seem to have hesitated about going to war. The Spartans charged this set price of two minas (200 drachmas) to ransom their prisoners, and when King Kleomenes I trapped a number of the Argive enemy in a wood sacred to the hero Argos in about 494, he enticed them out with the news that he had received their ransom money, and then killed them as they emerged (Hdt. 6.79.1: doc. 5.17). Two minas seems to have been the going rate: at the end of the sixth century the Athenians ransomed 700 Boeotian prisoners for two minas each (Hdt. 5.77.3), and in 420 the Eleians fined the Spartans two minas for every hoplite who crossed their borders during the Sacred Truce (Thuc. 5.49.1). Ransoming prisoners taken in war was common across the whole Greek world: the law code of Gortyn specified that if anyone paid the ransom for a prisoner who was away from his home city, the prisoner belonged to his ransomer until he had recompensed him for what he had spent (*Gortyn Law Code* VI.46: doc. 5.27).

Even the capture of a small town or island could be very profitable as a result of the slaves then sold or ransomed, and Athens' expansion during the fifth century, following the creation of the Delian League, ensured it regularly received good revenue from slaves. Soon after the creation of the League in 476 BC the Athenians, under the leadership of Kimon, enslaved the inhabitants of Eion, a town on the river Strymon which was occupied by the Persians. They did the same to the island Skyros and, after enslaving the inhabitants, they dispatched their own colony. When Brasidas was unable to come to the relief of Torone in 422 and it was captured by the Athenians, the women and children were enslaved by them, and the men taken to Athens: the Peloponnesians among them were returned to their homeland when peace was made and the people of Torone and Chalkis were exchanged for prisoners from Olynthos, captured by the Spartans (Thuc. 5.3.4–5). Thucydides also laconically records that during the same summer, and about this time, in 421, the Athenians reduced Skione, put to death all the adult males, enslaved the women and children and gave the land to the Plataeans, as

Figure 5.2 The marble grave stele of Hegeso, daughter of Proxenos (her name and her father's are inscribed along the lintel underneath the pediment), from the Kerameikos cemetery, Athens. She sits mournfully looking at something, probably a jewel or other small item, which she will never wear or use again now that she is dead. Her slave woman has brought her the box. Several vases show similar scenes in which girl and women slaves fetch and hold boxes for their mistress. This stele dates to about 410–400 BC. The original is in the Archaeological Museum, Athens – this copy now stands in situ in the Kerameikos. © Carlo B. Agulto.

their city had been destroyed by Sparta in 427 (Thuc. 5.32.1; cf. [Dem.] 59 *Against Neaira* 104: doc. 1.37).

Indeed, it was not just the Athenians who enslaved the populations they defeated, although they had greater opportunities for this type of conduct than most cities once the Delian League had given them subject allies who were prone to revolt. When Plataea was taken in 427 by the Spartans and Thebans, the Spartans asked each of the Plataeans separately whether they had done any service to the Spartans and their allies in the war. When each replied no, they took him away and killed him. Some 200 Plataeans were put to death, as well as twenty-five Athenians who had taken part in the siege; the women were enslaved (Thuc. 3.68.2–3). The Spartans acted similarly when they captured Hysiai in 417/16, putting to death all the free men whom they captured, and presumably enslaving any women and children who fell into their hands (Thuc. 5.83.2).

This behaviour continued throughout the Peloponnesian War. The island of Melos, which was previously non-aligned, decided to join forces with Sparta in 416/15. In response, the Athenians blockaded the island and on its surrender killed all the men and sold the women and children into slavery (Thuc. 5.116.2–4: doc. 5.4). They then settled 500 of their own colonists on the island. Some of the survivors were later restored by Lysander. The enslavement of even small towns could help a city's cash-flow in time of war quite considerably. Prior to the start of the Sicilian Expedition, the Athenians under Nikias' command took the small seaport of Hykkara in Sicily and enslaved the inhabitants, receiving 120 talents for them at the neighbouring town of Catana (Thuc. 6.62.3–4: doc. 5.5). In addition, the city itself was handed over to Egesta, Hykkara's enemy, and Nikias received 30 talents for this and 'other business'. The boot was also on the other foot: when the Sicilian Expedition failed spectacularly two years later in 413, the 7000 prisoners, except for the Athenians and Greeks from Italy and Sicily who were imprisoned in the stone quarries, were sold into slavery by the Syracusans. Thucydides considers this the greatest and most catastrophic action in the war:

> For those who were defeated were defeated utterly in every way and suffered on a vast scale in every respect – as the saying goes it was total ruin, with army, fleet and everything entirely destroyed and few of the many returning home. This is what took place in Sicily.
>
> (Thuc. 7.87: doc. 13.26)

When Philip of Macedon enslaved the inhabitants of Potidaea in 356 and those of Olynthos in 348, the entire population, including the Athenian garrison, was sold into slavery (docs 14.29–31), as was that of Thebes when it revolted against Alexander the Great in 335 BC. Alexander on this occasion exacted summary justice to quell any potential revolts elsewhere: 6000 Thebans were killed and 30,000 enslaved (doc. 15.4). Perhaps one of the quickest changes of fortune was when Philip II of Macedon destroyed Stageira (the birthplace of Aristotle) and enslaved its inhabitants in 348; it was later rebuilt and restored by his son and Aristotle's pupil Alexander (Plut. *Life of Alexander* 2.1–9, 7.1–8.3: doc. 15.1). Alexander's own conquests in the east resulted in the enslavement of huge populations; his campaign in Bactria alone involved the capturing of seven major fortresses, of which the male populations were massacred and the women and children enslaved.

Plutarch tells the tale of Alexander's sack of Thebes as an example of Alexander's magnanimity. A woman called Timokleia killed one of Alexander's Thracians, who had raped her and was looking to steal her valuables, by pushing him down a well. Alexander was impressed by her conduct and the fact that she was the sister of Theagenes who fell at Chaironeia, and allowed her and her children to go free (*Life of Alexander* 11.9–12.6: doc. 15.4). While this anecdote highlights Alexander's nobility in an isolated incident, it also demonstrates the normal misfortunes of women and children in warfare which could be horrific. The brutal sacking of Selinous in 409 by the Carthaginians in alliance with Selinous' enemy Egesta, in which 16,000 were killed and 5000 taken captive, shows how both Greeks and non-Greeks could behave in times of war. On this occasion the enslaved are even pitied by their Greek enemies:

> As the women reflected on the slavery they were to face in Libya, they saw themselves and their children in a condition where they would be without rights, subject to the insolent treatment of masters they would be forced to obey, and when they observed that these possessed unintelligible speech and a brutish character they mourned for their living children as if they were dead.
>
> (Diod. Sic. *Library of History* 13.57.1–58.2: doc. 13.32)

Despite the widespread practice of killing and enslaving rebellious allies, there were at times second thoughts about a rash decision made to exterminate an enemy, as in the Mytilene debate of 427, after the island of Lesbos, except for the city of Methymna, revolted against Athens (Thuc. 3.36.2–4, 39.1–4: doc. 13.9). Under the influence of the oratory of Kleon, a radical democrat and politician, the Athenian assembly decided to put all the males to death, whether they were involved in the revolt or not, and to enslave the women and children and sent a ship to convey the decision to the general Paches telling him to carry out the sentence. On the following day, however, the Athenians thought better of their decision: the vote was overturned in the assembly, which was persuaded by a speech of Diodotos, and a ship covered the 180 nautical miles in less than a day to ensure that the first instruction was countermanded. The Mytilenaean envoys provided them with wine and barley, and the rowers ate as they rowed and took turns at sleeping and rowing (Thuc. 3.49.1–4: doc. 13.9). These humanitarian considerations did not stop the execution of the chief authors of the revolt, but prevented a massacre of many hundreds of innocent people.

Pirates and kidnappers

Kidnapping and piracy were facts of life in the Greek world. They provided an alternative way of acquiring slaves for the market and were profitable professions. In fact, Thucydides calls piracy the 'old-fashioned' way of life, and still traditional to many parts of Greece especially in the remoter areas such as Arkarnania and Crete (Thuc. 1.5.3). The Phokaians when settled in the western Mediterranean also engaged heavily in piracy, competing with the Phoenicians and Etruscans in the area. Piracy on a large and small scale was a normal occurrence in many parts of the Mediterranean, and there were obviously smaller-scale kidnappers in the Greek world, targeting individuals in specific Greek cities. Lysias in his speech *Against Agoratos* taunts the defendant with the fact that his brother kidnapped a slave in Athens for the Corinthian market, and after being caught doing the same in Corinth, was imprisoned and put to death as a result (Lys. 13 *Against Agoratos* 67: doc. 5.8). It should be noted that the offence was not against the slave, but against the slave's owner who was losing a valuable piece of property.

Aristophanes, in his final play the *Ploutos* (Wealth), puts a comic spin on the important social role played by Thessalian 'kidnappers', or merchants dealing in slaves. The character of Poverty in the play argues that if the god Ploutos (who is blind) were to regain his sight and deal out wealth equitably as a result, it would be a disaster: because everyone would be equally wealthy, no one would work – why should anyone want to be 'a smith or build ships or sew or make wheels or shoes or bricks or do the laundry or tan hides, or farm,' if he didn't have to? Chremylos retorts that no one wants to cure Ploutos, because their slaves will do these jobs. But, Poverty tells him, with no one bothering to hold a profession any more there wouldn't even be any slavetraders or kidnappers, and so no slaves – hence Chremylos will have to do all the tasks himself and be far worse off than he is at present. This is a comic inversion of reality, but kidnappers and pirates did much to keep the slave markets operational (Ar. *Wealth* 509–26: doc. 5.9).

Despite warfare between Greek states, most slaves in Greece were non-Greek. Kephisodoros was one of the men accused of the mutilation of the hermai in 415 and as a result of his conviction his property was auctioned off including his sixteen slaves. Of these five were Thracian, one Scythian, two Illyrian and one from Colchis, suggesting a thriving slave trade from the area of northern Greece and the Black Sea; the others were from Syria, Lydia, Caria and Melittene. Four (or five) were women and two, both Carian, were children, perhaps suggesting a family group or part of one (*IG* I³ 421; doc. 5.18). Because slaves came from many different

Figure 5.3 Thracian tattooed women slaves collecting water from a fountain house at Athens: the tattoos are visible along their arms; a red-figure hydria (the women themselves are shown filling and carrying hydriai) 39 cm in height painted by the Egistos Painter, of around 470–460 BC. Louvre, Paris. Drawing by J. Etherington.

parts of the known world, they were often named within the household according to their ethnicity, and a Thracian woman, for example, might be known as 'Thratta' by her owners.

Slaves born into the household

The most privileged class of slaves were those who, having been born into a household, became part of the family. The loyalty and devotion of such slaves is stressed in dramatic works such as Euripides' *Helen*, where a slave recalls taking part in Helen's wedding procession, and feels it is part of his duty to empathise with the family to which he belongs (Eur. *Helen* 722–33: doc. 5.66). Laios' shepherd, who inadvertently set Oedipus' tragic chain of destiny in motion, proudly describes himself as 'not purchased but reared in his house' (*Oedipus Tyrannus* 1121–41: doc. 5.10; Fig. 5.4). The portrayal of such loyal slaves was popular in tragedies. Many of those born 'in the house' must have felt part of the family, having known no other life. Many of them too would have been biological children of men in the family, and hence half-siblings to the citizen children: however, they inherited the status of their mother and could be parted from the rest of the family and sold off at will.

Slave numbers

The number of slaves in Athens, in particular, is often overestimated: slaves were not a cheap commodity and not every citizen or metic family was able to purchase and maintain

187

a slave. At the beginning of the Peloponnesian War Athens may have comprised some 60,000 citizens, with another 120,000 living in Attica, and perhaps 25,000 metics, with 25,000 domestic slaves serving the citizens, and 10,000 the metics. There may also have been another 35,000 industrial slaves in the city and Piraeus, and another 60–80,000 slaves in the Attic countryside, some of whom were working the land and others the silver mines. Figures were somewhat higher in the fourth century, and every Greek city, depending on its prosperity, had a proportionate number of slaves: Chios was supposed to have had the largest number. While it is generally accepted that most Athenian households probably had one or more slaves, this has to be viewed with caution, and the cost of slaves may have been prohibitive for some families. Lysias wrote a speech for a disabled tradesman at the end of the fifth century who wished to continue to receive the government's social security payment of one obol a day to help him with his living expenses. This would not have been a living wage but was meant to assist him to keep 'his head above water'. The shopkeeper maintained that he had as yet no children who could help him out and that he could not afford to find someone, such as a slave, to give him any assistance. He was possibly one of a large number of citizen workers who had no slave support (Lys. 24: doc. 1.33).

It is difficult to estimate the actual numbers of slaves in Athens at any given time: Thucydides' comment that the 20,000 or so Attic slaves who deserted after the fortification of Dekeleia were mostly skilled manual workers gives no clue as to how many slaves in general were employed in the Attic countryside (Thuc. 7.27.5: 5.25). Athenaeus, citing works now lost, gives us some figures for slaves in the fourth century, and speaks of Mnason, a friend of Aristotle, who owned 1000 slaves, which was surely the exception. Indeed he states that Mnason was unpopular at Phokis because his slaves had taken on tasks previously performed by citizens; in contrast Plato in the *Republic* implies that it would be unusual for a family to possess fifty or more slaves (*Republic* 578e). Between 317 and 307 BC, when the tyrant Demetrios of Phaleron called for a general census of Attica, the totals supposedly arrived at were 21,000 Athenian citizens, 10,000 metics and 400,000 slaves, although this would not have borne any relationship to numbers in the fifth century, when citizen numbers were higher and seems incredible for the fourth century. Athenaeus also believed that slave numbers in Corinth and Aegina were similar to those in Athens: Timaios apparently recorded that Corinth was so rich that it had 460,000 slaves while Aristotle in his *Constitution of Aegina* stated that the island (which is only 85 km^2) had 470,000 (Ath. *Deipnosophistae* 272b–d). These figures can hardly be correct, but obviously the prevalent view was that there were extensive numbers of slaves at Corinth and Aegina.

Slaves: their occupations and training

Slavery and servile labour played a very important part in the economy and society of Greek city-states. Slaves, and in some states serfs, were a normal part of life in the Greek world. There were a range of day-to-day activities for which slaves were regarded as essential: as agricultural workers, shepherds, artisans, public slaves (the 'archers' being the Athenians' equivalent of the modern police force), in industry, and as domestic workers, managers and housekeepers within the household. Odysseus, in his palace on Ithaca had fifty female slaves, doubtless in the Homeric poems meant to signify an immense number (*Odyssey* 22.421), who worked wool, washed and cleaned, ground corn, made bread and served at table, prepared beds, made fires and fetched water (Fig. 5.3). These duties changed hardly at all throughout archaic and classical Greece civilisation. A fragment of a fifth-century play by the comic poet Krates lists the household utensils which performed some of the household tasks that slaves

Figure 5.4 A young shepherd is pursued by the god Pan; the god's intentions are made clear. Note the herm on the right. The scene is from an Athenian red-figure bell krater of about 470 BC by the Pan Painter; it is 37 cm high and has a diameter of 42.5 cm. Museum of Fine Arts 10.185, Boston. Drawing by J. Etherington.

were accustomed to undertake in the kitchen, such as setting the table, kneading bread, washing up, baking cakes and cooking vegetables and fish (*The Wild Animals F* 1: doc. 5.69).

Housekeepers and supervisors

One of the paradoxes in owning slaves was that the owners had to train slaves to oversee other slaves. When Ischomachos and his wife appointed a housekeeper they looked for a slave who was not given to overeating and drinking, did not spend all her time in bed, was not given to sexual relationships with male slaves, and who seemed most anxious to please her masters. Valuable qualities in such a housekeeper were a good memory, attention to detail and the anxiety to be rewarded for good work. The married couple trained her to share their joys and troubles, giving her an incentive to ensure that the household prospered by informing her of the state of affairs and letting her share in their success through a financial incentive (Xen. *Oeconomicus* 9.5, 9.11–12: doc. 5.13). As Xenophon comments in his conversation with Socrates, if a master wants to make his slaves into successful overseers, 'you have to oversee their work and examine it and be willing to reward those responsible for whatever is done well and not shrink from giving the punishment deserved to someone who has been careless'

189

(Xen. *Oeconomicus* 12.18–19: doc. 5.31). In her introduction to her new home, Ischomachos' wife promises to care for all sick slaves, in the hope that those who have been well treated will be even more grateful than before: the perception here is that slaves will be responsive to kind handling (Xen. *Oeconomicus* 7.37: doc. 4.63).

Prostitutes and concubines

Many enslaved women were put to work in brothels, like the concubine who accidentally poisoned her owner Philoneos in order to prevent this: he had grown tired of her and wanted to use her as a source of income (Antiph. 1 *Prosecution of the Stepmother* 14–17, 19–20: doc. 4.52). The same fate could happen to young men: the philosopher Phaedo of Elis was captured in war (perhaps in the war between Sparta and Elis in 402/1) and sold into slavery, ending up in the hands of an Athenian slave dealer who put him to work in a male brothel: he was freed by some of Socrates' friends and was present with the others at Socrates' execution. Plato names his dialogue, which describes the execution of Socrates, the *Phaedo* and after Socrates' death Phaedo returned to Elis to found a school of philosophy. New-born children who had been exposed by their parents could be raised by a slave-dealer for their monetary value once they were able to be put to work. Girls abandoned in this way, like others bought young in the slave market, were either trained as dancing or flute girls, or put to work in a brothel as prostitutes. Neaira, who was charged in court with falsifying her status as that of an Athenian citizen woman, was said to have been trained by such a professional called Nikarete, who 'was clever at spotting potential good-looks in young girls and knew from experience how to bring them up and educate them, as she practised this as her profession and made her living from them' ([Dem.] 59 *Against Neaira* 18–19, 28–32: doc. 4.98). She educated six others at the same time as Neaira, and procured money either from their services or by outright sale of them as slaves.

According to Plutarch, Aspasia, Perikles' partner, 'practised a calling that was neither decent nor respectable, since she brought up young girls as hetairai' (Plut. *Life of Perikles* 24.2–9: doc. 4.29). In this particular case Plutarch may have been misled by the many jibes by comic poets such as Aristophanes at Perikles' relationship with Aspasia, and while she was frequently attacked onstage as a concubine or hetaira this need not be taken literally (Ar. *Acharnians* 524–9: doc. 4.95). This training and hiring of young girls as hetairai or entertainers was, however, not unusual. Citizen girls, if not exposed shortly after birth, were legally protected from such treatment by their male relatives, with one important exception: although the reforms attributed to Solon in 594/3 prevented Athenians becoming enslaved for debt in Athens, he allowed the guardian of an unmarried woman (for example his sister or daughter) who had lost her virginity to sell her as a slave. There is no evidence as to whether this drastic measure was brought into play in Solon's time or later: at the least it must have helped deter Athenian girls from inappropriate behaviour. There is the clear implication that before Solon's time unwanted womenfolk could be disposed of in this way without criticism (Plut. *Life of Solon* 23.2: doc. 4.50).

Public slaves

Large cities with a sophisticated bureaucracy like Athens also had a need for public servants who belonged to the state. These would primarily have been professionals, such as secretaries and the drafters of documents, whose service to the city provided for higher-order duties which citizens elected by lot could not perform. There were also the Scythian archers, who essentially acted as a police force, since citizens were not allowed to lay hands on each other

(Figs 1.6, 3.5). Originally numbering 300, they were later increased to 1000 and from living in tents in the agora they moved to the Areiopagos (Schol. Ar. *Acharnians* 54: doc. 5.11). One of their duties was that of keeping order at the boule and assembly, dragging in procrastinating citizens with the vermilion-coloured rope (Ar. *Acharnians* 17–27: doc. 1.18), and keeping the peace generally: the weapon which they used against Athenian citizens was the whip and they clearly had powers of arrest. The orator Andocides (3.5) states that these Scythian archers were purchased shortly after the battle of Salamis, and were quite distinct from bowmen in the armed forces. While they may not all have been Scythians, it is clear that they are foreigners, as Aristophanes makes fun of their pronunciation of Greek in his *Thesmophoriazousai*.

Other public slaves included the public executioner and torturers, workmen employed on the roads ([Arist.] *Ath. Pol.* 54.1), clerks for the jury-courts, and workers in the mint and treasury. In the fourth century Athens made use of several hundred public slaves, many of whom were highly skilled, while others were employed in the less attractive roles of removing the bodies of those who died on the streets ([Arist.] *Ath. Pol.* 50.1–51.4: doc. 1.25). A particularly important public slave in the fourth century was the tester of silver coinage, and a decree of 375/4 specifies his duties which essentially are to test all foreign currency for counterfeit. He had great responsibilities, and if he failed to test properly or left his post he would receive fifty lashes. The decree also made provision for a similar tester for the Piraeus either to be appointed from among the existing public slaves or purchased. His salary was to be the same as that of the tester in the city and came from the same source as the salaries for workers in the mint (Bogaert *Epigraphica* 21: doc. 1.70). That these public slaves could be wealthy and live in their own houses is shown by Aeschines' speech *Against Timarchos*, where a public slave Pittalakos has plenty of money, and indulges in gambling and cock-fighting. Pittalakos actually brings a suit against Timarchos and his companion Hegesandros. Normally in the case of a slave his master would bring the suit: perhaps Pittalakos as a public slave had a prostates, a patron, who would speak on his behalf (Aeschin. 1 *Against Timarchos* 54–66).

Slaves and masters

Greek landowners never acquired the huge establishments of slaves that became a feature of Roman agriculture, especially in Sicily, and the majority of slaves worked alongside their masters, in workshops or on the farm, rather than in slave-gangs: the exception to this were the slave labourers in the silver mines at Laureion. Yet while many farmers in Attica and elsewhere may have had one or more slaves to help them in their work, this should not be considered the norm. Many Attic farmers possessed smallholdings which would not have been sufficiently productive to justify feeding a slave all year round. The norm was probably a single girl at best. Hesiod certainly advises a small farmer to start with a slave woman before he marries: 'First of all you should acquire a house and a woman and an ox for the plough, a female slave, not a wife, who can follow the oxen as well' (Hes. *Works and Days* 405–6: doc. 5.12). Her main duties, apart from helping on the farm, would have been the preparation of grain for bread and porridge, though she would doubtless have been expected to perform some of the functions of a wife in bed: Hesiod specifically advises against buying a woman nursing a child, for it makes her less handy around the place.

But even this scenario may have been beyond the capacity of a subsistence farmer, who would not have been able to afford an ox, or possessed enough land on which to use it if he had one. Solon's division of Athenians into timocratic classes suggests that few among the Athenians were really rich: his top class, the pentakosiomedimnoi, or 500 bushel men, would have needed 75–145 acres of grain producing land or 20–25 acres of vineyards or olive orchards to be included in that category; the second category had to make 300 bushels, the third 200, and the last, the thetes, anything under 200. A medimnos of barley was a month's supply for an adult. In reality, the poorest Athenians may well have been involved in small-scale low-status cultivation on as little as five acres, growing a mixture of cereals, grapes, olives and vegetables with perhaps a few small stock animals for cheese or for consumption by the family, and the farm would have been dependent on family, not slave, labour. The majority of citizens not on the land would similarly have been small-scale craftsmen in a family business.

When Dekeleia in central Attica was taken by the Spartans and occupied in 413, the Spartans had a continual presence in the countryside from which they were able to devastate the area routinely, and 20,000 Attic slaves are estimated by Thucydides to have deserted from Attica at this period. They are specifically called skilled workers (cheirotechnai), and while these may refer to slaves in the higher-level mining jobs at Laureion, they are far more likely to have been specialised farm workers – such as vine-dressers from the larger estates, rather than individuals each from one of several thousand different properties (Thuc. 7.27.5: doc. 5.25); they didn't get far, and were intercepted by the Boeotians and sold back into slavery. The agricultural slaves on Corcyra, who not surprisingly joined the democratic side in the civil war in 427 BC, might represent slaves owned by larger-scale farming interests (Thuc. 3.73: doc. 5.26). Larger-scale farmers in mountainous areas of Greece also employed slaves as shepherds to stay with the flocks in the summer months. The shepherd who failed to expose Oedipus as instructed proudly goes out of his way to describe himself as one of Laios' house-born slaves, and thus trustworthy. His occupation was to stay on the Kithairon hills for six months every summer with his flock, bringing them back to the homestead in the winter. It was here that he associated yearly with the Corinthian shepherd to whom

Figure 5.5 A fluted Ionic column, part of the Erechtheum; slaves, metics and citizens worked side by side on the fluting of these columns (doc. 5.42). Photo © Bryan Busovicki/iStock.

he had given Oedipus (Soph. *Oedipus Tyrannus* 1121–41: doc. 5.10). This position needed a fair degree of trustworthiness and commitment to protecting the sheep from predators and thieves, perhaps accompanied by a sheepdog who lived with the sheep to protect them from attack.

Citizens, metics and slaves column-fluting

An inscription regarding wages for fluting a column at the Erechtheion on the Athenian acropolis shows citizens, metics and slaves all working together, each receiving one drachma per day: 86 workers can be identified, and there are 24 citizens, 42 metics and 20 slaves recorded. Citizens are identified by their deme of origin, slaves by their owner's name, and metics by their deme of residence (*IG* I³ 476: doc. 5.42; Fig. 5.5). Citizens in this inscription also filled the positions of overseeing architect and under-secretary, and with the exception of one woodcarver and one labourer who laid roof-tiles, all the others were masons, carpenters and sculptors. The metics, while still outnumbering the citizens in these occupations, pursued all the minor specialised trades, while all the slaves were skilled, being either masons or carpenters. The rate of pay was one drachma per day for all skilled labour, and slaves worked for both citizens and metics.

Slaves with trade skills were also allowed to work on their own at their trade and be responsible for their own keep, while paying a regular sum to their masters and saving part of their wages to buy their freedom; the term for this was 'living apart'. The orator Aeschines gives an example of such slaves staffing a shoe-making shop and, from the income, paying their owner a daily proportion of their earnings

> There were nine or ten slaves who were skilled shoemakers, who each gave over to him [Timarchos] two obols a day, and the person in charge of the shop three obols. There was also a woman skilled in flax-working, who produced high-quality goods for the market, and a man skilled in embroidery.
>
> (Aeschin. 1 *Against Timarchos* 97)

Figure 5.6 A potter's workshop. On the left, a potter crafts a large pot; on the right, a man is inside a large cone of clay treading it to make a fine consistency, while another bends over the cone to take some clay from the mound and put it into his basket. The master is shown worshipping a herm. This is an Athenian black-figure skyphos 17.4 cm high of about 500 BC and attributed to the Theseus Painter. Harvard University Art Museums 1960.321 & 1958.19. Drawing by J. Etherington.

The shop and the slaves brought Timarchos a clear income of 15 minas (1500 drachmas) a year, and would have quickly recouped the cost of the outlay on the slaves and setting up the shop. Such slaves hoped to save enough to eventually purchase their freedom, with their master's permission. Slaves were also hired out to another employer, with the owner receiving the slave's wages. Because of the low cost of feeding and clothing slaves the profits from their work could be enormous, but against this must be set their purchase price.

When Chremylos in *Wealth* hopes that Ploutos will make everyone equally rich and therefore citizens will not want to work, he assumes that slaves will take over the necessary day-to-day jobs such as blacksmithing, building ships, sewing, making wheels, shoes and bricks, washing, tanning hides and farming. These were clearly occupations which could be performed by citizens or metics, but were also ones in which slaves assisted and for which it was possible to find slaves who were equally competent if other avenues failed. In fact the only occupations which citizens would not undertake were labouring in the mines at Laureion, and the more unpleasant duties of public slaves: the only role in which slaves could not serve alongside their masters was in warfare – and even then there were exceptions in times of real crisis.

Slave prices and earnings

Very few if any slaves were cheap, except those 'born in the house' at the discretion of the members of the family. Xenophon, in his *Memorabilia*, describes Socrates discussing the different prices of slaves:

> 'Antisthenes,' said Socrates, 'do friends have certain values, like servants? For one slave may be worth perhaps two minas, another less than half a mina, another five minas, and another even ten; Nikias, son of Nikeratos, is said to have paid a talent for an overseer for his silver-mine.'
>
> (*Memorabilia* 2.5.2: doc. 5.15)

This gives the range of prices which Athenians at the end of the fifth century expected to pay for a slave, depending on age and skill; in other words from between 50 drachmas for a cheap specimen, up to the exceptional price of 1000, with 200 drachmas (half a mina) appearing to be an average price. That Nikias paid a talent, or 6000 drachmas, for the overseer of his silver mine, a job with immense responsibilities and knowledge base, is meant to appear unprecedented. The customer paid for skill: Neaira the hetaira was allegedly bought from the owner who trained her in special skills by two young men at the cost of half a talent, or 3000 drachmas. When they decided to get married, they offered her her freedom, remitting her price by a third so she would only have to find 20 minas (2000 drachmas). With the help of some old friends, and what Neaira had been able to save for herself, she was able to find the money ([Dem.] 59 *Against Neaira* 18–19, 28–32: doc. 4.98). These prices were high and of course only paid for the most exclusive slaves.

After the mutilation of the hermai in 415 the property of one of the men involved, Kephisodoros, including his slaves, was publicly auctioned and the average price fetched per slave was 157 drachmas (nearly half a year's income for a skilled worker). This may seem a large sum of money, but parallels the normal rate for a ransomed prisoner of war at two minas (200 drachmas) per prisoner which is close to Xenophon's average price. Prices range from 301 drachmas for a Syrian (and 240 for another) to 72 drachmas for a little Carian child; the women's prices range from 220 drachmas down to 85 drachmas 1 obol (*IG* I³ 421: doc. 5.18).

Figure 5.7 A painted terracotta plaque from Penteskouphia, near Corinth showing slaves digging for clay. The holes are for hanging from the walls of the temple there. This plaque dates from 575–550 BC and there are several similar dedicated plaques from this site. Antikensammlung Museen Berlin F 871. Drawing by J. Etherington.

The Syrians may have been highly skilled professionals like secretaries or doctors, and the older child relatively expensive at 174 drachmas because it was old enough to be trained for a particular profession. It seems unlikely that it would have been easy for an Athenian craftsman to purchase a slave for domestic or work-related assistance; certainly a trained slave workman would have to be saved up for rather like an expensive car today, and might cost close to a year's income. Even an unskilled girl or woman must have been an investment.

The hire of slaves

Of course, for the wealthier Athenians, slaves were a profitable investment, and for those with large numbers of slaves hiring them out was clearly a good way to make money: slaves were hired out to work the mines, and Nikias was only one of a number of entrepreneurs who did so. Mines belonged to the state but were leased out to individuals, and Nikias was so wealthy that he was able to buy and hire out 1000 men to work for Sosias the Thracian, who paid him an obol a day for each (Xen. *Revenues* 4.14–15: doc. 15.15). Hiring out a single slave to work in the mines could therefore earn an owner over 60 drachmas per year and a 1000 of them 10 talents. The slaves' work must have been worth more than this to provide Sosias with a profit margin. But by the terms of the agreement Sosias was required to keep the numbers constant. In other words he was to replace any wastage, as in slaves who died, and it was therefore in his best interest not to maltreat the slaves or work them to death. It has been deduced from Xenophon (Xen. *Revenues* 4.4–16, 23; cf. doc. 5.16) that a typical Laureion slave miner cost 180 drachmas (which suggests that several of Kephisodoros' male slaves worth 161 or 171 drachmas were labourers or heavy-duty workers). It would, therefore, take nearly three years to recoup your expenditure at this rate of pay: it would only be economic for the very rich to buy slaves simply to hire them out for minework. Yet clearly this was considered by some an excellent investment: Xenophon relates that Hipponikos had 600 slaves let out on the same terms as Nikias. They brought him a clear mina a day, while Philemonides had 300 who brought him half a mina. There may have been as many as 30,000 slaves involved in the Athenian silver mines and their processing mills and Xenophon suggested in his *Revenues* that the city should buy a large number of slaves, up to three state slaves per citizen, so that their leasing would assure the state an income for all Athenians (Xen. *Revenues* 4.17).

Slave factories

Factories could be staffed by slaves, like the shield factory owned by the metics Lysias and his brother Polemarchos, which they had inherited from their father Kephalos who came to Athens when Perikles was in power. Under the pretext that some metics were hostile to the Thirty in 404–403, ten metic households were targeted by Theognis and Peison, and their goods appropriated. According to Lysias, he and his brother owned 120 slaves of whom they took the best and gave the rest to the state; the plunder also included 700 shields (Lys. 12 *Against Eratosthenes* 4–11, 19–20: doc. 5.41). The value of the slaves was considerable as many of them, if not all of them, were skilled workmen. Demosthenes' father, c. 380, similarly left his son a large estate including two productive factories, run by slaves who were skilled and valuable. These factories brought in a good income and were part of an extensive portfolio of earnings and investments, including sums of money out on loan at the usual rate of one drachma per mina per month. Demosthenes was engaged in a legal battle between 363 and 361 to recover his inheritance from his guardians. When reckoning up his father's assets he made it clear that the investment was primarily in skilled slaves. There was a sword-making factory with 32 or 33 slaves each worth five or six minas and none less than three, which brought in 30 minas a year, and twenty bed manufactur-ers, pledged for a 40 mina debt, which brought in a clear 12 minas a year. The furniture workmen here were held as pledges for a debt much less than their market value. This is assuming the workmen were of equivalent value to the sword-makers, who represented capital to the value of at least 150 minas, with each craftsman worth 500–600 drachmas, as opposed to the 180 drachmas for a unskilled labourer, such as a slave to work in the mines. Manufacturing overheads were, however, high: Demosthenes' father left ivory and iron, for use in the workshops, and wood for beds worth about 80 minas, and oak-gall and cop-per bought for 70 minas (Dem. 27 *Against Aphorbos* 1.9–11: doc. 5.19).

Factories staffed by slaves were, therefore, very profitable and represented a secure invest-ment. Socrates, on meeting a friend Aristarchos who had lost all his property in the Pelopon-nesian War and now had to support a number of female relatives, advised him to put the women of his family to productive work such as weaving – advice which turned out to be

Figure 5.8 An Athenian terracotta black-figure lekythos showing women at work in the household. In the centre of the obverse (left) of the vase, slaves work at the loom; the reverse shows women folding a cloth on the left, and on their right women spin wool into thread on drop-spindles. This vase is from 550–530 BC, probably painted by the Amasis Painter. Metropolian Museum of Fine Art 31.11.10, New York. Drawing by J. Etherington.

highly successful (Xen. *Memorabilia* 2.7.6–12: doc. 4.64). To persuade Aristarchos, Socrates lists a number of profitable slave-run businesses in Athens:

> Don't you know that from one of these occupations, making barley-groats, Nausikydes maintains not only himself and his household, but lots of pigs and cattle as well, and has enough left over to undertake liturgies for the city? That Kyrebos from baking keeps his whole household and lives in luxury, as does Demeas of Kollytos from making capes, and Menon by making cloaks, while most of the Megarians make a living out of tunic-making?

To be over the liturgy threshold, Nausikydes must have amassed capital worth at least three talents, and for those with capital to spare such investment in slaves would have paid well. However, skilled slaves were not a cheap commodity in Athens, although doubtless prices varied considerably, and, as already stated, even a relatively cheap slave would have been beyond the means of many Athenian or Attic families, the great majority of whom were not wealthy.

Slaves in war

Defence of the city was a citizen's duty, and only free men were expected to fight for the city by land or by sea: rowing the triremes was as important as being a hoplite and was the particular role of the thetes in Athens. Metics too were expected to serve as hoplites or in the fleet. Slaves of course served with the army, but not in a fighting capacity. They carried the baggage and prepared the food. At Potidaea in 428 each of the 3000 members of the Athenian garrison had a slave, and were paid two drachmas a day, one for themselves and one for the maintenance of their slaves. Theophrastos' coward, who does everything except actually fight, as soon as he sees battle commencing,

> Says to those standing next to him that in his haste he forgot to get his sword, runs to the tent and sends the slave out to see where the enemy are, hides the sword under the pillow and then wastes a lot of time pretending he is looking for it.
>
> (Theophr. *Characters* 25: doc. 1.41)

No doubt one of the attractions of victory was that the winning side would acquire the slaves of the losers.

It was only in real crises that slaves actually fought or rowed in war, and then they were freed, acquiring the status of metics. The first slaves who appear to have fought for Athens did so in 491 against Aegina, and those that died in battle were given a public burial with their individual names recorded on a stele stating that 'in the war they behaved bravely in respect of their masters' (Paus. *Description of Greece* 1.29.7: doc. 5.21). The other occasions when slaves were called on to serve with the Athenian army were at Marathon in 490, Arginousai in 406 and Chaironeia in 338; perhaps also at Aigospotamoi in 405. Herodotos does not mention slaves fighting at Marathon, perhaps because of the heroic nature of his account (and the Athenians may themselves have played down the slaves' involvement), but according to Pausanias the slaves who fought and died at Marathon had their own grave (Paus. *Description of Greece* 1.32.3: doc. 5.22). The situation prior to Arginousai, when the Athenian fleet was blockaded at Mytilene by the Spartans, was so desperate that in an unprecedented move every possible rower was mobilised – slaves and even hippeis (the cavalry). In reward for their victory the slaves who survived were made citizens, a decision which Aristophanes commends in the *Frogs* (Ar. *Frogs* 687–99: doc. 5.24). Other cities were less rigid, and there were slaves on the seven Chian ships blockading the enemy fleet in 411 (these too were later freed), and 800 on Corcyra's ships in 432 (Thuc. 8.15.2, 1.55.1).

On Corcyra during the civil war in 427 BC both sides invited slaves to join them by offering them their freedom: the point at issue was whether Corcyra remained allied to Corinth and the Peloponnesians as desired by the oligarchs, or joined Athens as desired by the democrats. The great majority of slaves joined the democratic side (Thuc. 3.73: doc. 5.26). Only in real emergencies were slaves used in land warfare. Obviously there were times when they formed the only manpower available in a crisis and their assistance was purchased at the cost of their freedom prior to the engagement. Spartan helots normally served with the army, with 35,000 present at the battle of Plataea. However, Sparta too was prepared to emancipate helots in a real military crisis, as when after the battle of Leuktra the Thebans invaded the

Peloponnese in 370 and threatened the city of Sparta itself. A call was made to the helots to enlist in return for their freedom and 6000 volunteered – so many that the Spartans were afraid and withdrew the offer (Xen. *Hellenika* 6.5.22–32: doc. 14.20).

The legal position of slaves

Gortyn in Crete

The legal position of slaves of course varied between different states and poleis. The Cretan serfs (apetairoi) mentioned in the law code of Gortyn had certain clear rights: if an estate was sold, they went with the property and could not be alienated from it. The code presents clear evidence about the status of slaves and serfs in Crete; these serfs, a class of hereditary workers tied to the land which did not exist in Attica, were akin to the Spartan helots. The law code lays down that persons accused of being slaves may not be seized before trial, and the penalties for so doing are very heavy. If the two sides do not agree about the status of the person under dispute, the matter is to be decided by witnesses, and if judged free the person must be released immediately or his captor was to pay heavy penalties. The code also clearly shows the status of children born to slaves or serfs, and of course a baby was automatically the possession of the master of the house to whom the woman belonged. Penalties for the rape of a serf or slave vary with the social class of the victim and offender and it was the master who was recompensed if the offence was committed against one of his slaves. Fines varied from 200 staters (400 drachmas) if a free woman was raped by a slave, down to one obol if a slave who was not a virgin was raped by another slave. In Athens sexual assault on a slave belonging to another citizen was punished by a fine half that laid down for rape of a free woman, probably of 50 drachmas, which was paid to the slave's owner (Plut. *Life of Solon* 23.1: doc. 4.50; cf. Lysias 1.32).

Slaves in Athens

Slaves were almost entirely within the power of their masters, who could sell them, give them or bequeath them, rent them out to work for others, and punish them in any way they chose short of killing them. There were certain limits on how slaves could be treated at Athens: like free men and women they were protected against hubris, and illegal treatment. Any citizen could bring an action (graphe hubreos) before the thesmothetai if they saw a slave being treated inappropriately. As Aeschines comments, however, the law was not intended to protect the slave, but to ensure that citizens did not become accustomed to outraging anyone in case they might find themselves behaving in the same way to free men, and that no one prepared to maltreat any person to extremes should have a place in a democracy (cf. doc. 1.42). Similarly, owners were not permitted to kill a slave, a ruling not made to protect the slave, but because the owner in killing the slave would commit hubris. If a slave deserved death then, officially, that was the role of the authorities – although there were undoubtedly cases where a slave was killed within the household and the incident was never reported. Even slaves guilty of killing their masters were not to be killed by the owner's relatives: their punishment was the duty of the state. Antiphon cites a case where a young slave boy, 11 years of age, tried to murder his owner: had he not run away and thus betrayed his guilt, all the slaves in the household would have been killed in response, as if they had shared in the crime (Antiph. 5 *On the Murder of Herodes* 46–8, 69: doc. 5.29).

While most misbehaviour by slaves was dealt with within the household, there were laws which forbade them from acting like citizens and just as they were not normally to serve in the army or navy (since it was the duty of a citizen to defend his city, except in the worst of crises), so they were not allowed to engage in an active sexual role with citizens. This did not, of course, refer only to citizen women: slaves were specifically forbidden by Solon to share the facilities of the gymnasia, or act as an erastes (lover) to a citizen boy, or importune him, on pain of 50 lashes (Aeschin. 1 *Against Timarchos* 138–9: doc. 5.34). Slaves were totally forbidden from being the lovers of free youths.

Evidence under torture

The difference in status between slaves and citizens can be seen in the legal status of slaves at Athens, where (because by definition they would lie) they could only give evidence in a court of law under torture, at the hands of both the prosecution and the defence. As part of the case the two sides would negotiate concerning the methods of torture to be used, and if the slave were disabled as a result of the proceedings the slave's master would receive compensation. A parody of such tortures in Aristophanes *Frogs* (lines 618–22) includes racking, hoisting,

Figure 5.9 A naked man, either a day labourer or (more likely given his nakedness while working) a slave, carries a large cylindrical sack. He is bent over by the weight and is clearly struggling to support it; he grasps it firmly in both hands to keep it in place. He walks past a herm. Aristocrats 'looked down' on such manual labour. The scene is on the inside of an Athenian red-figure vase dating to about 490 BC. Antikensammlung Staatliche Museen F2298, Berlin. Drawing by J. Etherington.

scourging, cudgelling, pouring vinegar up the nose and heaping bricks on the victim. It was possible for an owner to refuse the challenge to have his slave tortured, but his opponent would use that to his detriment in court since it would appear that he was deliberately with-holding evidence from a witness. One side could also give a slave an incentive to lie. Antiphon cites a speaker who claimed that his opponents had offered the slave his freedom if he gave the preferred response. Later he accused them of having a slave killed so the opposite side did not have an opportunity to torture him and extract his evidence (Antiph. 5 *On the Murder of Herodes* 29–32: doc. 5.28). Owners could also freely offer up a slave for torture to support their case, and in Lysias' fourth speech (*On a Wound by Premeditation* 5–10) the defendant offers to have a slave girl tortured who he says is co-owned by himself and the accuser and who is the cause of the quarrel between them.

The treatment of slaves

There was no concern felt about the fact that owners had the right to punish their slaves as they pleased, short of killing them. Plato in a discussion of his ideal civilisation states,

> Anyone who wishes, providing he is not mad, can seize his own slave and treat him as he wishes, within the limits of what is lawful; and he can seize a runaway on behalf of one of his relations or friends to keep him safe.
>
> (Pl. *Laws* 914e, 916a–c: doc. 5.20)

Xenophon records Socrates in his *Memorabilia* as discussing the ways in which masters treated slaves who were unwilling to do their work:

> Let us consider how masters treat such servants. Do they not control their lech-erousness by starving them? Prevent them stealing by locking up anywhere they might steal from? Stop them running away by putting them in fetters? Drive out their laziness with beatings? What do you do when you find one of your servants is like this?

His interlocutor's reply is forthright: 'I punish them with every kind of misery until I can compel them to behave like a slave should' (Xen. *Memorabilia* 2.1.15–17: doc. 5.30). In Lysias' speech on the killing of Eratosthenes, Euphiletos states that he discovered the adulterous liaison between his wife and Eratosthenes by threatening his slave-girl who had been acting as a go-between for the lovers:

> I went home and ordered the servant-girl to follow me to the market, where I took her to a friend's house and told her that I had full knowledge of what was going on in the house. And I said, 'So you can take your choice from two alternatives, either to be whipped and sent to the mill, where you will suffer the unrelieved miseries of that work, or to reveal the whole truth and suffer no harm. Do not lie at all, but tell the whole truth.
>
> (Lys. 1 *On the Murder of Eratosthenes* 18; cf. doc. 4.54)

Intent was not necessarily an issue: the concubine who gave her master poison, thinking that she was administering a love-potion (he was going to place her in a brothel so he could gain the income from her clients), was 'broken on the wheel and handed over to the public executioner' (Antiph. 1 *Prosecution of the Stepmother* 20: doc. 4.52).

Rewards for good behaviour

Xenophon understood that while punishment was one form of corrective, slaves who were farm-workers needed a system of rewards as well. Fair treatment of slaves meant that slaves were willing to work for their masters, while these should also set them a good example by being systematic in overseeing their work and rewarding or punishing as appropriate (Xen. *Oeconomicus* 12.18–19: doc. 5.31). The work ascribed to Aristotle defines the problem further: there are three areas of importance in dealing with slaves – work, punishment and food: as he states, 'the solution is to give him work and sufficient food. It is not possible to manage slaves without payment, and the payment for slaves is food'. However, he also clearly implies that slaves can be punished by withholding their rations ([Arist.] *Economics* 1344.a35–b21: doc. 5.32). Theophrastos' 'penny-pincher' takes it out of his rations if a slave breaks a pot or a plate (doc. 1.34). The author of the *Economics* admits that there should be incentives for good behaviour, with freedom as a possible reward once a particular goal is reached. He considers that letting slaves have children effectually means that the owner has hostages for the slave's good behaviour, while possessing too many slaves of the same ethnic background is dangerous, as the slaves can identify with each other.

Slaves had their own quarters in Greek homes and the women were firmly separated from the men. When choosing a housekeeper, Ischomachos and his wife 'considered which woman seemed to us to be the most temperate with regard to her stomach, wine, sleep and consorting with men'. As far as slave living conditions were concerned, female and male slaves had separate sleeping quarters and could only cohabit with the express permission of their owners: any children they might produce were of course the property of the oikos. One of the ways in which slave owners could control their slaves' behaviour was by allowing them to cohabit and have children, or conversely by preventing this. When Ischomachos showed his young wife round her new home, the slave quarters were an important part of the tour. The quarters for men and women were separated by a bolted door, so that the slaves were unable to cohabit except with permission and nothing could be removed or stolen (Xen. *Oeconomicus* 9.5, 9.11–12: doc. 5.13). Most female, and doubtless many male, slaves would also be in sexual servitude to the males of the family. Euphiletos, in defending himself against the accusation of entrapment and murder, comments to the jury that his wife, whom he allegedly caught in an affair, had accused him of molesting their slave-girl while drunk (*On the Murder of Eratosthenes* 12).

Household slaves might, however, be lucky enough to be cared for when sick and even given responsibility within the household (Xen. *Oeconomicus* 7.10–23, 7.35–7: doc. 4.63). Ischomachos' young wife maintained that she was happy to ensure that any sick slaves were cared for, and much of her married life would have been spent supervising her slave household: teaching them to weave (Fig. 5.8), keeping an eye on the cook, supervising the housekeeper when she was measuring out food, ensuring everything was kept in its right place, and helping the slaves with the baking and the shaking and folding of cloaks and bedding. That these were not necessarily easy tasks is shown by her husband's comment that the exercise ensured that she would 'eat better and be healthier, and have a better natural colour'. Elderly ex-slaves could be welcomed back into the household: in a speech attributed to Demosthenes the speaker states that his old nurse had been given her freedom, but that when her husband died and

Figure 5.10 The marble grave stele of an unknown young man in athletic pose. His father gazes at him contemplatively; his dog mourns him. His little slave boy, probably quite attached to his young master, has fallen asleep. This very fine relief dates to about 340 BC. National Archaeological Museum inv. No. 869, Athens. Photo © William McClung. All rights reserved.

she had no one to look after her, he took her back into his household so he could care for her, as he also did for his paidagogos, the slave who had been responsible for escorting him to school. This was obviously intended to impress the jurors with his sense of responsibility and gratitude for past favours: 'I couldn't bear to see either my nurse or the slave who attended me as a boy to be in want' ([Dem.] 47 *Against Evergos and Mnesiboulos* 55–6: doc. 5.14).

At certain times of the year slaves in Athens had their conditions temporarily ameliorated, and they were allowed a short break from servitude: they could take part in religious cults, such as the Eleusinian Mysteries (although presumably they needed their owner's permission) and were invited to join the banquet of the Choes, on the second day of the Anthesteria festival. Theophrastos' superstitious man attends the Orphic initiations every month with his children, and if his wife is too busy takes their slave-nurse instead (Theophr. *Characters* 16: doc. 3.72). If slaves were severely ill-treated, they were allowed to take sanctuary in the

Theseion (a sanctuary in which slaves were allowed to seek asylum; cf. Fig. 5.14) and demand resale, and of course if they were fortunate enough to have a craft they might be allowed to save up and purchase their own freedom.

For most, however, life would have been bleak, and even the possibility of manumission may not have been attractive, if freedom meant the freedom merely to starve. Yet the 'Old Oligarch' writing in about 425 was caustic about the amount of latitude given to slaves in Athens, grumbling that because of the general standard of dress one dare not hit a slave in passing in case he should turn out to be a citizen and summons you. He was also irate at seeing many slaves 'living in the lap of luxury' in Athens, and presumably these were slaves who were 'living apart'. He linked this with Athens' being a naval power – which made the Athenians 'slaves to their slaves' in as much as the owners took their earnings and eventually freed them, or the slaves were able to get themselves out of trouble with the money they earned. Clearly he thought much more highly of Sparta, where slaves were with good reason afraid of their masters ([Xen.] *Constitution of the Athenians* 1.10–12: doc. 5.35).

Manumission

When slaves were manumitted, or given their freedom, they were granted the status of metics, or resident aliens. Like metics, they had to have a prostates 'patron', who was usually their former owner and to whom they still owed some obligations. Some slaves, like Neaira, were able to save up enough money or take out a loan to buy their own freedom, while others could be manumitted by will. Ex-slaves in Athens were able to own property. In the classical period manumission could be performed informally, in the presence of witnesses, who were present at the emancipation of the slave before a public tribunal or in the theatre. Aristotle's will, quoted by Diogenes Laertius, states that certain slaves are to be freed at his death, and others on his daughter's marriage, while any slaves that looked after Aristotle are not to be sold but set free when at the appropriate age (Diog. Laert. 5.11–16).

Metics

Athens and a number of other Greek cities possessed a class of metics – resident foreigners, citizens from another polis who came to a new city to work. According to Plutarch, Solon actively encouraged foreign traders and craftsmen to settle in Athens (docs 8.27–8) and by the fifth century metics had become a large and important group of residents. Visitors from abroad were allowed to stay in Athens with the status of a parepidemos, or visitor, for a certain number of days; when this period had lapsed they were considered metics and liable to pay the metic tax (Aristophanes of Byzantium *F* 38: doc. 5.36). While not citizens, and unable to vote or own houses or land (they were known as 'resident in' not 'of' a deme), they had specific and very well-protected rights, including a citizen patron (prostates) who represented them in court if necessary. Xenophon, in his *Revenues*, speaks of them as 'one of the finest sources of revenue since they maintain themselves, and, though conferring many benefits on cities, they receive no payment but actually pay the metic tax' (Xen. *Revenues* 2.1: doc. 5.37). The metic tax, the metoikion, was paid to the state by metics at the rate of one drachma per month for a man and half that for a independent woman, that is one not living in her husband or son's household. That metic women did work independently is shown in Aristophanes' *Frogs*, by the metic lady innkeepers whom Dionysos meets in the underworld when dressed up as Herakles: one of the ladies sends off for her 'prostates' to make sure he pays up what

Figure 5.11 A marble thanksgiving relief. The size of the larger than life female figure on the left is an indication that she is a goddess and the remains of the right hand of a figure behind strongly suggests that this is the divine pair Asklepios and his daughter Hygieia. A mother sits slumped in her chair, while behind her a woman holds a small baby, apparently newly born. This is a thanksgiving relief in which the mother thanks these deities for the safe delivery of her child. The woman holding the infant is almost certainly a slave, assigned to looking after the baby after the mother's exhausting delivery; she may also have acted as a wet-nurse. The find spot is unknown but it seems to be from one of the Aegean islands; the relief is 26.7 cm high and 21.7 cm wide. Metropolian Museum of Fine Art 24.97.92, New York. Drawing by Tessa Rickards.

he owes from an earlier visit (Ar. *Frogs* 549–78: doc. 4.61). Similarly Euxitheos, in a speech of Demosthenes (*Against Euboulides* 30–1, 33–5, 40–2: doc. 5.63), argues passionately that just because his mother sells ribbons in the market and has acted as a wet-nurse to a citizen child, it does not necessarily mean that she is a metic. The 'Old Oligarch', while disapproving of the treatment of slaves in Athens, approves wholeheartedly of metics, because the city needed metics on account of its numerous trades and its fleet: 'for this reason we quite reasonably have given metics equal rights' ([Xen.] *Constitution of the Athenians* 1.10–12: doc. 5.35).

There may have been some 20–25,000 metics in Athens c. 431, although this number is only an estimate. It was obviously a privileged class and some metics became very wealthy, like the orator Lysias and his brother Polemarchos. Metics, along with their slaves, received the same wages as citizens for fluting a column of the Erechtheum, a drachma a day each (*IG* I³ 476: doc. 5.42). Under certain specific conditions, metics were granted citizenship: those metics who supported the democrat Thrasyboulos and helped restore the democracy in 403 were made citizens and their names and occupations were listed in a decree: several were farmers, and there was also a cook, carpenter, digger, baker, muleteer, builder, gardener, donkey-driver, olive-presser, fuller, statue-maker and hired labourer (IG II² 10: doc. 5.43). Citizenship was passed on to their descendents, but not, it seems, to their wives. Other metics who joined in the battle at Mounichia and protected the Piraeus only received isoteleia, exemption from paying the metic tax.

Metics were expected to participate in paying for liturgies (such as dramatic productions or the maintenance of a trireme for a year) if they were above the financial threshold, and this in itself shows how wealthy many metics became. They were also liable for the war-tax and helped to ransom state prisoners. Lysias and his brother Polemarchos were in this economic category and, when several metics were attacked on the grounds of being antagonistic to the Thirty, they lost all their goods. The plunderers accepted a talent of silver as a bribe, but then took three talents of silver and 400 cyzicenes, 100 darics and four silver cups, as well as 700 shields, 120 slaves and all the valuable paraphernalia of the household, including jewellery, furniture and women's cloaks. This despite the fact that the brothers had performed their duties to the city, defraying the cost of choruses (as choregoi), and contributing to many special taxes (eisphorai), as well as ransoming many Athenians from the enemy (Lys. 12 *Against Eratosthenes* 4–11, 19–20: doc. 5.41). The costs involved in some of these liturgies are outlined in another speech of Lysias (Lys. 21 *On a Charge of Taking Bribes* 1–5: doc. 1.30).

Metics' role in warfare

Another important contribution made by metics to the state was that they were liable for military service, and Perikles led a force of 10,000 citizens and 3000 metic hoplites into the Megarid in the first year of the Peloponnesian War (Thuc. 2.31.1–2: doc. 5.38). It does not appear to have been unusual for metics to have been part of the striking-force and the Athenians also had 16,000 men on garrison duty at Athens and elsewhere, a large proportion of whom were metics, serving alongside Athenians who were too old or young to be in the regular army. Metics also helped crew the triremes, and in his reply to Sparta's ultimatum Perikles specifically mentions that the fleet, crewed by Athenian citizens and metics, is more than a match for the Peloponnesians (Thuc. 1.143). In the last days of the Sicilian Expedition before the final crisis Nikias specifically addressed the metics in the fleet and urged them to remember what they have gained from being associated with Athens (Thuc. 7.63.3–4: doc. 5.40). He saw them as being in a position of great privilege and as having been envied throughout all Greece for their advantages in sharing the Athenians' empire and enjoying the respect and fear of Athens' allies. The Athenians were proud of their metics, and prouder still of the magnanimous way they themselves treated them. At the time of the Persian Wars, the Themistokles decree of 480 not only linked the metics with the Athenians who were to take ship to face the Persians at Salamis, but arranged for their children and wives to be taken to Troizen for safety (Meiggs and Lewis 23: doc. 11.35). While various duties were incumbent on Athenian citizens, metics were also seen as having obligations to the city of Athens, which sheltered them and gave them the opportunity to earn a good livelihood. In fact, if their services to the state warranted it, they might even be awarded citizenship, but this was rare and a great honour only awarded by the people in assembly.

Metics were so intrinsic to Athenian life that references to them frequently occur in drama, and three lost comedies entitled *Metics* were staged by Krates, Pherekrates and Plato the comic poet. Aeschylus also portrayed metics sympathetically in his tragedy the *Suppliant Women*. In this play, the fifty daughters of Danaos, the suppliant women of the title, took refuge in Argos and were granted metic status. Their father Danaos proudly proclaimed the privileged and protected status granted them by the Argive assembly, and his speech clearly reflected the Athenians' view of the position enjoyed by the metics in Athens, 'free and protected, with complete inviolability' (Aesch. *Suppliant Women* 600–14: doc. 5.39).

Helots, perioikoi and serfs

There seem to have been helots from an early stage in Spartan history, for when the Spartans subdued their neighbours in Lakonia some of these were forced into serfdom. Most of the helots, however, were Messenians, from the area in the south-west of the Peloponnese. During the great age of colonisation when many Greek cities sent out colonies to areas such as Sicily, Italy and the Black Sea, the Spartans sent out few colonies. Instead they solved their need for more land by turning their eyes to the territory of their Greek neighbours.

As early as the middle of the eighth century BC Sparta began a series of wars to extend its territory. According to Ephoros the city of Helos was reduced to serfdom and from this came the term helots, which was later applied to other people whom the Spartans reduced to the status of serfs, although the term helot is almost certainly derived from the city 'Helos' by false etymology, and in fact comes from the verb 'to capture' (Ephoros *F* 117: doc. 6.7). Tyrtaeus speaks of these helots, who were obliged to deliver a certain proportion of their agricultural produce to the Spartiates, as 'Just like donkeys oppressed with great burdens, bringing to their masters of grievous necessity half of all the produce their land bears . . .' (Tyrt. *Poem* 6: doc. 5.44). As well as working on the estates, helots also served in Sparta in the usual roles of slaves, both male and female, and they accompanied the Spartans on campaign.

According to Plutarch, the Spartan king Kleomenes was responsible for remarking that Homer was the poet of the Spartans, and Hesiod of the helots; for the first had given instructions on how to fight, and the second on how to farm (Plut. *Sayings of the Spartans* (*Moralia* 223a): doc. 5.45). The role of the helots was to engage in agricultural production on the Spartans' estates in Messenia and Lakonia, both to provide sufficient produce to allow the Spartan to contribute the necessary dues to his mess and to enable the Spartans to concentrate all their time and efforts on military training. Similarly, the Spartans were surrounded by the perioikoi, literally 'neighbours', who took care of all industrial production for the Spartans: they were politically subject to Sparta but had their own cities and some internal independence, while the helots from conquered Messenia possessed the status of serfs. They formed a self-perpetuating class of serfs, working their land in servitude to the Spartans. Sparta was not the only city to have a permanent class of serfs in place: there was a similar class, the penestai, in Thessaly and others in Asia Minor (Theopomp. *F* 122: doc. 5.51; Phylarchos *F* 8: doc. 5.52).

The helots were in essence public serfs, belonging not so much to an individual master as to the state, and Ephoros reports that Spartans were not allowed to give helots their freedom, or sell them outside Spartan territory (Ephoros *F* 117: doc. 6.7). Plutarch relates that the helots farmed the estates of their Spartan masters, paying them an amount that was settled in advance, while the Spartans were not allowed to demand a higher rent so the helots could make a profit and not be unhappy at working for their 'masters' (Plut. *Spartan Institutions* 239e). However, despite this, the helots were always a problem and likely to rebel, especially when the Spartans were engaged in theatres of war away from the Peloponnese.

An accurate estimate of helot numbers is almost impossible, but if it were assumed that the 35,000 helots at Plataea comprised 90 per cent of the helot males between 15 and 65 (with the remaining 10 per cent left behind to oversee the estates), the total adult males may have been approximately 40,000 and the entire helot population c. 120,000 at the beginning of the fifth century. It is however possible that a far greater proportion of helots remained on the land because the Spartans were concerned at mobilising and arming too many at any one time. At the most conservative estimate helots would probably have outnumbered Spartan citizens by 5:1. As a result, the Spartans considered that they needed to put in place a number of control mechanisms to prevent helot uprisings, such as constant brutal and humiliating treatment, a 'secret police' force and targeted murder of prominent helots. The whole Spartan system was governed by one overriding concern, the need to keep the helots under control. Despite the oaths that were exacted from the helots that they would never rebel or undertake any form of revolution, there were numerous helot revolts which crippled Sparta at the time they occurred and made the Spartans very cautious about going to war for fear they would be faced with a helot revolt in their absence. The rumour that a king or prominent Spartan was intriguing with the helots was taken very seriously indeed: this may have been one of the factors why Kleomenes was presented to Herodotos by his Spartan sources as of unsound mind (Hdt. 6.75.1–84.3: doc. 6.77), while the regent Pausanias was starved to death in the

Figure 5.12 A naked slave boy helps a bearded man to vomit; this is from the interior of an Athenian red-figure cup; the outside is decorated with scenes of drinking and dancing. Antikensammlung Staatliche Museen F2309, Berlin. Drawing by J. Etherington.

temple of Athena of the Brazen House after promising the helots freedom and citizenship if they joined in a revolt against Sparta (Thuc. 1.130.1–133.4: doc. 6.35). One of the reasons underlying the formation of the Peloponnesian League was so that Sparta was ringed with a network of allies who would come to its defence in the event of a helot revolution.

The treatment of the helots

The Spartans were harsh masters towards the helots, forcing them to behave in humiliating ways, such as compelling them to drink unmixed wine (all Greeks diluted wine with water) and then bringing them into the messes to show young boys the evils of drunkenness, as well as making them sing and dance in a ridiculous fashion. A famous quotation of Kritias, a Spartan sympathiser and associate of Socrates, stated that 'at Sparta a free man is really free and a slave really a slave' (Plut. *Life of Lykourgos* 28.8–12: doc. 5.46). Helots were demeaned in every possible way, and Myron of Priene may not be exaggerating when he records that helots were regularly flogged for no reason, made to wear dog's skin caps and leather, and if any of them appeared to be inappropriately robust, they would be put to death, while owners were expected to take to task any helots who were becoming fat (Myron of Priene *F* 2: doc. 5.47). There were some incentives in place for helots and in 421 the Spartans voted that the helots who had served with Brasidas in his capture of Amphipolis from the Athenians should be freed. Such helots received the status of neodameis (or new citizens) and were settled in a separate community. Brasidas' helots were settled at Lepreon, on the border between Lakonia and Elis, joining a community of neodameis that was already resident there. This settlement had the additional purpose of serving as a buffer state against Elis with whom the Spartans were at this point on terms of hostility (Thuc. 5.34.1: doc. 5.49). The Spartans were pleased to have an excuse on this occasion to send helots out on campaign: Pylos, on the west coast of the Peloponnese, was now in Athenian hands and this sent a clear message to helots that Sparta was no longer invincible.

Helots who were particularly experienced in warfare or had a reputation for courage and audacity were not always rewarded, and could be seen as potential rebel leaders. Fears that the helots would revolt, as they did on occasion, led the Spartans to undertake a series of measures against them. The Spartans were all the more concerned about possible helot revolts as they served in the army – and in large numbers: at the battle of Plataea, for instance, 35,000 helots served alongside 5000 Spartans (Hdt. 9.28.2). To counteract this potential for revolt, the Spartans had a secret police force, the krypteia ('kryptos' means hidden), supposedly one of Lykourgos' institutions. As part of their training, the supervisors of the young Spartans would send some of them out equipped only with daggers and basic provisions, and during the day they hid and rested. At night they came out and killed any helot that they caught. This in fact amounted to a de facto curfew, as the nocturnal killing of helots naturally encouraged them to stay indoors at night. Moreover, the Spartans went through the fields where the helots were working, and killed 'the sturdiest and most powerful of them'. But in order that these killings and murders of the helots would not bring down ritual, religious pollution on Sparta, the ephors, when they took up office each year, formally and officially declared war on the helots, so that killing them was an act of war and not murder as such – they were seen as a permanent enemy (Plut. *Lykourgos* 28.1–7: doc. 5.50).

Even more drastic measures could be taken. Thucydides records that, during the Peloponnesian war, the Spartans asked the helots to choose those they thought had done the Spartans the best service in their wars, implying that they would offer them their freedom as a reward. The helots picked out about 2000 men, who crowned themselves with garlands of leaves, a traditional Greek custom at celebrations, and visited religious sanctuaries in thanks for their freedom. Not long afterwards these 2000 helots disappeared and Thucydides writes that no one ever knew what happened to them (Thuc. 4.80.2–5: doc. 5.48). What the Spartans had done, writes Thucydides, was to conduct a test, 'as they considered that those with spirit who came forward first to claim their freedom would also be those most likely to turn against Sparta'. Those helots who were considered to be the most dangerous to the state were killed secretly and silently.

Sources that describe the Spartiate lifestyle imply that a citizen's presence was more or less continually required in Sparta, both so that he could engage in his military and civic duties and so that he could dine at his mess. Unless there was the possibility of Spartans travelling to visit their estates, it seems likely that they were essentially absentee landlords, and were probably even more disciplinarian on that account. There were presumably also some more trusted helots who acted as overseers, and with the helots giving half their produce to their masters, some may well have had a chance to become relatively wealthy from the portion that remained to them. Some helots may also have profited from plunder on the battlefield, as at Plataea, where they were detailed by Pausanias to collect all the Persians' gold and silver, much of which they sold to the Aeginetans (Hdt. 9.80.3). Some of this plunder, such as short Persian swords, may have ended up in the Parthenon treasury (*IG* I³ 351: doc. 1.11). While helots were responsible for working individual estates for specific masters, archaeological evidence seems to suggest that there were helot village communities in Messenia rather than isolated farmsteads. This possibly indicates that there could have been some type of centralised supervision that at the same time allowed the helots to develop some feeling of community, which would have encouraged a tendency to rebellion, and primitive decision-making processes. It appears from Thucydides' account that the 2000 prominent helots who vanished were selected by the helots themselves, which implies some type of political organisation, and when in 371 Sparta called for volunteers 6000 Lakonian helots offered to enlist (Xen. *Hellenika* 6.5.28–9).

The Spartans' treatment of the helots was brutal because of their fears of a revolt. Plutarch dates such harshness as particularly occurring after the helot revolt of the mid-460s, the 'great earthquake, when the helots are said to have risen up with the Messenians, did terrible damage to the country, and posed a serious threat to the city' (Plut. *Life of Lykourgos* 28.8–12: doc. 5.46; cf. Thucydides 1.102.1–103.3: doc. 12.11). They were joined by the perioikoi of Thouria and Aithaia and occupied Mount Ithome at the heart of Messenia. Nine years later they came to terms and the Athenians settled them at Naupaktos, which they had just taken from the Ozolian Lokrians, from where they could raid the Peloponnese. This was particularly viable after the Athenian occupation of Pylos, when the Messenians from Naupaktos sent their most suitable men to raid Lakonia, as they spoke the same dialect (Thuc. 4.41.2). The Spartans had no previous experience of such raiding, and, as the helots began to desert, they feared the spread of revolution. The Spartans' ability to maintain their social system, where Spartiates could give all their time to military training and service, depended on the subject helot population, and accordingly maintaining control over the helots was one of the Spartan state's main priorities.

Citizen labour

The poet Hesiod was writing in approximately 700 BC, just after the time at which the Homeric poems took their shape. While in his *Works and Days* he is apparently concerned with an almost purely agrarian economy, giving maxims for the survival of the farmer, he also gives evidence for the existence of crafts and trade (Hes. *Works and Days* 20–6: doc. 5.53). Hesiod sees nothing demeaning about hard work, and accepts that it is part of life in this age of the world and a disagreeable necessity, and while he assumes that the farmer will have some sort of slave labour, the farmer also has to work. Competition between workers and artisans is seen as natural – potters, craftsmen, beggars and minstrels – all envy each other and strive to do better than their rivals. The desire to acquire wealth was nothing to be ashamed of: Theognis of Megara warned his readers against poverty which 'overpowers a good man more than anything else'; moreover one who was poor was not listened to and clearly in seventh-century Megara such a person had no political power in Theognis' view. At the same time the gods helped those who acted justly to prosper and the inhabitants of a city that was justly ruled would 'with festivity reap the fruit of the work which is their care' and find that their enterprises – bees, oaks, sheep and children – will prosper – nor will they have to take to the sea – one of Hesiod's worse nightmares (Hes. *Works and Days* 225–37: doc. 5.55). Solon too in the early sixth century lists the ways in which wealth can be acquired justly: men can be traders, hired farmhands, farmers, craftsmen, 'trained by the Muses' and seers, all of which are seen as reputable professions: only doctors do not get his approval. Unlike Hesiod, as an aristocrat, Solon believed that the farmer's life was relatively idyllic (Solon *Poem* 13: doc. 5.56).

Agriculture versus craftsmanship

Later sources such as Xenophon in his portrait of Socrates make clear that, at least in certain classes of society, agriculture, rather than trade or salaried work, was considered the business of a 'gentleman', with farming leading to physical fitness and sufficient free time to fulfil the duties of a citizen (Xen. *Oeconomicus* 4.2–3, 6.8–9: doc. 5.58). He also believed that the Spartans were forbidden by Lykourgos to touch anything to do with making money, and that the Spartans were not alone in the Greek world in viewing trade as unsuitable for a citizen, although he does point out that in other states everyone makes as much money as they can – whether by farming, owing ships, trade or different crafts (Xen. *Constitution of the Spartan* s 7.1–2: doc. 5.57). According to Herodotos, the Kalasirians (a class of Egyptian warriors), Thracians, Scythians, Persians and Lydians and nearly all the barbarians consider that those who learn a craft are inferior to other citizens, while those exempted from manual work are noble. He continues by saying that the Spartans out of all the Greeks despise craftsmen the most and Corinth (that great commercial centre) the least (Hdt. 2.166–7: doc. 5.59). Naturally in Athens as in other Greek cities, many citizens had to support themselves by some sort of trade, with the assistance of their slaves if they had any. Farming may have remained the 'ideal' but judging by Solon's timocratic definition of classes, the thetes in particular struggled to make a subsistence living, as they made less than 200 measures of produce (such as barley) a year, while the minimum for the rich in Athens – the pentakosiomedimnoi – was 500 measures.

Socrates, as depicted by his biographers, may well have decried the indignities of being an artisan (poor posture, pale complexion, enervated constitution, and no leisure time to spend with friends), but he was not popular in Athens and perhaps this is one of the reasons why: he also attracted young men like Alkibiades, who had little else to do but engage in cultured and leisure activities. Even his view of farming is idealised with little reference to the subsistence farmer:

For this work seems to be both the easiest to learn and the most pleasant to work at, to make the body most beautiful and robust, and to leave the mind the greatest amount of spare time for looking after the interests of one's friends and city.

(Xen. *Oeconomicus* 4.2–3, 6.8–9: doc. 5.58)

211

He himself in the *Memorabilia* (3.7.6), when rebuking a shy friend, Charmides, points out that the assembly which Charmides is too timid to address is made up of 'fullers, cobblers, builders, smiths, farmers, merchants, and dealers in the agora who think of nothing but buying cheap and selling dear'.

Work for hire

To his friend Eutheros, who has obviously suffered some financial misfortune as a consequence of the Peloponnesian War and is now reduced to working as a labourer (as the only option instead of begging), Socrates suggests that he should hire himself out as an estate manager or overseer for some richer man. Eutheros initially equates working for another as 'slavery', clearly being of the class to whom labour is demeaning. Socrates points out that as he ages he will be unable to continue to work in this way and that it would be more expedient for him to take a job with 'someone who has more property who needs someone to assist him, and supervise his tasks and help bring in the crops and look after his estate' as the way to obtain a living in his old age (Xen. *Memorabilia* 2.8.1–6: doc. 5.60). Athenians did employ other Athenians: it was only to the aristocracy and ex-aristocracy that this seemed unpalatable. Certainly Perikles' building projects, even if the rationale behind them was not to provide jobs for citizens to prevent them from being idle as Plutarch suggests, would certainly have employed a range of citizens, metics and slaves in their construction. Plutarch (*Perikles* 12.5–6: doc. 5.61) lists those affected by this extensive programme (which included the Propylaia, the Parthenon, the temple of Athena Nike, the Erechtheum and the statue of Athena Promachos) as including carpenters, modellers, copper-smiths, stone-masons, gilders, workers in ivory, painters, embroiderers and engravers, as well as the carriers and suppliers of these materials – merchants, sailors and pilots by sea, and by land cartwrights, keepers of draught animals, muleteers, rope-makers, weavers, leatherworkers, road-makers and miners. These were comprised of a mixture of citizens, metics and slaves belonging to both.

Specialisation

In large cities such as Athens, according to Xenophon, there was obviously a high degree of specialisation while in a small town, he states, the same craftsmen make beds, doors, ploughs and tables – and anything else they are contracted to do. It is only in the large city that one sees very distinct lines of work: a maker of shoes for men, and another for women, and various artisans making the different component parts of shoes or simply assembling the whole. Similarly with the preparation of food: normally one slave was expected to prepare the couches, lay the table and cook all the dishes, resulting in a certain amount of pot luck regarding the success of the dinner, as opposed to the wealthy man who has a different slave attending to each component of the dinner, as in either poaching or baking the fish (Xen. *Education of Cyrus* 8.2.5–6: doc. 5.62).

Women and work

Some citizens, like Eutheros, may have been ashamed of their line of work. Demosthenes' speech, *Against Euboulides*, presents the case of a family, including the mother, who sold ribbons (tainiai, for sacrifices and decorating funerary stelai) in the market. The speaker, Euxitheos, states frankly: 'We admit that we sell ribbons and do not live in the manner we would

Figure 5.13 Four women bakers are busy kneading the dough for bread, while a musician plays his flute (missing). A small terracotta group, from Thebes, probably dating to about 600–575 BC. Louvre, Paris, CA804. Drawing by Tessa Rickards.

like' but argues cogently that they should not on those grounds be dismissed as non-citizens (Dem. 57 *Against Euboulides* 30–1, 33–5, 40–2: doc. 5.63). In fact he states that according to the laws 'anyone, who uses the fact that they work in the market against any male or female citizen, shall be liable to the penalties for slander'. Still worse, it has been brought up against his mother that as a result of reverses in the Peloponnesian War she had to take on the role of wet-nurse in another family, which the prosecution is asserting shows that she cannot have been a citizen (Fig. 5.11). Our speaker, however, affirms that he can name numerous Athenian citizens at the present time who are working as wet-nurses and claims that 'in terms of the poverty she was experiencing, what she did was perhaps both necessary and appropriate'. It was after all the norm that many citizen women worked, whatever the preferred stereotype of the secluded female. As well as working within the confines of the home, making an important contribution not only in weaving clothes and materials, but overseeing cooking, children and slaves, many citizen women worked in the agora as professional retailers.

Women in Greece played an extremely important part in the economy of the household: they were responsible not only for the care of the children and management of the slaves, but for overseeing all the production of clothes and materials. These contributed very significantly to the household's economy as a whole. As well as the duties within the home, there are examples of women doing a regular job outside, and this would have particularly been the case amongst the poor, where one wage was not enough, or where a woman was left widowed, such as the garland seller with five children whose husband died in Cyprus (Ar. *Thesmophoriazousai* 443–58: doc. 4.60). Women also sold ribbons in the market (doc. 5.63), and Euripides was constantly lampooned over the 'fact' that his mother used to sell vegetables. Lysistrata's citizen allies in her planned sex strike include 'you seed-pulse-and-vegetable-market-sellers, and garlic-innkeeping-bread-sellers' (Ar. *Lysistrata* 456–8: doc. 4.62). Two metic women even ran a tavern in the underworld (Ar. *Frogs* 549–78: doc. 4.61).

Even in the heyday of fifth-century democratic Athens traders in the sense of retail manufacturers – the term usually employed is artisans – could be looked down on. Many were metics, foreign immigrants, who had been encouraged to settle in Athens because of their skills in this regard. However, it is important not to consider the views of Socrates as typical of those of Athenian citizens as a whole. Many Athenian citizens were craftsmen and, apart from workers in the silver mines who were invariably slaves, there were no occupations in Athens reserved for slaves. Citizens, metics and slaves generally worked side-by-side just as Simias, a metic, had four slaves helping with column-fluting, more than quadrupling his day's income (*IG* I³ 476: doc. 5.42).

Moreover, there is clear evidence that many craftsmen were proud of their professions and a number of gravestones bear witness to the tools of the craft of the deceased, depicted by such items as wagon wheels, or smelting tools. And an unknown craftsman dedicated a tithe of his profits to Athena, asserting proudly in the inscription, 'It is good for the skilled to exercise their skill according to their craft; for he who has a craft has a better life' (*IG* I3 766: doc. 5.64).

The dramatic slave

The fact that slaves were a constant feature of both Athenian tragedy and comedy shows the extent to which they were considered absolutely central to the Greek family. Slaves were represented in various stereotypical ways in drama, reflecting the ways in which the audience wanted to see them. Tragedy frequently depicted loyal slaves, often born in the family, and trusted with the upbringing of children, who remain attached to their earlier charges, remembering them with fondness. The portrayal of these is often humorous, and occasionally whimsical, as in the case of Orestes' old nurse who remembers all the times he used to get her out of her bed when he was a baby and she laments over the tidings of his death (Aesch. *Libation Bearers* 747–65: doc. 5.65). A slave of Helen of Troy recalls her marriage to Menelaos, when he ran beside the chariot carrying a torch, and comments that 'it's a base slave that does not revere his masters' affairs and rejoice with them and share in their troubles' (Eur. *Helen* 726–7: doc. 5.66; cf. Fig. 4.7). He considers that being a slave is bad enough, but at least the 'noble' slave can be free in mind, and identify himself with his masters' fortunes. Tragedy rises to its greatest heights when picturing the fate of women in wartime, when the defeat of their menfolk leaves them defenceless, to be the slaves of their captors. This was something that every Greek could identify with, and the fate of the women of Troy was probably experienced or feared by a very high proportion of women in the Greek world at some point in their life (docs 5.67–8). Nevertheless, once enslaved, the slave became something less than human, depicted in reliefs as smaller than free citizens and male slaves have exaggeratedly large genitalia (Fig. 5.14). On stage they were treated with patronising humour or were the butt of demeaning jokes. Harsh treatment of slaves was considered amusing by the audience and, like Xanthias in the *Frogs*, they were often stock characters that were played for laughs, being beaten, carrying baggage that is excessively heavy, and being essentially a foil for their masters' humour (Ar. *Frogs* 1–20: doc. 5.70; cf. Fig. 5.9). Both in Sparta and in Athens slaves were made to look ridiculous to entertain their owners and other citizens, perhaps in order to ensure that they were seen as something less than human.

Figure 5.14 A terracotta model of an actor playing the role of a slave sitting on an altar where he has sought sanctuary and emptying the purse he just stole, presumably from his master. From Lokris (?), made in Boeotia, and dating to around 400–375 BC. Louvre CA 265, Paris. Drawing by Tessa Rickards.

A world without slaves?

When comic dramatists wished to present their audience with a topsy-turvy world, they hypothesised one without slaves – a situation unthinkable to Greek citizens. Krates, a contemporary of Aristophanes, dreamed up a state of affairs in which slaves were replaced by automation, with every piece of equipment doing its duty on command. One of the characters on stage is horrified by the thought of a city without slaves – 'will each man, even old people, have to look after themselves?' he inquires (Krates *The Wild Animals*: doc. 5.69). The Greeks had no concept of a civilisation without slaves, or if they did it was of one like that visualised by Aristophanes, a world without kidnappers and therefore without slaves – a world where everyone would have a much more painful life than the one that they currently enjoyed (Ar. *Wealth* 509–26: doc. 5.9).

6

SPARTA

Table 6.1 The kings of Sparta

Agiads	Eurypontids
Agis I (c. 930–c. 900)	
Echestratos (c. 900–c. 870)	Eurypon (c. 895–c. 865)
Leobotas (c. 870–c. 840)	Prytanis (c. 865–c. 835)
Dorrysos (c. 840–c. 815)	Polydektes (c. 835–c. 805)
Agesilaos I (c. 815–c. 785)	Eunomos (c. 805–c. 775)
Archilaos (c. 785–c. 760)	Charillos (c. 775–c. 750)
Teleklos (c. 760–c. 740)	Nikandros (c. 750–c. 720)
Alkamenes (c. 740–c. 700)	Theopompos (c. 720–c. 675)
Polydoros (c. 700–c. 665)	Anaxandridas I (c. 675–c. 660)
Eurykrates (c. 665–c. 640)	Archidamos I (c. 660–c. 645)
Anaxandros (c. 640–c. 615)	Anaxilas (c. 645–c. 625)
Eurykratidas (c. 615–c. 590)	Leotychidas I (c. 625–c. 600)
Leon (c. 590–c. 560)	Hippokratidas (c. 600–c. 575)
Anaxandridas I (c. 560–c. 520)	Agasikles (c. 575–c. 500)
	Ariston (c. 550–c. 515)
Kleomenes I, son of Anaxandridas I (c. 520–c. 490)	Demaratos, son of Ariston (c. 515–491)
Leonidas I, half-brother of Kleomenes I (c. 490–480)	Leotychidas II, cousin of Demaratos (491–476)
Kleombrotos (regent) (480)	
Pausanias (regent) (480/479)	
Pleistarchos, son of Leonidas I (480–458)	Archidamos II, grandson of Leotychidas II (476–427)
Pleistoanax, cousin of Pleistarchos, son of the regent Pausanias (458–408: in exile c. 445–c. 427)	Agis II, son of Archidamos II (427–399)
Pausanias, son of Pleistoanax 408–395 (regent, c. 445–c. 427)	Agesilaos II, half-brother of Agis II (399–360)
Agesipolis I, son of Pausanias (395–380)	
Kleombrotos I, brother of Agesipolis I (380–371)	
Agesipolis II, son of Kleombrotos I (371–370)	
Kleomenes II, brother of Agesipolis II (370–309)	Archidamos III, son of Agesilaos II (360–338)
	Agis III, son of Archidamos III (338–331)
	Eudamidas I, brother of Agis III (331–c. 305)
Araios I, grandson of Kleomenes II (309–265)	Archidamos IV, son of Eudamidas I (c. 305–c. 275)
Akrotatos, son of Araios I (265–c. 260)	Eudamidas II, son of Archidamos IV (c. 275–244)
Araios II, son of Akrotatos (c. 260–c. 251)	
Leonidas II, grandson of Kleomenes II (c. 251–236: in exile c. 243–c. 241)	Agis IV, son of Eudamidas II (244–241)

Kleombrotos II, son-in-law of Leonidas II
(c. 243–241)

Kleomenes III, son of Kleombrotos II (236–219)

Agesipolis III, grandson of Kleombrotos II
(219–215)

Eudamidas III, son of Agis IV (241–c. 228)

Archidamos V, brother of Agis IV (c. 228–227)
Eukleidas (Agiad), brother of Kleomenes III
(c. 227–222)
Lykourgos, descendent of Agis II (219–c. 210)
Pelops, son of Lykourgos (c. 210–c. 206)

'Stranger tell the Spartans that here
We lie, obeying their orders'
Simonides 22b: doc. 11.32

Introduction

The Spartans, renowned in antiquity for their courage and expertise in warfare, have been seen throughout history as the ultimate exponents of heroic last stands and glorious death in battle against overwhelming odds. This is demonstrated in the terse epitaph above for the Spartan dead at Thermopylai in 480. It describes the famous conflict in which King Leonidas and his 300 Spartan hoplites held the pass against Xerxes' mighty invasion force in order to allow the rest of the Greek army to withdraw in safety. For millennia it has epitomised the ideology of a splendid and noble death in the face of fierce opposition. The fact that the Persian spies and Xerxes himself were amazed that the Spartans calmly exercised and combed their long hair before the final engagement, and at their nonchalance at the point of certain death, simply adds to the 'romance' of the Spartan myth. This Spartan stand on the third day of the encounter allowed the other Greeks from the pass to retreat, but Leonidas doubtless felt that flight for the Spartans themselves was ignominious. After they were encircled by the Persians and Leonidas had fallen, the Spartans made several attempts to regain his body, succeeding on the fourth attempt. At the last stand the Thebans surrendered, but the rest, including the Thespiaians who had refused to leave the Spartans, fought with spears, swords and finally hands and teeth until all the Spartans were killed (Hdt. 7.204–22: doc. 11.27). As encapsulated so aptly by Simonides, the memorial for the dead merely states, with the Spartans' usual laconic brevity, that they had done their duty as Spartans.

Sparta and its territory

Sparta lies in the south-east of the Peloponnese, the southern part of mainland Greece, between two mountain ranges, the Taygetos range of mountains (Artemis' hunting-ground) separating it from Messenia in the west, and the Parnon range to the east dividing it from the eastern coastline of the Peloponnese (Fig. 6.1). The territory around Sparta was known as Lakonia, fertile, land-locked and essentially protected from invaders by its mountainous surrounds. Sparta's nearest neighbour Tegea lay some 57 kilometres to the north over the Arkadian hills and its port Gytheion 45 kilometres to the south. The Eurotas river, which ran past the city and ensured the fertility of the Lakonian plain, was used as a resource in the Spartan militaristic ethos, with the Spartan boys pulling reeds from its banks for their bedding; when a king of Pontos hired a Spartan cook so he could try the famous delicacy 'black broth' (made of pig's blood and vinegar), and disliked it, the cook's response was 'O King, those who appreciate this broth must first have bathed in the Eurotas' (Plut. *Life of Lykourgos* 12.13: doc.

217

THE ANCIENT GREEKS

6.46). The Spartans called themselves Lakedaimonians, and their city Lakedaimon; the Peloponnesian League dominated by Sparta was known as the alliance of 'the Lakedaimonians
and their allies'. Sparta is the modern name for the ancient Greek city, while the modern
town, refounded in AD 1834 by King Otto of Greece, is now called Sparti. The term Lakonian was also used by other Greeks, both for the Spartans themselves and the inhabitants of
the surrounding area. Hence the 'Lakonian' culture can be either that of the Spartans themselves or that of the perioikoi, the 'dwellers around', who lived in self-governing poleis, but
were subordinate to Sparta in foreign policy and had to serve in the army. It was the perioikoi
who engaged in most of the crafts and trades needed by the Spartans and who made the pottery and bronze-work known as Lakonian which was used at Sparta.

The term Lakedaimonian existed in the Bronze Age and is found in Linear B tablets at
Thebes as ra-ke-da-mi-ni-jo, referring to a 'Lakedaimonian' who may have played a cultic role
there. There was a Mycenaean palace situated at Therapne on a hill to the east of Sparta on
the banks of the Eurotas, which was destroyed with most of the rest of Mycenaean civilisation
around 1180 BC. The 'Catalogue of the Ships' in the *Iliad*, a section which arguably reflects
knowledge of Mycenaean topography and settlements, speaks of 'hollow Lakedaimon, with
its many ravines' (*Iliad* 2.582). In the Homeric poems Sparta was the home of Helen of Troy,
daughter of Zeus and Leda, and of her husband Menelaos, and it was from Sparta that she
was abducted by the Trojan prince Paris. Along with Menelaos and her brothers, the Dioskouroi (Castor and Pollux, sons of Zeus; Fig. 6.10), Helen was worshipped at Sparta in the his-

Figure 6.1 Modern Sparti at the foot of Mount Taygetos in the Eurotas valley, with ruins of the Hellenistic or Roman theatre in the foreground. Mount Taygetos dominated the Spartan landscape.
Photo © ulrichstill/commons.wikimedia.org.

218

torical period at a shrine named the Menelaion. When the Dorian invasion took place around 1000 BC, Sparta and most of the Peloponnese were, it was believed, settled by Dorians and the Spartans therefore shared the Doric dialect and customs with other Dorian societies such as Crete and Thera; the citizens were members of the three traditional Dorian tribes, the Hylleis, Pamphyloi and Dymanes. The Spartan kings considered themselves descendants of Herakles, whose great-great-great-grandsons Eurysthenes and Prokles were regarded as the fathers of the first two Spartan kings, Agis and Eurypon (Ephoros *F* 117: doc. 6.5). Tyrtaeus speaks of Sparta being founded from Erineus in Doris in northern Greece (Strabo *Geography* 8.4.10: doc. 6.52).

In prehistoric times, Sparta was comprised of four villages, Pitana, Mesoa, Limnai and Kynosoura, which at some point united as a civic entity (Map 6.1). Two of these villages may have possessed monarchies and this amalgamation of four communities provides a possible reason for Sparta's unique dual kingship, in which a member each of the Agiad and the Eury-pontid families ruled simultaneously, although the Agiad line was considered to be senior to the Eurypontid. At some time probably in the eighth century BC, Amyklai, another village five kilometres to the south, was added to the city. Amyklai, with its sanctuary of Apollo Amyklaios, a huge bronze statue of the god, and 'Throne of Apollo', was to become one of the main religious centres of the city of Sparta – a city without a wall. In practical terms it would have been a major task to fortify the five villages as one entity, and Sparta was never fortified in the archaic and classical periods. It was, however, well protected by its geographical location. The city itself resembled not so much an urban centre as a military camp, while the Spartans saw their army as the only defence needed. Plato said of Sparta that the organisation of the state (politeia) is that of an army camp, not of people who live in a city (*Laws* 666e).

The Spartans considered that their power was best demonstrated by their military campaigns and preparedness rather than through fortifications, monuments and buildings: after the final conquest of Messenia in the seventh century the Spartans controlled some 8000 square kilometres of territory, more than twice that of Syracuse and three times that of Athens, with a huge population of helots, a form of public indentured labour. The helots farmed the Spartans' estates and produced food on their behalf, thus freeing the Spartans themselves to concentrate on martial skills and training. Sparta itself was not walled until the hellenistic period.

At a later stage the ruins of Sparta's temples and buildings hardly gave the impression of a state that had inhabited two-fifths of the Peloponnese, controlling most of it and having many powerful allies elsewhere. Thucydides records a much-quoted contrast between the cities of Athens and Sparta in his own time and comments on Sparta: 'it has not been synoikised into a city, nor does it possess costly temples and buildings, but consists of a number of villages in the early Greek manner, and would seem an inferior place' (Thuc. 1.10: doc. 1.7). This lack of pomp and show was typical of Spartan understatement, as opposed to Athens' splendid and costly buildings and statues intended to impress their allies and the rest of Greece. Sparta had no 'city centre'; its shrines and monuments were scattered throughout the villages, and only a few sites within the city itself can today be identified with certainty: the shrines of Artemis Orthia and Athena Chalkioikos, and the Roman theatre. However, Thucydides' account cannot be taken quite literally: the city of Sparta may not have been particularly impressive, or left behind imposing buildings such as can be seen on the Athenian acropolis, or the magnificent temples to be found in the Greek cities of southern Italy or Sicily, but the Spartans did have important cult sanctuaries and shrines. Athena of the Brazen House was Sparta's patron deity and in her temple on the acropolis the interior was faced with bronze plaques (hence its name: Chalkioikos). As befitted a Dorian community Sparta's three greatest festivals were in honour of Apollo: the Gymnopaidiai, a celebration of unarmed dancing

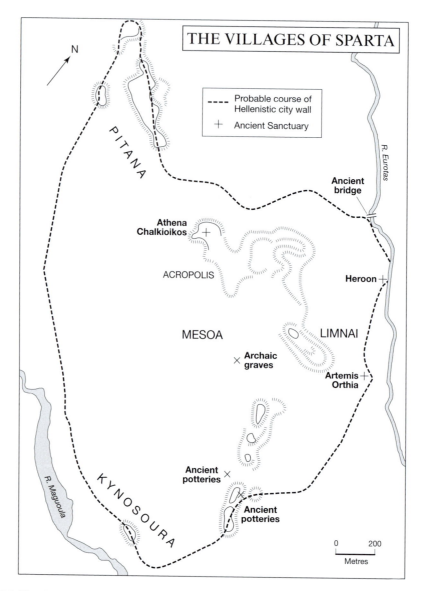

Map 6.1 The villages of Sparta. P. Cartledge, *Sparta and Lakonia*, second edition, Routledge, 2001, p. 91.

where choirs of different ages competed, the Karneia, and the Hyakinthia, celebrated outside the city at Amyklai in honour of Apollo and his beloved Hyakinthos whom Apollo accidentally killed with a discus. In the sixth century the Spartans invited Bathykles, an artist from Magnesia, to create a 'throne' of stone and precious metals there for Apollo's cult image. Little of the temple of Artemis Orthia survives today, but over 100,000 small dedications have been discovered at the site, as well as at the Menelaion to the east of the city, where Helen and her husband Menelaos had an important hero cult.

Sources on Spartan history and society

While various accounts of Spartan history and institutions exist, much of the information has to be treated with great caution. There is, for example, no extant work by a Spartan historian, or indeed anything other than the barest epigraphic record providing contemporary evidence from fifth-century Sparta. It has been suggested that Spartans laws were orally remembered rather than written down: one of the few inscriptions is that concerning the Spartan war fund (Meiggs and Lewis 67: doc. 14.7); another is the Erxadieis treaty, which is the earliest extant Spartan inscription (Meiggs and Lewis 67 (bis): doc. 6.61). Accounts are largely derived from Athenian authors and from periods later than Sparta's heyday. They were a reaction to what has been called the 'Spartan mirage' and were a response to the appeal of Spartan ideals rather than an accurate recording of the reality. As with other Greek states, the oral tradition was important, with poems such as those of Tyrtaeus learnt by heart by Spartan youths, and it was these oral traditions that Herodotos used. Herodotos is a valuable source of information on Sparta prior to his own time, most notably in terms of some anecdotal tales of Spartan kings. He visited Sparta and talked to the locals and is a reliable source for relatively recent history as it was remembered and interpreted at Sparta at the time. He does, however, occasionally conflate contradictory sources as in his account of Kleomenes I. It is in the context of Croesus of Lydia requesting allies from Greece in about 546 against Persia that Herodotos takes the opportunity to update his reader on early Spartan history (1.65–70). From Herodotos' account it is clear that in the fifth century there was no 'accepted' standard account of Spartan history. This can be seen in the contradictions regarding the date and genealogy of Lykourgos that he records (Hdt. 1.65.2–66.1: doc. 6.2). By his time, however, there clearly were king-lists available, probably compiled at the end of the sixth or beginning of the fifth century, which could be used to establish a chronology. There were also lists of ephors, not known to Herodotos, who simply has Demaratos mention that Chilon (an ephor) was the wisest of the Spartans (7.235.2; cf. 1.59.2–3; *Rylands Papyrus* 18: doc. 7.7).

Thucydides' narrative in the section in Book 1 of his history known as the 'Archaeology' deals briefly with the early history of Sparta. His account focuses specifically on Sparta as an antagonist of Athens in the Peloponnesian War: the conservative Dorian oligarchy against the flamboyant and enterprising Ionian democracy. Thucydides' twenty-year period of exile from Athens allowed him to give a relatively objective view of both sides. He does not expand on the details of Spartan institutions except parenthetically in his text, although he records that at the end of the Peloponnesian War these institutions had remained unchanged in his view for 400 years, so dating Sparta's constitutional reform to approximately 800 BC (Thuc. 1.18.1: doc. 6.57). In dating the beginning of the Peloponnesian War he cross-references it by stating that it began in the 48th year of office of Chrysis, the Argive priestess of Hera, and the ephorate of Ainesias at Sparta and the archonship of Pythodoros at Athens, in this way securely dating the year as 431 BC (Thuc. 2.2.1: doc. 3.60).

Xenophon (c. 430–c. 354) continued Thucydides' history from 411 to 362 in his *Hellenika*, and his account essentially charts the rise and fall of Sparta during this period. He was also the author of the earliest coherent, if sometimes misleading, source for Spartan society and institutions in his *Constitution of the Spartans*. Xenophon was an Athenian of good family born around 430, and a friend of Socrates sharing the pro-Spartan sympathies of his group, including Kritias and Kritias' cousin Plato. Plato frequently refers to Sparta's constitution and institutions in his dialogues, as would be expected given his exposure to the pro-Spartan circle of Socrates. In his *Republic* the Spartan constitution is the closest to his utopia, and falls only a little short of his ideal city (*Republic* 545a–c). Kritias also wrote in praise of Spartan customs, such as their drinking practices, and was known for his saying that 'at Sparta a free man is really free and a slave really a slave' (Kritias *FF* 6, 37: docs 5.46, 6.47).

After opposing the democratic restoration at Athens in 404–403, Xenophon served with the Persian prince Cyrus in Asia and then, after Cyrus' death in battle, with the Spartans in Asia under Agesilaos with whom he returned to Greece in 394. He was at Koroneia for Agesilaos' defeat of the Thebans and their Athenian allies. It is possible he was exiled from Athens following this event and in 394 settled near Sparta, where he erected a shrine to Artemis at his idyllic estate at Skillous near Olympia (Xen. *Anabasis* 5.3.7–13: doc. 3.52). His two sons were educated in the agoge with Spartan boys. It was here presumably that he wrote his *Constitution of the Spartans*. He was thus well acquainted with the Sparta of the first half of the fourth century and a close friend of Agesilaos and, while often considered naïve in his eulogy of Sparta's past history and 'Lykourgan' institutions, he is not uncritical in his account of Sparta's constitution in his own day: 'if anyone were to ask me, if still even now the laws of Lykourgos seem to me to remain unchanged, I could not, by Zeus, say this any longer with confidence' (Xen. *Const. Spart.*14.1–7: doc. 16.5). Nevertheless, despite this criticism, Xenophon waxes lyrical about 'the olden days of Sparta' and was the first to detail the 'myth' of the Spartans which has lasted to the present day.

Aristotle (384–322) was also intrigued by the Spartans and their constitution although he criticised Sparta for its loss of supremacy in Greece in the fourth century, especially after Messenia and the helots were liberated by the Thebans in 370, at a time when the number of Spartan citizens had fallen below 1000. He admires in Sparta what he sees as a good example of the 'mixed constitution' combining monarchy, oligarchy and democracy (cf. Arist. *Politics* 1294b19–34: doc. 6.25). However, he sees the system as essentially flawed, and his many criticisms include comments on the inequality of property ownership, financial insecurity and cash-flow problems, the 'savagery' engendered in Spartans by the agoge, and the problems inherent in the inherited kingship, gerousia and ephorate: 'it is clear that, since the Spartans' rule no longer exists today, they are not fortunate, nor was their lawgiver a good one' (*Politics* 1333b5–26: doc. 6.44). Unfortunately his *Constitution of the Spartans*, part of a voluminous project to examine the constitutions of the major Greek states as well as Carthage, only survives in fragments. Ephoros, an older contemporary of Aristotle, wrote a history of Greece in thirty books, most of which is now lost, but which was used as a source by many later writers and Strabo cites him in a passage on the Dorian occupation of Lakonia and the origin of the helots (Ephoros *F* 117: doc. 6.7).

Plutarch, priest, educator and biographer, was the writer most inspired by the Spartan ideal and in his biographical *Lives* of Lykourgos, Lysander, Agesilaos, Kleomenes III and Agis, he primarily writes character-building accounts or moral treatises (which were to the taste not only of his pupils and Roman audiences but, two millennia later, of many English schools) rather than a history: writing around AD 100 he may have been affected by the third-century BC reforms which attempted to restore Sparta to the status of a powerful city. In his biography of Lykourgos, the supposed founder of Sparta's institutions, he confesses that there is no certainty about Lykourgos' dates or reforms, but writes a life of him anyway (*Lykourgos* 1.1: doc. 6.1). Plutarch did, however, visit Sparta and his version of the Great Rhetra, with its difficulties of interpretation, appears to be an authentic decree (*Lykourgos* 6.1–4, 6.6–9: doc. 6.5), while much of his account is centred on an explanation and description of the laws and institutions attributed to Lykourgos. Along with Xenophon, Plutarch has been primarily responsible for the transmission of the Spartan 'mirage' to the present day.

In the mid-second century AD the geographer Pausanias travelled throughout Greece noting important facts about local topography, buildings, monuments and anything of interest such as festivals, recording the background history and traditions of these as far as he could research them. It is in this context that he records the rites of Artemis Orthia (*Description of Greece* 3.16.7, 3.16.9–11: doc. 6.51). His valuable account of Lakonia describes monuments and statues in Sparta no longer extant, such as the graves of Pausanias and Leonidas and the cenotaph of Brasidas. These descriptions help to round out the artistic and archaeological record.

Spartan sources

While most sources about Sparta were written by non-Spartans, there were some Spartan authors, if not historians, despite later writers' assertions that Sparta was culturally impoverished and unable to give rise to poetic or musical talents (Ael. *Varia Historia* 12.50: doc. 6.79). It is possible to use the works of Spartan poets, such as Tyrtaeus and Alcman, to round out the historical record, despite the later belief that the Spartans had no skilled poets. Tyrtaeus was clearly a Spartan general, commanding soldiers in what is known as the Second Messenian War, who wrote to exhort the Spartans to discipline, courage and victory (Tyrt. 5, 10–12: docs 6.8–11). While later Greeks believed that the Spartans were totally 'inartistic', Spartans did train in poetry and music, but their taste was for songs relating to military virtues and practices and choruses for performance at religious festivals (Plut. *Lykourgos* 21.1–2: doc. 6.13). Spartan choirs were well renowned and competed primarily at religious festivals such as the Gymnopaidiai, while works by Tyrtaeus' near contemporary Alcman, who was writing in about 630 BC, were sung by choruses at Sparta. Alcman was particularly famous for his partheneia, songs for girls' choirs, as in the dawn chorus celebrating the clothing of a cult statue (Alcm. 1: doc. 4.14). These choruses were part of the girls' education and rites of passage, their transition to womanhood. Alcman's poem was written specifically for this occasion, and there is the hint of a contest between the leaders Agido and Hagesichora. Even in Athens Sparta was well known for its choruses at festivals, and Aristophanes in his *Lysistrata* describes Sparta as famous for its choruses in honour of the gods, 'where the maidens, like fillies, beside the Eurotas, dance, with their feet often bounding and their tresses waving' (Ar. *Lysistrata* 1306–12: doc. 6.19).

Plutarch quotes a line of Alcman signifying the tension between art and militarism in Sparta: 'when weighed against the iron sweet lyre-playing tips the scales' (*F* 41; *Lykourgos* 21.5). In later years all Spartan professionals were thought to have been imported from other Greek cities, including Alcman, and Sparta was regarded as a cultural desert. This, however, was not the case (Ael. *Varia Historia* 12.50: doc. 6.79). Terpander, for example, was recorded as being a Spartan, and the best cithara-player of his time. Like Tyrtaeus he composed heroic songs, but was fined by the ephors (anachronistically, because there was no coinage at that time) because he added an extra string to create different melodies. The ephors argued that simple melodies were quite adequate for the Spartans (Plut. *Spartan Traditional Practices* 17: doc. 6.14).

Spartan art

Further evidence of Spartan culture and ritual practices is provided by Lakonian art, and the archaeological record shows that Lakonia in the archaic period was producing high-quality bronzes and ivories from the early seventh century to the first quarter of the sixth. Much of this would have been for Spartan use as shown by dedications at sanctuaries. The 'Lykourgan' regime of austerity was not yet a reality when Alcman was writing, for his partheneion for the chorus of Spartan girls speaks of their wearing purple cloth and gold snake bracelets, 'so much excess of purple is not enough to defend us, nor cunningly wrought serpent of solid gold, nor Lydian headband, adornment of dark-eyed girls' (Alcm. 1: doc. 4.14). His *partheneia*, and the works of Tyrtaeus and other poets, are evidence that at this period Sparta was home to its own brand of art and music, different from those elsewhere in Greece because uniquely channelled to fit Spartan martial and religious ideology. Indeed, it could be argued that the period between 650 and 500 was a golden age of Spartan art, music and culture generally (Figs 6.3, 6.8).

From about 750 BC Lakonian potters began to develop their own particular style and from the last quarter of the seventh century Lakonian pottery was exported to Samos, Taras and Cyrene in North Africa. The Spartans themselves, of course, did not engage in trade or crafts, and any craftsmanship would have been the work of the *perioikoi*, some of whose workshops may have been located in Sparta producing goods for a Spartan clientele. One of the most notable Lakonian productions is the 'Arkesilas cup' depicting King Arkesilas of Cyrene (Fig. 6.2). The cup, which is the work of the Arkesilas painter and dates to around 560 BC, depicts the king supervising the packing of silphium, the prime export of Cyrene (or alternatively wool). He is sitting under an awning, wearing a sunhat, with two servants packing the silphium into bags, a third weighing out the amounts, and the fourth recording the tally. In the lower register, men are carrying away the filled bags. Of the animals depicted, a cat is seated under the king's stool, a lizard is depicted on the wall and a monkey and birds on the cross-pole, while a stork flies past in the background.

Figure 6.2 The Arkesilas Cup: the inside of a Lakonian black-figure drinking cup with a scene of King Arkesilas of Cyrene overseeing the weighing of a product, identified either as wool or the herb silphium, for both of which Cyrene was famous. By the Arkesilas Painter, it dates to about 560 BC. Bibliothèque Nationale de France 189, Paris. Drawing by J. Etherington.

The majority of the subjects depicted on Lakonian cups feature hunting (Fig. 6.8), feasting and mythological scenes (Fig. 6.3), with Herakles a particular favourite. Odysseus, for example, blinds the Cyclops, Prometheus' liver is devoured by a vulture, and the heroes of Greece hunt the Calydonian boar. The Amyklaion was perhaps the most important cult centre associated with Sparta, and terracotta relief plaques from the sixth and fifth centuries at Amyklai are identified as 'hero reliefs', presumably depicting an underworld god and his consort, perhaps connected with the cult of Agamemnon and Cassandra. From the middle of the sixth century these hero reliefs also appear in stone. Generally a bearded male seated on a carved chair holds a kantharos, with a snake (symbol of the underworld) either behind the chair or in front of the figure. His consort often holds a pomegranate and miniature figures bring offerings to the couple (Fig. 6.7). Further items of cult significance are the clay masks found in large quantities at the shrine of Artemis Orthia. These are thought to be replicas of masks worn in cult rituals such as dances, and many are grotesque or humorous, depicting old women or gorgons. They perhaps are models of masks in wickerwork or cloth worn in ritual dances in honour of the goddess.

Lykourgos 'the Law-giver'

Sparta's institutions and the nature of its society, in which the Spartan citizens – known as Spartiates or homoioi, 'peers' or 'equals' – dedicated themselves to military training, are credited by most ancient sources to the figure of Lykourgos. Herodotos places him approximately in the ninth century as the regent for the young king Leobotas (or Charillos according to Aristotle and Plutarch), while Plutarch offers various theories such as that Lykourgos lived in about 776 or earlier, or might have been contemporary with the first kings, or indeed could have been two different people entirely (Plut. *Lykourgos* 1.1: doc. 6.1). Herodotos records that Lykourgos was consulting Delphi when the Pythia spontaneously proclaimed him a god, and perhaps at the same time revealed to him his future reforms. Alternatively, he may have brought them from Crete, which is the version that Aristotle also records (Hdt. 1.65.2–66.1: doc. 6.2; Arist. *Politics* 1271b24–6: doc. 6.3). Xenophon gives a more coherent account in which Lykourgos devised his reforms and then asked Delphi for ratification of his constitution before imposing it on Sparta (Xen. *Const. Spart.* 8.5: doc. 6.4). This plethora of contexts for Lykourgos and his reforms suggests that he may not have been historical and many scholars these days assume that Lykourgos was in fact a mythical figure: the name Lykourgos means 'Wolf-worker', the wolf being an attribute of Apollo, a major god in Dorian cities like Sparta. It therefore appears probable that at some point the Spartans attributed their political and social system to a mythical reforming figure to give more legitimacy to their change of constitution and social institutions.

Significantly, the poet Tyrtaeus, writing in the seventh century, does not mention Lykourgos, which he would certainly have done had the reforms been attributed to Lykourgos in his time. He considers that the kings Theopompos and Polydoros consulted Delphi over these reforms, and were thus responsible for the new constitution: on traditional dating Theopompos reigned from c. 720 to 675, Polydoros from 700 to 665. This would place the reforms in the first quarter of the seventh century (700–675) if the association of the kings with the constitutional reforms has any validity, perhaps in the period when they were jointly reigning following the First Messenian War in which victory was attributed to Theopompos (Tyrt. 4: doc. 6.6). It is now usual to date the so-called Lykourgan reforms to shortly after the 'Second Messenian War', as this provides a context in which the Spartans had a subject population, the Messenians (helots), who had to be kept permanently under control. The fact too that Lykourgos is described as having received the approval of Delphi for his reforms places these in the period when Delphi had acquired a panhellenic status. This did not take place until after 700 BC, and the oracles as reported were clearly invented retrospectively to legitimise the 'Lykourgan' system. Another reason to date these reforms to the seventh century, and not to some period of prehistory, is that they presuppose the citizenry fighting as a hoplite (heavy infantry) army, and hoplite armour and fighting techniques were developed around 650 BC (Fig. 6.4). It may therefore be assumed that 'Lykourgos' was a post-650 fiction, but one which became so integral a part of the Spartan lifestyle that by the fifth century his historicity was accepted without question. Whether or not Lykourgos was an actual person or a retrospective creation to give legitimacy to seventh-century reforms, the main impact was ideological – the creation of a state in which the good of the community transcended the interests of the individual. It was a state organised to ensure that civic duty and warfare were the main priorities of all citizens.

The fact that Tyrtaeus knows of the Great Rhetra but not of Lykourgos is conclusive evidence that it was after Tyrtaeus' time and before that of Herodotos that the reforms were attributed to 'Lykourgos', and that this was probably in the late seventh century. It is nevertheless convenient to speak of the reforms of 'Lykourgos'. The main pivot of these was the gerousia, perhaps originally a royal council, which was to consist of twenty-eight elders over the age of 60 in addition to the two Spartan kings, with the role of the gerousia being to prepare the agenda for and present political issues to the assembly of Spartan citizens. Lykourgos was also credited with the establishment of the compulsory public messes, and the system of military training for boys from the age of 7 to 18. Sparta now resembled an army camp, with all its citizens being full-time hoplites and with everything subordinated to the need to prevent and deal with helot uprisings. Sparta was the perfect example of the 'hoplite state', with a homogeneous citizen body, the 'homoioi' or peers. With the helots as their means of food production, the Spartans themselves had no need to work, and Spartan citizens were therefore able to concentrate on being permanent soldiers (Fig. 6.6). At the same time, the perioikoi, 'dwellers in the neighbourhood', lived in their own cities, provided military service in time of war, and carried out the manufacturing roles that were prohibited for the Spartans.

The Great Rhetra

The Great Rhetra was the cornerstone of the 'Lykourgan' reforms and according to Plutarch was delivered to Lykourgos by the Pythia as an oracle and was then put to the Spartans as a 'rhetra', or a law (Plut. *Lykourgos* 6.1–9: doc. 6.5). Tyrtaeus in the seventh century is clearly aware of this rhetra, but talks of the 'oracles of the god' brought from Delphi and the 'words of sure fulfilment proclaimed by Apollo for the city of Sparta', recording the tradition that the Spartans had consulted Delphi about their reforms including this law (Tyrt. 4: doc. 6.6). Tyrtaeus' version stresses the constitutional role of the kings, with the oracle proclaiming that the 'god-honoured kings' should be the first to advise the city, along with the gerousia, the 'first-born old men'. The people, or damos (demos in the Ionian dialect), are to answer these 'with straightforward ordinances', in other words the assembly is allowed to vote for or against a proposal put to them by the gerousia, without presumably being allowed to amend it. The rhetra as quoted by Plutarch, however, puts the gerousia in the place of pre-eminence: the Spartans are to set up a gerousia of thirty elders, which includes the archagetai (the 'founder-leaders' or kings), emphasising that the power given to the gerousia, and its incorporation of

226

the two kings, was the central reform. He also believes that a rider was later added to the rhetra by the kings Theopompos and Polydoros that if the people chose a 'crooked ordinance' the gerousia could discount it and dismiss the assembly. In Tyrtaeus' account, however, the rider is an implicit part of the original rhetra itself, giving the gerousia the power to override a decision of the assembly, if it was unsound or misguided.

Plutarch's version of the rhetra also states that a cult to Zeus Skyllanios and Athena Skyllania (the meaning of the epithet Skyllanios/a is uncertain) should be established, perhaps to allow the people more of a role in cult practice vis-à-vis the aristocracy, and to provide for regular meetings of the assembly. The term 'apellaze', which Plutarch uses here, means to celebrate the festival of Apollo, and also to summon the assembly, since Apollo had approved the reforms to the Spartan constitution. The assembly is to meet regularly at fixed times (not just at the whim of the kings) and is to have legal force. Presumably it met once a month, but in the classical period it may have been called as often as required. The people (damos) are divided into tribes (phylai), doubtless the three typically Dorian tribes, the Hylleis, Pamphyloi and Dymanes, and into obai, which may mean the four villages which constituted Sparta, plus Amyklai. The implication is that membership of the phylai and obai was a prerequisite for participation in civil duties and military service. Tyrtaeus (*F* 19) records that the Spartans fought in tribal units, and following the reforms, it appears that the Spartan army was also based on the obai (cf. Hdt. 9.53.2; Thuc. 1.20.3: doc. 6.28). The rhetra also defined the precise size of the royal council, now the gerousia, which was to introduce legislation to the assembly and have the power to reject any decision if it appeared to be unsound. From this point Sparta had what is sometimes called a mixed constitution: the kings were monarchical, the gerousia oligarchic, and the assembly democratic. The obvious power in the state rested now with the gerousia and the kings, with the people having an important but limited power of decision-making (Plut. *Lykourgos* 5.10–11: doc. 6.20; Pl. *Laws* 691d–692a: doc. 6.21).

Aristotle cites another poem of Tyrtaeus which speaks of internal unrest stemming from inequalities of wealth during the time of the Messenian Wars and leading to a redistribution of land (Tyrt. *Poem* 1: doc. 6.65). Whether or not this took place at the same time as the rhetra, Sparta's system was to depend on each citizen owning an estate (kleros, in the Dorian dialect 'klaros'), worked by helots, sufficient to meet his mess contribution. Later sources state that Lykourgos instituted an equitable distribution of land to all homoioi at birth which they could not alienate and which was handed down to the eldest son or reverted to the state (Plut. *Lykourgos* 8.1–8: doc. 6.66). It appears, however, that Spartans could dispose of land, which could be divided between sons and daughters (Plut. *Agis* 4.1–7: doc. 6.71). While sources, including Tyrtaeus, agree that Sparta did suffer from internal strife prior to these reforms, from around 630 Sparta avoided the political crises suffered by other Greek states and its constitution and prestige throughout Greece remained stable for nearly 300 years (Thuc. 1.18.1: doc. 6.57).

The Spartan ethos

Proud of their kings' descent from the great hero Herakles, the life of Spartan males was entirely devoted to the service of their state and to a career of military training in which each individual was expected to demonstrate, in the words of their general and poet Tyrtaeus, their willingness to lose their life in battle for the good of their state (Tyrt. *Poem* 11: doc. 6.10): 'You are descendants of invincible Herakles, so have courage . . . Let each man hold his shield straight towards the vanguard, reckoning life as hateful, and the black fates of death dear as the rays of the sun.' In a state where cowards were shunned and ridiculed, and where every-thing focused on producing fitness and inculcating courage in Spartans from the age of 7 until they were exempted from military service at the age of 60, there was an impressive and overt commitment to the values of the community. Tyrtaeus formulated the ideology in words, while the Persian Wars created the legend: in 425 when 120 Spartan hoplites surrendered to the Athenians at Sphakteria the report was greeted with shock and disbelief throughout the Greek world (Thuc. 38.5–39.3: doc. 13.11). Spartans were not expected to surrender.

There were, however, inherent paradoxes in Spartan society. The individual Spartan was typically presented as an expert in warfare and eager for death in battle, yet Sparta itself was generally reluctant to go to war. A community which did not even possess its own currency had a remarkable number of kings and magistrates prosecuted for corruption and avarice. A state which stressed above all else that all Spartan citizens were 'homoioi' or 'peers', sharing the same messes and education system, was remarkable for extremes of wealth which saw the acquisition of large estates and subsequent loss of citizen rights for a significant proportion of the citizenry. The city, whose only focus was on warfare, produced splendid vases, bronzes and ivories in the seventh and sixth centuries and was the home of major poets. The picture of the dour and austere Spartan and his values, enlivened only by the famous 'laconic wit', is seriously challenged in the archaeological record by the grotesque and humorous masks found at the shrine of Artemis Orthia (cf. Paus. *Description of Greece* 3.16.7–11: doc. 6.51).

Other Greeks saw the Spartans as maintaining a long-standing and conservative culture. When the Corinthians in 432 were trying (successfully as it turned out) to goad Sparta into war with the Athenians, they characterised their Spartan allies, in contrast with the Athenians, as typically pessimistic, cautious and inherently conservative: focusing on what they already possessed, coming up with no new ideas, and when taking action never achieving

Figure 6.3 The outside of a black-figure Lakonian style cup, by the Naukratis Painter. A dynamic scene of mythical creatures – griffins, sirens and sphinxes – is shown. With a diameter of 22.5 cm, it dates to the sixth century BC. This and similar vases are proof that Sparta was not a 'cultural desert' in the archaic period. Louvre E667, Paris. Drawing by J. Etherington.

as much as they should have done; mistrusting their own judgement; always imagining the worst; never taking risks; and preferring to stay at home in case they lost the possessions they already had. The Athenians, in contrast, are described as rash, acquisitive, optimistic and enthusiastic and 'incapable of leading a quiet life themselves or of allowing anyone else to do so' (Thuc. 1.70.1–8: doc. 13.3). While this Corinthian description of Spartan caution was obviously meant to rankle, it must have been close enough to the Spartans' own perceptions of themselves to spur them into action. And while the Spartan victory in the Peloponnesian War gave them a short period of supremacy in Greece, the truth of the Corinthians' criticisms was demonstrated in the ways Sparta then played its part as 'leader' of Greece. With the battle of Thermopylai in 480 the Spartan myth came vividly to life; with the surrender of Athens in 404 at the end of the Peloponnesian War Sparta was in reality the most powerful of all Greek states; by 370 it had lost its dominance and even most of its territorial holdings, as a result of the shortcomings of its political and social institutions, which had given rise to the Spartans' innate conservatism.

The Messenian Wars

Sparta had acquired a subject population, the helots, after a campaign against Messenia in the west of the Peloponnese across the Taygetos range: at this time they already possessed 'helotised' populations in Lakonia which farmed the fertile plains to the south-east of Sparta, centred around the city of Helos. It was from this city that ancient writers believed the helots took their name. According to Ephoros the capture of Helos took place in the reign of Agis, the initial Agiad king (Ephoros *F* 117: doc. 6.7). The original Messenian campaign, or 'First Messenian War', is stated by Tyrtaeus to have lasted twenty years, and to have taken place in the time of their 'fathers' fathers', or two generations (approximately sixty years) earlier than his own time, although this may be loose poetic licence rather than a statement of precise dating. At this point Messene may have referred to a settlement at the foot of Mount Ithome rather than the entire territory of Messenia. The war is said by Tyrtaeus to have been conducted by King Theopompos and is traditionally dated to approximately 740–720. This dating is suggested by the last Messenian victory at the Olympic festival which took place in 736 and demonstrated the Messenians' independence and prosperity. (Sparta's first Olympic victory was in 716.) A Second Messenian War, following a revolt of the subject population, is traditionally dated to approximately 650–630. If Theopompos was involved in the First Messenian War and the conflict took place two generations before Tyrtaeus' own time in the mid-seventh century, this would date the First Messenian War to the end of the eighth or beginning of the seventh century. If this scenario is accepted, towards the end of the eighth century Theopompos, or another Spartan king, defeated the Messenians and acquired their land for Sparta: 'they fought for it for fully nineteen years, unceasingly and always stout of heart, the spearmen fathers of our fathers' (Tyrt. 5: doc. 6.8).

If Theompompos and his younger colleague Polydoros consulted Delphi and introduced the Great Rhetra, as suggested by Tyrtaeus (Tyrt. 4: doc. 6.6), then this took place in their joint reign following Theopompos' victory, in the first quarter of the seventh century (700–675 BC). Later accounts, probably stemming primarily from Ephoros' *Universal History*, record that in Tyrtaeus' own time a second war was necessary, when the Messenians revolted and were supported by the Argives, Arkadians, Heleians and Pisatans (Strabo *Geography* 8.4.10: doc. 6.52). This appears to be supported by Tyrtaeus (*F* 23a), preserved in the fragmentary Oxyrhynchos papyrus. There is of course the possibility that a number of revolts may have later escalated into a full-blown war, but it is generally accepted that it was after this second victory that the Spartans divided up the Messenians' territory into estates farmed by the Messenians for the Spartan citizens, who received half of the helots' produce. In place of tribute, the Messenians had to send half their produce to Sparta and Tyrtaeus speaks of them as being 'Just like donkeys oppressed with great burdens, bringing to their masters of grievous necessity half of all the produce their land bears' (Tyrt. 6: doc. 5.44). This might, however, describe an earlier stage in conquest before the helots were reduced to serfdom, as Pausanias, who quotes this passage of Tyrtaeus, comments that the Messenians were compelled to take an oath that they would not rebel against the Spartans. If they were fully enserfed, there appears to be no reason why an oath would have been necessary.

The Partheniai

The period following the First Messenian War was apparently one of great prosperity, as evidenced by the artistic tradition. However, as this wealth was inequitably distributed it gave rise to dissent among the Spartan population. Up to this point Sparta was much like any other Greek city, except for the dual kingship, and was certainly known for its music and choirs, and fine artwork such as bronzes and ivories. But with newly acquired territory the extremes of wealth appear to have sparked discontent. One group, the Partheniai, or 'maidens' sons', who were plotting against the state, were encouraged to leave Sparta and found a colony at Taras around 706, although they were allowed to return and would be given land in Messenia if they were unsuccessful (Strabo *Geography* 6.3.2–3: doc. 2.23): Herodotos (4.145–8) also relates the story of an earlier group, the Minyans, who shortly after Sparta's foundation were absorbed into the population. However, when they started to stir up trouble they were dispatched to colonise the western Peloponnese and Thera. The details of the complaint of the Partheniani are not quite clear, but Antiochos sees them as citizens who were downgraded to helots, and Ephoros as illegitimate Spartans who did not have full citizen rights. Their settlement in Italy prospered, and their expulsion was obviously a symptom of some political struggle for power or rights within Sparta.

Eunomia

Both Herodotos (Hdt. 1.65.2: doc. 6.2) and Thucydides are aware of a period of political discord in Sparta (which Thucydides dates to 400 years before his own time), following which the city was under excellent government (Thuc. 1.18.1: doc. 6.57). The fact that Tyrtaeus too wrote a poem entitled *Eunomia*, 'Good Government', implies that there was or had been Spartan unrest, which Aristotle attributed to inequalities of wealth, and which had had a part in instigating the 'Lykourgan' reforms (Tyrt. 1: doc. 6.65). These need not have been a single package: it is possible that the reforms were introduced over an extended period during the seventh century. Once Messenia was under (and had to be kept under) Spartan control, Sparta began to have internal problems with dissident groups. The Messenian uprising, together with Sparta's defeat by Argos at the battle of Hysiai in 669 (Paus. *Description of Greece* 2.24.7: doc. 6.54), which might have incited the helots to revolt, was possibly the immediate catalyst for change and an increase in Spartan control in Messenia. Certainly, despite the ancient view that Spartan society remained unchanged for centuries, there was clearly an on-going process of change in response to different pressures from internal rebellion and external military engagements during the archaic period.

The works of Tyrtaeus

Tyrtaeus' poetry encapsulates much of the Spartan ethos: the concept of 'team spirit', respect for older men, and the glory of a noble death, along with indomitable courage and discipline even in the face of overwhelming odds: 'to die after falling in the vanguard is a good thing for a brave man doing battle on behalf of his native land' (Tyrt. 10: doc. 6.9). In these poems, he celebrates the Spartan conquest of Messenia which traditionally took twenty years to complete in the First Messenian War (Tyrt. 5: doc. 6.8), and exhorts the Spartans to victory in the Second Messenian War, reminding them of the dishonourable consequences of defeat and inciting his hearers to courage and steadfastness in the line of battle (Tyrt. 11: doc. 6.10). A noble death in warfare is presented as the most glorious of fates bringing honour to the Spartan's family and city, while the victorious warrior who returns to Sparta wins distinction and honour, and 'after much contentment goes to Hades' (Tyrt. 12: doc. 6.11). These poems remained central to Spartan education and training throughout the archaic and classical periods. They reflected the military character of Spartan ideology and were part of the harsh military lifestyle all Spartans were compelled to undertake following the Messenian Wars (Figs 6.4–6). Athenaeus records that the Spartans in their wars 'recited the poems of Tyrtaeus from memory and moved in time to them'. According to Philochoros, after the Spartans defeated the Messenians, they made it a custom in their expeditions to compete in singing the songs of Tyrtaeus at dinner, with the polemarch giving a prize of meat to the victor (Philoch. *F* 216: doc. 6.12). The emphasis on the glory associated with fighting and dying nobly for one's country is a central theme, and Tyrtaeus' works were used for generations to reinforce this dominant ethos. Spartan music in general was related to military virtues, and the ephors made sure that the traditional, simple, characteristics of Spartan music were maintained (Plut. *Spartan Traditional Practices* 17: doc. 6.14). As well as being valuable evidence for Spartan military ideology the poems are a useful means for dating the Messenian Wars and civic discord prior to the reforms.

The Spartans' reaction to defeat was similarly stoic: on the final day of the festival of the Gymnopaidiai in 371, when the men's choirs of different ages were competing in boasting of their bravery and noble deeds, past, present and future (Plut. *Lykourgos* 21.1–2: doc. 6.13), the news of the defeat at Leuktra arrived and the report that 400 Spartiates had fallen in battle. When the ephors learned of the catastrophe, they were deeply distressed, but allowed the contest to finish. And, in fact, on the following day it was the relatives of those who had died who looked cheerful, while those of the 300 still alive, who had technically acted as 'tresantes' (cowards) as they had recovered their dead under a truce with the Thebans, were downcast (Xen. *Hellenika* 6.4.13–16, 19–20: doc. 14.18).

The 'tresantes'

The penalties for cowards, 'tresantes' or 'tremblers', were severe and they were socially ostracised and formally ridiculed, rejected as messmates, or partners in team sports, put in the disgraceful positions in choruses, and made to give way to others on the streets. No one would marry a coward or his sisters, who shared his dishonour, and if he failed to behave in a properly humble manner he could be whipped. The coward, if unmarried, may even have been forbidden to marry, presumably because it was believed that he would pass on undesirable un-Spartan traits to his children. Penalties for cowardice were social rather than legal, though it appears that citizen rights were withdrawn, at least for a time. The 120 Spartiates who surrendered at Sphakteria lost the ability to stand for office and carry out financial trans-actions for a specified period of time (Thuc. 5.34.2). Among various degradations cowards had to wear a cloak with coloured patches and had their beard partially shaven; this was punishment indeed when we remember the pride which the Spartans placed on having their long hair neatly groomed before going into battle (Xen. *Const. Spart.* 11.3, 13.8–9: doc. 6.17). That death was better than the consequences of cowardice was the lesson that was continu-ally repeated in the works of Tyrtaeus and formed an integral part of the training for young Spartans (Tyrt. 11: doc. 6.10): 'no one would ever finish recounting each misery, all those that befall a man, if he should become disgraced'. As Xenophon astutely comments, 'when such dishonour is imposed upon cowards I do not wonder at their preferring death to such an ignominious and shameful life' (Xen. *Const. Spart.* 9.1–6: doc. 6.15).

Spartan men who failed to marry were fined, and like cowards were treated with dishon-our, being unable to watch the youngsters at their athletics. Furthermore in winter they were made to march round the agora, wearing only their tunics, while singing that they were being appropriately treated for breaking the law (Plut. *Lykourgos* 15.1–3: doc. 6.16). Bravery was expected to be shown by hand-to-hand combat in the vanguard, the front line, and the whole experience of battle was promoted as glorious: the Spartans wore long hair and red cloaks, with tall plumes on their helmets, to make themselves look taller, more noble and more ter-rifying to the enemy – a early form of psychological warfare perhaps – and their crimson cloaks, polished bronze armour and long, styled hair were respected throughout Greece.

Figure 6.4 The 'Chigi Vase', a Protocorinthian olpe, produced in Corinth in about 700–650 BC; it dates to when the hoplite form of warfare was being introduced throughout the Greek world. The flute players precede the army, as in the case of the Spartans, and the artist has tried to convey the idea of two lines of hoplites, the phalanx. The hoplites on each side jab each other with their spears. They wear breast-plates and greaves, carry shields and wear crested helmets but are barefoot. Villa Giulia 22679, Rome. Image © Soprintendenza per i beni archeologici dell'Etruria Meridionale.

Young men were not only to have their hair groomed but look both cheerful and noble prior to combat, as they marched to the sound of the army's flautists (Xen. *Const. Spart*.11.3, 13.8–9: doc. 6.17; Fig. 6.4).

It was considered unacceptable behaviour for a hoplite to throw away his shield, as this implied that it had been discarded so that he could flee from the enemy more expeditiously (this was also the case at Athens; Aeschin. 1 *Against Timarchos* 29: doc. 1.42). A famous saying was attributed by Plutarch to a Spartan mother as her son went into battle; she handed him a shield and said 'either on this or with this', which is a good example of laconic style, brief and to the point: the son either had to come back alive with his shield or come back, dead, carried on it. A Spartan mother would rather see her son dead than dishonoured. This sounds like true Spartan 'grit'– except for the fact that dead Spartans were actually buried on the battlefield and their bodies (except those of the kings) were not carried home. More trustworthy is another mother's comment recorded also by Plutarch: when told that her son had been killed in battle, she replied, 'Bury him, and let his brother fill his place' (Plut. *Sayings of Spartan Women* 16, 20: doc. 6.18; Figs 6.6, 6.11).

It was axiomatic of Spartans (like other Greeks) to pride themselves on wounds to the front of their bodies, while a wound to the back implied that the soldier had been running away. Plutarch attributes the same attitude to the Sacred Band at Thebes, when a soldier begged his enemy to run his sword through his breast, 'so that his beloved would not feel shame at seeing his body with a wound in its back' (Plut. *Life of Pelopidas* 18.3–4: doc. 14.17). And in Tyrtaeus' poems the Spartan who dies facing the enemy, pierced 'many times through his breast and bossed shield and breastplate', brings honour to his city and family and is nobly mourned and his name becomes immortal, even though he himself is underground (*F* 12: doc. 6.11). The fact that the Spartan dead were buried where they fell, as at Thermopylai, left a permanent record to other Greeks of the Spartans' indomitable prowess. Private memorials were also erected by families at Sparta: generally these consisted solely of the name of the deceased and the terse comment 'in war'. Spartan music as employed in the agoge and on campaign promoted exactly these values, being primarily, as in Tyrtaeus' songs, 'praises of those fortunate men who had died for Sparta, and censure of cowards, as living a wretched and miserable life' (Plut. *Lykourgos* 21.1–2: doc. 6.13).

Aristophanes in the *Lysistrata*, which was performed in 411 during the Peloponnesian War, concludes the play with a picture of Sparta in happier days when it was an ally of Athens, and not an enemy. He is trying to recall to his audience memories of Sparta before it became Athens' deadly enemy, and sees as particularly symbolic of Sparta its choruses in honour of the gods, in which the Spartan girls dance like the Bakchai in honour of Athena, the 'almighty, all-conquering goddess of the Brazen House' (Ar. *Lysistrata* 1296–1320: doc. 6.19). Many Athenians, perhaps all of them to some degree, admired Spartan ideology and commitment, and most would have remembered Sparta's past history when they confronted the Persians face-to-face and side-by-side.

Spartan martial ideology

Military preparedness and courage in battle were the Spartan ideal. But, of course, even in a system in which such emphasis was placed on martial qualities, there were bound to be some who failed to live up to these. In the Spartan system it was expected that the individual would conform to the Spartan ideal of bravery: to be a coward was to stand outside of society's norms. One example at Thermopylai was the seer Megistias, who was with the '300' at Thermopylai and stayed to die with his comrades despite having foreseen his own death. Simonides composed an epitaph for him individually to demonstrate his courage and loyalty to Sparta and the Greek cause (Hdt. 7.222.1: doc. 11.27; Simon. 6: doc. 11.28). A classic instance of Spartan reactions to impending death is that of two Spartans suffering from oph-thalmia at Thermopylai: Aristodemos decided not to fight at Thermopylai because of this eye infection. His fellow sufferer Eurytos, however, rushed blindly into battle with the help of his helot and was killed, and was the one who epitomised the Spartan ideal: there was no concept of living to fight another day. On his return to Sparta Aristodemos was ostracised and known as 'Aristodemos the trembler (i.e., coward)' until he vindicated himself in the next year with a noble death at Plataea. A third Spartan who had been sent with a message to Thessaly also failed to die with the Spartan corps: although this was not his fault he committed suicide after his return to Sparta (Hdt. 7.229.1–2, 7.231–2: doc. 11.30; cf. doc. 14.18).

Figure 6.5 A bronze statuette of Athena Promachos ('Athena the Warrior'), an important deity for the Spartans. It is of Lakonian workmanship of about 540 BC. Louvre Br 145, Paris. Drawing by Tessa Rickards.

It was only at Leuktra in 371 BC, after 400 Spartiates had fallen, that the remaining 300 were not visited with the consequences of their 'cowardice' in not fighting until the end. Agesilaos waived the loss of citizen rights for these, as they were essentially the last remaining citizens and expediency had to allow 'the laws to sleep': without them there would have been only a miniscule assembly and a non-existent Spartiate army (Plut. *Agesilaos* 30.5–6; cf. doc. 14.18).

The Spartan constitution

Sparta was an example of a 'mixed' constitution, with the kings, gerousia, assembly and ephorate having simultaneously monarchical, oligarchic and democratic features. Both Plutarch and Plato see the gerousia, the council of elders, as holding the constitution in balance, preventing it from swinging either towards tyranny or towards democracy, while Plato adds that the ephors acted as a 'kind of bridle', with this annual elected magistracy helping to keep the government under firm control (Plut. *Lykourgos* 5.10–11: doc. 6.20; Pl. *Laws* 691d–692a: doc. 6.21).

Spartan kingship

The two kings belonged to the Agiad (senior) and Eurypontid (junior) royal houses, and according to Herodotos the original kings were the twin sons of Aristodemos, great-great-grandson of Herakles. Herodotos (6.52.3–4) records the anecdotal account that their mother refused to say which of them was the elder so they would rule jointly. However, this dyarchy presumably represents the consequence of the union of different villages into 'Sparta', an amalgamation of four communities – although the dual kingship is unique in Greece. Sparta maintained its two distinct royal lines until the late third century BC; nevertheless the king's role never became completely formal or ritualised. They nearly always commanded the army on campaign, and had important religious duties, and were treated with the utmost respect: all citizens had to stand in their presence except the ephors (Xen. *Const. Spart.* 15.6–9: doc. 6.34). The kings no doubt had supreme powers to begin with, especially in times of dynamic conquest: later the aristocracy as epitomised in the gerousia gradually encroached on the kings' power until the state become more of an oligarchy, but one in which the kings had a clearly defined place. But, despite the powers of both gerousia and ephors, in practice a powerful and decisive king like Kleomenes I (520–491) could also wield a great deal of influence on matters technically outside of his sphere, such as foreign affairs. The successful commander of the army in a military state was bound to be potentially extremely powerful, and there was always the possibility in the monarchy of using wealth and status to influence others. The kings had access to considerable wealth and clearly had extensive estates, which Xenophon describes as 'enough good land belonging to the cities of the perioikoi to ensure moderate means without excessive wealth' (*Const. Spart.* 15.3). But over time the kings' powers became curtailed: after 506, they could not make war on their own initiative or together (Hdt. 5.75.2: doc. 6.31), while two ephors accompanied them on campaign to handle issues to do with foreign relations. The kings also had to exchange oaths with the ephors on a monthly basis, with the kings swearing that they would uphold the laws (Xen. *Const. Spart.* 15.6–9: doc. 6.34).

The kings' military role

As army commanders the kings exercised absolute power on the battlefield, including the right of summary execution for cowardice or treachery, but it was the ephors who treated with the enemy for peace. They could be held accountable for mishandling campaigns, and several kings were prosecuted for bribery by the ephors. The Agiad king Pleistoanax was forced into exile in 446 because he was unable to pay a 15 talent fine for allegedly accepting a bribe from Perikles to withdraw from an invasion of Attica (Thuc. 2.21.1). When Agis II failed to take Orchomenos in 418/17 the assembly voted that the ephors should raze his house to the ground and fine him 100,000 drachmas (Thuc. 5.63.1–4: doc. 6.33); from that point he had to take ten Spartiates as his advisers with him on campaign. Another king, Leotychidas, in 469 was caught red-handed with a glove full of Persian coins in his tent and was exiled from Sparta (Hdt. 6.70.3–72.2: doc. 6.76).

It was axiomatic that Spartans abroad went 'bad', as there were opportunities for personal enrichment and a more relaxed lifestyle. The regent Pausanias was the first to succumb to such temptation after the Persian campaigns and Thucydides gives a graphic account of his treachery and downfall (Thuc. 1.130.1–133.4: doc. 6.35). Pausanias was tricked into betraying his treachery, but before the ephors could arrest him he took refuge in the temple of Athena of the Brazen House on the Spartan acropolis, where they walled him up, removing him only when on the point of death, in around 470 BC (1.132.5–134.4). His arrogance was displayed by his dedications on the Serpent Column at Delphi and on a bronze bowl at Byzantium, on which he had himself described as 'ruler of spacious Greece' (Nymphis F 9: doc. 6.36). The rearing and training of horses for chariot events at the Olympic festival was particularly expensive: it is significant that the Spartan king Demaratos was said to have competed and won in the four-horse chariot race (Hdt. 6.70.3: doc. 6.76), as was Kyniska, daughter of King Archidamos in both 396 and 392 (Paus. *Description of Greece* 3.8.1: doc. 4.17). Clearly the kings and their families possessed considerable wealth and were able to use it overtly to enhance their personal prestige.

On campaign the king was protected by a special bodyguard of 100 hippeis (cavalry), and was allowed to sacrifice as many victims as he chose. The kings as leaders of the community had important religious functions, particularly connected with the rituals and conduct of warfare (Hdt. 6.56–60.1: doc. 6.26). Before setting out on campaign, a king sacrificed to the gods, to ensure that the expedition being undertaken had the gods' approval, and sacrificed again when he was crossing Sparta's border, to ensure that the gods supported the Spartans when they marched out of their country. On campaign it was their duty to sacrifice daily before dawn. They were particularly attentive to cosmological phenomena, and discontinued campaigns if an earthquake occurred, while they only engaged in battle when the omens were favourable. They had particular responsibility for Delphic oracular responses to Spartan enquiries, and appointed the Pythioi as consultants who went to Delphi on Sparta's behalf and guarded any oracular responses. They were also the kings' messmates. Delphi played an important role in Spartan affairs, as when the oracle allegedly instructed the Spartans to discover the bones of Orestes, Agamemnon's son, in order to have his aid in their war with Tegea (Hdt. 1.67.2–68.6: doc. 3.46). Kleomenes was also said to have bribed the Pythian priestess to convince the Spartans to depose his fellow king who disagreed with Kleomenes' foreign policy (Hdt. 6.66.2: doc. 6.75).

Aristotle considers Sparta a prime example of constitutional kingship, with limited powers except in time of war and in religious matters. In his view Spartan kingship was equivalent to an independent army command tenable for life, a 'perpetual generalship' and he records that while the kings were not generally supreme, they took the lead in warfare and had the power of summary execution over anyone considered a coward on the battlefield (Arist. *Politics* 1285a3–14: doc. 6.29). Xenophon too considered the Spartans to be 'craftsmen in warfare' and, as part of his discussion on the powers of kings on campaign, describes their religious duties and the rituals connected with their sacrifices on setting out from Sparta and at the frontier and the importance of their role in ascertaining the gods' will through the taking of omens (Xen. *Const. Spart.* 13.1–5: doc. 6.30).

The kings' powers in peacetime

Their powers in peace were rather less than in warfare. Part of the privileges of their rank was that the heir to the throne need not undergo the agoge, and kings were given double portions at the mess, of which the polemarchs and the three Spartiates, who took care of the provisions for the king and polemarchs, were also members so that they had close contact with the king. They were sent rations if they did not dine at the mess, but were expected to eat there unless they were entertaining foreign visitors. They were the first served, with double rations, at public sacrifices, and were given the skins of the sacrificed victims. Twice a month they performed a sacrifice at the shrine of Apollo, and had reserved seats at the games and festivals. Another important duty, considering the number of wealthy heiresses in Sparta, was that of determining to whom these girls should be married, and any adoption had to take place in their presence (Hdt. 6.56–60.1: doc. 6.26). The gradual lessening of the kings' powers was, in Aristotle's view, the main reason why Spartan kingship survived for so long: the diminution of the kings' authority, and the establishment of the ephorate in particular, ensured that kingship in Sparta lasted because it was not despotic (Arist. *Politics* 1313a18–33: doc. 6.32). He does, however, comment that the inherited nature of kingship meant that the office was not necessarily held by the best candidate, and notes that the kings' powers were kept in check by the fact that there were two of them and that they were overseen on campaign by the ephors (Arist. *Politics* 1271a18–26: doc. 6.38).

If the kings' powers were restricted in their lifetimes, after their deaths they were heroes. Unlike other Spartiates who died on campaign outside of Sparta, the bodies of kings were buried at Sparta with great ceremonial. Funerary practices for the kings involved the cessation of all business for ten days of mourning, in which helots and perioikoi had to join (Tyrt. 6–7: doc. 5.44). Herodotos records that the news of the death was carried throughout Lakonia and that two people from every household, one man and one woman, had to put on mourning, or incurred heavy penalties. The funeral itself was attended by thousands of citizens, perioikoi and helots all of whom lamented loudly, proclaiming that this was the best king ever to have ruled in Sparta (cf. Hdt. 6.58.3: doc. 6.26: Tyrt. 7: doc. 5.44).

The gerousia

Supposedly a 'Lykourgan' creation and the central pivot of 'his' reforms, as laid down in the Great Rhetra, the gerousia (council of elders) consisted of twenty-eight elected elders and the two kings. It may have previously existed as an advisory council for the kings and was perhaps drawn from an elite group of aristocratic families, but now had a clearly defined constitutional existence and function independent of the kings. Except for the kings, the minimum age for membership was 60 years of age, and members served for life, ensuring that, except under the influence of an extremely able king or kings, the body would be a conservative force in government. Herodotos believed that the kings had a double vote, but this is contradicted by Thucydides in one of his rare criticisms of Herodotos (Thuc. 1.20.3: doc. 6.28). The gerousia prepared the agenda for the assembly, deciding on what proposals should be brought before it, and was permitted by the rhetra to ignore popular decisions of which they did not approve. Essentially this made the gerousia the main political power in the state. The gerousia had the right of 'probouleusis', like the boule at Athens setting the agenda for the monthly meetings of the assembly and debating beforehand the measures which they put to the people. One of their duties was to supervise the laws and customs, and they had important judicial functions as a 'high court' in those cases relating to capital punishment and loss of citizen rights or exile. They also collaborated with the ephors in any cases connected with the kings. Not only may election to the gerousia have been restricted to an elite group within the citizens, voting was by acclamation, a method of election which was easy to manipulate and which Aristotle criticised: the electioneers were shut away from the assembly and judged the success of each candidate by the noise of the cheers they received as they appeared before the voters, a procedure which is described by Plutarch (*Lykourgos* 26.1–5: doc. 6.22). Aristotle has other criticisms too of the elders: their age, and the fact that the office was for life. He reported that some elders were guilty of taking bribes and giving away public property, and he considered that it was inappropriate that they should themselves canvas for the position as this meant that the gerousia would be comprised of Spartiates who were ambitious (Arist. *Politics* 1270b35–1271a18: doc. 6.40).

Both Plato and Plutarch, however, see the gerousia as Lykourgos' main achievement:

> [O]f all contests amongst mankind this seemed to be the most important and the one most worth fighting for . . . total authority in the state, with supreme powers over death and loss of citizen rights and the most important issues generally.
>
> (Plut. *Lykourgos* 26.2)

As the kings comprised only two out of thirty members, it is difficult to decide what degree of influence they exerted in general in the gerousia. Presumably a king (the senior one) chaired meetings of the gerousia, and in a body made up of twenty-eight men over the age of 60 the kings who were not subject to that age limit may have acquired a certain amount of authority: Kleomenes appears to be a case in point.

The Spartan ekklesia

All male citizens in good standing who were over the age of 30 belonged to the Spartan assembly, the 'ekklesia' (not the apella, as scholars sometimes term it). These were the 'homoioi' (peers) or Spartiates, regardless of birth or wealth. With the concurrence of the gerousia and under presidency of an ephor the assembly had the right to vote on laws, decide on peace and war and treaties, elect ephors and members of the gerousia, and emancipate helots, all by acclamation and not by counting of votes (Plut. *Lykourgos* 26.1–5: doc. 6.22). The assembly is clearly linked with the hoplite system, which arose in the first half of the seventh century (700–650 BC): this included the concept of every citizen fighting for his country with each being in possession of a klaros (allotment), being a member of a mess, and being educated through the agoge, the three criteria for being a Spartiate.

All major policy decisions, at least in foreign relations, were made by the assembly. However, its power was limited in comparison to that of Athens: it had no power to initiate or emend legislation but simply voted yes or no to items on the agenda prepared by the gerousia. By the fifth century the ephors convened the assembly and put matters to the vote which, given that they were elected by the assembly, was a democratic feature. Whether there was any right of debate

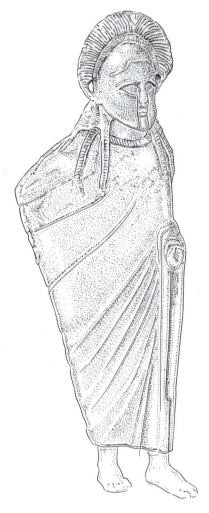

Figure 6.6 A bronze statuette traditionally identified as a draped Spartan hoplite. The height is 15.24 cm and it dates to about 500 BC. Wadsworth Atheneum Museum of Art 1917.815, Hartford, Connecticut. Drawing by Tessa Rickards.

is unclear, but it seems unlikely: while discussion is recorded for some meetings it seems primarily to have been between officials. The disagreement between King Archidamos and the ephor Sthenelaidas in 432 about whether to go to war with Athens was resoundingly settled in favour of war by the assembly (Thuc. 1.80.1–85.3), and in 415/14 Alkibiades persuaded the Spartan assembly that aid should be sent to assist Syracuse, despite the ephors' disapproval (Thuc. 6.88.10). King Agis in 418/17 was able to dissuade the assembly from fining him 10,000 drachmas and destroying his house as payment for failure to take Argos and his loss of Orchomenos, news which had incensed them. Instead they passed a law that he was to be accompanied by ten especially chosen Spartiates as his advisers whenever he led an army out of Sparta (Thuc. 5.63.1–4: doc. 6.33). In all cases the addresses to the assembly were given by someone with official standing, although the assembly clearly responded with enthusiasm and fervour to these various debates. The fact that all decisions were made by acclamation suggests that the practice allowed some possibility of manipulation of assembly decisions by the presiding magistrates. One rare departure from this practice was made by the ephor Sthenelaidas in order to demonstrate the Spartan enthusiasm for war against Athens. Pretending that he was unable to decide which side's shouts were louder, he called for an actual division to prove his point that the majority wanted war: peer pressure in competitive Spartan culture naturally ensured that many Spartiates did not want to be seen voting for peace (Thuc. 1.87.1–2). The assembly was regularly addressed by foreign ambassadors, and appears to have voted in favour of consulting Delphi to discover whether or not Kleomenes' fellow-king Demaratos was legitimate or not (Hdt. 6.66.1; cf. doc. 6.75). Moreover, it was the assembly that decided that Agesilaos rather than Leotychidas would succeed Agis II in 400 (Xen. *Hellenika* 3.3.4). It was the assembly too that voted that the Athenians had violated the Thirty Year Peace (Thuc. 1.87.1–2).

Membership of the ekklesia

Membership of the Spartan ekklesia directly paralleled that of the Spartan army, and Spartiates were by definition warriors (Figs 6.6, 6.11). To enjoy citizen rights, such as the ability to vote, Spartiates also had to possess an estate and be able to pay their mess contribution. Any failure to do so, or inability to complete the agoge, resulted in loss of citizenship. According to Xenophon, cowards also lost their citizen rights, such as the right to attend the assembly (*Const. Spart.*10.7); the Spartiates who surrendered at Sphakteria lost their citizen rights, although these were later restored. Younger sons may in many cases have been debarred from citizenship through lack of an estate, although this sits oddly with Aristotle's information that a father who had numerous sons was rewarded: Spartiates with three sons were exempted from military service, and those with four from taxation (Arist. *Politics* 1270a29–b6: doc. 6.37), which as Aristotle notes is a strange paradox for the militaristic state of Sparta. According to Plutarch, 'Lykourgos' divided the land into 9000 (Aristotle speaks of 10,000) estates, each supporting a hoplite and his family. While this figure may well be fictional and perhaps invented in the third century when such a redistribution was proposed to assist Sparta to regain its status as a military power, there does seem to have been at least a partial redistribution of land around the time of Tyrtaeus to resolve the civil unrest which occurred 'at the time of the Messenian Wars' (c. 700–675). Herodotos speaks of 8000 Spartiates in the army in 480 (7.234.2). Each of these must have possessed a klaros (estate) which fits well with the estimate of 9000 lots in total as does the figure of 5000 Spartiate hoplites serving at Plataea in 479; all these, plus older men or any others not called up for the campaign (the ephors proclaimed the age limit fixed for the campaign in question) would have fulfilled all requirements, including possession of an estate, for them to be members of the assembly.

Each man's estate had to be sufficient to produce enough grain for a Spartan to receive each year 70 medimnoi of barley for himself, and 12 for his wife (approximately 6050 litres in total), and proportionate amounts of liquid produce such as wine and oil (Plut. *Lykourgos* 8.1–7: doc. 6.66). According to Plutarch the monthly mess contribution for a Spartiate was one medimnos, or 74 litres of barley, some 36 litres of wine, three kilograms of cheese and one and a half of figs, plus some 'relishes' (Plut. *Lykourgos* 12.1–14: doc. 6.46). This would have left a considerable amount of barley for children, helot slaves in Sparta and recirculation by bartering if the estates were of sufficient size to produce such an amount. Obviously not all estates were equally productive, but in theory a Spartan could derive his mess allowance from less than a fifth of the 'ideal' estate. The members of the richest class in Athens were known as the pentakosiomedimoi (or 500 medimnoi men): allowing for the fact that the helots were supposed to give half their produce to a Spartiate (although in practice it may have been much higher, or of course lower), Spartan estates would have been roughly equivalent to those of the zeugitai in Athens, whose estates produced 200 medimnoi a year. It has been calculated that 75–145 acres were needed to produce 500 medimnoi of grain so a fertile Spartan klaros may have been as little as 30 acres (or 12 hectares), or proportionately more if Plutarch is recording Aeginetic measures as opposed to Attic. In this case the estates would have been equivalent to the Athenian hippeis (cavalry), and somewhat larger than estates for hoplites elsewhere than Sparta.

A century after the battle of Plataea in 479, there were less than 1000 Spartiates and 700 of these served at Leuktra where 400 fell. Aristotle blames this shortage of men, 'oliganthropia' on the fact that two-fifths of the land was in his time held by women. This was 'because of the large number of heiresses and the habit of granting large dowries' and the fact that property was not held on a basis of equity among male citizens. Many of these ex-citizens may have been reduced to the status of hypomeiones (inferiors), mentioned as discontents by Xenophon in the context of Kinadon's conspiracy in 397 BC (Xen. *Hellenika* 3.3.4–11: doc. 14.5), while helots who were granted freedom became neodameis, but were settled elsewhere and clearly did not attain citizen status.

Figure 6.7 Two diminutive worshippers in the right corner bringing offerings to an enthroned couple; the large snake indicates that the enthroned are chthonic (underworld) deities. The enthroned woman who looks at the viewer holds out a two-handled cup to receive a libation while both deities raise a hand in recognition of the offerings being made to them. This could be Menelaos and Helen, who were worshipped at Sparta, where there was a shrine called the Menelaion. Dating to about 550–530 BC, it has a height of 87 cm, and was found at Chrysapha near Sparta. Antikensammlung, Staatliche Museen SK 731, Berlin. Photo © bpk, Berlin/Jürgen Liepe.

The ephorate

While ephors were a feature of other Dorian societies, such as Thera, Cyrene and Taras, and may have existed in some form in early Sparta, their role as executive magistrates elected annually seems to have begun around or slightly before 550, a period when the ephor Chilon (traditionally 556/5 BC) was considered to have been extremely influential: although no contemporary evidence for his actions has survived he was later considered one of the Seven Sages. The mid-sixth-century date is also significant in that it was at this time that Sparta become involved in foreign relations, extending its power through the Peloponnesian League. Consequently there was a need for magistrates with an international or diplomatic role.

The five ephors functioned as a board of magistrates, with executive, disciplinary and judicial powers. They were elected annually from among all Spartiates over the age of 30, and could not be re-elected. The ephorate, as the last stage in the development of the Spartan constitution, was a democratic element, as the five ephors were elected by the assembly and, as they could only hold office once, there was an opportunity for most Spartiates to stand for the position. As at Athens, the senior ephor was eponymous (gave his name to the year) and Thucydides uses this office, together with the archonship at Athens and the tenure of the priestess of Hera at Argos as a method of cross-referencing his chronology for the start of the Peloponnesian War in 431. He is implying, perhaps, that the ephor at Sparta was as well known as the archon at Athens (Thuc. 2.2.1: doc. 3.60). Xenophon and Herodotos both believed that the ephorate was part of Lykourgos' package of reforms. Aristotle specifically puts it later, attributing it to Theopompos, as does Plato. The rationale here for a king introducing a democratically elected magistracy is that by carefully diminishing the king's power, Theopompos ensured that the monarchy would last in Sparta, as in fact it did, in contrast to monarchies in other Greek states (Plut. *Lykourgos* 7.1–3: doc. 6.23). Even if this account is incorrect, the decline in the power of the kings was mirrored by the increase in the powers of the ephors. Some scholars connect the ephors' number with the five villages which originally came together to form the Spartan state. However, the ephorate is not mentioned in the Great Rhetra, or in Tyrtaeus, and hence the ephors were clearly not important at that time, even if the office of ephor was already in existence. Both Tyrtaeus and the rhetra as quoted by Plutarch regarded the Spartan constitution as consisting of the two kings, the council or gerousia, and the assembly, so the ephors as an executive magistracy must post-date these.

The first appearance of ephors in the historical record is around 550, when Herodotos records that they instructed Anaxandridas II, the Agiad king, to divorce his current wife because she was childless. The ephors, in discussion with the gerousia, effected a compromise whereby he was allowed to marry a second wife concurrently. The implication was that if he did not do so then severer measures would be taken against him by the assembly under their direction: this second wife was to become the mother of Kleomenes. Similarly in approximately 515, when the Samian Maiandrios tried to bribe Kleomenes in order to be restored as tyrant in Samos, Kleomenes approached the ephors and, rather than taking executive action himself, advised them to banish Maiandrios from the city as a potentially dangerous element (Hdt. 3.148.1–2: doc. 6.73).

The powers of the ephors

The ephors had important judicial powers, and could levy fines on any Spartiate and expect immediate payment; they could also remove from office, imprison and bring to trial any official – although in the case of the kings they sat in judgement with the other king and the gerousia. The gerousia, however, was the usual court in the case of murder trials. In administrative matters the ephors negotiated with representatives of other states such as ambassadors and envoys, received embassies, expelled unwelcome foreigners (the term for this was xenelasia), convened and presided over the assembly and carried out its decisions. They also supervised the educational regime. When the assembly decided on war, the ephors ordered the mobilisation (involving the choice of appropriate age-groups) and dispatch of the army and channelled instructions to the generals who were to lead the campaign.

At least by the fifth century ephors monitored the kings' conduct, and they could prosecute them before the Spartan equivalent of a supreme court (the gerousia plus ephors) and settle disputes between the kings. Two ephors accompanied the kings on campaign to handle any matters relating to treaties and foreign affairs and to oversee his conduct. Each month the ephors exchanged oaths with the kings, swearing on behalf of the city to keep the kings' position unchallenged as long as they kept their oath to rule according to law (Xen. *Const. Spart.* 15.6–9: doc. 6.34). In major political trials they both presided and executed the sentence. One example of their executive powers was their ruthless suppression of the conspiracy of Kinadon who in 397 attempted to overthrow the Spartan constitution with the help of helots, hypomeiones (inferiors) and perioikoi (Xen. *Hellenika* 3.3.4–11: doc. 14.5). Another of their significant duties was that of formally declaring war on the helots each year, so that the killing of a helot was not a religious pollution. Because the ephorate was an annual magistracy, there was not necessarily a consistent policy from one board of ephors to the next, and the power of the board depended very much on the personalities involved in any year. Aristotle considers the ephorate another element, a democratic one, in the 'mixed' constitution, and levels further criticisms against it, considering that as many of the magistrates were poor they were amenable to bribery. He also regards the office powerful to the point of being even equal to that of a tyrant so that the kings themselves had to cultivate the support of the ephors (Arist. *Politics* 1270b6–35: doc. 6.39).

Aristotle's criticisms of the Spartan constitution

Aristotle makes a number of criticisms of the Spartan constitution, and comments on the oliganthropia, shortage of citizens, caused by the fact that fathers of large families of sons were exempted from military service or taxation. This resulted in the land being divided among too many Spartans who were therefore poor and unable to pay their mess dues (Arist. *Politics* 1270a29–b6: doc. 6.37). The kingship was inherited and kings not chosen on their merit (Arist. *Poiltics* 1271a18–26: doc. 6.38); the ephors were susceptible to bribery because many of them were poor since any Spartiate was a possible candidate for the office, and as even the kings had to curry favour with them they had made Sparta's government overly democratic (Arist. *Politics* 1270b6–35: doc. 6.39); and the elders were also susceptible to bribery and elected in a most inappropriate fashion. While the nature of the office encouraged the ambitious to stand for it, membership of the gerousia should not be held for life, in his view, 'as the mind, like the body, is subject to old age' (Arist. *Politics* 1270b35–1271a18: doc. 6.40). He also considers that the position of naval commander was so powerful as to be similar to a third kingship (Arist. *Politics* 1271 a37–41: doc. 6.41), while the state's finances were in an appalling state, with the city moneyless and the citizens greedy (Arist. *Politics* 1271a26–37, b10–17: doc. 6.42). Aristotle sums up the reasons for Sparta's failure to maintain supremacy in the fourth century as being due to the restricted nature of the training of Spartan citizens,

243

who were versed only in warfare and had no idea how to behave or govern others in times of peace. He also considers that as the constitution was designed with only conquest and warfare in mind this was one reason for its failure in the fourth century (Arist. *Politics* 1271 a41–1271b6, 1333b5–26: docs 6.43–4).

Clearly Sparta had, as Aristotle continues, a number of 'democratic' elements, such as its educational system, with the sons of the rich being brought up in the same way as those of the poor, and the common messes (syssitia) which were the same for everybody (with the kings a partial exception), while Spartiates were indistinguishable from each other by their clothing (Arist. *Politics* 1271a26–37, b10–17: doc. 6.42). They even borrowed horses, dogs or slaves from each other and chastised each other's children (Xen. *Const. Spart.* 6.1–3: doc. 6.48). However, despite certain 'democratic' rights, the power of political decision was carefully kept away from the populace as a whole, although in theory at least Spartiates had a quasi-communistic lifestyle, shared by all citizens.

Community life in Sparta

Following the 'Lykourgan' reforms Spartan citizens lived at Sparta, which resembled a military camp rather than a sophisticated urban settlement, with all Spartiates being obliged to take part in the state education system (agoge) and be a member of one of the common messes (pheiditia or syssitia). Only the heirs to the thrones were exempted from the agoge, and even the kings were not excused attendance at the mess, unless they were entertaining foreign dignitaries. For the Spartans military service was compulsory and full-time, from the age of 7 when boys entered the agoge up until the age of 60 years. This was possible because helots produced the food and the perioikoi (or 'dwellers-around') were employed in crafts and trades. Some redistribution of land must have taken place at the time of the Messenian Wars, for every Spartan citizen possessed an estate farmed by helots, which provided his mess-contribution. Without this he could not hold citizen status.

The common messes

The Spartan messes, syssitia (Herodotos and Aristotle), syskania (Xenophon), pheiditia (Aristotle and Plutarch cite this as the correct Spartan term) or andreia (the Cretan name according to Plutarch), were another intrinsic feature of the Spartan lifestyle and were supposedly instituted by Lykourgos himself. The ability to make the contribution to one's mess was essential for citizenship, but Aristotle points out that many were unable to make their food contribution (Arist. *Politics* 1271a26–37: doc. 6.42). This may have led to Spartans being demoted to the status of 'inferiors' and Aristotle suggests that, as the system was instituted with 'democracy' in mind, these dues should have been covered centrally. This issue was probably a contributing factor in the decline in citizen numbers to less than a thousand by the year 371, leading to Sparta's fall as a military power.

Xenophon provides an idealised view of these gatherings: a ration of grain (barley) for each member had been laid down by 'Lykourgos'. It was supplemented by hunting expeditions and wheaten bread from the richer members; sufficiency rather than extravagance was the expressed aim of the company at dinner; and – strange to the Greeks – there was no compulsory drinking of wine: the quenching of thirst, not deliberate intoxication, was the order of the day (Xen. *Const. Spart.* 5.2–4: doc. 6.45). In his *Life of Lykourgos* (doc. 6.46) Plutarch gives further details: messes customarily comprised fifteen or so members of mixed ages (although it is possible that Plutarch is mistaken in this number, as the messes in Crete were far larger); the messmates each contributed their rations monthly; everyone's presence was compulsory unless they were delayed by sacrificing or hunting; and even kings were bound by these rulings, although according to Herodotos (Hdt. 6.57.3: doc. 6.26) there were occasions on which they were able to eat at home. A single vote was enough to blackball a potential member. Boys attended the messes to learn the correct behaviour and hear adults singing Spartan songs and telling stories of successful combat; conversations were kept confidential. After moderate enjoyment of their food and drink, the messmates departed, without a light (Plut. *Lykourgos* 12.1–14: doc. 6.46). The pro-Spartan Kritias wrote in favour of drinking customs at Sparta and commented on the abstemious drinking habits in the messes: each man had his own goblet to drink from, and so did not need to empty the cup before passing it round as at Athens. Each man drank just enough for 'merriment' rather than drunkenness (Kritias *F* 6: doc. 6.47): 'the Spartan habit is evenly disposed, to eat and drink proportionately to prudence and capacity to work; there is no day appointed for intoxicating the body with unmeasured drinking.' To emphasise the virtues of sobriety and dissuade young men from drunkenness, the Spartans also brought helots into the mess and compelled them to drink a large quantity of unmixed wine. They would then 'order them to sing songs and perform dances which were ignoble and ridiculous' so that the boys could see the degrading and unmanly effects of excessive drinking (Plut. *Lykourgos* 28.8–9: doc. 5.46).

Eating together was a means of ensuring social conformity and control throughout Spartan society, and every citizen as he came of age joined a mess. This reinforced peer-bonding

Figure 6.8 Hunting was an important leisure sport for the Spartans and also a source of food. Here on the interior of a Lakonian black-figure, polychromatic cup, two hunters dressed as Spartans with elaborately braided long hair in tresses are shown having just speared the great boar of Kalydon in Aetolia: a myth told how Artemis sent the enormous boar to ravage Aetolia because the king of Kalydon had forgotten to sacrifice to her. Spartan depictions of this myth reflect their hunting interests. The scene is by the Naukratis Painter; the cup has a diameter of 19.5 cm, and dates to about 560 BC. Louvre E 670, Paris. Drawing by J. Etherington.

and emphasised the importance of state over family relations. However, there were exemptions, and as those who were occupied in hunting or sacrifices were excused from attendance (Plut. *Lykourgos* 12.4: doc. 6.46; Fig. 6.8) there must also have been strategies in place to allow Spartiates to travel abroad on embassies and compete in panhellenic festivals.

The agoge

The Spartan system was intended to produce boys who were obedient, respectful and self-controlled and soldiers who were tough and disciplined. It was idealised by Plutarch and Xenophon (who put his own sons through the system), while Aristotle criticised its limited nature and the way it inculcated habits of savagery and the inability to cope with crises outside of wartime (*Politics* 1338b9–19: doc. 6.81). It was unique within Greece, even though courage and physical fitness were considered essential for young men in all cities, and all boys in Sparta underwent the training involved in the agoge except for the heirs to the two thrones. Thucydides (2.38) has Perikles in the Funeral Oration speak of the difference in the educational systems of Sparta and Athens, of course to Athens' advantage: 'the Spartans, from their earliest boyhood, are submitted to the most laborious training in courage . . . yet we are just as ready to face the same dangers as they are.' This in itself demonstrates how remarkable the agoge appeared to other Greeks, and Xenophon, an enthusiastic exponent of the Spartan system, provides details about the training programme. The fact that successful completion was a prerequisite for citizenship says much about the minimum standard of fitness necessary in a Spartan; after all the weak and deformed had already been exposed at birth by the elders of the tribe (Plut. *Lykourgos* 16.1–2: doc. 4.23). Xenophon notes that in other Greek cities, boys were looked after by slaves, and that boys' feet were allowed to go soft because they could wear sandals; they were also coddled by being allowed to have changes of clothes and as much food as they could eat. In contrast to the liberal education and more comfortable lifestyle which the elite in other states received, Spartan boys spent their youth in rigorous training.

They did not, for example, have slaves to look after them, as elsewhere. Instead there was a paidonomos, a 'supervisor of education', who had powers similar to those of a general over an army. He was assisted by some of the older youths, who acted as scourge-bearers, flogging any boys who did not meet the exacting demands of Spartan training (Xen. *Const. Spart.* 2.1–8: doc. 6.49; Fig. 6.9). Xenophon notes that obedience was a Spartan characteristic as a result. In connection with this, the Spartan custom whereby any adult male could punish a boy whom he saw doing wrong implies that the discipline of all youths was the duty of every citizen. Furthermore, if the boy complained about this punishment to his father, the father was obliged to give him another beating (Xen. *Const. Spart.*6.1–3: doc. 6.48).

Unlike other Greeks who sent their sons (if they could afford it) to study reading and poetry, music and gymnastics, the emphasis in the agoge was on toughening up the young Spartans to make them all into professional soldiers. Only basic reading and writing was taught, and instruction was concerned primarily with bodily fitness, courage and obedience. They went barefoot and were allowed only one cloak (no tunic), regardless of the weather, so they would be able to endure heat and cold. Their diet also came under scrutiny. The boys were allowed only as much food as was necessary and Xenophon states that they were 'neither to be weighed down with repletion nor lack experience of going hungry'. Of course, this training, as Xenophon also relates, was not only so that they would be able to go without food when required, but also so that they could endure the same type of food for longer and 'be more tolerant of every kind of food and stay more healthy'. All this increased their ability to live off the land and rough it in enemy territory. But the boys were also encouraged to remedy their hunger by stealing, although, if caught, they were punished, in order to teach them to steal well – the idea being that anyone who was going to steal his food had to stay awake at night and wait in ambush during the day, thus learning good survival skills.

The nomenclature suggests the attitudes underlying the system: the paidonomos was a 'boy-herd' (as opposed to the paidagogos, or 'slave attendant' of other Greeks); the farming metaphor is carried on in the terminology of the groups into which boys were divided at different ages, such as bouai and agelai, terms used for herds of cattle: Plato (*Laws* 666e) speaks of the Spartans keeping their youths mustered together like a herd of colts at grass. The regimen was intentionally replicating that of an army camp and youths in the senior age class behaved like officers, organising war-games and presiding in the mess. Part of the ethos of not being caught is exemplified in the famous story of the boy and the fox. Plutarch tells how the boys took great care over their stealing; on this particular occasion a boy, who had stolen a fox-cub and hidden it under his cloak, endured having his stomach lacerated by the beast's claws and teeth, and died rather than be detected (Plut. *Lykourgos* 18.1: doc. 6.50). The endurance of physical pain was practised in the rites of Artemis Orthia, where boys were scourged so that their blood would besprinkle Artemis' altar; if the men wielding the scourges struck lightly, the cult statue 'would suddenly grow heavy', and the priestess who held it would warn them to strike the boys more severely. According to Plutarch boys actually died under this treatment, but this might refer to a later period (Paus. *Description of Greece* 3.16.7–11: doc. 6.51).

Spartan pederasty

Another feature of the educational regime was pederasty, which in Greece normally meant the love of an adult male, the erastes (lover) for an adolescent, the eromenos (beloved) who was the passive recipient of his affection. In Sparta this was an institutionalised part of the agoge for boys from the age of 12 years. Each was chosen by an older 'lover', probably in his twenties, who had completed the agoge but was not yet married. This older partner acted as a quasi-father figure and role model to his 'eromenos', mentoring the teenager in habits of courage and discipline, as part of the education and socialisation process of the agoge. Plutarch records an episode in which, when an adolescent cried out in pain, it was his older lover who was punished for not having taught him proper habits of self-restraint (Plut. *Lykourgos* 18.4). By convention in Athens, intercourse was supposed to take place between the thighs of the eromenos (this 'intercrural' copulation is frequently depicted on Attic vases, especially in the second half of the sixth century); but in Sparta anal penetration seems to have been the norm, with Aristophanes joking that the Spartans 'ploughed manure' (*Lysistrata* 1174).

Also in contrast to Athens, Spartans continued to participate in these pederastic associations into their twenties rather than terminating them with the adolescence of the eromenos, and the segregation of youths in barracks until the age of 30 encouraged such relationships, which were perhaps consolidated later by the mess system where homoioi dined together. The depth of such bonding can be seen in the case of the Sacred Band at Thebes, where lovers fought beside each other: Plutarch comments that 'a body of men held together by the affection between lovers is indissoluble and unbreakable, since the lovers and beloveds through shame stand firm to protect each other when in danger' (*Pelopidas* 18.3: doc. 14.17). The relationship of Apollo and the young Hyakinthos, his beloved, may have been symbolic

Figure 6.9 A bronze statuette of an athlete found at Sparta. Spartans competed in various athletic events both in Sparta and at the panhellenic festivals. Here the athlete is in the process of tying a victory headband, so the statuette commemorates a win. It stands at 12.4 cm high. Antikensammlung, Staatliche Museen 8576, Berlin. Photo © bpk / Antikensammlung, SMB / Johannes Laurentius.

of the ritualised pederastic relations practised by the Spartans, and the three-day festival, the Hyakinthia, was celebrated at Amyklai in the month of Hyakinthios (early summer) in their honour.

Xenophon attempts – unsuccessfully – to present the case that homosexual relationships in Sparta were purely platonic and spiritual, although he has to admit that this was not generally believed (Xen. *Const. Spart.* 2.12–14: doc. 4.79). Pederastic relations between youths and adolescents were a part of Dorian culture, as in the ritualised homosexual abduction that was practised on Crete (Ephoros *F* 149: doc. 4.78). According to Aelian (*Varia Historia* 3.10.12), any upstanding Spartan who did not act as an erastes to youths of good character was fined by the ephors, while the homosexual practices of Spartans were a constant joke in Attic comedy. The relationships thus formed could have potential political implications: in 400 Lysander played an important part in his lover's acquisition of the throne when Agesilaos became king instead of Agis' heir Leotychidas (Xen. *Hellenika* 3.3.1–4), while in 378

Sphrodias was acquitted of raiding Attica without the ephors' permission because of the relationship between his son and King Agesilaos (Diod. Sic. *Library of History* 29.5–8: doc. 14.14). This incident lead directly to the formation of the Second Athenian Confederacy (Diod. Sic. 15.28.1–5, 29.5–8, 30.2: doc. 14.14).

Spartan foreign affairs

By the sixth century Sparta was the most stable, powerful and internationally renowned state in Greece. When Croesus of Lydia sent to Greece in about 546 to seek allies against Persia, it was Sparta that he approached (Hdt. 1.69–70). In 525 some Samians, political opponents whom the tyrant Polykrates of Samos had sent to Egypt to get out of the way, detoured to Sparta and persuaded the Spartans to attempt to depose the tyrant. The expedition however was unsuccessful (Hdt. 3.39.1–4, 3.44.1–47.3, 54.1–2, 56.1–2: docs 7.32, 7.34). When Polykrates' successor Maiandrios was expelled by the Persians in about 515, he went to Sparta and attempted to bribe the king Kleomenes to support his return. Kleomenes refused this bribery and had the ephors expel Maiandrios from the city for fear he should find someone more amenable to corruption (Hdt. 3.148.1–2: doc. 6.73). In around 513, Sparta was visited by a Scythian embassy, requesting aid against Persia to revenge Darius' invasion of their territory (Hdt. 6.84.2–3: doc. 6.77). Kleomenes was still in power in 499 when Aristagoras visited Sparta to seek aid for the Ionian revolt (Sparta was his first port of call, even before Athens), but Kleomenes once again refused to be bribed (Hdt. 5.49.1–51.3, 6.73.1–84.3: docs 6.74, 6.77). Sparta did, however, send to Cyrus telling him to make no move against Greek cities (Hdt 1.152). Between these three appeals Sparta deposed Hippias, tyrant of Athens, in 511/10 and invaded Athenian territory twice more in 508–507. It went on to take action at the request of the Athenians against Aegina for medising in 491 (Hdt. 6.49.2–50.3: doc. 6.75). This series of foreign contacts and reliance on Sparta by other Greek states show that from 550 Sparta was generally seen both by the Greeks and others as the leading state in Greece.

Spartan and its Peloponnesian neighbours

This state of affairs did not come into being without certain struggles. Sparta had been defeated by Argos, the rival with whom it had been involved in continuous internecine warfare, at Hysiai in 669/8 (Paus. *Description of Greece* 2.24.7: doc. 6.54). Later, the Spartans initially failed to take Tegea in the 'battle of the fetters' around 560. The Spartans had optimistically taken with them fetters with which to bind their captives only to have them used on themselves (Hdt. 1.66.1–67.1: doc. 6.55). They also reached a stalemate in the battle of the Champions against Argos in about 545. Sparta won this battle on a technicality, but then followed it up by an outright victory (the initial conflict was fought between selected 'champions' from each side). Sparta then began to consolidate a series of alliances, and under the kings Anaxandridas II (560–520) and Ariston (550–515), and perhaps associated with the ephorship of Chilon, began a new policy, symbolised by the acquisition of Orestes' bones (who supposedly according to one tradition was a Spartan). By this means they attempted to gain mastery over the Peloponnese as a whole, legitimising their actions by claiming they were Orestes' descendants (Hdt. 1.67.2–68.6: doc. 3.46). Chilon and Anaxandridas together were credited with overthrowing tyrannies, including that of Aeschines of Sikyon (*Ryland Papyrus* 18: doc. 7.7). The cult of Agamemnon and Cassandra at Amyklai (both killed by

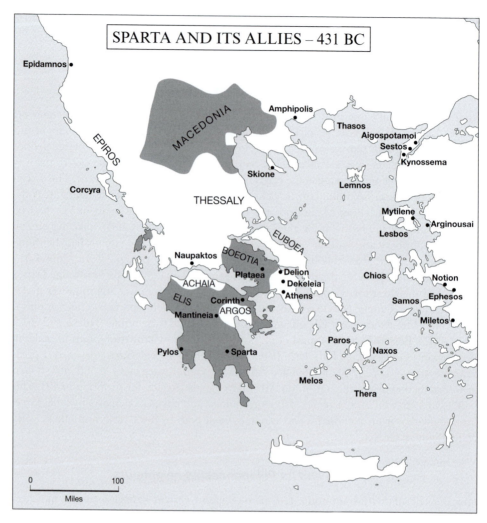

SPARTA AND ITS ALLIES – 431 BC

Map 6.2 Sparta and her allies in 431 BC. Based on M. Grant, *The Routledge Atlas of Classical History*, fifth edition, Routledge, 1994, p. 29.

Clytemnestra on their return from Troy; Aeschylus *Agamemnon* 1377–98: doc. 4.68) may have been refocused at this time for the same reason, in order to stress Sparta's relationship with Orestes' family, the Atreidai.

This policy culminated in the formation of the Peloponnesian League as a major factor in Sparta's foreign policy; Corinth was already an ally by 525. This League (the 'Lakedaimonioi and their allies') had a policy of defensive alliance in which the allies were autonomous but at League meetings, which only Sparta could convene, they were bound by a majority vote. Thucydides lists the allies of Sparta in 431 and again in 419/18, along with figures for the contingents each ally was able to put into the field against Argos (Thuc. 2.9.2–3, 5.57.1–2: docs 6.62–3). Sparta now had allies surrounding its territories that would come to its assistance in the case of a helot revolt. An example of a treaty between Sparta and its individual allies contains the clause that the ally must have 'the same friends and enemies' as the Spartans, while the ally has to come to Sparta's aid when requested (Meiggs and Lewis 67 (bis): doc. 6.61). Sparta also instituted a practice of supporting oligarchic governments, as opposed to tyrannies or democracies, and Sparta became a noted deposer of tyrants, who were replaced by oligarchic governments which surrounded Spartan territories (Thuc. 1.18.1: doc. 6.57; Plut. *On the Malignity of Herodotos* 21: doc. 6.58). States in which Sparta installed or attempted to install oligarchic governments included Athens, Megara, Sikyon, Argos, Elis, Corinth, Mantineia and Phleious. The Spartan system proved to be successful when Kleomenes defeated the Argives at Sepeia in 494, took punitive steps against Aegina which had 'medised' or agreed not to oppose the Persians in 491, and became by common consent the leader of the Hellenic League which opposed Xerxes in the Second Persian War. Plutarch describes Sparta at the peak of its power prior to the Peloponnesian War as 'Herakles', ruling a willing Greece with only a cloak and a dispatch-stick (the skytale was a cylindrical device used for sending messages on campaign), able to put down oligarchies and tyrannies simply by sending out a single envoy (Plut. *Lykourgos* 30.1–3: doc. 6.64).

The Spartan economy and Sparta's decline

The problems of inequality of wealth which caused Sparta to experience civil unrest at the time of the Messenian Wars were dealt with as part of the 'Lykourgan' reforms, perhaps by some form of redistribution of land as a result of which each Spartiate possessed an estate (Tyrt. *Poem* 1: doc. 6.65). However, there is no reason to accept Plutarch's statement that Lykourgos (or Lykourgos and then Polydoros) divided Spartan territory into 9000 inalienable lots (Plut. *Lykourgos* 8.1–8: doc. 6.66). Certainly Aristotle implies the contrary in his description of how large families had resulted in the land being divided to such an extent that many Spartans were poor (Arist. *Politics* 1270a29–b6: doc. 6.37). Certainly, one essential flaw in the Spartan system was the inability to maintain citizen numbers. This is particularly apparent from the middle of the fifth century. While Sparta was able to field an army of 8000 in 480 and 5000 at Plataea in 479, at Leuktra in 371 only 700 Spartiates were represented, 400 of whom were killed in battle. Numbers of Spartiates in the Second Persian War imply a total male population at that point of 10,000, and this may have grown until the Great Earthquake in the 460s, perhaps making it difficult to assign each Spartiate a klaros. There could of course have been attrition in war during the last few decades of the fifth century, although there are no records of huge Spartan losses in the Peloponnesian War: the capture, however, of 120 Spartiates in 425 at Pylos seems to have been a blow to Spartan manpower (and hence their loss of citizen rights on their return was only temporary).

A further problem throughout this period was that of the helots, who were certainly not accustomed to Spartan rule: an earthquake in 465 sparked a helot revolt, which is recorded as taking ten years to quell. When the helot rebels were finally allowed to leave under a truce, the Athenians settled them at Naupaktos, close to the Peloponnese (Thuc. 1.102.1–103.3: doc. 12.11). The earthquake and subsequent helot revolt may have had an impact on Spartiate numbers, both because of losses in battle and because their land was now not being adequately farmed. The primary problem, however, seems to have been a financial one: for whatever reasons, Spartans were unable to pay their dues to their messes and thus incurred a loss of citizen rights. This might have been the result of a decline in helot numbers, following the great revolt and resettlement at Naupaktos and continuing flight by helots.

Certainly Thucydides mentions this as a concern after the Athenian capture of Sphakteria (Thuc. 4.41.3, 5.14.3) and when Messene was founded by Epameinondas in 370 huge numbers of Messenian exiles are described as returning from Italy, Sicily and Libya (Paus. *Description of Greece* 4.26.5: doc. 14.22). Athenian raids on the coastline of the Peloponnese and from Pylos may also have had a negative effect on harvests, and Sparta's creation of a navy rowed by helots, and the use of helots on campaign may also have caused a decrease in agricultural production.

Spartiates who were no longer citizens were presumably downgraded to the status of hypomeiones (inferiors), and were no longer members of the assembly or true Spartiates, although they, like the helots and perioikoi, no doubt performed some form of military service. Xenophon represents the poorer Spartans as finding it difficult to pay their mess dues, even though these were not excessive, and on the evidence of Aristotle many no longer possessed an 'estate', as the land had become concentrated in the hands of a few, with two-fifths of the territory held by women. Hence, he records, a state which should have been able to support 30,000 hoplites and 1500 cavalry could field less than 1000 soldiers (Arist. *Politics* 1269b39–1270a8, 1270a23–a31: doc. 4.18). Plutarch gives an account, which should be treated with caution, of how a particular ephor, Epitadeus, changed the inheritance laws for personal reasons, possibly after the defeat at Leuktra. The result of this was that Spartans could leave their klaros and oikos to anyone and 'men in authority started acquiring estates unscrupulously, ejecting the true possessors from their inheritances, and very soon the wealth of the state flowed into the hands of a few and the city was impoverished' (Plut. *Agis* 5.5: doc. 6.71). At this point he records that only 700 Spartiates were left, of whom only 100 possessed an estate (and could therefore pay their mess dues): the rest of the people 'without resources or rights, remained in the city fighting off wars apathetically and unenthusiastically, but always looking for some opportunity for change and revolution.'

Spartan commanders abroad

However, there were other deep-rooted problems in terms of the Spartans' ability to interact with others in time of peace. Pausanias' behaviour as regent for Pleistarchos after the Second Persian War was a precursor to future problems. As commander of the naval forces in 478/7 he is described as arrogant, while following the capture of Byzantium he adopted Persian customs and dress. His two dedications, on the Serpent Column (Meiggs and Lewis 27: doc. 11.49) and at Byzantium (Nymphis *F* 9: doc. 6.36), inflamed resentment and distrust at Sparta. Indeed, the Spartans erased the couplet on the Serpent Column and were called to account by the Amphiktyonic Council and fined. It was at this point that the allies asked Athens to take leadership of the coalition and Pausanias was removed from command and recalled to face trial. Although acquitted on the charge of negotiating with the Persians, he was then thought to be conspiring with the helots while communicating with Persia and 'freelancing' as a Spartan commander in Asia until finally instructed to return. He was found to be intriguing with Persia and was tricked into revealing his plans, whereupon he was starved to death by the ephors after he took sanctuary in the temple of Athena Chalkioikos (Thuc. 1.130.1–133.4: doc. 6.35; Nymphis *F* 9: doc. 6.36).

Pausanias is a good example of the Spartan inability to deal with other free Greeks in a diplomatic manner: the Spartans were more at home with helots and inferiors. The other problem was one of greed: one aspect recorded of the 'Lykourgan' reforms was the prohibition of coinage. This of course is anachronistic, as the earliest regional mint, at Aegina, only

Figure 6.10 A marble stele of about 575–550 BC showing the twin Dioskouroi; the pediment indicates that the relief stood in a shrine. Archaeological Museum, Sparta. Drawing by Tessa Rickards.

began producing coins in 580–540, and such a ban on precious metal coins is more likely to have occurred at the end of that century in the time of Kleomenes. Mess contributions for example were made in kind. However, according to Plutarch, 'Lykourgos' made gold and silver coinage invalid, with only iron currency allowed. As a result Sparta was no longer able to engage in any form of external trade, and was visited by 'no rhetoric teacher, vaga-bond diviner, keeper of hetairai, or any craftsman of gold or silver ornaments, because there was no coinage' (Plut. *Lykourgos* 9.1–5: doc. 6.67). Of course, Spartans, and particularly the kings, did acquire coinage, and those who possessed money circumvented the regulation by depositing it at Tegea in Arkadia like Xouthias in the mid-fifth century, whose initial deposit of 200 minas was later replaced by one of 400. In the case of his death, his legitimate sons were to receive the money, when they were five years past the age of puberty. Should they not survive, his legitimate daughters were the next legatees, followed by his illegitimate sons and then his nearest relations (Bogaert *Epigraphica* III.29 A and B: doc. 6.69). The historian Poseidonios, whose work only survives in fragments, records that Spartans who did acquire money deposited it in Arkadia because they were not supposed to possess gold or silver, and that before this any gold or silver found in Sparta was dedicated to Apollo (Poseidonios *F* 48c: doc. 6.68). Perhaps because currency regulations were in place Spartiates, and especially the kings, are reported as potentially easy to bribe, as when in 476 Leotychidas, the Eurypontid king, was found with a Persian glove full of silver while on campaign in Thesssaly. Condemned at Sparta, his house was destroyed and he went into exile at Tegea where he died (Hdt. 6.72.1–2: doc. 6.76).

Lysander became as unpopular with the other Greeks as Pausanias had been, but for different reasons. Following Athens' defeat in 404 he put down democracies and established oligarchic dekarchies (boards of ten) in major Greek cities, composed of his friends and adherents, under the supervision of a Spartan harmost, or governor. But while Samian oligarchs gave him divine honours, Lysander's prestige seems to have gone to his head. He had his own epic poet in his retinue and made a huge dedication at Delphi which worried the Spartans. Sparta also for the first time collected more than 1000 talents from their conquests and this was a further concern when Gylippos, one of Lysander's commanders and the hero of Syracuse, was found trying to sneak 30 talents of silver from the revenue Lysander had sent back to Sparta. He starved himself to death after being convicted by the ephors (Poseidonios *F* 48c: doc. 6.68). Such was the ephors' concern about this influx of coinage that in 403 they prohibited private ownership of gold and silver coinage, and Sparta at the period of its supremacy was doomed to a coinage of iron, at exactly the time when cash was needed to pay allies and rowers for the navy (Plut. *Lysander* 17.1–6). Xenophon comments that the over-enthusiasm of Spartans at this period to serve abroad and their zeal for acquiring money was a serious problem (Xen. *Const. Spart.* 14.1–4: doc. 6.70). Lysander was recalled in 403/2 but escaped condemnation on the charge of bribing the oracle of Zeus Ammon, and was able to engineer the accession of his previous lover Agesilaos to the throne. He was killed at Haliartos in 395, but Plutarch gives an account of how papers were found afterwards which revealed that he was planning to rewrite the Spartan constitution, so that kings would be elected on merit and not birth (Plut. *Lysander* 13.1–7, 18.1–10, 24.1–25.3, 30.1–5: docs 13.38, 13.42).

Within thirty years Sparta was to lose its place on the world stage. At Leukra in 371 the myth of Spartan invincibility was smashed by the Theban general Epameinondas, who then proceeded to invade Lakonia. More damagingly, he entered Messenia and liberated the helots, recalled Messenian exiles and founded the city of Messene in 370: Sparta was stripped of the larger part of its territory and its workforce, losing simultaneously most of its productive farmland along with the helots who worked it. The perioikoi also defected as the Thebans marched into the Peloponnese. Epameinondas assisted the Arkadians in creating a new capital at Megalopolis, while Mantineia took the opportunity at this period to adopt a democratic government (Paus. *Description of Greece* 8.27.1–2: doc. 14.21). When the battle of Mantineia was won by the Boeotians in 362 BC, Sparta had clearly become a second-rate power.

Kleomenes: the 'mad' Spartan king

Kleomenes I (c. 521–490) was one of the most influential and controversial of Spartan kings. An Agiad, he dominated the gerousia and his fellow monarchs and did more than anyone to assure Sparta a position of supremacy in Greece by the time of the Persian Wars. It was during his reign that the Peloponnesian League ('Lakedaimon and its allies') became a working reality (cf. Thuc. 2.9.2–3: doc. 6.62). However, a number of contradictory traditions clearly existed in Sparta concerning his reign, and Herodotos, the main source for Kleomenes, utilises these uncritically. At different points in his *History* he calls him both 'the most upright of men' (Hdt. 3.148.2: doc. 6.73) and 'not of sound mind and on the verge of madness' (Hdt. 5.42.1: doc. 6.72). Kleomenes was the product of a double marriage, which was unusual for Sparta.

Table 6.2 The family of Kleomenes

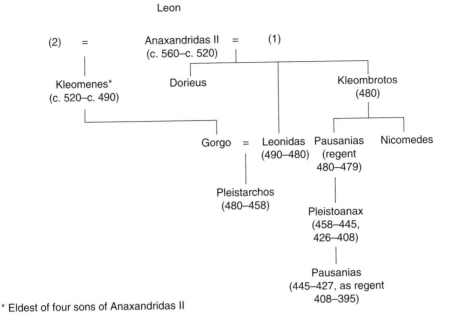

* Eldest of four sons of Anaxandridas II

Anaxandridas II (560–c.520) had long been married to his niece, of whom he was extremely fond, but was childless. When the ephors attempted to persuade him to divorce his wife and remarry, to continue the royal line, he refused, at which the ephors in consultation with the gerousia proposed that he be allowed, in most un-Spartan fashion, to take a second wife. The second wife, who came from the family of Chilon the ephor, gave birth to Kleomenes, after which the first wife presented Anaxandridas with Dorieus, Leonidas and Kleombrotos (Hdt. 5.39.1–42.2: doc. 6.72). There was clearly some rivalry between Kleomenes and Dorieus over who should become king, and Dorieus in his disappointment (Herodotos here in following the anti-Kleomenes tradition describes Dorieus as 'pre-eminent among all his age group and very confident that he would hold the kingship because of his merit') decided to lead a colony of Spartans overseas. He must have been supported in this enterprise by his half-brother, the new king Kleomenes. Herodotos describes Dorieus' two attempts to found a colony in the west as failing because of his lack of attention to the details of the Delphic oracle's instructions. He at first attempted a foundation in Libya, which failed in the third year, and then in western Sicily. However, before he reached Sicily he was killed in a battle in southern Italy between Croton and Sybaris (Hdt. 5.42.2–45.1: doc. 2.22). On both occasions he took with him the same body of men, which was granted him by the state. In other words, although leading a private colonisation venture Dorieus had Spartan support, including that of Kleomenes, in his attempt to found another Spartan colony to parallel that of Taras (Strabo *Geography* 6.3.2–3: doc. 2.23). Some of his companions are named by Herodotos, who records that one of them attempted to set up a tyranny at Selinous in Sicily, perhaps in 507/6 (Hdt. 5.46.1–2: doc. 7.42).

The hostile accounts recorded by Herodotos were derived from Kleomenes' half-brothers Leonidas and Kleombrotos, who felt that they had the best right to rule as they were the sons of Anaxandridas' first wife, even though Kleomenes, the son of Anaxandridas' second wife was technically the eldest son (Hdt. 5.39.1–42.2: doc. 6.72). The supporters of Demaratos, his fellow Eurypontid king whom Kleomenes had deposed in 491 BC on the grounds of illegitimacy, allegedly by bribing the Pythia, were also antagonistic to Kleomenes and scathing of his role in Spartan affairs (Hdt. 6.65.1–66.3: doc. 6.75). Perhaps Herodotos also talked to Kleomenes' daughter Gorgo and her son Pleistarchos: Gorgo was married to her half-uncle Leonidas, and it would be interesting to know with which side of the family her loyalties lay. Demaratos and Kleomenes fell out on campaign as early as 507 or 506 BC, when Demaratos refused to support Kleomenes' invasion of Attica to install Isagoras as tyrant (Hdt. 5.74.1–76: doc. 10.5). This marked a watershed in the relationship between the Spartan kings and from this point on, only one king was allowed to lead an army out of Sparta. The kings no longer campaigned together and instead one of the statues of the Tyndaridai (the Dioskouroi, castor and Pollux) accompanied the army while the other remained in Sparta (Hdt. 5.75.2: doc. 6.31; Fig. 6.10).

Kleomenes' and Spartan foreign affairs

Apart from the consolidation of Spartan power and influence through the Peloponnesian League, one of Kleomenes' main strengths was that of masterly inactivity. While Sparta during his reign was recognised as the pre-eminent state in Greece, he rejected with confidence suggestions that the Spartans should help to restore Maiandrios as tyrant of Samos in about 515 (Hdt. 3.148.1–2: doc. 6.73), assist the Scythians to invade Persia in 513, or campaign in Asia Minor in 499 in support of the Ionian Greeks, apparently making these decisions without any consultation (Hdt. 5.49.1–51.3: doc. 6.74). In hindsight, his lack of involvement in Asia Minor proved the right decision, as Athens' participation in the Ionian Revolt did nothing to help the Greek cities of the Asia coastline and only brought mainland Greece and its cities to the attention of the Persians. Herodotos comments that it was easier to fool 30,000 Athenians than one Spartan king (Hdt. 5.97.1–3: doc. 11.3). In two of these cases, Herodotos presents Kleomenes as incorruptible, untempted either by Maiandrios' gold and silver drinking cups, or Aristagoras' bribe of 50 talents, prompted by his daughter Gorgo's observation, 'Father, the stranger will corrupt you, if you don't go away'.

Kleomenes and Athens

While Kleomenes had no desire to involve Sparta in campaigns overseas, he showed no unwillingness to intervene in internal Greek affairs with the help of his Peloponnesian allies. Shortly after his accession he proposed in 519 an alliance between Athens and Plataea in the hope of stirring up trouble between Athens and the powerful Boeotian city of Thebes (Thuc. 3.55.1–3, 68.5). Kleomenes was also responsible for deposing the Athenian tyrant Hippias whom he besieged on the acropolis in 511/10, after an initially unsuccessful attack under the Spartan Anchimolos. Hippias' children were caught being smuggled out of the country and Hippias surrendered and went over to Persia (Hdt. 5.62.2–64.2, 5.65.1–5: docs 9.36–7). Following the restoration of the democracy, Isagoras, archon at Athens in 508/7, invited Kleomenes to Attica to 'drive out the curse', in other words his political rival Kleisthenes, a member of the Alkmeonidai who were responsible for the massacre of Kylon's supporters on the acropolis probably in 632 (Hdt. 5.71.1–2: doc. 7.21). Kleomenes successfully expelled 700 families from Athens, but was unable to disband the council, and was then besieged on the acropolis by the Athenians. Being unprepared to withstand a siege, he left on the third day under a truce (Hdt. 5.69.1–70.2, 5.73.1–3: docs 10.2–3). This incident was still considered amusing by the Athenians nearly a hundred years later, when Aristophanes in his *Lysistrata* has his chorus sing of the time when they 'savagely besieged that man, sleeping seventeen shields deep at the gates', after which Kleomenes delivered up his tiny threadbare cloak and departed for home (Ar. *Lysistrata* 256–85: doc. 6.78). While on the acropolis he was said to have discovered certain oracles, which he took back to Sparta despite the objections of the priestess of Athena Polias.

In 507 or 506 he returned again, on this occasion to install Isagoras as tyrant at Athens (the allegation that he had been having an affair with Isagoras' wife during the events of 508 can be dismissed as slanderous gossip). This attempt failed when his plans were revealed while on campaign and were opposed by his fellow-king Demaratos and the Corinthians (Hdt. 5.74.1–76: doc. 10.5). On this occasion Kleomenes had made arrangements for the Boeotians and Chalkidians to attack Athens simultaneously, and had clearly concealed the overall objective or overridden any concerns felt by the Spartiate government and his Peloponnesian allies. Later, learning that the Pythia had been bribed by the Alkmeonidai to persuade the Spartans to depose Hippias, Kleomenes considered leading another expedition into Attica in about 505–501 to restore him to power, but was not supported by his Peloponnesian allies. The Corinthians in particular opposed the proposal. One of the factors behind the plan to restore Hippias were the oracles which Kleomenes had 'discovered' on the Athenian acropolis in 508/7. These warned the Spartans of the future growth of Athenian power and the Spartans clearly felt that Athens would be weaker under a tyranny than under a democracy. Hippias was summoned to Sparta, but the allies remained unconvinced of the justice of the plan and it was aborted (Hdt. 5.90.1–93.2: doc. 6.59).

Kleomenes and Argos

Kleomenes was clearly a competent and ruthless general and in 494 defeated an Argive army at Sepeia, where he lured fifty survivors out of the forest on the grounds that their ransoms had arrived and then massacred them and burned the sacred grove with the rest of the survivors of the battle. His tactics were, at least in Greek eyes, unsporting, for he sounded the call to attack while the Argives were breakfasting. As a result his victory was total and the Argives reputedly lost 6000 men in this campaign. It was for this reason that they were unable to take part in the Persian Wars. Kleomenes, however, failed to take the city of Argos, which was reported to have been defended by Telesilla the poetess and the Argive women in male attire (Paus. 2.20.8–10; cf. Hdt. 6.75.3: doc. 6.77). On his return to Sparta he was prosecuted by the ephors for not taking Argos. However he argued persuasively that the 'Argos' mentioned in the oracle which foretold that Argos would be captured was not the city but the shrine of the hero Argos, to whom the forest was sacred (6.82.1).

Kleomenes and Persia

Shortly after the battle of Sepeia Persian envoys arrived in Greece in 491 (or perhaps earlier) to demand submission from all the Greek cities. The envoys to Athens and Sparta were thrown in one case into the pit for condemned criminals and in the other into a well from which they were told to take the king the earth and water which symbolised submission (Hdt. 7.133.1), although all of the islands and many cities submitted. Athens was concerned enough, when its ancient enemy Aegina medised, to request Spartan help, believing that the Aeginetans would fight on the side of the Persians. Kleomenes, therefore, went personally to Aegina to arrest those responsible for the decision. The episode was to be the breaking-point in the relationship between Kleomenes and his fellow king. The Aeginetans refused to obey one king without the other, and Kleomenes was now determined to depose Demaratos, who opposed his stance in Aegina and was supposedly maliciously discrediting Kleomenes. Once again, the Pythia was suborned and was bribed to state that Demaratos was not Ariston's son, but the son of his wife's previous husband. Consequently Demaratos was deposed and later fled to Persia, being succeeded by his cousin Leotychidas. The Persians gave Demaratos cities to rule in the Troad and he became an advisor of Xerxes during the Second Persian War. Kleomenes' plot was, however, discovered, and the Pythia, Periallos, whom he had bribed, was deposed as priestess (Hdt. 6.49.2–50.3, 6.61.1–66.3: doc. 6.75).

Kleomenes' downfall and death

Now that Kleomenes had a fellow-king with whom he could work harmoniously, he went with Leotychidas to Aegina and arrested ten of the most distinguished Aeginetans as hostages whom he sent to Athens for safe-keeping. However, his intrigues against Demaratos had become known, and he fled first to Thessaly (this might be a mistake for Sellasia in the Peloponnese), and then to Arkadia where it was alleged he was stirring up a rebellion against Sparta and may have created an anti-Spartan Arkadian League. He was still sufficiently powerful to be a concern at Sparta and was invited back, but soon took, according to the accounts on which Herodotos is relying at this point, to striking any Spartiates he met with his sceptre. His relatives – Leonidas and Kleombrotos, his half-brothers, and perhaps his daughter Gorgo – therefore put him in the stocks, where, it was said, that after acquiring a knife from his helot jailor, he committed suicide by self-mutilation. Herodotos records a number of possible reasons for his madness: the Argive view was that it was due to his massacre of Argives who had surrendered at Sepeia; the Spartiates said it was because he had acquired the habit of drinking unmixed wine from the Scythian envoys on their visit to Sparta; and Herodotos himself thought that the cause was his treatment of Demaratos and bribery of the Pythia (Hdt. 6.73.1–84.3: doc. 6.77). He had done much to put Sparta, and Greece as a whole, in a position of strength to face the oncoming Persian invasions, and the manner of his death has to remain an enigma. If he was thought to be intriguing with the Arkadians that might have been sufficient to cause concern in Sparta, and those with much to gain from his removal from power, namely his half-brother Leonidas, who was possibly already at this point married to Gorgo, may have seen advantages in disguising a murder under the pretence of suicide while of unsound mind.

Later views of the Spartans

As Aristotle puts it, the Spartans were only great when at war: they were unable to cope with leisure as their constitution was entirely focused on conquest and physical activities such as athletics. Accordingly he considers that while Sparta's government was stable during wartime, it started to decline once they inherited the Athenian empire in 404. This was because 'they did not know how to be at leisure and had never experienced any other training superior to that of warfare' (Arist. *Politics* 1271a41–b6: doc. 6.43). He even goes so far as to assert that the agoge, due to its emphasis on physical exertion and the importance of courage, produced

Figure 6.11 A bronze statuette from Dodona which was originally attached to a vessel; the hoplite is shown poised for an attack. His large crest probably indicates that this is meant to represent a Spartan warrior. Dating to around 500 BC, it is a superb piece of craftsmanship at just 12.8 cm high. Antikensammlung 7470, Staatliche Museen Berlin. Photo © b p k, Berlin/Johannes Laurentius.

'wild beasts' and that because of this focus on one particular virtue the Spartans ignored many others (Arist. *Politics* 1338b9–19: doc. 6.81). Certainly the Spartans at the end of the fifth century were not trained to run a large overseas empire, and this, together with severe financial problems, the accumulation of large estates and a decline in citizen numbers, along with the loss of Messenia, saw the end of Sparta's centuries as a major power in Greece.

Later Greeks saw the Spartans as typecast and committed only to warfare. They failed to acknowledge that in the archaic period Sparta had been home to poets and musicians of great renown, as well as a patron of crafts such as bronze- and ivory-working. To these Greeks it was unthinkable that Sparta produced composers such as Terpander, Tyrtaeus and Alcman, and they were considered to have imported professionals for their poetry and music (Ael. *Varia Historia* 12.50: doc. 6.79). In line with their apparent sole concern with athletics and music, the Spartans had a reputation for taciturnity and 'laconic' wit (the term of course comes from Lakonia, their homeland), and Plutarch in particular records examples of the 'brevity of speech and pointed utterances' which were typical of notable Spartans. These generally proved the superiority of Spartan customs to those of the other Greeks and Persians

(Plut. *Lykourgos* 19.6–20.8: doc. 6.80). Such anecdotes are attributed to most of the prominent Spartans, including Leonidas and Pausanias during the Persian Wars (Plut. *Sayings of the Spartans* (*Moralia* 225a–d, 230e–f): doc. 11.53), and Spartan women such as Gorgo are shown to be equally as witty as their menfolk (Plut. *Lykourgos* 14.8: doc. 4.19, cf. 6.18).

The Spartan myth was long-lasting: from the mid-seventh century Sparta had won the respect of all the Greeks, and been the dominant land power in Greece due to its possession of the most powerful land fighting force in the Greek world. The Spartans were the undisputed leaders of the Greek allies in the Second Persian War (480–479) and went on to defeat the Athenians and their allies in the Peloponnesian War (431–404). For a brief period they reigned supreme over Greece. This military supremacy collapsed with Sparta's defeat by Thebes at the battle of Leuktra in 371 and the loss of its subject territory in Messenia in 370. Nevertheless, despite its loss of prestige neither Philip of Macedon nor his son Alexander the Great attempted to conquer Sparta (although Philip did invade Lakonia and give some of its territory to his Peloponnesian allies), and Sparta was the only Greek state not to join the League of Corinth in 337. In 330 while Alexander the Great was in the east, Agis III rose against Macedon with some allied Greek states to assert Spartan independence, but the rising was crushed by Antipater, the regent of Macedon, at the Battle of Megalopolis, where Agis died fighting (Diod. Sic. 17.62.1–63.3: doc. 15.19). Alexander's inscription for his victory over the Persians at the Battle of the Granikos in 334 specifically mentions that the Spartans were the only Greeks who did not participate in his Persian campaign (Plut. *Alexander* 16.8): 'Alexander, son of Philip, and all the Greeks– except the Lakedaimonians– from the barbarians who dwell in Asia'.

7

TYRANTS AND TYRANNY

Table 7.1 Greek tyrants

Mainland

Name	Place of rule	Date ruled
Pheidon	Argos	c. 680–660
Theagenes	Megara	c. 640–620
Orthagoras	Sikyon	c. 656
Kleisthenes	Sikyon	c. 600–560
Aeschines	Sikyon	560–c. 556
Kypselos	Corinth	c. 658–627
Periander	Corinth	627–588
Psammetichos	Corinth	588–585
Kylon	Athens	attempt at tyranny c. 632
Peisistratos	Athens	561/0–556, 556/5, 546–27
Hipparchos	Athens	527–514
Hippias	Athens	527–510
Iason	Pherai	390–370
Alexander	Pherai	369–358

Islands and coastline of Asia Minor

Name	Place of rule	Date ruled
Melanchros	Mytilene	c. 612–608
Myrsilos	Mytilene	608–590
Pittakos	Mytilene	590–580
Thrasyboulos	Miletos	late 7th century
Histiaios	Miletos	c. 515–493
Aristagoras	Miletos	c. 505–496
Lygdamis	Naxos	546–c. 525
Polykrates	Samos	c. 532–522
Maiandrios	Samos	521–c. 520
Syloson	Samos	c. 520–514
Aiakes	Samos	514–499, 494–492
Artemisia	Halikarnassos	early 5th century

Sicily

Phalaris	Akragas	570 BC–554 BC
Euryleon	Selinous	508/7
Theron	Akragas, Selinous	c. 489 BC–473 BC
Anaxilas	Rhegium	494–476
Kleandros	Gela	c. 505–498
Hippokrates	Gela	498–491
Gelon	Gela	491–485
	Syracuse	485–478
Hieron I	Gela	485–466
	Syracuse	478–466
Deinomenes	Catana	470–465
Thrasyboulos	Syracuse	466–465
Dionysios I	Syracuse	c. 405–367
Dionysios II	Syracuse	367–357, 346–344
Dion	Syracuse	357–346
Timoleon	Syracuse	344–337

Introduction

Throughout the seventh and sixth centuries, ambitious men backed by armed force seized power throughout the cities of Greece, particularly in the Peloponnese. Overthrowing the existing political system (politeia) of their city-state, they ruled as individuals without the assistance of the aristocrats or citizenry. Frequently coming to power through force, they murdered, exiled or disarmed their opponents, often by making use of a wave of popular discontent against the ruling aristocrats. While their rule brought benefits in many cases to their cities, they were not necessarily altruistic figures: they did what was necessary to retain their own power, and could be ruthless in the accomplishment of this purpose. Certainly cities such as Corinth when ruled by tyrants benefited from public works, the establishment of colonies, and strong leadership. But tyranny was not a 'natural' form of government for the Greeks, whose historical preference, especially in the classical period, was for forms of collective governments, whether these were aristocracies, oligarchies or democracies. Many Greek cities experienced tyranny at some period of their existence, and Peisistratos and his sons Hippias and Hipparchos ruled Athens from 546 to 510 BC: because of their historical significance and importance in Athenian history they have a chapter to themselves. Tyranny was a widespread phenomenon not only in archaic Greece, particularly in the seventh and sixth centuries, but also in fourth-century Sicily.

Sources

Aristotle was concerned with tyranny in his *Politics*, discussing it along with the other forms of government practised by the Greeks, while to a lesser extent he also commented on it in his *Rhetoric*. In the *Politics*, his numerous examples of individual tyrants and discussion of the character of their rule are invaluable. But he is hostile to tyranny as a form of government, as in his opinion it combined the worst elements of oligarchy and democracy (Arist. *Politics* 1310b 3–7: docs 7.63–71). Yet it should also be noted that in the *Politics* generally he argues about the possible defects which could arise within all forms of Greek constitutions, and he gives many

262

historical examples of the political and social abuses that occurred in Greek cities under all types of government. His treatment of tyranny is relatively 'even-handed' when seen in context alongside the accounts he gives of other actual forms of government in practice in Greek cities. He does, however, emphasise the violent nature of tyranny, and there is a Machiavellian touch in his advice to tyrants about how to avoid giving offence (e.g., at *Politics* 1315a 5–24). Solon provides a perspective on tyranny in the archaic period (*Poem* 33: doc. 8.38), as do Theognis and Alcaeus from their personal points of view: Alcaeus was hostile to the tyrants who had ousted the aristocrats on Mytilene, while Theognis points to the conditions from which tyranny at Megara arose (Alc. 348, 429: docs 7.29–30; Thgn. 51–2, 891–4: docs 7.17, 7.19).

Herodotos is an important source for tyrannies, as tyrants were crucial players in the early history of Greece, and he recorded relatively full details of their rule at Corinth and Samos, while surprisingly saying little on the Peisistratidai at Athens. His discussions of the Kypselids are clearly affected by a later version of the events in which the Corinthians disclaimed Periander and his nephew, but they reveal a positive attitude towards Kypselos, the founder of the dynasty. Polykrates of Samos seems to have been admired by Herodotos as a successful ruler: perhaps the fact that his death took place at the hands of the Persians is relevant here. The modern historian, however, who would have liked to have more evidence about the tyranny at Sikyon itself is frustrated by the long story on the marriage of Kleisthenes of Sikyon's daughter, and the sparse details on his actual policies as tyrant. Herodotos' is the first account of tyrants in Greece, and his sources will have been oral in nature. Yet despite his clear opposition to tyranny, he provides a great deal of valuable information and Polykrates comes in for especial attention as the individual who was the first to wield control over the Ionians (Hdt. 3.39–60, with an excursus on why the Corinthians went to war with the Spartans against Samos, 3.120–5). Poets at the courts of the tyrants praised them – and were paid to do so: their positive comments about the tyrant's rule are therefore to be treated with caution. Thucydides judged tyrants on their results: most tyrants in his opinion achieved little, except for those in Sicily, though he demonstrates a very positive attitude towards the sons of Peisistratos: for him what mattered in this tyranny was the effectiveness of their government, and their political ideology came second.

Fourth-century Sicilian tyranny, that of Dionysios I and II, is known mainly from Diodorus, who made extensive use of Sicilian historians such as Philistos, and Timaios who based his own historical account on Philistos' work (the latter served under both tyrants and was very favourably disposed towards them). The generally positive accounts of their reigns in Diodorus stem from these sources, and from Didorus' own preference for the themes revealed in these tyrannies (and which he found in Philistos), such as the amorality and aggression of the Carthaginians against whom the Sicilian tyrants were the main bulwark. Plutarch, however, in his *Dion* and *Timoleon*, preserves a hostile historical tradition, especially with regard to Dionysios II. What is notable is that despite the bad reputation of tyranny in general, which was to some degree deserved, the accounts about individual tyrants allow the positive features of their reigns to be reconstructed, and to be set against the general negativity about Greek tyranny as expressed by Herodotos, Aristotle and Plutarch.

The first use of the word tyrannis

Gyges, a ruler of Lydia, was described by the poet Archilochos as 'rich in gold'. When the poet further states that he himself does not 'passionately desire great tyranny' or Gyges' wealth this is usually taken to imply that wealth was a characteristic generally ascribed to tyrants (Archil. 19: doc. 7.1). Gyges was a usurper, and so an understanding of the term tyrannis ('tyranny') –

which is not Greek – can be arrived at. 'Tyrannis' is a Lydian word and may have been Gyges' political title. For Archilochos and later Greeks the term came to have two main meanings: an individual who seized power and overthrew the existing political organisation of his city, and one who was also wealthy as a result of this, for the advantages of the position of tyrant included wealth and a luxurious style of living. Herodotos uses the term tyrant to describe Gyges in the context of his 'numerous dedicatory offerings to Delphi', and a tyrant was rich by definition (Hdt. 1.14.1: doc. 7.11). Alcaeus was the first writer to describe a specific Greek individual as a tyrant, namely Pittakos of Mytiline, whom he thoroughly despised (Alc. 348: doc. 7.29).

Typically but not universally (as Pheidon's case will indicate), aristocracies had replaced monarchies throughout most of Greece by the archaic period (Sparta provides the main exception), and it was this form of aristocratic government which the tyrants overthrew, replacing it with one-man rule. There was only one female tyrant in ancient Greece, and that was Artemisia of Halikarnassos, Herodotos' home town. At the battle of Salamis in 479 BC she escaped unscathed as captain of a trireme which sank a ship belonging to her own side, while the ships of the other Persian commanders were being destroyed or were in retreat. The Persian King Darius exclaimed, 'My men have become women, and my women have become men!' (Hdt. 8.88).

'Tyrant' and 'tyranny' were quite 'neutral' at first in the Greek language, and it was only when tyrants gained a reputation for blood-thirstiness and lawless rule that the terms became negative and pejorative. The term tyrannis and its corresponding noun tyrannos (tyrant) did not gain currency immediately after Archilochos' use of the word, and Theognis, for example, used the term mounarchoi ('monarchs') to refer to sole rulers (Thgn. line 52: doc. 7.19). In the source tradition some tyrants enjoyed a good reputation, such as Peisistratos at Athens and Kypselos at Corinth, but by the fourth century BC Aristotle certainly categorised tyranny as a debased system of government, and the Athenians had a specific law promulgated against it as late as 336 BC (*SEG* 12.87: doc. 14.52; Fig. 14.12).

The origins of tyranny

Much modern speculation surrounds the emergence of tyranny in the Greek world, but the ancient sources supply most of the answers as to why tyrannies arose (Arist. *Politics* 1310b14–31: doc. 7.2; Thuc. 1.13.1: doc. 7.3). Although Aristotle does not consider the background social, economic or political conditions in a particular city which led to the overthrow of the aristocracies throughout much of archaic mainland Greece from around 650 to 510 BC, he notes that the tyrants were 'popular leaders' (demagogoi) trusted by the people because they spoke against the 'distinguished': by which he must mean the aristocrats. By a reverse reading, they spoke for the interests of what can be called the non-distinguished: tyrants were the 'champions of the people' (Arist. *Politics* 1310b14–31: doc. 7.2; 1305a7–27: doc. 7.65) and certainly, once in power, they used various methods to curtail the power of the aristocracy. Both Thucydides and Aristotle agree that the growth in the size of cities was a crucial element in the emergence of tyranny as a phenomenon, for centralised power in the hands of one man rather than a collective aristocracy was now a real possibility, since cities were larger and had specific governmental needs. At places like Athens, already a large city in the mid-sixth century, the aristocrats were divided amongst themselves and engaged in a contest for political power which led to the emergence of Peisistratos as tyrant.

As for a motive, Aristotle saw tyrants inspired by naked ambition (Arist. *Politics* 1310b14–31: doc. 7.2). Many tyrants started their career in positions of power which they abrogated and distorted. Pheidon, like several other tyrants, began his political career as a hereditary king but seized more power than traditional monarchy allowed. Other tyrants had held political positions in their city and used these as a 'platform' from which to take complete control: Aristotle names several tyrants who started out as kings, magistrates or as popular leaders (doc. 7.65). They were aided in their grasp of power by the lack of a standing army or police force to defend the existing political structure (politeia), so that an individual already in a position of authority could use the assistance of armed associates, and the support of the people, to establish themselves as tyrants. Sometimes modern historians link the emergence of tyranny with the growth of the hoplite class in archaic Greece. This is in some ways indicated by the experience of Sparta: here the hoplite class agitated for reform but tyranny did not emerge, and instead a political compromise was achieved through the 'Lykourgan' reforms. Elsewhere, popular dissatisfaction may well have included that of this hoplite class, although both on Samos and at Athens the hoplite class was disarmed as a concomitant to the establishment of the tyranny. Tyrants came to power through armed force, but often it was a force of friends or associates, or of a bodyguard. So it seems unlikely that a new hoplite class emerged which supported tyrants against the aristocracy and in fact the hoplite class was clearly seen by tyrants as a potential cause of unrest, and in several cases, was disarmed by them when they came to power.

Tyranny and the achievements of tyranny

Thucydides notes that tyrannies arose at a period in which the cities of Greece were becoming 'more powerful and the acquisition of money still more important than before' (Thuc. 1.13.1: doc. 7.3). Revenues increased, cities began building navies, and tyrannies were established. It seems reasonable to link these developments with colonisation, and the trade, wealth and consequent power which accrued to cities as a result. Throughout the Greek world, the traditional aristocracy was tending to alienate the rest of society, and tyrannies should be seen in some sense as proto-democracies in which the tyrant had the tacit support of the population. Aristocratic rule had replaced that of kings, but cities were now 'prizes', wealthy and powerful, and as the aristocratic hold on authority grew weaker the perfect opportunity for individuals to seize power had arrived.

Thucydides' assessment of tyrants was that they were only concerned for their own safety and that they achieved nothing except in respect to their immediate neighbours. This is rather anachronistic as well as inaccurate. Poleis were still developing and it was not yet a period in which states were grouping together into leagues or possessed resources with which to employ large armies. Syracuse in Sicily was the exception, as noted by Thucydides (doc. 7.3). The tyranny at Athens challenged Mytiline for control of the Sigeion in the Troad, while the Corinthian tyrants clearly encouraged trade and established their control of the region of the Ambracian Gulf. Similarly Polykrates of Samos created a thalassocracy ruling over several islands and cities of the mainland of Asia Minor. Tyrants did engage in wars and achieved positions of power for their cities. In fact, Thucydides' own narrative is of a dynamic, expansionist Greece at this period with the tyrants playing an important role in Greece's historical development. The cultural and material legacy of certain tyrannies also contradicts Thucydides' assessment (Thuc. 1.13.1, 17.1: doc. 7.3.)

Pheidon of Argos

Pheidon of Argos is known from Herodotos as well as from Ephoros (*F* 115: doc. 7.4). Pheidon escaped the traditional constraints of his kingship (no doubt a council of aristocrats with whom he had to work in close conjunction) and reinvented his political position as a tyranny, becoming the most powerful man of his time. He ruled sometime in 700–650 BC and was the first of the Greek tyrants. While he is credited with the introduction of stamped coinage, this did not exist in Greece at this stage, but he may well have introduced a standard set of weights and measures, conducive to the trading which was now more widespread throughout the Greek world.

The Argives defeated Sparta in 669/8 BC at Hysiai (Paus. *Description of Greece* 2.24.7: doc. 6.54), and Ephoros states that Pheidon deprived the Spartans of their hegemony over the Peloponnese. Whether Sparta had control over the Peloponnese at this early stage is very doubtful, and this should be seen as a conflict between two neighbouring states. Pheidon's seizure of Olympia in 668 BC, however, indicates that he did have territorial ambitions, and control of the Olympic festival would have given him panhellenic status. Herodotos described the take-over of the Olympic sanctuary from Elis as 'the greatest outrage of all the Greeks' (Hdt. 6.127.3: doc. 7.6; cf. Ephoros *F* 115: doc. 7.4). Pheidon's transference of the control of the festival to the Pisatans (of the town of Pisa), who had long been Elis' rivals for this position, was however temporary, and the Eleians (with the help of the Spartans) were soon in charge again. Herodotos' account is the first reference to the long-running rivalry between Sparta and Argos which would continue for several centuries. While Sparta would come to dominate the Peloponnese, Argos remained independent and had to be taken into consideration by the Spartans when they made decisions about military expeditions. Pheidon's control of both Olympia and the Peloponnese (the extent of his dominance over it cannot be ascertained) was short-lived, but he must have provided an example for many other, unnamed kings and individuals throughout Greece (Ephoros *F* 115: doc. 7.4).

Tyranny at Sikyon: the Orthagorids 656/5?–556/5? BC

Orthagoras established a dynasty of tyrants at Sikyon, a city on the rich coastal plain somewhat west of Corinth, and as his tyranny seems to have been established only a few years after that of Kypselos in that city, he may well have been following Kypselos' example. This family of tyrants at Sikyon is referred to as the Orthagorids, but the identities of the tyrants between Orthagoras and his famous descendant Kleisthenes (his grandson) are uncertain. Orthagoras is described in one of the sources as a 'mageiros', sometimes translated as cook, but it could also refer to a religious official presiding over sacrifices. He was also a successful warrior who was elected polemarchos and from that position became tyrant (*FGH* 105 F2).

When Kleisthenes consulted the Delphic oracle, he was described as a mere 'stone-thrower', that is, one of the light-armed troops that accompanied the hoplites into battle, and as such not a real warrior (Hdt. 5.67.2: doc. 7.5). This is almost certainly a fabrication dating to some time after the tyranny was overthrown, for Kleisthenes – even if he did not engage personally in battle – pursued a militaristic aggressive policy against Sikyon's enemy, Argos. Sikyon was involved in war against its neighbour to the south, and it may well have been this military preoccupation which kept him and his successors in power. Kleisthenes was also involved in the 'First Sacred War', c. 595–591 BC, with the fleet he provided playing a role. Kirrha was just across the Corinthian Gulf and Kleisthenes assisted in the destruction of this city, because it was maltreating pilgrims who were on their way to Delphi. The oracle's sneer against him (if historical) did not mean that he did not take this opportunity to establish and display panhellenic status, a preoccupation of other tyrants, which was also manifested in the panhellenic nature of the competition for his daughter's hand in marriage (see below, p. 268).

Kleisthenes was perhaps the first Greek tyrant to purse a policy of both religious and literary censorship. After his war on Argos, he banned the rhapsodes (singers) from competing at Sikyon in the singing of the Homeric epics, for in these poems the Argives and Argos – Sikyon's enemies – were particularly praised. This somewhat Orwellian touch was then followed by an attempt at 'religious cleansing' and ethnic 'reidentification.' Delphi rejected his request to eject the Argive hero Adrastos from his sanctuary at Sikyon, so Kleisthenes employed a counter-device, introducing the worship of Adrastos' chief enemy Melanippos (who had killed some members of Adrastos' family), and transferring the sacrifices and festivals by which Adrastos was worshipped to Melanippos' newly established cult. In effect he terminated the veneration of Adrastos. He asked the permission of the Thebans to introduce Melanippos' cult, so as with all hero cults a transfer of Melanippos' bones from Thebes to Sikyon would have taken place. Adrastos had been one of the 'Seven' to invade his own city, Thebes, and been defeated by the Thebans, amongst them Melanippos. Religious allegory was presumably of some importance here too: the Argive Adrastos, representing Sikyon's enemy Argos, was in a sense being driven from Sikyon's religious life and replaced by the cult of a hero who had defended his city against an Argive (Hdt. 5.67.1–4: doc. 7.5).

Kleisthenes renames the tribes of Sikyon

Kleisthenes' renaming of the tribes at Sikyon appears to have arisen out of his anti-Argive attitude. Dorians in each of their cities were divided into three tribes: Argos and Sikyon therefore had the same Dorian names for the three tribes into which their citizens were divided. Kleisthenes wanted to distinguish the Sikyonian from the Argive tribes and so renamed those of his own city. His own tribe, which was not one of the three, and is therefore usually viewed as being non-Dorian, he named 'Rulers of the People' (Archelaoi). One of the reasons why Kleisthenes and his descendants stayed in power so long could well be because he had the strong support of this tribe. The other three tribes which were Dorian were renamed as Pig-men (Hyatai), Donkey-men (Oneatai) and Piglet-men (Choireatai). But it is also possible that the fourth tribe was a new creation, made up of Dorians, but those associated with Kleisthenes and families related to him. Traditional interpretations see Kleisthenes championing the pre-Dorian elements of the population (his own tribe) against the three Dorian tribes, but this paradigm is very problematic. It makes the tyranny one based along ethnic Dorian/non-Dorian lines, whereas all the evidence points to the conflict being not with Dorians but with Argos, the powerful neighbour to the south. The tribe named 'Rulers of the People' is better interpreted as an artificial creation composed of his own adherents, ensuring the security of tyrannical tenure which he and his descendants enjoyed in this longest lived of all the Greek tyrannies.

While Herodotos has Kleisthenes renaming the tribes in order to have a 'very good laugh', the reasons why he might have given these tribes such insulting names at the expense of his own citizens is unclear. It may well be that while these names of 'Pig-men', 'Donkey-men' and 'Piglet-men' later seemed insulting they originally had another shade of meaning. Kleisthenes was apparently ensuring that Sikyon was distinguished from Argos as much as possible. It must also be remembered that Herodotos compared the renaming of tribes by this Kleisthenes with that of the Athenian reformer Kleisthenes in Athens in 508 BC, and so shows his complete misunderstanding of the tribal reform at Athens. As a result his account of the tribal reform at Sikyon must also be treated with caution. Sixty years after Kleisthenes' death, and therefore not immediately at the end of the Orthagorid tyranny, the tribes were again renamed, with Kleisthenes' tribe 'the Archelaoi' renamed after Adrastos' son, so Kleisthenes' policies were changed at this point through this renaming of the tribes. The other three took on their original Dorian names (Hdt. 5.68.1–2: doc. 7.5). If this is dated to sixty years after Kleisthenes' death it must have taken place about 500 BC, and some sort of rapprochment with Argos must be assumed, or a desire to reassert Sikyon's solidarity with the Dorian ethnic group.

Agariste marries Megakles of Athens

Kleisthenes is the subject of a second lengthy narrative in Herodotos in the context of describing the Alkmeonidai family at Athens and its rise to fame. When Kleisthenes won the chariot race at Olympia, he invited the unmarried men amongst the assembled Greeks to come to Sikyon to see who would prove worthy of the hand of his daughter Agariste. For twelve months suitors from throughout the Greek world lived at Sikyon and were observed by their prospective father-in-law. If the list of the suitors' places of origin as given by Herodotos is any indication, winning the hand of Agariste, with a dowry of at least one talent (the compensation given to the unsuccessful suitors), reflecting the tyrant's wealth, was worth the time and the effort, and Kleisthenes' involvement at the panhellenic Olympic festival was reflected in the panhellenic atmosphere he created in Sikyon, though on chronological grounds the suitor Leokedes son of Pheidon cannot mean son of the tyrant Pheidon. Hippokleides was favoured above all, because of his connection with the Kypselid tyrants at Corinth, until he disgraced himself at the pre-wedding dinner by dancing on his head (the Greeks wore no underpants). Instead Kleisthenes opted for Megakles of Athens whose son Kleisthenes, named for his grandfather, would become the Athenian reformer of 508 BC. Kleisthenes' motives in choosing Megakles are unknown: the city of Athens was not particularly wealthy or powerful at this stage, but the family was one of the three most prominent in that city. It is also possible that Kleisthenes chose the man whom he thought was the best for his daughter: after all, the point of the twelve months was not to see who might be the best political ally, but to secure the best husband for his daughter and the best son-in-law for himself, taking into account as Herodotos notes the suitors' 'bravery, temper, education and manners' (Hdt. 6.126.1–131.1: doc. 7.6).

The deposition of the Orthagorid tyranny

The tyranny was one of Greece's most successful, lasting for a hundred years. That the tyranny endured for a century appears to be correct, but the figure is not necessarily precise. Kleisthenes' son Aischines was expelled by the Spartans, and the tyranny came to an end in about 556/5 BC. Aristotle attributed the length of the tyranny to the moderate manner in which the tyrants treated their subjects and their general compliance with the laws (Arist. *Politics* 1315b11–18: doc. 7.70). Herodotos' discussion of how Kleisthenes more or less insulted the Sikyonians through their tribal names therefore seems to warrant some modification. The basis on which Plutarch makes his comment that under the tyrants the Sikyonians 'ceased their wickedness' seems unclear either as to the basis for the report or its actual meaning, but it does seem to point to at least one version of history in which the tyrants ruled well, while Herodotos presents a more hostile account (Plut. *On Divine Vengeance* 7: doc. 7.72). As with other tyrannies this one met its end not through domestic dissatisfaction or internal politics, but because of the interference of the Spartans in about 556/5 BC (*Rylands Papyrus* 18:

doc. 7.7). The Spartans by the mid-sixth century were becoming a dominant power in the Peloponnese and their anti-tyranny policy also seems to have been in place by this period.

Tyranny at Corinth: the Kypselids c. 658–c. 585 BC

Corinth by the mid-seventh century BC had become wealthy and powerful through coloni-sation and trade; its unique position on the Isthmus between the Peloponnese and central Greece gave it an ideal location. Ruled by an oligarchy drawn from the Bakchiadai for nearly 200 years, then by the tyranny of the Kypselids, it would always be a major player in Greek affairs in the archaic and classical period. The Bakchiadai were so wealthy and powerful that Strabo could incorrectly refer to them as tyrants. He provides a brief history of the tyrants and the wealthy tyranny Kypselos established which lasted for three generations (Strabo *Geography* 8.6.20: doc. 7.8).

Oracles and the establishment of tyranny

Herodotos devotes two main sections of his narrative to a discussion of this tyranny: one to Kypselos who founded the tyranny in the early 650s (ruling probably 657–627 BC), and one to his successor Periander (627–587 BC). Quoting a Delphic oracle which refers to the Bak-chiadai as monarchoi (Theognis had also used the term mounarchoi: doc. 7.19) – sole rulers – he indicates that Kypselos belonged to this family on his mother's side. Herodotos records three oracles regarding Kypselos. The first was that Kypselos would crush the Bakchiadai and bring justice to Corinth and, as with the Orthagorids at Sikyon, the point is that the tyrant overthrew a corrupt political system. The oracles, with their hostility to the Bakchiadai and their support for Kypselos, are presumably inventions formulated after the overthrow of the Bakchiadai. The second oracle contained a warning that Kypselos would 'loose the knees of many' (Hdt. 5.92b.3), and according to Herodotos Kypselos exiled many Corinthians and confiscated the property of others, ruling for thirty years and ending his reign in prosperity. The third oracle declared that he would be a powerful ruler, with both Kypselos and his sons fortunate, but not his sons' sons. Clearly this refers to the demise of the tyranny under his grandson, and dates the oracle to after the overthrow of the tyranny (Hdt. 5.92b.1–92f.1: doc. 7.9).

Various stories about how the Bakchiadai attempted to do away with Kypselos as an infant are probably his own inventions to help justify overthrowing them, and serve in Herodotos (and his sources which would have gone back ultimately to Kypselos himself) as an excuse to record details about the oppressive nature of their regime. Kypselos' mother Labda, one of the Bakchiadai (his father Eetion was not), hid him in a wooden chest, which was later dedi-cated by one of his descendants (presumably his son Periander) at Olympia. It was of cedar decorated with gold and ivory, a famous artwork with various myths represented on it (Paus. 5.17.5–19.10). The story that he was in exile prior to becoming polemarch probably could belong to this parcel of historical fiction. In his capacity as polemarch and with popular sup-port as a champion of the people against this family, he seized power in around 650 BC.

Kypselos reported that he had an oracle from Delphi to support his claim to rule and he may well have received some such prediction, just as Kylon did later in the 630s BC which he used to justify his attempt at tyranny in Athens (Hdt. 1.126.4: doc. 7.22). That ambitious men consulted Delphi and received oracles which they interpreted as support for their political endeavours seems very plausible: the Spartans, for example, had received Delphi's support around this very time for their constitutional changes (Tyrt. *Poem* 4: doc. 6.6). It is difficult to assess the accuracy of the claims in the historical tradition as represented by both Herodotos and Nicholas of Damascus about the oppressiveness of the Bakchiadai. They may well have a kernel of historical truth but also be exaggerations propagated by Kypselos to help justify his seizure of power (Hdt. 5.92b.1–92f.1: doc. 7.9; Nic. Dam. *F* 57: doc. 7.10).

Kypselos and panhellenic sanctuaries

Engagement with panhellenic and other major religious sites was a preoccupation of tyrants; the participation of the Sicilian tyrants in panhellenic festivals will be discussed below (p. 291). Kypselos built a treasury house at Delphi to house various offerings which he made to the god Apollo on his behalf or that of Corinth. After the overthrow of the tyranny, the Corinthians engaged in a form of historical revisionism, claiming the treasury to be not his but 'Corinthian': Herodotos makes a point of noting that it was not the treasury of the Corinthians but that of Kypselos and hundreds of years later Plutarch also noted this rewriting of history. This treasury house was not just a means of expressing Kypselos' piety towards the god, but must be connected with his claim that he had an oracle from Delphi supporting his seizure of power. His dedications at Delphi will have taken the form of thanks-givings as well as reminders to the Corinthians of the prophetic support he had received (or claimed to have received). He was also publicly expressing his piety and indeed his wealth. Kypselos also dedicated a golden statue at Olympia, which later became the focus of a conflict between poleis. After the tyranny of Kypselos, his son and his grandson came to an end, the Corinthians were given permission by Delphi to inscribe the name of their city on the treasury, as well as on the golden statue: the Eleians who controlled Olympia were furious and refused them permission to do so, and so the Corinthians banned them from participating in the Isthmian Games organized by Corinth at the Isthmus (Hdt. 1.14.1–2: doc. 7.11; Plut. *The Oracles at Delphi* 13: doc. 7.12).

In addition to the chest of Kypselos, his sons dedicated a magnificent golden bowl at Olympia, to commemorate a victory at Herakleia. This is almost certainly the town on the Ambracian Gulf of western Greece founded by Corinth in around 625 BC and it must indicate military activity in the region for which the bowl was a thanks-giving dedication. Kypselos and his son Gorgos founded the colonies of Ambracia, Anaktorion and Leukas in the region of the Ambracian Gulf, digging a canal through Leukas to render it an island (Strabo 7.7.6, 10.2.8) and Periander served an apprenticeship as tyrant of Ambracia for a period. Potidaea, Athenian control of which was be a major factor in the outbreak of the Peloponnesian War in 431 BC, was founded by Corinth in around 600 BC and therefore almost certainly by Periander. He, like his father, was maintaining Corinth's active colonising role, extending its influence into other regions. Under the Kypselids, Corinth adopted coinage, the second Greek city (after Aegina) to do so: the wingèd horse Pegasos was the main motif on the coins. He had been captured at the fountain Peirene at Corinth by Bellerephon and the two had numerous mythical adventures together.

Apart from general comments about killing and exiling opponents, confiscating property and being a just ruler (perhaps somewhat contradictory statements), little in fact is known of the character of Kypselos' reign. Peisistratos at Athens in 546 BC would similarly kill many of his aristocratic opponents on the battlefield, and others went voluntarily into exile rather than be ruled by him, but yet he ruled mildly afterwards and received accolades from the *Athenaion Politeia* (16: doc. 9.16). How tyrants came to power is kept distinct in the sources from how they actually ruled. Thirty years in power, Corinthian prosperity, his public piety and the fact that he could hand the tyranny on to his son Periander in 627 BC, and Periander to his nephew Psammetichos in 588, must indicate something as to his abilities as a ruler.

Periander, Thrasyboulos and the ears of grain

The source tradition about Periander, Kypselos' successor, is very mixed, though the favourable elements cannot be entirely a fabrication by himself and his supporters. Herodotos focuses on the negative aspects of his tyranny, and according to his account Periander's reign (627–587 BC) was much harsher than his father's: 'Periander was initially milder than his father, but . . . became much more bloodthirsty than Kypselos.' The quotation comes from Herodotos' narrative of Periander's interaction with the tyrant of Miletos, Thrasyboulos (Hdt. 5.92f.1–92g.1: doc. 7.13; *Politics* 1313a34–1313b16: doc. 7.69; Arist. *Politics* 1311a20–2 has Periander giving the advice to Thrasyboulos). Thrasyboulos was a tyrant of Asia Minor, and when the Lydians and then Persians took over these Greek cities, they generally left the tyrants in power over the cities. The classic example was Histiaios, tyrant at Miletos and prime instigator of the Ionian Revolt against the Persians. Periander had sought Thrasyboulos' advice on how to govern Corinth by sending a messenger to Miletos. Thrasyboulos took the messenger through a field of grain and cut off the ears of any of the crop which were taller than the others. When the perplexed messenger reported this to Periander, the latter understood immediately that he should target any preeminent citizens. Observations can be made about this: within the world of the tyrants there were clear links and communications, as would be expected. Periander, for example, married the daughter of the tyrant of Epidauros, and though this was not to turn out well the marriage connection will have been politically motivated. While the Thrasyboulos narrative shows that there was communication between tyrants, there was otherwise rarely any communality of action amongst them. Lygdamis of Naxos assisted Peisistratos to become tyrant of Athens in 546 BC, and Peisistratos in turn assisted him to become tyrant of Naxos; Lygdamis then assisted Polykrates to become tyrant of Samos. However, in general, there often seems to have been a degree of rivalry between them, as, for instance, in the claims of Peisistratos and Polykrates regarding the island of Delos. Herodotos observed that Periander therefore followed Thrasyboulos' advice by continuing his father's policy of execution and exile.

Periander and the three hundred boys

The most significant historical event of Peridander's reign arose out of the murder of one of his sons by the people of Corcyra, a colony of Corinth. The story in Herodotos is convoluted and complicated. Not all the details may be true, for even after the tyranny at Corinth was overthrown the Corinthians blamed the Samians for their part in the overall affair and sent an expedition with Spartan assistance to overthrow the tyranny of Polykrates as a result. Periander according to Herodotos killed his wife Melissa, by whom he had two sons and a daughter, after which the two sons sought refuge with their grandfather Prokles, tyrant of Epidauros. Provoked by Prokles' accusations to his grandsons that their father had killed their mother, Periander attacked and captured his father-in-law. A falling out occurred between Periander and Lykophron, one of the sons, and Periander sent Lykophron to Corcyra. As Periander reached old age, he invited Lykophron back to Corinth to be tyrant, and they agreed that they would swap position and location: Lykophron would go to Corinth and

Periander to Corcyra (the other son was 'slow-witted'). At the news of this the Corcyraeans killed Lykophron, and Periander as punishment seized 300 of their young sons and sent them off to Sardis to be made into eunuchs, possibly intending them as a gift for the Lydian King Alyattes (reigned 610–560 BC), father of Croesus. Rumours that Periander had committed necrophilia with his wife were interwoven with the story of her murder (or she may well have died of natural causes). It is possible that, just as Periander had been tyrant of Ambracia prior to Corinth, Lykophron had been sent as tyrant to Corcyra, and that the population had assassinated him: Corinth and Corcyra were to be on bad terms throughout the classical period and this incident may well have been a reflection of, if not a cause of, that enmity (Hdt. 3.48.2–53.7: doc. 7.14).

Periander seems to have shared the general paranoia of tyrants throughout history. According to Nicholas of Damascus he kept the citizens busy, and those lounging around in the agora with nothing to do were fined, as they might be plotting against him. Acquiring

Figure 7.1 The diolkos, paved roadway, which ran along the Isthmus of Corinth (doc. 7.61). Goods from ships could be unloaded at one end of the Isthmus and transported by carts to ships waiting at the other end of the Isthmus, saving the time (and danger) of the sea voyage around the Peloponnese. Constructed by the Corinthian tyrants, it varies from 3.6 to 4.2 m wide; the wheel ruts in the stone, clearly visible, are about 1.5 m apart. Photo © Daniel P. Diffendale.

slaves was also prohibited so that everyone in the city would be fully occupied: other Greek tyrants, such as Peisistratos, also kept their subjects busy ([Ar.] *Ath. Pol.*16.3: doc. 9.16). Furthermore, while his father seemed not to require the services of a bodyguard, Periander had one of spear-bearers. Aristotle notes positive features of his rule: his revenue derived only from taxes levied in the agora and harbour and there were no other taxes. As Corinth was a prosperous trading city, these agora taxes were clearly enough for the day-to-day upkeep of the city. Periander also seems to have invented the notion of government fiscal responsibility and the balancing of government financial books: he established a council to ensure that expenditure did not exceed revenue. No public works are attested for his reign specifically, but the diolkos was either his work or that of his father (Fig. 7.1). But the Kypselids were involved in wars: he himself against Epidauros, as noted. There is also a reference in the poet Theognis (writing 640–600 BC) to the destruction of a city in Euboea and of vineyards in the Lelantine plain of that island being cut down, with an invocation that Zeus destroy the race of the Kypselids: whether this Corinthian military involvement occurred under Kypselos or Periander is unclear. Periander's action taken against Corcyra must have been carried out with a reasonable exertion of military force, and the dedication of the golden bowl at Olympia indicates activity in the Ambracian Gulf (Nic. Dam. *FGH* 90 *F* 58.1: doc. 7.15; Arist. *F* 611.20: doc. 7.16; Thgn. 891–4: doc. 7.17.)

Periander did not tolerate corruption, which hints that the bribery of any officials or revenue collectors was strictly prohibited. He also seems to have had a moral 'agenda', and all the prostitutes are reported as having been thrown into the sea, suggesting that Corinth's later reputation as a centre for expensive sex workers and home of Aphrodite's sacred prostitutes lay in the future (Nic. Dam. *FGH* 90 *F*58.1: doc. 7.15). He was included as one of the canon of 'Seven Sages' of ancient Greece and this could relate to his reputation for moral probity and also imply that the negative stories about him have been exaggerated. He was succeeded in 587 BC by his nephew, Psammetichos (also referred to as Kypselos), but his tyranny was overthrown in a popular uprising within a matter of years. It is recorded that the body of Kypselos was exhumed and exposed to the elements: the tyrants apparently had nothing more to offer Corinth, and they were succeeded by a powerful oligarchy (Nic. Dam. *F* 60.1: doc. 7.18).

Theagenes and tyranny in Megara, c. 640 BC

Changing socio-economic conditions and tension between the rich and the poor at Megara (in the northern Peloponnese, to the south of Athens) led to the establishment of a tyranny there by Theagenes in about 640 BC. He slaughtered the flocks of the wealthy and seized power, presumably because of popular support for this move. Aristotle specifically states that these flocks (presumably of sheep) owned by the wealthy were grazing by the river, and presumably the geographical location of the slaughter was of some significance (Arist. *Politics* 1305a7–27: doc. 7.65). Megara was an important wool and clothing exporter in the fifth century, and the city may well have been moving into the wool trade at this time. It is possible that there was competition for grazing and water rights between those who had built up large flocks and the poorer farmers with small holdings, with the economic security of the poor threatened because of competition. After such an action, Theagenes would have had the support of the poor, but he nevertheless, as tyrant, required the services of a bodyguard. This inversion of the traditional social order drew the attention of the poet Theognis of Megara, who like Solon provided a poetical social commentary on the affairs of his city (Thgn. 39–42, 43–52: doc. 7.19).

Theognis, apparently writing before Theagenes had come to power, had in a sense predicted that a tyrant would arise. He complained that Megara was 'pregnant' with hubris and he feared that a man would arise to correct the situation, and punish the city's leaders, complaints which echoed those of Solon about the excesses of the wealthy at Athens (*Poems* 4, 13: docs 8.5–6). Tyranny was already a widespread phenomenon in the Peloponnese at this time, and the excesses of city leaders were a clear point of complaint in the works of both Theognis and Solon and must point to a general dissatisfaction with aristocratic political leaders.

Involvement with Kylon's failed attempted tyranny at Athens in around 632 BC dates Theagenes' tyranny to the second half of the seventh century and Theagenes' overthrow perhaps occurred as a result of Kylon's failure to become tyrant in Athens. Theagenes' expulsion did not improve the relationship between the poor and the rich in Megara, apparently making it worse. A democratic government ensued and Plutarch records (perhaps correctly) that the poor demanded to be fed at the expense of the rich, and passed a decree for palintokia, by which they received back (palin) any interest (tokia) they had paid on loans made to them by the wealthy (Plut. *Moralia* 295d). This was not a radical cancellation of debts, but obviously an alleviation of the interest burden of the poor. While it is not described as a debt cancellation, it provided the same type of economic assistance and alleviation to the poor as had Solon's seisachtheia: the poor gained an economic reprieve from which they could then improve their lot, but not so far-reaching as that granted the Athenian farmers.

Theagenes' main legacy was his famous fountain-house, which Pausanias described as late as the second century AD as one of the main monuments of the city (Paus. *Description of Greece* 1.40.1: doc. 7.20; cf. Fig. 9.4). Tyrants were concerned to embellish their cities and this particular project remained important for centuries to come: two reservoirs of water in a fountain-house 14 by 21 metres which provided a crucial amenity for the city. Throughout the Peloponnese, and at Athens and on Samos, it was tyrants who were able to provide the civic organisation, resources and planning necessary for the establishment and provision of public works. Megara and Athens were neighbours and were to have a complex history and dispute with each other for the control of the island of Salamis (Athens was successful). Peisistratos was involved in a military conflict over Megara's main port Nisaia, and throughout the fifth century the states were alternatively allied and in conflict. Theagenes' lasting legacy, apart from his fountain-house, seems to have been to break down the traditional aristocratic order at Megara.

Kylon's attempted tyranny at Athens

In around 632 BC, Kylon attempted to seize power from the aristocrats at Athens and establish himself as tyrant; two main sources – Herodotos and Thucydides – give an account of the event, differing in certain details. These discrepancies arise because Herodotos' account is brief, whereas Thucydides' is lengthy, although both are digressions from their main narrative. Thucydides however seems, as on other occasions, to be making a special effort to point out where Herodotos' narrative is incorrect (Hdt. 5.71.1–2: doc. 7.21; Thuc. 1.126.3–12: doc. 7.22). An aristocrat from a powerful and wealthy family, Kylon had married the daughter of Theagenes, tyrant of nearby Megara. With a view to becoming tyrant he had consulted the Delphic oracle and received the response that he should seize the Athenian acropolis during 'the greatest festival of Zeus' (Thuc. 1.26.4: doc. 7.22). Clearly he must have asked the Pythia about seizing control of Athens, perhaps at the suggestion of his father-in-law or out of a desire to emulate him. Kylon had won a victory at the Olympic festival in 640 BC, and attempted to seize the acropolis in an Olympic year, taking the 'the greatest festival of Zeus' as a reference to the Olympic festival which was held every four years: this means that his attempt took place in 636, 632, 628 or 624 BC, but before Drakon's legislation in 621/0 ([Arist.] Ath. Pol. 4.1: doc. 8.2). The date 632 or a little later is usually preferred, on the hypothesis that when Kylon won his victory he will have been relatively young (and thus still too young in 636 to consider seizing power), but that he would not have waited too long lest his Olympic reputation fade. Athletes gained important status in ancient Greek cities, and, as in the modern West, could use a sporting career, though here it seems to be only one race, as a platform for political endeavour (Xen. Kol. *Poems F* 2: doc. 1.78). Pausanias describes a bronze statue of Kylon on the Athenian acropolis in his own time; the travel writer wondered why the Athenians left it there despite Kylon's attempt at tyranny, but considered that it commemorated his Olympic victory in 640 and he was 'kalos', beautiful to look at.

Using Megarian troops from Theagenes his father-in-law, and with the support of a hetaireia ('brotherhood') of young men his age, Kylon seized the Athenian acropolis at the time of the celebration of the Olympic festival: Thucydides stresses that his Olympic victory was foremost in Kylon's mind while, with his usual careful attention to the details of how oracles should be interpreted, he points out that the Athenians celebrated the festival of the Diasia, which was called the 'greatest festival of Zeus the Protector' (Thuc. 1.126.6). Having failed to interpret the oracle correctly, Kylon and his supporters were initially besieged on the acropolis by the Athenians as a whole, but most soon drifted away to get back to their daily lives, and officials were put in charge of the siege. Herodotos has the rebels besieged by the prytaneis of the naukraroi, Athens' main administrative officials at the time, while Thucydides has the archons responsible. One of the Alkmeonidai, Megakles, was apparently one of the archons, but neither Herodotos nor Thucydides mentions him, and, while Plutarch (*Solon* 12.1) states he was eponymous archon, this is probably an attempt by a later source to link the Alkmeonidai more specifically to the events.

The siege was ended when the besieged started to suffer from lack of food and water and Kylon and his brother literally made a run for it. His followers, which must have included the force from Theagenes of Megara, who were dying of starvation, took up position as suppliants at the altar on the acropolis, some of them apparently in Athena's temple. Their deaths there would have polluted the temple and they were persuaded to come out on the promise of safe conduct. Despite this, they were killed as they emerged, even though some of them, seeing what was going on, took up position as suppliants again, this time at the altars of the Erinyes, or Furies. Kylon's attempt at tyranny had failed and his Athenian supporters were presumably seen as traitors and the Megarians as invaders. However, sacrilege had been committed and the descendants of those responsible for the deaths of these suppliants – Herodotos (5.71.2) specifically notes the Alkmeonidai were held responsible – were later driven out as 'accursed'.

The Athenians rallied against Kylon, which suggests that the socio-economic divisions which were to appear in Attica at the latest by the 590s BC were not yet evident or at least not yet extreme, and Kylon's episode indicates that regionalism and disaffected aristocrats were not features of pre-Solonian Athens: while Plutarch places the regional squabbles in Attica prior to Solon, Herodotos and the *Athenaion Politeia* clearly date them to after Solon (*Solon* 13.1–2, *Mor.* 763d, 805d; Hdt. 1.59.1: doc. 9.1; *Athenaion Politeia* 13.4: doc. 9.2). Theagenes' support of his son-in-law indicates that tyrants did pursue foreign policies but, as Thucydides comments, it was usually for personal interest and in respect to their 'own immediate neighbours' (Thuc. 17.1: doc. 7.3). Theagenes was attempting to increase Megara's influence in the area by establishing his son-in-law as tyrant of Athens. Kylon's supporters would have included the most prominent young aristocrats, 'men of his own age' (Hdt. 5.71.1: doc. 7.21) with whom he would have associated in the gymnasia and palaistrai, and their sacrilegious murder probably gave rise to various blood feuds, which Drakon's law code addressed in its most famous section, that concerning homicide. In addition, after those who had committed the sacrilege were dead, the Athenians decided through a judicial process that sacrilege had in fact been committed and was to be punished: the bones of those had killed Kylon's supporters were cast out of Attica and their descendants were exiled, while Epimenides, a well-known religious expert, was brought from Crete to perform a purification of the city (*Athenaion Politeia* 1: doc. 7.23). Athens had now put the Kylonian affair behind it, but the issue of the 'accursed' would recur. The descendants of the Alkmeonidai must later have moved back to Athens because they were expelled by Isagoras and Kleomenes in 508 BC (Hdt. 5.70.2: doc. 10.2), and later again, just before the Peloponnesian War, the Spartans in 432 BC demanded that the 'accursed' be driven out: they aimed this at Perikles, a descendant of the Alkmeonidai (Perikles was the great-great-great-grandson of Megakles, who apparently brought the curse upon the Alkmeonidai: Thuc. 1.127.1, 1.139.1: doc. 13.4).

Tyranny at Mytilene

Successive tyrannies at Mytilene in the seventh century point to civic and political dysfunctionalism in the city. Historically, this city on Lesbos first appears to have been governed by the Penthilidai, led by Penthilos, apparently a family group (genos) which maintained power by hitting people with clubs (Peisistratos later at Athens would make use of club bearers during his first period of tyranny). Overthrown by a Megakles in the late seventh century BC, a tyranny emerged under Melanchros who lost his position when Pittakos, with the aid of the brothers of the poet Alcaeus, overthrew him in the 42nd Olympiad, i.e., 612–609 BC. However, Alcaeus went into exile when another tyrant took over, Myrsilos, with whom Pittakos made an alliance, apparently now thinking that this was the way to achieve political power in the city and Pittakos himself was to become tyrant in turn, 590–580 BC. Alcaeus as an aristocrat was ideologically opposed to tyranny, whether that of Mysilos or of Pittakos, and wanted to see an end to the division within the city, invoking the god Ares as the means by which he and his brothers could overthrow Pittakos (Alc. 70: doc. 7.24).

Much of what is known about events at Mytilene comes from the poems of Alcaeus, and his attitude to political events in his city is clear from his poetry. He spent much of his life in exile on Lesbos and elsewhere, but pinpointing these periods of exile chronologically is difficult. This absence from political life did, however, give him the leisure and motive to write poetry attacking both Myrsilos and then Pittakos. When Pittakos became tyrant after Melanchros and Myrsilos, Alcaeus and presumably his brothers and associates felt deeply wronged, and it appears that Pittakos had sworn an oath with Alcaeus and his brothers perhaps against there being any resumption of tyranny (Alc. 129: doc. 7.25), as their aim was to preserve the political power of the aristocracy to which they belonged. When Myrsilos died, Alcaeus celebrated the fact in song, urging everyone to drink 'with all their might' (Alc. 332: doc. 7.27), and seems to have returned from exile from the city of Pyrrha on Lesbos, but only briefly. Pittakos had became associated with Myrsilos, and 'devoured' the city with him, and then in turn by himself (Alc. 70: doc. 7.24, Alc. 129: doc. 7.25). This is presumably a reference to the capacity of tyrants to enrich themselves at the expense of the cities they governed.

For Alcaeus, Pittakos' involvement with Myrsilos and his assumption of power was betrayal and he prayed to the gods of Lesbos for revenge, insulting Pittakos for his 'pot-belly' and breaking of oaths (Alc. 129: doc. 7.25). The life of a Greek exile was not a happy one: most of them seem to have desperately missed their home city and to have deplored their lack of involvment in the political processes there: Alcaeus describes himself as a 'poor wretch' and compares himself to Onymakles, an otherwise unknown figure, but possibly a miserable exile from the mythology of Lesbos, yearning for the past, when the assembly and boule met – political organisations now in abeyance under tyranny (Alc. 130, lines 16–27: doc. 7.26).

Pittakos' path to tyrannical power was based not just on his relationship with Myrsilos but on two other factors, one of which is mentioned by Alcaeus: Pittakos had married into the Penthilidai, to whom in his poetry Alcaeus referred as the Atreidai, after Agamemnon, son of Atreus, from whom the family claimed descent (Alc. 70: doc. 7.24). Pittakos was also a successful warrior and when Athens and Mytilene were competing for the control of Sigeion in the Troad region Pittakos had defeated the Athenian general Phrynon in single combat, an encounter in which Alcaeus, so abusive of Pittakos, threw away his shield like the other Mytilenaeans and fled the battle (Hdt. 5.95.1: doc. 2.18; Alc. 428: doc. 2.19).

But the main factor that propelled Pittakos into the tyranny was the support of the people. It is generally assumed that Alcaeus, his brother Antimenidas, and the poet Sappho were exiled from Lesbos at this time. Antimenidas fought with the Babylonians, Alcaeus visited Egypt, and Sappho is said to have gone to Sicily (Alc. 350, 432; Marmor Parium *FGH* 239.36) and it may have been during this exile that Alcaeus and others attempted to gain control of Mytilene with the aid of the Lydians, who provided 2000 staters in assistance (Alc. 69: doc. 7.28). Pittakos' election as tyrant 'against the exiles' is generally linked with this, for Pittakos is an example of what Aristotle referred to as an aisymnetes, an 'elected' tyrant. For all of Alcaeus' abuse of Pittakos as a usurping autocrat, the situation in Mytilene seems to have been more complex, for the inhabitants chose to elect Pittakos to prevent the exiles from returning (Alc. 348: doc. 7.29). The rule of aristocrats like Alcaeus and his family, supported with Lydian gold, might not have been an attractive option, and the tyrannies of Melanchros and Myrsilos, and then that of Pittakos' elected as aisymnetes, seem to show a preference for rule by tyrants than by the aristocracy. The boule and assembly of Alcaeus' father's and grandfather's time must be imagined in Homeric terms, dominated by aristocrats with the people doing as they were instructed. While Alcaeus' judgement of Pittakos was negative and abusive (Alc. 429: doc. 7.30), after reigning as tyrant for ten years Pittakos relinquished office in 480 BC. His renown was such that he became known as one of the Seven Sages of ancient Greece, and various of his maxims or pithy sayings were preserved, or others attributed to him (Diog. Laert. 1.74–81).

Polykrates of Samos

Resting in the Aegean sea just two kilometres from the coastline of Asia Minor, the large island of Samos played an important part in the history of sixth-century tyranny, while later in the fifth century its demos was to be keenly loyal to Athens and the Delian League. Herodotos when writing of the conquest of the island by Darius referred to it as 'the first [most pre-eminent] of all Greek and non-Greek cities', a clear reference to how Polykrates' achievements and his public works on the island were generally viewed (Hdt. 3.139.1: doc. 7.36).

Polykrates seizes power

In about 600 BC the aristocrats (geomoroi) whose name indicates that they were the 'landowners' had been overthrown by the generals. This could well have been part of the phenomenon noted by both Alcaeus at Megara and Solon at Athens that the traditional aristocracy had become corrupt and was oppressing their social and economic inferiors. Following this, in the 530s, Polykrates and his two brothers Pantagnostos and Syloson seized power as tyrants on the island, but in 532 BC Polykrates sidelined his brothers, killing one and exiling the other, and assumed sole power for himself. It is possible that their father Aiakes had been tyrant before them, but there is not sufficient evidence to state this categorically. The lack of an aristocratic government and the military 'takeover' would have lent itself to the imposition of a tyranny. Polykrates then made himself the ruler of what could be described as a maritime empire, but it is also clear that he maintained power through bloodshed and the exile of opponents, and his successors Maiandros and Syloson were to devastate the population of the island.

According to Polyaenus, Polykrates and his brothers seized power during a religious festival (probably in the mid-530s given that he would assume sole rule in 532 BC). On this occasion all the Samians were involved in a religious procession to the temple of the goddess Hera on the island which, according to Herodotos, Polykrates was to make into one of the most magnificent temples in the Greek world. The male citizens processed to the temple with their weapons, but put them aside for the sacrifice to Hera. Polykrates' brothers (Syloson and Pantagnostos) and their supporters at the festival who had retained their weapons killed the other unarmed Samians, while Polykrates seized the most important parts of the city; the three brothers then fortified the acropolis. They sent a message to Lygdamis tyrant of Naxos to send them troops, and with the help of these they secured the tyranny. Key elements emerge in this seizure of power, as well as similarities with the tyranny of Peisistratos established about a decade earlier, with control in both cases based on the disarming of citizens before the tyranny could be established. How widespread the slaughter was at the festival of Hera is not made clear, but opponents in the hoplite class were clearly eliminated (Polyaenus *Strategemata* 1.23.2: doc. 7.31). After the battle of Pallene in 546 BC, in which Peisistratos had killed many of his opponents, he had had the weapons of the remaining citizens collected. It was obviously important in establishing a tyranny that potential resistance had to be disarmed or removed (*Athenaion Politeia* 15.4: doc. 9.13). Another key feature was that the brothers received the assistance of another tyrant, Lygdamis, who had also assisted Peisistratos at the battle of Pallene (*Athenaion Politeia* 15.3–5: doc. 9.13; Hdt. 1.64.2: doc. 9.14).

Polykrates comes to power

Polykrates, however, was not prepared to rule as a joint tyrant, unlike Hippias and Hipparchos later at Athens in 527–514 BC who constituted a successful team (and there were three other brothers as well). In 532 BC Polykrates murdered his brother Pantagnostos, while Syloson (the younger of the two) was sent into exile: perhaps Polykrates saw him as less of a threat, but he would play a role later in Samian affairs. An alliance was made with Amasis, king of Egypt, in the form of a 'treaty of friendship' involving gift exchange. Polykrates was militarily successful, and with a large naval force of 100 pentekonters and one thousand archers conquered many of the Aegean islands. In some ways, he was a precursor to the Athenians: whichever state had a large navy could dominate the islands. He even reached beyond the islands, capturing many of the cities of the mainland Asia Minor coast and was 'celebrated throughout Ionia and the rest of Greece' (Hdt 3.39.3). This naval success was what apparently brought him into conflict with the city of Miletos: its fleet and his engaged, but he defeated it as well as a large force from the island of Lesbos which had come to the assistance of the Milesians.

Herodotos describes Polykrates as robbing and plundering throughout the region, and this was probably how he gained material reward from his conquests, as there is no reference to any annual payments from islands he conquered. Miletos and Lesbos clearly resented this (Hdt. 3.39.3–4: doc. 7.32) and it is probable that Miletos, a large entrepreneurial city, contested his control of the region, especially as Miletos was a great coloniser and had sent out many emporia (docs 2.16–17), or he may even have set out to conquer the city outright. Alexis, a fourth-century historian from Samos refers to Polykrates constructing a new variety of ships, named the Samainai (after Samos), which perhaps gave him a maritime superiority over his opponents (Alexis of Samos *F* 2: doc. 7.37). While Herodotos earlier mentioned pentekonters, he also records that Polykrates (3.44.2) dispatched those Samians he considered untrustworthy to the Persian king Cambyses in forty triremes. Thucydides (1.13.2: doc. 1.61) states that the Corinthians constructed the first triremes in Greece (c. 700 BC) and Polykrates may have been instrumental in the switch from pentekonters to triremes in the Aegean. The Samainai may possibly have been a specially engineered version of a trireme, which could explain how he defeated the naval contingents of Lesbos and Miletos.

The thalassocracy of Polykrates

As tyrant Polykrates built up a thalassocracy, a 'rule over the seas'. Thucydides, like Herodotos, comments on his control of the islands and records that he took the island of Rheneia and dedicated it to Apollo by attaching the island to Delos by means of a chain (Thuc. 1.13.6, 3.104.2: doc. 7.33). This may have been in response to the actions of Peisistratos, tyrant of Athens, who had carried out a partial purification of the island (Hdt. 1.64.2: doc. 9.17). Delos was a crucial element in the Ionian identity, and Polykrates' conquest of this island, and various other Ionian islands and cities, was clearly an attempt to assert himself as ruler of the Ionian world, as Athens would later do in the fifth century. Herodotos also refers to important political developments in the wider world: the Ionians had a large fleet and contested the control of their territory with Cyrus, the first Persian King, who had conquered the Lydian king Croesus and subsumed his territory into what would become the expansionist Persian Empire under its rulers of the Achaemenid family.

The relationship between Polykrates and Cyrus' son and successor Cambyses (530–522 BC) is difficult to unravel from the source material available. Despite Polykrates' alliance with Amasis, king of Egypt (570–526 BC), he then sided with the Persians, who would soon be involved against Egypt. Herodotos has Amasis renounce the alliance and while the story concerning this in Herodotos has no historical value it does illustrate Herodotos' religious beliefs and those of the Greeks generally: Amasis, Herodotos narrates, warned Polykrates that his run of good luck could not go on forever and he should therefore throw away the thing dearest to him and thus 'break' his run of untramelled good luck. Polykrates threw a precious ring into the deep sea, but it was swallowed by a fish and caught by a fisherman, who proudly made a present of it to his tyrant; when the fish was prepared in the kitchen the ring was found and duly presented to Polykrates. He was thus informed that he could not escape his mortal fate and would come to a 'bad end' and Herodotos makes this the reason why Amasis broke off his friendship with Polykrates as he did not want to be distressed at what would happen to Polykrates if they were still allies. Clearly, however, Polykrates and Amasis could not remain allies once the tyrant had aided the Persian invasion of Egypt (for the story of Polykrates and the ring, see Hdt. 3.40.1–43.2, 3.125.4).

Polykrates' support of Cambyses has the appearance of a calculated decision to side with the Persians, who did conquer Egypt, with the assistance of a Samian fleet. Herodotos even has Polykrates asking Cambyses to invite him to send a military contingent, perhaps demonstrating that he was asserting himself as a powerful ruler and a major player in the affairs of the eastern Mediterranean by participating in the expedition. According to Herodotos he was motivated by the wish to deal with critics at home on Samos: he sent Cambyses forty triremes of those he suspected of 'rebellious tendencies', asking him not to send them back after the war (Hdt. 3.44.2: doc. 7.34). These, however, sailed off only as far as the island of Karpathos and turned back and defeated Polykrates' naval force at sea, though they were then defeated on land. Polykrates then showed the ruthlessness with which he and his brothers had taken power: seizing as hostages the children and wives of the citizens, he placed them in the boat sheds and prepared to set them alight if anyone on the island attempted to assist the exiles. This inflammatory threat deterred the Samian exiles, who proceeded to Sparta to request support (Hdt. 3.44.2–45.4: doc. 7.34).

In 525 BC the Samians at Sparta made a long appeal for assistance in response to which they encountered the famous Spartan taciturnity: the Spartans claimed not to be able to understand long speeches. When later invited to put their case again, the Samians, who had

Figure 7.2 The tunnel of Eupalinos that carried water from one side of the island of Samos to the city on the other side (doc. 7.60). It was probably constructed during Polykrates' tyranny. Photo © Kevin Whited.

learned their lesson, spoke briefly to secure Spartan involvement in their plot, producing an empty sack with the phrase: 'sack needs meal'. Even for this they were criticised, for they need not have used the word 'sack' since they had shown it, and hence could have used two words instead of three. Nevertheless, in their support, Sparta collected a large fleet from its Peloponnesian allies, particularly Corinth, which was still annoyed about how the Samians had prevented Periander's dispatch of 100 Corcyraean boys to Alyattes of Lydia for castration. Sparta had a general policy of opposition to tyrants and a preference for ousting them in favour of aristocratic governments which explains their willingness to become involved in a war to depose Polykrates. After initial success against the Samians loyal to Polykrates and the mercenaries in his employ, the situation degenerated into a siege, at which the Spartans throughout their history were to prove abysmal practitioners (as opposed to the Athenians). After forty days, the Spartans gave up and went home (Hdt. 3.44.1–47.3, 54.1–2, 56.1–2: doc. 7.34; cf. Plut. *On the Malignity of Herodotos* 21: doc. 6.58).

The murder of Polykrates

Polykrates' power over the islands and Ionian cities was bound to bring him into conflict with the Persians, despite his involvement with Cambyses. His plan to have Samos take part in the Persian conquest of Egypt may have been an attempt to ingratiate himself with the Persians and have his power over Greek islands and cities recognised and uncontested. In 522 BC, the year in which Cambyses died, the satrap ('viceroy') of Sardis, Oroites, apparently lured Polykrates to Sardis for a discussion about financing further of his conquests. This was probably arranged as a diplomatic meeting between Polykrates, the tyrant of Samos representing an Aegean power with plans to rule all Ionia and the Aegean, and the Persians who now in fact possessed most of Asia Minor. Although warned in a dream by his daughter not to take part he went, and was murdered and crucified by Oroites, whose intention had all along been to destroy Samian hegemony in the Aegean and pave the way for further Persian conquests. For Herodotos, Polykrates did not deserve such a fate and no other Greek tyrant could be compared to him for 'magnificence' (Hdt. 3.120.1–125.1: doc. 7.35).

Polykrates' successors

Maiandrios had been left in charge of Samos by Polykrates. He was rejected as tyrant by the people, but managed to hold on to power through imprisoning those opposed to him. When Maiandrios fell ill, his brother Lykaretos attempted to place himself in line for the succession by killing these prisoners. Darius was in Egypt, involved in completing Cambyses' work of conquest, and Syloson, Polykrates' surviving brother, made contact with him (the colourful story of Darius' desire for the red cloak he saw Syloson wearing in Memphis can be safely relegated to the annals of the charming and improbable history typical of Herodotos' anecdotes). What really happened is clear from Herodotos' account once the tale of the red cloak is set to one side: Syloson presented himself as an exile at Darius' court once Darius had become king by usurping the Persian throne, and gained his support for his reinstatement as tyrant of Samos. Syloson was apparently the first of many well-known Greeks who sought the assistance of Persian kings or dwelt at their court in the hope of receiving Persian assistance to return to their homeland with or without the aid of an army.

Maiandrios had not died of his sickness, but when the Persians conquered Samos under the command of Otanes he agreed under a truce to leave the island. At the ceremony to ratify the treaty, however, he had a number of important Persians killed. In revenge, the Persians engaged in an ethnic cleansing of the island, deporting its Greek population. Only later, when Otanes had a dream and suffered an illness of the genitalia did he repopulate the island (Hdt. 3.139.1–149.1: doc. 7.36). Samos serves as a useful case study for the increasing interaction between Persians and Greeks, and for the way in which the growth of Persian power deprived the Greeks of their independence until their conquest of the Persians in 480–479 BC. It is also an example of how bloody Greek history could be as Samos several times in this period experienced purges of its most important citizens. Polykrates was not a conscious role model for the Athenians after 479 BC, but he had shown what naval power could achieve: he was the first Greek 'who planned to dominate the sea' (Hdt. 3.122.2: doc. 7.35) and he had made Samos 'the first of all Greek and non-Greek cities' (Hdt. 3.139.1: doc. 7.36).

Polykrates' patronage of the arts

Of all the sixth-century tyrants Polykrates appears to have been the richest, or at the very least, the one who enjoyed the most extravagant lifestyle, even though tyrants were well known for their luxurious way of living (Arist. *Politics* 1311a8–11: doc. 7.66). From 532 BC to his death in 522 BC, extravagance prevailed at Polykrates' court and the poet Anacreon wrote there of love and wine, with his poems performed at drinking parties (symposia) attended by Polykrates and his court. Anacreon was born on Teos but helped found the colony at Abdera, and went to Athens after Polykrates' death at the invitation of Hipparchos (*Athenaion Politeia* 18.1: doc 9.22; [Pl.] *Hipparchos* 228c: doc. 9.23). It was important for tyrants to have around them famous poets who could sing their praises. Ibycus seems to have arrived on Samos prior to Anacreon, and might therefore have been the first of the court poets who composed works in honour of their tyrant patrons. Aelian stated that Polykrates was a particular patron of the arts, though he did not approve of his luxurious lifestyle (Ael. *Varia Historia* 9.4: doc. 7.39). Pythagoras left Samos in 531 BC (during Polykrates' tyranny) for Croton in southern Italy, but whether he did so because he objected to tyranny or because he sought a more fertile ground for his philosophy is unknown. Polykrates' goods came from all over the Greek world, just as Perikles was later to boast of Athens in 431 BC (Perikles: Thuc. 2.38.2: doc. 1.17; Samos: Alexis of Samos *F* 2: doc 7.37). Polykrates' imports, however, were not just for entertainment: in addition to hunting dogs from Molossia in northern Greece and Lakonia, Polykrates also bought goats from the islands of Skyros and Naxos, and sheep from Miletos and Attica. He was clearly aiming to improve the breeding stock of Samos, which would benefit animal husbandry and the economy of the island as a whole. His homoeroticism, too, was not in any sense tyrannical; it led merely to Polykrates' throwing a tantrum over one of his boyfriends being given a haircut (Alexis of Samos *F* 2: doc 7.37), whereas other tyrants' sexual behaviour led to much more violent situations, such as at Athens (Arist. *Politics*.1311a36–b6: doc. 7.67). According to Ibycus, Polykrates would have 'undying renown' (Ibycus 282: doc. 7.38).

Other tyrants were also patrons of the arts. Hieron's victories in the panhellenic festivals of 478–466 BC were celebrated by both Bacchylides of Keos and Pindar from Thebes, and Hipparchos at Athens was particularly noted as a patron of the poets, and it was he who apparently organised the editing of Homer's *Iliad* and *Odyssey* into a standard 'edition'. Simonides, Bacchylides' uncle, wrote at the court of Hipparchos but also, after the tyranny was overthrown, was thought to have sung the praises of the tyrannicides, perhaps in order to give such works equal status to his earlier compositions (*IG* I³ 502: doc. 9.42).

Xenophanes, the sixth-century poet most famous for his denunciation of the honours heaped on successful athletes (*Poem* 2: doc. 1.78), spent some time at Syracuse. Aeschylus was also a guest at Hieron's court and in 476 BC wrote his play *Women of Aetna* which honoured Hieron's establishment of this city, a refoundation of the older Greek colony at Catana (cf. Thuc. 6.5.3: doc. 2.12). For Hieron, this placed Aetna in the literary genre of city-foundation poems and epics, such as Pseudo-Skymnos' poem describing the foundation of colonies and cities (*Geographical Description* 986–97: doc. 2.17) and Pindar's *Pythian* 1 also celebrated the foundation of the city. Simonides was present at Hieron's court but nothing survives of any poetry he may have written particularly in honour of this tyrant. Poets of the sixth and fifth centuries therefore found an important source of inspiration – and of income – at the courts of tyrants, and some of the greatest Greek poetry was produced to celebrate their achievements. Xenophon even wrote an imaginary Socratic-style dialogue between Simonides and Hieron, named *Hieron*, but it is more of a discourse on the nature of tyranny and is of no historical value for Hieron's reign itself.

The earlier Sicilian tyrants

Sicily was home to tyrants in the sixth to fourth centuries to a degree that rivalled the number of tyrannies in the sixth-century Peloponnese, and tyranny persisted on that island – and was revived in the fourth century – long after it ceased to be the norm in Greece itself. Thucydides differentiates Sicilian from Greek tyrants in general: he considers that Sicilian tyrants rose to 'great power' and here he will have been thinking particularly of Gelon and Hieron, tyrants of Syracuse (Thuc. 1.17.1: doc. 7.3). The earlier Sicilian tyrants, especially the sixth-century tyrant Phalaris of Akragas, did much to help formulate the pejorative connotation of the word tyrant which was established at least by the time Herodotos was writing. Unlike the tyrants of mainland Greece or Ionia, the tyrants of Sicily engaged in carving out territorial dominions for themselves. This may well have been because of the nature of the island, as the indigenous Sikels and Carthaginians (of Phoenician descent) threatened the Greek cities, who were also constantly at war with each other. Sicilian tyrants also tended to be 'war-lords' because of the aggressive nature of the relationships between the inhabitants of the island, and the Syracusan tyrants in particular were energetic and aggressive conquerors and relocators of peoples.

Phalaris

Phalaris, tyrant of the city of Akragas (modern Agrigentum) on the island of Sicily, was infamous for roasting his enemies inside a specially made bronze bull. As the first of the Sicilian tyrants, like the others to follow, he came to power through force, ruling from about 570 to 554 BC. Having won the contract for the construction of the temple of Zeus Polieus ('of the city') on the acropolis, he took the opportunity to seize the acropolis and with his supporters took over the city, confiscating the weapons of the aristocracy. To consolidate his position he was chosen by the people of the city of Himera as a general with 'absolute powers' (though the city had been warned by the poet Stesichoros about the inherent dangers of this), and he extended his control over a large area of northern Sicily. He was deposed after sixteen years, and according to one tradition was roasted alive in his own bronze bull, but this may be a moralising embellishment. His career reflects the need both for the use of force in seizing power as a tyrant, and for the tyrant to be able to demonstrate ruthlessness towards potential enemies (Arist. *Rhetoric* 1393b10–22 [Stesichoros 281]: doc. 7.40, *Politics* 1310a28; Pind. *Pythian* 1.95–96: doc. 7.58; Diod. Sic. 9.19.1; Polyaenus *Strategemata* 5.1).

Theron, tyrant of Selinous

Under the pretext of using a body of 300 able-bodied slaves to bury warriors of the city who had fallen in battle against the Carthaginians Theron made himself tyrant of the Greek city of Selinous. Selinous had already experienced tyranny once before, when in 507/6 BC the Spartan Euryleon liberated the city from Peithagoras; Euryleon, who had been part of Dorieus' expedition, briefly established a tyranny, but was killed in a popular uprising (Polyaenus *Strategemata* 1.28.2: doc. 7.41; Hdt. 5.46.1–2: doc. 7.42). Theron also become tyrant of Akragas, where Phalaris had ruled a century earlier, in about 489 BC and he ruled until 473, and was succeeded briefly by his son Thrasydaios.

At the same time as Theron gained power, Gelon (son of Deinomenes) established a tyranny at Gela, which had founded Akragas as a colony, taking over from the brothers Kleander and Hippokrates; when Kleander died, he was succeeded by Hippokrates, who died in battle against the Sikels in 491 BC. Under these two brothers, the city of Gela had gained control of many of the Greek cities in Sicily. Gelon, who had established a reputation for military bravery and had served Hippokrates as hipparchos (cavalry commander), then took power in Gela, and marched on Syracuse, which surrendered. He transferred his seat of power to Syracuse in 485 BC and gave Gela to his brother Hieron to rule as tyrant (they and their descendants are known as the Deinomenides, sons of Deinomenes). Gelon transformed Syracuse into a great city by a synoecism involving population transfers which were to be a feature of Sicilian tyranny: the people of Camarina, after he had destroyed their city, were transplanted to Syracuse, along with half of the population of Gela and the wealthy men of Sicilian Megara which he had conquered (selling the rest of the population into slavery outside Sicily) and, on the same terms, the Euboeans in Sicily (Hdt. 7.153.1–156.3: doc. 7.43). This great increase in population would not necessarily in itself have made Syracuse the foremost city in Sicily, but the city also had the advantages of a series of harbours, especially the so-called Great Harbour where the Athenian navy would be spectacularly defeated in 413 BC. In an excellent position for commerce, it was also a defensible site, and Syracuse became one of the most populous of any of the Greek cities, not only in Sicily but anywhere in the Greek world.

Gelon as the most powerful of the Sicilian tyrants was, according to Herodotos, approached by the mainland Greeks in 481 BC to come to their aid against the imminent Persian invasion. He promised a huge force of men and provisions if he were made strategos and hegemon (leader) of the Greek forces, a condition he presumably felt he deserved as tyrant over many of the Greek cities of Sicily, but the condition was rejected. Herodotos also records that if the Persians were victorious, Gelon was prepared to surrender to them, presumably as a client-tyrant, and that he sent an envoy with a large sum of money to Delphi to be given to Xerxes if he defeated the Greeks. But the Sicilians were later able to claim that Gelon would have fought under the Spartans if the Carthaginians had not kept him occupied in Sicily at the battle of Himera in 480 BC (Hdt. 7.158–64; Pind. Pythian 1.71–5: doc. 11.55). Theron is best known for his role in the defeat of the Carthaginians in 480 BC. He had seized Himera in 483, where he was to install his son Thrasydaios as an unpopular and oppressive tyrant. After capturing Himera, Theron expelled its tyrant Terillos, a friend of the Carthaginian general Hamilcar who invaded Sicily in 480 BC and was spectacularly defeated by the combined forces of Theron and Gelon, assisted by Polyzelos and Thrasyboulos. Hamilcar and Terillos had brought a huge force of 300,000 Phoenicians and others to Sicily and tripods were dedicated at Delphi in thanksgiving but, while Simonides was active in Sicily and a friend of Hieron's, the inscription on the tripods does not seem to have been composed by the poet. Gelon dedicated in the temples, mainly those of Syracuse and Himera, the spoils of war taken from the huge invading force. The claim that the battle of Himera was fought on the same day as Salamis was no doubt invented to assuage Sicilian sensitivity over the fact that Gelon had not sent a force to aid the Greeks of the mainland, amongst whom stories circulated that he intended to medise (to go over to the Persians) if Xerxes won. Victory was due to the gods and they were thanked accordingly. A statue of Gelon was erected in Syracuse, and even when Dionysios II tyrant of Syracuse was deposed in 344 BC the statue was left intact, despite the Syracusan hatred of all of their tyrants, because of Gelon's victory at Himera (Simon. 34: doc. 7.45; Hdt. 7.166: doc. 7.44; Plut. *Timoleon* 23.8: doc. 7.55; Diod. Sic. 11.20–25.1).

When Gelon died in 478 BC his brother Hieron succeeded him as tyrant of Syracuse and ruled over most of Sicily's Greek cities. In 474 BC he assented to a request from the city of

Figure 7.3 The 'Charioteer of Delphi' is a life-size bronze statue dedicated at Delphi by Polyzalos, younger brother of Hieron tyrant of Syracuse, after a victory in the chariot races at the Pythian festival of 478 or 474 BC. As the rider holds reins, it was probably part of a statue group with horses and chariot; the driver has copper lips, glass eyes, and silver on his headband. At some stage it was damaged in an earthquake. An inscription on the limestone base of the statue reads in part, 'Polyzalos dedicated me, let him prosper, well-omened Apollo'. Courtesy of the Delphi Archaeological Museum. Photo © Cory George.

Cumae in Italy for assistance against the Etruscans who were attacking the city and defeated the Etruscans in a naval battle, dedicating at Olympia Etruscan helmets that still survive (Meiggs and Lewis 29: doc. 7.46; Diod. Sic. 11.51). This was only one of his interventions in Italy and it is clear that he had designs to extend his influence there. He increased Syracusan control of the Greek cities in Sicily, in particular razing Catana and Naxos to the ground and transferring their populations to the city of Leontinoi, and then refounded Catana as Aetna. Syracuse now dominated Greek Sicily, and the city should be considered as possessing a hegemony over this part of the Greek world.

Thrasydaios upon the death of his father Theron became tyrant of Akragas and made himself as unpopular there as he had been at Himera; he planned to attack Syracuse but Hieron struck first and launched an offensive against Akragas defeating Thrasydaios, who was expelled: he fled to Megara in Greece and was executed there (Diod. Sic. 11.48, 11.53). After ruling as tyrant for just over seven years, Gelon was succeeded by Hieron for ten years and by Thrasyboulos for less than a year. The Deinomenid family was then torn by internal dissension and the Syracusans took advantage of this to depose Thrasyboulos and end the tyranny in 466 BC (Arist. *Politics* 1312b9–16: doc. 7.47, 1315b34–8: doc. 7.70; Diod. Sic. 11.66–8). This meant the demise of Syracusan supremacy in Sicily: the Greek cities, without a war-lord at Syracuse controlling them and with the Carthaginians so recently pulverised in battle, asserted their independence. Syracusan rule over Greek Sicily – its epicracy – came to an end: the first great age of Sicilian tyranny was over, but a second would emerge in the fourth century.

The fourth-century Sicilian tyrants

The second period of tyranny in Sicily was that of Dionysius I (c. 405?–367 BC) and his son Dionysios II (367–357) in Syracuse. After the overthrow of the first wave of Syracusan tyrants in the fifth century Greek cities of the island enjoyed prosperity, and Diodorus comments that this was because the cities were no longer fighting amongst themselves (Diod. Sic. 11.72.1: doc. 7.48). This assertion needs some correction, because the context of the Athenian intervention in Sicily in the 420s and 415 was disputes between the different Greek cities. It is clear, however, that there were no longer the large-scale wars and population movements that there had been under the tyrants. In 405 BC Dionysios I was able to take control of Syracuse in the context of increasingly aggressive Carthaginian military activity against the Greek cities on the island. Carthage had conquered the Greek cities of Himera (the site of the previous Greek victory against them) and Selinous in 409, and even Akragas in 406 BC, where Dionysios himself had played a notable military role. In 405 BC Dionysios arrived with an army at Gela, which had appealed to Syracuse for military assistance, and proceeded to interfere in the internal affairs of the city, executing leading citizens and confiscating their property. The Sicilian Greeks in general seems to have blamed the Syracusans for allowing the Carthaginians to cause such devastation in Greek Sicily. In an assembly at Syracuse Dionysios denounced the generals and the Syracusans removed some of them from command, and chose Dionysios as strategos autokrator ('supreme general') because of the reputation he had gained from his battles against the Carthaginians.

Dionysios gains a bodyguard

Dionysios gathered his supporters at Leontinoi, a Syracusan outpost, and at an assembly of the Syracusans there asked for and was given a bodyguard: both Diodorus and Aristotle note that in this he was like Peisistratos and other tyrants. He filled Syracuse with mercenaries, originally in the employ of the Spartan Dexippos, whom Dionysios sent home, as he was afraid that he would oppose his plans to seize power, along with foreign exiles and troops which had been at Leontinoi. According to Diodorus he proclaimed himself tyrant at this stage, although it is more likely that he was still strategos autokrator and it was only later that he could first be termed a tyrant. The Syracusans, indignant about this seizure of control, were nevertheless in a state of alarm because of the danger represented by the Carthaginians, and so accepted the new political situation. To secure further his hold on power, he married the daughter of Hermokrates, who had played such an important role in organising Sicilian resistance to the Athenians in their invasion of Sicily, as well as marrying his sister to the brother of Hermokrates' wife, and he executed his two most important opponents, generals who were opposed to him (Diod. Sic. 13.92.1–96.4: doc. 7.49; Arist. *Rhetoric* 1357b30–36: doc. 7.64, cf. *Politics* 1286b 39–40).

Dionysios loses and regains power

When the Carthaginians attacked Gela in 405, Dionysios with a large maritime and land force was unable to save the city. His own criticisms of earlier generals now applied to himself, as he had done no better against the Carthaginian threat that the Syracusans feared so much. He evacuated the population of Gela, and on the way back to Syracuse, that of Camarina as well: the sight of this retreat turned Dionysios' troops against him. His Italian allies also deserted him and the Syracusan cavalry who were on the lookout for but missed an opportunity to assassinate him hurried back to Syracuse before him and pack-raped his wife, who committed suicide. Locked out of the city, he gained access by setting fire to the city gate, and with the troops loyal to him massacred or exiled his opposition. He took two new wives, marrying both on the same day, and one of these, Doris, gave birth to a son Dionysios, who would succeed his father as tyrant (Diod. Sic. 13.108–13; Plut. *Dion* 3).

Carthage in 405 BC offered Dionysios peace terms, as its army under Himilco was suffering from the plague. Under the terms of the treaty it retained its territory in Sicily, including the Greek cities it had captured. Selinous, Akragas, Himera, Gela and Camarina were to remain unwalled and pay tribute to Carthage, while Leontinoi, Messene and the Sikels were to be independent (Diod. Sic. 13.114). This had implications for Dionysios' position, as he had justification for maintaining his hold on power while he dangled, so to speak, the Carthaginian threat before the Syracusans, while peace undercut any rationale for his rule, particularly as the Carthaginians now held such a powerful position in eastern, traditionally Greek, Sicily. He began fortifying the Island (Ortygia) at Syracuse, with its own enclosed dockyards and space for sixty triremes, and foreigners and slaves were granted citizenship (Diod. Sic. 14.7.1–5: doc. 7.50). When he set out against the Sikels in 404 BC, Syracuse rebelled, but with the aid of mercenaries from Campania he retook the city (Diod. Sic. 14.7.4–9).

A series of wars waged by Dionysios against the Greek cities were successful and eastern Sicily came into his hands, with the treaty with the Carthaginians conveniently forgotten. Syracuse was enclosed by a massive fortification wall with regular towers, as part of the plans for a war against the Carthaginians in the west of Sicily (Diod. Sic. 18.1–8: doc. 7.50; Fig. 7.4). His campaigns from 397 to 392 in the Carthaginian part of the island resulted in a peace in 392 similar to the previous agreement, except that the Sikels now came under his authority: Carthage now recognised that the eastern part of the island was under Dionysios' control (Diod. Sic. 14.96). The Carthaginians even mounted a successful raid on Syracuse itself, but ultimately the Carthaginian drive into eastern Sicily faltered, even when a substantial force was sent under the Carthaginian Mago in 392 BC, and it had to accept Dionysios' suzerainty (Mago committed suicide but the Carthaginians were so angry at his failure that they impaled his corpse: Plut. *Timoleon* 22.8: doc. 7.55). Dionysios repopulated Messene (destroyed by the Carthaginians in 396 BC) on the Sicilian side of the strait separating the island from Italy, and Rhegium, the city on the Italian side of the strait, was destroyed in 386 (but refounded by Dionysios II in about 350 BC). These activities in southern Italy were partly a result of Dionysios' establishment of control over the Sicilian Greek cities, and also presumably part of a plan to have an Italian powerbase, to assist in the war against the Carthaginians.

The alliance with Athens

In 393 BC Athens had honoured Dionysios, possibly in order to draw him away from relations with Sparta; by this time the Peloponnesian War was firmly in Athens' past and the city was actively reasserting itself in Greek affairs. Athens and Sparta were to be on better terms, particularly after Thebes' defeat of Sparta at the battle of Leuktra in 371 BC. An Athenian decree of 368 BC made a mutual defensive-offensive alliance between Athens and Dionysos I (and his descendants). This was in addition to a grant of a golden crown and citizenship to him and his sons, presumably because Dionysios had aided Sparta against the Thebans in 369 and 368 BC, which would have met with Athens' approval (Xen. *Hellenika* 7.1.20–8; *IG* II² 105, 523: doc.

Figure 7.4 The Castello Eurialo, Syracuse. Dionysios I constructed this fortification in about 402–397 BC to both defend his own position and protect the city in case of a Carthaginian siege: its location was well-suited to defence. Photo © Kristina Jelinăč.

7.51). Soon afterwards, Dionysios sent a copy of a tragic play he had written, *The Ransom of Hector*, to Athens and at its performance at the festival of the Lenaia in 367 BC it was awarded first place. According to Diodorus, Dionysios on hearing the news – his literary merit at last acknowledged (note the incident at Olympia in 388 or 384 BC: see below, p. 293) – died from over-consumption of alcohol. Plato in 343 BC was to write scathingly of the Syracusan lifestyle: his hopes, initiated by Dion, that he could educate Dionysios II to be a 'philosopher-king' over a powerful Greek city had come to nothing (Pl. *Seventh Letter* 326b–d: doc. 7.52).

Dionysios I had been an effective military campaigner and, although the Carthaginians had achieved some stunning victories and subjugated various Greek cities, at the time of his death he was in control of eastern Sicily and had some territory in Italy. While aiming at dominion over the Greeks in Sicily he had also hoped to defeat the Carthaginians. He survived hostile attacks by his subjects more than once, and ruled for thirty-eight years. His empire was more than equivalent to that of the fifth-century Syracusan tyrants, and it could be argued that it was only his leadership which effectively thwarted the Carthaginian attempts against the eastern half of the island under their generals Himilco and Mago: otherwise the island could well have become an entirely Carthaginian possession.

Dionysios II

Dionysios II inherited the tyranny in 367 BC but in 357 BC was deposed by his uncle Dion. In that decade he had achieved notable successes: he made a peace with Carthage which secured the safety of the Greek cities, and another with the Lucanians in Italy after having defeated them twice and founding two cities in Italian Apulia. While Diodorus states that Dionysios II did all this in a state of apathy, this seems to be the product of a hostile source tradition: he was in fact adding a substantial part of Italy to his father's Sicilian territory. He was an effective ruler and if his uncle had not moved against him his tyranny may well have lasted much longer and Syracuse become even more powerful than it did.

Dion overthrew his nephew and was in turn killed, while a series of tyrants apparently took over power. Dionysios II was initially confined on Ortygia, but then went to Italian Lokris. From here in 346 BC he returned to capture Syracuse; while away, the Lokrians committed outrages against his wife and daughters, and killed both them and his sons. With Dionysios as tyrant over them again, the Syracusans turned for support to Hiketas tyrant of Leontinoi, and Dionysios II was ousted and again confined on Ortygia (Plut. *Timoleon* 1.1–6: doc. 7.53, 13.3–10: doc. 7.54; Diod. Sic. 16.5, 16.9–13; Plut. *Dion* 10–37).

Timoleon arrives from Corinth

Carthage, however, was watching events in Syracuse with great interest, and when the Sicilian Greeks sent an embassy to Corinth, Syracuse's mother-city, it sent out Timoleon as a commander, with seven ships (joined by another three ships en route) and 700 mercenaries. The Corinthians themselves did not send any hoplites, and what they expected Timoleon to achieve with such a small force is a matter for speculation. Apparently Timoleon's role was to be an organiser of the Syracusans, who needed leadership; it was a similar case to that of the Spartan Gylippos who by going to Syracuse single-handedly changed the course of the war in Sicily. Timoleon first attacked and defeated Hiketas, tyrant of Leontinoi, despite his role in deposing Dionysios; Hiketas had been engaged in a campaign against the city of Adranon, but was allowed to retain control of his city. Timoleon then went to Syracuse and Dionysios surrendered to him in 344, travelling to Corinth to live as an exile. Timoleon's policy in Sicily would be one of putting down tyrannies throughout the island, repopulating it, and confining Carthage to the island's western side. Carthage in response prepared a huge naval and land force, established good relationships with the Greek tyrants, and under Hanno crossed from Carthage to Sicily (Plut. *Timoleon* 2–3: doc. 7.53, 13.3–9: doc. 7.54, 22.8: doc. 7.55, also 12.3–5; Diod. Sic. 16.66–9).

The Carthaginians actually sailed into Syracuse's harbour but for unfathomable reasons departed. Timoleon reorganised Syracuse's political structure as a 'democracy', but this is probably simply political shorthand for the city no longer being ruled by a tyrant. Timoleon sent to Corinth for new settlers to come to Sicily to help rejuvenate the island's Greek population (Plut. *Timoleon* 22.7–23.8: doc. 7.55). He was not successful against Hiketas who had fled to Leontinoi, but captured Engyon and its tyrant Leptines, freeing Apollonia that had also been under Leptines' control. Timoleon adopted a deliberate policy of eradicating tyrannies throughout the Greek cities, which began to come over to his side due to his guarantees of autonomy, as too did Sikel and Sikanian cities, and others under Carthaginian control. Short of funds to pay his mercenaries, now numbering 4000 (1000 later deserted), he raided Carthaginian territory, with the result that he acquired a huge amount of money. Carthage, unhappy with its generals, sent out new ones with fresh forces (Diod. Sic. 16.70, 72–73; Plut. *Timoleon* 24.1–2: doc. 7.55, also *Timoleon* 25).

The battle at the river Krimisos in 340 BC

Coming to terms with Hiketas, Timoleon took over his forces, but later treacherously executed him. He then decided to take the war against the Carthaginians into their own territory, and assembled 12,000 men, being outnumbered by the enemy six to one. At Agrigentum (Akragas) 1000 of his mercenaries deserted (their ring-leader being a mercenary who had served with the Phokaians), but Timoleon advanced into the western part of the island and a great battle was fought at the river Krimisos in 340 BC. Ten thousand of the Carthaginians had crossed the river and Timoleon destroyed them first, taking up his own position in the centre of the line. The remaining Carthaginians, a huge force, then crossed and gained the advantage until a great storm blew up from behind the Greeks, whose backs were shielded from it, buffeting the Carthaginians full in the face. Taking advantage of this the Greeks renewed their attack and the enemy retreated, plunging into the river. Many were drowned or killed by their own side's swords or lances as they piled into the river, while others were herded there and struck down by Timoleon's cavalry. Tens of thousands of Carthaginians lost their lives including the 2500 members of the Carthagian Sacred Band and 15,000 were captured, along with 200 chariots, the rest being destroyed in the battle. A thousand breastplates and 10,000 shields were recovered which were dedicated in the temples of Syracuse, given to allies, and sent back to Corinth to be dedicated in the temple of Poseidon. Carthage, shocked by the scale of the defeat, sent ambassadors to Timoleon: a border was established, the Greek cities were to be free, and Carthage was not to give assistance to tyrants. Soon afterwards Timoleon killed the Etruscan pirate Postomios who chose the wrong time to put in to Syracuse. Greek settlers – some 60,000 – now arrived from the motherland and were settled with land grants at Syracuse, Agyrion, Akragas and Gela (Diod. Sic. 16.78–83; Plut. *Timoleon* 26–9, 35: doc. 7.56).

Timoleon's legacy

Timoleon ended tyranny in Sicily and confined the Carthaginians to the western part of the island. A combination of peace amongst the cities and the influx of new settlers led to a revival of Greek Sicily's prosperity and a return to its former glories. Timoleon laid down his position as commander voluntarily and died sometime in the 330s, being buried in Syracuse. Plutarch was in no doubt about the extent of Timoleon's achievements, and recorded the decree which the Syracusans passed on his death and which was read out at his funeral:

> The people of Syracuse here buries Timoleon, son of Timodemos, from Corinth at a public cost of 200 minas, and honours him for all time with musical, equestrian and athletic contests because he overthrew the tyrants, defeated the barbarians, refounded the greatest of the devastated cities, and gave the Greeks of Sicily back their laws.
>
> (Plut. *Timoleon* 39.5: doc. 7.56)

Sicilian tyrants and the panhellenic games

For the ancient Greeks, their panhellenic sanctuaries were an integral part of the elements that defined Greek culture (Hdt. 8.144.2: doc. 3.91). Many of the Greek colonies established abroad became important cities, and foremost amongst these was Syracuse in Sicily whose tyrants were anxious to maintain their Greek heritage and publicise their wealth, power and success by having their city represented in the various festivals of the mainland which were attended by great crowds of Greeks (up to 20,000 in the case of the Olympic festival). Athletes

Figure 7.5 The so-called Ear of Dionysios II, Syracuse. The story that its excellent acoustics enabled Dionysios to overhear the conversations of the prisoners kept here may be invention. Photo © James Meacock.

from the Greek cities of Sicily made their way to the panhellenic festivals and competed for honours, but of greatest importance were the horses and four-horse chariot teams sent by the tyrants to compete there (Figs 7.3, 7.6). Theron, tyrant of Akragas (489–473 BC), won a victory in the chariot race at Olympia in 476 BC, for which Pindar wrote two odes, *Olympian* 2 and 3. Theron's brother Xenokrates, associated with him in the tyranny, was a winner in the Pythian chariot race in 490 BC (before the tyranny) and at the Isthmian at an unknown date as well as at the Panathenaia in Athens (Pind. *Pythian* 6, *Isthmian* 2). Victories attest to these competitors' wealth and status even before they became tyrants: they were aristocrats who claimed one of the Theban heroes, Thersandros, as an ancestor.

Hieron, tyrant of Syracuse from 478 to 467 BC, had several of his victories immortalised in epinician ('victory') odes by Bacchylides of Keos, as well as by Pindar. He gained victories in the horse race at the Pythia in 482 and 478 BC, and in the horse race at Olympia in 476 BC (celebrated by Bacchylides 5 and Pindar *Olympian* 1: doc. 7.58) as well as in 472; there was another victory in the chariot race at the Pythia at some stage commemorated by Bacchylides 4 (doc. 7.57) and Pindar *Pythian* 1, and an Olympian chariot race victory in 468 (Bacchyl. 3: doc. 7.59). A third chariot win at an unknown contest was recorded by Pindar *Pythian* 2 (see also Paus. 8.42.9). Pherenikos was the name of the horse which won in 478 and 476 BC, and perhaps received special honours from Hieron as a result.

Hieron's victory in 470 BC

Bacchylides' fourth ode, for the victory of the chariot team Hieron sent to the Pythian festival at Delphi in 470 BC, served several purposes (this was Hieron's third victory at Delphi: 482, 478 and 470 BC). While, of course, glorifying the victory itself, like all such victory odes for tyrants it pointed to Hieron's wealth, for chariot racing was an expensive business. Much later in the same century, Alkibiades was in fact to boast that he had made the Greeks believe that Athens was far more prosperous and powerful than it really was by advertising the city's power through his entering seven chariot teams in the same Olympic contest (cf. Plut. *Alkibiades* 11.1–2: doc. 3.27). This fourth ode of Bacchylides also indicated the divine backing possessed by the tyranny: for 'golden-haired Apollo still loves the Syracusan city and honours Hieron' and it was through the god's patronage that Hieron had won victory. Moreover, the poem promotes Hieron's qualities as a 'just ruler'. In just a few lines Bacchylides provided a religious and political justification for Hieron's rule as tyrant (Bacchyl. 4: doc. 7.57).

Pindar's *Pythian* 1 (doc. 7.58) dealt with the same victory. The extravagance of Hieron is indicated by his commissioning two poems for the same event, but it should be noted that less important individuals occasionally also paid for poems by different writers (see Bacchyl. 6 and 7). This poem (*Pythian* 1) also displays political themes: the fame of Hieron is like that of Croesus, king of Lydia, known for his virtue, but is the antithesis of Phalaris, tyrant of Akragas (ruled 570–549 BC) who burnt his victims alive in a bronze bull. Hieron is well spoken of and has won the 'highest crown', drawing an allusion between the wreath with which the victorious chariot driver was crowned and Hieron's political integrity. Bacchylides' themes reveal much about perceptions of Hieron's tyranny. First he notes the extent of the tyrant's rule and its divine origin: it is from Zeus that Hieron has obtained 'widest sway over Greeks' (that is, he rules more Greeks than any other man). Moreover, he is a wealthy tyrant, who does not know how to hide his wealth, the implication being that it is so great he is unable to do so (Bacchyl. 4: doc. 7.57). Pindar's *Pythian* 3 introduces a cautionary note: that all mortal men are doomed to die (Hieron was ill at the time and died soon after, in 466 BC), perhaps a subtle way of stat-

Figure 7.6 A silver decadrachma (ten drachma) coin from Syracuse of about 425–400 BC. On the obverse it shows the head of the nymph Arethusa of the famous Syracusan spring of the same name, surrounded by four dolphins. The reverse shows a four-horse chariot with a winged Nike figure overhead, crowning the driver in his moment of victory. The prizes (athla) are visible in the exergue (lower register). The Syracusans were famous for their chariot victories. Yale University Art Gallery, 2001.87.121.

ing that even Hieron must not overstep his mortal bounds. The ode for the victory in 470 BC was sung at Delphi (Bacchyl. 3, lines 5, 9: doc. 7.57), but the ode was presumably sung again at Syracuse before an audience at Hieron's court. The tyrant clearly wanted to advertise his victories, as can be seen in coins decorated to advertise these victories (Fig. 7.6).

Dionysios I of Syracuse also participated in the Olympic festival, sending a group of four-horse chariot teams there in either 388 or 384 BC. Unlike the involvement of previous Sicilian tyrants, this was not a diplomatic success: the orator Lysias was present at Olympia and denounced Dionysios' tyranny over the Greeks. Dionysios had sent his own brother Thearides with a choir to sing his praises with songs Dionysios had composed himself. The Olympic crowd mocked the quality of the verses, while in the chariot racing, some of Dionysios' chariots exited the course and the others crashed amongst themselves. On the way back to Sicily, the vessel carrying them was wrecked at Taras. It was Dionysios' first and only foray into panhellenic sport (Diod. Sic. 14.109.1; Lys. 33). As an attempt to gain status amongst the Greeks, and at home, it was a spectacular but infamous failure.

Tyrants and public works

From reading Aristotle, it could be imagined that the tyrants of the Greek world were megalomaniac builders like the dictators of some modern totalitarian regimes. But the evidence points to a much more modest and targeted investment in public infrastructure. Specific examples indicate that tyrants did embellish their cities with architectural and engineering projects, thus dramatically improving the quality of life of their city's citizens. Thucydides, who clearly admired Hippias and Hipparchos as tyrants of Athens, specifically noted that they 'beautified their cities' (Thuc. 6.54.5: doc. 9.21). Herodotos was particularly fascinated by Samos, not only because of Polykrates, but because on that island were to be found in his estimation the greatest construction feats of the Greeks. What is striking about Greek tyrants is the predominance of water facilities in their construction portfolios: at Megara, Athens, and also on Samos. There, the architect Eupalinos of Megara designed a channel which ran beneath a mountain to bring water to the city of Samos. On Samos was also the 'greatest of known temples' the Heraion, the temple of Hera, designed by the Samian architect Rhoikos. To this day both the tunnel and the temple command respect, while in addition, there was a breakwater constructed around the harbour: Polykrates' naval interests would have made it easy to attribute this breakwater to him. While none of these three works are specifically attributed to Polykrates by Herodotos, they are of precisely the scale that required the civic organisation of a tyrant to execute, and Herodotos' narrative implies (but does not state specifically) that this tyrant was responsible for them, and it must inform Herodotos' judgement that Samos was the greatest of any city, Greek or non-Greek, of his time (Hdt. 3.60.1–4: doc. 7.60). Also according to Herodotos those made prisoner in the naval battle against Miletos and Lesbos were clapped in chains and put to work digging the moat which surrounded the city walls of Samos (Hdt. 3.39.1–4: doc. 7.32), and this defensive structure may have helped Polykrates withstand the later Spartan siege. It is often overlooked that Aristotle specifically refers to 'the works on Samos owed to Polykrates', so that at least by the fourth century there was an established tradition that the tyrant was a builder (Arist. *Politics* 1313b18–32: doc. 7.62). The original Heraion (temple to Hera) was destroyed by fire in Polykrates' reign, possibly during the Spartan attack of 525 BC, and it was Polykrates who began the rebuilding, though it was not completed until Hellenistic and Roman times. Of all the tyrants, he had the most extensive building programme.

A paved stone 'road' known as the diolkos ('passage through') ran from one side of the Isthmus (separating the Peloponnese from northern Greece) to the other, providing a six-kilometre road for wheeled traffic (Fig. 7.1). It was clearly constructed during the reign of the Kypselids, possibly under Periander, and there were wheeled grooves in the diolkos about one and a half metres apart, indicating that carts were specifically designed to be of this axle length for using the road. In some cases, the cargoes of ships arriving at one side of the Isthmus would be offloaded and transported by wagon to the other side. In this way, ships could stop at either side of the Isthmus (the Saronic or Corinthian Gulfs) without needing to sail around the Peloponnese, with its three extended prongs thrusting into the Mediterranean, to deliver their cargo. Whole ships could use the diolkos, and during the Peloponnesian War, triremes were transported across it on specially constructed wagons (Thuc. 3.15). The last recorded use of the diolkos for transporting ships across the diolkos comes in the ninth century AD. Much of the road still survives but conservation work on this monument is desperately needed. For Corinth, with its emphasis and reliance on trade, the diolkos was a great innovation requiring the organisational structure of a centralised government, that of tyranny, to see the project to completion (Strabo *Geography* 8.2.1: doc. 7.61). Corinth was not the only city to benefit from large-scale works under tyrants: after the battle of Himera in 480 BC, the tyrant Gelon of Syracuse distributed the captured prisoners of war throughout the Greek cities where they were employed on public works. Most of the prisoners were captured in the vicinity of Akragas, where they were put to work on the numerous temples still to be seen there today, as well as on an underground water drainage system (Diod. Sic. 11.25.3–4).

These various facilities were largely utilitarian: they benefited the city over which the tyrant ruled, and were obviously an important civic contribution which they could use to justify their rule. That many of these were water distribution projects indicates the somewhat primitive nature of Greek cities prior to the seventh century and these must be counted amongst the lasting legacies of the tyrants. Aristotle in one part of his long section on tyranny misinterprets these initiatives by tyrants (Arist. *Politics* 1313b18–32: doc. 7.62), but none of these works would have occupied large sections of the populations which the tyrant ruled. The Heraion on Samos was still being built in the Roman period, and so too was the example which Aristotle gives for the Peisistratidai, the temple of Olympian Zeus. Where Aristotle is correct is in the need for the population to be kept busy: at Athens there were several ways of ensuring this (*Athenaion Politeia* 16.2–3: doc. 9.16).

Aristotle on tyranny

Mercenaries, force and the championship of the demos

Aristotle wrote at length about tyranny in his *Politics*, while to a lesser extent it was also a subject of his *Rhetoric*. He was writing in the fourth century, and some of his comments on the nature of tyranny reflect conditions in the past, but when he gives contemporary or recent examples he draws on the Sicilian experience of tyranny; his examples from mainland Greece and Asia Minor belong to the earlier period of tyranny. For Aristotle, the main distinction between the two types of one-man rule – kingship and tyranny – was that the king ruled 'willing subjects according to the law' whereas the tyrant ruled the unwilling, and had a bodyguard of mercenaries, unlike a king who was protected by loyal armed citizens (Arist. *Politics* 1285a25–9: doc. 7.63). This correlates with his definition that kings' powers were limited by traditional customs and usages. In this way, Pheidon was king of Argos but when he accrued additional powers and became a one-man ruler (i.e., without the support of the traditional aristocracy) he was no longer a king but a tyrant (Arist. *Politics* 1310b14–31: doc. 7.2). Aristotle is able to use tyrants' use of force in coming to power as a means of rhetorical inductive reasoning: Peisistratos and Theagenes asked for a bodyguard and became tyrants, so when Dionysios (he is referring to Dionysios I of Syracuse) asked for a bodyguard it should have been clear from these previous examples that he was aiming at tyranny (Arist. *Rhetoric* 1357b30–6: doc. 7.64). In the past, Aristotle notes, popular leaders were also generals as well, making the usurpation of power easy. In his own day, rhetoric had become much more sophisticated, so that there was a distinction between the military man and the popular speaker who was a leader. Great powers in the past were entrusted to one person, allowing for the usurpation of these powers and their conversion into tyranny. Additionally, in the age of past tyranny there were no great cities but the people lived largely in the rural areas, and hatred of the wealthy allowed individuals such as Peisistratos and Megara to come to power. This might well have been the case with Theagenes, but at Athens the situation was more complicated and Aristotle's comment needs clarification: in a sense Peisistratos was a champion of the poor, but regional and aristocratic rivalry were also important factors.

The evils of tyranny

For Aristotle, tyranny was a degenerative form of government, a debasement of democracy, although this ignores the fact that the tyrannies of the seventh and sixth centuries tended to overthrow aristocratic rather than democratic constitutions. It did, however, apply to the tyranny of Dionysios I in the late fifth century, in which democracy was replaced by tyranny. The removal of the 'mob' and their dispersal from the city can find various examples amongst the tyrants: Peisistratos kept the Athenians in the countryside and took the judicial apparatus of the state to them to save them coming into the city (*Athenaion Politeia* 16.5: doc. 9.16), while Periander ensured that nobody sat around idle in the agora potentially plotting against him. But Aristotle ignores the great Syracusan synoikismoi; the removal of populations to Syracuse in order to create a large, populous city. What is also interesting here was Dionysios' fortification of the island, Ortygia, as a secure place of refuge if the need arose. Tyrants clashed with the leading citizens of a city as Aristotle correctly noted: from these citizens, plots against tyranny were most likely to arise. Aristotle observes the inimical nature of both democracies and tyrannies towards the leading citizens (that is, the aristocrats), and stasis (conflict) between democrats and aristocrats or oligarchs was a common feature of Greek history.

For Aristotle, tyrants were always hated. Solon at Athens warned of tyranny and the consequences it would have for the rich: the tyrant's enrichment at their expense (*Poem* 33: doc. 8.38; *Poem* 37.7–8: doc. 8.12). This was certainly not the case for many of the seventh and sixth century tyrants, such as Kypselos at Corinth and Peisistratos at Athens, though Aristotle argued that it was anger against tyrants, arising from their abuses of their position, which led to their downfall. He gives the example of Athens, where an insult by Hipparchos against Harmodios' sister led to the assassination of Hipparchos, although it was actually a more complex chain of events involving the Alkmeonidai and the Spartans that led to the overthrow of the tyranny in 510 BC (Arist. *Politics* 1312b17–23, 29–34: doc. 7.68).

How tyrants maintained their power

Aristotle provides almost a guide as to how to maintain oneself in power as a tyrant in his *Politics*. To dispose of potential trouble-makers, as several tyrants did, was a top priority. Citizens should be prevented from meeting in groups under any circumstances, and if they did, the tyrant should follow the example of Hieron and send 'eavesdroppers' amongst the crowds so that free speech was thereby curtailed and any potential organisation of a revolt difficult. The successful tyrant should also prevent people from becoming known to each other, for that would give them confidence and mutual support: a society full of strangers paranoid about what each other thinks is far more in a tyrant's interests, and all citizens must be kept under constant surveillance (Fig. 7.5). At Syracuse there were women spies called 'talebearers', amongst them, it seems, hetairai and prostitutes to whom men might confide their plots. Generally, the public should be prevented from meeting and if it did the tyrant must know what was discussed. Knowledge of the popular 'mood' was power (Arist. *Politics* 1313a34–b16: doc. 7.69).

The short-lived nature of tyranny

Tyranny and oligarchy alike were short-lived in the Greek world according to Aristotle. This certainly applied to tyranny, but states such as Corinth after the overthrow of tyranny appear to have been ruled by oligarchies for extensive periods of time. Orthagoras and his descendants at Sikyon constituted the longest-surviving tyranny, and Aristotle gives the mildness of their rule as the reason for their hundred-year reign. Kypselos, Periander and Psammetichos (Kypselos II) ruled for some 73 years: Kypselos was clearly popular, while Periander was 'more tyrant-like, but warlike too', and clearly kept a firm hand on government. Aristotle notes how it took Peisistratos three attempts to secure his power, after twice being deposed as tyrant. The first generation of Sicilian tyrants, too, did not rule for very long. But if the individual reigns of tyrants are compared with those of kings throughout history, it is not the individual length of reigns that are relatively short, for kings throughout history have had short reigns. Rather it was the nature of tyranny itself as a form of government in specific cities: tyranny did not have a 'long life' as a form of government as opposed to democracy or aristocracy (Arist. *Politics* 1315b11–18, 21–39: doc. 7.70). Aristotle sees oligarchies converting themselves into tyrannies, but here he might have been better advised to use the term aristocracies, for in most of the cases in archaic Greece the tyrant came to power as a member of an aristocracy that was ruling the city, and often not ruling well (Arist. *Politics* 1316a25–39: doc. 7.71). For Plutarch, tyranny was not a feature of the political development of the state; instead tyrants were 'chastisers' to improve the behaviour of the people they governed, or to punish them (Plut. *On Divine Vengeance* 7: doc. 7.72). His moralising attitude is also largely responsible for his praise of Timoleon and his role in freeing Sicily of its tyrants.

Tyrannies could come to an end through a popular uprising, as in Corinth, where the tyranny seems to have lost its purpose with Psammetichos not enjoying the popularity of Kypselos or possessing the aggressiveness of Periander. But in many places throughout Greece, the Spartans were responsible for the overthrow of tyrants. Sparta itself had experienced a period of 'bad government' (dysnomia) but had avoided tyranny, presumably because of the stability of its double monarchy and the central role of the gerousia in Sparta's constitution (Thuc. 1.18: doc. 6.57). Plutarch provides a specific list of examples of states liberated from tyranny by Sparta, and the examples should on the whole be accepted (Plut. *On the Malignity of Herodotos* 21: doc. 6.58). However, ideological opposition to tyranny did not prevent the Spartans from attempting to restore Hippias to power as tyrant over Athens in the last decade of the sixth century BC, and there were clear advantages for them if they had succeeded: closer involvement in Athenian affairs, and redress for Kleomenes' ungracious ejection from the city in 508 BC by the democracy instituted after he and the Spartans were forced to leave the city in that year. But Corinth was particularly opposed to this restoration, and its opposition effectively halted this attempt at reimposing a tyranny: they had ousted their own tyrants (Plutarch interestingly gives the Spartans a role in this) and now had a stake in ensuring that tyranny did not become an alternative, acceptable form of government in one of Greece's major cities (Hdt. 5.90.1–93.2: doc. 6.59). Aristocratic and oligarchic governments were more supportive of Sparta than tyrannies or democracies, and its fairly consistent anti-tyranny policy was a key factor in the spread of Spartan influence, particularly in the Peloponnese throughout the sixth century, while it became the basis for the Peloponnesian League, which was to prove such a formidable enemy to Athens in the Peloponnesian War (431–404 BC). By the fifth century tyrannies had been replaced by other forms of government in mainland Greece, but in the seventh and sixth centuries they had contributed much to Greek civilisation and were to give rise to a cultural renaissance in fourth-century Sicily.

8

THE LAW-GIVERS OF ATHENS
Drakon and Solon

Introduction

Attica in the last four decades of the seventh century (640–600 BC) and first decade of the sixth century (600–590 BC) was a society in a state of change. Kylon had attempted to establish a tyranny in about 632 BC and the Athenians had united to ensure that his attempt to seize power failed. By the 590s, however, they were disunited enough for the wealthy to be selling poor Athenians into slavery. The resulting discord in Athenian society led to Solon, a moderately wealthy aristocrat, being appointed as archon and mediator for 594 BC to solve Athens' political and economic problems. Solon came to the attention of the Athenians as a vocal social critic who wrote poetry focusing on the current state of affairs in Athens. He largely succeeded by transforming the political system, and his reforms became the cornerstone of Athenian politics for 300 years. Although he was by no means a democrat, his new system nevertheless opened the way for further constitutional development to take place in 508/7 BC, when another reformer, Kleisthenes, transferred the power of the state to the demos (the 'people').

Sources

Solon's own poetry provides the main ancient literary source for this period. While most of it is no longer extant, later historians, in particular the *Athenaion Politeia* and Plutarch in his *Life of Solon*, quoted sections, sometimes at some length, of his poems and provided a commentary on them. Only a few hundred of the original 5000 lines survive in the relevant chapters of the *Athenaion Politeia*, written around 330 BC and attributed to Aristotle. Plutarch's very unreliable *Life of Solon*, written 700 years after Solon's time, should be trusted only when Plutarch is drawing on Solon's own poetry or the works of fourth-century Athenian historians. Diogenes Laertius wrote a short biography of Solon in his collection of the 'Lives and Opinions of the Famous Philosophers', where he completely misunderstood the nature of the seisachtheia (the 'shaking off of burdens') and his work contains little of historical value.

Solon's poetry falls into two broad categories. Prior to becoming mediator and archon, he wrote several poems commenting in a very critical manner on the state of Athenian society, particularly the exploitation of the poor by the wealthy. He placed this in the context of the transgression of justice (dike), that he believed had resulted in a state of disorder (dysnomia) and hubristic behaviour (*Poems* 4, 13; docs 8.5–6). After his archonship, he felt the need to defend his actions as archon, and several poems both describe his achievements as archon, and justify his actions (for example, *Poem* 5: doc. 8.20). However, the poems are noteworthy for their lack of any detailed programme for the reforms he actually carried out. As Solon wrote in poetic form, there are many allegories, metaphors and similes in his work, and he does not explain the precise details of what occurred in the 590s at Athens, or the full scope of his activities. For example, one of his major reforms, the 'shaking off of burdens' (the *seisachtheia*) is described by him in allegorical terms: he cancelled the semi-feudal burdens of the smallholder farmers by removing the markers, which had enslaved 'the greatest mother of the Olympian gods and the best, black Earth' (*Poem* 36: doc. 8.12).

To understand the situation in early sixth-century Attica, modern historians have to interpret this allegory, assisted by the introductory comments made by the author of the fourth-century BC *Athenaion Politeia* when he quotes a particular poem. In the fourth century, various Athenian historians, including the author of the *Athenaion Politeia*, took an interest in Solon's reforms, although sometimes interpreting them from their own ideological point of view (Androt. *F* 34: doc. 8.13). It is also clear that many of the reforms which fourth-century writers attributed to Solon were probably not his, particular those associated with social practices and social reform. Furthermore, Solon was expressing his own opinions of his reforms and their aims, and then, after his archonship, justifying his achievements in the face of some criticism: his poems are, therefore, an autobiographical source on the political problems of his time with an inherent bias. Like writers such as Alcaeus and Theognis, he commented on the state of affairs in his own city, but is unique in being the only politician of the archaic or classical period to have left behind works which almost constitute a political manifesto-cum-autobiography. Plutarch's *Solon* gives the misleading impression that Greek history can be effectively studied through a series of biographies written by Plutarch hundreds of years after the event, but any study of Solon must commence with his poetry, followed by the *Athenaion Politeia*.

Drakon the Law-giver

During the seventh-century BC laws were written and inscribed throughout the Greek world. Literacy was an important factor in this, and the Homeric epics, written down in about the 750s BC, signal the beginning of a period when writing came to be used for a range of purposes. The formalisation of the political structures of the polis, which had emerged by this period as the basic political institution of the Greek world, encouraged the recording of laws by which the population of a city was to be governed. This was also a period of disturbance and social upheaval, in which explicitly recording the laws of the city was one way to prevent disputes about justice and its application. This was because written law was less likely to be overruled and distorted. Hesiod, for example, in the seventh century BC complained bitterly about the corruption of magistrates in Boeotia (*Works and Days* 38–9). The 'Lykourgan' reforms in Sparta were formulated in the same century, and the Delphic oracle granted its approval when they were presented there to the god Apollo for ratification. Sparta had undergone a period of dysnomia, 'bad-order', and the laws solved many of Sparta's problems, creating a society and constitution that was stable for centuries.

The promulgation of law-codes

A number of individuals promulgated law-codes in this period. Less well known than Solon or 'Lykourgos' is Zaleukos (Latin: Zaleucus), probably the first of the law-givers, who drew up laws for Lokris in Italy in about 650 BC. His laws had specific penalties for various offences, but they were known more specifically for their provisions which aimed to prevent crime through regulations governing individuals' behaviour. He was chosen as law-giver, nomoth-etes, possibly like Solon because of civic unrest, and his laws were still in force in the fourth century when Lokris was regarded as a model of a well-governed community. Similarly, Kharondas at Catana in Sicily towards the end of the sixth century BC, and thus closer in time to Solon, drew up laws for that city and the other Sicilian colonies of Chalkis, legislating in particular against the giving of false testimony in legal cases. In addition to the individu-als who drew up specific codes of law for their states, the appearance of individual decrees and laws inscribed on stone in the seventh century BC points to a general move towards the codification of laws, and to the desire of authorities to promulgate laws dealing with specific problems or ongoing issues in their communities. Drakon established his law-code for Athens in the archonship of Aristaichmos (621 BC) ([Arist.] *Ath. Pol.*4.1: doc. 8.2). The ancient sources do not give any particular reason for his legislation, but the proximity in time to the aftermath of Kylon's attempt at tyranny and the slaughter of his supporters, probably in 632 BC, sug-gests a connection with this event (docs 7.21–3).

Athenian pre-history

Archons were the main officials at Athens in archaic and classical times, with the record of these magistrates beginning in 682 BC. This is usually taken to indicate that the kingship had been abolished by that year. The chief archon was known as the eponymous archon, as he gave his name ('onoma') to the year in which he held office. The events of Solon's archonship were, therefore, referred to as taking place 'in the archonship of Solon'. The Athenians had a rich tradition about their origins: they were an autochthonous people, having 'sprung from the soil', literally, when the lame god of metallurgy Hephaistos attempted to rape the virgin goddess Athena. She wiped his semen off her thigh with a wad of wool, discarding it on the earth. This 'impregnated' the earth goddess, Gaia, and Erichthonios was born. Athenian vase paintings often show the myth, with Gaia as a woman emerging from the earth with the infant Erichthonios; Athena and Hephaistos both stand by and watch the scene (Fig. 8.1). Athenians, therefore, regarded themselves as indigenous to Attica: they were not invaders of Greece, unlike the Dorians (tradition puts the Dorians' arrival in Greece in about the twelfth or eleventh century BC).

Erichthonios' grandson Erechtheus became the first king of Athens (one of the new ten tribes instituted by the Athenian political reformer Kleisthenes in 508/7 BC (*Ath. Pol.* 21.1–6: doc. 10.7) was to be named after him). Later Theseus as king of Athens united, 'synoecised', all the territory of Attica under the city's control (Thuc. 2.15.1–2: doc. 1.56). The territorial integrity of Attica, some 1000 square kilometres, had a long history: Eleusis was conquered in the seventh century and fully incorporated into Attica politically as well as religiously through the annual celebration of the Great Mysteries of Eleusis, with the Eleusinian procession now setting out from Athens. Salamis was captured and added later, with Solon playing a part; later there were struggles over Megara concerning the port Nisaia, which earned Peisistratos his military credentials and popularity.

Immediately prior to Drakon, the city of Athens and its territory was primarily ruled by the council of the Areiopagos which 'had the task of keeping watch over the laws'. It took its name from its meeting place, 'The Hill of Ares' (Areiopagos), which was north-west of the acropolis. Membership of the council was open only to the aristocrats, who were known as the eupatridai, which can be translated as the 'well-born' or 'those of good parentage'; this remained the case until Solon's reforms (*Ath. Pol.* 8.2: doc. 8.17). These eupatridai were the leaders of the phylai

Figure 8.1 Hephaistos, visibly lame (his left leg is longer than his right), watching as Gaia, the earth goddess, gives the infant Erichthonios, with his hands stretched out, to Athena. The Athenians
considered themselves an autochthonous ('sprung from the earth') people because of this
myth. This scene is represented on several Athenian vases, in this case on a stamnos, dating
to about 460 BC. Munich Staatliche Antikensammlungen und Glyptothek, 2431. Drawing by
J. Etherington.

(tribes) and gene ('clans'), and belonged to the aristocratic hetaireiai (clubs), in Athens. These
laws over which the council of the Areiopagos had guardianship were unwritten, for Drakon
was the first to codify Athenian laws and have them inscribed. Nine archons ('chief officials')
were chosen 'by birth and wealth' for any one year by the Areiopagos and automatically
joined this council, although Solon was to change the criterion for their election from birth
to wealth (*Ath. Pol.* 7.3: doc. 8.16). This council had ancient origins; although it took over the
running of the state after the monarchy, there had presumably always been an aristocratic
council that advised the kings. It was the only office held for life in Athenian constitutional
history during the archaic and classical periods (*Ath. Pol.* 3.6: doc. 8.1).

Drakon's constitution

The *Athenaion Politeia* described a politeia (constitution) for Athens prior to Drakon, and attributed a new one to Drakon himself (*Ath. Pol.* 41.2: doc. 1.4). Other sources only deal with his
law-code; this does not mean that Drakon did not also establish a politeia, as constitutional
changes were something in which the author of the *Athenaion Politeia* took an especial interest
(4.1–5: doc. 8.2). However, many modern scholars reject this passage and its evidence for a
Drakonian constitution. To what extent, therefore, the statement that Drakon established a
new politeia is historically accurate is unknown: Drakon may have simply been formalising

the given political situation and clarifying details rather than introducing real changes. Certainly, prior to Solon, officials were chosen according to their position in society and their wealth, and there were probably nine archons at this point, as well as generals and cavalry commanders, as later. The Areiopagos clearly had guardianship of the laws, and ensured that officials ruled according to the law and existing constitution. These provided the basis from which Solon was to work some two decades later.

There are some problems with the account of the *Athenaion Politeia*, however, which suggest that perhaps it should be accepted only in its broadest details as reflecting the political situation in the late seventh century BC. The definition of property qualifications in monetary terms is an anachronism (there was no coinage in Greece at this time), an error of which the author of the *Athenaion Politeia* is also guilty in his account of Solon's reforms: ancient sources probably believed that there had always been coined money. The significant political role played by the cavalry and hoplite classes is an accurate representation of historical reality for the seventh century: 'those who supplied their own arms' were permitted to stand for the lesser magistracies, and Solon's classification of office according to wealth would have appeared less radical if Drakon had instituted or confirmed this privilege for hoplites. Generals are mentioned by the *Athenaion Politeia*, and, although they probably were not as important in 621 BC as they later became in the fifth century, there must have been generals to lead the army in military campaigns, such as the conquest of Eleusis, as well as the campaigns against Salamis which Solon sought (successfully) to reopen. The presence of generals in the *Athenaion Politeia*'s description of Drakon's constitution does not provide a reason to reject its authenticity. Although most scholars agree that the existence of a council of 401 members instituted by Drakon is plausible, this is improbable, given that the emphasis elsewhere in this section of the *Athenaion Politeia* is on the Areiopagos' control of the state. Solon introduced a council of 400 men and changed the election criteria for the Areiopagos, and it seems unlikely that this conservative council shared power with another council, of 401 members, in Drakon's day. Some historians do not accept that Drakon made any political changes at all, but it is at least clear that traditionally the Areiopagos and the wealthy ruled the state at that period, and that the hoplite class also played a significant part in politics.

Drakon's main task, however, appears to have been to codify the laws, only one of which is known. This is due to the fact that when he was appointed Solon repealed all of Drakon's laws except the one on homicide which remained in force (Plut. *Life of Solon* 17.1: doc. 8.4; *Athenaion Politeia* 7.1). There was a tradition, reported by Plutarch, that Drakon's laws were extremely harsh, written 'in blood, not ink'. This is part of a general ancient tradition which tended to see earlier laws as harsher than current ones (Plut. *Solon* 17.2–3: doc. 8.4). In fact Drakon's laws, if the law on homicide is taken as any indication, were not in fact 'draconian' (harsh) but very fair in legal terms.

This homicide law may well have been necessary because of Kylon's recent attempt to establish a tyranny. Many of his supporters were slain and the killers in turn sentenced to judgement. Drakon's law was possibly an attempt to put an end to revenge killings resulting from a blood feud between Kylon's supporters and relatives and those of the Alkmeonidai. There may also have been other private feuds taking place with similar outcomes, with families undertaking their own justice against the killer or killers of a family member. Alternatively, Drakon may have regarded murder as deserving special legislation as the most serious and destabilising crime in any state, undercutting all the values of the polis.

The law on homicide is known, in a fragmentary state, from a decree inscribed on stone in 409/8 BC (*IG* I³ 104: doc. 8.3). When the Athenians revised their laws in 411 BC after the fall of the oligarchic government of the Four Hundred (doc. 13.8), this law of Drakon remained and was inscribed as part of the Athenian legal code. Drakon's laws themselves when introduced in 621 BC were not inscribed on a stele (stone slab), but rather were written in paint on wooden tablets known as axones (singular axon; see Figure 8.2). In the inscription of 409/8 BC, the laws themselves are preceded by a preamble, giving the date of the republication of the law, the name of the person who proposed its republication, and financial details about defraying the expense of inscribing it. The archon is given as Diokles of 409/8 BC, and the anagrapheis (recorders) were instructed to inscribe Drakon's homicide law on a stone stele to be exhibited in front of the stoa basileios, the stoa of the basileus archon, in the agora (marketplace): it was from the basileus archon that the anagrapheis received the law for reinscribing, so the axones of Drakon were presumably also displayed in that stoa, just as Solon's laws were published there (*Ath. Pol.* 7.1: doc. 8.15). The actual stele survives.

The wooden tablets, the axones, are referred to in the inscription of 409/8 BC. Following the full text of the 'First Axon', the inscription breaks off at the words 'Second Axon' demonstrating that another law, now lost, followed. Laws of Solon are referred to as being inscribed on kyrbeis (*Ath. Pol.* 7.1: doc. 8.15), and while both ancient sources and modern authorities have dwelt at length on the precise meaning of both these terms, it seems that they refer more or less to the same object: Drakon's homicide law and Solon's laws were written on axones. These wooden tablets were set within a wooden framework which could be revolved by the reader (Fig. 8.2). So when Plutarch quotes the fourth-century BC comic poet Kratinos that those in the prytaneion (town hall) dine there and roast their barley (the main food in Athens) by virtue of the kyrbeis, it is in the sense that it is by law that they are accorded this privilege (Plut. *Solon* 25.1–2: doc. 8.33).

Drakon's first axon dealt with involuntary homicide, so presumably the second axon to which the inscription refers dealt with voluntary homicide, that is, wilful murder for whatever reason. The first axon states that, even for a homicide committed by accident, the penalty is exile: the killer must leave Attica and never return. This provision was strategic, for those who killed with premeditation might nevertheless argue that their crime had been involuntary, and so the punishment for such a category of homicide had to be an effective deterrent against even accidental manslaughter. Officials known as 'basileis' were 'to pass judgement' regarding the guilt of those accused of having committed or planned a murder, and if the accused was found guilty a group of fifty-one individuals known as the ephetai decided on the details of the actual punishment; in this sense both groups acted as a court of law. While exile was the prescribed (default) penalty, there was another option which shows the leniency of the law in one important respect: the relatives of the murder victim in a case of involuntary killing could exercise clemency, and if the father, brothers or sons of the deceased were alive and *all* of them agreed to pardon the murderer he would not be punished. However, this was not the case if even one of the relatives opposed it. This was important as, if even one of the close relatives was still aggrieved and resented the fact that the killer had escaped any form of penalty, there could be further violence and perhaps the institution of a vendetta. If all the relatives listed were deceased, then any male cousins and their sons had the same right, either to agree with the sentence of exile, or to pardon the killer. The wide range of relatives to be consulted perhaps indicates that blood feuds were taking their toll on Athenian families.

Several features of the law are crucial. It was fair and humanitarian, with the penalty imposed being exile not death. This suggests that the later traditions regarding the harshness of Drakon's laws and Plutarch's report that they were 'written in blood' are totally unreliable.

Figure 8.2 A young man before what appear to be wooden axones (doc. 8.33). Athenian red-figure drinking cup (kylix); dated to about 480–470 BC, and attributed to the Briseis Painter; diameter of cup: 23.2 cm. New York Metropolitan Museum of Arts, 27.74. Drawing by J. Etherington.

The more important point, however, is that the judgement on the case and the actual verdict were based on collective decision-making by two groups, the basileis, who ascertained guilt or innocence, and then the fifty-one ephetai, who determined the penalty. This arrangement foreshadowed not only Solon's later courts of appeal, the heliaia, but also the dikasteria (jury-courts) of fifth- and fourth-century Athens, in which large numbers of Athenian male citizens acted as a body of jurors in legal cases and made judicial decisions as to both the verdict and the penalty. Judicial decision-making was, therefore, a group process from early in Athens' history. The distinction between different types of homicide was developed further until in the fourth century BC (and perhaps earlier) there were five separate courts dealing with voluntary and involuntary homicide; one of the courts even dealt with deaths caused by animal attacks.

Another important aspect of Drakon's law on homicide was the fact that the state now legislated in matters over which families previously had competence, for by Drakon's law the state assumed authority over existing social usages in which families exercised their own retribution for murder of a family member. By the fourth century BC Athenian law gave the polis charge of a wide variety of private and family matters, ranging from the inheritance of property to prosecutions for adultery, sodomy and marriage to non-Athenians. Drakon's law resolved issues arising from homicide: Athens' next challenge was to deal with another serious problem faced by individual Athenians: that of enslavement for debt.

Poverty and inequality in Attica before Solon

In the 590s BC Attica was faced with serious problems with an underlying agrarian basis. Solon, the main source for this period, was an Athenian social critic who like the other writers of his time conveyed his own political and social concerns through poetry, as did Theognis at Megara (doc. 7.19) and Alcaeus at Mytilene (docs 7.24–30). In several poems Solon describes a state of affairs in which the Athenian state appears to be on the verge of civil war. He writes that it is not the 'decree of Zeus' or the will of the immortal gods that will destroy Athens, and here he is probably alluding to the Trojan War and the role gods such as Athena and Hera played in the doom and inescapable destruction of the city of Troy. Athens, in contrast, is protected by Pallas Athena (Solon *Poem* 4: lines 1–4: doc. 8.5), but the threat comes from the thoughtlessness and greed of Athenian citizens themselves who are bent on the destruction of their city. They do not know how to 'restrain excess' and the 'people's leaders' are unrighteous: in other words, the leaders of the state are themselves acting unjustly. Like a Biblical prophet, Solon predicts that they will suffer for their hubris, for 'civil discord and sleeping war', the killer of many in the prime of their lives, is about to visit Athens (*Poem* 4: lines 19–20). As a result of those who behave with presumption and lust after possessions, war will come to Athens, and it will apparently be a conflict between rich and poor, for 'evils are at large amongst the people' and many of the poor Athenians are being sold 'in chains' into slavery to foreign places (lines 23–5). The 'public evil', the greed of the people's leaders, affects everyone and there is no escaping it: all Athenians are at risk (lines 26–9). This enslavement of Athenians is the problem which will spark civic violence, and Solon clearly attempts to arouse awareness among those citizens who consider that the current injustices do not concern them. Solon returns to the theme of wealth, but this time gained honestly, in another poem (Solon *Poem* 13: doc. 8.6), where he prays that the Muses listen to his prayer that he be prosperous and wealthy, arguing that the wealth 'which the gods give' stays with a man (line 9), while other wealth comes from hubris, or presumption (lines 11–13; he criticised hubris also in *Poem* 4: doc. 8.5). Here he is criticising the unjust accumulation of wealth currently taking place at Athens and warns his auditors about the justice of Zeus and the inevitable downfall of those who gather riches unjustly.

Why does Solon write poems so critical of his city and country? He himself states that it is his 'spirit [that] bids me tell the Athenians' about what is happening (*Poem* 4: doc. 8.5, line 30). That is, his social conscience was stirred as he saw the problems afflicting Athens. These aroused his fears for the consequences, both for the city and its citizens. He was one of those champions in history who saw social, economic and political problems in his state and spoke out against them. His poems were not intended for the few literate citizens who could read. Rather, a clue as to how he presented his views to a wide audience is shown in the following anecdote: when the Athenians decreed that no one was to reopen the discussion about war with the neighbouring state of Megara over possession of the island of Salamis, Solon pretended to be mad and recited in the assembly a 100-line poem he had composed on the matter to encourage the Athenians to resume the war (Solon *Poems* 1–3: doc. 8.8). This is presumably how his other poems and their criticisms circulated: some were perhaps in written form for the literate, but he primarily recited them in public, when he addressed groups in the agora or in the assembly (as it is known poets later did at Olympia).

'Strife' between the rich and the poor

The *Athenaion Politeia* elaborates on the problem which Solon's poems outline, the 'strife' between the rich and the poor. The Greek word for 'strife' is stasis, which means serious political conflict or even civil war. The author of the *Athenaion Politeia* is writing from a fourth-century BC point of view and his account sometimes lacks clarity. He states that early sixth-century Athens was 'oligarchic', by which he means it was ruled by a few, the wealthy, while the poor were the 'slaves' of the rich. By this he cannot be referring literally to slavery: the term he uses does not necessarily imply that the poor were chattel-slaves although it was into enslavement that these previously free Athenians had been sold according to Solon. Rather the poor were forced to work their own land and give one-sixth of its produce to a wealthy landowner. Because they were bound to the rich by a system of serfdom or agricultural obligation, they were referred to as 'slaves' by the fourth-century source *Athenaion Politeia*. The poor farmers were actually known as 'pelatai' and 'hektemoroi' (*Ath. Pol.* 2.1–3: doc. 8.7). The hektemoroi ('sixth-parters') paid one-sixth of the agricultural produce from their own land to the wealthy; the pelatai, a word which seems to mean 'dependants', may well have been serfs in the fullest sense of the word, not owning any land and working the farms of the rich, or being in some way in a greater degree of obligation to the wealthy than the hektemoroi: unfortunately, while the *Athenaion Politeia* defines the hektemoroi, it does not do so for the pelatai. Clearly, however, if the hektemoroi failed to pay this one-sixth share of their produce, they were liable to be sold into slavery, both they and their children (wives are presumably meant as well, but being less important are not specifically mentioned). 'All the land was in the hands of a few' is a misunderstanding from a fourth-century perspective (*Ath. Pol.* 2.2: doc. 8.7): the best explanation is probably that the hektemoroi owned their farms, but one-sixth of their produce – not an inconsiderable amount in a subsistence economy – went to a wealthy landowner, and if they could not comply with this obligation their land was sequestered.

It is clear from Solon's reforms in response to this situation that the hektemoroi did own their land but that it had become encumbered with feudal-like obligations: originally in return for the one-sixth of their produce, the poor farmers probably received protection, arbitration in disputes, and assistance in hard times. This had developed into a rather one-sided arrangement, and the greed of the wealthy was enforcing payment of the obligation and sending the poor into slavery. Moreover the wealthy received the price for the slave and his family in goods (there was no coinage at this stage), and presumably in addition seized the now unoccupied land. For the *Athenaion Politeia*, the dissension in Athens was on a straightforward basis of class: the rich versus the poor, in which the poor were completely disempowered: 'they had no share in anything' (*Ath. Pol.*2.3: doc. 8.7). The crisis which Solon attempted to solve in 594/3 BC was, therefore, one between exploiters and exploited, rich against poor; there was at this stage no regional dysfunction or geopolitical disunity in Attica. This came later, in the 560s. Nor were there individual, identifiable families vying for power: Kylon had attempted to establish tyranny just a few decades earlier and Athens had successfully united against him.

How the situation came about in which the pelatai and hektemoroi could not meet their obligations and were being sold into slavery is unclear. It may have been that the custom of paying the one-sixth to the landlord had been in abeyance and was now being enforced. It has also been suggested that a growth in population saw the hektemoroi and pelatai needing more of their produce for themselves. However, there is no evidence for a significant boost in the number of Athenian 'mouths to feed' at this point. Certainly the fact that Athens was relatively uninterested in dispatching colonies during this period (doc. 2.11), and that the colonies which it did establish were modest affairs at Sigeion and the Chersonese (doc. 2.18), suggests that there were no concerns over surplus population. It was only in the fifth century BC that Athens had sufficient surplus population to send out significant numbers of colonists (docs 2.7, 12.31). There was no shortage of land in Attica, and the state was a good century away from relying on imports of grain from the Black Sea. The wealthy, rather, seem to have become zealous in exacting their 'one-sixths'.

The wrath of Zeus

At this stage, Solon could only warn the Athenians about civil war and threaten those who were treating others hubristically with the wrath of Zeus. He could neither invoke laws nor appeal to any officials (after all, he specifically criticises the 'leaders of the people'). Just before 594 BC, however, the situation changed, and Solon became the first 'champion of the people' (*Ath. Pol.* 2.3: doc. 8.7). With his poetry he had announced himself as a social commentator, and some of his lines made a critical impression on the Athenians: 'I look on, and pains lie within my breast, as I behold Ionia's oldest land being slain' (*Ath. Pol.* 5.1–2 (Solon *Poem* 4a): doc. 8.9). Having had enough of exploitation the poor 'rose up' against the rich; the stasis was 'fierce' and the state was in chaos 'for a long time', and both sides agreed to choose Solon as 'mediator and archon' for the year 594/3 BC. He implies that he was not himself particularly wealthy (Solon *Poem* 13.7–8: doc. 8.6) and he may well have had strong support from a 'middle' group in society, such as the hoplites, and those among the wealthy concerned at the state of affairs.

Solon, then, was not simply a typical archon. He was chosen as a 'mediator' and both sides agreed that he should deal with the sources of contention between them. He was well placed to do so: his poetry showed an awareness of the problems and a genuine concern with Athens' welfare. Well off and well educated, he was nevertheless not excessively wealthy. In fact, his main attacks were always against the wealthy and he did not see the poor as the cause of the problem (*Ath. Pol.* 5.3 (Solon *Poem* 4c): doc. 8.10). That the wealthy nevertheless chose him as 'mediator' indicates that there were a sufficient number in this group in agreement with Solon that some action was necessary. As a result Solon introduced a series of laws (his nomothesia: 'setting in place of laws') which solved many of Attica's problems and earned him a reputation as one of the wisest men of ancient Greece: he would later be numbered among Greece's 'Seven Sages'.

The seisachtheia

Solon's first reform in his nomothesia and perhaps his most important was the seisachtheia. It was the crucial step which stopped the rich from enslaving the poor and at a single stroke addressed the main problem behind the civil unrest in the state. There are three main ancient sources for this reform: a lengthy poem by Solon, and interpretations of the process by the *Athenaion Politeia* and by the fourth-century BC orator Androtion. Exactly what the seisachtheia was is partly problematic because Solon described the process poetically, rather than presenting the reform as a political manifesto.

Firstly, the seisachtheia means literally a 'shaking off of burdens'; it was not a 'cancellation of debts' as Androtion in particular claimed (see p. 308). The hektemoroi and the pelatai 'shook off' the burdens with which wealthy local landowners had encumbered them. Secondly, the measure did not involve a redistribution of land. Some of the poor expected this, but Solon pointed out that he had not promised that this would happen, and that he categorically did not wish to see the 'base and good' (poor and aristocrats) share the land equally. It may well have been the pelatai, if these were a class of landless dependants, who were mainly behind such agitation for land redistribution. As Solon notes, in a poem written during his archonship or afterwards, to redistribute the land would have required 'the force of tyranny'. It would have been a major upheaval and almost certainly would have led to violence and bloodshed, a worsening of the stasis he had been appointed to deal with as archon (Solon *Poem* 34: doc. 8.12). But it was necessary to guarantee the hektemoroi, who now became freehold farmers, full rights to their land and its produce. Aristotle in his *Politics* has it nearly right: Solon in his legislation realised that an equal distribution of property was an important part of the political community – not 'equal' in the sense of all citizens possessing the same amount of land, but with ownership of the land widely distributed among the social classes, and so guaranteeing the livelihoods of the majority of the population (Arist. *Politics* 1266b14–24: doc. 8.14).

To those angry at an absence of land redistribution in his nomothesia, Solon pointed out that he had accomplished everything he had promised. This included removing the horoi (markers) from 'black Earth', which was previously enslaved by them, but was now free. These horoi were presumably marker stones which indicated that the land which the hektemoroi owned was encumbered with an obligation to a local wealthy landlord. Now the hektemoroi were completely free citizens, and are heard of no more in the discourse of Athenian history: a free peasantry owning its own farms had emerged.

Those who had been enslaved in Attica were freed, and Solon somehow also managed to bring home many of those who had been sold overseas. Details of the process by which he did so are unclear, but his poetry indicates that a serious attempt was made to liberate such slaves (*Ath. Pol.* 12.4 (Solon *Poem* 36: doc. 8.12)). In addition, as well as the seisachtheia, Solon introduced a provision that loans could not be made on the security of the person: in other words, Athenians could not borrow money using themselves as collateral (*Ath. Pol.* 6.1: doc. 8.11). Debt slavery for Athenians was now abolished: unless enslaved in war, an Athenian citizen was born free and would remain so until death. This guarantee of the freedom of the citizen body was a cornerstone of Athenian society.

Solon's poetry makes it clear that the seisachtheia was a removing of agricultural obligations: the fourth-century accusations that he and his friends bought up large tracts of land by borrowing money before the seisachtheia and then benefited because it was a 'cancellation of debts' are simply erroneous. There was no coined money in existence at the time, and the idea that several large estates were 'up for sale' is improbable: the *Athenaion Politeia* finds the charge against Solon 'false' (*Ath. Pol.* 6.2–4: doc. 8.11). Androtion's idea that Solon reduced interest rates for the farmers is also improbable: the problem Solon solved was not that farmers were paying interest on debts but that they were paying a flat rate of one-sixth of their produce to the wealthy who were exploiting the situation to enslave the farmers and thereby make a greater profit (Plut. *Solon* 15.2–5 (Androt. *F* 34): doc. 8.13). Both the *Athenaion Politeia* and Plutarch agree that the usual interpretation of the seisachtheia as a 'shaking off of burdens' in connection with the land was the correct one. It is sometimes suggested that Solon's prohibition may also have made it more difficult for farmers to obtain credit; creditors who had previously lent on the security of the borrower's person would now have less security for their credit. But the notion that Solon's 'shaking off of burdens' harmed farmers by making it difficult for them to find anyone to give them assistance overlooks the nature of the status of the hektemoroi, who gave a proportion of their produce to the land-lords. Hektemoroi may *also* have borrowed from the landlord, but this is a separate issue.

Solon's constitutional reforms

In 411 BC, in the aftermath of the disastrous Sicilian Expedition, the Athenian politician Kleitophon recommended a return to Kleisthenes' constitution as being more conservative than that currently in place. In contrast, the preference for Solon's constitution was a fourth-century phenomenon, and fourth-century politicians viewed Solon as the founder of an Athenian democracy preferable to that of Kleisthenes. Solon's constitution was seen as 'democratic' and as ancestral (a 'patrios politeia'). For the conservative citizens in the state, it was preferable to the democracies of Kleisthenes or Ephialtes, mainly because the powers of the people (demos) were limited. Solon in fact believed strongly that the people should be content with only a partial say in Athenian affairs: 'To the people I gave as much privilege as was appropriate' (*Ath. Pol.* 12.1 (Solon *Poem* 5, line 1)). Solon's laws (in his poetry referred to as thesmoi) constituted a politeia (constitution), as many of his laws were political in nature and altered the political 'system'. They included changes in the competency of the Areiopagos and an extension of political privilege to a broader body of Athenians than before. Solon himself wrote that he set up 'straight justice' for 'good and bad alike' (*Ath. Pol.* 12.4 (Solon *Poem* 34: doc. 8.12)). This changed the political structure of Attica and left an indelible mark upon it for centuries to come. His system of the four classes, based on wealth, was always the basis for political privilege and rights in archaic and classical Athens, but over time the powers of the two lowest classes, the zeugitai and thetes, expanded. Solon's constitution was timocratic, a 'timokratia': a rule (kratia) based on wealth (time).

'Solon established a constitution and made other laws'

The Athenians no longer made use of Drakon's laws except for those concerning homicide, and Solon's legislation was inscribed on tablets, known as kyrbeis, and set up in the stoa of the basileus archon in the Athenian agora. All citizens at the time swore obedience to the laws, and even in the time of the *Athenaion Politeia* the nine archons swore on the stone outside the stoa that they would uphold them; this stone has been identified with the large limestone block discovered outside the stoa basileios (*Ath. Pol.* 7.1: doc. 8.15).

The four classes

A radical departure from the existing political system, and the main change in Solon's politeia, related to the four political classes. Every male Athenian citizen already belonged to one of four groups in Attica, based on landed wealth: these were the pentakosiomedimnoi, hippeis, zeugitai and the thetes, in descending order of wealth and prestige. Solon transformed these groups by making them the basis of political privilege: the officials (or magistrates) of the state were drawn from the first three of these classes, while the thetes, as the poorest, were not eligible for any political office. By the 330s BC thetes could hold office, not because the law was changed, but because it was ignored: 'when anyone is about to draw lots for a magistracy is asked what class he belongs to, he would never say the thetes' (*Ath. Pol.* 7.3–4: doc. 8.16). Yet that situation was more than two and a half centuries after Solon's reforms. Membership of a particular group was based on the amount of agricultural produce one's land yielded, measured in medimnoi (singular: one medimnos, a measure, which was 55 litres or approximately a month's allowance of barley for one person).

Table 8.1 Political classes in Attica

Pentakosiomedimnoi (singular: pentakosiomedimnos): their land produced 500 or more measures (medimnoi) of dry and liquid agricultural goods; they could be elected as treasurers, archons, poletai, and kolakretai (financial officials). The poletai acted as the sellers of state and confiscated property, and let out both contracts for collecting state taxes and the leases of the state owned silver mines.

Hippeis (singular: hippeus): their land produced between 300 and 500 measures of dry and liquid agricultural goods; they could be elected as archons, poletai, kolakretai.

Zeugitai (singular: zeugites): their land produced between 200 and 300 measures of dry and liquid agricultural goods; they could be elected as poletai and kolakretai and they became eligible for the archonship in 457/6.

Thetes (singular: thes): their land produced less than 200 measures of dry and liquid agricultural goods, or they were landless; they could hold no political office, but were members of the assembly and the law-courts. As members of the assembly they presumably were involved in the election of officials.

The classification of offices by wealth (timocracy) and not birth (aristocracy) suggests that there was a group of wealthy non-eupatridai in Attica, and that Solon thought that the extension of political power to this group would benefit the stability of the state. He may have given the wealthy non-eupatridai political power to offset that of the eupatridai. It was not the amount of land that one possessed that determined one's class but rather the yield a farmer could extract from his land. The pentakosiomedimnoi (500-bushel-men) as their name indicates, were those whose land could produce 500 medimnoi or above and they probably needed 75–145 acres of grain-producing land, or 20–5 acres of vineyards and olive orchards. So those belonging to the top group did not in fact need to possess large tracts of land: even the top group could include the moderately wealthy and in the pentakosiomedimnoi group, the eupatridai would have 'rubbed shoulders' with non-aristocratic fellow citizens. Etymology implies that the hippeis were originally those who kept horses, specifically a horse (hippos) to be used in the cavalry, while the term zeugitai, 'oxen-yokers', implies that these were smaller landowners who could afford oxen to plough the fields. Hesiod's advice to a farmer is to buy an ox as one of the most essential items: 'first of all you should acquire a house and a (slave) woman and an ox for the plough' (Hes. *Works and Days* 405: doc. 5.12). The word 'thes' in Homer usually refers to a labourer, but in Athens was used of the poorer farmers. The thetes in the fifth century BC became extremely important as the rowers in Athens' fleet of triremes with which it defeated the Persians at Salamis in 480 BC and afterwards maintained its hegemony over the Aegean.

Upward 'political mobility' through the classes is testified to by the example of Anthemion son of Diphilos: he was a thes who increased his wealth to the extent that he became a hippeus, skipping the zeugitai altogether. His dedication on the acropolis includes a statue of his father Diphilos and next to it that of a horse, confirming that hippeis were those who could afford a horse or horses (*Ath. Pol.* 7.4: doc. 8.16). This ability to move between classes was an incentive, either deliberate or accidental, to encourage farmers to work their land productively, and can be seen as part of Solon's agricultural measures (see below).

The empowerment of the poor was a crucial aspect of this political system, for they had been complaining bitterly that they had no share in the politeia (*Ath. Pol.* 2.3: doc. 8.7). Prior to Solon the Areiopagos simply summoned and appointed those it considered 'suitable' to hold the offices of state as magistrates. Under Solon's constitution each tribe elected ten candidates for the archonships, and the archons were chosen by lot from these. The treasurers were also chosen by lot, from the pentakosiomedimnoi, and this was presumably the case with the other officials as well (*Ath. Pol.* 8.2: doc. 8.17). Solon retained the existing four Ionian tribes (phylai), whose officials played a role in gathering and expending revenue (*Ath. Pol.* 8.3: doc. 8.18).

The Council of Four Hundred

Athens already had a council, the Areiopagos, but Solon created another, the Council of Four Hundred, simply known as the boule (literally 'council'). One hundred members were chosen from each of the four tribes, from the top three classes: so this boule was very representative of the Athenian citizen body. Under Kleisthenes' reforms of 508/7 BC its numbers were increased to 500. The *Athenaion Politeia* points out that Solon gave the Areiopagos guardianship of the laws (*Ath. Pol.* 8.4: doc. 8.19), which now became its main role given that it no longer appointed state officials. The function of the boule, Solon's Council of Four Hundred, is not made clear by the *Athenaion Politeia*, so the boule's role later in Athenian history must serve as a guide to the functions Solon intended for it. That role was to draw up the agenda for the assembly and to put into formal wording proposals for actions to be discussed and voted upon by the assembly. Why this role was not given to the Areiopagos seems clear: it was a conservative council, and although Solon's change to its membership, with archons joining it after their year of office, made it less aristocratic over time, Solon may have believed

Figure 8.3 In the foreground, the Areiopagos at Athens, where trials for homicide and some religious offences were held, with the Acropolis in the background. Photo © Colin Hepburn.

that making it responsible for the agenda-setting process for the assembly would undermine his other reforms which aimed to broaden out political participation. There were also two councils in Chios in the mid-sixth century BC (Meiggs and Lewis 8C: doc. 1.46), so the situation is not as unusual as it sounds. Retaining the Areiopagos, however, made good sense: it could continue its role as guardian of the state and serve as a pool of collective wisdom as each year's archons joined it. Furthermore, to abolish it would also have led to discontent from its members. It remained the only office in democratic Athens which was held for life: when the author of the *Athenaion Politeia* states that Solon made the Areiopagos responsible for judging those who might attempt to put down the democracy, he is being anachronistic, as this was not yet a democratic system. However, under Solon the Areiopagos was charged with guarding the constitution as a continuation of its existing political role (*Ath. Pol.* 8.4: doc. 8.19).

In constructing his new political system, Solon was guided by his own political beliefs: he gave the people power, but only as much as 'was appropriate' (*Ath. Pol.* 12.1–2: Solon *Poem* 5: doc. 8.20). He was no crypto-democratic, ushering in an era of democracy under the guise of a timocracy. He saw his system as a permanent solution to Athens' and Attica's problems. Moreover, it was a balanced system, in which he did not allow either the people or those in power to triumph over the other, as shown by one justly famous line of his poetry, 'I stood firm holding my strong shield in defence of both' (Solon *Poem* 5: doc. 8.20). For him, the people needed leaders which they would follow. They would only follow if they were neither oppressed nor allowed too much freedom. In his view the ordinary people were not of 'sound' mind, and he uses this word in the sense that the ordinary farming people were not intelligent enough to govern the state (*Ath. Pol.* 12.1–2: Solon *Poem* 5: doc. 8.20). This was a concept which democratic Athens from 508 BC was to reject completely.

The law against political apathy

Perhaps strangely, for a statesman concerned with civil strife and intent on preventing it, he introduced a law against political apathy, and was clearly concerned that some citizens took no active part in the political situation despite past events (the enslavement of farmers and the conflict between the rich and the poor). Those not willing to take up arms 'at the service of one side or the other' would now lose their citizen rights (*Ath. Pol.* 8.5: doc. 8.21). As Perikles said some 160 years later, the Athenians regarded the citizen who took 'no part in the affairs of the city not as one who minds his own business, but as one who is totally useless' (Thuc. 2.40.1: doc. 1.17).

Solon's social and judicial legislation

In the *Politics*, Aristotle notes that Solon established a 'traditional democracy' with mixed constitutional elements, the Areiopagos being oligarchic, the officials chosen from the wealthy aristocratic, and the law-courts democratic. Fourth-century critics of Solon claimed that giving power to the law-courts led inevitably to democracy, because these had supreme power. But Aristotle notes that it was not Solon's intention that Athens become a democracy, and that this phenomenon was caused by several later developments: the curtailment of the powers of the Areiopagos under Ephialtes, the introduction of pay for attendance as a juror in the law-courts by Perikles, and the people's growing power as a result of victory in the Persian Wars (because it was mainly the thetes who rowed the ships at Salamis and Mykale). What Aristotle fails to mention is that it was in fact Kleisthenes' democratic reforms of 508/7 BC which made Athens a democracy. Solon, therefore, did not found a fully fledged democracy, but by broadening political participation, and establishing law-courts, he created a system that was relatively democratic in many of its features as was recognised by the *Athenaion Politeia*. It was, moreover, a system that was able to metamorphose relatively easily into a democracy when historical conditions permitted this in 508/7 BC. Significantly, conservative Athenians citizens in fourth-century Athens looked back upon Solonian 'democracy' as preferable to 'Kleisthenic' democracy, as it was less radical, and Aristotle reflects this viewpoint (Arist. *Politics* 1273b35–1274a21: doc. 8.22).

The 'most democratic' aspects of the Solonian constitution

Three aspects of Solon's constitution struck the *Athenaion Politeia* as being the 'most democratic' of its elements (*Ath. Pol.* 9.1–2: doc. 8.23). Solon did not intend them to be 'democratic' as such, and the *Athenaion Politeia* is using the word more in the sense of 'popularist' or 'demos-oriented'. Firstly, loans could no longer be made on the security of the person: that is, Athenians could not borrow and give themselves as the guarantee (collateral) for any loan. Through his abolition of the hektemoroi Solon did away with obligations which if not met could lead to enslavement. To prevent any further such enslavement of Athenians was clearly one of his main concerns: the freedom of the citizen body was guaranteed.

The second and third most 'democratic' features related to the law-courts. Solon laid down that any individual could come to the legal assistance of another who was wronged. Athenian citizens as a whole were by this provision invited to take up the cause of those who were being unjustly treated and who did not have the confidence or ability to defend themselves. This was an extension of Solon's own authority as archon: he had taken up the cause of the poor, the enslaved and the disempowered, and he ensured that his stance could be followed by anyone who was interested in justice for all within the citizen body.

The third feature was the right of appeal (ephesis) to a law-court. If any Athenian citizen considered that a magistrate's verdict in a judicial case concerning him was unjust, he could then appeal to the courts against this verdict. That Athenians could now appeal against decisions of officials was meant to be a curb on the power of the wealthy and is a further indication that the main thrust of Solon's reforms was the protection of the poor. This was the first time that the ordinary people of Athens were given any judicial competence. Drakon's law on homicide had judicial groups of basileis and ephetai and did not allow for any participation by the people in general in murder trials. While the *Athenaion Politeia* uses the term dikasterion (plural: dikasteria) for the courts, Solon used the term heliaia for the court of appeal (see Lys. 10.16; Dem. 24.104). Precisely what the heliaia was is not clear from Solon's laws, but somehow it must have been a judicial body which was more representative than the magistrates in office. The *Athenaion Politeia* refers to Solon's heliaia by the term dikasteria, and sees Solon's reforms as eventually giving the demos power over the state, with the courts of the classical period drawn from all the four property classes and so represented Athenians in general. This must mean that the heliaia were somehow drawn from the citizen body. According to the *Athenaion Politeia* it was Solon who first gave the thetes a role in the assembly and the law-courts, so these heliaia ('courts') were somehow constituted from the whole citizen body. The usual interpretation that the heliaia was the assembly sitting in judgement in a legal capacity must be incorrect as that would have been too cumbersome a procedure. Some system similar to the procedure known from the fourth century, when jurors were chosen from the citizen body, must be assumed.

Some Athenians in the fourth century BC thought that Solon's laws were deliberately obscure to ensure that matters had to be taken to court, thus giving the people control of private and public decisions as they were the ones who sat as jurors in legal cases. But it is unlikely that Solon made his laws intentionally unclear: he was after all aiming for a peaceful society (*Ath. Pol.* 9.2: doc. 8.23). Only from a later perspective were the provisions of some of his laws difficult to understand, possibly because after a few centuries his vocabulary had become archaic. But the *Athenaion Politeia* was correct: the law-courts controlled by the demos came to have wide political and social power, especially in the fourth century BC when proposals related to decrees and the decrees passed in the assembly could themselves be challenged by recourse to the courts.

Solon was also credited by Athenians in the fifth and fourth centuries with a great deal of social legislation. One reform that referred to Athenian weights, measures and coinage is discussed by the *Athenaion Politeia* (10.1–2: doc. 8.24). Reforming weights and measures would have been important for Solon because his timocratic system which distributed power according to wealth depended on counting measures (medimnoi) of agricultural produce. It was, therefore, crucial that all Athenians used the same standard system of measurement. As for currency, there was no coinage in Attica at this time, and coins seem to have been first used in the 550s, in the 560s at the earliest. It was only under the sons of Peisistratos that they first came into widespread use at Athens. Until then, the system used was one of iron spits (originally known as 'obols'), which the Spartans continued to employ for a considerable time after the other Greeks had abandoned this system. But as Solon reformed weights and measures it seemed logical to the later Athenians to assume that he also reformed coinage.

Solon on trade and agriculture

Idleness, according to Herodotos, became an offence under Solon (Hdt. 2.177.1–2: doc. 8.25) and Plutarch is wrong in attributing this measure to Drakon (Plut. *Solon* 17.1–3: doc. 8.4). This law was still in force in the fourth century BC. Similar laws were found elsewhere in Greece, which was a society dominated by work and the 'daily grind': life was hard for most, and 'idlers' and 'spongers' were frowned upon. The idea that Solon introduced any specific legislation concerning agriculture apart from his seisachtheia, and whether he took any interest in increasing trade and promoting crafts, is more contentious. He himself writes nothing about this in his poetry.

Information on Solon's legislation on trade and agriculture is only given by Plutarch, and it should, therefore, be viewed with some caution. Athenian trade was relatively backward in the seventh century BC, the reason being the city's lack of colonies. This was in contrast to the great coloniser Corinth which was developing a flourishing commercial empire (docs 1.61–2). According to Plutarch, Solon encouraged manufacture in Athens but no other sources mention this (Plut. *Solon* 22.1: doc. 8.27), although it has long been assumed that Plutarch's picture of Solon encouraging crafts finds confirmation in the archaeological record of Athenian pottery. An increase in the distribution of Athenian pottery in the sixth century is often mentioned, but it is not a huge upsurge, and an expansion of the pottery industry hardly amounts to an industrialisation process. Athens was not to become in any sense a manufacturing centre until a good century or more after Solon's reforms. Athenian pottery starts to show distinct Corinthian influence in this period and this has been taken to suggest that Corinthian potters made their way to Attica, reflecting encouragement of trade by Solon. However, the evidence for the numbers of potters in Athens in the sixth and fifth centuries, possibly comprising 100 with about half of these being foreign in origin, seems to militate against a

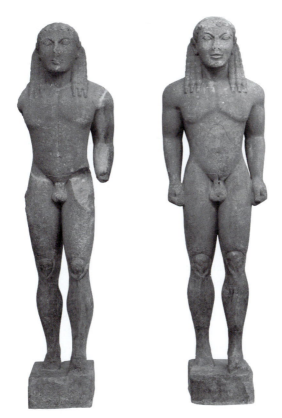

Figure 8.4 Life-size statues of Kleobis and Biton who, according to Solon, received the greatest possible blessing from Hera. Delphi Archaeological Museum. Photo © Hellenic Ministry of Culture and Tourism / Archaeological Receipts Fund.

large number of immigrants, although there were apparently some. These immigrant potters, and other craftsmen, were skilled workers (they were not farmers as only Athenian citizens could own land), and Solon is said by Plutarch to have given them citizenship (Plut. *Solon* 24.4: doc. 8.28). Furthermore, the spread of Attic black-figure ware throughout the Greek world from the early sixth century on cannot be taken to reflect (as it often is) an 'industrialisation' of Athens, because this is only one 'industry', which was carried out by small numbers of individuals. Essentially, the pots, used as containers, suggest a steady trade, probably in olive oil. Solon was concerned with agriculture rather than manufacturing, and Peisistratos' main 'economic' concern was also to be with farmers (doc. 9.16). Attica was always primarily a land of farmers, and this was especially true of the sixth century. Plutarch's quaint picture of Attica being swamped with immigrants from other cities is colourful, imaginative and totally unhistorical.

More importantly, Plutarch states that Solon prohibited the sale of all agricultural produce for export except that of olive oil. He states that the first axon of Solon recorded this law, although not all historians accept this as proof that from 594 BC only olive oil could be exported from Attica: rejection or acceptance of many of Solon's laws as reported by Plutarch and some earlier classical sources is often a case of simple faith. In reality, as the

315

Athenian population grew, demand for grain outstripped its production and within a century Attica was consuming boatloads of grain imported from the Black Sea region. Solon may well have prohibited the sale of grain outside Attica precisely because in 594 BC the population already needed every ear of grain it grew, and this law may have been passed in the context of an actual or potential food crisis. It is also possible that large landowners were selling grain abroad in a time of shortage for higher returns than they could receive in Attica. While this is his most famous law concerning agriculture as such, Solon is not known to have actually encouraged the planting of olive trees and the development of oleoculture. Rather, he was attempting to prevent the export of grain. It is possible, however, that with the prohibition on grain exports, olives, a much longer-term resource, may have been cultivated more extensively and/or intensively and this may explain the increase in Attic pottery exports. Olive trees were sacred to Athena and jars of sacred oil were presented as prizes at the Panathenaia (Dem. 43 *Against Makartatos* 71: doc. 1.15).

Solon's apodemia

Following the end of his archonship and perhaps tired of criticism of his reforms (see below, p. 318), Solon decided to leave Athens and travel: this was his apodemia, his 'journey abroad'. Herodotos presents him as visiting two kings: Croesus, king of Lydia, in Sardis (who reigned 560–546 BC) and Amasis (who reigned 570–526 BC) in Egypt. Solon himself writes in a poem that he visited Egypt (Plut. *Solon* 26.1 (Solon *Poem* 28): doc. 8.34) and that the man with friends in foreign countries was fortunate (Solon *Poem* 23: 8.39). His trip to Egypt is well known in other sources as well, and the *Athenaion Politeia* has Solon travelling there after his archonship 'for trade and to see the country' (*Ath. Pol.* 11.1–2: doc. 8.35). Herodotos notes that Solon's law on idleness was borrowed from Egypt (Hdt. 2.177.1–2: doc. 8.25), and, if this is true, perhaps Solon was curious to see the country; Greeks had resided there at least from the seventh century BC (Hdt. 2.152.3–154.5, 178.1–181.2: doc. 2.31).

Herodotos' account in which Solon visits Amasis and then Croesus immediately after his archonship presents chronological problems, for Solon as archon and law-giver in 594/3 cannot have visited Croesus and Amasis in a trip beginning soon after this date. This has led some scholars to 'downdate' Solon's archonship, that is, to place it in the period when these two kings were both in power. This is impossible, as his archonship and his reforms are firmly dated to 594 BC. In considering why Herodotos, or his sources, wished to set Solon alongside Amasis and Croesus, an understanding of Herodotos' portrayal of Croesus is crucial (the visit to Amasis is not described). In Herodotos' account, Solon inadvertently insulted Croesus, when Croesus showed Solon all his treasures and accoutrements of power and then asked him, having heard of Solon's wisdom, who was the happiest among mankind. Croesus was taken aback when Solon did not choose Croesus himself and instead named an Athenian, Tellos, who died in battle after a prosperous life leaving behind 'fine sons'. Croesus asked the question again, expecting to get second place. But Solon awarded this to Kleobis and Biton, two Argive youths who, when their mother was late for a festival of Hera because the oxen had not arrived home, dragged her themselves to the festival in the family ox-cart. The entire crowd at Hera's temple admired the sons when they arrived and the proud mother prayed to Hera that her sons receive the greatest possible blessing: in answer to her prayer, they fell asleep in the temple and never woke up. Statues were made of them and set up in Delphi, and two kouroi at Delphi sculpted in about 600 BC are conventionally named as this pair (Fig. 8.4).

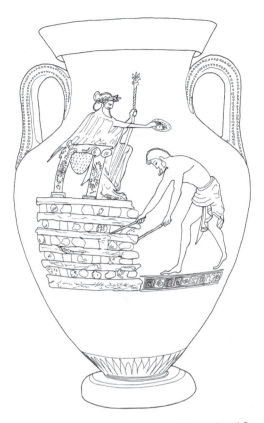

Figure 8.5 Croesus about to be burned to death on a pyre at the order of Cyrus; according to Herodotos as he was about to die Croesus spoke Solon's name three times. Athenian red-figure amphora, by the painter Myson; height: 59.5 cm; Louvre, G197, Paris. Drawing by J. Etherington.

Angered by this second response, Croesus asked Solon for an explanation as to why his wealth was not sufficient for him to be judged as the happiest of men. Solon replied that no man could be judged truly happy until he was dead. This was proved in the event in Croesus' own case, and when, having lost his empire to the Persians, he was about to be burned to death by his victor Cyrus, he spoke Solon's name aloud three times. Cyrus, curious, inquired why, and on hearing the explanation and realising the truth of Solon's words, ordered the fire to be extinguished. As it had taken too great a hold, Croesus called upon Apollo who sent rain to douse the flames and extinguish the pyre (Hdt. 1.30–33, 86–87). The incident is naturally not historical: Herodotos is here using the two contrasting characters of Croesus and Solon, a sage noted for his wisdom, to point to his own Herodotean philosophy about life, happiness and success. Solon was one of the Seven Sages, the others being Bias of Priene, the Spartan ephor Chilon, Kleoboulos of Rhodes, Periander the tyrant of Corinth, Pittakos the tyrant of Mytilene, and Thales of Miletos. This story of Solon and Croesus was known in Athens and is featured on a magnificent early fifth-century red-figure amphora (Fig. 8.5).

Reactions to Solon's legislation

When criticised over his legislation, Solon wrote additional poems in response to justify his actions. These poems defending his measures were probably composed after he completed his year as mediator and archon, although he may also have penned some during his archonship to convince the Athenians that his approach was the correct one and that his legislation was for the best. Solon's own view of his political reforms was that he had given the people as much political power as was appropriate, considering that the people should not be too free, yet not restrained too much. Moreover, he had also protected the powerful and the wealthy, defending both sides with his 'strong shield' (*Ath. Pol.*12.1–2 (Solon *Poems* 5, 6): doc. 8.20). However, in the event, he was criticised by both sides. He justified his actions by stating that the people had gained more than they had ever dreamed of, and that if someone else had been in charge, that person would not have restrained the people but allowed them to 'skim the cream off' the wealthy (*Ath. Pol.*2.3–5 [Solon *Poems* 34, 36, 37]: doc. 8.12).

According to Herodotos, the Athenians swore to observe Solon's laws for ten years; the *Athenaion Politeia* states for 100 years (Plut. *Solon* 25.1–2: doc. 8.33). Whichever was correct, within a few years the Athenians were at odds over the archonship, but it is not clear whether this implies that they were not observing Solon's laws and were ignoring his reforms. Certainly, when Peisistratos and his sons were in power as tyrants later in the century, they 'observed the laws', even those regarding the appointment of officials, although they somehow managed to ensure that their supporters were in office. When the tyranny ended in 510 and the Spartans attempted to install an oligarchy, the people rose up and besieged the Spartans on the acropolis: the demos was not willing at that point to give up its rights and privileges as guaranteed by the Solonian constitution.

Solon's policies, therefore, did not solve all Attica's problems immediately. In the fifth year after his archonship and reforms there was a period of anarchy, 'anarchia' (590/89 BC), that is, no archon was elected, and again in the fifth year after that (586/5 BC). Shortly afterwards the archon Damasias exceeded the year of his office. Presumably he initially had some support for this, but he was then ousted by force by his opponents, having held the office during 582/1, 581/0, and two months of 580/79. He may perhaps have been aiming to establish a tyranny. An unusual board of ten archons replaced him for the following year in 579/8 BC: five were eupatridai, three farmers, and two craftsmen. This differed from the arrangements which Solon had made for the election of the ten archons, and the three groups do not seem to match up with Solon's four classes. No mention is made of whether one of these was an eponymous archon and the account of the *Athenaion Politeia* seems against this (*Ath. Pol.* 13.1–3: doc. 8.36). There was apparently no further dissension over the archonship, so presumably the Athenians settled down to abiding by the Solonian constitution, and the archons were once again elected regularly.

Nothing is known of the years from 579/8 down to around 561, except for some general remarks by the *Athenaion Politeia* concerning general discontent in Attica due to a variety of reasons: the 'cancellation of debts' (the term seisachtheia is not used here) had made some Athenians poor (which seems unlikely and a fourth-century misunderstanding of what the seisachtheia actually involved as it was not a cancellation of debts); others were discontented by the great changes to the politeia; while yet others were engaged in personal rivalries (*Ath. Pol.*13.1–3: doc. 8.36). The last point related to the difficulties that first emerged in 561, which is the next topic considered by this source, when, following this passage, the *Athenaion Politeia* (doc. 9.2) goes on to describe the situation between Megakles, Lykourgos and Peisistratos, and the latter's seizing of power as a tyrant in 561. No precise chronological information is given for the years between c. 580 and 561, apart from the unrest among the Athenians.

Solon and tyranny

Solon specifically states that although he could have become tyrant he did not choose to do so, priding himself on repudiating tyranny, associating it with 'cruel violence', and on sparing his country tyrannical rule (Plut. *Solon* 14.4–9 [Solon *Poems* 32, 33]: doc. 8.38). Whatever he achieved, he did so without using the 'force of tyranny' (*Ath. Pol.*12.3 [Solon *Poem* 34]: doc. 8.12). Aristotle notes that many tyrants come to power through being elected to a magistracy or from being champions of the people (Arist. *Politics* 1305a7–27: doc. 7.65). When Peisistratos first seized power as tyrant in 561 BC, Solon was apparently still alive, and dramatically warned the boule, rushing into a meeting with his armour on; the Athenians had only themselves to blame, he stated, if they were now 'in servitude to a ruler' (Solon *Poems* 9–11: docs 8.37, 9.4). Above all, Solon claimed that he himself was a man of principle, attempting to do the 'right thing' politically by both poor and rich.

Solon's 'human side' is shown by his love of 'dear children', horses, hunting and friends in foreign places (Solon *Poem* 23: doc. 8.39), but it is for his political reforms that he is chiefly known. Solon prevented the enslavement of the people, provided the farmers with a fresh economic start, and reinvigorated Athenian political life. He had an immense impact on Athens socially and economically, paving the way for Athens to become the greatest city of the ancient Greek world. As a reformer, he is often considered to be the 'father of democracy'. This is true to some extent for he had empowered the demos and it now had real authority, although he himself considered that the people should follow its leaders and not grasp at too much power. Yet by allowing the demos an important and crucial role in the state he allowed for it to have certain political rights and when in 508 BC it seemed as if the citizens at large would lose these they reacted and ensured they retained these rights, with Kleisthenes building on Solon's consitution to turn Athens into a democracy.

9

PEISISTRATOS AND HIS SONS

Introduction

Solon's reforms resolved the dissension between the rich and the poor, and the latter now had political power, freehold title to their land, and a guarantee against enslavement. But such a radical change, as could be expected, resulted in an uneasy state of affairs in Athens and some degree of unrest. Solon's politeia, however, was generally accepted by the Athenian citizenry, and the next major phase of Athenian history did not concern such socio-economic issues as he had dealt with, but rather saw the emergence of political tension between three aristocrats vying for personal power over the state. This seems to be a manifestation of what was occurring generally across the Greek world during this period. Solon had been aware of this possible danger and stated his opposition to tyranny, although his friends pointed out that it was a phenomenon elsewhere (Solon *Poem* 32: doc. 8.38). In Athens at this time three men each sought to dominate the Athenian state: Lykourgos (not to be confused with the Spartan law-giver of the same name), Megakles and Peisistratos. The last – Peisistratos – emerged as the victor after a long struggle, and established a tyranny for himself and his sons. The period 561–510 BC is one of the most interesting and fascinating in Athenian history, involving club-wielding bodyguards, a faked murder attempt, impersonation of a goddess, sexual intercourse 'in an unnatural way', homoerotic relationships, an insulted aristocratic girl, and assassination and torture. Herodotos comments that the Athenians were supposed to be the wisest of all Greeks, but that they did not display much intelligence when they allowed themselves to be tricked by the Phye incident – the 'most simple-minded ruse' that Herodotos had ever encountered – although they were, of course, always amenable to good theatre (Hdt. 1.60.3: doc. 9.6).

Sources

Herodotos, Thucydides and the *Athenaion Politeia* provide the main sources for this period, which is quite well documented in the ancient literature, in addition to a range of archaeological and artistic evidence. Herodotos is concerned largely with the way in which Peisistratos eventually came to power, but it is the *Athenaion Politeia* which provides details about the tyranny itself. This text is quite favourable to Peisistratos' tyranny itself, but also reflects the popular tradition in which the reigns of his sons (Hippias and Hipparchos) were seen as being much harsher in character. Thucydides is not concerned with Peisistratos, but introduces a digression on the sons when he discusses the Athenian fear in 415 BC that there was a plot to overthrow the state. He provides a different view from that of the *Athenaion Politeia*, and rather than seeing the entire period of the sons' tyranny as negative, concentrates on the period before the assassination of Hipparchos in 514 BC. Moreover, he is concerned to correct what he views as popular misconceptions about the tyranny, and provides a valuable lesson for any historian in how events can be misremembered over time (Thuc. 6.55.1–3: doc. 9.20). This era also marks the beginning of an official epigraphic record for the Athenians, with the tyrants setting up public inscriptions. Another inscription, dating to the fourth century (which lists the eponymous archons of Athens), presents a controversial piece of evidence, for the first letters of the names of the archons for 527–522 are missing (see below, p. 333). This allows for the possibility that Kleisthenes as a member of the Alkmeonidai was archon in Athens in 525 BC (*IG* I³ 1031a: doc. 9.24), while the sources state that the family was in exile for the duration of the tyranny (Hdt. 1.64.1–3: doc. 9.14; [Arist.] *Ath. Pol.*20.1–5: doc. 10.6). The historian is, therefore, faced with several issues relating to the sources in dealing with this period.

The three 'parties'

Regionalism only emerged as a problem in Attica in the 560s BC. This term refers to the three main geographical areas of Attica which were led by three individuals, and Herodotos describes three staseis (singular: stasis), or factions, three groups in conflict with each other over the control of Athens and Attica. Lykourgos was the leader of the Athenians in the plain (those 'ek tou pediou': the pedieis, or 'plainsmen'); Megakles led those of the coast (the paralioi, 'coastal men'), and Peisistratos led the people who lived in the area behind the ridge running from Parnes to Brauron, in eastern Attica: they were referred to as those living 'beyond the hills', and the technical terms for these were the hyperakrioi ('those beyond the hills': Herodotos), or the diakrioi (the 'hillsmen': *Athenaion Politeia*). Peisistratos himself had estates at Brauron. But hyperakrioi, 'the men from beyond the hills', is a designation which would have been used by those for whom the hills were some distance away, and so would have been employed by the men of the coast and the plain to refer to the third group; diakrioi is probably the term which was used by Peisistratos and his supporters to describe themselves (Hdt. 1.59.3: doc. 9.1; *Ath. Pol.*13.4–5: doc. 9.2). In referring to the diakrioi the *Athenaion Politeia* is therefore more correct, in that diakria is the name of a specific geographical area, although the translation of diakrioi as 'hillsmen' requires some caution and major qualification: poor hillsmen existing on a subsistence livelihood is not an appropriate picture, as the diakria was as prosperous as the rest of Attica. The three regions were primarily agricultural-geographical regions: 'each group took its name from the area it farmed' (*Ath. Pol.*13.5: doc. 9.2). Attica was a land of farmers, as Solon's reforms had ensured.

Support for each of the three groups may also have come from outside of their specific area; Peisistratos certainly had support from malcontents, as well as from a group who were concerned about the possibility of losing citizen rights. Aristotle (*Politics* 1305a22–4: doc. 7.67) shows Peisistratos as a tyrant exploiting the hatred of the wealthy; this might over-state the case, but the sources agree that the poor were among his adherents. These three men led staseis which can be translated as factions, groups or very loosely as 'parties', but not in the modern political sense of the word. Based on regional areas, they had the potential to split Attica territorially, undoing the ancient synoikismos of Theseus (Thuc. 2.15.1–2: doc. 1.56); one of the main concerns of the later Athenian reformer Kleisthenes in 508/7 BC was to prevent geographical dysfunction within Attica by integrating disparate local areas into greater units so that there were no discrete, politically independent geographical units (see Chapter 10).

Lykourgos

Little is known of Lykourgos: he was the son of one Aristolaides, and after his role in the events which ousted Peisistratos from tyranny in 561 and again in 556 BC, nothing is known of his actions and he disappears from the historical record. According to the *Athenaion Politeia* he led the 'men of the plain' who wanted an oligarchy: presumably they were unhappy with Solon's politeia and the extension of power it had granted. This fertile agricultural plain was the area west of the city of Athens, where his descendants are known to have farmed.

Megakles

Megakles belonged to the Alkmeonidai family; he was the grandson of the Megakles who married Agariste, the daughter of the tyrant Kleisthenes of Sikyon (Hdt. 6.126.1–131.1: doc. 7.6). The Alkmeonidai were banished from Athens as polluted following the Kylonian affair (so c. 632 BC or soon after: Hdt. 5.71.1–2; Thuc. 1.126.3–12; *Ath. Pol.*1: docs 7.21–3). They were considered an 'accursed' family because of their role in killing the supporters of Kylon when these had taken sanctuary on hallowed ground. They were now clearly back in Attica, but were to go into exile again several times: when Peisistratos seized power for the third time, after Hipparchos' assassination, and after Kleomenes' second invasion of Attica. Megakles' son Kleisthenes was the Athenian political reformer of 508/7 BC. Perikles was related to the family and was 'tainted' too by the curse; when the Spartans in 432 BC demanded that the 'curse' be driven out, they were specifically aiming at the expulsion of Perikles (Thuc. 1.139.1: doc. 13.4). The land of Megakles and his supporters was centred on the south-eastern coastal region and extended close to Athens. Their 'middle-of-the-road' constitution may well have meant support for Solon's politeia (*Ath. Pol.*13.4: doc. 13.4). Megakles' political principles were, however, reasonably flexible: he could unite with Lykourgos in driving Peisistratos from his first tyranny, then ally himself with Peisistratos to set him up in a second tyranny, and then combine with Lykourgos again to end the second tyranny and drive Peisistratos from Attica.

Peisistratos

Peisistratos is better known than the other two, precisely because he emerged as the successful contender for power. He was clearly the most prominent aristocrat in his own particular area, and his status as a popular leader made him especially important. He had two sons, Hippias and Hipparchos, by a first Athenian wife (who is unnamed). Two other sons, Iophon and Hegesistratos (also known as Thettalos), were children by his wife Timonassa from Argos, who was previously married to one Archinos (from Ambracia) of the Kypselids, the family of tyrants at Corinth. Both these women must have been dead by the time Peisistratos married Megakles' daughter (see below, p. 325). It was on account of this relationship with the Argives that Hegesistratos was able to bring one thousand Argive mercenaries to the battle of Pallene in 546 BC when Peisistratos claimed the Athenian tyranny for the third time (*Ath. Pol.* 17.3–4: doc. 9.18); later Hegesistratos was sent to govern the Athenian possession Sigeion in the Troad region.

The *Athenaion Politeia* described Peisistratos as 'demotikotatos', 'a great friend to democracy', which probably means he was a popular leader who espoused the cause of the ordinary Athenian citizen: given that the poor were among his followers this is a reasonable

Table 9.1 The family of Peisistratos

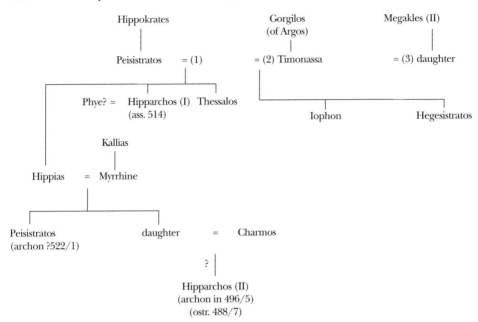

Source: Adapted from Davies (1971) Table I

description from a fourth-century BC point of view. He also attracted the support of those concerned about losing their citizen rights: these may well have been those made citizens by Solon, although the number of these cannot have been great (Plut. *Solon* 24.4: doc. 8.28). Certainly he seems to have protected their rights and possibly created new citizens: in 510 BC, after the overthrow of the tyranny of Peisistratos' sons, there was a review of the citizen body, and those who could not prove their citizenship were disenfranchised. This probably occurred because these individuals were guaranteed their citizenship by the tyrants who had now been expelled and were unpopular. It was presumably to this group that Kleisthenes gave back citizenship, once and for all (Arist. *Politics* 1275b34–8: doc. 10.15). Peisistratos also clearly had more of a 'public profile' than his two rivals: he was in a sense a 'national hero' because he had won a 'good reputation' in his command in the Athenian war against the neighbouring city of Megara to the south, having captured its main harbour Nisaia and performed other 'great deeds' of martial valour. There had been a long-running dispute between Athens and Megara which centred on the nearby island of Salamis; Solon had exhorted the Athenians not to give up the fight for the island. Peisistratos was presumably a general (strategos) in this command, indicating in itself that he must already have possessed an influential position in Athens (Hdt. 1.59.4: doc. 9.3; *Ath. Pol.*14.1: doc. 9.4; Solon *Poems* 1–3: doc. 8.8).

Peisistratos' first tyranny

In their bid for power Lykourgos desired oligarchy and Megakles a 'middle-of-the road' politeia, while Peisistratos wanted sole rule. In an age when Greece and its cities were dominated by tyranny, this requires no explanation. Kylon had attempted to establish a tyranny in Attica already, and Solon had ignored those who advised him to become tyrant. There was a clear possibility of a tyranny becoming established in Athens; all it needed was someone with sufficient support and ambition. In 561 BC, Peisistratos wounded himself and his mules, drove his cart into the Athenian agora, and convinced the people that he had been attacked by his political enemies. On the motion of Aristion he was awarded a bodyguard of citizen 'club-bearers' (korynephoroi) to protect him from his rivals; many tyrants had bodyguards and it was a common feature of their rule (docs 7.15–16, 7.19, 7.40, 7.43, 7.49, 7.62–5). An Athenian vase dating to c. 530–525 BC shows three club-bearers in single file preceding a fully clothed man wearing a himation (Fig. 9.1). This scene may well be a representation of Peisistratos and some of his club-bearers; these have their himatia draped over their left shoulders and arms and are ready for action, and are portrayed as solidly built and of splendid physique. His sons would later have spear-bearers, doryphoroi (Thuc. 6. 56.2, 56.4: doc. 9.30). When Peisistratos asked for a bodyguard, the *Athenaion Politeia* comments that 'it is said' that Solon spoke against it, and his poetry warning the Athenians against a monarchos, 'sole-ruler', may date to this time (Solon *Poems* 9–11: doc. 8.37). However, even the *Athenaion Politeia* seems to doubt that Solon was still alive in the 560s. Various anecdotal details of how Solon opposed Peisistratos before being won over by him are found, of course, only in Plutarch (*Solon* 30.5–31.5: doc. 9.5).

In the archonship of Komeas (561/0 BC) Peisistratos, with the assistance of his club-bearers, seized the acropolis which dominated the city and was easily defensible, in this way taking power. Both Herodotos and the *Athenaion Politeia* agree that he governed more in accordance with the existing (Solonian) politeia than as a tyrant, ruling moderately and managing public affairs with competence (Hdt. 1.59.6: doc. 9.3; *Ath. Pol.*14.3: doc. 9.4). Plutarch agrees, but seems to be writing of Peisistratos' tyranny in general rather than referring specifically to this first period (Plut. *Solon* 30.5–31.5: doc. 9.5). However, Megakles and Lykourgos, having lost

Figure 9.1 Three club-bearers, followed by a bearded man who is presumably Peisistratos (doc. 9.3). This is an Athenian black-figure vase of about 530 BC by the Swing Painter, with a height of 42 cm. National Archaeological Museum, Athens, inv. No. 15111. Photo © Hellenic Ministry of Culture and Tourism / Archaeological Receipts Fund.

out in the struggle (stasis) and obviously feeling disempowered, combined forces and in the archonship of Hegesias (556/5 BC) drove out Peisistratos after five years of power. Peisistratos then retired to his estates at Brauron.

Peisistratos' second tyranny

Megakles and Lykourgos soon fell out. Lykourgos was clearly the dominant partner, and as the disagreement between them was 'making life difficult' for Megakles he proposed a marriage alliance between his daughter and Peisistratos. Lykourgos' oligarchic views were clearly too narrow for Megakles' more moderate ones, and Megakles and his supporters may have felt they were being 'squeezed out' of political power. This marriage proposal took place 'not long after' the expulsion of 556/5 BC. It is known that Peisistratos returned for his third period of tyranny in 546 BC, ten years after being expelled from his second. His second reign as tyrant, therefore, which was not to last long, belongs to later in 556/5. Peisistratos came to power for the first time by faking wounds and a murder attack on himself, so his employing a charade in his attempt to win the tyranny for a second time is not surprising. Herodotos and the *Athenaion Politeia* both commented on the gullibility of the Athenians in falling for the drama enacted by Peisistratos and Megakles to achieve this return to power (Hdt. 1.60.1–5: doc. 9.6; *Ath. Pol.* 14.4–15.1: doc. 9.7).

Peisistratos returns with Athena

Megakles began the ruse by spreading a rumour that Athena, the goddess of Athens herself, was going to restore Peisistratos to power. Phye, a beautiful, tall young Athenian woman, was then dressed up in full armour to impersonate the goddess Athena Promachos ('Athena the Warrior'), the guardian of the city, who was worshipped on the acropolis. Standing in a war-chariot she struck up an imposing attitude, appropriate for a divinity, and messengers went ahead announcing that the Athenians were to accept Peisistratos back as Athena was restoring him to her own acropolis. Phye – as Athena – was driven into Athens by Peisistratos, with the people falling down in worship at the sight of her (Fig. 9.2). The Athenians in this way accepted Peisistratos back as tyrant. No evidence points to any cult ritual as the origin for this 'impersonation' and it was not customary for people to dress up as deities as part of religious festivals. Rather, the ruse was based on the belief that the gods could be present on earth and appear to mortals (a process known as an epiphany) and that they were interested in and participated in mortal affairs. The Athenians did not see Phye's chariot-ride as part of a festival ritual: they actually believed that she was the epiphany of Athena and they literally (and liberally) worshipped her as the goddess, believing the announcement made by the messengers whom Peisistratos had orchestrated in his own support (Hdt. 1.60.1–5: doc. 9.6; *Ath. Pol.* 14.4–15.1: doc. 9.7).

Megakles' support was on the condition that Peisistratos married Megakles' daughter, who, as an Athenian citizen woman, is not named (Hdt. 1.60.2: doc. 9.6). He did so, but within months (perhaps even weeks) he lost the tyranny for a second time as a result. Anxious mothers of newly wedded daughters throughout history in all societies where child-bearing is a woman's most important function naturally enquire about the possibility of a grand-child. Whether in answer to a question or not, Megakles' daughter admitted to her mother that her marriage had not been properly consummated. Peisistratos had adult sons already and apparently did not want any more children, presumably because he wanted his existing sons to inherit his tyranny. Moreover, the Alkmeonidai, including Megakles and his daughter, were said to be accursed because of the family's role in killing Kylon's supporters on sacred ground. Accordingly, to prevent the birth of further children, Peisistratos had not had intercourse with his wife 'in the normal way', as she finally informed her mother, who in turn told her husband Megakles. Megakles was so incensed at this insult to his daughter that he put aside his differences with his 'political opponents' (presumably Lykourgos and his followers are meant), and they took action, resulting in Peisistratos having to leave Attica altogether (Hdt. 1.61.1–2: doc. 9.8).

Herodotos' account is quite explicit and has raised some scholarly scepticism, and not a few eyebrows. Yet the details are intrinsically compatible with Peisistratos' circumstances, contemporary contraceptive practices, and the normal reactions of a Greek father to such a situation: the story is certainly true and no stranger than the other events with which Peisistratos was associated. His having intercourse with Megakles' daughter in an 'unnatural' way was a reference to anal intercourse, the method used by prostitutes in brothels and depicted frequently on Athenian vases. Peisistratos was treating his wife as a common whore, so avoiding the stigma of the curse of the Alkmeonidai. His father-in-law was, by ancient Greek standards, entitled to be extremely upset.

Figure 9.2 The goddess Athena. Dressed like this, with shield, spear, high crested helmet, and perhaps with the living snakes circling from her aegis, Phye impersonating Athena accompanied Peisistratos into Athens (doc. 9.6). This scene is from an Athenian red-figure vase dating to about 525 BC, probably by the Andokides Painter. Antikensammlung Staatliche Museen zu Berlin, F2159. Drawing by J. Etherington.

Peisistratos in exile

Leaving Attica, Peisistratos went to the city of Eretria on the nearby island of Euboea where he held a family council with his sons. Hippias, the eldest, who had probably gained a taste for power during his father's rule at Athens, persuaded his father that they should 'win back the tyranny'. Peisistratos was himself obviously a persistent character. He was to be away from Athens for ten years (556–546 BC) and his movements in that time are not altogether clear, but Herodotos and the *Athenaion Politeia* provide a framework of events prior to his returning to grasp the tyranny for a third time (Hdt. 1.61.3–4: doc. 9.9; *Ath. Pol.* 15.2: doc. 9.10).

From Eretria, Peisistratos helped to found a colony at Rhaikelos near the Gulf of Thermai in northern Greece. The nature of the assistance rendered is unclear: perhaps it involved helping to defeat some local peoples to ensure the security of the colony. Thrace was inhabited by warlike people, and an Athenian colony founded there in the fifth century was wiped out by the Thracians (Thuc. 1.100.2: doc. 12.9). Whether this Athenian colony consisted of the partisans who left Attica in exile with Peisistratos is unclear, but that he set out from Eretria to Rhaikelos and then at a late stage returned to Eretria suggests that he was helping the Eretrians establish a colony: they certainly showed their gratitude later in 546 BC. From Rhaikelos he first went to the region of Mount Pangaion in Thrace, an area rich in gold and silver, situated a few miles from the coast of Thrace and east of the river Strymon. Later in 437/6 BC the Athenians founded the colony Amphipolis on the Strymon, which was to play such a large part in Athenian affairs (Thuc. 1.100.3: doc. 12.9). Peisistratos must have been exploiting the Thracian mines and commenced a long Athenian interest in the area. With this gold and silver he hired mercenaries there (*Ath. Pol.*15.2: 9.10; cf. Hdt. 1.64.1: doc. 9.12), just as the Athenians employed Thracians as mercenaries in the Peloponnesian War.

Herodotos writes of Peisistratos and his sons raising money from cities that were in any way under obligation to them, especially from Thebes, Athens' powerful neighbour, which was presumably hoping to benefit should Peisistratos recover power at Athens (Hdt. 1.61.3–4: doc. 9.9). This suggests that in his two periods of tyranny and while in exile Peisistratos had been actively engaged in diplomatic relations with other cities, pursuing a 'foreign policy' with respect to other states. Nothing is known of what happened in Athens during his ten-year exile. He eventually returned to Attica in 546 BC, and with a considerable force, including the mercenaries he hired while in the Pangaion region, hippeis (cavalry) from Eretria, Thebans, Argive mercenaries and assistance from Lygdamis on the island of Naxos. This was clearly a considerable force. Lygdamis' presence is largely unexplained and he apparently 'turned up of his own accord'. He was later rewarded for this when Peisistratos established him as tyrant over the island of Naxos, which he used as a place to which to send hostages (Hdt. 1.64.2: doc. 9.14). On account of Peisistratos' friendship (philia) with the Argives, Hegesistratos, Peisistratos' son by his Argive wife, was able to bring 1000 Argive hoplites to his support (*Ath. Pol.* 17.4: doc. 9.18). The ties created by the marriage alliance were undoubtedly important, but some money may also have changed hands.

Peisistratos' third attempt at tyranny was not gained by rallying the populace, but through the use of military force, involving supporters from outside Attica. When he landed at Marathon, his supporters in the city and the countryside came out and joined him; Herodotos gives an account of the ensuing battle but curiously the *Athenaion Politeia* does not (Hdt. 1.62.1–63.2: doc. 9.11). That his popularity had survived his ten-year exile is a testimony to his personality and the favourable perception of his previous periods of tyranny. Sources do not reveal the course of events in Athens while he was away and the identity of those who served as archons in this period is largely unknown. The state of affairs in Attica may in fact have been quite unsettled. Marathon was chosen as his landing place both because of its proximity to Eretria, the hippeis of which were supporting his return, and because it was in Peisistratid territory; Peisistratos was clearly still popular in the region.

The battle of Pallene in 546 BC

The two sides met at the temple of Athena Pallenis, in the deme Pallene, where they took up opposing positions. Here a diviner named Amphilytos of Acarnania in southern Greece approached Peisistratos and under divine inspiration pronounced an oracle: 'the cast is thrown, the net is spread, the tuna-fish will come darting through the moonlit night.' This was not the first time an oracle had forecast Peisistratos' destiny, and his son Hippias also learned the future through consulting an oracular collection he kept on the Athenian acropolis, as well as by means of a dream he had in 490 BC.

Peisistratos 'accepted' the oracle, which validated it from the Greeks' point of view and 'made it come true', by attacking his opponents. Unfortunately for them they had just eaten lunch; some were enjoying a siesta and others playing dice and his forces fell upon them and routed them. It was hardly in the manner of the almost gentlemanly traditions of Greek warfare in which both sides lined up against each other and then commenced battle, but is a mark of the extraordinary combination of ruthlessness and mildness which comprised his character. Many of his opponents were slaughtered, and others began to run away, at which he put his sons on horseback and sent them to catch up with those fleeing the battle, with the message to tell the defeated 'to be of good courage and each return home'. In this way, while some did leave Athens, he prevented a large number of Athenians fleeing Attica who might later be a danger to his regime from a position of exile.

To ensure he did not lose power a third time, Peisistratos disarmed the citizens by means of a ruse (not his first). When he was addressing them as they stood equipped with their weapons at the Theseion (the temple of Theseus) in the agora, the people complained they were unable to hear him, so he told them to go to the gate (propylon) of the acropolis. While he was speaking there his supporters gathered up the Athenians' weapons, which they had obviously left at the Theseion so they would not have to walk the mile or so to the acropolis in full body armour. They stored the armour in buildings near the temple. The only time the Athenians were armed within the city in future was at the annual procession of the Panathenaia (Thuc. 6.58.2: doc. 9.30). At the acropolis, he told them he had confiscated their weapons but that they should not be worried: 'he was going to take care of all public business' (*Ath. Pol.*5.3–5: 9.13). Peisistratos' ruse can be accepted as historical given his previous success with the Athena charade, and throughout the events from 561 to 546 BC he appears in the guise of the Homeric Odysseus, full of wiles and stratagems.

Disarming the citizenry made ruling Athens easier. Moreover, most of his opponents on the battlefield were either dead or had accepted his sons' message to go home peacefully. But some had gone into exile, most notably the Alkmeonidai. One of the Alkmeonidai, Alkmeonides (Megakles' brother), had recently been victorious in the horse race at the Panathenaia, but had to make a dedication for this (inscribed on a marble Doric capital) at the sanctuary of Apollo Ptoios in Boeotia. This was because the family had gone into exile before he had a chance to make the dedication on the acropolis (*IG* I³ 1469: doc. 9.15). In addition, Peisistratos took as hostages the sons of the aristocrats who remained in Athens, and sent them to the island of Naxos, which he conquered, installing Lygdamis as tyrant as a reward for his assistance at Pallene (Hdt. 1.64.1–3: doc. 9.14). He also won over the aristocrats remaining in Athens by his fairness and by the fact that he mixed with them socially (*Ath. Pol.* 16.9: doc. 9.16). His was a mixture of force and leniency: the 'iron hand in the velvet glove'.

Peisistratos as tyrant

One entire chapter of the *Athenaion Politeia* is devoted to Peisistratos' reign as tyrant during the period 546–527 BC, and is the main source for his third tyranny (*Ath. Pol.* 16.1–10: doc. 9.16). Even in the fourth century BC, when tyranny had a negative reputation in Athens and the rest of Greece, the Athenians looked back to the rule of Peisistratos as a 'Golden Age', despite its bloody beginnings at the battle of Pallene. What the *Athenaion Politeia* actually states is that it was like 'life under Kronos', a mythical time when humans did not have to work, and the fields spontaneously bore crops, without the need for human effort. This is contrasted with the tyranny of the sons which was 'much harsher' than that of their father.

Many of Peisistratos' acts as recorded by the *Athenaion Politeia* were of an agricultural nature and benefited Attica's many farmers. He gained a reputation as a philanthropist by helping them survive any crises, so that they could make a living from their farms and stay on their land, scattered throughout the countryside. Because of this, they were able to farm in prosperity and not drift into the city, where they might have been in danger of becoming discontented and potentially the focus of unrest. Similarly Periander, as tyrant of Corinth, had not allowed people to lounge around in the agora doing nothing where they could possibly indulge in intrigue against his reign (Nicholas of Damascus *FGH* 90 *F* 58.1: doc. 7.15). But also, as the poor had supported Peisistratos, it was important to ensure the prosperity of this group, whose allegiance must now have been firmly with him more than ever before. Indeed, when the tyranny came to an abrupt end in 510 BC, the people gave no support to the aristocrats.

Taxation

Peisistratos exacted a 'dekate' from the Athenians, a tax of 10 per cent (otherwise known as a 'tithe'). Because the countryside was prosperous, the amount of state revenue was increased by the dekate levied from the farmers, whose self-sufficiency was one of Peisistratos' key concerns, and to which he contributed by supporting them in 'tough times'. An increase in the farmers' prosperity meant an increase in Peisistratos' revenues which was sizeable enough to be commented upon ('his revenue increased because the country was well-cultivated': *Ath. Pol.* 16.4: doc. 9.16). This suggests that during the third phase of the tyranny Peisistratos did not have revenue from silver or gold mines in Thrace as he had during his ten years of exile. The coins which seem to date to his reign vary markedly in their purity, indicating several sources for the silver, and at this period this coinage was modest with only a local circulation. The increase in the weight and the purity of the silver in the new coins which appear c. 525 BC after Peisistratos' death, the so-called 'owls', indicate that a new source of silver had been accessed (presumably Laureion, in Attica), which had been unavailable to Peisistratos.

This dekate and his regular visits to the countryside provide the context for one of the best-known incidents of Peisistratos' reign. When he was on Hymettos (presumably the slopes of Mount Hymettos are meant), he encountered a farmer trying to cultivate land that was extraordinarily rocky. Peisistratos sent his slave to ask the farmer what the farm produced: "'Nothing but aches and pains,'" replied the man, "and it's of these aches and pains that

Peisistratos ought to take his ten per cent!'" (*Ath. Pol.* 16.6: doc. 9.16). The farmer made this comment without recognising Peisistratos and the tyrant was impressed both by his outspokenness and his industry and declared the farm 'tax-free': the incident led to the farm actually being called 'the tax-free farm'.

Did this untaxed farm and its farmer exist? Even if they did not, the anecdote enabled the *Athenaion Politeia* to make some key points about Peisistratos. He rewarded the hard work of the farmer, but at the same time he was also pleased that the man spoke out against the tyrant and was prepared to criticise him openly. Peisistratos clearly did not impose strict censorship: there was no 'state-police' system as under Dionysios in Syracuse (Arist. *Politics* 1313a34–b16; doc. 7.69), and he did not deliberately 'impose burdens' on the people. This is in accordance with the details of his policy of supporting Attic farmers (*Ath. Pol.* 16.7: doc. 9.16).

Peisistratos and justice

Another important aspect of his rule was his attention to the law and legal processes. As part of his policy to keep the farmers prosperous, and in order to make them stay in their local area and out of Athens, he instituted a system of deme judges, so that each area had its own judicial system for settling disputes. More importantly, this meant that judicial authority was not in the hands of the local eupatridai and landowners, to whom the disputants probably would otherwise have turned. The *Athenaion Politeia* (26.3) states that the system of deme judges was instituted again in 453/2 BC, so apparently they were discontinued at some stage. Peisistratos himself often travelled throughout Attica dispensing justice, but with the emphasis on reconciling those who had disputes. He also possessed a reputation for mercy towards those who were convicted of wrongdoing (*Ath. Pol.* 16.2, 16.5: doc. 9.16). Herodotos writes of his first tyranny that he governed the state 'in accordance with the laws' (Hdt. 1.59.6: doc. 9.3), and the *Athenaion Politeia* confirms that it was his aim 'to administer everything in accordance with the laws'. Supporting the veracity of this aspect of his tyranny, the *Athenaion Politeia* recounts the story that when Peisistratos was accused of murder and summoned to the Areiopagos to answer the charge, he turned up, so recognising the importance and jurisdiction of this council (*Ath. Pol.* 16.8: doc. 9.16; Plut. *Solon* 31.3: doc. 9.5; see also Arist. *Politics* 1315b21–2), although Plutarch incorrectly places this incident in a passage which deals with Peisistratos' first tyranny.

The Solonian constitution

Peisistratos was also careful to observe the Solonian constitution – in so far as this was possible with one man in control of the state. Several comments are made about his constitutional rule in both the first and third of his periods of tyranny stating that he neither changed any law nor altered the magistracies: the second tyranny was too short for any verdict to be reached on its constitutional government (Hdt. 1.59.6: doc. 9.3; *Ath. Pol.* 14.3: doc. 9.4). Under Peisistratos the four Solonian classes (the pentakosiomedimnoi, hippeis, zeugitai and thetes) maintained their political powers, officials were elected, and Solon's laws observed, and the same was the case under his sons, with important political repercussions for Athenian constitutional development. That he ruled 'with moderation and constitutionally' rather than as a tyrant was the verdict given by the author of the *Athenaion Politeia* to this third period of tyranny, as he had to the first, despite the fact that Peisistratos had a more difficult task than other tyrants, for Attica was the largest state territorially on the Greek mainland and may well even at this stage have had the largest population.

Naxos was a notable conquest by Peisistratos, but otherwise he was known for keeping the peace (*Ath. Pol.*16.7: doc. 9.16). This may reflect not just the domestic but also the wider Greek situation, and Naxos may have been the only campaign of his reign. However, he had a very real interest in Delos, the sacred Aegean island of the Ionians, where Leto gave birth to the twins Apollo and Artemis. As the result of an oracle Peisistratos purified the island, by having the remains of all those who had been buried within sight of the temple dug up and moved elsewhere on Delos (Hdt. 1.64.2: doc. 9.17). Polykrates of Samos, who had established a thalassocracy ('sea power') over the Aegean, then conquered the island in what was clearly intended to be a display of his superior naval strength and ability as a tyrant (Thuc. 1.13.6, 3.104.2: doc. 7.33).

Religious policies

It is clear that religious concerns were a feature of Peisistratos' tyranny. The construction of the square telesterion at Eleusis, used for initiation into the Eleusinian Mysteries, is usually assigned to the period of his tyranny, and it was more than appropriate that he should pay Demeter such attention given his care for Athenian farmers. It was also a statement of ongoing Athenian control of Eleusis. Herodotos in his account of Peisistratos' first tyranny (Hdt. 1.59.6: doc. 9.3) writes that he made the city of Athens 'fine and beautiful', and his collection of the dekate contributed towards this policy later in his reign. While it is difficult to ascertain the exact details of his building programme it appears to have included at least one fountain-house (discussed below, p. 375).

Drama

It may also have been during Peisistratos' reign that the first dramatic performances were produced in Athens at the festival of the City Dionysia, in honour of the god Dionysos. Peisistratos may have overseen this development, and thus supported this festival and the development of tragic drama at Athens. Promotion and expansion of the Dionysia and Panathenaia, which were both celebrated in Athens itself, made the city a religious focal point and promoted it as the main centre of Attica. Problems of regionalism, which had been so evident in the 560s BC, may well have concerned Peisistratos. The Panathenaia, possibly established in 566 BC, was celebrated in the month Hekatombaion, with an especially magnificent, 'Great', celebration every fourth year. While there is only circumstantial evidence that Peisistratos instituted the Panathenaia, he certainly expanded it if it was already in existence after his seizure of power, and his sons, as can be seen in the account of the assassination of Hipparchos, took an active part in supporting it (see below, p. 338). Either Peisistratos or his sons had Homer's *Iliad* and *Odyssey* edited into its present literary form, and recited at each Panathenaia, and various lines about Athens seem to have made their way into the text. Peisistratos has also been credited with instituting the cult of Artemis Brauronia on the acropolis and the festival at Brauron, his home town.

The expansion of the Dionysia and Panathenaia indicate the development of 'civic cults'. These were promoted by the tyrants and, being organised by the state, lessened the influence of aristocratic cults. The family of the Boutadai (later the Eteoboutadai) continued to provide the priestess for the cult of Athena on the acropolis, but the Panathenaia lessened the significance of this as the state took the major lead in organising this birthday festival in the goddess's honour. It is also possible that Athena's escorting Peisistratos into Athens for his second tyranny may have been identified with the myth of Athena bringing Herakles to Mount Olympos in a chariot. This scene is shown on several vases of around 540–520 BC. It may point to a deliberate propagation of this myth as a means of recalling how Athena brought Peisistratos into the city in a chariot and commanded the Athenians to accept him as tyrant (above, p. 325). Peisistratos also seems to have stressed his ancestry while tyrant of Athens: the family claimed that they originated from Pylos in the western Peloponnese and were descended from Neleus, who was father of Nestor, the famous and aged king of Pylos portrayed in the *Iliad* as one of the chief advisors of the Greeks at Troy. Two Athenian kings, Kodros and Melanthos, were supposedly descendants of Neleus (Hdt. 5.65.3–4: doc. 9.37).

Peisistratos' family

Peisistratos died in 527 BC at an 'advanced age' (Thuc. 6.54.2: doc. 9.21) and there is nothing to indicate that he did not do so peacefully, as he was succeeded in a smooth transition of power by his sons. But having had three wives and at least four children, it is easy to understand that subsequent confusion arose in the Athenian oral tradition about Peisistratos' family. By his Athenian wife Peisistratos had two sons, Hippias and Hipparchos, who took over the tyranny as his successors when he died. Hippias was the senior partner in this tyranny (527–510 BC), but because it was Hipparchos who was assassinated in 514 BC, some Athenians came to think that he was the more important and elder of the brothers. Thucydides took some pains to correct this popular misconception, and dealt with it in two places in his history, the second time more fully. Hipparchos (despite his treatment of Harmodios' sister: see below, p. 338) was not the actual target of the assassination plot of 514 BC, which was aimed at Hippias, because he was the one who was the actual tyrant in charge of government (Thuc. 1.20.1–2: doc. 9.19). More importantly, Thucydides was able to examine the evidence of an altar and stele on the Athenian acropolis 'concerned with the injustice of the tyrants' (Thuc. 6.55.1–3: doc. 9.20). Clearly an altar was erected some time after the end of the tyranny in 510 BC to give thanks to the gods for Athens' liberation. The stele lists Peisistratos, then Hippias and his five children, before the other brothers and Thucydides specifically notes that the first son would naturally be married first. In any case, Hippias must have been the more important of the two brothers, for when Hipparchos was assassinated Hippias continued as tyrant without hesitation, for the citizens feared him and the mercenaries were obedient to him precisely because he was already in charge. If he had been a younger brother without experience in government his position would have been less secure.

The reign of the Peisistratidai

Hippias and Hipparchos – the Peisistratidai ('sons of Peisistratos') – took over the government of Athens in 527/6 BC, but Thucydides demonstrates that Hippias was the eldest and the one who was actually in charge. The writer of the *Athenaion Politeia*, who had presumably read Thucydides, agreed: Hippias was the elder and 'a natural politician', while Hipparchos was more interested in 'having a good time' and in homoerotic love affairs. He was deeply interested in the arts, sending a ship to bring the great poets Anacreon of Teos and Simonides of Keos, and their students, as well as other poets, to Athens (*Ath. Pol.*18.1: doc. 9.22; [Pl.] *Hipparchos* 228c: doc. 9.23). But there was more to running Athens than parties, poetry and love. Thucydides provides a crucial assessment of the tyranny of the two brothers, praising their wisdom, government, taxation, building projects, conduct of wars, piety and observance of the city's existing laws. Moreover he states that

Hipparchos, in the context of his assassination, is reported as having ruled lightly and 'without exciting hatred' (Thuc. 6.54.1–6: 9.21). It is almost as if Thucydides did not think he deserved assassination, and this is probably why he went to great lengths to prove that the assassination of Hipparchos was not in fact politically motivated but brought about through a personal love affair: 'a lover's distress' motivated the plot (Thuc. 6.59.1: doc. 9.32).

The archonship under the Peisistratidai

The control of Athens meant securing the political and military machinery of the state. Athenians still only had access to their arms on the day of the Panathenaic procession, and the tyrants possessed mercenaries and bodyguards, and were therefore relatively secure in power (Thuc. 6.55.3: doc. 9.20; 6.58.2: doc. 9.30). Hippias and Hipparchos observed the Solonian constitution but with an important caveat: 'they always made sure that one of their own people was in office' (Thuc. 6.54.6: doc. 9.21). Hippias' own son provides the best example of this: Peisistratos the Younger, named for his grandfather the tyrant, held the eponymous archonship in 522/1 (Thuc. 6.54.6–7: doc: 9.25; *IG* I³ 948: doc. 9.26). A stone fragment of the Athenian archon list gives the names of several archons for the period (*IG* I³ 1031a: doc. 9.24; Fig. 9.3). Not all of the names are fully preserved but one of them is clearly Miltiades, who is known to have been archon in 524/3 BC, while the name of the second archon after him can be reasonably restored as Peisistratos, who therefore held the archonship in 522/1 BC. Hippias himself is easily restored as the name of the archon in 526/5 BC. The other names, however, including that of Miltiades who was one of the Philaidai family, belong to non-family members, so when Thucydides wrote, 'one of their own people' he meant not just family members but also friends and supporters.

It is interesting that the name of Kleisthenes, who was a member of the Alkmeonid family, can be restored beside the year 525/4 BC in the archon list which has [.]leisthenes as the

Figure 9.3 The fragment of the archon list for the years 527/6–522/1 BC (doc. 9.24). In the third line, the Greek for the letters '-leisthen-' can be clearly read. Athens, Agora Museum I 4120. Drawing by J. Etherington.

archon for that year. If this is so, claims in the fifth century, reported by Herodotos (1.64.1: doc. 9.14), that the family, who had left Attica when Peisistratos returned for his third period of tyranny, had been in exile for the entire period from 546 (the battle of Pallene) until 510 BC are false. There are, however, other possibilities: the name Pleisthenes could be read in the list instead, or this archon may have been a Kleisthenes but not *the* Kleisthenes who was the political reformer of 508 BC. Alternatively, the Peisistratidai may have pursued a policy of reconciliation towards the Alkmeonidai and other exiles. This is perhaps supported by the fact that Peisistratos recalled Kimon from exile (Hdt. 6.103.2: doc. 9.27). If the Alkmeonidai had returned to Athens by 525 BC, they must have fallen out of favour once again, possibly as a result of the assassination of Hipparchos, when many Athenians were exiled (*Ath. Pol.* 19.1: doc. 9.33), for they were the most prominent family in the attempts to overthrow the tyranny subsequent to this event (*Ath. Pol.* 19.3: doc. 9.35). They were certainly in exile again soon after 514 BC and played a key role in overthrowing the tyranny of Hippias.

Miltiades ('the Younger'), archon in 524/3 BC, also belonged to an important Athenian family under the tyranny, that of the Philaidai. His uncle, Miltiades the Elder, had ruled the Chersonese as tyrant, as did his successors, his nephews Stesagoras and then Miltiades the Younger, who was later to flee the Chersonese in advance of the Persian invasion. His father Kimon had won two successive Olympic victories in the four-horse chariot race (in 536 BC and 532 BC), and had the second victory announced as that of Peisistratos, for which he was allowed to return to Athens from exile. He was victorious again in 528 BC, with the same team of mares who were accorded a prominent place of burial. Herodotos records a story that Kimon, the father of Miltiades the Younger, was murdered by the Peisistratidai when they succeeded to the tyranny (Hdt. 6.103.1–4: doc. 9.27). If this was the case, they may have thought that the presence of the head of the Philaidai in Attica was a political liability and,

Table 9.2 The Philaidai

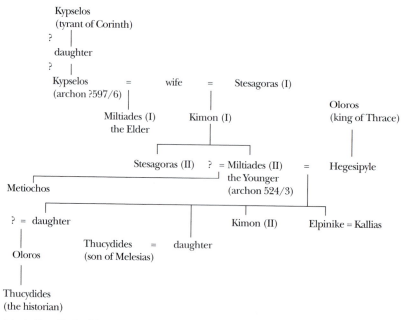

Source: Adapted from Davies (1971) Table I

when they allowed the younger Miltiades to leave Attica to succeed to the tyranny in the Chersonese, they presumably did so in order that he would be out of the way. On the other hand, Miltiades' rule as tyrant may be an indication that the Peisistratidai had not murdered Kimon. The fact that Miltiades the Younger was archon in 524/3 shortly after his father's 'murder' casts some doubt on Herodotos' story, especially since Miltiades was then sent officially to the Chersonese as tyrant. The Peisistratidai seemed to have continued their father's policy of enjoying a harmonious relationship with the aristocrats who stayed behind in the city after the battle of Pallene in 546 BC. The real hostility developed between these and the tyrants only with Hipparchos' assassination in 514 BC.

The tyrants and public works

A water-supply to households in Megara had been provided by the tyrant Theagenes when he built a 'fountain-house' (Paus. 1.40.1: doc. 7.20), a small building to which water was piped and from where it could be collected for domestic use. Similarly, the tunnel constructed under the mountain at Samos, which brought water to that city, appears to have been the work of the tyrant Polykrates (Hdt. 3.60.1–4: doc. 7.60). At Athens, a fountain-house known as the 'enneakrounos' ('Nine-Spouts'), was constructed, according to Thucydides, by 'the tyrants', while Pausanias specifically credits Peisistratos with this innovation (Thuc. 2.15.3–5: doc. 9.28). Pausanias describes the enneakrounos as situated in the agora, and it has been identified with a structure there, the south-east fountain-house: archaeological considerations date this construction to c. 520 BC. However, other fountain-houses were built in Athens in the same period and, while Pausanias places the enneakrounos in the agora, that is, west of the acropolis, Thucydides has it south of the acropolis. Thucydides' version is preferable given the archaeological date for the agora fountain-house, and Pausanias' fountain-house would therefore have been one of the several constructed by the Peisistratidai.

At the enneakrounos water was pumped through nine spouts and collected in large water jars (hydriai), usually by women and slaves. This water for the enneakrounos came from springs which were covered over in the building's construction. In ancient times and even in Thucydides' day the water from these springs was used at weddings and in religious rites (for purification). Many Athenian black-figure vases dating to the reign of the Peisistratidai show women collecting water at fountain-houses. They indicate that this provision of fresh, clean, running water was considered a great innovation in the city's amenities (Figs 5.3, 9.4).

Beautification of the city

Thucydides makes a particular point of recording that the Athenian tyrants 'beautified their city' (Thuc. 6.54.5: doc. 9.21). Other Greek tyrants did the same, and it is possible that there was some form of informal competition among tyrants as to who could best embellish their city. While it is unlikely that the building projects at Athens created widespread employment to stimulate the economy, they were important for the tyrants' 'public image'. They provided evidence that the tyrants were ruling for Athens' benefit and succeeding in this. The enlargement of the Eleusinian telesterion, the rebuilding of the temple of Athena Polias, the commencement of the Olympieion (the temple of Olympian Zeus), the wall Hipparchos constructed for the Academy precinct (proverbial for its expense), and the fortifications at Mounichia all belong to this period (*Ath. Pol.*19.2: doc. 9.35; Arist. *Politics* 1313b18–32: doc. 7.62; Fig. 9.7). The Olympieion was a long-term project and was completed some 600 years

Figure 9.4 Women collecting water from a fountain-house probably built by the tyrants (doc. 9.28); an Athenian black-figure vase of about 510–500 BC. New York Metropolitan Museum of Art 06.1021.77, New York. Drawing by J. Etherington.

later by the Roman emperor Hadrian. It is also possible that the remains of a building in the agora may be from the 'palace' of the tyrants.

Religious policies

To show their piety and religious leadership of the city, and so legitimate their rule, the Peisistratidai performed the prescribed sacrifices at Athens' temples (Thuc. 6.54.6: doc. 9.21). To commemorate his archonship in 522/1 BC Peisistratos the Younger (named after his grandfather the tyrant), the son of Hippias, dedicated two altars. One was an altar to the 'Twelve Gods' in the agora, the archaeological remains of which can be seen there today. Presumably, but not certainly, the twelve Olympian gods are meant. In addition, he erected an altar in the sanctuary of Pythian Apollo. The construction of both altars stresses that the family were concerned with religious practices, and the sacrifices made by the tyrants at these new altars provided a public, visible statement of their demonstrable piety towards the gods (Thuc. 6.54.6–7: doc. 9.25; *IG* I³ 948: doc. 9.26). The altar to the 'Twelve Gods' was a place of refuge and supplication, but was also important as the place from which distances were measured. A verse inscription nearby informs the reader that the distance from the harbour (at the Piraeus) to the altar was 45 stades.

Distances were also indicated by stone hermai (singular: herm), which Hipparchos set up throughout Attica, marking the distance between a deme (village) and the city of Athens. As well as serving this practical purpose, Hipparchos also sought to have the hermai enlighten those travelling within Attica by having pithy sayings carved on them, such as:

'A reminder of Hipparchos: do not deceive a friend'. Hermai such as these kept Hipparchos' name before the popular eye; perhaps they even played a part in the notion that he and not Hippias had been *the* tyrant. A herm was a short rectangular pillar with a head of Hermes (god of travellers) above it, with an ithyphallos carved on the front; not all of them measured distances and the best-known examples in classical Athens were those which stood outside houses and elsewhere as places of worship. Only one single actual distance-marking herm survives: it served as a marker on the road from the deme Kephale to Athens ([Pl.] *Hipparchos* 229a–b).

Financial policies

Peisistratos' 10 per cent tax did not impose financial burdens on the Athenians (*Ath. Pol.* 16.7: doc. 9.16). Even so, Thucydides notes that his sons levied a tax of only 5 per cent, a clear reduction (Thuc. 6.54.5: doc. 9.21). Despite this decrease in taxation, the sons clearly needed more money than their father: they had more extensive building projects, a court of poets to maintain, and wars to wage. However, the range of silver coinage, in terms of its quality and quantity, which was issued under their tyranny points to a new source of wealth. It is possible that the rich silver mines at Laureion, so important forty years later in 484 BC when these provided enough silver to build 200 triremes (warships), began to be worked during their tyranny and provided the state, which was always to own the mines throughout classical times, with enough silver to reduce taxation. The introduction of the fine 'owl' coin series seems to indicate that the tyranny of his sons had access to greater wealth than that of Peisistratos himself.

The assassination of Hipparchos

Despite Thucydides' positive comments about the tyranny, Hipparchos was assassinated in 514 BC and the tyranny came to an end a few years later in 510 BC. The main accounts are those of Thucydides, who clearly researched the matter closely and was interested in correcting popular misconceptions about the tyranny, and the *Athenaion Politeia*, which sometimes differs from Thucydides' account but not in any of the broad details (Thuc. 6.56.1–58.2: doc. 9.30; *Ath. Pol.* 18.2–6: doc. 9.31). The main difference is that the *Athenaion Politeia* incorrectly has Thettalos (Hippias and Hipparchos' younger brother) as the one whose behaviour triggered the plot against the tyranny. Thucydides' digression on the tyranny's downfall comes in the context of the investigation following the mutilation of the hermai in 415 BC, in his narration of events. The Athenians were suspicious that an attempt to overthrow the democracy was being planned: they remembered the stories about the tyranny and how harsh it had been in its later stages and were 'always afraid and suspicious of everything' (Thuc. 6.55.3: doc. 9.31). Both sources describe the original plan for the assassination and what went wrong with the conspirators' schemes.

Hipparchos, as noted, was fond of homoerotic love affairs, and sometime in 514 BC or shortly before he developed a sexual obsession for an aristocratic youth, Harmodios, who already had an older male lover, Aristogeiton. In Greek terms, Harmodios was the beloved, the eromenos, while Aristogeiton was the older lover, the erastes. Aristogeiton, 'suffering the pains of love and fearful of the power of Hipparchos in case he might procure Harmodios by force' (Thuc. 6.54.3: doc. 9.21), began to plan the downfall of the tyranny, clearly fearful that Hipparchos would gain access to Harmodios and rape him. Hipparchos did make further advances but made no progress, and clearly feeling slighted (as tyrant his love affairs had probably always proceeded smoothly), planned to insult Harmodios (Thuc. 6.54.1–6: doc. 9.21).

Matters came to a head at the celebration of the Panathenaia festival in 514 BC, which in that year was a Great Panathenaia, the especially magnificent celebration of the annual Panathenaia held every four years. Young unmarried women traditionally performed religious roles at festivals, and one of the most important of these was when a select few acted as 'basket-bearers' (kanephoroi, singular kanephoros) at the Panathenaia. They carried baskets which held ritual items needed for the sacrifice; an older woman in Aristophanes' play the *Lysistrata* recalls having been a kanephoros in her youth as one of her services to the state (lines 638–51: doc. 3.61). Hipparchos summoned Harmodios' sister (true to Athenian tradition, she is not named), but sent her away, spuriously arguing she had not been invited and that 'she was not fit to take part'. By saying this he insulted her and also her family: if she was 'not fit' to participate this was because she was not a virgin, and as an unmarried Athenian woman on the verge of marriage this was a great insult to her and her family. Aristogeiton, Harmodios' older lover, took this insinuation very badly on Harmodios' behalf, while the *Athenaion Politeia* also suggests that it was insinuated that Harmodios was effeminate, implying that, against all norms for well-born youths, he submitted to anal sex (*Ath. Pol.*18.2: doc. 9.31). In defending the honour of his beloved and that of his family, Aristogeiton was proving his love through his valour, as other male erastes did throughout Greek history (see docs 4.75–6).

Figure 9.5 In the centre of this Athenian red-figure stamnos dating to about 470 BC, Hipparchos is being assassinated by Aristogeiton on the left (bearded) who thrusts his sword into the tyrant, while on the right Harmodios (beardless), holds his sword up, ready for a downward thrust (docs 9.30–1). Three of Hipparchos' bodyguards (spear-bearers, the doryphoroi) are shown on the other side of the vase. Height of vase: 34.2 cm. Martin von Wagner Museum, University of Würzburg L515. Drawing by J. Etherington.

The two lovers chose the occasion of the celebration of the Great Panathenaia to be revenged for this insult as well as for the unwanted sexual approaches towards Harmodios: this timing made sense, firstly because this was the context of the insult to his sister and, secondly, because this was the only day of the year in which citizens could carry arms in the procession which was an integral part of the festival and which preceded the ceremonies on the acropolis (Peisistratos had confiscated the citizens' weapons in 546 BC and kept them locked away: *Ath. Pol.*15.4: doc. 9.13). To keep the conspiracy secret, only a few individuals were involved. Hippias was with his bodyguard at the Kerameikos, which was just outside the city-walls: it was the potters' quarters and a cemetery. The city gate here, the Dipylon ('Double Gate'), marked the beginning of the 'Sacred Way', the route from this entrance to the city to the acropolis where the Panathenaia would be celebrated. Hippias was organising the details of the procession and the order of its participants at the gate; clearly he was concerned that all the details of the festival went well. He was the conspirators' real target, and his death was to end the tyranny. Hipparchos was at a shrine nearby called the Leokoreion, organising proceedings at that point. The brothers expressed their piety as tyrants by paying meticulous attention to the celebration of the Panathenaia in honour of the state's (and hence the tyrants') protecting deity, Athena. Harmodios and Aristogeiton, armed with daggers, were near Hippias ready to kill him. But one of the conspirators approached Hippias and the two lovers thought their plan was foiled: they rushed away and coming upon Hipparchos stabbed him to death. Harmodios was killed on the spot by the tyrant's bodyguard, but Aristogeiton was captured alive.

Hippias reacted without panicking and instructed those in the procession who were bearing arms to put their weapons down, directing his mercenaries to seize the weapons. Anyone found with a dagger was arrested, for it was shields and spears that could be legitimately carried in the procession: those holding daggers were clearly part of the conspiracy. He wanted to disarm the citizens and to avoid a popular uprising. Although he was the senior tyrant and could take over power smoothly with his bodyguard, his exercise of that power was to change dramatically. Under torture Aristogeiton implicated numerous individuals in the conspiracy, both aristocrats and friends of the tyrants, wanting to make Hippias suspicious of everyone. And this is in fact what happened. Finally, in a slightly different account from Thucydides, the *Athenaion Politeia* recounts that under the duress of torture and wanting a quick death, Aristogeiton said that he would 'betray many others', convincing Hippias to shake his right hand as a sign of good faith. He then taunted him for taking the hand that had killed his brother; Hippias, enraged, drew his own dagger and killed him.

The tyranny becomes harsher

The assassination of Hipparchos was motivated, Thucydides insists, by a love affair (Thuc. 6.54.1, 6.59.1: docs 9.21, 9.32). There seems to have been no political agenda to it whatsoever, but the repercussions were wide and the ramifications crucial for Athenian history. Hippias was now frightened and executed many of the citizens, presumably those who had daggers in the procession along with the most likely of the suspects named by Aristogeiton. The tyrant became generally hated (according to the *Ath. Pol.*: doc. 9.33), but it must be stressed that crowds streamed out to Marathon to welcome Peisistratos back to Athens in 546 BC, and no ordinary Athenians took part in the deposition of Hippias in 510 BC. In his paranoia he began fortifying the famous hill, Mounichia, at Athens' port the Piraeus, while looking for some place of safety outside of Athens for fear of an uprising (Thuc. 6.53.3, 59.1–2: doc.

9.32; *Ath. Pol.* 19.2: doc. 9.35). In addition, he married his daughter to Aiantides, son of Hippokles, who was the tyrant of Lampsakos, on the eastern side of the Hellespont, and had great influence with the Persian king Darius (Thuc. 6.59.3: doc. 9.34). When he was ousted from the tyranny in 510 BC, Hippias went first to the Athenian colony at Sigeion, then to Lampsakos, and from there to Darius (Thuc. 6.59.4: doc. 9.39). Thucydides' comment that Hippias married his daughter to Aiantides 'though [she was] an Athenian' is out of context here and relates to the period after 451/0 BC when Perikles' citizenship law (*Ath. Pol.* 26.4: doc. 1.36) made marriages between Athenians and non-Athenians unattractive.

Hippias is said to have exiled many citizens, presumably aristocrats, as it was they who began a major armed campaign to oust him from power. The Alkmeonidai assumed the leadership of the Athenian exiles and made several attempts to attack Attica, all of which were unsuccessful, most spectacularly at Leipsydrion, below Mount Parnes. Here the exiles were joined by Athenians from the city, but they were forced to surrender. This event was commemorated in a skolion, drinking song, performed at symposia, from that time, by those on the side of the defeated (*Ath. Pol.*19.2–3: doc. 9.35). Another drinking song is recorded by the author of the *Athenaion Politeia*, who explains that, while the Alkmeonidai were mainly responsible for the expulsion of the tyrants, one Kedon (otherwise unknown) had also previously attacked them. The song therefore urges that he not be forgotten but be honoured as well by a libation poured in his honour as well as in honour of those involved in the battle of Leipsydrion (*Ath. Pol.* 20.5: doc. 10.6).

The overthrow of the tyranny by the Spartans

The Alkmeonidai and other aristocrats were certainly in exile after the assassination of Hipparchos, if not before, and even if Kleisthenes (now head of the Alkmeonid family) had been archon and in favour with the tyrants in 525 BC he was no longer so in 514 BC. Defeated in various battles, the Alkmeonidai sought different ways to accomplish the overthrow of the tyranny. It may well be these battles to which Thucydides was referring to when he stated that the tyrants 'prevailed in their wars' (Thuc. 6.54.5: doc. 9.21) but the Alkmeonidai were clearly not willing to accept exile. After military defeat, their new plan to ensure their return to Athens involved acquiring the assistance of Delphi and the Spartans. Thucydides is not interested in the details of how Hippias and his family were expelled, but notes merely that the Spartans and the Alkmeonidai drove out the tyrants in the fourth year after Hipparchos' assassination, that is, in 511/10 BC (Thuc. 6.59.4: doc. 9.39), a date with which the other sources agree, and the *Athenaion Politeia* specifically dates it to the archonship of Harpaktides (511/10 BC). Herodotos and the *Athenaion Politeia* both offer a similar account of the overthrow (Hdt. 5.62.2–64.2, 5.65.1–5, 5.66.1, 6.123.2: doc. 11.10).

The Alkmeonidai and Delphi

These two sources differ principally in the account of the rebuilding of the temple at Delphi by the Alkmeonidai and its significance. Herodotos describes the Alkmeonidai, who were awarded the contract to build a new temple for Apollo at Delphi after the previous one was destroyed by fire, as completing the temple 'better than the plan'; as they were wealthy they constructed the façade of marble from the Aegean island of Paros, whereas the plans had specified only conglomerate limestone. Marble from Paros is renowned for its shining whiteness but it also has a semi-translucent quality: the famous Venus de Milo was carved from it. The *Athenaion Politeia*, however, reports that the family made money on the contract, with which they then paid for the Spartans' assistance in overthrowing the tyrants. The second sounds very much like an anti-Spartan story of fifth-century origin, and there is otherwise no mention of the Spartans accepting money to depose the Athenian tyrants; Kleomenes of Sparta certainly refused to accept a bribe from Maiandrios to restore him as tyrant of Samos (Hdt. 3.148.1–2: doc. 6.73).

While the Alkmeonidai were rebuilding Apollo's temple at Delphi, according to the Athenians who themselves reported this to Herodotos, they bribed the Pythian priestess to make the same response to any Spartans who consulted the oracle. Perhaps, however, it was not a direct bribe but gratitude for the new marble as opposed to a temple of conglomerate limestone which made her and the Delphians generally well disposed towards them. This may well have been the motive of the Alkmeonidai for using this more expensive material. Accordingly, whenever Spartans came to enquire about any matters, public or private, they received the response that they were to 'liberate Athens'. Despite the fact that the Spartans had 'ties of hospitality' with the Athenians, their religiosity was such that obeying the oracle was more important to them. Another consideration was the Peisistratid tyranny's connections with Argos, Sparta's main enemy and rival in the Peloponnese. A first attempt to expel Hippias under the command of Anchimolos, a distinguished Spartan, failed when he landed troops by sea at Phaleron, Athens' main port of the time. The Peisistratidai cleared the plain of all its trees and crops and made it suitable for a cavalry attack: their allies the Thessalians had sent 1000 cavalry to assist them in response to a request for assistance. The Spartans were driven back by these into their ships and Anchimolos was killed (*Ath. Pol.*19.4–5: doc. 9.38).

Kleomenes, king of Sparta, and representative of the senior Spartan royal family, the Agiads, was sent by land with a larger force and was joined by the Athenian exiles. He defeated the Thessalians and then besieged the tyrants behind the ancient Pelargic wall on the acropolis. Hippias attempted to smuggle his children to safety: they were caught, and an arrangement made that the Peisistratidai leave Athens within five days under a truce guaranteeing their safe conduct (*Ath. Pol.* 19.5–6: doc. 9.38). Tyranny at Athens now came to an end after thirty-six years. The Spartans and the Alkmeonidai shared the credit for the expulsion of the tyrants (Thuc. 6.59.4: doc. 9.39), but later, when the Spartans learnt that the Pythia had been bribed, they came to regret having expelled the tyrants and set out to restore Hippias (Hdt. 5.91: doc. 6.59). Sparta was to attack Athens unsuccessfully in 508 BC and twice again between that year and 501 BC, while, in the aftermath of the Persian Wars, from 478 BC on, there was an uneasy relationship between the two cities, interrupted by outright war in 460 or 459. This finally terminated in the Peloponnesian War which broke out in 431 BC. Spartan involvement in the end of the tyranny was, if anything, an embarrassment in later Athenian history.

The cult of the tyrannicides

Whatever the role played by the Alkmeonidai and the Spartans, in the Athenian popular imagination in the fifth and fourth centuries it was Harmodios and Aristogeiton who were honoured for their role in bringing down the tyranny; they are always known as the tyrannicides, 'tyrant-slayers'. The role of the Alkmeonidai was intrinsically linked with the Spartans, for, without Spartan assistance, their previous attempts to oust the tyranny had failed

Figure 9.6 Statue group of the tyrant-slayers, Aristogeiton (left) and Harmodios (right), Roman marble copy of the Athenian bronze originals (doc. 9.42). Museo Archeologico Nazionale, Naples. Photo © Dennis Taylor.

and this association with the Spartans ensured that their role in deposing Hippias and his family was deliberately overlooked in an act of historical revisionism. This was despite the fact that it was one of the Alkmeonidai, Kleisthenes, who established democracy in Athens, despite further Spartan interference, in 508 BC. So while the tyrannicides had a fairly minor role, their role was glorified by later Athenians. In actuality, their assassination of Hipparchos and subsequent deaths did change the character of the tyranny, thus motivating the aristocrats in exile to overthrow the tyrants, but their cult was to magnify the part they played in these events. Herodotos points out that it was not the tyrannicides who brought about the downfall of the tyranny, and that they only aggravated Hippias and the other Peisistratidai and made their rule harsher: it was, to him, the Alkmeonidai who played the central role in the overthrow of the tyrants, while Thucydides argues that it was the Spartans who were ultimately responsible (Hdt. 6.121.1–123.2: doc. 11.10; Thuc. 6.53.3: doc. 9.32).

In subsequent Athenian tradition Harmodios and Aristogeiton overshadowed the Alkmeonidai to such an extent that it is impossible to believe that the Alkmeonidai promoted their cult. The popular view was certainly more concerned with magnifying the role of the tyrannicides, figures of heroic endeavour, than with that of the Alkmeonidai who bribed the Delphic oracle and encouraged the Spartans to invade Athens. Various honours, offered to heroes, were accorded to the tyrannicides, and offerings were made to them by the polemarch, one of the ten archons elected annually. He was the 'war-leader' archon, and the fact that he was made responsible for the offerings to the tyrannicides puts them on the same footing as those who gave their life in battle for the state (*Ath. Pol.*58.1: doc. 9.40). The tyrannicides were buried in the Kerameikos, the resting place of other important Athenians, particularly of the war dead, giving them another connection with those who gave their lives freely for their city; their bodies must have been reinterred here from their burial places of 514 BC (Paus. 1.29.15). Like the great heroes of the past, such as Achilles and Diomedes, Harmodios is addressed in a drinking song as not dead: he had gone to the 'Islands of the Blessed' to live eternally in the midst of plenty without toil or grief (Ath. *Deipnosophistae* 695b: doc. 9.44). The tyrannicides' descendants, the nearest in line if there were no legitimate sons, also received the privilege of dining in the town hall, the prytaneion, where they rubbed shoulders as they dined with athletic victors and successful Athenian generals (*IG* I^3 131, lines 1–15: doc. 9.41). According to Plutarch (*Aristeides* 27.6), Aristogeiton's grand-daughter, who was living in poverty on Lemnos, was later brought back to Athens, and given a husband of good family and an estate for a dowry.

Statues of the tyrannicides

The most notable and unprecedented honour accorded to the tyrannicides was that of having statues erected in their honour in the Athenian agora. Antenor made two bronze statues of the pair, probably soon after the expulsion of Hippias in 511/10 BC, but these were taken by Xerxes to Persia when he sacked Athens in 480 BC. Replacements were then made by Kritios and Nesiotes in 477/6 BC, an indication of the importance attached to the pair. Konon in the fourth century was to be the first Athenian since Harmodios and Aristogeiton who was considered important enough to have his statue set up by the state (Isoc. 12 *Evagoras* 51–6: doc. 14.4); throughout the fifth century, then, Harmodios and Aristogeiton were the only men to have official statues at Athens.

A pair of Roman marble statues at Naples has been confidently identified as copies of the bronze statues of Harmodios and Aristogeiton by Kritios and Nesiotes, and there are also fragments of other copies of the original statues (Fig. 9.6). Both in Greek and Roman antiquity the pair were a symbol of action against repression and tyrannical government. A statue base from Athens has an epigram which praises the two and probably belongs to one of the original pairs of statues. In ancient times the epigram was said to have been the work of Simonides; if so, it is ironic that he praises the men who killed his patron Hipparchos. The epigram refers to the tyrant-slayers as making their native Athens a land 'equal in laws', that is they introduced isonomia, legal equality for all citizens (*IG* I^3 502: doc. 9.42).

Drinking songs in praise of the tyrannicides

Equality in law – isonomia – is also mentioned in the drinking songs (skolia) concerning the tyrannicides. There are four of these songs preserved and there may well have been many others. Drinkers could also make clear their preference for songs on this topic over others: in a fragment of an Aristophanic play, when someone at a drinking-party was singing the 'Word of Admetos', another character forced him instead to sing the 'Song of Harmodios': Admetos was a mythical Thessalian king and the Thessalians had twice helped the Peisistratidai against the Spartans (Ar. *Pelargoi* F444: doc. 9.47). Harmodios was naturally preferred to Admetos in this new era of isonomia. Other versions of these songs existed, as one would expect given their oral transmission and delivery at symposia. In one of the skolia, the first two lines speak directly to Harmodios and Aristogeiton but the next two lines refer to 'the two of them'; the change of subject indicates that oral tradition has affected the transmission and that some couplets have been randomly tagged on to others (Ath. *Deipnosophistae* 695b: doc. 9.46). These drinking songs were probably very popular in the democratic period that commenced in 508 BC, and young boys would have been encouraged to perform them as part of the entertainment at symposia to reinforce their understanding of democratic ideology and the improving effects of homoerotic relationships.

Isonomia existed once the tyrants were expelled. This 'equality before the laws', or 'equal rights', was a term which probably had not previously existed, and had not been conceptualised until after the end of the tyranny. While the tyrants' observance of laws prior to 514 BC is praised by the sources, after that date the executions and expulsions of citizens were in stark contrast to the isonomia which was viewed as having been established by the tyrannicides. However, this in fact was not strictly true as it was another four years until the tyrants were expelled by the Alkmeonidai and the Spartans.

The tyranny of Peisistratos and his sons had a profound impact on the city of Athens and its history. The tyrants commenced the construction of civic buildings and the beautification of the city, a process that was continued during Athenian history and which culminated in the building of the magnificent Parthenon on the acropolis. Their provision of fountain-houses also marked the city's interest in this aspect of its amenities (*IG* I^3 49: doc. 1.14). During this

Figure 9.7 The temple of Olympian Zeus (the Olympieion) at Athens, with the Parthenon on the acropolis in the background. Commenced by Peisistratos' sons, the Olympieion was not completed until Roman times. Photo © Koorosh Nozad-Tehrani.

period Athens developed from a relatively unimportant city in the Greek world to one that was about to take its place on the stage of Mediterranean history. It was particularly significant that the tyrants more or less maintained the Solonian constitution, with its provision for the election of officials and a role for the thetes. When an attempt was made to do away with Solon's constitution in 508 BC, the Athenians who had lived under his system for some eighty years refused to let that happen and ensured, instead, the institution of the fully fledged Athenian democracy as envisaged by Kleisthenes.

10

KLEISTHENES THE REFORMER

Introduction

'Athens, which had previously been great, now became greater still after her deliverance from the tyrants': in these words Herodotos seems to be commending the reign of the Peisistratidai (Hdt. 5.66.1: doc. 10.1). However, in its next development, Athens became in his opinion even greater, no doubt because of his personal preference for democracy over tyranny. Before this was achieved, Athens was thrust back in 510 BC into the political stasis that preceded the tyranny. Just as three men, Megakles, Lykourgos and Peisistratos, vied for power in the 560s BC, the deposition of the tyranny created something of a 'power vacuum' in Athens, which led to a power contest between two individual aristocrats. In 508 BC, matters came to a head with open rivalry between Isagoras as eponymous archon and Kleisthenes, head of the Alkmeonidai (but without any position as an official). By the end of that year, Kleisthenes emerged as the most prominent person in Athens, with Isagoras in exile and Athens' Solonian timocratic constitution dramatically and yet also conservatively reformed under Kleisthenes' leadership to make Athens a radical democracy.

Kleisthenes' reforms had wide-ranging implications and created a democratic structure that lasted two centuries and coped with a complex series of historical events, from Spartan incursions, Persian invasions, the Peloponnesian War and the struggle with Macedon. Herodotos and the *Athenaion Politeia* are the main sources for Kleisthenes' changes to the constitution. Thucydides does not mention Kleisthenes: his interest in the tyrants concluded in 514 BC with the assassination of Hipparchos. His account of Hipparchos' assassination was simply a digression explaining the fears and paranoia about possible attempts to overthrow democracy in Athens during the Peloponnesian War.

Sources

Herodotos misinterprets aspects of Kleisthenes' reforms of the Athenian political system, specifically his tribal reforms, but is an invaluable source on the conflict between Isagoras and Kleisthenes, and Spartan interference in the city's affairs. But it is the *Athenaion Politeia* which, in a few chapters (21–2), provides basically all that is known about his changes to the constitution, while Aristotle in the *Politics* is interested in aspects of Kleisthenes' reforms as a paradigm for how democracies can be established. Unfortunately, the organisation of the new system of tribes and its constituent parts, the trittyes and demes, is not explained as fully as the modern historian would desire. Inscriptions from the fourth century BC indicate how aspects of the representational system operated by which demes sent members to the boule and how demes worked as 'mini-democracies' patterned on the democracy of the city itself. Thousands of terracotta sherds with the names of individuals scratched on them are evidence for the process of ostracism and indicate years in which individual political figures were unpopular. But given the importance of the changes Kleisthenes introduced, little is known about them or the man himself: in fact, after 508 BC, he quietly disappears from the historical record.

Kleisthenes, Isagoras and Kleomenes

It was the Agiad king Kleomenes with a force of Spartans that brought about the expulsion of the tyrants in 510 BC at the instigation of the Alkmeonidai. In the aftermath of this, two men came to prominence in Athens. One was Kleisthenes, the head of the Alkmeonid family, and Herodotos reports that it was he who according to rumour had bribed the Delphic oracle. Of the other, Isagoras, little is known: Herodotos reports that he was of a 'reputable family' and that his relatives sacrificed to Carian Zeus (Hdt. 5.66.1: doc. 10.1). Kleisthenes' popularity is easy to understand, as he had played a role in overthrowing the tyrants and was prominent among the Athenian aristocratic exiles during the tyranny.

Figure 10.1 A marble bust of Herodotos. This is from the famous 'paired bust' which has Thucydides on one side and Herodotos on the other (right). Museo Archeologico Nazionale, Naples. Photo © Caitlin M. Smith.

347

The hetaireiai

Isagoras, however, emerged as the leader of the wealthy aristocrats, and the struggle between the two men centred on their standing among the aristocratic clubs, known as hetaireiai (singular: hetaireia), for it was only when Kleisthenes 'was worsted by the hetaireiai' (*Ath. Pol.* 20.1: doc. 10.6; Hdt. 5.66.2: doc. 10.1) that he turned elsewhere for support. If it were not for the restoration of Kleisthenes' name as archon for 525 BC (*IG* I³ 1031a: doc. 9.24), suggesting that Kleisthenes had already held the archonship, it could be assumed that the struggle between the two men was over this office, and, when Isagoras was elected to the archonship for 508/7 BC, he presumably considered that he was now the pre-eminent political figure and would dominate Athenian politics for the forthcoming year.

Despite the fact that Kleisthenes had been the Athenian most responsible for overthrowing the tyranny, he was not popular among the hetaireiai, which supported Isagoras. In the immediate aftermath of 510 BC it must have been the Spartans who were seen as the real deliverers of Athens from the tyrants, and among the aristocratic political clubs, the hetaireiai, Isagoras gained proportionately more support, perhaps because of his connections with Sparta. The author of the *Athenaion Politeia* might well give the credit to the Alkmeonidai as 'primarily responsible' for the expulsion of the tyrants, but this did not translate into political influence at the time and Kleisthenes' disappointment must have been acute (*Ath. Pol.* 20.1–5: doc. 10.6). Isagoras' status and prominence is seen by the fact that when Kleomenes came to Athens to oust the tyrants, he stayed at the house of Isagoras, and Herodotos adds that gossip reported that Kleomenes had slept with Isagoras' wife (Hdt. 5.70.1: doc. 10.2). The *Athenaion Politeia* describes Isagoras as a 'friend of the tyrants' (*Ath. Pol.* 20.1: doc. 10.6): if this was the case, Isagoras was very flexible in his political principles. He had probably considered his best options for political success: the Spartans had been defeated once, but the arrival of a land force under Kleomenes and the flight of the Peisistratidai to the acropolis would easily have shown where the future of Athens lay (*Ath. Pol.* 20.1: doc. 10.6).

Kleisthenes turns to the people

Kleisthenes obviously thought that he had invested too much effort and too many resources in expelling the tyrants and returning to Athens to cede political leadership to Isagoras: years of exile, the defeat at Leipsydrion, the costly rebuilding of the temple at Delphi, and the manipulation of its oracles to persuade the Spartans to intervene in Athenian affairs were all considerable investments politically and financially. His family's opposition to the tyrants had seen him an exile for many years and he was clearly politically ambitious: his family had always been prominent in Athenian politics. He was not content to be worsted by the hetaireiai and have no political influence in the state after playing so important a role in overthrowing the tyranny. Both Herodotos and the *Athenaion Politeia* agree that what he did was to turn to the demos, abandoning the aristocratic hetaireiai altogether as a means to political power and influence, and taking the people into his own hetaireia (Hdt. 5.66.2: doc. 10.1, using the word 'moira' (party) at 5.69.2: doc. 10.2). This gives some idea of how these groups worked. The aristocrats of the Alkmeonidai apparently had their own hetaireia, and Isagoras' family their own as well. 'Hetairos' means 'companion', and the hetaireiai may well have represented different family groups and affiliations. The *Athenaion Politeia* is less specific than Herodotos and relates more simply that Kleisthenes 'brought over the people to his side' (20.1: doc. 10.6).

Given that Peisistratos had the poor and the Athenian citizenry in general among his adherents, Kleisthenes' approach to the people for political support is not as revolutionary as it sounds. As the demos had no say in the overthrow of the tyranny – it was the aristocrats, after all, who were killed or sent into exile by Hippias after 514 BC – they were relatively overlooked. Kleisthenes and Isagoras had both striven for political influence among the aristocratic clubs, taking no account of the ordinary people. The *Athenaion Politeia* then has Kleisthenes, when unsuccessful, coming to the fore by 'promising to hand the state over to the populace [demos]' (20.1: doc. 10.6). Herodotos dates Kleisthenes' most important reform, that of the tribes, to the time when he added the people to his moira (party), presumably early in 508 BC, and states that this resulted in Isagoras calling upon the Spartans (Hdt. 5.69.2: doc. 10.2). Kleisthenes' reforms made Athens a democracy, as promised, and Isagoras was left powerless as a result: his position as archon had not ensured him prominence for the year.

It is probable that as archon Isagoras had reforms of his own which he intended to introduce in the post-tyrant state, and when he found himself marginalised he sought Spartan assistance: he knew from the events of 510 how decisive their intervention could be. After his political defeat, Isagoras appears to have contacted Kleomenes, probably through a private messenger, and asked for his assistance in 'driving out the curse' (*Ath. Pol.* 20.2: doc. 10.6): the Alkmeonidai had been responsible for the murder of Kylon's supporters when they sought refuge on sanctified ground probably in 632 BC. In response to this request Kleomenes sent a Spartan herald to Athens and ordered the expulsion of Kleisthenes and other Athenians, presumably members of the Alkmeonid family and their supporters, as accursed (Hdt. 5.70.2: doc. 10.2).

Kleisthenes secretly left Athens, frightened off by the herald's communiqué and clearly apprehensive for the future. He was, after all, no stranger to exile or to the hostility of those in power. Kleomenes was obviously expecting no trouble in complying with Isagoras' request and arrived in Athens with only a small force, expelling 700 Athenian families as accursed and complicit in the final stage of the Kylonian affair (*Ath. Pol.* 20.3: doc. 10.6); this was his second invasion of the city. The fact that 700 families were singled out may give some indication of the size of Kleisthenes' hetaireia: apart from the Alkmeonidai themselves and their connections, these presumably included their supporters and families related to them by marriage. Isagoras was obviously seeking to destroy the influence of the Alkmeonidai genos (clan) in the state altogether.

Isagoras' attempted oligarchy

Kleomenes then attempted to turn Athens into an oligarchy, intending to give power in the state, not into the hands of the demos as Kleisthenes had promised, but very much the opposite. His plan was to put the government of Athens into the hands of Isagoras and 300 of his supporters and in this way to establish an oligarchy (Hdt. 5.72.1: doc. 10.3; *Ath. Pol.* 20.3: doc. 10.6). This was generally the Spartans' favoured type of government for their allies (docs 6.57–9). Clearly Athens would now be more or less an ally of Sparta and within the Spartan sphere of influence, with Isagoras and his supporters owing their position in government to Kleomenes.

The boule resists

Here Kleomenes and Isagoras encountered opposition to their plans. The demos stood by and watched the Spartans expel first the tyrants and then 700 'accursed' families. But now

349

Table 10.1 The Alkmeonidai family tree

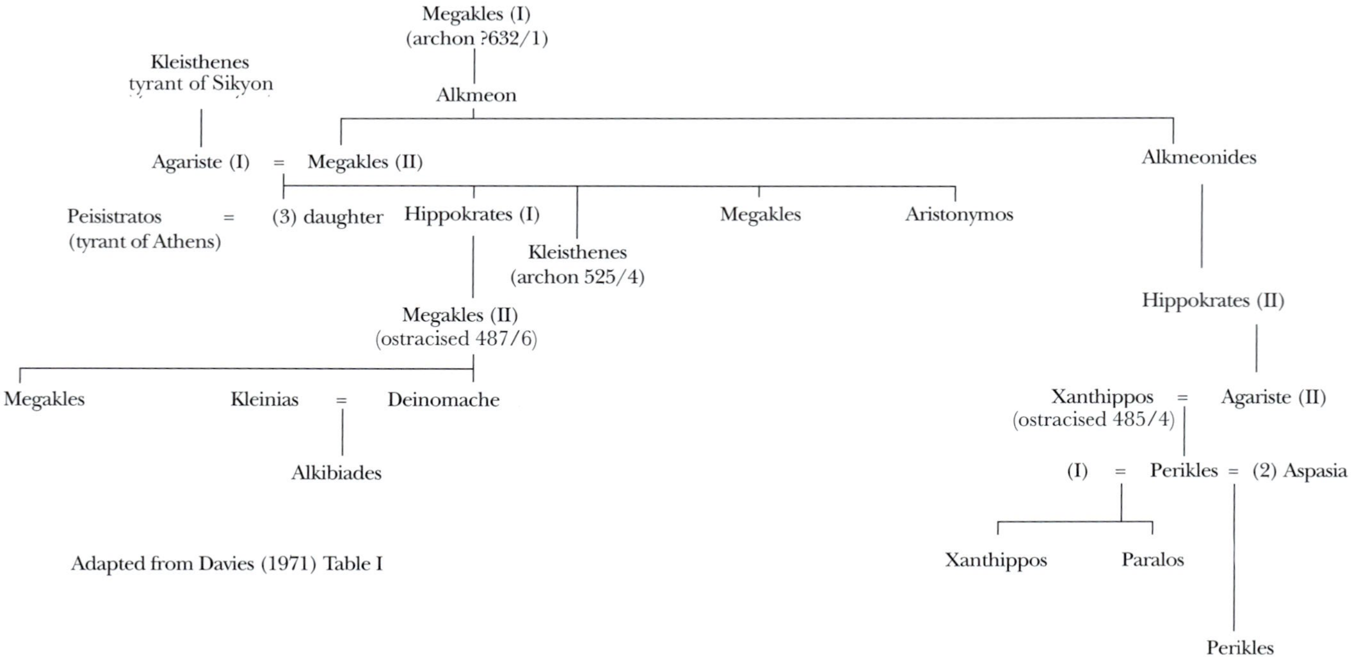

Kleisthenes
tyrant of Sikyon

Megakles (I)
(archon ?632/1)

Alkmeon

Alkmeonides

Agariste (I) = Megakles (II)

Peisistratos = (3) daughter   Hippokrates (I)
(tyrant of Athens)

Kleisthenes
(archon 525/4)

Hippokrates (II)

Megakles   Aristonymos

Megakles (II)
(ostracised 487/6)

Xanthippos =   Agariste (II)
(ostracised 485/4)

Megakles   Kleinias = Deinomache

(I) =   Perikles = (2) Aspasia

Alkibiades

Xanthippos   Paralos

Perikles

Adapted from Davies (1971) Table I

Kleomenes made the mistake of attempting to dissolve the Athenian council: both Herodotos and the *Athenaion Politeia* use the term boule (Hdt. 5.72.2: doc. 10.3; *Ath. Pol.* 20.3: doc. 10.6). There is debate about which council is meant, the Solonian council of 400, Kleisthenes' new council of 500 based on his tribal reform, or the Areiopagos. Kleisthenes is perhaps unlikely by this point to have had time to organise this new boule of 500, but it should be noted that Herodotos does date the tribal reform prior to Isagoras' appeal to the Spartans (Hdt. 5.69.2-70.1: doc. 10.2). If this new council, which represented Kleisthenes' democratic reforms, was already in place it would have been specifically targeted by Isagoras and Kleomenes as the main feature of the tribal reforms which had propelled Kleisthenes to the foremost position in the state. But this hypothesis depends on how quickly the complicated process for electing representatives to the new council could have been put in place. Otherwise, the boule referred to as being dissolved was either the Solonian council of 400 or the Areiopagos. The Areiopagos, with its membership moulded by decades of archons who had served under the tyranny, was more likely to have been hostile to Kleisthenes than to Isagoras, who is referred to as a friend of the tyrants. Both of the ancient sources link the attempt to dissolve the boule with the handing over of government to Isagoras and his supporters, and, as the Solonian boule was the organising body for the ekklesia, any attempt to create an oligarchy of 300 would have needed to override the ekklesia and the boule.

The boule and ekklesia had operated under the Solonian constitution from 594 to this point in 508 BC. The dissolution of the boule meant the end of that constitution and the imposition of an oligarchy upon Athens. The boule resisted this attempt: it was representative of the top three classes and its opposition to dissolution indicates that, while Isagoras had won the support of the hetaireiai and thus the archonship, his support did not extend to an overthrow of the constitution. Although elected as eponymous archon, he did not have the status of a law-giver such as Solon with powers to change the state's political structure, particularly not at the point of Spartan spears. This resistance of the boule was decisive and forced Kleomenes, Isagoras and his supporters to seize the acropolis in the age-old Athenian method of attempting to secure power over the city.

The accounts in Herodotos and the *Athenaion Politeia* are at this point slightly different: Herodotos has the boule resisting its own dissolution, and the acropolis being seized by Kleomenes as a result, whereas the *Athenaion Politeia* has the boule resisting and the demos gathering 'in force'. This resulted in the flight of Kleomenes and Isagoras and their supporters to the acropolis where they were then besieged by the Athenian people. The difference is slight, but the resistance of the boule was a crucial factor in both accounts. This, linked with Kleisthenes' promise to establish a democracy, ignited (despite Kleisthenes' own absence) a popular uprising in Athens, which saw the Spartans besieged on the acropolis for two days. Kleomenes had come with only a small force and may well have fled to the acropolis with limited provisions: at any rate after two days he left under a truce; the Athenians recalled Kleisthenes and the others who had been exiled (*Ath. Pol.* 20.3: doc. 10.6). In 411 BC the Athenians were still laughing at Kleomenes' discomfiture, remembering how 'though breathing Spartan fury [he] delivered up his arms to me and left, with his tiny threadbare cloak, hungry, filthy, unplucked, and unwashed for six years', after the Athenians had 'savagely besieged that man, sleeping seventeen shields deep at the gate' (Ar. *Lysistrata* 256–85: doc. 6.78).

What happened now was either a peaceful expulsion of the Spartans, Isagoras and his supporters, or the worst blood-bath Athens had ever seen, besides which the Kylonian incident pales into insignificance. Herodotos has the Spartans leaving the country under the truce, but the others, Isagoras and his 300 would-be oligarchs, imprisoned 'under sentence of death' and executed, although he also states that Kleomenes and Isagoras escaped (Hdt. 5.72.4, 5.73.1: docs 10.3–4). Included among those who died was Timesitheos of Delphi, about whom Herodotos notes 'of whose prowess and courage I could recount great things' (Hdt. 5.72.4: doc. 10.3). But as historians have noted, the *Athenaion Politeia*, in contrast, has Kleomenes and all those with him allowed to leave the country (*Ath. Pol.* 20.3: doc. 10.6). Perhaps by 'all' this source means all the Spartans and not 'all' in the sense of everyone on the acropolis, although Herodotos certainly has Isagoras escaping from the acropolis with Kleomenes (Hdt. 5.74.1: doc. 10.5).

Proposed alliance with Persia

Kleisthenes and the other exiles were recalled (*Ath. Pol.* 20.3: doc. 10.6), and an embassy sent to Sardis. With the Spartans now Athens' enemies, an alliance with Persia may well have made sense to the Alkmeonidai and other Athenians. But the Persian viceroy ('hipparchos') of Sardis was not only geographically ignorant of this small city, but was not interested in an alliance. Instead he demanded submission, to be given to the Persian king Darius in the symbolic form of earth and water from Athens, signifying the handing over to the Persians of the Athenian state. The Athenian messengers agreed to the terms, presumably preoccupied with thoughts of further Spartan intervention in Athenian affairs. But in this they took their own initiative without direct orders from the Athenians, who wanted an alliance and had not thought in terms of submission (just having expelled the Spartans). The ambassadors were accordingly 'severely blamed' when they returned to Athens (Hdt. 5.73.1–3: doc. 10.4); no earth and water was dispatched, and nearly twenty years later this issue of non-submission was to come to the fore again. Kleisthenes shared no responsibility for the embassy's actions in this matter and proceeded with his reforms; when he quietly disappears from the historical record after 508 BC it was not as some scholars have erroneously suggested because he incurred odium through this suggested alliance but because he just departed from the stage of Athenian history: if he had been archon in 525/4 he would now have been at a relatively advanced age.

Kleomenes returns to Attica

In either 507/6 or 506/5 BC, Kleomenes collected an army of Sparta's Peloponnesian allies and marched with a Spartan force to Eleusis in south-western Attica: his purpose was to return to Athens and install Isagoras as tyrant. In a prearranged plan, the Boeotians seized two Athenian frontier villages, while the Chalkidians of the island of Euboea off the coast of Attica attacked from the east. The Athenians made a crucial decision: although attacked on three sides, they marched against Kleomenes at Eleusis, seeing him as the main threat. However, he had his own problems as his Corinthian allies came to the conclusion that the attack on Attica was unjustified. This view was shared by Kleomenes' fellow Spartan king Demaratos, who was also participating in the campaign (until this point both Spartan kings went on campaign together: Hdt. 5.75.2: doc. 6.31). The other allies withdrew on seeing the two Spartan kings in disagreement (Hdt. 5.74.1–5.76: doc. 10.5), and Kleomenes' attack collapsed. Isagoras lost his chance of coming to power in Athens.

The Athenians now had to deal with their other invaders. They attacked the Boeotians, killing many of them, and took 700 prisoners, whom they kept in chains and later ransomed for 200 drachmas each: two minas was the standard Greek rate for ransoming a prisoner

(Hdt. 6.79.1: doc. 5.17). Herodotos saw the fetters which were still proudly displayed on the acropolis in his own time. One-tenth of the ransom money was dedicated by the Athenians to Athena, and was used to make a sculpture group of a chariot and four horses in bronze; Herodotos records the inscription accompanying the dedication, which is also known from two marble fragments (Hdt. 5.77). The Athenians then went to Euboea where they defeated the Chalkidians, and settled 4000 Athenians on their land: the age of Athens' overseas settlements had begun. Athenian victories on these two fronts indicated that the democracy could be militarily successful, and these were a prelude to their defeat of the Persians in 490 BC. The Spartans lost interest in Isagoras and his ambitions, and, on learning that the Pythia had been bribed to tell them to expel the tyrants from Athens, planned to restore Hippias as tyrant, probably sometime between 506 and 501, although the dates are not certain, and Kleomenes is not mentioned specifically as involved. Once again the Corinthians refused to follow the Spartans' lead, opposing the plan, and nothing eventuated (Hdt. 5.90.1–93.2: doc. 6.59). By the end of the sixth century, democratic Athens had defeated the Boeotians and Chalkidians and expelled a Spartan force from Athens, while the Corinthians had twice thwarted Spartan attempts to interfere with Athens' method of government. The city was free to pursue its own history.

Tribes, boule and strategia

The ten tribes

Since time immemorial the Athenians had been organised into four tribes (phylai; singular: phyle) named after the four sons of Ion, the mythical ancestor of the Ionian people to whom the Athenians belonged. The four tribes derived from the names of Ion's sons – Geleon, Aigikores, Argades and Hoples – were abolished, and in their place ten tribes were created named after Athenian heroes (Hdt. 5.65.5–67.1: doc. 10.1). According to the *Athenaion Politeia*, the Athenians chose the names of 100 heroes, and submitted these to the Pythia at Delphi, who chose ten of them, presumably through some form of inspired drawing of lots (*Ath. Pol.* 21.6: doc. 10.7). Herodotos, however, specifically notes that Ajax, while not an Athenian (but 'a neighbour of the city and an ally'), was one of the ten selected (Hdt. 5.66.2: doc. 10.1); how this accords with the version of the *Athenaion Politeia* in which the Pythia chose the ten from among 100 names is not clear, and has led some scholars to argue that the Pythia simply gave divine approval to ten heroes chosen by Kleisthenes. Ajax, in myth, was the son of the king of Salamis, and a mighty warrior who performed great deeds at the siege and sack of Troy. By naming one of their tribes after him, the Athenians were legitimising their right to possession of this island (Solon *Poems* 1–3: doc. 8.8).

These ten heroes became 'eponymous heroes' (the eponymoi), that is, each of the ten tribes was named after one of them, using the genitive form of the hero's name: the tribe named after Erechtheus, for example, was Erechtheis, '[the tribe] of Erechtheus'. In the official listing of the tribes in decrees and on monuments they were always given in the same order, and modern scholars give each of the tribes a Roman numeral to help identify them: Erechtheis (I), Aigeis (II), Pandionis (III), Leontis (IV), Akamantis (V), Oineis (VI), Kekropis (VII), Hippothontis (VIII), Aiantis (IX), Antiochis (X). From now on, each Athenian citizen belonged to one of these ten tribes and each tribe worshipped its eponymous hero: a decree of the deme Skambonidai of the tribe Leontis contains a provision that the deme officials were to sacrifice 'a perfect victim' to Leos, their tribal hero (*IG* I³ 244 (C): doc. 10.20).

Figure 10.2 The remains of the monument to the ten eponymous heroes in the agora. Photo © Timothy Hart

Table 10.2 The ten Athenian tribes instituted by Kleisthenes and the heroes after whom they were named

Erechtheis (I)	Erechtheus	King of Athens
Aigeis (II)	Aigeus	King of Athens, father of Theseus
Pandionis (III)	Pandion	King of Athens
Leontis (IV)	Leos	The father of three daughters who sacrificed themselves to save Athens
Akamantis (V)	Akamas	Son of Theseus, king of Athens
Oineis (VI)	Oineus	Son of Pandion (see above, Pandionis III)
Kekropis (VII)	Kekrops	King of Athens
Hippothontis (VIII)	Hippothoon	Hero, from Eleusis
Aiantis (IX)	Aias (Ajax)	Hero of Salamis; he fought in the Trojan War
Antiochis (X)	Antiochos	Son of Herakles

A monument to these heroes is referred to in the literary sources from the 420s that may date back to Kleisthenes; the remains of a later monument to the heroes constructed in the 330s when Lykourgos was refurbishing Athens can still be seen in the Athenian agora. A bronze life-size statue of each hero stood on an elevated stone base, nearly 17 metres long and almost 2 metres wide (Fig. 10.2). The base itself was over two and a half metres high. At either end of the base, flanking the ten statues, was a large tripod, obviously signifying the role which Delphi had played in the choice of the heroes. Surrounded by stone posts connected by wooden railings, these posts were in turn surmounted by lengths of stone acting as a sill, allowing individuals to rest against the fence and look at the notices posted on the base. Laws and decrees to be proposed to the Athenian ekklesia were displayed at the monument, so they could be read by the people, or be read to them by the literate, before the proposals came up for discussion in the ekklesia. Written notices concerning the tribes could also be posted there, and the degree regarding the appointment of tribute collectors in allied cities specifies that a copy was to be set up at this monument (*IG* I³ 68: doc. 13.15). Statues of seven of the heroes could also be seen at Delphi in the second century AD and presumably all ten were originally present (Pausanias 10.10.1).

Herodotos considered that the tribal rearrangement was inspired by Kleisthenes' grandfather, Kleisthenes of Sikyon, who had renamed the tribes of Sikyon and given the Dorians their insulting names: 'Pig-men', 'Donkey-men', and 'Piglet-men', while calling the tribe to whom he belonged the 'Rulers of the People' (Hdt. 5.68.1: doc. 7.5). Herodotos' view is that Kleisthenes of Athens similarly despised the Ionians and did not want the 'Athenians and Ionians to have the same tribes' (Hdt. 5.69.1: doc. 10.2). As a piece of historical reasoning, this leaves something to be desired. It is clear that Kleisthenes' intention was not to do away with the Ionian identity of Athens (an identity which the city in fact stressed in the second half of the fifth century), but rather, he sought to redistribute the Athenians into a series of new groupings which would facilitate the workings of the new Athenian democracy. Tribal reforms are known from other Greek city-states; Sparta at some stage abandoned the three tribes the citizens originally belonged to, and there was also a tribal reform at Argos, probably in the mid-fifth century. These tribal reforms seem aimed at either weakening or, conversely, emphasising the citizens' awareness of their origins: Kleisthenes' reforms aimed at the former.

The thirty trittyes

Attica was now divided into thirty trittyes ('parts' or 'thirds': singular trittys). Ten of these trittyes were in the city area (the asty), ten in the coastal area (the paralia), and ten in the inland area (the mesogeios). These thirty trittyes had their own names, not all of which are now known. Kleisthenes assigned three trittyes, one from each area, to each new tribe, using the system of selection by lot to randomise the distribution. In this way, each tribe had territory in each of the three regions: the city, coast and inland. Tribes were therefore not coherent territorial units, but made up of trittyes from throughout Attica. Kleisthenes' aim here was to break down regional tendencies (such as Athens experienced in the 560s BC) and to bring Athenians from various regions throughout Attica into each new tribe (*Ath. Pol.* 21.2–4: doc. 10.7).

The new citizens

The *Athenaion Politeia* gives a clearer account of this reform of the trittyes than Herodotos, and sets out (although with not as much detail as could be desired) the nature of these Athenian tribes, their constituent elements, and their purpose (doc. 10.7). Kleisthenes assigned all the Athenians to one of the ten completely new tribes in order to 'mix them up', so that more citizens would be actively involved in the politeia, the state, with no further inquiries into anyone's family background. As tribes were based on a citizen's place of residence, they did not represent family affiliations, which could not be discovered by looking into the

membership of the tribes themselves. In order to remove any political significance from family connections, Kleisthenes did not simply recycle the existing four tribes and twelve trittyes to which the Athenians had previously belonged. Rather, he started afresh with ten
new tribes and thirty new trittyes, with the aim of undermining existing regional loyalties.
The implementation of his reforms was made simpler by the fact that the Athenians were
accustomed to units called tribes and trittyes. The change for them was simply that the membership and geographical boundaries of these were radically redrawn. Similarly, the demes
became the basic building-block of the new system, but these were the villages, suburbs and
towns in which the Athenians already lived, and which must already have had some type of
local governance structures in place.

Each Athenian citizen now became a member of one of the 140 demes into which Attica
was divided, with a certain number of demes comprising each trittys. The number of demes
in each trittys (and therefore each tribe, made up of three of the trittyes) varied, and probably
some form of population count was made so that the number of Athenians in each trittys was
roughly the same. Members of each deme were meant from now on to address each other by
their given ('first') name and their deme name. Kleisthenes himself, as an example, would be
known as Kleisthenes of (the deme) Alopeke. But the Athenians were accustomed to addressing each other by their fathers' names and retained this practice, so Kleisthenes along with
all Athenians now ended up with a three-part name, as in Kleisthenes, son of Megakles, of
Alopeke.

Citizens of non-Athenian background had fathers with foreign names, and this is the reason why, according to the *Athenaion Politeia*, Kleisthenes wanted the Athenians to address each
other by their deme name and not their father's name, so that they would not 'show up the
new citizens' (21.4: doc. 10.7). It was no longer possible to use tribal membership to enquire
into a citizen's background and to be a member of a tribe did not mean that one's ancestors
had always been citizens. Solon had enfranchised new citizens, although not in great numbers, and Peisistratos and his sons must have guaranteed their rights, for the *Athenaion Politeia*
(13.5: doc. 10.2) notes that after the tyranny many who were not of pure Athenian descent,
and who had supported Peisistratos and his sons, were disenfranchised – this perhaps was one
of Isagoras' measures. Aristotle in the *Politics* writes that Kleisthenes gave Athenian citizenship to many metics 'both foreigners and slaves' (Arist. *Politics* 1275b34–8: doc. 10.15). The
slaves referred to by Aristotle were presumably manumitted (freed) slaves or their descendants; manumitted slaves received the status of metics. The foreigners would have come to
Attica of their own free will as traders or, more likely in this period, as craftsmen and been
granted metic status. Aristotle considered as a characteristic of an 'extreme' democracy the
policy of including as many new citizens as possible in the citizen body, whether illegitimate
or half-citizen. Why Kleisthenes enfranchised these 'foreigners and slaves' is unknown. Many
of these had perhaps been citizens in the past, if they were the descendants of the citizens
originally enfranchised by Solon, and this would therefore have been a means of ensuring
that this group was not dissatisfied with the new political system.

The oath of the boule

After Kleisthenes' major reforms of 508 BC, the Athenian constitution did not remain static,
and in the following decade some changes indicated that the Athenians were aware that
further improvements could be made. Although Athens had long had a boule – since Solon's
time –in 501/0 BC, in the archonship of Hermokreon, the Athenians decided that the mem-

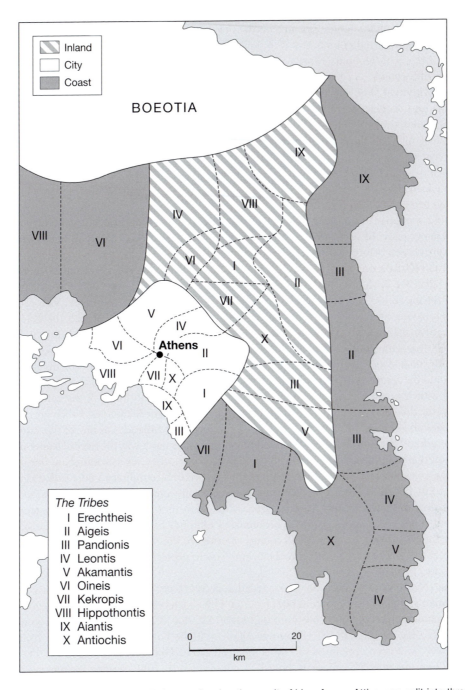

Inland
City
Coast

BOEOTIA

The Tribes
 I Erechtheis
 II Aigeis
 III Pandionis
 IV Leontis
 V Akamantis
 VI Oineis
 VII Kekropis
 VIII Hippothontis
 IX Aiantis
 X Antiochis

0   20
          km

Map 10.1 Kleisthenes' tribes and trittyes, showing the result of his reforms. Attica was split into three regions: the city (asty), the inland region (mesogeios) and the coast (paralia). Each region had ten trittyes, made up of demes. Each tribe, or phyle (represented here by Roman numerals), was made up of one trittys from each region. Based on R. Sowerby, *The Greeks: An Introduction to Their Culture*, second edition, Routledge, 2009, p. 46.

bers of the boule should swear an oath upon entering office. This was part of an overall pattern of Athenian democratic practice: at the deme level, the local deme officials also swore oaths and had to render an account of their office when they left it (*IG* I³ 244: doc. 10.20). The members of the boule swore to serve Athens' interests and to be free from corruption. By the fifth century a citizen could only serve on the boule twice, the second time after a ten-year interval. The role of the boule, as under Solon, consisted mainly of preparing the agenda for the ekklesia, organising and presiding over its sessions, and keeping order, while the prytaneis, the councillors who were members of one of the ten tribes, were responsible for executive duties for the tenth of the year for which they were in office. These duties included receiving foreign ambassadors and conducting the daily business of the state.

Strategia and strategoi (generals)

Another change in 501/0 BC was the introduction of a board of ten strategoi, generals (singular: strategos); the strategia was the office of strategos. There is no evidence as to how strategoi were chosen before this date. Each tribe now elected a strategos: 'they began electing the generals by tribes, one from each tribe, though the polemarch was in command of the whole army' (*Ath. Pol.* 22.2: doc. 10.8). In Herodotos' description of the battle of Marathon against the Persians in 490 BC (Hdt. 6.109.3–110: doc. 11.9), there were ten strategoi, with each of the ten having an equal say in the military decisions about how to deal with the Persians, while, in an arrangement similar to that for the chairperson for the boule (see below, p. 365), each strategos took it in turn on a day-by-day basis to be leader of the army (to hold the prytany for the army for the day: Hdt 6.110: doc. 11.9). This equality created problems at Marathon and the system only worked because four of the ten strategoi, as well as the polemarch, sided with Miltiades, giving six to five in favour of Miltiades' strategy; in the campaign in Sicily, the differences of a military nature between the strategoi Alkibiades, Nikias and Demosthenes also created problems. Despite the prominence of Miltiades as one of the strategoi in Herodotos' account, it is clear that Kallimachos as polemarch was the overall leader of the army at that point. But this situation changed in 487/6 BC when the polemarch, as one of the archons, was elected by lot, which meant that he ceased to be a military leader (*Ath. Pol.* 22.5: doc. 10.9). His duties after that date were primarily connected with military rituals, such as sacrificing to the war deities Artemis Agrotera and Enyalios, organising funeral contests to honour those who had died in war, and making offerings to Harmodios and Aristogeiton. Since they had freed the state from tyranny, offerings to them were of a quasi-military character, as one of the roles of the armed citizenry was to protect the democratic state (*Ath. Pol.* 58.1: doc. 9.40).

The office of strategos was not a new creation in 501/0 BC: Phrynon was a strategos in the Athenian campaign at Sigeion in 607/6 BC (cf. Hdt. 5.94.1–95.2: doc. 2.18); strategoi were also mentioned in Drakon's constitution (*Ath. Pol.* 4.2: doc. 8.2), while Peisistratos was also a strategos (*Ath. Pol.* 22.3: doc. 10.9), as was Alkmeon in the First Sacred War. These strategoi may well have been appointed simply as the need arose. The difference from 501/0 BC was that there was now a permanent 'board' of ten, elected by tribe, serving for one year at a time, and, in the fourth century at least, the prytaneis made the arrangements for the assembly to elect the strategoi in the sixth prytany of the year. The strategoi were not, however, responsible for the details of the military organisation of the tribes, which was the role of the ten elected taxiarchoi ('commanders of the tribal squadrons'; singular taxiarchos; sometimes transliterated as taxiarchs), one of whom was also elected from each tribe. It was the task of the taxiarchoi to lead their tribal contingents and to appoint the lochagoi (singular: lochagos), the commanders of individual lochoi (singular lochos: a group of soldiers). In addition, ten phylarchoi (singular: phylarchos; 'tribal leader') were elected, one from each tribe, to lead the cavalry into battle. They were the equivalent of the taxiarchoi who led the hoplites. Other military officials were also elected for various duties, and this allowed the strategoi to concentrate on strategy and tactics.

Through these arrangements, each tribe provided several military leaders and the tribe became the basis for the military organisation of the state. Citizens from all over Athens fought side by side in contingents which were based on the trittyes of each tribe, and in the casualty lists the dead were listed by their tribes (*IG* I^3 1147: doc. 12.14).

In the fifth century the office of strategos became increasingly politically significant as the prestige of the archonship diminished, and the importance of the strategoi was also a reflection of the number of wars which the Athenians waged in any given year. The strategia was an annual office, but, unusually for Athenian offices, one that could be held repeatedly. As a result it was a position from which individuals could gain prominence and influence in the state. Perikles held the strategia continuously from 443 to 429 BC, although the number of times he was elected to this office was unusual. However, all military positions could be held repeatedly.

Strategoi could punish treason or lapses of discipline by imprisonment, exile, fines or death (although the last was not usual). They rendered an account at the end of their office, just like all other Athenian officials, and underwent an audit or examination (euthynos). In fact, the conduct of military affairs was so important to the survival of the state that the assembly voted each prytany on whether or not individual strategoi should retain office. Even Perikles was dismissed from the strategia in 430 BC and fined when the Athenians decided to seek peace with Sparta (but he was re-elected for 429 BC). They were not held accountable as a group for their actions. The condemnation as a group of six of the eight strategoi who survived the Athenian victory at Arginousai but failed to pick up drowning Athenian sailors was in violation of the constitution (Xen. *Hellenika* 1.7.9–15: doc. 1.20). During times of war their role was clear, and distances from Athens meant that they had significant leeway in military decision-making while on campaign, but of course had to justify their actions at their end of office examination.

Table 10.3 The office of strategos

By the fourth century, the strategoi were allocated distinct spheres of activity by the vote of the ekklesia:

- One strategos was in charge of the hoplites and commanded them on military expeditions outside Athens;
- One strategos, a counterpart to the first, was charged with the defence of the Athenian countryside;
- Two strategoi guarded the Piraeus, Athens' port, which was vital for the import of food; one of these strategoi guarded Mounichia, the prominent hill at the Piraeus and crucial for its defence (docs 9.35, 13.40), and the other the Akte ('Point') to protect the population of the Piraeus;
- One strategos was in charge of the 'symmories' (created in 378/7, comprised of the 1200 most wealthy Athenians). He enrolled the trierarchs, the wealthy individuals who paid the expenses of running a trireme for one year (at a cost of about one talent), and introduced to the courts any claims to be made exempt from the role;
- Five further strategoi were to be sent on military expeditions as the need arose.

All the great leaders of the fifth century (Miltiades, Themistokles, Aristeides, Kimon, Perikles, Kleon, Alkibiades and Nikias) were engaged in the military sphere of operations, reflecting Athens' fight for survival in 490 and 480–479 BC and, later, its imperialistic aspirations. Direct election of the strategoi was unusual for Athens, as most offices, except the most important, were chosen by lot. The strategia, however, required military skill, which meant that the best candidates had to be chosen, and re-election was permitted so that those who had proved themselves in battle as the most successful generals could continue to employ their talents in the interests of the state. Theophrastos, in his discussion of the best ways of selecting officials, cites the general Hagnon's advice to the Athenians that the more experienced officials should be involved in training neophytes ('beginners'). This system was already in place for the strategia in other Greek states: 'as Hagnon once advised the Athenians to do in the case of their generals, using the example of hunting, where, he said, lovers of hunting always bring along puppies' (Theophr. *Laws for Eresos*: doc. 1.6).

While in 501/0 BC each tribe elected its own strategos this situation appears to have changed by the date of the casualty list for the tribe Erechtheis inscribed in 460 or 459 BC (*IG* I³ 1147: doc. 12.14), as this list includes two generals from the tribe Erechtheis, Phrynichos (line 6) and Hippodamas (line 63), although it is possible that Phrynichos was killed in battle and replaced by Hippodamas, who was then also killed. But in 441/0 BC there is a definite example of two strategoi from the same tribe, Akamantis (V), in a single year, namely Perikles and Glaukon, who served simultaneously. In 432/1 BC, there is an example of triple representation with three strategoi from the tribe Kekropis (VII). The election of one strategos from each tribe must, therefore, have been altered by at least 441/0 BC; presumably the ten candidates for the strategia who received the most votes were elected. In the fourth century strategoi were chosen not by tribes but from among all the Athenians collectively. Clearly, it was decided at some stage that it was more important to have the best possible strategoi than to ensure that each tribe had a strategos of its own. Significantly, the omens were observed when the election of the strategoi and other military officers took place: it was crucial not only to have the most militarily competent citizens in these roles, but the gods also must be seen to approve of their choice (*Ath. Pol.* 44.4).

Ostracism

The Athenaion Politeia on ostracism

Kleisthenes introduced the law on ostracism in Athens, and the most detailed account of its actual use in specific chronological years is that of the *Athenaion Politeia* (22.3–8, 43.5: docs 10.9–10). Ostracism was basically a process by which the citizens voted once a year to send one political figure into exile for ten years, without loss of citizenship or property. They voted by writing the name of the person they wished ostracised on a broken piece of pottery, known as an ostrakon (plural: ostraka), hence the name of the procedure, an ostrakophoria, or, in English, an ostracism. According to the *Athenaion Politeia*, Kleisthenes introduced the law specifically to send into exile Hipparchos, son of Charmos of the deme Kollytos. However, as it was not until 487 BC that the Athenians first made use of the law when they ostracised Hipparchos, this motive does not seem plausible. Moreover, the statement to the effect that the law was enacted due to 'suspicion of men in positions in power, because Peisistratos from being a popular leader and a general had set himself up as tyrant' seems more plausible as Kleisthenes' motive (*Ath. Pol.* 22.3: doc. 10.9; Philochoros gives a similar reason, that Kleisthenes introduced ostracism to expel the friends of the tyrants: *FGH* 328 *F* 30: doc. 10.11). Kleisthenes might also have had his own political struggles with Isagoras in mind when he framed the measure.

The *Athenaion Politeia* puts forward two reasons for the fact that the Athenians waited from the time of Kleisthenes' reforms in 508 until 487 BC to conduct the first ostracism: because the demos won the battle of Marathon against the Persians, which made it 'more confident', and because until this year they had been 'employing the tolerance characteristic of a democracy' and allowed the friends of the tyrants who were not implicated in any of Hippias' harsh measures to remain in the city (*Ath. Pol.* 22.4: doc. 10.9). The first three politicians to be ostracised, in 487, 486 and 485, are described as 'friends of the tyrants' (*Ath. Pol.* 22.6: doc. 10.9). Hipparchos, who was the first to be exiled, bears the same name as the Athenian tyrant assassinated in 514 BC, with the *Athenaion Politeia* specifically connecting him with the tyranny. Perhaps Hipparchos' father, Charmos, married a daughter of Hippias, and their child was given the name of his great-uncle. This Hipparchos is described as the leader and champion of the tyrants' friends in Athens after the tyrants themselves were expelled. That the tyrants' supporters were allowed to stay in Athens does reflect tolerance by the democracy, and is also an indication that the tyranny's crimes under Hippias, when his rule became harsh and he killed or exiled many Athenians, was seen as Hippias' personal responsibility. Many of the tyranny's supporters, if they had not been involved in this repressive regime, were allowed to stay on in the city. For example, Isagoras, elected as archon in 508 BC, was described as a 'friend of the tyrants' (*Ath. Pol.* 20.1: doc. 10.6). There was no 'purge' of the pro-tyrant citizens, unlike the expulsion of the Alkmeonidai under Isagoras and the Spartans, when 700 families were forced into exile.

The reform of the ten archonships

This greater confidence felt by the demos, which the *Athenaion Politeia* refers to in the first use of ostracism, was also reflected in a reform of the election of the board of ten archons in the following year, 487/6 BC. The archons were no longer directly elected by the tribes, and a process of partial sortition for their election was introduced. Five hundred candidates (prokritoi) were directly elected by the demes, and the archons were chosen out of these by lot. This measure greatly reduced the prestige of the archonship, and also made it less likely that an eponymous archon would become a 'leader' in the state (as Solon had been with a direct mandate from the demos, or like Isagoras, who was the eponymous archon but without being empowered to make any changes to the politeia). The demos was confident that there would always be 500 men eligible for and capable of holding the ten archonships: the democratic ethos was clearly growing.

In the same year (486 BC) the second ostracism was conducted, with Megakles, son of Hippokrates of Alopeke, one of the Alkmeonidai (he was Kleisthenes' nephew), being ostracised because of connections with the tyranny (*Ath. Pol.* 22.5: doc. 10.9): in handing power over to the people Kleisthenes had not secured his wider family group from political misfortunes. Megakles' ostracism may well have been connected with the allegation that the Alkmeonidai had signalled to the Persians during the battle at Marathon (Hdt. 6.120–124.2: doc. 11.10). Hippias' presence with the Persians there linked the tyrants with the invading Persians, and the story that the Alkmeonidai were responsible for the shield signal was probably the reason for Megakles' ostracism. Similarly, in 485, a third friend of the tyrants was ostracised, but – for whatever reason – he is not specifically named. This third victim of ostracism is often thought to be Kallias, son of Kratios of the deme Alopeke; he is represented by 763 ostraka, several of which accuse him of being a Mede, that is, a Persian. This was a damning accusation in the years after Marathon, particularly given the tyrant Hippias' return with the Persians to Marathon in 490 BC in the expectation of being restored as tyrant.

It was only in the fourth year after ostracism was first introduced that citizens unconnected with the tyranny fell victim to it: the demos 'started removing anyone else who appeared too powerful' (*Ath. Pol.* 22.6: doc. 10.9). In 484 BC it was Xanthippos, son of Ariphron of the deme Cholargeus, Perikles' father. The *Athenaion Politeia* (28.2) describes him as the 'champion of the people'. His ostracism can only be explained in terms of a political enmity other than that of connection with the tyranny. Although he may have been a 'champion of the people', clearly some type of power struggle was taking place in Athens, and, given that this is the period when Themistokles was achieving prominence, it is possible that the two democrats were rivals for the demos' political support. Themistokles may well have convinced the people that Xanthippos was becoming 'too powerful'. Several ostraka survive bearing Xanthippos' name but one in particular has his name and a message: he 'does most wrong of the accursed leaders' (Lang 134, no. 1065: doc. 10.14.i). This particular voter held all the leaders in contempt, but considered that Xanthippos was the worst. Xanthippos' son, Perikles, was also involved in an ostracism, but was more fortunate than his father and it was his opponent who went into exile. Certainly not long afterwards Themistokles seems to have used the demos' mistrust of Aristeides' influence to convince the people to ostracise him (Plut. *Aristeides* 7.1: doc. 10.12).

Aristeides was ostracised in 482 BC, the *Athenaion Politeia* stating that this was the same year that silver was discovered at Maroneia (22.7: doc. 10.9). This appears to have been the last ostracism prior to the Persian invasion of 480 BC. Themistokles according to Plutarch played a large role in Aristeides' ostracism (Plut. *Aristeides* 7.1: doc. 10.12; doc. 10.14.ii). However, Themistokles was able to put aside political differences in the face of the second Persian invasion and was responsible for the recall in 481 BC of 'all those who had been ostracised', so that they could help the Athenians face the Persians (*Ath. Pol.* 22.8: doc. 10.9; compare Meiggs and Lewis 23, line 45: doc. 11.35). Whether Hipparchos, a friend of the tyrants, is to be included in this 'all' is doubtful given that his status as the leader of the pro-tyrants in the city led to his ostracism. It is in the context of the recall of the ostracised that the *Athenaion Politeia* gives geographical parameters of where the ostracised could not live: 'within the limits of Geraistos (the cape of south-east Euboea) and Skyllaion (in Argos)'. This is confirmed by Philochoros (doc. 10.11). Aristeides seems to have spent his period of his ostracism at Aegina; Themistokles stayed at Argos; Hyperbolos (the last Athenian to be ostracised) was assassinated on Samos.

The procedure for an ostracism

Two fourth-century sources, as well as Plutarch and a scholiast, provide the information about the procedures for an ostracism. It should be noted, however, that while the situation in the fifth century was probably very much as they describe, there were no ostracisms conducted at Athens in the fourth century. In the sixth prytany of the year, the demos held a vote as to whether to hold an ostracism or not (*Ath. Pol.* 43.5: doc. 10.10). If the demos so decided, the vote was then held in the eighth prytany (Philoch. *FGH* 328 F30: doc. 10.11). While the physical preparations for an ostracism would not have taken much time, the period between the sixth and the eighth prytany in which the ostracism was to be held allowed time for lobbying within the demos to target a particular politician and for possible candidates for ostracism to protect themselves. Plutarch's account of the political rivalry between Thucydides, son of Melesias (not the historian), and Perikles seems to intimate that once the demos had decided that an ostracism would take place in 443 Thucydides and Perikles began orchestrating political campaigns against each other to ensure that the other was ostracised (Plut. *Perikles* 14.3: doc. 12.27; see examples of their ostraka at doc. 10.14.vi, xi).

The voting for the ostracism took place in the agora. According to Philochoros it was fenced off with planks for this purpose, while Plutarch has it fenced off with a 'circle of railings' (Plut. *Aristeides* 7.5: doc, 10.12), which could amount to more or less the same thing. According to Philochoros, ten gaps were left in the fencing, one for each tribe, presumably to give the chance for voters to be identified as citizens and to ensure that each voted only once. An official may well have had a list of names at each entrance and the members of the boule, who represented each and every single deme and kept the citizen lists, were present. Each citizen participating in an ostracism would scratch the name of the person he wished to be ostracised on a broken piece of pottery, and bring it into the agora via his tribe's entrance, holding the ostrakon upside down so that no one else could see what was written on it. This form of 'secret ballot' was obviously designed so that the citizens did not have to show anyone the name of the candidate against whom they were voting and so could not be intimidated by any of the proposed candidates for ostracism. The whole fencing off of the agora and its limited number of entrances, as well as the presence of the archons and boule, were designed to ensure that there would be no intimidation of the voters or miscounting of the votes (Philoch. *FGH* 328 F30: doc. 10.11; Schol. Ar. *Knights* 855: doc. 10.13).

As many Athenians were illiterate, they sought the assistance of those who could write. This is the origin of the charming, if fictitious, story in Plutarch that an illiterate citizen took one of the ostraka to Aristeides, without being aware of who he was, and asked Aristeides to inscribe 'Aristeides' on it. Aristeides asked the citizen why he wanted to have Aristeides ostracised and what Aristeides had ever done to him. The citizen replied that Aristeides had done him no harm, but he was 'tired of hearing him called "the Just" everywhere.' So Aristeides wrote his own name on the ostrakon and handed it back to his fellow-citizen (Plut. *Aristeides* 7.7: doc. 10.12).

Ostraka with names already scratched on them could be handed out to voters: a well on the north slope of the acropolis yielded a find of 190 ostraka inscribed with Themistokles' name, written in only fourteen different hands. Apparently the ostraka had been mass-produced, and were probably dumped in the well without having been used. This mass production of ostraka may have been intended for sale, but were more probably for free distribution to voters by Themistokles' political enemies. The ostraka often, but by no means always, included the name, the patronymic (that is, father's name), and the deme of the individual that the voter wished to be ostracised (see the examples at doc. 10.14; Fig. 10.3).

There is debate about the number of votes required to ostracise an individual. Philochoros has 6000 votes required against an individual as does the scholiast, while Plutarch has a quorum of 6000 in total, which seems more plausible, as it is known that 6000 was a quorum for other procedures in the assembly. Presumably he had a good source for this. The individual who received most of the 6000 votes would therefore be ostracised. The boule and the archon presided over the procedure, with the archons counting the ostraka to ensure that there were 6000 votes: if there were insufficient votes the ostracism was declared null and void. If there were 6000 or more whoever received the most votes 'lost' the ostracism and went into exile. He was given ten days to settle any law-suits he was engaged in and to organise his affairs (Philoch. *FGH* 328 F30: doc. 10.11; Plut. *Aristeides* 7.6: doc. 10.12).

Philochoros states that the period of ostracism was changed from ten years to five, but it is fairly certain that the ten-year period was always in force. The ostracised citizen did not lose his citizenship or property, and could receive income from his property (such as landed estates or businesses) while in exile (Philoch. *FGH* 328 *F* 30: doc. 10.11; Plut. *Aristeides* 7.6: doc. 10.12). After ten years' absence any ostracised figure was considered to be a 'spent' political force. However, Aristeides made a 'political comeback' after his ostracism although in his case he was only away for a few years, being one of the ostracised recalled to help the Athenians face the Persians. Another notable exception is Kimon who, after his ostracism in 461, returned to Athens ten years later and regained his political position, arranging a five-year truce with Sparta and taking part in a campaign against Persia on Cyprus where he died.

Hyperbolos, in either 417, 416 or 415, was the last victim of ostracism (doc. 10.14.xii). According to Plutarch, the demos wanted to ostracise either Nikias or Alkibiades because of their overt political differences, but in the face of this threat these two united and brought about Hyperbolos' ostracism instead. 'Incensed' at this corruption of the process, the demos no longer employed ostracism. But it was not abolished, for the *Athenaion Politeia* writing in the 330s (so some 80 years after the Athenians last used the practice), commented that every sixth prytany the demos still voted on whether or not to hold one (*Ath. Pol.* 43.5: 10.10). In the fourth century, political battles between rivals were fought in the ekklesia and the dikasteria instead, but in the fifth century it served Kleisthenes' purpose of removing rival leaders from the state and thus preventing civil dissension.

Demes and trittyes

Kleisthenes and religion

Aristotle advised that, in establishing democracy, 'other tribes and phratries should be created, more than before, and private religious rites should be channelled into a few public ones' (Arist. *Politics* 1319b19–27: doc. 10.16). Kleisthenes followed this advice in creating new tribes, but he did not touch the ancient religious rites of the Athenians or abolish their phratries ('brotherhoods'). Also everyone was allowed to 'retain their clans, phratries and priesthoods according to ancestral custom' (*Ath. Pol.* 21.6: doc. 10.7). To Aristotle the breakdown of private religious rites was significant for democratic cohesion because these gave the citizens a non-public, non-democratic orientation often associated with particular families, rather than with the state. For example, Isagoras' family had its own cult of Carian Zeus, providing them with a private religious identity (Hdt. 5.66.1: doc. 10.1). Clearly the idea of abolishing private religious rites did not occur to Kleisthenes. Alternatively, considering the problems Athens experienced with some of the aristocratic families over the attempted takeover of the state by Isagoras, he may have wanted to avoid annoying aristocratic families by tampering with their religious rites.

But Kleisthenes did ensure that religious loyalties at the local level did not interfere with his measures to unite the Athenians politically in the new democracy. For example, he did not put an end to the joint religious activities of the Marathonian tetrapolis ('four-city' association), but ensured that the tetrapolis did not also function as a political unit. From the earliest times right down to at least the first century BC the four towns of the tetrapolis, Marathon, Oinoe, Trikorynthos and Probalinthos, sent religious embassies to Delphi and Delos. These were distinct from those sent by the Athenian state. It was, therefore, always a unit with a distinct religious organisation, and Marathon certainly had Peisistratid associations. Kleisthenes broke up this unit: the deme of Probalinthos, which provided five members of the boule (bouleutai; singular: bouleutes), and was therefore reasonably populous, was detached from the other three and placed in a different coastal trittys; Rhamnous was joined to the other three to form a coastal trittys.

In this way the four centres of the tetrapolis were now split into two different tribes: Marathon, Oinoe, Trikorynthos in the tribe Aiantis (IX) and Probalinthos in the tribe Pandionis (III). While these four demes continued their religious, cultic activities as a unit, the important Probalinthos deme now had different political affiliations from the other three demes with regard to all the activities carried out on a tribal basis: it elected members of the boule, fought, and elected strategoi for a different tribe. Special effort was taken to detach Probalinthos, for it was an example of a deme geographically separated from its trittys: it belonged to the coastal trittys of Pandionis, but the coastal trittys of the tribe Aigeis intervened and split the demes of this trittys. Brauron, a Peisistratid centre, was in this Aigeis trittys, and it is significant that Probalinthos, with its Marathonian Peisistratid connection, was deliberately not attached to this trittys but was put with the Pandionis coastal trittys. The Tetrakomoi provides a similar example: the four demes involved, Piraeus, Phaleron, Xypete and Thymaitadai, were split into three different trittyes and so different tribes: Piraeus and Thymaitadai went to the tribe Hippothontis (VIII), Phaleron to Aiantis (IX) and Xypete to Kekropis (VII). Demes also celebrated the great festivals of the Athenian city at a local level: so the deme Skambonidai held the Athenian Dipoleia and Panathenaia at a local level at the same time as these festivals were celebrated in the city itself (*IG* I^3 244 (A): doc. 10.20).

The prytaneis

A consequence of the change to ten tribes was that the boule of Solon, with 100 members drawn from each of the four Ionian tribes, had to be changed in some way. Kleisthenes' solution was to have fifty men chosen by each tribe to serve on the council for one year, giving a boule of 500 members. He made no changes to the Council of the Areiopagos, leaving it with its Solonian functions, which were mainly the guardianship of the constitution. Each annual tribal contingent of fifty to the boule was given an executive role for one-tenth of the year; this one-tenth of the year was known as a prytany and the fifty members from each tribe were known as prytaneis during their term of office, their prytany. They then reverted to being ordinary members of the boule (bouleutai) for the remainder of the civic year. A different chairperson – epistates – for the boule was chosen for a single day and night by lot from among the fifty prytaneis. This epistates for that twenty-four hours had charge of the temple keys in which state monies and documents were kept, and of the state seal; he and one-third of the serving prytaneis spent the night in the prytaneion to be on hand in case of any state emergencies. The fifty members from each tribe were chosen by a system based on the demes which made up each tribe, with each deme electing a set number of men each year.

The number and character of the demes

The number of demes is now known to have been 140; Acharnai was once thought to be one deme and the total number of demes 139, but this populous area was actually two demes, bringing the number to 140. An inscription, which is now unfortunately fragmentary, listed the demes and is now referred to as the known as the 'great deme list' (*IG* II^2 2362). It provides evidence for reconstructing a list of demes and their tribes.

A deme was generally one village or town and its surrounding territory. Membership of a deme was hereditary, and an Athenian who moved to another deme retained membership in his original deme. All Athenians remained registered in the deme in which their ancestor in the time of Kleisthenes was enrolled. Many of the 'city' demes were not actually within the city-walls, but in its general vicinity. There were at least five demes within the walls: Koile, Kollytos, Kydathenaion, Melite and Skambonidai, which were presumably organised on quarters of the city. For an example of the arrangement of demes and trittyes within one particular tribe, see *Ancient Greece* Map IV.

The length of time required for Kleisthenes to organise the demes and trittyes into units is uncertain. Scholars agree that he would have carried out his reforms as soon as possible. The first year in which the boule took the oath, which became traditional when its members entered upon office for the year, was in 501/0, but this does not mean that the Kleisthenic boule first came into being in this year. Rather, the imposition of the oath needs to be seen as a further measure to ensure that the body was democratic and abided by its role in the new politeia (*Ath. Pol.* 22.2; doc. 10.8). The oath could easily date to several years after the intro-duction of the new boule. Kleisthenes came to prominence by promising the people power: to maintain this support at least some, and probably the majority, of his reforms needed to be carried out reasonably quickly. It is unlikely that precise surveying of the land of Attica took place or that teams of surveyors were sent out to divide Attica neatly into its 140 demes and thirty trittyes. As each deme was actually a village, town or suburb, it was simply this central location that mattered. Members of demes saw the nearest geographical urban unit as their local village, and this now became a deme centre which elected its quota of bouletai each year. Kleisthenes did not have to establish the physical boundaries of demes and the constituents of a particular deme were easy to determine.

Each of the thirty trittyes into which Kleisthenes divided Attica was made up of one or usu-ally more demes. These demes were clearly arranged systematically into trittyes, otherwise the populations of each individual trittys would have varied too much, and the representa-tion of demes on the boule would have been unequal and unrepresentative of the population of each deme. Trittyes could well have been assigned by lot to tribes, as the *Athenaion Politeia* states (21.4: doc. 10.7), but whether this happened is uncertain. A trittys was either a city, inland or coastal collection of demes, but the demes making up a trittys were not necessarily geographically contiguous: that is the demes in a trittys did not all border each other and did not need to be in the same geographical location. City demes as well could be non-contigu-ous with the other demes in a city trittys, as seems to have been the case with the city demes of Kollytos, Kolonos and Ankyle of the tribe Aigeis (II) (*Ancient Greece*, Map IV). Boundaries of demes within the city itself, however, probably needed to be more accurately defined than those of the other demes, as population areas in the city even in c. 508/7 presumably over-lapped. Boundaries were probably provided by roads and crossroads, rivers and streams, and possibly even major shrines. There were occasionally 'divided' demes, two separate demes of the same name, one 'Upper' and one 'Lower', i.e., Upper Lamptrai and Lower Lamptrai of Erechtheis (I), as well as Upper and Lower Ankyle of Aigeis (II).

The number of demes per trittys varied; the inland trittys of the tribe Aiantis (IX), for example, had only one deme, Aphidna, which provided a quota of sixteen bouleutai. Clearly Aphidna had a large population explaining why it was the only deme in this inland trit-tys. The number of demes per tribe also varied: from six demes in the tribe Aiantis (IX), to twenty-one demes in the tribe Aigeis (II) (see Map IV). Clearly, the system was organised so that the ten tribes were roughly equal in population to ensure equal representation on the boule. The registration of its members, the demotai, was the most important duty of the demes, especially after Perikles' citizenship law of 451/0 by which both parents had to be Athenians (*Ath. Pol.* 26.4: doc. 1.36); the list of demotai in each deme constituted a record of Athenian citizens. The fourth-century procedure for enrolment as a citizen is described by the *Athenaion Politeia* (42.1–2: doc. 1.38), and it seems reasonable that this procedure or a similar one was inaugurated by Kleisthenes.

Earlier scholarship erroneously argued that Kleisthenes devised a system of demes, trittyes and tribes to give prominence to his family, the Alkmeonidai. Basically, this theory suggests that the Alkmeonidai were able to dominate three tribes because their areas of influence south of the city were assigned to three tribes and were combined (in the same three tribes) with coastal areas in which they had influence. There is no substance in this suggestion: after Kleisthenes, the Alkmeonidai had no real prominence in the Athenian political system. Their most famous descendant – and not by direct descent – was Perikles who had prominence in Athens by virtue of his oratory and elected position as strategos, while his father Xanthippos achieved enough prominence as a political leader to be ostracised in 485/4 BC.

While the names of the tribes and demes are known, only eighteen names of the thirty trittyes are recorded, although several other possible identifications have been made. This is because they operated at a 'middle level' between demes and tribes, and, although serving to 'mix up' the Athenian citizen body thoroughly, did not have the same visible identity as the demes and tribes. The evidence for the names of trittyes comes largely from fifteen stone trittys markers found in Athens and the Piraeus. These do not actually mark boundaries between trittyes and their purpose was as marshalling-places where members of a trittys could assemble for military service (in the army and navy) when called upon to do so; citizens gathered at the appropriate marker when required.

Bouleutic quotas

A deme provided members to the council, boule, according to the population of that deme, with each deme being responsible for sending a certain number of men to the boule as its share of the fifty members for its tribe. This means that there were quotas for all the demes, which modern scholars refer to as bouleutic quotas. These quotas are known from inscriptions dating to the fourth century and later and these must have been set by Kleisthenes when devising the system by which demes sent members to the boule each year. When each of the ten groups of fifty took it in turns to run the boule for one-tenth of the year, this group of fifty men were known as prytaneis and were said 'to hold the prytany'. There are several fragmentary prytany lists, as well as some in an extant state of preservation, which provide evidence for the bouleutic quotas of certain demes. One, *Agora* xv.38 (doc. 10.18), gives the names of the fifty members of the tribe Aigeis (II) for the year 341/0 BC, listed according to their deme. The bouleutic quotas for the demes have been calculated from this and other inscriptions. In this prytany list for Aigeis (II) there are six names under the heading of the deme Erchia, indicating that this deme elected six members to the boule not just in 341/0 BC, the date of the inscription, but in every year presumably since Kleisthenes' reforms. Some demes, such as Bate, provided only one member of the boule, indicating that it was a much smaller deme than Erchia.

Larger demes provided a greater number of bouleutai: the inland part of the deme Acharnai, as opposed to the city part, provided a quota of fifteen (or possibly sixteen) bouleutai of the fifty bouleutai for its tribe, while the smallest demes might share a place on the boule with another deme, taking it in turns to provide the member for the boule in different years. This system, catering for the different sizes of each of the 140 demes, ensured that there was equal representation on the boule of the population throughout Attica.

Demes as mini-democracies

Each deme was a mini-polis. One inscription of about 420 BC records the financial details of one deme, Plotheia. The decree was passed by the members of the deme, the Plotheians, and the beginning of the decree reads exactly as if it were the beginning of a decree passed by the Athenian assembly itself: 'It was resolved by the Plotheians: Aristotimos proposed the motion' (IG I³ 258: doc. 10.19). Each deme acted as a mini-democracy modelled on the state democracy and had its own assembly of the citizens of the deme. They voted on proposals which became decrees regulating the deme's finances, religious activities and other local matters, such as those passed by the demes Plotheia and Skambonidai (docs 10.19–20). Demes had their own elected officials to administer their affairs, the most important of whom was the demarch ('deme official') whose financial role and religious duties and privileges are made clear by these two deme inscriptions. He also convened the deme assembly, organised its proceedings such as oath taking and voting, and ensured that the assembly's decisions, ratified by its decrees, were carried out. Such positions undoubtedly proved useful training for those who wished to engage in the wider arena of Athenian politics.

Plotheia as a deme serves as a useful example of how the demes operated politically. It elected its financial officials by lot – a demarch and two treasurers – and each were provided with the interest from capital funds to use for various deme expenses. This decree also refers to a previous decree of the deme concerning lending its money at the highest possible rate of interest. The deme's capital fund itself was not to be used for expenses. This ensured that the deme was in no danger of running out of money at some stage in the future; moreover the other forms of income besides the leases and interest on the capital are mentioned simply as 'what comes in from income' which was not to be spent, meaning that the capital fund of the deme could grow annually.

The financial priorities of the deme are made clear from the fact that a specific amount of capital is set aside for five festivals, the largest sum being for the Herakleion, with the interest from 7000 drachmas to supply the necessities of the festival. Another fund called the 'immunity' (with a balance of 5000 drachmas) provided the expenses for sacrifices at other festivals, including those held in common with the Athenians, and the nearby deme of the Epakreans. Members of the deme were provided with sweet wine at these sacrifices, in which they must have also eaten the meat from the sacrificial victims. While the deme carefully husbanded its resources, it also provided for festivals which ensured that the deme members worshipped the gods as a community and displayed their piety; these festivals also played a crucial role in defining the identity of the deme, with the demesmen (demotai) coming together as a group to celebrate these festivals, which also, of course, provided a welcome chance for relaxation, entertainment and feasting.

A similar decree, passed much earlier by the deme Skambonidai of the tribe Leontis (IV) in about 460 BC, has similar provisions but also indicates the financial safeguards which a deme could adopt to secure its capital reserves. The Skambonidai deme decree makes arrangements for the religious celebrations of the deme, ordering the demarch and the hieropoioi (sacred officials) to offer a perfect sacrificial victim to Leos, the eponymous hero of the tribe. The demarch was rewarded for his religious duties with the skin of the sacrificial victim at this festival. Meat and wine were shared out, and in this deme, the resident metics (foreigners) shared in the civic festivities, showing an understanding and appreciation of their role in Athenian society at a local level.

The middle section of this deme decree (Part B) also points to a mirroring at the deme level of the same mechanisms by which the Athenian state itself checked on its officials. While the context is unclear due to the fragmentary nature of the inscription, it seems as if an official or officials concerned with the deme finances had to swear an oath that he or they would render the required accounting or audit (euthynos) of the monies for which they had been responsible while they were in office. In other words the deme with its various concerns was organised along the same lines as the state itself and each deme as a democracy gave the citizens experience of how a democracy operated.

Kleisthenes' reforms radically altered the Solonian system: wealth was a criterion for political participation only with regard to the election of officials, and this saw further developments, when the third class, the zeugitai, became eligible for the archonship from 453/2. By the 330s even this regulation had fallen into abeyance and the thetes could stand for office – they simply did not admit to this when asked to which class they belonged when standing for election. The ekklesia, the body of citizens, became sovereign and the assembly decided on all important domestic and foreign political issues. The democracy was still led for the next eighty years or so by leaders drawn from the wealthy, but the emergence of political figures such as the non-aristocratic Kleon during the Peloponnesian War marked the emergence of a truly populist democracy in which ordinary Athenians proposed decrees, spoke in the ekklesia and voted on all issues of major importance. Kleisthenes was a pivotal figure in Athenian political history and the demos rallied behind his cause so that the Spartan attempt to impose a narrow oligarchy failed. Athens could have become Sparta's ally, but it was only a few generations later that they were bitter enemies and Athens was ignominiously defeated by the Spartans in the Peloponnesian War. But, before then, a great challenge lay ahead: the mighty Persian Empire in the east was gradually expanding westward and the fledging democracy was to face its first international crisis.

11

THE PERSIAN WARS

Table 11.1 The Achaemenid kings of Persia

Cyrus the Great, founder of the Persian Empire	c. 557–530
Cambyses, Cyrus' son	530–522
Smerdis, Cambyses' brother	522
Darius I the Great, son of Hystaspes	522–486
Xerxes the Great, son of Darius	486–465
Artaxerxes I, son of Xerxes	465–424
Xerxes II, son of Artaxerxes	424
Sogdianos, Xerxes II's half-brother	424
Darius II Nothus, Sogdianos' half-brother and rival	424–404
Artaxerxes II Memnon, Darius' son	404–358
Artaxerxes III Ochus, son of Artaxerxes II	358–338
Artaxerxes IV Arses, son of Artaxerxes III	338–336
Darius III, great-grandson of Darius II	336–330
Artaxerxes V Bessos	330–329

Introduction

Persia emerged as the major power in the east with the beginning of the reign of Cyrus 'the Great', who ruled from about 557 to 530 BC. Persia was an expansionist and imperialistic power, both ruthless towards its enemies and yet also committed to the worship of Auramazdâ, creator and defender of the 'Truth'. Persia's conquest of the Lydians in 546 BC brought it domination over the Greek city-states of Asia Minor, but half a century later in 499 BC these unsuccessfully revolted. The Persian king Darius and his son Xerxes both attempted to exact revenge against the Athenians for their role in this rebellion, which was squashed in 494 BC. Persia's lack of success ensured the freedom of Greece, and in particular the freedom of Athens, which went on to develop a maritime empire in the Aegean and a golden age of literature, learning and architecture.

Sources

The main source for the Persian wars is the *Histories* of Herodotos. In Book 4 he describes Darius I's campaigns against the Scythians, Books 5 and 6 narrate the history of the Ionian Revolt and Darius' attempt to conquer Athens, while Books 7 through to 9 deal with Xerxes' attack on Greece. Aeschylus in his play the *Persians* provides a valuable first-hand account of

Figure 11.1 Tomb of Cyrus the 'Great', founder of the Persian Empire, at Pasagardai, Iran. Photo © Alan D. Coogan.

the battle of Salamis, while Plutarch in various of his *Lives*, such as those of Themistokles and Aristeides, provides biographies of individual Athenian protagonists. These should, however, be used with caution. Various epitaphs and inscriptions relate to the war and glorify the achievements of the Greeks; what is missing is a Persian account of the conflict.

Darius and the Persians

Greek interaction with the Persians, and especially with the satrap (also hyparchos: 'governor' or 'viceroy') at Sardis, began in 546 BC and continued until the destruction of the Persian Empire in 331 BC with Alexander the Great's capture and burning of the Persian capital Persepolis. The Persians themselves were essentially an Iranian people, who under Cyrus 'the Great' acquired an empire. Cyrus first conquered the Medes who had previously controlled Persia, and then Lydia and Babylonia (Fig. 11.1; Map 11.1). By this he established the Persian Empire, which continued to grow, although conquest in Europe was checked in 480–479 BC when Xerxes was defeated by the mainland Greeks. Cyrus was succeeded by Cambyses II c. 530 BC, who conquered Egypt. Darius I came to power in 522 BC, but was not from this royal line, and faced a number of problems in securing his position as monarch.

The Bisitun rock inscription

This inscription, in which Darius speaks, is the chief non-Greek source for his reign ((*Bisitun Rock Inscription*: doc. 11.2). Carved 100 metres high up on a cliff face in Iran, between Teheran and Baghdad, on the ancient highway from Ekbatana (the capital of the Medes) and Babylon, it was inscribed in three languages: Elamite, Babylonian and Persian. The inscription is 25 metres wide and 15 metres high, and includes a relief showing a life-size Darius: he has a foot on a prostrate figure, usually identified as the pretender Gaumata (that is, Smerdis: doc.

371

11.2.52). Nine captive figures (one metre high) represent the peoples he conquered. Copies of the inscription were made 'on clay tablets and on parchment', and distributed throughout the Persian Empire (70: doc. 11.2): certainly no one could have read the Bisitun inscription itself given its position so high up the sheer cliff face. Darius attributes his various victories to the main Persian deity Auramazdâ (Ahura Mazda), the highest deity in the Zoroastrian religion and the creator of Truth (asha) which continually battles against the Lie (drug), until evil and the destructive spirit Angra Mainya are eventually destroyed by Auramazdâ (Fig. 11.2).

Darius and his successors ruled the Achaemenid Persian Empire (see Table 11.1) and Darius gives a detailed account of his own lineage, and how he was descended from Akhaemenes: 'King Darius says: For that reason we are called Akhaemenians; from of old we have been nobly born, from of old our family have been kings' (*Bisitun Rock Inscription* 3: doc. 11.2). Clearly one of the purposes of the inscription was to obscure the fact that he was not a descendant of Cyrus or Cambyses. His own succession, which was clearly an act of usurpation, led to various revolts and rival claims to the throne. In the course of 522 BC he fought nineteen battles and captured nine kings. He names all of these, describing them as liars who claimed kingship over their territories. Conquering them enabled him to describe himself in the inscription, as did subsequent Achaemenid kings, as 'Great King, King of Kings' (1: doc.11.2).

Darius founded the royal capital at Persepolis, with its public audience hall, the Apadana (Fig. 15.8), and his successors continued his building work here. Measuring 60 metres square, with 72 columns 19 metres high, the Apadana contains sculptured reliefs which famously show the Ten Thousand Immortals (the elite Persian troops described by Herodotos 7.83), tribute-bearers from twenty-three subject states, and Persian nobles (Fig. 11.3); Darius lists these twenty-three subject states in his Bisitun inscription (doc.11.2.6). Both Darius and Xerxes built a palace here, with splendid reliefs; additionally, the throne room built by Darius' successor Xerxes I shows the king giving audience. The complex was destroyed by Alexander and his companions in 331 BC in the aftermath of a drunken party (Diod. Sic. 17.72.1–6: doc. 15.20). Darius' naming of the twenty-three countries he subdued can be contrasted with Aeschylus' list of all the glorious conquests of Darius' reign in the *Persians* produced at Athens in 472 BC. In this list he individually named the Greek states in his empire, prior to Athens' crushing defeat at Marathon of the 'all-powerful, guileless, unconquerable King, God-like Darius' (*Persians* 852–907: doc. 11.1).

Persia's political system was absolutist and the king ruled directly over his empire. A religious ideology was a crucial aspect of this and the chief Persian deity Auramazdâ was said to have divinely appointed the king to reign (that is why Auramazdâ is mentioned so prominently in the Bisitun inscription). As such, the king's reign was part of Auramazdâ's plan for the universe and as the god's direct representative, all the king's subjects owed him direct obedience and (of course) tribute. Any rebellion was seen as denial of Auramazdâ. Herodotos at 3.89–94 lists these subject peoples and the tribute that they paid: the amounts, which seem accurate, add up to a staggering degree of wealth, especially when compared to the relative poverty of the Greek states.

The problem of communication within the vast territory ruled over by the king was partially overcome by the 'Royal Road' running from Susa to Sardis, with the section from Persepolis, the main capital, to Susa, the winter capital, in constant use (Map 11.1). Official couriers sent along this road could change horses and draw provisions from storerooms maintained by the state along the way. In addition, various other important roads connected the centre with the middle and periphery of the empire.

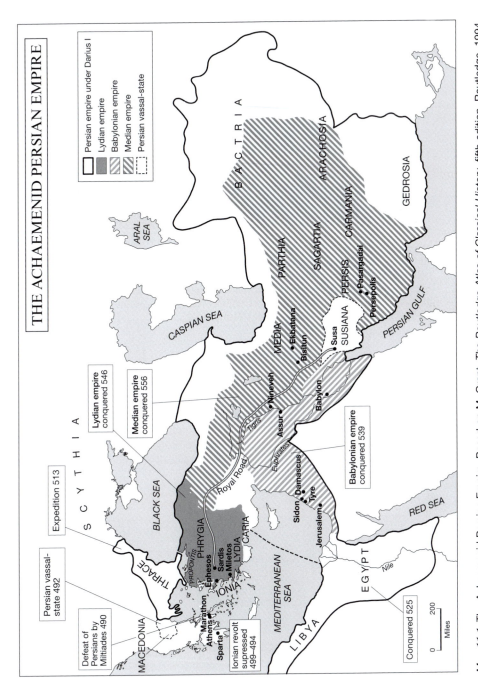

THE ACHAEMENID PERSIAN EMPIRE

Persian empire under Darius I
Lydian empire
Babylonian empire
Median empire
Persian vassal-state

Lydian empire
conquered 546

Median empire
conquered 556

Expedition 513

Persian vassal-
state 492

Defeat of
Persians by
Miltiades 490

Ionian revolt
supressed
499–494

Babylonian empire
conquered 539

Conquered 525

SCYTHIA

ARAL SEA

CASPIAN SEA

BACTRIA

ARACHOSIA

PARTHIA

SAGARTIA

CARMANIA

GEDROSIA

PERSIS

Pasargadai

Persepolis

SUSIANA

Susa

MEDIA

Ekbatana

Bisitun

PERSIAN GULF

BLACK SEA

THRACE

MACEDONIA

PROPONTIS

PHRYGIA

Ephesos

Sardis

Miletos

IONIA

LYDIA

CARIA

Marathon

Athens

Sparta

Royal Road

Tigris

Euphrates

Nineveh

Assur

Babylon

Damascus

Sidon

Tyre

Jerusalem

MEDITERRANEAN SEA

LIBYA

EGYPT

Nile

RED SEA

0   200

Miles

Map 11.1 The Achaemenid Persian Empire. Based on M. Grant, *The Routledge Atlas of Classical History*, fifth edition, Routledge, 1994, p. 21.

Figure 11.2 The Bisitun Rock Inscription, Iran, with inscriptions and relief sculptures (doc. 11.2). On the left Darius, shown life-size, stands on a prostrate figure while nine captive figures stand before him. Over the scene hovers the supreme god of the Persians, Auramazdâ (Ahura Mazda). The inscription and reliefs are 100 m up the cliff face, while the inscription itself is 15 m high and 25 m wide; Bisitun is a UNESCO World Heritage Site. Photo © Imagestate Media Partners Limited – Impact Photos/Alamy.

The Ionian Revolt

After Cyrus defeated Croesus (son of Alyattes), king of the Lydians, in 546 BC, Persia moved against the Greek cities of Asia Minor and conquered them. Lydia's chief city, Sardis, then became the Persian capital of a satrapy (province) controlling western Asia Minor, with its satrap governing numerous Greek city-states. These were left a degree of self-government, but usually under the immediate control of pro-Persian tyrants. In 499 BC the Ionian cities revolted against Persian rule, with the rebellion lasting until 494 BC when the Persians crushed the Ionians at the battle of Lade.

Figure 11.3 Bringing tribute to the Persian king, these tribute bearers are tentatively identified as Ionians. The carved relief scene is from the eastern staircase of the Apadana (audience hall, Persepolis. Photo © Alan D. Coogan

Naxos and the beginnings of the Ionian Revolt

Naxos was the catalyst for this revolt of the Ionian Greeks of Asia Minor against Persia. Peisistratos had seized the island for his supporter Lygdamis in return for his assistance at the battle of Pallene ([Arist.] *Ath. Pol.*15.3: doc. 9.13), but the Spartans had ousted Lygdamis in around 525 BC (Plut. *On the Malignity of Herodotos* 21 [859d]: doc. 6.58). After this the island, the wealthiest in the Aegean, was ruled by an aristocracy. The demos then took control and exiled the aristocrats, who went to Miletos, an Ionian city on the Asia Minor coast, ruled by Aristagoras, nephew and son-in-law of Histiaios, the previous tyrant of Miletos. He was now at Susa with Darius, somewhat unwillingly, as his counsellor. In response to the Naxians' request for assistance Aristagoras suggested to Artaphernes, the brother of Darius and the Persian satrap at Susa, that he be given a fleet and troops with which to capture the island of Naxos for the Persians and reinstate the aristocrats; he and the aristocrats would pay the expedition's expenses if the Persians advanced the necessary funds for the undertaking. These would then be repaid. Artaphernes consulted with Darius, who agreed to the plan. After a siege of four months, however, the city and island of Naxos remained unconquered. Aristagoras had failed, and now owed a large amount of money to the Persians. Histiaios, at Susa, therefore, sent a messenger to Aristagoras suggesting that he raise a revolt of the Ionian Greeks against the Persians. In order to ensure successful delivery of the message, the messenger's head was shaved, the message tattooed on his scalp, and his hair allowed to regrow before he was sent to Miletos. Histiaios, according to Herodotos, was hoping that Darius would release him from Susa and send him to Ionia to deal with this revolt.

All Aristagoras' supporters agreed with the plan to revolt from the Persians, except the writer Hekataios, who pointed out the resources of the Persian Empire and the number of countries under Persian domination (compare the list in Aesch. *Persians* 852–907: doc. 11.1; *The Bisitun Rock Inscription* 6: doc. 11.2). Aristagoras relinquished his position as tyrant at Miletos and isonomia ('equality') was introduced; this term, meaning, 'equal laws' meant equality before the law, or in simpler terms, democracy. He then deposed the pro-Persian tyrants throughout the Ionian cities, and isonomia was established in these cities as well. Herodotos emphasises the personal motives of both Histiaios and Aristagoras, but clearly the various Ionian cities had specific grievances against the Persians as well. Being ruled by pro-Persian tyrants was probably a primary reason to revolt given that the first act of the rebellion was to oust them; the tyrants were generally allowed to go into exile but one, Koes of the island of Mytilene, was stoned to death. The Ionian Greeks wanted freedom from external control, and this was achieved with the deposition of the tyrants and the establishment of isonomia. The people of Naxos had resisted the attempts of the Persians to reimpose the rule of the aristocrats, and if one island could defeat the Persians, the prospects of rebellion may have seemed sound to the Ionian Greeks.

Aristagoras, Sparta and Athens

Aristagoras then set out to Sparta to enlist its aid for the rebel cause. Kleomenes and Demaratos were kings there at the time and Herodotos has Aristagoras negotiating with Kleomenes. Although he was not sole ruler of Sparta, it is clear that he was a powerful and influential figure and does seem to have set the 'agenda' for Spartan military activities during his reign. Kleomenes rejected the request; Aristagoras then attempted to bribe Kleomenes, but was unsuccessful because Kleomenes' 8- or 9-year-old daughter Gorgo, later wife of king Leonidas, said to her father, 'Father, the stranger will corrupt you, if you don't go away' (Hdt. 5.49.1–51.3: doc. 6.74). According to Herodotos, Kleomenes' main objection was that Persepolis (the seat of the 'Great King') was three months' march from the Ionian coast. Aristagoras, however, was not asking Kleomenes to invade the Persian Empire and Herodotos should be understood as indicating that Kleomenes realised the extent of the Persian Empire and its powerful resources. Kleomenes was active in the political affairs of mainland Greece, but may have believed that Persia was too large to attack successfully. Previously, in about 515 BC, Kleomenes had also rejected Maiandros' attempt to bribe him to restore him as tyrant of Samos from which position the Persians had ejected him (Hdt. 3.148.1–2: doc. 6.73).

Aristagoras then went to Athens, where the Athenians were influenced by their own recent interaction with Persia. They had themselves, after Kleomenes was ejected from Athens in 508 BC, sent a delegation to Artaphernes, satrap of Susa, but had rejected its acceptance of Artaphernes' terms for an alliance: to give tokens of submission to the Persians (Hdt. 5.73.1–3: doc. 10.4). When later they discovered that Hippias was at Artaphernes' court scheming to be reinstalled as tyrant, with Athens under Persian rule, they sent another delegation to Artaphernes. He bluntly told them, in answer to their request that he should not listen to Hippias, to accept Hippias back as tyrant. So when Aristagoras requested assistance for the revolt against Persia, the Athenians promised twenty ships, with Melanthios as strategos (Hdt. 5.97.1–3: doc. 11.3). The city of Eretria on the island of Euboea also contributed five ships. These twenty-five vessels, along with the Ionian fleet, arrived at Ephesos in 498 BC and the crews and soldiers of the combined force marched inland to Sardis, where they captured and burnt the city, including a temple to Cybele 'which the Persians later used as an excuse for burning the temples in Greece in return' (Fig. 11.4). But Artaphernes the satrap still held the acropolis; as other Persian troops arrived the Greeks hastened to retreat, only to be severely defeated by the Persians at Ephesos. The mainland Greeks managed to escape and Athens no longer supported the rebellion, despite the fact that Aristagoras on several occasions asked for its assistance (Hdt. 5.100–103.1: doc. 11.4).

Figure 11.4 Sardis, in modern Turkey. This is the furthest the Ionians and Athenians penetrated into the Persian Empire after the Ionian Revolt broke out (doc. 11.4). Their burning of the temple of Cybele led to the Persian destruction of temples in their invasions of Greece in 490 and 480–479 BC. In the foreground is a temple of Artemis built in around 300 BC. Photo © Jeff Faust.

Darius was informed of events and according to Herodotos from this time forth had a servant remind him three times each day before dinner, 'Sire, remember the Athenians' (Hdt.
5.105.1–2: doc. 11.5). Despite the setbacks at Sardis and Ephesos, the revolt spread along
the Asia Minor coast and islands: Byzantium and nearby cities, the region of Caria, and
Cyprus all joined. Joint meetings of the Ionians were conducted at their ancestral political
and religious centre, the Panionion (Hdt. 1.142.1: doc. 1.59), but by 497 BC the Persian military machine was in full operation and Caria and Cyprus were reconquered. Histiaios, still
in virtual imprisonment at Susa with Darius, denied complicity in the rebellion and was sent
to Ionia to deal with the situation; at Sardis he quickly fled before Artaphernes' suspicions
and went over to the side of the Ionians. Miletos, however, where he had once been tyrant,
would not have him back, but the Lesbians gave him command of eight ships. Aristagoras
had been killed in Thrace in 496 BC, apparently trying to carve out a zone of influence for
himself there, shortly before Histiaios' arrival.

In 494 BC the crucial moment came for the revolt, when the Persian fleet mobilised.
Dionysios of the city of Phokaia (half of whose population had earlier fled from the coming
Persian conquest: Hdt. 1.163.1: doc. 2.13) was given command of an Ionian fleet numbering
some 353 triremes, against the Persian force of 600. Herodotos describes in detail how after
seven days of hard training under Dionysios the Ionian crews refused to exercise further, but
this seems belied by his own account of the very real success shown by those who stayed and
fought the Persians, for they were able to break the enemy's battle line at sea.

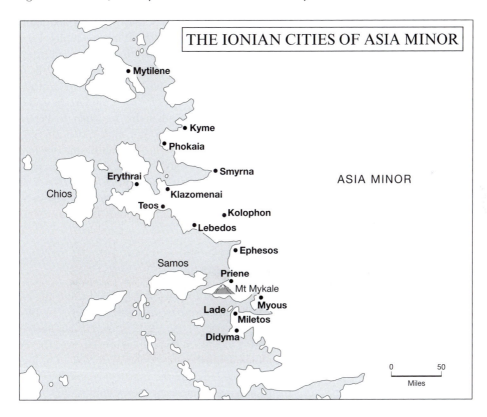

Map 11.2 The Ionian cities.

The end of the revolt

Battle was joined at Lade, an island off the coast of Miletos, but disunity reared its head among the Ionians. As the naval forces joined battle, the Samians deserted, followed by the Lesbians, and then other Ionians. The Chians and others fought on bravely but eventually retreated. A Persian siege of Miletos was commenced 'by land and sea' and the Persians 'dug under the walls' (Hdt. 6.18, 21.2: doc. 11.6). The city was taken and sacked and its people enslaved: a Delphic oracle about the city's fall was thus fulfilled, while the nearby temple of the oracle of Apollo at Didyma was pillaged and burnt to the ground. At Athens, the tragic playwright Phrynichos wrote and presented a play on the subject entitled *The Capture of Miletos*: the Athenian audience burst into tears during the performance, fined him for reminding them of the disaster, and in the first historical act of theatre censorship banned the subject as future material for theatrical performances (Hdt. 6.18, 21.2: doc. 11.6). Histiaios himself did not put in an appearance at the battle of Lade but pursued his own ambitions in the northern Aegean. Foraging for food in Persian territory in 493 BC, he was captured, impaled and decapitated, and his mummified head sent to Darius by Artaphernes. Darius was angered at this treatment of his former subject and gave the head an honourable burial.

The consequences of the Ionian Revolt

The Athenians' activities at Sardis brought them to the attention of Darius and in 490 BC he was to launch an expedition against the two Greek states not under Persian domination which had contributed to the sacking of Sardis: Athens and Eretria. While the Ionian Revolt probably accelerated the Persian drive westwards, it is often noted that the Persian Empire had been expanding, especially since Darius' expedition against the Scythians c. 513. But when Herodotos writes that the ships which the Athenians and Eretrians voted to send to aid the Ionians in their revolt, 'were the beginning of troubles for both the Greeks and the barbarians' (Hdt. 5.97.3: doc. 11.3), there is an element of truth in this, for when the Persians conquered the Greek cities of Asia Minor in the 540s they did not show much interest in the cities of mainland Greece. These had been on the edge of the Persian Empire for half a century, little known and arousing no curiosity, and they may well have continued in peace. When the Athenians sent an embassy to the Persian satrap Artaphernes at Sardis it is also interesting that he asked, 'who these men were and what part of the world they inhabited?' (Hdt. 5.73.2: doc. 10.4). The Ionian Revolt must be seen, as Herodotos saw it, as a major catalyst for the Persian interest in the Athenians.

Mardonios in 492 BC

In the aftermath of the defeat of the Athenians and Ionians in Asia Minor and the capture of Miletos, Darius turned his attention directly to the west, towards Greece. In 494/3 BC Mardonios, Darius' son-in-law, was placed in overall command of the Persian fleet and sailed with it from Cilicia to Ionia. But prior to the expedition against Greece, the Persians undertook two actions deliberately aimed at ameliorating political discontent in Ionia. First, Artaphernes as satrap of Sardis had representatives of the Ionian cities come to Sardis and settled the differences between them, making them swear they would no longer raid each other's territory but seek arbitration about disputes. He surveyed their territories and fixed their tribute (phoros) to the Persians, although it remained much the same as before.

378

Secondly, Mardonios after arriving in Ionia, established democracies in some of the Ionian cities, although tyrants continued to rule several cities after the revolt: Samos, Halikarnassos, Chios, Lampsakos and perhaps Kos. The establishment of democracies in some cities was, in fact, part of a Persian policy to obscure the reality of Persian rule partly.

Mardonios assembled a large naval fleet and army in 492 BC and sailed to the Hellespont, ferrying his troops across the strait, with Eretria and Athens as his goal. Macedonia under king Amyntas went over to the Persians when their troops reached his country, and the fleet took the island of Thasos without opposition. They then attempted to round the Athos promontory, where a great northerly storm inflicted massive losses, perhaps as many as 300 ships and 20,000 men. Meanwhile Mardonios was also attacked on land by the Thracians, whom he conquered, although with great losses, and both army and fleet returned to Persia.

Aegina, Athens and Kleomenes

Persian control of Thrace, Thasos and Macedonia meant that the north of Greece was now in Persian hands. This was not of great consequence for the moment, as the Persians decided to strike across the Aegean sea, but control of these areas was important in the second Persian invasion of 480–479 BC. In 491 BC, Darius sent heralds throughout Greece, seeking the Persian tokens of submission: earth and water. The Greeks referred to this as medism, going over to the Medes, a term they used (incorrectly) for the Persians (the Medes were in fact a separate people near Persia conquered by Cyrus). All of the islands and many of the Greek states visited by the heralds submitted to his demand, including the large island of Aegina, near Attica, and Athens' historical rival. The Athenians believed the Aeginetans did this out of hostility to Athens and that the island would join the Persian expedition against Athens. Accordingly they sent to Sparta, where king Kleomenes took up the matter. He went to Aegina and attempted to arrest the Aeginetans responsible.

This clearly indicates the importance of the Persian threat as the Athenians and Kleomenes were not on good terms after Kleomenes' earlier invasions of Attica when he attempted to install an oligarchy. Aegina opposed him: its spokesman Krios accused Kleomenes of accepting Athenian bribes, and of acting without authorisation from Sparta, as his fellow king Demaratos was not present. Krios means the animal 'ram', and Kleomenes warned him: 'You'd better cover your horns in bronze, Mr Ram, as you're going to meet big trouble!' (Hdt. 6.50.3: doc. 6.75). Demaratos in fact is said to have suggested these arguments to Krios: the two kings had been on bad terms for several years. Kleomenes, thwarted once already by Demaratos in his 507/6 BC invasion of Attica (Hdt. 5.74.1–76: doc. 10.5), decided to depose his colleague. Circulating a story that Demaratos was illegitimate, he bribed the Pythia priestess at Delphi to confirm this. He then deposed Demaratos and installed Leotychidas in his place as king (Hdt. 6.49.2–50.3, 6.61.1–66.3: doc. 6.75). Kleomenes, now in conjunction with Leotychidas, went to Aegina and ensured the island did not medise, and the kings took ten Aeginetans (including 'Mr Ram') as hostages to Athens, the 'Aeginetans' worst enemies' (Hdt. 6.73.2: doc. 6.77). Demaratos went to the Persians and accompanied them in their invasion of 480–479 BC. Herodotos writes that he gave Xerxes much useful advice and was negative about the chances of a Persian victory. For Herodotos' listeners and readers this all foreshadowed the inevitable defeat of Xerxes (Hdt. 6.70.3: doc. 6.76).

The Athenians hurled the heralds sent from Persia into 'The Pit', a place where those condemned to die were thrown, and the Spartans (famously) pushed them down a well, telling them that if they wanted earth and water to find it there, though, as heralds were sacred and

379

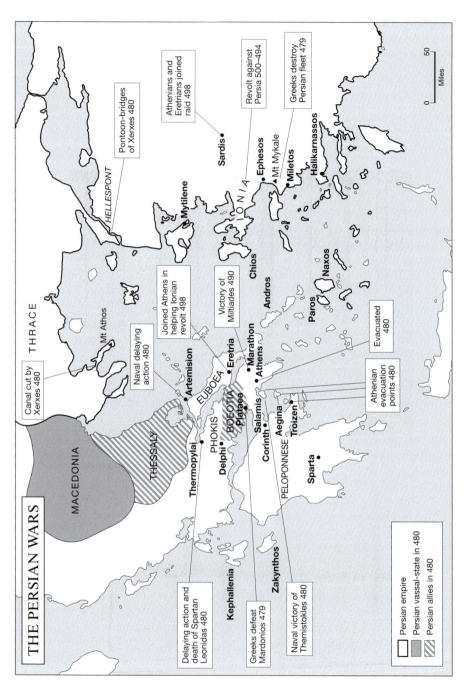

THE PERSIAN WARS

Canal cut by Xerxes 480

Pontoon-bridges of Xerxes 480

HELLESPONT

THRACE

MACEDONIA

Mt Athos

Athenians and Eretrians joined raid 498

Sardis

Revolt against Persia 500–494

Greeks destroy Persian fleet 479

Mytilene

Ephesos

Mt Mykale

IONIA

Miletos

Halikarnassos

Naval delaying action 480

Joined Athens in helping Ionian revolt 498

Chios

Artemision

THESSALY

EUBOEA

Eretria

Victory of Miltiades 490

Andros

Naxos

Thermopylai

PHOKIS

Marathon

Athens

Paros

Evacuated 480

Delphi

BOEOTIA

Plataea

Salamis

Aegina

Corinth

Troizen

Athenian evacuation points 480

Delaying action and death of Spartan Leonidas 480

Kephallenia

PELOPONNESE

Sparta

Greeks defeat Mardonios 479

Zakynthos

Naval victory of Themistokles 480

0   50
Miles

Persian empire

Persian vassal-state in 480

Persian allies in 480

Map 11.3 Key sites in the Persian Wars. Based on M. Grant, *The Routledge Atlas of Classical History*, fifth edition, Routledge, 1994, p. 22.

inviolable, they later saw their own action as impious. Xerxes requested the same tokens of submission from all the Greeks prior to his expedition of 480 BC, but deliberately not from either of these two states, as he intended to conquer them outright.

Naxos and Eretria captured in 490 BC

Mardonios was stripped of his command after the 492 campaign, and Darius appointed Datis and Artaphernes (son of the satrap of the same name), to take control of the attack against Eretria and Athens. Darius' servant was still repeating to him the injunction, 'Sire, remember the Athenians' (Hdt. 5.105.1–2: doc. 11.5), the Peisistratidai at the Persian court

Figure 11.5 'King of Kings' Darius, himself a usurper to the throne, shaded by attendants carrying a parasol and a fly-whisk. This is a relief sculpture from the 'Council Hall', Persepolis. Photo © Joyce McClure.

encouraged the attack on Athens, and Darius himself wanted vengeance. A huge naval force, complete with horse transports, therefore set out from Samos across the Aegean but deliberately avoided Athos. Naxos, which the Persians had failed to capture just prior to the Ionian Revolt and which had helped precipitate that revolt, was enslaved and the city burnt, including – Herodotos specifically notes – the temples. Delos was visited next, but treated leniently. An earthquake also occurred there which Herodotos suggested might have been a divine warning of all the troubles that the Greeks were to encounter (Hdt. 6.98.1–2: doc. 11.7). Datis moved against other Aegean islands, which were forced to surrender and took troops from them as well as hostages. Karystos briefly attempted resistance but was subdued.

The Persians sailed towards Eretria, which appealed to Athens for assistance. In response to this call, the Athenians sent the 4000 Athenian hoplites, who had been settled on the land of the wealthier citizens of Chalkis in the aftermath of the failed Chalkidian attack on Attica in conjunction with that of Kleomenes (Hdt. 5.74.2: doc. 10.5). Eretria was itself divided as to how to respond to the Persian attack: to defend the city or surrender, and one of the Eretrian political leaders advised the Athenians to go back to Attica, which they did. Once the Persian attack on the city began it lasted for six days, but on the seventh the city was betrayed to the Persians by two of its prominent citizens. The temples were pillaged and burnt in revenge for the burning of the temples in Sardis, and the inhabitants enslaved (Hdt. 6.101.1–102: doc. 11.8)

Marathon 490 BC

After a few days, the Persians sailed to Attica, a short distance away, landing at Marathon some time in September 490 BC. Herodotos explains this choice of destination: Marathon was closest to Eretria, it was the most suitable area for the cavalry, and Hippias the exiled tyrant of Athens guided the Persians here. This had been the place where Peisistratos and his sons had landed in 546 BC to launch their attack on Athens and resume power. According to Thucydides, Hippias was an 'old man' by 490 BC and this must have been the case as, according to Herodotos, he was already an adult in 556 BC (sixty-six years before the battle at Marathon) when he deliberated with his father about whether to make a third attempt at tyranny (Thuc. 6.59.4: doc. 9.39; Hdt. 1.61.2: doc. 9.8). Hippias' involvement with the Persian invasion, and his desire to be reinstalled as tyrant, led to a change in the fortunes of those at Athens who had been friends of the tyrants (Ath. Pol. 22.6: doc. 10.9). At Marathon the Athenians inflicted a humiliating defeat on the Persians with far-reaching consequences that would lead to the massive Persian invasion of 480–479 BC.

On hearing of the Persians' landing, the Athenian assembly met, ordered the army and strategoi to Marathon which lay some 42 kilometres (26 miles) from Athens, and immediately hurried to face the Persians on the plain there. Initially taking up their position in the foothills to the south-west of the Marathon plain, the Athenians sent an experienced runner, whom Herodotos calls Philippides (but other sources Pheidippides), to Sparta to seek that city's assistance. On the way Philippides met the god Pan who addressed him by name and asked why the Athenians did not worship him, despite his present services to them and those he would give in the future. When Philippides later told his story to the Athenians, they constructed a shrine for Pan beneath the acropolis, establishing an annual sacrifice and torch race in his honour (Hdt. 6.105.1–6.106.1: doc. 11.8). Miltiades, as one of the ten generals at Marathon, later set up a dedicatory statue of 'goat-footed' Pan, the god who was half-man and half-goat in form, and whose especial domain was the countryside, thanking him for being 'the enemy of the Persians and ally of the Athenians' (Simon. 5: doc. 11.12).

One of Herodotos' main themes in his narrative of the Persian Wars is that of the divine assistance granted on several occasions to the Greeks. Theseus and the hero Echtelos appeared at Marathon; several cults, such as that of Pan, grew out of both Persian invasions. Artemis as a hunter and warrior received especial honours and the Athenians vowed at Marathon to dedicate a goat to Artemis for every Persian killed: as it turned out they killed so many Persians that they did not have enough goats, so commuted the vow to a slaughter of 500 a year, and were still fulfilling this vow in the fourth century. Herodotos is at pains to note too that the Athenians encamped at Marathon on a piece of ground sacred to Herakles, and when they bivouacked outside Athens they also encamped on ground sacred to Herakles to deter the Persians from attacking the city during the second invasion (Hdt. 6.116). Themistokles established a cult of Artemis Aristoboule ('Best of Counsellors') after Salamis. Before that battle, the Greeks offered prayers to all the gods and to the heroes Telamon and his son Ajax, both from Salamis, while a dust cloud, as if made by 30,000 initiates in the Eleusinian Mysteries, all singing in honour of Dionysos, was seen and heard from Eleusis. Herodotos also gives several Delphic oracles concerning the war, such as the two given to the Athenians, in which Delphi provided advice that could be interpreted as support for Themistokles' naval strategy (Hdt. 7.140.1–143.2: docs 11.21–2). Furthermore, when the Greek fleet was backing water as the Persian ships advanced on them at Salamis, a phantom in the shape of a woman called out to the Greeks asking how much further they proposed to back water: in response they fell to the attack immediately and were successful. As the Greeks defeated the Persians against overwhelming odds, it was only natural for them to think that the gods had played a role in their victory, and thanksgiving to the gods for their success was only to be expected. During the second invasion the women of Corinth went to their acropolis to pray to the goddess Aphrodite who protected their city, and when the Persians were defeated, they dedicated statuettes of themselves praying (Simon. 14: doc. 11.43). Aphrodite's sacred prostitutes, owned by and earning revenue for her, participated in the prayers and they also seem to have made a separate dedication to the goddess on which their names were written.

Prior to Marathon, Philippides ran all the way to Sparta, arriving on the second day after leaving Athens, a distance of some 225 kilometres. This was an impressive but not impossible feat of physical endurance, with the need to gain assistance for his city a strong motivating force. He announced to the Spartans the destruction of Eretria and called upon them to defend Athens. Their reply must have astonished him along with the Athenians in their turn when they heard it: they could not come immediately as it was the ninth day of the month and they could not march out to war until the moon was full. Sparta frequently cancelled or broke off campaigns for religious reasons, and required good omens before crossing the borders of Sparta on military campaigns (Xen. *Const. Spart.*13.3–5: doc. 6.30), so their reason here is certainly to be accepted, although it is important to note that Leonidas broke Sparta's religious prescriptions to go to Thermopylai. It is often stated by modern historians that the Spartans were celebrating the Karneia festival in honour of Apollo when Philippides arrived, but this is not known.

Assistance was also sought from the nearby Boeotian city of Plataea. Herodotos narrates in the context of Marathon how Athens and this city came to be allies. Plataea was involved in a conflict with its powerful neighbouring city Thebes, and when Kleomenes, the Spartan king, was in the area they turned to him for possible support. He advised that as Sparta was too far distant they should seek a closer ally, Athens, and so the Plataeans allied themselves to Athens. A runner was dispatched from Athens to Plataea and the Plataeans sent hoplites to Marathon; they were to be stationed on the left wing at Marathon and afterwards, in gratitude, always 'at their four yearly festival [the Great Panathenaia] the Athenian herald prays that the Plataeans too, like the Athenians, will have good fortune' (Hdt. 6.111.2: doc. 11.9). The Plataean force at the battle of Plataea a little over a decade later numbered 600 hoplites.

By the reforms of 501/0 BC, Athens had ten democratically elected strategoi (generals), as well as the traditional polemarch – the war archon. Each general in turn held command for a day. They were evenly divided at Marathon as to their strategy: five agreed that they should stand and fight the Persians while the other five considered that the Athenian army was too small to join battle. One of the strategoi advocating attack was Miltiades. He had been sent by Hippias to be tyrant of the Athenian colony at the Chersonese and had served with Darius during the Persian invasion of Scythia. He had taken took part in the Ionian Revolt, after which he fled to Athens where he was tried for his role as tyrant of the Chersonese, but acquitted. Elected strategos, he now advocated attack and persuaded the war archon Kallimachos that the army should go on the offensive against the Persians. According to Herodotos, the war archon cast his vote, which made it six to five for fighting. However, at this stage in Athenian history it seems more likely that the war archon was in fact the supreme military leader who took advice from the generals but whose decision was the effective one. Miltiades' role here was to persuade the war archon of the best strategy (Hdt. 6.109.3–111.1: doc. 11.9). The strategoi who agreed with Miltiades each ceded to him their day of commanding the army but he did not undertake battle until his actual turn came. One reason that is sometimes given for the delay is that the Athenians were waiting for the Spartans to arrive so as to increase their numbers against the Persians and consequently their chance of victory. However they would have known when the moon was full and therefore when to expect the Spartans. It was clear that Miltiades did not intend to wait that long. On the day that Miltiades was the strategos, the presiding general, the army in accordance with Greek custom took up position on a hill above the Persians, probably at dawn and to make the most of the daylight.

Its front extended to the same length as the Persian line of battle in order to prevent the combined Plataean-Athenian force from being outflanked. Their centre was left deliberately weak in order to carry out this deposition of the troops, and as Herodotos notes the army was of course most vulnerable at this point. The Athenians were on the right wing, drawn up in their tribal contingents, with Kallimachos commanding. On the left wing were the Plataeans (Hdt. 6.111.1: doc. 11.9). Miltiades must have devised this strategy with the concurrence of Kallimachos as war archon as it was a complex manoeuvre and presumably the result of forward strategic planning.

As usual, when the army was drawn up, a sacrifice was made and as it gave favourable omens the army was given the order to advance. Between the Greeks and the Persians there was a distance of eight stades downhill (just under one and a half kilometres), and the Athenian and Plataean hoplites ran this in full armour to encounter the Persians who, according to Herodotos, thought that they were mad, as they had no supporting cavalry or archers. The momentum of their charge as they surged downhill, the adrenaline this must have produced, and the effect of their crashing into the static Persian line were all important factors in the outcome. Although September is a hot month in Greece, the Greeks were attacking early in the day and did not have to contend yet with heat and dust. As Herodotos notes, they were the first Greeks to charge at their enemy on the run like this, and the first not to be concerned or fearful at seeing the Persians whose very name had previously inspired the Greeks with fear (Hdt. 6.112.1–3: doc. 11.9).

In a drawn-out battle, the Persian soldiers crushed the hoplites in the weak Greek centre, pursuing these inland. But the Athenians and Plataeans on the wings defeated the Persians immediately in front of them, allowing those of the enemy they routed to escape and, after gradually pulling their own two wings together, turned to fight the Persians who had broken their centre and were still in their stations. With the Greeks victorious, the Persians fled to their ships, with the Athenians 'hot on their heels'. At the water's edge, the Greeks called for fire, and here some of the fiercest fighting took place as the Persians became desperate to

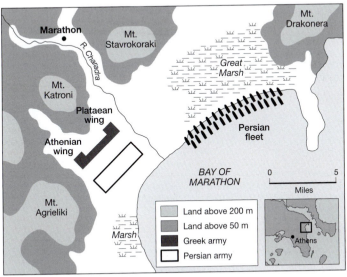

The armies are drawn up on the plain, the Greek forces on the higher ground. The Athenians are on the right wing, the Plataeans on the left.

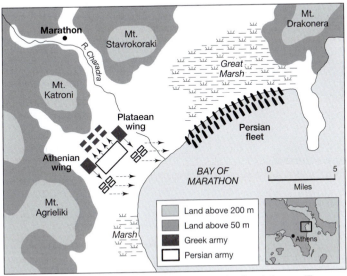

The Persians break through the weak centre of the Greek forces. The Athenian and Plataean wings defeat the Persian troops in front of them, who flee.

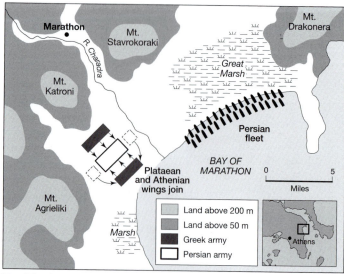

The Athenian and Plataean wings pull together, and turn to fight the Persians who have broken through the centre.

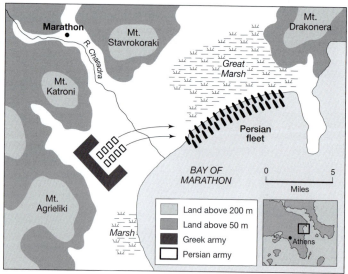

The Persians turn and flee for their ships, pursued by the Greek forces.

Map 11.4 The battle of Marathon, 490 BC.

escape. Kallimachos, having fought bravely, was killed; famously, one Kynegeiros, Aeschylus' brother, managed to grasp one of the Persian ships with his hand but it was cut off and he died while 'many other famous Athenians lost their lives' (Hdt. 6.113.1–114: doc. 11.9). Only seven Persian ships were captured. Herodotos' account is a little disappointing in that he does not really explain how the Athenians and Plataeans defeated the Persians, apart from giving the overall strategy and tactics. It has to be assumed that the Greek hoplite formation, armour and fighting skills were superior to those of the Persians, and it was these factors which he saw as contributing to the Greek successes at Thermopylai (at least initially) and at Plataea. The absence of the Persian cavalry in Herodotos' account of the actual battle remains a subject of debate among modern historians. This lack of cavalry is usually interpreted as one, if not the main, reason for the Greek success.

The Persian ships set sail from Marathon, rounding the point at Sounion (site of the famous temple of Poseidon) and headed for Phaleron, then Athens' main port, hoping to arrive before the Athenian army returned to the city. Nine of the ten tribal contingents in the Athenian army returned at full speed to the city immediately after the battle. They arrived there before nightfall (although the actual time is unknown) and before the Persians whose ships, however, were soon riding at anchor in the harbour. Antiochis, the tenth tribe (to which Aristeides belonged), guarded the Persian prisoners and considerable loot at Marathon.

The shield signal

Some time during the battle at Marathon, a shield was held up from within the Greek ranks as a signal of some kind to the Persians. At Athens, the Alkmeonidai were considered responsible for this and were accused of collaborating with the Persians. Herodotos, however, goes to some lengths to exonerate the family from the charge, arguing that they would not have wanted Athens to be subject to the Persians under the tyranny of a reinstated Hippias. He stressed the Alkmeonidai's hatred of the tyrants, their role in the overthrow of the tyranny (the bribing of the Delphic oracle to instruct the Spartans to expel the tyrants), and his view that they played a more important role in ousting the tyrants than Harmodios and Aristogeiton, who assassinated Hipparchos but did not bring down the tyranny. Herodotos comments that he does not deny that a shield signal was given (Hdt. 6.115, 6.121.1–124.2: docs 11.9–10), and such a signalling mechanism is not unknown from later Greek history: Lysander employed a shield signal at the battle of Aigospotamoi in 405. An alternative explanation (not provided by Herodotos) is that a pro-tyrant group at Athens made the signal at Marathon. There were still supporters of tyranny in Athens in the 490s, as demonstrated by the election of Hipparchos, probably the grandson of Hippias through a maternal line, as archon in 496/5 BC. Certainly, after Marathon political attacks on the 'friends of the tyrants' began and several were ostracised (*Ath. Pol.*22.5–6: doc. 10.09). If the Persians in their ships were waiting for someone or some group to betray the city, as at Eretria, they were disappointed, and they sailed back to Asia (Hdt. 6.116: doc. 11.9). They failed to capture Athens, but they established Persian control over many of the Aegean islands and punished Eretria. Back in Persia, Darius began plans for another invasion.

The Marathon mound

Herodotos gives the figures of 6400 Persian dead as opposed to 192 Athenians (Hdt. 6.117.1: doc. 11.9). These seem credible enough, and at least the 192 must be correct, for the names of the Athenian dead were probably inscribed on a monument at the site (Simon. 21: doc. 11.13). Athenian custom was that their war dead were accorded a public funeral, in which there was a procession with a coffin on each of ten wagons, with each coffin holding the cremated bones of the members of one of the ten tribes. These were then buried in a public grave in Athens' most beautiful suburb. While there are other examples of the Athenian war dead

Figure 11.6 Miltiades' bronze helmet which he wore into battle at Marathon. Afterwards, he dedicated it to Zeus at Olympia, having his own name inscribed along the lower left-hand jaw side. Photo © Olympia Archaeological Museum, Hellenic Ministry of Culture and Tourism, 7th Ephorate of Prehistoric and Classical Antiquities & Archaeological Receipts Fund.

being buried where they fell, Thucydides, who was aware of these, gave what he considered to be the most important example, those who died at Marathon (Thuc. 2.34.1–5: doc. 11.17). Here the Athenian dead were cremated and covered with a mound (soros) which can still be seen on the plain. The Plataeans were buried in a smaller mound, with the slaves (those of the Athenians; whether Plataean slaves participated is uncertain) who had been freed before the battle (Paus. *Description of Greece* 1.32.3: doc. 5.22). These mounds are presumably close to where the actual battle occurred. The Persian dead were buried by being dumped into a trench. After the full moon, the Spartans arrived, too late for the battle, and praised the Athenians for their achievement – and then returned home (Hdt. 6.120: doc. 11.10).

Following the successful outcome of the battle the Athenians thanked the gods for their deliverance from the Persians. They were particularly grateful to Pan and Artemis (see above. p. 382). Simonides, who had previously been employed by the tyrants ([Arist.] *Ath. Pol.*18.1: doc. 9.22), wrote of the Athenians as Greece's champions who laid low 'the might of the gold-apparelled Persians' (Simon. 5: doc. 11.12). From the spoils taken from the Persians at Marathon, the Athenians built a treasury house at Delphi and dedicated it to Apollo (Meiggs and Lewis 19: doc. 11.15). The Athenians had turned back the Persians 'by force' and an epigram honoured the Athenian dead at Marathon (*IG* I³ 503: doc. 11.16).

Participation at Marathon was a source of pride to all Athenians who took part. Aeschylus, the great Athenian tragedian, despite his numerous theatrical triumphs, mentioned the Athenian victory at Marathon and not his dramas in the epitaph he composed for himself, writing that 'the famous grove of Marathon can tell his valour, as can the long-haired Persian who knew it' (Aesch. *Poem* 2: doc. 11.11). His brother Kynegeiros also fought in the battle; as mentioned above, he lost his hand and his life in the climactic battle at the ships (Hdt. 6.114: doc. 11.9). 'First to endure seeing Persian dress and the men who wore it' was Herodotos' verdict on the bravery of these hoplites (Hdt. 6.112.3: doc. 11.9). Clearly the appearance of the Persians made a great impression on the Greeks given that it is referred to in these two separate epitaphs. Kallimachos died at Marathon, but he vowed a dedication to Athena before he went into battle, and after his death his family ensured that this was fulfilled (*IG* I³ 784: doc. 11.14).

Marathon lived on in the Athenian consciousness throughout the fifth and fourth centuries BC, and the conservative element in Athens in particular tended to praise the hoplite victory on land at Marathon over the thetes' victory at sea with the fleet at Salamis. As war veterans, the survivors of Marathon, the marathonomachoi, 'Marathon fighters', saw themselves as a special group, and in Aristophanes' play the *Acharnians* (produced in 425 BC) they protest about their treatment in the lawcourts (doc. 11.18), seeing themselves as representing the values of a nobler age, more virtuous and glorious. The Athenian ambassadors to Sparta in 432 BC reminded the Spartans that it was the Athenians alone – there was apparently no need to mention the Plataeans – who had stood against the Persians at Marathon (Thuc. 1.73.4: doc. 11.39). One myth can be disposed of here: the modern Marathon race is based on the 26-mile (about 42-kilometre) distance from Marathon to Athens which Philippides was said to have run to tell the news of the victory to the Athenians and warn them to prepare for the Persians coming by sea. This story is, however, a late invention that first appeared in the Greek author Lucian who wrote in the second century AD, some 600 years later. The account was made famous in modern times by the poem, *Pheidippides*, by Robert Browning (AD 1812–89).

Xerxes' campaigns

Darius was determined to have his revenge against Athens. The majority of his aims for the expedition had been fulfilled: the conquest of Naxos, subjection of the islands, and destruction of Eretria. But the final aim of the expedition, to conquer Athens, still eluded him. Organisation for a second expedition to Greece commenced immediately and simultaneously with one to Egypt, which had revolted in 486 BC. At his death in the same year, his son Xerxes inherited the Egyptian Revolt, which he crushed in the following year (485 BC), then commenced preparations for his conquest of Greece. Diodorus portrays Mardonios as playing a large role in persuading Xerxes to do so (Diod. Sic. *Library of History* 11.1.3: doc. 11.20). Mardonios was motivated by personal ambition and a desire to make up for his dismissal from the 490 BC expedition. Xerxes clearly wanted to complete what his father started, and the decision was made to assemble a huge expeditionary force, which included conscripts from throughout the Persian Empire, which would make its way by land through northern Greece and then southwards, conquering all in its path. It was accompanied by a massive fleet of war and supply ships.

To avoid repeating the earlier disaster at Mount Athos, a canal was dug through the peninsula connecting it to the Chalkidike. This was an immense engineering undertaking, and those who worked on it then built a bridge across the river Strymon in Thrace. Two bridges were also built across the Hellespont, from Abydos on the Asiatic side of the Hellespont to Sestos on the European side to make it easier and quicker for the Persian army to cross from Asia Minor into Europe. This saved time and the detailed organisation necessary to ferry the huge army across on boats and ships.

The Phoenicians in the Persian army were given the task of building a bridge of flax cables and the Egyptians one of papyrus cables, and when a storm soon afterwards destroyed both bridges Xerxes ordered that the Hellespont receive 300 lashes. He also threw a pair of fetters into it, even according to some branding it, while the construction overseers were

Map 11.5 Xerxes' route to Greece. Based on M. Grant, *The Routledge Atlas of Classical History*, fifth edition, Routledge, 1994, p. 23.

decapitated, a favourite form of Persian punishment while on military expeditions. Two new bridges were constructed, both using flax and papyrus cabling, and ships (pentekonters and triremes) were placed side-by-side and winched tightly together. Wooden planking was placed over the cabling with brushwood and tightly packed soil laid over the top, with a high railing. This prevented the horses being led across from seeing the open sea. Once this was accomplished, the army set out from Abydos, with Xerxes in charge of the expedition which he intended to lead all the way to its objective, Athens. It took seven days and nights for the huge force to cross the two bridges into Europe, where it joined the fleet of 1207 warships and the transport ships waiting at Cape Sarpedon; the fleet then made its way safely through the canal at Athos. Greeks under Persian rule (Ionians, Dorians and the islanders) contributed 147 ships to Xerxes' fleet.

Having arrived at Therme (modern Thessalonika), Xerxes sent his demands for earth and water to all the Greek cities, except the Athenians and Spartans. Prominent among those who went over to the Persians, who 'medised', were the Thessalians, Lokrians, Thebans, and in fact all the Boeotians except for the Plataeans and Thespiaians. In response to this, the Greeks who did not medise but who were determined to fight the Persians swore an oath that those Greeks who had voluntarily medised would be made to surrender a tithe of their property to Delphi if the Greeks defeated the Persians (Hdt. 7.32, 131–133.1: doc. 11.19). This oath was probably taken at a meeting of the Hellenic League, an organisation of those states 'loyal to the Greek cause' (Hdt. 7.145.1: doc. 11.24). Xerxes, according to Diodorus, made an alliance with the Carthaginians that they would attack the Greeks in southern Italy and Sicily, to keep them busy and thereby prevent them from coming to the assistance of the mainland Greeks (Diod. Sic. *Library of History* 11.1.2: doc. 11.20). Herodotos does not mention such an alliance, and ascribes the absence of the western Greeks either to the fact that Gelon of Syracuse refused to place himself under Spartan command, because he wanted to lead the Greek campaign itself, or, possibly a rather truer picture, to the fact that the Greeks in Sicily were preoccupied with fighting the Carthaginians. Gelon defeated a huge force of 300,000 Carthaginians and their allies in 480 BC at the battle of Himera. The claim that this occurred on the same day as the battle of Salamis was probably an attempt by the western Greeks to ensure that their contribution to the struggle for Greek freedom was recognised by the cities of the mainland (Hdt. 7.165–6: doc. 7.44; compare Pindar *Pythian* 1.71–5: doc. 11.55).

Greece prepares for the attack

In Greece, various preparations took place. Athens sent an embassy to consult the Delphic oracle as to what course to pursue; so too did Argos. The Argives knew that the Greeks would call upon them for assistance, and therefore sent to Delphi for advice, and received an oracle to sit out the war. Kleomenes had wiped out 6000 Argive warriors a generation ago, burning them to death after they sought shelter in a sacred grove of Apollo at Sepeia. Despite this, the Argives were willing to participate if the Spartans granted them a thirty-year truce and shared the command of the Greek forces with them. The Spartans refused the latter request, and the Argives declined to join the Greeks: without a truce they considered they would end up under Spartan domination, and they preferred to be under Persian rule. Crete, as with the Argives, received an oracle at Delphi not to become involved.

The wooden wall

The Athenians were given an oracle from the Pythian priestess that advised them to flee before the Persians. However, in an unprecedented move the Athenian envoys asked for a second, more hopeful oracle (Hdt. 7.140.1–143.2: docs 11.21–2). This was granted after their threat to remain there until they died: this would have polluted the temple with their corpses. Some historians doubt the historicity of the two oracles as quoted by Herodotos, but the unusual nature of the double response is good evidence for its authenticity. Delphi was not afterwards blamed for its negative attitude and the Greeks in general did not view it as having medised. It was consulted after Plataea and thanksgivings such as the Serpent Column were made at Delphi (Meiggs and Lewis 27: doc. 11.49; Fig. 11.1). The account that the Persians were driven off from Delphi by supernatural forces accords with the impression that Delphi was loyal to the Greek cause: no doubt some local colouring was added later, but the oracular site clearly wanted some share in the glory of the Persian defeat.

Debate broke out at Athens concerning the meaning of the second oracular response given to the Athenian ambassadors by the Pythia. It promised that Athena would intervene with

Figure 11.7 An enthroned Darius (or Xerxes?), his heir standing behind the throne, with Persian Immortals with spears, far left and right, approached by an official performing proskynesis (bowing
from the hips and touching his right hand to his lips). He is probably announcing the arrival
of the tribute bearers, who are approaching (not shown here). The two Immortals on the far
right are Melophoroi (literally, 'Apple Bearers'), whose spears ended not in a normal butt at
the base but in an 'apple' shape (not visible here); they were an elite of one thousand chosen from the ten thousand Immortals, the special guard of the king (see Arrian 7.29.4: doc.
15.45). Originally decorating the Treasury in Persepolis, now in the National Archaeological
Museum of Iran, Tehran. Photo © Alan D. Coogan.

Zeus to save the Athenians, stating that all of Attica would be destroyed by the Persians, and
the Athenians should at this point flee Attica, but that the 'wooden wall' would not fall. The
Athenians would meet the Persian enemy 'face-to-face' later on. Some of the older Athenians took this 'wooden wall' to refer to the acropolis which was surrounded in the past by a
hedge of thorn bushes. Others thought that the 'wooden wall' referred to the ships, that is,
to the Athenian fleet of triremes. They were concerned by two lines in the oracle which they
thought portended defeat at sea: 'O divine Salamis, you will destroy women's children, either
when corn is scattered or when it comes together.' This was the interpretation advanced by
the professional diviners.

Themistokles, son of Neokles, at the time the most prominent politician in Athens, disputed this. Salamis would not be referred to as 'divine', he argued, if the Athenian ships
were going to be defeated there; rather, it was the enemies of Athens who would suffer at
Salamis. The Athenians agreed with him rather than with the diviners, for in the democracy that now was Athens even the interpretation of oracles was a matter decided by the
Athenian assembly. Themistokles, in fact, had been the inspiration behind the creation of a
large Athenian fleet of warships. When in 483/2 BC a vein of silver was discovered in Attica
at Maroneia, the city had 100 talents unexpectedly at its disposal. Rather than distribute
this money among the citizens, Themistokles had argued that it be used for the creation of
a fleet of 100 triremes (200: Hdt. 7.144), to be used in their conflict with Aegina ([Arist.]
*Ath. Pol.*22.7: doc. 11.23). In the event, they never saw battle against their neighbour,
and both Aegina and Athens fought together at Salamis against the Persians, with these
Athenian triremes forming the backbone of the Greek naval opposition to the Persians
(Thuc. 1.74.1: doc. 11.39).

The trireme

At 36.5 metres long and 4.5 metres wide the trireme was a long, narrow wooden ship specifically designed as an instrument of naval warfare (Fig. 11.9). Its narrowness increased its speed and was the crucial element in its effectiveness as its principal weapon was the bronze ram attached to the front of the vessel at water level. The oarsmen generated sufficient speed to ram their trireme into an opposing ship and render the enemy unseaworthy. The object was not so much to sink the opposing vessel, although this could happen, but to disable it. Athenian triremes were rowed by 170 men drawn primarily from the thetes class, the poor citizens who could not afford bronze armour to fight as hoplites, as well as by metics (and, only in an extreme crisis, slaves). A complement of marines, archers and sailors brought the crew of a trireme to 200. Sails were also fitted to them for long journeys, but were not used when the triremes were actually engaged in battle. Rowers were organised into groups of three, seated one above each other and each with their own oar; however, some details of trireme construction are disputed. It is assumed that the trireme originated in Phoenicia, and it was the Phoenicians who had the fastest ships in the Persian navy. Early Greeks made use of the pentekonter, a smaller vessel rowed by fifty oarsmen, some of which were still in service at Salamis.

The Hellenic League

Faced with the medism of so many Greeks, those 'loyal to the Greek cause' assembled together and formed the Hellenic League. The conflict between Athens and Aegina was formally ended, spies were sent to Sardis, and envoys to Argos and Sicily to request help (Hdt. 7.145.1–2: doc. 11.24). When the spies were captured Xerxes allowed them to see all of his preparations and then released them so they would report the size of his forces to the Greeks in the hope that this would weaken opposition. Greek unity is sometimes used as an explanation for the Greeks' ability to defeat the superior Persian force. However, many of the Greek states medised and others such as Argos and Crete sent no assistance at all. Of all the numerous Greek states, a mere handful – thirty-one – were inscribed on the 'Serpent Column' under the rubric: 'These the war fought', although there were a few minor omissions from the list (Meiggs and Lewis 27: doc. 11.49). Athens ceded military leadership, even of the fleet, to the Spartans, as the Peloponnesian states refused to serve under Athens, and the Athenians also put themselves under Spartan command at Plataea in 479 BC. This led to the incongruous situation in which the fleet was under the command of Eurybiades, a Spartan from a state possessing only ten triremes. The Greek fleet was plagued by disunity with major differences over strategy. More logically and understandably, the land forces were under the control of one of the Spartan kings, Leonidas. Nevertheless, Plato pointed out that the Greeks won despite all their dissensions and disputes with each other (Pl. *Laws* 692d–693a: doc. 11.56).

The first meeting of the Hellenic League was held in 481 BC, several years after Xerxes began his preparations against Greece. It was the threat of the gathering of the Persian forces at Sardis that motivated the Greeks to hold a meeting and subsequently form the league. It remained in existence for some decades, and the Athenians only renounced their membership after the Spartans dismissed them from Mount Ithome (Thuc. 1.102.4: doc. 12.11). The Hellenic League and the Peloponnesian League were two different entities, although it is possible that the later Delian League was modelled on the Hellenic.

The Persian army and navy

Soon after the Hellenic League sent its spies to Sardis, the 'wondrous army' of the *Persians*, described in poetic terms by Aeschylus, set forth in 481 BC (Aeschylus *Persians* 73–91, 101–14: doc. 11.25). In this play, a chorus of Persian elders and Queen Atossa (widow of Darius, and Xerxes' mother) discuss Xerxes' actions in invading Greece and hear the news of his defeat. Aeschylus' description emphasises the past military successes of the Persians, their martial prowess and their confidence in their power on land and at sea. Clearly these lines were composed to magnify the extent of the Greek victory over the Persians. Later in the play the chorus of Persian elders discuss Athens with Atossa: it is a place with a 'spring of silver', its warriors fight not with the bow but with the spear and armour; they have no overlord but nevertheless had successfully destroyed Darius' army (Aesch. *Persians* 230–55: doc. 11.26).

The Athenians and other Greeks faced a numerically superior Persian navy and army. In the Persian navy, 1207 triremes opposed the Greek fleet, and although some of these had been lost in the storm of Artemision, the Greeks must still have been heavily outnumbered at Salamis with their 271 triremes and nine pentekonters (fifty-oared ships). Ascertaining the reality behind the numbers in the Persian army is difficult, if not impossible. Herodotos' figures are always seen as too high, and he gives the numbers for Xerxes' army when it reached Thermopylai as 1,700,000 infantry and 80,000 cavalry that came with him from Asia Minor; he then estimates the numbers of Thracians and Greeks who joined Xerxes, bringing the total to 2,641,610, and argues that there was an equal number of warship and supply-ship crewmen, servants and camp followers, giving a grand total of 5,283,220 (Hdt. 7.186). Herodotos himself made clear that his additions to the original force of 1,700,000 and 80,000 were estimates, and the origin of these two figures is uncertain. Modern scholars cannot agree on the size of the Persian force, but to suggest that Xerxes had a force of some 250,000 infantry and 20,000 cavalry would not be too far wide of the mark. What is important is that the army was a large one and that Xerxes and his advisors planned to suppress opposition or completely destroy it with this force. Comments in Herodotos that the Persian troops drank whole rivers dry need not be taken literally, but do indicate that this was a force that greatly impressed the Greeks with its size. The comment also underlines the logistical problems of feeding, watering and otherwise supplying this huge group of combatants in enemy territory.

Thermopylai and Artemision

The pass at Tempe

The Hellenic League, influenced by a delegation from the Thessalians, who had not yet medised, took the decision to defend the pass at Tempe, which led from lower Macedonia into Thessaly. Here the Greeks hoped to halt the Persian advance. Ten thousand Greek hoplites and the Thessalian cavalry took up position in May 480 BC, with the Athenian contingent commanded by Themistokles and the Spartans by Euainetos, a Spartan polemarch. Alexander I (498–454 BC), king of Macedonia, sent them a message that the Greeks would be well advised to retreat as they would be unable to stop the huge approaching force. However, there was at least one other pass into the area and this may have prompted the Greeks to withdraw. As a result Thessaly quickly medised. After discussion the Greeks decided to make a stand at Thermopylai, hoping to halt the Persian advance into Greece there: it was a narrower pass than that at Tempe and closer to home. At the same time, the Greek fleet went to Artemision on the northern coast of the island of Euboea, opposite Thermopylai. This allowed for easy communication between the army and fleet and a boat was kept at each place specifically for this purpose.

Thermopylai

At Thermopylai the Persians were unable to make use of their cavalry or even of their large numbers of infantry, as the pass was too narrow and close to the seashore. As Xerxes marched there with all his land forces, a small Greek force of 4200 hoplites, all Peloponnesians except for 700 Thespiaians and 400 Thebans, awaited them: Leonidas called upon the Thebans to participate to test their loyalty to the Greek cause. The Spartans were celebrating the Karneia at the time and it is a sign of the urgency felt about the need to halt the Persians that the Spartans put aside their religious scruples and sent these men; other Spartan hoplites followed later. Other Greeks were busy celebrating the Olympic festival, and also delayed in sending more troops (Hdt. 7.204–206.2: doc. 11.27). While waiting for the Persians to arrive, the Spartans and the other Greeks rebuilt the wall across the Thermopylai pass.

When the Persian forces arrived at Thermopylai, the Greeks there held a conference and the Peloponnesians on the whole thought a retreat to the Isthmus was advisable, but Leonidas successfully argued that they stay in place and request reinforcements from the Greeks. Xerxes sent a spy who returned astonished with the news that the Spartans who were on guard outside the wall were exercising and grooming their hair: before battle the Spartans always groomed themselves (Hdt. 7.208.2, 7.209.3: doc. 11.29; Xen. *Const. Spart.*13.9: doc. 6.17). According to Herodotos an astounded Xerxes summoned Demaratos, who had been deprived of kingship at Sparta by Kleomenes, and questioned him about the spy's report. There is some doubt as to whether this conversation took place, but Herodotos uses conversations between Demaratos and the Persians as a means to express the valour of the Spartans and the difficulties the Persians encountered in attempting to conquer them (Hdt. 7.209.2–3: doc. 11.29).

Leonidas and the three hundred Spartans

For four days the Persians attacked the Greeks at Thermopylai; on the fifth, Xerxes sent in the Immortals. They too failed: they had shorter spears than the Greeks and in the confined space their superior numbers did not count. A sixth day of fighting made no difference. Then Xerxes' luck changed and Ephialtes, son of Eurydemos, turned traitor to the Greek cause and revealed to Xerxes a track leading over the hills to Thermopylai. The Phokaians were guarding the track but the Persians came upon them after a forced overnight march and took them by surprise; the Phokaians withdrew up the mountain, but the Persians left them behind in their haste to reach Thermopylai and to catch the Greeks in the rear. According to Herodotos, the Spartans had a prophecy from Delphi before the invasion that either their city would be destroyed or one of the kings be killed in battle. Megistias the diviner foresaw the destruction of the Greek force in the sacrificial entrails and Simonides wrote an epitaph in his honour, praising him for choosing to remain and die despite having foreseen his own death (Hdt. 7.221: doc. 11.27; Simon. 6: 11.28).

Leonidas was informed by deserters from Xerxes' army that the Persians had made this encircling movement, after which the Greek lookouts came running down from the hills with the news that the Persians were coming. Knowing the Persians would soon be behind them, Leonidas sent the rest of Greeks away except for the Thespiaians and the Thebans: the first

Figure 11.8 A Greek hoplite, with shield, crested helmet, body armour and spear stabing a lightly clad betrousered Persian in the midriff; the Persian is armed with a bow and a sword. The scene is on an Athenian red-figure terracotta amphora dating to about 480–470 BC. The vase stands at 34.8 cm. The Metropolitan Museum of Art 06.1021.117, New York. Drawing by J. Etherington.

refused to leave while the second were virtual hostages due to their suspected pro-Persian sympathies. Instead of making forays from behind the wall, the Greeks now changed their fighting tactics and came out further into the pass, knowing that they were going to their doom. Persian commanders whipped their troops into the assault; many Persians fell into the sea next to the pass and drowned, while others were trampled to death by one another. Aware that the Persians would soon be arriving behind the wall, the remaining Greeks fought with the desperation of men going to inevitable death. Their spears were now mostly broken and they used their swords. Leonidas was killed, and a desperate struggle ensued over his body: four times the Greeks advanced before they claimed it.

When Ephialtes arrived with the force he had guided behind the wall, the Greeks withdrew there too, and were soon an isolated island of troops attacked from behind and in front. They made their stand on the hillock in front of the wall. The Thebans surrendered to the Persians, but were rewarded later by being branded with the 'king's marks'. So desperate was the struggle that when the Greeks lost hold of their swords in the fighting they were reduced to using their bare hands and their teeth in the final impossible struggle against their opponents.

These 300 Spartans became the stuff of legend. Two of the 300 were suffering from an eye illness, ophthalmia. One, however, insisted on being led into the battle and died heroically, the other shirked the battle and returned to Sparta. Branded a coward, he retrieved his reputation only by fighting and dying at Plataea. Another of the 300 had been sent as a messenger to Thessaly: he also survived, but because he was disgraced he hanged himself (Hdt. 7.229.1–232: doc. 11.30). Simonides wrote several epitaphs for those who participated in this glorious defeat: the role of Leonidas was of course celebrated, as was that of the 4000 who served with him and that of the Lokrians who fought with Leonidas but who were not at the

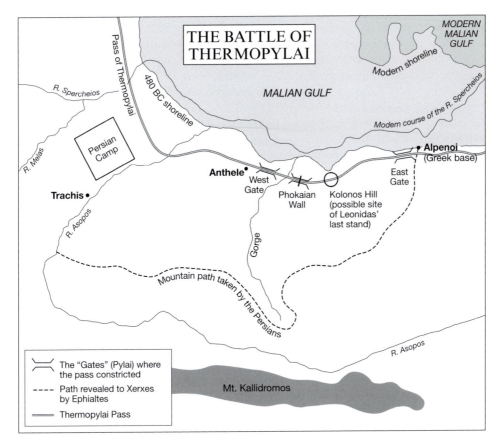

Map 11.6 The battle of Thermopylai, 480 BC.

final stand. Most famous of all are Simonides' lines for the 300 (or perhaps more correctly the 298) Spartiates, 'Stranger, tell the Spartans that here we lie, obeying their orders' (Simon. 7, 22a and b, 23: docs 11.31–3).

Every one of the Greeks at Thermopylai, apart from those who had been instructed to withdraw by Leonidas or indeed had withdrawn without such instructions, died in the last vicious round of fighting: 300 (or so) Spartans, 700 Thespiaians, and possibly some 900 helots. (Herodotos admits that he is not quite clear about events at this point.) The significance of Thermopylai for the Greek cause was that the Persians were not permitted to march into central Greece and Attica without a fight, and the rest of the Greek army at Thermopylai were given the chance to retreat, so saving some 3000 Greeks to live and fight against the Persians another day. Leonidas and his troops held up the Persians only for a matter of days, and so this was not a significant victory from a practical viewpoint, yet it was an important 'moral victory': the Persians paid dearly for their advance, with perhaps the loss of some 20,000 men, while the Greeks indicated that they would and could fight for their freedom, whatever the cost.

Artemision

Xerxes' navy, while anchored along the Magnesian coast of northern Greece between Kasthanaie and Cape Sepias, was severely damaged by a storm, with a loss of about 400 ships. While the Athenians claimed that they prayed to the god of the north wind, Boreas, to repeat the disaster encountered at Athos by Mardonios, the Persian fleet was nevertheless still largely intact and made its way to Artemision, named after a temple of the goddess Artemis there, close to Thermopylai. Here the Greeks, under the command of the Spartan Eurybiades, contested with the Persians for the passage of the Euripos, the stretch of water between Euboea and Attica, at the same time as the struggle at Thermopylai was taking place. The battle lasted three days, and on the first of these the Greeks came out to fight only late in the day, as they did on the second, while on the third the Persians took the initiative and attacked at midday as they were anxious at their lack of progress, and Xerxes' reaction to it. The Greeks were (more or less) victorious but suffered considerable losses and hearing of the annihilation of the Spartan forces at Thermopylai, which occurred that very day, the Greek fleet retreated (Hdt. 8.16.1–18: doc. 11.34). Artemision and the Greek naval successes there were, however, significant as the first real indication in this invasion that major losses could be inflicted on the Persian fleet.

Salamis 480 BC

When Xerxes' land force passed through Thermopylai and entered Boeotia, which medised except for Plataea and Thespiai, he made for Athens. The Greek fleet sailed from Artemision to Athens at the request of the Athenians, who to their consternation had found that the Peloponnesians were not going to defend Boeotia but were building a wall across the Isthmus of Corinth and leaving the rest of mainland Greece to its fate. At Athens, an emergency evacuation began.

The Themistokles Decree

An inscription dating to the third century BC (but sometimes dated, less probably, to the late fourth), known to modern scholars and students as the 'Themistokles Decree', seems to be an authentic copy of a decree proposed by Themistokles to the Athenian assembly, to organise the evacuation of Athens and to make naval preparations against the Persians (Meiggs and Lewis 23: doc. 11.35). A single word, 'Gods', opens this Athenian decree (and all others), thereby invoking the gods' support and good will, as well as inviting them to witness the decree. Just as at the Delphic oracle Zeus granted to Athena that the 'wooden wall only shall be unsacked' (Hdt. 7.141.1: doc. 11.22), the decree shows the Athenians placing their trust in their goddess. All the Athenians and the metics in the city were to send their children to Troizen, an island south of Athens and Salamis, the spot where the decree was discovered. Some of the women and children also went to Aegina and to the nearby island of Salamis; the decree specifically notes that the old people went to Salamis. Plutarch draws an imaginative scene of the evacuation, but the story that Xanthippos' dog swam alongside his master's trireme all the way to Salamis and then died of exhaustion might even be true (Plut. *Themistokles* 10.8–10: doc. 11.36). Thucydides notes that the Athenians displayed the 'most audacious courage' of all those who fought at Salamis, for they deliberately abandoned their city to Persian occupation (Thuc. 1.74.2: doc. 11.39).

In this evacuation of Athens, the treasurers and the priestesses, presumably those of both Athena Polias and Athena Promachos, remained behind on the acropolis to look after the gods' possessions: in the event they met their deaths at the hands of the Persians. The Athenians should have realised this from the fate of the temples on Naxos and in Eretria in 490 BC, but some of those who stayed in the city on the acropolis believed the 'wooden wall' referred to the acropolis and that the 'wooden wall' around this would keep them safe. Apart from these, the able-bodied Athenians and the metics in the city embarked on the 200 triremes to 'resist the barbarian on behalf of freedom', along with the other Greek allies.

The arrangements given concerning the ships that carried the evacuees are very detailed: the strategoi appointed 200 trierarchs to captain the ships, and lists were drawn up of who was to serve on which ship. Ten marines between the age of 20 and 30, that is fighting men in the prime of their lives, were allocated to each ship, and four archers: these fourteen men could be used in any close fighting between ships. The trierarchs of each ship were legitimate Athenians, owning both land and houses in Attica, and had children: clearly it was envisaged that the casualty rate among them would be high and, to ensure their family line did not die out, only those with children were chosen: the Spartans made the same decision regarding the 300 Spartiates who accompanied Leonidas to Thermopylai. Once all arrangements were made, the boule and strategoi had the ships manned, making a propitiatory sacrifice to Zeus Pankrates ('Almighty Zeus'), Athena and the goddess of Victory, Nike. Poseidon in his guise of Asphaleios ('Preserver') also received a sacrifice; he had an important cult on the acropolis and according to myth vied with Athena for the position of chief god of Athens. Hence he was now invoked to preserve the city. One hundred ships set out for Artemision, and 100 were to wait near Salamis. It was after the battle at Artemision that the evacuation began in earnest.

The ostracised return

To ensure a united front and to make best use of Athens' political and military talents, but also to have any potential leaders nearby and not with the Persians, those who had been ostracised (obliquely referred to at the end of the decree as it survives as 'those who have changed their residence for ten years'), went to Salamis while the people decided what to do with them (see also *Ath. Pol.* 22.3–8: doc. 10.9). Aristides, ostracised in 483/2 BC, played an important role at Salamis and both he and Xanthippos, ostracised in 484/3 BC, were elected as Athenian strategoi (generals) for 479 BC. Themistokles was instrumental in having Aristeides recalled, seeing that the Athenians wanted him back (despite being said to have been responsible for the ostracism in the first place). Hipparchos, the first to be ostracised as a 'friend of the tyrants' in 488/7, presumably did not return given that Hippias accompanied the Persians to Marathon in the hope of being reinstalled as tyrant and this was the presumed reason behind Hipparchos' ostracism in the first place (*Ath. Pol.* 22.3: doc. 10.9).

Allied disunity before Salamis

Aeschylus provides the earliest account of the battle of Salamis in his play, the *Persai*, performed in 472 BC, and there is also an extensive account in Herodotos, and also in Plutarch (Aesch. *Persians* 348–471: doc. 11.38; Hdt. 8.49–96; Plut. *Themistokles* 11–17, *Aristeides* 8–9; also Diod. Sic. 11.16–19). As noted above the Peloponnesian army was stationed at the Isthmus of Corinth which they planned to fortify with a wall, from behind which they hoped to defeat the Persian army. The Isthmus is 6.3 kilometres (four miles) wide, and so walling it would not have been an impossible task, although it left out of account the fact that the Persians had a perfectly serviceable fleet which could land a Persian force anywhere around the Peloponnesian coastline. Eurybiades was in command of the Greek fleet, as he had been at Artemision, and summoned the leaders of the various contingents supplied by each allied state. The Peloponnesians argued that the fleet should sail to the Isthmus and join the army there, rather than stay and fight a naval battle at Salamis as Themistokles planned. They objected to the choice of Salamis on the grounds that if their ships were defeated there they would be entrapped, while if they fought at the Isthmus they could retreat to wherever the army was positioned. This must have seemed a sound strategy to the Peloponnesians and when news of the sack of Athens and the burning of the acropolis by the Persians arrived, some of the Peloponnesians immediately fled. In contrast the news must have galvanised the rest who decided to stay and fight at Salamis.

At a second war council Themistokles argued that battle at the Isthmus would be on the open sea, which would disadvantage the Greeks with their fewer ships. He argued that fighting in the narrow straits between Attica and Salamis would give the Greeks a distinct advantage while the open sea, where the Persians could manoeuvre leisurely and bring their numbers to bear, disadvantaged the Greek triremes. Moreover, retreating to the Isthmus automatically ceded Aegina, Salamis and Attica to the Persians without a fight. The naval battle had to take place somewhere, and fighting at Salamis was the best option.

While Themistokles argued for his proposed strategy, he was twice interrupted by Adeimantos, the leader of the Corinthian naval contingent (Plut. *Themistokles* 11.2–5: doc. 11.37). In Herodotos' account of the battle as a whole, the Corinthians are given a 'bad press' and this is obviously because by the time Herodotos was in Athens and listening to Athenian accounts of events at Salamis, the two states were enemies, and the Athenians used every opportunity to attack the Corinthians' war record. Themistokles apparently threatened that if battle was not joined the Athenians would withdraw their fleet: they had 180 ships, half the Greek naval contingent (Plutarch mentions 200: *Themistokles* 11.5: doc. 11.37). Eurybiades was probably as much convinced by this threat as by any strategic considerations, and adopted Themistokles' strategy, but not all were convinced and a third tactical meeting was held.

In Aeschylus' account one of the Greeks apparently deserted, informing Xerxes that the Greek ships intended to slip away from Salamis and that 'each would save his life in secret flight' (Aesch. *Persians* 355–84). Herodotos ascribes this ploy directly to Themistokles who, fearing that he could not win the argument a third time, used one of his slaves, named Sikinnos, to give Xerxes the news that the Greeks were about to retreat from Salamis and that he was going to lose his best chance of defeating them. In both Herodotos' and Aeschylus' accounts, Xerxes accepted this report and made his fleet row through the night from Phaleron to Salamis. Consequently the rowers in the Persian fleet were tired when they arrived and the Greeks awoke to find the Persian fleet at hand. It was then too late for the Greeks to debate any longer about strategy (Hdt. 8.75–76).

The battle of Salamis

Word was brought to the Greeks (apparently by Aristeides, although this could be a later invention to magnify his role at Salamis) that the Persian fleet had arrived. On this unknown day in late September 480 BC, the two forces confronted each other at dawn. The Greeks fielded 378 triremes and an unspecified number of pentekonters, perhaps twenty-two, as Thucydides gives the number of Greek ships as 400 (Thuc. 1.74.1: doc. 11.39, although he

Figure 11.9 A modern reconstruction of an Athenian trireme. The Athenian fleet was the 'backbone' of the Greek fleet at Salamis, and, combined with Themistokles' strategy, it was the Athenian navy which was largely responsible for Greek victory at Salamis. This reconstructed vessel can reach speeds of 18 km an hour: the use of such speed and the bronze ram explain the trireme's effectiveness in naval warfare. Photo © Paul Lipke, The Trireme Trust.

might be 'rounding up' the number involved). Xerxes' fleet probably numbered about 1200 in all, but it was not possible for all the ships to fit into the straits of Salamis at the same time and so during the course of the battle the Greeks probably opposed a Persian force roughly the same size as their own. The Greeks backed water – presumably to entice the Persians further into the straits – and joined battle. Working as one unit the Greeks were to defeat the Persians, whose ships quickly lost formation and whose rowers were tired.

Yet the chief factor in defeating the Persians was that the Greeks could operate well in these restricted conditions in their smaller, shallower ships while the Persians could not bring their whole force to bear. The Greeks did not have to face the full Persian navy but only that proportion of it which could fight in the straits. Even these limited numbers of Persian ships kept running foul of each other. Aeschylus describes the Persians ramming each other due to the limited space available and because they were eager to be seen by Xerxes to be fighting. At the same time they were rammed by the Greek ships, which circled individual Persian vessels, attacking them from every side. Thucydides makes the point very clearly that the choice of Salamis as the battle site was successful: not only were some two-thirds of the Greek ships Athenian, but more importantly these were commanded by Themistokles, and it was he who 'saved the situation' by organising it so that the battle took place 'in the narrow straits' of Salamis. Thucydides notes too that the Athenians did not withdraw their ships despite the fact that they had abandoned their city, but stayed and fought (Thuc. 1.74.1–2: doc. 11.39).

Near Salamis was another smaller island, Psyttaleia, and Aeschylus describes how the Persians who survived the battle went there as a Persian force had been stationed there: but the Greeks landed troops, and all the Persians there were killed (Aesch. *Persians* 457–64: doc.

11.38; see also Plut. *Aristeides* 9). Notably the Greeks could swim but the sailors of the Persian fleet apparently could not. This added to the Persian losses whenever one of their ships was taken or sunk and the crew dived overboard. Aristides is said to have played a notable role on the island, but this was not an important engagement, and once again his role here may be the result of later embellishment: the true architect of victory that day was of course Themistokles. What remained of the Persian fleet turned to sail back to Athens' harbour Phaleron, but Aegina's fleet was waiting for them in the narrow southern exit and destroyed many of them; only a few escaped and joined the Persian army at Phaleron.

Xerxes at Salamis

Xerxes watched the battle from the base of a hill across from Salamis, sitting on a diphros (stool): an argyropous diphros (silver-footed stool) was among the barbarian loot later dedicated on the acropolis and may well have belonged to Xerxes himself (*IG* I³ 351: doc 1.11). Xerxes did not sit on a throne watching the battle, but drove around in a chariot, and when the action became critical at a particular point, alighted from his chariot, and sat on this stool. According to Herodotos, he noted carefully what was going on in the engagement, with his secretaries keeping a list of those whom he saw fighting bravely. He could also be critical: the Phoenicians had lost their ships and came to Xerxes to try to blame the Ionians for this, but despite earlier Greek overtures to them to desert, the Ionians, like Artemisia, tyrant of Dorian Halikarnassos, remained largely loyal to Persia. Even as the Phoenicians spoke Xerxes saw a ship from Samothrace, one of the Ionian islands, ramming an Athenian trireme: convinced by the evidence of his own eyes, he gave orders that the Phoenicians' heads should be cut off.

When Xerxes saw that his fleet was defeated, the surviving ships were instructed to make for Phaleron, but although he still had numerous ships he did not, as the Greeks expected, undertake a second engagement with them on the following day. From this it seems clear that despite the huge army he had with him Xerxes primarily saw this as a naval campaign, like his father Darius in 490 BC, with the backbone of Greek power being its navy. This had certainly been the case with the Ionian Greeks, who once defeated at sea quickly surrendered to the Persians in the Ionian Revolt. Why Xerxes did not renew the attack is not at all clear, as his navy was still relatively intact and still greatly outnumbered that of the Greeks. Perhaps he did not comprehend the factors leading to his defeat, and saw the Greek victory over his navy as final and crushing. On the other hand, he made preparations as if he meant to continue the fighting, and while Herodotos sees these as feints to occupy the Greeks while he escaped via the Hellespont, it is possible that initially Xerxes did consider continuing the fight, but changed his mind.

Xerxes sent news ahead of him to Persia, and ships were sent to sail with all speed to prevent the destruction of the bridges at the Hellespont (compare Plutarch *Themistokles* 16). After staying a few days in Athens, he then began the land march back to Sardis and the Persian Empire. In Thessaly, he left Mardonios in charge of the army of 300,000 men who wintered in that country. During the 45-day march to the Hellespont the remainder of the army endured shocking losses, as often occurs with retreating armies. Food supplies completely failed and many of the ordinary soldiers died of hunger and thirst. They attempted to sustain themselves by eating the bark and leaves of trees and, while crossing the unseasonably frozen river Strymon, the ice gave way under their weight, sending large numbers to a chilly grave (Hdt. 8.115; Aesch. *Persians* 495–507).

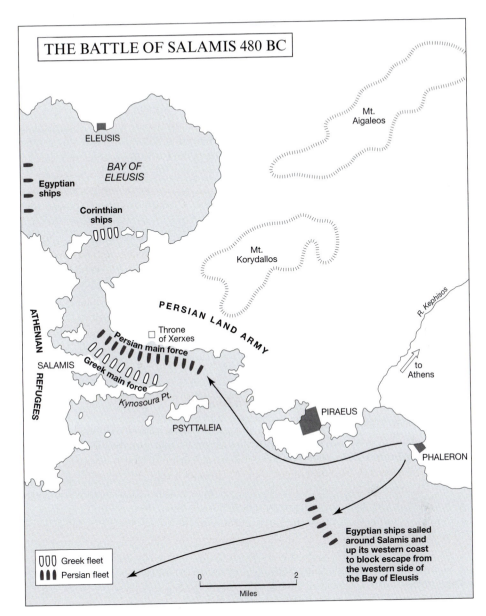

Map 11.7 The battle of Salamis, 480 BC. Based on M. Grant, *The Routledge Atlas of Classical History*, fifth edition, Routledge, 1994, p. 23.

The epigrams on the battle of Salamis

Simonides wrote several epigrams for the Greek victors, extolling their virtues and achievements. An epigram for the Athenians refers to the foot-soldiers – probably the hoplites on the island of Psyttaleia, or perhaps the marines on each ship – and those in the ships 'who both as foot soldiers and in quick-sailing ships prevented all Greece from seeing the day of slavery' (Simon. 20a: doc. 11.40). The Athenians were well aware that the Persians had enslaved the populations of Naxos and Eretria in 490 BC, and that they could expect no less from Xerxes in 480 BC. But 'slavery' here perhaps has a wider connotation as well; to be ruled by the Persians was, to the Athenians, a form of enslavement, Persian absolutism as opposed to democracy. The epigram in praise of the Corinthian commander Adeimantos makes this clear: 'through him all Greece put on a garland of freedom' (Simon. 10: doc. 11.41). Despite Herodotos' description of Adeimantos' jibes against Themistokles, and his statement that the Corinthians sailed away just as battle was commenced at Salamis, clearly this was later Athenian propaganda. According to Simonides many of the Corinthians died and were buried on Salamis and they had played their part in capturing 'Phoenician ships and Persians and Medes and saved holy Greece' (Simon. 11: doc. 11.42). In the period leading up to the Peloponnesian War, the animosity between Athens and Corinth was clearly played out in the manipulation of the historical record regarding Salamis. Even the women of Corinth played their part, in their prayers for Greek victory (Simon. 14: doc. 11.43). The Naxians, initially fighting for Persia, changed sides, and the Naxian Demokritos captured five Persian ships, and saved a Greek one from the Persians (Simon. 19a: doc. 11.44). While the Greeks of the west did not participate, the city of Croton in southernmost Italy sent a ship under the command of the athlete Phayllos, who 'captured ships which Asia sent forth' and a statue of him was erected on the Athenian acropolis to honour his role (*IG* I³ 822: doc. 11.45). After the battle of Gaugamela, Alexander sent part of the booty to Croton in commemoration of Phayllos' role in combating the Persians at Salamis: this led to Phayllos becoming a symbol of the Greek struggle against Persia (Plut. *Life of Alexander* 34.3: doc. 15.18).

Plataea 479 BC

When the Persians failed to attack again after the battle of Salamis, the Greek fleet sailed to the Aegean island of Andros. Here Themistokles proposed that it make for the Hellespont and destroy the bridges; Eurybiades opposed this on the grounds that it was better to assist Xerxes and his forces in leaving Greece than to prevent it (Hdt. 8.108; Plut. *Aristeides* 9). Themistokles turned the situation to his benefit by sending another message to Xerxes, again via Sikinnos, that Themistokles had prevented the Greeks from destroying the bridges over the Hellespont. On the basis of this message and the previous one, Xerxes was later to give Themistokles refuge in Persia when he was ostracised by the Athenians in the late 470s BC. While some historians reject one or both of these messages carried by Sikinnos as later inventions, Themistokles' intelligence and planning is praised by both Herodotos and Thucydides and these stories can be accepted as reliable. The Greeks besieged Andros as pro-Persian, but failed to take it, and returned to Salamis, after which they made their way to the Isthmus.

Mardonios in 479 BC made peace overtures and an offer of alliance to the Athenians through the Macedonian king Alexander I. Alarmed at this possibility the Spartans sent an embassy to Athens, but they need not have been concerned: the Athenians rejected the possibility of coming to terms with the Persians, stressing to the Spartans their solidarity with the other Greeks and their commitment to the cause of Greek freedom (Hdt. 8.136, 140–144: doc. 3.90). Mardonios himself came to Athens, ten months after Xerxes first captured it, but the Athenians now on Salamis, having abandoned Athens for the second time, would not listen to this second proposal. One of the members of the Athenian boule proposed accepting Mardonios' terms but was stoned to death by the Athenians without trial,

Figure 11.10 Scene from an Athenian fifth-century BC red-figure pelike (jug) showing a confrontation between a Persian cavalryman and a heroically nude Greek hoplite; the cavalryman indicates that this could represent the battle at Plataea. National Museum, Warsaw, Poland. Drawing by J. Etherington.

after which their wives stoned his wife and children (Hdt. 5.87.1–88.3: doc. 4.26). Failing to win over the Athenians, Mardonios burnt anything that remained standing in Athens from Xerxes' first sacking of the city in 480 BC, and returned into central Greece. The Athenians worked hard to persuade the Spartans to send a force north, and as the isthmian wall was nearing completion the Athenians suspected that the Spartans and other Peloponnesians would use it as an excuse not to come to Athens' assistance. Nevertheless, a Spartan force was duly sent north under Pausanias, acting as regent for Leonidas' son Pleistarchos until he came of age to reign in Sparta. At the Isthmus Pausanias was joined by other Peloponnesian troops. Having obtained favourable omens for continuing the expedition, he marched north into Attica.

The Peloponnesians, joined by Athenian hoplites, then took up position at Plataea in Boeotia, with Mardonios and the Persians based at a wooden palisade encampment outside Thebes. The Thebans were active supporters of the Persians, and the other Greeks who had medised sent troops to Mardonios there. Plataea itself was loyal to the Greek cause, and the uneven terrain in the foothills in its vicinity impeded Mardonios' cavalry (which, however, played a major role before the battle itself). There were 5000 Spartans and 35,000 light-armed helots, seven each attending each Spartan hoplite, and 8000 Athenian hoplites: the Athenians and Spartans formed the core of the 38,700 strong Greek hoplite force. Herodotos gives the total Greek force, including helots and other light-armed troops, as 110,000. Mardonios moved his army – 300,000 Persians and the medising Greeks (Herodotos admits that he is guessing that there were 50,000 of them) – up to the river Asopos at Plataea, where the Persians faced the Spartans. The extent of Mardonios' force is often considered by modern historians to be exaggerated, but the Greeks were clearly well outnumbered. An oath was sworn by the Athenians prior to the battle that their wives should give birth to monsters and various other misfortunes occur if they did not keep their oath not to desert, follow commands, bury the allied dead, give a portion of the spoils (a tithe) from Thebes to the gods, and not harm Athens, Plataea or Sparta (Tod 2.204: doc. 11.46).

The Greeks remained on the high ground and Mardonios sent a cavalry charge against them, after which the Athenians, in a notable action, went to the assistance of the Megarians, who held the point in the line most vulnerable to the Persian cavalry. With this move the Persian force was beaten off with the loss of its commander Masistios. Probably emboldened by this success, the Greeks moved down to Plataea to a spring called Gargaphie near the sanctuary of the local hero Androkrates, which gave them better access to water. A dispute between the Tegeates and Athenians as to who should have one of the positions on the wing was settled by the Spartans in Athens' favour.

For ten days, the omens from the sacrifices made by both sides were unpropitious. Mardonios used the services of a Greek diviner, Hegesistratos, who was later caught and killed by the Spartans, and also consulted Artabazos (son of Pharnakes) about a suitable course of action. The latter urged a retreat to Thebes, but Mardonios decided to commit the army to battle on the basis of its numerical superiority over the Greek forces and to ignore the omens. Seeing that Mardonios had put his Persian wing opposite the Spartans, these changed places with the Athenians, on the grounds that the Athenians had fought the Persians successfully at Marathon. But Mardonios, in response to this, switched his own wing dispositions around, so that the Persian troops themselves faced the Spartans (Hdt. 9.46.1–48.1: doc. 11.47). Once again, Alexander I of Macedon made an appearance to warn the Greeks that Mardonios had decided to attack.

The Greek troops soon suffered from the activities of the Persian cavalry, which harassed them and cut them off from water, as well as intercepting the servants who brought them supplies from the Peloponnese. They decided to move again, falling back to the river Oeroe and take up the ground known as 'The Island' between two branches of the river. But when the move began during the night most of the Greeks panicked and fled to Plataea, stopping at the temple of Hera outside the city. Pausanias saw what had happened and moved his Spartan troops along the higher ground. The Athenians followed, but went down into the plain. When news of this move was brought to Mardonios in the morning, he moved to the attack. He himself advanced against the Spartans and Tegeates, while the Greek troops fighting with him attacked the Athenians, who were therefore unable to come to the assistance of the Spartans.

Reasons for the Greek success at Plataea

Pausanias tried once more to obtain favourable omens from the sacrificial victims, but to no avail, and his troops were soon being killed and wounded by Persian arrows. It was only after he turned his eyes to the temple of Hera and prayed that he finally received a favourable sacrificial omen, just as the Tegeates surged forward to defend themselves (Hdt. 9.62.1: doc. 11.47). Modern readers may wonder whether the good omen was a coincidence or Pausanias' decision that the sacrifice *had* at this point to be propitious. Fighting now became hand-to-hand, and fiercest around the temple of Demeter, with the Spartans and Tegeates outnumbered. While courageous and determined, the Persians lacked the Greeks' armour, training and skill (Hdt. 9.62.1–2: doc. 11.47). Mardonios fought from a white horse with his 1000 best Persian troops, but both he and those around him were killed. This broke the Persians, who fled. Herodotos notes that their greatest disadvantage was their lack of armour: 'for they were fighting without armour against hoplites' (Hdt. 9.63.2: doc. 11.47).

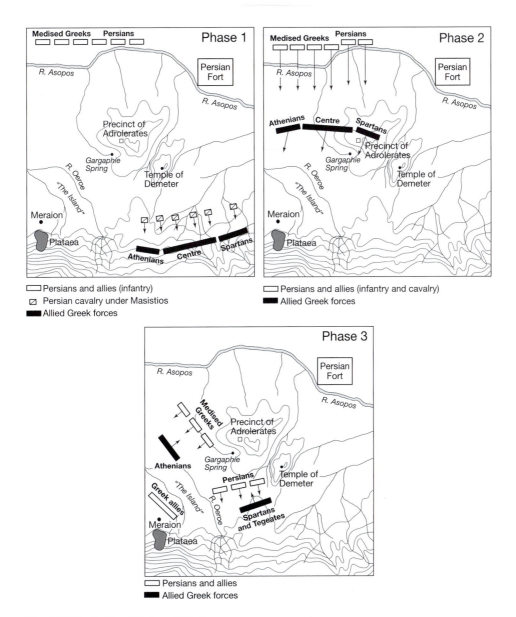

Map 11.8 The battle of Plataea, 479 BC.

The Greeks' success at Plataea, despite the numerical odds, can be explained by their hoplite armour, training, and discipline.

Herodotos also gave credit to the gods: Hera's assistance with the omens was 'in the nick of time', and he mentions the temples of Hera and Demeter not just as topographical markers but as indicating the sacred geography within which the Greeks fought. The river Asopos was itself a god and Plataea was named after his daughter, a nymph. Moreover, Mardonios' death fulfilled the prophecy that his death would requite that of Leonidas. It was the Spartans, separated from the other Greeks, who were attacked by Mardonios and whose defeat of the Persians was conclusive: a fragment of an elegy by Simonides praises their role (*Elegy* 11: doc. 11.48). Artabazos led the remaining Persians, some 40,000, directly to the Hellespont. Hunger, thirst and the Thracians took a heavy toll but he reached Byzantium and sailed safely to Asia Minor. Other Persians took refuge in their wooden fort, which the Greeks overcame with great slaughter. Thebes (after being unsuccessfully besieged by the victorious Greeks) handed over its traitors, who were taken to Corinth and executed.

The Serpent Column

A tenth (tithe) of the booty from the battle at Plataea was dedicated to Apollo at Delphi, whose many oracles played a major role in the war and which the Greeks believed had been fulfilled in their victory over the Persians. Some of the booty was also set aside for a five metre (15 feet) high bronze statue of Zeus at Olympia, as well as for a three and a half metre one for Poseidon, god of the sea, at the Isthmus (where he had a sanctuary and where the Isthmian festival was celebrated every two years). The rest was shared out among the Greeks. Significantly, Pausanias received ten of every item from the booty: women, horses, talents of silver, camels, and everything else. To celebrate their victory the Greeks dedicated the Serpent Column at Delphi, made, according to Herodotos, from melting down captured Persian weapons. It comprised three intertwined bronze serpents reaching to six metres high, surmounted by a gold tripod (which was later melted down by the Phokaians in 354 BC during the Third Sacred War). Constantine the Great (reigned AD 306–37) took the column to his new capital

Figure 11.11 The bronze 'Serpent Column' in its present location in Istanbul (doc. 11.49). Photo © Önder Çakoğlu.

Constantinople (ancient Byzantium, modern Istanbul) for his hippodrome; there it remains today, without its heads. The names of thirty-one states were inscribed on its coils: these refer not just to those who fought at Plataea but in the war of 480–479 BC as a whole. Some states, for whatever reason, did not have their names inscribed: Croton, Pale, Seriphos, Mantineia and the Lokrians. Mantineia can be explained: their hoplites turned up too late for the battle and so when they returned home the city exiled the leaders of the hoplites. Perhaps the role of the others was deemed insufficiently meritorious or important. The Tenians (from the Aegean island of Tenos) were inscribed later, in recognition of their trireme which deserted to the Greeks and brought news that confirmed Aristeides' report on the eve of the battle of Salamis: the Persian fleet had indeed sailed to Salamis.

Pausanias had a couplet composed by Simonides and inscribed on the Serpent Column: 'Since as leader of the Greeks he destroyed the Persian army, Pausanias dedicated this memorial to Phoibos [Apollo]', but the Spartans immediately erased this egocentric boast (Thuc. 1.132.1–2: doc. 6.35). In a further attempt to promote his achievements Pausanias had also added his own dedication as 'ruler of spacious Greece' to a bronze bowl that stood at the entrance to the Black Sea (Nymphis *F* 9: doc. 6.36). These were the first indications of the problems they and the other Greeks would have with him later ([Arist.] *Ath. Pol.*23.4: doc. 12.2). Simonides' other poems fared better, and their praise still conveys, even to a modern readership, the glory seen as won by those heroic citizens who gave their lives 'to crown Greece with freedom' (Simon. 8 and 9: doc. 11.50). The Megarians who had died at Artemision and Plataea were honoured with an epigram inscribed on stone and set up in the agora of their port Nisaia (Simon. 16: doc. 11.52) and the Megarians also appear on the Serpent Column. There was a mass grave at Megara for the Megarians who died in the Persian Wars, but those who died fighting off the Persian cavalry attack at Plataea were entombed there in a mound. There were many such mounds at Plataea: those of the Megarians, Athenians and Tegeates actually contained the bones of the slain, while others were erected as empty cenotaphs to commemorate the dead. Various laconic sayings of the Spartans paid tribute both to their courage and pithiness of expression. Some may have been invented after the event but nevertheless capture the Spartan spirit of defiance in the face of unprovoked Persian aggression. Best known is the anecdote that, when told that the Persians' arrows were so numerous that they hid the sun, Leonidas was said to have quipped: 'How nice, then, to fight in the shade' (Plut. *Sayings of the Spartans* 6: doc. 11.53).

Mykale 479 BC

On the same day as the battle of Plataea the Greek fleet, under the command of the Spartan king Leotychidas II (who had succeeded the deposed Demaratos: doc. 6.47), inflicted a massive defeat on the Persian naval forces at Mykale, not far from Lade where in 494 BC the Ionians were defeated by the Persians and their revolt crushed. The Greeks sailed to Delos, then to Samos, where the Persian fleet was stationed. It took flight at the approach of the Greeks, who followed it to Mykale, where they beached their ships and attacked the Persians, who drew up their ships on land. This, in fact, was a battle fought solely on land, the ships beached, with the Persians fighting behind their interlocked shields in front of their fortification there; the Ionians and Aeolians deserted to the Greeks. Attacking the Persians, the Athenians, Corinthians, Sikyonians and Troizenians forced their way through the shield barrier, and drove the Persians back into the fortification where they then followed them. Those with the Persians fled, but the Persians themselves remained and fought it out and it was only with considerable losses that the Greeks defeated them. The Athenians and those with them fought their hardest as they wanted the victory to be theirs alone. They were unwilling to share the successful outcome of this conflict on land with the Spartans who were still making their way to the battlefield (Hdt. 9.101.3–102.3: doc. 11.51).

After Mykale, the Greeks sailed back to the island of Samos. The Peloponnesians proposed that the Ionians be transplanted to mainland Greece and live on the land of 'medisers', who would be removed, but the Athenians opposed the suggestion. The Peloponnesians dropped the idea and Samos, Chios, Lesbos and other islands joined the Hellenic League. The fleet then sailed to destroy Xerxes' bridges over the Hellespont, but at Abydos found the locals had already removed them. The Spartan king Leotychidas and the Peloponnesians returned to Greece, while the Athenians under Xanthippos successfully besieged Sestos, on the opposite side of the Hellespont, and then returned to Athens. At this point Herodotos ended his narrative of the Persian Wars. In the following year (or 477 BC), Leotychidas campaigned in Thessaly and was disgraced, ending his reign in exile (Hdt. 6.72.1: doc. 6.76).

Who won the war against the Persians?

After Salamis the Spartans awarded Themistokles several honours when he came to their country: a crown of olive for wisdom, the best chariot in the city, and when leaving an escort to the border of Sparta by a special guard of honour comprised of 300 of the best Spartan hoplites. The ships from Aegina were given the credit for excellent fighting followed by the Athenians. But as rivalry emerged between Sparta and Athens in the following decades, and especially before and during the Peloponnesian War, the Athenians developed strong opinions about who had contributed the most to Greek victory, quite naturally believing this to be themselves. As far as Herodotos was concerned, and he was possibly strongly influenced by the Athenians in his view, it was they who won the war, although he writes that 'most people' would resent his opinion. For him the Athenians, by placing their fleet at the disposal of the Greeks, and not going over to the Persians, had saved Greece. He dismisses as unworkable the strategy of a Peloponnesian defence behind the Isthmus wall, as the Persian ships would

Figure 11.12 A marble relief from the temple of Athena Nike on the Athenian acropolis. On the left, a hoplite is slaughtering a Persian on his knees, while in the middle a Persian in baggy clothing lies prostrate on the ground and the hoplite who has just killed him prepares to meet the onslaught of a Persian cavalryman; a Persian and hoplite are engaged on the right. This is often taken to be a depiction of Marathon but the presence of the Persian horseman is against this: it is either Plataea or may even represent a campaign against the Persians in Asia Minor. The relief is 183 cm long and 44.5 cm high and dates to the 420s BC. British Museum 1816,0610.159, London. Image © The Trustees of the British Museum.

simply have sailed around the Peloponnese (Hdt. 7.139.1–6: doc. 11.54). Thucydides was of a like mind: in his view the Athenians were the only ones who had fought the Persians at Marathon, and without the naval strategy of Themistokles – and he points out that the Athenians provided most of the ships in the Salamis campaign – the Persians would have conquered the Greeks (Thuc. 1.73.2–74.3: doc. 11.39).

Sparta clearly played the major role at the battle of Plataea, and it is difficult to say what would have happened if Mardonios had not been defeated. Attica may have remained free, or at least the Peloponnese, but central Greece could have been irrevocably lost to the Persians. In addition, the western Greeks should not be forgotten, for they were fighting at the same time against the Etruscans and Carthaginians, thus keeping the Greeks of the eastern part of Sicily free. This was sufficiently important for Pindar to honour the achievement in a *Pythian* ode celebrating the fact that the Syracusans delivered Greece 'from grievous slavery' (Pind. *Pythian* 1.71–5: doc. 11.55). Certainly Plato was not eulogistic about the Greek performance as a whole, as the Greeks had lacked unity, and it was Sparta and Athens who in reality warded off 'approaching slavery'. Had it not been for them the Greeks and the barbarians would 'all be mixed up with each other', here referring to the Persian policy of deporting populations to other places (Pl. *Laws* 692d–693a: doc. 11.56). Yet for Aristophanes in 411 these had been grand days, and he puts on stage a Spartan praising the imaginary peace treaty coming into effect between Sparta and Athens ending the Peloponnesian War, after which everything would be like the 'good old days' when they fought together to defeat the Persians (Ar. *Lysistrata* 1242–70: doc. 11.57).

The effects of the Persian Wars

For Xerxes, as King of Kings over Persia and its subject lands, there were no repercussions within his empire, and despite the huge force sent out, this was in many ways a minor setback for the Persians. Even when the Greeks won back his Greek possessions, including those of western Asia Minor, his power and tribute were not greatly affected. The Athenians won at Marathon, Salamis and Mykale, and as a result they became increasingly powerful, partly because they had proved that democracy worked. Aeschylus' depiction of Salamis and the role of the fleet there was intended to extol the virtues of Athens and the rule of the many who governed it: democracy. When Queen Atossa asked the chorus of Persian elders who commanded the Athenian forces, she received the reply: 'of no man are they called the slaves or subjects' (Aesch. *Persians* lines 241–2: doc. 11.26). Conservatives at Athens on the other hand preferred to extol the virtues of Marathon, won by hoplites. Athens with its naval power went on to develop an empire, but even more importantly brought into being a 'Golden Age' of art, architecture, literature, philosophy and freedom, none of which could have occurred if the Persians had conquered mainland Greece. Athens has contributed more to, and had a greater impact on, western civilisation than any other city or people, and had Athens not survived the Persian invasion the world today would be a greatly diminished place culturally. The part that the Athenians played in 490 and 480–479 BC in saving Greece from Persian domination had been one of the most important turning points in world history.

12

THE DELIAN LEAGUE AND THE PENTEKONTAETIA

Introduction

After the Persian land forces were defeated at Plataea in 479 BC, and their navy worsted by the Greek fleet at Mykale, the surviving Persian forces fled from Greece. The Greeks followed them and liberated the islands of the Aegean and the Greek cities of Asia Minor. Athens became the leader of these Greek states and founded what modern historians refer to as the Delian League. It met on the island of Delos (hence the name). Athens was probably at first on relatively equal terms with its allies in the league. Soon, however, Athens came to dominate the alliance, and the league developed into what modern scholars grandiosely call the 'Athenian empire'. It was in fact more a hybrid of the two: a loose confederation of states, paying 'tribute' which Athens collected, using force to make the allies comply with the terms of the alliance, and imposing treaties and democratic constitutions on those that rebelled. Athens had ceded leadership in the struggle against the Persians to the Spartans in 480–479 BC, but by the 450s the two cities were in conflict and on a collision course to all-out warfare in 431 BC.

Sources

In his history of the Peloponnesian War (for the 'title', see Thucydides 1.1), Thucydides includes a section named by an ancient commentator on his work the 'pentekontaetia', meaning the roughly fifty-year period between the end of the Persian Wars (479 BC) and the outbreak of the Peloponnesian War (431 BC). Thucydides himself comments that apart from Hellanikos other historians failed to write about this period. Hellanikos, however, only did so briefly and without 'chronological accuracy'. Thucydides, in his account, provides few clues with respect to absolute chronology, although he does make clear that he is discussing events in their correct sequential order (Thuc. 1.97.2: doc. 12.4). This section on the pentekontaetia is crucial for knowledge of the Delian League and events in Greece during this period. The *Athenaion Politeia* provides an account of the establishment of the Delian League and some of the political issues, but it is disappointingly brief and contains errors (such as claiming that Themistokles was involved with Ephialtes in stripping the Areiopagos of its powers; *Ath. Pol.* 25: doc. 12.12). Diodorus also provides a chronological account of events and is reasonably trustworthy when he follows his sources closely. Plutarch wrote *Lives* of the major protagonists of this period, Themistokles, Kimon, Aristeides and Perikles, all of whom played an important part in the development of the Delian League. Unfortunately his account is heavily interlaced with misconceptions and moralising anecdotes. In particular he misunderstands the nature of

Athenian politics so it is necessary, as always, to use him with caution; the lengthy dialogues between characters in his lives are simply the product of the over-active workings of his historical imagination. Inscriptions recording decrees of the Athenian assembly are crucial for an understanding of this period, especially with regard to Athens' relationship with its allies, although there is disagreement among scholars as to the dating of many of these decrees.

The Athenians rebuild their walls

After the battle of Mykale in 479 BC, the allied fleet sailed to the Hellespont to break down the Persian-made bridges there. Finding that this was already accomplished, the Spartan king Leotychidas II, who commanded the Greek forces at Mykale, returned to the Peloponnese with Sparta's Peloponnesian allies, and the fleet then dispersed. Its next engagement was under the Spartan regent Pausanias against Cyprus and then Byzantium (see below, p. 415). The Athenians, however, remained, and with the Greeks of the Hellespont and the Ionians who had been liberated went on to besiege the Persian-held city of Sestos. With this development, the Athenians began to act independently of the Spartans. Clearly after the victory at Salamis the Athenians were keen to follow up their naval successes against the Persians (Thuc. 1.89). The Athenian fleet then sailed to Andros, which had medised, and besieged it, but it would not capitulate, refusing to pay 'tribute' because of the island's poverty, although it did become a member of the Delian League a few years later (Herodotos 8.111.1–3: doc. 12.3).

First priority for the Athenians when they returned to Athens was to fortify their city, the walls of which the Persians had destroyed. The city's original fortifications, which were normal for such cities, had probably been built by the beginning of the sixth century, but little remained of these now. Sparta was a notable exception in terms of fortifications as it depended on its hoplites for defence. The Athenians constructed new walls in haste. They were longer than the previous fortifications and nothing was spared in walling the city: material from damaged or destroyed buildings, both public or private, was utilised and the new walls contained column drums, funerary stelai, pieces of sculpture (damaged in the Persian sackings of the city) and whatever stone came to hand (for example *IG* I^3 1226: doc. 4.39; Fig. 12.1). Thucydides' narrative indicates that the reason for the rapid construction was not fear of the Persians returning but concerns regarding Sparta. These were confirmed when the Spartans were informed by their allies, who were afraid of the size of Athens' fleet and 'the courage which they had displayed in fighting the Persians', that the Athenians planned to rebuild their walls, and the Spartans sent a delegation to Athens to protest (Thuc. 1.89.3–93.7: doc. 12.1).

The Spartan delegation proposed that the Athenians should not refortify their city, and also recommended that all cities outside the Peloponnese which possessed walls should tear them down, so that in the event of another Persian invasion the Persians would not possess a base of operations, as they had at Thebes. Clearly this was against Athenian interests, and Themistokles advised the Athenians to send the Spartans away with the promise that they would soon dispatch an embassy to Sparta to discuss the issue. On Themistokles' own recommendation the Athenians then sent him to Sparta, where he kept delaying any decision on the matter until other ambassadors from Athens arrived. They had been instructed not to leave Athens until the walls were of defensible height. When reports reached the Spartans that the Athenians were rebuilding their walls, Themistokles suggested they send an embassy to Athens to see for themselves. He secretly sent a message to Athens that these Spartan ambassadors should be detained in Athens. Aristeides and Abronikos, as Athenian ambassadors, then arrived in Sparta with the news that the walls were of sufficient height to protect

Figure 12.1 Part of Athens' walls, which were rebuilt in haste after the end of the Persian Wars. This portion is in the Kerameikos. Photo © Antigoni Gouras Manzi.

Athens from attack, and Themistokles addressed the Spartans on the matter of Athens' walls, informing them that the city was now fortified, and able to defend itself. From now on, he continued, the Athenians would decide for themselves what was in their own best interests. For the good of Greece as a whole they had abandoned their city and taken to their ships without consulting anyone, and had always given the best advice possible when conferring with the Spartans during the Persian Wars. Similarly, they thought it better for the city to be fortified both for their own sake and for that of the allies as this would strengthen the Hellenic League. Athens, after all, would not be able to have an equal say in the deliberations of the alliance (the Hellenic league) unless it argued from a position of strength (Thuc. 1.89–92).

Themistokles was perhaps remembering here the Peloponnesians' jibe in 480 that the Athenians could not insist on what strategy should be employed at Salamis as they no longer possessed a city, as Athens was under Persian domination (Plut. *Themistokles* 11.2–5: doc. 11.37). But, more importantly, Thucydides' account makes it clear that the Spartans responded positively to the Athenian decision to rebuild: their original embassy they said had given advice, not orders, and they showed no open resentment towards Athens, making clear that they were on good terms with the Athenians because of the part they had played in the Persian Wars. They were nevertheless secretly piqued that the Athenians had not listened to them on this occasion. If, however, Thucydides' account is correct, Sparta's allies were already concerned about Athens' potential power, and Themistokles would hardly have invented this sophisticated strategy to deceive the Spartans about Athens' fortifications until they were actually in place unless he felt it possible that the Spartans would again attack Athens. Athens had, after all, been the subject of several invasions in the last decade of the

500s, and more importantly the Peloponnesians' focus both now and during the Persian Wars on the importance of defending the Isthmus and protecting the Peloponnese may have suggested to the Athenians that the Spartans would be quite happy to see Athens, and other cities north of the Isthmus, left without defences if they could have their way.

The fortification of the Piraeus

The 10-kilometre wall around the Piraeus and Mounichia was begun in Themistokles' archonship (493/2), and protected a good swathe of territory, including the urban and mercantile areas there. Later, in 461 to 457 BC, the Athenians built a pair of 'Long Walls' as they termed them, the northern one running from Athens to the Piraeus, the southern one from Athens to Phaleron. Sometime in 450–445 BC the Athenians constructed a third long wall, parallel to the northern one, from Athens to the Piraeus. This new Long Wall meant that the road to the Piraeus was between a pair of walls, securing this route in case the Long Wall to Phaleron was taken. These walls were famously demolished at the command of the Spartans in 403 BC, to the accompaniment of music by flute-girls (Xen. *Hellenika* 2.18–23: doc. 13.35). Konon was to rebuild them in 393 BC as a sign of Athens' resurgence (Tod 2.107: doc. 14.10).

The origins of the Delian League

Victory at Mykale took the conflict into Persian territory and in the immediate aftermath of the war Aristeides and Themistokles emerged as the two main leaders of the Athenian demos, working together to organise the rebuilding of the walls. Depite Themistokles' prominence, it was Aristeides who actually organised the Delian League, while it was the high-handed and Persian-like behaviour of the Spartan regent and commander Pausanias at Byzantium which provided the main impetus behind this development of a new alliance.

Pausanias aims to become ruler of Greece

Shortly after the Athenians rebuilt their walls, the Spartans sent Pausanias, regent for the young Agiad king Pleistarchos, abroad in command of the Greek forces with twenty Peloponnesian, thirty Athenian and many allied ships. These captured most of Cyprus, an island with many Greek cities, and then the strategic site of Byzantium. Here Pausanias became unpopular with the Greeks due to his arrogance, which had already revealed itself in 479 BC when he disgraced himself in Spartan eyes by having his name engraved on the Serpent Column dedicated to Apollo at Delphi, as responsible for the victory against the Persians: 'Since as leader of the Greeks he destroyed the Persian army Pausanias dedicated this memorial to Phoibos (Apollo)' (Simon. 17: doc. 6.35). He also returned to Xerxes some of his relatives and friends who were taken prisoner at Byzantium, along with a letter containing a proposal of alliance, which offered Xerxes the chance to gain control of Sparta and the rest of Greece. Xerxes responded with a letter delivered to Pausanias through Artabazos, which encouraged Pausanias in his plans.

This letter caused Pausanias to adopt even more Persian customs, dressing in Persian garments, being escorted on his journeys through Thrace by a Persian and Egyptian bodyguard, holding Persian-style banquets, and restricting access to himself like a monarch. As a result of their concern over Pausanias' conduct, the Ionians and others, who after all had only just been liberated from the control of the Persian king, approached the Athenians with the request that Athens become their leader, as they were 'kin', part of the same ethnic group: the Athenians were also Ionians, while the Spartans, of course, were Dorians. Pausanias was at this point recalled to Sparta to face charges that he was behaving more like a tyrant than a general. He was acquitted, but not reinstated, and instead the Spartans sent out Dorkis and some other officers with a small force to replace him. When, however, they arrived at Byzantium, the allies would not accept their assistance – leadership of the Ionian Greeks had clearly passed to the Athenians. The Spartans returned home but with, as yet, no ill-feeling towards the Athenians whom they considered as their allies and fully capable of continuing the war against the Persians. Moreover, the Spartans were apprehensive that other Spartans would become as corrupt as Pausanias if they served outside Sparta, a phenomenon which other Greeks noticed with concern (Xen. *Const. Spart.*14.1–4: doc. 6.70).

Pausanias returned to the Hellespont on his own initiative, but was driven out of Byzantium by the Athenians. He then went to Kolonai in the Troad (the region around Troy), and again began intriguing with the Persian king Xerxes, with the aim of becoming ruler of Greece. He was no doubt motivated by the fact that, despite being the victor of Plataea and commander of all the allied forces, once his regency concluded he would lose his official standing at Sparta and influence abroad. The ephors recalled him to Sparta, where he was thrown into prison, but released. Pausanias was then tricked into revealing everything he was planning in a conversation overheard by the ephors. However, when they went to arrest him he realised what was going to happen and fled to the temple of Athena Chalkioikos (Athena of the Bronze House). The ephors walled him up inside and only brought him out when he was about to die of starvation. This brought a curse upon the Spartans, which they appeased with the aid of an oracle from Delphi (Thuc. 1.130.1–133.4: doc. 6.35). The Eurypontid kind, Leotychidas II (491–476) was also found to have taken huge bribes from the Thessalians and was exiled from Sparta (Hdt. 6.72.1–2: doc. 6.76; for Pausanias: Thuc 1.94–95, 128–35).

The founding of the Delian League and its organisation

The allies asked the Athenians to become their leaders because of their concerns over Pausanias' behaviour, and this led to the alliance known as the Delian League. Two main ancient sources deal with the organisation of the league, Thucydides and the *Athenaion Politeia* (Thuc. 1.96.1–97.2: doc. 12.4; *Ath. Pol.*23.3–24.3: doc. 12.2; cf. Plut. *Aristeides* 24–5; Diod. Sic. 11.47). Athens' allies agreed to make annual contributions of money and ships to continue the war against the Persians. The pretext was that they were retaliating 'for what they had lost by ravaging the king's country' (Thuc. 1.96.1). Aristeides was responsible for calculating the assessment which prescribed the annual contribution of each ally, doing so in 478/7 BC, the third year after the battle of Salamis. The monetary contribution which each allied state agreed to pay annually was known as the 'phoros' and is referred to by modern scholars as the tribute. Aristeides also administered the oaths taken by the Ionians, that they would have the same friends and enemies as the Athenians. Lumps of iron were thrown into the sea to make the oath binding: the alliance was to last until the iron floated, or, in other words, forever. From the very beginning of the league the Athenians had numerous allies, and were joined by all the liberated islands and cities.

Thucydides notes that the Athenians were the league leaders (after all, they possessed the largest fleet and were the most populous city), and the allies were 'at first autonomous' (Thuc. 1.97.1), with the league making its decisions in general meetings. Each of the allies probably had one vote in these meetings. The alliance was probably unicameral in nature, with the

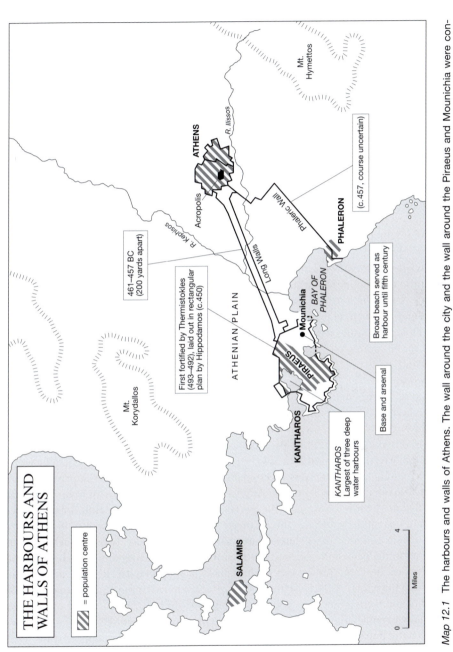

THE HARBOURS AND WALLS OF ATHENS

= population centre

SALAMIS

Mt. Korydallos

ATHENIAN PLAIN

461–457 BC (200 yards apart)

First fortified by Thermistokles (493–492), laid out in rectangular plan by Hippodamos (c.450)

KANTHAROS

KANTHAROS Largest of three deep water harbours

Base and arsenal

PIRAEUS

Mounichia

BAY OF PHALERON

Broad beach served as harbour until fifth century

Long Walls

R. Kephsos

Acropolis

ATHENS

R. Ilissos

Phaleric Wall

PHALERON

(c.457, course uncertain)

Mt. Hymettos

0 — 4 Miles

Map 12.1 The harbours and walls of Athens. The wall around the city and the wall around the Piraeus and Mounichia were constructed in 479 BC. The 'Long Walls' from the city to the Piraeus were constructed between 461 and 457 BC. Based on M. Grant, *The Routledge Atlas of Classical History*, fifth edition, Routledge, 1994, p. 27.

allies and Athens meeting as one body, rather than bicameral, in which the allies would have met separately from Athens. The Athenians organised a new group of 'treasurers of Greece', the hellenotamiai, to handle the financial affairs of the league and its treasury was also located at Delos, with the first annual tribute collection amounting to 460 talents.

While the overt purpose of the alliance was to retaliate against the Persians by plundering their territory (Thuc. 1.96.1), the Athenians and their allies had from the beginning of the alliance an equally important aim of liberating those Greeks who were still under Persian authority and domination. Thucydides places an emphasis on the Athenians' subjugation of their allies, using the pentekontaetia to describe how Athens became powerful enough to challenge Sparta. Yet he also gives an account of the Athenian and allied campaigns against the Persians, which is particularly detailed in the case of their military activity in Egypt. The Athenians with their allies vigorously prosecuted the war against the Persians (see docs 12.4, 12.7–8, 12.13–15), and during this time also dealt seriously with revolts from within the league. It would be surprising if the Athenians in 478/7 BC had not realised the benefits which leadership of the allies, a large fleet and the potential for booty would bring them. Aristeides pointed out precisely these advantages to the Athenians (*Ath. Pol.* 23.3–24.3: doc. 12.2).

Revolts from the Delian League

Once the league was established, the Athenians under the command of Kimon, son of Miltiades (one of the strategoi at Marathon in 490 BC and architect of the Athenian strategy that led to victory there), in 476 BC besieged the Persian fortress of Eion on the river Strymon in Thrace, and enslaved its inhabitants. Next they attacked Skyros (an island off Euboea), where the Dolopian pirates who inhabited it were enslaved and replaced with Athenian settlers. Karystos (in south-west Euboea) which medised after the battle of Artemision was then conquered and made to become a member of the Delian League. Thucydides at this point indicates how quickly the character of the alliance changed (Thuc. 1.98.1–99.3: doc. 12.4). After Karystos, the Athenians besieged Naxos, a member of the alliance which had revolted, and made it accept surrender terms, possibly in 465 BC. Thucydides comments that 'this was the first allied city that was enslaved against the terms of the existing agreement, and then it happened to others as well' (1.98.1). By 'enslaved' he does not mean literal enslavement but rather that the Naxians were now forced to be subject to Athenian authority. When he writes 'against the existing agreement' this must mean that the alliance included a provision that allied states remained independent from Athens. As the alliance was meant to be perpetual, it appears that no provision was made for members to secede, and so he cannot be referring to a provision that allies could leave the alliance.

Various revolts against Athens' leadership occurred in the period before the Peloponnesian War and in the pentekontaetia section Thucydides explicitly mentions Naxos, Thasos, Boeotia, Euboea, Megara, Samos and Byzantium as having rebelled. Revolts were caused according to Thucydides (1.99.1) by the failure of states to make the agreed contributions, for the Athenians were punctilious about collecting the phoros (tribute). Some of the allies commuted their contribution of ships and money to one simply of money, and the effect was that the power of the Athenian navy grew as they used these funds to build more ships. With this ever-increasing navy the Athenians came to take a more prominent part in expeditions, while Chios, Lesbos and Samos, powerful states with their own navies, were accorded different treatment from the other allies according to the *Athenaion Politeia* (24.2: doc. 12.2), and retained a degree of autonomy that other allies were to lose.

The ostracism of Themistokles

A major change in Athenian politics occurred in the late 470s when Themistokles was ostracised. He was also a candidate for ostracism in the 480s (doc. 10.14.vii). The reasons behind his ostracism are unclear, but what is apparent is that, after rebuilding Athens' walls and playing some role in organising the tribute collection for the new league, Themistokles seems to have gradually ceded influence to his old rival Aristeides and also to Kimon, who emerged in this period as a successful general. Thucydides provides a detailed account of Themistokles' later flight to Persia, and a eulogy on him as one of Athens' most successful political and military leaders (Thuc. 1.135.2–138.6: doc. 12.5). When Pausanias' treasonous correspondence and dealings with the Persians came to light, the Spartans accused Themistokles of also being involved. It does not appear that they had any grounds for this charge but the Athenians were willing to believe it to the extent that they decided to recall Themistokles to Athens. After being ostracised Themistokles took up residence in Argos, which was well disposed towards him as he had successfully opposed the Spartan suggestion that those who had failed to fight against the Persians not be allowed to be members of the Amphiktyonic League. While in Argos Themistokles may have helped stir up democratic feeling, as Mantineia, Elis and perhaps Tegea installed democracies at this time. Sparta was both Argos' implacable enemy and an opponent of democracies generally, preferring its allies in the Peloponnesian League to be controlled by oligarchies, and may have resented Themistokles' presence in the Peloponnese for this reason. Themistokles took no chances in the face of this hostility, and fled to Corcyra, after which he took refuge with his enemy the king (Admetos) of Molossia, and then travelled on a merchant ship to Ephesos on the Asia Minor coast, passing the siege of Naxos en route. From Ephesos he travelled inland and sent a letter to Artaxerxes, who had succeeded his father Xerxes as king of Persia. The siege of Naxos has been dated anywhere between 471 to 465; but a late date for Naxos' revolt, c. 465 (the date of Artaxerxes' accession), suits Thucydides' narrative. Themistokles reminded Artaxerxes, writes Thucydides, of the two benefactions which he had given Artaxerxes' father Xerxes: he had warned him that the Greek fleet was about to leave Salamis and that he should hasten if he wanted to waylay it there, and he had prevented the destruction of the bridges across the Hellespont (although this statement was patently untrue). When his arguments were accepted by the Persian king in a return letter, Themistokles travelled inland learning the Persian language and customs and 'arrived at court more important than any other Greek had ever been' (Thuc. 1.138.2: doc. 12.5; Diod. Sic. 11.55–58; Plut. *Themistokles* 25–31).

Partly because of his reputation (as victor at Salamis) and the fact that he was holding out to Artaxerxes the hope of conquering Greece, but primarily because of his obvious intelligence, Artaxerxes gave him lands to rule: Magnesia in Asia Minor on the river Maeander for his bread, Lampsakos for his wine and Myous for his meat. There was a monument to him in Magnesia, which still honoured the descendants of Themistokles in Plutarch's time. His relatives secretly brought his bones back to Attica, since he could not legally be buried there as he had been convicted of treason in his absence. He was buried in the Piraeus, where he seems to have been the object of a private cult. Some ancient authors preferred to believe that Themistokles met Xerxes, not Artaxerxes, but this is an invention by those who preferred a meeting with the man Themistokles actually defeated, rather than his successor; Thucydides can be trusted to be correct on this detail. As sources for his life, there are also the twenty-one 'Letters of Themistokles'; although inauthentic, being written in the second century AD, they provide a framework of historical truth insofar as Themistokles did send several messages and letters in the course of his career and these letters are based on the historical record.

Both Pausanias and Themistokles, the two main heroes of the Persian Wars, were found guilty of dealing treasonably with the Persians. For Pausanias this seems to have been a reasonable conclusion, but Themistokles was clearly the victim both of Spartan suspicion (and delayed anger at their being duped over the rebuilding of Athens' walls) and of rivalry within Athenian politics. Thucydides' treatment of Themistokles is very eulogistic, the most detailed of any protagonist in his history, and its commendatory tone is unusual for that work. Herodotos gives a positive account of Themistokles' career, but is aware of reports that he was susceptible to both giving and taking bribes: he supposedly accepted a bribe of 30 talents from the Euboeans to make the Greek fleet stay and fight at Artemision (on the tip of Euboea) and not abandon Euboea to the Persians without a fight, after Eurybiades refused to fight there; Themistokles then bribed Eurybiades with five of the talents, and Adeimantos the Corinthian with three talents, keeping the rest for himself. Timokreon of Rhodes vilifies Themistokles for his general self-interest and for taking a bribe not to restore him (Timokreon) from exile for medising, despite the fact that he and Themistokles were friends (Timokreon 727: doc. 12.6). Pausanias' death and Themistokles' ostracism and then exile marked the end of the period of the Persian Wars and Greek history moved on to other concerns.

The aftermath of the Persian Wars

The battle of Euymedon

After the siege of Naxos, the Athenians and their allies were involved in a battle at the river Eurymedon in Pamphylia in southern Asia Minor, which took place both on land and sea, perhaps c. 469–466, although the date is disputed; despite only a brief notice in Thucydides this was a battle with important consequences, as the Phoenician fleet of 200 triremes was captured. Kimon commanded the entire Greek navy and the backbone of his force was the fleet of 200 triremes built by Themistokles (Thuc. 1.100.1: doc. 12.7). Simonides praised the prowess of the Greeks who died 'on foot and in their swift ships' (Simon. 46: doc. 12.8). The Athenian war dead from this engagement were buried in the Kerameikos cemetery at Athens, the first time this seems to have occurred. A direct consequence of the campaign was that the Greek cities of Asia Minor were freed from the Persians, and the coast from Ionia to Pamphylia was in Greek hands. Its cities became members of the Delian League and new members joined the alliance, especially from the region of Caria.

At Athens, victory was celebrated by establishing in the Piraeus a hero-cult of the river Eurymedon, a bronze palm with a gilded figure of Athena on the top was dedicated at Delphi, and the southern wall of the acropolis was constructed from the spoils. On one red-figured Athenian vase a Persian is depicted bending over, offering himself for anal intercourse to an athletic naked Greek who has his own erect male organ in his hand: the accompanying inscription reads, 'I am Eurymedon', and 'I stand bent over'. Defeat is here represented in sexual form: the masculine Greeks had defeated the 'effeminate Persians' and put an end to any future threat of Persian invasion of the mainland.

The revolt and siege of Thasos

This took place after the battle of Eurymedon, possibly in the same year. Impressive as the victory over the Persians at Eurymedon had been, Thasos rebelled soon afterwards from Athens and its allies. The revolt seems to have stemmed primarily from a trading dispute concerning the trading stations (emporia) on the coast of Thrace opposite Thasos, and the gold mine Thasos worked there. Athens established a presence in the region with the capture of Eion from the Persians: Thasos may well have considered that its economic interests were at risk and that defeating the Persians was a lesser consideration than more immediate economic concerns closer to home. The Thasians were besieged, after being defeated in a sea battle, and finally came to terms in the third year of the siege. While the revolt and its suppression are sometimes seen as acts of 'economic imperialism' on the part of Athens, especially when Athens took control of Thasos' emporia and gold mine, returning Thasos to its status as a member of the league must have been Athens' primary concern in crushing the revolt.

Athens also had an interest in colonising the mainland nearly, and at this time sent 10,000 colonists to 'Nine Ways' (Ennea Hodoi) on the river Strymon, later known as Amphipolis. However, a force which advanced further into the interior was destroyed at Drabeskos by the Thracians, who considered this settlement as 'an act of hostility' (Thuc. 1.100.2–3: doc. 12.9). On its surrender Thasos was forced to demolish its wall (rebellious allies were often required to tear down their city walls, as this prevented the possibility of another siege, and also made them dependent on Athens' protection in case of invasion), hand over its ships, and not only cede to Athens their emporia on the mainland and the mine, but pay 'whatever they had to immediately as well as tribute for the future'. This very much reads like the tribute they had not paid since they revolted. They were also to pay tribute regularly and annually from then on. Such measures were surely intended not only to punish Thasos, but to serve as an example to the other allies who had assisted Athens in crushing the revolt.

Consequences followed from this revolt. When Thasos was under siege, it appealed to Sparta for assistance. According to Diodorus, the Spartans in 475/4 BC regretted having lost their command of the sea (Diod. Sic. 11.50.1–3: doc. 12.10), and certainly the revolt of Thasos now gave them the opportunity to intervene in the affairs of the Delian League. Without the knowledge of the Athenians they therefore considered invading Attica and were about to do so when an earthquake in Sparta demolished most of the houses in the city. Taking advantage of the situation, the helots and some of the perioikoi rebelled against the Spartans and withdrew to Mount Ithome (in 465/4 or 464/3 BC). The Spartans besieged them there, and in consequence no Spartan invasion of Attica occurred at this time.

Kimon was in command at Thasos, but on his return he was charged at his euthyna (the accounting at the end of term of office) with having been bribed by Alexander of Macedonia, who was still on the throne, not to invade his country (Plut. *Kimon* 14). Given that Kimon conquered the Chersonese as part of this campaign and expelled the Persians there, this may seem unfair, but at Athens it seemed logical to some that from the Chersonese one could invade and conquer a large part of Macedonia. There was clearly a political agenda in this accusation and Perikles was involved in the prosecution. It is often assumed by scholars that Kimon's trial may have been before the Areiopagos, and that it was possibly Kimon's acquittal which encouraged Ephialtes to curtail its powers in 462/1 BC. However, given the ongoing further democratisation of Athens' political system in the 460s and 450s BC, the trial need not be seen as any form of catalyst or motivating factor for further change.

The revolt of the helots and perioikoi

Sparta had considered invading Attica prior to the revolt of the helots and some of the perioikoi, but in 462 BC, when the siege of Mount Ithome failed to make progress, the Spartans called on their allies, including Athens, for assistance. The Athenians were considered to be very proficient at siege warfare but, as it turned out, they were not successful on this occasion. This was the last military undertaking of the Hellenic League, acting in this case not against Persians but fellow Greeks who were under Spartan domination. Athens sent a force of 4000 hoplites under Kimon's leadership, but this became the cause of the first 'open dispute' between the two cities (Thuc. 1.102.3: doc. 12.11; Plut. *Kimon* 16–17). Kimon was a 'philo-Lakonian', a friend of Sparta, while Ephialtes who makes his first appearance in the historical narrative at around this time argued against sending this expedition to Sparta. (Plut. *Kimon* 16–17 has two Athenian expeditions to Sparta but this contradicts Thucydides.)

Events played into Ephialtes' hands, for, even with the Athenians' assistance, the Spartans failed to take Ithome. According to Thucydides, the Spartans became afraid of the 'Athenians' boldness and revolutionary spirit' and were concerned in case the Athenians took sides with the besieged at Ithome, who after all as Messenians were Greeks themselves, and 'attempt some sort of revolution'. Accordingly Sparta sent the Athenians home saying that they had no further need of their services, while retaining those of their other allies. Thucydides notes that the Spartans took into consideration the fact that the Athenians were not of the 'same race' as themselves: the Athenians were Ionians, the Spartans Dorian. This reflects the divide which was now evident in the Greek world, between Sparta with its league of Peloponnesian allies, and Athens with its mainly Ionian allies in the Delian League. This rejection of their help roused Athenian anger as they realised they had not been discharged on any reasonable grounds. When the hoplites arrived back at Athens the Athenians therefore renounced their membership of the Hellenic League and allied themselves with Sparta's main enemy, Argos, as well as with the Thessalians in a triple alliance. Aeschylus refers, obviously with approval, to the new alliance with Argos in his play the *Eumenides*, and at Athens there was clearly an anti-Spartan group which gained a political advantage as a result of Sparta's treatment of Athens at Ithome. Ephialtes' reforms at Athens (see below, p. 423), were perhaps enacted during Kimon's absence with the army, and news of these democratic reforms had possibly reached Sparta, but recent Athenian activities against Naxos and Thasos were also evidence of the Athenians' 'boldness and revolutionary spirit' and were sufficient to cause Sparta to mistrust the Athenians' assistance.

In the long run, the Messenian rebels surrendered, but only after a ten-year siege. They were allowed to depart on the terms that they were never to set foot in the Peloponnese again. Due to their enmity with the Spartans the Athenians settled the rebels at Naupaktos, which they had captured from the Lokrians and which developed into an important Athenian naval base. The Spartans expelled the settlers from there after the Peloponnesian War. If the helots

Figure 12.2 A bronze spear-head dedicated at Olympia by the Messenians, taken from the Spartans and Athenians besieging Mt. Ithome (doc. 12.11). The inscription reads, 'The Methanioi (i.e. Messenians) [took this] from the Lakedaimonians (i.e. Spartans)'. Olympia Museum Br 219, Olympia. Photo © Olympia Archaeological Museum, Hellenic Ministry of Culture and Tourism, 7th Ephorate of Prehistoric and Classical Antiquities & Archaeological Receipts Fund.

revolted in 465/4 or 464/3 BC and surrendered in 456/5 or 455/54 BC, Thucydides' narrative is not chronological, for he continues by narrating Megara's alliance with Athens in 460–459 BC; the easiest solution is to assume that in narrating the end of the revolt, he got ahead of the chronological sequence of events. Two bronze spear butts dedicated by the 'Methanioi' were possibly dedications of spears taken from the Spartans and Athenians besieging Mount Ithome; Methanioi appears to be the 'Messenian' spelling for Messenians, the helots long enserfed by the Spartans, whose day of freedom eventually came in 369 BC.

Ephialtes' reforms

After the Persian Wars there were no major constitutional changes at Athens for seventeen years, but in 462/1 BC Ephialtes introduced reform legislation to reduce greatly the powers of the Areiopagos Council. The *Athenaion Politeia* is the main source for these reforms (25.1–4: doc. 12.12). As a governing council the Areiopagos was 'gradually declining' (*Ath. Pol.*25.1), presumably in importance and influence. According to Plutarch (*Kimon* 15), during the absence of Kimon and the 4000 hoplites at Mount Ithome, Ephialtes put through legislation in the assembly to curb the powers of the Areiopagos. The absence of these hoplites may have tipped the balance in the ekklesia in favour of the poor, the thetes, despite the majority of the hoplites having remained in Athens. As he was absent Kimon was unable to speak against the reforms and they were passed by the assembly. On his return he tried to reverse these changes, but both he and his pro-Spartan policy had been discredited by the hostility of the Spartans at Mount Ithome, and he was ostracised at the next opportunity, probably in 461 BC (doc. 10.14.ix). At this point it can be noted that while the *Athenaion Politeia* has Themistokles present at the time of these reforms, he was in fact already in exile in Persia. One Archestratos, of whom nothing else is known, was associated with Ephialtes in these reforms, for the Thirty Tyrants in 404 BC erased their laws (*Ath. Pol.*35.2: doc. 13.40). While Perikles was also apparently involved in these constitutional changes, Ephialtes was clearly the main mover behind them. Indeed, after introducing the reforms, Ephialtes was assassinated, an indication of the antagonism which the reforms created as well as their very real constitutional significance.

Ephialtes systematically prepared the ground for his reforms, firstly by attempting to discredit the Areiopagos by bringing many of its members to trial for 'administrative misconduct'. Through legislation passed by the assembly, he removed the Areiopagos' 'additionally acquired powers, through which it was the guardian of the constitution', and gave some of these powers to the Council of Five Hundred, some to the demos (in its capacity as the assembly), and some to the lawcourts. Prior to Ephialtes' reforms, the Areiopagos had several political responsibilities, which included guardianship of the laws, oversight of the officials (conducting the dokimasia and euthyna for each official on their entering and leaving office), and a general 'supervision' of the citizens (compare docs 8.1–2, 8.17). This dokimasia was the 'inspection' of an official conducted before he took up office to see if he was capable of fulfilling its functions and duties, and the euthyna the report he gave of his office when its term expired, at which his accounts were audited. These would now be conducted by the lawcourts, giving the demos great power over the city's officials.

In many ways the Areiopagos council was an anomaly in a democracy, as its members, who were all current or previous archons, were drawn only from the top two property classes, the pentakosiomedimnoi and the hippeis, although the method of election for archons introduced in 487/6 BC meant that membership of this council was less prestigious than previously: 500 candidates from that date on were directly elected by the people and from these ten were chosen by lot ([Arist.] *Ath. Pol.*22.5: doc. 10.9). Under Ephialtes the Areiopagos was deprived of all but a few areas of jurisdiction: trials for deliberate homicide, arson and poisoning, and the protection of the sacred olive trees and other religious cases. It retained the right of prosodos (introducing motions) to the boule and ekklesia, but this right was possibly little exercised. It is often assumed that Aeschylus in the *Eumenides* (produced in 458), which deals to a great degree with Orestes' trial for homicide before the Areiopagos for the murder of his mother Clytemnestra, shows support for Ephialtes' reforms. The role of the Areiopagos as a court of homicide is stressed in the play and this may reflect Aeschylus' point of view that the council should possess only this function, although Aeschylus also emphasises that the Areiopagos fulfils an important role as a guardian of the state and that the Athenians must avoid civil conflict.

Following Ephialtes' reforms, the Areiopagos was left with its jurisdiction over homicide and religious issues, and a general oversight of the constitution. However, it no longer possessed any political power. These changes paved the way for a further alteration to its membership when in 458/7 BC the zeugitai were made eligible for election to the archonship, and so became members of the Areiopagos. From this point this council was no longer the preserve of the aristocrats or the prosperous but of quite ordinary farmers and hoplites as well. Athens' conservative council was stripped of its powers, and the further reforms by Perikles which introduced pay for jury service extended the political participation of the demos even further. This was especially significant as many of the Areiopagos' powers were now in the hands of the jury-courts (see below, p. 432).

Athenian military campaigns

Athenian disaster in Egypt

After the Athenian return from Ithome, Athens and its allies continued to conduct campaigns against the Persians, this being the rationale for the league's existence. As a result they became embroiled in a major military disaster in Egypt. This country had become a Persian satrapy in 525 BC, and by revolting in 486 delayed the second Persian invasion of mainland Greece. Xerxes crushed this rebellion, but it revolted again, under the leadership of Inaros, king of the Libyans, and the Athenians and their allies who had been involved with 200 ships in a campaign in Cyprus became his allies. This occurred in about 460 BC and Thucydides provides a detailed account of events (Thuc. 1.104.1–2, 109.1–110.4: doc. 12.13). Egypt was an important part of the Persian empire and the Athenians supported Inaros in the hope that Egypt might be detached from the Persian sphere of influence. There was no reason not to be confident of success given that Egypt was already in revolt, the Athenian and allied fleet was large, and they had already liberated the Greek cities of Asia Minor from Persian rule. The Athenians achieved initial successes, gaining control of the Delta and two-thirds of Memphis, the ancient Egyptian capital situated where the Nile starts to branch out to form the Delta.

After this initial success, the Persian king Artaxerxes sent Megabazos to Sparta, to bribe the Spartans to invade Attica. When this approach did not work, he was recalled, and Artaxerxes sent another (similarly named) Persian, Megabyzos son of Zopyros, with a large army into Egypt. He was able to defeat the Egyptians and Greeks, and these were expelled from Memphis and surrounded on the island of Prosopitis. After besieging it for eighteen months Megabyzos then drained the water around the island and, leaving the 200 Greek ships stranded on land, he crossed over the strait and took the island. Inaros was crucified by the Persians. After six years the Greek venture came to nothing and incurred heavy casualties, although some Greeks escaped via Libya to the Greek city of Cyrene (see docs 2.28–9). This disaster was compounded when the Athenians and allies sent a fleet of fifty triremes to relieve those on the island of Prosopitis: this force was attacked and most of the ships destroyed. Thucydides comments drily: 'So ended the great expedition of the Athenians and their allies to Egypt' (1.109.4).

Thucydides is quite clear on the extent of the Hellenic disaster in Egypt: 200 ships initially took part and these were followed by a relief force of fifty more, most of which were destroyed with few survivors (250 ships with crews of 180–200 men meant casualties of up to 50,000, a disaster comparable to the Sicilian Expedition). Another historian Ktesias, however, whose work is now lost, recorded that only forty ships, not 200, went to Egypt from Cyprus and that they surrendered and their crews returned home. These two accounts cannot be reconciled despite attempts to do so. Thucydides clearly gives the reader the impression that 250 ships and crews were lost, although the disaster had little apparent effect on Athenian resources and Thucydides' sources may have been exaggerating, with more ships and their crews escaping than he suggests.

A casualty list of the Erechtheid tribe

Although this defeat in Egypt was a major one, it was not the only field of military engagement for the Athenians at this time. A casualty list of one of Athens' ten tribes, Erechtheis (I), lists the dead who died in one year, either in 460 or in 459 BC (*IG* I³ 1147: doc. 12.14; Fig. 12.3). The extensive nature of Athens' campaigns is clear with the Athenians engaged in fighting in Cyprus, Egypt, Phoenicia, Halieis, Aegina and Megara all in the same year. Two generals (strategoi), both from this one tribe (see above, p. 360) and 176 soldiers lost their lives in these campaigns. The first three expeditions named involved activities against the Persians, but the last three were against Greeks. The Athenians, however, used the same expression for both spheres of activity, against the Persians and other Greeks, referring to both of these simply as 'the war': they saw themselves as fighting on many fronts, against both Greeks and Persians. An epigram was written for those who fell on Cyprus. While it is attributed to Simonides it cannot be his work as he was dead by the 460s, and it may well refer to any of the various Athenian expeditions there, including the one that the Athenians and their allies were engaged in when they went to the aid of Inaros in Egypt (Simon. 45: doc. 12.15).

The First Peloponnesian War

The Greek campaigns at Halieis, Aegina and Megara named in the casualty list of the tribe Erechtheis deserve further mention, although in their correct chronological order these should read Megara, Halieis and then Aegina. These conflicts formed part of the so-called 'First Peloponnesian War', a modern term, which involved several conflicts between Athens and its allies, and the Spartans and their allies. The Athenians soundly defeated the Corinthians at Megara, while the Peloponnesians prevailed at Tanagra, and the Athenians in turn were victorious at Oionophyta, leading to their conquest of all Boeotia. When Corinth complained in 432 BC of the Spartans' slowness to go to war (Thuc. 1.70.1–8: doc. 13.3), this was probably an allusion to the First Peloponnesian War, in which Corinth and other allies of Sparta did most of the fighting rather than the Spartans themselves.

Figure 12.3 An inscribed list carved on marble of the citizens of the tribe Erechtheis who were killed on the field of battle, dating to around 460 or 459 BC (doc. 12.14). Dimensions: 59 cm × 144 cm. Louvre MA863, Paris. Drawing by J. Etherington.

Megara and Halieis

In 460 or 459 BC the Megarians allied themselves with the Athenians because the Corinthians had invaded their territory as the result of a dispute over the boundary between the two states. Their abrupt dismissal from Mount Ithome made this alliance against Corinth welcome to the Athenians. Diodorus (11.78–9: doc. 12.19) gives the date as 458 BC but the engagement is generally believed to have taken place in 460 or 459 BC. Megara controlled the strip of territory immediately north of the Isthmus through which any army moving north from the Peloponnese had to pass: it therefore had immense strategic value for the Athenians and the Athenians took advantage of this opportunity. Megara also had two ports, one of these (Pegai) at the eastern end of the Corinthian Gulf, use of which meant that the Athenians could avoid the long sail around the Peloponnese, as in Perikles' Corinthian Gulf expedition of 455/4 or 454/3 BC. Nisaia, the other port was near the city of Megara itself and the Athenians had earlier contested its possession with the Megarians in the sixth century. The Athenians also stationed a force there, after building for the Megarians the 'Long Walls' (similar to those at Athens) from Megara to the port Nisaia, which they manned themselves. Thucydides notes that 'it was primarily from this alliance with the Megarians that the Corinthians' violent hatred for the Athenians first came into being' (Thuc. 1.103.4: doc. 12.18; Diod. 11.78–9: doc. 12.19). They had previously been on good terms, with the Corinthians twice opposing and thwarting Spartan invasions of Attica in the last decade of the sixth century. In 460 or 459 BC, the Athenians made a landing at Halieis but were opposed by the Corinthians and Epidaurians and were defeated, while a little later the Athenian and Peloponnesian fleets had an encounter at Kekryphaleia in which the Athenians were victorious (Diod. Sic. 11.78.1–2: doc. 12.19, incorrectly stating that the Athenians won against the Corinthians and Epidaurians). These two obscure events, passed over quickly by Thucydides (1.105), are pointers to the larger outbreak of war that soon followed.

Aegina

Athens and the nearby island of Aegina co-operated at the battle of Salamis but there was a long history of animosity between the two states and a major naval engagement was fought off Aegina between these two and their respective allies in which the Athenians captured seventy ships. Reasons for the outbreak of war are not made clear except for the long-standing rivalry between the two states, which Athens probably considered sufficient cause for war. In addition, Aegina as an island and naval power was suitable in both respects as a candidate for (forced) entry into the Delian League. At this time, the Corinthians and their allies invaded Megara, capturing the heights of Geraneia and moving into the plain (the Megarid): they reasoned that as the Athenians had two large military forces occupied in Egypt and on Aegina they would not be able to assist Megara. They underestimated the Athenians to their peril: these raised an army from among the older and younger men, marched to Megara under the command of the strategos Myronides and engaged the Corinthians in an inconclusive battle, but one in which the Athenians fared rather better than their opponents. Faced with the taunts of the old men at Corinth, the Corinthians marched back and were soundly defeated. Meanwhile a large number of the troops retreating from the battle became trapped in a field surrounded by a deep ditch and were stoned to death by the Athenians. About this time the Athenians began constructing their two Long Walls, to the Piraeus and Phaleron (Thuc. 1.107.4: doc. 12.20; Diod. 11.78.3–5: doc. 12.19). When Athens defeated the Boeotians at Oionophyta (see below, p. 428), and there was clearly no chance of assistance from

Sparta, the Aeginetans surrendered to the Athenians, destroyed their walls, handed their navy over to Athens, and became a tributary member of the Delian League, and according to the tribute quota lists contributed 30 talents annually (Thuc. 1.108.4: doc. 12.20).

Tanagra 458/7 BC

In 458/7 BC the Spartans went to the rescue of Doris, the mother-city of the Spartans, after one of its towns was captured by Phokis. The Spartans, with 1500 of their own hoplites and 10,000 of their allies, forced the Phokaians to make peace. They then had to deliberate about how to return home, as the Athenians now controlled the Megarid. Accordingly they decided to stay in Boeotia waiting on developments in Athens, as they had been contacted by some Athenians who wanted to overthrow the democracy and prevent the building of the Long Walls. Athens and its allies, including 1000 hoplites from Argos, marched out with a total force of 14,000 to meet the Spartans, suspecting a plot to overthrow the democracy. At Tanagra in Boeotia the Spartans were victorious, but both sides sustained heavy losses and the Spartans returned to the Peloponnese via Geraneia and the Isthmus. Kimon is said to have put in an appearance at the battle, wishing to fight with his tribe Oineis (VI), but the boule forbade this, mindful of the rumour of the plan to overthrow the democracy. That he was then officially recalled from ostracism (with Perikles, who fought at Tanagra, proposing the decree himself) is unlikely as he is next seen in Athenian military service against Cyprus in 451, when his period of ostracism would have been officially over. A golden shield was dedicated at Olympia by the Spartans and their allies in thanks for this victory, which they clearly considered a significant one (Meiggs and Lewis 36: doc. 6.60).

Oionophyta 458/7 BC

On the sixty-second day after the battle at Tanagra, the Athenians returned to Boeotia under the command of Myronides, who had shown his military talents in Megara. They defeated the Boeotians at Oionophyta, so gaining territorial control of all Boeotia and Phokis while the walls of Tanagra were torn down as a reaction against the Spartan victory there. Capture of Boeotia led to a ten-year Athenian domination of the region (referred to as the 'land empire'). It is uncertain whether the Boeotians paid tribute as the names of any of their cities cannot with certainty be identified in the tribute lists, but like other allies, they provided military contingents, until the Athenians lost control of the area in 447 BC.

Five-year truce between Athens and Sparta 451 BC

With Boeotia defeated, Sparta quiet, and Aegina's navy now their own, the Athenians in 456/5 BC under the command of Tolmides sailed around the Peloponnese, burnt the Spartan dockyards (at Gytheon), captured Chalkis, a Corinthian city on the northern side of the Corinthian Gulf, and landed at Sikyon, defeating the Sikyonians in battle (Thuc. 1.108.5: doc. 12.20). In 454 BC, the treasury of the Delian League was moved from Delos to Athens in the aftermath of the Persian defeat of the Athenian and allied force in Egypt, to ensure its security. In 451 BC, a five-year truce was made between Athens and the Peloponnese, which was somewhat ineffective. Not long after the truce was made, the Spartans, in what is known as the 'Second Sacred War', gained control of Delphi and its oracular sanctuary in 449 BC and made it independent of Phokis, which had been in control of the oracle. In response, the Athenians, allied to Phokis, marched there after the Spartans left and gave Delphi back to the Phokaians. There was no direct military conflict between Sparta and Athens, but this action can hardly have pleased the Spartans (Thuc. 1.112.5: doc. 12.21). Kimon is said to have arranged the five-year truce on his return from ostracism in 451 BC, and then immediately left in command of a naval expedition against Cyprus, where he died. Following this, the Athenians fought and won a land and sea battle off Salamis in Cyprus against an army of Phoenicians, Cypriotes and Cilicians (Thuc. 1.112; Diod. 12.3–4; Plut. *Kimon* 18–19). The major defeat in Egypt of a few years ago had obviously not affected the Athenians' naval capacity or capability.

The Peace of Kallias of 449/8 BC

Athens and its allies apparently made a peace treaty in 449/8 BC with Persia, which was named after the Athenian ambassador who negotiated it, the Peace of Kallias. But about this there is some dispute. There is no fifth-century evidence for such a peace treaty, although Herodotos does mention that Kallias son of Hipponikos was in Susa on an embassy during the reign of the Persian king Artaxerxes (7.151). Thucydides, who mentions various peace treaties between Athens and Sparta and records the treaties between Persia and the Spartans verbatim, nevertheless makes no mention of a peace made between Athens and Persia. If there were a Peace of Kallias, Thucydides' silence is interesting, but not decisive. An absence of reported hostilities between Persia and Athens after Kimon's campaign with 200 ships against Cyprus in 451 BC supports but does not convincingly prove the statements that a peace was concluded there between the two states at this time. After 451, the Athenians conducted no further military activities against Persian possessions and their preoccupation in subsequent decades with affairs in Greece and the commitment to domestic building programmes suggests that a formal peace was signed, perhaps in recognition of Persian power in the aftermath of the Athenian defeat in Egypt. Also in favour of the Peace of Kallias is the treaty of 424/3 BC agreed with Artaxerxes' successor, Darius II, who came to the throne in that year. As treaties with Persia were made specifically with the king himself, they were renegotiated on the accession of a new king, and this treaty could, therefore, have been a renewal of the earlier one, that of Kallias. Certainly, the current scholarly consensus is firmly in favour of the existence of this peace.

Isocrates in his speech *Panegyricus* of 380 BC is the first ancient source to refer specifically to the Peace of Kallias, and he draws a contrast between the situation in 480 BC, when the Persians invaded Greece with 1200 warships, and the terms of this peace which allowed no Persian warships past Phaselis, on the southern coast of Lycia (Isoc. 4 *Panegyricus* 117–18: doc. 12.16). As part of its conditions, the Persians were to keep the distance of one day's journey by horse from the coast, were not to sail past the Kyaneai (Blue Rocks) at the entrance of the Black Sea, thus guaranteeing the safety of the Greek cities along the shore of the Black Sea, and not to sail past the Chelidoniai, the islands between Lycia and Pamphylia, so keeping their navy out of the waters along the Aegean coastline. Plutarch reports that Kallisthenes, Alexander the Great's historian, specifically stated that no such peace existed, and that the Persians kept away from the Greek cities of Asia Minor and the Black Sea simply because they feared further defeats at the hands of the Athenians and their allies. Kallisthenes may have been motivated to write this because he wanted to deny that there was any formal peace treaty between Athens and Persia as this might undermine the legitimacy of Alexander's invasion of Persia. Plutarch is also able to quote the evidence of Krateros (perhaps in the first half of the third century BC), who collected fifth-century decrees and commented in detail on them in his work *Decrees* (Plut. *Kimon* 13.4–5: doc. 12.17).

A crisis in tribute payment?

The Peace of Kallias is thought by modern historians to have caused a crisis in the empire in the 440s BC. This is reflected in the tribute-quota lists, which record the proportion of the tribute dedicated to Athena (see below, p. 439). There was one year in which tribute was not paid, perhaps because the reason for it, war against the Persians, no longer existed, and 449/8 BC is usually viewed as the missing year. The year 447/6, the second possibility, may indicate that there was widespread disaffection among the allies following the defeat of the Athenians at Koroneia in Boeotia. It has also been suggested that the quota of the tribute for 449/8 was not recorded because the entire tribute was allocated to a specific project. However, it seems implausible that the Athenians would have deprived Athena of its quota, whatever the way in which the money was expended. It can perhaps be assumed that in 449/8 the allies refused to pay tribute because peace with Persia had been made. Collection of tribute certainly took place after the 'missing year', and the tribute-quota list for the following year, 448/7, indicates many partial payments, perhaps indicating difficulty in collecting the tribute. Whatever the circumstances, tribute remained crucial to the Athenians, and although campaigns were no longer conducted against the Persians, the tribute from their allies was still collected.

End of the land empire in Boeotia 446 BC

Athens was soon in trouble in Boeotia where exiles and their allies were successful in regaining control of some Boeotian cities. The Athenians were obliged to send a force under Tolmides that captured, enslaved and garrisoned Chaeroneia and which was then, on its return to Attica, attacked by the Boeotians at Koroneia in 446. Here the Boeotians were victorious, killing some of the Athenian hoplites, and capturing others, and the Athenians made a treaty with the Boeotians as the price for the prisoners' return. As part of this treaty they evacuated all of Boeotia. The ten-year old land empire was at an end and Athens was once again the controller of a largely Ionian and island-based empire with few 'footholds' in mainland Greece (Thuc. 1.114.1–115.1: doc. 12.22; also Thuc. 1.113).

The revolts of Euboea and Megara in 446 BC

Boeotia's revolt seemed to act as a signal for other rebellions against the Athenians, and Euboea revolted, although Thucydides gives no indication why (but Euboean exiles were among those supporting the Boeotians at Koroneia). His general statements about some allies' unwillingness to meet Athenian financial and military requirements may provide a clue to account for the dissatisfaction (Thuc. 1.98.4–99.2: doc. 12.4). It has also been suggested that the establishment of a cleruchy on Euboea c. 450 helped provoke the revolt: a cleruchy was a colony settled on land taken from a conquered city-state. Perikles in his role as strategos had already crossed over to the island when news was brought that the Megarians had revolted and called in the Corinthians, Sikyonians and Epidaurians as allies. Perikles then brought the Athenian army back from Euboea to deal with this situation, but king Pleistoanax of Sparta (459–409 BC) invaded Attica through the territory of Megara, which was now no longer hostile to the Spartans, advancing as far as Eleusis and Thria (Thuc. 1.114.1–2: doc. 12.22). A memorial was set up at Athens to honour Pythion of Megara who led three military tribal contingents of the Athenians safely back through Boeotia to Athens (*IG* I³ 1353: doc. 12.23). The reasons behind Megara's revolt are not explained, but this city and Athens had long been enemies, and as a Dorian city it belonged more naturally in the Peloponnesian 'camp'. Athens had now lost the strategic advantage of controlling the Peloponnesian invasion route to Attica, and Spartan invasions into Attica could now reach its borders unchecked. Pleistoanax was sent into exile when he returned to Sparta for not pressing home his attack, and was accused of being bribed, perhaps by Perikles. Clearly there was now a group at Sparta willing to confront Athens openly and on its own soil. Later an oracle from Delphi caused the Spartans to restore Pleistoanax as king, but his enemies accused him of having bribed the Pythia (Thuc. 2.21, 5.16).

Megara was lost, but Perikles and the Athenians were not going to let go of Euboea. When the Spartans retreated, Perikles led the army back to the island, subdued it and signed treaties with all of its cities, except for that of the Hestiaians, who had captured an Athenian trireme and massacred its crew. As punishment they were expelled from their land and Athenians were settled on it. The terms of these treaties can probably be judged by that of one of the

Figure 12.4 The 'Mourning Athena'. The goddess sadly contemplates a casualty list of the dead soldiers from Athens' various conflicts. The original relief is of marble, dating to around 470 BC; 48 cm high, now in the Acropolis Museum, Athens. This is a nineteenth-century copy in the Blanton Museum of Art, the University of Texas at Austin, the Willian J. Battle Collection of Plaster Casts (2004.15). Photo © Steven Bach.

Euboean cities, Chalkis, in which Athens imposed strict but not burdensome conditions: this decree, however, may not date to 446 but to 424 BC. In this treaty the people of Chalkis swore not to revolt from Athens and to pay tribute, while the city retained control of its legal system, apart from the fact that no one could be sent into exile (in this way supporters of Athens would be protected), and in its turn Athens swore not to expel the Chalkidians from Chalkis, not to destroy the city or confiscate property, and not to exile anyone or vote on any proposals about Chalkis without giving 'due notice' (*IG* I³ 40: doc. 13.19).

Thirty years' peace with Sparta

In 446/5 BC, the Athenians made a Thirty Years' Peace with Sparta and its allies, giving back Nisaia and Pegai (Megara's two harbours), Troizen and Achaea, which they had taken from the Peloponnesians (Thuc. 1.114.3–115.1: doc. 12.22); in 425 Athens demanded that these four places, surrendered by the terms of the truce, be returned. Athens had now relinquished its control of Boeotia and of any possessions in the Peloponnese.

Perikles 'the Olympian'

Perikles (who lived from c. 495 to 429 BC) was the son of Xanthippos and Agariste, the niece of the reformer Kleisthenes. His nickname 'Olympian' was probably earned because of his extraordinary role in Athenian affairs and as a result of his having been the main political figure during the period that saw both the flowering of Athenian art, architecture, culture, and the growth of the Athenian empire. His oratory, encouragement of the Athenian building programme, and prowess as both a statesman and general, all contributed to this eulogistic description. He was the choregos for Aeschylus' play *Persians* when it was produced in 472 BC, and as such paid for all the costs associated with the performance. It was a significant choice of play in view of his later political career. His first political role was in the prosecution of Kimon in 463/2 BC for not taking advantage of his victories in Thrace to invade Macedonia. More importantly he supported Ephialtes in his reforms of the Areiopagos in 462/1 BC. Perikles became increasingly prominent after the assassination of Ephialtes, and emerged as the main democratic leader, with his policies oriented towards the demos rather than towards a conservative 'agenda'.

Kimon's ostracism from Athens in 461–451 BC and his death soon after left the conservatives without a leader until Thucydides son of Melesias took up this role. Perikles' institution of jury pay and his citizenship law of 451/0 were his two known political reforms ([Arist.] *Ath. Pol.* 26.4: doc. 1.36; 27.3–4: doc. 12.26). He was apparently strategos for a campaign in the Gulf of Corinth in 454 BC, but came to particular military prominence as strategos for the command against Euboea in 446/5 BC, after which he held the strategia continuously until his death in 429 BC. This position cemented his influence in Athenian affairs, particularly after the ostracism of his main rival Thucydides son of Melesias in 443 BC. His achievements show him to have been both a brilliant military leader and civic organiser. He was born with a disproportionate head, and as a result nearly all his portraits showed him wearing a helmet. This was a constant target for jokes from the comic poets who called him 'squill-head'.

The Congress Decree

In the early 440s BC, according to Plutarch (*Perikles* 17), Perikles proposed what modern historians call the 'Congress Decree', which involved organising a panhellenic congress at

Athens to discuss the rebuilding of the temples destroyed by the Persians, the sacrifices vowed when the Persians invaded, and the keeping of the peace generally. All Greeks states were invited, and the ambassadors were dispatched, but the Spartans opposed the congress, possibly because it implied Athenian leadership of the Greeks, and it came to nothing. It is possible that with the Peace of Kallias (although the date of Perikles' Congress Decree is uncertain), Perikles sought a new rationale for the Delian League, or it was possible that Perikles sought to revive the Hellenic League, which was created to oppose the Persians in 480–479 BC. Whether he was really interested in Greek unity is doubtful, given his involvement in various military actions against other Greek states and his bellicosity in 432 BC when war with the Peloponnesians was imminent.

The revolt of Samos 440 BC

Samos and Miletos went to war in 440 BC over the possession of the city-state of Priene, to the north of Miletos, and when the Milesians found themselves defeated by the Samians, they went to Athens to complain. There they were joined by some Samians (described by Thucydides as 'private individuals'), who wanted to establish a democracy on Samos, which at the time had an aristocratic government. When Samos refused to discontinue its attacks on Miletos, the Athenians, led by Perikles with forty triremes, overthrew the government and set up a democracy. They also took fifty men and children as hostages and sent them to the island of Lemnos before returning to Athens leaving a garrison behind on Samos: Miltiades the Younger had captured Lemnos, which became an Athenian cleruchy. The Athenians were clearly motivated to support the Samian democrats who wanted a change in government, not simply on the ideological grounds that a Samian democracy would be more amenable to Athens' interests, but also because the 'private individuals' were presumably of sufficient prominence to be potentially powerful friends in the new political arrangement. Certainly Plutarch's statement that Perikles' actions against Samos were inspired by Aspasia, who was a Milesian (Plut. *Life of Perikles* 24.2–9: doc. 4.29), can be safely rejected: he was primarily prompted by imperial considerations (Thuc. 1.115–117: doc. 12.24; Thucydides does not mention Aspasia anywhere in his narrative).

The Samian oligarchs in exile, however, requested Persian assistance and were returned to power with the help of Pissouthnes, the Persian satrap (governor) of Sardis and some 700 mercenaries they had collected. They crossed over to Samos at night, seized most of the democratic leaders, and handed the Athenian officials and garrison over to Pissouthnes; they also recovered the hostages from Lemnos. So while there *may* have been a Peace of Kallias with a cessation of formal hostilities, Persian interference continued and the Persian satraps at Sardis played an important role in Greek affairs, with both the Athenians and the Spartans courting their assistance. The returned exiles made immediate preparations to attack Miletos, as they obviously considered that this matter was not closed and probably saw this conflict as a way of asserting their independence against Athenian interference. At about the same time, Byzantium revolted from the Delian League, despite the fact that it was one of the first members and that Pausanias' arrogant and treacherous behaviour there had been one of the main reasons for the league's creation.

Perikles and the other strategoi for the year sailed with sixty ships to deal with the various emergencies in the Aegean and defeated the Samian fleet off the island of Tragia. Further Athenian ships arrived and Samos was blockaded by land and sea. Perikles left with sixty of the Athenian ships to ensure that the Phoenician fleet would not interfere, as one of the Samians, Stesagoras, had left with five ships to enlist the support of the Phoenician fleet which was in Persian employ. The Samians took advantage of the absence of Perikles and his ships to launch a surprise attack in which they defeated the Athenian fleet and gained control of the sea for two weeks. Perikles then returned, resuming the blockade of the Samians with the help of more ships sent out from Athens, under the command of Thucydides (the historian), Hagnon and Phormio. Ships also were sent by Chios and Lesbos, members of the Delian League, to assist the Athenians.

End of the revolt of Samos and Athenian expenses

The Samians endured a nine-month blockade and siege of their city but finally had no option but to come to terms. They tore down their walls, provided hostages, and agreed to pay back in instalments the money that the Athenians had spent on suppressing their revolt. Thucydides notes that the Byzantines now also returned to the Delian League. The Athenian expenses for the Samian campaign had been paid out of the fund of the Treasurers of Athena, providing the first example of the borrowing of temple funds for the prosecution of a war. The cost was the enormous sum of some 1200 or 1400 talents, and the Potidaea campaign cost the Athenians 2000 talents: warfare was not a cheap business. Scholars have debated how long it took the Samians to pay off the indemnity and suggestions range from before 431, to 414/3, but it must have taken the Samians well over a decade or two to pay off this amount and the latter time-frame, a period of some twenty-six years, is far more realistic. Samos had been one of the chief members of the Delian League, with a large navy of its own, and its revolt encouraged Byzantium to revolt in turn. Clearly the Athenians needed to act against it in order to keep the league together whatever the cost. The assistance of allies, such as Chios and Lesbos, also played an important part in the Athenians' eventual success (Thuc. 1.115.2–117.3: doc. 12.24; Plut. *Perikles* 24–8).

Perikles sends out colonies and cleruchies

Groups of Athenian citizens were sent out to occupy land taken from allies who had revolted and as a result numerous settlements were sent out in the fifth century, to Naxos, Andros, the Chersonese, Chalkis, Mytilene, Thrace, Potidaea, Sinope, Amisos, Skyros, Eion, Aegina, Melos, Brea, Thourioi, Amphipolis and perhaps Karystos. Hestiaia is a well-known case of a cleruchy: when Euboea revolted the people of Hestiaia were expelled from their territory and Athenians took their land (Thuc. 1.114.3: doc. 12.22). Plutarch gives the figures of 1000 Athenian settlers sent to the Chersonese, and 500 to Naxos, 250 to Andros, 1000 to Thrace 'to live alongside the Bisaltai', and some to Thourioi in Italy, stating that this colonisation policy was the work of Perikles. The cleruchy among the Bisaltai is often identified with Brea (see *IG* I³ 46: doc. 12.31), and the foundation of the colony of Thourioi in southern Italy took place in 444/3 BC (a refoundation on the site of Sybaris). It was a panhellenic colony, with Athenian settlers and an Athenian founder Lampon the chresmologos (diviner), but a greater number of other Greek colonists, including Herodotos the historian. These settlements, however, were made by decree of the people, and Plutarch is guilty of ascribing everything that happened in Athens from the 450s to the 430s to Perikles as if he were the only influential figure of the time (Plut. *Perikles* 11.4–6: doc. 12.25). It was, however, Perikles who personally led the military expedition to the Black Sea that brought about the establishment of the colonies at Sinope and Amisos, and Lemnos and Imbros were other cleruchies established with Athenian settlers. The Athenians who were sent out to cleruchies retained their Athenian citizenship, and could

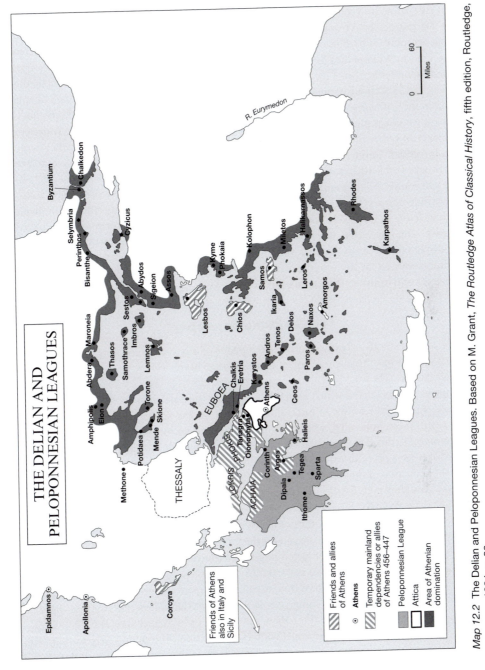

THE DELIAN AND
PELOPONNESIAN LEAGUES

R. Eurymedon

Byzantium
Chalkedon
Selymbria
Perinthos
Bisanthe
Cyzicus
Abydos
Sestos
Sigeion
Assos
Imbros
Maroneia
Abdera
Thasos
Samothrace
Lemnos
Torone
Skione
Mende
Potidaea
Eion
Amphipolis
Methone

Lesbos

Kyme
Phokaia
Kolophon
Samos
Miletos
Halikarnassos
Rhodes
Karpathos
Leros
Amorgos

Chios
Ikaria
Naxos
Paros
Delos
Tenos
Andros
Karystos
Ceos
Chalkis
Eretria
EUBOEA
THESSALY

Athens
Tanagra
Oinophyta
Megara
LOKRIS
PHOKIS
Plataea
Corinth
Argos
Halieis
Dipaia
Tegea
Sparta
Ithome
ACHAIA

Corcyra

Epidamnos
Apollonia

Miles
0   60

Friends and allies
of Athens

Athens

Temporary mainland
dependencies or allies
of Athens 456–447

Peloponnesian League

Attica

Area of Athenian
domination

Friends of Athens
also in Italy and
Sicily

Map 12.2 The Delian and Peloponnesian Leagues. Based on M. Grant, *The Routledge Atlas of Classical History*, fifth edition, Routledge, 1994, p. 28.

act as garrisons for the Athens in those allied states. Most of these settlers probably improved their economic situation, and if they were thetes settled on prosperous land they could become hoplites. Unlike colonies which were self-governing, members of cleruchies still retained their Athenian citizenship and the cleruchies were dependencies of Athens.

When Strepsiades in Aristophanes' play the *Clouds* (line 203) is told by one of Socrates' pupils that geometry is used to measure land, he automatically assumes that it will be used to divide up land into cleruchies for Athenian citizens. The establishment of cleruchies seems to have led to the reduction of the tribute assessed from the region involved: for example, the Chersonese in 453 BC paid 18 talents but less than 3 talents in 446, and Andros paid 12 talents in 450 but in the following year only 6; Skyros, settled by Athenians, never paid tribute. Such cleruchies were not popular with Athens' allies, and by the terms of the Second Athenian Confederacy in 377, which was a fourth-century revival of the Delian League, they were expressly forbidden, and no Athenian from then on was allowed to possess a house or land in allied territory (Tod 2.123: doc. 14.15). While Plutarch gives various motives for the cleruch-ies these can mostly be discounted, along with many of his interpretative comments about sixth- and fifth-century BC Greek affairs. Perikles did not aim to 'gratify' the people with festivals and feasts as if he were some earlier version of a Roman emperor providing 'bread and circuses', and the settlers were not drawn from some 'idle mob': there was no such thing in Athens in the fifth century. Rather, with its large population, there was a sufficient surplus of inhabitants who, as throughout the period of Greek colonisation, sought to gain more land for themselves and improve their condition in life (see pp. 63–4).

Perikles institutes jury pay

Ephilates' reforms in 461 BC stripped the Areiopagos of any remnants of its political power and much of its legal jurisdiction (apart from hearing homicide and religious cases), and as a result Athens was a radical democracy (*Ath. Pol.* 25.1–4: doc. 12.12). Further demo-cratic reforms then occurred which aimed at increasing the participatory nature of Athenian democracy. Ephialtes' transfer of judicial functions from the Areiopagos to the jury-courts gave the courts more political power and importance. Perikles introduced jury pay, by bring-ing the proposal to the ekklesia which voted in support. The date of this reform is not known, but it probably took place shortly after 461 as the lawcourts had more judicial work to do as a result of the reduction of the Areiopagos' jurisdiction. Initially two obols per day, the amount of jury pay was later increased to three, perhaps in 425 or 424: three obols was about half the average daily wage for hired workers (see docs 1.24, 1.26–8). Solon's reforms to Athens' judicial system laid the foundation for popular participation and Perikles' reform meant that the citizens were now paid for their service on the jury-courts, compensating them for the loss of a day's income (legal cases never lasted more than one day).

That all citizens have the right to serve on juries and be paid for doing so to compensate them for their loss of wages remains a fundamental feature of western-style democracy. The *Athenaion Politeia*'s comment that 'some people allege that the courts deteriorated' because ordinary people acted as jurors rather than the 'better off' ([Arist.] *Ath. Pol.* 27.3–4: doc. 12.26) reflects the prejudices of the conservatives of that time: it was precisely so that ordi-nary citizens could participate fully in the judicial process that pay was introduced. In his comic play the *Wasps*, Aristophanes parodies the juries as being dominated by cranky old men, hell-bent on supporting the prosecution and imposing the harshest penalties (Ar. *Wasps* 836–62, 894–7: doc. 1.26). This criticism can be easily dismissed, and, while no doubt there was a substantial representation of older Athenians serving on the juries to draw the stipend, other Athenian sources do not support the notion that it was simply the elderly who served as jurors. Evidence in fact points in the opposite direction: the juries represented a cross-section of the Athenian male citizen population, which was Perikles' intention in proposing jury pay. Perikles' citizenship law of 451 BC was designed to ensure that citizen rights would only be granted to those whose parents were both Athenian citizens, and the penalties for marrying a non-citizen or attempting to pass off a non-citizen as an Athenian became increasingly severe. There may have been a problem for Athenian fathers in finding suitable husbands for their daughters, but, more significantly, now that important financial privileges were extended to the whole citizen body, it was essential to ensure that these duties and privileges were only enjoyed by members of the citizenry (Ath. Pol. 26.4: doc. 1.36).

Perikles and Kimon

Kimon lost influence after the helot revolt and the Athenian dismissal from Mount Ithome, and had spent from 461 to 451 in exile after being ostracised. Shortly after his return to Athens he was sent on campaign to Cyprus where he died soon afterwards. The *Athenaion Politeia* comments that Perikles' introduction of jury pay was a deliberate attempt to counteract Kimon's generosity since Kimon, who was as rich 'as a tyrant', performed his liturgies munificently and was extraordinarily generous to his demesmen. This, however, can be discounted as Perikles would have been motivated by ideological grounds in wishing to strengthen the democratic element of the constitution. Moreover, even if Kimon did support his fellow demesmen financially, this would only have had an impact on one deme out of 140, and the anecdote that he permitted any Athenians to help themselves to the produce of his land is hardly convincing evidence that he was able to assist any great proportion of the 30,000 or so citizens at the time. Perhaps Kimon's reputation for generosity, which enhanced his political reputation, inspired Perikles to find some way of his own through which the demos would be financially beholden to him (*Ath. Pol.* 27.3–4: doc. 12.26). The careers of these two statesmen do not really overlap, and if the introduction of jury pay took place shortly after Ephialtes' reforms, it would actually have occurred while Kimon was in exile and so could not have been brought in to counteract Kimon's benefactions to the demos. Kimon's death in about 450 BC made Perikles the dominant political figure in Athens, until he was challenged by Thucydides, son of Melesias.

Perikles and Thucydides, son of Melesias

The actual date when this rivalry between Perikles and Thucydides commenced cannot be ascertained, but Thucydides was according to Plutarch (*Perikles* 11, 12, 14) a relative of Kimon's and formed an aristocratic faction against Perikles. Thucydides seems to have gathered around him a large number of aristocrats who perhaps opposed the current antagonism in Athens towards Sparta, and were opposed to the overtly democratic nature of Athenian politics. Thucydides does not seem to have held any military commands, and was the champion (prostates) of the aristocrats. His main point of attack against Perikles seems to have been the misuse of allied funds for the adornment of Athens, in particular the expenditure outlaid on the Parthenon, but these accusations were doubtless greatly exaggerated as political invective. Perikles had taken a leading role in organising the rebuilding of the temples on the Athenian acropolis, which had been deliberately left in its sacked and looted condition to remind the Athenians of the menace of Persia.

Perikles was accused by his critics of 'squandering money and wasting revenues', but his response according to Plutarch was to offer to have all the expenses put down to his name, and to take the credit as well (Plut. *Perikles* 11.1–2, 14.1–3: doc. 12.27). This is nonsense even for Plutarch, as Perikles could hardly afford to pay for the costs of the construction of the Parthenon (see the expense accounts at docs 1.12–13). He and his sons did offer to pay for some improvements to Athens' water supply – modest in comparison with the cost of the Parthenon – but that was a much smaller project. Even then the demos commended them but did not take up the offer and covered the costs from the tribute instead (*IG* I³ 49: doc. 1.14). There is also the question of whether the tribute from the allies in fact paid for the temples on the acropolis. The total amount involved was immense, but it could be argued that the cost, spread over two decades in the 440s and 430s, could have been met from Athenian internal revenues without touching the tribute. Perikles must, however, have felt threatened by Thucydides, who was organising aristocratic opposition against him. An ostracism was held in 443 BC, at which Thucydides, as the loser, was sent into exile, never to be heard of again (doc. 10.14.xi). After this, Perikles was the pre-eminent figure in Athenian politics, and was elected as strategos for each subsequent year (for the strategia at Athens, see p. 358).

Opposition to Perikles after 443 BC

Despite the ostracism of his political opponent Thucydides son of Melesias, Perikles still faced opposition. When Pheidias, a friend of Perikles and the greatest sculptor of the ancient world, was prosecuted in around 438 BC for embezzling gold and ivory intended for the chryselephantine statue of Athena (see *IG* I³ 458a: doc. 1.12), Perikles was implicated. Pheidias was acquitted of embezzlement, but actually prosecuted for impiety (asebeia) for including the likeness of Perikles and himself in the Amazonomachia (battle of the Amazons) on Athena's shield in the Parthenon (Plut. *Perikles* 31). He was imprisoned and although, until recently, it was thought that Pheidias died in prison soon after this incident it is now thought that he was exiled to Elis, where he worked on the Olympian Zeus. A 'workroom' thought to have belonged to Pheidias, has been found in Olympia. It contains a number of terracotta moulds believed to have been used for the drapery of the Olympian Zeus. Diopeithes passed a decree against those who did not believe in the gods, and Anaxagoras of Klazomenai, a natural philosopher and another of Perikles' friends, was on this occasion the target. This charge can be interpreted as an indirect attack on Perikles, who perhaps arranged for Anaxagoras to leave the city, or he was prosecuted and fined (Anaxag. *F* 12: doc. 3.76). Perikles himself was deposed from the strategia in 430 as the war with Sparta, which he did so much to encourage, was not going well; he seems to have been fined as well, but was re-elected.

Perikles and Aspasia

After amicably divorcing his wife, Perikles lived with Aspasia, a hetaira from Miletos, probably from about 445 BC. He had two sons by his Athenian wife (Xanthippos and Paralos), and one son by Aspasia (also called Perikles). His two sons are chiefly known for their involvement in their father's waterworks project (doc. 1.14), but both died in the plague that broke out in Athens in 429 BC. As Perikles junior was born of a non-Athenian mother he could not be a citizen under the terms of the citizenship law of 451 BC that Perikles had himself proposed to the assembly. But Perikles requested in 429 that his illegitimate son be made a citizen and this was ratified; this son was one of the strategoi at the battle of Arginousai in 406 BC in which the Athenians were victorious but many of the sailors drowned. As a result the assembly, in a highly unconstitutional move, condemned the strategoi (including Perikles junior) to death en bloc (Xen. *Hellenika* 1.7.9–15: doc. 1.20). Socrates, a member of the boule at the time, was the only councillor to object.

Aspasia and Perikles' relationship was quite an open one (Plutarch relates that he kissed her every day on leaving for the agora: Plut. *Perikles* 24.9: doc. 4.19), and she was highly intelligent and mixed with his male friends. That Aspasia was prosecuted, at about the same time as Pheidias, for impiety, and for procuring free women for Perikles, is doubted by scholars as a misinterpretation of jokes in Aristophanes, and should be seen in the context of these other attacks. There was, however, certainly nothing in any way inappropriate in her training hetairai, although Aristophanes makes much of this, as this was a perfectly acceptable occupation for metics (see docs 4.29, 4.95). The idea that Perikles went to war against Samos in 440 because Aspasia incited him to do so because she was from Miletos, Samos' enemy, can be safely discounted, as can the hilarious anecdote in Aristophanes that the Peloponnesian War started because some Megarians stole three prostitutes owned by Aspasia. It is however quite possible that she was unpopular in Athens following the Samian War, and that Perikles' opponents attacked her as well as Perikles' friends to discredit him as a politician.

The tribute

Aristeides had assessed the tribute that the allies paid to Athens to cover the cost of the war against Persia. This money was at first kept on the island of Delos and used for war expenses (including forcing rebellious allies back into the alliance), but from 454/3 BC the treasury of the league was at Athens. The major defeat suffered at the hands of the Persians in Egypt may have led to the treasury being moved, for fear of the Persians renewing their presence in the Aegean. This is known because it was in this year that the Athenians erected the first of a series of inscribed marble slabs which relate to the amounts of tribute paid, with the first list referring to the quotas as 'the first to be audited' (*IG* I³ 259: doc. 12.28). The term 'tribute lists' is in fact a misnomer as the lists do not in fact record how much tribute was paid, and they should be more correctly referred to as 'tribute-quota lists' because they record the portion (quota) of the tribute (actually the phoros or 'contribution') which was paid to the goddess Athena, who received one-sixtieth of each allied state's contribution (Fig. 13.2). Whether the allies had a say in this is unclear but they were probably not consulted. Modern scholars can multiply each of the recorded amounts of Athena's quota by 60 to arrive at the total that a particular state paid in any one year.

The first tribute-quota list, 454/3 BC

Naturally not all these stelai survive intact, and a few years are missing. The lists of the first fifteen years from 454/3 were recorded on a single massive stele (3.663m × 1.109m × 0.385m) and there are also fragments of a second smaller stele for the lists of 438/7–432/1 BC. The preamble to the first year and the names of contributing states indicates the character of all the lists (*IG* I³ 259: doc. 12.28). After 454 BC, the tribute was reassessed every four years and changes in the tribute generally occur in years in which the Great Panathenaia was celebrated (450, 446, 434 BC; but see *IG* I³ 71: doc. 13.16); payments were made by the allies at the festival of the Dionysia (see *IG* I³ 34: doc. 13.17). From 443/2 BC, cities were grouped according to region: Ionia, the Hellespont, Thrace, Caria and the Islanders; the Ionians and Carians were placed together from 438/7 BC. Cities paying the phoros were listed by their ethnicity rather than by the name of their cities (for example, the 'Byzantines' rather than 'Byzantium'). During the Peloponnesian War, the payment of the phoros was tightened up by the Athenians to ensure that there were sufficient funds for the war's prosecution.

Athenian decrees concerning Athens' allies

Athens regulated its affairs with the allies through decrees promulgated by the Athenian assembly. Some of these were specifically directed at individual allies after they revolted, while others, such as those concerning tribute payments and the imposition of uniform currency, weights and measures, were decrees covering the allies as a whole. The dating of many decrees is subject to debate, but the dates adopted here are accepted by an increasing number of scholars. The fact that all of the decrees were passed by the Athenian assembly demonstrates the degree to which the alliance had grown into an empire: it was Athens that passed the resolutions which organised the political arrangements in cities which rebelled, and Athens alone that controlled every aspect of the tribute payment.

Relations with Phaselis

An early decree, dating to between 469 and 450 BC, deals with Phaselis, an unwilling member of the league which, left to its own devices, would not have joined the alliance. A colony of Rhodes on the eastern coast of Lycia, it had a triple harbour and was prosperous as a consequence. Kimon was responsible for conducting a siege against it after the battle of Eurymedon but the Chians interposed on behalf of Phaselis. An Athenian named Leon successfully proposed a decree regulating legal matters between the two cities, and such judicial arrangements are dealt with in several similar decrees. Legal actions concerning the Phaselites which arose at Athens were heard before the polemarch, the archon with jurisdiction over foreigners at Athens. There is also a reference to other cases, which were to be tried according to the terms of an existing treaty. It appears that other judicial cases, which had no reference to Athens, were dealt with at Phaselis. Clearly some point of clarification was required and this decree was passed to deal with it. The decree is not punitive and in fact awards the Phaselites the same rights as the Chians, who were favoured members of the league. Having the case brought before the polemarch was a privilege in that the Phaselites did not then need to arrange for an Athenian to represent their interests as they would have had to do if it was done in an ordinary lawcourt. Additionally a trial before the polemarch possibly took place sooner than in the ordinary courts, and was less inconvenient to a Phaselite trader. This privilege indicates a process of transition and an evolution in the relationship between Athens and its at first unwilling ally: the Phaselites were forced into the league but their rights were regulated by a treaty, and this decree now accorded them legal privileges at Athens and established a positive relationship between the two states (*IG* I^3 10: doc. 12.29).

Regulations for Erythrai

In about 453/2 BC, the Athenians passed a decree concerning Erythrai, an Ionian city on the Asia Minor coast. As the stele on which the decree was inscribed is now lost there are many uncertain readings. What is clear is that the decree sets down the obligation of Erythrai to bring grain, or victims for sacrifice (depending on the restoration of the inscription), to the Great Panathenaia at Athens. As such, it foreshadows the later participation in this festival that the Athenians came to expect from all its allies. The offering of a cow and panoply (a set of armour) at the Panathenaia, while not mentioned in this particular case, became a standard obligation for the allies (see *IG* I³ 46: doc. 12.31). This involvement in Athens' religious festivals, especially the Panathenaia, its greatest festival, was a way of asserting control over the allies but also an attempt to establish a common religious identity for all members of the league.

That no arrangements for an alliance are mentioned in this decree is usually taken to mean that Erythrai was a member of the league that revolted (possibly a pro-Persian group was responsible), for the decree refers to those who 'fled to the Persians'. As in the case of the revolt of Samos, Persia provided a sympathetic home for Greek rebels and a potential source of aid. Erythrai, in fact, may have revolted on the basis of a promise of Persian support. In 454/3 and 453/2 BC Boutheia (about 10 kilometres north of Erythrai), part of the Erythrai-ian peraia (district), is listed by itself with a quota of 300 drachmas and so paid a tribute of three talents, whereas later it paid 1000 drachmas as part of the Erythraian 'syntely', when Erythrai and the nearby towns in its peraia were listed as one tribute-paying entity (a syntely roughly means a 'syndicate' or group of towns assessed together for an amount of phoros). Usually it is assumed that Erythrai was in revolt, but that those loyal to Athens fled from Erythrai to Boutheia, and paid their dues from there to Athens.

When Erythrai was brought back into the Athenian fold, the Athenians took measures to ensure that a revolt did not occur again. The instigators of the revolt fled to the Persians and so the Athenians now imposed a democratic regime. A council of 120 members was established, with the Athenian supervisors (episkopoi) and the garrison commander (phrour-arch) hand-picking the first members. The membership of the council was annual, and after this first year Erythrai chose its own council members. In a measure similar to that which regulated the council at Athens, members could not serve another term until four years had passed, which ensured that membership of the council rotated among the citizens. The coun-cil swore an oath to make decisions for the benefit of the demos of Erythrai, Athens and its allies, and not to rebel against Athens or its allies, or to receive back those who had fled to the Persians, without the permission of the Athenian boule and demos. In addition, no one was to be banished without specific approval from the Athenian boule and demos. An Erythraian who killed another Erythraian was to be executed if found guilty, or if a sentence of exile was passed the convicted person was to be exiled from the Athenian alliance as a whole, which sounds as if some political crime was envisaged in this provision. These measures can be interpreted as being aimed against civil disturbance which might have led to revolt against Athens. That no one was to be banished without reference to Athens protected pro-Athe-nians and democrats, and anyone committing murder in an attempt to overthrow the new democracy was to be punished. The final fragmentary section of the inscription appears to make reference to tyrants, support of whom would incur a death penalty. Erythrai had possi-bly been ruled by a dynasty of tyrants and this regulation may have been specifically designed to forbid Erythrai from reinstalling them. Apart from the Athenian supervisors and garrison commander at Erythrai the fragmentary conclusion of the inscription refers to a garrison and archers: it appears that Athens was backing up its decree and the new democratic regime with military support. Such supervisors and garrisons were a common occurrence among the allies. It is also significant that the decree refers to 'Athens and its allies', and not yet to 'Ath-ens and the cities that it rules'. While a democratic government and religious prescriptions that the city must participate in the Panathenaia were imposed, the language of Athenian imperialism was not yet in use (*IG* I³ 14: doc. 12.30).

The foundation of the colony at Brea

Sometime between 445 and 430 BC, the Athenians established a colony in Thrace called Brea, and it is perhaps the colony settled among the local people, the Bisaltai, near Amphipolis which is mentioned by Plutarch (Plut. *Perikles* 11.4–6: doc. 12.25). Significantly in this settlement the colonists were chosen from the zeugitai and the thetes, obviously because they were the citizens who would gain the most benefit from taking up land in the colony (*IG* I³ 46: doc. 12.31). That the colony was in danger of being attacked is made clear by the provision in the decree that the local allies were to come to its assistance when it was threatened. The decree also laid down that the colonists were to bring a cow (for sacrifice) and panoply of armour to the Great Panathenaia, and a model phallus to the Dionysia festival. These religious requirements, like those imposed on the people of Erythrai, indicate how these Athenian festivals were developing as imperial occasions. They pointed to Athens' pre-eminence in the alliance as demonstrated by the presence of the allies with their contributions at these great festivals.

An Athenian alliance with Rhegium, 433/2 BC

In 433/2 BC the Athenians renewed a treaty which they had made some years earlier with Rhegium, in southern Italy, which overlooked the strait separating Italy from Sicily, and was thereby always of strategic importance (*IG* ³ 53: doc. 12.32). In the same year, the Athenians renewed their treaty with Leontinoi in Sicily. The Greek settlements in Sicily and southern Italy were by this time not only more prosperous but frequently far most sophisticated in lifestyle than many of the cities of the mainland and gave birth to and were the home of many philosophers, athletes and poets: Sicily in particular was seen as the home of an extravagant and luxurious lifestyle (Diod. Sic. 13.82.5–8: doc. 1.76). In 427 BC Gorgias from Leontinoi visited Athens and caused what can only be described as a sensation with his style of rhetoric. One of the ambassadors who travelled from Rhegium to renegotiate the treaty died and was buried in Athens (*IG* I³ 1178: doc. 12.33). These alliances with the west reflect Athenian interests in this area, and while it is the Athenian expedition to Sicily in 415 BC which is best known, they campaigned there in 427 and the following years, and their interest in the Greek coastal cities of Sicily and southern Sicily is understandable.

Conclusion

Athens and its allies were engaged in numerous conflicts after 479 BC: with the Peloponnesians, the Persians and their own allies. Athenian power continued to grow, and from its allies Athens collected enough phoros to fight these wars and maintain control over the Aegean and the coast of Asia Minor. For Athens, and its allies, it was a 'Golden Age' of architecture, literature and philosophy. The city grew and prospered, being able to send out thousands of colonists while still maintaining a large population. During this period open warfare with the Peloponnesians became increasingly confrontational, but Athens was determined not to exist in Sparta's shadow.

13

THE PELOPONNESIAN WAR AND ITS AFTERMATH

Introduction

In 431 BC the Peloponnesian War broke out, a conflict that lasted until 404 BC and ultimately saw Athens' defeat by Sparta and the loss of both its allies and most of its navy. It was not, however, these two states alone that were involved: both Athens and Sparta had their allies, the 'Delian' League and the Peloponnesian League. As a result of the conflict between these two 'super-powers' the Greek world was convulsed by warfare for some three decades. The result was certainly not a foregone conclusion, despite Sparta's military reputation as invincible on land and Athenian supremacy on the sea. There were various causes of conflict, but matters came to a head when in 432 BC the Corinthians sent a delegation to Sparta to complain that Athens had violated the terms of the truce of 446 BC (Thuc. 1.114.1–115.1: doc. 12.22). An Athenian embassy responded, reminding the Spartans of the Athenians' services against Persia and the forces they could currently mobilise. Sparta was neither convinced nor was its belligerent attitude softened: it sent an ultimatum to Athens warning the city that unless the various Peloponnesian grievances were addressed Sparta would go to war. Perikles persuaded the Athenians not to give in to Spartan pressure, rejecting the Spartan demand that the Athenians should 'allow the Greeks to be autonomous'. In response Sparta and its allies declared war on Athens and invaded Athenian territory in the summer of 431 BC (Thuc. 1.139.1–3: doc. 13.4). Whether Perikles' decision in convincing the Athenian assembly to go to war – and clearly many Athenians opposed this at the time – was the correct one can only be answered with the benefit of hindsight.

Sources

Thucydides is the main source for the events of the Peloponnesian War, and he commences in the pentekontaetia (see Chapter 12, p. 412) with an outline of the history of the period from the end of the Persian Wars until the capture of Samos in 440 BC (1.89–117). Prior to these chapters, at the very beginning of his work, he explains the reasons why he was impelled to write a history of the war. When it broke out in 431 BC, he states that he believed it would be the greatest of all wars ever fought by the Greeks to date: 'This disturbance was the greatest which ever affected the Greeks, as well as affecting a great part of the barbarian world, and thus, so to speak, most of mankind' (Thuc. 1.1.2: doc. 13.1). He provides an extremely detailed, chronological account and allows the scope, atrocities and vicissitudes of the war to be clearly understood from the perspective of both sides. His history is praiseworthy in historiographical terms and provides an extremely accurate and lucid narrative.

He primarily relates events as they happened, and certainly spares the reader the trite moralisms of Diodorus and Plutarch. Eyewitnesses, his own experiences, and decrees make up his sources. There is little overt editorial intervention, except in some cases: his adulation of Perikles and dislike of Kleon are clear, and the Sicilian Expedition is written up as a tragedy in which he perhaps overemphasises the scale of the disaster.

Unfortunately Thucydides' narrative breaks off in 411 BC, and it is at this chronological point that Xenophon began his *Hellenika* ('Greek Affairs'), which covers the rest of the history of the war down to 404 BC (Books 1–2), and then subsequent Greek events to 362 BC. The Aristotelean *Athenaion Politeia* (29–37) provides a brief synopsis of the period, but is particularly crucial for the two periods of oligarchy in Athens, the Four Hundred and especially the Thirty Tyrants, while Diodorus gives a chronological treatment of uneven quality (12.39–14.9). Plutarch wrote *Lives* of some of the major protagonists, such as Perikles, Alkibiades, Nikias and Lysander, more anecdotal than historical, but he was making use of some valuable sources that are now lost.

Inscriptions from Athens provide valuable evidence for the Athenian conduct of the war and, despite scholarly dispute on the dating of these decrees, they clearly belong to this period. Domestic events at Athens which had an impact on the course of the war, such as the affair of the mutilation of the hermai and the profanation of the Eleusinian Mysteries, are not only covered by Thucydides, but supplemented by Andokides' surviving lawcourt speech *On the Mysteries*, while the metic Lysias' experiences and those of his family, at the hands of the Thirty Tyrants who took power at Athens in 404 BC, make disturbing reading in his *Against Eratosthenes* (4–20: doc. 5.41). Athenian playwrights produced dramas throughout the war years, which directly or indirectly commented on events, and are crucial sources for Athenian perceptions of the war. Aristophanes, for example, in his play the *Knights*, as well as in the *Wasps*, vilifies Kleon (Ar. *Knights* 162–7: doc. 1.29; *Wasps* 836–62, 894–7: doc. 1.26), while his *Lysistrata* portrays the women of Greece uniting in a sex-strike against their husbands to force them to bring the war to an end (Ar. *Lysistrata* 77–82, 507–20, 565–97: docs 4.21, 4.66). Euripides' *Trojan Women* produced in 415 BC must be a commentary on the victims of war, especially the enslavement of women and their fate, and, perhaps significantly, postdates the capture of Melos whose male citizens were massacred and the women and children enslaved (Eur. *Trojan Women* 235–52, 272–8: doc. 5.68). The Peloponnesian War is the most studied conflict of the ancient world due to this wealth of sources, and Thucydides' account remains a model of how the history of a military conflict should be written.

The outbreak of the Peloponnesian War

The 'truest cause of the war'

If the Spartans thought of intervening in Athens' conflict with Samos in 440 BC (Thuc. 1.115.2–117.3: doc. 12.24), in the end they did not do so, and the terms of the Thirty Years' Peace of 446 BC between Athens and the Peloponnesians, agreed after the Athenians put down the revolt in Euboea, remained in force (Thuc. 1.23.4: doc. 13.2). The war arose from a variety of reasons according to Thucydides, and he specifically recorded the various complaints and disputes between the two sides, 'so that no-one ever has to ask why such a great war came upon the Greeks' (Thuc. 1.23.5: doc. 13.2). These causes were the incidents over the Corinthian colonies, Epidamnos, Corcyra and Potidaea (see Thuc. 1.24–65, docs 2.8–9). For Thucydides, however, these were mere pretexts for war on the part of the Peloponnesians, and the catalyst was the fact that the Spartans had come to fear the growing power of Athens and that this fear compelled them to go to war against the Athenians. So the 'truest cause' (alethestate prophasis) of the war was Spartan fear of Athens, and the specific causes of complaint (aitiai) were particular incidents contributing to this concern of the Spartans.

Corcyra and Epidamnus – Corinth and Athens

One of the disputes leading up to war was Athenian involvement with Corcyra (modern Corfu). Epidamnos in Illyria was a colony founded jointly by Corinth and Corcyra, which had in its turn been a colony of Corinth. Whereas, however, Corinth had good relations with its other colonies, it was on bad terms with Corcyra. In contrast, Potidaea, a colony of Corinth founded in about 600 BC, was still receiving Corinthian officials when it came into conflict with Athens (Thuc. 1.56.1: doc. 2.9). Epidamnos had been a prosperous state, but just prior to the Peloponnesian War the democrats expelled the aristocrats, who joined the local Taulantians, who were Illyrian 'barbarians'. The Epidamnians were hard pressed in the ensuing conflict and therefore requested help from their mother-city Corcyra, which refused to give any form of assistance. Epidamnos as a result enquired of Delphi what course of action to take, and was advised to seek help from Corinth. In this the Epidamnians were successful, as Corinth was on bad terms with Corcyra because although it was their colony it failed in the view of the Corinthians to give them appropriate respect: Corcyra was a powerful city in its own right, with a large navy, and held Corinth in contempt. Corinth sent out colonists and troops to Epidamnos, at which Corcyra reacted swiftly, dispatching a force of twenty-five ships, with another fleet following soon after, demanding that Epidamnos receive the exiles back and send the Corinthian settlers and troops home.

When this was refused the Corcyraean fleet, now consisting of forty ships, besieged the city, and the Corinthians in turn organised a fleet of thirty triremes and 3000 hoplites, supported by naval contingents from various Peloponnesian allies (Megara, Pale, Epidauros, Hermione, Troezen, Leukas and Ambracia). At this, the scope of the conflict suddenly became much broader. Funds were requested from Thebes and the Phliasians, and ship hulls from Elis. Corcyra asked Corinth to accept arbitration in the matter or to refer it to Delphi (Thucydides, as elsewhere in his history, is careful to point out the political role of the religious centre of the Greek world, Delphi). Corinth sailed with a fleet of seventy-five triremes to Actium near Anaktoria, at the mouth of the Ambracian Gulf, and the Corcyraeans sent a herald urging them to desist from war, but were rebuffed. With a further eighty triremes (in addition to the forty besieging Epidamnos) the Corcyraeans defeated this fleet at Actium (where centuries later Octavian would defeat Antony and Cleopatra), and set up a trophy at Leukimme, a headland off Corcyra (but not the battle-site itself). Fifteen Corinthian ships were destroyed, and on the same day the Epidamnians surrendered on condition that the colonists and troops were sold as slaves (they were in fact put to death), and the Corinthians kept as prisoners of war (Thuc. 1.24–30 [1.24.1–26.2: doc. 2.8]). Corcyra then attacked some Corinthian allies which had supported Corinth in this conflict, and now were in possession of the local sea. In the following year, 434 BC, the Corinthian navy took up position at Leukimme but no further action eventuated.

Corcyra becomes an Athenian ally

The Corinthians, however, were not prepared to submit to this defeat and began to make intensive naval preparations. Corcyra, despite its large fleet, grew alarmed and in 433 BC took an initiative that had wide-ranging consequences. They were not at this point a member of either the Peloponnesian or the Delian League, and decided to send a delegation to Athens to see if they could join the Delian League, as their Corinthian enemies were part of the Spartan alliance. Corinth, on hearing of this, also sent representatives to Athens. Thucydides records the speeches made by both the Corcyraean and the Corinthian delegates, in which the Corcyraeans portrayed themselves as victims of Corinthian aggression, inasmuch as they were now threatened by a large Peloponnesian force (including Megara once more). An alliance with Corcyra, it was pointed out, would benefit the Athenians because they would thus secure Corcyra's large navy for themselves, which would be useful in the coming war against Sparta. Corinthian delegates countered with the argument that the Corcyraeans were in the wrong and, while any Greek state was free to join either alliance, the Corcyraeans only wanted to join the Athenians in order to harm Corinth. Corinth meanwhile ensured that the other Peloponnesian states did not interfere with Athens over Samos despite the desire of some of these to do so.

Two assembly meetings were devoted to debating the matter, and the Athenians at first inclined towards the Corinthian point of view, but then sided with Corcyra in a limited defensive alliance, considering that an Athenian attack on Corinth in conjunction with Corcyra would break the Thirty Years' Peace. But they were unwilling to forego the opportunity of gaining access to Corcyra's large navy (at least 120 triremes). Perikles' influence can almost certainly be seen in this desire to expand Athens' influence in western Greece and to include Corcyra's navy in Athens' naval forces. Whatever the reason, through this decision Athens became embroiled in open conflict with Corinth.

Open warfare between Corinth and Athens

Ten Athenian ships went to support Corcyra and a battle took place near a group of islands known as 'Sybota' in which Corinth mobilised 150 triremes, ninety from Corinth itself and the remainder from its allies (twelve came from Megara), while Corcyra put 110 ships to sea. At first the Athenians only came to the aid of the Corcyreans when these were hard pressed by the Corinthians and other Peloponnesian allies, and did not openly join battle. Matters, however, escalated when the Corinthians were clearly on the point of victory, and the Athenians then joined the battle in earnest. Despite this the Corinthians were victorious and battle was broken off. It was about to be rejoined later in the day when the Corinthians retreated at the sight of the approach of twenty more Athenian ships. Corcyra was reprieved and the Corinthian fleet went home, but Athens and Corinth had met in battle, and this was to be the first of Corinth's grievances against the Athenians (see Thuc. 1.24–55).

Potidaea, Corinth and Athens

Almost immediately after these events involving Athenian military action in support of Corcyra against several Peloponnesian states, the episode concerning Potidaea took place. This city was a colony of Corinth, located on the Isthmus of Pallene in Chalkidike in northern Greece and founded in about c. 625–585 BC, but was a tribute-paying member of the Athenian alliance. The Athenians, who thought that Corinth was 'planning how to revenge themselves' on them, demanded that Potidaea tear down its walls, provide hostages, expel the Corinthian officials they received every year as Corinth's colony, and refuse to receive any more in the future. Athens seems also to have been concerned about the king of Macedon,

Perdikkas, and his influence in the area, as he was currently hostile to Athens (which was supporting his brother Philip, and one Derdas, in a claim for the Macedonian throne) and attempting both to interest Sparta in war against Athens and to persuade Corinth to support a revolt in Potidaea. An Athenian force was sent out under Archestratos to ensure that the demands made against Potidaea were met and also to prevent revolts among the allies in the region. Potidaea sent representatives to Athens to request that matters be left as they were, and to Sparta to win its support. The Athenians remained unconvinced, but Sparta promised to invade Attica in the case of Athenian hostility towards Potidaea (Thuc. 1.56–8).

Perdikkas persuaded the Chalkidians to destroy and abandon their coastal cities and to make one large inland settlement at Olynthos about 11 kilometres from Potidaea (which became prominent as part of the history of the rise to power of Philip II of Macedon in the fourth century). When the Athenians arrived, Potidaea and Athens' other allies in the area revolted. The Corinthians sent a force under the command of Aristeus (the son of the famous Adeimantos of Salamis) composed of volunteers from Corinth and mercenaries from throughout the rest of the Peloponnese, and so not an 'official' force as such, supported by the Peloponnesian League. Archestratos had captured Therme for Athens, when a fresh Athenian force under the strategos Kallias arrived to assist him in his siege of Pydna: as this went on too long the Athenians made an alliance with Perdikkas and then moved on to their main objective, Potidaea. Macedonian forces loyal to Perdikkas' brother Philip assisted the Athenians and Aristeus and the Peloponnesians were defeated and then besieged in Potidaea, while Kallias was killed in action. Another Athenian force was sent to Potidaea under the general Phormio to assist with the siege and ensure that the city was completely blockaded. Phormio had participated with Perikles (and Sophocles) in the Athenian siege of Samos in 440 BC, and in 429 BC blockaded Corinthian shipping from Naupaktos and defeated two Peloponnesian fleets. He is often overlooked in the narrative because of the prominence of Perikles and Kleon at this period, but clearly like Demosthenes later in the war he was one of the Athenian generals who combined initiative and military skill in his ability to take the war to the Peloponnesians.

About this time, with Potidaea under siege by the Athenians, the famous debate over Athens took place at Sparta, with the Corinthians comparing the Athenians' ambition and energy with the Spartans' general inactivity and lack of confidence (Thuc. 1.70.1–8:

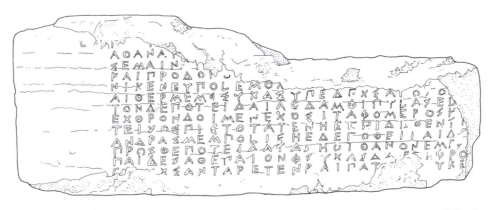

Figure 13.1 A fragmentary marble inscription listing the Athenians killed in action at Potidaea, dating to about 432 BC. British Museum 1816,0610.348, London. Drawing by J. Etherington.

447

doc. 13.3). Whether this helped to goad the Spartans into open hostility against Athens is difficult to determine, but after this meeting the Spartan assembly made the decision to declare war. Potidaea was later forced to surrender to the Athenians, in 430 BC, and an Athenian cleruchy was founded on the site (Thuc. 1.56–65; 1.56.1–57.1: doc. 2.9). An inscription honoured the Athenians who died at Potidaea; it includes an epitaph, and lists the fallen, including the strategos Kallias (*IG* I³ 1179 II: doc. 3.56; Fig. 13.1).

The Megarian decrees

At the urging of the Corinthians a number of Sparta's allies visited Sparta in 432 BC to lodge complaints against the Athenians. Among them were the Megarians, who stated that, contrary to the terms of the Thirty Years' Peace of 446 BC, they had been excluded from all the ports within the Athenian empire, and from the agora of Athens itself. A series of Athenian decrees seems to have been imposed against the Megarians to enforce these sanctions. It is difficult to ascertain exactly how this form of economic 'warfare' contravened the peace, but from the Megarian point of view it could be seen as an act of hostility and hardly conducive to peaceful relations. Athens, for its part, accused Megara of cultivating sacred ground at Eleusis which lay on the border with Megara. This land in the Athenians' view was dedicated to the two goddesses, Demeter and Persephone. They also accused Megara of harbouring runaway slaves from Attica. Megara had revolted from the Athenian empire in 446 BC, and also aided the Corinthians against the Corcyraeans in both of the naval encounters of 435 and 433. This issue became a key demand of the Spartans in 432 BC and Aristophanes' *Acharnians* features the theme as part of Dikaiopolis' private negotiation of a peace treaty with Sparta, after which he sets up a private market where he can trade with the enemies of Athens, including a starving Megarian who sells off his daughters, disguised as pigs.

Aegina

The Aeginetans, out of fear of Athens, sent no formal embassy to Sparta, but secretly attempted to stir up war on the grounds that they had not been granted the independence they believed was guaranteed to them by the Thirty Years' Peace. How they could argue this is unknown, but that Athens should allow Aegina to be independent became one of the key Spartan demands in 432 BC. Athens took revenge in 431 once war broke out by expelling the inhabitants from the island and establishing an Athenian cleruchy. This was a decision not to be taken lightly from a financial point of view, as Aegina had paid 30 talents of tribute in the 440s, but in 432 BC their contribution amounted to less than 15 talents, perhaps a sign of growing unwillingness to accept Athens' leadership. Certainly, in 431 BC, the Athenians blamed the Aeginetans for being largely responsible for the outbreak of the war.

Athens versus Sparta: the Corinthian view

The Athenians and Peloponnesians had various causes of complaint against each other. Potidaea was a key issue of contention as Athens considered Corinth to be interfering in its relationship with one of Athens' tribute-paying allies and assisting it in its revolt. From the Corinthians' perspective the Athenians were besieging a city where Corinthians and Peloponnesians were resident. Athens now had access to the large fleet which Corcyra contributed to the Peloponnesian League, and control of Potidaea gave Athens a base from which to launch operations in Thrace. Corinth's concerns over Corcyra and Potidaea were one of the main factors that impelled it in 432 BC to urge Sparta's allies to send representatives to Sparta.

When in Sparta the Corinthians made a speech accusing the Athenians of depriving Greek states of their freedom, and of formulating long-term plans to do the same to others, including Sparta's allies. The most interesting aspect of this speech, however, is that the Corinthians blamed the Spartans for letting the situation arise in the first place. It was Sparta that had let Athens rebuild its walls after 479 BC, and which had stood by and allowed Athens to 'enslave' Greek states. The Corinthians contrasted in very significant terms the characteristics of the Spartans and the Athenians and, while the Corinthians probably did make these points, Thucydides was also using the speech as a vehicle to express what he saw as the fundamental differences between the two leading powers of Greece (Thuc. 1.66–78).

According to the Corinthians, the Athenians were 'quick thinkers', while the Spartans had 'no new ideas'. The Athenians wanted always to acquire more, the Spartans to hang on to what they had. Athens is portrayed as a city in which the citizens gave little thought to their bodies, which were not really their own but were used for the city. For them, 'peace and inactivity' were 'a greater calamity than hardship and action' (Thuc. 1.70.1–8: doc. 13.3). The Corinthians argued that Spartan hesitation must come to an end and that it was time for them to engage in decisive action. After this speech, some Athenians who were present in Sparta on other business were allowed to speak. They tried to point out how powerful Athens was and to make the Spartan assembly think twice before acquiescing to the Corinthian demands for mobilisation against Athens.

King Archidamos and the ephor Sthenelaidas

The Spartans then requested that their allies and the Athenians leave the meeting and they held an assembly to debate the issue, with most of the Spartans considering that the Athenians had been the aggressors and that war should be declared. King Archidamos, however, made a speech urging that the Spartans consider the situation with great care. He reminded them of the Athenians' wealth and resources in terms of ships, cavalry, hoplites and its tribute-paying allies. He pointed out the major disadvantage facing the Spartans, which was that they had no available money in the treasury or from taxation to spend on warfare. While he commented that Sparta could invade Attica's agricultural land, it was also the case that Athens was able to import its food, and he urged the Spartans now to wait. For the moment they should send envoys to lodge a protest against the Athenians' actions and watch closely how events turned out over the next two or three years, using this time to gather resources and make appropriate preparations for war against Athens.

But he was succeeded in the debate by Sthenelaidas, one of the ephors, whose speech urged the assembly to consider Sparta's dignity and take immediate action against the aggression Athens had shown towards Sparta's allies. Sparta should not allow Athens to grow any stronger – the matter was not to be resolved by words but by action. He put his own motion to the vote, declaring that he could not clearly determine from the shouting the assembly's decision: the Spartans voted by acclamation (Plut. *Life of Lykourgos* 26.3–5: doc. 6.22). He then took the unusual step of making the Spartans divide into two groups depending on whether or not they believed that Athens had broken the Thirty Years' Peace: the majority were of the opinion that the Athenians had done so, which was hardly surprising in a culture that thought so highly of courage and discipline. The allies' representatives in Sparta were recalled to the assembly to hear for themselves the Spartans' decision to go to war before returning to their cities. Thucydides comments that the Spartans voted for war, not because of the persuasiveness of their allies' speeches, but because they saw the extent to which Athens now dominated Greece and were afraid of the growth of Athenian power (Thuc. 1.79–88).

All of Sparta's allies meet at Sparta 432 BC

War did not break out immediately. Sparta consulted the Delphic oracle about the advisability of going to war and received the much-quoted advice that Apollo would be on their side and that they would win if they fought as strongly as they could. They then called a formal meeting of all their allies in the Peloponnesian League to vote on whether or not to declare war. This was a necessary procedure as, while Sparta was the leader of its allies, the league was not a hegemony like that of Athens. Sparta had to take its allies' interests and opinions into account, and the allies were not bound to follow Sparta into war simply because Sparta wished it. Once again the Corinthians were the most vocal about declaring war, as they wanted action taken over Potidaea as quickly as possible (Thuc. 1.118–24). Most of the allies voted in favour of war, and without delay, as soon as they had made the necessary preparations. These took nearly a year and war did not break out until 431 BC (1.125).

Sparta's ultimatum in 432 BC

Various Spartan embassies were sent to Athens because according to Thucydides they wanted to make sure that they had the best possible pretext for war if the Athenians continued to ignore their demands (Thuc. 1.126). This is an unexpected comment from Thucydides and a curious proceeding on the part of the Spartans, as they had already declared war on a number of grounds. The first of the Spartan demands, which were made over the course of several embassies to Athens, was that the Athenians drive out the 'accursed'. This was a reference to Athenian history when Kylon's supporters had been slaughtered after taking sanctuary at the altars on the acropolis (docs 7.21–3). Perikles was among the descendants of the Alkmeonidai involved and this must have been a deliberate ploy of the Spartans in the hope of having Perikles exiled from Athens. The Athenians refused, pointing in reply to two curses on the Spartan side: the slaying of helots who took refuge at the altar of Poseidon at Tainaron, and the death of the regent Pausanias who took refuge in the temple of Athena Chalkioiokos (Athena of the Bronze House) and was barricaded inside until he was on the point of starving to death (Thuc. 1.128, 1.134: doc. 6.35). Further Spartan demands were that the siege of Potidaea be abandoned, that Aegina be allowed autonomy, and that the Megarian decree be revoked. Athens refused to comply with any of these, pointing for their part to the Megarians' cultivation of sacred ground at Eleusis. Thucydides (scrupulous as ever on matters of religion) makes a specific point of recording these religious reasons put forward by both sides to give their case moral authority (Thuc. 1.126–8).

A final embassy from Sparta summed up their position most clearly: 'The Spartans want the peace to continue, and it will, if you would allow the Greeks to be autonomous' (Thuc. 1.139.1–3: doc. 13.4). This was surely the crux of the matter: Thucydides gave as the pretexts (the aitiai) for the war the conflicts concerning Potidaea and Corcyra and other matters (such as Megara and Aegina), but the truest cause (alethestate prophasis) was the Spartan fear of the growing power of the Athenians, which would be broken if Athens renounced leadership of its hegemony and control of its allies.

Perikles and the Athenian response

At Athens an assembly was held to discuss the Spartan demand for Greek autonomy. Some speakers were in favour of revoking the Megarian decree on the grounds that it was an impediment to peace, while others believed that it was necessary to go to war. The Athenian assembly was clearly divided over the issue, but at this point Thucydides reports that Perikles spoke in favour of war and convinced the Athenians that they should vote to take up arms against the Spartans. This they did on his advice (Thuc. 1.140–5). He began by stating that his own view, that no concessions should be made to the Spartans, was unchanged. The Athenians should not allow Sparta to dictate to them and any differences between them, he argued, should be settled by arbitration as set out in the peace of 446 BC, rather than by war, which was how the Spartans wanted to resolve them – later in the war, in fact, the Spartans held themselves at fault for the outbreak of hostilities in 431 BC and for their lack of success because they refused arbitration (Thuc. 7.18.2–3). If the Athenians gave in over the Megarian decree, other demands would follow, and it was up to the Athenians to ensure that the Spartans treated them as an equal power. But it is also important to note that Perikles was willing to make concessions: Athens would give Megara access to Athens' agora and its ports if Sparta exempted Athens and its allies from Spartan xenelasiai (regular expulsions of foreigners from Sparta), gave independence to its allies if they were independent when the treaty was made, and allowed its allies to have their own government rather than one that was conducive to Spartan interests and ideology (Thuc. 1.144). Later, in 431 BC, he reminded the assembly of Athens' resources, including hoplites, cavalry, ships, money and sacred treasures (including the 40 talents of gold on the statue of Athena Parthenos), and convinced them that Athens possessed sufficient resources to wage a successful war. Sparta in comparison, as Archidamos had argued, would be hampered by a lack of money (Thuc. 2.13.3–5: doc. 1.10).

Assigning the responsibility for the outbreak of the war is difficult, and perhaps is not historically appropriate. It is impossible now to determine whether Sparta should have accepted arbitration over the points at issue, or whether, had Athens given in and rescinded the Megarian degree, more demands would have followed from Sparta, as argued by Perikles. On the one hand, Sparta already had a number of other demands on the table, and rescission of the Megarian degree alone was unlikely to satisfy the war-mongers among Sparta's allies. On the other hand, the Athenians would never have taken seriously the demand that they abandon their empire and allow their allies to become autonomous. While the Spartans may have been genuinely afraid that Athens was 'swallowing up' Greece and destroying Greek autonomy, they must also have been concerned about their own position vis-à-vis Athens. Their lack of altruism is shown by the fact that in 404 BC Sparta did not give Athens' allies autonomy but took them over and developed its own (short-lived) hegemony in the Aegean and along the coast of Asia Minor. Perikles always argued that no concessions should be made to the Spartans, a political stance that could perhaps be seen as provocative, and on both sides there was a majority view that war was necessary. Perhaps the crux of the matter was simply that Sparta was until recently Greece's leading power and Athens now successfully challenged that position. They had two very different political systems and two very different alliances, and in the event a conflict was perhaps inevitable.

The Archidamian War, 431–421 BC

The first phase of the Peloponnesian War is known as the Archidamian War (431–421 BC), named after King Archidamos of Sparta (who reigned about 476 to 427). While he was lukewarm over the question of war and urged the Spartans to wait for a few years in order to husband their resources and seek a peaceful resolution of the situation, he was the king who now invaded Attica on several occasions. Thucydides and modern historians see the conflict between Athens and Sparta as one continuous war, but the Greeks themselves generally saw it as a series of conflicts. When war finally came, it did not at first involve conflict between Athens and Sparta, but, as Thucydides notes, the actual outbreak or war and termination of the Thirty Years' Peace of 446 BC occurred when Thebes attacked Athens' old and loyal ally Plataea in central Greece (Thuc. 2.1–5).

Abandoning rural Attica

As Archidamos had stated in his speech to the Spartan assembly, the Athenians regarded their land as something so valuable that they would fight for it rather than sue for peace. Moreover, they were able, in any case, to import any supplies they needed (Thuc. 1.81). Perikles, in fact, advised the Athenians to concede that the Spartans were superior on land and refrain from going out to meet them in battle when they invaded Attica. Instead he persuaded the Athenians to adopt a defensive strategy. Many of those who lived in the Attic countryside moved into the city, to be out of the way of the invading Spartans and the other Peloponnesians (presumably not all the rural Athenians moved in, but mainly those whose land was within the path of the Spartan invasions). They took up residence wherever they could, even in temples and sanctuaries. This was normally forbidden and some places such as the acropolis were too sacred for this to be countenanced. They took their furniture and even the woodwork decorations from their houses with them while the farms were abandoned to the invading forces and the sheep and cattle sent across to nearby Euboea and other islands (Thuc. 2.14, 65.6–7: doc. 13.5).

The Athenian financial and military position

Perikles assured the Athenians of the strength of their financial and military situation: there were 6000 talents of silver on the acropolis, and 600 talents coming in annually from the tribute, as well as various dedications made by individuals and the state, and spoils taken from the Persians, adding up to another 500 talents. There were also 40 talents of pure gold in removable plates on the statue of Athena herself. Athens possessed 29,000 hoplites (including the resident foreigners, the metics), 1200 cavalry, and 300 triremes (Thuc. 2.13.3–5: doc. 1.10). But while this no doubt sounded impressive to the assembly, the fact that the siege of Samos cost between 1200 and 1400 talents should have been a warning of the possible costs involved, and Perikles' comment about the 600 talents of tribute each year depended on the allies remaining loyal while Athens itself was under attack – after all, to equip and man a trireme for one year cost a talent. However, he gave crucial advice: the Athenians should not try to extend their empire while the war was on, but look after the fleet, do nothing to endanger the city, and bide their time. This was all good advice and in the event the Athenians more or less abided by it until 415 and the launching of the Sicilian Expedition. Furthermore, no consideration was given as to whether the hostile Persian Empire across the Aegean might

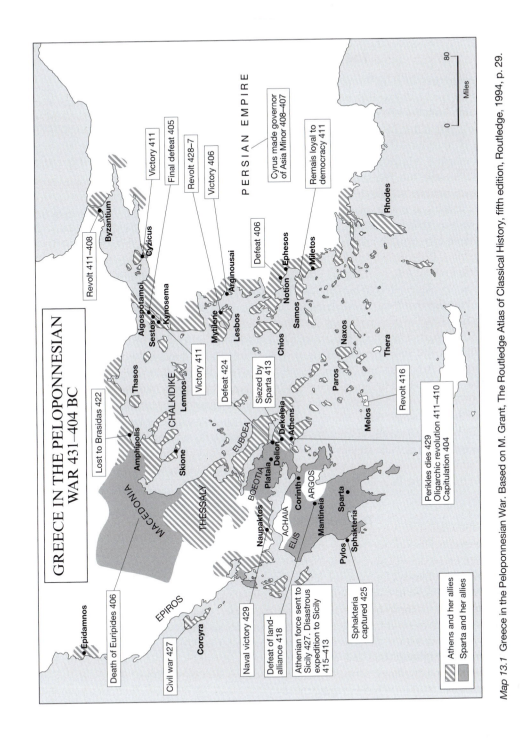

GREECE IN THE PELOPONNESIAN WAR 431–404 BC

Epidamnos

Death of Euripides 406

EPIROS

Corcyra

Civil war 427

MACEDONIA

THESSALY

Amphipolis

Lost to Brasidas 422

CHALKIDIKE

Skione

Thasos

Lemnos

Victory 411

Defeat 424

EUBOEA

BOEOTIA

Plataia

Delion

Dekeleia

Athens

Siezed by
Sparta 413

Naupaktos

Naval victory 429

Defeat of land-
alliance 418

Athenian force sent to
Sicily 427. Disastrous
expedition to Sicily
415–413

ACHAIA

ELIS

Corinth

ARGOS

Mantineia

Sparta

Pylos

Sphakteria

Sphakteria
captured 425

Perikles dies 429
Oligarchic revolution 411–410
Capitulation 404

Byzantium

Revolt 411–408

Cyzicus

Victory 411

Final defeat 405

Revolt 428–7

Victory 406

Aigospotamoi

Sestos

Kynosema

Mytilene

Lesbos

Arginousai

Samos

Chios

Notion

Ephesos

Defeat 406

Miletos

Naxos

Paros

Thera

Rhodes

Melos

Revolt 416

PERSIAN EMPIRE

Cyrus made governor
of Asia Minor 408–407

Remais loyal to
democracy 411

0   80

Miles

Athens and her allies

Sparta and her allies

Map 13.1 Greece in the Peloponnesian War. Based on M. Grant, The Routledge Atlas of Classical History, fifth edition, Routledge, 1994, p. 29.

become involved (Thuc. 2.62, cf. 6.17). Leaving Persia out of account was probably the most fatal mistake the Athenians made in their preparations for war.

The first Spartan invasion, 431 BC

Archidamos marched up through the Isthmus, unsuccessfully besieging the Athenian fortress Oenoe on the border with Boeotia. He was criticised, however, for making slow progress on the march from the Isthmus to Oenoe, and then for the lack of success there, which was taken as an indication that he did not really want to wage war on Attica and still held out hopes for peace. He then moved into Attica itself, in mid-summer when the grain was ready for harvest, devastating the area around Eleusis and Acharnai (the largest Athenian deme). This occurred eighty days after the Thebans attacked Plataea. Many Athenians, especially the young hoplites, were anxious to march out to meet the invaders, but Perikles was able to enforce his advice, which was not to offer battle. While the Athenians allowed the Spartans to take the initiative, they then launched a significant counter-offensive, sending a fleet of 100 triremes to the Peloponnese, plus an additional fifty ships later from their new ally Corcyra, and pillaged the coastline. Brasidas, who makes his first appearance in the war at this stage, saved the city of Methone from an Athenian siege (Thuc. 2.18–25). At the end of the first campaigning season, in 431 BC, Perikles delivered his famous 'Funeral Oration', emphasising the greatness of Athens and the fact that it was worth dying for, and reiterating the democratic ideology that every citizen had a part to play in running the state (Thuc. 2.37.1–40.2: doc. 1.17).

Another Spartan invasion of Attica followed in 430 BC, and again the Athenians did not go out to meet them. This Spartan strategy was therefore of limited success, for they were unable to entice the Athenians into a land battle from which they could emerge victorious and end the war quickly. The Spartans obviously put limited planning into the war, apparently envisaging, despite Archidamos' advice, that an annual invasion of Attica, and destruction of some of its crops, would bring Athens to its knees. Athens was secure, as long as the Athenians could be persuaded to refrain from meeting the Spartan army on land. Sparta lacked the skill to besiege a huge city like Athens (as they themselves admitted), and Athens' system of walls and fortifications meant that it was essentially impregnable to siege, as it was able to import its food through the Piraeus as long as the fleet was operational.

The plague strikes Athens, 430 BC

Sparta and its allies invaded Attica in 430, again with limited success, only a few days before a plague broke out in Athens. It was already prevalent in other places in the Greek world, such as on the island of Lemnos, but it was at Athens that it was to prove particularly virulent; the plague was said to have originated in Ethiopia. Thucydides gives a graphic and detailed description of it, and modern scholars have speculated endlessly on what it was, without success. Suffice to say the plague was extremely infectious, and very few survived once they came in contact with it: Perikles was himself to die of it in 429 BC. Its greatest impact and severity was on those who came in from the countryside and were living in temporary huts and shanty-type dwellings: corpses lay on top of corpses, and the half-dead staggered around, possessed by an unquenchable, raging thirst.

A burning sensation in the head was followed by red and inflamed eyes, bleeding from the throat, and difficulty in breathing, after which the pain spread to the chest accompanied by coughing. Painful vomiting or dry retching from the throat with violent spasms then occurred, and the skin turned a livid red with pustules, which ulcerated. If the victims lived to the seventh or eighth day, the disease spread to the bowels, and the constant diarrhoea became the cause of death. Thucydides was interested not so much in the symptoms, but in the breakdown in custom that the plague gave rise to in Athens: many people died neglected, corpses were thrown onto unlit funerary pyres that were meant for others, or if lit, piled on top of other corpses, and many Athenians lived riotously as if it was their last day (Thuc. 2.47.2–3, 52.1–53.4: doc. 13.6). With his usual careful attention to religious matters as they pertained to his narrative, Thucydides notes that many recalled the oracle that death would come when there was war with the Dorians. While the Athenians were preoccupied with their problems within the city, the Spartans laid waste to the Attic plain and then moved down to the silver mines at Laureion and ravaged the area.

The financial decrees of Kallias

Either just prior to the Peloponnesian War in 434/3, or perhaps as late as 422/1, an individual named Kallias proposed two decrees to the Athenian demos relating to Athens' finances, specifically as they concerned the money of the gods, and in particular that belonging to Athena. His first decree is generally considered to have provided for the moving of the treasures of the gods from their shrines throughout Attica to the acropolis for safekeeping. The second decree concerns building works on the acropolis and the use of Athena's money, with penalties for those proposing a decree to this effect without a prior decree ratifying that such a decree could be proposed. The Athenians were making doubly certain that expenditure of Athena's money should not be decided upon lightly. What is important in both decrees is the scrutiny paid to the money belonging to the gods. Permanent records of these amounts were made so that the gods could be repaid, along with a provision that the record of the treasurers must be checked by auditors (*IG* I³ 52: doc. 13.7).

Kolophon swears loyalty to Athens, 427 BC

Athens had problems in its relationships with one of its allies in 427 BC. Kolophon was seized by a pro-Persian group, and the pro-Athenians in the city fled to Kolophon's port Notion, where there was a further split, with one side aided by the pro-Persian group from Kolophon. The pro-Athenian group then called on the assistance of the Athenian strategos Paches, who was in the area. He captured Notion through treachery with the assistance of the leader of the Arkadian mercenaries who were in the employ of the pro-Persian group. Paches handed Notion over to the Kolophonians, with the exception of the pro-Persian group, and the Athenians sent out additional settlers and encouraged Kolophonians who were resident elsewhere to join the settlement. An inscription deals with arrangements for a democratic constitution to be put in place, with the provision that Kolophon not rebel from Athens and 'not desert to the enemy', a clear reference to the pro-Persian group. Thucydides records all the events as taking place in 427 BC (Thuc. 3.34) and this inscription can only belong to this year, when there were historically attested troubles at Kolophon (*IG* I³ 37: doc. 13.8).

Dating Athenian decrees

Traditionally, however, this decree concerning Kolophon has been dated by scholars to 447/6 BC, although no historical evidence supports this. The reason for this judgement is based on the letter-forms used as dating criteria for Athenian decrees when the archon's name is missing or when the archon's name is known but the date of his archonship is not. In Athenian inscriptions the sigma (the letter 's') with three bars was eventually superseded by a four-barred form. The three-barred sigma last appears in a firmly dated inscription in 447/6 (*IG* I³ 265), so around 445 is usually taken as the date at which these sigmas went out of use, and on this criterion undated inscriptions with three-barred sigmas are dated to before 445. Four-barred sigmas first appear in *IG* I³ 264, in 448/7, but there is an isolated single example in the casualty list for the Erechtheid tribe dated to 460 or 459 BC (*IG* I³ 1147: doc. 12.14) at line 67, and in the prescript of *IG* I³ 264 (453/2 BC). The tailed rho (the letter 'r', with a 'tail') last appears in a firmly dated inscription in 438/7 (*IG* I³ 445). The Greek epigraphist Harold Mattingly has long questioned these formal dating criteria by letter-form on both historical and epigraphic grounds, and while, on the traditional dating advocated by a previous generation of scholars, all absolutely dated decrees with a three-barred sigma date to before c. 445 BC, this does not mean that all inscriptions with three-barred sigmas must automatically fall within this period. This is especially true, given that the sample is small, and the criterion does not possess the status of indubitable proof. While many of Mattingly's arguments have been criticised, the use of laser technology now seems to prove that three-barred sigmas and tailed rhos appear as late as 418/17 BC, strengthening his previous arguments, and when decrees with these letter-forms seem to fall appropriately into the period after 447/6 BC they must be dated accordingly.

The destruction of Plataea 427 BC

Athens recovered quickly from the plague, and, despite Thucydides' commentary on the extensive loss of life, hoplite numbers and Athens' military capacity do not seem to have been affected. In 430 BC the Spartans made their first overtures to the Persians for aid. Potidaea came to terms with Athens, without receiving any Spartan assistance. In 429 BC, instead of invading Attica, which was still suffering from the effects of the plague, Archidamos besieged the Boeotian city of Plataea, which had already endured a siege in 431 at the hands of the Thebans in the first action of the Peloponnesian War. The Plataeans sought assistance from Athens, and sent most of their population there, except for 400 men, 80 Athenians, and 110 women to prepare and cook meals. The Peloponnesians surrounded the city with a stockade and the Plataeans initially held out but, soon after the Mytilene revolt was crushed by Athens in 427 BC, surrendered to the Spartans. At the suggestion of the Thebans each individual Plataean was asked by the Spartans what contribution they had made to the Spartan war effort. When they answered that they had made no contribution, the men were put to death and the women sold into slavery. Athens did not come to Plataea's assistance except for the small token force of eighty men, perhaps too preoccupied at that point with Mytilene to do so, but most of the Plataeans were already in Athens at this stage and were granted citizenship ([Dem.] 59 *Against Neaira* 104: doc. 1.37). Significantly, Athens was to spare the Mytileneans despite the fact that they revolted from an alliance into which they had willingly entered, but the Plataeans as allies of Athens were besieged and then executed by the Spartans, while the city of Plataea itself was destroyed (Thuc. 2.71–8, 3.51–68).

The Mytilene debate 427 BC

In 428 BC Lesbos revolted (except for the town of Methymna), with its main city Mytilene taking the lead: it was one of Athens' main allies and unlike the 'subject allies' it possessed a reasonable degree of independence. Chios was the other ally with similar privileges and status, and while Samos was originally in a similar position, its revolt in 440 BC reduced the island to the class of an ordinary tribute-paying ally. The revolt on Lesbos was crushed in 427 BC, when the demos of Mytilene was armed by the oligarchs and then turned on them so that they had no option but to surrender to the strategos Paches who was besieging the island. A debate took place in the assembly at Athens about the fate of Mytilene, and the decision was made to kill all the adult men and to sell the women and children into slavery. What prompted this harsh punishment was the fact that Mytilene possessed special status as an ally of Athens, and that Spartan ships sailed to Ionia in support of the revolt after Mytilene sent a delegation asking Sparta for assistance. Thucydides comments that this made the Athenians think that the revolt was premeditated, but more important was the consideration that enemy ships had 'trespassed' into territory – the Aegean – which the Athenians regarded as especially their own. A trireme was sent to Mytilene to inform Paches of the assembly's decision.

By the next day, many Athenians regretted this decision, and a second assembly was held. Famously, it is at this point that Thucydides introduces the politician Kleon, who proposed and carried the motion to sentence the adult males of Mytilene to death: 'the most violent of all the citizens and by far the most persuasive over the demos' (Thuc. 3.36.6). In arguing for the death penalty he accused the Athenian democracy of being incapable of running an empire and of not realising that their empire was in fact a tyranny. An individual named Diodotos, who is not otherwise known, successfully spoke for the repeal of the decree, not on humanitarian grounds (which had led to the reconvening of the assembly to reconsider its decision) but in an appeal to the self-interest of the Athenians, arguing that extermination now would compel all other rebels from the empire to hold out to the end and that execution of the demos, which was not responsible for the revolt, would send the wrong message to other democracies, which now counted on Athenian support (Thuc. 3.36.2–4, 39.1–4: doc. 13.9). Reversing their previous decision, the assembly voted to send a trireme with all speed to overtake the one dispatched the day before: it arrived, literally, 'in the nick of time' and saved Mytilene's population. The 1000 ringleaders were, however, sent to Athens and executed on Kleon's decree and the walls of Mytilene were demolished. Athens also took possession of its fleet and installed 3000 cleruchs.

The popularity of the Athenian empire

Diodotos argued that the democracies among the allies were loyal to Athens, and that revolts were caused by oligarchs, whom the democrats did not support, or who, if they were forced to, still remained pro-Athenian. In the case of Mytilene, it was the democrats in that city who enabled the revolt to be crushed. Thucydides uses the Mytilene debate to give two perspectives on the empire: those of Kleon and Diodotos, as well as to provide perceptions about the popularity of the empire. Kleon is the cynic, Diodotos pragmatic, and the latter's views seem to have been more rooted in reality as events at Mytilene showed. In most cities the demos did tend to support Athens and the alliance, while the richer citizens in allied states wanted to establish oligarchies, and took the chance to revolt when it presented itself: it was therefore important that Athens send the 'right message' to the democrats among its allies. Kleon for his part echoes Perikles, who had earlier stated that the empire was 'like a tyranny' (compare Thuc. 2.63.2 with 3.37.2, 3.40.4; 2.61.2 with 3.38.1), and tells the Athenians that the empire was a tyranny over subjects who disliked Athens and would take any opportunity to rebel, and that it would be dangerous for them to let the empire go. This was in fact not true, as many of Athens' allies remained loyal, even to the bitter end, and the cases of Neapolis (doc. 13.31) and Samos (doc. 13.34) are good examples of allies who remained loyal, even late in the war.

There is no doubt that the Athenians committed atrocities, narrowly avoided in the case of Mytilene, but put into practice elsewhere, as at Melos, where all the men were killed and the women and children enslaved in 416/15 (Thuc. 5.116.2–4: doc. 5.4). The Spartans, however, were no better, as the case of Plataea exemplifies. Thucydides' view, that when the war broke out the allies wanted to revolt, and that the whole hellenic world was opposed to Athens after the Sicilian Expedition, is inaccurate (Thuc. 8.2). But however popular the empire may have been with some of its allies, Athens during the war maintained a tight control over them, and various decrees regulated their affairs, most notably the coins, weights and measures decree (see below, p. 460). For some reason in 426/5 BC, Athens regulated the judicial affairs of Miletos, and a reference to a garrison points, as in the case of Erythrai in 453/2 (*IG* I^3 14: 12.30), to the ways in which Athens used a combination of judicial authority, oaths of loyalty and a military presence to maintain control and vigilance over the allies (*IG* I^3 21: doc. 13.10).

Herakleia established in 426 BC

When both the Trachinians and Doris, Sparta's ancestral mother-city, appealed to Sparta on the grounds that they were being attacked by the Oitaians, the Spartans established a colony at Herakleia in Trachis not far from Thermopylai. This was close to Thrace but, more importantly, a naval fleet could be prepared there for an expedition against Euboea, which was not just an Athenian ally but the place to which the Athenians had sent much of their livestock. At first the Athenians were anxious about this development, but as it turned out, the Thessalians were equally concerned at having this large settlement on their doorstep and continually attacked it. Large numbers of settlers were initially attracted to the colony, thinking that it would be a safe place under the protection of Spartan founders, but the Thessalians massacred many of them, while the Spartan magistrates 'through their harsh and often unjust government' drove many settlers away. Herakleia's strategic potential was as a consequence never fully realised (Thuc. 3.92.1–93.2: doc. 2.24).

Pylos and Sphakteria, 425 BC

A spectacular victory for the Athenians, the campaign at Pylos, was the handiwork initially of Demosthenes and then of Kleon (Thuc. 4.2–41; Diod. Sic. 12.61–63; Plut. *Nikias* 7). A foray into Sicilian affairs in 427–424 BC had not been a success, and Eurymedon and Sophocles were sailing to Sicily with a further naval force, with instructions while en route to give what help they could to Corcyra where civil war had broken out. Demosthenes, although having no official position as strategos, was granted permission at his own request to make use of this fleet as it made its way around the Peloponnese, while the Spartan army was in Attica pillaging and disrupting the harvest. Demosthenes wanted to sail to Pylos, and although the other two strategoi preferred to push on to Corcyra, where a Peloponnesian fleet had preceded them, a storm forced them to seek shelter in Pylos anyway. Demosthenes urged them to fortify the position but was unable to convince either the strategoi or the company commanders of the strategic value of this move, until the soldiers, bored by the inclement weather which prevented them from sailing away, began building fortifications of their own accord, despite their lack of suitable tools. A wall to the landward side of Pylos was completed in six days and the fleet then continued on to Corcyra, leaving Demosthenes with five ships to defend it.

Pylos is about 70 kilometres west of Sparta in Messenia, and Demosthenes saw its advantages for Athens, as it had an excellent harbour while an Athenian outpost here could count on helot support. King Agis and the Spartans, concerned at this development, returned from Attica after only fifteen days and proceeded to Pylos where the Peloponnesian fleet at Corcyra was summoned to meet them. Demosthenes was able to get word to Athens when the Spartans attacked the Athenian fortification and attempted to block the harbour. After the arrival of the Athenian fleet, a body of Spartans became trapped on the nearby island of Sphakteria, to the south of the Athenian fortifications. An initial armistice was agreed while the Spartans sent envoys to Athens, but Kleon opposed making peace with the Spartans and the Athenian blockade on the island continued. Now, however, the Athenians faced their own difficulties. It was taking a long time to subdue the Spartans trapped on the island as they were maintained by supplies smuggled in by loyal helots. The Athenian troops and sailors, however, were short of food and water. As a result, back at home the Athenians began to regret they had not made peace.

Kleon was becoming unpopular as a result of the situation at Pylos, and in an assembly meeting attacked Nikias, with the comment that if the generals had any initiative, they would have been able to take Pylos – if he, Kleon, were in command he would have done so. Nikias replied that Kleon was welcome to take a force and try his own luck, and although Kleon tried to back out of the situation the assembly forced him into accepting it. While Thucydides' hostility to Kleon is clear in this passage, Kleon obviously saw this as an opportunity, and perhaps his reluctance about going to Pylos was merely a pretence and he intended to go there all along. He certainly had immediate plans to hand, and declared to the assembly that he would not take any more Athenians with him, but instead would command some troops from Lemnos and Imbros who were currently in Athens, peltasts from Ainos, and 400 archers from other places. He was either thinking very quickly 'on his feet' or he tricked Nikias and the assembly into awarding him the command. While Thucydides describes him as a 'strategos' he was not one of the strategoi elected for the year and this must be seen as an 'extra-ordinary' military appointment. Kleon also seems to have been in contact with Demosthenes and had 'learned' that he was planning a landing on the island of Sphakteria, and so chose him as his colleague in the command.

Kleon promised the assembly he would be back in twenty days with the Spartans dead or alive, and so he was. Prior to his arrival the dense brushwood on Sphakteria was accidentally burnt off in a fire lit by an Athenian soldier and this made conditions easier for an Athenian attack. On Kleon's arrival the generals offered the Spartans the chance to surrender, which they declined. Eight hundred hoplites were then landed on the island and advanced at a run against the Spartan guardposts, followed by the crews of seventy ships and 1600 archers and peltasts. Overwhelmingly outnumbered, the majority of the Spartans managed to withdraw to a fortification at the far end of the island, but a Messenian managed to bring round a light-armed force to their rear, at which point Kleon and Demosthenes, who wished to take them alive to Athens, offered the chance of surrender. Of the original Peloponnesian force of 420 hoplites, 292 were taken to Athens and imprisoned, of whom 120 were Spartiates (Thuc. 4.27.5–28.5, 38.5–39.3: doc. 13.11). The Greek world was stunned by this unprecedented surrender by Spartan hoplites, and the shields taken from them were dedicated on the acropolis. One badly damaged one still survives (*Agora* B, 262: doc. 13.12). The Spartan desire for the return of those captured was an important theme in the years to come and assisted in the

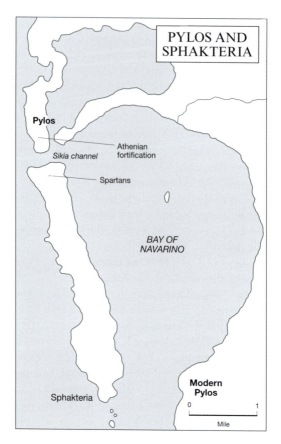

Map 13.2 Pylos and Sphakteria.

Spartan agreement to the Peace of Nikias. Pylos was garrisoned, and the Messenians who settled at Naupaktos after the helot revolt at Ithome sent troops there, who used it as a base for carrying out raids in Spartan territory, aided by the fact that they spoke the same dialect as the Messenian helots (Thuc. 4.41).

The Athenian decree on coins, weights and measures

In the year 425 BC the Athenians imposed a monetary decree throughout their empire forbidding the minting of coinage in allied cities. Numismatic evidence indicates that continuous minting of local coins was taking place in the north Aegean mints of Abdera, Akanthos, Mende, Maroneia and Ainos through the 440s, 430s and into the 420s. The coinage decree can be set alongside the decree which reassessed Athenian tribute in 425/4 BC ($IG\,I^3$ 71: doc. 13.16). It was also imperialistic in tone, and reflected the hard-line attitude adopted by Kleon and his successors. Certainly the parodying of the coinage decree by Aristophanes in his play *Birds* suggests a date relatively close to the performance of this drama which was produced in 414 BC, although earlier scholars preferred to date the decree prior to 445 (Ar. *Birds* 1035–42: doc. 13.14). The inscription $IG\,I^3$ 90, probably dated to the 420s (its mason cut several other

460

decrees in the 420s), is a 'supplement' to the coinage decree, and may well have been passed within a few years of the original decree. Evidence of vase container types is also important: these seem to indicate that the new measures were not in use in the 440s and 430s, although this evidence needs further examination.

This decree, along with the reassessment of tribute, points to tighter Athenian control over the empire and a grander ideological vision of empire itself. Stricter assessment of tribute payment was now made. This was assisted by the fact that the coinage decree made tribute collection easier as all the allied states had to use Athenian silver coins. Now that allied cities were prohibited from minting their own coinage, they lost a crucial element of their identity as independent states, although Athenian coins were already in wide circulation throughout the empire as a result of Athenian trade. A single, shared coinage was an important way of stamping a unified identity on the empire and impressing its cities with the reality of Athenian control (IG I^3 1453: doc. 13.13). References in the decree to Athenian governors (archontes) in some of the allied cities show the extent of Athenian supervision over these states, but when no Athenian governors were present local officials were responsible for ensuring the decree's implementation. That the decree was to stay in force permanently was ensured by the provision that, if anyone at Athens proposed in future that it should be permissible to make use of or to lend foreign currency, he would be executed in Athens by the 'Eleven', the board responsible for carrying out such punishments.

The tribute in the Peloponnesian War

Perikles told the Athenians that they could rely on an annual income of 600 talents a year from the phoros of the allies. By 426 BC the war had been going on for six years, although whether Perikles had thought that it would last this long (and it was to continue for another two decades) is unclear. The number of decrees on tribute payment and the sophisticated and detailed procedures for collecting it show that finance was a major preoccupation of the Athenians, and punishments were in place for both allied states and Athenians responsible for tribute collection who failed to comply with the regulations, with specific schedules laid down for the procedures involved.

The appointment of tribute collectors in 426 BC

In this year, in a securely dated decree, Kleonymos successfully proposed to the Athenian assembly that the tribute collection be organised more effectively (IG I^3 68: doc. 13.15). He was persistently vilified by Aristophanes (*Wasps* 19–20, 592–3, *Acharnians* 88–9), and these attacks made before the public in drama, and his role in the tribute collection as evidenced by this decree, indicate that he was an important figure in Athenian politics. Like Kleon and others (doc. 13.18), he was clearly concerned to ensure that tribute payment was maximised, while the Athenian assembly must have been aware of the crucial significance which tribute played in the financing of the Athenian war effort. A relief depicting the jars and sacks in which the tribute was brought to Athens surmounts the inscription (Fig. 13.2).

All the allied states were to elect tribute collectors in their cities, who were responsible for the collection of all the tribute required of that state. Clearly, hitherto, the collections were organised in a piece-meal manner, and if some of the local citizens defaulted on taxes earmarked for the tribute the full amount was not collected. The tribute was paid at the Dionysia and twenty days later the hellenotamiai ('Greek treasurers', actually Athenian but

Figure 13.2 Inscriptiones Graecae I³ 68 (doc. 13.15) surmounted by an engraving showing the vessels in which tribute was brought to Athens. Athens Epigraphical Museum. Drawing by J. Etherington.

still known by this title from the early days of the Delian League) announced to the ekklesia the cities which had paid and those which had not, or not in full, so that action could be taken against those that had not made the full payment. Delegations of five men were sent out to those cities defaulting on their payment. The hellenotamiai placed the names of the defaulting cities on the notice-board in front of the shrine of the Eponymous Heroes in the agora.

There was to be a similar decree for the Samians and Therans, not regarding their tribute payment but concerning monies owed by these cities to Athens: presumably Samos was still paying off its war indemnity from 440 BC, and Thera that from its conquest by the Athenians in 430 BC (both cities would, of course, also be paying their tribute). An amendment to Kleonymos' original decree makes explicit the connection between tribute and war: the decree is to ensure 'that the Athenians may as well and as easily as possible carry on the war'. It also lays down that one of the strategoi sit with the epimeletai (superintendents) in cases involving a defaulting city. Athens was clearly ensuring that the allies would realise that it was prepared to use military force over the issue of tribute payment. In the amendment, any allied citizen could indict in court a fellow citizen who either tried to prevent the effectiveness of the decree or prevent the tribute being brought to Athens. The boule elected heralds and sent these to the allied cities to organise each city's election of men who would be responsible for collecting the tribute. These men had their names recorded in the council chamber (bouleuterion).

The reassessment of Athenian tribute, 425/4 BC

Kleonymos' decree was followed by a reassessment of tribute payments proposed by Thoudippos, 'as the tribute has become too little' (*IG* I³ 71: doc. 13.16). The reassessment was not a 'one-off' measure but from now on was to take place regularly every four years at the Great Panathenaia. Allied states were now required to bring a cow for sacrifice and a full suit of armour (probably for dedication to the goddess Athena) to the Great Panathenaia, which had truly become an imperial festival and a religious obligation for allied cities. These had to participate 'in the same way as colonists' (line 58): Athens was now the mother-city of all its allies, whether they were Ionians or Dorians. When the allied representatives attended they were informed of the new tribute assessments. A severe penalty, a fine of 10,000 drachmas, was meted out to the Athenian prytaneis if they did not ensure the process occurred correctly (other fines for them were also stipulated). It was the responsibility of the strategoi to ensure that the tribute was paid.

'Optimistic' is the only word that can be used to describe the amounts the Athenians calculated that they could collect: tribute payments were greatly increased, and the total seems to have come to 1460 talents. But while Thoudippos' assessment shows between 380 to 400 cities being assessed, the aparchai (tribute-quota lists) for the 430s BC never list more than 175 paying states. Many of the 'missing' names were small cities, such as Carian cities – ones known not to have paid tribute since the 440s. The aim of the comprehensive reassessment was that the increase from cities that paid regularly would have the desired effect of raising more tribute. The tribute quota list for 418/17 BC shows that about 1000 talents were collected in that year (*IG* I³ 287: 13.21) approximately two-thirds of the assessment expected under the provisions of Thoudippos' decree (*IG* I³ 71: 13.16).

Kleinias' decree on tribute payment, 420s BC

Further regulations were imposed to ensure that when the tribute arrived it comprised the correct amount and no sums had been siphoned off en route. Kleinias' decree arranged for special seals for the containers that held the tribute, and each city was to write on a tablet the amount of tribute it was sending to Athens and seal the tablet with its official seal. The tablet would then be opened and read out in the council at Athens when the tribute was paid. The treasurers (hellenotamiai) would then report to the assembly which cities had, or had not paid in full, and four men would be sent through the allied cities to give receipts for the tribute and demand the payment of any that was still outstanding. A 10,000 drachma fine was imposed on each of the prytaneis (as in *IG* I³ 71: doc. 13.16) if they failed to bring before the council any indictment concerning irregularities in tribute payment. The decree is not securely dated, but Thoudippos' decree made the bringing of a cow and panoply to the Great Panathenaia compulsory and Kleinias' decree reinforces this by providing penalties for failing to do so (lines 34, 41–3). It can therefore be argued that Kleinias' decree logically follows on from that of Thoudippos. Kleinias' decree was also passed after Kleonymos' tribute decree of 426 BC, as the method of collecting tribute in Kleinias' decree is more sophisticated than that prescribed by Kleonymos (*IG* I³ 34: doc. 13.17). Aristophanes mocked Kleon in his comedy *Knights* in 424 BC for his vigilance over the tribute payments, describing him as keeping 'a lookout for tribute as if it were tuna-fish' (Ar. *Knights*, 303–27, 1030–4, 1067–72: doc. 13.18), but the decrees proposed and passed by the people show that Aristophanes' mockery is unfair: Athens needed the tribute and without it the Athenians would have been unable to continue the war.

Athenian regulations for Chalkis, 424/3 BC

Athens' treatment of Mytilene, which Kleon saw as too lenient, was in a sense reflected in the arrangements it made in 424/3 BC with Chalkis on the nearby island of Euboea. The whole island rebelled in 446 BC, and the decree of 424/3 BC proposed by Diognetos refers to an earlier decree which presumably related to the earlier revolt. By the terms of Diognetos' decree, Athens guaranteed Chalkis important rights, while asserting Athenian control, and it seems probable that at this stage of the conflict in the Peloponnesian War Athens' treatment of allies that had previously rebelled was driven by arguments similar to those put forward by Diodotos concerning Mytilene: that it was in the Athenians' best interests to treat their allies firmly but leniently. In the case of Chalkis, the Athenian council and the (6000) jurors swore that they would not expel the inhabitants from their city, nor harm any individual citizen, without a trial at Athens. Chalkis for its part swore not to revolt and that it would help to defend and 'obey' the Athenian people. The Athenians, however, were holding Chalkidian hostages at Athens, and would not comply with Chalkis' request that they be returned, although they left the matter open for consideration at a later date. An amendment guaranteed the judicial independence of Chalkis, except in cases of 'exile, death or loss of civic rights' for which there was a right of appeal. Clearly this was a measure to protect pro-Athenians in case of internal strife within the city (*IG* I³ 40: doc. 13.19). In the previous year (425 BC), the Athenians had forced the city of Chios, which enjoyed special status as an ally, to tear down its new fortifications as the Athenians thought the inhabitants were planning a revolt. However, the city was able to secure guarantees from Athens that there would be no changes in the existing relationship with the Athenians (Thuc. 4.51). It is within this imperial context that the decree concerning Chalkis can be understood.

Athenian success and reverses in 425 BC

The Athenians kept up the pressure on the Peloponnesians with a daring attack on Corinth in 425 in which 212 Corinthians were killed (Thuc. 4.42–4). The Corcyraean democrats prevailed in their civil war with the aristocrats, with the aid of the Athenians (the fleet of Eurymedon and Sophocles which now continued on its way to Sicily: Thuc. 4.46–8) and Athens also made a successful expedition against Kythera, an island near Sparta off the Peloponnesian coast, garrisoning it to use as a base from which it lay waste to parts of the Peloponnesian coast (4.54–6). Athens also captured the island of Aegina, as the Spartan force there did not take part in its rebellion and executed all Aeginetan prisoners (4.57). The Athenian expedition to Sicily ended when the Sicilians made peace among themselves: back at Athens, two of the Athenian strategoi involved, Pythodoros and Sophocles, were exiled, and the third, Eurymedon, was fined. Athens at this time was also involved in a conflict with Megara: they had invaded their neighbour twice a year every year since the war began, and Megara was suffering both from this and raids from Megarian exiles at Pegai. A pro-Athenian party attempted to betray the city to the Athenians who seized the Long Walls and Nisaia, but the arrival of the Spartan general Brasidas, while on his way north to Thrace, prevented the Athenians from capturing Megara itself (4.66–74).

Athenian losses at Delion and Amhipolis

In 424 BC the Athenians, who were encouraged to campaign in the area by pro-Athenian Boeotians, were defeated at Delion in a battle which resulted in the deaths of 500 Boeotians and 1000 Athenians; Socrates served as a hoplite (Thuc. 4.89–101). In the same year, the Spartans sent Brasidas to Thrace, hoping that since Athens was attacking the Peloponnese they might be able to divert the Athenians' attention by threatening their possessions in Thrace, particularly as Athens' allies in the area were in a state of rebellion. Sparta was also alarmed at the possibility that the helots might revolt, and sent 700 of them with Brasidas to Thrace via a land march through Thessaly. It was at this time that the famous massacre of prominent helots occurred at Sparta (Thuc. 4.80.2–5: doc. 5.48). Brasidas then successfully attacked Amphipolis, Athens' colony on the river Strymon (Thuc. 5.11.1: doc. 2.7). Most of the population were non-Athenians and when the city was besieged by Brasidas, who captured many of the relatives of those inside and offered the besieged reasonable terms, the city accepted and the Athenians in the city were allowed to leave for nearby Eion. Thucydides the historian, as strategos, arrived too late with a fleet to save Amphipolis, but ensured that Eion did not fall into Brasidas' hands. This rankled with the Athenians far into the next century. The loss of Amphipolis was felt deeply at Athens, which relied on timber for ship-building, as well as tribute, from this region. Because of Brasidas' successes Athens' allies in the area became restive, and the Athenians sent garrisons as quickly as it could to the area, but was unable to recapture Amphipolis (which fell to Philip of Macedon in 357), while Brasidas succeeded in capturing Torone and Lekythos (Thuc. 4.102–16). Thucydides was exiled for his failure to save Amphipolis and his history deteriorates from this point as he no longer had first-hand access to events in Athens until he returned to the city twenty years later.

The death of Brasidas and Kleon

An armistice was made in 423 BC between Athens and Sparta (Thuc. 4.117–18), which was a prelude to the Peace of Nikias in 421 BC. Hostilities recommenced, however, in 422 BC when the Athenians determined to recapture Amphipolis. Kleon went north, retaking Torone despite the presence of a Spartan garrison, and the women and children were enslaved, while the men, together with the Spartans, were sent back to Athens as prisoners. They were later released under the terms of the peace of Nikias in 421 BC. Kleon and Brasidas met in battle outside Amphipolis, where both were killed: Thucydides described Kleon as running away from the battle and being killed in flight, but this was probably coloured by his hostility: he had after all done no better in the region himself (Thuc. 5.1–12). Both sides now wanted peace. The Athenians had been defeated at Delion and Amphipolis and were worried about revolts among their allies. For Sparta the war had gone on much longer than they had envisaged, its territory was being raided from Pylos and Kythera, the helots were deserting, and the thirty-year peace with Argos was about to come to an end. Sparta was aware that it could not fight both Argos and Athens simultaneously, and – most importantly – it wanted the return of the prisoners from Pylos (Thuc. 5.14).

Kleon as Perikles

According to Thucydides, Brasidas and Kleon were the most opposed to peace, Brasidas because war brought him 'success and honour', Kleon because 'in peace time his villainy would be more obvious' (Thuc. 5.16.1: doc. 13.20). Perikles, according to Thucydides, was able to keep the assembly under control, and Kleon was very much Perikles' successor. Although he did not become a strategos until towards the end of his career, he pursued the same Periklean vision of Athenian imperialism, keeping the allies under firm Athenian control and refusing to negotiate with the Spartans. Under Perikles' immediate successors, such as Kleon, Athens fared extremely well against Sparta. It was only the events of 415 BC and the military and political ambitions of Alkibiades that set Athens on the path to defeat. Sparta, for its part, achieved notable successes under Archidamos and Brasidas, but the policy of invading Attica was a failure.

The end of the Archidamian War, 421 BC

Nikias at Athens and King Pleistoanax of Sparta were the foremost proponents of peace, and in 421 Athens and Sparta made a peace-treaty, known by scholars as the 'Peace of Nikias'. According to Thucydides, Nikias wished to 'rest on his laurels' and finish his career on a high note, although he was also concerned to put an end to the troubles of his fellow citizens. Pleistoanax, son of the regent Pausanias, was deposed following an accusation of being bribed to retreat from the invasion of Attica in 446 BC, but was recalled in 428 after an oracle from Delphi. There were of course accusations that the Pythia had been bribed to ensure his recall and his enemies blamed him for Spartan reverses in the war, so peace was also in his interests. Some of Sparta's allies were unhappy at the terms of the treaty and did not accept it, including the Boeotians, Corinthians, Eleians and Megarians. The Spartans, however, were motivated by the fact that Argos refused to renew its treaty with Sparta, and therefore agreed to the terms which laid down that Sparta and Athens would be allies for fifty years, with mutual provisions that they come to each other's aid if their territory were invaded. Each side was to return to the other any of its territory which was captured, but this in fact did not occur and was one reason why the peace failed. The Spartan prisoners whom the Athenians captured at Sphakteria were returned (Thuc. 5.23–4), and significantly the very first clause of the peace terms guaranteed access to panhellenic sanctuaries throughout Greece (Thuc. 5.18.1–3: doc. 3.26). Thucydides, however, noted that while both sides did not invade each other's territory, the war continued in other theatres (5.26), and this is one of the reasons why he treated the conflict between 431 and 404 as one single war rather than a series of wars interrupted by the peace of 421 BC.

Alliances with Argos

After they rejected the Fifty Year Peace of 421 BC, the Corinthians left Sparta and sent ambassadors to Argos, complaining that by signing this truce Sparta was enslaving Greece through allying themselves with Athens. They suggested that the Argives invite independent states, except for Athens and Sparta, to join in a defensive alliance. Mantineia, a democracy which had conquered most of Arkadia while Sparta was preoccupied with the Peloponnesian War, left the Peloponnesian League and joined Argos, worried that Sparta would intervene in its affairs. This caused the other Peloponnesian states to consider the benefits of an alliance with Argos. Like the Corinthians they suspected that Sparta was planning to dominate them with Athens' connivance, and Elis, the Corinthians and the Chalcidians in Thrace joined the Argive alliance, while Boeotia and Megara remained allied with Sparta as they felt that Sparta had not intervened in their affairs and they had a good working relationship with Sparta's government. A Spartan proposal that Boeotia join the Argive alliance, and that

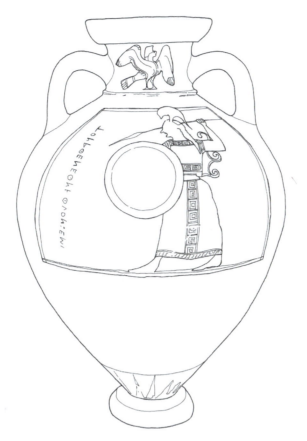

Figure 13.3 The Burgon amphora from the British Museum, dated to c. 565 BC, depicts Athena Promachos with her spear and aegis and her owl. The inscription reads 'One of the prizes from
Athens'. Panathenaic amphorai, which were 60–70 cm in height, were filled with olive oil
from the sacred grove of Athena, and awarded as prizes at the Panathenaic games. They
depicted on one side Athena Promachos and on the other the competition in which the victory had been gained. Drawing by J. Etherington.

the new coalition in its entirety then be brought within Sparta's sphere of influence, came to
nothing. Argos, however, as a result began to feel that the alliance was in danger of collapsing, and sent an embassy to Sparta to seek a renewal of their treaty (Thuc. 5.27–42).

   There was a party at Athens that was opposed to the peace. Alkibiades was particularly
prominent among them and at this point he sent a personal message to the Argives in order
to promote the idea of an Athenian–Argive alliance. According to Thucydides he was jealous
that the peace had been negotiated through Nikias and that he was left out of the discussions. The Argives, therefore, put no more effort into renewing their treaty with Sparta, but
began considering Athens as a possible ally in the event of war against Sparta: Athens was
a long-time friend, a sister democracy and had a large navy (Thuc. 5.44). Elis, Mantineia
and Sparta in their turn all sent representatives to Athens. Spartan ambassadors came with
full powers to make decisions in regard to the disputes between Athens and Sparta over the

exchange of conquered territories under the terms of their alliance. However, by secretly promising them the return of Pylos, Alkibiades tricked them into denying in a meeting of the Athenian assembly that they came with full powers. This caused uproar among the Athenian citizens, who felt that there was no point in discussion unless the Spartans were empowered to make decisions. Next day the assembly met again and Nikias strove to ensure that the peace with Sparta was continued as it was in Athens' best interests. Despite this, Elis, Mantineia, Argos and Athens signed a treaty, although Corinth, despite remaining Argos' ally, did not (Thuc. 5.45–8).

The battle of Mantineia in 418 BC

Events in the Peloponnese led to a conflict between Sparta and Athens and their allies at the battle of Mantineia in 418 BC, when a party at Tegea wanted to turn Mantineia over to the Athenians. Sparta was warned of this by the pro-Spartans in the city. Under King Agis the Spartans marched with a large force to Tegea, then turned and attacked Mantineia. The Spartans and Tegeates faced the Argives, Athenians, Mantineians and Arkadians, and the Mantineians on the right wing broke through the Spartan line. Under Agis, however, the Spartan centre was more successful and routed the Argives and Athenians. The Athenians were rescued by their cavalry, but lost both their generals in battle and the result was a conclusive victory for the Spartans (Thuc. 5.66–82). Thucydides makes no comment on the actual repercussions of the battle, beyond a comment that this was one of the largest engagements fought in the war. Mantineia went back to an alliance with Sparta and surrendered all those areas of Arkadia it had conquered. A pro-Spartan faction took control of Argos, but the city was soon back in democratic hands and remained allied with the Athenians. The battle showed that Sparta was still the most important power in the Peloponnese, although Alkibiades' plan of establishing a large alliance to offset Sparta's power forced it to risk its primacy at Mantineia. Corinth, however, was now back in the Spartan fold, and the Argives were unable to demonstrate that they could provide a viable alternative for leadership in the Peloponnese.

Melos enslaved in 416 BC

Thucydides does not explain why in 416 BC the Athenians made an expedition, with thirty ships of their own and others from Chios and Lesbos, against the island of Melos which claimed to be a colony of Sparta. It had previously refused to join the Athenian alliance, its territory was subject to Athenian raids, and it was now the only island in the Aegean apart from Thera which was not in Athenian hands. The Athenians began their attempt to control the island in 416 BC by negotiating with the council of Melos, which refused to allow the Athenian envoys to address the people. Thucydides records the discussion, which is now called the 'Melian Dialogue', in which the Athenians and Melians argued over Athens' right to force Melos into its alliance. Melos hoped for Spartan assistance but this was not forthcoming, and the Athenians and their allies built a wall around the city and besieged it (Thuc. 5.84–116). Treachery from within led the Melians to surrender and all the men of military age were put to death, and the women and children sold into slavery (Thuc. 5.116.2–4: doc. 5.4). When in 405 BC the fall of Athens to the Spartans was inevitable, this particular atrocity was remembered, and the Athenians feared that they would share the fate they had meted out to Melos (Xen. *Hellenika* 2.2.3–4: doc. 5.7).

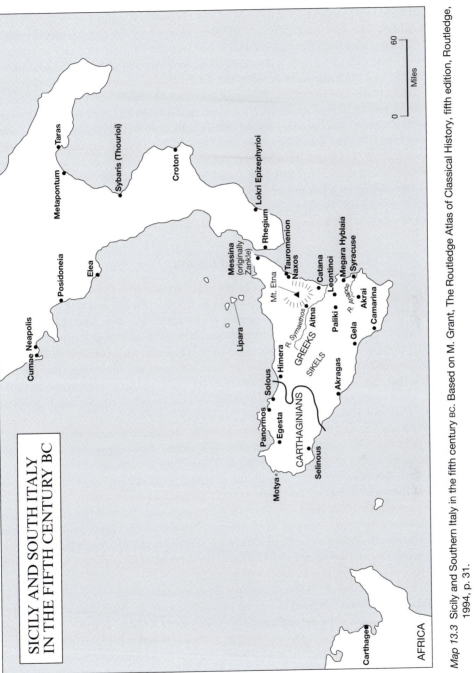

SICILY AND SOUTH ITALY
IN THE FIFTH CENTURY BC

Taras

Metapontum

Sybaris (Thourioi)

Croton

Posidoneia

Elea

Lokri Epizephyrioi

Cumae Neapolis

Rhegium

Lipara

Messina (originally Zankle)

Tauromenion

Naxos

Mt. Etna

Catana

R. Symaethos

Leontinoi

GREEKS

Aitna

Megara Hyblaia

Paliki

Syracuse

R. Anapos

SIKELS

Akrai

Gela

Camarina

Himera

Akragas

Solous

Panormos

Egesta

CARTHAGINIANS

Motya

Selinous

AFRICA

Carthage

0   60

Miles

Map 13.3 Sicily and Southern Italy in the fifth century BC. Based on M. Grant, The Routledge Atlas of Classical History, fifth edition, Routledge, 1994, p. 31.

The Sicilian Expedition and its aftermath

Books 6 and 7 of Thucydides concern the Athenian expedition against Sicily, which began in 415 and ended with disaster for Athens in 413 BC. It played a major role in the eventual defeat of Athens. The east coast of Sicily had been colonised by the Greeks, and the initial chapters of Thucydides Book 6 are an invaluable source on how the Greeks came to establish cities on the island (Thuc. 6.3.1–5.3: doc. 2.12). The western coast of Sicily was held by the Carthaginians, and the indigenous peoples, the Sikels, largely controlled the interior, with the Greek cities frequently engaged in fighting each other, the Sikels and the Carthaginians. Athens had shown an interest in the area for some time, and in 427–424 BC sent out expeditions with a view to gaining allies on the island, although a panhellenic feeling among the Sicilian Greeks meant that these plans came to nothing, despite Athens alliances with Rhegium in Italy (*IG* I³ 53: doc. 12.32) and initial success in winning over some of the cities. In 415 BC the Athenians decided that they would set out to conquer the island, not realising 'that they were taking on a war not much less in scope than that against the Peloponnesians' (Thuc. 6.1.1: doc. 13.23). Perikles' advice not to attempt to expand the empire while the war with the Spartans was still in progress had been quite forgotten.

Athens and Egesta

Athens made an alliance with Egesta in Sicily in 418/17 BC (probably a renewal of an alliance made in 427/6 BC when Laches as strategos was in Sicily), one of many in a long series of such alliances (*IG* I³ 11: doc. 13.22). Athens' interest in the island was clear, and these alliances and the campaigns of the 420s presumably gave the Athenians some awareness of the size of Sicily and the power and prosperity of the cities there. However, their criticism of the limited success of the generals sent there at the time perhaps indicates that Thucydides had grounds for arguing that the Athenians were not aware of the scale and size of the island or of the enormity of the enterprise they were undertaking with the launch of the Sicilian Expedition in 415 BC (Thuc. 6.1.1: doc. 13.23).

Egesta was the key to Athens' involvement in Sicily. Because it was engaged in war with Selinous, a Dorian city which had the support of Syracuse, Egesta appealed to Athens for assistance, in the winter of 416/15 according to Thucydides' chronology. Its envoys at Athens argued for Athenian intervention, with the tempting proposal that Egesta would pay for the costs of the war. Moreover they argued that Syracuse had driven out the population of Leontinoi, an Athenian ally from the time when Laches was in Sicily in the 420s, and that if Athens allowed Syracuse to defeat all of Athens' allies the whole island would soon be in Syracusan hands. An Athenian embassy which was sent to check on Egesta's financial situation was, according to Thucydides, deceived as to the amount of silver the city had available (Thuc. 6.6, 8, 46).

In 415, with Alkibiades as its foremost proponent and financed by sixty talents of silver from Egesta, the Athenians decided to send an expedition to Sicily. Alkibiades was motivated by ambition; he wanted to be the conqueror of Sicily – and Carthage as well – and opposed Nikias when he attacked him in the assembly over the proposed expedition. At that assembly meeting the Athenians voted to send a force of sixty ships, with Alkibiades, Nikias and Lamachos in command, in order to assist Egesta, re-establish Leontinoi, and generally to act to secure Athenian interests on the island (Thuc. 6.8).

Nikias attempts to dissuade the Athenians

Just a mere five days later, the assembly met again to make further arrangements for the campaign. Nikias, who thought that the expedition to Sicily was an error of judgement, took this opportunity to reopen the debate and ask whether it really was a good idea for the Athenians to sail against Sicily at all at this juncture. He pointed to the fact that Athens was leaving many enemies behind in Greece. The treaty with Sparta was now, following Mantineia, merely nominal – a treaty in name only – and these enemies would support Syracuse in its struggle against Athens. Moreover, the Athenians were ill advised to aim at a new empire when their existing one was far from secure: a clear echo of Perikles' advice from the beginning of the war. He argued that the increases in manpower and resources that they were seeing, now that Athens had had a few years to recover from the plague and the war, should be spent on their enemies in Greece and not in Sicily. He accused Alkibiades of being motivated purely by personal considerations and of wanting to make money from the war to pay for his expensive lifestyle (cf. Thuc. 6.1.1, 15.2–4: doc. 13.23).

Some speakers supported Nikias, but the majority were in favour of going to war, and when Alkibiades rose to speak it was to defend his reputation, reminding the Athenians that he was responsible for bringing together the coalition at Mantineia which forced the Spartans to risk everything in one battle, and to argue for an aggressive imperialistic policy (Thuc. 6.8–18). Among other points he stated that he spent his wealth to benefit the city, as when he entered seven chariot teams at the Olympic Games (in 420 BC), winning first, second and fourth places, thus giving the Greeks in general the impression that Athens was even greater than it actually was (Plut. *Alkibiades* 11.1–12.1: doc. 3.27). As the Athenians were more enthusiastic than ever in favour of the war, Nikias accepted the inevitable, but made a speech arguing that if the Athenians did go to Sicily they would be up against considerable forces and that they should therefore take a large force of hoplites, along with an even greater fleet of 100 triremes. In this he was, according to Thucydides, hoping to dissuade the Athenians by the enormity of the forces involved, but if so he did not succeed and the Athenians voted even more eagerly for the expedition to Sicily (Thuc. 6.19–26). Athens had regained its prosperity after the devastating effects of the plague and some years of relative peace. Nikias succeeded, in fact, in increasing the size of the Athenian commitment and this force, later augmented by reinforcements, eventually meant that by the time Athens was defeated in 413 BC, over half its fleet had been committed and destroyed.

The mutilation of the Hermai in 415 BC

It was at this point that Athens was plunged into a religious crisis when it was discovered that the stone hermai throughout Athens had been mutilated: their phalloi had been smashed off overnight. This was considered to be a bad omen and also 'part of a revolutionary conspiracy to overthrow the democracy' (Thuc. 6.27.3: doc. 13.24). While this was investigated, allegations were also made that the Eleusinian Mysteries had been celebrated in private houses, with Alkibiades named as one of those involved (Andoc. 1 *On the Mysteries* 11–12: doc. 3.34). His opponents made a great deal of the whole affair, but it was decided that he should still sail with the expedition (Thuc. 6.27.1–28.2: doc. 13.24).

The Athenian armada sails

In mid-summer 415 BC a huge Athenian armada set forth and all of Athens turned out to see it off: prayers were said and libations poured from vessels of gold and silver, a hymn was sung and the ships then raced each other as far as Aegina (Thuc. 6.32). Making its way to Corcyra, and joined by various allies, it crossed over to Italy. This force consisted of 100 Athenian triremes, 60 for naval battles and 40 for transport, and 34 allied triremes, with 5100 hoplites, 1500 of them Athenians, and 700 thetes serving as marines, supported by 1180 bowmen and slingers, and a horse-transport with 30 cavalry. At the time it was the largest force ever sent out by a Greek city (Thuc. 6.30, 6.43).

At Syracuse, news of the expedition arrived and a debate took place, with some speakers even denying that any expedition was on its way. Hermokrates, who as Thucydides noted was a man of extraordinary intelligence and courage, argued that preparations be made, and, while the pro-Athenian speaker Athenagoras spoke on Athens' behalf, an unnamed Syracusan general cut short debate by arguing that preparations against the invasion should go ahead (Thuc. 6.41). Despite this, there is very little to indicate that the Syracusans did in fact take any measures for their defence until 414 BC.

The lack of Athenian strategy

Immediately upon the expedition's arrival in Sicily, the lack of any overall Athenian strategy became clear. The Athenians' motive for sailing to Sicily was to aid Egesta against Selinous, but the report was brought back by three Athenian triremes sent to Egesta that it did not, after all, have the money to pay for all the expenses of the war and that the Athenians had been duped in this financial aspect. Nikias' plan was therefore to see whether the conflict between Egesta and Selinous could be resolved, to sail along the coast making alliances, to make a show of strength, and then to return home.

Alkibiades disagreed: to go home without any conquests after having set sail with such a massive force would be a disgrace, and they should win over those cities, starting with Messina, which could serve as a base for the war in Sicily. Lamachos in his turn argued that they should go directly to Syracuse, the most powerful city, and attack it before it was prepared. As there was no agreement, Lamachos eventually supported Alkibades' plan (Thuc. 6.46, 6.49). In fact, it was not until the first (abortive) attack on Syracuse in 414 BC that the Syracusans built new fortifications and became proactive in their own defence, and Lamachos' plan may well have worked in 415 BC, although it did not later, as the element of surprise had been lost.

Alkibiades had no luck with Messina, although the Athenians did manage to make Catana their base, but at this point one of the special state triremes, the Salaminia, arrived to return Alkibiades to Athens to stand trial for the mutilation of the hermai and profanation of the Mysteries. A number of other suspected participants had been arrested and executed. He followed the state trireme in his own ship, but absconded at Thourioi, and eventually reached Sparta where he stirred up trouble against the Athenians. A sentence of death was passed at Athens against him and those with him (Thuc. 6.60–1).

A year passed in Sicily with very little to show for it. Alkibiades' departure meant that his strategy was abandoned and that of Lamachos adopted, and the Athenians spent the winter preparing to attack Syracuse. Lamachos and Nikias devised a successful stratagem to lure the Syracusans north to Catana, and when they heard that the Syracusans were on their way there the Athenians sailed south to Syracuse with their entire army, made their way into Syracuse's great harbour, and set up a stockade. Here they won a land battle, but the Syracusan cavalry returned and prevented the Athenians from making anything of their victory. The Athenians retired back to Catana, on the grounds that as it was winter they did not think their foothold at Syracuse a suitable base. This whole episode is a little hard to understand, in that after establishing a 'beachhead' in Syracuse the Athenians then abandoned it, and wintered at Sicilian Naxos and Catana (Thuc. 6.63–72).

Hermokrates and Syracuse

At Syracuse Hermokrates successfully persuaded the Syracusans to set their house in order and three generals (including himself) were elected with wide military powers, with ambassadors sent to Corinth and Sparta to request assistance. A new wall was built onto Syracuse's existing city walls, running along the ground that overlooked Epipolai ('the heights'), taking in the temple of Apollo Temenites, and forts were constructed at both the Olympieion and Megara, so that it would be harder to surround their city by a blockading wall if they were defeated; stakes were also driven into the sea at possible landing places (Thuc. 6.72–5). The Athenians made overtures to the city of Kamarina, which had made an alliance with the Athenians when Laches was in Sicily. The Syracusans also sent ambassadors to Kamarina, where Hermokrates attacked the Athenians who in turn, in a speech delivered by the Athenian Euphemos, justified their position. Kamarina remained neutral as a result of the pressure from both sides, but the speeches as recorded by Thucydides serve to highlight Athens' imperialism and the need for Sicily to unite against it (Hermokrates' speech) and the Athenians' defence of their right to have an empire and of their actions in Sicily (Euphemos' speech, whose name, incidentally, means 'well-spoken': Thuc. 6.73–88).

Alkibiades at Sparta

Athens sent representatives to Carthage and Eretria (on Euboea, the mother-city of a number of Sicilian cities) to see if any assistance would be forthcoming from them, for the first time turning their attention to the other powers in the region. Syracusan delegates received a warm welcome at Corinth and the Corinthians voted that they should receive all possible assistance that Corinth could give (Thuc. 6.88). The Syracusans then went to Sparta, to which the Corinthians also sent ambassadors. Alkibiades was now resident in Sparta (where he was said to have seduced and made pregnant queen Timaia, king Agis' wife: doc. 4.24), and made a speech in which he sketched the Athenians' ambition to conquer Sicily, the Greeks in Italy, and Carthage and its entire empire (Thuc. 6.89–92). Athens would then be powerful enough to attack the Peloponnese with all the forces gained from the conquest of the west and a far greater navy. Obviously this was calculated to rouse the Spartans and to stir them to greater military efforts. He then suggested ways of defeating Athens, including the dispatch of a force to Sicily and the fortification of Dekeleia in Attica, to harm Athens by depriving it of the silver mines at Laureion and the tribute, which would be reduced as its allies would have less fear of Athens as a result of this move. The Spartans were in fact already considering these ideas, but Alkibiades helped to persuade them to put them into effect (Thuc. 6.93). His ideas were not original and he was not a decisive influence: his arguments simply confirmed the Spartans' existing intentions.

The Athenians at Syracuse

Athenian cavalry reinforcements arrived in Sicily as requested by the generals, and in summer 414 BC, after some campaigning in the spring, the Athenian forces sailed from Catana, landed in Syracusan territory at Leon north of the city, marched straight for Epipolai, and defeated a Syracusan force hastily sent against them. The next day the Athenians marched to the city of Syracuse itself, but no force was sent out to meet them. They built a fort at Labdalon on Epipolai and then another fort there known as 'The Circle', and after winning another skirmish against the Syracusans began constructing a wall to reach from the Great Harbour to Trogilos on the opposite northern coast. The Syracusans attempted to obstruct the Athenian wall from the Circle down to the Great Harbour by building a counter-wall at right angles from their city wall to interrupt the Athenian construction. The Syracusan counter-wall was destroyed by the Athenians, and the Syracusans began a second wall, around which another engagement took place, in which the Athenians were victorious, but Lamachos was killed. The Circle fort was attacked, but Nikias, who was lying there sick from a kidney illness, saved the situation, and at this point the Athenian fleet sailed into the Great Harbour (Thuc. 6.99–103). It looked as if the encirclement of Syracuse would continue.

Gylippos

In response to the Syracusan appeal for help, the Spartans sent no actual troops, but instead sent Gylippos, who was a mothax (that is, not a 'pure' Spartiate). He was either the child of a disenfranchised Spartan (who could not, for example, afford the contributions to the mess), or his mother may have been a helot. His talents proved remarkable, and his ability to rally the Syracusans and provide leadership against the Athenians were major contributing factors in the eventual Syracusan victory in 413 BC. He arrived from Sparta, energetic and determined, with Corinthian triremes, but fearing that Syracuse was already lost sailed first to Italy, although he was soon back in Sicily to galvanise the Syracusans and their allies (Thuc. 6.104). Nikias fortified Plemmyrion, a promontory on the southern side of the Great Harbour, as a convenient base closer to the Great Harbour which allowed for quicker action against the enemy fleet if it moved. For some reason, however, while Nikias had commenced the fortification wall from the Circle to Trogilos he had not yet completed it, so Syracuse was not enveloped in an Athenian besieging wall. Gylippos was defeated in one battle but not a second, and the Syracusan counter-wall proceeded, cutting across the Athenians' construction (and even managing to use some of the stones which the Athenians laid for their own wall), and so putting an end to the Athenians' chance of encircling Syracuse (Thuc. 7.1–8). Nikias, seeing the situation deteriorate, with the Syracusans attracting reinforcements, wrote to Athens requesting to be relieved of the command and asking for a further naval force. The Athenians would not let him resign his command, but sent two generals, Eurymedon and Demosthenes (known for his success at Pylos and his general energy), to assist him, while a further 82 ships and 5000 hoplites joined the original force (Thuc. 7.7–17, 7.42). The Athenians had now committed a large proportion of their fleet to the Sicilian war.

Gylippos meanwhile gathered reinforcements from throughout Sicily, and encouraged them to consider seriously the prospect that Athens could be defeated at sea, especially as the Athenian encircling wall had been interrupted and Syracuse could not now be besieged by land. The Syracusans launched their ships, and although defeated, managed to capture the fort at Plemmyrion while the Athenians were distracted. This caused difficulties for the

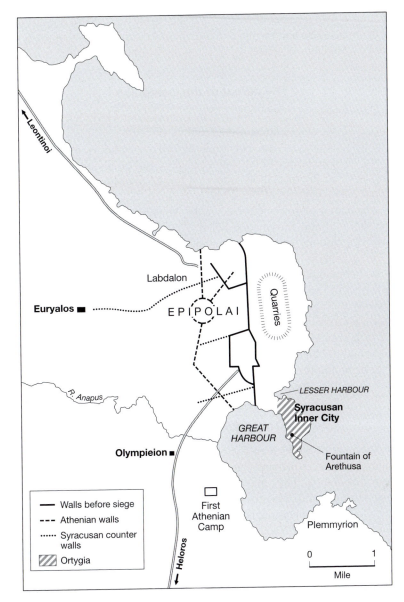

Map 13.4 The siege of Syracuse 415–413 BC. The construction of the Athenian siege walls progressed to the north of the city but were intercepted by the Syracusan counterwall. Based on M. Grant, The *Routledge Atlas of Classical History*, fifth edition, Routledge, 1994, p. 30.

Athenians as they were using the area as a supply depot and lost a great deal of foodstuffs and equipment (Thuc. 7.24). Syracuse launched another naval attack, this time successfully (Thuc. 7. 36–41), and a major defeat occurred when Demosthenes, attempting to rectify the situation, attacked via Epipolai with great loss of Athenian life (Thuc. 7.42–4). As a consequence, realising that the campaign was doomed, Demosthenes suggested withdrawing the entire force from Sicily, returning to Athens and confronting those building the fortification at Dekeleia in their own territory of Attica (7.47). The army was short of supplies and demoralised, and the Syracusans had the upper hand. Sparta's contribution to the war – Gylippos – had proved devastatingly effective.

The defeat of the expedition

Nikias, however, was waiting for a betrayal by traitors from within Syracuse (which never came; Thuc. 7.47–9), and sickness spread among the Athenian forces while the enemy forces continued to increase. Nikias eventually agreed to a withdrawal, but a speedy retreat was prevented when an eclipse of the moon occurred and his diviners advised him to wait 'thrice nine days', an interpretation supported by the majority of the Athenians (Thuc. 7.50.3–4: doc. 3.24). Because of the delay in escaping, a great battle took place in the harbour in which after a protracted struggle the Athenians, who fought tenaciously, were nevertheless defeated and Eurymedon killed (7.50–71). Thucydides provides a detailed and dramatic description, which must be based on the accounts of participants and eyewitnesses. The Athenians lost their fleet and began a retreat by land, with two contingents led by Demosthenes and Nikias, but both were forced to surrender. They were executed against the wishes of Gylippos and Hermokrates, and Thucydides writes a lengthy encomium for Nikias (but neglects Demosthenes: presumably because of his close connections with Kleon earlier in his career). Seven thousand captives were kept in the stone quarries at Syracuse in horrendous conditions. After ten weeks many were sold into slavery, but the Athenians and the Sicilian and Italian Greeks who fought on the Athenian side were kept there for eight months, with many dying of exposure, hunger and sickness during this period (Thuc. 7.87.1–6: doc. 13.26).

Thucydides' assessment

Thucydides' account of the Sicilian Expedition has often been compared to the plot of a Greek tragedy, with the Athenians convicted of hubris for the part that they played and meeting their just deserts. They may perhaps have been foolhardy in setting out on the expedition and had no right to be so confident. However, defeat at the hands of the Syracusans was not a foregone conclusion, for Athens possessed a large navy and land forces. One of the major factors was that Nikias lost the initiative by failing to complete the siege wall, and the Athenians, if they were going to attack Syracuse, should have done so immediately in 415 BC, rather than frittering away their time and resources with very little to show for it. Alkibiades' policy was a clear failure and Nikias was unwell at crucial moments and perhaps not up to the task. The arrival of Gylippos inspired the Syracusans to resistance and they were eventually able to call on many allies. The Athenian failure to surround Syracuse with a wall, the deteriorating supply situation and spreading sickness were major elements in their defeat. In addition, the whole expedition was planned haphazardly, with a mighty armada sailing off with very little direction, disagreement among the strategoi, and no overall campaign strategy. The Athenians suffered enormous losses and Thucydides saw it as the greatest military action of the war and of all Greek history: 'as the saying goes it was total ruin, with army, fleet and everything entirely destroyed and few of the many returning home' (Thuc. 7.87.6: doc. 13.26).

The fortification of Dekeleia in 413 BC

Under the command of King Agis in 413 the Spartans invaded Attica earlier in the campaign season than they had ever done before, and proceeded to fortify Dekeleia at about the time that Demosthenes was sent to Sicily to assist Nikias. The Corinthians in 432 BC had mentioned the possibility of establishing fortresses in Attica (Thuc. 1.122), and Alkibiades as noted urged the Spartans to carry out their plan to do so. Dekeleia in northern Attica was close to Euboea, which was important for Athens as it had moved many of its flocks there because of the war. Now instead of supplies from Euboea coming to Oropos and through Dekeleia, they had to be transported by sea around the cape at Sounion. Dekeleia was a mere 22 kilometres from Athens, from where it was clearly visible, and the Spartans could and did ravage the rich central plain of Attica from this base, which they occupied permanently. Thucydides viewed the occupation as one of the main reasons for a lessening of Athenian power, as all the flocks from the area were lost, and it was constantly raided, while land that was in use in between the previous Spartan invasions was now subject to regular attack (Thuc. 7.19.1–2, 27.3–4: doc. 13.25).

Athenian cavalry was employed continuously in Attica against the Spartans. This had debilitating effects on the horses, through their being lamed, or wounded by the enemy (Thuc. 7.27). But despite this, the effect of the permanent Spartan presence in Attica was limited in one major sense: Agis, in 410 BC, saw many grain ships sailing into the Piraeus and commented that there was no point wasting time denying the Athenians access to their land if grain was coming in by sea (Xen. *Hellenika* 1.1.35). In fact Lysander in 405, prior to the defeat of the Athenians at Aigospotamoi, sailed to the Hellespont to prevent grain ships sailing to Athens, and planned to bring the war to an end by starving Athens into submission. Another major effect of the occupation of Dekeleia was that 20,000 slaves, mostly skilled workmen, deserted from Attica (although how Thucydides arrived at this number is difficult to say; Thuc. 7.27.5: doc. 5.25). Falling into Spartan and Theban hands, they were then immediately resold into slavery. Despite Alkibiades' opinion that the flow of silver from Laureion in the south of Attica would be interrupted by the fortification of Dekeleia, this does not seem to have happened. The slaves who deserted as a result of the occupation were 'skilled', and it is unclear what effects this had on silver production, in which presumably most of the slaves were unskilled.

When news reached Athens of the Sicilian disaster, the result was shock, disbelief, and then an attempt to find others to bear the blame. Thucydides aptly sums up the reactions of the Athenians to the incredible news that the huge force sent to Sicily had not only achieved nothing but been completely annihilated. Athens realised that it was in very real danger and took some immediate steps to secure its situation. The democracy proved very resilient and organised the construction of a new fleet, a close watch was kept on Euboea and the other allies, and a body of 'preliminary advisors', the probouloi, was appointed. According to Thucydides, as news spread throughout the Greek world, the Greeks turned against Athens and their allies looked for an opportunity to revolt (Thuc. 8.1.1–2.2: doc. 13.27), although those who thought this was the end of Athens were mistaken. Chios revolted in 412 causing Athens to fear for the loyalty of the other allies but (perhaps surprisingly) many allies remained loyal: Chios was besieged. It was the revolt of Euboea in the following year that particularly worried Athens.

The Four Hundred take over Athens in 411 BC

Athens may well have survived, but a new threat was looming. Alkibiades had told the Athenians in 415 BC not to concern themselves about the Persians, as their forefathers in the past fought them and their fellow Greeks simultaneously (Thuc. 6.17). However, while the Persians had no intention of becoming militarily involved in the situation, they were prepared to use their gold to undermine Athens. Darius II was king of Persia, but it was his satraps, Pharnabazos in Dascylium and Tissaphernes at Sardis, who dealt with the Greeks. The Spartans and their allies made an agreement in 411 with the Persian king and Tissaphernes, recognising Persian control over all the cities possessed by Darius II, as well as those that had been under the control of his forefathers (that is, the Greek cities of Asia Minor and the islands freed by the Athenians and their allies in 479 BC and afterwards: Thuc. 8.37). Alkibiades, however, was at the court of Tissaphernes after losing favour at Sparta (his alleged indiscretion with Agis' wife is a possible factor here), and briefed him on Greek affairs, criticising the Spartans but also advising Tissaphernes not to give aid which would allow either side to prevail over the other, as this was not in the interests of the Persians (8.45).

Alkibiades also advised the leaders of the Athenian fleet, which was at Samos, that Tissaphernes would give them his friendship if their constitution was less democratic. Peisander, who was with the fleet, set sail from Samos with the support of its leaders, and stopped at various allied states along the way, including Thasos, installing non-democratic regimes. Thasos revolted from Athens two months later, seeing no point in remaining as Athens' ally and paying tribute. Peisander went to Athens and argued to the assembly that the Persian king would be their ally and that they could defeat the Peloponnesians if they recalled Alkibiades and changed the constitution. There was a great deal of opposition to this political proposal, and the families in charge of the Eleusinian Mysteries were vehemently opposed to the recall of Alkibiades. They were doubtless encouraged by Kallias, the dadouchos (torch-bearer) at the Mysteries, and Alkibiades' brother-in-law. Peisander gained the support of the hetaireiai (political clubs) in Athens, and the democracy was abolished, along with one of its main features, payment for political office. An oligarchic council of Four Hundred was set up, and it was proposed that 5000 citizens, those who were 'most capable of serving the state physically and financially' would take over the administration. But the Five Thousand were chosen only in name and the Four Hundred ran the state ([Arist.] *Ath. Pol. a* 29.5–30.2, 31.1, 32.3: doc. 13.28). Alkibiades was not involved in the overthrow of the democracy, as he was not trusted by the oligarchs. At Athens these were chiefly led by Peisander, Phrynichos, Theramenes, Aristarchos and Antiphon (Thuc. 8.45–97), aided in particular by 120 'Hellenic youths' who did any 'dirty work' that needed doing (Thuc. 8.69).

The rowers in the fleet at Samos, however, were not present at the ekklesia meeting in Athens, which abolished both itself and the democracy. Two individuals, Thrasyboulos and Thrasyllos, led the democrats in the fleet, and convinced it to stay at Samos and make sure the democracy on that island was preserved, and to face off the enemy fleet. This was despite the news brought to them that the oligarchy of the Four Hundred was engaging in violence against Athenian citizens, who were being executed, imprisoned and exiled (Thuc. 8.70, 74). Thrasyboulos persuaded the fleet to recall Alkibiades and he was elected as one of the generals. The Four Hundred, however, were not prosecuting the war but making peace overtures, with Phrynichos and Antiphon sent on an embassy to Sparta to make peace on any terms which were reasonably acceptable (Thuc. 8.71, 8.90). The Four Hundred also began fortifying Eetioneia, a mole of the Piraeus alongside the harbour's entrance, and it was suspected in the city that, as the Piraeus could be controlled from here, they intended to use it as base to betray the city to the Spartans. On his return to Athens in the autumn of 411 BC Phrynichos was assassinated, and when the democracy was later restored it honoured his assassins (*IG* I³ 102: doc. 13.30; Thuc. 8.92).

The deposition of the Four Hundred

Dissension arose among the Four Hundred, stirred up by Theramenes, who was unhappy with the excesses of the regime and the fortification of Eetioneia. Those hoplites who comprised the Five Thousand were also increasingly critical of the state of affairs, not wanting peace with Sparta on any terms. They agitated to be put in control, tearing down the fortification at Eetioneia with Theramenes' approval: the term 'Five Thousand' was now used almost as a 'code-word' for democracy and its return (Thuc. 8.92). Under the Spartan admiral Agesandridas the Spartans defeated thirty-six Athenian ships off Eretria in the summer of 411 BC. This sparked a revolt on Euboea, and an inscription from the city of Eretria on the island refers to the liberation of the city from the Athenians (Meiggs and Lewis 82: doc. 13.29). It caused great panic at Athens, as the island was more useful to them than Attica itself now the Spartans occupied Dekeleia (Thuc. 8.96). The ekklesia met, deposed the Four Hundred, and put the Five Thousand in control at Athens, and Thucydides approved of their moderate constitution and government (Thuc. 8.97). Democracy itself was fully restored in 410 BC. Athens' allies were more important to it than ever before, and the city honoured Neapolis for its support (whose mother-city Thasos had rebelled in 411 BC), which included manpower and money (*IG* I³ 101: 13.31).

Alkibiades returns to Athens

This period of civil conflict damaged Athens, but the city recovered quickly. Any hope of Persian assistance evaporated with the signing of an accord between Tissaphernes and the Spartans, the first of several such agreements by which the Persians assisted the Spartans with gold (Thuc. 8.18; other agreements: 8.37, 8.58). In Sicily in 409 BC, the city of Selinous, which had threatened Egesta, and so helped spark the Sicilian Expedition, was attacked and captured by the Carthaginians on the island (Diod. Sic. 13.57.1–58: doc. 13.32). But Athens itself was still powerful, and it won two notable naval successes against the Spartan fleet, first at Kynossema in 411 BC (Thuc. 8.102–6), and then spectacularly under the generalship of Alkibiades at Cyzicus in 410 BC (Xen. *Hellenika* 1.1.11–18). In 407 BC Alkibiades returned to Athens, as general, where he received a rapturous welcome and an extraordinary command, and conducted the Eleusinian procession to Eleusis from Athens by land. Since the occupation of Dekeleia the procession had taken place by sea because of the Spartan presence in Attica (Xen. *Hellenika* 1.4.20–1: doc. 3.35; the major source for the period is no longer Thucydides, whose account breaks off after recounting the events of the battle of Kynossema and is taken up by Xenophon). Accusations of impiety against Alkibiades were dropped, and his escort of the procession was obviously meant to vindicate his protestations of innocence over the affair, and to be a 'slap in the face' to those who accused him of profaning the Mysteries. He recaptured Selymbria for Athens, probably in 408 BC, and in 407 BC proposed a decree concerning new arrangements for the defeated ally (*IG* I³ 118: doc. 13.33). Alkibiades was definitely back on the political stage and the decree advertised his military role even while he was absent from Athens. Thrasyboulos recovered Thasos (with help from Neapolis) as well as other cities in the area which revolted in 411 BC.

Alkibiades disgraced and the emergence of Lysander

Alkibiades was soon to be in disgrace again, and Athens was on the slippery road to ruin. Victory at Kynossema and Cyzicus must have reinvigorated the Athenians through the success of the Athenian fleet. When, however, Alkibiades was in charge of the fleet at Notion, with powers over the other strategoi, he left the captain of his own ship Antiochos in command, with strict orders not to engage the nearby enemy fleet, which was under the command of Lysander at Ephesos. With some of the Athenian ships, however, Antiochos sailed past Lysander's very prow, and an engagement ensued. Lysander defeated the Athenian fleet, which lost fifteen triremes, largely because Antiochos was killed and the Athenians panicked. When Alkibiades returned he attempted to engage Lysander in battle, but the Spartan refused. At Athens, Alkibiades was held responsible and deposed; he had already retired to the Chersonnese to avoid the inevitable. Athens elected new generals, including Konon, who became very prominent in the 390s BC, when he took over command of the Athenian fleet (Xen. *Hellenika* 1.5.10–14; cf. doc. 14.4).

Lysander, unlike Gylippos, was probably not a mothax, and this 'information' derives from sources at Sparta hostile to him. He seems to have had 'royal blood', as he belonged to the line of the kings at Sparta, the Herakleidai, but was from an obscure branch. He was also the lover (erastes) of Agesilaos II, who became king of Sparta from around 401/0 to 360 BC, and played an important part in ensuring his succession to the throne. Lysander's ability to establish a working relationship with the Persians was the key to eventual Spartan success in the war, but he made enemies at Sparta. Athens had made overtures to the Persians in the spring of 407 BC, but they were already committed to an alliance with Sparta. There had been several treaties between the Persians and Spartans, who were more natural allies for the Persians than the Athenians, both because of their type of government and the history of Athenian anti-Persian military activity after 479 BC.

An agreement was struck between Sparta and Persia in 408 BC and Darius II sent his son Cyrus as karanos ('Lord') to reorganise Persian involvement in the war between the Greeks in support of Sparta. Cyrus was a younger son, but hoped to become king, and later led a revolt against his brother Artaxerxes II who succeeded their father Darius in 405/4 BC. Cyrus and Lysander became friends, and Lysander successfully urged Cyrus to prosecute the war vigorously: the old enemies of Thermopylai and Plataea were now allies and friends in a war to crush Athens, the victor at Marathon and architect of the naval victory against the Persians at Salamis. Lysander was also able to win an increase in pay for the rowers of the Peloponnesian fleet, and the Persians and Spartans co-operated against the Athenians. Tissaphernes' policy (suggested by Alkibiades) of playing one side off against the other and maintaining diplomatic links with the Athenians was superseded by all-out support for Sparta (Xen. *Hellenika* 1.4.1–7).

The Athenian victory at Arginousai

While Lysander was Spartan nauarchos (overall naval commander) in 407 BC, he was not reappointed to the position in 406 BC but was succeeded by Kallikratidas (the position could only be held once). Kallikratidas did not enjoy a good relationship with Cyrus (to whom Lysander returned the Persian gold he had not yet spent), and disliked the fact that Sparta was being assisted by Persian aid in a war against fellow Greeks. Lysander's supporters in the fleet also undermined Kallikratidas' position by belittling his abilities and spreading talk that it was a mistake to replace Lysander. Kallikratidas started his campaigning by capturing Methymna

Figure 13.4 Samos and Athens renewed their alliance in 405/4 BC, and the inscription recording this was surmounted by a relief showing Hera (on the left), the goddess of Samos, shaking hands with Athena on the right. Athena's military attributes (spear, helmet, shield) are to indicate that Athens will take military action if necessary for Samos' sake (doc. 13.34). Photo © Acropolis Museum, Athens.

on Lesbos and enslaving its Athenian garrison (Xen. *Hellenika* 1.6.13–15: doc. 5.6).

Following this Kallikratidas with 170 ships blockaded Konon and the Athenian fleet at Mytilene on the island of Lesbos. Persian gold had increased the size of the Peloponnesian navy, and Athens' fleet had lost its numerical superiority. The consequences of the Sicilian Expedition, in which so many ships were lost, were still having an impact on Athens. A ship escaped from the blockade and took the news to the Athenians, who mobilised all their resources as far as was humanly possible: slaves were freed to row in the fleet, and even the cavalry went on board as rowers. They managed to man 110 ships, and were assisted by forty more from the allies, including ten from Samos, whose loyalty persevered and was soon recognised by a decree (Fig. 13.4). Gold dedications were melted down to provide the necessary funds: Perikles' confident estimate of Athenian financial reserves was but now a memory.

Kallikratidas left fifty ships under the command of Eteonikos blockading Konon, and sailed to Lesbos with 120 ships. At the Arginousai islands opposite Mytilene the recently mobilised Athenian fleet lay at anchor. Kallikratidas therefore moved to Arginousai, and the Athenians extended their left wing out to sea under the overall command of Aristokrates, with Perikles son of Perikles (and Aspasia) one of the strategoi on this left wing, and Protomachos as over-all commander on the right. The ships were arranged so that the Peloponnesians could not break through the line, for the Athenians were aware that they were less experienced than the Peloponnesian fleet as their own crews had been hastily recruited. Kallikratidas decided to attack despite being warned by his ship's captain that he lacked numerical superiority. The Athenians arranged their ships into small contingents, while the Spartans arranged theirs in a single line. At first the ships fought at close range, although the battle soon broke down into individual engagements. Two factors proved decisive: Kallikratidas fell overboard and drowned as his ship rammed another, and the Athenian right wing under Protomachos defeated the Peloponnesian left, at which the Peloponnesians fled. Seventy Peloponnesian ships were lost in the action, compared to twenty-five of the Athenians (Xen. *Hellenika* 1.6.24–38). Conditions were stormy, and the Athenian generals failed in their attempt to rescue their survivors who had fallen into the sea: for this six of the eight generals present (two did not return to Athens) were later condemned and put to death by the Athenian assembly in an unconstitutional procedure which Socrates opposed and which the Athenians later regretted (Xen. *Hellenika* 1.7.9–15: doc. 1.20; Diod. Sic. 13.101–3); one of those executed was Perikles' son Perikles. This victory at sea destroyed over half the Peloponnesian fleet and once again proved Athenian superiority at sea (despite the fact that their fleet was assembled hastily). The Spartans as a result decided to propose peace terms, including the abandonment of Dekeleia and the continuation of the status quo, thereby tacitly accepting Athens' leadership of its allies. Athens however refused to make peace, perhaps considering that a truce would only give Sparta a chance to equip a new fleet, and decided to continue to oppose Sparta with a view to overcoming its naval power, so that Sparta would lose Persia's support.

The fall of Athens

Lysander returns

The Spartans were well aware that Lysander, who was no longer in command, needed to return to the campaign, and Cyrus and the Peloponnesian allies requested his reappointment. As he could not be appointed nauarchos for a second time, he was made epistoleus ('second-in-command') to the new commander, Arakos, for 405 BC, and Cyrus provided Lysander with more funds before departing to visit his father. Ostensibly this was because Darius claimed he was ill, but rather it was to lure his son home to punish him as he had killed two of Darius' nephews who had failed to honour him (Cyrus) as king (Xen. *Hellenika* 2.1.7–8; Diod. Sic. 13.100.8).

Aigospotamoi 405 BC

The final and decisive battle of the war took place in 405 BC. The Athenian fleet of some 180 ships lay anchored at Aigospotamoi on the Hellespont, and at this point Alkibiades arrived from Thrace to offer his services to his state, as well as the support of a Thracian army, and the advice that the fleet should move to Sestos where supplies would be available. These offers were rejected and he was reminded that he was no longer in command (Xen. *Hellenika* 2.1.25–6; Plut. *Alkibiades* 36–7). Lysander, who had taken the city of Lampsakos and was threatening to cut off the Athenians' grain supply from the Black Sea, kept refusing over four days to join battle with the Athenians. As they were suffering from hunger the Athenian general Philokles, who was in command for that day, set out with thirty triremes, either to tempt

Lysander into battle or make for Sestos to find provisions. Lysander forced him back to the other Athenian triremes, which were now without their crews as the Athenians after offering battle had scattered to find food on shore. Lysander put Eteonikos onshore with troops who seized part of the Athenian camp, while Lysander sailed in and dragged off the unmanned Athenian ships with grappling hooks. The Athenians could not escape by land or sea and took flight, most fleeing to Sestos; only nine triremes escaped with Konon, while the state ship the *Paralos* took the grave news to Athens. Lysander executed the prisoners he caught (Xen. *Hellenika* 2.1.31–2: doc. 13.36), perhaps amounting to as many as 3000 (Plut. *Lysander* 13.1: doc. 13.38). Philokles, who as an Athenian strategos had ordered the crews of two triremes, one from Corinth and one from Andros, to be thrown overboard alive, was accorded the special treatment of having his throat publicly cut. Konon escaped and, too sensible to return to Athens with the news, went to Evagoras in Cyprus, with whom he was friendly (doc. 14.4). Lysander captured Sestos but allowed the Athenians to return to Athens, and proceeded to besiege Samos. As a historical footnote, it should be noted that Gylippos, architect of the victory of Syracuse in 413 BC, was sent by Lysander to Sparta with 1500 talents, and helped himself to 300 en route. However, his theft was detected at Sparta, and he fled and was condemned to death in absentia (Diod. Sic. 13.106.8–10)

Athens besieged

Except for the handful of ships which escaped with Konon, the Athenian fleet was effectively destroyed. When the report of the disaster reached Athens it brought consternation and panic: 'lamentation passed from the Piraeus along the Long Walls to the city, one man telling the news to another' and the Athenians feared that they would now be treated in the same way as they had earlier treated the Melians and others (Xen. *Hellenika* 2.2.3–4: doc. 5.7). Both Spartan kings, Agis and Pausanias, invaded Attica and camped beneath its walls, denying the city the opportunity of importing of food by land, while Lysander captured Byzantium and Chalcedon, allowing the Athenian garrisons to return to Athens, and cut off the supply of grain from the Black Sea. He went through the Aegean, freeing cities from Athenian control, and continued his policy of sending the Athenian garrisons home, so that they swelled the population of the city the sooner to starve it out (Plut. *Lysander* 13.3: doc. 13.38).

Lysander 'who crowned unsacked Sparta'

Lysander attacked Samos with no success and it refused to surrender to him. For this Athens honoured the island in a decree for its loyalty as an ally (*IG* I³ 127: doc. 13.34). Lysander succeeded later in capturing Samos and imposed a dekarchy (rule by a group of ten), and when Samos overthrew this in 403 BC, Athens reaffirmed its honorary decree of 405 BC. All Athens' other allies went over to Sparta after the defeat at Aigospotamoi, and Lysander, acting under orders from Sparta, imposed a Spartan governor (harmost) on each state that had been an Athenian ally. He abolished democracies and put in place a dekarchy to rule each city, choosing these ten officials from political clubs (hetaireiai), with the men selected being his personal associates and partisans (Diod. Sic. 14.10.1–2: doc. 13.37; Plut. *Lysander* 13.5–7: doc. 13.38). One of the Spartan demands at the outset of the war was that the Athenian allies be 'autonomous': this now seems to have meant, in 405–404 BC, that they were to be ruled by pro-Spartan oligarchic regimes. Additionally, the tribute was not abolished and Sparta now collected 1000 talents from those who had been Athens' allies (Diod. Sic. 14.10. 2: doc. 13.37).

Meanwhile, Lysander sailed to Aegina and restored it to the Aeginetans, laid waste to Salamis, and sailed into the Piraeus with 150 triremes. Athens was besieged by land and sea, and its population gradually began to starve. First Agis at Athens, and then the ephors at Sparta, rejected the Athenian offer to become Sparta's allies if they could keep their walls and the Piraeus; the Athenians feared that if they gave up the walls they would be enslaved (Xen. *Hellenika* 2.2.10–15: doc. 13.35).

Theramenes

At this point Theramenes proposed to the assembly that he should be sent to Lysander to see whether the Spartans wanted the Athenians to destroy the walls so that the city could be enslaved. There are two different accounts of this: one in which he waited three months with Lysander, so that by the time of his return the Athenians were starving so severely they would agree to anything, and he then went back to the assembly which granted him full powers to make peace with Sparta on any terms; the other version records that he spent all this time at Sparta, where political divisions concerning how to deal with Athens delayed his return. At Sparta an assembly of its allies discussed the future of Athens, and whereas Corinth, Thebes and many other cities wanted to destroy Athens, Sparta itself refused on the grounds that the Athenians 'had done great service at the time of Greece's greatest danger'. Athens had reminded the Spartans of this back in 432 BC, and the Spartans had not forgotten the Persian Wars, especially that Athens was now at its mercy. Terms were agreed upon: the Long Walls and those of the Piraeus were to be torn down, and the Athenians would only retain twelve ships, take back their exiles (primarily those exiled after the rule of the Four Hundred), and be Sparta's allies, meaning that they would 'have the same enemies and friends as the Spartans and follow them by land and sea wherever they should lead'; furthermore, the Athenians would be governed by their traditional (i.e., non-democratic) constitution. Returning to Athens, where large numbers were dying of starvation, the Athenians agreed to the Spartan terms that Theramenes announced. Their walls were destroyed to the music of flute girls, with the exiles who returned 'thinking that that day was for Greece the beginning of freedom' (Xen. *Hellenika* 2.2.16–23: doc. 13.35; [Arist.] *Ath. Pol.* 34.3: doc. 13.40).

Lysander is honoured and honours himself

Lysander's achievement was momentous and he erected statues of himself and his admirals at Delphi. He was the first living person to whom cities 'erected statues and made sacrifices as if to a god'. When he conquered Samos, the festival of the Heraia there was renamed the Lysandreia and poets sang his praises (Plut. *Life of Lysander* 13.1–7, 18.1–10: doc. 13.38). This was the first time the line between a living man and a god had been blurred, and later Philip and Alexander, and then the Hellenistic kings, followed suit. He inscribed on the dedication of the statue of himself – a living man – at Delphi, that it was he who had destroyed the ships of Athens and broken its power, he was the victor who 'crowned unsacked Sparta' (*Fouilles de Delphes* 3.1 50: doc. 13.39): contrast Pausanias' self-glorification in 479 BC which was not tolerated by the Spartans (Thuc. 1.132.3: doc. 6.35). Sparta won the war, largely through Lysander's efforts in its closing stages, but his arrogance made him enemies.

The rule of the Thirty Tyrants

For a second time the Athenian democracy abolished itself. Once peace was made in 404 BC, and the other democracies throughout what had been Athens' empire were abolished, Lysander did not allow Athens to remain a democracy. Those exiles who returned to Athens under the terms of the peace and the aristocratic hetaireiai (political clubs) wanted the abolition of democratic rule. Their main spokesman was at first Theramenes, but Kritias soon emerged as their real leader. Intimidated by Lysander and Spartan force, the assembly voted to elect a group of Athenians to codify the ancient laws of Athens into a system of government: by 'ancient' they meant laws prior to Solon's reforms. Thirty were chosen (including Theramenes and Kritias), and because their rule was violent, lawless and excessive they became known as the Thirty Tyrants; the term is first found in Diodorus' description of them (14.3.7), and may come from his source, which was possibly Ephoros.

These Thirty appointed 500 Councillors and officials from a pre-chosen group of 1000, ten supporters as governors of the Piraeus, eleven prison guards ('the Eleven' had always existed and presumably they appointed these from their particular supporters), and 300 whip-bearers. At first their rule was moderate: the laws of Ephialtes and Archestratos, which curtailed the powers of the Areiopagos, were repealed, the 'ambiguous' laws of Solon removed, and the jury system abolished. They also did away with the professional informants (the sycophants), which was a popular move (their only one). They then sent to Lysander at Sparta and he assisted them by installing a Spartan garrison of 700 men and a harmost, Kallibios; the Athenians covered all the financial costs. Now firmly in control the Thirty began what can only be described as a reign of terror. Theramenes disagreed with Kritias when the latter embarked on a killing spree to even up the scores because earlier he had been exiled by the democracy. The Thirty confiscated the weapons and armour of all, except for 3000 of their supporters, and 1500 men were killed for their property and on account of their public reputation: the Thirty did not want any opposition ([Arist.] *Ath. Pol.* 34.2–35.4: doc. 13.40). Metics, including the orator Lysias, were also attacked because of their wealth, with each of the Thirty allotted a target of one rich metic to pay for the expenses of the Spartan garrison (Lys. 12 *Against Eratosthenes* 4–20: doc. 5.41). When Theramenes objected, he was forced to drink hemlock. Socrates refused to participate in the wrongful arrest of one of the chosen victims and simply went home (Pl. *Apology* 31c–32d: doc. 3.85, cf. 13.43; see also Xen. *Hellenika* 2.2–3; Diod. Sic. 14.4–6.)

Return of the democrats

Some of the democrats went into exile, chief among them Thrasyboulos, the prominent strategos of the later stages of the war, who took refuge at Thebes. Now that Athens was a Spartan outpost, Thebes welcomed exiled democrats opposed to the Spartan occupation. With his supporters Thrasyboulos seized the border fortress of Phyle and defeated a force sent against them, while Kritias and the rest of the Thirty prepared for a move to Eleusis in the eventuality of being overthrown. When Thrasyboulos and the democrats, whose forces by now numbered about 1000, seized the Piraeus, the Thirty attacked them with the Spartan garrison, at which the democrats, now supported by many in the Piraeus, took up their stand on the hill of Mounichia. In the ensuing battle Kritias was killed, and on the next day the Five Thousand deposed the Thirty, who retired to Eleusis, and chose ten men to carry on government and the war against the democrats. Civil war now broke out between the city and the Piraeus, and Lysander went to Eleusis to assist, lending the oligarchs 100 talents and planning to besiege the Piraeus by land and sea. But king Pausanias, annoyed at Lysander' prominence and fearful that he was going to capture Athens, persuaded the ephors that he should instead take a Spartan and allied army to Attica. Both the Boeotians and Corinthians pointedly refused to participate, an indication of events to come. They were unsure of Spartan intentions and were concerned in case the Spartans intended to annex Athens and become even more powerful (Xen. *Hellenika* 2.4–30).

The amnesty of 403 BC

Reluctant to engage the democrats in the Piraeus, Pausanias nevertheless found himself in a deteriorating situation in which the Spartans were forced to take part in an engagement in which many on both sides were killed and the democrats narrowly defeated. Later the Spartans who died were accorded a public common grave in the Kerameikos, still to be seen, to honour them for their role in restoring democracy. At some stage, the Athenians in the city elected a second group of ten men, less hard-line than the Thirty, but still opposed to the democrats (the first ten were put into power in the Piraeus). With these and the democrats at the Piraeus, Pausanias set about organising a truce, in which the Athenian Rhinon (one of the second group of ten) was prominent, having been already engaged in communications with the men in the Piraeus as to how to end the conflict. Pausanias was supported by three of the ephors who were with him; as they disagreed with Lysander's policy they worked towards a reconciliation and an amnesty was agreed upon. The terms are set out in detail by the *Athenaion Politeia* (39.6: doc. 13.40; 38.4–40.4: doc. 13.41; Xen. *Hellenika.* 2.4.31–43). Pausanias rejected Lysander's policy of a large-scale attack on the Piraeus, which would have led to extensive bloodshed in the pursuit of his individual ambition.

This amnesty covered all but those oligarchs who committed the most heinous crimes: the Thirty, the first group of Ten elected after the Thirty were deposed, the Eleven, and those who governed the Piraeus (although these last could submit their accounts and await judgement if they chose). Each party was to make its own repayments for any sums borrowed, but in the interests of unity and reconciliation the newly restored democracy later repaid the money the Thirty had borrowed from the Spartans. Many of those who supported the Thirty were allowed to emigrate to Eleusis, and these were subject to a special reconciliation in 401 BC (*Ath. Pol.*40.1, 40.4: doc. 13.41). Archinos in fact in 403 BC shortened the agreed time to register for emigration, and so reduced the number of citizens who left for Eleusis. He also persuaded the council (boule) to execute without trial anyone who was talking against the amnesty, and indicted as unconstitutional Thrasyboulos' decree to enfranchise all who were at the Piraeus: some were obviously slaves, although metics who supported Thrasyboulos were granted citizenship (*IG* II² 10: doc. 5.43; *Ath. Pol.*40.1–2: doc. 13.41).

Archinos' action and the amnesty ensured that life in Athens returned to normal and the citizen body was reunited. In all, the democracy took a very lenient approach to the short-lived oligarchy of 404–403 BC in the interest of the unity of the state. Plato had been invited to join the Thirty, the Eleven and the Ten in the Piraeus as he had relatives and friends among them. He was initially flattered, but soon he saw that their government made the democracy 'seem like a Golden Age' and when the democracy was restored he noted that it 'showed great moderation' (Pl. *Seventh Letter* 324b8–325a7: doc. 13.43). But when Socrates was tried and executed, he became disillusioned about government and whether it was possible for any government truly to administer justice.

End of Lysander's career

Lysander gained Agesilaos' support and agreement at Sparta to take a force to Asia Minor in 396 BC to accompany Agesilaos; he hoped to restore the dekarchies which had failed, probably as early as 402 BC. In Ephesos, Lysander was treated by the inhabitants of the region as a go-between with Agesilaos, and crowds thronged to his door. This created tensions between the two men, despite their previous homoerotic relationship, and Agesilaos sent Lysander off to the Hellespont. Lysander – brilliant and energetic – played a secondary military role, but extended Spartan influence, and organised the defection of the Persian Spithridates from Pharnabazos. Agesilaos in Asia Minor and Lysander in the north Aegean made Sparta's presence felt.

In Plutarch's account a disillusioned Lysander returned to Sparta and contemplated changing the Spartan constitution and abolishing the kingship. In 395 BC he helped stir up war against Thebes, and while invading Boeotia he was killed in a surprise attack at Haliartos. Agesilaos then 'discovered' among Lysander's papers a speech concerning the abolition of the Spartan kingship. This 'discovery' was almost certainly invented: Lysander was the victim of political jealousy, and perhaps also an object of fear to the Spartans, whose kings were military leaders while the rest of society was meant to remain fairly 'anonymous'. Those who became or were perceived to be too powerful tended to be exiled. At the end of the Peloponnesian War he was clearly the most powerful man in Greece and his reputation among the Spartans suffered accordingly (Plut. *Lysander* 24.1–25.3, 30.1–5: doc. 13.42). As for Alkibiades, he attempted to give sound military advice to the Athenian fleet at Aigospotamoi in 405 BC and then made his way first to Bithynia and then Phrygia, which was ruled by the satrap Pharnabazos, with the intention of going to the court of the Great King. The Spartans, however, ordered his death, thinking he was a threat to the security of Spartan-occupied Athens. Lysander organised the details of his assassination and the house in a village of Phrygia where he was staying was set on fire: as Alkibiades emerged he was slain (Plut. *Alkibiades* 37–9).

Effects of the Peloponnesian War

Athens lost its empire and the tribute which came with it. Two oligarchic governments in the city overturned the rule of law and executed citizens for their political affiliations or simply for their money. Thousands of hoplites and thetes died in the various campaigns, especially in the Sicilian Expedition, and not only Athenians but their allies. The Spartans and their allies also experienced great loss of life, and Sparta was soon to go into a decline of manpower from which it did not recover. The destruction of olive trees, vines and crops not just in Attica but in Athenian raids on the Peloponnese, and in the campaigns in the Thracian hinterland and elsewhere, must have had an effect on the supply of food and general prosperity. Attica bore the brunt of the loss of life and agricultural damage, and its people were starving to death in 404 BC as the result of the Spartan blockade. There was also the plague at the beginning of the war taking its toll of thousands of lives, including that of Perikles. Perhaps the outcome of the war would have been different if he had lived, though his immediate successor Kleon followed Periklean policies. On the whole Athens showed remarkable resilience through various misfortunes, including its recovery from the Sicilian Expedition, but this should not be overrated: that the outcome of the war depended on just one battle at Aigospotamoi in 405 BC showed how dramatically Athenian resources had been reduced, but already by 403 BC Athens was recovering, and renewed its alliance with Samos, as well as finding new friends in Corinth and Thebes.

Sparta managed to win the war without the helots rising in revolt, but took various measures to prevent this, such as Brasidas marching a force of them with him to Thrace, and the mysterious 'disappearance' of the helots who could have acted as potential leaders (Thuc. 4.80.2–5: doc. 5.48). Perikles' strategy was to use the Athenian navy to help Athens survive and win the war. With the aid of Persian gold the Spartans overturned this strategy when they themselves built up a strong and experienced fleet. This overcame the problem which Sparta had at the beginning of the war, that of limited financial resources. Goaded by Corinth and others into war, Sparta chose willingly to confront Athens in order to free the Greeks, and then imposed oligarchic government on Athens' ex-allies and exacted tribute. In 404 BC, Sparta dominated more of the Greek world than any other state had hitherto done before and was the arbiter of Greek affairs for the next few decades. Now it was to move against Persia: 'Cyrus sent messengers to Sparta requesting that the Spartans should do the same for him as he had done for them in the war against the Athenians' (Xen. *Hellenika* 3.1.1).

14

THE RISE OF MACEDON

Table 14.1 The kings of Macedon

Amyntas I	c. 547–c. 498
Alexander I	c. 498–454
Alketas II	454–448
Perdikkas II	448–413
Archelaos I	413–399
Krateros	399
Orestes, son of Archelaos I	399–396
Archelaos II, son of Archelaos I	396–393
Amyntas II	393
Pausanias	393
Amyntas III	393
Argaios II, pretender	393–392
Amyntas III	393–370
Alexander II, son of Amyntas III	370–368
Perdikkas III, son of Amyntas III	368–359
Amyntas IV, son of Perdikkas III	359–356
Philip II, son of Amyntas III	359–336
Alexander III 'the Great', son of Philip II	336–323
Antipater, regent of Macedon	334–323
Philip III Arrhidaios, son of Philip II	323–317
Alexander IV, son of Alexander III	323–311
Perdikkas, regent of Macedon	323–321
Antipater, regent of Macedon	321–319
Polyperchon, regent of Macedon	319–317
Kassander, regent of Macedon	317–305

Introduction

Sparta was supreme in Greece in 404 BC, but disagreements with its allies such as Thebes and Corinth which refused to join Pausanias' expedition to Attica in 403 BC soon took place and led to open hostility. Persia played an important role in events in this period and, while initially attacked by Sparta after the Peloponnesian War, arbitrated peace amongst the Greek states in 386 BC. A period of hegemonies emerged, with Sparta more or less dominating events down to its defeat in 371 BC by the Thebans, who then had a brief decade of prominence. Athens attempted to resurrect its maritime empire but failed, and yet in the long run emerged as the main bulwark against the growing power of Macedon. Thebes joined Athens in a final showdown against Philip in 338 BC at Chaironeia (Fig. 14.1): his victory was followed by the foundation of the League of Corinth left Macedonia in charge of Greek affairs, with Philip's plans to attack the Persian empire cut short by his assassination in 336 BC.

Sources

Xenophon took up Thucydides' account where it left off in 411 BC, and narrated Greek affairs down to 362 BC in the seven books of his *Hellenika* (*Greek Affairs*). He was in exile from Athens (at Sparta) for most of this period, and on the whole his work is written from the Spartan perspective, concentrating on events in which Sparta was involved. He is also very selective in his account: clearly he did not approve of the rise of Thebes and its virtual destruction of Spartan power (but on the other hand he saw the Spartan seizure of the Theban acropolis in 382 BC as something which the gods later punished: Xen. *Hellenika* 5.4.1). Thebes' leaders Epameinondas and Pelopidas are hardly mentioned in his history, and the formation of the Second Athenian Confederacy, which had such a large impact on the resurgence of Athenian power and on events in the Aegean, is not dealt with. Xenophon's biography of *Agesilaos* is closely followed by Plutarch's *Life* of this king. Xenophon deliberately omits various events which did not reflect well on Agesilaos, especially his response to Phoibidas and Sphodrias' actions, and the second half (actually a little over half) of the work is pure eulogy. However, while an admirer of Sparta (Plut. *Agesilaos* 1.3), Xenophon was also capable of criticising it. His *Constitution of the Spartans*, a contemporary eyewitness account of the workings of the Spartan political system and society, is an invaluable source, and in his *Anabasis* he wrote an account of Cyrus' rebellion against his brother and the return journey of the Greek mercenaries to Greece.

Diodorus' account in Books 14–17 of his *Library of History* relies heavily on Ephoros, and deals with a wider variety of events than does Xenophon (who omits the Theban defeat of the Spartans at Tegyra in 375 BC entirely, and has no role for Epameinondas). The aim of Diodorus' history was to praise the good and criticise the bad, and at the beginning of Book 15 (1.1–5) he has a few hundred words of censure of the Spartans for their behaviour leading to their loss of hegemony. The Oxyrhynchus historian's work survives on some scraps of papyrus and what remains covers the period 409–407 and 396–394 BC. Theopompos' lost *History of Philip* expressed both admiration and criticism of the king, but various other histories dealing with Philip, such as Satyros' *Life of Philip*, have not survived (Ath. 557b: doc. 14.37).

Athenian speechwriters and orators provide valuable evidence for this period, with Isocrates, Aeschines and especially Demosthenes delivering speeches on political affairs. These should not be accepted uncritically and Aechines and Demosthenes give different versions of the events of 346 BC in which they were involved. There are inscriptions, primarily from Athens, but the number of these which bear on historical matters is much reduced from those of the heyday of Athens' fifth-century empire; epigraphic highlights include the decree for the foundation of the Second Athenian Confederacy, and a rare inscription from Sparta on contributions to the Spartan war fund. Plutarch in his *Moralia* (835–51) wrote biographies of the main orators of this period (including Isocrates, Aeschines and Demosthenes), as well as *Lives* of Spartan and Theban leaders such as Lysander, whose career was to end in 395 BC, Agesilaos II the Spartan king of the Eurypontid branch (reigned 401/400–360 BC), and Pelopidas. He also wrote a biography of the other great Theban leader Epameinondas, but this is now lost, while his biographies of Phokion, Artaxerxes and Demosthenes are also useful. Though they should be read with caution these biographies are invaluable for information not in other sources, especially the *Pelopidas*, given Xenophon' neglect of his role in events.

490

Figure 14.1 Ivory head of (perhaps) Philip II, from one of the tombs in the 'Great Tumulus' at Aigai (modern Vergina). Museum of the Royal Tombs at Aigai. Photo © Hellenic Ministry of Culture and Tourism, 17th Ephorate of Prehistoric and Classical Antiquities & Archaeological Receipts Fund.

Sparta versus Persia 401–387 BC

Darius II died in 404 BC and was succeeded by his elder son Artaxerxes II. Cyrus, Darius' younger son, was not willing to submit to this, and in 401 BC raised a revolt against his brother, for which he requested Spartan support. The Spartans agreed as he had aided them in their war against the Athenians, and their admiral (navarchos) Samios was instructed to follow Cyrus' orders (Xen. *Hellenika* 3.1.1–8: doc. 14.1). In addition, Cyrus employed a large number – 10,000 – of Greek mercenaries, amongst them Xenophon. On the plain of Cunaxa, Cyrus who did not enjoy the support of the Persians as a whole, was killed in battle but his Greek force were successful in defeating the Persians. They were then in the ignominious position of being a victorious army in Persia without a Persian leader, and Xenophon's *Anabasis* described the vicissitudes of their journey through the hostile territory of the Persian Empire back to the Black Sea and the Greek world. A famous passage relates their excitement at seeing the sea after months of marching inland through the Persian Empire (Xen. *Anabasis* 4.7.21–6: doc. 14.2; Map 14.1).

Tissaphernes was made satrap by Artaxerxes and demanded that the Ionian cities, which had previously been allies of Athens but now were part of the Spartan hegemony, be his subjects: that is, they should return to Persian rule. These cities had supported Cyrus, and now they both were frightened of the consequences of this and wanted to remain free. Lysander's

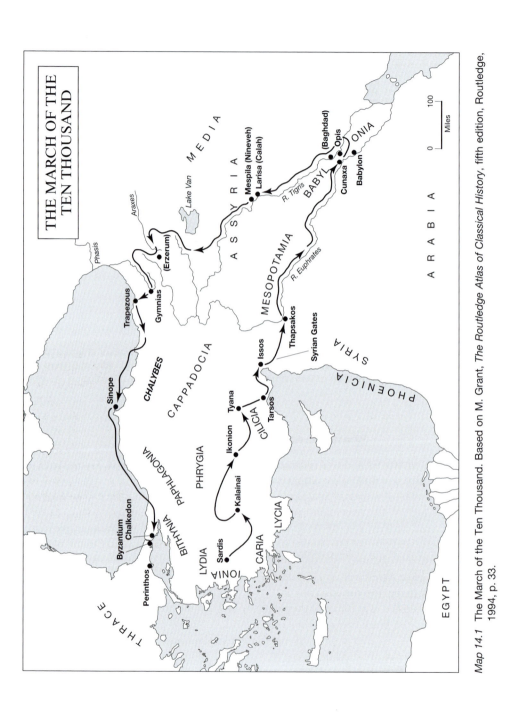

Map 14.1 The March of the Ten Thousand. Based on M. Grant, *The Routledge Atlas of Classical History*, fifth edition, Routledge, 1994, p. 33.

various dekarchies in Greek cities seem to have collapsed by 402 BC. These Ionian cities appealed to Sparta as the 'champions of Greece . . . to ensure their liberty' and Thibron was sent out as their harmost in 400 BC and was successful in taking Magnesia but not Tralles. He then occupied himself in preventing Tissaphernes' forces from ravaging Ionia and when in 399 BC the mercenaries who had served under Cyrus joined him, he became more proactive and took control of various Persian-held cities. After he had besieged Larisa unsuccessfully, the ephors sent him orders to move against Caria, but while he was at Ephesos preparing to do so Derkylidas was sent out to take over command. When Thibron returned home, he was fined and exiled on the grounds that he had permitted his army to plunder the allies he was meant to protect (Xen. *Hellenika* 3.1.1–8: doc. 14.1). Throughout the fifth century and into the next, Spartans abroad showed a propensity to become corrupt and amass wealth, but the need to plunder may been the result of insufficient war funding from Sparta.

Derkylidas was nicknamed 'Sisyphos' because of his energy: Sisyphos was the mythical figure in Hades who was punished by having to roll a huge rock up a hill without success for all eternity. Clearly the Spartans intended to protect the Greek cities of Asia Minor and were taking the campaign against the Persians seriously: this was the first time they had engaged the Persians in warfare since 479 BC. Derkylidas turned his attention to the territory of the satrap Pharnabazos, against whom he held a personal grudge because of an earlier incident in the Peloponnesian War, and seized many cities held by the Persians, at one stage capturing nine cities in eight days (Xen. *Hellenika* 3.1.8–2.20).

Sparta's war on Elis

The Spartans also took the opportunity to settle some old scores: Elis, the city in charge of the Olympic games, had debarred Sparta from the Olympics from 420 BC, had flogged the elderly Spartan Lichas for entering a chariot race despite the fact that Spartans were excluded, had sided with Argos, Athens and Mantineia in 418 BC, and had refused to let King Agis sacrifice at Olympia. So in 399 BC Agis went there, sacrificed, and made war on the city of Elis, which resulted in an agreement of alliance being reached in 397 BC (Xen. *Hellenika* 3.2.21–2: doc. 14.3). Sparta had a long memory, but it was precisely this long memory that saved Athens from enslavement in 404 BC, when Sparta recalled Athens' services in the Persian Wars and refused to enslave it on that ground. A serious conspiracy to overthrow the Spartan state in 397 by Kinadon, who did not belong to the Spartiate class, was successfully thwarted but underlined the social tensions in the city between full and part Spartiates (Xen. *Hellenika* 3.3.4–11: doc. 14.5).

The enemies of Sparta fight back

Konon had escaped with nine triremes from the Athenian defeat at Aigospotamoi in 405 BC, and made his way to King Evagoras of Cyprus, where he remained until 397 BC. He then in that year became a commander in the Persian fleet, persuading the Persians that the way to defeat Sparta was to fight them at sea. A long passage in the Athenian orator Isocrates eulogises both men, and gives a brief summary of how Konon with Persian assistance began to implement attacks upon the Spartans (Isoc. 12 *Evagoras* 51–6: doc. 14.4). News arrived at Sparta in 396 BC that Artaxerxes and Tissaphernes were preparing a fleet of 300 ships in Phoenicia, at which Agesilaos, who had just succeeded to the throne on the death of his brother Agis, took a force of thirty Spartans, 2000 neodameis and 6000 allies to Asia Minor in 396 BC (Xen. *Agesilaos* 1.7). He was committed in his approach to the campaign and before leaving Greece had attempted to imitate Agamemnon who had sacrificed at Aulis before sailing to Troy. However on this occasion Agesilaos had just made the sacrifice when a group of Boeotian officials (Boeotarchs) came and overthrew his sacrifices (Xen. *Hellenika* 3.4.4).

In Asia Minor Agesilaos made a three-month truce with Tissaphernes, who according to Xenophon was merely aiming at gaining time for further military preparations against the Spartans. After initial Spartan looting and pillaging of Persian territory in 395 BC, a battle took place near Sardis: Tissaphernes (who was at Sardis as satrap) was blamed for the Persian defeat and Artaxerxes had him beheaded. He was replaced as satrap at Sardis by Tithraustes, who demanded again that the Greek cities be returned to Persian control. Agesilaos refused, but suggested that Tithraustes pay him to leave his satrapy. Tithraustes therefore gave him 30 talents and Agesilaos went and pillaged Pharnabazos' satrapy of Phrygia instead. Spartan finances in Asia Minor had always been a problem, resulting in Thibron's downfall, and an inscription of this period indicates that Sparta was relying on contributions from its allies to carry on the war effort (Meiggs and Lewis 67: doc. 14.7). Tithraustes then sent Timokrates of Rhodes to Greece with gold to the value of 50 talents of silver to bribe the Greek states to make war on Sparta. Leading individuals at Thebes, Corinth and Argos took the gold, swearing to make war on Sparta, and while Athens did not receive a share the Athenians were also eager for war, as they wanted to recover their empire (Xen. *Hellenika* 3.5.1–2: doc. 14.6). At Athens, two figures, Epikrates and Kephalos, were particularly in favour of war against Sparta, and Thrasyboulos, who had played the leading role in the return of the democrats, although initially lukewarm, later came over to the idea when military success seemed relatively certain.

The outbreak of the Corinthian War (395–387 BC)

Tithraustes' money did not cause war to break out against Sparta but it was a notable inducement and generated anti-Spartan sentiment in the various Greek cities. In 395 BC the Athenians had allied themselves with Boeotia (*SIG³*122: doc. 14.9), as well as with Corinth, both of which had been their enemies in the Peloponnesian War. The two cities were apprehensive about Spartan power as Sparta was still leader of the Peloponnesian League and in addition was in control of Athens' previous allies, and nominally Athens as well. The Spartans were achieving successes against Persia, and Agesilaos had conquered several cities under Persian control, been victorious in an important battle near Sardis, and obviously had hopes of conquering the western satrapies and perhaps even the Persian empire itself.

The opportunity for war with Sparta occurred as a result of one of the apparently endless series of disputes which Phokis apparently enjoyed having with its neighbours over territory. It was precisely the pretext which the Thebans needed in order to engage with the Spartans. Lokris appealed for help from Thebes against Phokis, while Phokis appealed to Sparta, and Athens joined Thebes and Lokris. The resulting conflict from 393 BC on was fought primarily in the territory of Corinth, hence the name of the war. Agesilaos was bitterly disappointed at being recalled from Asia Minor as he had looked forward to further conquests there against Persia. He promised the cities there that he would be back but he was never to return (Xen. *Hellenika* 4.2.1–4: doc. 14.8).

The battle of Knidos in 394 BC

A major naval confrontation in the Aegean took place near Knidos, a city on a peninsula opposite the island of Kos. Here in 394 BC, after Agesilaos had left for Greece, the Spartans

Figure 14.2 The funerary monument of the Athenian cavalryman Dexileos, erected in the Kerameikos at Athens; he was killed in action in 394 BC as one of the Athenian cavalry at Corinth in the Corinthian War. Here he is shown killing an opponent; the monument is 1.75 m high, with an inscription giving the date of his birth (414 BC) and death (394 BC). The original is in the National Museum, Athens. This copy is in situ on the Street of the Tombs in the Kerameikos cemetery. Photo © Tara Atkinson.

were defeated by a combined Greek and Persian fleet: Konon commanded the Greek ships and Pharnabazos the Phoenician. Peisander the Spartan commander (who was the brother of Agesilaos' wife; Agesilaos had appointed him) was outnumbered even by the Greek ships alone, and the allies on his left wing deserted. His remaining triremes were driven ashore and their crews escaped to Knidos, while Peisander died fighting on his ship, which had been rammed. Spartan naval supremacy had been annihilated: 'the Spartans were defeated at sea, and they lost their empire while the Greeks were liberated and our city [Athens] recovered part of its old glory' (Isoc. 12 *Evagoras* 55–6: doc. 14.4; Knidos is not directly named: Xen. *Hellenika* 3.10–12; Diod. Sic. 14.82.4–7; Plut. *Agesilaos* 17.2–3). Persia now promised to guarantee the autonomy of the Greek cities. The destruction of any remaining Spartan influence was Pharnabazos' main priority, and he even sailed east in 393 BC and briefly raided the Peloponnese. He left Konon with the combined fleet at the Isthmus of Corinth, and gave him funds for rebuilding the walls of Athens (Xen. *Hellenika* 4.8.8–9: doc. 14.11), while he also gave money to Corinth which it spent on the construction of ships. The Athenians had already begun rebuilding the Piraeus walls in 395/4 BC and Persian funds were no doubt a welcome addition to the refortification project. Thebes had wanted Athens completely destroyed in 404 BC but a contractor from Boeotia is specifically named in the decree that organised the rebuilding (Tod 2.107: doc. 14.10). But Spartan naval power, despite Isocrates' comments, was not yet entirely finished.

The battle of Koroneia in 394 BC

After an initial victory under Agesilaos at Koroneia in central Boeotia in 394 BC, the Corinthian War was to go badly for Sparta. Xenophon was present at Koroneia ('there has been no battle like it in our times': Xen. *Agesilaos* 2.9). Boeotians, Athenians, Argives, Corinthians, Euboeans and Lokrians fought against the Spartans and their allies, who included troops from the Greek (and Ionian) cities in Asia Minor, as well as Phokaians. The Thebans on the right wing smashed through the enemy's left wing, while Agesilaos and his right wing were victorious against the enemy left opposite, the Argives, who fled to Mount Helikon. Agesilaos wheeled his wing around to fight the Thebans who were looting the Spartan baggage train. Seeing this the Thebans formed up against him, wishing also to escape to Mount Helikon, the escape to which Agesilaos was now blocking. Some of the Thebans broke through, though many were killed and Agesilaos was wounded in the action. He was victorious, and went to Delphi and made an offering, but as his army departed under the command of Gylis it was continuously harassed by Lokrian peltasts, and several were killed by stones and javelins, including Gylis himself (Xen. *Hellenika* 4.3.15–20). Corinth, now united with Argos as a political entity, became the base for the anti-Spartan coalition, and Sikyon for the Spartans' allies (Fig. 14.2).

First Spartan overtures to Persia for peace

In 392 BC Sparta turned to Persia for support. Just a few years after Agesilaos had been devastating the king's territory, the Spartan Antalkidas attempted to negotiate a peace with the Persian King through Tiribazos, that all the mainland cities and most of the islands be autonomous but that Klazomenai and Cyprus and the cities of Asia Minor should come under Persian control. When the other Greek states learnt of this they also sent representatives to Tiribazos, not wanting to agree that all the Greek cities be autonomous: Thebes did not want to lose control of the Boeotian confederacy, Athens wanted to retain the islands Lembros, Imbros and Skyros, and Argos wanted to keep the union between itself and Corinth intact.

Artaxerxes himself stripped Tiribazos of his satrapy, because of his support of Sparta which had recently done so much damage to Persian territory, and sent Strouthas in his stead, who once in Asia Minor supported the Athenians. Sparta dispatched Thibron to campaign against Strouthas, and Thibron ended up being killed by Strouthas and his cavalry while discus-throwing in enemy territory (Xen. *Hellenika* 4.8.12–19). His successor Diphridas had more luck, capturing and ransoming Strouthas' daughter and son-in-law.

Spartan disaster at Lechaion in 390 BC

In 390 BC the Athenians under Iphikrates and Kallias had annihilated a Spartan regiment (mora) at Lechaion, Corinth's port, largely because the mercenary peltasts under Iphikrates were able to manoeuvre more quickly in the battle and inflict large losses on the Spartan hoplites, who could fight well against hoplites in a traditional pitched battle but who were unsuited for the running, attack, then retreat tactics of Iphikrates' peltasts (the Spartans had used peltasts at Koroneia in 394 but not in this engagement). Two hundred and fifty Spartans died: a heavy blow for their city (Xen. *Hellenika* 4.5.7–19).

Athenian actions caused Artaxerxes to change his mind about whom to support amongst the Greeks. Athens had long been involved with Evagoras on Cyprus which Persia saw as its own and which it was to reconquer; Athens was also in alliance with Egypt, which was in rebellion against Persia. In 389 BC Thrasyboulos had been enjoying successes for Athens in the Hellespont, including installing a democracy at Byzantium and collecting a tax on ships sailing down the Hellespont, and was soon also busy detaching the cities of Asia Minor and the islands from Spartan control, but he was killed at Aspendos (Xen. *Hellenika* 4.8.25–31). Iphikrates in the same year defeated and killed the Spartan Anaxibios who had been sent as navarchos to the Hellespont (Xen. *Hellenika* 4.8.32–9).

The King's Peace of 386 BC

In 388 BC, however, the Spartans appointed Teleutias as navarchos in Greek waters and he conceived the brilliant plan of a raid on the Piraeus; he captured numerous grain ships, disabled triremes and even landed in the Piraeus and carried off merchants and ship owners in broad daylight. Sailing to Sounion he then captured grain and other merchant vessels (Xen. *Hellenika* 5.1.19–24). In the same year (388/7 BC) Antalkidas was appointed navarchos of the Spartan forces in Asia Minor and had an audience with the Great King and the pro-Spartan Tiribazos, who was reappointed as satrap at Sardis. Antalkidas returned to Greece in 387 BC with the terms of what is known as the 'King's Peace' and with his fleet of eighty triremes at the Hellespont prevented the grain ships from sailing from the Pontos to Athens. Once again Athens faced the situation which led to the Spartan domination of 404 BC and Athens' consquent starvation (Xen. *Hellenika* 5.1.25–9).

Tiribazos ordered those Greek states which wished to hear the terms of the King's Peace to send delegates to him, and early in 386 (rather than late 387) the Greeks accepted what is called the 'King's Peace' or the 'Peace of Antalkidas', which Xenophon baldly reports (he refers to it as the 'Peace of Antalkidas': Xen. *Hellenika* 5.1.36): Artaxerxes claimed all the Greek cities in Asia Minor and the islands of Klazomenai and Cyprus; the mainland cities and the other islands were to be autonomous, except that by allowing the Athenians to keep the islands of Lemnos, Imbros and Skyros the terms were made partly accetable to Athens. The king threatened war on anyone who would not accept the peace but his instruments of oppression were made clear: he would give 'both ships and money' for the purpose of keeping the peace to those who accepted it – in other words, he would rearm and finance the Spartans (Xen. *Hellenika* 5.1.30–1: doc. 14.12; Diod. Sic. 14.110; cf. Plut. *Agesilaos* 23, *Artaxerxes* 21).

The Greek states agree to the peace

In return for the cessation of the Corinthian War, the termination of the Argive–Corinthian union, the dissolution of the Boeotian league dominated by Thebes (cf. docs 1.57–8), and the discontinuation of Athenian imperialistic ambitions in Thrace, the Hellespont, the islands and Asia Minor, all Sparta had to do was to stop making war on Persia and abandon the Greeks of Asia Minor, who had been freed by the Athenians from 478 BC onwards, but were now in 386 BC sacrificed to the Persians. Agesilaos' plans for conquering Persia or at least its western satrapies had come to nothing; this task would fall to the Macedonians. Greece accepted the truce: Athens feared disruption to its grain supply, and Argos that Sparta would now turn its full attention to attacking it, which left Corinth no alternative, with its union with Argos dissolved, but to accept the terms as well. Thebes agreed to sign, but only in the name of all the Boeotians and not just Thebes, which Agesilaos saw as flouting the terms of autonomy of Greek cities laid down by the peace of Antalkidas. When he threatened invasion, the Thebans gave way and the Boeotian league was dissolved, and exiles from Thebes returned (Xen. *Hellenika* 5.1.32–3, *Agesilaos* 2.21). The Thebans would not be so accommodating at a later stage.

Mantineia punished by Sparta

Sparta now had the upper hand in Greece and decided, despite the clause of autonomy in the peace, to punish the Mantineians, attacking them in 385 BC under the command of king Agesipolis, and splitting their city into villages, and next returning the pro-Spartan exiles of Phlious to their city in the northwestern Argolid (Xen. *Hellenika* 5.2.1–10; cf. 4.4.15). Further trouble occurred at Phlious when the exiles complained to Sparta, and Agesilaos led an expedition against the city which was besieged, starved and finally surrendered in 379 BC. In 382 BC the Spartans had been approached by ambassadors from the cities of Akanthos and Apollonia to deal with the growing power of Olynthos in northern Greece, which was taking over all the neighbouring cities: Sparta eventually forced the city to surrender in 379 BC (5.2.11–23, 37–43, 5.3.1–9, 18–26).

Sparta captures Olynthos and the Theban Kadmeia

As part of this episode, the Spartan Eudamidas had set off to Olynthos while his brother Phoibidas stayed behind to organise a larger force, with which he then marched north in 382 BC. Phoibidas came to Thebes, which on hearing of the planned campaign against Olynthos had shown its hostility to Sparta by making an alliance with that city. Thebes was divided into factions with the Theban pro-Spartans, including the exiles who had returned under the terms of the peace, led by Leontiades, and the anti-Spartans by Ismenias, both of whom were Theban polemarchs ('war-leaders': the office of Boeotarch had been abolished along with the Boeotian alliance in 387 BC). Phoibidas, encouraged by Leontiades, seized the Theban acropolis (the Kadmeia) when Leontiades gave him the keys to the gates in 381 BC (Xen. *Hellenika* 5.2.25–36). Ismenias was imprisoned, tried and executed, and some of the anti-Spartan party fled to Athens where they were welcomed. Xenophon saw this as the height of Sparta's authority in Greece: the Thebans and Boeotians were in their power, Argos was frightened of Spartan invasion, and Athens had no allies, while Sparta has all its allies firmly under its control (5.3.27).

Thebes freed from Spartan control in 379 BC

At Sparta the news met with a mixed reaction. Phoibidas had acted without authority from Sparta, but it was decided to maintain a Spartan garrison in Thebes, which was a flagrant violation of the peace of 386 BC. Pelopidas, in exile at Athens, returned and freed the city in 379 BC (Cornelius Nepos *Pelopidas* 16.2.5–3.3: doc. 14.13), but it is interesting that Xenophon assigns him no role in the liberation of the city. In Xenophon's account, some of the Theban exiles, led by Melon, arrived at Thebes dressed up as women and gained entry to where the Theban polemarchs were celebrating a festival of Aphrodite. After killing them and then Leontiades they roused the citizenry, which at dawn approved the events that had taken place. Two Athenian generals on the Attic border had arrived with assistance, having been forewarned as to what would happen, and helped the Thebans in their attack on the Kadmeia. A truce was made with the pro-Spartans, but as these left the city many were butchered and the Spartan governor (harmost), who had surrendered and left Thebes, was executed on his return to Sparta. Sparta called out its army to invade under king Kleombrotos, but he achieved nothing notable, except that his march near to Attica on his way to attack Thebes scared the Athenians, who were clearly impressed by the show of Spartan strength, into wondering if the actions of their generals had been well advised. As a result they executed one, while the other who had fled was formally exiled (Xen. *Hellenika* 5.4.1–19).

Foundation of the Second Athenian Confederacy in 378 BC

Thebes' independence, however, encouraged Athens to establish a new alliance and Spartan control of Greece did not rest easily with many cities. Prominent amongst the first members of the new Athenian alliance were Chios, Byzantium, Rhodes, Mytilene and other islanders. A council (synedrion) was established, with each city having its own single vote. Xenophon does not mention the new alliance but seventy cities joined: Sparta and Athens 'were now well matched' (Diod. Sic. 15.28.1–5, 29.5–8, 30.2: doc. 14.14).

At Athens it was Aristoteles who in 377 BC successfully proposed the decree to establish what modern scholars call the 'Second Athenian Confederacy'. The actual decree lists sixty states, as opposed to the seventy Diodorus gives, or the seventy-five which Aeschines mentions (2.70), and some cities who were late in joining might not have had their names engraved on the stele. The Athenians' purpose in establishing the new alliance was stated in the inscription: 'so that the Spartans may allow the Greeks, free and autonomous, to live in peace' (Tod 2.123: doc 14.15). It was now the Athenians who were the champions of Greek autonomy. Athenian governors and garrisons were forbidden in the territory of Athens' allies, and tribute was not to be exacted. Furthermore, Athenians were not allowed to own property in allied states and any who did so had now to relinquish it. Athens was attempting to ensure that the unpopular elements of its fifth-century empire were not part of the new alliance. It was a mutual defence treaty: if any ally was attacked, all the other allies were to attack the aggressor. The new alliance made a good beginning, but in the end Athens would end up fighting against some of these same allies.

Sphodrias attacks the Piraeus in 378 BC

Sphodrias was the Spartan harmost at Thespiai, and Xenophon has an absurd theory that the Thebans persuaded him to attack Athens so that the Athenians would become opposed to the Spartans and take sides with the Thebans. At any rate, Sphodrias set out late one afternoon, and slowly made his way towards the Piraeus (which at this stage still did not have any gates), planning to be there by daylight on the next day. But the Athenians were forewarned of his coming as his troops plundered the countryside, and guarded their city. The

Athenians seized some Spartan ambassadors at Athens on the grounds that they must have known of the plot, but these reasonably argued that if they had known an attack was coming they would not have stayed in the city. In Diodorus' account Kleombrotos gave Sphodrias orders to attack the Piraeus: this might have been his reaction to the Athenians gathering together a coalition of allies. The ephors recalled Sphodrias and condemned him to death, but he was acquitted (Diod. Sic. 15.29.5–6: doc. 14.14; Xen. *Hellenika* 5.4.20–4). Apparently, Spartan homoeroticism had something to do with Sphodrias' acquittal: Sphodrias' son Kleonymos was the young beloved of Archidamos, the son of Agesilaos. After taking several days to screw up the courage to do so, Archidamos approached his father and interceded for Sphodrias for Kleonymos' sake (Xen. *Hellenika* 5.4.25–33; Plut. *Agesilaos* 24–5, *Pelopidas* 14).

The decision to execute Sphodrias would have been the right one: Sparta had no quarrel with Athens and had just lost possession of Thebes. Kleombrotos had obviously deliberately avoided marching through Attica on his way to Thebes to prevent angering the Athenians, who attempted to keep peace with Sparta through their execution and exile respectively of their two generals who had assisted the Thebans. But the acquittal of Sphodrias, after marching through and plundering Attica in broad daylight, brought serious consequences. Athens voted that Sparta had broken the truce, and sent troops under Chabrias to support the Thebans (Diod. Sic. 15.29.7: doc. 14.14). Agesilaos campaigned against the Thebans in 377 and 376, and despite privations at Thebes (they could not sow their land for two consecutive seasons) they gradually re-established their control of Boeotia (Xen. *Hellenika* 5.4, esp. 14, 64; *Agesilaos* 2.22). Defeat awaited the Spartans and their allies in 375 BC when they launched a fleet to deprive Athens of its grain supplies: Chabrias defeated the Spartan admiral Pollis off the island of Naxos and thereby re-established Athens' naval supremacy in the Aegean (Xen. *Hellenika* 5.4.60–1).

Sparta, Thebes, and the battle of Leuktra in 371 BC

Thebes defeats Sparta at Tegyra, 375 BC

On land, too, the Spartans were about to face a major military reversal. In 375 BC, two entire divisions, morai, of the Spartan army (about one-third of its full strength) were defeated by the Thebans under Pelopidas at Tegyra (Plut. *Agesilaos* 27.4: doc. 14.16; Plut. *Pelopidas* 16–17). Xenophon neglected to tell his readers of this calamity, but he did record a direct result of it: Athens became wary of Thebes' growing power and made a short-lived peace with Sparta in 374 BC which ended when the Spartans attempted to interfere in Corcyra. Athens sent a fleet there under the command of Timotheos. When he failed to achieve any successes he was replaced by Iphikrates (Xen. *Hellenika* 6.2), and Sparta's fleet sailed away, not wishing to be trapped at the island by the Athenians. Thebes in 373 BC attacked and destroyed Plataea, whose citizens fled to Athens, its ally, where they were accepted as Athenian citizens, with some qualifications on their enfranchisement, and Thespiai was captured by Thebes in the same year. Thebes then began attacking Phokis, a long-standing ally of Athens, and Athens in 371 BC sent ambassadors to Thebes to invite them in turn to send envoys to Sparta, like Athens, to seek a general peace amongst the Greek states (Xen. *Hellenika* 6.3.1–2). Isocrates' treatise *Plataikos*, written as if spoken by a Plataean (but it was almost certainly not delivered as a speech), was composed soon after the destruction of the city, as an attempt to justify both Athenian aggression as a defence of Greek autonomy and the Second Athenian Confederacy (esp. *Plataikos* 17, 21).

The peace conference at Sparta in 371 BC

A consequence of this was the famous confrontation between Agesilaos and Epameinondas, one of the Theban ambassadors at Sparta, who at this stage had as yet no military victories to his credit. That Sparta was the venue was significant, for it had been Sparta which had initiated and in a very real sense guarded the peace of 386 BC, however imperfectly and to a great extent for its own advantage. The Greeks were in agreement with Agesilaos about the need for peace and autonomy amongst the various states, and Epameinondas spoke up to make the point that war made Sparta great at the expense of Greece as a whole, and that peace should be made on the terms that all states be equal. Agesilaos challenged this: Thebes ruled the cities of Boeotia which were not free. Nor, retorted Epameinondas, were the cities ruled by Sparta in Lakonia free. As a result all the Greek states made peace except for Sparta and Thebes (Plut. *Agesilaos* 27.5–28.4: doc. 14.16). Xenophon has a slightly different account with no mention of Epameinondas but with the same result: Thebes did not want to have to give up control of Boeotia, and Agesilaos and the Spartans were determined that it would. Athens, however, withdrew its garrisons from the cities it controlled, and the Spartans their governors (harmosts) and garrisons likewise (Xen. *Hellenika* 6.3.3–4.1).

The lead-up to Leuktra in 371 BC

Kleombrotos as king had a force consisting of four of the six Spartan morai, companies under arms in Phokis, and the Spartan assembly ordered him to Boeotia. He did not enter the country at the point where the Thebans had expected, and encamped at Leuktra, in the vicinity of Thespiai. Xenophon has a fairly detailed description of the battle and its aftermath, but excludes Pelopidas and Epameinondas from the narrative, while both Diodorus and Plutarch stress their role (*Hellenika* 6.4.3–26: partly doc. 14.18; see also Plut. *Pelopidas* 20–3; Diod. Sic. 15.51–6). Thebes only had other Boeotians as allies, while the Spartans had various allies and mercenaries, and considerably outnumbered the Thebans. Various omens and oracles encouraged the Thebans to fight the Spartans (when they were interpreted in a favourable light by Epameinondas). Pelopidas was the first to agree with Epameinondas that the Thebans had to fight the Spartans, and the vote to engage was by four Boeotarchs in favour to three against. Pelopidas was in command of the Theban 'Sacred Band', a group of 150 pairs of male lovers, which had been conspicuous in defeating the Spartans at Tegyra (Plut. *Pelopidas* 19.4: doc. 14.17). Kleombrotos stationed his cavalry in front of their phalanx and the Thebans followed suit: the Theban cavalry was in a high state of efficiency because of its use in the recent war against Orchomenos, while the Spartan was not (having had no regular practice). As for the infantry, the Spartans placed theirs twelve men deep, but the Thebans fifty deep opposite Kleombrotos as king, considering that if they broke the Spartan army here they would easily be able to vanquish the remaining enemy forces.

Spartan defeat at Leuktra

The two forces of cavalry met and the Thebans easily routed the Spartan horse, which then fell back on the Spartan hoplites creating confusion amongst their ranks and upsetting the ordered phalanx; at this point the Theban infantry began attacking. With the Theban phalanx fifty men deep, the Sacred Band under Pelopidas on the left wing, and Epameinondas (as one of the seven Boeotarchs) drawing the Thebans' phalanx towards their own left, so that the Spartan right wing would bear the brunt of the assault, the Thebans overcame the Spartan right. The polemarch Deinon, as well as Sphodrias and his son Kleonymos, were killed, and Kleombrotos was wounded and had to be carried off the field, dying soon afterwards; Agesilaos' son Archidamos was also fighting. Seeing their right collapsing, the Spartan left wing also gave way and the Spartans were defeated; they retreated across a trench in front of their own camp and here stopped, some of them thinking that they should make a stand to prevent the Thebans from erecting a victory trophy, and to fight to recover the bodies of the dead, rather than to have to ask for them under a truce. As the camp was on sloping ground, a defence here would have appeared practicable.

But 1000 of the Lakedaimonian army were dead and of 700 Spartiates who had fought 400 had been killed. The shortage of Spartan manpower is nowhere more clearly illustrated than at this battle, and it was Leuktra which caused the downfall of Sparta as a military power, as Aristotle recognised (Arist. *Politics* 1270a 31–3). Yet the Spartan force as a whole had been larger than the Theban: it was the Theban superiority in cavalry, the massed depth of their phalanx, and their tactics which defeated the superior Spartan force. A discussion initiated by the polemarchs led to the decision to request, successfully, a truce (Xen. *Hellenika* 6.4.13–16, 19–20: doc. 14.18). While the written ancient sources (except for Xenophon) focus on the

Figure 14.3 An exquisite carved gem of the stone chalcedony, showing an archer testing his arrow; he holds the bow by its string between his lower legs. The artist has captured magnificently the dynamics of the archer's musculature. While the Spartans disdained archery, many Greek armies included archers as an important component of their forces. This gem has a scaraboid shape (that is, the same shape as the scarab [dung-beetle] rings of ancient Egypt); it is believed to be the work of Epimenes of about 500 BC; it is 1.7 cm high. Metropolitan Museum of Art 31.11.5, New York. Drawing by Tessa Rickards.

role of Pelopidas and Epameinondas, other Theban leaders played their part and desired to be remembered: in an inscription three of the Thebans who fought that day asserted that their role was not 'second to Epameinondas', while more importantly they asserted that, 'The Thebans are greater in war [than the Spartans]', a claim that the Thebans would confirm and validate in the following years (Tod 2.130: doc. 14.19).

News of the defeat reaches Sparta

Back at Sparta the festival of the Gymnopaidiai was being celebrated and, when news was brought to the ephors of the disaster at Leuktra, in true Spartan fashion they did not interrupt the contests between the men's choruses that were a central part of the festival. Later, the ephors gave out the names of the dead, and the women were instructed to mourn silently, while on the next day the relatives of those who had been killed appeared with cheerful countenances in public, while the relatives of the survivors went around as if in mourning. Not only the defeat, but the fact that the survivors were seen to have surrendered in recovering the bodies of their dead under a truce was a great psychological blow. Though this was just one battle, the Thebans had already defeated the Spartans at Tegyra in 375 BC, and this defeat in 371 was a decisive one, with so many Spartiates killed. Nevertheless, the ephors called up the last two of the Spartan companies, including all the men up to 60 years of age (those up to 55 years of age had fought at Leuktra), such was the emergency, to meet up with the survivors from Kleombrotos' force; Archidamos was appointed to command. Sparta was not deserted by its allies and the force was brought back safely from Leuktra (Xen. *Hellenika* 6.4.19–20).

News of the defeat reaches Athens

When at Athens, which was currently at peace with Sparta, the news of the victory was announced by a Theban herald it was listened to in silence by the Athenian boule, which made no answer to the Theban request for assistance. The Thebans' defeat of Sparta had made Thebes the dominant force in Greece, a situation about which the Athenians could hardly be pleased (Xen. *Hellenika* 6.4.19–20: doc. 14.18), and later in the year they organised that all those states that wanted to participate in the King's Peace should send envoys to Athens. Many agreed to this, though Elis abstained, and the Thebans were almost certainly not invited and did not participate. Because of this renewal of the Peace of 386 BC, Mantineia felt it had the right to reconstitute itself as a single city and did so: Sparta had violated the treaty immediately after its ratification by destroying Mantineia's walls and forcing it to separate into villages. Agesilaos led out a force to Arkadia in 370 BC but achieved little and returned home to Sparta; Mantineia stayed 'sitting tight' waiting for the arrival of the Thebans who supported their cause and assisted Arkadia in unifying its various cities into a federation.

The Thebans invade the Peloponnese in 370 BC

Soon after Agesilaos' departure from Arkadia the Thebans arrived, and the Arkadians, who had been punishing the city of Heraia by burning down its houses and felling its trees because it had supported the Spartan invasion of Arkadia, joined forces with the Thebans, and persuaded them to invade Lakonia along with troops from Argos and Elis. Many Greek states were happy to join them as allies. Victory at Leuktra had encouraged the Thebans to become professional soldiers and since then they had trained constantly. In their invasion of Lakonia they burned and looted the Spartan houses along the right side of the river Eurotas, distressing the women of Sparta who could not even bear to look at the smoke from the burning houses, as they had never seen an enemy in Sparta before – nor had Sparta in its long history. A proclamation by the Spartans offering freedom to any helots who were willing to come to the aid of the city was answered by some 6000 volunteers, which at first alarmed the Spartan authorities, but as their allies remained loyal the Spartans considered the situation stable. Although the Thebans crossed the Eurotas at Amyklai, one of the villages which made up the city, the Spartans and their allies were able to drive them off and the Thebans withdrew, burning the unwalled cities of the region, and attacking Sparta's port at Gytheion for a period of three days (Xen. *Hellenika* 6.5.22–32: doc. 14.20). This intrusion into the heart of Sparta itself was without parallel and resulted in two major developments: the liberation of Messenia and the founding of an Arkadian league.

Messene re-established and the Messenian helots freed

In the two Messenian Wars of the seventh century BC, Sparta had conquered Messenia and enserfed its population. They had not been enslaved and went on living in their town and villages, but were subject to the Spartans, and gave over to them half of all their produce (Tyrt. *F* 6: doc. 5.44). After attacking the city of Sparta in 370 BC, Epameinondas persuaded his allies to refound the city of Messene near Mount Ithome, as an ideal base from which to attack Sparta, as it was situated relatively close by and was eminently defensible. This must in fact have been one of his main goals in entering the Peloponnese. The Messenian helots were freed, and they were now independent, no longer having to support the Spartans with either produce or manpower. After the great helot revolt on Mount Ithome in the 460s (Thucydides 1.102.1–103.3: doc. 12.11), some of the helots had been settled by the Athenians at Naupaktos, others had gone to Kephallenia, and yet others to Sicily. These exiles now returned and with the liberated helots constructed and populated the new settlement of Messene, of which Pausanias provides a detailed description. It was the foundation of Messene as the Messenian capital and the liberation of the Messenians even more than the battle of Leuktra that brought about the demise of Spartan power, as these emasculated and empoverished the Spartan state. It was also the case that the actual population of male adult Spartans was very much in decline in this period, a phenomenon Aristotle referred to as oliganthropia, 'shortage of men' (Aristot. *Politics* 1270a29–b6: doc. 6.37). Sparta called on Athens for aid and the Athenians sent a force under Iphikrates to assist the Spartans, but Epameinondas was able to make his way safely back to Thebes (Paus. *Description of Greece* 4.26.5–27.11: doc. 14.22; Diod. Sic. 15.66.1: doc. 14.23).

Foundation of Megalopolis

Thebes had supported the Arkadians against the Spartans, and now a unified Arkadia decided to found a 'federal' capital, with Epameinondas' encouragement. The dating is insecure, and it is one of the omissions from Xenophon's narrative, but it occurred sometime between 370 and 367 BC. The establishment of a united Arkadia meant that Spartan interference in that area was at an end, and as a state situated in the centre of the Peloponnese it could form an important bulwark against Sparta (Paus. 8.27.1–2: doc. 14.21). Arkadia played an important role in the lead-up to the battle of Mantineia in 362 BC, after which Mantineia, whose walls had been destroyed by Sparta in 385, reconstituted itself. Agesilaos' attempt to prevent this

Figure 14.4 The impressive remains of the theatre at Megalopolis (doc. 14.21). Photo © Daniel P. Diffendale.

had failed and it became a prime player in the events of the next few years. The foundation of Megalopolis and the refounding of Mantineia and Messene were all a consequence of the Theban invasion of Lakonia, which showed that Sparta's power was no longer sufficient to protect its own territory and that Sparta had lost military supremacy in its immediate neighbourhood (Fig. 14.4).

Peace attempts in 369–368 BC

Although Thebes was now the main power in Greece, Sparta was not entirely a spent force as yet. When Epameinondas invaded Sparta in 369 BC, Dionysios tyrant of Syracuse arrived with twenty triremes and a force of Celts and Iberians (Spaniards) and the Thebans withdrew after some skirmishing. Dionysios' forces attacked and defeated Sikyon, and then returned home, while a second force sent by Dionysios in 368 BC later went to Lakonia. In 368 BC an attempt at a peace, brokered by the Persians, foundered at Delphi as the Thebans would not agree that Messenia should once again be subject to Sparta (Xen. *Hellenika* 7.1.27). Arkadia pursued its own independent path without the Thebans, and a combined Arkadian-Argive force was defeated as it approached Lakonia in 368 BC without the loss of one Spartan life: the Thebans were as happy at this as were the Spartans, who were reassured at achieving a victory after their recent disasters (Xen. *Hellenika* 7.1.28–32). In 367 BC various Greek ambassadors were present at the court of the Persian king at Susa taking part in a discussion concerning peace (Xen. *Hellenika* 7.1.30–40). Pelopidas represented the Thebans and posed as a friend of the Persians: the Thebans had fought alongside the Persians at Plataea in 479 BC and had never attacked them. But for Xenophon the Thebans' motives were plain: had they been successful they would then like the Spartans in 386 BC have secured their place as the leaders of Greece (Xen. *Hellenika* 7.1.40). A further attempt at a peace congress at Thebes in 366 was a total failure.

In 366 BC Thebes seized the border town and sanctuary of the healing hero Amphiaraos from Athens, which was an act of deliberate provocation, and the Arkadians and Thebans became allies again in the same year. Thebes launched a fleet in 364 BC and fomented discord between Athens and its allies Rhodes, Chios and Byzantium, which appears to have resulted in Byzantium leaving the Second Athenian Confederacy. Trouble was brewing between Athens and its allies (Diod. Sic. 15.78–9). Pelopidas was killed at Kynoskephalai in 364 BC while in northern Greece on a military mission against the tyrant of Pherai, Alexander, who had been attacking cities in Thessaly. Pelopidas won the battle but paid the ultimate price. Another second battle saw Alexander completely defeated, and he had to surrender the Thessalian cities he had conquered, and to become an ally of Thebes and rule only over Pherai (Diod. Sic. 15.80).

Arkadia was meanwhile at war with Elis, and had been 'borrowing' money from the treasuries at Olympia to pay for the Eparitoi, a group of Arkadian soldiers, something to which the Mantineians objected. The Arkadians as a whole decided to stop this borrowing of funds, but those responsible for it feared that they would be punished and asked the Thebans for assistance. In 363 BC, however, a peace was arranged between Elis and Arkadia which was ratified at Tegea by various Arkadian delegates as well as by a Theban commander who had been sent there with 300 hoplites. The Arkadians who feared they would be held to account for the sacred treasures seized Tegea with the help of the Boeotian hoplites and the various Arkadian ambassadors who had just sworn to the peace. The Mantineians came to an agreement with the other Arkadian cities, and the Boeotians were allowed to leave Tegea (Xen. *Hellenika* 7.4.33–40).

The battle of Mantineia in 362 BC

Soon afterwards in 362 BC Epameinondas marched to Tegea with a force of Boeotians, Euboeans, Tegeans, Megalopolitans, Messenians, Argives, some of the Arkadians, and the Thessalians. Having heard that Agesilaos had set out for Tegea and that Sparta was undefended, Epameinondas marched to Sparta, but Agesilaos was informed of this in time and returned. His son Archidamas played a key role in its successful defence, and set up a victory trophy, an indication of 'how the mighty state had fallen' in that there was seen to be glory in publicising a battle against enemies who had attacked the city of Sparta itself. Epameinondas withdrew to Tegea and, as it was nearly the appointed time for him to finish the campaign and he was concerned that he would be besieged at Tegea, he led his army to Mantineia. Awaiting him there in the plain were the Spartans, Athenians, Achaeans, Eleians and other Arkadians, including the Mantineians, supported by a mercenary force.

The Theban and their allies comprised 30,000 infantry and 3000 cavalry, while ranged against them were 20,000 infantry and 2000 cavalry. This was the greatest battle in terms of sheer numbers of troops yet fought in classical Greece. Epameinondas on the left wing faced the entire force of Spartans except for the 6000 Athenians who were on their own left wing.

The Thebans were successful in battle with regards to their cavalry, but not without facing a strong resistance from the cavalry of Elis. With neither side prepared to yield, the foot battle lasted a long time with the armies interlocked. Once their spears were thrown (such were the number thrown that many shattered as they met each other in the air), they fought with their swords. Epameinondas realised that an extra effort would be needed, and taking his best troops directly assaulted the Spartans breaking their phalanx through sheer pressure of numbers, aided in this by the reputation as a great warrior he had amongst the Spartans, who were clearly frightened of him. As the Spartans fell back the Boeotians kept killing, and mounds of corpses piled up. But when the Spartans saw Epameinondas too far forward in front of his line, they threw their spears directly at him and eventually one hit home and he collapsed. Fierce struggles ensued around him but the Boeotians beat off the Spartans who fled, and Epameinondas was carried from the battle, to die when the spear point stuck in his body was extracted. On their left wing, the Athenians had defeated the Euboeans and the mercenaries and this Athenian victory meant that the result of the battle was unclear. Because of this the participants agreed to a peace, but the Spartans refused to sign because the Messenians were included in its terms. Xenophon's description of the battle of Mantineia is the last section of his *Hellenika*, and his final paragraph sums up the situation: neither side could really claim victory, nothing had been settled, and the affairs of Greece were more undecided and disordered than ever before (Xen. *Hellenika* 7.5; Diod. Sic. 15.84–7, 89.1; Plut. *Agesilaos* 34–5).

Events in northern Greece

Iason of Pherai

Iason of Pherai in north-eastern Greece had inherited a tyranny from his father Lykophron, and had extended his power over numerous cities of Thessaly and over the king of Epiros, partly through the employment of a force of 6000 mercenaries. In 374 BC, Polydamos of Pharsalos, who had been defeated in battle by Iason, had gone to the Spartans and requested their assistance, but they had pointed out the realities of what was clearly their own over-stretched position: their forces were already committed against their Athenian and other enemies, and they could give him no aid. Polydamos returned to Thessaly and secured a peace with Iason, with Pharsalos willingly became his ally. Soon after, Iason became tagos (commander) of Thessaly, assessing the military forces that the Thessalians would provide him with as 8000 cavalry, 20,000 hoplites and numerous peltasts; in addition, they were to pay tribute to him (Xen. *Hellenika* 6.1.1–19, esp. 19).

Iason was an enemy of Phokis and so naturally an ally of Thebes, and after Leuktra in 371 BC the Thebans sent him news of their victory. Arriving at the battle scene, he advised them not to go ahead with their plan to attempt to engage the remaining Spartan forces in a further battle: desperation would make the Spartans fight to the death. He also advised the Spartans to desist from further battle and reserve their forces for the next encounter. Xenophon considers Iason's advice as stemming from the fact that, with the Spartans and Thebans in conflict, both sides would have need of him. He was also setting himself up as a mediator in Greek affairs: as Xenophon notes, he was the most powerful single Greek individual of the time and his intervention between Sparta and Thebes was a reflection of his power. On his way back to Thessaly, his destruction of the city-wall of the Herakleiots meant that no other state would be able to take this city and block his path south into Greece (Xen. *Hellenika*

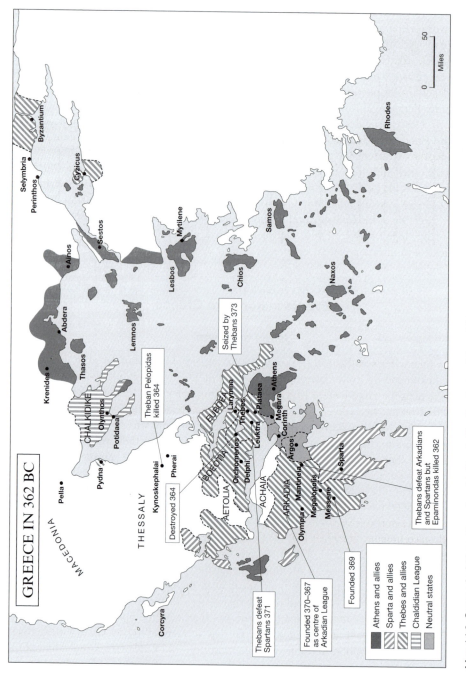

Map 14.2 Greece in 362 BC. Based on M. Grant, *The Routledge Atlas of Classical History*, fifth edition, Routledge, 1994, pp. 34–35.

GREECE IN 362 BC

MACEDONIA

Pella

Pydna

THESSALY

Kynoskephalai

Pherai

Corcyra

Destroyed 364

Theban Pelopidas
killed 364

CHALKIDIKE

Olynthos

Potidaea

Krenides

Thasos

Abdera

Ainos

Lemnos

Sestos

Perinthos

Selymbria

Byzantium

Cyzicus

Mytilene

Lesbos

Chios

Samos

Naxos

Rhodes

Seized by
Thebans 373

EUBOEA

Larymna

Orchomenos

Thebes

Delphi

Leuktra

Plataea

Athens

Megara

Corinth

Argos

Mantineia

Sparta

AETOLIA

BOEOTIA

ACHAIA

ARKADIA

Olympia

Megalopolis

Messene

Thebans defeat
Spartans 371

Founded 370–367
as centre of
Arkadian League

Founded 369

Thebans defeat Arkadians
and Spartans but
Epaminondas killed 362

Athens and allies

Sparta and allies

Thebes and allies

Chaldidian League

Neutral states

0 50

Miles

Figure 14.5 Pella, capital of Macedonia, where Alexander was born to Philip and Olympias, founded by Archelaos I of Macedon who reigned 413–399 BC; it replaced the earlier capital of Vergina, which remained an important city. Photo © bilwander (www.bilwander.blogspot.com).

6.4.22–5). He clearly had further military activity in central Greece in mind, just as Philip of Macedon was later to seize Thermopylai to guarantee his access to Greece. Any plans Iason had to increase his territory were cut short in 370 BC, when he planned a religious-military offensive, ordering the Thessalian cities to prepare contributions for the celebration of the Pythian festival, while he at the same time gathered the Thessalian forces for a march on Delphi. His intentions were never quite clear, but presumably he intended to wrest control of Delphi for himself as part of his campaign against the Phokaians, and to win himself a seat on the prestigious Amphiktyonic Council, a Greek council which managed the affairs of Delphi. His membership of it would have marked his, like Philip's later, acceptance into the Greek world. But there were grievances against him and he was assassinated in 370 BC. The killers were welcomed as tyrant-slayers and liberators wherever they went afterwards, and Xenophon comments, 'it is clear that the Greeks were extremely afraid in case Iason became a tyrant' (Xen. *Hellenika* 6.4.27–32: doc. 14.24; Diod. Sic. 15.60).

The accession of Philip II of Macedon

Macedon in northern Greece had played a part in Greek affairs in the Persian Wars of the fifth century, in which its king Alexander had proved a friend of the Greeks. Otherwise, it was a relatively 'backward' area which played little role in Greek affairs. This was to change when Philip II came to the Macedonian throne. Amyntas of Macedon (reigned c. 393–370 BC) had three sons: Alexander, Perdikkas and Philip. Amyntas was defeated by his warlike neighbours the Illyrians in 369, and made to pay tribute, and his youngest

509

son Philip was handed over to them as a hostage. The Illyrians in turn entrusted him to the care of their allies, the Thebans, and Philip in 369 or 368 BC came into the charge of Epameinondas' father who had him educated with his son in philosophy and other forms of liberal education. It was also at Thebes that Philip was first exposed to the Theban military tactics and strategy involving the deployment of the phalanx. Philip was an ambitious and aggressive ruler: in 359 BC, starting his career as regent, his plans were clearly to preserve Macedonia's territorial integrity, but he was to be continuously presented by the Greek cities with opportunities which would allow him to expand his power until he became hegemon of Greece.

Amyntas III (393–370 BC) was succeeded by his eldest son Alexander II (370–368 BC), who was murdered by Ptolemy of Oloros (368–365), who acted as regent until killed in his turn by the rightful heir Perdikkas III (368–359 BC). Perdikkas was defeated and killed (along with 4000 Macedonians) in 359 BC when the Illyrians invaded under their King Bardylis. This brought his brother Philip II to the fore; Perdikkas had a young son, Amyntas IV, who was technically ruler but a minor (359–356 BC), and Philip displaced him when he had himself crowned as king in 356 BC (Amyntas would later be killed by Alexander in 336 BC). Macedonia was under threat: the Illyrians had won a decisive engagement against the Macedonians and had begun preparing for another invasion, while the Paionians near Macedonia were taking advantage of the situation to pillage the country. In addition a pretender, Pausanias, who was related to the ruling family (the Argead dynasty), was plotting with the Thracians to be put on the throne, while the Athenians were planning to install their own preferred candidate, Argaios. Against this backdrop of potential disasters, Philip rallied the Macedonians to support his regime (Diod. Sic. 16.2.1–3.3: doc. 14.25).

Philip secures Macedonia

A series of quick successes over the next few years secured Macedonia from outside threats and expanded its power and influence. Justin and Diodorus are the main sources for these early years of Philip's reign (Just. *Epitome Historiarum* 7.5.1–6.16: doc. 14.26; Diod. Sic. 16.1–4). In 359 BC, Philip dealt with the Athenian force under the general Mantias, whose aim was to put Argaios on the Macedonian throne with the aid of a large fleet and 3000 hoplites, by withdrawing the Macedonian garrison from Amphipolis; the Athenian force therefore accompanied Argaios only as far as Methone, while Argaios went ahead to Aigai, where the population did not support him. While he was returning to Methone Philip defeated his forces in battle. Philip dealt with the other rival to the throne, Pausanias, by concluding peace through gifts with the Thracian king who was supporting him. With regard to the Paionians Philip at first made peace with them through the use of gifts and bribery, but when their king died in 359 BC he attacked them and forced them to become his allies. In the same year, with 10,000 soldiers and 600 cavalry, he marched into Illyria and defeated its king, Bardylis, who commanded a force of similar size. After the Macedonians slaughtered 7000 Illyrians they made peace and withdrew their forces from Macedonian cities. Philip's control of Macedonia was now secure and Diodorus' assessment of Philip is worth noting. For him, securing Macedonia from further Illyrian attacks was a key factor in Philip's success, as the elimination of the threat from this powerful neighbour gave Philip the opportunity to use Macedonian resources to the full for other ventures (Diod. Sic. 16.1.3–6: doc. 14.27; also 16.2–4).

Amphipolis, Olynthos and Potidaea

Philip captured Amphipolis in 357 BC, having withdrawn from there to deceive Mantias and the Athenians in their attempt to install the pretender Argaios on the Macedonian throne. Amphipolis was a powerful, strategically placed city that had opposed him and he besieged it successfully and exiled his opponents in the city. He next conquered Pydna, and made an alliance with Olynthos, one of the many Greek cities on the Chalkidice peninsula, capturing Potidaea for the Olynthians as part of the deal. Potidaea had an Athenian garrison, which he allowed to leave in safety, but he enslaved the inhabitants, and handed over the site to Olynthos (Diod. Sic. 16.8.1–5: doc. 14.29). In the same year, Philip allied himself with the Chalkidian league as a whole: Macedonia had become a major player in the affairs of northern Greece.

Philip's resources in 356 BC

Philip's resources were greatly enhanced when he took control of the city of Krenides (in Thrace), founded only a few years earlier by settlers from the island of Thasos (Diod. Sic. 16.3.7). It was now renamed Philippoi and he increased its population dramatically, heavily fortifying it as a base against the Thracians. Proclaimed by the Macedonian assembly as king in this year, on the basis of his successes and his salvation of the country, he now pursued a vigorous foreign policy. It was at this stage that Philip gained access to financial resources which were to prove crucial in the years to come, when he fully exploited the hitherto neglected gold mines of the region. Coins struck from this gold displaying his image were

Figure 14.6 A gold coin minted at Amphipolis. The obverse shows the god Apollo wearing a wreath. The reverse shows a man in a two-horse chariot with the legend, 'Of Philip'. Such coins attest to Philip's panhellenic aspirations through his sending of chariot teams to compete in the festivals of mainland Greece, and is also a testimony to his personal wealth which played a major factor in his political and military success (doc. 14.29). It weighs 8.57 g. Yale University Art Gallery, 2001.87.9716

known as Philippeioi and these were used to pay for mercenaries and later were very useful in bribing politicians in the cities of mainland Greece (Diod. Sic. 16.8.6–7: doc. 14.29; Arr, *Expedition of Alexander* 7.9.2–3: doc. 14.55; Fig. 14.6). He marked his arrival on the panhellenic religio-cultural scene in 356 BC with a victory at Olympia in the four horse chariot race, with further victories in 352 and 348 BC.

The revolt of Athens' allies in 357 BC

Athens meanwhile was preoccupied with what scholars call, particularly in the older literature, the Social War (from the Latin noun socii, meaning allies), which lasted from 357 to 355 BC. Athens had set up the Second Athenian Confederacy as a counter to Spartan power and it had reinvigorated Athenian control of the Aegean (docs 14.14–15). This was challenged when Euboea was torn by civil conflict in 357 BC for thirty days with great loss of life on both sides. Athens was involved, supporting one side against the other, which had the support of the Thebans. Athens prevailed and a peace was signed, which was to result in Athens' domination of the island for the next eight years. Through this Thebes had been dealt a telling blow, and its activities would henceforth be directed against a closer neighbour and old enemy, Phokis.

At approximately the same time Athens' allies decided to revolt, when Chios, Rhodes, Kos and Byzantium all left the Athenian alliance in 357 BC. The Athenian generals Chares and Chabrias were sent with a fleet of sixty triremes to Chios, where they were met by a fleet of rebel states assisted by the independent ruler of Caria, Mausolos. Chabrias was killed in the defeat that the allies inflicted on Athens, but most of the Athenian fleet escaped, though as a result of the defeat more allies left the alliance. In 356 BC Chares was joined by Timotheos and Iphikrates with another sixty triremes and the size of the Athenian fleet was considerable. The rebels with a fleet of one hundred triremes sacked the Athenian islands of Imbros and Lemnos and proceeded to ravage the island of Samos and besiege its city, which had always been loyal to the Athenian cause, while other islands were plundered to provide the rebels with funds. Athens attempted a counter-stroke by investing Byzantium, which lured the allied fleet from Samos, and Chares insisted on giving battle despite a storm. Timotheos and Iphikrates refused to engage, and when the Athenians heard of this from Chares they deposed them from their command and fined them several talents (Diod. Sic. 16.7.2–4: docs 14.28, 16.21).

Peace with the allies

The Athenians, however, were short of funds (which was an ongoing problem), so Chares took service in 356 BC with Artabazos, the satrap of Phrygia, who was in revolt against the Persian king. Chares defeated the armies of several satraps of Artaxerxes III (358–338 BC), who had recently come to the Persian throne, and Artabazos gave him a huge amount of money. The Athenians at first approved of all of this, until the Great King sent ambassadors to Athens to complain about Chares' actions and they also heard that the king was promising to give Athens' allies the assistance of 300 triremes. At this point the assembly voted for peace and Athens lost control of Chios, Kos and Rhodes; Byzantium, which had been an unwilling member of the alliance since 364 BC, was also independent. But the situation was not the same as it had been in 404 BC: Athens still possessed the support of several allies and remained a powerful force, though it would be plagued by a shortage of funds in its future war against Philip. Moreover, the interference of Persia and the fear this aroused was to be a significant factor in future: the king merely needed to spread the rumour that he was offering assistance to Athens' disaffected allies to put an end to Athenian intervention in the affairs of his empire (Diod. Sic. 16.22).

At Athens, Euboulos took control of Athens' finances soon after the war with the allies and gradually built these up, increasing Athenian revenues from 130 to 400 talents a year. Revenues were focused on the construction of new triremes and improvements to the naval dockyards, as well as the fortifications of the city. The theoric fund (theorika), which assisted the poor in paying entrance fees to public festivals such as the Dionysia where theatrical productions took place, was also probably established by Euboulos, and it was allocated a fixed sum of money annually and any surplus revenue. Sometimes criticised for gratuitously distributing money to the poor, this was only part of its portfolio, and it was used for various projects. The city had been fighting wars in several places, in particular at Amphipolis and in the Chersonese, and the war with the allies had not only cost money, but lost them allies. Athens needed careful financial management and Euboulos provided this, as Lykourgos did later, from 338 to 326 BC. Xenophon recognised the financial difficulties facing the city, and in his *Poroi (Revenues)* he advocated that Athens encourage foreigners to relocate to Athens, and that the silver mines at Laureion should be worked more efficiently. Similarly, the Athenian speech writer Isocrates penned his *On the Peace* (probably in 355 BC), in which he argued that peace was necessary not just with Chios, Rhodes, Byzantium and Kos, against whom the war with the allies had just been fought, but with all states, and that the Athenians should return to the terms of the King's Peace of 386 BC (Isoc. 1 *On the Peace* 16), and abandon costly wars.

Philip, Athens and Olynthos

In 356 BC, a coalition of Thracians, Paionians and Illyrians began assembling their forces against Philip but before they were prepared he was there confronting their troops. The mere sight of him was apparently sufficient inducement for them to join his army (Diod. Sic. 16.22.3). In 355 BC he attacked Methone (an Athenian ally) on the coast of the Thermaic Gulf, not far from Pydna. The city was besieged and the siege ended in the following year. At the siege of Methone Philip famously lost his right eye when struck by an arrow (Just. 7.6.14–16: doc. 14.26; Diod. Sic. 16.31.6, 34.4–5). Athens now had no allies in this region, which Philip now dominated, with Olynthos and the Chalkidike his allies. The loss of Potidaea and Methone, not to mention Amphipolis, meant that Macedonian rather than Athenian influence predominated in northern Greece. Athens, however, prevented him descending into central Greece in 352 BC by holding the pass at Thermopylai against him (Dem. 19.310; Diod. Sic. 16.38.1), for which he retaliated.

In 351 BC, Philip attacked Athens' grain ships as they rounded the south of Euboea, and carried off one of the state triremes from Marathon itself. In the same year, in the first of his four speeches called the *Philippics*, Demosthenes warned the Athenians against Philip's aggression, versatility, martial energy and territorial aggrandisement. In 349 BC Demosthenes summed up the situation as it appeared at that juncture: Philip had captured Amphipolis, Pydna, Potidaea and Methone, taken control of Thessaly, Pherai, Pagasai and Magnesia, and dominated Thrace by appointing its rulers (Dem. *First Olynthiac* 11–13: doc. 14.30).

Olynthos had joined Philip in 357 BC but as his influence and power continued to grow in the region it came to have second thoughts. He was clearly aiming at complete domination of the

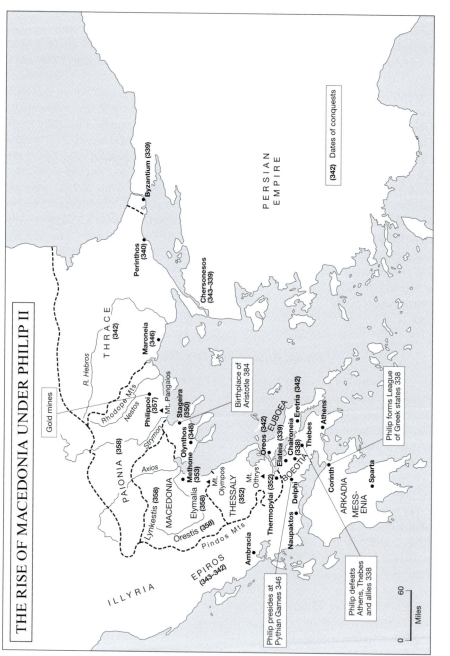

THE RISE OF MACEDONIA UNDER PHILIP II

ILLYRIA

PAIONIA (358)

Lynkestis (358)
MACEDONIA
Orestis (358)
Elymalia (358)

EPIROS (343–342)

Ambracia

THESSALY (352)
Mt. Othrys
Mt. Olympos

Pindos Mts

Axios
Strymon

Gold mines

THRACE (342)

Rhodope Mts
Nestos
R. Hebros

Maroneia (346)

Mt. Pangaios
Philippoi (357)
Stageira (350)

Olynthos (348)
Methone (353)

Chersonesos (343–339)

Perinthos (340)

Byzantium (339)

PERSIAN EMPIRE

Birthplace of Aristotle 384

Thermopylai (352)

Naupaktos

Delphi

Oreos (342)
Elateia (339)
Chaironeia (338)
BOEOTIA
Thebes

EUBOEA

Eretria (342)

Athens

Corinth

ARKADIA
MESS-
ENIA

Sparta

Philip presides at Pythian Games 346

Philip defeats Athens, Thebes and allies 338

Philip forms League of Greek states 338

(342) Dates of conquests

0   60
Miles

Map 14.3 The rise of Macedonia under Philip II. Based on M. Grant, *The Routledge Atlas of Classical History*, fifth edition, Routledge, 1994, p. 35.

coastal region to the south of Macedonia: Olynthos and the Chalkidian cities, while his allies, stood in his way. In 352 BC Olynthos and Athens signed a peace treaty, and in 349 this developed into a full alliance. Philip had sent to Olynthos demanding that it return to him his two half-brothers who had fled there; they were perhaps intriguing to be placed on the Macedonian throne. Thirty-eight triremes and 2000 peltasts were sent by Athens under Chares, who had been in northern waters, but nothing was achieved. Charidamos, operating in the Hellespont, was then sent with eighteen triremes and 4000 peltasts. This force, though conducting some successful raids in the area, did not assist the Olynthians, who requested another force, not of peltast mercenaries but of Athenians themselves. Chares was then dispatched, with seventeen triremes, 2000 Athenian hoplites and 300 Athenian cavalry, but these were to arrive too late, after the fall of Olynthos. Philip began his siege of Olynthos that same year and captured and enslaved it in 348 BC; frontal assaults and battles in which he lost many men failed, but bribery and corruption of two of Olynthos' officials succeeded and the gates were opened to him (Dem. *Olynthiacs* 1–3; Diod. Sic. 16.52.1–3: doc. 14.31); immediately prior to capturing Olynthos he had taken Mekyberna (Olynthos' port) and Torone (on the second peninsula of the Chalkidike). For Athens, the loss should not be exaggerated: Olynthos and Athens were not close allies, and assistance from the Athenian seems to have been relatively insignificant and almost half-hearted. The city had its eyes on events closer to home.

The Third Sacred War

Delphi and its temple were controlled by the amphiktyony, a council made up of representatives from several Greek states, largely in the region, each of which sent one or two members; these representatives were known as hieromnemones. The amphiktyony also seems to have considered that it had a role in wider Greek affairs, and after the battle of Leuktra in 371 BC the Thebans brought a complaint to the council about Sparta's seizure of the Kadmeia in 382 BC, which had violated the terms of the King's Peace which the Spartans themselves had sponsored. A heavy fine of 500 talents was levied against the Spartans but they ignored it, and the fine was later doubled to 1000 at the instigation of the Thebans (Diod. Sic. 16.23.2–3: doc. 14.32; cf. 16.29). Closer to home, the council in 357 BC condemned the Phokaians (who had two votes on the council) and imposed a large fine on them for having cultivated the sacred land of Delphi, the Kirrhaian plain. Thebes, Phokis' traditional enemy, was almost certainly behind this prosecution, which should be seen as part of a Theban attempt to gain even more influence and control in central Greece.

When Phokis refused to pay the fine the amphiktyones decided to consecrate as sacred land all Phokaian territory, amounting to a massive confiscation of land, which could not be cultivated because it was sacred, and as such dedicated to the god. The Phokaian leader Philomelos argued to his countrymen that the fine was too heavy a penalty for the offence of having cultivated a small amount of sacred land, arguing – on the basis of some lines from Homer – that Delphi had once belonged to the Phokaians (Diod. Sic. 16.23.2–3: doc. 14.32). Elected as supreme commander (autokrator strategos) of Phokis, Philomelos went to Sparta where Archidamos, persuaded by Philomelos that he would have the amphiktyonic judgement against the Spartans annulled, secretly gave him 15 talents with which to hire mercenaries and cover war expenses. Philomelos seized Delphi, killing some of the Delphians, defeated the Lokrians who took to the field against him, and then cut out from the Delphic stelai the amphiktyonic decrees as well as destroying the written records. The Boeotians, with the Lokrians and various other Greeks, especially those in the region, took up Delphi's – or

Figure 14.7 The circular Philippeion at Olympia, commenced in 338 BC and probably completed by Alexander, which housed chryselephantine (gold and ivory) statues of Philip, his parents, Olympias, and Alexander, by the sculptor Leochares. Originally there were eighteen Ionic columns and the circular building was 18 m in diameter. Photo © Lee L. Brice.

Thebes' – cause, while Athens and Sparta aligned themselves on the other side: Athens and Phokis had long been allies but Thebes and Athens had been estranged after the battle of Leuktra. With most of Greece on one side or the other, the war convulsed the entire mainland (Diod. Sic. 16.24–29).

Philomelos drew on the sacred treasures of Delphi and hired mercenaries at one and a half the times the normal rate of pay. After some successes, he threw himself off a cliff when trapped after a battle in which the Thebans defeated the Phokaians in 354 BC. Onomarchos then took over as supreme commander, and invaded Lokris and Boeotia, but was forced out of the latter. The year 353 saw Philip, in support of the Thessalians, attacking Lykophron tyrant of Pherai who called upon his allies the Phokaians. Phayllos, Onomarchos' brother, was sent to Lykophron's assistance with a force of 7000 men but was defeated by Philip. Onomarchos then led the Phokaian army in person and twice defeated Philip, while in the next year, 352, he captured Koroneia in Boeotia. Philip marched against Lykophron once more, but on this occasion when Onomarchos came to Lykophron's support, Philip defeated him and hanged him as a temple-robber. Onomarchos' brother Phayllos then took over command of the Phokaians, also using the sacred treasures to hire mercenaries at double pay. Philip conquered Pherai, and in 352 made for the pass at Thermopylai but here the Athenians blocked his passage. Phayllos lost three battles to the Boeotians, but successfully captured many cities in Lokris. On his death, Onomachos' son Phalaikos took over leadership of the Phokaians. Meanwhile, Sparta and Megalopolis had a major confrontation in 352

516

BC which ended in a truce, while Mausolos, ruler of Caria, died and his sister-wife Artemisia took control of the region for two years (Diod. Sic. 16.30–7; Dem. 19.84).

The Thebans requested financial assistance from Artaxerxes, probably in return for the help they gave him in 351 BC, when they sent 1000 hoplites to help Persia reconquer Egypt (Diod. Sic. 16.44.1–2; see 44–51 for the crushing of the Egyptian revolt with Greek assistance). Their involvement was largely due to financial considerations: in 353/2 BC they had fought for Artabazos in his rebellion against the king (16.34.1–2); similarly in 356/5 the Athenian Chares had entered Artabazos' employ for money for his ships and men (16.22: he was recalled by Athens when the king protested). Phalaikos and the Phokaians in 347 BC seized several Boeotian cities, in particular Orchomenos and Koroneia, constantly campaigning with their mercenaries against the Boeotians, and plundering their territory. Phalaikos, however, was accused of embezzling sacred treasures and was removed from his command, though soon reinstated. The Boeotians, who had lost a great number of soldiers and were now short of money, asked for Philip's help and in 346 he descended into central Greece and encountered Phalaikos near Thermopylai. The Phokaians, outnumbered, surrendered to Philip rather unexpectedly, and the Third Sacred War came to a close with Philip able to take credit for the cessation of hostilities.

Philip garrisoned Nicaea, a town from which the pass of Thermopylai could be controlled, and was awarded the two seats on the Amphiktyonic Council which had been held by the Phokaians. Their cities were destroyed and they were forced to live in villages of no more than fifty houses; those who had robbed the temple at Delphi were cursed. The Phokaians also had to repay 60 talents a year until the stolen Delphic treasures were all accounted for, a total sum of some 10,000 talents (Diod. Sic. 16.38–60; 16.59.4–60.5: doc. 14.34; Just. 8.2.5–9: doc. 14.35; Tod 2.172A: doc. 14.36). Significantly the Phokaians and their mercenaries, well generalled, determined and with access to the treasures at Delphi, had managed to defeat Philip more than once, as well as overcoming the Boeotians and Lokrians several times and overrunning their territory: had they perhaps received a little more help from Sparta and Athens (though Phailakos in 346 had rejected an offer from Athens), Phokis might have joined Sparta, Athens and Thebes as one of the hegemons of classical Greece. Furthermore it was precisely this struggle with Phokis which wore Thebes down and made it look to Philip for assistance, which gave him a pretext for entering central Greece and eventually led to the destruction of Theban power.

'A wife with each war'

In determining the secret of Philip's success the matrimonial aspect should not be overlooked. Marriage alliances were a deliberate part of his strategy, and he took several wives, engaging in polygamy throughout his reign. Most important of these wives was Olympias (his fourth), with her status due to the fact that she brought him control of the Molossian kingdom. By her he had two children, Alexander and Kleopatra. Though of less importance, the other wives also created ties which helped to cement his control of northern Greece: Illyria, Thessaly and Thrace were bound to him in this way. None of these wives were Macedonians, until the seventh and last, one Kleopatra Eurydike, the niece of Attalos (Ath. *Deipnosophistae* 13.557b–e: doc. 14.37), and it was this marriage which would lead to a break in his relationship with Alexander.

Companions and Pages

Philip also built up a body of loyal followers at court. These included the so-called Companions, drawn not just from Macedonia but from throughout his possessions, and thus helping

Table 14.2 The immediate family and marriage alliances of Philip II of Macedon

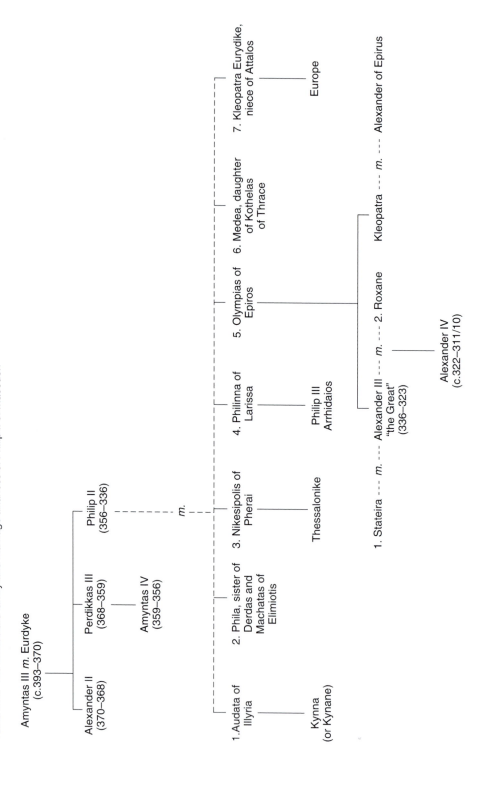

Figure 14.8 A gold medallion of Olympias, wearing a diadem and headdress, with a sceptre in her right hand. It dates to 300–250 BC, with a diameter of 5.8 cm and weighs 81.86 g. Münzkabinett 18200020, Staatliche Museen, Berlin. Drawing by Tessa Rickards.

to draw these places further into the Macedonian orbit; there were 800 Companions all told and they were rewarded with a place at court and estates. Theopompos criticised their lifestyle, and it appears that Philip's court was fairly extravagant and high-spirited; gambling and drinking (sometimes accompanied by brawls and deadly insults) appear to have been a feature of both his and his son's reign (Theopomp. *The History of Philip: FF*224–5: doc. 14.39). Adolescent sons of the Macedonian Companions served the king as 'Pages', guarding him while he slept and generally waiting on his person; they were to play a key role in a conspiracy against Alexander (Arr. 4.13.1: doc. 14.38; conspiracy: doc. 15.25).

Philip and the art of warfare

Gold from Philippoi and the booty of war (including slaves, from cities that he captured and enslaved like Olynthos) enriched Philip and enabled him to fight a different type of warfare against the Greeks. They waged war according to specific rules and out in the open (perhaps a slight exaggeration as there were always those in Greek cities willing to negotiate with the enemy). But Philip had a particular flair for spending money with a view to influencing the key political figures in Greek cities. Many cities, such as Olynthos, were betrayed from within, or had pro-Philip factions. Demosthenes points out that whereas the Greeks traditionally had one campaigning season a year, of four to five months' duration, Philip campaigned all year

519

round, making 'no distinction between summer and winter' and employed not just the phalanx but also light-armed troops (peltasts), mercenaries, cavalry and archers (Dem. 9 *Third Philippic* 47–50: doc. 14.40, doc. 14.3). This was not in fact so very different from other Greek armies, and even the Spartans had employed hoplite mercenaries and peltasts. The key to Philip's success was rather in the continual nature of his campaigning (as Demosthenes notes), in the size of the forces he used, and most particularly in the effectivness of his Macedonian phalanx.

The phalanx and the sarissa

According to Diodorus, as early as 358 BC shortly after his accession, Philip improved the organisation of the Macedonian forces, equipped them with superior weapons and drilled his forces continuously, making them compete against each other in training, and it was in this way that he defeated the Illyrians. Diodorus also places the adoption of the phalanx to this period (Diod. Sic. 16.3.1–2: doc. 14.25). Polybios explains the phalanx in detail, and Asklepiodotos agrees with his account. Its main features were the depth of men employed and the type of weapon. Sarissas, the Macedonian long pikes, were made from cornel wood, common in Macedonia, and well known for its strength and density. The first five rows of men in the phalanx held their sarissas horizontally, so that all five spears extended beyond the first rank of men, with each man in the front rank having five spears between him and the enemy. As each spear projected a different distance in front of the first rank, it had a different effective length. Each soldier in the first rank was effectively protected by his own and four other spears, giving him ideal cover while he used his own spear to attack the enemy.

The ranks behind the first five held their spears slanting over the heads of the men in front of them in order to ward off any aerial missiles heading in their direction. In addition, the enemy was faced with a bristling array of spears that held even if men in the first rank were killed, as the soldiers in the sixth rank could then lower their spears. The sarissas at 6 metres (19 to 20 feet) long needed to be held with both hands. There were of course less positive aspects to the formation, as Polybios notes: the formation needed to remain intact and so had to fight on level ground, without obstacles such as 'ditches, ravines, stream-junctions, ridges and river beds' for these would detract from its effectiveness and break up the phalanx formation (12.20.2–6: doc. 15.12). Shields were round, about 60 centimetres or two feet in diameter, large enough to afford protection but small enough not to be too heavy. Infantry and cavalry worked in conjunction: Alexander made devastatingly effective use of the phalanx against Persia, and it was this formation which was responsible for the destruction of the Persian empire and its armies (Polyb. *Histories* 18.29.1–30.4, 31.5–7: doc. 14.41; Asklepiodotos *Tactics* 5.1–2: doc. 14.42).

Demosthenes

Philip brought the Third Sacred War to an end in 346. But at the same time, just prior to the surrender of the Phokaians and the penalty imposed on them, other events had been in train, in which Demosthenes, Aeschines and Philokrates were the key players (Fig. 14.9). Demosthenes' guardians had defrauded him of his estate, so as a young man he practised oratory in order to win back his patrimony through the courts: he did not succeed in this but took to politics instead and put his oratorical skills to use in public life (Plut. *Demosthenes* 6.1–5, 11.1: doc 14.43). He had warned the Athenians against Philip and his ambitions in his speeches, the *First Philippic* in 351, and the *Olynthiacs* in 349.

Figure 14.9 Roman marble copy of the bronze statue of Demosthenes by Polyeuktos of 280 BC. Vatican Museum, Vatican. Drawing by Tessa Rickards.

The Peace of Philokrates in 346 BC

When Olynthos was captured in 348 some Athenians there fell into Philip's hands, and Athens requested their return, sending an ambassador Aristodemos to this effect; after Aristodemos' return to Athens, one of the prisoners was released and both he and Aristodemos reported to the Athenians that Philip desired peace. Philokrates therefore proposed a decree that ten Athenians be sent to Philip to seek peace terms: Aeschines and Philokrates were amongst those chosen, as well as Demosthenes, whose name was proposed by Philokrates. What had brought about this mission for peace, with the support of Demosthenes? Firstly, Athens had supported Phokis, but when the Phokaian leader Phalaikos was reinstated, he declined the Athenians' offer of assistance to help him hold Thermopylai (Aeschin. 2. 37, 130–4; Dem. 19.322: fifty triremes had been readied). In addition, Euboulos had successfully proposed that Athenian ambassadors be sent throughout Greece to seek support against Philip, and Aeschines had been sent to Arkadia in the Peloponnese, where, as he claimed, he did his best to unite the Arkadians and the Greeks generally against Philip (Aesch. 2.60, 2.79, 3.65, 3.67; Dem 19.303–4, cf. 305–7). Nothing came of this, and in fact, some of the ambassadors had not yet returned when Athens began considering the possibility of making peace with Philip. Athens was also still concerned with Thebes' power, and hoped that Philip would counteract this (Dem. 6.30).

This embassy in March 346 BC negotiated peace terms with Philip, the 'Peace of Philokrates', and it was agreed that both sides would keep their current possessions (so the Athenians would have to accept that Amphipolis was lost), while Philip undertook not to attack the Chersonese, an area in which Athens had had involvement since the time of Peisistratos; its cities had been members of the Athenian empire, and the region, the western side of the Hellespont, was strategically important for Athens as the grain ships from the Black Sea passed through the Hellespont. When the embassy returned to report their discussions Aeschines claimed that he had taken the leading role in establishing a peace and that Demosthenes had become nervous before Philip and botched his prepared speech (Aeschin. 2 *On the Embassy* 34–9: doc. 14.44; see also Aeschin. 2, esp. 15–20, 34–5, 45–54; Dem. 19.12–13, 19.234).

The Athenian assembly met over two days on the embassy's return (the 18th and 19th of the month Elaphebolion, 15th and 16th of April: it is rare to be able to pinpoint crucial events in Greek history as accurately as this). It should be noted that Athens' allies, in their separate council, voted to accept whatever decision Athens should come to about making peace with Philip. The Athenian assembly considered the issues at the first assembly, and after further discussion voted for peace at the second, a peace between Athens and its allies, and Philip. There was still talk of claiming Amphipolis but realism prevailed, and a second embassy was dispatched to Philip in late April to receive his oath swearing to ratify the peace; he swore to peace terms after returning from his campaigns, and the second embassy returned in July. A few days later the assembly decided to call on Phokis to surrender to the amphiktyony. A third embassy was sent to Philip a few days later, but he soon arrived at Thermopylai. Athens had blocked his entrance to the pass in 352 BC, but on this occasion he successfully entered central Greece. The third embassy turned back to Athens when it heard the news that the Phokaians had surrendered to Philip (for which see Diod. Sic. 16.59), ending, as noted above, the Third Sacred War of some ten years' duration.

At Athens there was consternation at the thought of Philip's arrival in central Greece: the walls were strengthened, and the women and children brought into the city from the countryside for safety. Technically, Philip had not agreed to anything specifically or generally about Phokis, but his appearance at the gates to central Greece and the fact that he had received the surrender of Phokis made him the dominant player in the region. A fourth embassy sent to him achieved little. While Athens had made peace with Philip in the 'Peace of Philokrates', the Athenians were immediately disillusioned by Philip's behaviour. At the time, all Athens could do to register its anger at Philip's destruction of Phokis (via the amphiktyony) was to boycott the Pythian festival at Delphi that year (Dem. 19.128: Aeschines attended in a private capacity and drank to Philip's health). Some time later (in 343 BC, though Demosthenes reports it as 'recently') some Thessalians and ambassadors from Philip came to Athens to request that it vote for Philip to become a member of the Amphiktyonic Council; Aeschines attempted to speak in support of this, but was howled down by the assembly (Dem. 19.112–13). In 344 BC Philip sent envoys to Athens to reinvigorate the peace, but the Athenians were still angry over his treatment of Phokis and his control of Thermopylai, and ambassadors from Messenia and Argos arrived at the same time to complain of Athens' support for Sparta. At this point Demosthenes delivered his *Second Philippic* in the assembly, arguing that Philip had used the peace of 346 to gain control of Thermopylai and Phokis, and that he had acted in Thebes' interests, not Athens'. As a result, Philip's overtures were rebuffed, and the Athenians even raised the issue of Amphipolis once again (Dem. 6.7, 6.17; a keen sense of betrayal by Philip and the fact that he was seen as having broken his promises is indicated at 29–30).

The events of these two main embassies and the peace of 346 BC are principally known from two speeches, one by Demosthenes (Dem. 19) and one by Aeschines (Aeschin. 2), and to a lesser extent from Demosthenes (Dem. 18) and Aeschines (Aeschin. 3) (see below, p. 524). In 343 BC, Demosthenes, regretting the peace with Philip and clearly attempting to minimalise his role in it, prosecuted Aeschines for his conduct on the embassy (Dem. 19); Aeschines defended himself (Aeschin. 2), but was barely acquitted by a margin of thirty of the 1501 jurors' votes. Accusations that Aeschines had been bribed may simply reflect the fact that he may have rather naïvely accepted diplomatic gifts from the king. Philokrates, a few weeks before, had been summoned to trial by the orator Hypereides, but had fled Athens: his guilt in having accepted bribes from Philip for helping to organise the peace seems clear. But Aeschines, whatever Demosthenes' allegations, seems to have been sincere in his attempt to reach a peaceful agreement with Philip and at this stage was not discredited.

Demosthenes' opposition to Philip after 346 BC was to be vindicated by the battle of Chaironeia in 338 BC and in 336 BC Ktesiphon proposed to the ekklesia that Demosthenes be

Figure 14.10 The lion commemorating and guarding the Theban dead from the battle of Chaironeia (doc. 14.49). Photo © John Sie Yuen Lee.

awarded a golden crown in honour of his services to the state, a proposal Aeschines indicted as against the laws (a graphe paranomon). For reasons largely unknown, the case against Ktesiphon did not come to court until 330 BC, when Demosthenes delivered his speech, *On the Crown* (Dem. 18). Aeschines lost the case, and failed to convince even one-fifth of the jurors, a result which at Athens meant that the unsuccessful prosecutor was fined, while in his speech Demosthenes presented a brilliant defence of his career and of his overall opposition to Philip (Dem. 18 *On the Crown* 60–9: doc. 14.46).

Philip and Athens

Philip and Phokion; Perinthos and Byzantium

Philip was preoccupied in northern Greece in 345–341 BC, particularly in Thrace in 342–341 BC. In 342 BC he intervened in the island of Euboea, as democrats at Eretria had expelled their tyrant and then deliberated as to whether to call on the help of Athens or Philip. They decided on the latter, who commenced his involvement in Euboean affairs with an initial force of 1000 mercenaries; a similar situation arose on the island at Oreos. Demosthenes spoke against Philip's Euboean campaign in the *Third Philippic* in 341 BC (Dem. 9.57–8). Athens drove out his mercenaries in 340 BC, but his forces had come rather close to their city. In 341 BC, Demosthenes had also delivered his *On the Chersonese* defending Athenian expeditions in the area against Philip.

In 340 BC Philip besieged Perinthos (to the north of the Chersonese, on the west side of the Hellespont), which was pro-Athenian, and also close to Byzantium, the gateway from the Black Sea into the Hellespont. He was obviously intending to conquer the area, from where he could threaten to control the flow of grain to Athens, and would in fact be able to cut off supplies from the Black Sea. Philip had a huge force of 30,000 men and employed siege towers that overlooked Perinthos' wall and ramming engines, undermined the fortifications, and drove the defenders from the walls with catapults. Byzantium sent assistance including reinforcements of manpower, missiles and artillery equipment. Just when it appeared that Philip would succeed, the Persian king Artaxerxes III instructed his coastal satraps to assist the Perinthians, and they sent mercenaries, money, food, missiles and whatever else was required. Philip was now operating very close to the frontier of the Persian Empire, which explains Artaxerxes' involvement against him. Philip therefore decided to split his force in two and proceeded to besiege Byzantium, which had sent its men, weapons and military machines to Perinthos. Chios, Kos, Rhodes and other cities sent assistance to Byzantium and though Athens sent Chares with a force he was distrusted and achieved nothing. At some stage, Philip seized 230 grain ships at the entrance to the Bosphoros. Phokion was sent by Athens to Byzantium's aid in 339 BC and was welcomed into the city. He forced Philip to retreat from Byzantium, captured some of his ships and even some of the cities he had garrisoned, and raided and plundered Philip's territory until he was wounded and forced to return home to Athens. This was evidence that Philip was not as invincible as he had appeared, and open warfare had now broken out between Athens and Philip (Dem. 18.87; Plut. *Phokion* 14; Diod. Sic. 16.74–7; Philochoros FF 54, 162). While Philip was in this region, his 16-year old son Alexander gained his first military experience against the Maidoi in Thrace, capturing their city, settling colonists, and in a taste of the city founding and naming that was to come later in his career, called it Alexandropolis (Plut. *Alexander* 9).

The Fourth Sacred War

This war provided Philip with another opportunity to intervene in Greek affairs: the Delphic amphiktyony (of which he was now a member) invited him in 339 BC to lead it in a (Fourth) Sacred War against Amphissa, which had been accused by Aeschines of cultivating the sacred plain of Kirrha. Philip occupied Elateia in Phokis with his troops, with the result that he was just two days' march from Athens. News of this reached Athens in the evening and the city was soon in an uproar. At dawn, the citizens, summoned by the trumpets on the instruction of the strategoi, were already in the assembly. All the citizens, at a loss as to what actions to take, turned to Demosthenes, who proposed an alliance with Thebes, where he was then sent as ambassador. Philip also sought Thebes' alliance, but Demosthenes' oratory prevailed at Thebes over Philip's spokesman Pytho (Dem. 18.169–80, 18.230, cf. 18.136; Diod. Sic. 16.84.1–85.1: doc. 14.48).

The battle of Chaironeia in 338 BC

Philip decided to attack both the Boeotians and the Athenians, marching into Boeotia and meeting them at Chaironeia in 338 BC in a lengthy and hard-fought battle. Alexander fought on the left wing, Philip on the right, with the Athenians on the left wing facing Philip and the Boeotians on the right facing Alexander. Philip with 30,000 soldiers seems to have had about the same number of troops as the Thebans and Athenians, and he had great military experience, having been continually at war since his succession: the Greeks had no leader to match him, and Chares and Lysikles were the best generals the Athenians could put into the field. Yet the battle was hotly contested and the Athenians and Thebans held out against Philip for a considerable period. Alexander and the Macedonian Companions first broke the Greek line and caused it to flee. The entire Theban Sacred Band showed its bravery and loyalty to their city by perishing to a man (Plut. *Pelopidas* 18.7: doc. 14.17). That night Philip held a komos (Fig. 14.11), gloating over his victory, chanting the preamble of the decree proposed by Demosthenes to seek alliance with the Thebans, dividing it into lines and beating time to the rhythm, 'Demósthenes, son of Demósthenes of Paianía, here móves the mótion' (Plut. *Demosthenes* 20.3: doc. 14.47; cf. Diod. Sic. 16.85.1: doc. 14.48). However, Demades, an Athenian orator who had been captured, called him to his senses (Diod. Sic. 16.87.1–3: doc. 14.48; Map 14.4).

Over 1000 Athenians fell in battle (2000 had been taken as prisoners, whom Philip later released), and they were commemorated for dying 'to save the sacred land of Greece' from the Macedonians (*IG* II² 5226: doc. 14.49), and Demosthenes was chosen to deliver the eulogy. As a result of a decree by Lykourgos the Athenian general Lysikles was executed for his lack of success as commander at Chaironeia. The Thebans erected a stone lion, just over 6 metres high, to guard a common grave to commemorate their dead, some of whom were buried there: archaeologists have discovered 254 skeletons arranged in seven rows (Fig. 14.12).

Peace terms

Demosthenes hastened back to Athens to organise the defence of the city – not running away from the battle as alleged in Plutarch. Philip realised that it was this orator who had compelled him to risk everything on one battle (Plut. *Demosthenes* 20.3: doc. 14.47). Hypereides proposed that the Athenians take emergency measures, including a decree to give citizenship

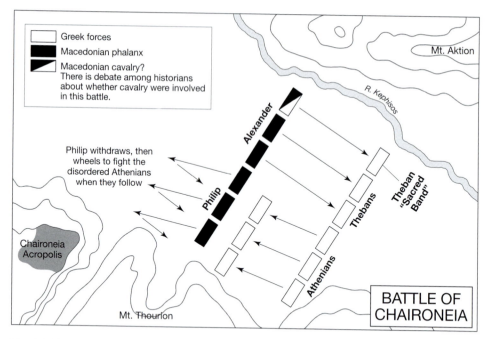

Map 14.4 The battle of Chaironeia, 338 BC.

to the metics and freedom to the slaves (Plut. *Moralia* 849; Hyper. *F* 18.3), but in the event Athens was not attacked. There was extreme tension and anxiety in the city, however, and Lykourgos later in 330 BC prosecuted an Athenian citizen Leokrates for deserting his city at this point. Phokaian was appointed commander at Athens and Demades, who had been released by Philip, and Aeschines were sent to Philip for peace terms. The terms imposed by Philip were that Athens had to disband the Second Athenian Confederacy but was allowed to keep its fleet and retained Samos and Delos, and the islands Lembros, Imbros and Skyros, which had been guaranteed to them by the King's Peace of 386 BC. Peace was made with other Greek states, also on an individual basis. Thebes received a garrison on the Kadmeia and pro-Macedonian Thebans took control of the city. Corinth also received a garrison, as did Ambracia and possibly Chalkis on Euboea (Diod. Sic. 16.87.3, 17.3.3; Paus. 1.25.1: Polyb. 38.3.3; Plut. *Aratos* 23.4). At this stage, the Athenian orator Lykourgos was given command of Athenian finances, which he would control from 338 to 326 BC (Plut. *Moralia* 841), greatly improving Athens' financial situation and its defences.

The League of Corinth

In the winter of 338/7 BC, Philip reqested that all the Greek states send representatives to Corinth. Sparta alone declined, but it was now a political irrelevancy and easily ignored, while Archidamos III of Sparta (who had been the lover of Sphodrias' son Kleonymos) had been killed at the same time as the battle of Chaeironeia fighting for Tarentum, a Spartan colony, against the local Lucanians: Diod. Sic. 16.88.3). Philip forced peace on the Greek cities, and established a council of all the Greeks, of which he was hegemon

Figure 14.11 A komos such as Philip celebrated after his victory at Chaeroneia (doc. 14.48). Museum of Fine Arts 98.930, Boston. Drawing by J. Etherington.

(leader). Modern scholars have dubbed this council the 'League of Corinth', and it was here Philip that announced his planned campaign against the Persian Empire, confirming Artaxerxes' suspicions at the time of the siege of Perinthos. The Greek states were forced to swear to a treaty, the oath of which survives. Warfare amongst the signatories to the treaty was forbidden and if any state broke the treaty, war would be made against it by all the other states involved. None of the governments of these cities could be overthrown, so Philip's pro-Macedonian governments were safeguarded, while the cities also had to swear loyalty to Philip and his descendants. Strife within cities was also prevented by the fact that there were to be no debt-cancellations, confiscations or redistributions of land, nor freeing of slaves to bring about changes to a city's constitution: in short, democrats would not be allowed to overthrow aristocratic or oligarchic governments (Just. 9.5.1–6: doc. 14.50; *IG* II² 236: doc. 14.51; Diod. Sic. 16.89).

By this treaty and oath Philip directly intervened in a basic concept of Greek freedom, the choice of government. After the oath follows a list of states that swore the oath, with a numeral against each name. Not only had the Greek states lost their autonomy, they also had to provide military contingents, as subservient allies, for Philip's military enterprises, in particular – now that he had conquered the Greeks – for his planned attack on Persia, which had been revealed at the congress. Isocrates had promoted the panhellenic idea of a crusade against the Persians as an idea in his *Panegyricus* of 380 BC in which he proposed that Athens and Sparta should unite the Greeks against the Persians (4.17). It was not a new idea but he took a long time to write the piece, suggesting that he intended it to survive as some kind of a manifesto of the Greek destiny. Initially, it was Philip's potential to unite the Greeks against the barbarians that had excited Isocrates' interest and in 346 he wrote the *Philippos*, a revisiting of the *Panegyricus*, not only calling on Philip to lead the Greeks against the Persians, but also, as is sometimes overlooked, to champion concord amongst the Greeks (5.16; cf. 9, 30, 50, 89). He also wrote two letters to Philip on the same theme, though the authenticity of the second can be doubted if it was written after Chaironeia, for there is another tradition that, hearing of Philip's success there, Isocrates starved himself to death. Philip was probably not influenced by Isocrates' vision of Philip at the head of a group of united Greeks, for Philip in reality had conquered the Greeks and his intention was now to lead them into his war with Persia, not as allies or equals but as dependants.

At Athens in 336 BC a law was passed against tyranny. This seems strange given that, by the terms of the League of Corinth, no state was meant to alter its constitution. At the top of the stele, Demokratia is shown crowning a seated Demos (the people). The main purport of the decree was that if the demos was overthrown, the Areiopagos was prohibited to meet: it was not to set itself up as an alternative method of governing, or co-operate with the regime which displaced the democracy. By 'tyranny', of course, the Athenians could have had in mind a potential pro-Macedonian oligarchic government (*SEG* 12.87: doc. 14.52; Fig. 14.12).

Philip takes another wife

In 338 or 337 BC Philip decided to take another wife: Kleopatra Eurydike, niece of the Macedonian noble Attalos. There was a violent, drunken scene at the wedding in which the inebriated Attalos called upon the Macedonian guests to pray to the gods that this union should

Figure 14.12 The Athenian law against tyranny in 336 BC (doc. 14.52): Demokratia (democracy) is shown crowning Demos (the people). Photo © Athenian Agora Museum I 6524, Athens.

Figure 14.13 The ruins of the theatre at Vergina, site of Philip's murder. © Kyoko Nomura.

produce a legitimate (Macedonian) heir. Alexander shouted back to the effect that Attalos was implying that he was a bastard. Philip, drunk, drew his sword against his son but fell over (Plut. *Alexander* 9.4–5). Alexander took his mother to her home in Epiros while he went to Illyria, though he did later return to court. He must, however, have had concerns about the situation for any offspring of Philip and Kleopatra would be full-blooded Macedonian, and Attalos' sentiments cannot have been his alone.

Philip's murder in 336 BC

Another matrimonial festivity provided the stage for Philip's assassination. He was marrying his daughter by Olympia (also called Kleopatra, like his new wife) to the girl's uncle, Alexander king of Epiros. A festival and athletic contests were to be held at Aigeai (modern Vergina) in Macedonia and the crowd assembled in the theatre before dawn, when proceedings began with a procession in which the statues of the twelve Olympian gods were carried. There was also a thirteenth statue, as Diodorus notes, 'appropriate for a god', which was of Philip himself. Philip had already in 337 planned to construct at Olympia a circular building to house chryselephantine statues (a material reserved for statues of the gods) of himself, as well as of Alexander, Olympias and his parents Amyntas III and Eurydike (Fig. 14.7). Eresos on Lesbos erected altars to Zeus Philippios, clearly associating Philip with the god Zeus, and at Ephesos a statue of Philip had been set up in the temple of Artemis.

On the evening of these celebrations in October 336 BC, according to the sources, Attalos allowed his drunken muleteers to sexually assault one Pausanias, who complained about the incident to Philip – he had been one of Philip's lovers but had been supplanted by another

Pausanias, which he had resented: Philip did not want to offend Attalos, and attempted to placate Pausanias with gifts and by making him one of his bodyguards. But he was not to be placated, and as Philip entered the theatre Pausanias stabbed him through the ribs with a Celtic dagger (Fig. 14.13). Rushing for his waiting horse, Pausanias' boot caught on a creeper and he fell, giving his pursuers Leonnatos, Perdikkas and Attalos the chance to run him through with their javelins (Diod. Sic. 16.92.5, 16.93.7–95.1: doc. 14.53; he calls Attalos Kleopatra's nephew but he was in fact her uncle). Suspicion immediately extended to others apart from Pausanias himself. Olympias had motives for seeing her husband dead, and so too did Alexander, though Plutarch absolved him from blame. Olympias took her vengeance by murdering Philip's wife Kleopatra and her baby daughter, while Attalos who was in Asia Minor was also murdered through the agency of Parmenion who was leading the expeditionary force there: Alexander must have been involved in this decision to execute Attalos (Plut. *Alexander* 10.6–8: doc. 14.54).

Alexander's view of Philip's achievements

Philip had taken the Macedonians from the status of vagabonds 'mostly clothed in skins', worn down by the attacks of their neigbours, especially the Illyrians, and turned them into rulers: such was Alexander's assessment of his father's achievements (Arr. 7.9.1–5: doc. 14.55; cf. Diod. Sic. 16.1). Philip had indeed taken Macedonia, always a prey to those around it, and made it the ruler of Greece. He had destroyed Greek liberty and ensured that its great states, Thebes and Athens, and to a lesser degree (the already declining) Sparta, would never again hold sway over Greek affairs. Motivated by ambition and territorial acquisitiveness, he left Macedonia and his heir with the resources with which to conquer the Persian Empire, while his divinisation of himself would find a reflection in his son's own quest for godhead. The Macedonian royal family had their tombs within a huge earthen mound at Aigea, including the tombs of Amyntas and Eurydike. The great earthen mound at Aigea contained one tomb with various items such as a larnax of ashes and small ivory heads identified by scholars as those of Philip and Alexander (Fig. 14.1). It is argued that this is the tomb of either Philip's son Arrhidaios, later Philip III, by Philip II's fifth wife Philinna, of Larissa, or as argued by the modern excavator Andronikos Philip's tomb, and so it may have been the burial place of the leader who 'conferred renown not so much upon himself as upon the Macedonian state' (Arr. 7.9.5).

15

ALEXANDER 'THE GREAT' OF MACEDON, 336–323 BC

Introduction

Following Philip's assassination in 336 BC, Alexander came to the Macedonian throne. With possible sources of Macedonian opposition eliminated, he entered Greece and succeeded Philip as hegemon of the League of Corinth. He then embarked on a campaign against the Triballoi and Getai on Macedonia's northern borders, as much to prove his worth as king as to secure the frontiers; Illyria revolted but he dealt with this rebellion successfully. While Greece considered revolting, only Thebes and Athens took the risk and Thebes paid for this with its total destruction, and the massacre and enslavement of its inhabitants in 335 BC. Alexander then proceeded with a relatively modest force to Asia Minor, intent on conquering the Persians. Spectacular successes in battles at Granikos, Issos and Gaugamela gave him control of the Persian Empire, but he pushed further east and fought one last major campaign at the river Hydaspes. His empire now stretched from Greece to northern India; although it fell apart on his death, this empire had a profound significance on the ancient world in both cultural and historical terms. However, it also destroyed a magnificent civilisation and led to numerous wars between his 'successors' in the centuries to come.

Sources

Arrian, whose *Anabasis of Alexander* (generally shortened to *Anabasis*, meaning 'expedition up-country') is the best extant ancient source for Alexander, but is also the most removed in time from Alexander's career. Writing in the second century AD Arrian made use of two main sources in his own history of Alexander, the works of Ptolemy son of Lagos and the works of Aristoboulos, with his preference being for Ptolemy. He considered that, of the many accounts of Alexander, these were the two most reliable. He remarks that they differed on some points and under these circumstances he made a decision having considered which was 'the most reliable and also the best worth recounting' (Arr. *Anabasis of Alexander* 1.1: doc. 16.9). Both Ptolemy and Aristoboulos were present on Alexander's campaigns and so their accounts (neither of which survives) provide eyewitness descriptions of events. Although Nearchos, one of Alexander's naval commanders, is best known for his maritime voyages, especially from India to the northern tip of the Persian Gulf, he too wrote an account, also lost, of Alexander's conquests of which Arrian made use (Arr. 6.13.4: doc. 15.30); Nearchos' description of India forms the basis for Arrian's own *Indika*. Onesikritos accompanied Nearchos (the two disagreed about who played the greater role in the naval expedition) and wrote his own account of Alexander's campaigns and the voyage.

Arrian was also aware of another body of sources and commented that these 'have given very different accounts of Alexander' (Arr. 1.2: doc. 16.9). This is probably a reference to what is known by modern scholars as the 'vulgate tradition', or 'popular tradition' concerning Alexander. Into this category fall the works written by Diodorus, Justin and Curtius, the last two writing in Latin. Justin's work (of the second or third century AD) is an epitome of Pompeius Trogus' earlier *Historiae Philippicae*, a Latin historian of Augustus' reign. Curtius' account, which dates to the first or early second century AD, is detailed; lengthy passages recording speeches detract from the work, but it has value in providing information (particularly points of detail) not found elsewhere. The first two of his ten books are lost, and his extant narrative commences in 333 BC. Diodorus provides a continuous narrative, not as detailed as Arrian's, but one which is particularly useful for specific episodes in Alexander's campaigns.

Plutarch wrote *a Life* of Alexander, pairing it with one of Caesar. Any reader of Plutarch's *Alexander* will agree with Plutarch's own assessment of his work, that owing to the numerous events in Alexander's life exhaustive details are out of the question and only a summary of these is feasible: Plutarch is, as he himself notes, writing biography, not history. As such, character traits and behaviour are in his view just as important as the actual history of an individual and his *Alexander* is in fact more useful for Alexander's early life than for actual details of campaigns and events (Plut. *Alexander* 1.1–3: doc. 16.10). It is from these five main literary sources (Arrian, Diodorus, Plutarch, Curtius, Justin) that the historical events of the reign can be reconstructed, while inscriptions provide an invaluable source for Alexander's relationship with the Greek cities and islands.

In addition, the Greek writer Kallisthenes, Aristotle's nephew, travelled with Alexander as his court historian until his execution for involvement in the Page Boys' Conspiracy in 327 BC. His *Deeds of Alexander* was presumably accurate (although see Polyb. *Histories* 12.20.1–6, 22.1–7: doc. 15.12), but also encomiastic as Alexander would have read the account as it was being written. There were also the Royal Diaries (*Basileioi Ephemerides*), consulted by Arrian for his description of Alexander's death, but the keeper of these daily records is unknown (Arr. 7.25.1: doc. 15.43; cf. Diod. Sic. Sic. 3.38.1; Plut. *Alexander* 76.1, 77.1). There were numerous other authors followed particularly by the three 'vulgate' historians Diodorus, Curtius and Justin. In the third century AD *The Alexander Romance* emerged, attributed to Kallisthenes despite the fact it narrates events after his death. Hence it is sometimes referred to as Pseudo-Kallisthenes. The least trustworthy of all accounts, including numerous mythical exploits of Alexander, it was also the most popular, being translated into several languages from the fourth century AD. While all the literary sources are at times critical of Alexander, even that of Arrian his most ardent admirer, the accounts are generally favourable, and he excited admiration among his biographers and their readers.

Inscriptions provide pragmatic records of some of Alexander's activities, particularly his arrangements for Eresos, and his piety at Priene, while the details concerning the career of Gorgos are extremely illuminating in terms of Alexander's relationship with the Greeks. Athenian oratory is a disappointing source: the great days of independent politics and Demosthenes' speeches against Philip were over. Demosthenes was still alive, a narrow escapee from Alexander's demands for the surrender of Athenian orators after the destruction of Thebes. He delivered the Funeral Oration over the Athenian dead of 338 BC. Aeschines and he battled it out in the courts over events in the 340s and Demosthenes emerged triumphant in the courts with Aeschines exiled to Rhodes in 330 BC. Hypereides and Deinarchos prosecuted him for his role in the Harpalos affair (both of their speeches were entitled *Against Demosthenes*). As a source Demosthenes is not important for Alexander's reign: the speech

On the Treaty with Alexander attributed to him which provides details of the peace imposed by Alexander on Greece is certainly not his work.

Alexander's parentage and education

Descended from Herakles on Philip's side, Alexander was the product of a romantic marriage, resulting from Philip's meeting with Olympias on the island of Samothrace, where she had gone from her native Epiros to take part in the Samothracian mysteries. Various omens are said to have attended Alexander's conception and birth, all later fabrications developed after he became a mighty warrior and the world's most successful conqueror (Fig. 15.1). Olympias, in one story, on the night just before she went into the marriage chamber saw a bolt of lightning strike her womb; this lightning then kindled a huge conflagration. In another Philip dreamed that he set a seal, marked with the image of a lion, on his wife's womb: Aristander of Telmessos, the diviner who was to accompany Alexander on his travels and who gave a favourable interpretation of so many portents and omens, saw this as a sign that she was pregnant with a son who would be 'lion-like'. On another occasion Philip's marital ardour was apparently cooled when he saw a giant snake lying by Olympias' side, symbolising her union with Alexander's divine father (Plut. *Alexander* 2.1–9: doc. 15.1). The relationship between Philip and Olympias, who was given to maenadic religious practices, seems to have been an uneasy one: Philip had other wives and his last marriage in 338/7 to Kleopatra Eurydike led

Figure 15.1 A marble head of Alexander dating to the first half of the second century BC, found at Pergamon in modern Turkey. The copying of statues of Alexander in Hellenistic and Roman times indicates his importance to the Graeco-Roman world. Archaeological Museum, Istanbul, Turkey.

to a total estrangement with Olympias (Ath. *Deipnosophistae* 13.557b–e: doc. 14.37). Alexander, however, was the unquestioned heir to the throne. Olympias sent many letters of advice to Alexander while he was on campaign, and clearly kept him informed in his absence of Antipater's activities as regent of Macedon. However, her threatening attitude towards Athens over Harpalos in 324 probably represented her most important involvement in politics (Diod. Sic. 17.108.7: doc. 15.37), for she remained in Epiros after Alexander's departure to Asia Minor and ruled it almost as a separate kingdom.

When Alexander was 14 years of age Aristotle was summoned to the Macedonian court to tutor him: the nymphaion (shrine of the nymphs) at Mieza became the venue for their study. He apparently read all the Greek 'classics', and while in central Asia sent for copies of the works of Euripides, Sophocles and Aeschylus among others. His favourite work was Homer's *Iliad*, and he possessed Aristotle's edition of this, which he kept with him at all times, considering it the 'essential guide to the art of warfare' (Plut. *Alexander* 8.2–3: doc. 15.1). From the *Iliad*, as well as from the example of his own father's exploits as a warrior, he must have imbibed heroic notions of individual combat: the pursuit of excellence (arete) was a crucial part of his identity and he excelled in warfare (Arr. 1.12.5).

Alexander's first tasks as a ruler

Alexander was not without military and administrative experience when he came to the throne. In 340 BC, when only 16 years old, he was left in command as regent of Macedonia while Philip campaigned against Byzantium, and at Chaironeia in 338 BC his role was crucial to the Macedonian victory (Diod. Sic. 16.84.1–87.3: doc. 14.48). Immediately upon Philip's assassination, Alexander was proclaimed king by the Macedonian assembly, and he executed those implicated in the plot against his father. Olympias also took her revenge on Philip's new wife Kleopatra and her baby daughter and Parmenion executed Attalos, her uncle, in Asia Minor. Alexander also took the opportunity to rid himself of his cousin Amyntas, son of Perdikkas III (Philip's predecessor), as well as the two brothers of Alexander of Lynkestis, although Alexander himself was spared for the time being as one of the friends who had first rallied to the new king (Arr. 1.25.2). He was even given various commands before being executed as part of the purge of those involved in the conspiracy of Philotas in 330 BC. Various friends who were exiled when Alexander and Philip were estranged after Philip's marriage to Kleopatra returned, notably Nearchos, Harpalos and Ptolemy (Diod. Sic.17.2.1–3, 17.3.1–6: doc. 15.2; Arr. 3.6.6; Plut. *Alexander* 10).

Alexander and the League of Corinth

Greece was naturally agitated at the news of Philip's death: the battle of Chaironeia in 338 BC and the formation of the League of Corinth and the oath that had been imposed upon the Greeks was at this time fresh in their memory. Athens, Thebes and the Aetolians in particular weighed up the chances of a rebellion against Macedonian control; in addition, tribes across the Macedonian frontiers were on the point of revolt (Diod. Sic. 17.3.1–6: doc. 15.2). Deciding to deal with Greece first, Alexander entered the Peloponnese with a Macedonian force and was voted hegemon and strategos autokrator of the League of Corinth. Command of an expedition against the Persians, a campaign his father had planned, was also granted by the League at his request. Only the Spartans refused to accept Alexander's leadership, while Athens, which had been in a state of unrest, was quick to vote him various honours when he actually approached the city (Arr. 1.1.1–3: doc. 15.3).

Unrest in Greece and the revolt and destruction of Thebes in 335 BC

After securing Greece Alexander campaigned against the Triballoi and Getai in Thrace and put down revolts in Illyria (Arr. 1.1–6). While he was engaged in these military activities in the north, Greek cities continued to consider the possibility of rebellion. Thebes decided to revolt after exiles from Thebes re-entered the city and surprised and killed two of the Macedonian garrison leaders; Philip had garrisoned the Kadmeia, and the Macedonian force itself under Philotas there held firm. By overturning its oligarchic pro-Macedonian government, Thebes was also breaking one of the terms of the League of Corinth (Arr. 1.7; Diod. Sic. 17.8.1–2; Plut. *Alexander* 11.3). News of Thebes' revolt concerned Alexander, as Thebes and Athens had resisted his father in 338 BC. It was possible that Sparta, the other Peloponnesians and the Aetolians might also join in the revolt compounding the problems he was facing in the north. It took him only seven days to reach Pelinna in Thessaly, and in another five days he was in Boeotia itself, at Onchestos; even at this stage the Theban rebel leaders insisted that he had been killed in action in the north and that the news of his arrival nearby was untrue. The ancient sources concur that Alexander did not attack Thebes immediately but camped outside the city to give the Thebans time to reconsider their revolt: they, however, called on the Greeks to join them and the Great King, who had helped finance the revolt, in freeing the Greeks from 'tyranny'. Thebes freed its slaves and these and the metics guarded the walls while the Theban hoplites themselves prepared to repel the Macedonian attack when it came: the Thebans had been in constant training in the city gymnasia. Women and children thronged the temples praying to the gods who according to our sources only sent an array of prophetic warnings of the city's impending doom (Arr. 1.7.7; Diod. Sic. 17.9–11; Plut. *Alexander* 11).

The Thebans themselves blockaded the Kadmeia with a double stockade so that the Macedonian force there could not link up with Alexander's forces even if he broke into the city. A delay of a few days occurred with Alexander encamped outside the city as near to the Kadmeia as possible in order to be able to support the garrison there. In the account of Ptolemy as recorded by Arrian, Perdikkas initiated a Macedonian attack against the Theban palisade apparently without direct orders; Diodorus, however, has Alexander order an attack on the palisade with the battle fully under way (he does not specifically name Perdikkas), and it was in this way that the Macedonians broke through into the city. Arrian's account gives Alexander a greater role in the capture of Thebes as he had to come to the rescue of the reckless Perdikkas. After being initially successful against the Macedonians the Thebans were eventually driven back to their city gates which they could not close in time due to the crush of numbers. The Macedonians were thereby able to rush in hot on their heels. Inside the city, Alexander then led a phalanx charge against the Thebans. He soon overcame the infantry, while the Theban cavalry fled to the plains outside. All was over very quickly: the Phokaians, Plataeans and other Boeotians serving with Alexander were particularly keen to settle old scores and the Theban hoplites were slaughtered indiscriminately (Arr. 1.8; Diod. Sic. 17.11; Plut. *Alexander* 11.5–6).

The Greeks of the time, according to Arrian, were so struck by the suddenness and completeness of the destruction of Thebes, an event the like of which, he argues, the Greek world had never seen, that they considered it as an act of divine retribution for the Thebans having sided with the Persians in 480–479 BC. Diodorus considers that the decision to enslave and destroy the city was decided by the council of the allies who were with Alexander, and Alexander seems to have seen this as a meeting of, and decision by, the League of Corinth. While the Kadmeia itself was to remain garrisoned, the rest of the city was razed to the ground with the exception of the poet Pindar's house; 6000 Thebans were executed, and 30,000 sold into slavery: by this action Alexander made a profit of 440 talents (Plut. *Alexander* 11.12: doc. 15.4; Arr. 1.9; Diod. Sic. 17.14.1; Aeschin. 3.133).

Plutarch records a charming story of Timokleia, which is not in Arrian's account: after she was raped by a Thracian who then asked her if she had any gold or silver hidden, she led him to a well and said she had thrown all her valuables in there: as he leaned over to look she threw him in. The other Thracians took her to Alexander to decide on her fate, but when she told him she was the sister of Theagenes who had led the Thebans against Philip in 338 at Chaironeia he allowed her and her children to depart in freedom (Plut. *Alexander* 12.1–6: doc. 15.4; Plut. *Moralia* 259–60). This is the sort of story that attracted Plutarch's attention and its historicity can be safely set aside. The destruction of Thebes, one of Greece's greatest cities, was just the beginning of the history of Alexander's ruthless treatment of local populations that defied him. Timokleia's role is simply part of a tradition which attempts to downplay Alexander's destruction of this and other cities by emphasising instead his personal charisma and magnanimity in individual cases.

Alexander and Diogenes the Cynic

Plutarch narrates a further anecdote, depicting Alexander's unusual respect for the values of others. While at Corinth in 336 Alexander received the fulsome congratulations of statesmen and philosophers, with one notable exception: he fully expected that the famous philosopher Diogenes the Cynic would come to meet him: the cynics (the 'dog-like') were philosophers who believed in following the dictates of nature and living a simple life free from normal conventions and without possessions or ambitions. When he did not Alexander decided to visit him instead. Lazing in the sun Diogenes merely raised himself a little off the ground at seeing so many people approach. Alexander enquired if there was anything Diogenes wanted and received the reply: 'Stand a little out of my sun.' Alexander was impressed with his philosophical attitude and told his companions who were laughing about the incident as they left, that were he not Alexander, he would be Diogenes. The companions were the hetairoi, many of which Alexander 'inherited' from Philip (Theopomp. *FF* 224–5: doc. 14.40), along with some of his friends, such as Kleitos and Hephaistion (Plut. *Alexander* 14.1–5: doc. 15.5; Arr. 7.2.1). Plutarch dates this story to after the destruction of Thebes, but Alexander was at Corinth in 336 and did not visit it again in 335 BC.

Greece pacified

Alexander's destruction of Thebes had its desired effect, with the Greeks now pacified and malleable. The Arkadians who had set out to aid Thebes turned back and condemned to death all those who had persuaded them to vote to send this assistance, while the Aetolians sought Alexander's clemency for revolting from Macedonian rule. Athens was celebrating the Eleusinian Mysteries but actually abandoned the festival in panic at the news. An assembly was held and Demades successfully proposed that ten ambassadors be sent to Alexander to congratulate him on defeating the Illyrians and Triballians (as Arrian notes, a little belatedly), and for squashing the Theban revolt. The Athenians in 336 and 335 had no intention of repeating their opposition of 338 BC. But they still possessed some resolve: Alexander accepted their letter but demanded the city send him Demosthenes, Lykourgos, Hypereides,

Chares, Charidemos and various other Athenian politicians (probably ten in all, but the number varies according to different sources) whom he saw as responsible for the Athenian participation at Chaironeia in 338 BC. Phokion argued that these should give themselves up for the good of the city, but Demades (bribed with 5 talents from those whose surrender was demanded) proposed a decree sending himself and others as envoys to Alexander to ask him to spare the orators from being handed over – his eloquence saved them; Alexander only insisted on Charidemos being exiled (Arr. 1.10; Diod. Sic. 17. 15; Plut. *Alexander* 13, *Demosthenes* 23, *Phokion* 17).

As Alexander's next major move was to cross over into Asia, it is probable that with Thebes destroyed and the other Greeks submissive he accepted Athens' response in order to commence what he considered to be his real business. On his way north he consulted the Delphic oracle about his planned campaign against Persia. The day was one usually inauspicious for consulting the oracle, and when he attempted to drag the Pythia into the temple to prophesy she announced that he was invincible (Plut. *Alexander* 14.4). Omens accompanied his forces when they set out against Persia (and throughout his campaigns), indicating the gods' support for his activities; most famously the statue of Orpheus at Leibethra in Pieria made of cypress wood was reported to be sweating continuously (Arr. 1.11; Plut. *Alexander* 14). One of Alexander's various diviners, Aristander of Telmissos, interpreted the sign to mean that Orpheus as a deity of music and all composers and writers of victory odes would be kept hard at work singing of Alexander's many exploits. In fact, Arrian noted that whereas the tyrants Hieron, Gelon and Theron had their exploits recorded in poetry, Alexander did not (Arr. 1.11.2). Aristander was in Macedonian employ since at least the birth of Alexander and was Alexander's most prominent diviner in his expedition. When Alexander returned to Macedonia in 335 he celebrated the Macedonian festival in honour of Olympian Zeus and then over winter put together his invasion force for Asia Minor to avenge the Persian invasions of Greece and, symbolically, to continue the Greeks' war against Troy.

The Macedonian assault on Asia

Antipater in charge of Macedon and Greece

Antipater, who served under Philip, especially in ambassadorial roles at Athens during the momentous events of 346 and 338 BC, was left in charge of Greece by Alexander with 12,000 infantry and 1500 horse (Diod. Sic. 17.5). He governed for Alexander until 324 BC, and played a notable role in 331 BC in crushing the revolt of Thrace followed by that of Agis III in Sparta. It was crucial for Alexander to have an experienced and loyal military commander in Macedonia and Greece while he was attacking Persia. In a few years, Alexander would be too far from these places to be able to hurry back and deal with any problems or crises. Alexander later came to suspect Antipater, and in 324 BC while Alexander was at Opis (see below, p. 569) he sent Krateros to replace him; Antipater, however, was not replaced as Krateros was still in Asia Minor at the time of Alexander's death.

Alexander's forces and the symbolic capture of Asia

In spring 334 BC, Alexander crossed the Hellespont, marching along the route which Xerxes took in his invasion of Greece in 480 BC, retracing Xerxes' steps in twenty days from Pella to Sestos, where the force was shipped across the Hellespont to Abydos. Nothing as dramatic as

Xerxes' bridges of ships were needed, as Alexander's force was much smaller. Alexander's military force was not a large one, and different accounts, as Plutarch notes, put the troops between 30,000 and 43,000 infantry and 4000 to 5000 cavalry. Parmenion, who was sent to Asia Minor in 336 by Philip, oversaw the ferrying of the troops across the Hellespont; his own troops numbered some several thousand, while his son Philotas was in charge of the Companions' cavalry. Alexander's war chest was also a small one, holding a mere 70 talents: his intention was clearly to 'live off the land' and in this he was successful, as the treasures of the Persian Empire soon fell into his hands. To maintain the loyalty of his Companions, he distributed land to them before leaving although some, like Perdikkas, refused to accept it, exclaiming that Alexander would not have anything left of his own (Plut. *Alexander* 15.1–7: doc. 15.6; cf. *Moralia* 327; Arr. 1.11.3; Diod. Sic. 17.17.3–4). This is clearly an exaggerated version of events as Philip would have left Alexander well endowed with resources: the point is that Alexander was setting out to conquer Persia and would find what he and his army needed to survive there. Antigonos 'the One-Eyed' was in charge of the allied troops (Arr. 1.29.3); he had ably served under Philip II, and emerged as one of the main contenders for Alexander's conquests after 323 BC.

On the European side of the Hellespont Alexander sacrificed to the Greek hero Protesilaos who in the *Iliad* was the first to step on Trojan soil (Arr. 1.11.5). On landing on the Asian side Alexander like him was the first to disembark and he plunged his spear into the soil there as a sign that he had received Asia from the gods themselves as a 'spear-prize'. From Abydos, he marched to Troy (Ilion), where he visited the tombs of Achilles, Ajax and other Greek heroes. He consciously took upon himself the mantle of the heroic epic tradition of the fight against

Figure 15.2 A mosaic dating to around 120 BC from the House of the Faun at Pompeii, a copy of the Greek painting by Philoxenos of Eretria, commissioned by Kassander of Macedon. Darius in his chariot and Alexander on his horse make eye contact above the melee of the battle of Issos (doc. 15.11). There are over one and a half million separate coloured tiles in the composition. Museo Archeologico Nazionale NM 10020, Naples. Photo © Rita Willaert.

Asia, signifying that the Greeks had returned to continue the ten-year campaign against Troy they had waged in their early history. This campaign was not myth to them but historical reality. Alexander sacrificed at Athena's temple at Troy and dedicated his own armour to the goddess there, and then took for himself the finest set of armour said to have been dedicated at the temple at the time of the Trojan War. He wore this at the battle of Granikos (Diod. Sic. 17.17.1–18.1; 17.21.2: doc. 15.7; Arr. 1.11.7).

Darius III

Persia at this point was ruled by Darius III (336–330), the last surviving member of the Achaemenid house, as his predecessors Artaxerxes III (who crushed revolts in Phoenicia in 345 BC and in Egypt in 343 and 335 BC) and his son Artaxerxes IV had been assassinated by the Grand Vizier Bagoas, who placed Darius III on the throne in 336 BC; Bagoas then also attempted to assassinate Darius, but was himself forced to drink the poison intended for Darius. Darius' accession brought stability to the empire, but he also came to the throne when it faced its greatest crisis. His reign saw the end of the Achaemenid Empire after more than two centuries, but he fought Alexander aggressively and personally encountered him in battle.

The battle of Granikos, May 334 BC

Alexander then retraced his steps from Troy to Abydos, and marched with his forces inland to the river Granikos, which flowed into the Propontis. Memnon of Rhodes, Darius' most experienced general, advised a scorched-earth policy so that Alexander could not supply his troops through plunder, but the other Persian satraps did not follow his advice. A Persian army was waiting at the Granikos, clearly in a strategy to block Alexander's path into the empire. It was drawn from the forces commanded by Darius' satraps (Spithridates satrap of Ionia and Lydia, Arsamenes satrap of Cilicia, and Arsites satrap of Hellespontine Phrygia) and comprised 20,000 Persian cavalry and 20,000 Greek mercenaries. Alexander's original force with which he crossed into Asia was still intact. On the eastern side the banks of the Granikos were steep, uneven and slippery with mud. This proved to be a problem for the Macedonian horses and infantry once they reached the further bank. The site was therefore well chosen and the Persians hoped that the Macedonian phalanx would be less effective here, for it would lose formation in crossing the river and climbing the difficult banks. Darius himself was not present but important Persian commanders were, particularly Rhoisakes and Spithridates, who played notable roles in the action. Diodorus and Arrian's accounts are markedly different. In Diodorus' narrative Alexander, after noting the difficulties of the terrain, had his army cross at dawn to meet the Persians unexpectedly on level ground (Diod. Sic. 17.19.1– 21.6: doc. 15.7). In Arrian's account, Alexander arrives on the opposite side of the river in the afternoon; Parmenion – as at Philip's death – is said to have given Alexander cautious advice not to risk battle that afternoon, pointing out that the Macedonian army formation would be broken up as it crossed the river and climbed the river banks. Parmenion's role in the historical narrative is to act as a 'foil' to Alexander whose daring, initiative and risk-taking is contrasted with the other's caution and conservative strategy. This portrayal was naturally a result, too, of Parmenion's later assassination at Alexander's orders in 330 BC. Parmenion's advice was sound, but Alexander saw his opportunity and was prepared to take the risk. Moreover, he had left Macedonia several months ago, and was probably anxious for some action, especially while he was wearing the armour from Athena's temple.

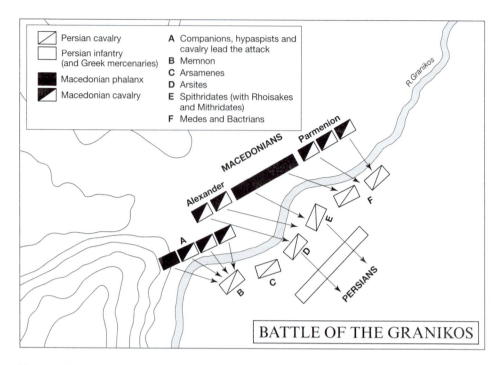

Map 15.1 The battle of Granikos, 334 BC.

Parmenion led the left wing, Alexander the right, with the infantry in the centre; on this right wing Alexander also placed Philotas and the Companion cavalry (Map 15.1). When the Persians saw Alexander on the Macedonian right wing, made conspicuous by the helmet he was wearing, they placed a contingent of the elite Persian cavalry and their commanders to face him; with them were Memnon and his son. Next to these elite horsemen was an extended line of Persian cavalry, and behind that the Persian infantry and the hoplite force of Greek mercenaries in Persian employ. Alexander ordered a mixed group of cavalry, hypaspists (elite infantry attached to the king), Paionians and Companions to cross the river, and Arrian has the Macedonians struggling from the river under attack from a volley of javelins by the Persian cavalry, with Alexander and his cavalry pushing the Persians back from the bank.

Arrian notes that it was more like an infantry battle fought on horseback, with the Macedonians proving more effective against the Persians because they had lances made of cornel wood in contrast to the Persian cavalry's short javelins. Experience also counted, and the Macedonian cavalry was superior to the Persian in this respect. Alexander had a chance for personal glory when he noticed Darius' son-in-law Mithridates charging with a wedge-shaped company of cavalry (and so at least at some distance from the river) against the Macedonians; making straight for him Alexander lanced him in the face. Rhoisakes then riding towards Alexander struck him on the helmet and split it open, but did no harm to Alexander. Spithridates, Rhoisakes' brother, meanwhile charged Alexander, raising his scimitar to attack, but 'Black' Kleitos came to Alexander's rescue, chopping off Spithridates' right shoulder (in Diodorus' account Kleitos saves Alexander from Rhoisakes; Diodorus spells the name as Rhosakes).

Meanwhile the Macedonian phalanx began successfully to cross the river, their task easier now that Alexander's cavalry was engaging with the Persian horse, and once across the Macedonian foot managed to regroup, foiling one of the Persians' strategies in their choice of the Granikos as the site for the battle. The Persian cavalry was massacred, and several of their prominent leaders fell. As for the Persian infantry, the combined Macedonian cavalry and infantry slaughtered them. Calling for quarter, the Greek mercenaries were nevertheless put to the sword, except for a group of 2000: they were enchained and dispatched to Macedonia, as slave labour in Macedonia, for contravening the common decisions of the Greeks – in the League of Corinth – to fight against the Persians. Bronze statues of the twenty-five Companions who fell in battle were sculptured at Alexander's orders by Lysippos and set up at Dion, while 300 sets of Persian armour were sent to Athens as dedications for Athena's temple on the acropolis, with an inscription that Alexander and the Greeks – with the pointed notice 'except for the Spartans' – had captured the armour from the barbarians. Spartan aloofness from the panhellenic crusade obviously still rankled, and Alexander was also attempting to send a message that this was not just a Macedonian campaign but a Greek one; few would have been convinced as the numbers of Greeks fighting against him outnumbered those who fought for him. However, Aeolia, Ionia, Phrygia, Lydia and Caria (except for Halikarnassos) were now or soon to become Alexander's (Diod. Sic. 17.19.1–21.6: doc. 15.7; Arr. 1.13.1–16.7, 3.21.3; Plut. *Alexander* 16).

Lydia, Magnesia and Tralles surrender

After the battle Alexander marched through Lydia, and Sardis was surrendered to him with the enormous treasury of wealth from this prosperous province; the Argive troops with Alexander were left behind to garrison Sardis' citadel; Asander, son of Philotas was made satrap of Lydia. At Ephesos Alexander disbanded the pro-Persian oligarchy and some of the oligarchs were put to death, though he prevented extensive blood-letting and established a democracy. He sacrificed to Artemis in Ephesos and held a great military parade there; Magnesia and Tralles sent ambassadors to surrender their territory to him. Alexander also sent Alkimachos son of Agathokles to Aeolia and Ionia to overthrow oligarchies and establish democracies in the cities. Priene surrendered to Antigonos 'the One-Eyed', who was accorded various honours, clearly not just to flatter him but Alexander as well, who had rededicated the temple of Athena Polias in the city (Tod 2.184: doc. 15.8; Tod 2.186: doc. 15.9; Fig. 15.3). Memnon and other survivors from Granikos fled to Miletos, where they were besieged by Alexander, with the Greek fleet arriving there before the Persian fleet, which was unable to influence the tide of events. Alexander's siege engines forced the city to surrender, but Memnon made good his escape. Alexander disbanded his fleet, but did so too early and had to commission a new one in 333 BC to oppose the still active Persian naval contingents (Diod. Sic. 17.22–23.3; Arr. 1.17–20.1).

The campaigns before the battle of Issos

Memnon was appointed chief commander of the Persians in the area and prepared to make a stand at Halikarnassos along with the Greek mercenaries. Two Athenians, Ephialtes and Thrasyboulos, were prominent in its defence: they were among the politicians whose surrender Alexander had demanded from the Athenians in 335 BC after the destruction of Thebes. With Memnon was Orontobates, satrap of Caria. Alexander, as at Miletos, prosecuted the

Figure 15.3 The inscription of Alexander dedicating Athena's temple at Priene: 'King Alexander dedicated this temple to Athena Polias' (doc. 15.8). British Museum, London GR 1870.3–20.88 (Inscription 399 and 400). Drawing by J. Etherington.

siege vigorously with the usual array of Macedonian siege machinery, so that Memnon abandoned the city in 334 BC, taking the Persian army to Kos. Halikarnassos was razed to the ground, but the citadel was still held by the Persians under Orontobates. Alexander did not concern himself with Memnon but continued his campaign of conquest in Asia Minor, setting out for Phrygia. Now in control of Caria, Alexander appointed a woman called Ada as satrap; she was the sister of the satrap Mausiolos who had aided the islands against Athens in the Social War during the Second Athenian Confederacy. After his death, as widow of the satrap Idrieus, who was also her brother, she had ruled for a few years; she was deposed by her brother Pixodaros, who in turn was succeeded by Orontobates. Now with Alexander's backing she was back in charge, having surrendered her city to Alexander and adopted him as her son, thus making him her successor (Diod. Sic. 17.23.4–27.6; Arr. 1.20.2–23). Ptolemaios (not the son of Lagos) was left to conquer the rest of Caria. Orontobates did not surrender, and although he was defeated by the Macedonians in 333 BC prior to the battle of Issos the entire satrapy was not subdued until 332 BC.

The newly married Macedonian men were sent home to have families, a move which made Alexander popular, and he also sent Kleander to the Peloponnese to enlist more troops (Arr. 1.24; Curt. 3.1.1). In the event, only 150 soldiers came (from Elis) to join him at Gordion. In general Greek participation in Alexander's conquests was relatively slight (Arr. 1.29.4). In 333 BC Parmenion was sent to Sardis and then on to campaign in Phrygia with the allied troops, as the Persian satrap Atizyes remained active there with a force under his command. Meanwhile Alexander entered Lycia, where Pinara and Patara and the city of Xanthos surrendered; Phaselis and other towns of lower Lycia sent ambassadors offering to surrender their cities to him (Arr. 1.24; cf. Diod. Sic. 17.28). At Phaselis in the winter of 333 BC he had a communication from Parmenion: a certain Persian named Sisines had been sent by Darius with a letter to Alexander the Lynkestian, who was now commander of Alexander's Thessalian cavalry. It proposed that he assassinate king Alexander and in return Darius would give him 1000 talents and the Macedonian throne: this Alexander's brothers had been implicated in the murder of Philip. Parmenion captured Sisines and sent him to Alexander at Phaselis and Alexander the Lyncestian was put under close arrest (Diod. Sic. 17.32.1: doc. 15.11; Arr. 1.25). In view of Alexander of Lyncestis' execution later, the episode was either held against him or was a later fabrication to support his fall from favour.

Alexander then entered Pamphylia, where Perge surrendered. Nearchos of Crete was later installed as satrap of Lycia and Pamphylia with Perge as his capital (Arr. 3.6.6). On his march away from this city Alexander received the surrender of Aspendos, which soon revolted but was later reduced by him (Arr. 1.26–27.4; Diod. Sic. 17.32). In spring 333 he marched into Pisidia where various tribes were subdued, and while at first he had to bypass the city of Telmissos (also Termessos), perched high on a hill with magnificent views and the command of local passes, it fell to him later. Western Pisidia was added to Nearchos' satrapy. Alexander then proceeded into Phrygia, the capital of which was Kelainai and held by the Phrygian satrap with Carian and Greek mercenaries. It surrendered and Antigonos 'the One-Eyed' was made satrap of Phrygia, a position he held until Alexander's death (Arr. 1.27.5–29.6; Curt. 3.1.6–8).

The prophecy of the Gordian knot

Alexander then set out for Gordion in Phrygia, where he met up by prior arrangement with Parmenion. Here the Macedonians who had gone home to beget children with their young wives rejoined the army with a small number of reinforcements, 3150 foot and 500 cavalry. The Athenians requested that the Athenian mercenaries captured at Granikos and transported to Macedonia for hard labour be released. This was turned down: the Athenians would be able to ask again at a later date, and according to Arrian, Alexander considered them as hostages for the good behaviour of the Greeks. Here at Gordion the famous knot on the ox-cart dedicated to Zeus by King Midas, and the prophecy regarding it, awaited him: whoever undid the knot of the wagon's yoke, so the prophecy ran, would become ruler of Asia. Alexander succeeded in doing so, either by cutting the knot or by removing the pole pin of the yoke, and the gods sent favourable omens to him that night (Arr. 2.3.6–8: doc. 15.10; Plut. *Alexander* 18; Curt. 3.1.9). Alexander then turned south, accepting the surrender of the Paphlagonians, and marched to Cappadocia, and thence into Cilicia.

Elsewhere, Memnon, whom Darius had put in charge of the Persian navy and Asia Minor coastline, was still active with the Persian fleet and in 333 BC it took a number of islands, including Chios and Lesbos except for the city of Mytiline. The islands of the Cyclades sent

Memnon ambassadors to negotiate surrender, and it seemed as if Alexander might be caught between two groups of Persians, one controlling the Aegean and its islands, and the other that part of the Persian Empire still unconquered (Diod. Sic. 17.28–9). Memnon died of an illness, which Arrian considered to be one of the severest blows to the Persian cause, but other Persian commanders succeeded him, and Mytilene surrendered to them on terms, while a Persian fleet of ten ships under Datames went to the Cyclades where Tenedos surrendered: both Mytilene and Tenedos were forced to destroy the stele on which were inscribed their agreements with Alexander, and to agree to abide by the King's Peace of 386 BC. This provides an interesting perspective on the Persian point of view and how they viewed the Macedonian invasion: it was for them in contravention of the agreement between the Persians and the Greeks. Antipater was forced in haste to put together a Greek fleet which succeeded in defeating the Persians: Alexander had been premature in disbanding the Greek fleet (Arr. 2.1–2).

Persian defeat at Issos

Darius at Issos

Meanwhile Alexander marched through Cappadocia, conquering on both sides of the Halys river, and seized the Cilician gates. He then proceeded through Cilicia to Tarsos which was abandoned by its Persian commander Arsames who fled to Darius. At Tarsos, Alexander fell extremely ill and only one physician dared (successfully) to treat him. Parmenion was sent with the allied infantry, Greek mercenaries, Thracians and Thessalian cavalry to seize the other 'Gates' between Cilicia and Assyria (Arr. 2.4–5; Diod. Sic. 17.31.4–6; Plut. *Alexander* 19; Curt. 3.5–6). Darius had brought a large force into Assyria and was in fact encamped in an area ideal for a Persian battle, an open plain where his cavalry had room to manoeuvre and his large number of infantry had sufficient space in which to be effective. But Alexander's prolonged stay at Tarsos because of his sickness, and then at Soli (where he sacrificed in gratitude to Asklepios and held athletic and musical competitions: he was obviously still recovering), unnerved the Great King. Consequently he decided to move his forces to confront Alexander, and in his advance arrived at Issos in the rear of Alexander's army; Alexander at first refused to believe this. From Soli, news had also reached Alexander – and no doubt Darius as well – that Orontobates who controlled the citadel at Halikarnassos and several islands had been defeated (Arr. 2.5–7; Diod. Sic. 17.32).

The battle of Issos

Issos is on the coast in the very south-east of Cilicia, near the Cilician gates: exactly the opposite type of position to that which Darius had originally chosen. In Assyria he waited on a plain suited to the Persian style of warfare, where his huge numbers of infantry and his cavalry had plenty of room to manoeuvre. While Alexander tarried at Tarsos and Soli, Darius became restless and eager to confront Alexander, and moved his troops to the north-west of Alexander, with the river Pinaros dividing them from Alexander's forces to the south. At first Alexander did not believe that Darius was in his rear to the north, but this was confirmed. The actual battle took place on a narrow strip of coastal land, only about four kilometres wide. As at Granikos, Alexander was clearly outnumbered but he realised that the narrowness of the battle area at Issos was in his favour. With the sea on one side and the mountains on the other (west and east

Figure 15.4 The so-called Alexander Sarcophagus, showing an intricately carved marble bas-relief scene which reproduces a painting of the battle of Issos (doc. 15.11). On the far left Alexander, his right arm raised, which would have held a spear, is shown on his horse (at this stage this would still be Boukephalas) putting to flight a Persian cavalry man, whose horse stumbles; Alexander prepares for the kill. Alexander is shown wearing a lion skin in a clear allusion to his imitation of Herakles. The defeat of the Persians is in progress. On the far right the final horseman may well be Perdikkas who always commanded the left wing opposite Alexander. Possibly made for Abdalonymos, king of Sidon, who was appointed by Alexander (Curt. 4.1.22; he died in 311 BC) in the late fourth century BC, the sarcophagus comes from the Sidon necropolis where it was discovered in AD 1887. The other long side depicts Alexander with both Macedonians and Persians in a lion-hunt. It measures 318 cm long, with a width of 167 cm, and a height of 195 cm. Archaeological Museum Istanbul 370T, Turkey. Photo © Nickmard Khoey.

respectively) hemming in the Persian forces, their numbers were of no advantage; 'Alexander realised that the gods had given him the chance to destroy the Persian power' (Diod. Sic. 17.33.1). He fully realised this as he led his troops to where Darius' forces were located through a relatively narrow corridor of land about one kilometre in width, widening out to about two, before entering into what could loosely be called the plain of Issos; Arrian records Alexander telling his generals, squadron leaders (ilarchoi) and allies that the relatively small space suited them rather than the Persians. (For the battle, see Diod. Sic. 17.32.1–34.9, 17.36.6: doc. 15.11; Arr. 2.6.1–12.1; Plut. *Alexander* 20; Curt. 3.7–12; Just. 11.8–9; Figs 15.2, 15.4, 15.5.)

Disposition of the forces

Both armies had their cavalry on their wings, with the infantry in the centre. Alexander was on the right wing, while once again Parmenion commanded the left wing, with orders not to move away from the coastal shore. This tactic and the mountains ensured that no Persians broke through past Alexander's forces, although a few did actually get around via the base of the mountain. Darius was in the Persian centre, as was customary for the Persian king and most of the Persian cavalry were on the right wing (opposite Alexander's left). A Persian force was to the north-east of Alexander's army, obviously in an attempt to outflank his right wing, but the Agrianians under Attalos, with some cavalry and archers, chased them into the foot-hills where they could play no role in the battle. Darius remained on his side of the Pinaros, and had the river, the banks of which were steep in some places but not all the way along its length, reinforced with a palisade. Alexander ordered the phalanx to advance, but with all the hoplites at the same pace, so that its line was unbroken. This tactic only worked until the banks on the other side were reached.

Alexander and those with him on the right wing charged against the Persian infantry opposite him, which gave way as soon as the contest became a 'hand-to-hand' one. But the Macedonian centre, the phalanx, was broken up in its advance when some of it encountered steep banks, and the Greek mercenaries on the Persian side attacked them mercilessly. Having routed the Persian left wing, the Macedonian cavalry on the right turned towards these mercenaries and attacked their flank. Their defeat was almost inevitable, and they joined in the general rout. Meanwhile, the Persian cavalry squadron charged the Thessalian cavalry across the river, taking the initiative, and here there was a major cavalry engagement which continued, with the Thessalians not gaining the upper hand, until it became apparent that Darius had fled the field (Map 15.2).

Darius flees

Arrian writes that Darius deserted the field when he saw his left wing crushed. However, Diodorus gives a more probable account: that the king came to Issos to fight Alexander and that he did so. Plutarch even records a version of events in which Darius personally wounded Alexander in the thigh. When Alexander made for Darius, Darius' brother Oxathres rode with the elite Persian cavalry to protect his brother, and fought in front of Darius' chariot. Piles of bodies formed around Darius and the horses of the king's chariots took fright; Darius grabbed the reins himself, but could not extricate the chariot and another vehicle was brought up into which the Great King jumped as the enemy pressed upon him. When the Persians saw this they also fled. Eventually he abandoned the chariot and all his weaponry and fled on horseback. Arrian gives the numbers of the Persian dead as 100,000 infantry and 1000 cavalry, and it appears that at one place the fleeing Persians fell into a deep defile, so many in fact that their pursuers were able to use the bodies as a bridge. The mosaic illustrating the battle of Issos from the House of the Faun at Pompeii shows Alexander and Darius in close proximity, and the depiction of the two main protagonists of the battle in conflict need not merely be an artistic device: Alexander and Darius undoubtedly met face-to-face, for Alexander certainly wanted to kill or capture Darius if he could (Fig. 15.2).

Kallisthenes' ignorance of military matters?

Polybios criticised Kallisthenes' account of the battle, but Kallisthenes was there and one can presume that Alexander read or had read to him the journal which Kallisthenes kept. Kallisthenes has the Macedonian phalanx extended over an area of some 40 stades: about three and a half kilometres. The terrain at Issos in fact allows for such a length of line. In addition, the crevices which Polybios complains of are clearly those gullies behind the Persian line into which the fleeing Persians fell: the Macedonian phalanx did not break up until some of it encountered

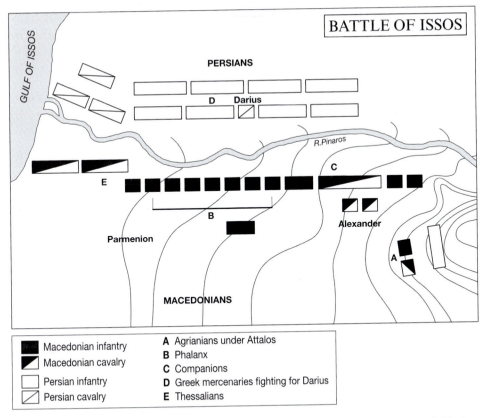

Map 15.2 The battle of Issos, 333 BC. Based on D.J. Lonsdale, *Alexander the Great: Lessons in Strategy*, Routledge, 2007.

the steep banks of the Pinaros. As at the Granikos, Alexander relied on the impact of a cavalry charge to force his way against and into the Persian lines. Polybios criticises Kallisthenes' account for describing Alexander as having the Macedonian phalanx attack a river bank which was steep and 'full of brambles'. But this was exactly what Alexander did do, as at Granikos. What he relied on was that his cavalry assault would break up the enemy's line sufficiently to enable the phalanx to scale the bank: some of the phalanx managed to do so, while others did encounter difficulties (Polyb. *Histories* 12.20.1–6, 12.22.1–7: doc. 15.12).

Darius had gone to war with a superior force and fully expected victory. In his mind, he probably did not view fighting at another river (as at Granikos) as a potential failure: he heavily outnumbered Alexander and he had the element of surprise. But as at Thermopylai, the Persians did not give themselves enough room to manoeuvre, and Alexander took the initiative. He had a specific strategy, to force the left Persian wing to collapse, and the tactic he used to effect this was to cross the river and engage the enemy at speed and with aggression, confident in his army's superiority in weaponry, experience and training. Cilicia was now Alexander's, and he appointed Balakros as Macedonian satrap of the country (Arr. 2.12.2; Diod. Sic. 18.22.1). As in Phrygia, Caria and elsewhere, Alexander took over the existing administrative units, generally imposing a Macedonian as satrap.

As he did not envisage defeat, Darius had travelled in style: his mother, wife and two of his daughters were with him, along with a huge array of treasures to make life comfortable, all of which were captured by the Macedonians, including 3000 talents of gold. This is the setting of the charming anecdote in which Hephaistion and Alexander visited Darius' family after the battle, and the Great King's mother and wife mistook Hephaistion, who was the taller of the two, for Alexander, and made proskynesis to him. As Arrian specifically implies that the superior sources of Ptolemy and Aristoboulos did not record this story, it can be discounted as a vignette of dubious historical value (Arr. 2.12.6–8; Diod. Sic. 17.37.3–38.3; Curt. 3.11.24–6, 3.12.1–26; cf. Plut. *Alexander* 21), but in the popular imagination it is one of the best-known incidents in Alexander's conquests.

Darius' response to defeat

Darius crossed over the river Euphrates with the remainder of his force, some 4000 troops. The Greek mercenaries escaped by land to Phoenicia and then by ship to Cyprus and on to Egypt. Alexander appointed Menon son of Kerdimnas as satrap of 'Hollow Syria', and then proceeded down the coast to Phoenicia. At Marathos, he received a Persian envoy and a let-ter from Darius offering peace terms: just how many peace overtures Darius did make and at what dates remains unclear. Arrian has two: one at Marathos in early 332 and one at Tyre later in the summer of 332. He is followed in this by Curtius, while Plutarch has one in 331 in Phoenicia, and both Diodorus and Justin have peace offers from Darius from Babylon in 332. The most reliable tradition is Arrian, and it is probable that Darius made two offers, one after Issos, and one while the siege of Tyre was in progress (Arr. 2.14, 2.25; Diod. Sic. 17.39, cf. 17.54; Plut. *Alexander* 29; Curt. 4.1, 4.5; Justin 11.12).

Figure 15.5 A detail from the Alexander sarcophagus: Alexander prepares to kill a Persian cavalryman in the battle of Issos. Photo © N. Croll.

The peace offer made by Darius was in the form of a letter, perhaps an original, copied into Kallisthenes' journal of events. Darius wrote that Philip and the Great King had been at peace when Philip invaded (in 338 BC) and that he had merely been defending his country, and asked for the return of his family and for an alliance. Alexander's reply was meant as much for panhellenic consumption as for Darius. Persia had aided the Greeks at Perinthos (cf. Diod. Sic. 16.84.1–87.3: doc. 14.48), Darius had murdered Artaxerxes IV (Arses) and was therefore a usurper, and after Philip's death had incited the Greeks to revolt. Alexander was now master as 'lord of the whole of Asia', and in future Darius was to address him as 'King of Asia': if Darius wanted to contest this he would have to stand and fight – 'because wherever you are I will come after you' (Arr. 2.14.1–9: doc. 15.13).

Alexander increases his grip on the Persian Empire

The siege of Tyre

Alexander's reply to Darius showed him supremely confident of his right to rule Asia. However, for the moment, Alexander did not pursue Darius into the interior as the coast of the Mediterranean still needed to be secured against the Persian fleet. He therefore moved down the Phoenician coast and received the surrender of all cities except one, Tyre, which decided it would obey all Alexander's commands but allow no Persians or Macedonians within the city, presumably hoping that in this way it would avoid annoying the Great King while appearing to Alexander as a neutral city. But Alexander was aware that the Persian fleet could use Tyre as a base of operations, and he was attempting to deprive the Persians of all coastal ports: Persia still controlled some of the islands and parts of the Aegean. Moreover, while he initially bypassed Telmissos as impossible to take by siege, he captured the city eventually, and as there was no reason not to attempt the capture of Tyre he undertook a protracted siege of the city in the spring of 332 BC. Why Tyre chose not to surrender to Alexander seems unclear, but Arrian depicts its inhabitants as still uncertain of the course of the war. After all, a Persian fleet was still operating in the area and Darius himself had been defeated only once, and it must have been known that he was preparing a fresh army against Alexander.

Tyre was actually located on an island, nearly a kilometre off the coast, and heavily fortified with high walls, and its capture excited the imagination of several ancient sources who give detailed accounts of the difficulties of Alexander's siege operation (Arr. 2.18–24, 2.18.1–19.6: doc. 15.14; Diod. Sic. 17.40–7; Plut. *Alexander* 24; Curt. 4.3.11–12). As Arrian notes, 'it was obvious that besieging Tyre would be a massive operation' (Arr. 2.18.1). Alexander constructed a mole out to the island, a task easy enough when the water was shallow but increasingly difficult as the water deepened. Alexander supervised the work in person, which encouraged the troops, as did the gifts he bestowed for exceptional work. As the mole neared the city, the Tyrians were able to attack the workers with missiles. Two towers with siege engines were therefore constructed at the end of the mole, but the Tyrians used the 'fire-ship' method to deal with these, filling a ship with combustible material, towing it close to the towers, and setting it alight: when the ship hit the end of the mole the towers burst into flame.

Alexander was not deterred: the mole was made broader, so it could accommodate more towers and he sent for his ships to contest Tyre's control of the sea. When his fleet arrived, the city refused a naval battle but used their own ships to block up their harbours. The city was now blockaded. When the mole was very close to the city, the Tyrians did put out for a naval battle, but they were comprehensively defeated. Siege engines on the mole now attacked

Figure 15.6 A silver tetradrachma coin (four drachmas) from Amphipolis. Alexander on the obverse is shown as the god Herakles wearing a lion skin, its claws tied around his neck; he emulated Herakles and increasingly identified himself with this god as his reign progressed. On the reverse is an enthroned Zeus with his bird of prophecy, an eagle; the inscription reads 'Of Alexander'. Dating to 315–308 BC, it weighs 17.2g with a diameter of 15mm. Yale University Art Gallery, 2001.87.3697.

the city's fortifications but with little success. However, siege machines mounted on ships proved more effective, and a breach was made in Tyre's wall. Alexander ordered an all-out assault around the city to keep the Tyrians busy. Admetos leading the hypaspists was the first to breach the wall and was killed but the Macedonians soon captured the city. The Tyrians who fled to the temple of Herakles, including the king of Tyre, were spared: it was this very temple which was the reason for Alexander's visit to Tyre and the Tyrians' refusal to allow him to worship there as one of Herakles' descendants was part of the pretext for his attack. Some 30,000 inhabitants were sold into slavery, and Alexander had his wish and sacrificed at the temple of Herakles (see Fig. 15.6).

Darius attempts to make terms

While at Tyre, Darius sent envoys to Alexander with a second offer of peace. Darius was facing unpleasant realities, now that his satraps' army had been defeated at Granikos, and the huge force he led in person at Issos was annihilated. His family was also in Macedonian hands. Envoys from Darius now offered to Alexander what he practically already possessed in terms of conquest: all of the Persian Empire from the Mediterranean to the river Euphrates (although there was still a Persia fleet in the Aegean); a ransom of 10,000 talents for the return of his family; and a marriage alliance with his daughter by which Alexander could become his son-in-law. Parmenion, as ever, is said to have taken the cautious line, and advised Alexander to accept the terms, at which Alexander quipped that he would too, if he were Parmenion. Alexander's reply to the Persian envoys neatly summed up the historical situation: he had no need of Darius' money, he intended to control all of the Persian Empire and not merely the part that he had so far conquered, and he would marry Darius' daughter if he wanted to. Most humiliating for Darius was the request that if he wanted terms he would need to come and discuss them with Alexander himself (Arr. 2.25.1–3: doc. 15.15; cf. Diod. Sic. 18.22.1).

After he completed the siege of Tyre in July or August of 332 BC Alexander moved further down the coast. All of Syria had now revolted from the Persians except the city of Gaza, which was heavily fortified. It was the last major city before Egypt to the south. About now, ambassadors from the League of Corinth arrived with a golden wreath to honour Alexander for his victory at Issos: Antipater made sure that Greece was kept up to date with the news of Alexander's conquests, including that of the defeat of the Persian King, which had excellent propaganda value. Now they could take back news of the capture of Tyre as well, which was equally useful to keep the Greeks under control. As the city of Gaza was built on a mound, Alexander suggested building a mound of corresponding height against the south wall, and the siege engines, which had done good service at Tyre, were brought up and the walls were battered and sapped. After the Macedonians stormed in, all the men of Gaza fought to the death, after which the women and children were sold into slavery. The entire operation took two months and Gaza was repopulated with indigenous locals to act as a frontier fortress settlement controlling access into Egypt. Amyntas son of Andromenes was now sent by ship to Macedonia for reinforcements, returning with them in late 331 BC (Arr. 2.25.4–27.7, 3.16.10–11; Diod. Sic. 17.48.7–49.1, 17.65.1; Plut. *Alexander* 25.3).

From Gaza to Egypt

From Gaza it was logical to travel to and conquer the next and last of the Persian satrapies along the shores of the Mediterranean. Alexander marched to Pelousion at the eastern delta of the Nile, where his fleet anchored, and he moved on to Heliopolis, sacred to the sun god, and to Memphis, the ancient Old Kingdom capital of Egypt with its nearby pyramids at Giza and Saqqara. The Persians had reinstated Memphis as the capital and it was here that the Persian satrap Mazakes surrendered and Alexander was welcomed by the local population. Resistance by the Persians was futile, as Egypt had risen several times in revolt against them, most recently in 343–342 BC. Mazakes also took into account the extent of Alexander's territorial conquests and the consequences of Darius' flight (Arr. 3.1; Diod. Sic. 17.49.1–2; Curt. 4.7.1–5). Alexander as ruler of Egypt was now, of course, its king (or pharaoh, a term not actually used by the Egyptians themselves), and as such he was the god Horus incarnate on earth and the son of the sun god Amen-Re. As the new ruler he was given a specific titulature of five names reflecting his relationship with the land of Egypt and its gods. A coronation ceremony was presumably held for him at Memphis and the Egyptian priests proclaimed him son of Ra and the incarnation of Horus. While at Memphis he sacrificed to the gods, including the Egyptian Apis bull. Alexander was depicted on temple reliefs at Luxor (known to the Greeks as Egyptian Thebes) in the company of the Egyptian gods, and to the priests he was fully assimilated as an Egyptian god-king. His Egyptian throne name was Setep-en-Re Meri-amen: 'The chosen one of Re, blessed of Amen' (Fig. 15.9).

The foundation of Alexandria in 331 BC

Alexander sailed downstream from Memphis to the western delta and founded the city of Alexandria, before marching across the desert to the oracle of Ammon at the oasis of Siwah.

The first Greeks in Egypt were mercenaries and traders in the seventh century BC (Hdt. 2.152.3–154.5, 178.1–181.2: doc. 2.31; Fig. 2.10), but now the Macedonians had come to stay – as rulers. Ptolemy, son of Lagos, upon Alexander's death would hold Egypt for himself and his descendants, establishing the Ptolemaic dynasty which only ended when Cleopatra VII committed suicide after Octavian (later Augustus) defeated Anthony and herself in the great naval battle at Actium in 31 BC. Good omens attended the laying out of the city, which Alexander intended to be a great Greek city, named after himself (an eponymous city), with typical Greek institutions. In fact Alexandria became one of the great cities of the ancient world and Alexander himself was buried there. Throughout his conquests, Alexander named cities after himself: some were new establishments, while others were reinvigorations of existing cities. Perhaps the most famous after Alexandria in Egypt was Alexandria on the river Oxos, modern Khanoum in Afghanistan (above the border of north-west India), which lay thousands of kilometres from Greece but possessed all the necessities of Greek civilisation, including a gymnasium and theatre. It was probably actually founded by Hephaistion when he was campaigning in this area and both Greek and Persian veteran soldiers were settled here (Plut. *Alexander* 26.1–10: doc. 15.16; Arr. 3.1–2.2; Diod. Sic. 17.52; Curt. 4.8.1–6; Just. 11.11.13).

While in Egypt news came of success in the Aegean. The Macedonian fleet had been active and the islands of Tenedos and Chios had revolted from the Persians, while Mytilene had been captured from Chares (the Athenian politician) and the other cities on Lesbos had come over to Alexander. Kos had also joined the Macedonian side when a fleet of sixty ships under the Macedonian Amphoteros appeared and appealed to the island to join Macedon. Persian naval strategy in the Aegean was in tatters and its fleet no longer a threat. News also came that Sparta had revolted and Amphoteros was sent with a fleet, including Phoenician and Cypriot ships, to assist the other Peloponnesians against the Spartans (Arr. 3.2.3–7, cf. 2.13.6; Diod. Sic. 17.48.1; Curt. 4.5.14–22).

Consultation of Ammon in 331 BC

Alexander was then 'overwhelmed by a desire to visit the oracle of Ammon in Libya' at Siwah (Arr. 3.3.1), which had been consulted earlier by Greeks, including Alkibiades who received a positive response about whether the Sicilian expedition should go ahead. As the force travelled over 400 kilometres across sandy desert, the god Ammon sent rain, and according to the ancient sources, dispatched either crows or serpents to show the way. Alexander had consulted Delphi before leaving Greece, engaged in a form of oracular enquiry at Gordion, and now he actively sought oracular guidance in Egypt. Otherwise, he generally relied on the Greek form of divination, which involved the interpretation of various signs sent by the gods, in particular oionomanteia, or bird divination. This is particularly stressed by the sources for Alexander presumably because it was the type of divination found in Homer, whose work had a profound significance for Alexander. Ammon's oracle was according to Greek belief consulted by Herakles and Perseus, and Alexander was a descendant of both – the importance of his relationship with Herakles, also a son of Zeus (and as Zeus was also Zeus-Ammon, he had a relationship with Ammon as well), is once again clear, as most recently demonstrated at Tyre. Arrian simply states that Alexander 'heard the response he desired'. Other sources are more forthcoming, or perhaps more speculative and record that Alexander was told he was the son of Zeus (Arr. 3.3.1–4.5: doc. 15.17; Diod. Sic. 17.49.2–51.4; Plut. *Alexander* 26.6–27.6; Curt. 4.7.5–32; Figs 15.7, 15.12). At some stage Cyrene and its subsidiary towns willingly surrendered themselves to him (cf. docs 2.28–30).

Figure 15.7 The ruins of the Oracle of Ammon, Siwah, Egypt. Photo © Prof. Richard T. Mortel, Riyadh, Saudi Arabia.

The final conquest of Persia

In spring 331 BC Alexander marched north to the coast, then eastwards to Alexandria, and retraced his steps to Tyre, where once again he sacrificed to Herakles. Here he was met by Athenian ambassadors who again asked for the release of the Athenian mercenaries captured at Granikos and this time he acquiesced. As Darius showed no desire to bring the war to Syria, Alexander travelled inland northwards, and then eastwards, crossing the Euphrates and then the Tigris rivers into the heartland of the Persian Empire. Darius waited for Alexander at Gaugamela with an army perhaps some 250,000 strong (Arrian estimates 1,000,000 infantry), and four days' march from the enemy Alexander's troops sighted Persian cavalry; some were captured and from them the news was learnt that Darius was nearby with a large force (Arr. 3.7). This was Alexander's third major pitched battle against the Persians, and the second in which he fought Darius. The outcome of the battle decided the fate of the Persian Empire – and ultimately of Darius.

The battle at Gaugamela in 331 BC

There are differences in all of the versions of the battle of Gaugamela, which took place on 1 October 331 BC. Darius had learned the lesson of Issos, and he chose his battleground carefully. For several days his troops trained in the same area, and attention was paid to the level of the ground which was smoothed over where necessary so that chariots – with scythes attached – could be employed effectively; Alexander inspected the area as well. According to Arrian, Darius' forces numbered 40,000 cavalry, 1,000,000 foot soldiers, 200 scythe chariots and even some elephants. He also specifically records that according to Aristoboulos Darius' battle dispositions were written up after the battle, presumably by Kallisthenes. This was *the* crucial battle of the war against Persia, which gave Alexander the entire empire and no doubt extra care went into recording all of its details (for Gaugamela, see Plut. *Alexander* 33.4–8, 34.1–4: doc. 15.18; Arr. 3.7.3–15; Diod. Sic. 17.58–61; Curt. 4.12–13; for the date: Plut. *Camillus* 19.4).

The disposition of the Persian forces

On Darius' far left wing were stationed Bactrian cavalry, then Dahai and Arachotians, then a mixed force of Persian cavalry and infantry, the Susians and Cadusians. In the centre was a force of Greek mercenaries, comprising some 2000 on either side of Darius, while Darius himself was stationed in the middle of the centre, with the Kinsmen and Melophoroi. The 'Kinsmen' were the cream of the Persian cavalry, some 1000 strong drawn from the Persian aristocracy, while the Melophoroi (literally, 'Apple Bearers': the Persians whose spears ended not in a normal butt at the base but in a golden 'apple') were an elite of 1000 chosen from the 10,000 Immortals, the special guard of the King. They were part of a long-standing Persian tradition and marched out with Xerxes from Sardis on his way to Greece (Herodotos 7.41; cf. Arr. 7.29.3: doc. 15.45). Eventually, Alexander too had a similar guard, made up of 500 Persian Melophoroi and 500 Macedonian Argyraspides. With them were the Indians, the 'transplanted' Carians and the Mardian archers, and on his far right wing were the forces from Hollow Syria, then Mesopotamians, Medians, Parthians, Sakians, Topeirians, Hyrkanians, Albanians and Sakesinians, right up to the centre phalanx. Behind both wings and the centre was a large group of Uxians, Babylonians and Red Sea Sittakenoi as an in-depth formation. In front of the left wing was a force of Scythian cavalry, and about 1000 Bactrian and 100 scythed chariots; they faced Alexander's right wing, where he himself was stationed. A group of elephants and fifty scythed chariots were in the middle of the centre. Armenian and Cappadocian cavalry were in front of the left wing and fifty scythed chariots in front of the right wing. Mazaios commanded the right wing, Darius the centre, and Bessos the left. The numbers involved, and the range of major ethnic groups represented, indicate that Darius had by no means lost his empire: in fact he still held about two-thirds of it. This was a force to be reckoned with (Map 15.3).

Alexander's dispositions

Parmenion commanded the left, a force of cavalry and the Thracian javelin throwers. In the centre was the phalanx (commanded by Simmias), and to its right the hypaspists and further right the hypaspist guard (the agema). There was also a subsidiary or secondary phalanx behind the centre, which played a vital role in beating off a Persian attack from the rear. Alexander commanded the right wing, positioning himself in fact on its very extremity, as part of a strategy to avoid Darius' scythed chariots. Here also was the Companion Cavalry (commanded by Parmenion's son Philotas), with Alexander and its royal squadron, commanded by Kleitos the Black, in front.

As the armies approached each other Alexander moved his wing over to the right, so the Persians moved correspondingly to their left, greatly outflanking Alexander's wing because of their sheer numbers. The Scythian cavalry attacked Alexander's front line, but Alexander kept pushing his line towards the right, nearly leaving the ground prepared by the Persians. Darius, noticing this and anxious that his chariots would not be able to operate effectively if the Macedonians reached uneven ground, ordered his cavalry to envelope Alexander's forces to stop them proceeding any further in that direction. At this Alexander ordered his mercenary cavalry, commanded by Menidas, to charge, at which the Scythian and Bactrian cavalry counter-charged and pushed them back. Persian cavalry gained the upper hand and killed numerous Macedonians but in the long run the discipline of the Macedonians prevailed and they broke up the attacking cavalry formation.

Failure of the scythed chariots

To counter this the scythed chariots were sent against Alexander, in an attempt to break up his line of battle, but the Agrianians and the javelin throwers under Balakros' command threw volleys of spears at them, even reaching up to snatch the reins of the horses, and the Macedonian ranks then parted to allow the remaining chariots to pass through (rendering the scythes ineffective): these were finished off by Alexander's grooms (hippokomoi) and the royal hypaspists. Darius now ordered all his line to attack, while the Macedonian cavalry managed to make a 'dent' in the Persian line. Alexander made for this and with a wedge of the Companion cavalry and some of the phalanx that was on the spot made straight for Darius, screaming out a lusty war cry. Here the Macedonian cavalry thrust against the Persian infantry near the Great King, the Macedonian cavalry stabbing the Persian infantry in the face with their spears, and the Macedonian phalanx with their long sarissas playing havoc with the Persians. All this was at close quarters to Darius and aiming for him: he fled the scene.

But on the Macedonian left, Parmenion and his men were in difficulties, as the front line of the phalanx on the Macedonian left wing was broken, and some of the Indian and Persian cavalry had made their way through to the Macedonian baggage camp. Alexander, however, had his reserve phalanx force in the rear, which wheeled about and attacked these Persians according to previous instruction if this were to happen. Oblivious of Darius' departure the Persian right wing was still fighting, and wheeled around the left wing so that Parmenion's troops were attacked on two sides. At this point Parmenion – famously – sent an urgent message to Alexander to come to his assistance and Alexander and the Companions swiftly arrived, charging at the enemy cavalry. Hand-to-hand combat on horseback ensued in which Hephaistion was wounded and sixty Companions killed. Alexander prevailed and soon the entire Persian cavalry and infantry were in flight. He now resumed his pursuit of the fleeing Darius, hoping to capture him at Arbela about 110 kilometres away, but unable to rally resistance Darius did not stop and made for Media as a refugee. Darius the Great King had now fled from his second battle. Alexander did not pursue him but, as after Issos, he made for the major urban centres in the region to take control of the wealth and resources of Persia.

Alexander's strategy

Alexander had planned to avoid the Persian scythed chariots by moving his wing eastwards and to the right across the battleground, and then to exploit a gap opened up in front of Darius by the extension of the two lines. He knew that combat with the king himself was at the heart of the matter and to fight it out with him was crucial. Darius' strategy of using scythed chariots to break up the formidable phalanx was a sound one, but the Macedonians dealt with this fairly easily and more chariots were needed for the task than Darius had estimated: Alexander's forces avoided the chariots and succeeded in reaching Darius without having to cope with them, although Macedonian victory was not a foregone conclusion. The fighting was fierce and the Persians fought very well, especially their cavalry, but the battle was in the heart of the empire, and Babylon, Susa and Persepolis lay in a southerly direction and were undefended by Darius, who was fleeing eastwards into Media and away from the centre of power. Alexander was now truly king of the Persian Empire. The sources give a huge number of Persian dead at 300,000, with a large number of wounded, as compared to 500 or 1000 Macedonian dead. Modern historians here are dealing with sources operating in the realm of fantasy, and the number of Persian dead is incredible, while Macedonian casualties must have been far greater than recorded, with losses on the left wing particularly severe.

The consequences of Gaugamela

This battle more or less secured the Persian Empire for Alexander but ironically led to unrest and encouraged rebellion in Greece. For many it must have seemed a 'now or never' situation, in which there was a chance to have a last gamble for freedom. Rebellion broke out in Thrace under Memnon (not Memnon of Rhodes), its governor, who had his own army. This was dealt with by Antipater, in charge of Macedonia and Greece. Most of the Macedonian army was with Alexander, but Antipater was able to come to terms with the rebels. News of the revolt in Thrace, however, sparked rebellion in Greece in 331 BC. King Agis and the Spartans made preparations for a military confrontation with the Macedonians, and sent embassies throughout Greece appealing for support; they apparently thought that Darius was still in a position to provide financial assistance to their cause. Many Peloponnesians, although not Messene or Megalopolis, joined them, while Athens was undecided. Demosthenes did not support the Spartan cause, and Demades pointed to the financial implications of an uprising, while Athens may well have remained wary of a Sparta that could become powerful again through a coalition of allies, especially as the Spartan rebels besieged Megalopolis, unable to let go of their fixation with their historical primacy in the south-western Peloponnese. By early 330 BC Antipater was in the Peloponnese: he had a force of 40,000, made up of Macedonians and Greeks loyal to Alexander whom he collected en route, as opposed to the 20,000 Peloponnesians with their 2000 cavalry led by Agis, who was killed in the fighting. The battle took place near Megalopolis in 330 BC. It was still under siege and a few thousand died on each side. It was not an easy victory for the Macedonians, but an important one as it wiped out large numbers of the Spartans and showed the Greeks that rebellion against Alexander was futile. Agis may have been confident of victory, for he chose a restricted plain on which to fight where Antipater could not bring his force to bear simultaneously. However, Antipater's superior numbers told, for as the rebels were killed or wounded in fighting they could not be replaced, whereas Antipater had men to make up for the losses in the front line throughout the course of the battle. The Peloponnesian rebels were then disciplined by the League of Corinth: Greece was not technically ruled by Alexander and the Macedonians, rather the league had elected him as their supreme leader (strategos autokrator). Only Sparta had not joined the league and fifty important Spartans were demanded as hostages and sent to Alexander: their fate is unknown (see Diod. Sic. 17.62.1–63.2: doc. 15.19, 17.73.5; Curt. 6.1; Plut. *Moralia* 235b, 818e–f; Aeschin. 3.133; the revolt is curiously omitted by Arrian).

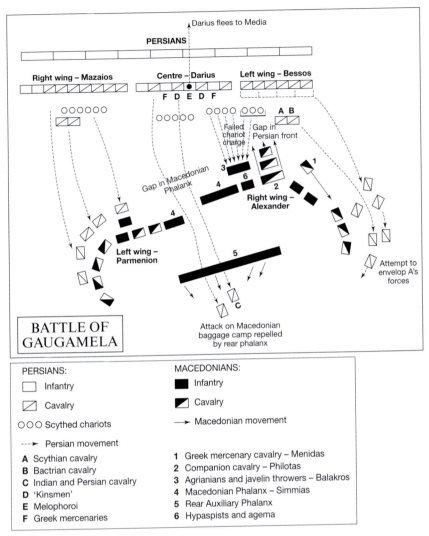

Map 15.3 The battle of Gaugamela, 331 BC. Based on D.J. Lonsdale, *Alexander the Great: Lessons in Strategy*, Routledge, 2007.

Alexander's appointment of Persian satraps

After Gaugamela, Alexander advanced towards the ancient city of Babylon where Mazaios, who commanded the Persian wing at Gaugamela, had taken refuge. He surrendered to Alexander and was appointed satrap, but with a Greek and a Macedonian – Apollodoros of Amphipolis and Menes of Pella – in charge of the garrison which Alexander stationed there. Asklepiodoros was responsible for taxation. Alexander rebuilt the temples destroyed by Xerxes, especially that of the city's main god, Baal (Arr. 3.16.3–5; Diod. Sic. 17.64.5–6; Curt. 5.1.19–44). The Persian Mithrenes (who had surrendered Sardis to Alexander) was sent as satrap to Armenia. Other Persian satraps were also installed: Phrasaortes son of Rheomithras in Persia, Oxydates

557

in Media, and Aboulites in the region of Susiana. When Alexander returned from the far east in 324 he was to execute Aboulites and his son for maladministration (Arr. 7.4.1). Amminapes (a Parthyaian) was made satrap of the Parthyaians and Hyrkanians, and Satibarzanes confirmed as satrap of the Areians, although he was replaced by Arsakes, another Persian, when he revolted (Arr. 3.16.9, 3.20.3, 3.22.1, 3.25.1, 3.25.7; also 3.28.4, 3.29.1). Previously, Sabiktas had been left in place as the Persian satrap of Cappadocia (Arr. 2.4.2) and Ada reinstalled in Caria (see above, p. 542). Clearly Alexander was following a policy of leaving administration to members of the empire's ethnic groups, although the satraps were assisted by Macedonian-Greek garrisons with hand-picked commanders generally chosen from the Companions.

The fact that the existing civil administration was left in the hands of Persian and indigenous satraps was not just convenient for Alexander but also made good sense, as the satrapal system had worked well for the Achaemenid rulers and would now do the same for Alexander. In addition, the Persian nobility were involved as an integral part of Alexander's system of government rather than being marginalised into disaffected and dispossessed outcasts. Alexander had of course freed the Greek cities of Asia Minor and granted them their independence. With regard to the rest of the Persian Empire, local and satrapal government were left to others while he was still pursuing his conquests. Whatever his long-term plans were (if there were any) remains of course unknown because of his premature death.

From Babylon he made his way to Susa, receiving on his march a letter from Philoxenos whom he had sent on ahead reporting that the city had surrendered. A huge quantity of treasure awaited Alexander there, including 50,000 talents of silver and all the royal paraphernalia. Famously, the bronze statues of the tyrannicides Harmodios and Aristogeiton which Xerxes had pillaged from Athens were now returned (cf. *IG* I³ 502: doc. 9.42; Fig. 9.6), and Alexander's goodwill towards Athens should be noted. While at Susa, reinforcements led by Amyntas arrived from Macedonia (Arr. 3.16.9; Diod. Sic. 17.65.5–66; Plut. *Alexander* 36; Curt. 5.2.8).

The burning of Persepolis in 330 BC

From Susa, Alexander made his way to Persepolis, fighting en route a devastating campaign against the Uxian hillsmen. He then made a forced march to Persepolis, the capital of the Persian Empire (Persepolis meaning in Greek: 'city of the Persians'). His path was blocked by Ariobarzanes the satrap of Persis at the 'Persian Gates' with a force of 25,000 or 40,000 infantry and 300 or 700 cavalry (the sources give different numbers), but a guide showed him a way around. He left Krateros to face Ariobarzanes, who was then successfully attacked from both front and rear and his force almost totally annihilated (Arr. 3.18; Diod. Sic. 17.68; Curt. 5.3–4). At Persepolis, Alexander's men, who had now marched some 7000 miles, looted and pillaged, and apparently spent most of their time for the next four months partying, while Alexander, who according to Plutarch (*Alexander* 37.1–2) had the inhabitants massacred, had most of the treasury – some 120,000 talents – carried off on 10,000 pairs of mules and 5000 camels. These enormous resources would secure for Alexander anything that he needed from now on.

On the eve of their departure there was a huge drinking bout, with female musicians and courtesans present (as was usual in Alexander's revels). Thais, an Athenian prostitute, who was later the hetaira of Ptolemy son of Lagos when he became king of Egypt, was said to have suggested that the palaces, commenced by Darius and completed by Xerxes, be burned to the ground. Alexander was purported to have led the party off on their act of vandalism,

Figure 15.8 The Apadana at Persepolis, captured and later burned down by the Macedonians in what was apparently a drunken orgy (doc. 15.20). Photo © Mary Loosemore.

telling them all to form a 'victory komos in honour of Dionysos'. The palaces were then set on fire. Whether the destruction of the main buildings of the world's greatest ancient city was the consequence of an overenthusiastic symposium, or was in fact premeditated, is an issue raised by the ancient sources themselves. Arrian barely touches on the episode, and is clearly embarrassed by it (he has Parmenion attempting to persuade Alexander to protect what was now his), and suggests that Alexander's motive was to take revenge on the Persians for their destruction of Athens and their burning of its temples on the acropolis. However, this sounds very much like an explanation made up retrospectively to excuse the act of recklessness. Whatever the cause, the destruction of the palace complex was a sign that the Persian Empire had been well and truly captured (Diod. Sic. 17.70–2 (72.1–6: doc. 15.20); Arr. 3.18.10–12; Plut. *Alexander* 37–8; Curt. 5.7; Fig. 15.8).

The murder of Darius III, Great King of Persia

Alexander now set out for the city of Ekbatana, capital of Media, having learnt that Darius was there, but the Great King escaped from the city with his treasure a mere four days before Alexander arrived. Here a significant development occurred. Alexander sent home his Greek allies and Thessalian cavalry after paying them large bonuses, although allowing them to re-enrol as mercenaries, an option which many of them took. His army was now primarily Macedonian. Parmenion was instructed to move the royal treasure to Ekbatana, where it was placed in the care of Harpalos (a friend of Alexander's boyhood) with a garrison of 6000 Macedonians. Alexander continued his pursuit of Darius, who had already passed through the Caspian Gates, when the news arrived that Darius had been arrested by Bessos (satrap of Bactria, who had commanded the Persian left wing at Gaugamela), and some fellow conspirators. Next came the news that he had been murdered. Alexander recovered the body and had it sent to Persepolis for royal burial, the appropriate action for the successor of a Great King.

A campaign against the Mardians ensued as he passed through their territory. At Zadrakarta, capital of the Hyrkanians, he was told the news that Bessos, accompanied by a court of Persians who had escaped to Bactria, had assumed the 'upright tiara', the crown of the Persian Great Kings, and the name Artaxerxes V. Around this time while in Hyrka-nia, Alexander's horse Boukephalas was captured by some of the inhabitants: Alexander was furious but his threats were enough to have the horse safely returned (Arr. 5.19.6: doc. 15.27). The queen of the Amazons was said to have visited him here, apparently for the purposes of procreation with Alexander to which he acquiesced. Some of the sources relate that Alexander at this point 'went Persian', which was perhaps a reaction against Bessos' self-acclamation as king. He began to dress in the Persian way, in white, except for their baggy trousers, assumed the Persian tiara, and selected Persian bodyguards for himself, including Oxathres, Darius' own brother (Arr. 3.19–25; Diod. Sic. 17.73–8; Plut. *Alexander* 42–7; Curt. 5.8–13).

Philotas, Parmenion and conspiracy in 330 BC

Knowledge of a conspiracy unfolded in an unusual way in 330 BC. Dimnos, one of the king's 'friends' (probably one of the Companions) apparently for some personal reason conspired with others to kill Alexander. He revealed this to his young lover Nikomachos, who in turn told his brother Kebalinos, who informed Philotas. He, despite seeing Alexander twice in his tent every day, gave him no warning. So Kebalinos told one of the Royal Pages who informed Alexander of the plot: the Royal Pages were of noble birth or sons of the Compan-ions and acted as the king's attendants, in particular guarding him while he slept (Arr. 4.13.1: doc. 14.38). Philotas was brought before Alexander and when he admitted to knowledge of the conspiracy was condemned for having done nothing to prevent it. Initially protesting his innocence, under torture he confessed to being part of the conspiracy. He and those others implicated were executed by having javelins hurled at them – the usual Macedonian method of execution. Dimnos had committed suicide.

Alexander decided that Parmenion, Philotas' father, should be executed and orders were sent to the Macedonian generals in Media to carry this out. As the sources note, Alexander presumably believed that Philotas had his father's support for the plot, or that Parmenion would be dangerous now that his son had been executed by Alexander. The somewhat nega-tive attitude towards Parmenion in the sources was presumably the result of his execution. He was consistently portrayed as cautious, as in the episode when he advised Alexander to settle with Darius for less than half the empire. One of Alexander's bodyguards, Demetrios, was also executed as having been part of the plot and replaced with Ptolemy son of Lagos, and Alexander now put two of the hipparchoi in charge of the Companion Cavalry, Hep-haistion and Kleitos the son of Dropides. It is difficult to avoid the conclusion that this was a serious conspiracy against Alexander which was politically motivated. At the same time

Alexander the Lyncestian, who had been under 'house-arrest', was executed in the atmosphere of paranoia and suspicion that must have developed as a result of Philotas' plot (Arr. 3.26–7 [3.26.1–4: doc. 15.21]; Diod. Sic. 17.79–80; Plut. *Alexander* 48–9 (differing from Diodorus' account); Curt. 6.7–11).

The death of Bessos in 329 BC

Alexander then pursued the 'Great King' Bessos through the Hindu Kush into Bactria, despite its being winter, and when Bessos crossed the river Oxos into Sogdiana Alexander followed. Bessos was deserted by some of the leading Persians, in particular Spitamenes (a Sogdian aristocrat), and he fell into Alexander's hands: he handed Bessos over to Darius' relatives who put him to death. Alexander was now undisputed 'Great King' of Persia (Arr. 3.28–30.5; Diod. Sic. 17.83.7–9; Plut. *Alexander* 43; Curt. 7.3.1–10.11). Alexander then pursued his campaigns in Bactria, where Spitamenes, despite betraying Bessos, did not surrender himself, and led the remaining opposition to Alexander in Bactria and Sogdiana. He had some success against the Macedonian forces and even advanced on the capital Baktra but did not attack it. His downfall came when 3000 Masegetai, Scythian tribesmen, decided to make peace with Alexander by decapitating Spitamenes and sending Alexander the kephalic trophy (Arr. 4.17). Seleukos, one of Alexander's generals, married Spitamenes' daughter Apame at the Susa weddings of 324 BC, and together they founded the Seleucid dynasty which ruled over the bulk of what had been the Persian Achaemenid Empire.

Alexander murders Kleitos in 328 BC

At a festival of Dionysos at Samarkand, when Alexander and his friends had been drinking heavily, comments were made that Alexander's achievements outdid those of Castor and Pollux, while others said that Alexander could be compared to Herakles himself. Kleitos the Black, who saved Alexander's life at Granikos in 334 by chopping off Spithridates' right shoulder just as he was about to strike Alexander and who disapproved of Alexander's Persianisation, took offence at these comparisons of a mortal to divine beings, and pointed out that Alexander had not conquered the Persians single-handed, but with the assistance of his Macedonians. This did not prevent further comparisons, with some of those present claiming that Philip's achievements were nothing in comparison with those of his son Alexander. Kleitos who was very drunk at this stage furiously defended Philip's reputation and taunted Alexander by holding out his own right hand that had saved Alexander's life at Granikos. Alexander jumped up to strike Kleitos but was restrained by the Companions, and when he called for the hypaspists no-one obeyed. He shouted out dramatically that he was now as helpless as Darius when he was captured by Bessos. The Companions were no longer able to restrain him, and he snatched a spear from one of the bodyguards and drove it through Kleitos' body. An attempt was made retrospectively to justify Kleitos' murder: the army as an assembly decreed Kleitos had been justly killed, his death had been foretold, and that all the deeds of a king were by definition just. Alexander's regrets at murdering Kleitos were suitably exaggerated by the ancient sources and accounts state that he attempted to commit suicide and took to his bed without food or drink for three days. Kleitos seems to have taken issue with two main items: Alexander's adoption of Persian dress, and the undue credit Alexander was given for his achievements. There is more than a hint too that the semi-deification of Alexander in the comparisons between him and the Dioskouroi and Herakles offended

561

Kleitos. His critical views of the presence of Persians at court and as satraps, and of Alexander's semi-Persian dress, were ones held by others, and would recur as other events unfolded (Arr. 4.8.1–9.4: doc. 15.22; Plut. *Alexander* 50–2; Curt. 8.1.22–2.12; Justin 12.6; Diodorus' narrative is missing for this period).

'Soldiers with wings' in 327 BC

Spitamenes was killed in Bactria in 329 BC but the opposition to Alexander there only ended in 327 BC. Supposedly impregnable and seemingly unscaleable, the last remaining independent stronghold in the region was the Rock of Sogdiana, where Alexander managed the impossible. The inhabitants jeered that he would only capture the place if he could find 'soldiers with wings'. By offering massive rewards he managed to have a group of soldiers scale the rock with ropes and iron pegs, many, of course, falling to their deaths in the attempt. When the Macedonian climbers on the Rock were seen, the besieged, thinking there were more Macedonians than there were in fact, were deceived into surrendering. Alexander here met the beautiful Roxane, daughter of the Bactrian king Oxyartes; he married her having apparently genuinely fallen in love with her, but it was a move that would have been popular in Bactria. She bore him a son after Alexander's death: Alexander IV; both she and her son were murdered, probably in 311, at Amphipolis. Nevertheless he still had to capture one last stronghold, the Rock of Chorienes, which was holding out, and with its surrender he left Krateros to mop up any remaining rebels in Bactria and Sogdiana. The most north-eastern parts of the Achaemenid Empire were now in his hands and he prepared to move towards India (Arr. 4.18.4–19.6: doc. 15.23; 4.21–2; Plut. *Alexander* 47.4; Curt. 7.11).

'Having missed out on a kiss'

After the Sogdians' revolt commenced and sometime after Kleitos' murder there was further internal dissension among the Macedonians. Clearly Kleitos was reflecting not just his own concerns but those of other Macedonians as well, for soon afterwards a further incident was sparked off by the introduction of another Persian custom, proskynesis: the Persian practice of bowing or prostrating oneself before the Great King (Fig. 11.7). By the time of this incident, Alexander was master of the entire Persian Empire and it was obviously in his interests that his new subjects saw him being treated in a way appropriate for their King. In Arrian, the initiative came from Alexander himself who wanted people to bow before him, his motive being his belief that Ammon rather than Philip was his father, although Arrian adds that Alexander had already started to indicate his admiration for Persian and Median customs both in dress and court etiquette. What is also clear is that this behaviour was natural to the Persians who wished in this way to acknowledge Alexander as their Great King. To test the general feeling on the issue a staged debate took place, with sophists (Anaxarchos and Agis the Argive), Macedonians, and prominent Persians and Medes present on the occasion. The sophists argued that Alexander was greater even than Herakles and Dionysos; moreover, neither of these was Macedonian, and it would be more justifiable for them to honour Alexander who was their own king than non-Macedonian deities. Their propositions, however, were refuted by Kallisthenes, who argued that the distinction between gods and men should remain clear (in Greek eyes, obeisance was made only to the gods), and that the Greeks, let alone the Macedonians, should not be dishonoured by making proskynesis to a living man.

In addition, Kallisthenes apparently claimed (Arrian seems doubtful) that Alexander's fame would rely in the future on what Kallisthenes wrote about him, not on Olympias' stories about his birth. It also appears that Kallisthenes had encouraged Philotas, and his associates, to be critical of Alexander.

The Macedonians were more accustomed to a freer Macedonian-style court than to Persian protocol and they were pleased by Kallisthenes' arguments, so Alexander told them to think no more of bowing before him. But the Persians present then rose and prostrated themselves before Alexander as he was now their Great King. To the Persians their king had never been a god, but they nevertheless paid him this honour as the living representative of their chief deity, Auramazdâ (Ahura Mazda). On a subsequent occasion at a feast, Alexander sent around a golden cup, which was given first to those who had agreed to make obeisance to him, so clearly there had been discussions at court among Alexander's supporters on this topic. Those who were part of the plan drank from the cup, went forward and bowed to Alexander, and received their kiss. Kallisthenes drank and went up for his kiss, without having made proskynesis; Alexander did not notice the omission as he was talking to Hephaistion at the time, but one Demetrios did and pointed it out to Alexander, who refused to kiss him; hence the famous line of Kallisthenes: 'So – I go away, having missed out on a kiss' (Arr. 4.9.9–12.5: doc. 15.24; Plut. *Alexander* 54; Justin 12.7).

The Royal Pages' conspiracy in 327 BC

Arrian's narrative on the proskynesis incident is followed immediately by the so-called 'Royal Pages' Conspiracy', also linked with Kallisthenes' and Macedonian dissatisfaction with the Persianisation of Alexander's court. The Macedonian elite were clearly dividing into groups: those who supported the Macedonian style of kingship and resented the adoption of Persian ways, and those willing to embrace a degree of Persianisation and accept Alexander's assimilation of the trappings of a Persian king. The story has overtones reminiscent of the Harmodios and Aristogeiton affair at Athens in 514 BC, and in fact when Philotas once asked Kallisthenes whom in particular he honoured among the Athenians Kallisthenes replied the tyrannicides Harmodios and Aristogeiton (docs 9.30–1). Homoerotic issues also played their part in the Royal Pages' conspiracy, for Arrian describes one of the Royal Pages, Hermolaos, being publicly whipped by Alexander for killing a boar during a hunt before Alexander could spear the beast. In consequence Hermolaos and his lover Sostratos formed a conspiracy which drew in other Pages. It was discovered when one of the conspirators told his lover, who told his brother, who informed Ptolemy, who told Alexander. All those named were put on the rack and tortured and Hermolaos admitted to the conspiracy before the Macedonian assembly: significantly despite the Persianisation of customs at court, this institution was still in existence.

Hermolaos in a speech to the assembly attacked proskynesis and Alexander's adoption of Persian dress, as well as his heavy drinking at night and his consequent late hours on the next day. Kallisthenes was considered to be implicated for having encouraged the Pages to see themselves as liberators, as in his idealisation of Harmodios and Aristogeiton, and in some way they saw themselves as the preservers of the Macedonian tradition in which the king did not exercise autocratic powers. Kallisthenes was either (according to Aristoboulos) chained and dragged around with the army until he died of illness, possibly exposure, or (according to Ptolemy) he was tortured and then executed by hanging. There was now no court historian (Arr. 4.13.7–14.3: doc. 15.25; Curt. 8.6.7–8.8.23).

Poros and his faithful elephant: Alexander in India

Alexander had still not finished his conquests. The Persian Empire extended to the Indus river with India beyond its southern frontier, and Alexander naturally wanted to add this area to his conquests, especially as the Greeks believed that the great river Ocean – and thus the end of the world – lay just beyond the Indus river, while the region was full of marvels such as dog-headed men. Whether he would have attempted the conquest of the entire sub-continent is unclear, for events unfolded to prevent this being an option. At any rate, in 326 BC, leaving Bactria and the various dramas at court behind him as history, he began his Indian campaign. When Alexander reached the Kabul river, Hephaistion and Perdikkas set out with half of the Macedonians and mercenaries towards the Indus river, which they were to bridge and cross in preparation for Alexander's arrival. Alexander himself engaged in various bloody campaigns against local peoples, making his way roughly eastwards before reaching Aornos, another 'impregnable' rock – which he took (Arrian 4.28.2 notes the story that not even Herakles was able to capture Aornos) – and sailed down the Indus to join forces with Hephaistion at the bridge. Taxilas, king or ruler of an area probably identified with that between the Indus and Hydaspes rivers, had already made his surrender through envoys to Alexander at Sogdiana, and at Taxilas' capital, Taxila, Alexander sent various embassies to Indian rulers and soon learned that Poros, one of the major kings of the Punjab, refused to submit and had assembled a large army to contest Alexander's further progress. At the Hydaspes (Jhelum), a tributary of the Indus, the last major set-piece battle of Alexander's career was fought.

Alexander advanced away from the main camp where he left Krateros, and sought a crossing place, bringing his forces (6000 infantry and cavalry) at night and with difficulty by rafts and boats across the river which was swollen by the monsoon to nearly a mile in width. Poros' son failed to stop him when Alexander reached the opposite bank, and Alexander pushed on towards Poros' forces. Warned of this development, Poros moved his forces towards Alexander, found a place he thought suitable for battle and organised his forces in battle formation. There were forces of cavalry and chariots on Poros' left and right wings. Alexander regrouped his own forces opposite those of Poros. He posted a force of cavalry on his right wing, with the infantry in the centre but behind the line of the cavalry, and on the right wing a small force of cavalry. This was, essentially, because of the presence of the elephants immediately in front of Poros' infantry force, to be a cavalry battle. Alexander's dispositions were therefore more unusual than in the past (Map 15.4).

Alexander began the attack, taking his cavalry and mounted archers, and advancing against Poros' left, with Koinos' and Demetrios' detachments of cavalry apparently sent round to the extreme right, to go behind the enemy line, and to attack the cavalry on Poros' left wing in the rear. The Macedonian infantry was ordered to go on the attack only after the Macedonian cavalry had disrupted Poros' cavalry and infantry. Engaging Poros' cavalry Alexander threw them into confusion, especially as they were then attacked by him from the front and also from behind (by Koinos' force), and they retreated to the line of elephants. These were brought forward to attack the Macedonian cavalry, and the Macedonian phalanx advanced against the elephants, throwing javelins at their riders, and surrounding the beasts and attacking them. These responded violently, charging the Macedonians, goring them with their tusks, or grabbing them in their trunks, lifting them up and throwing them to the ground. The Indian cavalry were therefore given time to reform and charged the Macedonian cavalry, but Alexander routed them a second time with catastrophic results for the Indians. Poros' cavalry now became entangled with their own elephants and infantry, where chaos ensued, as elephants had lost their riders; wounded, angered and tired, the massive beasts rampaged against those around them, indiscriminately and regardless of whether friend or foe. With room to manoeuvre, the Macedonians fell back from the elephants when necessary, and then hurled javelins at them, while Alexander formed up his cavalry and infantry around Poros' forces and cut them down.

Poros' elephant loyally defended his badly wounded master, who in fact recovered and later had his kingdom extended in size by Alexander and given back to him to rule. Krateros who was left with a force on the other side of the river now crossed it and helped with the 'mopping up'; a break in the Macedonian lines allowed some Indians to flee but they were now cut down by Krateros. Battle losses for the Indians were therefore heavy, amounting to 20,000 infantry and 3000 cavalry according to Arrian, with Alexander losing eighty men out of his force of 6000 infantry, ten mounted archers and some 220 cavalry. Two cities were founded, one (Nikaia: 'Victory') where Alexander set out for the battle and one where it was fought, called Boukephala, after Alexander's horse, which had died of old age, although according to some accounts he died after being wounded by Poros' son: he was an important part of Alexander's

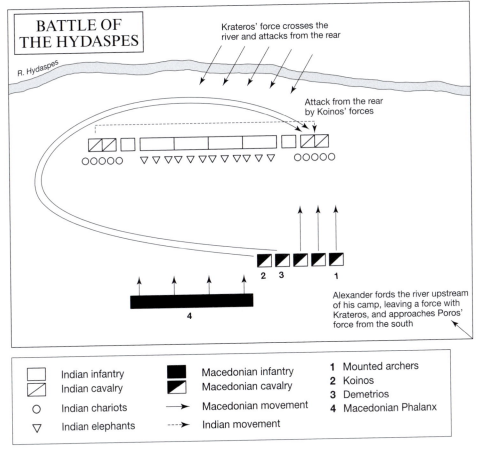

Map 15.4 The battle of Hydaspes, 326 BC Based on D.J. Lonsdale, *Alexander the Great: Lessons in Strategy*, Routledge, 2007.

legendary achievements and the city still exists today (Arr. 5.14.4, 5.19.4–6: doc. 15.27). After this, Alexander intended to attack Sopeithes, king of a neighbouring kingdom in India, but he willingly surrendered (Diod. Sic. 17.91.7–92.3: doc. 15.28). At the Babylonian mint, a series of tetradrachma coins were struck showing Alexander with a javelin on horseback attacking Poros on his elephant. The Hydaspes, as well as being Alexander's last major set-battle campaign, was also the most easterly and clearly he wanted it to be appropriately commemorated (for the Hydaspes' campaign: Curt. 8.14.31–4, 8.38–40, 8.44–6: doc. 15.26; Plut. *Alexander* 60, 62.1: doc. 15.29; Arr. 4.30.7–9, 5.8–21; Diod. Sic. 17.87–9; Just. 12.8–9).

The turning-point: the Hyphasis river in 326 BC

Alexander now controlled the northern Punjab and he marched across its rivers, campaigning against the local kingdoms, while Hephaistion was sent off against Gandara. But when they reached the Hyphasis river his forces decided that they had gone far enough and rumours that another huge battle awaited them combined with general fatigue to trigger a mutiny. His forces refused to go further, although this was demonstrated not by rioting but by a general disaffection and malaise: geography had deceived them and they had not arrived at the river Ocean as expected; they were experiencing the season of the heaviest rains, and they had been marching for eight years. Koinos, so crucial at the battle of the Hydaspes, pleaded for the army and advanced their case, although Alexander threatened that he would go on alone if necessary. Alexander then did 'an Achilles', and sulked in his tent for three days refusing to see even the Companions, but he had reached the easternmost point of his conquests – his only defeat. When the omens for crossing the Hyphasis were unfavourable, he finally gave way, to his men's great joy, and after building twelve large altars they returned to the Hydaspes river to sail to the Great Sea. At this point they were joined by reinforcements of 30,000 infantry and 6000 cavalry. In November 326 Alexander embarked most of the cavalry, as well as the archers and the hypaspists, on a fleet commanded by Nearchos, a friend since childhood, who served as satrap of Lycia until 329 and then accompanied Alexander on campaign. The remainder went with Hephaistion and Krateros along each bank of the river. Sailing south, encountering a number of hostile tribes, the Macedonians reached the confluence of the river Akesines, where the turbulence of the water upset some of the vessels. Alexander and Perdik-kas left the fleet to attack the Mallians, who were generally massacred or enslaved while the remainder made a last-ditch stand in a citadel. Alexander thought that the Macedonians bringing up the ladders to scale the walls of the citadel were too slow, so he seized a ladder and climbed up it, followed by some of his men, soon joined by the hypaspists, whose weight collapsed the ladder: Alexander was now by himself inside the wall. He was wounded and came very close to being killed before his men came up, after which followed the usual mas-sacre of all inhabitants when his forces captured a place with difficulty (Plut. *Alexander* 62.1–8: doc. 15.29; Arr. 6.1–11, 6.25–9; Diod. Sic. 17.94–9; Curt. 9.2–3; Just. 12.9).

The army's devotion to Alexander

Lamentation at the (incorrect) news that Alexander was dead broke out among the army back at the main camp (where the Chenab and Ravi rivers met). A letter from him was supposed to have been forged by his generals, but he made his way to them by boat. Emotional scenes broke out at the sight of him still alive and even able to ride on horseback. His troops' loyalty and their affection for him was real, but it was time to head back west, and he continued his

Indus river journey southwards. He met troubled conditions along the way, where various revolts had to be quashed, and the Indian ascetics, the gymnosophists, 'naked philosophers', sometimes referred to as 'Brahma philosophers' by modern scholars, encouraged opposition to Alexander. Krateros was ordered off on a separate expedition through Arachosia to quell unrest, and met up later with Alexander at Karmania. Reaching Pattala by boat in mid-325 BC, Alexander then went westwards, as only one-third of his force could be transported by the fleet, and crossed the Gadrosian desert. Here apparently some two-thirds of his force of 85,000 perished from thirst in what was clearly a horrific journey. At Persepolis Hephaistion rejoined him, and then they proceeded on to Susa, which they reached in March 324 BC.

At the capital of Gadrosia, and then as he travelled further west, back towards the heart of the Persian Empire, Alexander executed or replaced various satraps and generals for maladministration. He executed his general Kleander and Sitalkes, as both the army and the inhabitants brought charges against them, and he removed the satrap of Gadrosia for disobeying orders. A Mede, Baryaxes, had assumed the upright tiara and title 'King of Persians and the Medes' and was executed along with his associates when Alexander was at Pasargadai. Here Alexander was distressed at the plundering and damage to Cyrus' tomb (Fig. 11.1), which Aristoboulos was commanded to repair. At nearby Persepolis the Persian Aboulites who had been appointed satrap of Susa and its territory was executed, and Orxines, who had replaced Phrasaortes as Persian satrap, was hanged for plundering temples and tombs and executing many unjustly. Arrian notes that because Alexander had been away so long, and many did not believe that he would return alive, some of the satraps behaved as they pleased: they were clearly administering their territories as personal fiefdoms (Arr. 6.27–30, 7.4.3). Harpalos, who was in charge of the treasury, fled to Greece. Nearchos' fleet continued along the coast up the Persian Gulf, having met up with Alexander in Karmania (Nearchos had briefly left the fleet and travelled inland), then up the Tigris (Arr. 6.12.1–13.4: doc. 15.30; also 6.3–30, 7.1–4.3; Diod. Sic. 17.100–107.5, 17.108.6; Plut. *Alexander* 64; Curt. 9.4.15–19.10.1, 10.30).

Marriage with princess Stateira in 324 BC

At Susa a large joint wedding ceremony occurred in which Alexander and ninety-one Companions (eighty in Arrian) married well-born Persian women. A feast attended by some 9000 guests was held for the couples and all those Macedonians who had already married women in Persia (10,000 in Arrian) were given wedding gifts. Alexander married Stateira, daughter of Darius, and Hephaistion her sister Drypetis; Nearchos also took a Persian wife. Arrian on the authority of Aristoboulos states that Alexander also married a daughter of Ochos. Like his father, he was a polygamist – and like Philip, he chose his wives carefully: he may have married Roxane for love but she was also the daughter of the king of an important region. The marriages were celebrated in the Persian style, but this was a Macedonian affair and Persian male dignitaries were notably absent. Through these marriages Alexander was asserting the rights of the conqueror over the women of the conquered. Alexander discharged the debts of his soldiers as part of the celebrations (Plut. Alexander 70.3: doc. 15.31; Arr. 7.4.4–8; Diod. Sic. 17.107.6).

Thirty thousand boys

Alexander had previously chosen 30,000 Persian boys to be trained to fight in the Macedonian style, who now arrived having grown to manhood. They were called the Epigonoi ('Successors'), a name which sounded ominous to Alexander's Macedonian troops. The Persian-style marriages,

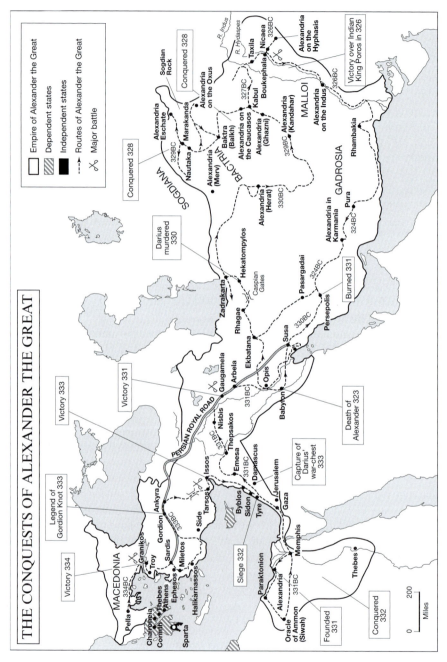

THE CONQUESTS OF ALEXANDER THE GREAT

Empire of Alexander the Great
Dependent states
Independent states
Routes of Alexander the Great
Major battle

Victory 334
Legend of Gordion Knot 333
Victory 333
Victory 331
Conquered 328
Conquered 328

MACEDONIA
Pella
Chaironeia 338BC
Corinth
Athens
Thebes
Sparta
Ephesos
Halikarnassos
Troy
Granikos 334BC
Sardis
Gordion
Miletos
Side
Ankyra
333BC

Tarsos
Issos
333BC
Nisibis
Thepsakos
Emesa 331BC
Damascus
Byblos
Sidon
Tyre
Jerusalem
Gaza

Siege 332
Paraktonion
Memphis
Alexandria 331BC
Oracle of Ammon (Siwah)
Founded 331
Conquered 332
Thebes

Capture of Darius' war-chest 333

PERSIAN ROYAL ROAD

Gaugameia
Arbela 331BC
Ekbatana
Opis
Babylon
Susa
330BC
Persepolis
Burned 331
Pasargadai 324BC

Death of Alexander 323

Rhagae
Zadrakarta
Hekatompylos
Caspian Gates

Darius murdered 330

SOGDIANA
329BC
Nautaka
Marakanda
Alexandria Eschate
Sogdian Rock
Alexandria on the Oxus
Baktra (Balkh)
BACTRIA
Alexandria (Merv)

Alexandria on the Caucasos
Kabul 327BC
Alexandria (Ghazni)
329BC
Alexandria (Kandahar)
Alexandria (Herat)
330BC

Taxila
Boukephala
Nicaea
326BC
Alexandria on the Hyphasis
Victory over Indian King Poros in 326
326BC
MALLOI
Alexandria on the Indus

GADROSIA
Alexandria in Karmania
Pura
Rhambakia
324BC

R. Indus
R. Hydaspes

0   200
Miles

Map 15.5 The conquests of Alexander the Great. Based on M. Grant, *The Routledge Atlas of Classical History*, fifth edition, Routledge, 1994, pp. 38–39.

Alexander's adoption of Persian dress and his appointment of Peukestas as satrap of Persia after the execution of Orxines sent a warning message: although Peukestas saved Alexander's life in the battle against the Mallians, he was the only Macedonian who 'went native' and adopted Persian dress and learnt to speak Persian. Some of the cavalry of the Persian Empire were even enrolled in the Companion cavalry (Plut. *Alexander* 71.1–3: doc. 15.31, also 47.3; Arr. 7.6; Diod. Sic. 17.108.1–3). Veteran Macedonians became very uneasy. They considered that Alexander had become a 'barbarian' at heart and was treating the Macedonians and their customs with disrespect – perhaps with reason, given what he is reported to have said at Opis.

Mutiny at Opis

Alexander travelled from Susa to Opis in 324 BC, where he discharged his senior veterans and those unfit for military service due to their battle wounds, giving them all huge bonuses. Those who stayed would also be greatly rewarded. Somehow this struck the wrong chord with his Macedonian troops. They were already discontented with Alexander's own 'Persianisation' and that of the army. The 30,000 Epigonoi and the 'other races' enrolled in the Companion cavalry were seen as replacements for the Macedonians and as evidence that Alexander no longer needed them. These concerns had obviously been festering for some time, and a spontaneous mutiny erupted: when he announced their discharge his troops called out to him to discharge them all and go on campaign with his father Ammon, not with them. Arrian in fact blames the Persianisation of the court for Alexander's changed attitude, as he was accustomed to 'barbarian obsequiousness'. He leapt from the speaking platform, pointed out the thirteen or so ringleaders to the hypaspists and had them led away and executed. He then listed all his great achievements, blamed them once again for refusing the cross the Hyphasis, and accused them of deserting him, telling them to 'Go!'

Again, as at the Hyphasis, Alexander sulked, this time in a palace, with the Companions refused access to him. On the third day he summoned selected Persians, who were given the command of the battalions. Only those he declared his 'kinsmen' were allowed to kiss him. He announced that barbarians were to be enrolled in the army, and there was in fact to be a new Persian agema, division, in the Companion cavalry. As at the Hyphasis his troops pleaded with him, and demanded to be kinsmen and be allowed to kiss him, like the Persians. They offered to hand over the ringleaders of the mutiny and those that had incited them, refusing to leave the doors until Alexander agreed. He gave way and a huge banquet of reconciliation was held with both Greek diviners and Persian Magi initiating the ceremony: Alexander prayed that Macedonians and Persians would share the government harmoniously. However, the veteran Macedonians and those unfit for service were discharged and sent home, each with a bonus of one talent. They left their foreign wives behind, as well as their sons to be trained in the Macedonian style of warfare. Krateros took the veterans back to Macedonia to assume control of Macedonia, Thrace, Thessaly and the 'freedom of the Greeks', and replace Antipater, who had been put in charge when Alexander left Macedonia. Antipater was to come to Alexander with fresh recruits. Olympias was said to have wanted Antipater out of Macedonia and had been writing to Alexander to this effect (for the mutiny at Opis: Plut. *Alexander* 71.2–3: doc. 15.31; Arr. 7.8–12 (sections at docs 14.56, 15.32); Arr. 7.29.4: doc. 15.45; Diod. Sic. 17.109.2; Curt. 10.2–4).

What exactly was meant by the 'freedom of the Greeks' in this context? Presumably Krateros' main role was to protect the freedom of government and the democracies that Alexander had established. Alexander was hegemon of the Greek cities of the mainland and established democracies and abolished tyrannies in the islands and cities of Asia Minor as he liberated them. Chios was one beneficiary of this, when in 334 BC a democracy was established there. There was another change of government in 333 BC when the city was betrayed by pro-Persians (despite having been exiled in 334 BC) and the island came under the control of Memnon of Rhodes, but it was liberated again in 332 BC. Chios under the terms of the agreement with Alexander in 334 BC had to supply Alexander with a fleet of twenty triremes (S*IG*³ 283: doc. 15.33). Persia's war in the Aegean at this stage was not entirely over, but Alexander was successful in capturing the mainland cities and islands, even if some of them had to be won back, and the Persian navy was ultimately defeated.

Largely the Greek cities were not Alexander's concern as he was fully engaged in conquering the Persian Empire. It was Antipater's role to deal with the Greek cities, especially the revolt of the Peloponnesians under Agis. In 332 BC Alexander allowed the people of Eresos on Lesbos to decide for themselves what actions to take against the tyrants who had ruled their city and others on the island of Lesbos (*IG* XII 526, lines 4–28: doc. 15.36). Greek cultural and athletic life continued as before, and Aristotle and Kallisthenes put together a list of the victors in the Pythian festival held at Delphi since 591/0 BC (Tod 2.187: doc. 15.34). Many Greeks served the Macedonian king, such as Philoneides, who acted as a courier and surveyor for Alexander (Tod 2.188: doc. 15.35).

The Harpalos affair at Athens in 324 BC

When Alexander returned from India, various Macedonian and Persian satraps met with his displeasure and sometimes execution (Diod. Sic. 17.108.56: doc. 15.37). He had left his childhood friend Harpalos (he was banished along with other friends of Alexander's at the time of the estrangement between Philip and Alexander when Philip married Kleopatra Eurydike) in charge of a huge treasury at Babylon, despite the fact that he had previously absconded with funds left in his charge. He was, however, forgiven and accepted back into Alexander's retinue. At Babylon, Harpalos made the most of the opportunity, treating the treasure as his own. Alexander's imminent return frightened him, and he fled to Athens with the huge sum of 5000 talents. He arrived there in 324 BC (when news had reached the city of the Exiles Decree, see below, p. 571) with a large mercenary force of 6000 he had hired. Initially he was denied entry, but later was allowed in with only three ships (with which he could not pose a threat to the city), and proceeded to bribe various Athenian politicians to support his cause, including Demosthenes and Demades. Antipater, however, demanded the extradition of Harpalos, as did Olympias, and also Philoxenos, the Macedonian satrap of Caria. Harpalos was arrested by the demos and the money he brought with him to Athens was placed on the Athenian acropolis. Somehow he escaped; collusion was suspected, and the Areiopagos investigated the matter. Of the 700 talents deposited on the acropolis (the estimate was his own), only some 350 were there when counted after his hasty departure.

The Areiopagos delivered its report over six months later and the matter came to court. Demosthenes was exiled in 323 BC for accepting 20 talents from Harpalos, and spent his time at Troezen and in Aegina (when Alexander died the orator supported the revolt of the Greek states from the Macedonians). Harpalos fled to Crete, where murder awaited him at the hands of his second-in-charge, Thibron (a Spartan mercenary); the incident had led to severe tension between Macedon and Athens (for the Harpalos affair: Diod. Sic. 17.108.6–8: doc. 15.37; Plut. *Demosthenes* 25–6, *Phokion* 21, *Moralia* 846; Curt. 10.2.1–3; Hyper. 5, esp. 5–13; Dein. 1, esp. 61–70; Paus. 2.33.4; not mentioned by Arrian.)

The 'Exiles Decree'

The Harpalos affair nearly brought Athens and Macedon into collision, but the demos acted sensibly in not supporting him. Alexander wanted Harpalos back, and no matter how much money Harpalos might offer the city as a whole – and its politicians individually – it was not the time to rebel against Alexander, although there obviously was some discussion along these lines. How Alexander perceived his relationship with the Greeks is made very clear by the 'Exiles Decree' which was proclaimed at the Olympic festival of 324 BC, and of which Athens was aware when Harpalos arrived at their city. At the festival Nikanor of Stageira read out a letter from Alexander which stated that all exiles from Greek cities – except those who had been exiled for impiety – were to be allowed to return to their home cities. Antipater would use force against any cities refusing to comply. This decree threatened chaos: not only would those with views which were ideologically opposed to those of the majority of their fellow citizens be allowed to return, but their return was bound to cause disputes over property, with the potential for other 'old scores' to be settled. Diodorus goes so far as to argue that this interference of Alexander's in Greek affairs was one of the main causes of revolt in Greece when Alexander died in the next year, 323 BC. The Aitolians had already been threatened by Alexander over their destruction of the city of the Oiniadai and their expulsion of its inhabitants, and had begun secret dealings with the Athenians, who were unhappy both about the prospective return of Athenian exiles and the situation on Samos where an Athenian cleruchy had been established. After Alexander's death the Aitolians and Athenians rebelled largely because of this issue of the exiles, while the return of exiles to Thessaly tipped the country into anti-Macedonian sentiment, leading it to join the revolt (Diod. Sic. 18.8.6, cf. 11.1; Plut. *Alexander* 49.8). The number of Greek exiles whom this decree affected was huge: 20,000 of them attended the Olympic festival in anticipation of the announcement (Diod. Sic. 18.8.1–7: doc. 15.38; Curt. 10.2.4–7).

Athens' fears were justified, for Gorgos of Iasos, a 'guardian of arms' and one of Alexander's officials who played an important part in seeing that the Exiles Decree was carried out, aided the return of the Samian exiles. The Athenians had established a cleruchy on Samos in 366 and expelled pro-Persian landowners, who fled to Iasos, a town on the mainland opposite. Gorgos of Iasos, who was at Alexander's court when the decision on the exiles was made, assisted the return of these exiles, and seems to have played a similar role at Kos, where a dedication to him was erected in gratitude for his loyalty to the 'godlike king'. He also supported Alexander's belligerent threat to set Antipater upon the Greeks if they disobeyed the ruling, and after consulting with Alexander he had a herald proclaim at the festival of Dionysos at Ekbatana that he, Gorgos, would not only crown Alexander with a crown worth 3000 gold pieces, but would give him 10,000 suits of armour, and the same number of catapults along with the appropriate number of missiles, to undertake an assault on Athens. Athens, however, was quiet for the moment (*SIG*³312: doc. 15.39; *IG* IV² 616: doc. 15.40; Ephippos *FF* 4–5: doc. 15.41).

Alexander's death: 'he drank and partied'

After the mutiny at Opis was dealt with, Alexander celebrated a festival at Ekbatana where he staged musical and athletic competitions. He had reason to celebrate: the Opis mutiny, the Harpalos affair, the Exiles Decree were all successfully concluded. The Persian Empire was under his control and his central authority had been imposed on the satrapies and the

Greek cities of Greece and Asia Minor. Soon, however, he would be dead, and his Exiles Decree had upset the balance which Philip created in the League of Corinth, for the Greek cities could not now be said to be autonomous. Although the support of the Macedonian army, as demonstrated in both the mutinies, lay firmly with him, he was endangering the Macedonian control of Greece won at Chaironeia in 338 and at Thebes in 335 BC.

The death of Hephaistion in 324 BC

While at Ekbatana, Alexander's closest friend Hephaistion fell ill during one of Alexander's drinking bouts with his Companions which are mentioned by Arrian as having become increasingly frequent. On the seventh day Alexander was told that Hephaistion was gravely ill, and he left the stadium where an athletic contest for boys was scheduled, and hurried to Hephaistion's side only to find him already dead. According to all the ancient sources Alexander was deeply

Figure 15.9 Alexander's name in hieroglyphs in a royal cartouche, Egypt. Louvre Museum E30890, Paris. Drawing by J. Etherington.

affected and emotionally traumatised: until the third day after Hephaistion's death he fasted and neglected his own person. Arrian is dubious about some of the details recorded of Alexander's grief, such as his execution of the doctor, his destruction of the temple of Asklepios at Ekbatana, and the suggestion that Alexander himself drove the vehicle in which the deceased was carried, but accepts that Alexander cut off his own hair in emulation of Achilles, who also grieved excessively when his lover Patroklos was killed in battle by Hektor.

One of the many embassies from Greece that met Alexander as he was travelling to Babylon was from Epidauros, and he granted the wish of the delegation by giving an offering to Asklepios' temple there, but nevertheless censured the god for not saving Hephaistion (cf. docs 3.42–4). Some writers recorded that Alexander instituted regular sacrifices to Hephaistion as to a hero, according him semi-divine honours, and that Alexander sent to the oracle of Ammon at Siwah asking whether sacrifices could be made to Hephaistion as a god. This was refused, although Hephaistion could be given the honours befitting a hero. A funeral pyre costing 10,000 or 12,000 talents was constructed at Babylon, and athletic and musical competitions with 3000 participants were organised in imitation of the funeral contests in honour of Patroklos: the same competitors were to compete not long afterwards at Alexander's own funeral. Hephaistion had been chiliarch of the Companion cavalry, and Alexander never appointed any one in his place, so that it was still called after Hephaistion and carried his standard (for Hephaistion's death: Arr. 7.14.1–10: doc. 15.42; also 7.23.6; Diod. Sic. 17.114–15 [Siwah's response]; Plut. *Alexander* 72; Curt. 10.5.20; Just. 12.13–15).

Alexander's death

After an extensive period of mourning Alexander resumed his campaigns and undertook a successful expedition against the Kossaians who bordered Uxian territory, and ordered the construction of a fleet of warships to explore the Caspian Sea. He also had a fleet built in Babylonia and a number of Phoenician ships dismantled and carried overland to the Persian Gulf to explore its coastline and to take part in a future campaign against Arabia. According to Aristoboulos a harbour at Babylon was excavated which was large enough to accommodate 1000 warships. Arrian comments that there were reports that Alexander planned to sail beyond Gibraltar and into the Black Sea and Sea of Azov, and envisages him adding Europe to Asia and the Britannic isles to Europe (Arr. 7.1.1–4). Alexander was always sensitive to diviners, and the Chaldeans warned Alexander not to enter the city of Babylon, as they had an oracle from their god Baal that entering the city would be harmful to him. He followed their advice as far as was possible and the visit on this occasion was uneventful, but after exploring the Euphrates a further omen occurred as he was returning upstream to Babylon when his cap and diadem were blown into the water, signifying that his kingdom would be transferred to others.

In Babylon there was court business to attend to though the drinking-parties continued. On one such occasion on 29 May 323 Alexander drank far into the night, and was leaving the symposium when one of his favourites among the Companions, Medios, persuaded him to stay. Arrian even cites the entry in the Royal Diaries that Alexander 'drank and partied with Medios' (Arr. 7.25.1). The next day after bathing, he again went drinking with Medios and in early June a fever set in from which the king never recovered. He continued to plan a naval voyage, but became progressively weaker over several days and had to be carried out on a couch to perform the usual daily sacrifices. Both Plutarch and Arrian in their accounts of his death cite the Royal Diaries and clearly a day-by-day report was kept of his condition.

Eventually, at their request, the soldiers were allowed to process past the dying king who was now incapable of speech but was just able to raise his head and acknowledge them. Some accounts recorded that when the Companions asked him to whom he was leaving the empire, he replied 'To the strongest'. Alexander died on 10 June without nominating a successor: his son by Roxane was not yet born. Rumours that the king had been poisoned spread easily, and that Medios was part of the plot. Others implicated Antipater, whose son Kassander had just arrived at court, bringing, it was said, a poison concocted by Aristotle (Plut. *Alexander* 77). Clearly, Alexander suffered a natural death brought on by a long night of drinking, and a consequent fever which he was unable to shake off due to the weakening of his constitution by prolonged hard living (Arr. 7.24.4–27.3: doc. 15.43; cf. 7.16.5–24.3; Diod. Sic. 17.117; Plut. *Alexander* 73–6; Curt. 10.5).

Praise for Alexander's reign

What, if anything, did Alexander achieve? His empire soon fell apart in territorial squabbles among his generals, leading to the formation of the great hellenistic kingdoms which dominated the history of the next few centuries until the coming of Rome to the east. Did he deserve his epithet 'Great'? Arrian was in no doubt as to the achievements of his twelve years and eight months of rule as Macedonian king, and while his empire fell apart at his death, he could not have anticipated dying so young (Arr. 7.28.1–3: doc. 15.44; 7.29.4: doc. 15.45). In essence he ruled over the Persian Empire with the addition of mainland Greece, and the apparatus of the Persian Empire was left largely intact, with an administrative system in place which an adult successor could successfully have inherited. The hellenisation of some of the Persian troops and the involvement of the Persian nobility in government were only natural given the size of the empire he conquered. But despite criticisms of his adoption of Persian customs, these went only so far, and he remained essentially Macedonian. There was to be no 'brotherhood of man' in his scheme of government, but the creation of a ruling Macedonian-Persian elite, and the weddings at Susa and training of the Epigonoi were a move in that direction. Modern scholars concur with Arrian's statements concerning Alexander's physical courage and intelligence, and

Figure 15.10 A gold stater with the head of Alexander the Great, who wears a diadem (not quite visible) and ram's horns (indicating his identification with the god Ammon); issued by Lysimachos, the coin dates to about 297–281 BC. Photo courtesy of CNG Coins.

his ability to organise his army. Yet the late-night drinking, the murderous rage which led to Kleitos' demise, his ruthless crushing of opposition among the Greeks in general and certain Macedonians, and the frequent massacres and enslavements of civilian populations lead the unbiased observer to consider a different side of Alexander. Yet in all this he acted as a man of his times, and in the same way as other leaders and generals throughout history; this conduct in battle and conquest was second nature both to him and to his army.

Alexander's divinity

Alexander's belief in his own divinity was not a Persian concept but rather derived from Greek models: the Persian king was an instrument of Auramazdâ, but not a god himself. Philip demonstrated that he aspired to divinity when he had his statue carried as a thirteenth along with those of the twelve Olympians (Diod. Sic.16.92.5: doc. 14.53). Alexander saw himself as akin to Herakles and the Dioskouroi and also to a less divine figure, Achilles. He was a descendant himself of Herakles (Plut. *Alexander* 2.1: doc. 15.1). Individuals such as athletes and oikistai (founders of colonies) were often made 'heroes' after death and worshipped in Greek cities, and the Spartan Lysander received a form of veneration while alive. Alexander, however, was the first to seek divine status for himself, as in his expedition to Siwah where Ammon encouraged a belief in his divinity, and as king of Egypt Alexander was automatically a god. His desire for proskynesis was an aspect of his belief in his divine status: for the Persians it was a gesture of respect, but it was alien to the Greeks and Macedonians to bow before a human being. Greeks rarely even bowed to the statues of the gods but instead raised their hands in prayer before them. The Greeks, however, did encourage Alexander's belief in his own divinity and at Babylon in 323 embassies from Greece crowned Alexander with golden crowns, as if they were on a theoria – a sacred embassy – to a god (Arr. 7.23.2). In fact the year before, in 324, he requested that he be honoured as a god: Demosthenes said that Alexander could be the son of Zeus or Poseidon if he wished, while the Spartans' laconic reply was, 'As Alexander desires to be a god, let him be so'. Stories that a bolt of lightning struck Olympias' womb and that Alexander was conceived from this, and that Philip once saw her asleep with a serpent lying next to her are part of the parcel of stories and legends that grew up around notions of his divinity. But, in truth, Alexander in fact achieved more than any other Greek: he conquered the entire Persian Empire and travelled as far as the gods Herakles and Dionysos before him: only the god Dionysos had crossed the Indus (Arr. 7.10.6: doc. 15.32). By the late 320s his belief in his suprahumanness is perhaps understandable, and it is reflected in his requests for divine honours and revealed in coins of his reign showing him grasping a thunderbolt and crowned by the winged goddess of victory, Nike (Arr. 7.29.3–4, 7.30.2–3: doc. 15.45; Plut. *Moralia* 842d, *Alexander* 2.3–6: doc. 15.1; Ael. *Varia Historia* 2.19; Hyper. 5.31, 33; Dein. 1.94)

At his death, his empire quickly fell apart: Alexander's generals quarrelled and carved up his possessions. Greece rebelled almost immediately and nearly freed itself from Macedonian control in the so-called Lamian War, with Athens and Aetolia leading the Greeks unsuccessfully against Antipater (323–322 BC). Demosthenes committed suicide rather than fall into his hands. Greek culture spread across the territories of the Persian Empire, and the Classical period closes with Alexander's death and the Hellenistic period begins. Ptolemy established a kingdom in Egypt, and managed to capture Alexander's body, installing it with pomp in Alexandria where he wrote an account of the king he had served. Roxane, pregnant with Alexander's unborn child, came under the protection of Perdikkas: he had the young child

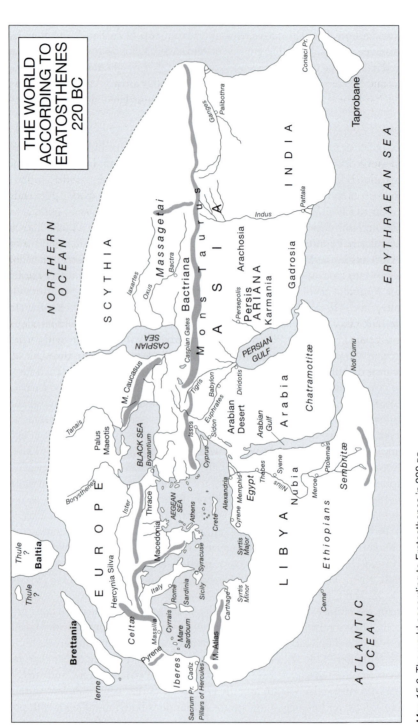

Map 15.6 The world according to Eratosthenes in 220 BC.

proclaimed king Alexander (IV), probably in 322 BC or a little later, but the other claimants to sections of the empire did not respect his position as Alexander's son and heir. Perdikkas, who murdered Krateros in 320, was killed in battle in Egypt by Ptolemy's forces in the same year. Antigonos (satrap of Phrygia) and his son Demetrios were briefly kings of Macedon and Greece in 306 BC, but Antigonos was killed at the battle of Ipsos in Phrygia in 301 BC by Lysimachos and Seleucus. Going to Greece in 319 BC, Roxane was captured by Kassander in 316 at the battle of Pydna, and she and her child were murdered at Amphipolis probably in 311 (or possibly 310) BC. Olympias and Kassander met in battle at Pydna in Greece in 316 but her troops deserted and she was executed. Philip Arrhidaios, Philip's son by Philinna of Larisa (Ath. *Deipnosophistae* 13.557c: doc. 14.37) had been murdered by Olympias in 317 BC. Kassander emerged as king of Macedonia and Greece (305–297 BC); Lysimachos, a member of the Companion bodyguard, had received Thrace to govern from Alexander, and he established a kingdom based on it and Asia Minor; Seleucus, one of Alexander's generals, held most of the central Persian Empire barring Asia Minor; and Ptolemy kept Egypt. The various wars of these successors (the Diadochoi) are complex but ensured the break-up of Alexander's kingdom and that none of Philip's or Alexander's descendants inherited the territories these two conquerors subjugated. Greece endured over a solid century of misery; Macedonia by 167 BC was split into four sections and by 146 BC was merely another Roman province. Rome gradually incorporated Alexander's semi-hellenised conquests into its empire, particularly in the first century BC. More than any other person in the ancient world, Alexander changed the character and culture of Europe and Asia. His fame at the time was extensive, his exploits known throughout the known world, and Arrian's words ring as true today as when he wrote them: 'there was no nation and no city – not even a single person – whom the name of Alexander at that time had not reached' (Arr. 7.30.2: doc. 15.45).

BIBLIOGRAPHY

Abbreviations

New series of journals are not indicated in the bibliography.

ABSA	Annual of the British School at Athens
AC	L'antiquité classique
AClass	Acta Classica
AD	*Archaiologikon Deltion*
AE	*Archaiologike Ephemeris*
AHB	The Ancient History Bulletin
AHR	American Historical Review
AJA	American Journal of Archaeology
AJAH	American Journal of Ancient History
AJPh	American Journal of Philology
AncSoc	Ancient Society
AncW	The Ancient World
ANSMusN	American Numismatic Society Museum Notes
APhs	American Philosophical Society
BCH	Bulletin de correspondance hellénique
BICS	Bulletin of the Institute of Classical Studies
C&M	Classica et Mediaevalia
CAH	*Cambridge Ancient History*
CAH III.3²	Boardman, J. and N.G.L. Hammond (eds) (1982) *The Expansion of the Greek World, Eighth to Sixth Centuries B.C.*, *CAH* III.3, Cambridge, second edition
CAH IV²	Boardman, J., N.G.L. Hammond, D.M. Lewis and M. Ostwald (eds) (1988) *Persia, Greece and the Western Mediterranean, c. 525 to 479 B.C.*, *CAH* IV, Cambridge, second edition
CAH V²	Lewis, D.M., J. Boardman, J.K. Davies and M. Ostwald (eds) (1992) *The Fifth Century B.C.*, *CAH* V, Cambridge, second edition
CJ	The Classical Journal
ClAnt	Californian Studies in Classical Antiquity
Classical Contributions	Shrimpton, G.S. and D.J. McCargar (eds) (1981) *Classical Contributions: Studies in Honour of Malcolm Francis McGregor*, New York
Classical Sparta	Powell, A. (ed.) (1989) *Classical Sparta: Techniques Behind her Success*, London
CPh	Classical Philology
CQ	Classical Quarterly
CRDAC	Atti del centro ricerche e documentazione sull'antichità classica
Crux	Cartledge, P.A. and F.D. Harvey (eds) (1985) *Crux: Essays in Greek History Presented to G.E.M. de Ste Croix* = *History of Greek Political Thought* 6

BIBLIOGRAPHY

EMC	Échos du monde classique (Classical Views)
G&R	Greece and Rome
GRBS	Greek, Roman and Byzantine Studies
HSPh	Harvard Studies in Classical Philology
HThR	Harvard Theological Review
ICS	Illinois Classical Studies
IG I²	De Gaertringen, F.H. (1924) *Inscriptiones Graecae. Inscriptiones Atticae Euclidis anno anteriores*, Berlin, second edition
IG I³	Lewis, D.M. (1981) *Inscriptiones Graecae. Inscriptiones Atticae Euclidis anno anteriores, fasc. 1* (nos 1–500), Berlin, third edition; Lewis, D.M. and L. Jeffery (1994) *Inscriptiones Graecae. Inscriptiones Atticae Euclidis anno anteriores, fasc. 2* (nos 501–1517), Berlin, third edition
IG II²	Kirchner, J. (1913–40) *Inscriptiones Graecae. Inscriptiones Atticae Euclidis anno posteriores, fasc. 1*, Berlin, second edition
IG IV	Fraenkel, M. (1902) *Inscriptiones Graecae. Inscriptiones Argolidis*, Berlin.
IG IV²	Von Gaertringen, F.H. (1929) *Inscriptiones Graecae. Inscriptiones Argolidis*, Berlin, second edition
IG V	Kolbe, G. (1913) *Inscriptiones Graecae. Inscriptiones Laconiae Messeniae Arcadiae*, Berlin
JHS	Journal of Hellenic Studies
JRS	Journal of Roman Studies
LCM	Liverpool Classical Monthly
LSAG	Jeffery, L.H. (1961) *The Local Scripts of Archaic Greece*, Oxford; and A.W. Johnstone (1990) rev. edn *Supplement*
LSAM	Sokolowski, F. (1955) *Lois sacrées de l'Asie mineure*, Paris
LSCG	Sokolowski, F. (1969) *Lois sacrées des cités grecques*, Paris
LSCG Suppl.	Sokolowski, F. (1962) *Lois sacrées des cités grecques: Supplément*, Paris
MH	Museum Helveticum
ML	Meiggs, R. and D.M. Lewis (1988) *A Selection of Greek Historical Inscriptions: To the End of the Fifth Century BC*, Oxford, second edition
NC	Numismatic Chronicle
NOMOS	Cartledge, P., P. Millett and S. Todd (eds) (1990) *NOMOS: Essays in Athenian Law, Society and Politics*, Cambridge
OJA	Oxford Journal of Archaeology
P&P	Past and Present
PACA	Proceedings of the African Classical Association
PAPhS	Proceedings of the American Philosophical Society
PCPhS	Proceedings of the Cambridge Philological Society
PP	La Parola del Passato
QUCC	Quaderni Urbinati di Cultura classica
RA	Revue Archéologique
RBN	Revue Belge de Numismatique et de Sigillographie
REA	Revue des Études Anciennes
REG	Revue des Études Grecques
RhM	Rheinisches Museum
RIDA	Revue Internationale des Droits de l'Antiquité
RSA	Rivista storica dell'Antichità
SEG	*Supplementum Epigraphicum Graecum*
*SIG*³	Dittenberger, W. (1915–24) *Sylloge Inscriptionum Graecarum* I–IV, Leipzig
SO	Symbolae Osloenses
TAPhA	Transactions and Proceedings of the American Philological Association

BIBLIOGRAPHY

Tod   Tod, M.N. *A Selection of Greek Historical Inscriptions*, I² (1946); II (1948), Oxford
YClS   Yale Classical Studies
ZPE   Zeitschrift für Papyrologie und Epigraphik

General bibliography

The chapter bibliographies are not intended to be exhaustive. Listed immediately below are works which serve as a useful introduction to Greek history. These generally do not reappear in the chapter bibliographies which follow.

Buckley, T. (1996) *Aspects of Greek History 750–323 BC. A Source-Based Approach*, London.
Burn, A.R. (1960) *The Lyric Age of Greece*, London.
Bury, J.B. and R. Meiggs (1975) *A History of Greece: To the Death of Alexander the Great*, Petersfield, fourth edition.
Cartledge, P. (1993) *The Greeks: A Portrait of Self and Others*, Oxford.
—— (ed.) (1998) *The Cambridge Illustrated History of Ancient Greece*, Cambridge.
—— (2011) *Ancient Greece: A Very Short Introduction*, New York.
Davies, J.K. (1993) *Democracy and Classical Greece*, London, second edition.
Demand, N. (1996) *A History of Ancient Greece*, New York.
Ehrenberg, V. (1960) *The Greek State*, Oxford.
—— (1973) *From Solon to Socrates*, London, second edition.
Fine, J.V.A. (1983) *The Ancient Greeks: A Critical History*, Cambridge, Mass.
Finley, M.I. (1963) *The Ancient Greeks*, London.
Fisher, N. and H. van Wees (1998) *Archaic Greece*, London.
Fornara, C.W. and L.J. Samons (1991) *Athens from Cleisthenes to Pericles*, Berkeley.
Forrest, W.G. (1966) *The Emergence of Greek Democracy: The Character of Greek Politics, 800–400 B.C.*, London.
Hammond, N.G.L. (1986) *A History of Greece to 322 B.C.*, Oxford, third edition.
Hornblower, S. and A. Spawforth (eds) (1996) *The Oxford Classical Dictionary*, Oxford, third edition.
Jeffery, L.H. (1976) *Archaic Greece: The City-States c. 700–500 B.C.*, New York.
Jones, A.H.M. (1957) *Athenian Democracy*, Oxford.
Kitto, H.D.F. (1957) *The Greeks*, Harmondsworth, second edition.
Levi, P. (1984) *Atlas of the Greek World*, Oxford.
Meier, C. (1998) *Athens: A Portrait of the City in Its Golden Age*, New York.
Murray, O. (1993) *Early Greece*, London, second edition.
Osborne, R. (1996) *Greece in the Making, 1200–479 BC*, London.
Pomeroy, S., S. Burstein, W. Dolan and J. Roberts (eds) (2008) *Ancient Greece: A Political, Social, and Cultural History*, Oxford, second edition.
Powell, A. (1988) *Athens and Sparta: Constructing Greek Political and Social History from 478 B.C.*, London.
Roberts, J.W. (1984) *City of Sokrates: An Introduction to Classical Athens*, London.
Sealey, R. (1976) *A History of the Greek City States ca. 700–338 B.C.*, Berkeley.
Starr, C.G. (1977) *The Economic and Social Growth of Early Greece*, New York.

Chapter 1 The polis: the Greek city-state

Introductory reading:
Adkins, A.W.H. and P. White (eds) (1986) *The Greek Polis*, Chicago.
Carter, L.B. (1986) *The Quiet Athenian*, Oxford.
Cartledge, P. (2010) *Ancient Greece: A History in Eleven Cities*, Oxford.
Dynneson, T.L. (2008) *City-State Civism in Ancient Athens: Its Real and Ideal Expressions*, New York.
Freeman, K. (1950) *Greek City-States*, London.

Hansen, M.H. (2006) *Polis: An Introduction to the Ancient Greek City-State*, Oxford.

Murray, O. and S. Price (eds) (1991) *The Greek City from Homer to Alexander*, Oxford.

Rich, J. and A. Wallace-Hadrill (eds) (1991) *City and Country in the Ancient World*, London: 97–118.

Stockton, D. (1990) *The Classical Athenian Democracy*, Oxford.

Adeleye, G. (1983) 'The Purpose of the *Dokimasia*' *GRBS* 24: 295–306.

Alston, R. and O.M. Nijf (eds) (2008) *Feeding the Ancient Greek City*, Leuven.

Andrewes, A. (1961) 'Philochorus on Phratries' *JHS* 81: 1–15.

—— (1974) 'The Arginousai Trial' *Phoenix* 28: 112–22.

—— (1978) 'The Opposition to Perikles' *JHS* 98: 1–8.

Austin, M.M. and P. Vidal-Nacquet (1977) *Economic and Social History of Ancient Greece: An Introduction*, tr. M.M. Austin, Berkeley.

Bauman, R.A. (1990) *Political Trials in Ancient Greece*, London.

Bogaert, R. (1976) *Epigraphica III: Texts on Bankers, Banking and Credit in the Greek World*, Leiden.

Borza, E.N. (1987) 'Timber and Politics in the Ancient World: Macedon and the Greeks' *PAPhS* 131: 32–52.

Bowie, A.M. (1997) 'Thinking with Drinking: Wine and the Symposium in Aristophanes' *JHS* 117: 1–21.

Bravo, B. (1974) 'Une lettre sur plomb de Berezan: colonisation et modes de contact dans le Pont' in *Dialogues d'histoire ancienne* I, Centre de recherches d'histoire ancienne, XII, Paris: 111–87.

Buck, C.D. (1955) *The Greek Dialects*, Chicago, second edition.

Burford, A. (1963) 'The Builders of the Parthenon' in G.T.W. Hooker (ed.) *Parthenos and Parthenon*, Oxford: 23–45.

Burke, E.M. (1990) 'Athens after the Peloponnesian War: Restoration Efforts and the Role of Maritime Commerce' *ClAnt* 9: 1–13.

—— (1992) 'The Economy of Athens in the Classical Era: Some Adjustments to the Primitivist Model' *TAPhA* 122: 199–226.

Camp, J.M. (1986) *The Athenian Agora: Excavations in the Heart of Classical Athens*, London.

Cartledge, P., E.E. Cohen and L. Foxhall (2002) *Money, Labour and Land: Approaches to the Economies of Ancient Greece*, London.

Caspari, M.O.B. (1915) 'The Ionian Confederacy' *JHS* 35: 173–88.

Castriota, D. (1992) *Myth, Ethos and Actuality: Official Art in Fifth-Century B.C.*, Madison.

Cavanagh, W.G. (1991) 'Surveys, Cities and Synoecism' in J. Rich and A. Wallace-Hadrill (eds) *City and Country in the Ancient World*, London: 97–118.

Chadwick, J. (1973) 'The Berezan Lead Letter' *PCPhS* 19: 35–7.

Cohen, D. (1995) *Law, Violence and Community in Classical Athens*, Cambridge.

Cooper, A.B. (1977–78) 'The Family Farm in Ancient Greece' *CJ* 73: 162–75.

Davidson, J. (1997) 'A Ban on Public Bars in Thasos?' *CQ* 47: 392–5.

Davies, J.K. (1967) 'Demosthenes on Liturgies: A Note' *JHS* 87: 33–40.

—— (1971) *Athenian Propertied Families 600–300 B.C.*, Oxford.

—— (1977–78) 'Athenian Citizenship: The Descent Group and the Alternatives' *CJ* 73: 105–21.

—— (1981) *Wealth and the Power of Wealth in Classical Athens*, New York.

Demand, N.H. (1982) *Thebes in the Fifth Century*, London.

De Ste Croix, G.E.M. (1981) *The Class Struggle in the Ancient World*, London.

Dillon, M.P.J. (1995) 'Payments to the Disabled at Athens: Social Justice or Fear of Aristocratic Patronage?' *AncSoc* 26: 27–57.

—— (1996) 'The Importance of the Water Supply at Athens' *Hermes* 124: 192–204.

Emlyn-Jones C.J. (1980) *The Ionians and Hellenism: A Study of the Cultural Achievements of the Early Greek Inhabitants of Asia Minor*, London.

Errington, R.M. (1994) '*Ekklesia kyria* in Athens' *Chiron* 24: 135–60.

Farrar, C. (1988) *The Origins of Democratic Thinking: The Invention of Politics in Classical Athens*, Cambridge.

581

Finley, M.I. (1951) *Studies in Land and Credit in Ancient Athens 500–200 B.C.: The Horos-Inscriptions*, New Brunswick.

—— (1968) *A History of Sicily: Ancient Sicily to the Arab Conquest*, London.

—— (1985) *The Ancient Economy*, London, second edition.

Fisher, N.R.E. (1990) 'The Law of *Hubris* in Athens' in *NOMOS*: 123–38.

—— (1992) *Hybris: A Study in the Values of Honour and Shame in Ancient Greece*, Warminster.

Flower, M.A. (1985) '*IG* II².2344 and the Size of Phratries in Classical Athens' *CQ* 35: 232–5.

Forrest, W.G.G. (1966) *The Emergence of Greek Democracy, 800–400 BC*, Ann Arbor.

French, A. (1964) *The Growth of the Athenian Economy*, London.

Garland, R. (1987) *The Piraeus: From the Fifth to the First Century BC*, Bristol.

—— (1990) *The Greek Way of Life: From Conception to Old Age*, Ithaca.

—— (1995) *The Eye of the Beholder: Deformity and Disability in the Graeco-Roman World*, London.

Garnsey, P. (1988) *Famine and Food Supply in the Graeco-Roman World: Responses to Risk and Crisis*, Cambridge.

Gates, C. (2011) *Ancient Cities: The Archaeology of Urban Life in the Ancient Near East and Egypt, Greece and Rome*, London.

Glass, S.L. (1988) 'The Greek Gymnasium' in W.J. Raschke (ed.) *The Archaeology of the Olympics: The Olympics and Other Festivals in Antiquity*, Madison: 155–73.

Gomme, A. (1933) *The Population of Athens in the Fifth and Fourth Centuries B.C.*, Oxford.

Graham, A.J. (1984) 'Commercial Interchanges between Greeks and Natives' *AncW* 10: 3–10.

Hahn, I. (1983) 'Foreign Trade and Foreign Policy in Archaic Greece' in P. Garnsey and C.R. Whittaker (eds) *Trade and Famine in Classical Antiquity*, Cambridge: 31–6.

Halliwell, S. (1991) 'Comic Satire and Freedom of Speech in Classical Athens' *JHS* 111: 48–70.

Hansen, M.H. (1976) 'How Many Athenians Attended the Ecclesia?' *GRBS* 17: 115–34.

—— (1979) 'Misthos for Magistrates in Classical Athens' *SO* 54: 5–22.

—— (1979) 'The Duration of a Meeting of the Athenian Ecclesia' *CPh* 74: 43–9.

—— (1980) 'Seven Hundred Archai in Classical Athens' *GRBS* 21: 151–73.

—— (1983) *The Athenian Ecclesia: A Collection of Articles: 1976–83*, Copenhagen.

—— (1987) *The Athenian Assembly in the Age of Demosthenes*, Oxford.

—— (1990) 'The Political Powers of the People's Court in Fourth-Century Athens' in O. Murray and S. Price (eds) *The Greek City from Homer to Alexander*, Oxford: 215–43.

—— (1991) *The Athenian Democracy in the Age of Demosthenes: Structure, Principles and Ideology*, Oxford.

—— (2005) *An Inventory of Archaic and Classical Poleis*, Oxford.

Hanson, V.D. (1983) *Warfare and Agriculture in Classical Greece*, Pisa.

Harris, D. (1995) *The Treasures of the Parthenon and the Erechtheion*, Oxford.

Harris, E.M. (1992) 'Perikles' Praise of Athenian Democracy: Thucydides 2.37.1' *HSPh* 94: 157–67.

Herman, G. (2002) *Ritualised Friendship and the Greek City*, Cambridge.

Highnett, C. (1952) *A History of the Athenian Constitution to the End of the Fifth Century B.C.*, Oxford.

Hodkinson, S. (1988) 'Animal Husbandry in the Greek Polis' in C.R. Whittaker (ed.) *Pastoral Economies in Classical Antiquity, Cambridge Philological Society* Suppl. 14, Cambridge: 35–74.

Hunter, V. (1992) 'Constructing the Body of the Citizen: Corporal Punishment in Classical Athens' *EMC* 11: 271–91.

Hurwit, J.M. (2004) *The Acropolis in the Age of Pericles*, Cambridge.

Isager, S. and M.H. Hansen (1975) *Aspects of Athenian Society in the Fourth Century B.C.*, tr. J.H. Rosenmeier, Odense.

Jameson, M.H. (1983) 'Famine in the Greek World' in P. Garnsey and C.R. Whittaker (eds) *Trade and Famine in Classical Antiquity*, Cambridge: 6–16.

—— (1990) 'Private Space and the Greek City' in O. Murray and S. Price (eds) *The Greek City from Homer to Alexander*, Oxford: 171–95.

Kagan, D. (1991) *Pericles of Athens and the Birth of Democracy*, New York.

Kallet-Marx, L. (1989) 'Did Tribute Fund the Parthenon?' *ClAnt* 8: 252–66.

—— (1993) *Money, Expense, and Naval Power in Thucydides' History 1–5.24*, Berkeley.

Kapparis, K. (1995) 'The Athenian Decree for the Naturalisation of the Plataeans' *GRBS* 36: 359–78.

Laix, de R.A. (1973) *Probouleusis at Athens: A Study of Political Decision-Making*, Berkeley.

Lang, M.L. (1990) 'Illegal Execution in Athens' *PAPhS* 36: 24–9.

Larsen, J.A.O. (1955) *Representative Government in Greek and Roman History*, Berkeley.

—— (1968) *Greek Federal States*, Oxford.

Legon, R.P. (1981) *Megara: The Political History of a Greek City-State to 336 B.C.*, Ithaca.

Lewis, D. (1990) 'Public Property in the City' in O. Murray and S. Price (eds) *The Greek City from Homer to Alexander*, Oxford: 245–63.

Loraux, N. (1986) *The Invention of Athens: The Funeral Oration in the Classical City*, Cambridge, Mass.

Low, P. (2009) *Interstate Relations in Classical Greece: Morality and Power*, Cambridge.

MacDowell, D.M. (1976) 'Bastards as Athenian Citizens' *CQ* 26: 88–91.

—— (1978) *The Law in Classical Athens*, London.

McKechnie, P. (1989) *Outsiders in the Greek Cities in the Fourth Century*, London.

Markle, M.M. (1985) 'Jury Pay and Assembly Pay at Athens' in *Crux*: 265–97.

—— (1990) 'Participation of Farmers in Athenian Juries and Assemblies' *AncSoc* 21: 149–65.

Meiggs, R. (1982) *Trees and Timber in the Ancient Mediterranean World*, Oxford.

Meritt, B.D. (1976) 'Normal Lengths of Prytany in the Athenian Year' *GRBS* 17: 147–52.

—— and H.T. Wade-Gery (1963) 'Dating of Documents to the Mid-Fifth Century' *JHS* 83: 100–17.

Merrill, W.P. (1991) '*To Plethos* in a Treaty concerning the Affairs of Argos, Knossos and Tylissos' *CQ* 41: 16–25.

Migeotte, L. and J. Lloyd (2009) *The Economy of the Greek Cities: From the Archaic Period to the Early Roman Empire*, Berkeley.

Mikalson, J.D. (1977) 'Religion in the Attic Demes' *AJPh* 98: 424–35.

Miller, A.P. (1975) 'Notes on the Berezan Lead Letter' *ZPE* 17: 157–60.

Miller, S.G. (1978) *The Prytaneion: Its Function and Architectural Form*, Berkeley.

Millett, P. (1989) 'Patronage and Its Avoidance in Classical Athens' in A. Wallace-Hadrill (ed.) *Patronage in Ancient Society*, London: 1–47.

—— (1991) *Lending and Borrowing in Ancient Athens*, Cambridge.

Morley, N. (2007) *Trade in Classical Antiquity*, Cambridge.

Morris, I. (1991) 'The Early Polis as City and State' in J. Rich and A. Wallace-Hadrill (eds) *City and Country in the Ancient World*, London: 25–57.

Murray, O. (1990) 'The Solonian Law of *Hybris*' in *NOMOS*: 139–45.

Nixon, L. and S. Price (1990) 'The Size and Resources of Greek Cities' in O. Murray and S. Price (eds) *The Greek City from Homer to Alexander*, Oxford: 137–70.

Ober, J. (2008) *Democracy and Knowledge: Innovation and Learning in Classical Athens*, Princeton.

Osborne, R. (1985) *Demos: The Discovery of Classical Attika*, Cambridge.

—— (1990) 'The Demos and Its Divisions in Classical Athens' in O. Murray and S. Price (eds) *The Greek City from Homer to Alexander*, Oxford: 265–93.

—— (1991) 'Pride and Prejudice, Sense and Subsistence: Exchange and Society in the Greek City', in J. Rich and A. Wallace-Hadrill (eds) *City and Country in the Ancient World*, London: 119–45.

Ostwald, M. (1969) *Nomos and the Beginnings of the Athenian Democracy*, Oxford.

—— (1986) *From Popular Sovereignty to the Sovereignty of Law: Law, Society and Politics in Fifth-Century Athens*, Berkeley.

Patterson, C.B. (1981) *Perikles' Citizenship Law of 451/50 B.C.*, New York.

—— (1990) 'Those Athenian Bastards' *ClAnt* 9: 40–73.

Polignac, F. de (1995) *Cults, Territory, and the Origins of the Greek City-State*, Chicago.

Powell, A. (1995) 'Athens' Pretty Face: Anti-feminine Rhetoric and Fifth-Century Controversy over the Parthenon' in A. Powell (ed.) *The Greek World*, London: 245–70.

Raaflaub, K.A. (1990) 'Contemporary Perceptions of Democracy in Fifth-Century Athens' in W.R. Connor, M.H. Hansen, K.A. Raaflaub and B.S. Strauss (eds) *Aspects of Athenian Democracy (Classica et Mediaevalia. Dissertationes* XI), Copenhagen: 33–70.

BIBLIOGRAPHY

Rhodes, P.J. (1972) *The Athenian Boule*, Oxford.

—— (1981) *A Commentary on the Aristotelian Athenaion Politeia*, with (1993) *Select Addenda*, Oxford.

—— (1982) 'Problems in Athenian Eisphora and Liturgies' *AJAH* 7: 1–19.

—— (1986) 'Political Activity in Classical Athens' *JHS* 106: 132–44.

—— (1995) 'Ekklesia Kyria and the Schedule of Assemblies in Athens' *Chiron* 25: 187–98.

—— (2007) *The Greek City States: A Source Book*, Cambridge.

Salmon, J.B. (1997) *Wealthy Corinth: A History of the City to 338 BC*, Oxford.

Schmitt-Pantel, P. (1990) 'Collective Activities and the Political in the Greek City' in O. Murray and S. Price (eds) *The Greek City from Homer to Alexander*, Oxford: 199–213.

Sealey, R. (1983) 'How Citizenship and the City Began in Athens' *AJAH* 8: 97–129.

—— (1987) *The Athenian Republic: Democracy or the Rule of Law?*, University Park, Pa.

Sinclair, R.K. (1988) *Democracy and Participation in Athens*, Cambridge.

Stanier, R.S. (1953) 'The Cost of the Parthenon' *JHS* 73: 68–76.

Starr, C.G. (1987) 'Athens and Its Empire' *CJ* 83: 114–23.

Tandy, D.W. (1997) *Warriors into Traders. The Power of the Market in Early Greece*, Berkeley.

Thomas, R. (1989) *Oral Tradition and Written Record in Classical Athens*, Cambridge.

Todd, S. (1990) 'The Purpose of Evidence in Athenian Courts' in *NOMOS*: 19–39.

—— (1990) 'Lady Chatterley's Lover and the Attic Orators: The Social Composition of the Athenian Jury' *JHS* 110: 146–73.

Tomlinson, R.A. (1972) *Argos and the Argolid*, Ithaca.

Van Wees, H. (2004) *Greek Warfare: Myths and Realities*, London.

Vlassopoulos, K. (2011) *Unthinking the Greek Polis: Ancient Greek History beyond Eurocentrism*, Cambridge.

Walker, K. (2004) *Ancient Eretria*, London.

Walters, K.R. (1983) 'Perikles' Citizenship Law' *ClAnt* 2: 314–36.

Webster, T.B.L. (1969) *Everyday Life in Classical Athens*, London.

—— (1973) *Athenian Culture and Society*, Berkeley.

Whitehead, D. (1986) *The Demes of Attica: 508/7 – ca. 250 B.C.*, Princeton.

Wood, E.M. (1988) *Peasant-Citizen and Slave: The Foundations of Athenian Democracy*, London.

Zimmern, A. (1931) *The Greek Commonwealth: Politics and Economics in Fifth-Century Athens*, Oxford, fifth edition.

Chapter 2 Colonisation

Introductory reading:

Austin, M.M. (1970) *Greece and Egypt in the Archaic Age*, Cambridge.

Carratelli, G.P. (ed.) (1996) *The Western Greeks. Classical Civilization in the Western Mediterranean*, London.

Cawkwell, G.L. (1992) 'Early Colonisation' *CQ* 42: 289–303.

Demand, N.H. (1990) *Urban Relocation in Archaic and Classical Greece: Flight and Consolidation*, Norman.

Dunbabin, T.J. (1948) *The Western Greeks: The History of Sicily and South Italy from the Foundation of the Greek Colonies to 480 B.C.*, Oxford.

Graham, A.J. (1983) *Colony and Mother City in Ancient Greece*, Chicago, second edition.

—— (2001) *Collected Papers on Greek Colonization*, Leiden.

Sjöqvist, E. (1973) *Sicily and the Greeks*, Ann Arbor.

Tsetskhladze, G.R. (ed.) (2008) *Greek Colonisation: An Account of Greek Colonies and other Settlements Overseas*, Leiden.

Adamesteanu, D. (1967) 'Problèmes de la zone archéologique de Métaponte' *RA* 1: 3–38.

Asheri, D. (1988) 'Carthaginians and Greeks' in *CAH* IV²: 739–80.

Austin, M.M. (1970) *Greece and Egypt in the Archaic Age*, Cambridge.

—— and P. Vidal-Naquet (1977) *Economic and Social History of Ancient Greece: An Introduction*, tr. M.M. Austin, Berkeley.

Beaumont, R.C. (1936) 'Greek Influence in the Adriatic Sea before the Fourth Century B.C.' *JHS* 56: 159–204.

Bérard, J. (1957) *La colonisation grecque. De l'Italie méridionale et de la Sicile dans l'antiquité: l'histoire et la légend*, Paris, second edition.

Boardman, J. (1965) 'Tarsus, Al Mina and Greek Chronology' *JHS* 85: 5–15.

—— (1966) 'Evidence for the Dating of Greek Settlements in Cyrenaica' *ABSA* 61: 149–56.

—— (1980) *The Greeks Overseas: Their Early Colonies and Trade*, London, second edition.

—— (1982) 'An Inscribed Sherd from Al Mina' *OJA* 1: 365–7.

—— (1990) 'Al Mina and History' *OJA* 9: 169–90.

—— (1994) 'Settlement for Trade and Land in North Africa: Problems of Identity' in G.R. Tsetskhladze and F. De Angelis: 137–49.

Bradeen, D.W. (1952) 'The Chalcidians in Thrace' *AJPh* 73: 356–80.

Bradley, G.J. and J.P. Wilson (eds) (2006) *Greek and Roman Colonisation: Origins, Ideologies and Interactions*, Swansea.

Brauer, G.C. (1986) *Taras: Its History and Coinage*, New York.

Braun, T.F.G.R. (1982) 'The Greeks in the Near East' in *CAH* III.3²: 1–31.

—— (1982) 'The Greeks in Egypt' in *CAH* III.3²: 32–56.

Braund, D. (2005) *Scythians and Greeks: Cultural Interactions in Scythia, Athens and the Early Roman Empire (sixth century BC – first century AD)*, Exeter.

Brinkman, J.A. (1989) 'The Akkadian Words for "Ionia" and "Ionian"' in R.F. Sutton (ed.) *Daidalikon: Studies in Memory of R.V. Schoder*, Wauconda: 53–71.

Buck, R.J. (1959) 'Communalism on the Lipari Islands (Diod. 5.9.4)' *CPh* 54: 35–9.

Calame, C. (1990) 'Narrating the Foundation of a City: The Symbolic Birth of Cyrene' in L. Edmunds (ed.) *Approaches to Greek Myth*, Baltimore: 277–341.

Carawan, E.M. (1987) '*Eisangelia* and *Euthyna*: The Trials of Miltiades, Themistokles, and Cimon' *GRBS* 28: 167–208.

Cartledge, P. (1979) *Sparta and Lakonia: A Regional History 1300–362 BC*, London.

Coja, M. (1990) 'Greek Colonists and Native Populations in Dobruja (Moesia Inferior): The Archaeological Evidence' in J.-P. Descoeudres (ed.) *Greek Colonists and Native Populations*, Oxford: 157–68.

Coldstream, J.N. (1994) 'Prospectors and Pioneers: Pithekoussai, Kyme and Central Italy' in G.R. Tsetskhladze and F. De Angelis (eds) *The Archaeology of Greek Colonisation*, Oxford: 47–59.

Cook, J.M. (1982) 'The Eastern Greeks' in *CAH* III.3²: 196–221.

Cook, R.M. (1937) 'Amasis and the Greeks in Egypt' *JHS* 57: 227–37.

—— (1946) 'Ionia and Greece in the Eighth and Seventh Centuries B.C.' *JHS* 66: 67–98.

—— (1962) 'Reasons for the Foundation of Ischia and Cumae' *Historia* 11: 113–14.

Cunliffe, B. (1988) *Greeks, Romans and Barbarians: Spheres of Interaction*, London.

Danov, C.M. (1990) 'Greek Colonization in Thrace' in J.-P. Descoeudres (ed.) *Greek Colonists and Native Populations*, Oxford: 151–5.

De Angelis, F. (1994) 'The Foundation of Selinous: Overpopulation or Opportunities?' in G.R. Tsetskhladze and F. De Angelis (eds) *The Archaeology of Greek Colonisation*, Oxford: 87–110.

—— (2003) *Megara Hyblaia and Selinous: Two Greek City-states in Archaic Sicily*, Oxford.

Demand, N.H. (1990) *Urban Relocation in Archaic and Classical Greece: Flight and Consolidation*, Norman.

Dillon, M.P.J. (1997) 'A Homeric Pun from Abu Simbel (Meiggs and Lewis 7a)' *ZPE* 118: 128–30.

Dougherty, C. (1994) 'Archaic Greek Foundation Poetry: Questions of Genre and Occasion' *JHS* 114: 35–46.

Drews, R. (1976) 'The Earliest Greek Settlements on the Black Sea' *JHS* 96: 18–31.

Dushanic, S. (1978) 'The ORKION TWN OIKISTERON and Fourth-Century Cyrene' *Chiron* 8: 55–76.

Ehrenberg, V. (1948) 'The Foundation of Thurii' *AJPh* 69: 149–70.

Faraone, C.A. (1993) 'Molten Wax, Spilt Wine and Mutilated Animals: Sympathetic Magic in Near Eastern and Early Greek Oath Ceremonies' *JHS* 113: 60–80.

—— (1996) 'Taking the "Nestor's Cup Inscription" Seriously: Erotic Magic and Conditional Curses in the Earliest Inscribed Hexameters' *ClAnt* 15: 77–112.

Finley, M.I. (1979) *Ancient Sicily*, London, second edition.

Forrest, W.G. (1957) 'Colonisation and the Rise of Delphi' *Historia* 6: 160–75.

—— (1982) 'Euboia and the Islands' in *CAH* III.3²: 249–60.

Freeman, K. (1950) *Greek City-States*, London.

Gabrielsen, V. and J. Lund (2008) *The Black Sea in Antiquity: Regional and Interregional Economic Exchanges*, Aarhus.

Graham, A.J. (1958) 'The Date of the Greek Penetration of the Black Sea' *BICS* 5: 25–39.

—— (1960) 'The Authenticity of the ORKION TWN OIKISTHRWN of Cyrene' *JHS* 80: 94–111.

—— (1962) 'Corinthian Colonies and Thucydides' Terminology' *Historia* 11: 246–52.

—— (1971) 'Patterns in Early Greek Colonization' *JHS* 91: 35–47.

—— (1978) 'The Foundation of Thasos' *ABSA* 73: 61–98.

—— (1980–81) 'Religion, Women and Greek Colonization' *CRDAC* 11: 293–314.

—— (1982) 'The Colonial Expansion of Greece' in *CAH* III.3²: 83–162.

—— (1982) 'The Western Greeks' in *CAH* III.3²: 163–95.

—— (1984) 'Commercial Interchanges between Greeks and Natives' *AncW* 10: 3–10.

—— (1992) 'Abdera and Teos' *JHS* 112: 44–73.

Gwynn, A. (1918) 'The Character of Greek Colonisation' *JHS* 38: 88–123.

Huxley, G. (1962) *Early Sparta*, London.

Jameson, M.H. (1983) 'Famine in the Greek World' in P. Garnsey and C.R. Whittaker (eds) *Trade and Famine in Classical Antiquity*, Cambridge: 6–16.

Jeffery, L.H. (1961) 'The Pact of the First Settlers at Cyrene' *CQ* 10: 139–47.

Jones, A.H.M. (1967) *Sparta*, Oxford.

Labaree, B.W. (1957) 'How the Greeks Sailed into the Black Sea' *AJA* 61: 29–33.

Laronde, A. (1990) 'Greeks and Libyans in Cyrenaica' in J.-P. Descoeudres (ed.) *Greek Colonists and Native Populations*, Oxford: 169–80.

Legon, R.P. (1981) *Megara: The Political History of a Greek City-State to 336 B.C.*, Ithaca.

Lewis, D.M. (1992) 'Sources, Chronology, Method' and 'The Thirty Years' Peace' in *CAH* V²: 1–14, 121–46.

Lewis, N. (1986) *Greeks in Ptolemaic Egypt*, Oxford.

Londey, P. (1990) 'Greek Colonists and Delphi' in J.-P. Descoeudres (ed.) *Greek Colonists and Native Populations*, Oxford: 117–27.

Malkin, I. (1985) 'What's in a Name? The Eponymous Founders of Greek Colonies' *Athenaeum* 63: 114–30.

—— (1987) *Religion and Colonization in Ancient Greece*, Leiden.

—— (1994) *Myth and Territory in the Spartan Mediterranean*, Cambridge.

Meiggs, R. (1972) *The Athenian Empire*, Oxford.

Millar, F. (1983) 'Epigraphy' in M. Crawford (ed.) *Sources for Ancient History*, Cambridge: 80–136.

Miller, M. (1970) *The Sicilian Colony Dates: Studies in Chronography* I, Albany.

Mitchell, B.M. (1966) 'Cyrene and Persia' *JHS* 86: 99–113.

Morgan, C. (1990) *Athletes and Oracles: The Transformation of Olympia and Delphi in the Eighth Century BC*, Cambridge.

Noonan, T.S. (1973) 'The Grain Trade of the Northern Black Sea in Antiquity' *AJPh* 94: 231–42.

Oliver, J.H. (1966) 'Herodotus 4.153 and *SEG* IX 3' *GRBS* 7: 25–9.

Paget, R.F. (1968) 'The Ancient Ports of Cumae' *JRS* 58: 151–69.

Parker, R. (1985) 'Greek States and Greek Oracles' in *Crux*: 298–326.

—— (2011) *On Greek Religion*, Ithaca.

Parker, V. (1991) 'The Dates of the Messenian Wars' *Chiron* 21: 25–47.

Pease, A.S. (1917) 'Notes on the Delphic Oracle and Greek Colonization' *CPh* 12: 1–20.

Pesely, G.E. (1989) 'Hagnon' *Athenaeum* 67: 191–209.

Petropoulos, E.K. (2005) *Hellenic Colonization in Euxeinos Pontos. Penetration, Early Establishment and the Problem of the 'Emporion' Revisited*, Oxford.

Polignac, F. de (1995) *Cults, Territory, and the Origins of the Greek City-State*, Chicago.

Powell, B.B. (1989) 'Why Was the Greek Alphabet Invented? The Epigraphical Evidence' *ClAnt* 8: 321–50.

Ridgway, D. (1973) 'The First Western Greeks: Campanian Coasts and Southern Etruria' in C. and S. Hawkes (eds) *Greeks, Celts and Romans*, London: 5–38.

—— (1992) *The First Western Greeks*, Cambridge.

Rihll, T. (1993) 'War, Slavery and Settlement in Early Greece' in J. Rich and G. Shipley (eds) *War and Society in the Greek World*, London: 77–107.

Robb, K. (1994) *Literacy and Paideia in Ancient Greece*, New York.

Roebuck, C. (1951) 'The Organization of Naukratis' *CPh* 46: 212–20.

—— (1959) *Ionian Trade and Colonization*, New York.

Rougé, J. (1970) 'La colonisation grecque et les femmes' *Cahiers d'Histoire* 15: 307–17.

Schlotzhauer, U. and A. Villing (2006) *Naukratis: Greek Diversity in Egypt. Studies on East Greek Pottery and Exchange in the Eastern Mediterranean*, London.

Shefton, B.B. (1994) 'Massalia and Colonization in the North-Western Mediterranean' in G.R. Tsetskhladze and F. De Angelis (eds) *The Archaeology of Greek Colonisation*, Oxford: 61–86.

Snodgrass, A. (1983) 'Archaeology' in M. Crawford (ed.) *Sources for Ancient History*, Cambridge: 137–84.

—— and G.R. Tsetskhladze (eds) (2002) *Greek Settlements in the Eastern Mediterranean and Black Sea*, Oxford.

Tandy, D.W. (1997) *Warriors into Traders. The Power of the Market in Early Greece*, Berkeley.

Tsetskhladze, G.R. (ed.) (1998) *The Greek Colonisation of the Black Sea Area: Historical Interpretation of Archaeology*, Stuttgart.

—— and F. De Angelis (eds) (1994) *The Archaeology of Greek Colonisation*, Oxford.

Woodhead, A.G. (1952) 'The Site of Brea: Thucydides 1.61.4' *CQ* 2: 57–62.

—— (1962) *The Greeks in the West*, London.

Woolley, C.L. (1938) 'Excavations at Al Mina, Sueidia' *JHS* 58: 1–30.

Chapter 3 Religion in the Greek world

Introductory reading:

Bremmer, J.N. (2006) *Greek Religion*, Oxford.

Burkert, W. (1985) *Greek Religion: Archaic and Classical*, tr. J. Raffan, Oxford.

Dillon, M.P.J. (1997) *Pilgrims and Pilgrimage in Ancient Greece*, London.

Guthrie, W.K.C. (1950) *The Greeks and Their Gods*, Boston.

Mikalson, J. (2004) *Ancient Greek Religion*, Oxford.

Ogden, D. (ed.) (2010) *A Companion to Greek Religion*, Oxford.

Parker, R. (2005) *Polytheism and Society at Athens*, Oxford.

Pedley, J.G. (2005) *Sanctuaries and the Sacred in the Ancient Greek World*, Cambridge.

Price, S. (1999) *Religions of the Ancient Greeks*, Cambridge.

Simon, E. (1983) *Festivals of Attika: An Archaeological Commentary*, Madison.

Zaidman, L.B. and P.S. Pantel (1992) *Religion in the Ancient Greek City*, tr. P. Cartledge, Cambridge.

Aleshire, S.B. (1989) *The Athenian Asklepieion: The People, Their Dedications, and the Inventories*, Amsterdam.

—— (1991) *Asklepios at Athens: Epigraphic and Prosopographic Essays on the Athenian Healing Cults*, Amsterdam.

Barnes, J. (1982) *The Presocratic Philosophers*, London.

Barringer, J.M. (2008) *Art, Myth, and Ritual in Classical Greece*, Cambridge.

Behr, C.A. (1968) *Aelius Aristides and the Sacred Tales*, Amsterdam.

Bloch, R. (1963) *Les Prodiges dans l'antiquité classique (Grèce, Étrurie et Rome)*, Paris.

Blum, A.F. (1978) *Socrates: The Original and Its Images*, London.

Blundell, S. and M. Williamson (eds) (1998) *The Sacred and the Feminine in Ancient Greece*, London.

Boedeker, D. (1993) 'Hero Cult and Politics in Herodotos: The Bones of Orestes' in C. Dougherty and L. Kurke (eds) *Cultural Poetics in Archaic Greece. Cult, Performance, Politics*, Cambridge: 164–77.

Bouché-Leclercq, A. (1879–82) *Histoire de la divination dans l'antiquité* I–IV, Paris.

Brickhouse T.C. and N.D. Smith (1989) *Socrates on Trial*, Princeton.

—— (1992) 'The Formal Charges against Socrates' in H.H. Benson (ed.) *Essays on the Philosophy of Socrates*, Oxford: 14–34.

Brumfield, A.C. (1981) *The Attic Festivals of Demeter and Their Relationship to the Agricultural Year*, Salem.

Burford, A. (1969) *The Greek Temples at Epidauros: A Social and Economic Study of Building in the Asklepian Sanctuary*, Liverpool.

Burkert, W. (1979) *Structure and History in Greek Mythology and Ritual*, Berkeley.

—— (1983) *Homo Necans: The Anthropology of Ancient Greek Sacrificial Ritual and Myth*, tr. P. Bing, Berkeley.

—— (1987) *Ancient Mystery Cults*, Cambridge, Mass.

—— (1992) 'Athenian Cults and Festivals' in *CAH* V²: 245–67.

Calame, C. (1997) *Choruses of Young Women in Ancient Greece*, Lanham.

Caldwell, R. (1989) *The Origin of the Gods: A Psychoanalytic Study of Greek Theogenic Myth*, New York.

Castriota, D. (1992) *Myth, Ethos and Actuality: Official Art in Fifth-Century B.C. Athens*, Madison.

Clairmont, C.W. (1979) 'The Lekythos of Myrrhine' in G. Kopcke and M.B. Moore (eds) *Studies in Classical Art and Archaeology: A Tribute to Peter Heinrich von Blanckenhagen*, New York: 103–10.

—— (1983) *Patrios Nomos: Public Burial in Athens during the Fifth and Fourth Centuries B.C.* Parts I–II, Oxford.

Clark, R.J. (1968) 'Trophonios: The Manner of His Revelation' *TAPhA* 99: 63–75.

Clinton, K. (1971) 'Inscriptions from Eleusis' *AE*: 81–136.

—— (1974) *The Sacred Officials of the Eleusinian Mysteries*, Philadelphia.

—— (1980) 'A Law in the City Eleusinion Concerning the Mysteries' *Hesperia* 49: 258–88.

—— (1993) 'The Sanctuary of Demeter and Kore at Eleusis' in N. Marinatos and R. Hägg (eds) *Greek Sanctuaries: New Approaches*, London: 110–24.

Coldstream, J.N. (1985) 'Greek Temples: Why and Where?' in P.E. Easterling and J.V. Muir (eds) *Greek Religion and Society*, Cambridge: 67–97.

Cole, S.G. (1992) '*Gynaiki ou themis:* Gender Difference in the Greek *Leges Sacrae*' *Helios* 19: 104–22.

—— (1995) 'Women, Dogs and Flies' *AncW* 26: 182–91.

Connor, W.R. (1987) 'Tribes, Festivals and Processions: Civic Ceremonial and Political Manipulation in Archaic Greece' *JHS* 107: 40–50.

—— (1988) 'Seized by the Nymphs: Nympholepsy and Symbolic Expression in Classical Greece' *ClAnt* 7: 155–89.

Culham, P. (1986) 'Again, What Meaning Lies in Colour!' *ZPE* 64: 235–45.

Daux, G. (1949) 'Un règlement cultuel d'Andros (Vème siècle avant J.-C.)' *Hesperia* 18: 58–72.

Davies, J.K. (1967) 'Demosthenes on Liturgies: A Note' *JHS* 87: 33–40.

De Romilly, J. (1992) *The Great Sophists in Periclean Athens*, tr. J. Lloyd, Oxford.

Den Adel, R. (1983) 'Apollo's Prophecies at Delos' *CW* 76: 288–90.

Detienne M. and J.-P. Vernant (1978) *Cunning Intelligence in Greek Culture and Society*, tr. J. Lloyd, Sussex.

Detienne, M. and J.-P. Vernant (eds) (1989) *The Cuisine of Sacrifice among the Greeks*, tr. P. Wissing, Chicago.

Dillon, M.P.J. (1990) '"The House of the Thebans" (*FD* iii.1 357–58) and Accommodation for Greek Pilgrims' *ZPE* 83: 64–88.

—— (1993) 'Restoring a Manuscript Reading at Paus. 9.3.7', *CQ* 43: 327–9.

—— (1994) 'The Didactic Nature of the Epidaurian Iamata' *ZPE* 101: 239–60.

—— (1996) 'Oionomanteia: Divination by the Birds in Ancient Greece' in M.P.J. Dillon (ed.) *Religion in the Ancient World*, Amsterdam: 99–121.

—— (1997) 'The Ecology of the Greek Sanctuary', *ZPE* 118: 113–27.

—— (1999) 'Post-Nuptial Sacrifices on Kos (Segre, *ED* 178) and Ancient Greek Marriage Rites' *ZPE* 124: 63–80.

—— (1999) 'Did Parthenoi Attend the Olympic Games? Female Athletes and Spectators at Greek Religious Festivals' *Hermes* 128: 457–80.

—— (2002) *Girls and Women in Classical Greek Religion*, London.

—— (2008) '"Xenophon Sacrificed on account of an Expedition" (Xenophon *Anabasis* 6.5.2): Divination and the Sphagia before Ancient Greek Battles' in P. Brulé and V. Mehl (eds), *Le sacrifice antique. Vestiges, procédures et stratégies*, Rennes: 235–51.

—— (2009) 'Kassandra: Mantic, Maenadic or Manic? Gender and the Nature of Prophetic Experience in Ancient Greece' in *Annual Conference Proceedings of the Australian Association for the Study of Religions (2008)*: 1–21.

Dodds, E.R. (1956) *The Greeks and the Irrational*, Berkeley.

—— (1971) *The Ancient Concept of Progress and Other Essays on Greek Literature and Belief*, Oxford.

Dover, K.J. (1971) 'Socrates in the Clouds' in G. Vlastos (ed.) *The Philosophy of Socrates: A Collection of Critical Essays*, New York: 50–77.

Dowden, K. (1989) *Death and the Maiden: Girls' Initiation Rites in Greek Mythology*, London.

Ducrey, P. (1986) *Warfare in Ancient Greece*, tr. J. Lloyd, New York.

Easterling, P.E. and J.V. Muir (eds) (1985) *Greek Religion and Society*, Cambridge.

Edelstein, E.J. and L. Edelstein (1945) *Asclepius: A Collection and Interpretation of the Testimonies* I–II, Baltimore.

Eidinow, E. (2011) *Luck, Fate and Fortune: Antiquity and Its Legacy*, London.

Ekroth, G. (2002) *The Sacrificial Rituals of Greek Hero-Cults*, Liège.

Emerson, M. (2007) *Greek Sanctuaries: An Introduction*, New York.

Emlyn-Jones, C.J. (1980) *The Ionians and Hellenism: A Study of the Cultural Achievement of the Early Greek Inhabitants of Asia Minor*, London.

Fantham, E., H.P. Foley, N.B. Kampen, S.B. Pomeroy and H.A. Shapiro (eds) (1994) *Women in the Classical World: Image and Text*, Oxford.

Farnell, L.R. (1896–1909) *The Cults of the Greek States* I–V, Oxford.

—— (1921) *Greek Hero Cults and Ideas of Immortality*, Oxford.

Ferguson, J. (1970) *Socrates: A Source Book*, London.

—— (1989) *Among the Gods: An Archaeological Exploration of Ancient Greek Religion*, London.

Festugière, A.J. (1954) *Personal Religion among the Greeks*, Berkeley.

Finley, M. (1985) 'Foreword' in P.E. Easterling and J.V. Muir (eds) *Greek Religion and Society*, Cambridge: xiii–xx.

Fisher, N.R.E. (1992) *Hybris: A Study in the Values of Honour and Shame in Ancient Greece*, Warminster.

Flacelière, R. (1965) *Greek Oracles*, tr. D. Garman, London.

Flower, M.A. (2008) *The Seer in Ancient Greece*, Berkeley.

Foley, H.P. (1994) *The Homeric Hymn to Demeter. Translation, Commentary, and Interpretive Essays*, Princeton.

Fontenrose, J. (1968) 'The Hero as Athlete' *ClAnt* 1: 73–104.

—— (1978) *The Delphic Oracle*, Berkeley.

—— (1988) *Didyma: Apollo's Oracle, Cult and Companions*, Berkeley.

—— (1988) 'The Cult of Apollo and the Games at Delphi' in W.J. Raschke (ed.) *The Archaeology of the Olympics. The Olympics and Other Festivals in Antiquity*, Madison: 121–40.

Foxhall, L. (1995) 'Women's Ritual and Men's Work in Ancient Athens' in R. Hawley and B. Levick (eds) *Women in Antiquity. New Assessments*, London: 97–110.

Freeman, K. (1971) *Ancilla to the Pre-Socratic Philosophers*, Oxford.

Gagarin, M. (2002) *Antiphon the Athenian. Oratory, Law and Justice in the Age of the Sophists*, Austin: 9–92.

Garland, R.S.J. (1984) 'Religious Authority in Archaic and Classical Athens' *ABSA* 79: 75–123.

—— (1985) *The Greek Way of Death*, Ithaca.

—— (1989) 'The Well-Ordered Corpse: An Investigation into the Motives behind Greek Funerary Legislation' *BICS* 36: 1–15.

—— (1990) *The Greek Way of Life*, London.

—— (1990) 'Priests and Power in Classical Athens' in M. Beard and J. North (eds) *Pagan Priests: Religion and Power in the Ancient World*, London: 75–91.

—— (1992) *Introducing New Gods*, London.

Goff, B. (2004) *Citizen Bacchae: Women's Ritual Practice in Ancient Greece*, Berkeley.

Golden, M. (1990) *Children and Childhood in Classical Athens*, Baltimore.

Gould, J. (1994) 'Herodotus and Religion' in S. Hornblower (ed.) *Greek Historiography*, London: 91–106.

Gray, V.J. (1989) 'Xenophon's *Defence of Socrates*: The Rhetorical Background to the Socratic Problem' *CQ* 39: 136–40.

Green, P. (1989) *Classical Bearings: Interpreting Ancient History and Culture*, London.

Guthrie, W.K.C. (1967) *The Greek Philosophers from Thales to Aristotle*, London.

—— (1971) *The Sophists*, Cambridge = (1969) *A History of Greek Philosophy* III: *The Fifth Century Enlightenment*, Cambridge: 3–319.

—— (1971) *Socrates*, Cambridge = (1969) *A History of Greek Philosophy* III: *The Fifth Century Enlightenment*, Cambridge: 323–507.

Hägg, R. (ed.) (1999) *Ancient Greek Hero Cult*, Stockholm.

Halliday, W.R. (1913) *Greek Divination*, London.

Hamilton, M. (1906) *Incubation, or the Cure of Disease in Pagan Temples and Christian Churches*, London.

Harrison, J. (1922) *Prolegomena to the Study of Greek Religion*, Cambridge, third edition.

—— (1925) *Themis: A Study of the Social Origins of Greek Religion*, London, second edition.

Harrison, J. (2000) *Divinity and History: The Religion of Herodotus*, Oxford.

Henrichs, A. (1993) 'The Tomb of Aias and the Prospect of Hero Cult in Sophokles' *ClAnt* 12: 165–80.

Hewitt, J.W. (1909) 'The Major Restrictions on Access to Greek Temples' *TAPhA* 40: 83–91.

Hodkinson, S. (1983) 'Social Order and the Conflict of Values in Classical Sparta' *Chiron* 13: 239–81.

Hornblower, S. (1982) 'Thucydides, the Panionian Festival, and the Ephesia (III.104)' *Historia* 31: 241–5.

Hughes, J.D. (1980) 'Early Greek and Roman Environmentalists' in L.J. Bilsky (ed.) *Historical Ecology: Essays on Environment and Social Change*, New York: 45–59.

Humphreys, S.C. (1980) 'Family Tombs and Tomb Cult in Ancient Athens: Tradition or Traditionalism?' *JHS* 100: 96–126.

Hurwit, J.M. (2004) *The Acropolis in the Age of Pericles*, Cambridge.

Huxley, G. (1979) 'Bones for Orestes' *GRBS* 2: 145–8.

Irwin, T.H. (1985–86) 'Socratic Inquiry and Politics' *Ethics* 96: 400–15.

Jameson, M. (1983) 'Famine in the Greek World' in P. Garnsey and C.R. Whittaker (eds) *Trade and Famine in Classical Antiquity*, Cambridge: 6–16.

Johnston, S.I. (2008) *Ancient Greek Divination*, Oxford.

Jordon, B. (1979) *Servants of the Gods: A Study in the Religion, History and Literature of Fifth-Century Athens*, Hypomnemata 55, Göttingen.

—— (1986) 'Religion in Thucydides' *TAPhA* 116: 119–47.

—— and J. Perlin (1984) 'On the Protection of Sacred Groves' in K.J. Rigsby (ed.) *Studies Presented to Sterling Dow*, *GRBS* Mono. 10: 153–9.

Kearns, E. (1989) *The Heroes of Attica*, *BICS* Suppl. 57, London.

Kerényi, C. (1960) *Asklepios: Archetypal Image of the Physician's Existence*, tr. R. Manheim, London.

—— (1967) *Eleusis: Archetypal Image of Mother and Daughter*, tr. R. Manheim, New York.

Kirk, G.S. and J.E. Raven (1960) *The Presocratic Philosophers: A Critical History with a Selection of Texts*, Cambridge.

Kraut, R. (1984) *Socrates and the State*, Princeton.

Krug, A. (1984) *Heilkunst und Heilkult: Medizin in der Antike*, Munich.

Kurtz, D.C. and J. Boardman (1971) *Greek Burial Customs*, London.

Lambridis, H. (1976) *Empedocles: A Philosophical Investigation*, Albama.

Larson, J. (1995) *Greek Heroine Cults*, Wisconsin.

—— (2001) *Greek Nymphs: Myth, Cult, Lore*, Oxford.

Lauenstein, D. (1989) *Die Mysterien von Eleusis*, Stuttgart.

Lefkowitz, M.R. (1986) *Women in Greek Myth*, Baltimore.

—— (1996) 'Women in the Panathenaic and Other Festivals' in J. Neils (ed.) *Worshipping Athena: Panathenaia and Parthenon*, Wisconsin: 78–91.

Lesher, J.H. (2001) *Xenophanes of Colophon*, Toronto.

Lloyd-Jones, H. (1976) 'The Delphic Oracle' *G&R* 23: 60–73.

Luck, G. (1985) *Arcana Mundi: Magic and the Occult in the Greek and Roman Worlds*, Baltimore.

Lyons, D. (1997) *Gender and Immortality. Heroines in Ancient Greek Myth and Cult*, Princeton.

Marinatos, N. and R. Hägg (1993) *Greek Sanctuaries. New Approaches*, London.

Martin, L.H. (1987) *Hellenistic Religions: An Introduction*, Oxford.

Mattingly, H.B. (1961) 'The Athenian Coinage Decree' *Historia* 10: 148–88 = Mattingly (1996) 5–52.

—— (1974) 'Athens and Eleusis: Some New Ideas' in D.W. Bradeen and M.F. McGregor (eds) *FOROS: Tribute to Benjamin Dean Meritt*, Locust Valley: 90–103 = Mattingly (1996) 325–45.

—— (1982) 'The Athenian Nike Temple Reconsidered' *AJA* 86: 381–5 = Mattingly (1996) 461–71.

Meritt, B.D. (1945) 'Attic Inscriptions of the Fifth Century' *Hesperia* 14: 61–133.

—— (1946) 'Greek Inscriptions' *Hesperia* 15: 169–263.

Meritt, B.D. and H.T. Wade-Gery (1963) 'Dating of Documents to the Mid-Fifth Century' *JHS* 83: 100–17.

Meyer, E.A. (1993) 'Epitaphs and Citizenship in Classical Athens' *JHS* 113: 99–121.

Mikalson, J.D. (1975) *The Sacred and Civil Calendar of the Athenian Year*, Princeton.

—— (1983) *Athenian Popular Religion*, Chapel Hill.

—— (1991) *Honor Thy Gods: Popular Religion in Greek Tragedy*, Chapel Hill.

—— (1998) *Religion in Hellenistic Athens*, Berkeley.

—— (2003) *Herodotos and Religion in the Persian Wars*, Chapel Hill.

Mills, H. (1984) 'Greek Clothing Regulations: Sacred and Profane' *ZPE* 55: 255–65.

Mitchell-Boyask, R. (2008) *Plague and the Athenian Imagination: Drama, History and the Cult of Asclepius*, Cambridge.

Momigliano, A. (1978) 'Freedom of Speech and Religious Tolerance in the Ancient World' in S.C. Humphreys (ed.) *Anthropology and the Greeks*, London: 179–93.

Montuori, M. (1981) *Socrates: Physiology of a Myth*, Amsterdam.

—— (1990) 'The Oracle Given to Chaerephon on the Wisdom of Socrates. An Invention by Plato' *Kernos* 3: 251–9.

Morgan, C. (1990) *Athletes and Oracles: The Transformation of Olympia and Delphi in the Eighth Century BC*, Cambridge.

Morgan, M.L. (1992) 'Plato and Greek Religion' in R. Kraut (ed.) *The Cambridge Companion to Plato*, Cambridge: 227–47.

Morris, I. (1992) *Death-Ritual and Social Structure in Classical Antiquity*, Cambridge.

Most, G.W. (1993) '"A Cock for Asclepius"' *CQ* 43: 96–111.

Muir, J.V. (1985) 'Religion and the New Education' in P.E. Easterling and J.V. Muir (eds) *Greek Religion and Society*, Cambridge: 191–218.

Mylonas, G.E. (1961) *Eleusis and the Eleusinian Mysteries*, Princeton.

Nichols, M.P. (1987) *Socrates and the Political Community*, New York.

Nilsson, M.P. (1925) *Greek Religion*, Oxford.

—— (1961) *Greek Folk Religion*, New York = (1940) *Greek Popular Religion*, Columbia.

Nixon, L. (1995) 'The Cults of Demeter and Kore' in R. Hawley and B. Levick (eds) *Women in Antiquity. New Assessments*, London: 75–96.

Nock, A.D. (1942) 'Religious Attitudes of the Ancient Greeks' *APhS* 85: 472–82 = (1972) Z. Stewart (ed.) *A.D. Nock: Essays on Religion and the Ancient World* I–II, Oxford: 534–50.

—— (1944) 'The Cult of Heroes' *HThR* 37: 141–74 = (1972) Z. Stewart (ed.) *A.D. Nock: Essays on Religion and the Ancient World* I–II, Oxford: 575–602.

Nussbaum, M. (1980) 'Aristophanes and Socrates on Learning Practical Wisdom' in J. Henderson (ed.) *Aristophanes: Essays in Interpretation* (*YClS* 26): 43–97.

O'Brien, D. (1968) 'The Relation of Anaxagoras and Empedocles' *JHS* 88: 93–113.

Osborne, R. (1985) *Demos: The Discovery of Classical Attika*, Cambridge.

—— (1993) 'Women and Sacrifice in Classical Greece' *CQ* 43: 392–405.

Parke, H.W. (1939) 'Notes on Some Delphic Charges' *Hermathena* 28: 59–65.

—— (1967) *Greek Oracles*, London.

—— (1977) *Festivals of the Athenians*, London.

—— (1984) 'Croesus and Delphi' *GRBS* 25: 209–32.

—— and Wormell, D.E.W. (1956) *The Delphic Oracle* I–II, Oxford.

Parker, R. (1983) *Miasma: Pollution and Purification in Early Greek Religion*, Oxford.

—— (1985) 'Greek States and Greek Oracles' in *Crux*: 298–326.

—— (1989) 'Spartan Religion' in *Classical Sparta*: 142–72.

—— (1996) *Athenian Religion. A History*, Oxford.

Peppa-Delmousou, D. (1988) 'The Theoria of Brauron' in R. Hagg, N. Marinatos and G.C. Nordquist (eds) *Early Greek Cult Practice*, Stockholm: 255–8.

Petropoulou, A. (1981) 'The *Eparche* Documents and the Early Oracle at Oropus' *GRBS* 22: 39–63.

Podlecki, A. (1971) 'Cimon, Skyros and Theseus' Bones' *JHS* 91: 141–3.

Pollard, J. (1965) *Seers, Shrines and Sirens*, London.

—— (1977) *Birds in Greek Life and Myth*, London.

Pomeroy, S. (1975) *Goddesses, Whores, Wives and Slaves*, New York.

—— (1997) *Families in Classical and Hellenistic Greece. Representations and Realities*, Oxford.

Powell, C.A. (1979) 'Religion and the Sicilian Expedition' *Historia* 28: 15–31.

Price, S. (1985) 'Delphi and Divination' in P.E. Easterling and J.V. Muir (eds) *Greek Religion and Society*, Cambridge: 128–54.

Pritchett, W.K. (1979) *The Greek State at War. Part III: Religion*, Berkeley.

Purvis, A. (2003) *Singular Dedications: Founders and Innovators of Private Cults in Classical Greece*, London.

Rankin, H.D. (1983) *Sophists, Socratics and Cynics*, London.

Richardson, N.J. (1974) *The Homeric Hymn to Demeter*, Oxford.

—— (1992) 'Panhellenic Cults and Panhellenic Poets' in *CAH* V²: 223–44.

Richter, G.M.A. (1961) *Archaic Gravestones of Attica*, London.

Robertson, N. (1992) *Festivals and Legends: The Formation of Greek Cities in the Light of Public Ritual*, Toronto.

—— (1995) 'The Magic Properties of Female Age-Groups in Greek Ritual' *AncW* 26: 193–203.

Robinson, T.M. (1987) *Heraclitus: Fragments*, Toronto.

Roebuck, C. (1941) *Corinth* XIV: *The Asklepieion and Lerna*, Princeton.

Rosen, R.M. (1987) 'Hipponax fr. 48 Dg. and the Eleusinian *Kykeon*' *AJPh* 108: 416–26.

Rougement, G. (1973) 'La hiéroménie des Pythia et les "trêves sacrées" d'Éleusis, de Delphes et d'Olympie' *BCH* 97: 75–106.

Santas, G.X. (1979) *Socrates: Philosophy in Plato's Early Dialogues*, London.

Schachter, A. (1981) *Cults of Boiotia* I: *Acheloos to Hera*, London.

Simms, R.M. (1990) '*Myesis, Telete,* and *Mysteria*' *GRBS* 31: 183–95.

Sokolowski, F. (1954) 'On Prothysia and Promanteia in Greek Cults' *HThR* 47: 165–71.

—— (1959) 'On the Rules Regulating the Celebration of the Eleusinian Mysteries' *HTR* 52: 1–4.

—— (1960) 'On the Episode of Onchestus in the Homeric Hymn to Apollo' *TAPhA* 91: 376–80.

—— (1973) 'On the New Pergamene *Lex Sacra*' *GRBS* 14: 407–13.

Sordi, M. (1984) 'Il Santuario di Olimpia e la Guerra d'Elide' in M. Sordi (ed.) *I Santuari e la Guerra nel Mondo Classico*, Milan: 20–30

Sourvinou-Inwood, C. (1988) *Studies in Girls' Transitions. Aspects of the Arkteia and Age Representation in Attic Iconography*, Athens.

—— (1990) 'What Is Polis Religion?' in O. Murray and S. Price (eds) *The Greek City from Homer to Alexander*, Oxford: 295–322.

—— (1995) *'Reading' Greek Death to the End of the Classical Period*, Oxford.

Stone, I.F. (1988) *The Trial of Socrates*, Boston.

Strauss, L. (1966) *Socrates and Aristophanes*, Chicago.

Symeonoglou, S. (1985) 'The Oracles of Thebes' in *La Béotie Antique: Lyon-St. Étienne 16–20 mai 1983 (Colloques Internationaux du Centre National de la Recherche Scientifique)*, Paris: 155–8.

Tarrant, H. (1988) 'Midwifery and the *Clouds*' *CQ* 38: 116–22.

Tomlinson, R.A. (1976) *Greek Sanctuaries*, London.

—— (1983) *Epidauros*, London.

Turner, J.A. (1988), 'Greek Priesthoods' in M. Grant and R. Kitzinger (eds) *Civilization of the Ancient Mediterranean: Greece and Rome*, New York: 925–31.

Tyrrell, W.B. (1984) *Amazons: A Study in Athenian Mythmaking*, Baltimore.

Van Straten, F.T. (1981) 'Gifts for the Gods' in H.S. Versnel (ed.) *Faith, Hope and Worship: Aspects of Religious Mentality in the Ancient World*, Leiden: 65–193.

Versnel, H.S. (1994) *Inconsistencies in Greek and Roman Religion II. Transition and Reversal in Myth and Ritual*, Leiden.

Vlastos, G. (1991) *Socrates. Ironist and Moral Philosopher*, Cambridge.

Walcot, P. (1978) *Envy and the Greeks: A Study of Human Behaviour*, Warminster.

Warner, R. (1958) *The Greek Philosophers*, New York.

Wasson, R.G., A. Hoffman and C.A.P. Ruck (1978) *The Road to Eleusis: Unveiling the Secret of Their Mysteries*, New York.

——, Kramrisch, S., J. Ott and C.A.P. Ruck (1986) *Persephone's Quest: Entheogens and the Origins of Religion*, New Haven.

Watkins, C. (1978) 'Let us Now Praise Famous Grains' *PAPhS* 122: 7–17.

West, M.L. (1978) *Hesiod: Works and Days*, Oxford.

Willetts, R.F. (1962) *Cretan Cults and Festivals*, London.

Winkler, J. (1990) *The Constraints of Desire: The Anthropology of Sex and Gender in Ancient Greece*, New York.

Woodbury, L. (1965) 'The Date and Atheism of Diagoras of Melos' *Phoenix* 19: 178–211.

Woodward, A.M. (1962) 'Athens and the Oracle of Ammon' *ABSA* 57: 5–13.

Woozley, A.D. (1971) 'Socrates on Disobeying the Law' in G. Vlastos (ed.) *The Philosophy of Socrates: A Collection of Critical Essays*, New York: 299–318.

Chapter 4 Women, sexuality, and the family

Introductory reading:

Blundell, S. (1995) *Women in Ancient Greece*, Cambridge MA.

Cantarella, E. (1987) *Pandora's Daughters: The Role and Status of Women in Greek and Roman Antiquity*, Baltimore.

Clark, G. (1989) *Women in the Ancient World*, Oxford.

Cohen, D. (1991) *Law, Sexuality, and Society: The Enforcement of Morals in Classical Athens*, Cambridge.

Demand, N. (1994) *Birth, Death and Motherhood in Classical Greece*, Baltimore.

Dillon, M.P.J. (2002) *Girls and Women in Classical Greek Religion*, London.

Dover, K.J. (1978) *Greek Homosexuality*, London.

Golden, M. (1990) *Children and Childhood in Classical Athens*, Baltimore.

Just, R. (1989) *Women in Athenian Life and Law*, London.

Pomeroy, S.B. (2002) *Spartan Women*, Oxford.

Andersen, O. (1987) 'The Widows, the City and Thucydides (II,45,2)' *SO* 62: 33–49.

Arthur, M.B. (1973) 'Origins of the Western Attitude towards Women' *Arethusa* 6: 7–58.

Bremmer, J.N. (1990) 'Adolescents, Symposion, and Pederasty' in O. Murray (ed.) *Sympotica. A Symposium on the Symposion*, Oxford: 135–48.

Brock, R. (1994) 'The Labour of Women in Classical Athens' *CQ* 44: 336–46.

Budin, S. (2008) *The Myth of Sacred Prostitution in Antiquity*, Cambridge.

Calame, C. (2001) *Choruses of Young Women in Ancient Greece*, Lanham, second edition.

Carey, C. (1995) 'Rape and Adultery in Athenian Law' *CQ* 45: 407–17.

Cartledge, P.A. (1981) 'The Politics of Spartan Pederasty' *PCPhS* 27: 17–36.

—— (1981) 'Spartan Wives: Liberation or Licence?' *CQ* 31: 84–105.

Clarke, W.M. (1978) 'Achilles and Patroclus in Love' *CQ* 106: 381–96.

Cohen, A. and J.B. Rutter (eds) (2007) *Constructions of Childhood in Ancient Greece and Italy*, Princeton.

Cohen, D. (1984) 'The Athenian Law of Adultery' *RIDA* 31: 147–65.

—— (1987) 'Law, Society and Homosexuality in Classical Athens' *P&P* 117: 3–21.

—— (1989) 'Seclusion, Separation, and the Status of Women in Classical Athens' *G&R* 36: 3–15 = I. McAuslan and P. Walcot (eds) (1996): 134–45.

—— (1990) 'The Social Context of Adultery at Athens' in *NOMOS*: 147–65.

—— (1993) 'Consent and Sexual Relations in Classical Athens' in A.E. Laiou (ed.) *Consent and Coercion to Sex and Marriage in Ancient and Medieval Societies*, Washington, D.C.: 5–16.

Cohn-Haft, L. (1995) 'Divorce in Classical Athens' *JHS* 115: 1–14.

Cole, S.G. (1984) 'Greek Sanctions against Sexual Assault' *CPh* 79: 97–113.

Connelly, J.B. (2008) *Portrait of a Priestess: Women and Ritual in Ancient Greece*, Princeton.

Cox, C.A. (1998) *Household Interests. Property, Marriage Strategies, and Family Dynamics in Ancient Athens*, Princeton.

Davies, J.K. (1977–78) 'Athenian Citizenship: The Descent Group and the Alternatives' *CJ* 73: 105–21.

De Quesne, T. (1989) *Sappho of Lesbos: The Poems*, Thame.

Des Bouvrie, S. (1990) *Women in Greek Tragedy*, Norwegian University Press (*SO* Suppl. 27).

Dewald, C. (1981) 'Women and Culture in Herodotus' Histories' in H.P. Foley (ed.) *Reflections of Women in Antiquity*, New York: 91–125.

Dillon, M.P.J. (1999) 'Post-Nuptial Sacrifices on Kos (Segre, *ED* 178) and Ancient Greek Marriage Rites' *ZPE* 124: 63–80.

—— (2003) 'Woe for Adonis – But in Spring, Not Summer' *Hermer* 131: 1–16.

—— (2012) 'Educating Sappho's Daughters. Girls' and Women's Literacy in Classical Greece' in T. Parkin and J. Evans-Grubbs (eds) *The Oxford Handbook of Childhood and Education in The Ancient World*, New York, forthcoming.

Dover, K.J. (1973) 'Classical Greek Attitudes to Sexual Behaviour' *Arethusa* 6: 59–73.

—— (1988) 'Greek Homosexuality and Initiation' in *The Greeks and Their Legacy*, Oxford: 115–34.

Dué, C. (2004) *The Captive Woman's Lament in Greek Tragedy*, Houston.

Dynes, W.R. and S. Donaldson (eds) (1992) *Homosexuality in the Ancient World I*, New York.

Edwards, M.L. (1998) 'Women and Physical Disability in Ancient Greece' *AncW* 29: 3–9.

Engels, D. (1980) 'The Problem of Female Infanticide in the Greco-Roman World' *CPh* 75: 112–20.

Fantham, E., H.P. Foley, N.B. Kampen, S.B. Pomeroy and H.A. Shapiro (eds) (1994) *Women in the Classical World: Image and Text*, Oxford.

Ferrari, G. (2002) *Figures of Speech: Men and Maidens in Ancient Greece*, Chicago.

—— (2008) *Alcman and the Cosmos of Sparta*, Chicago.

Foley, H.P. (1981) 'The Concept of Women in Athenian Drama' in H.P. Foley (ed.) *Reflections of Women in Antiquity*, New York: 127–68.

—— (2002) *Female Acts in Greek Tragedy*, Princeton.

Frontisi-Ducroux, F. (1996) 'Eros, Desire, and the Gaze' in N.B. Kampen (ed.) *Sexuality in Ancient Art: Near East, Egypt, Greece, and Italy*, Cambridge: 81–100.

Gardner, J.F. (1989) 'Aristophanes and Male Anxiety – the Defence of the Oikos' *G&R* 36: 51–62 = I. McAuslan and P. Walcot (eds) (1996): 146–57.

Garland, R.S.J. (1990) *The Greek Way of Life: From Conception to Old Age*, Ithaca.

Geddes, A. (1975) 'The Philosophic Notion of Women in Antiquity' *Antichthon* 9: 35–40.

Glazebrook, A. and M.M. Henry (eds) (2011) *Greek Prostitutes in the Ancient Mediterranean 800 BCE–200 CE*, Madison.

Goff, B. (2004) *Citizen Bacchae. Women's Ritual Practice in Ancient Greece*, Berkeley.

Golden, M. (1981) 'Demography and the Exposure of Girls at Athens' *Phoenix* 35: 316–31.

—— (1984) 'Slavery and Homosexuality at Athens' *Phoenix* 38: 308–24.

—— (1988) 'Did the Ancients Care When Their Children Died?' *G&R* 35: 152–63.

—— (1991) 'Thirteen Years of Homosexuality (and other recent works on Sex, Gender and the Body) in Ancient Greece' *EMC* 10: 327–40.

Goldhill, S. (1995) 'Representing Democracy: Women at the Great Dionysia' in R. Osborne and S. Hornblower (eds) *Ritual, Finance, Politics*, Oxford: 347–69.

Gomme, A.W. (1925) 'The Position of Women in Athens in the Fifth and Fourth Centuries BC' *CPh* 20: 1–25 = (1937) *Essays in Greek History and Literature* 89–115.

Gould, J. (1980) 'Law, Custom and Myth: Aspects of the Social Position of Women in Classical Athens' *JHS* 100: 38–59.

Greene, E. (2005) *Women Poets in Ancient Greece and Rome*, Norman.

Harris, E.M. (1990) 'Did the Athenians Regard Seduction as a Worse Crime than Rape?' *CQ* 40: 370–7.

Harris, W.V. (1982) 'The Theoretical Possibility of Extensive Infanticide in the Graeco-Roman World' *CQ* 32: 114–16.

Harvey, D. (1985) 'Women in Thucydides' *Arethusa* 18: 67–90.

Henderson, J. (1980) 'Lysistrate: The Play and Its Themes' in J. Henderson (ed.) *Aristophanes: Essays in Interpretation*, *YClS* 26: 153–218.

—— (1991) *The Maculate Muse. Obscene Language in Attic Comedy*, Oxford, second edition.

—— (1991) 'Women and the Athenian Dramatic Festivals' *TAPhA* 121: 133–47.

Henry, M.M. (1995) *Prisoner of History. Aspasia of Miletus and her Biographical Tradition*, Oxford.

Hubbard, T.K. (2003) *Homosexuality in Greece and Rome: A Sourcebook of Basic Documents*, Berkeley.

Hunter, R. (ed.) (2005) *The Hesiodic Catalogue of Women. Constructions and Reconstructions*, Cambridge.

Huys, M. (1996) 'The Spartan Practice of Selective Infanticide and Its Parallels in Ancient Utopian Tradition' *AncSoc* 27: 47–74.

Katz, M.A. (1994) 'The Character of Tragedy: Women and the Greek Imagination' *Arethusa* 27: 81–103.

—— (1995) 'Ideology and "the Status of Women" in Ancient Greece' in R. Hawley and B. Levick (eds) *Women in Antiquity. New Assessments*, London: 22–43.

Keuls, E.C. (1993) *The Reign of the Phallus: Sexual Politics in Ancient Athens*, Berkeley, second edition.

Kilmer, M.F. (1993) *Greek Erotica on Attic Red-Figure Vases*, London.

King, H. (1998) *Hippocrates' Woman: Reading the Female Body in Ancient Greece*, London.

Klinck, A.L. (2008) *Women's Songs in Ancient Greece*, Montreal.

Kunstler, B. (1987) 'Family Dynamics and Female Power in Ancient Sparta' in M. Skinner (ed.) *Rescuing Creusa: New Methodological Approaches to Women in Antiquity*: 31–48 (= *Helios* n.s. 13), Texas University Press.

Kurke, L. (1995) 'Pindar and the Prostitutes, or Reading Ancient "Pornography"' *Arion* 4: 49–75.

—— 'Inventing the Hetaira: Sex, Politics, and Discursive Conflict in Archaic Greece' *ClAnt* 16: 106–50.

Lacey, W.K. (1964) 'Thucydides II, 45, 2' *PCPhS* 10: 47–9.

—— (1968) *The Family in Classical Greece*, London.

Lardinois, A.P.M.H. and L. McClure (eds) (2001) *Making Silence Speak: Women's Voices in Greek Literature and Society*, Princeton.

Leader, R.E. (1997) 'In Death not Divided: Gender, Family, and State on Classical Athenian Grave Stelae' *AJA* 101: 683–99.

Lear, A. and E. Cantarella (2009) *Images of Ancient Greek Pederasty: Boys Were Their Gods*, London.

Lefkowitz, M.R. (1983) 'Wives and Husbands' *G&R* 30: 31–47 = I. McAuslan and P. Walcot (eds) (1996): 67–82.

—— (2007) *Women in Greek Myth*, Baltimore, second edition.

—— and Fant, M.B. (1992) *Women's Life in Greece and Rome*, Baltimore, second edition.

Lewis, S. (2002) *The Athenian Woman: An Iconographic Handbook*, London.

Llewellyn-Jones, L. (2003) *Aphrodite's Tortoise: The Veiled Woman of Ancient Greece*, Swansea.

Lloyd-Jones, H. (1975) *Females of the Species: Semonides on Women*, London.

Loraux, N. (1993) *The Children of Athena. Athenian Ideas about Citizenship and the Division between the Sexes*, tr. C. Levine, Princeton, N.J.

McAuslan, I. and P. Walcot (eds) (1996) *Women in Antiquity*, Oxford.

MacDowell, D.M. (1976) 'Bastards as Athenian Citizens' *CQ* 26: 88–91.

—— (1978) *The Law in Classical Athens*, London.

—— (1989) 'The Oikos in Athenian Law' *CQ* 39: 10–21.

Mertens, J.R. (2011) *How to Read Greek Vases*, New York.

Munson, R.V. (1988) 'Artemisia in Herodotos' *ClAnt* 7: 91–106.

Neils, J., J.H. Oakley and L.A. Beaumont (2003) *Coming of Age in Ancient Greece: Images of Childhood from the Classical Past*, Hanover, N.H.

Nevett, L.C. (1995) 'Gender Relations in the Classical Greek Household: The Archaeological Evidence' *ABSA* 90: 363–81.

—— (2001) *House and Society in the Ancient Greek World*, Cambridge.

Newmyer, S.T. (2010) *Animals in Greek and Roman Thought: A Sourcebook*, London.

Nielsen, T.H., L. Bjerstrup, M.H. Hansen, L. Rubinstein and T. Vestergard (1989) 'Athenian Grave Monuments and Social Class' *GRBS* 30: 411–20.

O'Higgins, L. (2003) *Women and Humor in Classical Greece*, Cambridge.

Page, D. (1955) *Sappho and Alcaeus: An Introduction to the Study of Ancient Lesbian Poetry*, Oxford.

Parker, H.N. (1993) 'Sappho Schoolmistress' *TAPhA* 123: 309–51.

Patterson, C.B. (1981) *Perikles' Citizenship Law of 451/50 B.C.*, New York.

—— (1985) '"Not Worth the Rearing": The Causes of Infant Exposure in Ancient Greece' *TAPhA* 115: 103–23.

—— (1987) 'Hai Attikai: The Other Athenians' in M. Skinner (ed.) *Rescuing Creusa: New Methodological Approaches to Women in Antiquity*, Lubbock: 49–67.

—— (1990) 'Those Athenian Bastards' *ClAnt* 9: 40–73.

—— (1991) 'Marriage and the Married Woman in Athenian Law' in S.B. Pomeroy (ed.) *Women's History and Ancient History*, Chapel Hill: 48–72.

Percy, W.A. (1996) *Pederasty and Pedagogy in Archaic Greece*, Urbana.

Plant, I.A. (2004) *Women Writers of Greece and Rome*, Norman.

Podlecki, A.J. (1990) 'Could Women Attend the Theater in Ancient Athens? A Collection of Testimonia' *AncW* 21: 27–43.

Pomeroy, S.B. (1974) 'Feminism in Book V of Plato's Republic' *Apeiron* 8: 33–5.

—— (1975) *Goddesses, Whores, Wives and Slaves*, New York.

—— (1982) 'Charities for Greek Women' *Mnemosyne* 35: 115–35.

—— (1994) *Xenophon's Oeconomicus. A Social and Historical Commentary*, Oxford.

—— (1995) 'Women's Identity and the Family in the Classical Polis' in R. Hawley and B. Levick (eds) *Women in Antiquity. New Assessments*, London: 111–21.

—— (1997) *Families in Classical and Hellenistic Greece. Representations and Realities*, Oxford.

Redfield, J. (1977–78) 'The Women of Sparta' *CJ* 73: 146–61.

Reese, A. and I. Vallera-Rickerson (2003) *Athletries: The Untold History of Ancient Greek Women Athletes*, Costa Mesa.

Richter, D.C. (1971) 'The Position of Women in Classical Athens' *CJ* 67: 1–8.

Rouselle, A. (1988) *Porneia: On Desire and the Body in Antiquity*, Oxford.

Roy, J. (1997) 'An Alternative Sexual Morality for Classical Athenians' *G&R* 44: 11–22.

Scanlon, T.F. (1988) 'Virgineum Gymnasium: Spartan Females and Early Greek Athletics' in W.J. Raschke (ed.) *The Archaeology of the Olympics: The Olympics and Other Festivals in Antiquity*, Madison: 185–216.

—— (2002) *Eros and Greek Athletics*, Oxford.

Schaps, D. (1975) 'Women in Greek Inheritance Law' *CQ* 25: 53–7.

—— (1977) 'The Women Least Mentioned' *CQ* 27: 323–30.

—— (1979) *Economic Rights of Women in Ancient Greece*, Edinburgh.

—— (1982) 'The Women of Greece in Wartime' *CPh* 77: 193–213.

Scheidel, W. (1995) 'The Most Silent Women of Greece and Rome: Rural Labour and Women's Life in the Ancient World, I' *G&R* 42: 202–17.

—— (1996) 'The Most Silent Women of Greece and Rome: Rural Labour and Women's Life in the Ancient World, II' *G&R* 43: 1–10.

Seaford, R. (1990) 'The Imprisonment of Women in Greek Tragedy' *JHS* 110: 76–90.

Sealey, R. (1984) 'On Lawful Concubinage in Athens' *ClAnt* 3: 111–33.

—— (1990) *Women and Law in Classical Greece*, Chapel Hill.

Seltman, C. (1955) 'The Status of Women in Athens' *G&R* 2: 119–24.

—— (1957) *Women in Antiquity*, London.

Shapiro, H.A. (1992) 'Eros in Love: Pederasty and Pornography in Greece' in A. Richlin (ed.) *Pornography and Representation in Greece and Rome*, Oxford: 53–72.

Shaw, M. (1975) 'The Female Intruder: Women in Fifth Century Drama' *CPh* 70: 255–68.

Snyder, J.M. (1989) *The Woman and the Lyre: Women Writers in Classical Greece and Rome*, Carbondale.

—— (1991) 'Public Occasion and Private Passion in the Lyrics of Sappho of Lesbos' in S.B. Pomeroy (ed.) *Women's History and Ancient History*, Chapel Hill: 1–19.

—— (1997) *Lesbian Desire in the Lyrics of Sappho*, New York.

Stewart, A. (1997) *Art, Desire, and the Body in Ancient Greece*, Cambridge.

Stigers, E.S. (1981) 'Sappho's Private World' in H.P. Foley (ed.) *Reflections of Women in Antiquity*, New York: 45–61.

Strauss, B.S. (1990) 'Oikos/Polis: Towards a Theory of Athenian Paternal Ideology 450–399 B.C.' in W.R. Connor, M.H. Hansen, K.A. Raaflaub and B.S. Strauss (eds) *Aspects of Athenian Democracy (Classica et Mediaevalia. Dissertationes XI)*, Copenhagen: 101–27.

Sussman, L.S. (1984) 'Workers and Crones: Labor, Idleness and Gender Definition in Hesiod's Beehive' in J. Peradotto and J.P. Sullivan (eds) *Women in the Ancient World: The Arethusa Papers*, Albany: 79–93.

Sutton, R.F., Jr. (1992) 'Pornography and Persuasion on Attic Pottery' in A. Richlin (ed.) *Pornography and Representation in Greece and Rome*, Oxford: 3–35.

Svenbro, J. (1993) *Phrasikleia: An Anthropology of Reading in Ancient Greece*, tr. J. Lloyd, Ithaca.

Taaffe, L.K. (1993) *Aristophanes and Women*, London.

Thompson, W.E. (1967) 'The Marriage of First Cousins in Athenian Society' *Phoenix* 21: 273–82.

—— (1972) 'Athenian Marriage Patterns: Remarriage' *ClAnt* 5: 211–25.

Thornton, B.S. (1997) *Eros. The Myth of Ancient Greek Sexuality*, Boulder and Oxford.

Venit, S.M. (1988) 'The Caput Hydria and Working Women in Classical Athens' *CW* 81: 265–72.

Walcot, P. (1984) 'Greek Attitudes Towards Women: The Mythological Evidence' *G&R* 31: 37–47 = I. McAuslan and P. Walcot (eds) (1996): 91–102.

Walker, S. (1983) 'Women and Housing in Classical Greece: The Archaeological Evidence' in A. Cameron and A. Kurht (eds) *Images of Women in Antiquity*, London: 81–91.

Webster, T.B.L. (1969) *Everyday Life in Classical Athens*, London.

—— (1973) *Athenian Culture and Society*, Berkeley.

Wender, D. (1973) 'Plato: Misogynist, Paedophile, and Feminist' *Arethusa* 6: 75–90.

Williams, D. (1983) 'Women on Athenian Vases: Problems of Interpretation' in A. Cameron and A. Kurht (eds) *Images of Women in Antiquity*, London: 92–106.

Williams, C.K. (1986) 'Corinth and the Cult of Aphrodite', in M.A. del Chiaro (ed.), *Corinthiaca. Studies in Honor of D.A. Amyx*, Columbia: 12–24.

Winkler, J. (1981) 'Gardens of Nymphs: Public and Private in Sappho's Lyrics' in H.P. Foley (ed.) *Reflections of Women in Antiquity*, New York: 63–89.

—— (1990) *The Constraints of Desire: The Anthropology of Sex and Gender in Ancient Greece*, London.

—— (1990) 'Laying Down the Law: The Oversight of Men's Sexual Behavior in Classical Athens' in D.M. Halperin, J. Winkler, and F. Zeitlin (eds), *The Construction of Erotic Experience in the Ancient Greek World*, Princeton: 171–209.

Zeitlin, F.I. (1981) 'Travesties of Gender and Genre in Aristophanes' Thesmophoriazousae' in H.P. Foley (ed.) *Reflections of Women in Antiquity*, New York: 169–217.

—— (1995) 'Signifying Difference: The Myth of Pandora' in R. Hawley and B. Levick (eds) *Women in Antiquity. New Assessments*, London: 58–74.

—— (1996) *Playing the Other. Gender and Society in Classical Greek Literature*, Chicago.

Chapter 5 Labour: slaves, serfs and citizens

Introductory reading:

Finley, M.I. (1980) *Ancient Slavery and Modern Ideology*, Harmondsworth.

—— (1981) *Economy and Society in Ancient Greece*, London.

Fisher, N.R.E. (1993) *Slavery in Classical Greece*, London.

Garlan, Y. (1988) *Slavery in Ancient Greece*, Ithaca.

Garnsey, P. (1996) *Ideas of Slavery from Aristotle to Augustine*, Cambridge.

McKeown, N. (2007) *The Invention of Ancient Slavery*, London.

Thompson, F.H. (2003) *The Archaeology of Greek and Roman Slavery*, London.

Whitehead, D. (1977) *The Ideology of the Athenian Metic*, Cambridge.

Wiedemann, T.E.J. (1987) *Slavery*, Oxford.

Wood, E.M. (1988) *Peasant-Citizen and Slave: The Foundations of Athenian Democracy*, London.

Andrewes, A. (1971) *Greek Society*, Harmondsworth.

Austin, M.M. and P. Vidal-Nacquet (1977) *Economic and Social History of Ancient Greece: An Introduction*, Berkeley.

Balme, M. (1984) 'Attitudes to Work and Leisure in Ancient Greece' *G&R* 31: 140–52.

Beringer, W. (1982) '"Servile Status" in the Sources for Early Greek History' *Historia* 31: 13–32.

Bicknell, P.J. (1968) 'Demosthenes 24, 197 and the Domestic Slaves of Athens' *Mnemosyne* 21: 74.

Bradley, K. and P. Cartledge (2011) *The Cambridge World History of Slavery. Vol. 1: The Ancient Mediterranean World*, Cambridge.

Carey, C. (1991) 'Apollodoros' Mother: The Wives of Enfranchised Aliens in Athens' *CQ* 41: 84–9.

Cartledge, P. (1976) 'Did Spartan Citizens Ever Practise a Manual Techne?' *LCM* 1: 115–19.

—— (1993) 'Like a Worm i' the Bud? A Heterology of Classical Greek Slavery' *G&R* 40: 163–80.

Christensen, K.A. (1984) 'The Theseion: A Slave Refuge at Athens' *AJAH* 9: 23–32.

Cooper, A.B. (1996) '"Deconstructing Gortyn": When Is a Code a Code?' in L. Foxhall and A.D.E. Lewis (eds) *Greek Law in Its Political Setting: Justifications not Justice*, Oxford: 33–56.

De Souza, P. (1995) 'Greek Piracy' in A. Powell (ed.) *The Greek World*, London: 179–98.

De Ste Croix, G.E.M. (1981) *The Class Struggle in the Ancient World*, London.

Demand, N.H. (2011) *The Mediterranean Context of Early Greek History*, Bloomington.

DuBois, P. (2003) *Slaves and Other Objects*, Chicago.

Dué, C. (2004) *The Captive Woman's Lament in Greek Tragedy*, Houston.

Duncan-Jones, R.P. (1980) 'Metic Numbers in Periclean Athens' *Chiron* 10: 101–9.

Finley, M.I. (1959) 'Was Greek Civilization Based on Slave Labour?' *Historia* 8: 145–64.

—— (ed.) (1960) *Slavery in Classical Athens*, Cambridge.

—— (1962) 'The Black Sea and Danubian Regions and Slave Trade in Antiquity' *Klio* 40: 51–9.

Fisher, N.R.E. (1995) 'Hybris, Status and Slavery' in A. Powell (ed.) *The Greek World*, London: 44–84.

Gagarin, M. (1995) 'The First Law of the Gortyn Code Revisited' *GRBS* 36: 7–15.

—— (1996) 'The Torture of Slaves in Athenian Law' *CPh* 91: 1–18.

Garlan, Y. (1980) 'Le travail libre en Grèce ancienne' in P. Garnsey (ed.) *Non-Slave Labour in the Greco-Roman World*, Cambridge: 6–22.

Golden, M. (1984) 'Slavery and Homosexuality at Athens' *Phoenix* 38: 308–24.

Hanson, V.D. (1992) 'Thucydides and the Desertion of Attic Slaves during the Decelean War' *ClAnt* 11: 210–28.

Hunt, P. (1998) *Slaves, Warfare, and Ideology in the Greek Historians*, Cambridge.

Isager, S. and M.H. Hansen (1975) *Aspects of Athenian Society in the Fourth Century B.C.*, tr. J.H. Rosenmeier, Odense.

Jameson, M.H. (1977–78) 'Agriculture and Slavery in Classical Athens' *CJ* 73: 122–45.

Johnstone, S. (1994) 'Virtuous Toil, Vicious Work: Xenophon on Aristocratic Style' *CPh* 89: 219–40.

Jordan, B. (1990) 'The Ceremony of the Helots in Thucydides, IV, 80' *AC* 59: 37–69.

Kagan, D. (1963) 'The Enfranchisement of Aliens by Cleisthenes' *Historia* 12: 41–6.

Lavelle, B.M. (1992) 'Herodotos, Skythian Archers, and the doryphoroi of the Peisistratids' *Klio* 74: 78–97.

Mirhady, D.C. (1996) 'Torture and Rhetoric in Athens' *JHS* 116: 119–31.

Nussbaum, G. (1960) 'Labour and Status in the Works and Days' *CQ* 10: 213–20.

Osborne, R. (1995) 'The Economics and Politics of Slavery at Athens' in A. Powell (ed.) *The Greek World*, London: 27–43.

Pomeroy, S.B. (1994) *Xenophon's Oeconomicus. A Social and Historical Commentary*, Oxford.

Randall, R.H. (1953) 'The Erechtheum Workmen' *AJA* 57: 199–210.

Rihll, T. (1993) 'War, Slavery and Settlement in Early Greece' in J. Rich and G. Shipley (eds) *War and Society in the Greek World*, London: 77–107.

Sargent, R.L. (1927) 'The Use of Slaves by the Athenians in Warfare' *CPh* 22: 201–12, 264–79.

Seaman, M.G. (1997) 'The Athenian Expedition to Melos in 416 B.C.' *Historia* 46: 385–418.

Vogt, J. (1975) *Ancient Slavery and the Ideal of Man*, tr. T. Wiedemann, Cambridge.

Welskopf, E.C. (1980) 'Free Labour in the City of Athens' in P. Garnsey (ed.) *Non-Slave Labour in the Greco-Roman World, Cambridge Philological Society* Suppl. 6, Cambridge: 23–5.

Westermann, W.L. (1955) *Slave Systems of Greek and Roman Antiquity*, Philadelphia.

Whitehead, D. (1984) 'A Thousand New Athenians: IG II².10+' *LCM* 9: 8–10.

Wood, E.M. (1983) 'Agricultural Slavery in Classical Athens' *AJAH* 8: 1–47.

Zelnick-Abramovitz, R. (2005) *Not Wholly Free: The Concept of Manumission and the Status of Manumitted Slaves in the Ancient Greek World*, Leiden.

Chapter 6 Sparta

Introductory reading:

Cartledge, P. (1979) *Sparta and Lakonia; a Regional History 1300–362 BC*, London.

—— (2004) *The Spartans: The World of the Warrior-Heroes of Ancient Greece: from Utopia to Crisis and Collapse*, New York.

Fitzhardinge, L.F. (1980) *The Spartans*, London.

Jones, A.H.M. (1967) *Sparta*, Oxford.

Kennel, N.M. (2010) *Spartans: A New History*, New York.

Lazenby, J.F. (1985) *The Spartan Army*, Warminster.

Lewis, D.M. (1977) *Sparta and Persia*, Leiden.

Powell, A. (ed.) (1989) *Classical Sparta: Techniques Behind Her Success*, London.

——. and S. Hodkinson (eds) (1994) *The Shadow of Sparta*, London.

Rusch, S. (2011) *Sparta at War: Strategy, Tactics and Campaigns 950–362 BC*, Barnsley.

Whitby, M. (ed.) (2001) *Sparta*, Edinburgh.

Allison, J.W. (1984) 'Sthenelaidas' Speech: Thucydides 1.86' *Hermes* 112: 9–16.

Anderson, J.K. (1970) *Military Theory and Practice in the Age of Xenophon*, Berkeley.

Andrewes, A. (1978) 'Spartan Imperialism' in P.D.A. Garnsey and C.R. Whittaker (eds) *Imperialism in the Ancient World*, Cambridge: 91–102.

Bloedow, E.F. (1987) 'Sthenelaidas the Persuasive Spartan' *Hermes* 115: 60–66.

Boring, T.A. (1979) *Literacy in Ancient Sparta*, Leiden.

Bradford, A.S. (1994) 'The Duplicitous Spartan' in A. Powell and S. Hodkinson (eds) *The Shadow of Sparta*, London: 59–85.

Butler, D. (1962) 'Competence of the Demos in the Spartan Rhetra' *Historia* 11: 385–96.

Cartledge, P. (1976) 'A New 5th-Century Spartan Treaty' *LCM* 1: 87–92.

—— (1977) 'Hoplites and Heroes: Sparta's Contribution to the Technique of Ancient Warfare' *JHS* 97: 11–27.

—— (1978) 'Literacy in the Spartan Oligarchy' *JHS* 98: 25–37.

—— (1981) 'Spartan Wives: Liberation or Licence?' *CQ* 31: 84–105.

—— (1987) *Agesilaos and the Crisis of Sparta*, London.

—— (2003) *Spartan Reflections*, Berkeley.

Cawkwell, G.L. (1983) 'The Decline of Sparta' *CQ* 33: 385–400.

—— (1989) 'Orthodoxy and Hoplites' *CQ* 39: 375–89.

(1993) 'Cleomenes' *Mnemosyne* 46: 506–27.

Christesen, P. (2006) 'Xenophon's "Cyropaedia" and Military Reform in Sparta' *JHS* 126: 47–65.

Connor, W.R. (1988) 'Early Greek Land Warfare as Symbolic Expression' *P&P* 119: 3–29.

David, E. (1984) 'The Trial of Spartan Kings' *RIDA* 32: 131–40.

—— (1989) 'Dress in Spartan Society' *AncW* 19: 3–13.

—— (1989) 'Laughter in Spartan Society' in *Classical Sparta*: 1–25.

—— (1991) *Old Age in Sparta*, Amsterdam.

—— (1992) 'Sparta's Social Hair' *Eranos* 90: 11–21.

—— (1993) 'Hunting in Spartan Society and Consciousness' *EMC* 12: 393–413.

De Ste Croix, G.E.M. (1972) *The Origins of the Peloponnesian War*, London.

Dillon, M.P.J. (1995) 'The Lakedaimonian Dedication to Olympian Zeus: The Date of *Meiggs & Lewis* 22 (*SEG* 11, 123A)' *ZPE* 107: 60–8.

—— (2007) 'Were Spartan Women who Died in Childbirth Honoured with Grave Inscriptions? Whether to Read *Hieron* or *Lechous* at Plutarch *Lykourgos* 27.3' *Hermes* 135: 149–65.

Ducrey, P. (1986) *Warfare in Ancient Greece*, New York.

Figueira, T.J. (1984) 'Mess Contributions and Subsistence at Sparta' *TAPhA* 114: 87–109.

(1986) 'Population Patterns in Late Archaic and Classical Sparta' *TAPhA* 116: 165–213. Finley, M.I. (1975) 'Sparta' in *The Use and Abuse of History*, London: 161–77 = (1968) in P. Vernant (ed.) *Problèmes de la guerre en Grèce ancienne*, Paris: 143–60.

Fornara, C.W. (1966) 'Some Aspects of the Career of Pausanias of Sparta' *Historia* 15: 257–71.

Fornis, C. and J. Casillas (1997) 'An Appreciation of the Social Function of the Spartan *Syssitia*' *AHB* 11: 37–46.

Forrest, W.G. (1963) 'The Date of the Lykourgan Reforms in Sparta' *Phoenix* 17: 157–79.

—— (1980) *A History of Sparta*, London, second edition.

French, V. (1997) 'The Spartan Family and the Spartan Decline: Changes in Child-Rearing Practices and Failure to Reform' in C.D. Hamilton and P. Krentz (eds) *Polis and Polemos*, Claremont: 241–74.

Gerber, D.E. (1997) 'Elegy' in D.E. Gerber (ed.) *A Companion to the Greek Lyric Poets*, Leiden: 89–132.

Griffiths, A. (1989) 'Was Kleomenes Mad?' in *Classical Sparta*: 51–78.

Hammond, N.G.L. (1950) 'The Lycurgean Reform at Sparta' *JHS* 70: 42–64.

—— (1982) 'The Peloponnese' in *CAH* III.3²: 321–59.

—— (1992) 'Plataea's Relations with Thebes, Sparta and Athens' *JHS* 112: 143–50.

Hansen, O. (1990) 'The Date of the Archaic Dedication of the Lacedaemonians to Olympian Zeus' *Kadmos* 29: 170.

Harvey, D. (1994) 'Lacomica: Aristophanes and the Spartans' in A. Powell and S. Hodkinson (eds) *The Shadow of Sparta*, London: 35–58.

Hodkinson, S. (1983) 'Social Order and the Conflict of Values in Classical Sparta' *Chiron* 13: 239–81.

—— (1986) 'Land Tenure and Inheritance in Classical Sparta' *CQ* 36: 378–406.

—— (1989) 'Inheritance, Marriage and Demography: Perspectives upon the Success and Decline of Classical Sparta' in *Classical Sparta*: 79–121.

—— (1993) 'Warfare, Wealth, and the Crisis of Spartiate Society' in J. Rich and G. Shipley (eds) *War and Society in the Greek World*, London: 146–76.

—— (2009) *Sparta: Comparative Approaches*, Swansea

—— and A. Powell (eds) (2003) *Sparta Beyond the Mirage*, London.

—— and A. Powell (eds) (2009) *Sparta: New Perspectives*, London.

—— and A. Powell (eds) (2010) *Sparta: The Body Politic*, Swansea.

Holladay, A.J. (1977) 'Spartan Austerity' *CQ* 27: 111–26.

Hooker, J.T. (1980) *The Ancient Spartans*, London.

Hunt, P. (1997) 'Helots at the Battle of Plataea' *Historia* 46: 129–44.

Huxley, G. (1962) *Early Sparta*, London.

Jameson, M.H. (1991) 'Sacrifice before Battle' in V.D. Hanson (ed.) *Hoplites: The Classical Greek Battle Experience*, London: 197–227.

Jeffery, L.H. (1988) 'Greece before the Persian Invasion' in *CAH* IV²: 347–67.

Kelly, T. (1985) 'The Spartan Scytale' in J.W. Eadie and J. Ober (eds) *The Craft of the Ancient Historian. Essays in Honor of Chester G. Starr*, Lanham: 141–69.

Kennell, N.M. (2004) *The Gymnasium of Virtue: Education and Culture in Ancient Sparta*, Chapel Hill.

Koiv, M. (2005) 'The Origins, Development and Reliability of the Ancient Tradition about the Formation of the Spartan Constitution' *Historia* 54: 233–64.

Larsen, J.A.O. (1932) 'Sparta and the Ionian Revolt: A Study of Spartan Foreign Policy and the Genesis of the Peloponnesian League' *CPh* 27: 136–50.

—— (1933) 'The Constitution of the Peloponnesian League' *CPh* 28: 257–76.

—— (1934) 'The Constitution of the Peloponnesian League, II' *CPh* 29: 1–19.

Lendon, J.E. (1997) 'Spartan Honor' in C.D. Hamilton and P. Krentz (eds) *Polis and Polemos*, Claremont: 105–26.

Lewis, D.M. (1992) 'Mainland Greece, 479–451 B.C.' in *CAH* V²: 96–120.

Luraghi, N. and S. Alcock (2004) *Helots and Their Masters in Laconia and Messenia: Histories, Ideologies, Structures*, Cambridge, Mass.

MacDowell, D.M. (1986) *Spartan Law*, Edinburgh.

Miller, D.A. (1998) 'The Spartan Kingship: Some Extended Notes on Complex Duality' *Arethusa* 31: 1–17.

Mitchell, H. (1952) *Sparta*, Cambridge.

Parker, R. (1988) 'Were Spartan Kings Heroized?' *LCM* 13.1: 9–10.

—— (1989) 'Spartan Religion' in *Classical Sparta*: 142–72.

Parker, V. (1991) 'The Dates of the Messenian Wars' *Chiron* 21: 25–47.

—— (1993) 'Some Dates in Early Spartan History' *Klio* 75: 45–60.

Powell, A. (1989) 'Mendacity and Sparta's Use of the Visual' in *Classical Sparta*: 173–92.

—— (2001) *Athens and Sparta: Constructing Greek Social and Political History from 478BC*, London.

Proietti, G. (1987) *Xenophon's Sparta: An Introduction*, Leiden.

Redfield, J. (1977–78) 'The Women of Sparta' *CJ* 73: 146–61.

Ridley, R.T. (1974) 'The Economic Activities of the Perioikoi' *Mnemosyne* 27: 281–92.

Scanlon, T.F. (1988) '*Virgineum Gymnasium*: Spartan Females and Early Greek Athletics' in W.J. Raschke (ed.) *The Archaeology of the Olympics: The Olympics and Other Festivals in Antiquity*, Madison: 185–216.

Schütrumpf, E. (1994) 'Aristotle on Sparta' in A. Powell and S. Hodkinson (eds) *The Shadow of Sparta*, London: 323–45.

Snodgrass, A.M. (1964) *Early Greek Armour and Weapons from the End of the Bronze Age to 600 B.C.*, Edinburgh.

—— (1965) 'The Hoplite Reform and History' *JHS* 85: 110–22.

—— (1967) *Arms and Armour of the Greeks*, London.

Talbert, R.J.A. (1989) 'The Role of the Helots in the Class Struggle at Sparta' *Historia* 38: 22–40.

Thomas, C.G. (1974) 'On the Role of the Spartan Kings' *Historia* 23: 257–70.

Wheeler, E.L. (1982) '*Hoplomachia* and Greek Dances in Arms' *GRBS* 23: 223–33.

Whitby, M. (1994) 'Two Shadows: Images of Spartans and Helots' in A. Powell and S. Hodkinson (eds) *The Shadow of Sparta*, London: 87–126.

Yates, D.C. (2005) 'The Archaic Treaties between the Spartans and Their Allies' *CQ* 55: 65–76.

Chapter 7 Tyrants and tyranny

Introductory reading:

Andrewes, A. (1956) *The Greek Tyrants*, London.

Austin, M.M. (1990) 'Greek Tyrants and the Persians, 546–479 B.C.' *CQ* 40: 289–306.

Caven, B. (1990) *Dionysius I: Warlord of Sicily*, New Haven.

Cawkwell, G.L. (1995) 'Early Greek Tyranny and the People' *CQ* 45: 73–86.

Drews, R. (1972) 'The First Tyrants in Greece' *Historia* 21: 127–44.

Lewis, S. (2009) *Greek Tyranny*, Bristol.

McGlew, J. (1993) *Tyranny and Political Culture in Ancient Greece*, New York.

Starr, C.G. (1977) *The Economic and Social Growth of Early Greece*, New York.

Andrewes, A. (1949) 'The Corinthian Actaeon and Pheidon of Argos' *CQ* 43: 70–8.

Asheri, D. (1988) 'Carthaginians and Greeks' in *CAH* IV²: 739–80.

—— (1992) 'Sicily, 478–431 B.C.' in *CAH* V2: 147–70.

Barron, J.P. (1964) 'The Sixth-Century Tyranny at Samos' *CQ* 14: 210–29.

—— (1969) 'Ibycus: *To Polycrates*' *BICS* 16: 119–49.

Berger, S. (1992) *Revolution and Society in Greek Sicily and Southern Italy*, Historia Einzelschrift 71, Stuttgart.

Berve, H. (1967) *Die Tyrannis bei den Griechen* I–II, Munich.

Billigmeier J.-C. and A.S. Dusing (1981) 'The Origin and Function of the *Naukraroi* at Athens: An Etymological and Historical Explanation' *TAPhA* 111: 11–16.

Boardman, J. (1982) 'The Material Culture of Archaic Greece' in *CAH* III.3²: 442–62.

Bowen, A. (1992) *Plutarch: The Malice of Herodotus*, Warminster.

Burnett, A.P. (1983) *Three Archaic Poets: Archilochus, Alcaeus, Sappho*, London.

Campbell, D.A. (1982–91) *Greek Lyric* I–III, London.

Champion, J. (2010) *Tyrants of Syracuse: War in Ancient Sicily, 480–367 BC*, Barnsley.

Cook, J.M. (1982) 'The Eastern Greeks' in *CAH* III.3²: 196–221.

De Ste Croix, G.E.M. (1981) *The Class Struggle in the Ancient World*, London.

Demand, N.H. (1990) *Urban Relocation in Archaic and Classical Greece: Flight and Consolidation*, Norman.

Drijvers, J.W. (1992) 'Strabo VIII 2,1 (C335): PORTHMEIA and the *Diolkos*' *Mnemosyne* 45: 75–8.

Dunbabin, T.J. (1948) *The Western Greeks: The History of Sicily and South Italy from the Foundation of the Greek Colonies to 480 B.C.*, Oxford.

Ferrill, A. (1978) 'Herodotus on Tyranny' *Historia* 27: 385–98.

Figueira, T.J. (1985) 'A Chronological Table of Archaic Megara, 800–500 BC' in T.J. Figueira and G. Nagy (eds), *Theognis of Megara. Poetry and the Polis*, Baltimore: 261–303.

Finley, M.I. (1979) *Ancient Sicily*, London.

Fisher, N.R.E. (1992) *Hybris: A Study in the Values of Honour and Shame in Ancient Greece*, Warminster.

Fol, A. and N.G.L. Hammond (1988) 'Persia in Europe, apart from Greece' in *CAH* IV²: 234–53.

Gerber, D.E. (1997) 'Elegy' in D.E. Gerber (ed.) *A Companion to the Greek Lyric Poets*, Leiden: 89–132.

Graf, D. (1985) 'Greek Tyrants and Achaemenid Politics' in J.W. Eadie and J. Ober (eds) *The Craft of the Ancient Historian. Essays in Honor of Chester G. Starr*, Lanham: 79–123.

Graham, A.J. (1982) 'The Western Greeks' in *CAH* III.32: 163–95.

Gray, V.J. (1996) 'Herodotus and Images of Tyranny: The Tyrants of Corinth' *AJPh* 117: 361–89.

Griffin, A. (1982) *Sikyon*, Oxford.

Hammond, N.G.L. (1956) 'The Family of Orthagoras' *CQ* 6: 45–53.

—— (1982) 'The Peloponnese' in *CAH* III.32: 321–59.

Herington, C.J. (1967) 'Aeschylus in Sicily' *JHS* 87: 74–85.

Hershbell, J.P. (1993) 'Plutarch and Herodotus – The Beetle in the Rose' *RhM* 136: 143–63.

Hornblower, S. (1992) 'The Religious Dimension to the Peloponnesian War, or, What Thucydides does not tell us' *HSPh* 94: 169–97.

Huxley, G. (1958) 'Argos et les derniers Téménides' *BCH* 82: 588–601.

—— (1962) *Early Sparta*, London.

Jones, N.F. (1980) 'The Civic Organisation of Corinth' *TAPhA* 110: 161–93.

Jordan, B. (1970) 'Herodotos 5.71.2 and the Naukraroi of Athens' *ClAnt* 3: 153–75.

Kelly, T. (1976) *A History of Argos to 500 B.C.*, Minneapolis.

Lambert, S.D. (1986) 'Herodotus, the Cylonian Conspiracy and the PRYTANIES TON NAUKRARON' *Historia* 35: 105–12.

Lang, M.L. (1967) 'The Kylonian Conspiracy' *CPh* 62: 243–9.

Leahy, D.M. (1956) 'Chilon and Aeschines: A Further Consideration of the Rylands Greek Papyrus fr. 18' *Bulletin of the John Rylands Library* 38: 406–35.

—— (1957) 'The Spartan Embassy to Lygdamis' *JHS* 77: 272–5.

—— (1959) 'Chilon and Aeschines Again' *Phoenix* 13: 31–7.

—— (1968) 'The Dating of the Orthagorid Dynasty' *Historia* 17: 1–23.

Legon, R.P. (1981) *Megara: The Political History of a Greek City-State to 336 B.C.*, Ithaca.

Marinatos, N. (1981) 'Thucydides and Oracles' *JHS* 101: 138–40.

Mitchell, B.M. (1975) 'Herodotus and Samos' *JHS* 95: 75–91.

Morgan, C. (1990) *Athletes and Oracles: The Transformation of Olympia and Delphi in the Eighth Century BC*, Cambridge.

Morgan, K.A. (ed.) (2009) *Popular Tyranny: Sovereignty and Its Discontents in Ancient Greece*, Austin.

Mossé, C. (1969) *La tyrannie dans la Grèce antique*, Paris.

Nagy, G. (1985) 'Theognis and Megara: A Poet's Vision of His City' in T.J. Figueira and G. Nagy (eds), *Theognis of Megara. Poetry and the Polis*, Baltimore: 22–81.

Oost, S.I. (1972) 'Cypselus the Bacchiad' *CPh* 67: 10–30.

—— (1974) 'Two Notes on the Orthagorids of Sicyon' *CPh* 69: 118–20.

Page, D. (1955) *Sappho and Alcaeus: An Introduction to the Study of Ancient Lesbian Poetry*, Oxford.

Parke, H.W. (1946) 'Polycrates and Delos' *CQ* 40: 105–8.

Parker, V. (1992) 'The Dates of the Orthagorids of Sicyon' *Tyche* 7: 165–75.

Podlecki, A.J. (1984) *Early Greek Poets and Their Times*, Vancouver.

Rihll, T.E. and V.J. Tucker (1995) 'Greek Engineering: The Case of Eupalinos' Tunnel' in A. Powell (ed.) *The Greek World*, London: 403–31.

Robertson, N. (1978) 'The Myth of the First Sacred War' *CQ* 28: 38–73.

Salmon, J.B. (1984) *Wealthy Corinth: A History of the City to 338 BC*, Oxford.

Sanders, L.J. (1987) *Dionysios I of Syracuse and Greek Tyranny*, London.

Scanlon, T.F. (1987) 'Thucydides and Tyranny' *ClAnt* 6: 286–301.

Shipley, G. (1987) *A History of Samos 800–188 BC*, Oxford.

Snodgrass, A.M. (1965) 'The Hoplite Reform and History' *JHS* 85: 110–22.

Toher, M. (1989) 'On the Use of Nicolaus' Historical Fragments' *ClAnt* 8: 159–72.

Ure, P.N. (1922) *The Origin of Tyranny*, New York.

Van der Veen, J.E. (1993) 'The Lord of the Ring: Narrative Technique in Herodotus' Story on Polycrates' Ring' *Mnemosyne* 46: 433–57.

Wade-Gery, H.T. (1925) 'The Growth of the Dorian States' in J.B. Bury, S.A. Cook and F.E. Adcock (eds) *CAH* III: *The Assyrian Empire*: 527–70.

Walcot, P. (1978) *Envy and the Greeks: A Study of Human Behaviour*, Warminster.

White, M. (1954) 'The Duration of the Samian Tyranny' *JHS* 74: 36–43.

—— (1955) 'Greek Tyranny' *Phoenix* 9: 1–18.
—— (1958) 'The Dates of the Orthagorids' *Phoenix* 12: 2–14.

Chapter 8 The law-givers: Drakon and Solon

Introductory reading:
Almeida, J.A. (2003) *Justice as an Aspect of the Polis Idea in Solon's Political Poems*, Leiden.
Anhalt, E.K. (1993) *Solon the Singer: Politics and Poetics*, Lanham.
Blok, J.H. and A.P.M.H. Lardinois (eds) (2006) *Solon of Athens: New Historical and Philological Approaches*, Leiden.
Freeman, K. (1926) *The Work and Life of Solon*, Cardiff.
Gagarin, M. (1981) *Drakon and Early Athenian Homicide Law*, New Haven.
Lewis, J. (2008) *Solon the Thinker: Political Thought in Archaic Athens*, London.
Owens, R. (2010) *Solon of Athens: Poet, Philosopher, Soldier, Statesman*, Brighton.

Adkins, A.W.H. (1972) *Moral Values and Political Behaviour in Ancient Greece*, New York.
Andrewes, A. (1974) 'The Survival of Solon's *Axones*' in D.W. Bradeen and M.F. McGregor (eds) *FOROS: Tribute to Benjamin Dean Meritt*, New York: 21–8.
—— (1982) 'The Growth of the Athenian State' in *CAH* III.3²: 360–91.
Bailey, B.L. (1940) 'The Export of Attic Black-Figure Ware' *JHS* 60: 60–70.
Bérard, C. and C. Bron (1989) *A City of Images: Iconography and Society in Ancient Greece*, tr. D. Lyons, Princeton.
Bers, V. (1975) 'Solon's Law Forbidding Neutrality and Lysias 31' *Historia* 24: 493–8.
Camp, J.M. (1979) 'A Drought in the Late Eighth Century B.C.' *Hesperia* 48: 397–411.
Carawan, E. (1998) *Rhetoric and the Law of Draco*, Oxford.
Chambers, M. (1973) 'Aristotle on Solon's Reform of Coinage and Weights' *ClAnt* 6: 1–16.
Chiasson, C.C. (1986) 'The Herodotean Solon' *GRBS* 27: 249–62.
Cook, R.M. (1958) 'Speculations on the Origins of Coinage' *Historia* 7: 257–62.
David, E. (1984) 'Solon, Neutrality and Partisan Literature of Late Fifth-Century Athens' *MH* 41: 129–38.
Day, J. and M. Chambers (1962) *Aristotle's History of Athenian Democracy*, Berkeley.
De Ste Croix, G.E.M. (1981) *The Class Struggle in the Ancient Greek World: From the Archaic Age to the Arab Conquests*, London.
Develin, R. (1977) 'Solon's Law on Stasis' *Historia* 26: 507–8.
— (1979) 'The Election of Archons From Solon to Telesinos' *AC* 48: 455–68.
— (1989) *Athenian Officials 684–321 B.C.*, Cambridge.
Dillon, M. P. J. (2011) 'Solon as Prophet and Diviner: Was the Athenian Archon and Mediator of 594 BC Inspired by Mania?' in J. Che. and N.C.J. Pappas (eds) *The Traditional Mediterranean: Essays from the Ancient to the Early Modern Era*, Athens Institute for Education and Research, Athens: 63–76.
Ducrey, P. (1986) *Warfare in Ancient Greece*, New York.
Dunbabin, T.J. (1948) *The Western Greeks: The History of Sicily and South Italy from the Foundation of the Greek Colonies to 480 B.C.*, Oxford.
Eliot, C.W.T. (1967) 'Where Did the Alkmaionidai Live?' *Historia* 16: 279–86.
Ellis, J. and G.R. Stanton (1968) 'Factional Conflict and Solon's Reforms' *Phoenix* 22: 95–110.
Figueira, T.J. (1984) 'The Ten Archontes of 579/8 at Athens' *Hesperia* 53: 447–73.
Fine, J.V.A. (1951) *Horoi: Studies in Mortgage, Real Security, and Land Tenure in Ancient Athens*, Princeton.
Finley, M.I. (1951) *Studies in Land and Credit in Ancient Athens 500–200 B.C.: The Horos-Inscriptions*, New Brunswick.
—— (1968) 'The Alienability of Land in Ancient Greece: A Point of View' *Eirene* 7: 25–32.
—— (1971) 'The Ancestral Constitution' in M.I. Finley (ed.) *The Use and Abuse of History*, London: 34–59.

—— (1985) *The Ancient Economy*, London, second edition.

Forrest, W.G. and D.L. Stockton (1987) 'The Athenian Archons: A Note' *Historia* 36: 235–40.

Freeman, K. (1926) *The Work and Life of Solon*, Cardiff.

French, A. (1956) 'The Economic Background to Solon's Reforms' *CQ* 6: 11–25.

—— (1957) 'Solon and the Megarian Question' *JHS* 77: 238–46.

—— (1963) 'Land Tenure and the Solon Problem' *Historia* 12: 242–7.

—— (1964) *The Growth of the Athenian Economy*, London.

Frost, F.J. (1981) 'Politics in Early Athens' in *Classical Contributions*: 33–9.

Fuks, A. (1953) *The Ancestral Constitution: Four Studies in Athenian Party Politics at the End of the Fifth Century B.C.*, London.

—— (1986) *Early Greek Law*, Berkeley.

Gallant, T.W. (1982) 'Agricultural Systems, Land Tenure, and the Reforms of Solon' *ABSA* 77: 111–24.

Garland, R.S.J. (1989) 'The Well-Ordered Corpse: An Investigation into the Motives behind Greek Funerary Legislation' *BICS* 36: 1–15.

Garnsey, P. (1988) *Famine and Food Supply in the Graeco-Roman World: Responses to Risk and Crisis*, Cambridge.

Gill, D.W.J. (1991) 'Pots and Trade: Spacefillers or Objets d'Art?' *JHS* 111: 29–47.

Goldstein, J.A. (1972) 'Solon's Law for an Activist Citizenry' *Historia* 21: 538–45.

Hammond, N.G.L. (1940) 'The Seisachtheia and the Nomothesia of Solon' *JHS* 60: 71–83.

—— (1961) 'Land Tenure in Athens and Solon's Seisachtheia' *JHS* 81: 76–98.

Hansen, M.H. (1975) *Eisangelia: The Sovereignty of the People's Court in Athens in the Fourth Century BC and the Impeachment of the Generals and Politicians*, Odense.

—— (1978) 'Demos, Ecclesia and Dicasterion in Classical Athens' *GRBS* 19: 127–46.

—— (1981–82) 'The Athenian Heliaia from Solon to Aristotle' *C&M* 33: 9–47 = Hansen, M.H. (1989) *The Athenian Ecclesia II. A Collection of Articles 1983–89*, Copenhagen: 219–57.

—— (1989) 'Solonian Democracy in Fourth-Century Athens' in W.R. Connor, M.H. Hansen, K.A. Raaflaub and B.S. Strauss (eds) *Aspects of Athenian Democracy* (*Classica et Mediaevalia. Dissertationes* XI), Copenhagen: 71–99.

—— (1991) *The Athenian Democracy in the Age of Demosthenes: Structure, Principles and Ideology*, Oxford.

Hanson, V.D. (1995) *The Other Greeks. The Family Farm and the Agrarian Roots of Western Civilization*, New York.

Harding, P. (1974) 'Androtion's View of Solon's Seisachtheia' *Phoenix* 28: 282–9.

—— (1994) *Androtion and the Atthis. The Fragments, Translated with Introduction and Commentary*, Oxford.

Harris, E. (1997) 'A New Solution to the Riddle of the Seisachtheia' in L. Mitchell and P. Rhodes (eds), *The Development of the Polis in Ancient Greece*, London: 103–12.

Hölkeskamp, K.-J. (1992) 'Written Law in Archaic Greece' *PCPhS* 38: 87–117.

Holloway, R. (1984) 'The Date of the First Greek Coins: Some Arguments from Style and Hoards' *RBN* 130: 5–18.

Hopper, R.J. (1968) 'Observations on the *Wappenmünzen*' in C.M. Kraay and G.K. Jenkins (eds) *Essays in Greek Coinage Presented to S. Robinson*, Oxford 1968: 16–39.

Isager, S. and J.E. Skydsgaard (1992) *Ancient Greek Agriculture: An Introduction*, London.

Jacoby, F. (1949) *Atthis: The Local Chronicles of Ancient Athens*, Oxford.

Jameson, M. (1983) 'Famine in the Greek World' in P. Garnsey and C.R. Whittaker (eds) *Trade and Famine in Classical Antiquity*, Cambridge: 6–16.

Kagan, D. (1960) 'Pheidon's Aeginetan Coinage' *TAPhA* 91: 121–36.

—— (1982) 'The Dates of the Earliest Coins' *AJA* 88: 343–60.

Knox, B.M.W. (1978) 'Literature' in W.A.P. Childs (ed.) *Athens Comes of Age: From Solon to Salamis*, Princeton: 43–52.

Kraay, C.M. (1964) 'Hoards, Small Change and the Origin of Coinage' *JHS* 84: 76–91.

—— (1968) 'An Interpretation of *Ath. Pol.*, Ch. 10' in C.M. Kraay and G.K. Jenkins (eds) *Essays in Greek Coinage Presented to S. Robinson*, Oxford 1968: 1–9.

—— (1976) *Archaic and Classical Greek Coins*, Berkeley.

—— (1988) 'Coinage' in *CAH* IV²: 431–45.

Kroll, J.H. (1981) 'From *Wappenmünzen* to Gorgoneia to Owls' *ANSMusN* 26: 1–32.

Kroll, J.H. and N.M. Waggoner (1984) 'Dating the Earliest Coins of Athens, Corinth and Aegina' *AJA* 88: 325–40.

Laix, de R.A. (1973) *Probouleusis at Athens: A Study of Political Decision-Making*, Berkeley.

Legon, R.P. (1981) *Megara: The Political History of a Greek City-State to 336 B.C.*, London.

Linforth, I.M. (1919) *Solon the Athenian*, Berkeley.

MacDowell, D.M. (1978) *The Law in Classical Athens*, London.

McGlew, J.F. (1993) *Tyranny and Political Culture in Ancient Greece*, Ithaca.

Manville, P.B. (1980) 'Solon's Law of Stasis and *Atimia* in Archaic Athens' *TAPhA* 110: 213–21.

—— (1990) *The Origins of Citizenship in Ancient Athens*, Princeton.

Markianos, S.S. (1974) 'The Chronology of the Herodotean Solon' *Historia* 23: 1–20.

Martin, T.R. (1996) 'Why did the Greek *Polis* Originally Need Coins?' *Historia* 45: 257–83.

Miller, M. (1969) 'The Accepted Date for Solon: Precise, but Wrong?' *Arethusa* 2: 62–86.

Millett, P. (1989) 'Patronage and Its Avoidance in Classical Athens' in A. Wallace-Hadrill (ed.) *Patronage in Ancient Society*, London: 1–47.

Moore, J.M. (1983) *Aristotle and Xenophon on Democracy and Oligarchy*, London, second edition.

Morris, I. (1991) 'The Early Polis as City and State' in J. Rich and A. Wallace-Hadrill (eds) *City and Country in the Ancient World*, London: 25–58.

Murray, O. (1990) 'The Solonian Law of *hubris*' in *NOMOS*: 139–46.

Reden, S. von (1997) 'Money, Law and Exchange: Coinage in the Greek Polis' *JHS* 117: 154–76.

Rhodes, P.J. (1979) Eisangelia in Athens' *JHS* 99: 103–14.

—— (1984) *Aristotle: The Athenian Constitution*, Harmondsworth.

—— (1991) 'The Athenian Code of Laws, 410–399 B.C.' *JHS* 111: 87–100.

Rihll, T.E. (1989) 'Lawgivers and Tyrants (Solon, FRR. 9–11 West)' *CQ* 39: 277–86.

—— (1991) '*Ektemoroi*: Partners in Crime?' *JHS* 111: 101–27.

Robertson, N. (1986) 'Solon's Axones and Kyrbeis, and the Sixth-Century Background' *Historia* 35: 147–76.

—— (1990) 'The Laws of Athens, 410–399 BC: The Evidence for Review and Publication' *JHS* 110: 43–75.

Rosivach, V.J. (1992) 'Redistribution of Land in Solon, fragment 34 West' *JHS* 112: 153–7.

Ruschenbusch, E. (1958) '*Patrios politeia*' *Historia* 7: 398–424.

—— (1966) SOLONOS NOMOI: *Die Fragmente des Solonischen Gesetzwerkes*, *Historia* Einzelschrift 9, Wiesbaden.

Sallares, R. (1991) *The Ecology of the Ancient Greek World*, London.

Samuel, A.E. (1972) *Greek and Roman Chronology: Calendars and Years in Classical Antiquity*, Munich.

Sealey, R. (1960) 'Regionalism in Archaic Athens' *Historia* 9: 155–80.

—— (1983) 'How Citizenship and the City Began in Athens' *AJAH* 8: 97–129.

Shapiro, S.O. (1996) 'Herodotus and Solon' *ClAnt* 15: 348–64.

Snodgrass, A. (1980) *Archaic Greece: The Age of Experiment*, London.

Starr, C.G. (1982) 'Economic and Social Conditions in the Greek World' in *CAH* III.3²: 417–41.

—— (1990) *The Birth of Athenian Democracy: The Assembly in the Fifth Century B.C.*, Oxford.

Staveley, E.S. (1972) *Greek and Roman Voting and Elections*, London.

Stroud, R. (1968) *Drakon's Law on Homicide*, Berkeley.

—— (1978) 'State Documents in Archaic Athens' in W.A.P. Childs (ed.) *Athens Comes of Age: From Solon to Salamis*, Princeton: 20–42.

—— (1979) *The Axones and Kyrbeis of Drakon and Solon*, Berkeley.

Sumner, G.V. (1961) 'Notes on Chronological Problems in the Aristotelian *Athenaion Politeia*' *CQ* 11: 31–54.

Thompson, H.A. (1976) *The Athenian Agora*, Athens, third edition.

—— and R.E. Wycherley (1972) *The Athenian Agora* XIV. *The Agora of Athens: The History, Shape and Uses of an Ancient City Centre*, Princeton.

Vickers, M. (1985) 'Early Greek Coinage, a Reassessment' *NC* 145: 1–44.

Vlastos, G. (1946) 'Solonian Justice' *CPh* 41: 65–83.

von Fritz, K. (1954) 'The Composition of Aristotle's *Constitution of Athens* and the So-called Dracontian Constitution' *CPh* 49: 73–93.

Wallace, R.W. (1983) 'The Date of Solon's Reforms' *AJAH* 8: 81–95.

—— (1985) *The Areopagos Council, to 307 B.C.*, Baltimore.

Waters, K.H. (1960) 'Solon's Price "Equalisation"' *JHS* 80: 181–90.

Woodhouse, W.J. (1938) *Solon the Liberator*, Oxford.

Wycherley, R.E. (1957) *The Athenian Agora* III: *Literary and Epigraphical Testimonia*, Princeton.

—— (1978) *The Stones of Athens*, Princeton.

Chapter 9 Peisistratos and his sons

Introductory reading:

Lavelle, B. (1993) *The Sorrow and the Pity: A Prolegomenon to a History of Athens under the Peisisitratids*, c. 560–510 BC, Stuttgart.

—— (2005) *Fame, Money, and Power: The Rise of Peisistratos and 'Democratic' Tyranny at Athens*, Ann Arbor.

Sancisi-Weerdenburg, H. (ed.) (2000) *Peisistratos and the Tyranny: A Reappraisal of the Evidence*, Amsterdam.

Shapiro, H.A. (1989) *Art and Cult under the Tyrants in Athens*, Mainz.

Smith, J.A. (1989) *Athens under the Tyrants*, Bristol.

Taylor, M.W. (1991) *The Tyrant Slayers: The Heroic Image in Fifth Century B.C. Athenian Art and Politics*, Salem, second edition.

Andrewes, A. (1982) 'The Tyranny of Pisistratus' in *CAH* III.3^2: 392–416.

Arnush, M.F. (1995) 'The Career of Peisistratos son of Hippias' *Hesperia* 64: 135–62.

Berve, H. (1967) *Die Tyrannis bei den Griechen* I–II, Munich.

Boardman, J. (1972) 'Herakles, Peisistratos and Sons' *RA*: 57–72.

—— (1975) 'Herakles, Peisisitratos and Eleusis' *JHS* 95: 1–12.

Boersma, J.S. (1970) *Athenian Building Policy from 561/0–405/4 B.C.*, Groningen.

Brunnsker, S. (1971) *The Tyrant Slayers of Kritios and Nesiotes*, Stockholm, second edition.

Cawkwell, G.L. (1995) 'Early Greek Tyranny and the People' *CQ* 45: 73–86.

Cole, J.W. (1975) 'Peisistratus on the Strymon' *G&R* 22: 42–4.

Connor, W.R. (1987) 'Tribes, Festivals, and Processions; Civil Ceremonial and Political Manipulation in Archaic Greece' *JHS* 107: 40–50.

—— (1990) 'City Dionysia and Athenian Democracy' in W.R. Connor, M.H. Hansen, K.A. Raaflaub and B.S. Strauss (eds) *Aspects of Athenian Democracy* (*Classica et Mediaevalia. Dissertationes* XI), Copenhagen: 7–32.

Cook, R.M. (1987) 'Pots and Pisistratan Propaganda' *JHS* 107: 167–9.

Crosby, M. (1949) 'The Altar of the Twelve Gods in Athens' in *Commemorative Studies in Honor of T.L. Shear, Hesperia* Suppl. VIII, Princeton: 82–103.

Davison, J.A. (1955) 'Peisistratos and Homer' *TAPhA* 86: 1–21.

Day, J. (1985) 'Epigrams and History: The Athenian Tyrannicides, a Case in Point' in M. Jameson (ed.) *The Greek Historians: Literature and History. Papers Presented to A.E. Raubitschek*, Stanford: 25–46.

Dover, K.J. (1978) *Greek Homosexuality*, London.

Dunkley, B. (1935–36) 'Greek Fountain-Buildings before 300 B.C.' *ABSA* 36: 142–204.

Ehrenberg, V. (1950) 'Origins of Democracy' *Historia* 1: 515–48.

Finley, M.I. (1981) *Economy and Society in Ancient Greece*, London.

Fitzgerald, T.R. (1957) 'The Murder of Hipparchus: A Reply' *Historia* 6: 275–86.

Fornara, C.W. (1968) 'The "Tradition" about the Murder of Hipparchus' *Historia* 17: 400–24.

—— (1970) 'The Cult of Harmodius and Aristogeiton' *Philologus* 114: 155–80.

Forrest, W.G. (1969) 'The Tradition of Hippias' Expulsion from Athens' *GRBS* 10: 277–86.

French, A. (1957) 'Solon and the Megarian Question' *JHS* 77: 238–46.

—— (1959) 'The Party of Peisistratos' *G&R* 6: 46–57.

Frost, F.J. (1990) 'Peisistratos, the Cults, and the Unification of Attica' *AncW* 21: 3–9.

Harvey, D. (1985) 'Women in Thucydides' *Arethusa* 18: 67–90.

Hind, J.G.F. (1974) 'The "Tyrannis" and the Exiles of Pisistratus' *CQ* 24: 1–18.

Holladay, J. (1977) 'The Followers of Peisistratus' *G&R* 24: 40–56.

Hopper, R.J. (1961) '"Plain", "Shore", and "Hill" in Early Athens' *ABSA* 56: 189–219.

Jacoby, F. (1949) *Atthis: The Local Chronicles of Ancient Athens*, Oxford.

Jordan, B. (1975) *The Athenian Navy in the Classical Period*, Berkeley.

Kinzl, K.H. (1989) 'Regionalism in Classical Athens? (Or: An Anachronism in Herodotos 1.59.3?)' *AHB* 3: 5–9.

Knox, B.M.W. (1978) 'Literature' in W.A.P. Childs (ed.) *Athens Comes of Age: From Solon to Salamis*, Princeton: 43–52.

Lang, M.L. (1968) *Waterworks in the Athenian Agora*, Princeton.

Lavelle, B.M. (1984) 'Thucydides VI.55.1 and Adikia' *ZPE* 54: 17–19.

—— (1986) 'Herodotus on Argive Misthotoi' *LCM* 11: 150.

—— (1989) 'Thucydides and *IG* I³ 948: *amudrois grammasi*' in R.F. Sutton (ed.) *Daidalikon: Studies in Memory of Raymond V. Schoder*, Wauconda: 207–12.

—— (1991) 'The Compleat Angler: Observations on the Rise of Peisistratos in Herodotos (1.59–64)' *CQ* 41: 317–24.

—— (1992) 'Herodotos, Skythian Archers, and the *doryphoroi* of the Peisistratids' *Klio* 74: 78–97.

—— (1992) 'The Pisistratids and the Mines of Thrace' *GRBS* 33: 5–23.

Legon, R.P. (1981) *Megara: The Political History of a Greek City-State to 336 B.C.*, London.

Lewis, D.M. (1963) 'Cleisthenes and Attica' *Historia* 12: 22–40.

—— (1988) 'The Tyranny of the Peisistratidai' in *CAH* IV²: 287–302.

Lintott, A. (1982) *Violence, Civil Strife and Revolution in the Classical City: 750–330 BC*, London.

McGlew, J.F. (1993) *Tyranny and Political Culture in Ancient Greece*, Ithaca.

Millett, P. (1989) 'Patronage and Its Avoidance in Classical Athens' in A. Wallace-Hadrill (ed.) *Patronage in Ancient Society*, London: 1–47.

Moretti, L. (1953) *Iscrizioni Agonistiche Greche*, Rome.

Morgan, C. (1990) *Athletes and Oracles: The Transformation of Olympia and Delphi in the Eighth Century BC*, Cambridge.

Mossé, C. (1969) *La tyrannie dans la Grèce antique*, Paris.

Mylonas, G. (1961) *Eleusis and the Eleusinian Mysteries*, Princeton.

Nock, A.D. (1944) 'The Cult of Heroes' *HThR* 37: 141–74 = (1972) Z. Stewart (ed.) *A.D. Nock: Essays on Religion and the Ancient World I–II*, Oxford: 575–602.

Ostwald, M. (1991) 'Herodotus and Athens' *ICS* 11: 137–48.

Owens, E.J. (1982) 'The Enneakrounos Fountain-house' *JHS* 102: 222–5.

Parke, H.W. (1946) 'Polycrates and Delos' *CQ* 40: 105–8.

Podlecki, A.J. (1966) 'The Political Significance of the Athenian "Tyrannicide-Cult"' *Historia* 15: 129–41.

Pritchett, W.K. (1980) *Studies in Ancient Greek Topography* III: *Roads*, Berkeley.

Rhodes, P.J. (1976) 'Pisistratid Chronology Again' *Phoenix* 30: 219–33.

Richter, G.M.A. (1961) *Archaic Gravestones of Attica*, London.

Ruebel, J.S. (1973) 'The Tyrannies of Peisistratos' *GRBS* 14: 125–36.

Schachter, A. (1994) 'The Politics of Dedication: Two Athenian Dedications at the Sanctuary of Apollo Ptoieus in Boeotia' in R. Osborne and S. Hornblower (eds) *Ritual, Finance, Politics*, Oxford: 291–306.

Sealey, R. (1960) 'Regionalism in Archaic Athens' *Historia* 9: 155–80.

Shapiro, H.A. (1990) 'Oracle-Mongers in Peisistratid Athens' *Kernos* 3: 335–45.

Shear, T.L. (1978) 'Tyrants and Buildings in Archaic Athens' in W.A.P. Childs (ed.) *Athens Comes of Age: From Solon to Salamis*, Princeton: 1–19.

Sinos, R.H. (1993) 'Divine Selection: Epiphany and Politics in Archaic Greece' in C. Dougherty and L. Kurke (eds) *Cultural Poetics in Archaic Greece. Cult, Performance, Politics*, Cambridge: 73–91.

Stahl, M. (1987) *Aristokraten und Tyrannen im Archaischen Athen*, Stuttgart.

Stockton, D. (1990) *The Classical Athenian Democracy*, Oxford.

Stroud, R.S. (1971) 'Greek Inscriptions: Theozotides and the Athenian Orphans' *Hesperia* 40: 280–301.

Sumner, G.V. (1961) 'Notes on Chronological Problems in the Aristotelian *Athenaion Politeia*' *CQ* 11: 31–54.

Thompson, H.A. (1976) *The Athenian Agora*, Athens, third edition.

—— (1978) 'Some Hero Shrines in Early Athens' in W.A.P. Childs (ed.) *Athens Comes of Age: From Solon to Salamis*, Princeton: 96–108.

Thompson, H.A. and R.E. Wycherley (1972) *The Athenian Agora* XIV. *The Agora of Athens: The History, Shape and Uses of an Ancient City Centre*, Princeton.

Thompson, W.E. (1971) 'The Prytaneion Decree' *AJPh* 92: 226–37.

Viviers, D. (1987) 'Pisistratus' Settlement on the Thermaic Gulf: A Connection with Eretrian Colonization' *JHS* 107: 193–5.

Ure, P.N. (1922) *The Origin of Tyranny*, New York.

Wade-Gery, H.T. (1958) 'Miltiades' in *Essays in Greek History*, London: 155–70 = (1951) *JHS* 71: 212–21.

White, M.E. (1974) 'Hippias and the Athenian Archon List' in J.A.S. Evans (ed.) *Polis and Imperium: Studies in Honour of Edward Togo Salmon*, Toronto: 81–95.

Whitehead, D. (1986) *The Demes of Attica 508/7–ca. 250 B.C.: A Political and Social Study*, Princeton.

Wright, J.H. (1892) 'The Date of Cylon' *HSPh* 3: 1–74.

Wycherley, R.E. (1957) *The Athenian Agora* III: *Literary and Epigraphical Testimonia*, Princeton.

—— (1964) 'The Olympieion at Athens' *GRBS* 5: 161–79.

—— (1978) *The Stones of Athens*, Princeton.

Chapter 10 Kleisthenes the reformer

Introductory reading:

Andrewes, A. (1977) 'Kleisthenes' Reform Bill' *CQ* 27: 241–8.

Bicknell, P.J. (1972) *Studies in Athenian Politics and Genealogy*, Wiesbaden.

Develin, R. and M. Kilmer (1997) 'What Kleisthenes Did' *Historia* 46: 3–18.

Eliot, C.W.J. (1962) *Coastal Demes of Attika: A Study of the Policy of Kleisthenes*, Toronto.

Traill, J.S. (1975) *The Political Organization of Attica: A Study of the Demes, Trittyes, and Phylai, and Their Representation in the Athenian Council*, Princeton.

—— (1986) *Demos and Trittys: Epigraphical and Topographical Studies in the Organization of Attica*, Toronto.

Whitehead, D. (1986) *The Demes of Attica 508/7–ca. 250 B.C.: A Political and Social Study*, Princeton.

Bicknell, P.J. (1969) 'Whom Did Kleisthenes Enfranchise?' *PP* 24: 34–7.

—— (1974) 'Athenian Politics and Genealogy; Some Pendants' *Historia* 23: 146–63.

—— (1975) 'Was Megakles Hippokratous Alopekethen Ostracised Twice?' *AC*: 172–5.

—— (1989) 'Athenians Politically Active in Pynx II' *GRBS* 30: 83–100.

Bowra, C.M. (1961) *Greek Lyric Poetry from Alcman to Simonides*, Oxford, second edition.

Broneer, O. (1938) 'Excavations on the North Slope of the Acropolis' *Hesperia* 7: 161–263.

Carawan, E.M. (1987) '*Eisangelia* and *Euthyna*: The Trials of Miltiades, Themistocles and Cimon' *GRBS* 28: 167–208.

Christ, M.R. (1992) 'Ostracism, Sycophancy, and Deception of the Demos: [Arist.] *Ath. Pol.* 43.5' *CQ* 42: 336–46.

Connor, W.R. and J.J. Keaney (1969) 'Theophrastus on the End of Ostracism' *AJPh* 90: 313–19.

Cromey, R.D. (1979) 'Kleisthenes' Fate' *Historia* 28: 129–47.

Develin, R. (1977) 'Cleisthenes and Ostracism: Precedents and Intentions' *Antichthon* 11: 10–21.

—— (1985) 'Bouleutic Ostracism Again' *Antichthon* 19: 7–15.

Dillon, M.P.J. (2006) 'Was Kleisthenes or Pleisthenes Archon at Athens in 525 BC?' *ZPE* 155: 91–107.

Doenges, N.A. (1996) 'Ostracism and the *Boulai* of Kleisthenes' *Historia* 45: 387–404.

Dover, K.J. (1960) 'DEKATOS AUTOS' *JHS* 80: 61–77.

Ehrenberg, V. (1945) 'Pericles and His Colleagues between 441 and 429 B.C.' *AJPh* 66: 113–34.

—— (1950) 'Origins of Democracy' *Historia* 1: 515–48.

Eliot, C.W.J. (1968) 'Kleisthenes and the Creation of the Ten Phylai' *Phoenix* 22: 1–17.

Figueira, T.J. (1987) 'Residential Restrictions on the Athenian Ostracized' *GRBS* 28: 281–305 = Figueira, T.J. (1993) *Excursions in Epichoric History. Aiginetan Essays*, Lanham: 173–96.

Finley, M.I. (1952) *Studies in Land and Credit in Ancient Athens 500–200 B.C.: The Horos-Inscriptions*, New Brunswick.

Fornara, C.W. (1971) *The Athenian Board of Generals from 501 to 404*, Historia Einzelschrift 16, Wiesbaden.

Forsén, B. (1993) 'The Sanctuary of Zeus Hypsistos and the Assembly Place on the Pnyx' *Hesperia* 62: 507–21.

Grace, E. (1974) 'Aristotle on the "Enfranchisement of Aliens" by Cleisthenes (a Note)' *Klio* 56: 353–68.

Hands, A.R. (1959) 'Ostraka and the Law of Ostracism – Some Possibilities and Assumptions' *JHS* 79: 69–79.

Hansen, M.H. (1982) 'The Athenian *Ecclesia* and the Assembly-Place on the Pnyx' *GRBS* 23: 241–49 = Hansen, M.H. (1983) *The Athenian Ecclesia: A Collection of Articles 1976–1983*: 25–34.

—— (1987) *The Athenian Assembly in the Age of Demosthenes*, Oxford.

—— (1988) 'The Organization of the Athenian Assembly: A Reply' *GRBS* 29: 51–58 = (1989): 155–62.

—— (1989) 'The Organization of the Athenian Assembly: A Reply. Addenda' in Hansen, M.H. *The Athenian Ecclesia II. A Collection of Articles 1983–89*, Copenhagen: 163–65.

—— (1991) *The Athenian Democracy in the Age of Demosthenes: Structure, Principles and Ideology*, Oxford.

Harding, P. (1994) *Androtion and the Atthis. The Fragments, Translated with Introduction and Commentary*, Oxford.

Jameson, M.H. (1955) 'Seniority in the *Strategia*' *TAPhA* 86: 63–87.

Kagan, D. (1961) 'The Origin and Purposes of Ostracism' *Hesperia* 30: 393–401.

—— (1963) 'The Enfranchisement of Aliens by Cleisthenes' *Historia* 12: 41–6.

Karavites, P. (1974) 'Cleisthenes and Ostracism Again' *Athenaeum* 52: 326–35.

Keaney, J.J. (1970) 'The Text of Androtion F 6 and the Origin of Ostracism' *Historia* 19: 1–11.

—— (1995) 'Androtion F6 and Methodology' *Klio* 77: 126–31.

—— and A.E. Raubitschek (1972) 'A Late Byzantine Account of Ostracism' *AJPh* 93: 87–91.

Kearns, E. (1985) 'Change and Continuity in Religious Structures after Cleisthenes' in *Crux*: 189–207.

—— (1989) *The Heroes of Attica*, BICS Suppl. 57, London.

Kinzl, K.H. (1987) 'On the Consequences of Following *AP* 21.4 (on the Trittyes of Attika)' *AHB* 1: 25–33.

Kron, U. (1976) *Die zehn attischen Phylenheroen: Geschichte, Mythos, Kult und Darstellungen*, Berlin.

Lang, M.L. (1982) 'Writing and Spelling on Ostraka' in *Studies in Attic Epigraphy, History and Topography Presented to E. Vanderpool*, Hesperia Supplement 19, Princeton: 75–87.

—— (1990) *The Athenian Agora XXV: Ostraka*, Princeton.

Langdon, M.K. (1985) 'The Territorial Basis of the Attic Demes' *SO* 60: 5–15.

Lavelle, B.M. (1988) 'A Note on the First Three Victims of Ostracism (Athenaion Politeia 22.4)' *CPh* 83: 131–5.

—— (1992) 'Herodotos, Skythian Archers, and the *doryphoroi* of the Peisistratids' *Klio* 74: 78–97.

Lewis, D.M. (1961) 'Double Representation in the Strategia' *JHS* 81: 118–23.

—— (1963) 'Cleisthenes and Attica' *Historia* 12: 22–40.

—— (1974) 'The Kerameikos Ostraka' *ZPE* 14: 1–4.

Longo, C.P. (1980) 'La Bulé e la Procedura dell' Ostracismo: Considerazioni su *Vat. Gr.* 1144' *Historia* 29: 257–81.

Manville, P.B. (1990) *The Origins of Citizenship in Ancient Athens*, Princeton.

Martin, A. (1989) 'L'ostracisme Athénien: Un demi-siècle de découvertes et de recherches' *REG* 102: 124–45.

Mattingly, H.B. (1971) 'Facts and Artifacts: The Researcher and His Tools' *Leeds University Review* 14: 277–97.

—— (1991) 'The Practice of Ostracism at Athens' *Antichthon* 25: 1–26.

Mikalson, J.D. (1975) *The Sacred and Civil Calendar of the Athenian Year*, Princeton.

—— (1977) 'Religion in the Attic Demes' *AJPh* 98: 424–35.

Mirhady, D.C. (1997) 'The Ritual Background to Athenian Ostracism' *AHB* 11: 13–19.

Ober, J. (1993) 'The Athenian Revolution of 508/7 B.C.: Violence, Authority and the Origins of Democracy' in C. Dougherty and L. Kurke (eds) *Cultural Poetics in Ancient Greece: Cult, Performance, Politics*, Cambridge: 215–32 = Ober, J. (1996) *The Athenian Revolution. Essays on Ancient Greek Democracy and Political Theory*, Princeton: 32–52.

Osborne, R. (1985) *Demos: The Discovery of Classical Attika*, Cambridge.

Oliver, J.H. (1960) 'Reforms of Cleisthenes' *Historia* 9: 503–7.

Ostwald, M. (1986) 'New Ostraka from the Athenian Agora' *Hesperia* 37: 117–20.

—— (1988) 'The Reform of the Athenian State by Cleisthenes' in *CAH* IV²: 303–46.

Parke, H.W. (1977) *Festivals of the Athenians*, London.

Parker, R. (1987) 'Festivals of the Attic Demes' in T. Linders and G. Norquist (eds) *Gifts to the Gods. Boreas: Uppsala Studies in Ancient Mediterranean and Near Eastern Civilizations* 15, Stockholm: 137–47.

Patterson, C.B. (1981) *Perikles' Citizenship Law of 451/50 BC*, New York.

Phillips, D. (1990) 'Some Ostraka from the Athenian Agora' *ZPE* 83: 123–48.

Rapke, T.T. (1989) 'Cleisthenes the Tyrant Manqué' *AHB* 3: 47–51.

Raubitschek, A.E. (1947) 'The Ostracism of Xanthippos' *AJA* 51: 257–62.

—— (1953) 'Athenian Ostracism' *CJ* 48: 113–22.

Rhodes, P.J. (1986) 'Political Activity in Classical Athens' *JHS* 106: 132–44.

—— (1994) 'The Ostracism of Hyperbolus' in R. Osborne and S. Hornblower (eds) *Ritual, Finance, Politics*, Oxford: 85–98.

—— (1995) 'The "Acephalous" Polis?' *Historia* 44: 153–67.

Rocchi, G.R. (1972) 'Politica di famiglia e politica di tribù nella polis ateniese (V secolo)' *Acme* 24: 13–44.

Sealey, R. (1960) 'Regionalism in Archaic Athens' *Historia* 9: 155–80.

Siewert, P. (1982) *Die Trittyen Attikas und die Heeresreform des Kleisthenes*, Munich.

Sinclair, R.K. (1988) *Democracy and Participation in Athens*, Cambridge.

Stanton, G.R. (1984) 'The Tribal Reform of Kleisthenes the Alkmeonid' *Chiron* 14: 1–41.

—— and P.J. Bicknell (1987) 'Voting in Tribal Groups in the Athenian Assembly' *GRBS* 28: 51–92.

Staveley, E.S. (1966) 'Voting Procedure at the Election of Strategoi' in E. Badian (ed.) *Ancient Society and Institutions: Studies Presented to V. Ehrenberg*, Oxford: 275–88.

—— (1972) *Greek and Roman Voting and Elections*, London.

Stockton, D. (1990) *The Classical Athenian Democracy*, Oxford.

Thompson, W.E. (1971) 'The Deme in Kleisthenes' Reforms' *SO* 46: 72–9.

Thomsen, R. (1972) *The Origin of Ostracism: A Synthesis*, Copenhagen.

Thorley, J. (1996) *Athenian Democracy*, London.

Traill, J.S. (1982) 'An Interpretation of Six Rock-cut Inscriptions in the Attic Demes of Lamptrai' in *Studies in Attic Epigraphy, History and Topography Presented to E. Vanderpool*, Princeton: 162–71.

Vanderpool, E. (1968) 'New Ostraka from the Athenian Agora' *Hesperia* 37: 117–20.

—— (1970) *Ostracism at Athens*, Lectures in Memory of Louise Taft Semple, Cincinnati.

—— (1974) 'Ostraka from the Athenian Agora, 1970–1972' *Hesperia* 43: 189–93.

Wade-Gery, H.T. (1958) 'The Laws of Kleisthenes' in *Essays in Greek History*, Oxford: 135–54 = (1933) *CQ* 27: 17–29.

West, A.B. (1924) 'Notes on Certain Athenian Generals of the Year 424–3 B.C.' *AJPh* 45: 141–60.

Whitehead, D. (1977) *The Ideology of the Athenian Metic*, Cambridge.

Williams, G.M.E. (1978) 'The Kerameikos Ostraka' *ZPE* 31: 103–13.

Winters, T.F. (1993) 'Kleisthenes and Athenian Nomenclature' *JHS* 113: 162–5.

Woodhead, A.G. (1949) 'I.G., I², 95, and the Ostracism of Hyperbolus' *Hesperia* 18: 78–83.

Zaidman, L.B. and P.S. Pantel (1992) *Religion in the Ancient Greek City*, tr. P. Cartledge, Cambridge.

Chapter 11 The Persian Wars

Introductory reading:

Balcer, J.M. (1995) *The Persian Conquest of the Greeks, 545–450 B.C.*, Konstanz.

Burn, A.R. (1962) *Persia and the Greeks*, with postscript by D.M. Lewis (1984) London.

Cawkwell, G. (2006) *The Greek Wars: The Failure of Persia*, Oxford.

Green, P. (1996) *The Greco-Persian Wars*, Berkeley = (1970) *The Year of Salamis, 480–479 BC*, London = (1970) *Xerxes at Salamis*, New York.

Krentz, P. (2010) *The Battle of Marathon*, New Haven.

Lazenby, J.F. (1993) *The Defence of Greece 490–79 B.C.*, Warminster.

Lenardon, R.J. (1978) *The Saga of Themistocles*, London.

Strausss, B. (2002) *The Battle of Salamis*, New York.

Szemler, G.J., W.J. Cherf and J.C. Kraft (1996) *Thermopylai. Myth and Reality in 480 B.C.*, Chicago.

Allen, L. (2005) *The Persian Empire*, Chicago.

Austin, M.M. (1990) 'Greek Tyrants and the Persians, 546–479 B.C.' *CQ* 40: 289–306.

Armayor, O.K. (1978) 'Herodotus' Catalogues of the Persian Empire in the Light of the Monuments and the Greek Literary Tradition' *TAPhA* 108: 1–9.

Avery, H.C. (1972) 'Herodotus 6.112.2' *TAPhA* 103: 15–22.

—— (1973) 'The Number of Persian Dead at Marathon' *Historia* 22: 757.

Balcer, J.M. (1989) 'The Persian Wars Against Greece: A Reassessment' *Historia* 38: 127–43.

Bengtson, H. (1968) *The Greeks and the Persians from the Sixth to the Fourth Centuries*, tr. J. Conway, London.

Bicknell, P. (1970) 'The Command Structure and Generals of the Marathon Campaign' *AC* 39: 427–442.

Billows, R.A. (2010) *Marathon: The Battle that Changed Western Civilization*, London.

Boedeker, D. (1995) 'Simonides on Plataea: Narrative Elegy, Mythodic History' *ZPE* 107: 217–29.

—— and D. Sider (eds) (1996) *The New Simonides: Arethusa* 29.2.

Bonner, C. (1906) 'The Omen in Herodotus VI.107' *CPh* 1: 235–38.

Borgeaud, P. (1988) *The Cult of Pan in Ancient Greece*, tr. K. Atlass and J. Redfield, Chicago.

Bowden, H. (1993) 'Hoplites and Homer: Warfare, Hero Cult, and the Ideology of the Polis' in J. Rich and G. Shipley (eds) *War and Society in the Greek World*, London: 45–63.

Bradford, A.S. (1992) 'Plataea and the Soothsayer' *AncW* 23: 27–33.

Bridges, E., E. Hall and P. Rhodes (2007) *Cultural Responses to the Persian Wars*, Oxford.

Brown, T.S. (1981) 'Aeneas Tacticus, Herodotus and the Ionian Revolt' *Historia* 30: 383–93.

Brunt, P.A. (1953–54) 'The Hellenic League Against Persia' *Historia* 2: 135–63.

Buck, R.J. (1987) 'Boiotians at Thermopylae' *AHB* 1: 54–60.

Burn, A.R. (1969) 'Hammond on Marathon: A Few Notes' *JHS* 89: 118–20.

Burstein, S.M. (1971) 'The Recall of the Ostracized and the Themistocles Decree' *ClAnt* 4: 94–110.

Bury, J.B. (1896) 'Aristides at Salamis' *CR* 10: 414–18.

Caspari, M.O.B. (1915) 'The Ionian Confederacy' *JHS* 35: 173–88.

Castriota, D. (1992) *Myth, Ethos and Actuality: Official Art in Fifth-Century B.C. Athens*, Wisconsin.

Cartledge, P. (2007) *Thermopylae: The Battle that Changed the World*, New York.

Chambers, M. (1961–62) 'The Authenticity of the Themistocles Decree' *AHR* 67: 306–16.

—— (1967) 'The Significance of the Themistocles Decree' *Philologus* 111: 157–67.

Chapman, G.A.H. (1972) 'Herodotus and Histiaeus' Role in the Ionian Revolt' *Historia* 21: 546–68.

Clairmont, C.W. (1983) *Patrios Nomos: Public Burial in Athens during the Fifth and Fourth Centuries B.C. Parts I–II*, Oxford.

Connor, W.R. (1993) 'The Ionian Era of Athenian Civic Identity' *PAPhS* 194–206.

Detienne M. and J.-P. Vernant (1978) *Cunning Intelligence in Greek Culture and Society*, tr. J. Lloyd, Sussex.

Dillon, M.P.J. (2008) '"Xenophon Sacrificed on account of an Expedition" (Xenophon *Anabasis* 6.5.2): Divination and the Sphagia before Ancient Greek Battles' in P. Brulè and V. Mehl (eds), *Le sacrifice antique. Vestiges, procédures et stratégies*, Rennes: 235–51.

Doenges, N.A. (1998) 'The Campaign and the Battle of Marathon' *Historia* 47: 1–17.

Dow, S. (1962) 'The Purported Decree of Themistokles: Stele and Inscription' *AJA* 66: 353–68.

Evans, J.A.S. (1963) 'Histiaeus and Aristagoras: Notes on the Ionian Revolt' *AJPh* 84: 113–28.

—— (1976) 'Herodotus and the Ionian Revolt' *Historia* 25: 31–37.

—— (1982) 'The Oracle of the "Wooden Wall"' *CJ* 78: 24–29.

—— (1984) 'Herodotus and Marathon' *Florilegium* 6: 1–27.

—— (1988) 'The "Wooden Wall" Again' *AHB* 2: 25–30.

—— (1993) 'Herodotus and the Battle of Marathon' *Historia* 42: 279–307.

Fornara, C.W. (1966) 'The Hoplite Achievement at Psyttaleia' *JHS* 86: 51–54.

—— (1971) *The Athenian Board of Generals from 501 to 404*, Historia Einzelschrift 16, Wiesbaden.

Forrest, W.G. (1984) 'Herodotus and Athens' *Phoenix* 38: 1–11.

Francis, E.D. and M. Vickers (1985) 'The Oenoe Painting in the Stoa Poikile, and Herodotus' Account of Marathon' *ABSA* 80: 99–113.

Frost, F.J. (1973) 'A Note on Xerxes at Salamis' *Historia* 22: 118–19.

—— (1980) *Plutarch's Themistokles: A Historical Commentary*, Princeton.

Garland, R.S.J. (1985) *The Greek Way of Death*, London.

Gillis, D. (1969) 'Marathon and the Alkmeonids' *GRBS* 10: 133–45.

Georges, P.B. (1986) 'Saving Herodotus' Phenomena: The Oracles and Events of 480 B.C.' *ClAnt* 5: 14–59.

Goldhill, S. (1988) 'Battle Narrative and Politics in Aeschylus' *Persai*' *JHS* 108: 189–93.

Gomme, A.W. (1952) 'Herodotos and Marathon' *Phoenix* 6: 77–83.

Graf, D.F. (1984) 'Medism: The Origin and Significance of the Term' *JHS* 104: 15–30.

Grant, J.R. (1961) 'Leonidas' Last Stand' *Phoenix* 15: 14–27.

Hall, E. (1993) 'Asia Unmanned: Images of Victory in Classical Athens' in J. Rich and G. Shipley (eds) *War and Society in the Greek World*, London: 108–33.

Hammond, N.G.L. (1968) 'The Campaign and the Battle of Marathon' *JHS* 88: 13–57.

—— (1982) 'The Narrative of Herodotus VII and the Decree of Themistocles at Troezen' *JHS* 102: 75–93.

—— (1986) 'The Manning of the Fleet in the Decree of Themistokles' *Phoenix* 40: 143–48.

—— (1988) 'The Expedition of Datis and Artaphernes' in *CAH* IV²: 491–517.

—— (1988) 'The Expedition of Xerxes' in *CAH* IV²: 518–91.

—— (1996) 'Sparta at Thermopylae' *Historia* 45: 1–20.

Harrison, E.B. (1972) 'The South Frieze of the Nike Temple and the Marathon Painting in the Painted Stoa' *AJA* 76: 353–78.

Herington, C.J. (1967) 'Aeschylus in Sicily' *JHS* 87: 74–85.

Hignett, C. (1963) *Xerxes' Invasion of Greece*, Oxford.

Hodge, A.T. and L.A. Losada (1970) 'The Time of the Shield Signal at Marathon' *AJA* 74: 31–36.

Hodge, A.T. (1975) 'Marathon: The Persians' Voyage' *TAPhA* 105: 155–73.

—— (1975) 'Marathon to Phaleron' *JHS* 95: 169–71.

Holladay, A.J. and M.D. Goodman (1986) 'Religious Scruples in Ancient Warfare' *CQ* 36: 151–71.

Holland, T. (2010) 'Propaganda and Imperial Overreach in the Greco-Persian Wars' in V.C. Hanson (ed.) *Makers of Ancient Strategy: From the Persian Wars to the Fall of Rome*, Princeton: 11–30.

Hudson, H.G. (1936–37) 'The Shield Signal at Marathon' *AHR* 12: 443–59.

Hughes, D.D. (1991) *Human Sacrifice in Ancient Greece*, London.

Jameson, M.H. (1960) 'A Decree of Themistokles from Troizen' *Hesperia* 29: 198–223.

—— (1962) 'A Revised Text of the Decree of Themistokles from Troizen' *Hesperia* 31: 310–15.

—— (1963) 'The Provisions for Mobilization in the Decree of Themistokles' *Historia* 12: 385–404.

—— (1991) 'Sacrifice before Battle' in V.D. Hanson (ed.) *Hoplites: The Classical Greek Battle Experience*, London: 197–227.

Isserlin, B.S.J. (1991) 'The Canal of Xerxes: Facts and Problems' *ABSA* 86: 83–91.

Jordan, B. (1979) *Servants of the Gods: A Study in the Religion, History and Literature of Fifth-Century Athens*, Göttingen.

—— (1988) 'The Honors for Themistocles after Salamis' *AJPh* 109: 547–71.

Keaveney, A. (1988) 'The Attack on Naxos: A "Forgotten Cause" of the Ionian Revolt' *CQ* 38: 76–81.

Kurht, A. (2007) *The Persian Empire: A Corpus of Sources from the Achaemenid Period*, London.

Lang, M.L. (1968) 'Herodotus and the Ionian Revolt' *Historia* 17: 24–36.

Lateiner, D. (1982) 'The Failure of the Ionian Revolt' *Historia* 31: 129–60.

—— (1974) 'Again the Marathon Epigram' in D.W. Bradeen and M.F. McGregor (eds) *FOROS: Tribute to B.D. Meritt*, Locust Valley: 80.

Larsen, J.A.O. (1932) 'Sparta and the Ionian Revolt: A Study of Spartan Foreign Policy and the Genesis of the Peloponnesian League' *CPh* 27: 136–50.

—— (1944) 'Federation for Peace in Ancient Greece' *CPh* 39: 145–62.

—— (1955) *Representative Government in Greek and Roman History*, Berkeley.

Lewis, D.M. (1980) 'Datis the Mede' *JHS* 100: 194–95.

—— (1985) 'Persians in Herodotus' in *The Greek Historians: Literature and History. Papers Presented to A.E. Raubitschek*, Stanford: 101–17.

Lloyd-Jones, H. (1976) 'The Delphic Oracle' *G&R* 23: 60–73.

Manville, P.B. (1977) 'Aristagoras and Histiaios' *CQ* 27: 80–91.

Mattingly, H.B. (1981) 'The Themistokles Decree from Troizen: Transmission and Status' in *Classical Contributions*: 79–87.

Mikalson, J.D. (2003) *Herodotus and Religion in the Persian Wars*, Chapel Hill.

Miller, M.C. (2004) *Athens and Persia in the Fourth Century BC: A Study in Cultural Receptivity*, Cambridge.

Mitchell, B.M. (1975) 'Herodotus and Samos' *JHS* 95: 75–91.

Mosley, D.J. (1973) *Envoys and Diplomacy*, Weisbaden.

Murray, O. (1988) 'The Ionian Revolt' in *CAH* IV²: 461–90.

Notopoulos, J.A. (1941) 'The Slaves at the Battle of Marathon' *AJPh* 62: 352–54.

Nyland, R. (1992) 'Herodotos' Sources for the Plataiai Campaign' *AC* 61: 80–97.

Parker, R. (1989) 'Spartan Religion' in *Classical Sparta*: 142–72.

Parsons, P.J. (1992) '3965. Simonides, Elegies' in E.W. Handley, H.G. Ioannidou, P.J. Parsons and J.E.G. Whitehorne (eds), *The Oxyrhynchus Papyri* 59, London.

Pemberton, E.G. (1972) 'The East and West Friezes of the Temple of Athena Nike' *AJA* 76: 303–10.

Podlecki, A.J. (1968) 'Simonides: 480' *Historia* 17: 257–75.

Pritchett, W.K. (1962) 'Herodotos and the Themistokles Decree' *AJA* 66: 43–47.

—— (1974) *The Greek State at War. Part* II, Berkeley.

—— (1979) *The Greek State at War. Part* III: *Religion*, Berkeley.

—— (1985) *The Greek State at War. Part* IV, Berkeley.

Raubitschek, A.E. (1940) 'Two Monuments Erected after the Victory of Marathon' *AJA* 44: 53–59.

—— (1960) 'The Covenant of Plataea' *TAPhA* 91: 178–83.

Robertson, N. (1976) 'The Thessalian Expedition of 480 BC' *JHS* 96: 100–20.

—— (1982) 'The Decree of Themistocles in Its Contemporary Setting' *Phoenix* 36: 1–44.

—— (1987) 'The True Meaning of the "Wooden Wall"' *CPh* 82: 1–20.

Roebuck, C. (1955) 'The Early Ionian League' *CPh* 50: 26–40.

Rosenbloom, D. (1993) 'Shouting "Fire" in a Crowded Theatre: Phrynichos's *Capture of Miletos* and the Politics of Fear in Early Attic Tragedy' *Philologus* 137: 159–96.

Rosivach, V.J. (1987) 'Execution by Stoning in Athens' *ClAnt* 6: 232–48.

Rung, E. (2008) 'War, Peace and Diplomacy in Graeco-Persian Relations' in P. de Souza and J. France (eds) *War and Peace in Ancient and Medieval History*, Berkeley: 28–50.

Sacks, K.S. (1976) 'Herodotus and the Dating of the Battle of Thermopylai' *CQ* 26: 232–48.

Sargent, R.L. (1927) 'The Use of Slaves by the Athenians in Warfare' *CPh* 22: 201–12, 264–79.

Schachter, A. (1998) 'Simonides' Elegy on Plataia: The Occasion of Its Performance' *ZPE* 123: 25–30.

Schreiner, J.H. (1970) 'The Battles of 490 BC' *PCPhS* 16: 97–112.

Sealey, R. (1972) 'Again the Siege of the Acropolis' *ClAnt* 5: 183–94.

Shear, T.L. (1993) 'The Persian Destruction of Athens. Evidence from Agora Deposits' *Hesperia* 62: 383–482.

Shipley, G. (1987) *A History of Samos 800–188 BC*, Oxford.

Simpson, R.H. (1972) 'Leonidas' Decision' *Phoenix* 26: 1–11.

Shrimpton, G. (1980) 'The Persian Cavalry at Marathon' *Phoenix* 34: 20–37.

Stronk, J.P. (2010) *Ctesias' Persian History: Introduction, Text and Translation*, Düsseldorf.

Thomas, R. (1989) *Oral Tradition and Written Record in Classical Athens*, Cambridge.

Thompson, H.A. (1976) *The Athenian Agora*, Athens, third edition.

Tronson, A. (1991) 'The Hellenic League of 480 BC – Fact or Ideological Fiction?' *AClass* 34: 93–110.

Vanderpool, E. (1966) 'A Monument to the Battle of Marathon' *Hesperia* 35: 93–106.

van der Veer, J.A.G. (1982) 'The Battle of Marathon: A Topographical Survey' *Mnemosyne* 35: 290–321.

Vidal-Nacquet, P. (1986) *The Black Hunter: Forms of Thought and Forms of Society in the Greek World*, tr. A. Szegedy-Maszak, Baltimore.

Wade-Gery, H.T. (1933) 'Classical Epigrams and Epitaphs' *JHS* 53: 71–104.

Wallace, P.W. (1969) 'Psyttaleia and the Trophies of the Battle of Salamis' *AJA* 73: 293–303.

Walters, K.R. (1981) 'Four Hundred Athenian Ships at Salamis?' *RhM* 124: 199–203.

—— (1981) '"We Fought Alone at Marathon": Historical Falsification in the Attic Funeral Oration' *RhM* 124: 204–11.

Wardman, A.E. (1959) 'Tactics and the Tradition of the Persian Wars' *Historia* 8: 49–60.

Waters, K.H. (1970) 'Herodotus and the Ionian Revolt' *Historia* 19: 504–08.

Wéry, L. (1966) 'Le meurtre des hérauts de Darius en 491 et l'inviolabilité du héraut' *AC* 35: 468–86.

West, M.L. (1992) *Iambi et Elegi Graeci* II, Oxford, second edition.

—— (1993) *Greek Lyric Poetry*, Oxford.

—— (1993) 'Simonides Redivivus' *ZPE* 98: 1–14.

West, S. (1991) 'Herodotus' Portrait of Hecataeus' *JHS* 111: 144–60.

West, W.C. (1969) 'The Trophies of the Persian Wars' *CPh* 64: 7–19.

—— (1970) 'Saviors of Greece' *GRBS* 11: 271–82.

Wycherley, R.E. (1957) *The Athenian Agora* III: *Literary and Epigraphical Testimonia*, Princeton.

Chapters 12 and 13 The Delian League and the Peloponnesian War

Introductory reading:

Connor, W.R. (1971) *The New Politicians of Fifth-Century Athens*, Princeton.

De Ste Croix, G.E.M. (1954–55) 'The Character of the Athenian Empire' *Historia* 3: 1–41.

—— (1972) *The Origins of the Peloponnesian War*, London.

Due, B. (1987) 'Lysander in Xenophon's *Hellenica*' *C&M* 38: 53–62.

Kagan, D. (1969) *The Outbreak of the Peloponnesian War*, Ithaca.

—— (1987) *The Fall of the Athenian Empire*, Ithaca.

—— (1991) *Pericles of Athens and the Birth of Democracy*, New York.

Low, P. (2008) *The Athenian Empire*, Edinburgh.

Meiggs, R. (1972) *The Athenian Empire*, Oxford.

Podlecki, A.J. (1998) *Perikles and His Circle*, London.

Rhodes, P.J. (1985) *The Athenian Empire*, Oxford.

—— (1987) 'Thucydides on the Causes of the Peloponnesian War' *Hermes* 115: 154–65.

Westlake, H.D. (1968) *Individuals in Thucydides*, Cambridge.

Adkins, A.W.H. (1960) *Merit and Responsibility. A Study in Greek Values*, Oxford.

Adshead, K. (1986) *Politics of the Archaic Peloponnese*, Aldershot.

Allison, J.W. (1983) 'Pericles' Policy and the Plague' *Historia* 32: 14–23.

Anderson, J.K. (1965) 'Cleon's Orders at Amphipolis' *JHS* 85: 1–4.

—— (1974) *Xenophon*, London.

Andrewes, A. (1959) 'Thucydides on the Causes of the War' *CQ* 9: 223–39.

—— (1962) 'The Mytilene Debate: Thucydides 3.36–49' *Phoenix* 16: 64–85.

—— (1978) 'The Opposition to Perikles' *JHS* 98: 1–8.

—— (1992) 'The Peace of Nikias and the Sicilian Expedition' in *CAH* V²: 433–63.

Asheri, D. (1969) 'Note on the Site of Brea: Theopompus, F 145' *AJPh* 90: 337–40.

Badian, E. (1987) 'The Peace of Kallias' *JHS* 107: 1–39.

—— (1988) 'Towards a Chronology of the Pentekontaetia down to the Renewal of the Peace of Callias' *EMC* 7: 289–310.

—— (1990) 'Athens, the Locrians and Naupactus' *CQ* 40: 364–9.

—— (1993) *From Plataea to Potidaea: Studies in the History and Historiography of the Pentekontaetia*, Baltimore.

Bagnall, N. (2004) *The Peloponnesian War: Athens, Sparta and the Struggle for Greece*, London.

Balcer, J.M. (1974) 'Separatism and Anti-Separatism in the Athenian Empire (478–433 B.C.)' *Historia* 23: 21–39.

—— (1978) *The Athenian Regulations for Chalkis: Studies in Athenian Imperial Law*, Historia Einzelschrift 33, Wiesbaden.

—— (1995) *The Persian Conquest of the Greeks, 545–450 B.C.*, Konstanz.

Barron, J.P. (1964) 'Religious Propaganda of the Delian League' *JHS* 84: 35–48.

Bauer, A. and F.J. Frost (1967) *Themistokles: Literary, Epigraphical and Archaeological Testimonia*, Chicago, second edition.

Bauman, R.A. (1990) *Political Trials in Ancient Greece*, London.

Bauslaugh, R.A. (1990) 'Messenian Dialect and Dedications of the "Methanioi"' *Hesperia* 59: 661–8.

Bicknell, P.J. (1974) 'Athenian Politics and Genealogy: Some Pendants' *Historia* 23: 146–63.

Bloedow, E.F. (1987) 'Pericles' Powers in the Counter-Strategy of 431' *Historia* 36: 9–27.

—— (1990) '"Not the Son of Achilles, but Achilles Himself": Alcibiades' Entry on the Political Stage at Athens II' *Historia* 39: 1–19.

—— (1992) 'The Peaces of Kallias' *SO* 67: 41–68.

—— (1992) 'Alcibiades "Brilliant" or "Intelligent"?' *Historia* 41: 139–57.

Boedeker, D. and K.A. Raaflaub (eds) (2003) *Democracy, Empire and the Arts in Fifth-Century Athens*, Washington, D.C.

Boersma, J.S. (1970) *Athenian Building Policy from 561/0–405/4 B.C.*, Groningen.

Bosworth, A.B. (1990) 'Plutarch, Callisthenes and the Peace of Callias' *JHS* 110: 1–13.

Bowra, C.M. (1971) *Periclean Athens*, London.

Bradeen, D.W. (1960) 'The Popularity of the Athenian Empire' *Historia* 9: 257–69.

Bridges, A.P. (1980) 'The Athenian Treaty with Samos, ML 56' *JHS* 100: 185–8.

Brunt, P.A. (1953–54) 'The Hellenic League against Persia' *Historia* 2: 135–63.

—— (1965) 'Spartan Policy and Strategy in the Archidamian War' *Phoenix* 19: 255–80.

—— (1966) 'Athenian Settlements Abroad in the Fifth Century B.C.' in E. Badian (ed.) *Ancient Society and Institutions: Studies Presented to V. Ehrenberg*, Oxford: 71–92.

Buck, R.J. (1970) 'The Athenian Domination of Boeotia' *CPh* 65: 217–27.

—— (1988) 'The Sicilian Expedition' *AHB* 2: 73–9.

Bugh, G.R. (1988) *The Horsemen of Athens*, Princeton.

Burke, E.M. (1992) 'The Economy of Athens in the Classical Era: Some Adjustments to the Primitivist Model' *TAPhA* 122: 199–226.

Burn, A.R. (1960) *Pericles and Athens*, London.

Cairns, F. (1982) 'Cleon and Pericles: A Suggestion' *JHS* 102: 203–4.

Carawan, E.M. (1985) '*Apophasis* and *Eisangelia*: The Role of the Areopagus in Athenian Political Trials' *GRBS* 26: 115–39.

—— (1987) '*Eisangelia* and *Euthyna*: The Trials of Miltiades, Themistocles and Cimon' *GRBS* 28: 167–208.

—— (1990) 'The Five Talents Cleon Coughed up (schol. Ar. *Ach.* 6)' *CQ* 40: 137–47.

Cargill, J. (1981) *The Second Athenian League*, Berkeley.

—— (1995) *Athenian Settlements of the Fourth Century B.C.*, Leiden.

Cartledge, P. (1979) *Sparta and Lakonia: A Regional History 1300–362 BC*, London.

Castriota, D. (1992) *Myth, Ethos and Actuality: Official Art in Fifth-Century B.C. Athens*, Madison.

Cawkwell, G.L. (1970) 'The Fall of Themistokles' in B.F. Harris (ed.) *Auckland Classical Essays Presented to E.M. Blaiklock*, Auckland: 39–58.

—— (1975) 'Thucydides' Judgement of Periclean Strategy' *YCS* 24: 53–70.

—— (1988) 'Nomophulakia and the Areopagus' *JHS* 108: 1–12.

—— (1997) 'The Peace between Athens and Persia' *Phoenix* 51: 115–30.

—— (1997) *Thucydides and the Peloponnesian War*, London.

Chambers, M. (1982) 'Thucydides and Pericles' *HSCP* 62: 79–82.

—— (1992) 'Photographic Enhancement and a Greek Inscription' *CJ* 88: 25–31.

—— (1993) 'The Archon's Name in the Athens-Egesta Alliance (*IG* I³ 11)' *ZPE* 98: 171–4.

——, R. Gallucci and P. Spanos (1990) 'Athens' Alliance with Egesta' *ZPE* 83: 38–63.

Champion, J. (2010) *Tyrants of Syracuse: War in Ancient Sicily, 480–367 BC*, Barnsley.

Christ, M.R. (1990) 'Liturgy Avoidance and *Antidosis* in Classical Athens' *TAPhA* 120: 147–69.

Christensen, J. and M.H. Hansen (1983) 'What Is *Syllogos* at Thukydides 2.22.1?' *C&M* 34: 17–31.

—— (1989) 'What Is *Syllogos* at Thukydides 2.22.1? Addenda' in M.H. Hansen *The Athenian Ecclesia II. A Collection of Articles 1983–89*, Copenhagen: 210–11.

Cohen, E.E. (1973) *Ancient Athenian Maritime Courts*, Princeton.

Connor, W.R. (1968) *Theopompos and Fifth Century Athens*, Washington.

—— (1984) *Thucydides*, Princeton.

Cornford, F.M. (1907) *Thucydides Mythistoricus*, London.

Crane, G. (1992) 'The Fear and Pursuit of Risk: Corinth on Athens, Sparta and the Peloponnesians (Thucydides 1.68–71, 120–121)' *TAPhA* 122: 227–56.

Culham, P. (1978) 'The Delian League: Bicameral or Unicameral?' *AJAH* 3: 27–31.

Daniel, J. and R. Polansky (1979) 'The Tale of the Delphic Oracle in Plato's Apology' *AncW* 2: 83–5.

Davison, J.A. (1953) 'Protagoras, Democritus, and Anaxagoras' *CQ* 3: 33–45.

—— (1966) 'Aeschylus and Athenian Politics, 472–456 B.C.' in E. Badian (ed.) *Ancient Society and Institutions: Studies Presented to V. Ehrenberg*, Oxford: 93–107.

Dawson, S. (1996) 'The Egesta Decree *IG* I³ 11' *ZPE* 112: 248–52.

Debnar, P. (2001) *Speaking the Same Language: Speech and Audience in Thucydides' Spartan Debates*, Ann Arbor.

De Romilly, J. (1963) *Thucydides and Athenian Imperialism*, tr. P. Thody, Oxford.

De Ste Croix, G.E.M. (1956) 'The Constitution of the Five Thousand' *Historia* 5: 1–23.

—— (1961) 'Notes on Jurisdiction in the Athenian Empire' *CQ* 11: 94–112, 268–80.

Detienne M. and J.-P. Vernant (1978) *Cunning Intelligence in Greek Culture and Society*, tr. J. Lloyd, Sussex.

Dewald, C. (2005) *Thucydides' War Narrative: A Structural Study*, Berkeley.

Dorey, T.A. (1956) 'Aristophanes and Cleon' *G&R* 3: 132–9.

Edmunds, L. (1975) *Chance and Intelligence in Thucydides*, Cambridge, Mass.

Ehrenberg, V. (1948) 'The Foundation of Thurii' *AJPh* 69: 149–70.

—— (1952) 'Thucydides on Athenian Colonization' *CPh* 47: 143–49.

Ellis, W.M. (1989) *Alcibiades*, London.

Evans, J.A.S. (1976) 'The Settlement of Artaphrenes' *CPh* 71: 344–8.

Falkner, C. (1999) 'Sparta's Colony at Herakleia Trachinia and Spartan Strategy in 426' *Classical Views* 43: 45–58.

Figueira, T.J. (1991) *Athens and Aigina in the Age of Imperial Colonization*, Baltimore.

—— (1998) *The Power of Money: Coinage and Politics in the Athenian Empire*, Philadelphia.

Finley, M.I. (1965) 'Trade and Politics in the Ancient World' in *Second International Congress of Economic History* I, Paris: 11–35.

—— (1974) 'Athenian Demagogues' in M.I. Finley (ed.) *Studies in Ancient Society*, London: 1–25.

—— (1977) *Aspects of Antiquity: Discoveries and Controversies*, Harmondsworth, second edition.

Flower, H.I. (1992) 'Thucydides and the Pylos Debate (4.27–29)' *Historia* 41: 40–57.

Forde, S. (1989) *The Ambition to Rule: Alcibiades and the Politics of Imperialism in Thucydides*, Ithaca.

Fornara, C.W. (1971) *The Athenian Board of Generals from 501 to 404*, Historia Einzelschrift 16, Wiesbaden.

—— (1977) *Archaic Times to the End of the Peloponnesian War*, Baltimore.

—— (1979) 'On the Chronology of the Samian War' *JHS* 99: 7–19.

Forrest, W.G. (1960) 'Themistokles and Argos' *CQ* 10: 221–41.

French, A. (1976) 'The Megarian Decree' *Historia* 25: 235–49.

—— (1979) 'Athenian Ambitions and the Delian Alliance' *Phoenix* 33: 134–41.

—— (1988) 'The Guidelines of the Delian Alliance' *Antichthon* 22: 12–25.

Frost, F.J. (1968) 'Themistocles' Place in Athenian Politics' *ClAnt* 1: 105–24.

—— (1980) *Plutarch's Themistocles: A Historical Commentary*, Princeton.

Garland, R.S.J. (1987) *The Piraeus: From the Fifth to the First Century B.C.*, London.

Gomme, A.W. (1939–81) *A Historical Commentary on Thucydides* vols I–V, Oxford; IV–V with A. Andrewes and K.J. Dover.

—— (1962) 'Thucydides and Kleon' in *More Essays in Greek History and Literature*, Oxford: 112–21.

Green, P. (1989) *Classical Bearings: Interpreting Ancient History and Culture*, London.

Hall, E. (1993) 'Asia Unmanned: Images of Victory in Classical Athens' in J. Rich and G. Shipley (eds) *War and Society in the Greek World*, London: 108–33.

Hall, L.G.H. (1990) 'Ephialtes, the Areopagus and the Thirty' *CQ* 40: 319–28.

Hamilton, C.D. (1979) 'On the Perils of Extraordinary Honors: The Case of Lysander and Conon' *AncW* 2: 87–90.

Hammond, N.G.L. (1955) 'Studies in Greek Chronology of the Sixth and Fifth Centuries B.C.' *Historia* 4: 371–411.

—— (1967) 'The Origins and the Nature of the Athenian Alliance of 478/7 B.C.' *JHS* 87: 41–61.

Hansen, M.H. (1975) *Eisangelia: The Sovereignty of the People's Court in Athens in the Fourth Century BC and the Impeachment of Generals and Politicians*, Odense University Classical Studies 6, Odense.

—— (1987) *The Athenian Assembly in the Age of Demosthenes*, Oxford.

—— (1991) *The Athenian Democracy in the Age of Demosthenes: Structure, Principles and Ideology*, Oxford.

Harding, P. (1988) 'King Pausanias and the Restoration of Democracy at Athens' *Hermes* 116: 186–93.

Harris, E.M. (1993) 'The Constitution of the Five Thousand' *HSPh* 95: 243–80.

Henry, A.S. (1978) 'The Dating of Fifth-Century Attic Inscriptions' *ClAnt* 11: 75–108.

—— (1992) 'Through a Laser Beam Darkly: Space-age Technology and the Egesta Decree (*IG* I³ 11)' *ZPE* 91: 137–45.

—— (1993) 'Athens and Egesta (*IG* I³ 11)' *AHB* 7: 49–53.

—— (1995) 'Pour Encourager les autres: Athens and Egesta Encore' *CQ* 45: 237–40.

—— (1998) 'The Sigma Enigma' *ZPE* 120: 45–8.

Herman, G. (1990) 'Treaties and Alliances in the World of Thucydides' *PCPhS* 36: 83–102.

Higgins, W.E. (1977) *Xenophon the Athenian: The Problem of the Individual and the Society of the Polis*, Albany.

Holladay, A.J. (1977) 'Sparta's Role in the First Peloponnesian War' *JHS* 97: 54–63.

—— (1978) 'Athenian Strategy in the Archidamian War' *Historia* 27: 399–426.

—— (1985) 'Sparta and the First Peloponnesian War' *JHS* 105: 161–2.

—— (1986) 'The Détente of Kallias?' *Historia* 35: 503–7.

—— (1989) 'The Hellenic Disaster in Egypt' *JHS* 109: 176–82.

Hornblower, S. (1987) *Thucydides*, Baltimore.

—— (1991) *The Greek World 479–323 BC*, London, second edition.

—— (1991) *A Commentary on Thucydides, vol. I, Books I–III*, Oxford; (1996) *A Commentary on Thucydides, vol. II, Books IV–V.24*, Oxford.

—— (1992) 'The Religious Dimension to the Peloponnesian War, or, What Thucydides Does not Tell Us' *HSPh* 94: 169–97.

—— and M.C. Greenstock (1984) *The Athenian Empire: Sources Translated from Index III of Hill's Sources for Greek History*, London.

Hunt, P. (1998) *Slaves, Warfare, and Ideology in the Greek Historians*, Cambridge.

Hunter, V.J. (1973) *Thucydides the Artful Reporter*, Toronto.

Hussey, E. (1985) 'Thucydidean History' in *Crux*: 118–38.

Immerwahr, H.R. (1973) 'Pathology of Power and the Speeches in Thucydides' in P.A. Stadter (ed.) *The Speeches in Thucydides*, Chapel Hill: 16–31.

Jackson, A.H. (1969) 'The Original Purpose of the Delian League' *Historia* 18: 12–16.

Jacobsen, H. (1975) 'The Oath of the Delian League' *Philologus* 119: 256–8.

Jensen, S.R. (2011) *Rethinking Athenian Imperialism: Sub-hegemony in the Delian League*, UMI Dissertation Publishing.

Jones, L.A. (1987) 'The Role of Ephialtes in the Rise of Athenian Democracy' *ClAnt* 6: 53–76.

Jordan, B. (1986) 'Religion in Thucydides' *TAPhA* 116: 119–47.

Kagan, D. (1974) *The Archidamian War*, Ithaca.

—— (1981) *The Peace of Nicias and the Sicilian Expedition*, Ithaca.

Kallet-Marx, L. (1989) 'The Kallias Decree, Thucydides, and the Outbreak of the Peloponnesian War' *CQ* 39: 94–113.

—— (1989) 'Did Tribute Fund the Parthenon?' *ClAnt* 8: 252–66.

—— (1993) *Money, Expense, and Naval Power in Thucydides' History 1–5.24*, Berkeley.

Kearns, E. (1989) *The Heroes of Attica*, *BICS* Suppl. 57, London.

Krentz, P. (1982) *The Thirty at Athens*, Ithaca.

—— (1984) 'The Ostracism of Thoukydides, son of Melesias' *Historia* 33: 499–504.

—— (1993) 'Athens' Allies and the Phallophoria' *AHB* 7: 12–16.

—— (1997) 'The Strategic Culture of Periklean Athens' in C. Hamilton and P. Krentz (eds) *Polis and Polemos: Essays on Politics, War and History in Ancient Greece in Honor of Donald Kagan*, Claremon: 55–72.

Lang, M.L. (1990) 'Illegal Execution in Ancient Athens' *PAPhS* 134: 24–9.

Lateiner, D. (1977) 'Heralds and Corpses in Thucydides' *CW* 71: 97–106.

Lazenby, J.F. (2004) *The Peloponnesian War: A Military Study*, London.

Lenardon, R.J. (1956) 'The Archonship of Themistokles, 493/2' *Historia* 5: 401–19.

—— (1959) 'The Chronology of Themistokles' Ostracism and Exile' *Historia* 8: 23–48.

—— (1961) 'Charon, Thucydides, and "Themistokles"' *Phoenix* 15: 28–40.

—— (1978) *The Saga of Themistocles*, London.

—— (1981) 'Thucydides and Hellanikos' in *Classical Contributions*: 59–70.

Lewis, D.M. (1961) 'Double Representation in the Strategia' *JHS* 81: 118–23.

—— (1966) 'After the Profanation of the Mysteries' in E. Badian (ed.) *Ancient Society and Institutions: Studies Presented to V. Ehrenberg*, Oxford: 177–91.

—— (1977) *Sparta and Persia*, Leiden.

—— (1981) 'The Origins of the First Peloponnesian War' in *Classical Contributions*: 71–8.

—— (1989) 'Persian Gold in Greek International Relations' *REA* 91.1–2: 227–35.

—— (1992) 'Mainland Greece, 479–451 B.C.' in *CAH* V²: 96–120.

Lewis, R.G. (1997) 'Themistokles and Ephialtes' *CQ* 47: 358–62.

Libourel, J.M. (1971) 'The Athenian Disaster in Egypt' *AJPh* 92: 605–15.

Lintott, A. (1982) *Violence, Civil Strife and Revolution in the Classical City, 750–330 BC*, London.

Loening, T.C. (1987) *The Reconciliation Agreement of 403/402 B.C. in Athens*, Historia Einzelschrift 53, Stuttgart.

Loomis, W.T. (1990) 'Pausanias, Byzantion and the Formation of the Delian League: A Chronological Note' *Historia* 39: 487–92.

—— (1992) *The Spartan War Fund. IG V 1, 1 and a New Fragment*, Historia Einzelschrift 74, Stuttgart.

Luginbill, R.D. (1997) 'Thucydides' Evaluation of the Sicilian Expedition: 2.65.11' *AncW* 28: 127–32.

—— (2011) *Author of Illusions: Thucydides' Rewriting of the History of the Peloponnesian War*, Cambridge.

Ma, J., N. Papzarkadas and R. Parker (eds) (2009) *Interpreting the Athenian Empire*, London.

MacDonald, B.R. (1983) 'The Megarian Decree' *Historia* 32: 385–410.

MacDowell, D.M. (1962) *Andokides: On the Mysteries*, Oxford.

McGregor, M.F. (1987) *The Athenians and Their Empire*, Vancouver.

Macleod, C.W. (1978) 'Reason and Necessity: Thucydides III.9–14, 37–48' *JHS* 98: 64–78.

McNeal, R.A. (1970) 'Historical Methods and Thucydides I.103.1' *Historia* 19: 306–25.

McPherran, M.L. (1997) *The Religion of Socrates*, University Park, Pa.

Mansfeld, J. (1979) 'The Chronology of Anaxagoras' Athenian Period and the Date of His Trial, I' *Mnemosyne* 32: 39–69.

—— (1980) 'The Chronology of Anaxagoras' Athenian Period and the Date of His Trial, II' *Mnemosyne* 33: 17–95.

Manville, P.B. (1997) 'Pericles and the "Both/And" Vision for Democratic Athens' in C.D. Hamilton and P. Krentz (eds) *Polis and Polemos*, Claremont: 73–84.

Marinatos, J. (1981) 'Thucydides and Oracles' *JHS* 101: 138–40.

—— (1981) *Thucydides and Religion*, Königstein.

Marr, J.L. (1993) 'Ephialtes the Moderate?' *G&R* 40: 11–19.

—— (1995) 'The Death of Themistocles' *G&R* 42 (1995) 159–67.

—— (1998) 'What Did the Athenians Demand in 432 BC?' *Phoenix* 52: 120–4.

Marshall, F.H. (1905) *The Second Athenian Confederacy*, Cambridge.

Marshall, M.H.B. (1984) 'Cleon and Pericles: Sphacteria' *G&R* 31: 19–36.

Marshall, M. (1990) 'Pericles and the Plague' in E.M. Craik (ed.) *'Owls to Athens': Essays on Classical Subjects Presented to Sir Kenneth Dover*, Oxford: 163–70.

Mattingly, H.B. (1996) *The Athenian Empire Restored: Epigraphic and Historical Studies*, Detroit.

Meiggs, R. (1963) 'The Crisis of Athenian Imperialism' *HSPh* 67: 1–36.

—— (1966) 'The Dating of Fifth-Century Attic Inscriptions' *JHS* 86: 86–98.

Meritt, B.D. (1984) 'The Samian Revolt from Athens in 440–439 B.C.' *PAPhS* 128: 123–33.

—— H.T. Wade-Gery and M.F. McGregor (1939–53) *The Athenian Tribute Lists I–IV*, Cambridge, Mass.

Meyer, E.A. (1997) 'The Outbreak of the Peloponnesian War after Twenty-Five Years' in C.D. Hamilton and P. Krentz (eds) *Polis and Polemos*, Claremont: 23–54.

Mikalson, J.D. (1984) 'Religion and the Plague in Athens, 431–423 B.C.' in K.J. Rigsby (ed.) *Studies Presented to Sterling Dow*, GRBS Monograph 10: 217–25.

Milton, M.P. (1979) 'The Date of Thucydides' Synchronism of the Siege of Naxos with Themistokles' Flight' *Historia* 28: 257–75.

Missiou-Ladi, A. (1987) 'Coercive Diplomacy in Greek Interstate Relations' *CQ* 37: 336–45.

Mitchell, B. (1991) 'Kleon's Amphipolitan Campaign: Aims and Results' *Historia* 40: 170–92.

Morens, D.M. and R.J. Littman (1992) 'Epidemiology of the Plague of Athens' *TAPhA* 122: 271–304.

Morgan, T.E. (1994) 'Plague or Poetry? Thucydides on the Epidemic at Athens' *TAPhA* 124: 197–209.

Nichols, M.P. (1987) *Socrates and the Political Community*, New York.

Ober, J. (1985) 'Thucydides, Pericles, and the Strategy of Defense' in J.W. Eadie and J. Ober, *The Craft of the Ancient Historian*, Lanham: 171–88 = Ober, J. (1996) *The Athenian Revolution. Essays on Ancient Greek Democracy and Political Theory*, Princeton: 72–85.

—— (1989) *Mass and Elite in Democratic Athens: Rhetoric, Ideology, and the Power of the People*, Princeton.

O'Neil, J.L. (1981) 'The Exile of Themistokles and Democracy in the Peloponnese' *CQ* 31: 335–46.

Oost, S.I. (1975) 'Thucydides and the Irrational: Sundry Passages' *CPh* 70: 186–96.

Osborne, R. (1985) 'The Erection and Mutilation of the Hermai' *PCPhS* 31: 47–73.

Ostwald, M. (1979) 'Diodotus, Son of Eucrates' *GRBS* 20: 5–13.

—— (1982) *Autonomia: Its Genesis and Early History*, Chico.

—— (1986) *From Popular Sovereignty to the Sovereignty of Law: Law, Society and Politics in Fifth-Century Athens*, Berkeley.

Page, D.L. (1953) 'Thucydides' Description of the Great Plague at Athens' *CQ* 3: 97–119.

Palagia, O. (2009) *Art in Athens during the Peloponnesian War*, Cambridge.

Philippides, M. (1985) 'King Pleistoanax and the Spartan Invasion of Attica in 446' *AncW* 11: 33–41.

Pinney, G.F. (1984) 'For the Heroes Are at Hand' *JHS* 104: 181–3.

Plant, I.M. (1994) 'The Battle of Tanagra: A Spartan Initiative?' *Historia* 43: 259–74.

Pleket, H.W. (1963) 'Thasos and the Popularity of the Athenian Empire' *Historia* 12: 70–7.

Podlecki, A.J. (1966) *The Political Background of Aeschylean Tragedy*, Ann Arbor.

—— (1975) *The Life of Themistocles: A Critical Survey of the Literary and Archaeological Evidence*, Montreal.

Poole, J.C.F. and A.J. Holladay (1979) 'Thucydides and the Plague of Athens' *CQ* 29: 282–300.

—— (1984) 'Thucydides and the Plague' *CQ* 34: 483–5.

Pope, M. (1988) 'Thucydides and Democracy' *Historia* 37: 276–96.

Powell, C.A. (1979) 'Religion and the Sicilian Expedition' *Historia* 28: 15–31.

—— (1979) 'Thucydides and Divination' *BICS* 26: 45–50.

Price, J.J. (2001) *Thucydides and Internal War*, Cambridge.

Pritchett, W.K. (1985) *The Greek State at War* IV, Princeton.

—— (1995) *Thucydides' Pentekontaetia and Other Essays*, Amsterdam.

Proietti, G. (1987) *Xenophon's Sparta: An Introduction*, Leiden.

Quinn, T.J. (1964) 'Thucydides and the Unpopularity of the Athenian Empire' *Historia* 13: 257–66.

—— (1981) *Athens, and Samos, Lesbos and Chios: 478–404 B.C.*, Manchester.

Rankin, D.I. (1987) 'Sokrates, an Oligarch?' *AC* 56: 68–87.

Rawlings, H.R. (1977) 'Thucydides on the Purpose of the Delian League' *Phoenix* 31: 1–8.

Reger, G. (1990) 'Some Remarks on "IG XII 8, 262 complété" and the Restoration of Thasian Democracy' *Klio* 72: 396–401.

Rhodes, P.J. (1970) 'Thucydides on Pausanias and Themistocles' *Historia* 19: 387–400.

—— (1972) 'The Five Thousand in the Athenian Revolution of 411' *JHS* 92: 115–27.

Richardson, J. (1990) 'Thucydides I.23.6 and the Debate about the Peloponnesian War' in E.M. Craik (ed.) *'Owls to Athens': Essays on Classical Subjects Presented to Sir Kenneth Dover*, Oxford: 155–61.

Rihll, T.E. (1995) 'Democracy Denied: Why Ephialtes Attacked the Areiopagus' *JHS* 115: 87–98.

Roberts, J.T. (1988) 'The Teflon Empire? Chester Starr and the Invulnerability of the Delian League' *AHB* 2: 49–53.

Robertson, N. (1980) 'The True Nature of the "Delian League" 478–61 BC' *AJAH* 5: 64–96.

Roller, D.W. (1989) 'Who Murdered Ephialtes?' *Historia* 38: 257–66.

Rood, T. (1998) *Thucydides. Narrative and Explanation*, Oxford.

Rutter, N.K. (1973) 'Diodorus and the Foundation of Thurii' *Historia* 22: 155–76.

Ryder, T.T.B. (1965) *Koine Eirene*, Oxford.

Samons, L.J. (1996) 'The "Kallias Decrees" (*IG* I³ 52) and the Inventories of Athena's Treasure in the Parthenon' *CQ* 46: 91–102.

—— (1998) 'Kimon, Kallias and Peace with Persia' *Historia* 47: 129–40.

Scarrow, G.D. (1988) 'The Athenian Plague: A Possible Diagnosis' *AHB* 2: 4–8.

Seager, R. (1967) 'Alcibiades and the Charge of Aiming at Tyranny' *Historia* 16: 6–18.

Sealey, R. (1964) 'Ephialtes' *CPh* 59: 11–22 = (1968) *Essays in Greek Politics*, New York: 42–58.

—— (1966) 'The Origin of the Delian League' in E. Badian (ed.) *Ancient Society and Institutions: Studies Presented to V. Ehrenberg*, Oxford: 235–55.

—— (1975) 'The Causes of the Peloponnesian War' *CPh* 70: 89–109.

—— (1981) 'Ephialtes, *Eisangelia*, and the Council' in *Classical Contributions:* 125–34.

—— (1987) *The Athenian Republic: Democracy or the Rule of Law?*, University Park, Pa.

Shipley, G. (1987) *A History of Samos 800–188 BC*, Oxford.

Sidwell, K. (2009) *Aristophanes the Democrat: The Politics of Satirical Comedy during the Peloponnesian War*, Cambridge.

Sinclair, R.K. (1988) *Democracy and Participation in Athens*, Cambridge.

Smart, J.D. (1967) 'Kimon's Capture of Eion' *JHS* 87: 136–38.

Spence, I.G. (1995) 'Thucydides, Woodhead, and Kleon' *Mnemosyne* 48: 411–37.

Stadter, P.A. (1983) 'The Motives for Athens' Alliance with Corcya (Thuc. 1.44)' *GRBS* 24: 131–6.

—— (1989) *A Commentary on Plutarch's Pericles*, Chapel Hill.

—— (1991) 'Pericles among the Intellectuals' *ICS* 16: 111–24.

Stahl, H.-P. (2003) *Thucydides: Man's Place in History*, Swansea.

Starr, C.G. (1988) 'Athens and Its Empire' *CJ* 83: 114–23.

—— (1990) *The Birth of Athenian Democracy: The Assembly in the Fifth Century B.C.*, Oxford.

Staveley, E.S. (1972) *Greek and Roman Voting and Elections*, London.

Stern, R. (2003) 'The Thirty at Athens in the Summer of 404' *Phoenix* 52: 18–34.

Stockton, D. (1982) 'The Death of Ephialtes' *CQ* 32: 227–28.

—— (1990) *The Classical Athenian Democracy*, Oxford.

Strassler, R.B. (1988) 'The Harbor at Pylos' *JHS* 108: 198–203.

—— (1990) 'The Opening of the Pylos Campaign' *JHS* 110: 110–25.

Strauss, B.S. (1983) 'Aegospotami Reexamined' *AJPh* 104: 24–35.

—— (1986) *Athens after the Peloponnesian War: Class, Faction and Policy 403–386 BC*, London.

—— (1993) *Fathers and Sons in Athens: Ideology and Society in the Era of the Peloponnesian War*, Princeton.

Talbert, R.J.A. (1989) 'The Role of the Helots in the Class Struggle at Sparta' *Historia* 38: 22–40.

Taylor, M. (2010) *Thucydides, Pericles and the Idea of Athens in the Peloponnesian War*, Cambridge.

Thompson, W.E. (1981) 'The Peace of Callias in the Fourth Century' *Historia* 30: 164–77.

Tréheux, J. (1991) 'Bulletin Épigraphique' *REG* 104: 469.

Tritle, L.A. (2010) *A New History of the Peloponnesian War*, Oxford.

Unz, R.K. (1986) 'The Chronology of the Pentekontaetia' *CQ* 36: 68–85.

Usher, S. (1979) '"This to the Fair Critias"' *Eranos* 77: 39–42.

Vanderpool, E. (1974) 'The Date of the Pre-Persian Wall of Athens' in D.W. Bradeen and M.F. McGregor (eds) *Phoros: Tribute to B.D. Meritt*, Locust Valley: 156–60.

Vickers, M. (1989) 'Alcibiades on Stage: Aristophanes' *Birds*' *Historia* 38: 267–99.

—— (1995) 'Alcibiades at Sparta: Aristophanes *Birds*' *CQ* 45: 339–54.

—— (1996) 'Fifth Century Chronology and the Coinage Decree' *JHS* 116: 171–4.

Wade-Gery, H.T. (1933) 'Classical Epigrams and Epitaphs' *JHS* 53: 71–104.

—— (1958) 'Thucydides the Son of Melesias' in H.T. Wade-Gery (ed.) *Essays in Greek History*, Oxford: 239–70 = (1932) *JHS* 52: 205–27.

—— (1958) 'The Peace of Kallias' in H.T. Wade-Gery (ed.) *Essays in Greek History*, Oxford: 201–33 = (1940) *Athenian Studies Presented to W.S. Ferguson*: *HSPh* Suppl. 1: 121–56.

—— (1958) 'The Judicial Treaty with Phaselis and the History of the Athenian Courts' in H.T. Wade-Gery (ed.) *Essays in Greek History*, Oxford: 180–200.

Walbank, M.B. (1982) 'The Confiscation and Sale by the Poletai in 402/1 of the Property of the Thirty Tyrants' *Hesperia* 51: 74–98.

Wallace, R.W. (1974) 'Ephialtes and the Areopagos' *GRBS* 15: 259–69.

—— (1985) *The Areopagos Council, to 307 B.C.*, Baltimore.

Walsh, J. (1981) 'The Authenticity and the Dates of the Peace of Callias and the Congress Decree' *Chiron* 11: 31–63.

Wartenberg, U. (1995) *After Marathon. War, Society and Money in Fifth-Century Greece*, London.

Westlake, H.D. (1950) 'Thucydides and the Athenian Disaster in Egypt' *CPh* 45: 209–16.

—— (1962) 'Thucydides and the Fall of Amphipolis' *Hermes* 90: 276–87.

—— (1977) 'Thucydides on Pausanias and Themistokles: A Written Source?' *CQ* 27: 95–110 = H.D. Westlake (ed.) (1989) *Studies in Thucydides and Greek History*, Bristol: 1–18.

Whitehead, D. (1982/83) 'Sparta and the Thirty Tyrants' *AncSoc* 13/14: 105–30.

—— (1998) 'O NEOS DASMOS: "Tribute" in Classical Athens' *Hermes* 126: 173–88.

Wilson, J.B. (1979) *Pylos 425 BC*, Warminster.

Winnington-Ingram, R.P. (1965) 'TA DEONTA EIPEIN: Cleon and Diodotos' *BICS* 12: 70–82.

Winton, R.I. (1981) 'Thucydides 1, 97, 2: The "Arche of the Athenians" and the "Athenian Empire"' *MH* 38: 147–52.

Woodhead, A.G. (1952) 'The Site of Brea: Thucydides I.61.4' *CQ* 2: 57–62.

—— (1960) 'Thucydides' Portrait of Cleon' *Mnemosyne* 13: 289–317.

Wycherley, R.E. (1978) *The Stones of Athens*, Princeton.

Wylie, J.A.H. and J. Stubbs (1983) 'The Plague of Athens: 430–428 B.C.: Epidemic and Epizoötic' *CQ* 33: 6–11.

Chapters 14 and 15 The rise of Macedon; Alexander the Great, 336–323 bc

Introductory reading:

Ashley, J.R. (2004) *The Macedonian Empire. The Era of Warfare under Philip II and Alexander the Great, 359–323 BC*, Jefferson.

Bosworth, A.B. (1988) *Conquest and Empire. The Reign of Alexander the Great*, Cambridge.

Cargill, J. (1981) *The Second Athenian League*, Berkeley.

Cartledge, P. (1987) *Agesilaos and the Crisis of Sparta*, Baltimore.

Ellis, J.R. (1976) *Philip II and Macedonian Imperialism*, London.

Green, P. (1991) *Alexander of Macedon: 356–323 BC. A Historical Biography*, Berkeley, revised edition.

Hammond, N.G.L. (1994) *Philip of Macedon*, London.

—— and G.T. Griffith (1979) *A History of Macedonia* ii, Oxford.

—— and F.W. Walbank (1988) *A History of Macedonia* iii, Oxford.

Lane Fox, R. (1973) *Alexander the Great*, London.

Roismann, J. (ed.) (2003) *Brill's Companion to Alexander the Great*, Leiden.

Sealey, R. (1993) *Demosthenes and His Time: A Study in Defeat*, New York.

Strauss, B. (1986) *Athens after the Peloponnesian War*, Ithaca.

Adams, W.L. and E.N. Borza (eds) (1982) *Philip II, Alexander the Great, and the Macedonian Heritage*, Washington, D.C.

Adcock, F.E. (1957) *The Greek and Macedonian Art of War*, Berkeley.

Allen, L. (2005) *The Persian Empire*, Chicago.

Andronikos, M. (1992) *Philip of Macedon*, Athens.

Anson, E.M. (1991) 'The Evolution of the Macedonian Army Assembly, 330–315 BC' *Historia* 40: 230–47.

Austin, M.M. (1981) *The Hellenistic World from Alexander to the Roman Conquest. A Selection of Ancient Sources in Translation*, Cambridge.

Badian, E. (1958) 'Alexander the Great and the Unity of Mankind' *Historia* 7: 425–44.

—— (1962) 'Alexander the Great and the Loneliness of Power' *Journal of the Australasian Universities Language and Literature Association* 17: 80–91.

—— (1963) 'The Death of Philip II' *Phoenix* 17: 244–50.

—— (1971) 'Alexander the Great, 1948–1961' *Classical World* 65: 37–56, 77–83.

—— (1982) 'Greeks and Macedonians' in B. Barr-Sharrar and E.N. Borza (eds) *Macedonia and Greece in Late Classical and Early Hellenistic Times*, Washington, D.C.: 33–51.

—— (1991) 'The King's Peace' in M.A. Flower and M. Toler (eds) *Georgia. Greek Studies in Honour of George Cawkwell*, London: 25–48.

—— (2006) *Collected Papers on Alexander the Great*, London.

Barr-Sharrar B. and E. N. Borza (eds) (1982) *Macedonia and Greece in Late Classical and Early Hellenistic Times*, Washington.

Baynham, E. (2004) *Alexander the Great: The Unique History of Quintus Curtius*, Ann Arbor.

Bengtson, H. (1969) *The Greeks and the Persians*, London.

Billows, R.A. (1990) *Antigonos the One-eyed and the Creation of the Hellenistic State*, Berkeley.

—— (1995) *Kings and Colonists: Aspects of Macedonian Imperialism*, Leiden.

Bloedow, E. (2003) 'Why did Philip and Alexander Launch a War Against the Persian Empire?' *AC* 72: 261–74.

Borza, E.N. (1987) 'Malaria in Alexander's Army' *AHB* 1: 36–8.

—— (1992) *In the Shadow of Olympus: The Emergence of Macedon*, Princeton.

—— (1995) *Makedonica: Essays by Eugene N. Borza*, Claremont.

—— (1999) *Before Alexander: Constructing Early Macedonia*, Claremont.

Bosworth, A.B. (1980) *A Historical Commentary on Arrian's History of Alexander*, Oxford.

—— (1988) *From Arrian to Alexander: Studies in Historical Interpretation*, Oxford.

—— (1996) *Alexander and the East: The Tragedy of Triumph*, Oxford.

—— (1996) 'The Tumult and the Shouting: Two Interpretations of the Cleitus Episode' *AHB* 10.1: 19–30.

—— (1997) 'A Cut Too Many? Occam's Razor and Alexander's Footguard' *AHB* 11: 47–56.

—— and E. Baynham (2002) *Alexander the Great in Fact and Fiction*, New York.

Bradford, A.S. (1992) *Philip II of Macedon: A Life from the Ancient Sources*, Westport.

Briant, P. (2010) *Alexander the Great and His Empire: A Short History*, tr. A. Kuhrt, Princeton.

Buckler, J. (1980) *The Theban Hegemony, 371–362 BC*, Cambridge, Mass.

—— (1989) *Philip and the Sacred War*, Leiden.

Burn, A.R. (1962) *Alexander the Great and the Hellenistic World*, New York, second edition.

—— (1965) 'The Generalship of Alexander' *G&R* 12: 140–54.

Carney, E.D. (2000) *Women and Monarchy in Macedonia*, Norman.

—— (2006) *Olympias: Mother of Alexander the Great*, New York.

—— and D. Ogden (2010) *Philip II and Alexander the Great: Father and Son, Lives and Afterlives*, New York.

Cartledge, P. (2004) *Alexander the Great: The Hunt for a New Past*, New York.

Cawkwell, G.L. (1969) 'The Crowning of Demosthenes' *CQ* 19: 163–80.

—— (1972) 'Epaminondas and Thebes' *CQ* 22: 254–78.

—— (1973) 'The Foundation of the Second Athenian Confederacy' *CQ* 23: 47–59.

—— (1976) 'Agesilaus and Sparta' *CQ* 26: 62–84.

—— (1977) *Philip of Macedon*, London.

—— (1981) 'Notes on the Failure of the Second Athenian Confederacy' *JHS* 101: 40–55.

—— (1983) 'The Decline of Sparta' *CQ* 33.2: 385–400.

—— (1984) 'Athenian Naval Power in the Fourth Century' *CQ* 34.2: 334–45.

—— (2006) *The Greek Wars: The Failure of Persia*, Oxford.

Cohen, A. (2010) *Art in the Era of Alexander the Great: Paradigms of Manhood and Their Cultural Traditions*, Cambridge.

Cook, J.M. (1983) *The Persian Empire*, London.

David, E. (1980) 'Revolutionary Agitation in Sparta after Leuctra' *Athenaeum* 68: 299–308.

Devine, A.M. 'The Strategies of Alexander the Great and Darius III in the Issus Campaign (333 BC)' *AncW* 12: 25–38.

Dillery, J. (1995) *Xenophon and the History of His Times*, London.

Dillon, M. P. J. (1995) 'Phryon of Rhamnous and the Macedonian Pirates: The Political Significance of the Sacred Truces' *Historia* 44: 250–540.

Engles, D.W. (1978) *Alexander the Great and the Logistics of the Macedonian Army*, London.

—— (1980) 'Alexander's Intelligence System' *CQ* 30: 327–40.

Errington, R.M. (1981) 'Alexander the Philhellene and Persia' in H.J. Dell (ed.) *Ancient Macedonian Studies in Honor of C. Edson*, Thessaloniki: 139–43.

—— (1990) *A History of Macedonia*, New York.

Fraser, P.M. (1996) *Cities of Alexander the Great*, Oxford.

Freeman, P. (2010) *Alexander the Great*, New York.

Fuller, J.F.C. (1960) *The Generalship of Alexander the Great*, New Brunswick.

Garlan, Y. (1975) *War in the Ancient World. A Social History*, London.

Garnsey, P. and C.R. Whittaker (eds) (1987) *Imperialism in the Ancient World*, Cambridge.

Ginouves, R. (ed.) (1994) *Macedonia: From Philip II to the Roman Conquest*, Princeton.

Hack, H. (1978) 'Thebes and the Spartan Hegemony' *AJP* 99: 210–23.

Hamilton, C.D. (1979) *Sparta's Bitter Victories: Politics and Diplomacy in the Corinthian War*, Ithaca.

—— (1991) *Agesilaus and the Failure of the Spartan Hegemony*, Ithaca.

Hamilton, J.R. (1982) *Alexander the Great*, Pittsburgh.

Hammond, N.G.L. (1980) 'Training in the Use of a Sarissa and Its Effect in Battle, 339–333 B.C.' *Antichthon* 14: 53–63.

—— (1989) *The Macedonian State: Origins, Institutions, and History*, Oxford.

—— (1989) *Alexander the Great: King, Commander and Statesman*, Park Ridge, second edition.

—— (1992) 'Alexander's Charge at the Battle of Issus' *Historia* 41: 395–406.

—— (1993–97) *Collected Studies*, Amsterdam.

—— (1995) 'Alexander's Order during the Cleitus Episode' *AHB* 9: 111–16.

—— (1997) *The Genius of Alexander the Great*, London.

—— (2007) *Three Historians of Alexander the Great: The So-called Vulgate Authors, Diodorus, Justin, and Curtius*, Cambridge.

—— (2007) *Sources for Alexander the Great: An Analysis of Plutarch's 'Life' and Arrian's 'Anabasis'*, Cambridge.

Hansen, M.H. (1991) *The Athenian Democracy in the Age of Demosthenes: Structure, Principles, Ideology*, Oxford.

Hanson, V.D. (1990) *The Western Way of War: Infantry Battle in Classical Greece*, London.

Harris, E.M. (1995) *Aeschines and Athenian Politics*, Oxford.

Hatzopoulos, M.B. (1996) *Macedonian Institutions under the Kings*, Athens.

—— and L.D. Loukopoulos, (1980) *Philip of Macedon*, Athens.

Heckel, W. (1992) *The Marshals of Alexander's Empire*, London.

—— and L.A. Tritle (eds) (2003) *Crossroads of History. The Age of Alexander the Great*, Claremont.

—— and L.A. Tritle (eds) (2009) *Alexander the Great: A New History*, Chicester.

——, L.A. Tritle and P. Wheatley (eds) (2007) *Alexander's Empire: Formulation to Decay*, Claremont.

Heisserer, A.J. (1980) *Alexander the Great and the Greeks: The Epigraphic Evidence*, Norman.

Holt, F.L (2006) *Into the Land of Bones: Alexander the Great in Afghanistan*, Berkeley.

Hornblower, S. (1982) *Mausolus*, Oxford.

Jaeger, W. (1963) *Demosthenes: The Origin and Growth of His Policy*, New York.

Jordan, B. (1975) *The Athenian Navy in the Classical Period*, Berkeley.

Keyser, P.T. (1994) 'The Use of Artillery by Philip II and Alexander the Great' *AncW* 25: 25–59.

Kuhrt, A. and S. Sherwin-White (eds) (1987) *Hellenism in the East: The Interaction of Greek and Non-Greek Civilizations from Syria to Central Asia under Alexander*, Berkeley.

Larsen, J.A.O. (1968) *Greek Federal States*, Oxford.

Lendon, J.E. (1989) 'The Oxyrhynchus Historian and the Origins of the Corinthian War' *Historia* 38: 300–13.

Lewis, D.M. (1977) *Sparta and Persia*, Leiden.

Lonsdale, D.J. (2007) *Alexander the Great: Lessons in Strategy*, New York.

McDowell, D.M. (2010) *Demosthenes the Orator*, Oxford.

Mader, G. (2005) '*Pax duello mixta*: Demosthenes and the Rhetoric of War and Peace' *CQ* 55: 11–35.

Markle, M.M. (1974) 'The Strategy of Philip in 346 B.C.' *CQ* ns 24: 253–68.

—— (1977) 'The Macedonian Sarissa, Spear, and Related Armor' *AJA* 81: 323–39.

—— (1978) 'Use of the Sarissa by Philip and Alexander of Macedon' *AJA* 82: 483–97.

—— (1981) 'Demosthenes' *Second Philippic*: A Valid Policy for the Athenians against Philip' *Antichthon* 15: 62–85.

Montgomery, H. (1985) *The Way to Chaeronea: Foreign Policy, Decision Making and Political Influence in Demosthenes' Speeches*, Oxford.

Mossé, C. (2004) *Alexander: Destiny and Myth*, Edinburgh.

Mueller, K. (1979) *The Fragments of the Lost Historians of Alexander the Great*, Chicago.

Munn, M.H. (1993) *The Defense of Attica: The Dema Wall and the Boiotian War of 378–375 B.C.*, Berkeley.

Pearson, L. (1960) *The Lost Histories of Alexander the Great*, New York.

Perlman, S. (1973) *Philip and Athens*, Cambridge.

Price, M.J. (1974) *Coins of the Macedonians*, London.

Rice, D.G. (1974) 'Agesilaus, Agesipolis and Spartan Politics, 386–379' *Historia* 23: 164–82.

Roisman, J. (ed.) (2003) *Alexander the Great*, Leiden.

—— and I. Worthington (eds) (2010) *A Companion to Ancient Macedonia*, Oxford.

Romane, P. (1988) 'Alexander's Siege of Gaza in 332 BC' *AncW* 18: 21–30.

Roy, J. 'Diodorus Siculus 15.40: The Peloponnesian Revolutions of 374 BC' *Klio* 55: 135–9.

Ryder, T.T.B. (1965) *Koine Eirene*, Oxford.

Savill, A. (1993) *Alexander the Great and His Time*, New York.

Seager, R. (1974) 'The King's Peace and the Balance of Power in Greece, 386–362' *Athenaeum* 52: 36–63.

Stoneman, R. (2004) *Alexander the Great*, London.

—— (2008) *Alexander the Great: A Life in Legend*, New Haven.

Talbert, R.J. (1974) *Timoleon and the Revival of Greek Sicily, 344–317 BC*, Cambridge.

Tarn, W.W. (1948) *Alexander the Great*, Cambridge.

Thomas, C.G. (1968) 'Alexander the Great and the Unity of Mankind' *CJ* 63: 258–60.

—— (2006) *Alexander the Great in His World*, Oxford.

Traxell, H. (1997) *Studies in the Macedonian Coinage of Alexander the Great*, New York.

Trevett, J.C. (1999) 'Demosthenes and Thebes' *Historia* 48: 184–202.

Tritle, L.A. (ed.) (1997) *The Greek World in the Fourth Century: From the Fall of the Athenian Empire to the Successors of Alexander*, London.

Waterfield, R. (2009) *Xenophon's Retreat: Greece, Persia and the End of the Golden Age*, Boston.

Wickersham, J. (1994) *Hegemony and Greek Historians*, Lanham.

Wilcken, U. (1967) *Alexander the Great*, tr. G.C. Richards, New York.

Worthington, I. (1999) 'Alexander and the "Interests of Historical Accuracy"' *AHB* 13.4: 136–40.

—— (1999) 'How "Great" Was Alexander?' *AHB* 13.2: 39–55.

—— (ed.) (2000) *Demosthenes, Statesman and Orator*, London.

—— (2002) *Alexander the Great: A Reader*, New York.

—— (2004) *Alexander the Great: Man and God*, London, revised edition.

—— (2008) *Philip II of Macedonia*, New Haven.

INDEX